The Grants Register®

1997

D1363544

ST. MARTIN'S
PRESS

Editor: Ruth Austin

Published in the United States and Canada by
ST. MARTIN'S PRESS, INC.
257 Park Avenue South, New York
NY 10010

Fifteenth edition
ISBN 0-312-15898-X
ISSN 0072-5471

A catalog record for this book is available from the Library of Congress

Published in Great Britain by
MACMILLAN PRESS LTD
25 Eccleston Place, London, SW1W 9NF
and Basingstoke
Companies and representatives throughout the world.

Fifteenth edition
ISBN 0-333-60699X

A catalogue record for this book is available from the British Library

Typeset by Macmillan Press Ltd

Printed and bound in Great Britain by The Bath Press
Printed on acid-free paper

LIST OF CONTENTS

HOW TO USE THE GRANTS REGISTER

For ease of use, The Grants Register 1997 is divided into four sections:

Subject and Eligibility Guide to Awards
The Grants Register
Index of Awards
Index of Discontinued Awards

Subject and Eligibility Guide to Awards

Awards can be located through the Subject and Eligibility Guide to Awards. This section allows the user to find an award within a specific subject area. The Grants Register uses a list of subjects endorsed by the International Association of Universities (IAU), the information centre on higher education, located at UNESCO, Paris (please see pp. 3-4 for the complete subject list). It is further subdivided into eligibility by nationality. Thereafter awards are listed alphabetically within their designated category, along with a page reference where full details of the award can be found.

The Grants Register

Information in this section is supplied directly by the awarding organisations. Entries are arranged alphabetically by name of organisation, and awards are listed alphabetically within the awarding organisation. This section has been reorganised and information significantly expanded to include details on subject area, eligibility, purpose, type, numbers offered, frequency, value, length of study, study establishment, country of study, and application procedure. Full contact details appear with each awarding organisation and also appended to individual awards where additional addresses are given.

Where we have not been notified of changes, the award details are repeated as in the previous edition and each award is prefixed by an asterisk.

THE US-UK FULBRIGHT COMMISSION

US-UK Fulbright Commission, Fulbright House, 62 Doughty Street, London, WC1N 2LS, England
Tel: 0171 404 6880
Fax: 0171 404 6834
Email: education@fulbright.co.uk
Contact: Programme Director

Academic Administrator in Veterinary Education

Subjects: Veterinary education.

Eligibility: Applicants must hold a veterinary degree and be actively involved in veterinary education.

Level of Study: Professional development.

Purpose: To enable an administrator to conduct research into an aspect of veterinary education in the UK.

No. of awards offered: One.

Frequency: Every two years.

Value: £7,500 (inclusive of round-trip travel).

Length of Study: A minimum of four months.

Study Establishment: One of the six UK veterinary schools.

Country of Study: UK.

Applications Procedure: Please apply to CIES with four references and a proposal.

Closing Date: November 1st.

Index of Awards

All awards are indexed alphabetically with a page reference.

Index of Discontinued Awards

This Index lists awards previously included within The Grants Register which are no longer being offered, have been replaced by another program, or are no longer relevant for inclusion in the publication.

PUBLISHER'S FOREWORD

Wayne Perrin

The Grants Register, now in its fifteenth edition, continues to be the most comprehensive worldwide source on the current availability of grants for individuals. In response to changes in the marketplace and specific requests from our customers, this edition sees a number of changes from previous editions.

Most significantly, this edition sees an increase in coverage to the whole world, making The Grants Register the only truly worldwide source of its kind. Grants from a total of 86 different countries are listed in this 1997 edition.

Users familiar with The Grants Register will notice the change in format from previous editions and the complete revision of entry format. A number of new fields have been introduced to make access to the information more straightforward and to reflect the growing importance of electronic communication in today's world.

If this is the first time you have used The Grants Register then please refer to the How to Use section for a full description of the entries in The Grants Register and how you can most easily find the information which you require.

We are grateful to all those institutions which have supplied information for inclusion in The Grants Register 1997. We would also like to thank, in particular, the International Association of Universities for permission to use their subject index in this edition.

The Grants Register database is updated continually and if your organisation provides grants eligible for inclusion and you would like to be listed in the world's leading grants resource or alternatively if you have any suggestions for improvements to our product then please contact the Editor, Ruth Austin at:

Macmillan Press Ltd
Reference Division
25 Eccleston Place
London SW1W 9NF
United Kingdom

St. Martins Press, Inc.
257 Park Avenue South
New York, NY10010
United States of America

Email: Grants_Register@macmillan.co.uk

SUBJECT AND ELIGIBILITY GUIDE TO AWARDS

AGRICULTURE, FORESTRY AND FISHERY

General
Agronomy
Animal husbandry and animal production
  Sericulture
Horticulture and viticulture
Crop husbandry and crop production
Agriculture and farm management
Agricultural economics
Food science and production
  Meat and poultry
  Dairy
  Fish
  Oenology
  Brewing
  Harvest technology
Soil and water science
  Water management
  Soil conservation
Veterinary medicine
Tropical/Sub-tropical agriculture
Forestry
  Forest soils
  Forest biology
  Forest pathology
  Forest products
  Forest economics
  Forest management
Fishery
  Aquaculture

ARCHITECTURE AND TOWN PLANNING

General
Structural architecture
Architectural restoration
Environmental design
Landscape architecture
Town and community planning
Regional planning

ARTS AND HUMANITIES

General
Interpretation and translation
Writing (authorship)
Native language and literature
Modern languages and literatures
  English
  French
  Spanish
  Germanic languages
  German
  Swedish
  Danish
  Norwegian
  Italian
  Portuguese
  Romance languages
  Modern Greek
  Dutch
  Baltic languages
  Celtic languages
  Finnish
  Russian
  Slavonic languages (others)
  Hungarian
  Fino Ugrian languages
  European languages (others)
  Altaic languages
  Arabic
  Hebrew
  Chinese
  Korean
  Japanese
  Indian languages
  Iranic languages
  African languages
  Amerindian languages
  Austronesian and oceanic languages
Classical languages and literatures
  Latin
  Classical Greek
  Sanskrit
Linguistics and philology
  Applied linguistics
  Psycholinguistics
  Grammar
  Semantics and terminology
  Phonetics
  Logopedics
Comparative literature
History
  Prehistory
  Ancient civilisations
  Medieval history
  Modern history
  Contemporary history
Archaeology
Philosophy
  Philosophical schools
  Metaphysics
  Logic
  Ethics

BUSINESS ADMINISTRATION AND MANAGEMENT

General
Business studies
International business
Secretarial studies
Business machine operation
Business computing
Management systems and techniques
Accountancy
Real estate
Marketing and sales management
Insurance management
Finance, banking and investment
Personnel management
Labour/industrial relations
Public administration
Institutional administration

EDUCATION AND TEACHER TRAINING

General
Nonvocational subjects education
  Education in native language
  Foreign languages education
  Mathematics education
  Science education
  Humanities and social science education
  Physical education
  Literacy education
Vocational subjects education
  Agricultural education
  Art education
  Commerce/business education
  Computer education
  Technology education
  Health education
  Home economics education
  Industrial arts education
  Music education
Pre-school education
Primary education
Secondary education
Adult education
Special education
  Education of the gifted
  Education of the handicapped
  Education of specific learning disabilities
  Education of foreigners
  Education of natives
  Education of the socially disadvantaged
  Bilingual/bicultural education
Teacher trainers education
Higher education teacher training
Educational science
  International and comparative education
  Philosophy of education
  Curriculum
  Teaching and learning
  Educational research
  Educational technology
  Educational and student counselling
  Educational administration
  Educational testing and evaluation
  Distance education

ENGINEERING

General
Surveying and mapping science
Engineering drawing/design
Chemical engineering
Civil, construction and transportation engineering
Environmental and sanitary engineering
Safety engineering
Electrical/electronic and telecommunications engineering
Computer engineering
Industrial and management engineering
Metallurgical engineering
Production engineering
Materials engineering
Mining and minerals engineering
Petroleum engineering
Energy engineering
Nuclear engineering
Mechanical/electromechanical engineering
Hydraulic/pneumatic engineering
Sound engineering
Automotive engineering
Measurement/precision engineering
Control engineering (robotics)
Aeronautical and aerospace engineering
Marine engineering and naval architecture
Agricultural engineering
Forestry engineering
Bioengineering and biomedical engineering

FINE AND APPLIED ARTS

General
History and philosophy of art
  Aesthetics
Art management
Drawing and painting
Sculpture
Handicrafts
Music
  Musicology
  Music theory and composition
  Conducting
  Singing
  Musical instruments (performance)
  Religious music
  Jazz and popular music
  Opera
Drama
Dancing
Photography
Cinema and television
Design
  Interior design
  Furniture design
  Fashion design
  Textile design
  Graphic design
  Industrial design
  Display and stage design

HOME ECONOMICS

General
Household management
Clothing and sewing
Nutrition
Child care/child development
House arts and environment

LAW

General
History of law
Comparative law
International law
Human rights
Labour law
Maritime law
Law of the air
Notary studies
Civil law
Commercial law
Public law
  Constitutional law
  Administrative law
  Fiscal law
Criminal law
Canon law
Islamic law
European community law

MASS COMMUNICATION AND INFORMATION SCIENCE

General

Journalism
Radio/television broadcasting
Public relations and publicity
Mass communication
Media studies
Communications skills
Library science
Museum studies and
  conservation
Museum management
Restoration of works of art
Documentation techniques and
  archiving

MATHEMATICS AND COMPUTER SCIENCE

General
Statistics
Actuarial science
Applied mathematics
Computer science
Artificial intelligence
Systems analysis

MEDICAL SCIENCES

General
Public health and hygiene
  Social/preventive medicine
  Dietetics
  Sports medicine
Health administration
Medicine and surgery
  Anaesthesiology
  Cardiology
  Dermatology
  Endocrinology
  Epidemiology
  Gastroenterology
  Geriatrics
  Gynaecology and obstetrics
  Haematology
  Hepatology
  Nephrology
  Neurology
  Oncology
  Ophthalmology
  Otorhinolaryngology
  Parasitology
  Pathology
  Paediatrics
  Plastic surgery
  Pneumology
  Psychiatry and mental health
  Rheumatology
  Urology
  Virology
  Tropical medicine
  Venereology
Rehabilitation medicine and
  therapy
Nursing
Medical auxiliaries
Midwifery
Radiology
Treatment techniques
Medical technology
Dentistry and stomatology
  Oral pathology
  Orthodontics
  Periodontics
  Community dentistry
Dental technology
  Prosthetic dentistry

Pharmacy
Biomedicine
Optometry
Podiatry
Forensic medicine and dentistry
Acupuncture
Homeopathy
Chiropractic
Osteopathy
Traditional eastern medicine

NATURAL SCIENCES

General
Biological and life sciences
  Anatomy
  Biochemistry
  Biology
  Histology
  Biophysics and molecular biology
  Biotechnology
  Botany
  Plant pathology
  Embryology and reproduction
   biology
  Genetics
  Immunology
  Marine biology
  Limnology
  Microbiology
  Neurosciences
  Parasitology
  Pharmacology
  Physiology
  Toxicology
  Zoology
Chemistry
  Analytical chemistry
  Inorganic chemistry
  Organic chemistry
  Physical chemistry
Earth and geological sciences
  Geochemistry
  Geography (Scientific)
  Geology
  Mineralogy and crystallography
  Petrology
  Geophysics and seismology
  Palaeontology
Physics
  Atomic and molecular physics
  Nuclear physics
  Optics
  Solid state physics
  Thermal physics
Astronomy and astrophysics
Atmosphere science/
  meteorology
  Arctic studies
  Arid land studies
Oceanography

RECREATION, WELFARE, PROTECTIVE SERVICES

General
Police and law enforcement
Criminology
Fire protection/control
Military science
Civil security
Peace and disarmament
Social welfare and social work
  Public and community services

Vocational counselling
Environmental studies
  Ecology
  Natural resources
  Environmental management
  Wildlife and pest management
Physical education and sports
  Sports management
  Sociology of sports
Leisure studies
Parks and recreation

RELIGION AND THEOLOGY

General
Religious studies
  Christian
  Jewish
  Islam
  Asian religious studies
  Agnosticism and Atheism
  Ancient religions
Religious education
Holy writings
Religious practice
Church administration (pastoral
  work)
Theological studies
Comparative religion
Sociology of religion
History of religion
Esoteric practices

SERVICE TRADES

General
Hotel and restaurant
Hotel management
Cooking and catering
Retailing
Tourism

SOCIAL AND BEHAVIOURAL SCIENCES

General
  Economics
  Economic history
  Economic and finance policy
  Taxation
  Econometrics
  Industrial and production
   economics
Political science and
  government
  Comparative politics
International relations
Sociology
  History of societies
  Comparative sociology
  Social policy
  Social institutions
  Social communication problems
  Futurology
Demography
Anthropology
  Ethnology
  Folklore
Women's studies
Urban studies
Rural studies
Cognitive sciences
Psychology
  Experimental psychology

Social and community psychology
Clinical psychology
Personality psychology
Industrial/organisational
 psychology
Psychometrics
Educational psychology
Geography (social and
  economic)
Development studies
Area and cultural studies
  North African
  Subsahara African
  African studies
  African American
  Native American
  Hispanic American
  American
  Canadian
  Asian
  South Asian
  East Asian
  Southeast Asian
  European (EC)
  Eastern European
  Western European
  Nordic
  Caribbean
  Latin American
  Pacific area
  Aboriginal
  Middle Eastern
  Islamic
  Jewish
Preservation of cultural heritage
Ancient civilisations (Egyptology,
  Assyriology)

TRADE, CRAFT AND INDUSTRIAL TECHNIQUES

General
Food processing techniques
Building trades
Electrical/electronic equipment
  and maintenance techniques
Metal trades techniques
Mechanical equipment and
  maintenance techniques
Wood technology
Heating, air conditioning and
  refrigeration technology
Leather techniques
Textile techniques
Paper and packaging
  technology
Graphic arts techniques
  Printing
  Publishing and book trade
Laboratory techniques
Optical technology

TRANSPORT AND COMMUNICATIONS

General
Air transport
Marine transport and nautical
  science
Railway transport
Road transport
Transport management
Transport economics
Postal services
Telecommunications services

AGRICULTURE, FORESTRY AND FISHERY

GENERAL

ARCHITECTURE AND TOWN PLANNING

GENERAL

STRUCTURAL ARCHITECTURE

ARCHITECTURAL RESTORATION

ENVIRONMENTAL DESIGN

African Nations

Australia

Canada

East European Countries

West European non-EC Countries

INTERPRETATION AND TRANSLATION

African Nations

Australia

Canada

East European Countries

West European non-EC Countries

EC Countries

Far East

Indian Sub-Continent

Middle East

New Zealand

South Africa

South America

Former Soviet Republics

United States

WRITING (AUTHORSHIP)

Any Country

New Zealand

United Kingdom

United States

NATIVE LANGUAGE AND LITERATURE

Any Country

Canada

New Zealand

South America

United States

MODERN LANGUAGES AND LITERATURES

Any Country

CLASSICAL GREEK

LINGUISTICS AND PHILOLOGY

MEDIEVAL HISTORY

MODERN HISTORY

ARCHAEOLOGY

PHILOSOPHY

BUSINESS ADMINISTRATION AND MANAGEMENT

GENERAL

BUSINESS STUDIES

EDUCATION AND TEACHER TRAINING

GENERAL

NONVOCATIONAL SUBJECTS EDUCATION

MATHEMATICS EDUCATION

SCIENCE EDUCATION

HUMANITIES AND SOCIAL SCIENCE EDUCATION

PHYSICAL EDUCATION

LITERACY EDUCATION

VOCATIONAL SUBJECTS EDUCATION

EDUCATIONAL ADMINISTRATION

EDUCATIONAL TESTING AND EVALUATION

ENGINEERING

GENERAL

African Nations

Australia

Canada

East European Countries

West European non-EC Countries

EC Countries

Far East

SURVEYING AND MAPPING SCIENCE

Any Country

ENGINEERING DRAWING/DESIGN

Any Country

CHEMICAL ENGINEERING

Any Country

African Nations

Australia

Canada

East European Countries

EC Countries

Far East

Indian Sub-Continent

Middle East

New Zealand

South Africa

South America

Former Soviet Republics

CIVIL, CONSTRUCTION AND TRANSPORTATION ENGINEERING

Any Country

African Nations

Australia

Canada

East European Countries

EC Countries

Far East

Indian Sub-Continent

Indian Sub-Continent

Middle East

New Zealand

South Africa

South America

Former Soviet Republics

United Kingdom

COMPUTER ENGINEERING

Any Country

African Nations

Australia

Canada

East European Countries

EC Countries

Far East

Indian Sub-Continent

Middle East

New Zealand

South Africa

South America

Former Soviet Republics

United Kingdom

INDUSTRIAL AND MANAGEMENT ENGINEERING

Any Country

African Nations

Australia

Canada

East European Countries

EC Countries

Far East

Indian Sub-Continent

Middle East

New Zealand

South Africa

South America

Former Soviet Republics

United Kingdom

METALLURGICAL ENGINEERING

Any Country

African Nations

Australia

Canada

East European Countries

EC Countries

Far East

PRODUCTION ENGINEERING

MATERIALS ENGINEERING

MINING AND MINERALS ENGINEERING

PETROLEUM ENGINEERING

ENERGY ENGINEERING

NUCLEAR ENGINEERING

MECHANICAL/ELECTROMECHANICAL ENGINEERING

HYDRAULIC/PNEUMATIC ENGINEERING

SOUND ENGINEERING

AUTOMOTIVE ENGINEERING

MEASUREMENT/PRECISION ENGINEERING

CONTROL ENGINEERING (ROBOTICS)

AERONAUTICAL AND AEROSPACE ENGINEERING

MARINE ENGINEERING AND NAVAL ARCHITECTURE

AGRICULTURAL ENGINEERING

BIOENGINEERING AND BIOMEDICAL ENGINEERING

FINE AND APPLIED ARTS

GENERAL

African Nations

Australia

Canada

East European Countries

HISTORY AND PHILOSOPHY OF ART

Canada

EC Countries

United Kingdom

United States

JAZZ AND POPULAR MUSIC

Any Country

OPERA

Any Country

United States

DRAMA

Any Country

Far East

New Zealand

United States

DANCING

Any Country

Far East

United States

PHOTOGRAPHY

Any Country

Australia

Far East

HOME ECONOMICS

GENERAL

NUTRITION

Any Country

LAW

GENERAL

HISTORY OF LAW

CONSTITUTIONAL LAW

Any Country

ADMINISTRATIVE LAW

Canada

United States

CRIMINAL LAW

Any Country

Canada

East European Countries

Far East

Former Soviet Republics

United Kingdom

EUROPEAN COMMUNITY LAW

Any Country

Canada

United States

MASS COMMUNICATION AND INFORMATION SCIENCE

GENERAL

Any Country

African Nations

Australia

Canada

East European Countries

JOURNALISM

Any Country

MATHEMATICS AND COMPUTER SCIENCE

GENERAL

African Nations

Australia

Canada

East European Countries

West European non-EC Countries

STATISTICS

APPLIED MATHEMATICS

COMPUTER SCIENCE

ARTIFICIAL INTELLIGENCE

SYSTEMS ANALYSIS

MEDICAL SCIENCES

GENERAL

African Nations

Australia

PUBLIC HEALTH AND HYGIENE

SOCIAL/PREVENTIVE MEDICINE

BIOLOGICAL AND LIFE SCIENCES

PHARMACOLOGY

PHYSIOLOGY

TOXICOLOGY

ZOOLOGY

CHEMISTRY

Lindemann Trust Fellowships 309

Canada
ACS - PRF Type AC Grants 132
ACS - PRF Type B Grants 132
British (General) Fellowship 499
Corday-Morgan Memorial Fund 528
Lindemann Trust Fellowships 309
Sloan (Alfred P) Foundation Research Fellowships 541

East European Countries
ACS - PRF Type AC Grants 132

West European non-EC Countries
ACS - PRF Type AC Grants 132

EC Countries
ACS - PRF Type AC Grants 132
EPSRC Research Studentships 306

Far East
ACS - PRF Type AC Grants 132
British (General) Fellowship 499
Corday-Morgan Memorial Fund 528
Lindemann Trust Fellowships 309

Indian Sub-Continent
British (General) Fellowship 499
Corday-Morgan Memorial Fund 528
Lindemann Trust Fellowships 309

New Zealand
ACS - PRF Type AC Grants 132
Australian National University - Kodak Research Scholarship 620
Australian National University - PhD Research Scholarship...... 620
British (General) Fellowship 499
Corday-Morgan Memorial Fund 528
Lindemann Trust Fellowships 309

South Africa
ACS - PRF Type AC Grants 132
AECI Postgraduate Research Fellowship.................. 120
British (General) Fellowship 499
Corday-Morgan Memorial Fund 528
Lindemann Trust Fellowships 309

South America
ACS - PRF Type AC Grants 132

United Kingdom
ACS - PRF Type AC Grants 132
British (General) Fellowship 499
Corday-Morgan Memorial Fund 528
EPSRC Research Studentships 306
Lindemann Trust Fellowships 309
Musgrave Research Studentships 498

United States
ACS - PRF Type AC Grants 132
ACS - PRF Type B Grants 132
COBASE- Collaboration in Basic Science and Engineering (long term) 458
COBASE-Collaboration in Basic Science and Engineering 459
Hertz (Fannie and John) Foundation Fellowships.............. 350
McDonnell Astronaut Fellowship in the Space Sciences......... 411
Sloan (Alfred P) Foundation Research Fellowships 541

ANALYTICAL CHEMISTRY

Any Country
CIRES Visiting Fellowships............................... 284
JILA Postdoctoral Research Associateship and Visiting Fellowships 395

Krasnoyarsk State Academy Scholarship 402

INORGANIC CHEMISTRY

Any Country
Manipur University Scholar 414

New Zealand
Australian National University - PhD Research Scholarship...... 620

ORGANIC CHEMISTRY

Any Country
Ciba Foundation Symposium Bursaries 273
Ichikizaki Fund for Young Chemists 256
Manipur University Scholar.............................. 414
Wieland (Heinrich) Prize 213

New Zealand
Australian National University - PhD Research Scholarship...... 620

United Kingdom
Hickenbottom/Briggs Fellowship 529

PHYSICAL CHEMISTRY

Any Country
CIRES Visiting Fellowships............................... 284
JILA Postdoctoral Research Associateship and Visiting Fellowships 395
Manipur University Scholar.............................. 414
Welch Foundation Scholarship 390

EARTH AND GEOLOGICAL SCIENCES

Any Country
ACS - PRF Type G 'Starter' Grants........................ 133
American Association of Petroleum Geologists Grant-in-Aid 131
American Museum of Natural History Collection Study Grants.... 152
American Museum of Natural History Research and Museum Fellowships 153
Atomic Energy of Canada Ltd Research Associateships 197
Farmy (Hossein) Scholarships 616
Helmich (Janson Johan) Scholarships and Travel Grants 392
Royal Society European Science Exchange Programme........ 521
SEG Scholarships 557
Smithsonian Institution Graduate Student Fellowships.......... 542
Smithsonian Institution Senior Fellowships.................. 543
Stone (Ralph W) Graduate Research Award 462
Targeted Research Awards: Competitive Industry Theme 322
Vickery (Joyce W) Scientific Research Fund 410

African Nations
Association of Commonwealth Universities Development Fellowships 191

Australia
ACS - PRF Type AC Grants 132
Association of Commonwealth Universities Development Fellowships 191

Canada
ACS - PRF Type AC Grants 132
ACS - PRF Type B Grants 132
Association of Commonwealth Universities Development Fellowships 191
Emergency Preparedness Canada Research Fellowship in Honour of Stuart Nesbitt White 194

East European Countries
ACS - PRF Type AC Grants 132

NATURAL SCIENCES

RECREATION, WELFARE, PROTECTIVE SERVICES

GENERAL

POLICE AND LAW ENFORCEMENT

United Kingdom

CRIMINOLOGY

Any Country

MILITARY SCIENCE

New Zealand

PEACE AND DISARMAMENT

Any Country

WILDLIFE AND PEST MANAGEMENT

New Zealand

United States

PHYSICAL EDUCATION AND SPORTS

Any Country

United States

RELIGION AND THEOLOGY

GENERAL

Any Country

African Nations

Australia

Canada

East European Countries

West European non-EC Countries

RELIGIOUS STUDIES

Any Country

CHRISTIAN

Any Country

Canada

United States

COOKING AND CATERING

Any Country

TOURISM

Any Country

African Nations

East European Countries

Far East

Indian Sub-Continent

Middle East

South Africa

South America

Former Soviet Republics

SOCIAL AND BEHAVIOURAL SCIENCES

GENERAL

Any Country

African Nations

Australia

Canada

East European Countries

West European non-EC Countries

TRADE, CRAFT AND INDUSTRIAL TECHNIQUES

GENERAL

BUILDING TRADES

United States

ELECTRICAL/ELECTRONIC EQUIPMENT AND MAINTENANCE TECHNIQUES

United States

METAL TRADES TECHNIQUES

United States

MECHANICAL EQUIPMENT AND MAINTENANCE TECHNIQUES

United States

HEATING, AIR CONDITIONING AND REFRIGERATION TECHNOLOGY

Any Country

GRAPHIC ARTS TECHNIQUES

Any Country

PRINTING

Any Country

PUBLISHING AND BOOK TRADE

Any Country

TRANSPORT AND COMMUNICATIONS

GENERAL

Any Country

African Nations

Australia

Canada

East European Countries

AIR TRANSPORT

MARINE TRANSPORT AND NAUTICAL SCIENCE

RAILWAY TRANSPORT

ROAD TRANSPORT

TRANSPORT MANAGEMENT

TRANSPORT ECONOMICS

THE GRANTS REGISTER

AAUW EDUCATIONAL FOUNDATION

AAUW Educational Foundation, PO Box 4030, Iowa City, IA, 52243, USA
Tel: 319 337 1716
www: www.aauw.org

American Fellowships

Subjects: All subjects.

Eligibility: Applicants must be US citizens.

Level of Study: Doctorate, Postdoctorate.

Purpose: To offset a scholar's living expenses while she completes her final year of dissertation writing; or, to increase the number of women in tenure-track faculty positions and promote equality for women in higher education.

Type: Fellowship.

Frequency: Annual.

Value: US$14,500 for the Dissertation Fellowship; US$20,000-US$25,000 for Postdoctoral Fellowship; and US$5,000 for the Summer Fellowship.

Length of Study: One year.

Country of Study: USA.

Applications Procedure: Application package includes an application form, narrative autobiography, CV, statement of project, transcripts, three letters of recommendation and a filing fee.

Closing Date: November 15th.

International Fellowships Program

Subjects: All areas of study.

Eligibility: Open to women who are not US citizens or permanent residents. Must hold a US bachelor's degree or equivalent. Must be planning to return to their home country upon completion of degree/research. English proficiency required.

Level of Study: Postgraduate, Doctorate, Postdoctorate, Professional development.

Purpose: To award women who are not US citizens or permanent residents studying at the graduate or postgraduate level or for research beyond the bachelor's level. These women must have the intention to return to their home countries upon the completion of their degree/research. Preference is given to applicants who provide verification of a career position upon their return home.

Type: Fellowship.

No. of awards offered: 42.

Frequency: Annual.

Value: $US15,065.

Length of Study: One year.

Study Establishment: Any accredited institution.

Country of Study: USA.

Applications Procedure: Application must be filled out for each year applying. Applications must be obtained through our customer service centre in Iowa (AUWW Educational Foundation, PO Box 4030, Iowa City, IA 52243: phone 319 337 1716) between August 1st and November 15th. Application postmark deadline December 2nd. Three letters of recommendation, transcripts, TOEFL scores (min 550) are also required.

Closing Date: Application request: November 15th; application postmark: December 2nd.

Additional Information: These awards are non-renewable.

ACADEMY OF MARKETING SCIENCE FOUNDATION

AMS Executive Office, University of Miami, PO Box 248012, Coral Gables, FL, 33124, USA
Tel: 305 284 6673
Fax: 305 284 3762
Contact: Harold W Berkman

*Alpha Kappa Psi Doctoral Dissertation

Subjects: Marketing.

Eligibility: Open to individuals of any nationality.

Purpose: To recognize a research contribution to the discipline of marketing.

Type: Prize.

No. of awards offered: Two.

Frequency: Annual.

Value: 1st Prize US$1,000; 2nd Prize US$500.

Country of Study: Any country.

Closing Date: December 1st.

*Dr M Wayne DeLozier Best Paper Award

Subjects: Marketing.

Eligibility: Open to individuals of any nationality.

Purpose: To recognize a research contribution to the discipline of marketing.

Type: Fellowship.

No. of awards offered: One.

Frequency: Annual.

Value: US$500.

Country of Study: Any country.

Closing Date: December 1st.

*Mary Kay Doctoral Dissertation Award

Subjects: In areas related to the discipline of marketing, i.e. buyer behavior, channels of distribution, advertising and promotion, etc.

Eligibility: Open to individuals of any nationality.

Level of Study: Doctorate.

Purpose: To recognize a research contribution to the discipline of marketing.

No. of awards offered: One.

Frequency: Annual.

Value: US$500 cash prize; conference registration fee waived.

Country of Study: Any country.

Closing Date: December 1st.

*Dr Jagdish N Sheth Best Article Award for the Journal of the Academy of Marketing Science

Subjects: Marketing.

Eligibility: Open to individuals of any nationality.

Purpose: To recognize a research contribution to the discipline of marketing.

No. of awards offered: One.

Frequency: Annual.

Value: US$1,000.

Country of Study: Any country.

Closing Date: December 1st.

ACADEMY OF MOTION PICTURE ARTS AND SCIENCES

Academy of Motion Picture Arts and Sciences, 8949 Wilshire
Boulevard, Beverly Hills, CA, 90211-1972, USA
Tel: 213 247 3059
www: http://www.oscars.org

Don and Gee Nicholl Fellowships in Screenwriting

Subjects: Screenwriting.

Eligibility: Open to writers in English who have not sold or optioned a screen or teleplay or the story for a screen or teleplay.

Purpose: To foster the development of new writers.

Type: Fellowship.

No. of awards offered: Up to five.

Frequency: Annual.

Value: US$25,000.

Applications Procedure: Send a stamped, self-addressed business-size envelope for further details.

Closing Date: May 1st.

Additional Information: The Fellowships are not to be used to pursue undergraduate or graduate college degrees. In addition to the Academy Awards or Oscars (no monetary value) and the Nicholl Fellowships, the Academy offers Student Film Awards for films completed by students at an accredited college or university.

ACADEMY OF NATURAL SCIENCES

Academy of Natural Sciences, 1900 Benjamin Franklin Parkway,
Philadelphia, PA, 19103-1195, USA
Tel: 215 299 1000
Fax: 215 299 1028
Contact: Dr A E Schuyler, Chairman

Jessup and McHenry Awards

Subjects: Jessup award is non-specific. McHenry award is for Botany.

Eligibility: Students commuting within the Philadelphia area are ineligible.

Level of Study: Postgraduate, Doctorate, Postdoctorate.

Purpose: These awards are intended to assist predoctoral and postdoctoral students within several years of receiving their PhDs.

Type: Travel costs and stipends, Grant.

Frequency: Annual.

Value: Round trip travel costs up to a total of US$500, for North American (including Mexico and the Caribbean) applicants, and US$1,000 for applicants form other parts of the world, are allowed. The stipend for subsistence is US$250, per week.

Length of Study: Two to 16 weeks.

Study Establishment: Academy of Natural Sciences.

Country of Study: USA.

Applications Procedure: Send queries, requests for information and supporting information to the given address.

Closing Date: March 1st, November 31st.

Additional Information: The provision of scientific supplies and equipment is the responsibility of the student and the sponsoring curator.

ACADEMY OF SCIENCES OF THE CZECH REPUBLIC

UNESCO-ROSTE Course, Institute of Microbiology, Academy of
Sciences of the Czech Republic, Videnská 1083, 142 20 Prague 4,
Czech Republic
Tel: 422 475 2379
Fax: 422 475 2384
Email: nerud@biomed.cas.cz

Long-term Postgraduate Training Course on Modern Problems in Biology and Microbial Technology

Subjects: Microbiology (physiology and biochemistry of microorganisms, microbial ecology, molecular biology, bioengineering, immunology).

Eligibility: Open especially to young scientists from Central and Eastern European countries and a limited number of students from other regions, who hold an MSc, PhD or equivalent degree, and who have two to three years' practical experience in their field. Candidates should be not more than 35 years of age, and should possess a good knowledge of English.

Level of Study: Postgraduate.

Purpose: To enable young scientists to obtain a more profound education and methodical preparation for a research career.

Type: Training.

No. of awards offered: 15.

Frequency: Annual.

Value: 3,200-3,600 Czech crowns, plus lodging.

Length of Study: 11 months.

Study Establishment: Institutes and laboratories of the Academy of Sciences of the Czech Republic.

Country of Study: Czech Republic.

Applications Procedure: Application form must be completed.

Closing Date: March 31st.

Additional Information: The Courses are given in cooperation with the Czech Commission for UNESCO, and sponsored by UNESCO-ROSTE and Academy of Sciences of the Czech Republic.

ACTION RESEARCH

Action Research, Vincent House, North Parade, Horsham, West
Sussex, RH12 2DA, England
Tel: 01403 210406
Fax: 01403 210541
Contact: Dr Kate Walsh, MA PhD

Capital Grants

Subjects: With the exception of cancer, cardiovascular and HIV/AIDS research, the charity supports basic and clinical research leading to the (a) prevention of disability, regardless of cause or age group, with an emphasis on genetic and developmental factors, and (b) alleviation of existing physical handicap.

Eligibility: Open only to researchers in the UK.

Level of Study: Unrestricted.

Purpose: To assist the erection of research laboratories or the provision of a major item of research equipment.

Type: Grants.

No. of awards offered: Variable.

Frequency: Varies.

Value: Varies.

Country of Study: UK.

Applications Procedure: Completed application form must be submitted by the closing date.

Closing Date: March 15, July 20, November 15.

Additional Information: The assessment period is dependent on the scale and complexity of the application.

Longer-Term Grants

Subjects: With the exception of cancer, cardiovascular and HIV/AIDS research, the charity supports basic and clinical research leading to the (a) prevention of disability, regardless of cause or age group, with an emphasis on genetic and developmental factors, and (b) alleviation of existing physical handicap.

Eligibility: Open only to researchers in the UK.

Purpose: To create and/or maintain a research department or research unit by funding the core staff.

Type: Grant.

No. of awards offered: Variable.

Frequency: Varies.

Value: Varies.

Length of Study: At least five years.

Country of Study: UK.

Applications Procedure: Completed application forms must be submitted by the closing date.

Closing Date: March 15th, July 20th, November 15th.

Additional Information: Assessment usually takes one year.

Programme Grants

Subjects: With the exception of cancer, cardiovascular and HIV/AIDS research, the charity supports basic and clinical research leading to the (a) prevention of disability, regardless of cause or age group, with an emphasis on genetic and developmental factors, and (b) alleviation of existing physical handicap.

Eligibility: Open only to researchers in the UK.

Purpose: To support coherent proposals based on an established line of enquiry.

Type: Grant.

No. of awards offered: Variable.

Frequency: Varies.

Value: Varies.

Length of Study: Normally for five years, possibly renewable.

Country of Study: UK.

Closing Date: March 15th, July 20th, November 15th.

Additional Information: Assessment usually takes one year.

Project Grants

Subjects: With the exception of cancer, cardiovascular and HIV/AIDS research, the charity supports basic and clinical research leading to the (a) prevention of disability, regardless of cause or age group, with an emphasis on genetic and developmental factors, and (b) alleviation of existing physical handicap.

Eligibility: Open only to researchers in the UK. No grants are made for higher education.

Purpose: To support one precisely formulated line of research.

Type: Grant.

No. of awards offered: Variable.

Frequency: Three times yearly.

Value: Varies.

Length of Study: Up to three years; assessed every four months.

Country of Study: UK.

Applications Procedure: Completed application forms to be submitted by the closing date.

Closing Date: March 15th, July 20th, November 15th.

Research Training Fellowship

Subjects: With the exception of cancer, cardiovascular and HIV/AIDS research, the charity supports basic and clinical research leading to the (a) prevention of disability, regardless of cause or age group, with an emphasis on genetic and developmental factors, and (b) alleviation of existing physical handicap.

Eligibility: Open to medical and non-medical graduates, usually between 23-32 years old, in the UK. Although not limited to UK citizens, consideration will only be given to those applicants from abroad who are to remain in the UK following the period of training.

Level of Study: Postgraduate, Doctorate, Professional development.

Purpose: To enable the training of young medical and non-medical graduates in research techniques and methodology in areas of interest to the charity.

Type: Fellowship.

No. of awards offered: Variable.

Frequency: Annual.

Value: Varies.

Length of Study: Up to three years.

Country of Study: UK.

Applications Procedure: The appropriate application should be submitted.

Closing Date: Last friday in January.

Additional Information: Fellowships are advertised separately each year in November.

THE ADA ENDOWMENT AND ASSISTANCE FUND, INC

The ADA Endowment and Assistance Fund, Inc, 211 East Chicago Avenue, Chicago, IL, 60611-2678, USA
Tel: 312 440 2567
Fax: 312 440 2822
Contact: Ms Marsha L Mountz

Allied Dental Health Scholarship (Hygiene, Assisting, Laboratory Technology)

Subjects: Dental technology.

Eligibility: Open to US citizens only.

Level of Study: Professional development.

Purpose: To defray school expenses which include tuition, fees, books, supplies and living expenses.

Type: Scholarship.

No. of awards offered: 45.

Frequency: Annual.

Value: US$1,000.

Country of Study: USA.

Applications Procedure: Application forms are available at allied health programs and are disbursed by school officials. Application forms must be original, typed, current academic year, completed and signed with the help of school officials. Forms must be embossed with school's official seal on the academic achievement record form.

Closing Date: August 15th (Hygiene Lab.Tech) or September 15th (Assisting).

Dental Student Scholarship

Subjects: Dentistry.

Eligibility: Open to US citizens only.

Level of Study: Postgraduate.

Purpose: To defray school expenses which include tuition, fees, books, supplies and living expenses..

Type: Scholarship.

No. of awards offered: 25.

Frequency: Annual.

Value: US$2,500.

Country of Study: USA.

Applications Procedure: Application forms are available at dental schools. Application forms must be original, typed, current academic year, completed and signed with the assistance of school officials. Forms must be embossed with schools official seal on the academic achievement record form.

Closing Date: June 15th.

Minority Dental Student Scholarship

Subjects: Dentistry.

Eligibility: Applicants must be a member of one of the following groups: Black African American, Native American or Hispanic.

Level of Study: Postgraduate.

Purpose: To defray school expenses which include tuition, fees, books, supplies and living expenses.

Type: Scholarship.

No. of awards offered: 25.

Frequency: Annual.

Value: US$2,000.

Country of Study: USA.

Applications Procedure: Application forms are available at dental schools and disbursed by school officials. Applications must be original, typed, current academic year, completed and signed with the assistance of school officials. Forms must be embossed with schools official seal on the academic achievement record form.

Closing Date: July 1st.

AECI LIMITED

AECI Limited, PO Box 1122, Johannesburg, 2000, South Africa
Tel: 011 223 9111
Contact: The Scholarships Officer

Postgraduate Research Fellowship

Subjects: Chemistry, physics, metallurgy, biochemistry, microbiology; chemical, civil, industrial, electrical, mechanical or instrument engineering; accountancy, business science, economics; pure, applied and statistical mathematics; computer and social sciences.

Eligibility: Open to South African citizens with four-year or higher degree, towards a masters or doctorate degree.

Level of Study: Postgraduate, Doctorate.

Purpose: To strengthen postgraduate study and research in South Africa, particularly in the fields in which AECI has interests.

Type: Fellowship.

No. of awards offered: Varies.

Frequency: Annual.

Value: Annual allowance which is sufficient to cover all fees, equipment, books, etc. The Fellow is responsible for own university fees.

Length of Study: Two years; renewable for up to one further year, subject to satisfactory progress.

Study Establishment: Any recognized university in South Africa.

Country of Study: South Africa.

Applications Procedure: Application form must be completed and submitted with academic results and references.

Closing Date: September 30th.

Additional Information: Research projects will preferably be in line with AECI interests and will bring Fellowship holders into contact with AECI staff. The orientation of the project thus suggests that Fellowship holders will be readily eligible and will certainly be considered for employment in AECI on completion of their studies. However, the granting of a Fellowship implies no obligation on either party to the other.

AFRICA EDUCATIONAL TRUST

Africa Educational Trust, 38 King Street, London, WC2E 8JS, England
Tel: 0171 836 5075/7940
Fax: 0171 379 0090
Email: mbrophy@aet.win-uk.net
Contact: Dr M Brophy

Emergency Grants

Subjects: Unrestricted and at all levels.

Eligibility: Open to students from Africa studying in the UK. The applicant must have run into unexpected difficulties at the end of his/her course for which the small level of grant will, by itself or in conjunction with other grants, solve the problem. Most awards are made on a humanitarian basis. Academic considerations are more important at the postgraduate and research levels.

Level of Study: Unrestricted.

Purpose: To provide one-off grants on an emergency basis to students from Africa studying in the UK.

Type: Emergency Grant.

No. of awards offered: 10-15.

Frequency: Monthly.

Value: £100-£600.

Country of Study: UK.

Additional Information: Applications should be made by post or via a third party (such as a student welfare officer). Emergency Grants are provided at any time of year. The Trust will also consider contributions towards conference fees.

For further information contact:
Africa Educational Trust, 38 King Street, London, WC2E 8JS, England
Tel: 0171 836 5075
Fax: 0171 379 0090
Email: mbrophy@aet.win-uk.net
Contact: Director, Small Grants Project

Scholarships

Subjects: All subjects, but emphasis on those linked or relevant to development.

Eligibility: Open to people of African descent. The Scholarships are aimed mainly at refugees from Africa.

Level of Study: Postgraduate.

Purpose: To fund general education, mainly of refugees from Africa.

Type: Scholarship.

No. of awards offered: Varies, but depends on funding.

Frequency: Annually, but dependent on funds available.

Value: Full and partial Scholarships awarded: full may cover fees, maintenance, transport, and fieldwork costs.

Country of Study: EC countries but mainly UK.

AFRICAN NETWORK OF SCIENTIFIC AND TECHNOLOGICAL INSTITUTIONS

African Network of Scientific and Technological Institutions, PO Box 30592, Nairobi, Kenya
Tel: 254 2 622620
Fax: 254 2 215991
Email: J.MASSAQUOI@UNESCO.ORG
Telex: 22275
Contact: Professor J G M Massaquoi

Postgraduate Fellowships

Subjects: Engineering and science.

Eligibility: Open to African nationals only.

Level of Study: Postgraduate, Postdoctorate.

Purpose: To enable students to pursue master's and PhD courses in the basic and engineering sciences.

Type: Fellowship.

Frequency: Annual, depending on funds available.

Value: $12,000.

Length of Study: 18 months.

Country of Study: African countries.

Applications Procedure: Application form must be completed.

Closing Date: July 31st.

Additional Information: The applicant is responsible for gaining admission into the university of his/her choice. Preference is given to graduates with a few years' experience.

AFRO-ASIAN INSTITUTE IN VIENNA AND CATHOLIC WOMEN'S LEAGUE OF AUSTRIA

Student Division, Afro-Asian Institute in Vienna, Türkenstrasse 3, Vienna, A-1090, Austria
Tel: 0222 31 05 145 213
Fax: 0222 31 05 145 312
Email: aai.wien@magnet.at.internet
Contact: Dr Ruth Gamsjäger or Mag Markus Pleschko

Scholarships

Subjects: Any subject.

Eligibility: Open to nationals of developing countries in Africa, Asia and Latin America who are between the ages of 18 and 35 and have had adequate previous study or vocational practice in the specific field for which the Scholarship is applied.

Level of Study: Unrestricted.

Purpose: To promote cultural exchange, international development and international cooperation aid.

Type: Scholarship.

No. of awards offered: Variable.

Frequency: Annual.

Value: 2,500 - 7,500 Austrian Schillings monthly.

Study Establishment: Universities (Vienna, Linz, Innsbruck).

Country of Study: Austria.

Applications Procedure: Contact the Institute for application form.

Closing Date: 1 - 30 April for the following academic year.

Additional Information: It is preferred that candidates be able to speak German. Only those in financial need will be considered, and applicability of the special branch of study or training in the applicant's home country is essential. It is expected that scholars will return to their home country after studying. Good, and sometimes excellent, study results are also required. Preference is given to applicants from the least developed countries. It is one of AAI's essential aims to establish a 'partnership' contact between assisted students and the Scholarship donor which continues beyond the termination of studies. Only personal applications will be considered. Only about 10% of the applicants can be accepted. Only written applications are accepted.

AGRICULTURAL HISTORY SOCIETY

Center for Agricultural History, 603 Ross, Iowa State University, Ames, IA, 50011-1202, USA
Tel: 515 294 5620
Fax: 515 294 6390
Email: rdhurt@iastate.edu
Contact: R. Douglas Hurt, Editor

Vernon Carstenson Award in Agricultural History

Subjects: Agricultural history as broadly defined.

Eligibility: Open to any author who wishes to enter an article published in the quarterly journal Agricultural History.

Level of Study: Doctorate, Postdoctorate.

Purpose: To promote research and publication.

No. of awards offered: One.

Frequency: Annual.

Value: US$200.

Country of Study: Any country.

Applications Procedure: All published articles per issue and year are considered.

Closing Date: The December issue of the journal of each year.

Theodore Sabutos Award

Subjects: Agricultural history.

Eligibility: Open to nationals of any country.

Purpose: To award the best book published annually in USA agricultural history.

Type: Prize.

Frequency: Annual.

Value: US$500.

Applications Procedure: Send four copies of the book to the Editor (details as shown).

For further information contact:
Agricultural History Society, 603 Ross, Iowa State University, Ames, IA, 50011-1202, USA
Tel: 515 294 5620
Fax: 515 294 6390
Email: rdhurt@iastate.edu
Contact: R. Douglas Hurt, Editor

AGRICULTURAL RESEARCH COUNCIL OF NORWAY

The Research Council of Norway, PO Box 2700, St Hanshaugen, Oslo, 0130, Norway
Tel: 47 22 03 7000
Fax: 47 22 03 7104

Contact: Liv Jenssen Daling

Senior Scientist Visiting Programme

Subjects: Agriculture, forestry, veterinary medicine, and related fields.

Eligibility: Open to well-established and internationally recognized scientists who are at the professional or equivalent level.

Purpose: To enable Norwegian research institutions to receive foreign scientists to participate in research groups, discuss research arrangements and give lectures within their special fields.

No. of awards offered: On average 2-10 grants.

Frequency: Annual.

Value: NOK20,000 per month for the first two months, NOK15,000 for the third month and NOK10,000 per month thereafter. Travelling expenses may also be defrayed.

Length of Study: Up to six months.

Country of Study: Norway.

Applications Procedure: A scientist who wishes to come to Norway will have to contact one of the departments at the Agricultural University of Norway, the Norwegian College of Veterinary Medicine or one of the independent agricultural research institutions, at the addresses shown. The department/institution may then submit an application to the Research Council on behalf of the scientist.

Closing Date: April 1st and October 1st.

For further information contact:
Agricultural University of Norway (NLH), PO Box 5003, N-1432 AS, Norway
Tel: 64 94 7500
Fax: 64 94 7505

or

Norwegian Forest Research Institute (NISK), Hegsholem 12, N-1430 AS, Norway
Tel: 64 94 9000
Fax: 64 94 2980

or

Norwegian Plant Protection Institute, Fellesbygget, N-1432 AS, Norway
Tel: 64 94 9400
Fax: 64 94 9226

or

MATFORSK Norwegian Food Research Institute, Osloveien 1, N-1430 AS, Norway
Tel: 64 97 0100
Fax: 64 97 0333

or

The Norwegian State Agricultural Research Stations (SFL), PO Box 100, N-1430 AS, Norway
Tel: 64 94 2060
Fax: 64 94 2229

or

Norwegian Agricultural Economics Research Institute (NILF), PO Box 8024 Dep, Oslo, N-0030 1, Norway
Tel: 22 17 3540
Fax: 22 17 3538

or

NLVF-Institute of Aquaculture Research (AKVAFORSK) A/S, PO Box 5010, N-1432 AS, Norway
Tel: 64 94 9532
Fax: 64 94 9502

or

JORDFORSK Centre for Soil and Environmental Research, Jordforskbygget, N-1432, Norway

Tel: 64 94 8154
Fax: 64 94 8110

or

Norwegian College of Veterinary Medicine (NVH), PO Box 8146 Dep, Oslo, N 003301, Norway
Tel: 22 96 4505

or

National Veterinary Institute (VI), PO Box 8156 Dep, Oslo, N 0033 1, Norway
Tel: 22 96 4613
Fax: 22 46 0034

EDWARD F ALBEE FOUNDATION, INC

Edward F Albee Foundation, Inc, 14 Harrison Street, New York, NY, 10013, USA
Tel: 212 226 2020
Contact: Foundation Secretary

William Flanagan Memorial Creative Persons Center

Subjects: Writing; painting.

Eligibility: Open to artists and writers of talent and need.

Level of Study: Unrestricted.

Purpose: To provide accommodation.

Type: Accommodation only.

No. of awards offered: 18 places.

Frequency: Annual.

Value: No financial aid or grants; accommodation only.

Length of Study: Four months between June 1st and October 1st.

Study Establishment: The Center in Montauk, Long Island.

Country of Study: USA.

Applications Procedure: Application form must be completed. Forms are available upon request, and should be accompanied by a pre-paid return envelope. Other materials are also required - please write for further details.

Closing Date: January 1st to April 1st.

Additional Information: The environment is communal and residents are expected to do their share in maintaining the conditions of the Center.

ALBERTA HERITAGE FOUNDATION FOR MEDICAL RESEARCH

Alberta Heritage Foundation for Medical Research, 3125 Manulife Place, 10180-101 Street, Edmonton, Alberta, T5J 3S4, Canada
Tel: 403 423 5727
Fax: 403 429 3509
Contact: Grants Administration

Full-Time Fellowships

Subjects: Medical research.

Eligibility: Open to graduates of science programs relevant to AHFMR objectives or of health progressional programs who received the PhD not more than five years prior to application. Professional health degrees should not have been received more than ten years prior to application.

Level of Study: Postdoctorate.

Purpose: To enable doctoral graduates to prepare for careers as independent investigators.

Type: Fellowship.

No. of awards offered: One.

Frequency: Twice yearly.

Value: C$2,000 research allowance plus stipend.

Study Establishment: Normally at an Alberta university.

Country of Study: Canada.

Applications Procedure: Application forms must be submitted by the deadline.

Closing Date: March 1st; October 1st.

Heritage Clinical Fellowships

Subjects: Medical research.

Eligibility: Open to candidates who hold an MD or DDS and have received a significant portion of postgraduate training in Alberta.

Level of Study: Post MD,DDS.

Purpose: To provide an opportunity for research training to candidates who have completed clinical subspecialty training requirements.

Type: Fellowship.

No. of awards offered: Approximately ten.

Frequency: Twice yearly.

Value: C$3,000 research allowance, plus stipend.

Study Establishment: An appropriate institution, normally in Alberta.

Country of Study: Canada.

Applications Procedure: Application form must be completed.

Closing Date: March 1st; October 1st.

Heritage Clinical Investigatorships

Subjects: Medical research.

Eligibility: Open to candidates who hold an MD or DDS, have completed all requirements for clinical speciality recognition, and who are eligible to hold a full-time position in a clinical department of the sponsoring institution.

Level of Study: Professional development.

Purpose: To provide funding for highly qualified clinicians to further their research experience beyond the fellowship level in a setting providing guidance and supervision by an established scientist.

Type: Investigatorship.

No. of awards offered: One.

Frequency: Annual.

Value: A stipend plus an establishment grant; values are negotiated individually.

Length of Study: Three years, may be extended for a further three years.

Study Establishment: An Alberta university or an affiliated hospital/institution.

Country of Study: Canada.

Applications Procedure: Application form must be completed.

Closing Date: September 15th.

Additional Information: Candidates must be prepared to commit up to 75% of their time to medical research.

Heritage Full-Time Studentships

Subjects: Medical research.

Eligibility: Open to academically superior students who wish to undertake full-time graduate studies in a discipline relevant to AHFMR objectives.

Level of Study: Graduate.

Type: Studentships.

No. of awards offered: 50-70.

Frequency: Twice yearly.

Value: C$15,500 stipend plus C$1,000 research allowance.

Length of Study: One year; renewable four times.

Study Establishment: An Alberta university.

Country of Study: Canada.

Applications Procedure: Application form must be completed.

Closing Date: March 1st; October 1st.

Heritage Medical Scholarships

Subjects: Medical Research.

Eligibility: Open to candidates who hold an MD, DDS, DVM or PhD (or equivalent) in a discipline important to AHFMR objectives and are eligible for a full-time appointment at the sponsoring institution.

Level of Study: Professional development.

Purpose: To assist in the recruitment and establishment of scientists in Alberta.

Type: Scholarship.

No. of awards offered: One.

Frequency: Annual.

Value: Stipend plus establishment grant; negotiated individually.

Length of Study: Five years; renewable once only.

Study Establishment: An Alberta university or affiliate.

Country of Study: Canada.

Applications Procedure: Application form must be completed.

Closing Date: September 15th.

Additional Information: Up to 75% of the candidate's time may be devoted to medical research.

Heritage Medical Scientist Awards

Subjects: Medical research.

Eligibility: Open to candidates who hold an MD, DDS, DVM or PhD (or equivalent) in a discipline important to AHFMR objectives and are eligible for a full-time appointment at the sponsoring institution.

Level of Study: Professional development.

Purpose: To assist in the recruitment and establishment of nationally or internationally recognized medical scientists in Alberta.

Type: Award.

No. of awards offered: One.

Frequency: Annual.

Value: Stipend plus establishment grant; negotiated individually.

Length of Study: Five years; renewable.

Study Establishment: An Alberta university or affiliate.

Country of Study: Canada.

Applications Procedure: Application form must be completed.

Closing Date: October 1st.

Additional Information: Up to 75% of the candidate's time may be devoted to medical research.

Heritage Part-Time Fellowships

Subjects: Medical research.

Eligibility: Open to graduates holding a PhD in a science relevant to AHFMR objectives or who are registered in a health professional program in Alberta.

Level of Study: Postdoctorate.

Purpose: To enable continuing active participation in research during professional education.

Type: Fellowship.

No. of awards offered: Approximately 15.

Frequency: Twice yearly.

Value: C$6,000 plus C$1,000 research allowance.

Length of Study: One year; renewable.

Study Establishment: An Alberta university.

Country of Study: Canada.

Applications Procedure: Application form must be completed.

Closing Date: March 1st; October 1st.

Heritage Part-Time Studentship

Subjects: Medical research.

Eligibility: Open to students enrolled in a full-time professional degree program who wish to continue research training on a part-time basis during the regular academic year.

Level of Study: Graduate.

Type: Studentship.

No. of awards offered: One.

Frequency: Twice yearly.

Value: C$3,100 (honorarium).

Length of Study: One year; renewable twice.

Study Establishment: An Alberta university.

Country of Study: Canada.

Applications Procedure: Application form must be completed.

Closing Date: March 1st; October 1st.

Additional Information: The Foundation also offers the 'Visiting Professor' and 'Visiting Scientist Awards', which primarily provide travel assistance, as well as a number of awards for individuals currently resident in Alberta.

ALCAN ALUMINIUM LIMITED

Alcan Aluminium Limited, 1188 Sherbrooke Street West, Montreal, Quebec, H3A 3G2, Canada
Tel: 514 848 8494
Fax: 514 848 1536
Contact: Chairman, Central Donations Committee

*Alcan Fellowship in Industrial Relations

Subjects: Industrial relations.

Eligibility: Open to suitably qualified scholars.

Type: Fellowship.

No. of awards offered: One.

Frequency: Annual.

Value: C$1,000.

Study Establishment: Laval University.

Country of Study: Canada.

*Alcan Fellowships in Applied Mathematical and Physical Sciences

Subjects: Applied mathematical and physical sciences.

Eligibility: Open to suitably qualified scholars.

Purpose: To foster increased academic/industrial interaction.

Type: Fellowship.

No. of awards offered: Seven.

Frequency: Annual.

Value: C$10,000 per annum.

Length of Study: One year; renewable annually.

Study Establishment: At one of seven institutions (listed with their respective preferred fields): University of British Columbia, metallurgy; Laval University, chemical engineering; McGill University, metallurgy; Queen's University, chemistry/metallurgical engineering; University of Toronto, metallurgy; University of Montreal, chemistry/metallurgy; and McMaster University, material science.

Country of Study: Canada.

*Alcan Fellowships in Canadian Studies

Subjects: Canadian studies.

Eligibility: Open to suitably qualified scholars.

Type: Fellowship.

No. of awards offered: One.

Frequency: Annual.

Value: US$6,000.

Study Establishment: The Paul H Nitze School of Advanced International Studies, Johns Hopkins University, Washington, DC.

Country of Study: USA.

*Alcan Fellowships in Japanese Studies

Subjects: Japanese studies.

Eligibility: Open to suitably qualified scholars.

Type: Fellowship.

No. of awards offered: Varies.

Frequency: Annual.

Value: C$10,000.

Study Establishment: University of British Columbia.

Country of Study: Canada.

ALCOHOL BEVERAGE MEDICAL RESEARCH FOUNDATION

Alcohol Beverage Medical Research Foundation, 1122 Kenilworth Drive, Suite 407, Baltimore, MD, 21204, USA
Tel: 410 821 7066
Fax: 410 821 7065
Contact: A A Pawlowski, PhD

Research Project Grant

Subjects: Medical and behavioural sciences.

Eligibility: Open to US and Canadian citizens.

Purpose: To acquire new knowledge in order to prevent alcohol-related problems.

Type: Research Grant.

Frequency: Twice a year.

Value: Up to $40,000.

Length of Study: Up to two years.

Study Establishment: Non-profit university, research institutions.

Country of Study: USA or Canada.

Applications Procedure: Application form must be completed - these are available upon request.

Closing Date: February 15th and September 15th (annual recurring submission dates).

ALL SAINTS EDUCATIONAL TRUST

All Saints Educational Trust, St Katherine Cree Church, 86 Leadenhall Street, London, EC3A 3DH, England

Tel: 0171 283 4485
Contact: The Secretary

Grants

Subjects: Religious education, home economics, multicultural education, pastoral care and counselling, nutrition.

Eligibility: Open to individuals over 18 years of age who are, or intend to become, teachers. For research, grants are open to individuals and corporate bodies. Study must take place in UK.

Level of Study: Unrestricted.

Purpose: To enable persons who are, or intend to become, teachers to become qualified or better qualified. In the application of income, the Trustees seek to advance education in accordance with the doctrines of the Church of England or of a Church in communion with it.

Type: Grant.

No. of awards offered: Approximately 80 individual grants and 6 corporate grants.

Frequency: Annual.

Value: Varies but normally in the range of £500-£2,000.

Length of Study: 1-3 years.

Country of Study: UK.

Applications Procedure: Application form must be completed.

Closing Date: December 31st.

Additional Information: Enquiries should not be delayed until the offer of a place on a course of study has been confirmed. Late applications cannot be considered.

ALZHEIMER'S ASSOCIATION

Medical & Scientific Affairs, Alzheimer's Association, 919 North Michigan Avenue, Suite 1000, Chicago, IL, 60611-1676, USA
Tel: 312 335 5779
Contact: Grants Coordinator

*Faculty Scholar Awards

Subjects: Alzheimer's disease and related disorders.

Eligibility: Open to qualified investigators from non-profit institutions, who have at least two years' postdoctoral experience by July, previous to the year of the award.

Level of Study: Postdoctorate.

Purpose: To provide sustained salary support to experienced junior faculty level (or equivalent) investigators.

No. of awards offered: Varies.

Frequency: Annual.

Value: Up to US$50,000 per annum.

Length of Study: Three years.

Country of Study: Unrestricted.

Closing Date: January (deadline changes each year).

*Investigator-Initiated Research Grants

Subjects: Alzheimer's disease and related disorders.

Eligibility: Open to qualified investigators from non-profit institutions.

Purpose: To build on the success of established investigators, by providing sustained support for independent research projects.

Type: Research Grant.

No. of awards offered: Varies.

Frequency: Annual.

Value: Up to US$50,000 per annum.

Length of Study: 2 or 3 years.

Country of Study: Unrestricted.

Closing Date: January (deadline changes each year).

*Pilot Research Grants

Subjects: Alzheimer's disease and related disorders.

Eligibility: Open to qualified investigators from non-profit institutions.

Purpose: To stimulate interest by new investigators, to enable new and established investigators to test the feasibility of new ideas on a small scale, and to enable investigators to generate pilot data to support proposals to NIH foundations, or the Association for larger grants.

Type: Research Grant.

No. of awards offered: Varies.

Frequency: Annual.

Value: Up to US$30,000.

Length of Study: One year; non-renewable.

Country of Study: Unrestricted.

Closing Date: June (deadline changes each year).

*Zenith Awards

Subjects: Alzheimer's disease.

Eligibility: Open to projects that will test new and innovative ideas that are likely to lead to fundamental findings related to the biology of Alzheimer's disease.

Purpose: To provide major support to qualified scientists in basic biomedical research who have already made substantial contributions in the field of Alzheimer's.

No. of awards offered: Varies.

Frequency: Annual.

Value: US$100,000 per annum.

Length of Study: Two years; with possible competitive renewal upon review of research progress.

Country of Study: Unrestricted.

Closing Date: August (deadline changes each year).

Additional Information: Applications will be evaluated by an expert panel of senior scientists, already well recognized for their own accomplishments in Alzheimer research. Detailed eligibility and application requirements are available on request.

AMERICAN ACADEMY IN ROME

American Academy in Rome, 41 East 65th Street, New York, NY, 10021, USA
Tel: 212 517 4200

*Kress Fellowships in Art History

Subjects: Classical art history (1 Fellowship); Italian art history (1 Fellowship).

Eligibility: Open to US citizens.

Type: Fellowship.

No. of awards offered: Two.

Frequency: Annual.

Value: Varies.

Length of Study: Two years.

Study Establishment: American Academy in Rome.

Country of Study: Italy.

Closing Date: November 15th.

Rome Prize Fellowship

Subjects: Fine and applied arts, humanities.

Eligibility: All applicants must be US citizens.

Level of Study: Professional development, Postdoctorate, Doctorate.

Purpose: To allow the winner the time to pursue independent study, research and creative work at the American Academy in Rome.

Type: Fellowship.

No. of awards offered: Varies.

Frequency: Annual.

Value: Varies; up to US$17,800 plus room, board and study.

Length of Study: Varies, from six months to one year.

Study Establishment: American Academy in Rome.

Country of Study: Italy.

Applications Procedure: Please submit application, support materials and $40 fee.

Closing Date: November 15th.

AMERICAN ACADEMY OF ARTS AND LETTERS

American Academy of Arts and Letters, 633 West 155th Street, New York, NY, 10032, USA
Tel: 212 368 5900
Fax: 212 491 4615

Richard Rodgers Awards for the Musical Theater

Subjects: Musical theater.

Eligibility: Open to US citizens or permanent residents.

Purpose: To encourage the development of the musical theater by subsidizing a production by a not-for-profit theater group of a work by composers and writers who are not already established in the field of musical theater.

Type: Varies.

No. of awards offered: Varies.

Frequency: Annual.

Value: Varies.

Country of Study: USA.

Applications Procedure: A self-addressed stamped envelope should accompany requests for further information. Applications are available in the spring.

Closing Date: Usually November 1st.

AMERICAN ACADEMY OF FACIAL PLASTIC AND RECONSTRUCTIVE SURGERY

Educational and Research Foundation for AAFPRS, 1110 Vermont Avenue, NW, Suite 220, Washington, DC, 20005, USA
Tel: 202 842 4500
Fax: 202 371 1514
Contact: Fatima Porter-EL, Fellowship & Research Programs Coordinator

Bernstein Award

Subjects: Original research with direct application to facial plastic and reconstructive surgery.

Eligibility: Open to AAFPRS Fellow members.

Level of Study: Professional development.

Purpose: To encourage original research projects which will advance facial plastic and reconstructive surgery.

No. of awards offered: One.

Frequency: From time to time.

Value: US$25,000.

Length of Study: Two years.

Applications Procedure: Application form and other documentation must be submitted (to include CV and research proposal).

Closing Date: February 28th.

Additional Information: Application forms and guidelines are available on request.

For further information contact:
Educational and Research Foundation for AAFPRS, 1110 Vermont Avenue, NW, Suite 220, Washington, DC, 20005, USA
Tel: 202 842 4500
Fax: 202 371 1514
Contact: Fatima Porter-EL, Fellowship & Research Programs Coordinator

Investigator Development Award

Subjects: Facial plastic surgery; clinical or laboratory research.

Eligibility: Open to AAFPRS members.

Level of Study: Postgraduate.

Purpose: To support the work of a young faculty member conducting significant clinical or laboratory research and the training of resident surgeons in research.

No. of awards offered: One.

Frequency: Annual, dependent on funds available.

Value: US$15,000.

Length of Study: One year.

Study Establishment: The recipient's institution.

Country of Study: USA.

Applications Procedure: Application form and other documentation must be submitted (to include CV and research plans).

Closing Date: February 28th.

Additional Information: Application forms and guidelines are available on request.

For further information contact:
Educational and Research Foundation for AAFPRS, 1110 Vermont Avenue, NW, Suite 220, Washington, DC, 20005, USA
Tel: 202 842 4500
Fax: 202 371 1514
Contact: Fatima Porter-EL, Fellowship & Research Programs Coordinator

Resident Research Awards

Subjects: Facial plastic surgery.

Eligibility: Open to residents who are AAFPRS members. Residents at any level may apply even if the research work will be done during their fellowship year.

Level of Study: Postgraduate.

Purpose: To stimulate resident research in projects that are well conceived and scientifically valid.

Type: Research grant.

No. of awards offered: Up to three.

Frequency: Annual, dependent on funds available.

Value: US$5,000 - each award.

Length of Study: One year.

Study Establishment: The recipient's institution.

Applications Procedure: Application form and other documentation must be submitted (to include CV and comprehensive research proposal).

Closing Date: February 28th.

Additional Information: Residents are encouraged to enter early in their training so that their applications may be revised and resubmitted if not accepted the first time. Application forms and guidelines are available on request.

For further information contact:
Educational and Research Foundation for AAFPRS, 1110 Vermont Avenue, NW, Suite 220, Washington, DC, 20005, USA
Tel: 202 842 4500
Fax: 202 371 1514

AMERICAN ACADEMY OF FAMILY PHYSICIANS

American Academy of Family Physicians, 8880 Ward Parkway, Kansas City, MO, 64114-2797, USA
Tel: 816 333 9700
Contact: Chairman, Mead Johnson Awards Committee

Mead Johnson Awards for Graduate Education in Family Practice

Subjects: Residency training in family practice.

Eligibility: Open to physicians who are second-year residents in an approved practice residency program. They must express the intention to enter the family practice of medicine in the USA. Applicants must be resident members of the American Academy of Family Physicians.

Level of Study: Graduate.

Purpose: To provide financial assistance for outstanding young physicians planning careers in the family practice of medicine in the US.

Type: Monetary.

No. of awards offered: 20.

Frequency: Annual.

Value: US$2,000 per annum.

Length of Study: 12 months; not renewable.

Study Establishment: Hospital training programs accredited by the Accreditation Council for Graduate Medical Education.

Country of Study: USA.

Applications Procedure: Formal application must be submitted. Application to include: CV and personal statement, reference letter and form from residency program director, reference letter and form from active member of AAFP.

Closing Date: March 15th.

Additional Information: Recipients will be guest of honor at an Awards Breakfast hosted by Mead Johnson during the Annual AAFP Meeting.

THE AMERICAN ACADEMY OF FIXED PROSTHODONTICS

The American Academy of Fixed Prosthodontics, 917 W Dickens Ave, Chicago, IL, 60614-4231, USA
Tel: 312 413 1181
Fax: 312 996 3535
Contact: Dr Peter S Lund

Tylman Research Grant Program

Eligibility: Open to all graduate prosthodontic students studying in an accredited USA dental school and in an accredited prosthodontic graduate specialty program.

Level of Study: Postgraduate, Postdoctorate.

Purpose: To promote and support research by graduate students in the speciality of Prosthodontics.

Type: Grant.

No. of awards offered: Six.

Frequency: Annual.

Value: US$2,000.

Study Establishment: An accredited Dental School.

Country of Study: USA.

Applications Procedure: Protocol of research project submitted to the Academy Research Committee. The six best protocols are funded. The student must submit progress reports and final manuscript of completed project.

Closing Date: April 1st.

Additional Information: From the finalists, three awards are given to the first three winning manuscripts. First place wins $US1,000 and trip to annual AAFP meeting to present research on program and receive a plaque. 2nd place wins $US500 and third place $US300. This is a competitive process.

AMERICAN ACADEMY OF NEUROLOGY

IAC Foreign Scholarship Award Subcommittee, American Academy of Neurology, 2221 University Ave, SE, Suite 335, Minneapolis, MN, 55414, USA
Tel: 612 623 8115
Fax: 612 623 3504
Contact: Kathleen James

International Affairs Committee Foreign Scholarship Award

Subjects: Neurology.

Eligibility: Open to residents of countries other than the USA and Canada who are under 35 years of age and investigators of neurology. Applicants from underdeveloped countries are encouraged to submit.

Purpose: To enable a young investigator to attend the Academy's annual meeting in order to deliver a platform or poster presentation at the scientific sessions.

Type: Scholarship.

No. of awards offered: One.

Frequency: Annual.

Value: Stipend for travel, lodging and admission to educational programs offered at the Academy's annual meeting.

Country of Study: USA.

Applications Procedure: Applicants should submit a copy of the abstract submitted to the Scientific Program; a current curriculum vitae including date of birth, nationality and country of permanent residence; a letter from the program director under whose guidance the work was performed, describing the teaching or research program and the personal characteristics of the applicant.

Closing Date: December 31st of the year preceding the award.

AMERICAN ACADEMY OF PEDIATRICS

AMERICAN ACADEMY OF PEDIATRICS

Department of Education, American Academy of Pediatrics, PO Box 927, 141 Northwest Point Boulevard, Elk Grove Village, IL, 60009-0927, USA
Tel: 708 228 5005
Contact: Jackie Bucko, Sections Manager

Residency Scholarships

Subjects: Pediatrics.

Eligibility: Open to legal residents of the USA, Puerto Rico or Canada who have completed, or will have completed by 1 July, a qualifying approved internship (PL-O) or have completed a PL-1 year and have a definite commitment for a first-year pediatric residency (PL-1 or PL-2) accredited by the Residency Review Committee for Pediatrics, and who are pediatric residents (PL-1, PL-2, or PL-3) in a training program and have made a definite commitment for another year of residency (not Fellowship) in a program accredited by the Residency Review Committee for Pediatrics, and who have a real need for financial assistance.

Purpose: To enable young physicians to complete their training.

Type: Scholarship.

No. of awards offered: Varies.

Frequency: Annual.

Value: Varies: US$1,000; US$3,000; US$5,000.

Applications Procedure: Please write for details.

Closing Date: February 9th.

Additional Information: Applicants must support their applications with a letter from the department head or the chief of service as well as the Residency Program Director substantiating the requirements outlined under eligibility. The letter must address the financial need, commitment to pediatrics and performance in the program. If a change in residency program is contemplated (i.e. moving to another institution), a letter from the Residency Program Director certifying acceptance into the new program will also be necessary.

AMERICAN ACCORDION MUSICOLOGICAL SOCIETY

American Accordion Musicological Society, 334 South Broadway, Pitman, NJ, 08071, USA
Tel: 609 854 6628
Contact: Stanley Darrow, Secretary

Music Competition Contest

Subjects: Musical composition.

Eligibility: Open to any composer acquainted with the various types of accordion. There are no restrictions in regard to age or nationality.

Level of Study: Professional development.

Purpose: To encourage composers to write classical accordion music.

No. of awards offered: Two.

Frequency: Annual.

Value: Amateur Award of US$100 and Professional Award of US$500; paid in a lump sum.

Closing Date: September 30th.

Additional Information: Applicants competing for the Professional Award should have at least one composition already published.

AMERICAN ACCOUNTING ASSOCIATION

American Accounting Association, 5717 Bessie Drive, Sarasota, FL, 34233-2399, USA
Contact: Marie Hamilton, Office Manager

*Arthur H Carter Scholarship

Subjects: Accounting.

Eligibility: Open to US citizens who have satisfactorily completed at least two years of study at an accredited college or university and have a minimum of one more year of study at the time the award is made. During the scholarship period the recipient must be enrolled a minimum of 12 semester hours (or equivalent) of classroom work per semester, of which two courses should be accounting related. The school must be an Assembly Member of the AACSB. Awards may be made to students at undergraduate level or to candidates for masters degrees. PhD candidates are not eligible.

Type: Scholarship.

Frequency: Annual.

Value: US$2,500.

Length of Study: One year.

Study Establishment: An accredited college or university.

Country of Study: USA.

Applications Procedure: The application for the Arthur H Carter Scholarship must be obtained from the Department of Accounting Chairman of the school attended by the applicant.

Closing Date: April 1st.

*AAA Fellowship Program in Accounting

Subjects: Accounting.

Eligibility: Open to US and Canadian citizens who have expressed interest in and outstanding promise for a career in teaching accounting, and have been accepted into a doctoral program at a school accredited by the AACSB at the master's level. Only candidates entering the doctoral program are eligible. Actual awards will go only to students in the first year of their doctoral program. Foreign students are eligible for Fellowships if a resident of the USA or Canada at the time of application, enrolled in or with a degree from a US or Canadian accredited graduate program and planning to teach in the USA or Canada. Candidates' minority status will be considered when selecting recipients of Fellowships.

Level of Study: Doctorate.

Type: Fellowship.

No. of awards offered: Varies.

Frequency: Annual.

Value: Up to US$5,000.

Length of Study: One academic year.

Study Establishment: A school accredited by the AACSB.

Country of Study: USA and Canada.

Closing Date: February 1st.

THE AMERICAN ALPINE CLUB

The American Alpine Club, 710 Tenth Street, Ste 100, Golden, CO, 80701, USA
Tel: 303 384 0110
Fax: 303 384 0111
Email: amalpine@ix.netcom.com
Contact: Heidi Pomfret

Mountaineering Fellowship Fund Grants

Eligibility: Must be under 26 years of age.

Purpose: To encourage young American climbers to go into remote ares and seek out climbs more difficult than they normally do.

Type: Grant.

No. of awards offered: Five to 16.

Frequency: Twice per year.

Value: Usually between US$300, and US$600.

Country of Study: USA.

Applications Procedure: Write for application form.

Closing Date: April 1st and November 1st.

Additional Information: Grants will be based on the excellence of the proposed project and evidence of mountaineering experience. Membership in The American Alpine Club is not a prerequisite.

AMERICAN ANTIQUARIAN SOCIETY

American Antiquarian Society, 185 Salisbury Street, Worcester, MA, 01609, USA
Tel: 508 752 5813
Fax: 508 754 9069
Email: CFS@mwa.org
Contact: John B Hench, Director of Research and Publication

AAS/American Society for Eighteenth-Century Studies Fellowships

Subjects: American eighteenth-century studies.

Eligibility: Open to suitably qualified scholars. Degree candidates are not eligible. Membership in ASECS is required upon taking up an award, but not for making an application.

Type: Fellowship.

No. of awards offered: One.

Frequency: Annual.

Value: US$950 per month.

Length of Study: One to two months.

Study Establishment: The Society's library in Worcester, Massachusetts.

Country of Study: USA.

Closing Date: January 15th.

AAS/National Endowment for the Humanities Visiting Fellowships

Subjects: Early American history and culture.

Eligibility: Fellowships may not be awarded to degree candidates or for study leading to advanced degrees; nor may they be granted to foreign nationals unless they have been resident in the USA for at least three years immediately prior to receiving the award.

Purpose: To make the Society's research facilities more readily available to qualified scholars.

Type: Fellowship.

No. of awards offered: Two or more.

Frequency: Annual.

Value: The maximum available stipend is US$30,000.

Length of Study: Six to 12 months.

Study Establishment: The Society's library in Worcester, Massachusetts.

Country of Study: USA.

Closing Date: January 15th.

Additional Information: Fellows may not accept teaching assignments or undertake any other major activities during the tenure of the award. Other major fellowships, except sabbaticals or grants from the Fellow's own institution, may not be held concurrently with a Fellowship.

Stephen Botein Fellowship

Subjects: The history of the book in American culture: research.

Eligibility: Open to suitably qualified scholars.

Type: Fellowship.

No. of awards offered: One.

Frequency: Annual.

Value: US$950 per month.

Length of Study: Up to two months.

Study Establishment: The Society's library.

Country of Study: USA.

Closing Date: January 15th.

Kate B and Hall J Peterson Fellowships

Subjects: Early American history through 1876.

Eligibility: Open to individuals engaged in scholarly research and writing, including foreign nationals and persons at work on doctoral theses.

Purpose: To enable persons who might not otherwise be able to do so, to travel to the Society to make use of its research facilities.

Type: Fellowship.

No. of awards offered: Six to ten.

Frequency: Annual.

Value: US$850 per month.

Length of Study: One to three months.

Study Establishment: The Society.

Country of Study: USA.

Closing Date: January 15th.

AMERICAN ASSOCIATION FOR DENTAL RESEARCH

American Association for Dental Research, 1619 Duke Street, Alexandria, VA, 22314-3406, USA
Tel: 703 548 0066
Fax: 703 548 1883
Email: PAT@IADR.COM
Contact: Patricia J Reynolds, Executive Secretary

Student Research Fellowships

Subjects: Basic and clinical research related to oral health.

Eligibility: Open to students enrolled in an accredited DDS/DMD or hygiene program in a dental (health-associated) institution within the USA who are sponsored by a faculty member at that institution. Students should not have received their degree, nor should they be due to receive their degree in the year of the award. Applicants may have an advanced degree in a basic science subject.

Purpose: To encourage dental students living in the United States to consider careers in oral health research.

Type: Fellowship.

No. of awards offered: A variable number (30 in 1996).

Frequency: Annual.

Value: US$2,100, plus US$300 for supplies.

Study Establishment: Two years.

Country of Study: USA.

Applications Procedure: Application guidelines are available on request.

Closing Date: January 15th.

Additional Information: Recipients will present their research at the AADR meeting, by submitting abstracts for poster or oral presentations..

AMERICAN ASSOCIATION FOR WOMEN RADIOLOGISTS

American Association for Women Radiologists, 1891 Preston White Drive, Reston, VA, 22091, USA
Tel: 703 648 8939
Fax: 703 391 0397
Contact: Ann W Rosser

Distinguished Resident Award

Eligibility: Nominees must be members of the AAWR as of January 1st of the year the award is presented and must be in an acccredited radiology or radiation oncology resident program.

Level of Study: Radiation/radiology oncology resident.

Purpose: To recognise outstanding residents on the basis of contributions in clinical care, teaching, research or public service.

Type: Recognition/monetary.

No. of awards offered: Two.

Frequency: Annual.

Value: US$500, Plus per diem expenses to accept award.

Applications Procedure: Submit application, nominating letter from residency director, letter of concurrence from department chair, curriculum vitae and personal statement of nominee.

Closing Date: July 1st.

*Distinguished Resident Award (Diagnostic Radiology)

Subjects: Radiology.

Eligibility: Open to residents in the field of diagnostic radiology who are members of AAWR as of 1 January of the year of the award.

Purpose: To honor a resident diagnostic radiologist on the basis of outstanding contributions in clinical care, teaching, research and/or public service.

No. of awards offered: One.

Frequency: Annual.

Value: US$500 and reimbursement of expenses (travel, lodging, and per diem).

Applications Procedure: Applications should include a CV, a letter of nomination and a letter of concurrence.

Closing Date: July 1st.

*Distinguished Resident Award (Radiation Oncology)

Subjects: Radiology.

Eligibility: Open to residents in the field of radiation oncology who are members of AAWR as of 1 January of the year of the award.

Purpose: To honor a resident radiation oncologist on the basis of outstanding contributions in clinical care, teaching, research and/or public service.

No. of awards offered: One.

Frequency: Annual.

Value: US$500 and reimbursement of expenses (travel, lodging, and per diem).

Applications Procedure: Applications should include a CV, a letter of nomination and a letter of concurrence.

Closing Date: July 1st.

Marie Curie Award

Subjects: Radiology.

Eligibility: Open to practitioners in the field of radiology.

Level of Study: Unrestricted.

Purpose: To honor a radiologist, radiation oncologist, or other person who has been a mentor, role model or leader in radiology.

Type: Award.

No. of awards offered: One.

Frequency: Annual.

Value: Reimbursement of expenses (travel, lodging and per diem).

Applications Procedure: Submit letter of nomination, at least one letter of support, & curriculum vitae.

Closing Date: 1 July.

Additional Information: Applications should include a letter of nomination, a letter of support and a cv.

AMERICAN ASSOCIATION OF LAW LIBRARIES

Scholarship Committee, American Association of Law Libraries, Suite 940, 53 West Jackson Boulevard, Chicago, IL, 60604, USA
Contact: Executive Director

*Final Year of Law School for Library School Graduates

Subjects: Law.

Eligibility: Open to library school graduates who have successfully completed two years, or the equivalent, in accredited law schools and have law library experience.

No. of awards offered: Varies.

Frequency: Annual.

Value: Up to US$2,000 for tuition and school-related expenses.

Study Establishment: Accredited law schools.

Closing Date: April 1st.

*Library Degree Scholarships for Law Graduates

Subjects: Law librarianship.

Eligibility: Open to law graduates who are candidates for a library degree.

Type: Scholarship.

No. of awards offered: Varies.

Frequency: Annual.

Value: Up to US$2,000 for tuition and school-related expenses.

Study Establishment: Accredited library schools.

Closing Date: April 1st.

*Library Degree Scholarships for Non-Law Graduates

Subjects: Law librarianship.

Eligibility: Open to college graduates with meaningful law library experience who are library degree candidates.

No. of awards offered: Varies.

Frequency: Annual.

Value: Up to US$2,000 for tuition and school-related expenses.

Study Establishment: Accredited library schools.

Closing Date: April 1st.

*Minority Group Stipend

Subjects: Law librarianship: advanced studies.

Eligibility: Open to college graduates who are members of a minority group. Preference is given to experienced law librarians.

No. of awards offered: Varies.

Frequency: Annual.

Value: Up to US$3,500 for tuition and school-related expenses.

Study Establishment: Accredited library schools.

Closing Date: April 1st.

*Special Course in Law Librarianship

Subjects: Law librarianship.

Eligibility: Open to law librarians.

No. of awards offered: Varies.

Frequency: Annual.

Value: Up to US$500 for tuition.

Closing Date: April 1st.

THE AMERICAN ASSOCIATION OF PETROLEUM GEOLOGISTS FOUNDATION

The American Association of Petroleum Geologists Foundation, PO Box 979, Tulsa, Oklahoma, 74101-0979, USA
Tel: 918 560 2644
Fax: 918 560 2642
Contact: William Morgan, Chairman

American Association of Petroleum Geologists Grant-in-Aid

Subjects: Earth and geological sciences.

Eligibility: Open to nationals of any country.

Level of Study: Masters, Doctorate.

Purpose: To support graduate students in studies related to earth science aspects of the petroleum industry who plan careers that will contribute to the practice of petroleum geology in a broad sense.

Type: Grant.

Frequency: Annual.

Value: Maximum US$2,000; merit awards in the form of certificates redeemable for AAPG publications.

Country of Study: Unrestricted.

Applications Procedure: 1) complete application form, 2) submit copy of college academic transcripts or signed statements from professor commenting on applicants acdemic credentials, and 3) submit endorsements.

Closing Date: January 15th.

Additional Information: Grants are to be applied to expenses directly related to the students thesis work, such as summer field work, analytical analyses etc. Funds are not to be used to purchase capital equipment, or to pay salaries, tuition or room and board during the school year.

AMERICAN ASTRONOMICAL SOCIETY

American Astronomical Society, 2000 Florida Ave, NW, Suite 400, Washington, DC, 20009, USA
Tel: 202 328 2010
Fax: 202 234 2560
Email: aas@aas.org

www: www.aas.org
Contact: Diana Alexander

Chrétien International Research Grants

Subjects: Observational astronomy.

Eligibility: Open to astronomers throughout the world.

Purpose: To further international collaborative projects in observational astronomy.

Type: Research Grant.

Value: To cover any reasonable costs associated with astronomical observational research including travel costs, salary, publication costs, and small pieces of research equipment.

Applications Procedure: Applications should include a description of the proposed research project, a proposed budget, CV, and two letters of recommendation from astronomers who know the applicant's work.

Additional Information: At the conclusion of the research project, a short report and a simple financial statement will be required.

International Travel Grants

Subjects: Astronomy.

Eligibility: Open to astronomers working in the USA. Applicants must have a PhD or equivalent.

Level of Study: Postdoctorate.

Purpose: The AAS administers a grant from the National Science Foundation for the purpose of supporting US attendance at selected foreign astronomical meetings.

Type: Travel Grant.

No. of awards offered: One.

Value: The maximum award will cover tourist class round trip air fare. Preference will be given to those applicants who request partial support.

Applications Procedure: Applications should include a letter of invitation, an abstract of the paper to be presented at the meeting and any other relevant materials.

Additional Information: Each recipient will be required to submit a Meeting Report Form to the Executive Office upon his/her return.

Small Research Grants

Subjects: Astronomy.

Eligibility: Open to astronomers with a PhD or equivalent. Astronomers from smaller, less endowed institutions will be given priority; however, proposals will be accepted from individuals not associated with an institution.

Level of Study: Postdoctorate.

Purpose: To cover costs associated with any type of astronomical research.

Type: Research Grant.

Value: Varies.

Applications Procedure: Proposal must include CV and budget. Please send original and four copies.

Closing Date: December.

Additional Information: Awards will not be made to investigators holding other federal research grants except under special circumstances.

AMERICAN BAR FOUNDATION

American Bar Foundation, 750 N. Lake Shore Drive, Chicago, IL, 60611, USA
Tel: 312 988 6500
Fax: 312 988 6579
Email: at-abf@nwu.edu
Contact: Anne Tatalovich

The American Bar Foundation is committed to developing the next generation of scholars in the field of law and social science

Doctoral Dissertation Fellowship in Law and Social Science

Subjects: Law.

Eligibility: There are no restrictions, except that candidates must be writing a dissertation. Proposed research must be in the general area of sociolegal studies or in social scientific approaches to law, the legal profession, or legal institutions.

Level of Study: Doctorate.

Purpose: To encourage original and significant research on law, the legal profession, and legal institutions.

Type: Fellowship-residential.

No. of awards offered: Two.

Frequency: Annual.

Value: $14,000 +.

Length of Study: Two years.

Study Establishment: ABF.

Country of Study: USA.

Applications Procedure: Applications must include: (1) a dissertation prospectus or proposal with an outline of the subsatnce and methods of the intended research; (2) two letters of reference, one of which must be from a supervisor of the dissertation; (3) a curriculum vitae; and (4) a transcript of graduate record. In addition, at the applicant's option, a short sample of written work may be submitted.

Closing Date: February.

AMERICAN CHEMICAL SOCIETY

The Petroleum Research Fund, American Chemical Society, 1155 Sixteenth Street NW, Washington, DC, 20036, USA
Tel: 202 872 4481
Fax: 202 872 6319
Email: j_rogers@acs.org
Contact: Dr Joseph E Rogers Jr, Program Administrator

The Petroleum Research Fund is a Trust established in 1944 by seven major oil companies. ACS, as income beneficiary under the Trust, must use the income "for advanced scientific education and fundamental research in the petroleum field", which may include any field of pure science which ... may afford a basis for subsequent research directly connected with the petroleum field'. Since the first ACS-PRF grants were approved in 1954, several grant programs have evolved to serve segments of the scientific community. PRF funding commitments in 1993 totalled $13.9 million

ACS - PRF Scientific Education Grants

Subjects: Projects designed to enhance '... advanced scientific education and fundamental research in the petroleum field ...'.

Eligibility: Open to non-profit institutions in the USA and other countries. Speakers coming to conferences in USA, Canada and Mexico.

Purpose: To provide partial funding for foreign speakers at major symposia in the USA or Canada.

Type: Grant.

Value: Up to US$1,000 per speaker or up to US$2,000 per symposium.

Applications Procedure: Must use DRF "SE" form.

Closing Date: Throughout the year.

ACS - PRF Type AC Grants

Subjects: Fundamental research is currently supported in chemistry, the earth sciences, chemical engineering, and in related fields such as polymers and materials science.

Eligibility: Open to non-profit institutions in the USA and other countries. Grants are made in response to proposals. Recently, PRF support has been restricted to faculty holding tenure or a tenure-track appointment. This is the largest PRF grant program and usually funds proposals from graduate departments. Undergraduate faculty may also apply.

Level of Study: Professional development.

Type: Grant.

No. of awards offered: 153 grants in 1995.

Frequency: Usually three times yearly.

Value: A total of US$7,600,423 in 1995. Most AC grants provide US$50,000 over two years; the budget may include stipends for graduate students, undergraduates or postdoctoral fellows, summer faculty, research supplies, travel costs and a US$500 annual departmental allocation. No overhead costs may be charged to the grant; travel may be reimbursed up to US$1,000 per annum (this limit does not apply to field research); principal investigators may receive no more than US$5,000 per annum in summer salary and benefits from a PRF grant. As PRF prefers to support people rather than purchase capital equipment, there is a limited budget for such equipment and funding will only be supplied if requested funds are matched by institutional funds.

Applications Procedure: DRF "AC" form must be used.

Closing Date: Throughout the year.

Additional Information: Most grants begin 1 September, but an earlier start can be negotiated. The PRF Advisory Board normally meets to review proposals in February, May and November. Prospective applicants should call the PRF office for current information on dates of submission and consideration.

ACS - PRF Type B Grants

Subjects: Fundamental research is currently supported in chemistry, the earth sciences, chemical engineering, and in related fields such as polymers and materials science.

Eligibility: Open to non-profit institutions in the USA and other countries. Grants are made in response to proposals. Recently, PRF support has been restricted to faculty holding tenure or a tenure-track appointment. Type B grants are restricted to departments which do not award the PhD. The fundamental research proposed must include participation by undergraduate students, and graduate students may not be supported by Type B funds.

Level of Study: Professional development.

Type: Grant.

No. of awards offered: 52 grants in 1995.

Frequency: Usually three times yearly.

Value: A total of US$1,287,603 in 1995. Up to US$25,000 over two years; budget may include undergraduate student stipends, summer faculty salary, supplies and equipment, travel costs and a US$500 annual departmental allocation. No overhead costs may be charged to the grant; travel may be reimbursed up to US$1,000 per annum (this limit does not apply to field research); principal investigators may receive no more than US$5,000 per annum in summer salary and benefits from a PRF grant. As PRF prefers to support people rather than purchase capital equipment, there is a limited budget for such equipment and funding will only be supplied if requested funds are matched by institutional funds.

Applications Procedure: Must use DRF "B" application.

Closing Date: Throughout the year.

Additional Information: Most grants begin 1 September, but an earlier start can be negotiated. The PRF Advisory Board normally meets to review proposals in February, May and November. Prospective applicants should call the PRF office for current information on dates of submission and consideration.

ACS - PRF Type G 'Starter' Grants

Subjects: Fundamental research is currently supported in chemistry, the earth sciences, chemical engineering, and in related fields such as polymers and materials science.

Eligibility: Open to non-profit institutions in the USA only. Grants are made in response to proposals. Recently, PRF support has been restricted to faculty holding tenure or a tenure-track appointment. These grants are intended for new faculty within the first three years of teaching and without 'extensive' postdoctoral research experience.

Level of Study: Professional development.

Type: Grant.

No. of awards offered: 123 grants in 1995.

Frequency: Usually three times yearly.

Value: A total of US$2,460,000 in 1995. US$20,000 over two years; may fund student stipends, summer faculty salary, supplies and equipment, and travel costs. No overhead costs may be charged to the grant; travel may be reimbursed up to US$1,000 per annum (this limit does not apply to field research); principal investigators may receive no more than US$5,000 per annum in summer salary and benefits from a PRF grant. As PRF prefers to support people rather than purchase capital equipment, there is a limited budget for such equipment and funding will only be supplied if requested funds are matched by institutional funds.

Length of Study: Two years.

Applications Procedure: Must use DRF "G" form.

Closing Date: Throughout the year.

Additional Information: Most grants begin 1 September, but an earlier start can be negotiated. The PRF Advisory Board normally meets to review proposals in February, May and November. Prospective applicants should call the PRF office for current information on dates of submission and consideration. A detailed budget is not required.

AMERICAN COLLEGE OF PHYSICIANS

American College of Physicians, Independence Mall West, Sixth Street at Race, Philadelphia, PA, 19106-1572, USA
Tel: 215 351 2732/800 523 1546
Fax: 215 351 2759
Contact: Ana Santoyo, International Medicine Coordinator

ACP International Speakers' Program

Eligibility: Restricted to support members of ACP..

Level of Study: Professional development.

Purpose: To provide an ACP member as faculty to medical meeting in countries other than the USA (or airfare expenses up to $1,500 per speaker). This will broaden ACP's outreach and contribute to the exchange of medical knowledge amongst nations.

Type: Faculty support.

No. of awards offered: Approximately 15.

Frequency: Annual.

Value: Airfare up to $1,500.

Applications Procedure: Application for an ACP speaker must be submitted by the individual responsible for planning the conference.

Closing Date: January 30th of each year.

Additional Information: Program selections will be announced in May. The Program usually supports one speaker per event, but requests for more will be considered if increased benefits are demonstrated.

For further information contact:
Independence Mall West, Sixth Street at Race, Philadelphia, PA, 19106-1572, USA
Tel: 215 351 2520
Fax: 215 351 2759

Email: CompuServe 75364,2740
Contact: Ana Santoyo

AMERICAN COUNCIL OF LEARNED SOCIETIES

American Council of Learned Societies, 228 E.45th Street, New York, NY, 10017, USA
Tel: 212 697 1505
Fax: 212 949 8058

The China Program: Fellowships for Doctoral Research

Subjects: Research or writing on any topic or problem of importance in the study of China.

Eligibility: Open to US citizens and foreign nationals who have resided In the USA for a minimum period of two consecutive years at the time of application. Applicants must hold the PhD or its equivalent as of the deadline.

Level of Study: Doctorate, Postdoctorate.

Type: Scholarship.

No. of awards offered: Varies.

Frequency: Annual.

Value: Up to US$25,000.

Length of Study: Six to 12 months.

Country of Study: Any country except the Peoples Republic of China.

Closing Date: December 1st.

Additional Information: Support is available for original research on Chinese culture or society, including research designed to synthesize or reinterpret the applicants past research in order to produce an original overview of scholarship. Support is not given for translation projects unless such work is part of a broader study. These programs are not intended to support research in the Peoples Republic of China. Scholars wanting such support should write to the Committee on Scholarly Communication with China, Suite 2103, Thomas Jefferson Street, NW, Washington, DC 20007, USA. This program is supported by the Chiang Ching-kuo Foundation.

The Eastern European Program: Fellowships for Doctoral Research

Subjects: The social sciences and humanities relating to Albania, Bulgaria, the Czech Republic, the eastern part of Germany, Hungary, Poland, Romania, Slovakia, and the former Yugoslavia. Proposals dealing with Germany should focus on the culture and society of the communist period, and its antecedents or consequences.

Eligibility: Open to US citizens or permanent legal residents who hold PhD or its equivalent as of the application deadline. Candidates should be senior scholars and, in special circumstances, to untenured scholars or younger independent scholars without an academic appointment who may use the support over any period of one to three years.

Level of Study: Doctorate.

Purpose: To provide free time for research.

Type: Fellowship.

No. of awards offered: Varies.

Frequency: Annual.

Value: Up to US$30,000. The funds may be used to supplement sabbatical salaries or awards from other sources, provided they would intensify or extend the contemplated research.

Length of Study: For a period of 6-12 months full-time research.

Country of Study: Any country outside Eastern Europe.

Closing Date: December 1st.

Additional Information: The product of the proposed work must be disseminated in English.

For further information contact:
American Council of Learned Societies, 228 E 45th Street, New York, NY, 10017, USA
Tel: 212 697 1505
Fax: 212 949 8058

The China Program: Fellowships for Dissertation Research Abroad

Eligibility: Open to regular PhD candidates who will have completed all requirements for the doctorate except the dissertation by June 30th. There are no citizenship restrictions, but non US nationals must be enrolled as full-time PhD candidates in US institutions.

Purpose: To enable doctoral degree candidates to undertake a period of dissertation research.

Type: Fellowship.

No. of awards offered: Varies.

Frequency: Annual.

Value: Up to US$20,000 to cover living and research expenses.

Length of Study: One year.

Country of Study: Any country outside the USA, with the exception of the Peoples Repulic of China.

Closing Date: Decmber 1st.

Additional Information: The choice of location must be carefully and fully justified. These programs are not intended to support research within the Peoples Republic of China. Scholars wanting such support should write to the Committee on Scholarly Communication with China, Suite 2013, 1055 Thomas Jefferson Street, NW, Washington, DC 20007, US. Successful applicants may be eligible for the Louis Dupree Prize for research on Afghanistan and/or Central Asia. This program is supported by the Chiang Ching-kuo Foundation.

For further information contact:
American Council of Learned Societies, 228 E 45th Street, New York, NY, 10017, USA
Tel: 212 697 1505
Fax: 212 949 8058

The Eastern Europe Program: Dissertation Fellowships

Subjects: The social sciences and humanities relating to Albania, Bulgaria , the Czech republic, the Eastern part of Germany, Hungary, Poland, Romania, Slovakia, and the former Yugoslavia. Proposals for dealing with Germany should focus on the culture and society of the communist period, its antecedents or consequences.

Eligibility: Open to US citizens or permanent legal residents.

Type: Fellowship.

No. of awards offered: Varies.

Frequency: Annual.

Value: Up to US$15,000. plus expenses.

Length of Study: One year.

Study Establishment: Any university or institution for one academic year.

Country of Study: Any country outside Eastern Europe.

Closing Date: December 1st.

Additional Information: The product of the proposed work must be disseminated in English.

For further information contact:
American Council of Learned Societies, 228 E 45th Street, New York, NY, 10017, USA
Tel: 212 697 1505
Fax: 212 949 8058

The Eastern Europe Program: East European Language Training Grants

Subjects: Any East European Language (except the languages of the Commonwealth of Independent States).

Eligibility: Open to US citizens or permanent residents who are graduating college seniors, graduate students, or postdoctoral Scholars.

Level of Study: Postgraduate, Doctorate.

Purpose: To support summer language training for students and scholars who cannot receive such training at their home institutions.

Type: Grant.

No. of awards offered: Varies.

Frequency: Annual.

Value: US$2,000 for first or second year study; US$2,500 for intermediate or advanced training.

Country of Study: USA for first or second year study; Eastern Europe for intermediate or advanced training.

Closing Date: March 1st.

Additional Information: In cases of special need tutorial instruction during the acdemic year may be suported. Institutional Language Grants of up to US$7,500 are offered to schools willing to offer intensive summer language programs in Albanian, Bulgarian, Czech, Hungarian, Macedonian, Polish, Romanian, Serbo-Croatian, Slovak, or Slovenian.

For further information contact:
American Council of Learned Societies, 228 E 45th Street, New York, NY, 10017, USA
Tel: 212 697 1505
Fax: 212 949 8058

The Eastern Europe Program: Fellowships for Advanced Graduate Training

Subjects: The social sciences and humanities relating to Albania, Bulgaria the Czech Republic, the eastern part of Germany, Hungary, Poland, Romania, Slovakia and the former Yugoslavia. Proposals dealing with Germany should focus on the culture and society of the communist period, its antecedents or consequences.

Eligibility: Open to graduate students who are US citizens or permanent residents currently enrolled in a degree program who will have completed at least two academic years of work toward the doctorate by June 30th.

Level of Study: Postgraduate, Doctorate.

Purpose: To allow graduate students to undertake an extra year of training before beginning the PhD dissertaion, because of the difficulties combining area studies with work in a discipline.

Type: Fellowship.

No. of awards offered: Varies.

Frequency: Annual.

Value: Up to US$15,000, plus expenses.

Length of Study: One academic year.

Study Establishment: At any university or research institute.

Country of Study: Any country outside Eastern Europe, although brief trips to Eastern Europe of up to two months, especially for advanced language training, may be supported when they are part of a coherent overall program.

Closing Date: December 1st.

Additional Information: The product of the proposed work must be disseminated in English.

For further information contact:
American Council of Learned Societies, 228 E 45th Street, New York, NY, 10017, USA
Tel: 212 697 1505
Fax: 212 949 8058

The Eastern Europe Program : Predissertation Travel Grants

Subjects: The Social Sciences and Humanities relating to Albania, Bulgaria, and the Czech Republic, the eastern part of Germany, Hungary, Poland, Romania, Slovakia and the former Yugoslavia. Proposals dealing with Germany should focus on the culture of the communist period, its antecedents or consequences.

Eligibility: Open to US citizens and permanent residents enrolled in full-time grauate training programs. Applicants must have completed one year of full-time graduate study and have been accepted into a PhD program before applying for the grant.

Level of Study: Doctorate.

Purpose: To improve the quality of dissertation research on Eastern Europe by supporting students who have begun to formulate research ideas for a dissertation on Eastern Europe but who lack the necessary field experince.

Type: Travel Grant.

No. of awards offered: Varies.

Frequency: Annual.

Value: US$25,00 for travel.

Length of Study: For a summer trip of two months or more.

Country of Study: Eastern Europe.

Closing Date: March 1st.

Additional Information: The grants are to be used to travel to Eastern Europe to examine the resources available for research on possible topics and are intended to help students define and shape their dissertation programs and possibly to begin their research. The product of the proposed work must be disseminated in English.

For further information contact:
American Council of Learned Societies, 228 E 45th Street, New York, NY, 10017, USA
Tel: 212 697 1505
Fax: 212 949 8058

AMERICAN COUNCIL OF THE BLIND

American Council of the Blind, 1155 15th Street, NW, Ste 720, Washington, DC, 20005, USA
Tel: 202 467 5081
Fax: 202 467 5085
Email: jbeach@access.digex.net
www: http://www.acb.org
Contact: Jessica Beach

ACB Scholarship Program

Subjects: Any subject.

Eligibility: Eligible applicants must be US citizens and be legally blind in both eyes.

Level of Study: Postgraduate, Doctorate, Postsecondary.

Purpose: To provide scholarships to legally blind postsecondary students.

Type: Scholarship.

No. of awards offered: 25.

Frequency: Annual.

Value: $500 to $4,000.

Length of Study: One year.

Country of Study: USA.

Applications Procedure: Application to include: application form, two-page autobiographical sketch, transcripts, letter of recommendation, and proof of legal blindness.

Closing Date: March 1st.

AMERICAN COUNCIL ON EDUCATION

American Council on Education, One Dupont Circle, NW, Suite 800, Washington, DC, 20036-1193, USA
Tel: 202 939 9420
Fax: 202 785 8056

ACE Fellows Program

Subjects: Administration in higher education; leadership and governance of higher education; management of colleges and universities.

Eligibility: Open to senior members of a college faculty or mid-level staff with a minimum of five years' teaching or administrative experience who show evidence of potential for senior level administration. English is the language of instruction.

Level of Study: Professional development.

Purpose: To strengthen leadership in American higher education by identifying and preparing individuals who have shown promise for responsible positions in higher education administration.

Type: Fellowship.

No. of awards offered: 30-35.

Frequency: Annual.

Value: The nominating institution supports the salaries and benefits. The host institution supports the seminar and travel costs of the ACE Fellows and the Council provides support for programmatic costs.

Study Establishment: At a host college or university, for 1 academic year.

Applications Procedure: Applications must be submitted with nomination form along with four confidential letters of reference.

Closing Date: 1 November.

Additional Information: Candidates must be nominated by the president or vice-president of a college or university. Non-ACE member institutions are charged a US $4,500 tuition fee. ACE Fellows work with a mentor, normally a president or other senior officer, at policy and practical levels. The Fellowship experience is supplemented with national and regional seminars and meetings.

AMERICAN DANCE GUILD

American Dance Guild, 31 West 21st Street, 3rd Floor, New York, NY, 10010, USA
Tel: 212 627 3790
Fax: 212 675 9657
Contact: Karen Deaver

*Fannie Weiss Student Scholarship

Subjects: Dance.

Eligibility: Open to American Dance Guild members (or those recommended by ADG members), who are 18-24 years of age and have at least two years of training (preferably in modern dance).

Purpose: To fund further study for a dance student interested in pursuing a career in dance.

Type: Scholarship.

No. of awards offered: One.

Frequency: Annual.

Value: US$300-US$600.

Length of Study: 6-8 weeks of summer study.

Study Establishment: Past sucordees have studied at The Ballet Hispanico, Martha Graham School, Joffrey Ballet, Nikolais-Louis Danceclub, Fieldston School.

Country of Study: USA.

Closing Date: May 15th.

Additional Information: Must provide own transportation to and from New York as well as accommodation.

AMERICAN DENTAL HYGIENISTS' ASSOCIATION INSTITUTE FOR ORAL HEALTH

ADHA Institute Scholarship Program, Suite 3400, 444 North Michigan Avenue, Chicago, IL, 60611, USA
Contact: Beatrice Pedersen, Associate Administrator

ADHA Institute Scholarship Program

Subjects: Dental hygiene.

Eligibility: Open to full-time students at the certificate/associate, baccalaureate and graduate levels. Scholars must currently be enrolled as full-time students in a dental hygiene program in the USA, have completed a minimum of one year with a grade point average of at least 3.0, and be able to demonstrate financial need. Additional requirements vary depending upon degree level.

Type: Scholarship.

No. of awards offered: Approximately twenty.

Frequency: Annual.

Value: Up to US$1,500.

Length of Study: One year; not renewable.

Country of Study: USA.

Closing Date: May 1st.

AMERICAN DIABETES ASSOCIATION

American Diabetes Association, 1660 Duke Street, Alexandria, VA, 22314, USA
Tel: 703 549 1500 ext.2376
Fax: 703 683 1839
Contact: Matt Peterson

Career Development Awards

Subjects: Diabetes-related research.

Eligibility: Open to US citizens or permanent residents (or those who have applied for permanent resident status) who have MD or PhD degrees or, in the case of other health professions, an appropriate health or science related degree, and who hold full-time faculty positions or the equivalent at university-affiliated institutions within the US and US possessions. At the time of the award applicants must have at least two, but not more than five, years of postdoctoral or postfellowship research experience in a diabetes-related field with relevant accomplishments and publications.

Level of Study: Postdoctorate.

Purpose: To assist exceptionally promising new investigators to conduct diabetes-related research.

Type: Development award.

No. of awards offered: Varies; dependent on funds available.

Frequency: Twice yearly.

Value: Up to US$75,000 per annum. Payment is made quarterly. Awards carry no commitment for overhead costs or tuition. The funds are to be divided by the recipient between the salary of the principal investigator and other grant support. The salary stipend for the principal investigator, paid from ADA funds, cannot exceed $50,000 per year, which includes any fringe benefits of the sponsoring institution for which the recipient of the award qualifies. Grant support may be used to defray the support of a technician and/or for supplies. Travel support is restrict-

ed to a maximum of $1,000 per year and equipment to a maximum of $5,000 per year.

Length of Study: Four years; non-renewable.

Country of Study: USA.

Closing Date: February 1st (for July 1st funding); August 1st (for January 1st funding).

Additional Information: Each year of funding, after the first, is contingent upon approval by the ADA of the recipient's research progress report, and the availability of funds.

Clinical Research Grants

Subjects: Diabetes: for the purpose of this program, clinical research is defined as research involving humans directly. Support will be provided for studies that focus on intact human subjects in which the effects of a change in the individual's external or internal environment is evaluated.

Eligibility: Open to US citizens or permanent residents (or those who have applied for permanent resident status) who have MD or PhD degrees or, in the case of other health professions, an appropriate health or science related degree, and who hold full-time faculty positions or the equivalent at university-affiliated institutions within the US and US possessions.

Level of Study: Postdoctorate.

Purpose: To support patient-oriented research in diabetes.

Type: Research Grant.

No. of awards offered: Varies; dependent on funds available.

Frequency: Twice yearly.

Value: Up to US$60,000 per annum. Payment is made quarterly. Awards carry no commitment for overhead costs or tuition. Applications for three years of support for amounts up to $60,000 per year will be considered. Up to $20,000 of the funds may be used as salary support. The funds may be used for equipment (up to $5,000), supplies, or technician salary support.

Length of Study: Three years.

Country of Study: USA.

Closing Date: February 1st (for July 1st funding); August 1st (for January 1st funding).

Additional Information: Each year of funding, after the first, is contingent upon approval by the ADA of the recipient's research progress report, and the availability of funds.

For further information contact:
American Diabetes Association, 1660 Duke Street, Alexandria, VA, 22314, USA
Tel: 703 549 1500 ext.2376
Fax: 703 683 1839
Contact: Matt Petersen

LCIF Clinical Research Grant Program

Subjects: New treatment regimens, epidemiology, and translation research in the area of diabetic retinopathy.

Eligibility: Open to holders of an MD or PhD degree or, in the case of other health professions, an appropriate health or science related degree. The applicant must hold a faculty-level appointment or its equivalent at a research institution. The program is intended for any investigator with or without NIH or other significant support.

Level of Study: Postdoctorate.

Purpose: To support clinical or applied research in diabetic retinopathy in the USA and throughout the world.

Type: Research Grant.

No. of awards offered: Varies; dependent on funds available.

Frequency: Annual.

Value: Up to US$40,000 per annum. The Grants carry no commitment for overhead costs or tuition. The funds may be used for equipment and/or supplies and/or salary support. The funds may not be used for the principal investigator's salary. Travel, to diabetic retinopathy-related scientific meetings, is restricted to a maximum of US$1,000 per year.

Length of Study: Two years.

Country of Study: USA or abroad.

Closing Date: February 1st.

Additional Information: This program is part of the Lions SightFirst Diabetic Retinopathy Research Program, funded by the Lions Club International Foundation.

For further information contact:
The Lions SightFirst Diabetic Retinopathy Research Program, c/o American Diabetes Association, Division of Scientific Affairs, 1660 Duke Street, Alexandria, VA, 22314
Tel: 703 549 1500 ext.2362
Fax: 703 683 1839
Contact: Odette Brown

LCIF Equipment Grant Program

Subjects: Clinical research in diabetic retinopathy.

Eligibility: Open to holders of an MD or PhD degree or, in the case of other health professions, an appropriate health or science related degree. The applicant must hold a faculty-level appointment at a research institution.

Level of Study: Postdoctorate.

Type: Equipment Grant.

No. of awards offered: Varies; dependent on funds available.

Frequency: Annual.

Value: US$15,000 for the purchase of equipment (one July payment - final disposition due within six months of receipt).

Country of Study: USA or abroad.

Applications Procedure: A detailed justification for the need to purchase the equipment and an explanation of its intended use must be submitted.

Closing Date: February 1st.

Additional Information: This program is part of the Lions SightFirst Diabetic Rectinopathy Research Program, funded by the Lions Club International Foundation.

For further information contact:
The Lions SightFirst Diabetic Retinopathy Research Program, c/o American Diabetes Association, Division of Scientific Affairs, 1660 Duke Street, Alexandria, VA, 22314, USA
Tel: 703 549 1500 ext.2362
Fax: 703 683 1839
Contact: Odette Brown

LCIF Training Grant Program

Subjects: Diabetic retinopathy.

Eligibility: Open to US citizens who have an MD or PhD degree or, in the case of other health professions, an appropriate health or science related degree, and hold a faculty-level appointment at a US research institution; and to non-US citizens who have an MD or PhD degree or, in the case of other health professions, an appropriate advanced degree and hold a faculty-level appointment at a research institution outside the USA.

Level of Study: Postdoctorate.

Purpose: To enable foreign investigators to visit USA research institutions and receive training in clinical research, implementation of public health programs (e.g. screening), or epidemiology; and to enable US investigators to visit foreign institutions (particularly institutions in underdeveloped countries) to conduct training programs in clinical research and implement public health programs.

No. of awards offered: Varies; dependent on funds available.

Frequency: Annual.

Value: Up to US$40,000.

Length of Study: Two years.

Study Establishment: An approved institution.

Country of Study: USA or abroad.

Closing Date: February 1st.

Additional Information: This program is part of the Lions SightFirst Diabetic Retinopathy Research Program, funded by the Lions Club International Foundation.

For further information contact:
The Lions SightFirst Diabetic Retinopathy Research Program, c/o American Diabetes Association, Division of Scientific Affairs, 1660 Duke Street, Alexandria, VA, 22314, USA
Tel: 703 549 1500 ext.2362
Fax: 703 683 1839
Contact: Odette Brown

Medical Student Diabetes Research Fellowship Program

Subjects: Diabetes.

Eligibility: Open to institutions within the USA and USA possessions. The application must be initiated by the student, and the student must have a qualified sponsor. The student must have completed at least one year of medical school. The student's sponsor must hold a faculty position within an accredited medical school in the USA and must be a US citizen or have (or have applied for) permanent resident status.

Purpose: To promote medical student interest in careers of diabetes-related clinical investigation or basic research.

Type: Fellowship.

No. of awards offered: Up to eight.

Frequency: Annual.

Value: The total award stipend given to the student will be US$3,000. An additional US$1,000 will be made available to the student's sponsor to help to defray the cost of supplies, animals, etc. related to the student's research project. Funds will be paid to the institution in one sum after the student has begun his/her research experience.

Length of Study: 3-6 months.

Closing Date: March 1st.

For further information contact:
American Diabetes Association, 1660 Duke Street, Alexandria, VA, 22314, USA
Tel: 703 549 1500 ext.2376
Fax: 703 683 1839
Contact: Matt Petersen

Mentor-Based Postdoctoral Fellowship Program

Subjects: Diabetes.

Eligibility: There are no citizenship requirements for the Fellow. However, the applicant investigator must be a US citizen or permanent resident. The applicant investigator must also hold an appointment at a US research institution and have sufficient research support to provide an appropriate training environment for the Fellow. The Fellow selected by the awarded investigator must hold a MD or PhD degree and must not be serving an internship or residency during the fellowship period. The fellow must not have more than three years of postdoctoral research experience in the field of diabetes/endocrinology at the commencement of this fellowship.

Level of Study: Postdoctorate.

Purpose: To support the training of scientists in an environment most conducive to beginning a career in diabetes research. An award will be given to an established and active investigator in diabetes research for the annual stipend support of a postdoctoral fellow to work closely with the mentor.

Type: Fellowship.

No. of awards offered: Varies; dependent on funds available.

Frequency: Annual.

Value: For the stipend support of a single Postdoctoral Fellow in a given year, as well as laboratory supplies and travel costs. The salary of the Fellow is to be determined by the applicant investigator, but the total amount of the award cannot exceed US$30,000 per annum. Laboratory supply costs are restricted to a maximum of US$3,000 per annum and travel for the Fellow to attend diabetes-related scientific meetings is restricted to a maximum of US$1,000. The salary portion of the award may include health insurance and social security benefits, if applicable. The American Diabetes Association does not pay indirect costs. Funds will be paid to the institution in quarterly payments.

Length of Study: Up to three years.

Country of Study: USA.

Applications Procedure: Application form must be completed.

Closing Date: Usually first Friday in October for appointment July 1st.

For further information contact:
American Diabetes Association, 1660 Duke Street, Alexandria, VA, 22314, USA
Tel: 703 549 1500 ext.2376
Fax: 703 683 1839
Email: obrown@diabetes.org
Contact: Matt Petersen

Research Awards

Subjects: Any aspect of diabetes research.

Eligibility: Open to US citizens or permanent residents (or those who have applied for permanent resident status) who have MD or PhD degrees or, in the case of other health professions, an appropriate health or science related degree, and who hold full-time faculty positions or the equivalent at university-affiliated institutions within the US and US possessions.

Level of Study: Postdoctorate.

Purpose: To assist investigators, new or established, who have a particularly novel and exciting idea for which they need support.

Type: Research Grant.

No. of awards offered: Varies; dependent on funds available.

Frequency: Twice yearly.

Value: US$20,000-US$40,000 per annum. Payment is made quarterly. The funds may not be used for training stipends, postdoctoral fellowships, or non-technical salaries (i.e. administrative personnel, etc.) The funds may be used for equipment and/or supplies and/or salary for technical assistance.

Length of Study: Up to three years.

Country of Study: USA.

Closing Date: February 1st (for July 1st funding); August 1st (for January 1st funding).

Additional Information: Each year of funding, after the first, is contingent upon approval by the ADA of the recipient's research progress report, and the availability of funds.

For further information contact:
American Diabetes Association, 1660 Duke Street, Alexandria, VA, 22314, USA
Tel: 703 549 1500 ext.2376
Fax: 703 683 1839
Contact: Matt Petersen

AMERICAN FOUNDATION FOR AGING RESEARCH

American Foundation for Aging Research, North Carolina State University, Biochemistry Department, Polk Hall, Box 7622, Raleigh, NC, 27695, USA
Tel: 919 515 5679
Fax: 919 515 2047

Email: AFAR@BCHserver.BCH.NCSU.EDU
Contact: Dr Paul F Agris, President

Wilson-Fulton and Robertson Awards in Aging Research, Cecille Gould Memorial Fund Award in Cancer Research, Richard Shepherd Fellowship

Subjects: Aging and cancer research.

Eligibility: Open to students enrolled in undergraduate and graduate (MS, PhD, MD or DDS) degree programs at US institutions who are working on specific projects in the fields of aging or cancer.

Level of Study: Postgraduate, Doctorate, Undergraduate.

Purpose: To encourage young people to pursue research.

Type: Fellowship.

No. of awards offered: Five to ten.

Frequency: Annual.

Value: US$500-US$1,000 per semester or summer.

Study Establishment: Educational institutions.

Country of Study: USA.

Applications Procedure: There are two levels of review: a pre-application form to determine eligibility, and a full application. Applicants should submit a request for pre-application and enclose a check or money order to AFAR for $3.00 to cover handling and postage of both pre- and full applications.

Additional Information: Projects should be biological in nature. Sociological and psychological research is not accepted in this program. AFAR is a national, tax-exempt, non-profit, educational and scientific charity not associated with North Carolina State University.

AMERICAN FOUNDATION FOR AIDS RESEARCH (AMFAR)

American Foundation for AIDS Research, Grants Administration Department, 5900 Wilshire Boulevard, 23rd Floor, Los Angeles, CA, 90036, USA
Tel: 213 857 5900
Fax: 213 857 5920

*AIDS Research Grants

Subjects: AIDS: laboratory and clinical investigations of new and/or unfunded high quality research; a portion of AmFAR's resources is allocated to grants for research on the ethical, psychological, legal and socio-economic implication of the AIDS epidemic.

Eligibility: Open to suitably qualified researchers.

Type: Research Grant.

No. of awards offered: Varies.

Frequency: Annual.

Value: Up to US$50,000 in direct costs, plus a maximum of 20% of that amount for indirect costs.

Length of Study: One year; renewable for one additional year.

Closing Date: Mid-April.

*AmFAR Scholar Awards

Subjects: AIDS research.

Eligibility: Open primarily to postdoctoral investigators at non-profit institutions located within the USA, its territories, and the Commonwealth of Puerto Rico. Exceptionally Scholar Awards may be awarded in other geographic areas when the investigator is uniquely qualified and the institution is uniquely capable of providing the facilities and resources necessary for the execution of a particular research program. AmFAR welcomes Scholar Awards enquiries from investigators willing to dedicate their careers to research bearing on AIDS and its associated disorders. AmFAR Scholars are scientists who have completed more than basic training and education in their chosen field but do not have a tenured position. In general, a typical AmFAR Scholar has had at least two to three years of postdoctoral training at the time of application.

Level of Study: Postdoctorate.

Type: Research Grant.

No. of awards offered: Varies.

Frequency: Annual.

Value: Up to US$102,000 in direct costs, plus a maximum of 10% of that amount for indirect costs.

Length of Study: Three years.

Closing Date: Mid-April.

*Pediatric Short-Term Scientific Awards

Subjects: Any project or portion of a project, directly relevant to pediatric AIDS, that can be accomplished with US$5,000.

Eligibility: Open primarily to institutionally affiliated US investigators, although foreign investigators may also apply.

Type: Research Grant.

No. of awards offered: Varies.

Frequency: Annual.

Value: US$5,000 for travel, per diem and housing.

Length of Study: The awards are made for a 1-year period and travel and training may be done at any time within that period.

Study Establishment: A US institution other than that to which the awardee is affiliated.

Closing Date: Mid-April.

Additional Information: These awards are funded by the Pediatric AIDS Foundation.

*Short-Term Scientific Awards

Subjects: AIDS.

Eligibility: Open to established investigators qualified in the sciences, medicine or the humanities.

Purpose: To allow established investigators to travel to another institution for the purpose of study or specialized training.

No. of awards offered: Varies.

Frequency: Annual.

Value: Up to US$5,000.

Closing Date: Mid-April.

*Special Two-year Pediatric Scholar Awards

Subjects: AIDS research: especially, but not exclusively, related to the targeted areas listed in the program announcement.

Eligibility: Open to pediatric researchers with two to three years of postdoctoral experience.

Level of Study: Postdoctorate.

Type: Research Grant.

No. of awards offered: Varies.

Frequency: Annual.

Value: Up to US$66,000 salary and fringe benefits over two years: US$32,000 in year one, US$34,000 in year two; if renewed, US$36,000 in year three.

Length of Study: Two years; exceptionally renewable for a third additional year.

Closing Date: Mid-April.

Additional Information: These awards are funded by the Pediatric AIDS Foundation.

*Targeted Pediatric Research Grants

Subjects: AIDS research: targeted areas are listed in the program announcement.

Eligibility: Open to institutionally affiliated investigators.

Type: Research Grant.

No. of awards offered: Varies.

Frequency: Annual.

Value: Up to US$65,000 direct costs.

Length of Study: One year; renewable for one additional year.

Closing Date: Mid-April.

Additional Information: These grants are funded by the Pediatric AIDS Foundation.

AMERICAN FOUNDATION FOR PHARMACEUTICAL EDUCATION

American Foundation for Pharmaceutical Education, 1 Church Street, Suite 202, Rockville, MD, 20850-4158, USA
Contact: Dr Richard Faust

*AACP-AFPC Gateway Scholarships for Minorities

Subjects: Pharmaceutical sciences.

Eligibility: Open to students who have participated in the American Association of Colleges of Pharmacy (AACP) Undergraduate Research Participation Program for Minorities. Candidates should be US citizens or permanent residents and demonstrate proof of acceptance into a graduate program leading to a PhD degree in any pharmaceutical discipline.

Purpose: To encourage minority undergraduates in pharmacy colleges to continue their education and pursue a PhD.

Type: Scholarship.

No. of awards offered: Four.

Frequency: Annual.

Value: US$5,000.

Study Establishment: A college of pharmacy.

Country of Study: USA.

Additional Information: The Scholarships are funded through a grant from Glaxo, Inc.

*AAPS-AFPE Gateway Scholarships

Subjects: Pharmaceutics.

Eligibility: Open to undergraduates of any nationality who are enrolled in the last three years of either: (a) a baccalaureate or doctor of pharmacy degree program in an accredited school of pharmacy; or (b) a baccalaureate degree program in a related field of scientific study. Candidates should have demonstrated interest in and potential for a career in any of the pharmaceutical sciences.

Purpose: To encourage undergraduates from any discipline to pursue a PhD in a pharmacy graduate program.

Type: Scholarship.

No. of awards offered: Four.

Frequency: Annual.

Value: US$9,250.

Length of Study: One year.

Closing Date: December 1st.

*First-Year Graduate Scholarship Program

Subjects: Any pharmaceutical discipline.

Eligibility: Open to US citizens or permanent residents who hold a BS PharmD or equivalent degree and are planning to pursue the PhD in any pharmaceutical discipline.

Purpose: To encourage undergraduate students or recent graduates to continue their education in a graduate program for the PhD in one of the nation's pharmacy colleges.

Type: Scholarship.

No. of awards offered: Five.

Frequency: Annual.

Value: US$5,000.

Country of Study: USA.

Applications Procedure: A dean may select a senior or recent student who intends to study in a pharmacy college graduate program. The basis for selection should be both academic excellence and financial need. The student may be one from the institution's graduating senior class and/or one who will be enrolled in an institution's pharmacy graduate program. In addition to a letter of recommendation from the dean (either the dean where the student is graduating, or has graduated, or the dean where the student is enrolling), the following information must be provided by the student nominated: name of the Graduate School the student plans to attend and the major areas of study to be undertaken (if known); a transcript of all grades for undergraduate work; special honors, awards, accomplishments in high school and college that reflect the excellence of the candidate and their ability to succeed in graduate school (this information can be a vital part of the application); Graduate Record Examination (GRE) and SAT scores, if available, as well as any other national achievement tests; a one- or two-page statement elaborating reasons for wishing to attend graduate school; a letter from a faculty member acquainted with the student and their potential for graduate study. This program includes the following Scholarships: Ortho/McNeil-AFPE First Year Graduate Scholarship, Sandoz-AFPE First Year Graduate Scholarship (2), Smithkline Beecham-AFPE First Year Graduate Scholarship, and Upjohn-AFPE First Year Graduate Scholarship.

Closing Date: May 1st for all documentation, for notification by June 15th. Funds are provided September 1st.

*Gateway Scholarship Program

Subjects: Pharmaceutics.

Eligibility: Open to US citizens or permanent residents who are undergraduates enrolled in the last three years of a BS or PharmD program in a college of pharmacy.

Purpose: To encourage undergraduates in a pharmacy college to pursue the PhD in a graduate program within a pharmacy college.

Type: Scholarship.

No. of awards offered: Five.

Frequency: Annual.

Value: US$9,250: US$4,250 is provided for an undergraduate research project and then US$5,000 when the student enrols in a graduate program in a pharmacy college. The US$4,250 may be used for any purpose decided by the awardee and faculty sponsor that will enable the student to have a successful program, i.e. student stipend, laboratory supplies or materials related to the project, travel, etc. None of the funds shall be used for indirect costs by the institution.

Study Establishment: A college of pharmacy.

Country of Study: USA.

Applications Procedure: Application documents must include: a letter from a faculty sponsor who will supervise the research experience (a brief description of the research to be carried out and the time period involved must be provided); a letter from the dean of the college or one other faculty member supporting the application; a letter from the student outlining career goals and reasons for applying for the Scholarship; a list of special honors, awards, accomplishments in high school and college reflecting achievement and an ability to carry out the research project and succeed in graduate school; an official transcript of all collegiate grades and, if available, copies of GPA and SAT and/or other national

achievement test scores. Successful candidates must submit a brief final report of their accomplishments at the conclusion of the undergraduate research experience. If students go on to graduate school they may receive the balance of the award, US$5,000, anytime within two years after completion of their undergraduate program. This program includes the following Scholarships: Hoechst Roussel-AFPE Gateway Scholarship, Merck-AFPE Gateway Scholarship, Sandoz-AFPE Gateway Scholarship, Schein-AFPE Gateway Scholarship, and Syntex-AFPE Gateway Scholarship.

Closing Date: December 1st for all documentation, for notification by January 15th. The Scholarship itself will begin any time after February 1st.

*Glaxo-AFPE Graduate Studies Scholarship

Subjects: Pharmaceutical sciences, or business administration, law, public health, engineering, etc.

Eligibility: Open to individuals in the final year of a BS or PharmD program in a pharmacy college and planning to continue their education in pursuit of any graduate or professional degree (except a PharmD).

Purpose: To encourage undergraduate students in pharmacy colleges to continue their education in a graduate or professional program leading to an advanced degree providing a valuable background for careers in the pharmaceutical industry.

Type: Scholarship.

No. of awards offered: Eight.

Frequency: Annual.

Value: US$5,000.

Country of Study: USA.

Closing Date: May 1st.

*Graduate Fellowships and Scholarships

Subjects: Any of the pharmaceutical sciences, including pharmaceutics, pharmacology, manufacturing pharmacy and medicinal chemistry.

Eligibility: Open to US citizens or permanent residents currently enrolled in a graduate program in the pharmaceutical sciences.

Purpose: To offer Fellowship support leading to a PhD degree.

No. of awards offered: Approximately 125.

Frequency: Annual.

Value: US$10,000 for 32 Fellowships; US$6,000 or US$7,500 for the remainder. Payments are made to the university in twice yearly installments.

Length of Study: One year; renewable for two additional years.

Study Establishment: An appropriate university.

Country of Study: USA.

Closing Date: March 1st for Fellowships beginning in September.

*G D Searle & Co Postdoctoral Research Fellowship in Pharmacoeconomics

Subjects: Pharmacoeconomics.

Eligibility: Open to all pharmacy faculty members having a strong record of research in an area encompassing such topics as cost-benefit and cost-effectiveness of pharmaceuticals, the impact of current or future legislation on drug innovation and/or healthcare in the nation, the economics of healthcare and the quality of life in changing patterns of healthcare delivery systems, the contribution of the pharmaceutical industry and the economic impact of research and new drugs, healthcare cost-containment issues, etc.

Level of Study: Postdoctorate.

Type: Fellowship.

No. of awards offered: One.

Frequency: Annual.

Value: Up to US$22,500.

Study Establishment: An institution of higher learning.

Country of Study: USA.

Closing Date: March 1st.

*United States Pharmacopeial Convention-AFPE Fellowship in Drug Information

Subjects: Pharmacy practice or pharmacy administration.

Eligibility: Open to either graduate students pursuing the PhD in pharmacy practice or pharmacy administration or individuals having the PharmD degree and a postgraduate research appointment with a project that could include such areas as drug information technology, information handling, practitioner or patient use of information, or clinical studies that are targeted to expand upon the existing information data base.

Type: Fellowship.

No. of awards offered: One.

Frequency: Annual.

Value: US$7,500.

Study Establishment: An institution of higher learning or other appropriate research institution.

Country of Study: USA.

Closing Date: March 1st.

AMERICAN FOUNDATION FOR UROLOGIC DISEASE, INC

Research Program Division, American Foundation for Urologic Disease, Inc, 300 West Pratt Street, Suite 401, Baltimore, MD, 21202-2463, USA

*AFUD/NKF Resident Fellowship

Subjects: Urologic or nephrologic diseases.

Eligibility: Open to urology residents.

Type: Fellowship.

Frequency: Annual.

Value: US$25,000 per annum.

Length of Study: One year; renewable.

Study Establishment: An accredited medical research institution.

Closing Date: October 15th.

Additional Information: An accredited medical research institution must sponsor the candidate by guaranteeing adequate support, including responsibility for the adequacy of the environment, laboratory equipment and the supplies to perform the proposed research and development. The preceptor must be a senior PhD or MD engaged in urological research in an established laboratory who will make a one year commitment to sponsor the Scholar. Application forms are available on request. The Fellowship is jointly funded by the National Kidney Foundation.

*New Investigator Urology Research Award

Subjects: Proposals involving the areas of stones, obstruction, infection, surgical prophylaxis, neurourology, impotence, infertility and outcomes will be given special attention.

Eligibility: Open to suitably qualified urologists.

Purpose: To support new, unfunded innovative urological research.

Frequency: Annual.

Value: Up to US$50,000 per annum. Matching funds must be provided by the sponsoring institution.

Length of Study: Two years.

Study Establishment: An accredited medical research institution.

Closing Date: October 15th.

Additional Information: The award cannot be used to supplement or duplicate any work which is being supported by other physicians, co-investigators, agencies, institutions or pharmaceutical/medical companies.

For further information contact:
Research Program Division, American Foundation for Urologic Disease, Inc, 300 West Pratt Street, Suite 401, Baltimore, MD 21202-2463, USA

*Office-Based Urology Research Award

Subjects: Urology: stones, infection, impotence, infertility, neurourology, outcomes, information system technology, surgical prophylaxis and surgical instrumentation.

Eligibility: Open to office-based urologists.

Purpose: To fund novel previously unfunded research proposals.

Frequency: Annual.

Value: Up to US$50,000 per annum.

Length of Study: Up to 12 months.

Closing Date: October 15th.

*PhD Research Scholars Program

Subjects: Urologic or related diseases and dysfunctions.

Eligibility: Open to postdoctoral basic scientists, enrolled in approved urological residency programs.

Level of Study: Postdoctorate.

No. of awards offered: Varies.

Frequency: Annual.

Value: A stipend of US$23,000 per annum. Funds must be matched by the host institution.

Length of Study: Two years.

Study Establishment: An accredited medical research institution.

Applications Procedure: Application form must be completed.

Closing Date: October 15th.

Additional Information: The preceptor should be a senior PhD or MD engaged in urological research in an established laboratory who will undertake direct responsibility for the Scholar. The sponsoring Urology Department is required to provide space, laboratory equipment and supplies to perform the proposed research. Continued support is subject to yearly review and evaluation by the Scientific and Education Committee.

*Practising Urologist's Research Award

Subjects: Urology.

Eligibility: Open to practising urologists with research ideas suitable for collaborative investigations.

Frequency: Annual.

Value: US$5,000. The sponsoring institution is expected to provide matching funds.

Length of Study: One year.

Study Establishment: An accredited medical research institution.

Closing Date: October 15th.

Additional Information: Application forms are available on request.

*Research Scholar Program

Subjects: Urology.

Eligibility: Open to young urologists, in residency or within five years of post-residency, who are committed to a career in research, and who are able to provide evidence of their capabilities in research.

Frequency: Annual.

Value: A stipend of US$22,000 will be paid directly to the scholar in monthly instalments. The sponsor must provide matching funds.

Length of Study: Two years.

Study Establishment: An accredited medical research institution.

Applications Procedure: Application form must be completed.

Closing Date: October 15th.

Additional Information: An accredited medical research institution must sponsor the candidate by guaranteeing adequate support, including responsibility for the adequacy of the environment for research and development.

*Summer Medical Student Fellowship

Subjects: Urology.

Eligibility: Open to medical students.

Type: Fellowship.

No. of awards offered: 10.

Frequency: Annual.

Value: A stipend of US$2,000.

Length of Study: Two months.

Study Establishment: Urology research laboratories.

Applications Procedure: Application form must be completed.

Closing Date: April 15th.

Additional Information: An accredited medical research institution must sponsor the candidate by guaranteeing adequate support, including responsibility for the adequacy of the environment for research and development.

AMERICAN FOUNDATION FOR VISION AWARENESS (AFVA)

American Foundation for Vision Awareness, 243 North Lindbergh Boulevard, St Louis, MO, 63141, USA
Tel: 314 991 4100
Fax: 314 991 4101
Contact: Huck Roberts, Executive Director

*Research Grant

Subjects: Vision or related areas of study.

Eligibility: Open to citizens and permanent residents of the United States.

Purpose: To provide funds for projects which will add to and enhance the body of vision research.

Value: US$6,000-US$10,000.

Length of Study: One year.

Applications Procedure: To apply candidates should write to the AFVA for an application form and guidelines (available October through December) and submit all completed forms, along with a brief narrative describing the project, and a budget outline.

Closing Date: February 1st for notification by July 1st.

Additional Information: Candidates must submit research results for publication in an appropriate journal.

AMERICAN HEALTH ASSISTANCE FOUNDATION

American Health Assistance Foundation, 15825 Shady Grove Road, Rockville, Maryland, 20850, USA
Tel: 301 948 3244

Fax: 301 258 9454
Contact: Dr Sherry Marts

Alzheimer's Disease Research

Subjects: Neurology.

Eligibility: The principal investigator must hold the rank of assistant professor (or equivalent) or higher.

Level of Study: Professional development.

Purpose: To enable basic research on the causes of and/or treatments for Alzheimer's Disease.

Type: Grant.

No. of awards offered: Varies.

Frequency: Annual.

Value: Up to $US200,000 per year.

Length of Study: One to two years.

Country of Study: Any.

Applications Procedure: Application form required.

Closing Date: October 31st.

For further information contact:
American Health Assistance Foundation, 15825 Shady Grove Road, Suite 140, Rockville, Maryland, 20850, USA
Tel: 301 948 3244
Fax: 301 258 9454
Contact: Dr Sherry Marts

National Glaucoma Research

Subjects: Ophthalmology.

Eligibility: The principal investigator must hold the rank of assistant professor (or equivalent) or higher.

Level of Study: Professional development.

Purpose: To enable basic research on the causes of, or treatments for, Glaucoma.

Type: Grant.

No. of awards offered: Varies.

Frequency: Annual.

Value: Up to $US50,000.

Length of Study: One to two years.

Country of Study: Any.

Applications Procedure: Application form required.

Closing Date: November 30th.

For further information contact:
American Health Assistance Foundation, 15825 Shady Grove Road, Suite 140, Rockville, Maryland, 20850, USA
Tel: 301 948 3244
Fax: 301 258 9454
Contact: Dr Sherry Marts

AMERICAN HEART ASSOCIATION, INC

American Heart Association, Inc, 7272 Greenville Avenue, Dallas, TX, 75231, USA
Tel: 1 214 706 1453
Fax: 1 214 706 1341
Contact: Division of Research Administration

Grants-in-Aid

Subjects: All basic disciplines, such as physiology, biochemistry, pathology, as well as epidemiological and clinical investigations which bear on cardiovascular problems, including stroke.

Eligibility: Open to US citizens or foreign nationals with an exchange visitor or permanent residence visa, who hold an MD, DO, PhD, DSc, DVM or equivalent domestic or foreign degree and will be engaged in essentially full-time research.

Purpose: To support research activities broadly related to cardiovascular function and disease or to related science, clinical and public health problems.

Frequency: Annual.

Value: Approximately US$40,000 maximum, plus 10% for overheads.

Length of Study: 1-3 years.

Study Establishment: Accredited institutions.

Country of Study: USA or abroad.

Closing Date: July 1st.

Additional Information: Limited funds are available for support of research in the basic sciences irrespective of apparent direct application to the field of cardiovascular disease.

AMERICAN HISTORICAL ASSOCIATION

American Historical Association, 400 A Street S.E, Washington, DC, 20003, USA
Tel: 202 544 2422
Fax: 202 544 8307
Email: aha@gmu.edu
Contact: Administrative Assistant

Albert J Beveridge Grant

Eligibility: Open to AHA members only.

Purpose: Modest grants not to exceed $US1,000 are offered annually to support research in the history of the Western hemisphere.

Type: Grant.

No. of awards offered: Varies.

Frequency: Dependent on funds available, annually.

Value: Not to exceed $US1,000.

Country of Study: Western Hemisphere.

Applications Procedure: Please contact the AHA.

Closing Date: February 1st.

J Franklin Jameson Fellowship

Purpose: Sponsored jointly by the Library of Congress and the AHA to support significant scholarly research in the collections of the Library of Congress by young historians.

Type: Fellowship.

No. of awards offered: One.

Frequency: Dependent on funds available, annually.

Value: $US10,000.

Length of Study: One semester.

Country of Study: USA.

Applications Procedure: Contact the AHA.

Closing Date: January 15th.

Littleton-Griswold Research Grant

Eligibility: Open to AHA members only.

Purpose: Grants up to $US1,000 are offered to support research in American legal history and the field of law and society.

Type: Research Grant.

No. of awards offered: Varies.

Frequency: Annual.

Value: Up to $US1,000.

Applications Procedure: Contact the AHA.

Closing Date: February 1st.

Bernadette E Schmitt Grants

Eligibility: Open to AHA members only.

Level of Study: Postgraduate, Doctorate, Postdoctorate.

Purpose: Established in 1988 through a bequest from Bernadette Schmitt, President of the Association in 1960, modest grants of up to $US1,000 aim to support research in the history of Europe, Asia and Africa.

Type: Grant.

No. of awards offered: Varies.

Frequency: Dependent on funds available, annually.

Value: Up to $US1,000.

Country of Study: Varies.

Applications Procedure: Contact the American Historical Association.

Closing Date: September 15th.

AMERICAN HOME ECONOMICS ASSOCIATION FOUNDATION

American Home Economics Association Foundation, 1555 King Street, Alexandria, VA, 22314, USA

*AHEAF General Fellowship

Subjects: Home economics.

Eligibility: Open to US citizens or permanent residents of the US who are members of AHEA. Applicants must have completed at least one year of professional home economics experience by the beginning of the academic year for which the award is made.

Type: Fellowship.

No. of awards offered: One.

Frequency: As available.

Value: US$3,000.

Country of Study: USA.

Applications Procedure: Six copies of the completed application form should be submitted.

Closing Date: January 15th.

Additional Information: There is an application fee of US$15 for AHEA members or US$30 for non-members.

*Borden Award

Subjects: Nutrition and/or experimental foods.

Eligibility: Open to any home economist in the USA or Canada who has published research. Preference is given to AHEA members.

Purpose: To recognize significant research.

No. of awards offered: One.

Frequency: Annual.

Value: US$2,000 and a gold medal.

Closing Date: February 1st.

*Carley-Canoyer-Cutler Fellowship

Subjects: Consumer studies.

Eligibility: Open to members of minority groups or non-US citizens.

Type: Fellowship.

No. of awards offered: One.

Frequency: As available, about once every four years.

Value: US$3,000.

Country of Study: USA.

Closing Date: January 15th.

Additional Information: A US$15 application fee for AHEA members or US$30 for non-members must accompany any request from US citizens and those international students who may be currently residing in the USA.

*Gladys Branegan Chalkley Public Policy Internship

Subjects: Home economics; public policy and policy-making.

Eligibility: Open to home economists with a baccalaureate degree in home economics or any of its specialities who have demonstrated leadership in AHEA at state and/or national level and have a strong interest in public policy.

Purpose: To stimulate interest in public policy as it affects the home economics profession, to train interns in various aspects of policy-making and to provide avenues for interaction with members of the US Congress and leaders of various home economics-related organizations.

No. of awards offered: One.

Frequency: Annual.

Value: US$3,000.

Length of Study: 10-week internship.

Country of Study: USA.

Closing Date: February 1st.

*Mary Josephine Cochran Fellowship

Subjects: Textiles and clothing.

Eligibility: Open to US citizens or permanent residents of the US who are members of AHEA. Applicants must have completed at least one year of professional home economics experience by the beginning of the academic year for which the award is made.

Type: Fellowship.

No. of awards offered: One.

Frequency: As available.

Value: US$3,000.

Country of Study: USA.

Applications Procedure: Six copies of the completed application form should be submitted.

Closing Date: January 15th.

Additional Information: There is an application fee of US$15 for AHEA members or US$30 for non-members.

*Jeannette H Crum Fellowship

Subjects: Home economics.

Eligibility: Open to US citizens or permanent residents of the USA who are members of AHEA. Applicants must have completed at least one year of professional home economics experience by the beginning of the academic year for which the award is made.

Type: Fellowship.

No. of awards offered: One.

Frequency: As available.

Value: US$3,000.

Country of Study: USA.

Applications Procedure: Six copies of the completed application form should be submitted.

Closing Date: January 15th.

Additional Information: There is an application fee of US$15 for AHEA members or US$30 for non-members.

*Mildred B Davis Memorial Fellowship

Subjects: Nutrition.

Eligibility: Open to US citizens or permanent residents of the US who are members of AHEA. Applicants must have completed at least one year of professional home economics experience by the beginning of the academic year for which the award is made.

Type: Fellowship.

No. of awards offered: One.

Frequency: As available.

Value: US$3,000.

Country of Study: USA.

Applications Procedure: Six copies of the completed application form should be submitted.

Closing Date: January 15th.

Additional Information: There is an application fee of US$15 for AHEA members or US$30 for non-members.

*Freda A DeKnight Memorial Fellowship

Subjects: Home economics communication or cooperative extension.

Eligibility: Open to Black American graduate students.

Type: Fellowship.

No. of awards offered: One.

Frequency: As available.

Value: US$3,000.

Country of Study: USA.

Closing Date: January 15th.

Additional Information: A US$15 application fee for AHEA members or US$30 for non-members must accompany any request from US citizens and those international students who may be currently residing in the USA.

*Marie Dye Memorial Fellowship

Subjects: Home economics.

Eligibility: Open to US citizens or permanent residents of the USA who are members of AHEA. Applicants must have completed at least one year of professional home economics experience by the beginning of the academic year for which the award is made.

Level of Study: Doctorate.

Type: Fellowship.

No. of awards offered: One.

Frequency: As available.

Value: US$3,000.

Country of Study: USA.

Applications Procedure: Six copies of the completed application form should be submitted.

Closing Date: January 15th.

Additional Information: There is an application fee of US$15.

*Fellowships

Subjects: Home economics.

Eligibility: Open to US citizens or permanent residents for National Fellowships, and to non-US citizens for International Fellowships.

Purpose: To assist graduate study in home economics and its related fields.

Type: Fellowship.

No. of awards offered: 7-10.

Frequency: Annual.

Value: US$3,000.

Country of Study: USA.

Closing Date: January 15th.

*Flemmie P Kittrell Fellowship for Minorities

Subjects: Home economics.

Eligibility: Open to members of minority groups in the USA and to students from developing countries.

Type: Fellowship.

No. of awards offered: One.

Frequency: As available.

Value: US$3,000.

Country of Study: USA.

Closing Date: January 15th.

Additional Information: A US$15 application fee for AHEA members or US$30 for non-members must accompany any request from US citizens and those international students who may be currently residing in the USA.

*Ruth O'Brien Project Grant

Subjects: Home economics.

Eligibility: Open to suitably qualified individuals.

No. of awards offered: One or more.

Value: US$3,000.

Closing Date: November 15th.

*Ethel L Parker International Fellowship

Subjects: Home economics.

Eligibility: Open to non-US citizens.

Type: Fellowship.

No. of awards offered: One.

Frequency: As available.

Value: US$3,000.

Country of Study: USA.

Applications Procedure: Six copies of the completed application form should be submitted.

Closing Date: January 15th.

Additional Information: Although the International Fellowships are intended for graduate-level study, exceptions may be made for applicants whose home country offers little or no training in home economics. International students residing in the USA at the time of application must submit a US$15 fee. Those students residing outside the USA are not required to submit an application fee, and need complete only one copy of the application form.

*Marion K Piper International Fellowship

Subjects: Home economics.

Eligibility: Open to non-US citizens.

Type: Fellowship.

No. of awards offered: One.

Frequency: Annual.

Value: US$3,000.

Country of Study: USA.

Applications Procedure: Six copies of the completed application form should be submitted.

Closing Date: January 15th.

Additional Information: Although the International Fellowships are intended for graduate-level study, exceptions may be made for applicants whose home country offers little or no training in home economics. International students residing in the USA at the time of application must submit a US$15 fee. Those students residing outside the USA are not required to submit an application fee, and need complete only one copy of the application form.

*Inez Eleanor Radell Memorial Fellowship

Subjects: The design, construction and/or marketing of clothing for the ageing and/or handicapped adult.

Eligibility: Open to US citizens or permanent residents of the USA who are members of AHEA. Applicants must have completed at least one year of professional home economics experience by the beginning of the academic year for which the award is made.

Type: Fellowship.

No. of awards offered: One.

Frequency: As available.

Value: US$3,000.

Country of Study: USA.

Applications Procedure: Six copies of the completed application form should be submitted.

Closing Date: January 15th.

Additional Information: There is an application fee of US$15 for AHEA members or US$30 for non-members.

*Ellen H Richards Fellowship

Subjects: Home economics, with emphasis on administration.

Eligibility: Open to US citizens or permanent residents of the USA who are members of AHEA. Applicants must have completed at least one year of professional home economics experience by the beginning of the academic year for which the award is made. Applicants should be home economics graduates who have had work experience in an administrative area such as supervision, college or university administration, cooperative extension work or business.

No. of awards offered: One.

Frequency: As available.

Value: US$3,000.

Country of Study: USA.

Applications Procedure: Six copies of the completed application form should be submitted.

Closing Date: January 15th.

Additional Information: There is an application fee of US$15 for AHEA members or US$30 for non-members.

*Jewell L Taylor Fellowships

Subjects: Home economics.

Eligibility: Open to US citizens or permanent residents of the USA who are members of AHEA. Applicants must have completed at least one year of professional home economics experience by the beginning of the academic year for which the award is made.

Type: Fellowship.

No. of awards offered: Two.

Frequency: As available.

Value: US$5,000.

Country of Study: USA.

Applications Procedure: Six copies of the completed application form should be submitted.

Closing Date: January 15th.

Additional Information: There is an application fee of US$15 for AHEA members or US$30 for non-members.

*D Elizabeth Williams Fellowship

Subjects: Home economics.

Eligibility: Open to non-US citizens.

No. of awards offered: One.

Frequency: As available.

Value: US$3,000.

Country of Study: USA.

Closing Date: January 15th.

Additional Information: Although the International Fellowships are intended for graduate-level study, exceptions may be made for applicants whose home country offers little or no training in home economics. International students residing in the USA at the time of application must submit a US$15 fee. Six copies of the completed application form should be submitted. Those students residing outside the USA are not required to submit an application fee, and need complete only one copy of the application form.

AMERICAN INDIAN GRADUATE CENTER

American Indian Graduate Center, 4520 Montgomery Blvd, NE, Suite 1-B, Albuquerque, NM, 87109, USA
Tel: 505 881 4584
Fax: 505 884 0427
Contact: Reginald Rodriguez, Executive Director

AIGC Fellowship

Subjects: Any subject.

Eligibility: American Indians - enrolled members of federally recognized tribes only, attending accredited institutions and programs. Degree granting programs only.

Level of Study: Postgraduate, Baccalaureate.

Purpose: To support American Indian graduate students in all professional degree programs.

Type: Fellowship grant.

No. of awards offered: 400.

Frequency: Dependent on funds available.

Value: Need-based program; must apply to financial aid office to determine need.

Length of Study: Depends on degree program.

Country of Study: USA.

Applications Procedure: Application must be requested by individual student. Application to be submitted by June 1st each year.

Closing Date: June 1st.

Additional Information: Applications are sent to individuals only. Application form indicates the length of time for eligibility for each program - PhD, MD, LAW, MA, MFA.

AMERICAN INDIAN SCIENCE AND ENGINEERING SOCIETY

American Indian Science and Engineering Society, 1630 30th Street Suite 301, Boulder, CO, 80301-1014, USA

Tel: 303 939 0023
Fax: 303 939 8150
Email: ascholar@spot.colorado.edu
Contact: Sonya Todacheene

A T Anderson Memorial Scholarship

Eligibility: Open to Native Americans and Alaskan Natives.

Level of Study: Unrestricted.

Purpose: To award academic excellence and leadership.

Type: Scholarship.

No. of awards offered: 400.

Frequency: Annual.

Value: US$1,000-US$2,000.

Study Establishment: An accredited School.

Country of Study: USA.

Applications Procedure: Applicants must submit an application, an official transcript, a personal statement, a certificate of Indian Blood, and two letters of recommendation.

Closing Date: June 15th.

EPA Tribal Lands Environmental Science Scholarship

Eligibility: Open to US citizens.

Level of Study: Postgraduate, Doctorate.

Purpose: To award academic excellence and leadership.

Type: Scholarship.

No. of awards offered: Fifty.

Frequency: Annual.

Value: US$4,000.

Study Establishment: An accredited school.

Country of Study: USA.

Applications Procedure: Please submit two letters of recommendation, application form, official transcript and personal statement.

Closing Date: June.

Santa Fe Pacific Foundation Scholarship

Eligibility: Open to Native Americans or Alaskan Natives.

Level of Study: College Freshman.

Purpose: To award excellence and leadership.

Type: Scholarship.

No. of awards offered: Four.

Frequency: Annual.

Value: US$1,000-US$2,500.

Study Establishment: An accredited School.

Country of Study: USA.

Applications Procedure: Applicants must submit two letters of recommendation, a personal statement, a high school transcript, an application, and a certificate of Indian blood.

Closing Date: March 15th.

AMERICAN INSTITUTE FOR ECONOMIC RESEARCH

American Institute for Economic Research, PO Box 1000, Great Barrington, MA, 01230-1000, USA
Tel: 413 528 1216
Fax: 413 528 0103
Email: aier@world.std.com
www: http://world.std.com/~aier/

Contact: Kerry A Lynch, Associate Director of Research

Summer Fellowship Program

Subjects: Economic research, primarily scientific procedures of enquiry and monetary economics.

Eligibility: Open to graduate students majoring in economics. Undergraduates who have completed their junior year may also apply, although preference is given to graduates. US citizens are given first priority. Foreign nationals must be fluent in written and spoken English.

Level of Study: Postgraduate, Doctorate.

Purpose: To further the development of economic scientists.

Type: Fellowship.

No. of awards offered: 10-12.

Frequency: Annual.

Value: US$125 per week, plus room and board. Supplementary stipends of US$25 per dependant are provided to Fellows with family responsibilities. Awardees become eligible for tuition support following successful completion of the summer fellowship.

Length of Study: 8 weeks.

Study Establishment: At the Institute.

Country of Study: USA.

Applications Procedure: Application form must be completed and submitted with school transcript, a copy of a recent term paper, a biography and two scholastic references.

Closing Date: March 31st.

Additional Information: The Institute is unable to assist with transportation costs, visas, insurance or any of the other technicalities necessary for students, foreign or US, to participate in the program.

AMERICAN INSTITUTE OF BAKING

American Institute of Baking, 1213 Bakers Way, Manhattan, KS, 66502, USA
Tel: 1 800 633 5137
Fax: 1 913 537 1493
Email: aibakers@inc.org
Contact: Ken Embers, Registrar, or Marilyn Thomas

Scholarships for Advanced Study in Baking Science and Technology and/or Maintenance Engineering

Subjects: The scientific basis of baking and the technology of modern bakery production. The ten-week maintenance engineering course emphasizes electricity, electronics, motor controls, programmable controllers and computers.

Eligibility: Open to candidates who meet entrance requirements for baking science and technology class or for maintenance engineering.

Level of Study: Professional development.

Purpose: To enable scholars to advance rapidly in the baking and allied industries.

Type: Scholarship.

No. of awards offered: At least 20.

Frequency: Twice yearly.

Value: US$500-US$3,700.

Length of Study: 16 weeks (baking science and technology) or 10 weeks (maintenance engineering) of comprehensive instruction.

Study Establishment: The Institute.

Country of Study: USA.

Closing Date: May 1st and November 1st. Late applications are accepted prior to the beginning of classes in February and May.

Scholarships for Study in Maintenance Engineering

Subjects: Maintenance engineering.

Eligibility: Open to candidates who meet the requirements for maintenance engineering.

Level of Study: Professional development.

Purpose: To train promising individuals for positions of responsibility.

Type: Scholarship.

No. of awards offered: Four.

Frequency: Throughout the year.

Value: US$500-US$2,000.

Length of Study: Ten weeks of comprehensive instruction.

Study Establishment: The Institute.

Country of Study: USA.

Additional Information: The classes are held twice a year and commence September 1st and February 1st.

AMERICAN INSTITUTE OF CERTIFIED PUBLIC ACCOUNTANTS

Academic & Career Development, American Institute of Certified Public Accountants, 1211 Avenue of the Americas, New York, NY, 10036, USA
Tel: 212 596 6221
Fax: 212 596 6292
Contact: Leticia B Romeo

Doctoral Fellowships

Subjects: Accounting.

Eligibility: Open to US citizens who hold a valid CPA certificate, and have at least five years of professional accounting experience. Candidates must be accepted into or be in the process of applying to a doctoral program in accounting at a college or university whose business administration programs are accredited by the AACSB. Applicants should have the intention to pursue an academic career in accounting in the US. All applicants are expected to exhibit fluency in English appropriate to teaching.

Level of Study: Doctorate.

Purpose: To encourage practising CPAs to consider a career change to academe.

Type: Fellowship.

Frequency: Annual.

Value: US$5,000 per annum.

Length of Study: A maximum of three years.

Study Establishment: A college or university whose business administration programs are accredited by the American Assembly of Collegiate Schools of Business.

Country of Study: USA.

Applications Procedure: An official academic transcript is required, in addition to references from three individuals, and the completion of an application form.

Closing Date: April 1st.

AMERICAN JEWISH ARCHIVES

American Jewish Archives, 3101 Clifton Avenue, Cincinnati, OH, 45220, USA
Contact: Administrative Director

147

*Rabbi Frederic A Doppelt Memorial Fellowship

Subjects: American Jewish studies.

Eligibility: Open to ABDs.

Type: Fellowship.

Value: US$1,000.

Length of Study: One month.

Study Establishment: The Archives.

Applications Procedure: Applicants must provide an up-to-date curriculum vitae, a research proposal and three faculty recommendations (including dissertation supervisors'). These will constitute the application forms.

Closing Date: April 1st.

Additional Information: Preference will be given to candidates from Eastern Europe or those working on a topic related to East European Jewry in the American context.

*Marguerite R Jacobs Memorial Award

Subjects: American Jewish studies.

Eligibility: Open to postdoctoral candidates.

Level of Study: Postdoctorate.

Value: US$2,000.

Length of Study: One month.

Study Establishment: The Archives.

Applications Procedure: Applicants must provide an up-to-date curriculum vitae, a research proposal, evidence of published research, where possible, and two recommendations from academic colleagues. These will constitute the application forms.

Closing Date: April 1st.

*Rabbi Theodore S Levy Tribute Fellowship

Subjects: American Jewish Studies.

Eligibility: Open to ABDs.

Type: Fellowship.

Value: US$1,000.

Length of Study: One month.

Study Establishment: The Archives.

Applications Procedure: Applicants must provide an up-to-date curriculum vitae, a research proposal and three faculty recommendations (including dissertation supervisors'). These will constitute the application forms.

Closing Date: April 1st.

*Loewenstein-Wiener Fellowship Awards

Subjects: American Jewish studies.

Eligibility: Open to ABDs who have completed all but the dissertation requirement and to postdoctoral candidates.

Type: Fellowship.

Value: US$1,000 for ABDs; US$2,000 for postdoctoral candidates.

Length of Study: One month.

Study Establishment: The Archives.

Applications Procedure: Applicants must provide an up-to-date curriculum vitae, a research proposal, and evidence of published research, where possible. ABDs must provide three faculty recommendations (including dissertation supervisors') and postdoctoral candidates must provide two recommendations from academic colleagues. These will constitute the application forms.

Closing Date: April 1st.

*Ethel Marcus Memorial Fellowship

Subjects: American Jewish studies.

Eligibility: Open to ABDs.

Type: Fellowship.

Value: US$1,000.

Length of Study: One month.

Study Establishment: The Archives.

Applications Procedure: Applicants must provide an up-to-date curriculum vitae, a research proposal and three faculty recommendations (including dissertation supervisors'). These will constitute the application forms.

Closing Date: April 1st.

*Bernard and Audre Rapoport Fellowships

Subjects: American Jewish studies.

Eligibility: Open to postdoctoral candidates.

Level of Study: Postdoctorate.

Type: Fellowship.

Value: US$2,000.

Length of Study: One month.

Study Establishment: The Archives.

Applications Procedure: Applicants must provide an up-to-date curriculum vitae, a research proposal, evidence of published research, and two recommendations from academic colleagues. These will constitute the application forms.

Closing Date: April 1st.

AMERICAN LIBRARY ASSOCIATION

50 East Huron Street, Chicago, IL, 60611, USA
Tel: 312 280 4273
Fax: 312 280 3256
Email: mjlynch@ala.org
Contact: Mary Jo Lynch

Carroll Preston Baber Research Grant

Subjects: Library service.

Eligibility: Open to members of the American Library Association.

Level of Study: Unrestricted.

Purpose: To encourage innovative research that could lead to an improvement in library services to any specific groups of people.

Type: Research Grant.

No. of awards offered: One.

Frequency: Annual.

Value: Up to US$7,500.

Applications Procedure: Application must include research proposal.

Closing Date: March 1st.

Additional Information: The project should aim to answer a question that is of vital importance to the library community, and the researchers should plan to provide documentation of the results of their work. The jury would welcome proposals that involve innovative uses of technology and proposals that involve co-operation between libraries, between libraries and other agencies, or between librarians and persons in other disciplines.

For further information contact:
American Library Association, 50 East Huron Street, Chicago, IL, 60611-2795, USA
Tel: 312 280 4273
Fax: 312 280 3256
Email: mjlynch@ala.org

Contact: Mary Jo Lynch, Staff Liaison

Beta Phi Mu Award

Subjects: Education for librarianship.

Eligibility: Open to library school faculty members or others in the library profession.

Level of Study: Professional development.

Purpose: To recognise distinguished service to education for librarianship.

No. of awards offered: One.

Frequency: Annual.

Value: US$500 and a citation.

Applications Procedure: Nominations should be submitted to Beta Phi Mu Award, Jury Chair.

Closing Date: December 1st.

For further information contact:
American Library Association, MPS, 50 East Huron Street, Chicago, IL, 60611-2795, USA
Tel: 312 280 3247
Fax: 312 280 3257
Contact: Awards Committee

CIS/GODORT/ALA Documents to the People Award

Subjects: Library science.

Eligibility: Open to individuals and/or libraries, organizations and other appropriate non-commercial groups.

Purpose: To promote professional advancement in the field of librarianship and to recognize the most effective encouragement of the use of federal documents in support of library services.

No. of awards offered: One.

Frequency: Annual.

Value: US$2,000.

Closing Date: December 15th.

Additional Information: Nominations should be submitted to GODORT Staff Liaison, ALA. The award is sponsored by the Congressional Information Service, Inc.

For further information contact:
American Library Association, 1301 Pennsylvania Ave.,NW, Washington, DC, 20004, USA
Tel: 202 628 8410
Fax: 202 628 8419
Contact: Patricia Muir, Staff Liaison

Equality Award

Subjects: The contribution may be either a sustained one or a single outstanding accomplishment in such areas as pay equity, affirmative action, legislative work and non-sexist education.

Eligibility: Open to members of the library profession.

Level of Study: Professional development.

Purpose: To recognize an outstanding contribution towards the promotion of equality between men and women in the library profession.

No. of awards offered: One.

Frequency: Annual.

Value: US$500 plus a certificate.

Closing Date: December 1st.

Additional Information: Nominations should be submitted to ALA Awards Committee, c/o Equality Jury Chair.

Facts on File Grant

Subjects: Library science.

Eligibility: Open to adult librarians.

Level of Study: Professional development.

Purpose: Awarded to a library for imaginative programming which would make current affairs more meaningful to an adult audience.

Type: Grant.

No. of awards offered: One.

Frequency: Annual.

Value: US$2,000.

Applications Procedure: A proposal must be submitted accompanied by a statement of objectives; identification of the current issue(s), the target audience and the extent of community involvement planned; an outline of planned activities for conducting and promoting the project; budget summary and how the project will be evaluated.

Closing Date: December 15th.

Additional Information: Programs, bibliographics, pamphlets, and innovative approaches of all types and in all media will apply.

For further information contact:
American Library Association, 50 East Huron Street, Chicago, IL, 60611-2795, USA
Tel: 800 545 2433 ext 4398
Fax: 312 944 8085
Contact: RASD

The Loleta D. Fyan Grant

Subjects: Library service.

Eligibility: Applicants can include but are not limited to: local, regional or state libraries, associations or organizations, including units of the American Library Association; library schools; or individuals.

Level of Study: Unrestricted.

Purpose: Loleta Fyan, 1951-52 ALA President, bequeathed funds to ALA with the intent that 'these funds be used for the development and improvement of public libraries and the services they provide'.

Type: Research grant.

No. of awards offered: One.

Frequency: Annual.

Value: Up to $10,000.

Applications Procedure: Application form must be submitted in addition to a proposal and budget.

Additional Information: The project(s) 1] must result in the development and improvement of public libraries and the services they provide, 2] must have the potential fro broader impact and application beyond meeting a specific local need, 3] should be designed to effect changes in public library services that are innovative and responsive to the future, and 4] should be capable of completion within one year.

Grolier Foundation Award

Subjects: The Award is given for outstanding work with children and young people through high school age, for continuing service, or in recognition of one particular contribution of lasting value.

Eligibility: Open to community and school librarians.

Level of Study: Professional development.

Purpose: To recognize a librarian whose "unusual contribution to the stimulation and guidance of reading by children and young people" exemplifies outstanding achievement in the profession.

No. of awards offered: One.

Frequency: Annual.

Value: US$1,000 plus a citation.

Closing Date: December 1st.

Additional Information: Nominations and five copies of the statement should be submitted to Grolier Award, Jury Chair, ALA Awards Committee.

G K Hall Award for Library Literature

Subjects: Library literature.

Eligibility: Open to American librarians.

Level of Study: Professional development.

Purpose: Presented to one author and/or co-authors to recognize an outstanding contribution to library literature issued during the three years preceding the presentation. The book might emphasise management principles and practices, understanding and applications of new technologies and education for librarians or other information specialists.

No. of awards offered: One.

Frequency: Annual.

Value: US$500 plus a citation.

Applications Procedure: Nominations should be submitted to G K Hall Award Jury Chair.

Closing Date: December 1st.

John Philip Immroth Award for Intellectual Freedom

Subjects: Intellectual freedom.

Eligibility: Open to intellectual freedom fighters.

Purpose: To recognize a notable contribution and the demonstration of remarkable courage.

No. of awards offered: One.

Frequency: Annual.

Value: US$500 plus a plaque.

Applications Procedure: A detailed statement must be submitted to state why the nominator believes that the nominee should receive the award.

Closing Date: December 1st.

Additional Information: Nominations should be submitted to IFRT Staff Liaison, ALA.

For further information contact:
American Library Association, 50 East Huron Street, Chicago, IL, 60611-2795, USA
Tel: 312 280 4224
Fax: 312 280 4227
Email: dliebow@ala.org
Contact: Deborah Liebow

Library Research Round Table Research Award

Subjects: Library science.

Eligibility: Open to library science researchers.

Level of Study: Unrestricted.

Purpose: To encourage excellence in research.

Type: Research Award.

No. of awards offered: One.

Frequency: Annual.

Value: US$1,000.

Applications Procedure: Please request guidelines from ALA.

Closing Date: February 2nd.

Additional Information: Papers must not exceed 50 pages in length and will be judged on the definition of the research problem, application of research methods, clarity of reporting and the significance of conclusions. Research papers completed in pursuit of an academic degree are not eligible. Candidates should submit their entries to the jury chair, whose name is available each year from ALA.

For further information contact:
American Library Association, 50 East Huron Street, Chicago, IL, 60611--2795, USA
Tel: 312 280 4273
Fax: 312 280 3256
Email: mjlynch@ala.org
Contact: ORS

Joseph W Lippincott Award

Subjects: Service should include outstanding participation in the activities of professional library associations, notable published professional writing, or other significant activity on behalf of the profession and its aims.

Eligibility: Open to librarians.

Level of Study: Professional development.

Purpose: To recognize distinguished service in the profession of librarianship.

No. of awards offered: One.

Frequency: Annual.

Value: US$1,000 plus a citation.

Applications Procedure: Nominations should be submitted to Lippincott Award Jury Chair, ALA Awards Committee.

Closing Date: December 1st.

Frederick G Melcher Scholarships

Subjects: Library service to children.

Eligibility: Open to qualified young persons who have been accepted for admission to an appropriate school.

Level of Study: Professional development.

Purpose: To provide financial assistance for the professional education of men and women who intend to pursue children's librarianship.

Type: Scholarship.

No. of awards offered: Two.

Frequency: Annual.

Value: US$5,000.

Study Establishment: An ALA-accredited school.

Closing Date: March 1st.

For further information contact:
American Library Association, 50 East Huron Street, Chicago, IL, 60611-2795, USA
Tel: 312 280 2163
Fax: 312 280 3257

*NMRT Professional Development Grant

Subjects: Library studies.

Eligibility: Open to members of the ALA and the New Members Round Table.

Purpose: To allow librarians to attend the annual conference of the ALA.

No. of awards offered: Varies.

Frequency: Annual.

Value: Varies.

Applications Procedure: Nominations should be submitted to NMRT Professional Development Grant, c/o ALA.

Closing Date: November 15th.

For further information contact:
Colorado Schools of Mines, Arthur Lakes Library, 1400 Illinois Street, Golden, CO, 80401-1887, USA
Contact: Susan A Benjamin

Eli M Oboler Memorial Award

Subjects: Intellectual freedom, freedom to read.

Eligibility: There are no eligibility restrictions.

Purpose: To award the best published work in the area of intellectual freedom.

No. of awards offered: One.

Frequency: Every two years.

Value: US$1,500 award plus citation.

Applications Procedure: Please submit the nominated documents with nominating form.

Closing Date: December 1st.

*Shirley Olofson Memorial Awards

Subjects: Library science.

Eligibility: Open to members of the ALA who are also current or potential members of the New Members Round Table.

Purpose: To allow individuals to attend their second conference of the ALA.

No. of awards offered: Varies.

Frequency: Annual.

Value: Varies.

Closing Date: December 1st.

For further information contact:
Marquette University, Memorial Library, 1415 West Wisconsin Avenue, Milwaukee, WI, 53233, USA
Contact: Ann M Gordon

Putnam & Grosset Group Award

Subjects: Library science.

Eligibility: Open to members of the Association for Library Service to Children with between one and ten years' experience who have never attended an ALA annual conference.

Level of Study: Professional development.

Purpose: To allow two school librarians and two public library children's librarians to attend the annual conference of the ALA.

Type: Award.

No. of awards offered: Four.

Frequency: Annual.

Value: US$600.

Closing Date: December 1st.

For further information contact:
American Library Association, 50 East Huron Street, Chicago, IL, 60611-2795, USA
Tel: 312 280 2163
Fax: 312 280 3257
Contact: Executive Director, ALSC

Herbert W Putnam Awards

Subjects: Studies related to the library service.

Eligibility: Open to American librarians.

Level of Study: Professional development.

Type: Grant-in-aid.

No. of awards offered: One.

Frequency: Whenever the Putnam Fund has accumulated US$500.

Value: US$500 towards travel writing or other use that might improve the recipient's service to the library profession or to society.

Additional Information: Inquiries should be addressed to ALA Awards Staff Liaison, ALA.

*YALSA/Baker and Taylor Conference Grants

Subjects: Library science.

Eligibility: Open to members of the Young Adult Services Division with 1-10 years of library experience who have never attended an ALA annual conference.

Purpose: To allow young adult librarians who work directly with young adults in either a public library or a school library, to attend the annual conference of the ALA.

No. of awards offered: Two.

Frequency: Annual.

Value: US$1,000.

Closing Date: December 1st.

Additional Information: Applications should be submitted to Young Adult Services Division, ALA. The ALA offers a number of other awards in various fields related to library science, including the following medals and citations with no cash prizes: (medals) Randolph Caldecott Medal; James Bennett Childs Award; Dartmouth Medal, Melvil Dewey Medal; John Newberry Medal; Laura Ingalls Wilder Medal; (citations) ASCLA Exceptional Service Award; Armed Forces Librarians Achievement Citation; Francis Joseph Campbell Citation; Margaret Mann Citation; Isadore Gilbert Mudge Citation; Esther J Piercy Award; Distinguished Library Service Award for School Administrators; Trustees Citations. A full list of awards is available from the Association.

AMERICAN LIVER FOUNDATION

American Liver Foundation, 1425 Pompton Avenue, Cedar Grove, NJ, 07009, USA
Tel: 1 800 223 0179
Fax: 1 201 256 3214
Contact: Research Awards

Naomi Judd Pediatric Liver Scholar Research Award

Subjects: Pediatric liver diseases.

Level of Study: Postdoctorate, Professional development.

Purpose: To fund MD/PhD research into biliary atresia and other pediatric liver diseases.

Type: Research Grant.

No. of awards offered: One.

Frequency: Annual.

Length of Study: Three years.

For further information contact:
American Liver Foundation, 1425 Pompton Avenue, Cedar Grove, NJ, 07009, USA
Tel: 800 223 0179
Fax: 201 256 3214
Contact: Research Awards

Liver Scholar Award

Subjects: Liver research.

Eligibility: Open to junior faculty.

Type: Research Grant.

Frequency: Annual.

Value: US$30,000 per annum.

Length of Study: Three years.

Closing Date: December 15th.

Postdoctoral Supplementary Fellowship

Subjects: Liver research.

Eligibility: Open to MD and PhD candidates.

Level of Study: Doctorate, Postgraduate.

Type: Fellowship.

Frequency: Annual.

Value: US$7,500.

Length of Study: One year.

Closing Date: December 15th.

Student Research Fellowship

Subjects: Liver research.

Eligibility: Open to MD, PhD and veterinary candidates.

Level of Study: Postgraduate, Doctorate.

Type: Fellowship.

Frequency: Annual.

Value: US$2,500.

Length of Study: Three months.

Closing Date: December 15th.

For further information contact:
American Liver Research, 1425 Pompton Avenue, Cedar Grove, NJ, 07009, USA
Tel: 1 800 223 0179
Fax: 1 201 256 3214
Contact: Research Awards

AMERICAN MATHEMATICAL SOCIETY

American Mathematical Society, PO Box 6248, Providence, RI, 09240, USA
Tel: 401 455 4000
Fax: 401 331 3842
Email: ams@ams.org
www: http://www.ams.org/
Contact: Executive Director

AMS Centennial Fellowship

Subjects: Mathematics.

Eligibility: Applicants must be citizens or permanent residents of a country in North America; must have held their doctoral degrees for at least two years at the time of the award; must not have permanent tenure; and must have held less than two years of research support at the time of the award. Recipients may not hold this fellowship concurrently with other research fellowships; they may not use the stipend solely to reduce the teaching at the home institution; and they are expected to spend some of the fellowship period at another institution which has a stimulating research environment suited to the applicants' research development.

Level of Study: Postdoctorate.

Purpose: To provide funds for research mathematicians during the early developmental stage of their careers.

Type: Fellowship.

No. of awards offered: At least one.

Frequency: Annual.

Value: A stipend of US$36,000 (in 1996/97) plus an expense allowance of US$1,400.

Length of Study: Nine months.

Study Establishment: At any institution selected by the Fellow or at more than one in succession.

Country of Study: Any country.

Applications Procedure: Application form plus three letters of reference on special reference form, provided with the application packet.

Closing Date: December 1st.

AMERICAN MUSEUM OF NATURAL HISTORY

American Museum of Natural History, Central Park West at 79th Street, New York, NY, 10024, USA
Tel: 212 769 5040
Contact: Office of Grants and Fellowships

Chapman and Naumberg Fellowships

Subjects: Ornithology.

Eligibility: Open to postgraduate scholars and distinguished ornithologists.

Level of Study: Postgraduate.

Type: Fellowship.

No. of awards offered: One or two.

Frequency: Annual.

Value: Support includes a stipend and possible contributions toward research expenses.

Length of Study: One year.

Study Establishment: The Museum or one of its field stations.

Country of Study: USA.

Closing Date: January 15th.

Additional Information: One of those Fellowships, to be called the Elsie Binger Naumberg Fellowship, will be restricted to the general field of tropical American ornithology.

Chapman Memorial Fund Grants

Subjects: Ornithology.

Eligibility: Grants are primarily designed to encourage and aid less experienced individuals with recent graduate degrees, although there are no restrictions as to age, the formal qualifications of applicants or the locality in which research is to be conducted. In this regard, grant proposals are encouraged from graduate students and visiting scientists from outside the USA.

Level of Study: Postgraduate.

Purpose: To support and foster research from a broad and international point of view.

Type: Grant.

No. of awards offered: Varies.

Value: Approximately US$750 on average.

Study Establishment: The Museum or one of its field stations.

Country of Study: USA.

Closing Date: January 15th.

Additional Information: Proposals for museum, field and laboratory investigations are invited. Consideration is seldom given to projects which foster research more indirectly, such as publication subsidies, travel expenses to attend ornithological meetings, and temporary field assistance.

Collection Study Grants

Subjects: Any of the fields covered by the scientific collections at the American Museum: zoology, anthropology; mineral science.

Eligibility: Open to predoctoral and recent postdoctoral investigators.

Level of Study: Predoctoral, Postdoctorate.

Type: Study grant.

No. of awards offered: Varies.

Frequency: Varies.

Value: Up to US$500 partially to support travel and subsistence while visiting the American Museum.

Study Establishment: The Museum.

Country of Study: USA.

Applications Procedure: Applicants must contact the appropriate Museum department to discuss the feasibility of the project and obtain written approval of the Chairman. A special application form is required and it should be requested by name from the Office of Grants and Fellowships. A final report is required.

Additional Information: These grants are not available to investigators residing within daily commuting distance of the Museum.

For further information contact:
American Museum of Natural History, Central Park West at 79th Street, New York, NY, 10024, USA
Contact: Office of Grants and Fellowships

Lerner-Gray Fund Grants for Marine Research

Subjects: Marine biology, exclusive of botany.

Eligibility: Open to applicants at the graduate or postdoctoral level. There are no other restrictions.

Level of Study: Postdoctorate, Graduate.

Purpose: To support scientists beginning careers where funding from large foundations and granting agencies is unavailable.

Type: Grant.

No. of awards offered: Varies.

Value: An average of US$650 towards transportation costs, living expenses, expendable equipment and supplies.

Length of Study: One year.

Study Establishment: Field work.

Country of Study: Unrestricted.

Closing Date: March 15th.

Additional Information: The grants may not be applied to salaries or used for the purchase of non-expendable equipment.

Research and Museum Fellowships

Subjects: Research in any field of zoology; anthropology; mineral sciences; astronomy or museum education.

Eligibility: Open to recent postdoctoral investigators and established scientists.

Level of Study: Postdoctorate.

Purpose: To advance the training of the participant by having him pursue a project in association with museum professionals in a museum setting.

Type: Fellowship.

No. of awards offered: Varies.

Frequency: Annual.

Value: Varies. Limited relocation, research and publication support is often also available.

Length of Study: Generally for one year; possibly renewable.

Study Establishment: The Museum.

Country of Study: USA.

Applications Procedure: Applications may be obtained from the Office of Grants and Fellowships and should include project description, budget, bibliography, curriculum vitae, and letters of reference.

Closing Date: January 15th.

Additional Information: At the time of appointment the Museum names the Fellow after the primary source of funding, for example Kalbfleisch Research Fellow.

Theodore Roosevelt Memorial Fund Grants

Subjects: North American fauna; any phase of wildlife conservation or natural history related to the activities of the Museum.

Eligibility: Preference is given to graduate students and individuals with recent graduate degrees.

Level of Study: Graduate.

Purpose: To help finance research where funds are not usually available from large foundations or granting agencies.

Type: Grant.

No. of awards offered: Varies.

Value: An average of US$750 in support of field work, including transportation, subsistence, expendable supplies and equipment.

Country of Study: North American continent.

Closing Date: February 15th.

Additional Information: Grant recipients are expected to submit a project report and statement of expenses at the end of the project period. The report may be waived if results are to be published within one year.

AMERICAN MUSIC CENTER, INC

Jory Program, American Music Center, 30 West 26th Street, 10th Floor, New York, NY, 10010-2011, USA
Tel: 212 366 5260
Fax: 212 366 5265
Email: center@amc.net
www: http://www.ingress.com/amc/
Contact: The Director

Margaret Fairbank Jory Copying Assistance Program

Subjects: Musical composition.

Eligibility: Open to American composers/members of the American Music Center, who have composed musical works which require at least four performers. The composer must have a commitment in writing for at least one public performance of the work by a professional ensemble of recognized artistic merit.

Level of Study: Professional development.

Purpose: To assist composers with copying expenses for a premiere performance.

Type: Bursary.

No. of awards offered: Varies.

Frequency: Three times yearly.

Applications Procedure: Application form must be completed.

Closing Date: February 1st; May 1st; October 1st.

AMERICAN MUSICOLOGICAL SOCIETY

American Musicological Society, Department of Music, University of Illnois, Urbana, IL, 61801, USA
Tel: 217 333 0371
Fax: 217 244 4585
Contact: John W Hill

AMS 50 Dissertation Fellowship

Subjects: Any field of musical research.

Eligibility: Open to full-time students registered for a doctorate at a North American university, in good standing, who have completed all formal degree requirements except the dissertation at the time of full application. Open to all students without regard to nationality, race, religion or sex.

Purpose: To encourage research in the various fields of music as a branch of learning and scholarship.

Type: Fellowship.

No. of awards offered: Variable number of Fellowships (6 in 1993).

Frequency: Annual.

Value: US$10,000.

Country of Study: US or Canada.

Closing Date: 1 October.

Additional Information: Any submission for a doctoral degree in which the emphasis is on musical scholarship is eligible. The award is not intended for support of early stages of research; it is expected that a recipient's dissertation will be completed within the fellowship year. An equivalent major award from another source may not normally be held concurrently unless the AMS award is accepted on an honorary basis.

For further information contact:
American Musicological Society, Department of Music, New York University, 268 Waverly Building, Washington Square, New York, NY, 10003, USA
Contact: Rena Charnin Mueller

or
American Musicological Society, 201 South 34th Street, Philadelphia, PA 19104--6313, USA

The Paul A Pisk Prize

Subjects: Any field of musicology.

Eligibility: Open to graduate students whose abstracts have been submitted to the Program Committee of the Society and the papers accepted for inclusion in the Annual Meeting. Open to all students without regard to nationality, race, religion, or sex.

Purpose: To encourage scholarship by graduate students in musicology.

Type: Prize.

No. of awards offered: One.

Frequency: Annual.

Value: US$1,000.

Country of Study: USA or Canada.

Closing Date: 1 August.

For further information contact:
American Musicological Society, 201 South 34th Street, Philadelphia, PA, 19104-6313, USA

AMERICAN MUSIC SCHOLARSHIP ASSOCIATION

American Music Scholarship Association, 1030 Carew Tower, Cincinnati, OH, 45202, USA
Tel: 513 421 2672
Contact: Gloria Ackerman, Chief Executive Officer

*International Piano Competition

Subjects: Musical performance: piano.

Eligibility: Open to piano students of any nationality who are between the ages of 5 and 30.

Purpose: To encourage the careers of aspiring young pianists and expose them to the performances of great musicians.

No. of awards offered: 11.

Frequency: Annually, depending on funds available.

Value: Artists Division: 1st prize US$12,500, 2nd prize US$3,000, 3rd prize US$2,000, 4th prize US$1,000, 5th prize US$500, 6th prize

US$300; Young Artists Division: precollege grand prizes levels 9-12 US$750 and US$250, levels 5-6 US$500; plus US$50 in each of the 12 levels; regional awards of US$400 in each of the eight regional areas; Grand Prizes: 9-12 solo US$1,500, concerto US$1,500.

Closing Date: January 1st.

Additional Information: Full competition rules and regulations are available on request.

AMERICAN NUMISMATIC SOCIETY

American Numismatic Society, Broadway at 155th Street, New York, NY, 10032, USA
Tel: 212 234 3130
Fax: 212 234 3381
Contact: Chief Curator

ANS Graduate Fellowship

Subjects: A dissertation topic in which the use of numismatics plays a significant part.

Eligibility: Open to persons enrolled at universities in the USA or Canada who have completed the general examinations (or the equivalent) for the doctoral degree and have attended one of the Society's summer seminars.

Level of Study: Doctorate.

Purpose: To further the study of numismatics as an ancillary discipline.

Type: Fellowship.

No. of awards offered: One.

Frequency: Annual.

Value: US$3,500.

Study Establishment: An appropriate university.

Closing Date: March 1st.

Fellowship in Roman Studies

Subjects: Ancient Civilisations.

Eligibility: Open to nationals of Canada and the United States.

Level of Study: Professional development, Unrestricted.

Purpose: To promote the use of the ANS collection and library in connection with studies of the Roman world.

Type: Fellowship.

No. of awards offered: One.

Frequency: Annual.

Value: Up to $5,000.

Length of Study: One year.

Country of Study: USA.

Applications Procedure: Application form and references are required.

Closing Date: March 1st.

For further information contact:
American Numismatic Society, Broadway at 155th Street, New York, NY, 10032, USA
Tel: 212 234 3130
Fax: 212 234 3381
Contact: William E. Metcalf

Grants for ANS Summer Seminar in Numismatics

Subjects: Numismatics.

Eligibility: Open to persons who have had at least one year's graduate study at a university in the USA or Canada, and are students of classical studies, history, Near Eastern studies or other humanistic fields.

Level of Study: Postgraduate.

Purpose: To provide a selected number of graduate students with a deeper understanding of the contribution this subject makes to other fields.

Type: Grant.

No. of awards offered: Approximately ten.

Frequency: Annual.

Value: US$2,000.

Length of Study: Nine weeks during the summer.

Study Establishment: The Society.

Country of Study: USA.

Closing Date: March 1st.

For further information contact:
American Numismatic Society, Broadway at 155th Street, New York, NY, 10032, USA
Tel: 212 234 3130
Fax: 212 234 3381
Contact: Chief Curator

Frances M Schwartz Fellowship

Subjects: Numismatic methodology and museum practice.

Eligibility: Open to students of numismatics who possess a BA or equivalent degree.

Level of Study: Postgraduate.

Purpose: To assist the Fellow in the study of Greek and Roman fields relevant to the subject.

Type: Fellowship.

No. of awards offered: Variable.

Frequency: Varies.

Value: Up to US$2,000.

Country of Study: USA.

Closing Date: March 1st.

AMERICAN NURSES FOUNDATION

American Nurses Foundation, 600 Maryland Avenue, SW, Suite 100W, Washington, DC, 20024-2571, USA
Tel: 202 651 7298
Fax: 202 651 7001
Email: ANF@ANA.ORG
Contact: Grants Program Manager

Nursing Research Grant

Subjects: Nursing.

Eligibility: Open to registered nurses of any nationality.

Level of Study: Postgraduate, Doctorate, Postdoctorate.

Type: Research Grant.

No. of awards offered: Twenty.

Frequency: Annual.

Value: Minimum of $3,500.

Length of Study: One year.

Applications Procedure: Application form must be completed.

Closing Date: May 1st each year.

AMERICAN ORCHID SOCIETY

6000 South Olive Avenue, West Palm Beach, FL, 33405, USA
Contact: Lee S Cooke

Grants for Orchid Research

Eligibility: No restrictions.

Level of Study: Postgraduate.

Purpose: To advance scientific study of orchids in every respect and to assist in publication of scholarly and popular scientific literature on orchids.

Type: Grant.

Frequency: Semi-annual.

Value: $US500-$US12,000.

Length of Study: Up to three years.

Country of Study: Not restricted.

Applications Procedure: Write for guidelines.

Closing Date: January 1st and August 1st.

Additional Information: Telephone or fax to Jennifer Letourneau; tel: 407 5845 8666 or fax: 407 585 0654.

AMERICAN ORIENTAL SOCIETY

American Oriental Society, Hatcher Graduate Library, University of Michigan, Ann Arbor, MI, 48109-1205, USA
Tel: 313 747 4760
Contact: Secretary-Treasurer

*Louise Wallace Hackney Fellowship

Subjects: Chinese art, with special relation to painting, and the translation into English of works on the subject.

Eligibility: Open to US citizens who are doctoral or postdoctoral students and have successfully completed at least three years of Chinese language study at a recognized university and have some knowledge or training in art.

Level of Study: Doctorate, Postdoctorate.

Purpose: To remind scholars that Chinese art, like all art, is not a disembodied creation, but the outgrowth of the life and culture from which it has sprung, and it is requested that scholars give special attention to this approach in their study.

Type: Fellowship.

No. of awards offered: One.

Frequency: Annual.

Value: US$8,000.

Length of Study: One year.

Study Establishment: Any institution where paintings and adequate language guidance are available.

Closing Date: February 1st.

Additional Information: In no case shall a Fellowship be awarded to scholars of well recognized standing, but shall be given to either men or women who show aptitude or promise in the said field of learning.

AMERICAN ORNITHOLOGISTS' UNION

American Ornithologists' Union, National Museum of Natural History, Smithsonian Institution, Washington, DC, 20560, USA
Tel: 202 357 2334
Contact: James Dean

Student Research Awards

Subjects: Avian biology.

Eligibility: Open to students or others without recourse to regular funding. Applicants must be members of the AOU.

Level of Study: Doctorate, Postgraduate.

Type: Research Award.

No. of awards offered: Varies.

Frequency: Annual.

Value: Varies; usually US$200-US$500.

Country of Study: USA.

Applications Procedure: Application forms are available from the Union. Applicants should also submit letters of recommendation and a proposed budget.

Closing Date: February 1st.

For further information contact:
Department of Wildlife and Fisheries Sciences, Texas A & M University, College Station, TX, 77843, USA
Tel: 409 845 5765
Fax: 409 845 3786
Contact: Dr Paul J Dubowy

Marcia Brady Tucker Travel Award

Subjects: Ornithology.

Eligibility: Open to students in a relevant discipline.

Purpose: To assist students planning to give a paper to attend the annual meeting.

Type: Travel Award.

No. of awards offered: Varies.

Frequency: Annual.

Value: Travel expenses.

Country of Study: USA.

Closing Date: Three months prior to the meeting.

For further information contact:
Bell Museum of Natural History, Ecology Building, University of Minnesota, St Paul, MN, 55110, USA
Tel: 612 624 7207
Fax: 612 624 6777
Contact: Dr Robert Zink

AMERICAN OSTEOPATHIC ASSOCIATION

American Osteopathic Association, 142 E.Ontario Street, Chicago, Illinois, 60611, USA
Tel: 312 280 5804
Fax: 312 280 3860
Contact: Sharon L McGill, Research Services Manager

AOA Research Grants

Subjects: Osteopathy.

Eligibility: Open to an osteopathic physician or biomedical researcher holding a faculty or staff appointment at an AOA accredited, affiliated, or approved osteopathic institution.

Level of Study: Doctorate.

Purpose: To support clinical and basic science projects that lead to a better understanding and a more effective application of the philosophy and concepts of osteopathic medicine.

Type: Research Grant.

No. of awards offered: Dependent on funds available.

Frequency: Annual, dependent on funds available.

Value: Varies.

Length of Study: One to two years.

Study Establishment: University/hospital.

Country of Study: USA.

Applications Procedure: The AOA Oseopathic Research Handbook contains grant applications and describes the programs and eligibility requirements in greater detail.

Closing Date: December 1st.

For further information contact:
American Osteopathic Association, 142 E. Ontario Street, Chicago, Illinois, 60611, USA
Tel: 312 280 5804
Fax: 312 280 3860
Contact: Sharon L McGill, Research Services Manager

AMERICAN OTOLOGICAL SOCIETY

Research Fund, American Otological Society, 702 Barnhill Drive, Room 0860, Indianapolis, IN, 46202-5230, USA
Tel: 317 630 8966
Fax: 317 630 8958
Email: rmiyamotx@Indyvex.iupui.edu
Contact: Richard T Miyamoto, MD, Secretary-Treasurer

Research Grants

Subjects: All aspects of otosclerosis, Meniere's Disease and related disorders.

Eligibility: Open to physicians and doctoral-level investigators.

Level of Study: Postgraduate, Postdoctorate.

Type: Research Grant.

No. of awards offered: Varies.

Frequency: Annual.

Value: Up to US$40,000 per annum; no funding for the investigator's salary.

Length of Study: One year; renewable.

Country of Study: USA or Canada.

Closing Date: January 31st.

Research Training Fellowships

Subjects: Ostosclerosis, Meniere's disease and related disorders.

Eligibility: Open to physicians (residents and medical students) in the USA and Canada.

Purpose: To study otosclerosis, Meniere's disease and related disorders.

Type: Fellowship.

No. of awards offered: Varies.

Frequency: Annual.

Value: Up to US$40,000 depending on position and institutional norms.

Length of Study: 1-2 years.

Country of Study: USA and Canada.

Closing Date: January 31st.

Additional Information: Requires institutional documentation that facilities and faculty are appropriate for requested research.

AMERICAN PHILOSOPHICAL ASSOCIATION

University of Delaware, Newark, DE, 19716, USA
Tel: 302 451 1112
Contact: American Philosophical Association

*Baumgardt Memorial Lecture

Subjects: Philosophy.

Eligibility: Open to candidates of any nationality, working in any country, whose work has some bearing on the philosophical interests of the late David Baumgardt.

No. of awards offered: One.

Frequency: Every five years (next 1997).

Value: US$5,000.

*Edinburgh Fellowship

Subjects: Philosophy.

Eligibility: Open to suitably qualified scholars.

Type: Fellowship.

No. of awards offered: One.

Frequency: Annual.

Value: To cover the cost of a study and secretarial support.

Length of Study: 3-5 months.

Study Establishment: Institute for Advanced Studies in the Humanities, University of Edinburgh, Scotland.

Country of Study: Scotland.

*Rockefeller Prize

Subjects: Philosophy.

Eligibility: Open to non-academically affiliated philosophers.

Purpose: To recognize unpublished work in philosophy by non-academically affiliated philosophers.

No. of awards offered: One.

Frequency: Annual.

Value: US$500.

Additional Information: The prize is funded by the Rockefeller Foundation.

*Frank Chapman Sharp Memorial Prize

Subjects: The philosophy of war and peace.

Eligibility: Open to writers of unpublished essays or monographs.

Purpose: To recognize unpublished work in philosophy.

No. of awards offered: One.

Frequency: Biennially (odd-numbered years).

Value: US$1,500.

AMERICAN PLANNING ASSOCIATION

Fellowships & Council Administration, American Planning Association,
1776 Massachusetts Avenue, NW, Washington, DC, 20036, USA
Tel: 202 872 0611 ext.332
Fax: 1 800 800 1589
Contact: Assistant for Divisions

APA Fellowships

Subjects: Planning: the rational and equitable distribution of resources and opportunities.

Eligibility: Open to US citizens who are African-American, Hispanic or Native American students enrolled in a PAB-accredited graduate planning program. The program is open to first- and second-year graduate students. First-year students who receive Fellowships are eligible to compete for an award the following year as well. Preference will be shown to full-time students. Candidates must be able to document the need for financial assistance.

Level of Study: Postdoctorate, Masters.

Purpose: To encourage students of certain minority backgrounds to enter the planning profession and to help such students who would otherwise be unable to continue their studies in planning.

Type: Fellowship.

No. of awards offered: Varies.

Frequency: Annual.

Value: US$1,000-US$4,000, paid to the school in two equal instalments.

Applications Procedure: Call FAX-ON-DEMAND 1-800-800-1589 for application and information.

Closing Date: May 15th.

Additional Information: Applications should include a two- to five-page personal and background statement written by the student, describing how the student's graduate education will be applied to career goals and why planning was chosen as a career; a resume providing an overview of the student's background (a resume is optional if the information is supplied in the student's personal statement); letter(s) of recommendation (one letter of recommendation is required, with a maximum of two being accepted to enhance an application); an APA financial aid application form completed and signed by the applicant; official transcripts of all previous collegiate and graduate academic work (sent directly from the office of the registrar); a photocopy of the university's letter indicating that the student has been accepted for graduate study in planning; and written verification from the university's financial officer or copies of a school publication indicating the average cost of one academic year of graduate school.

For further information contact:
Fellowships & Council Administration, American Planning Association,
1776 Massachusetts Avenue, NW, Washington, DC, 20036, USA
Tel: 202 872 0611 ext.324
Contact: Assistant for Divisions

Charles Abrams Scholarship

Subjects: Planning.

Eligibility: Open to US citizens who have been accepted into the graduate planning program of one of the five eligible schools. Incoming students are eligible. Applicants must be in need of financial assistance as determined by a review of the applicant's financial needs.

Level of Study: Postgraduate.

Purpose: To aid students who will pursue careers as practising planners.

Type: Scholarship.

No. of awards offered: One.

Frequency: Annual.

Value: US$2,000.

Study Establishment: Columbia University, Harvard University Graduate School of Architecture and Design, Massachusetts Institute of Technology, the New School for Social Research or the University of Pennsylvania, for study leading to a masters degree in city and regional planning or urban planning.

Country of Study: USA.

Applications Procedure: Call 1 800 800 1589 for FAX-ON-DEMAND applications and information.

Closing Date: April 30th.

Additional Information: Applications should include a one- to two-page statement written by the applicant containing a description of the applicant's commitment to complete the planning curriculum of the university and to pursue a career in the planning profession and an outline of the applicant's academic qualifications, extra-curricular activities, and reasons for believing a scholarship award is justified; as well as a short statement by the department chair discussing the reasons why the sudent was chosen, including comments on the student's strengths, areas of interest, and other abilities, as appropriate; official transcripts of all previus collegiate and graduate academic work; and an official copy of GRE scores. An eligible applicant should apply through one of the five designated schools on forms supplied to the participating university by APA.

AMERICAN PODIATRIC MEDICAL ASSOCIATION

American Podiatric Medical Association, 9312 Old Georgetown Road, Bethesda, MD, 20814, USA
Tel: 301 571 9200
Fax: 301 530 2752
Contact: Anne Martinez, CMP

*APMA Research Grants

Subjects: Podiatric medicine: biomechanics, podiatric epidemiology, cost effectiveness, outcomes research.

Eligibility: Open to suitably qualified researchers.

Purpose: To further develop research which contributes to the advancement of podiatric medicine.

Type: Research Grant.

No. of awards offered: Varies.

Frequency: Annual.

Value: Varies; dependent on funds available.

AMERICAN POLITICAL SCIENCE ASSOCIATION

American Political Science Association, 1527 New Hampshire Avenue, NW, Washington, DC, 20036, USA
Tel: 202 483 2512
Fax: 202 483 2657
Contact: Kay Sterling, Administrative Director

APSA-MCI Communications Congressional Fellowships

Subjects: Experiential program: work in unpaid positions for Members of Congress or congressional committees.

Eligibility: Open to mid-career professionals who are PhD-level scholars of any discipline or journalists with demonstrated professional interest in telecommunications and who show promise of making significant contribution to the public's understanding of the political process. Journalists must have a bachelor's degree and two to ten years' full-time professional experience in print or broadcast reporting, which may be as writers, producers, directors or researchers.

Level of Study: Postdoctorate, Professional development.

Purpose: To allow participants to learn more about the legislative process through direct participation.

Type: Fellowship.

No. of awards offered: Varies.

Frequency: Annual.

Value: US$28,000 stipend paid over a 12-month period.

Length of Study: Ten months.

Country of Study: USA.

Applications Procedure: Contact APSA for application procedures.

Closing Date: December 1st for entry in the following November.

Additional Information: Applicants living outside the USA must fund their own travel to and from Washington if selected as finalists for interview.

Congressional Fellowship Program

Subjects: Experiential program: work in unpaid positions as legislative aides for Members of Congress or congressional committees.

Eligibility: Open to mid-career political scientists with a PhD completed within the past 15 years or near completion who can show scholarly interest in Congress and the policy-making process. Minorities are encouraged to apply.

Level of Study: Postdoctorate.

Purpose: To allow participants to learn more about the legislative process through direct participation.

Type: Fellowship.

No. of awards offered: Varies.

Frequency: Annual.

Value: US$28,000 stipend paid over a 12-month period.

Length of Study: Ten months.

Country of Study: USA.

Applications Procedure: Call or write for application procedure information. There is no application form.

Closing Date: December 1st for entry in the following November.

Additional Information: Applicants living outside the USA must pay for their own transportation to and from Washington if selected as finalists for interview.

For further information contact:
American Politcal Science Association, 1527 New Hampshire Avenue, NW, Washington, DC, 20036, USA
Tel: 202 483 2512
Fax: 202 483 2657
Contact: Kay Sterling, Administrative Director

Congressional Fellowships for Journalists

Subjects: Experiential program: work in unpaid positions as legislative aides for Members of Congress or congressional committees.

Eligibility: Open to mid-career professionals with a bachelor's degree and an interest in Congress; preference is given to candidates with a background in political reporting but without extensive experience in Washington. Candidates should have an absolute minimum of two years' full-time professional-level experience in newspaper, magazine, radio or TV reporting at the time of application. Candidates with more than ten years' experience will not be considered. Broadcast journalists' reporting may be as producers, directors, writers or researchers.

Level of Study: Professional development.

Purpose: To allow participants to learn more about the legislative process through direct participation.

Type: Fellowship.

No. of awards offered: Varies.

Frequency: Annual.

Value: US$28,000 stipend paid over a 12-month period.

Length of Study: Ten months.

Country of Study: USA.

Applications Procedure: Write to APSA for application procedure.

Closing Date: December 1st for entry in the following November.

Additional Information: Applicants living outside the USA must fund their own travel to Washington for interview if selected as finalists.

AMERICAN PSYCHIATRIC ASSOCIATION

American Psychiatric Association, 1400 K Street NW, Washington, DC, 20005, USA
Tel: 202 682 6097

Fax: 202 682 6352
Email: jtaylor@id.psych.org
Contact: Janice Taylor

APA/Burroughs Wellcome Fellowship

Subjects: Medical Sciences, Psychiatry and mental health.

Eligibility: Candidates should be in their PGY-second year of psychiatric residency training. Candidates must be either a member of the American Psychiatric Association or have applied for membership.

Level of Study: Professional development.

Purpose: To promote professional education in psychiatry. To inform psychiatric residents of the work of the association and to contribute to the professional development of the residents.

Type: Fellowship.

No. of awards offered: Ten.

Frequency: Annual.

Length of Study: Two years.

Applications Procedure: Application form required. Training directors letter of recomendation.

Closing Date: March 31st.

Additional Information: Candidates are not required to be USA citizens or a graduate of a USA medical school.

AMERICAN PSYCHOLOGICAL ASSOCIATION MINORITY FELLOWSHIPS PROGRAM

American Psychological Association Minority Fellowships Program, 750 First Street NE, Washington, DC, 20002-4242, USA
Tel: 202 336 6026
Fax: 202 336 6012
Email: MFP@APA.ORG
Contact: James M Jones PhD

MFP Aging Traineeship

Subjects: The MFP Aging Traineeship is geared to those pursuing careers as research scientists in gerontology and ethnic minority poulations.

Eligibility: A member of an ethnic minority group including but not limited to, African Americans, Alaskan Natives, American Indians, Asian Americans, Hispanics and Pacific Islanders. Applicants must demonstrate commitment to a career in psychology with a speciality in gerontology research related to ethnic minority populations.

Level of Study: Doctorate.

Purpose: Provides financial support and professional guidance to individuals pursuing doctoral degrees in psychology.

Type: Traineeship.

Frequency: Annual.

Closing Date: January 15th.

For further information contact:
American Psychological Association Minority Fellowships Program, 750 First Street NE, Washington, DC, 20002-4242, USA
Tel: 202 336 6026
Fax: 202 336 6012
Email: MFP@APA.ORG
Contact: James M Jones, PhD

MFP Clinical Training Fellowship

Subjects: MFP Clinical Training Fellowship is geared to those pursuing careers as practitioners and as researchers specialising in clinical concerns such as prevention and treatment of problems affecting ethnic minority populations.

Eligibility: Open to members of an ethnic minority group including but not limited to African Americans, Alaskan Americans, American Indians, Hispanics, Pacific Islanders. Applicants must demonstrate a commitment to careers in psychology related to mental health.

Level of Study: Doctorate.

Purpose: To provide financial support and professional guidance to individuals pursuing doctoral degrees in psychology.

Type: Fellowship.

Frequency: Annual.

Closing Date: January 15th.

MFP Neurosciences Training Fellowship

Subjects: The MFP Neurosciences Training Fellowship is geared to those pursuing careers in neuroscience.

Eligibility: An additional important factor for selection is that members be of an under-represented minority group, including but not limited to African Americans, Alaskan Natives, Mexican Americans, Native Americans, Pacific Islanders and Puerto Ricans.

Level of Study: Doctorate.

Purpose: To provide financial support and professional guidance to individuals pursuing doctoral degrees in psychology.

Type: Fellowship.

Frequency: Annual.

Closing Date: January 15th.

MFP Research Training Fellowship

Subjects: The MFP Research Training Fellowship is geared to those pursuing careers as research scientists on mental health issues related to minority populations.

Eligibility: Open to members of an ethnic minority group including but not limited to: African Americans, Alaskan Natives, American Indians, Asian Americans, Hispanics, Pacific Islanders. Applicants must demonstrate a commitment to careers in psychology related to minority mental health.

Level of Study: Doctorate.

Purpose: To provide financial support and professional guidance to individuals pursuing doctoral degrees in psychology.

Type: Fellowship.

Frequency: Annual.

MFP Substance Abuse Training Fellowship

Subjects: Substance abuse.

Eligibility: Open to members of an ethnic minority group but not limited to, African Americans, Alaskan Natives, American Indians, Asian Americans, Hispanics, Pacific Islanders. Applicants must demonstrate a commitment to careers in psychology related to ethnic minority mental health and substance abuse issues.

Level of Study: Doctorate.

Purpose: To provide financial support and professional guidance to individuals pursuing doctoral degrees in psychology.

Type: Fellowship.

Frequency: Annual.

Closing Date: January 15th.

AMERICAN RESEARCH CENTER IN EGYPT

American Research Center in Egypt, 30 East 20th Street, Suite 401,
New York, NY, 10003-1310, USA
Tel: 212 529 6661
Fax: 212 529 6856
Email: Walz@is.nyu.edu

ARCE Fellowships

Subjects: Arts and humanities; Near Eastern studies.

Eligibility: Open to US nationals only for pre-doctoral candidates; post-doctoral candidates should be US nationals or foreign nationals who have been teaching at an American university for three years or more.

Level of Study: Doctorate, Postdoctorate.

Purpose: For dissertation or postdoctoral research in Egypt.

Type: Fellowship.

No. of awards offered: Fifteen.

Frequency: Annual.

Value: Varies.

Length of Study: 3-12 months.

Study Establishment: ARCE.

Country of Study: Egypt.

Applications Procedure: Applicants should write to the office for materials.

Closing Date: November 1st.

Egyptian Development Fellowships

Subjects: Development studies.

Eligibility: Open to Egyptian nationals only.

Level of Study: Doctorate.

Purpose: To enable Egyptian graduate students enrolled in a PhD program at an American or Canadian university to conduct dissertation research in Egypt on subjects related to development.

Type: Fellowship.

No. of awards offered: Four.

Frequency: Annual.

Value: Varies.

Length of Study: 3-12 months.

Study Establishment: ARCE.

Country of Study: Egypt.

Applications Procedure: Applicants should write for materials.

Closing Date: November 1st.

Kress Fellowship in Egyptian Art

Subjects: Egyptian art.

Eligibility: Open to PhD candidates in the all-but-dissertation stage, who are US nationals.

Level of Study: Doctorate.

Purpose: For research on any period or aspect of Egyptian art.

Type: Fellowship.

No. of awards offered: One.

Frequency: Annual.

Value: Varies.

Country of Study: Egypt.

Applications Procedure: Applicants must write for materials.

Closing Date: November 1st annually.

AMERICAN RESEARCH INSTITUTE IN TURKEY

American Research Institute in Turkey, c/o University Museum, 33rd and Spruce Streets, Philadelphia, PA, 19104-6324, USA
Tel: 215 898 3474
Fax: 215 898 0657
Email: leinwand@sas.upenn.edu
Contact: Nancy Leinwand

ARIT/NEH Fellowships for the Humanities in Turkey

Subjects: All subjects of the humanities and interdisciplinary approaches: art, archaeology, language, history, etc.

Eligibility: Open to US citizens or permanent residents who have completed a doctoral degree. Independent scholars are considered.

Level of Study: Postdoctorate.

Purpose: To fund research in all fields of the humanities in Turkey; to support longer-term projects by scholars in the early years of their careers.

Type: Fellowship.

No. of awards offered: Two to four.

Frequency: Annuall, pending NEH renewal.

Value: Salary replacement of up to US$30,000 for 12 months.

Length of Study: Four or 12 months.

Study Establishment: ARIT maintains two research institutes in Turkey: ARIT-Istanbul and ARIT-Ankara.

Country of Study: Turkey.

Applications Procedure: Application form, project statement and references.

Closing Date: November 15th.

Humanities and Social Science Fellowships

Subjects: All fields of the humanities and social sciences.

Eligibility: Open to US citizens and permanent residents, or others, affiliated with USA or Canadian institutions of higher learning.

Level of Study: Postgraduate, Doctorate, Postdoctorate.

Purpose: To encourage research on Turkey in ancient, medieval and modern times.

Type: Fellowship.

No. of awards offered: Six to 12.

Frequency: Annual.

Value: Varies; dependant on the length of the study period.

Length of Study: Two to 12 months; renewable only in exceptional cases.

Country of Study: Turkey.

Applications Procedure: Application form, transcript (where relevant), references, and project statement.

Closing Date: November 15th.

Language Fellowships

Subjects: (Spoken) Turkish language.

Eligibility: Open to instructors of and undergraduate and graduate students enrolled in a degree program of Turkish or related language and area studies. Applicants must be US citizens or permanent residents and have at least two years of college-level Turkish language study or its equivalent.

Level of Study: Unrestricted.

Purpose: To provide students the opportunity of studying at an advanced level in Turkey.

Type: Fellowship.

No. of awards offered: 10-15.

Frequency: Annual.

Value: Tuition, travel and a maintenance stipend of varying amounts.

Length of Study: Eight weeks during July and August, plus additional travel time.

Study Establishment: Bosphorus University, Istanbul.

Country of Study: Turkey.

Applications Procedure: Application form, statement, references and exam.

Closing Date: February 15th.

For further information contact:
ARIT Summer Fellowship Program, Center for the Study of Islamic Societies and Civilizations, Washington University, Campus Box 1230, One Brookings Drive, St. Louis, MO, 63130-4899, USA
Tel: 314 935 7462
Fax: 014 905 5100
Email: sandrew@artsci.wustl.edu
Contact: Sheila Andrew

Mellon Research Fellowship

Subjects: Humanities and social sciences.

Eligibility: Czech, Slovak, Polish, Hungarian nationals residing in same countries.

Level of Study: Postdoctorate.

Purpose: To bring East-Central European scholars to Turkey to carry out research in humanities and social sciences.

Type: Fellowships.

No. of awards offered: Three.

Frequency: Dependent on funds available.

Value: Up to $10,500.

Length of Study: Three months.

Study Establishment: Open.

Country of Study: Turkey.

Applications Procedure: Application form, project statement, and references.

Closing Date: May 3rd.

For further information contact:
American Research Institute in Turkey, University of Pennsylvania Museum, 33rd and Spruce Streets, Philadelphia, PA, 19104-6324, USA
Tel: 215 898 3474
Fax: 215 898 0657
Email: leinwand@sas.upenn.edu
Contact: The Administrator

THE AMERICAN-SCANDINAVIAN FOUNDATION

The American-Scandinavian Foundation, 725 Park Avenue, New York, NY, 10021, USA
Tel: 212 879 9779
Fax: 212 249 3444
Email: grants@amscan.org
Contact: Ellen McKey

Fellowships and Grants for Study and Research

Subjects: All Fields.

Eligibility: Open to US citizens and permanent residents.

Level of Study: Doctorate, Postdoctorate, Professional development.

Purpose: To encourage advanced study and research, and increase understanding between the USA and Scandinavia.

Type: Fellowship, Grant.

No. of awards offered: 25-30.

Frequency: Annual.

Value: US$3,000-US$15,000.

Length of Study: 1-12 months.

Country of Study: Denmark, Finland, Iceland, Norway, Sweden.

Applications Procedure: Application form, three references plus US$10 application fee.

Closing Date: November 1st.

Translation Prize

Subjects: Translation.

Eligibility: Open to translators of any nationality.

Purpose: To award the best English translation of poetry, fiction, drama or literary prose written by a Scandinavian author since 1800.

Type: Translation prize.

No. of awards offered: One.

Frequency: Annual.

Value: US$2,000, plus publication of an excerpt in an issue of 'Scandinavian Review' and a commemorative bronze medallion.

Country of Study: Scandinavia.

Applications Procedure: An entry should consist of: four legible copies of the translation, including a title page and a table of contents for the proposed book of which the manuscript submitted is a part; one copy of the work(s) in the original language; a separate sheet containing the name, address and telephone number of the translator and the title and author of the manuscript with the original language specified; and a letter or other document signed by the author, the author's agent or the author's estate granting permission for the translation to be entered in this competition and published in 'Scandinavian Review'.

Closing Date: June 3rd.

Additional Information: The Inger Sjoberg Prize of US$500 will be offered annually for the Honorable Mention entry.

AMERICAN SCHOOL OF CLASSICAL STUDIES AT ATHENS

American School of Classical Studies at Athens, 993 Lenox Drive, Suite 101, Lawrenceville, NJ, 08648, USA
Tel: 609 844 7577
Fax: 609 844 7527

ASCSA Fellowships

Subjects: Classical philology and archaeology; post-classical Greek studies.

Eligibility: Open to US or Canadian citizens who have a BA degree with a major in classics or classical archaeology. Non-US and non-Canadian citizens may apply if they have received an appropriate degree from one of the 148 US and Canadian colleges and universities which support the school.

Level of Study: Postgraduate.

Type: Fellowship.

No. of awards offered: Four.

Frequency: Annual.

Value: US$6,640 stipend plus fees, room and partial board.

Length of Study: One academic year.

Study Establishment: At the American school of Classical Studies at Athens.

Country of Study: Greece.

Applications Procedure: Applications are judged on the basis of examinations and credentials. Fulbright Fellowships are also sometimes available for work at the School. Application to the School must be made simultaneously with the application for a Fulbright grant. Two Fellowships may not be held concurrently.

Closing Date: January 5th.

Gennadeion Fellowship

Subjects: Post-classical studies.

Eligibility: Open to US or Canadian citizens.

Level of Study: Postgraduate, Doctorate.

Type: Fellowship.

No. of awards offered: One.

Frequency: Annual.

Value: US$6,640 stipend plus fees, room and partial board.

Length of Study: One academic year.

Study Establishment: The American School of Classical Studies at Athens.

Country of Study: Greece.

Applications Procedure: Please submit CV, project description, and two letters of support.

Closing Date: January 31st.

Jacob Hirsh Fellowship

Subjects: Pre-classical, classical, or post-classical archaeology.

Eligibility: Open to US or Israeli graduate students writing a dissertation, or to recent PhD graduates completing a project, such as a dissertation for publication. Applications will be judged on the basis of appropriate credentials, including referees.

Type: Fellowship.

No. of awards offered: One.

Frequency: Annual.

Value: US$6,640 stipend plus room and partial board.

Length of Study: One academic year; not renewable.

Country of Study: Greece.

Applications Procedure: Please submit application form, letters of recommendation, and transcripts.

Closing Date: January 31st.

Kress Fellowship in Classical Art History

Subjects: Classical art history.

Eligibility: Open to US citizens.

Type: Fellowship.

No. of awards offered: One.

Frequency: Annual.

Value: Varies.

Length of Study: Academic year.

Study Establishment: The American School of Classical Studies in Athens.

Country of Study: Greece.

Closing Date: January 5th.

Summer Sessions

Subjects: Archaeology, with emphasis on the topography and antiquities of Greece.

Eligibility: Open to graduate and advanced undergraduate students and high school and college teachers.

Type: Scholarship.

No. of awards offered: Five.

Frequency: Annual.

Value: To cover tuition, room and partial board.

Length of Study: Six weeks.

Study Establishment: At one of the two Summer Sessions of the School in Athens.

Country of Study: Greece.

Applications Procedure: Please submit application form, transcripts, and letters of recommendation.

Closing Date: February 15th.

Additional Information: Applications should be made to the Committee on the Summer Sessions.

For further information contact:
American School of Classical Studies at Athens, 993 Lenox Drive, Suite 101, Lawrenceville, NJ, 08648, USA
Tel: 609 844 7577
Fax: 609 844 7527
Contact: Committee on the Summer Sessions

AMERICAN SOCIAL HEALTH ASSOCIATION

ASHA Research Fund, PO Box 13827, Research Triangle Park, NC, 27709, USA
Tel: 919 361 8400
Fax: 919 361 8425
Contact: Kay Flaminio

*ASHA Research Fellowship Fund

Subjects: Sexually transmitted diseases including behavioral, clinical, epidemiological and policy issues as well as basic science.

Eligibility: Open to recent recipients of a PhD, MD, or DSc degree in a relevant field who are resident in the USA.

Level of Study: Postdoctorate.

Purpose: To provide postdoctoral candidates with the opportunity to spend two years in a research environment under the sponsorship of an established STD researcher. The projects undertaken must make a substantive contribution to the body of medical knowledge.

No. of awards offered: Varies.

Frequency: Biennially pending availability of funds.

Value: Stipend based on years of postdoctoral work completed.

Length of Study: Two years.

Study Establishment: US research institutions.

Country of Study: USA.

Closing Date: April 15th.

Additional Information: Candidates must seek the sponsorship of an established investigator at the host institution, who is willing to supervise research training during the award term.

AMERICAN SOCIETY FOR EIGHTEENTH-CENTURY STUDIES

Center for 17th- and 18th-Century Studies, 1100 Glendon Avenue, Suite 1548, Los Angeles, CA, 90024-1404, USA
Tel: 310 206 8552
Fax: 310 206 8577
Contact: Fellowship Coordinator

*Ahmanson and Getty Postdoctoral Fellowships

Subjects: Themes of an interdisciplinary, cross-cultural nature. The theme is announced in the fall.

Eligibility: Open to postdoctoral scholars.

Level of Study: Postdoctorate.

Type: Fellowship.

No. of awards offered: Varies.

Frequency: Annual.

Value: US$9,200 per quarter.

Length of Study: 2-3 academic quarters.

Country of Study: USA.

Closing Date: March 15th.

*ASECS/Clark Library Fellowships

Subjects: The Restoration or the eighteenth century.

Eligibility: Open to members of ASECS who are postdoctoral scholars and hold a PhD or equivalent degree at the time of application.

Level of Study: Postdoctorate.

Type: Fellowship.

No. of awards offered: Varies.

Frequency: Annual.

Value: US$1,500.

Length of Study: One month.

Study Establishment: William Andrews Clark Memorial Library of the University of California, Los Angeles.

Country of Study: USA.

Closing Date: March 15th.

For further information contact:
William Andrews Clark Memorial Library, UCLA, 2520 Cimarron Street, Los Angeles, CA, 90018, USA
Tel: 213 735 7605
Fax: 213 731 8617
Contact: Ms Beverly Onley, Fellowships Coordinator

*Clark Library Short-Term Resident Fellowships

Subjects: Research relevant to the Library's holdings.

Eligibility: Open to scholars holding the PhD or equivalent degree who are involved in advanced research.

Level of Study: Postdoctorate.

Type: Fellowship.

No. of awards offered: Varies.

Frequency: Annual.

Value: US$1,500 per month.

Length of Study: 1-3 months.

Study Establishment: William Andrews Clark Memorial Library of the University of California, Los Angeles.

Country of Study: USA.

Closing Date: March 15th.

For further information contact:
William Andrews Clark Memorial Library, UCLA, 2520 Cimarron Street, Los Angeles, CA, 90018, USA
Tel: 213 735 7605
Fax: 213 731 8617
Contact: Ms Beverly Onley, Fellowships Coordinator

*Predoctoral Fellowships

Subjects: Any area represented in the Clark's collections or linked to Center/Clerk programs supported by these collections or by others at UCLA.

Eligibility: Open to advanced doctoral students whose dissertation concerns an area appropriate to the available collections.

Level of Study: Postgraduate, Doctorate.

Type: Fellowship.

No. of awards offered: Varies.

Frequency: Annual.

Value: US$4,500.

Length of Study: Three months.

Study Establishment: Clark Library.

Country of Study: USA.

Closing Date: March 15th.

For further information contact:
William Andrews Clark Memorial Library, UCLA, 2520 Cimarron Street, Los Angeles, CA, 90018, USA
Tel: 213 735 7605
Fax: 213 731 8617
Contact: Ms Beverly Onley, Fellowship Coordinator

AMERICAN SOCIETY FOR ENGINEERING EDUCATION

American Society for Engineering Education, Suite 600, 1818 N Street NW, Washington, DC, 20036, USA
Tel: 202 331 3525
Contact: Jeffrey Jarosz, Program Manager

*Office of Naval Research (ONR) Fellowships

Subjects: Electrical and mechanical engineering, computer science, naval architecture and ocean engineering, materials science, chemistry, physics, oceanography and biological sciences, mathematics, and cognitive and neural science.

Eligibility: Open to US citizens who will receive the baccalaureate by the year of application. Applicants already in graduate school are ineligible.

Purpose: To encourage students to study in subject areas crucial to the US Navy.

Type: Fellowship.

No. of awards offered: Fifty.

Frequency: Annual.

Value: US$16,000, plus cost of tuition and other fees.

Length of Study: Three years.

Country of Study: USA.

Closing Date: January 19th.

Additional Information: A booklet on the ONR Fellowship Program is available from the Society.

AMERICAN SOCIETY FOR MEDICAL TECHNOLOGY EDUCATION AND RESEARCH FUND, INC

Executive Secretary, ASMT Education and Research Fund, Inc, Suite 400, 2021 L Street NW, Washington, DC, 20036, USA

*Baxter Healthcare Scientific Products Division Graduate Scholarship

Subjects: Clinical laboratory science.

Eligibility: Open to citizens or permanent residents of the USA who are clinical laboratory practitioners or educators. Applicants must fulfil requirements for admission or be currently enrolled in a program leading to masters or PhD degree in clinical laboratory science or a related field, and must have performed clinical laboratory functions for at least one year.

Level of Study: Postgraduate, Doctorate.

Purpose: To assist clinical laboratory practitioners and educators in pursuing graduate or advanced studies.

Type: Scholarship.

No. of awards offered: One.

Frequency: Annual.

Value: US$1,000.

Closing Date: February 1st.

Additional Information: This Scholarship was donated by Baxter Healthcare Scientific Products Division.

*Gloria F 'Mike' Gilbert Memorial Trustee Award

Subjects: Laboratory administration.

Eligibility: Open to any clinical laboratory practitioner who has been engaged in the practice of clinical laboratory science for at least three years, and has position responsibilities including supervision, administration, or management or has established goals consistent with professional development including these responsibilities.

Level of Study: Professional development.

Purpose: To recognize professional excellence and to assist individuals within the profession of clinical laboratory science in their development or improvement of skills through continuing education in structured or independent modes of study.

No. of awards offered: One.

Frequency: Annual.

Value: US$300.

Closing Date: February 1st.

*Ruth I Heinemann Memorial Trustee Award for Educational Development

Subjects: Clinical laboratory science education.

Eligibility: Open to any citizen or permanent resident of the USA who is an educator in a structured education program in clinical laboratory science or its specialities or a graduate student preparing to become an educator, and has been involved in an instructional role for at least one year.

Purpose: To asist individuals within the profession of clinical laboratory science in developing educational strategies, preparing educational media, or designing innovative methods of instruction.

No. of awards offered: One.

Frequency: Annual.

Value: Up to US$500.

Closing Date: February 1st.

Additional Information: This Award was established by Founders Group.

*Joseph J Kleiner Memorial Awards

Subjects: Clinical laboratory science.

Eligibility: Open to writers of papers published in Clinical Laboratory Science.

Purpose: To recognize authors of outstanding articles published in Clinical Laboratory Science.

No. of awards offered: Two.

Frequency: Annual.

Value: US$1,000.

*John C Lang Memorial Award for Health Care Administration

Subjects: The award is given for a completed innovative project in health-care administration or managements such as cost-analysis, computer applications, staffing management, cost containment, innovative resource management, or strategic management technique.

Eligibility: Open to any individual within the profession of health-care administration.

Purpose: To recognize outstanding performance in administration and laboratory management and to encourage individuals to disseminate their knowledge to the profession.

No. of awards offered: One.

Frequency: Annual.

Value: US$250.

Applications Procedure: In addition to filing an application, the applicant shall submit a project description that outlines the rationale for the project, the steps in completing the project, delineates any costs, and describes the project's application to other health-care facilities. Material for publication is not required: however, it is encouraged that an article describing and evaluating the project be submitted for consideration by an appropriate peer-reviewed journal. This award was established by ASMT-CMU Students and Alumni.

Closing Date: February 1st.

*Robin H Mendelson Memorial Awards

Subjects: Clinical laboratory science.

Eligibility: Open to all elected or appointed officers, committee chairs and members, and employees of the ASMT or the ASMT Education and Research Fund, Inc, ASMT representatives, or such other persons whose contributions have been particularly commendable and deserving of recognition for a particular service or position during a designated period of time.

Purpose: To honor outstanding service and contributions to the ASMT, the ASMT Education and Research Fund, Inc, or clinical laboratory science in general.

Applications Procedure: Letters of nomination should be sent to Julie Gaucher, Chairperson, ASMT Awards Committee, Suite 400, 2021 L Street, NW, Washington, DC 20036, USA, stating the specific contribution for which the nominee is being commended and the year(s) of this outstanding service.

*Ortho Diagnostic Systems Scholarship in Immunohematology

Subjects: Immunohematology.

Eligibility: Open to any clinical laboratory practitioner or educator who fulfils requirements for admission into a program leading to SBB (ASCP) certification or for admission into a program leading to a master's or PhD degree in an area of study relevant to immunohematology and has performed clinical laboratory functions for at least one year.

Level of Study: Postgraduate, Doctorate.

Purpose: To assist clinical laboratory practitioners or educators in pursuing a program of study leading to SBB (ASCP) certification or an advanced degree.

Type: Scholarship.

No. of awards offered: One.

Frequency: Annual.

Value: US$1,000.

Closing Date: February 1st.

AMERICAN SOCIETY OF CIVIL ENGINEERS

American Society of Civil Engineers, United Engineering Center, 345 East 47th Street, New York, NY, 10017, USA
Tel: 1-800-548-ASCE ext.7222
Email: mperalta@ny.asce.org
Contact: Student Services

O H Ammann Research Fellowship in Structural Engineering

Subjects: Structural design and construction.

Eligibility: Open to citizens of any country who are members of the Society in any grade and to applicants for membership.

Purpose: To encourage the creation of new knowledge in the field of structural design and construction.

Type: Fellowship.

No. of awards offered: One.

Frequency: Annual.

Value: US$5,000; the recipient may apply for an additional stipend in the following year.

Length of Study: One year; renewable.

Study Establishment: An approved institution.

Closing Date: February 15th for notification in June.

Additional Information: Selection for the Fellowship is made on the basis of transcripts of scholastic records; evidence indicating ability to conceive and explore original ideas in the field of structural engineering; description of proposed research and its objectives, including a statement from the institution at which the research is to be done that the applicant and proposed research are acceptable to the institution.

For further information contact:
American Society of Civil Engineers, United Engineering Center, 345 East 47th Street, New York, NY, 10017, USA
Tel: 1 800 548 ASCE ext.7222
Email: mperalta@ny.asce.org
Contact: Student Services

Freeman Fellowship

Subjects: Hydraulics.

Eligibility: Open to members of the Society in any grade and to applicants for membership. Preference is given to young engineers.

Purpose: To assist with expenses for experiments, observations and compilations to discover new and accurate data that will be useful in engineering.

Type: Fellowship.

No. of awards offered: Variable.

Frequency: Annual.

Value: Varies, based upon funds available from an endowment. Past awards in the range of $3,000-$5,000.

Closing Date: February 15th for notification in June.

Additional Information: Each application must include a statement, in general terms, of the purpose for which funds are expected to be used.

For further information contact:
American Society of Civil Engineers, United Engineering Center, 345 East 47th Street, New York, NY, 10017, USA
Tel: 1 800 548 ASCE ext.7222
Email: mperalta@ny.asce.org
Contact: Student Services

*J Waldo Smith Hydraulic Fellowship

Subjects: Experimental hydraulics.

Eligibility: Open to graduate students who are members, preferably associate members, of the Society. The Fellow will be selected on the basis of the quality of the application.

Purpose: To encourage research.

Type: Fellowship.

No. of awards offered: One.

Frequency: Triennially (1997).

Value: US$4,000 per annum, plus an additional amount not in excess of US$1,000 as may be required for physical equipment connected with the research. Equipment becomes the property of the institution upon completion of the work.

Length of Study: One academic year.

Study Establishment: Approved institutions.

Closing Date: February 15th for notification in June.

Arthur S Tuttle Memorial National Scholarship Fund

Subjects: Civil engineering.

Eligibility: Open to members of the Society. Financial need and educational standing will be considered.

Level of Study: Graduate.

Purpose: To provide tuition assistance to students during the first year of graduate studies.

Type: Scholarship.

No. of awards offered: Variable.

Frequency: Annual.

Value: Varies, depending on earnings available from the endowment. Past awards in the range of $3,000-$5,000.

Length of Study: One year.

Study Establishment: An approved institution.

Closing Date: February 15th for notification in June.

For further information contact:
American Society of Civil Engineers, United Engineering Center, 345 East 47th Street, New York, NY, 10017, USA
Tel: 1 800 548 ASCE ext.7222
Email: mperalta@ny.asce.org
Contact: Student Services

AMERICAN SOCIETY OF HEATING, REFRIGERATING AND AIR CONDITIONING ENGINEERS, INC

1791 Tullie Circle, NE, Atlanta, GA, 30329, USA
Tel: 404 636 8400
Fax: 404 321 5478
www: WWW.ASHRAE.ORG
Contact: Manager of Research

Grants-in-Aid for Graduate Students

Subjects: Heating, refrigeration, air conditioning and ventilation.

Eligibility: Open to graduate engineering students capable of undertaking appropriate and scholarly research. Grants are not restricted to US citizens.

Level of Study: Doctorate.

Purpose: To stimulate interest through the encouragement of original research.

Type: Grant.

No. of awards offered: Usually 12-18.

Frequency: Annual.

Value: Up to US$7,500 depending upon needs and nature of request.

Length of Study: Usually for one year or less; non-renewable.

Study Establishment: The Grantee's institution.

Applications Procedure: Application form must be obtained, completed and returned by applicant and faculty advisor.

Closing Date: December 15th for consideration later.

AMERICAN SOCIETY OF INTERIOR DESIGNERS EDUCATIONAL FOUNDATION, INC

American Society of Interior Designers Educational Foundation, Inc, 608 Massachusetts Avenue, NE, Washington, DC, 20002-6006, USA
Tel: 202 546 3480

ASID/Mabelle Wilhelmina Boldt Memorial Scholarship

Subjects: Interior design.

Eligibility: Applicants must have been practising designers for a period of at least five years prior to returning to graduate level.

Level of Study: Graduate.

Type: Scholarship.

No. of awards offered: One.

Frequency: Annual.

Value: US$1,800.

Study Establishment: A degree-granting institution.

Closing Date: April.

Additional Information: The scholarship will be awarded on the basis of academic/creative accomplishment, as demonstrated by school transcripts and a letter of recommendation.

ASID/Joel Polsky-Fixtures Furniture Academic Achievement Award

Subjects: Interior design.

Level of Study: Postgraduate, Undergraduate.

Purpose: To recognize an outstanding undergraduate or graduate student's interior design research or thesis project.

Type: Prize.

No. of awards offered: One.

Frequency: Annual.

Value: US$1,000.

Closing Date: January.

Additional Information: Entries will be judged on actual content, breadth of material, comprehensive coverage of topic, innovative subject matter and bibliography/references.

ASID/Joel Polsky-Fixtures Furniture Prize

Subjects: Interior design.

Purpose: To recognize outstanding academic contributions to the discipline of interior design through literature or visual communication.

Type: Prize.

No. of awards offered: One.

Frequency: Annual.

Value: US$1,000.

Closing Date: January.

Additional Information: Entires should address the needs of the public, designers, and students on such topics as educational research,

behavioral science, business practice, design process, theory, or other technical subjects. Material will be judged on innovative subject matter, comprehensive coverage of topic, organization, graphic presentation, and bibliography/references.

AMERICAN SOCIETY OF MECHANICAL ENGINEERS

American Society of Mechanical Engineers, 345 East 47th Street, New York, NY, 10017, USA
Tel: 212 705 8131
Fax: 212 705 7143
Email: perryt@asme.org
Contact: Thomas J Perry, PE, Director, Engineering Education

ASME Graduate Teaching Fellowship Program

Eligibility: Applicant must be US citizen or permanent resident, have an undergraduate degree from an ABET accredited program, and be a student member of ASME.

Level of Study: Doctorate, Postgraduate.

Purpose: The ASME Graduate Teaching Fellowship Program was established to encourage outstanding graduate students, especially women and minorities, to pursue the doctorate in Mechanical Engineering and encourage engineering education as a profession.

Type: Fellowship.

No. of awards offered: Four.

Frequency: Annual.

Value: From US$1,500 to US$5,000 depending on the award.

Length of Study: One to three years.

Country of Study: USA.

Applications Procedure: Applicant must be a PhD student in Mechanical Engineering, with a demonstrated interest in a teaching career. Applicant must submit an undergraduate GPS, GRE scores, two letters of recommendation from faculty or their M.S committee, a graduate transcript, and a statement about a faculty career.

Closing Date: April 15th.

Additional Information: In the terms of the fellowship, the awardee must teach at least two lecture courses if the fellowship term is three years and one course if the term is one or two years.

AMERICAN SOCIETY OF NAVAL ENGINEERS

American Society of Naval Engineers, 1452 Duke Street, Alexandria, VA, 22314-3458, USA
Tel: 703 836 6727
Fax: 703 836 7491
Email: ANSEHQ.ASNE@MCIMAIL.COM

Scholarships

Subjects: Engineering or physical sciences. The following are some of the programs which apply: naval architecture; marine, ocean, mechanical, civil, aeronautical, electrical and electronic engineering; the physical sciences; as well as other programs leading to careers with both military and civilian organizations requiring these educational backgrounds.

Eligibility: Open to US citizens who are about to enter either the last year of a full-time or co-op undergraduate program or one year of graduate study leading to a designated engineering or physical science degree. A Scholarship will not be awarded to a doctoral candidate or to a person already having an advanced degree. Candidates must have demonstrated or expressed a genuine interest in a career in naval engineering.

Level of Study: Senior year on undergraduate level, Postgraduate.

Purpose: To encourage college students to enter the field of naval engineering and to support naval engineers seeking advanced education in the field.

Type: Scholarship.

No. of awards offered: Varies (11-17).

Frequency: Annual.

Value: US$2,000 per annum.

Length of Study: One year; renewable.

Study Establishment: An accredited college or university.

Country of Study: USA.

Applications Procedure: Please submit an application form, transcripts, and letters of recommendation.

Closing Date: February 15th.

Additional Information: The selection criteria are the candidate's academic record, work history, professional promise and interest in naval engineering, extra-curricular activities, and recommendations of college faculty, employers, and other character references. Financial need may also be considered.

AMERICAN SOCIOLOGICAL ASSOCIATION

American Sociological Association, 1722 North Street, NW,
Washington, DC, 20036, USA
Tel: 202 833 3410
Fax: 202 785 0146

Minority Fellowship Program

Subjects: Sociological research on mental health and mental illness is germane to core areas of emphasis within the National Institute of Mental Health specifically, and the National Institutes of Health more generally. Research on the social dimensions of mental health includes attention to prevention and to causes, consequences, adaptations and interventions.

Eligibility: Open to citizens or non-citizen nationals of the United States, or those who have been lawfully admitted to the United States for permanent residence and have in their possession an Alien Registration Card, who have been accepted and/or enrolled in a full-time sociology doctoral program in the United States. In addition, applicants must be members of a racial and ethnic group, including Blacks/African-Americans, Latinos (e.g. Chicano, Cuban, Puerto Rican), American Indians or Alaskan Natives, and Asians (e.g. Chinese, Japanese, Korean, Southeast Asian) or Pacific Islanders (e.g. Hawaiian, Guamanian, Samoan, Filipino). Seniors in colleges or universities, students in master only programs who have been accepted by or are applying to doctoral programs and have strong interests in the sociology of mental health are encouraged to apply. If, however, a candidate is selected for an award, but not enrolled in an appropriate doctoral program by the time the funding year begins, he/she will not be eligible to receive the award. Students already enrolled in a graduate program can apply, provided that they fulfil the eligibility criteria and demonstrate research interests in mental health and mental illness.

Level of Study: Doctorate.

Purpose: To support the development and training of minority sociologists in mental health. Funded by a grant from the National Institute of Mental Health (NIMH), the MFP seeks to attract talented minorities students interested in mental health issues and to facilitate their placement, work and success in an appropriate graduate program.

Type: Fellowship.

No. of awards offered: Varies.

Frequency: Annual.

Value: Annual stipend of US$10,008.

Length of Study: Twelve months; renewable, upon reapplication, for up to 3 years.

Closing Date: December 31st for announcement by April 15th.

Additional Information: Students who accept the award are obligated to engage in mental health and mental illness research and/or teaching for a period equal to the length of time they receive the award. For example, if a Fellow receives funding for three years, there is a pay back period of two years in the sociology of mental health. Dissertation support is available to Fellows who have completed all course work and who have been advanced to degree candidacy. However, Fellows who request dissertation support are required to demonstrate that the added support will facilitate progress towards the completion of their degree.

AMERICAN TINNITUS ASSOCIATION

American Tinnitus Association, PO Box 5, Portland, OR, 97207-0005,
USA
Tel: 503 248 9985
Fax: 503 248 0024
Contact: Gloria E Reich, PhD

Scientific and Medical Research Grants

Subjects: Tinnitus.

Eligibility: Open to non-profit tax-exempt institutions.

Purpose: To identify the mechanism(s) of tinnitus or improve tinnitus treatments.

Type: Research Grant.

No. of awards offered: Varies.

Frequency: Annual.

Value: Varies.

Country of Study: Unrestricted.

Applications Procedure: Write for grant application policies and procedures brochure.

Closing Date: Proposals may be sent at any time.

THE AMERICAN UNIVERSITY IN CAIRO

The American University in Cairo, 113 Kasr El Aini Street, Cairo, Egypt
Tel: 20 2 357 5530
Fax: 20 2 355 7565
Email: kimmer@auc-acs.eun.eg
www: http://www.auc-acs.eun.eg
Contact: Kimberlee Bell

African Graduate Fellowship

Subjects: Arts and humanities, business administration, engineering and information science.

Eligibility: Open to sub-Saharan nationals with a bachelors degree. Must be proficient in the English language.

Level of Study: Postgraduate.

Purpose: To enable outstanding young men and women from sub-Saharan Africa to study at AUC.

Type: Tuition waiver.

No. of awards offered: Ten.

Frequency: Annual.

Value: US$9,250 per academic year.

Length of Study: Two years.

Study Establishment: AUC only.

Country of Study: Egypt.

Applications Procedure: Application form and supporting documents are available from address shown.

Closing Date: February 1st.

Ryoichi Sasakawa Young Leaders Graduate Scholarship

Subjects: Arts and humanities.

Eligibility: Applicants should have a bachelors degree, 3.0 GPA or above.

Level of Study: Postgraduate.

Purpose: To award grants to outstanding young men and women for the pursuit of graduate studies at AUC.

Type: Tuition waiver and stipend.

No. of awards offered: Three.

Frequency: Annual.

Value: $9,250 per academic year.

Length of Study: Two years.

Study Establishment: AUC only.

Country of Study: Egypt.

Applications Procedure: Faculty nominations are required in the first instance.

Closing Date: February 1st.

AMERICAN WATER WORKS ASSOCIATION

American Water Works Association, 6666 West Quincy Avenue, Denver, CO, 80235, USA
Tel: 303 794 7711
Fax: 303 794 8915
Contact: Scholarships Coordinator

Academic Achievement Award

Subjects: Public water supply.

Eligibility: Open to all master's theses and doctoral dissertations that are relevant to the water supply industry. The manuscript must reflect the work of a single author and be submitted during the competition year in which it was submitted for the degree. The competition is open to students majoring in any subject provided the work is directly related to the drinking water supply industry.

Level of Study: Doctorate, Postgraduate.

Purpose: To encourage academic excellence by recognizing contributions to the field.

No. of awards offered: 4 awards, 2 for doctoral dissertations and 2 for masters theses.

Frequency: Annual.

Value: Two first prizes of US$1,000; two second prizes of US$500.

Country of Study: USA.

Closing Date: October 1st.

Thomas R Camp Scholarship

Subjects: Planning applied research in the drinking water field.

Eligibility: Open to PhD or master's students (in alternate years).

Level of Study: Postgraduate, Doctorate.

Purpose: To honor the memory of Dr Thomas R Camp by supporting and encouraging outstanding graduate students doing applied research in the drinking water field.

Type: Scholarship.

No. of awards offered: One.

Frequency: Annual.

Value: US$5,000.

Country of Study: USA, Canada, Guam, Puerto Rico or Mexico.

Applications Procedure: Application form must be completed - forms are available on request.

Closing Date: January 15th.

Holly A Cornell Scholarship

Subjects: Water supply and treatment.

Eligibility: Open to female and/or minority master's students.

Level of Study: Postgraduate.

Purpose: To encourage outstanding female and/or minority students to pursue advanced training in the field of water supply and treatment.

Type: Scholarship.

No. of awards offered: One.

Frequency: Annual.

Value: US$5,000.

Applications Procedure: Application form must be completed - forms are available on request.

Closing Date: December 15th.

Larson Aquatic Research Support Scholarships

Subjects: Including but not limited to corrosion control, treatment and distribution of domestic and industrial water supplies, aquatic chemistry, analytical chemistry and environmental chemistry.

Eligibility: Open to candidates pursuing an advanced degree, MS or PhD, at an institution of higher education located in Canada, Guam, Puerto Rico, Mexico or the USA. Also the requirements for the degree must be completed in the year of the award. Selection of Scholarship recipients is based upon the excellence of their academic record and their potential to provide leadership in one of the fields served by Dr Larson.

Level of Study: Postgraduate, Doctorate.

Purpose: To provide support and encouragement to outstanding graduate students preparing for a career in one of the fields of science or engineering to which Dr Thurston E Larson made significant contributions.

Type: Scholarship.

No. of awards offered: Two.

Frequency: Annual.

Value: US$3,000 for an MS student and US$5,000 for a PhD student.

Country of Study: Canada, Guam, Puerto Rico, Mexico or the USA.

Closing Date: December 15th for the MS for receipt the following year; January 15th for the PhD for receipt the same year.

Additional Information: The Scholarship recipients will be publicly recognized at the annual conference of the American Water Works Association in June.

Abel Wolman Doctoral Fellowship

Subjects: Water supply and treatment.

Eligibility: Open to candidates who anticipate completing the requirements for their PhD degree by the fall of the second year after the award has been made. Applicants must be citizens of a country that has an AWWA section (USA, Canada, or Mexico).

Level of Study: Doctorate.

Purpose: To encourage promising students to pursue advanced training and research.

Type: Fellowship.

No. of awards offered: One.

Frequency: Annual.

Value: A stipend of US$10,000 distributed over 12 months, US$1,000 for research supplies and equipment, and an education allowance of up to US$4,000 to cover the cost of tuition and other fees.

Length of Study: Initially one year; renewable for one further year on submission of evidence of satisfactory progress and approval by a review committee.

Country of Study: Canada, USA or Mexico.

Closing Date: January 15th; the recipient will be notified by May 1st and support will be available for the fall.

ANATOMICAL SOCIETY OF GREAT BRITAIN AND IRELAND

Anatomical Society of Great Britain and Ireland, Department of Anatomy and Cell Biology, Imperial College School of Medicine at St Mary's, Norfolk Place, London, W2 1PG, England
Tel: 0171 594 3764
Fax: 0171 723 7349
Email: j.p.bennett@sm.ic.ac.uk
Contact: Dr J P Bennett

Anatomical Society Research Studentships

Subjects: Anatomical sciences.

Eligibility: Students must be UK or Irish nationals with degree from British or Irish University.

Level of Study: Doctorate.

Purpose: To provide support for graduates to pursue a research degree in the anatomical sciences.

Type: Fellowship.

No. of awards offered: Three to four.

Frequency: Annual.

Value: Standard MRC studentship rates.

Length of Study: Three years.

Study Establishment: University.

Country of Study: UK or Republic of Ireland.

Applications Procedure: Application by academic staff member (prospective supervisor) on appropriate forms.

Closing Date: Early October, as advertised.

Additional Information: Please see advertisements in 'Nature' and 'Journal of Anatomy' in August each year.

For further information contact:
Anatomical Society of Great Britain and Ireland, Department of Anatomy and Cell Biology, Imperial College School of Medicine at St Mary's, Norfolk Place, London, W2 1PG, England
Tel: 0171 594 3764
Fax: 0171 724 7349
Email: j.p.bennett@sm.ic.ac.uk
Contact: Dr J P Bennett

Anatomical Society Senior Visiting Fellowship

Subjects: Anatomy.

Eligibility: Any qualified person normally living and working outside of the UK and Republic of Ireland.

Level of Study: Professional development.

Purpose: To enable a senior scientist from overseas with an established reputation in the anatomical sciences to visit the UK or Republic of Ireland to engage in collaborative research.

Type: Fellowship.

No. of awards offered: One.

Frequency: Annual.

Value: Contribution to expenses (by individual negotiation).

Length of Study: Up to one year.

Study Establishment: University.

Country of Study: UK or Republic of Ireland.

Applications Procedure: Apply by letter and curriculum vitae, supported by letter of invitation from host department.

Closing Date: Early October, as advertised.

Additional Information: Please see advertisements in 'Nature' and 'Journal of Anatomy' in August each year.

GÉZA ANDA FOUNDATION

Géza Anda International Piano Competition, Bleicherweg 18, Zurich, CH-8002, Switzerland
Tel: 1 205 14 23
Fax: 1 205 14 20
Contact: Ruth Bossart

Géza Anda International Piano Competition

Subjects: Piano.

Eligibility: Open to young pianists of up to 32 years of age.

Purpose: To sponsor young pianists in the musical spirit of Géza Anda.

Type: Prizes.

No. of awards offered: Three.

Frequency: Triennially (1997).

Value: Cash prizes of SwFr60,000, concert engagements, Audience Prize sponsored by Bally, a Mozart Prize awarded by the Zurich Tonhalle-Gesellschaft, free management services during three years.

Country of Study: Switzerland.

Closing Date: March 1st.

ANGLO-AUSTRIAN MUSIC SOCIETY

Richard Tauber Memorial Scholarship Committee, Anglo-Austrian Music Society, 46 Queen Anne's Gate, London, SW1H 9AU, England
Tel: 0171 222 0366
Fax: 0171 233 0293
Contact: The Secretary

Richard Tauber Prize

Subjects: Vocal musical performance.

Eligibility: Open to British and Austrian residents, singers who are men between the ages of 21 and 32 or women between the ages of 21 and 30.

Level of Study: Postgraduate.

Purpose: To enable a British or Austrian singer to travel and study in order to broaden his or her musical experience prior to giving a public recital in London under the auspices of the Anglo-Austrian Music Society.

Type: Prize.

No. of awards offered: One.

Frequency: Biennially (Next 1997).

Value: A cash prize of £2,500 to be used in whatever way the winner prefers to further his/her career as a singer, or to study a language, or become acquainted with the Austrian or British musical scene. Advice to this end will be available from the Anglo-Austrian Music Society if required. There will also be a Wigmore hall recital for the winner.

Length of Study: An unlimited period.

Country of Study: Unrestricted.

Applications Procedure: Application form must be completed.

Closing Date: February 1997.

Additional Information: Preliminary auditions are held in London and Vienna in March. A public final audition is held in London in April or May. Applicants attend the preliminary auditions at their own expense.

ANGLO-BRAZILIAN SOCIETY

Anglo-Brazilian Society, 32 Green Street, London, W1Y 3FD, England
Tel: 0171 493 8493
Fax: 0171 493 5105
Contact: Secretary

BAT/Souza Cruz Scholarship

Subjects: Any aspect of Brazil: cultural, historical, geographical, literature, economy and medical.

Eligibility: Open to British citizens at postgraduate or undergraduate level.

Level of Study: Undergraduate, Postgraduate.

Purpose: To promote close and friendly relations between Brazil and Great Britain.

Type: Scholarship.

No. of awards offered: One.

Frequency: Annual.

Value: Return air fare to Brazil and local currency equivalent of £800 for expenses in Brazil.

Country of Study: Brazil.

Applications Procedure: Selection of candidates is by means of an essay competition or presentation of a detailed plan of the proposed study in Brazil, of approximately 3,000 words. Recipients travel to Brazil later in the same year and are expected to deliver a lecture to the Society on their return. Final selection is by interview in London (fare paid) in April.

Closing Date: March 1st.

Additional Information: The Society administers this scholarship on behalf of BAT Industries PLC.

Scholarship

Subjects: Any aspect of Brazil: cultural, historical, geographical, literature, economy and medical.

Eligibility: Open to British citizens at postgraduate or undergraduate level.

Level of Study: Undergraduate, Postgraduate.

Purpose: To promote close and friendly relations between Brazil and Great Britain.

Type: Scholarship.

No. of awards offered: One.

Frequency: Annual.

Value: £1,000.

Country of Study: Brazil.

Applications Procedure: Selection of candidates is by means of an essay competition or presentation of a detailed plan of the proposed study in Brazil, of approximately 3,000 words. Recipients travel to Brazil later in the same year and are expected to deliver a lecture to the Society on their return. Final selection is by interview in London (fare paid) in April.

Closing Date: 1 March.

For further information contact:
Anglo-Brazilian Society, 32 Green Street, London, W1Y 3FD, England
Tel: 0171 493 8493
Fax: 0171 493 5105
Contact: The Secretary

THE ANGLO-DANISH SOCIETY

The Anglo-Danish Society, 25 New Street Square, London, EC4A 3LN, England
Tel: 01753 884846
Contact: Mrs A M Eastwood, Secretary

The Anglo-Danish (London) Scholarships - The Hambros Bank Award

Subjects: Other things being equal, candidates whose study topics are of specific value to Anglo-Danish cultural/scientific interests will be preferred.

Eligibility: Graduates of Danish nationality.

Level of Study: Postgraduate.

Type: Scholarship.

No. of awards offered: 3-4.

Frequency: Dependent on funds available.

Value: £175 per month for a maximum of six months.

Length of Study: Maximum 6 month grant.

Study Establishment: UK university.

Country of Study: UK.

Applications Procedure: Application forms are required. These are available from the Secretary, between October 1st and December 31st.

Closing Date: January 12th.

Additional Information: Application forms can be obtained by writing to Mrs A-M Eastwood, 'Danewood', 4 Daleside, Gerrards Cross, Bucks, England SL9 7JF.

The Denmark Liberation Scholarships

Subjects: Other things being equal, candidates whose study topics are of specific value to Anglo-Danish cultural/scientific interests will be preferred.

Eligibility: Open to graduates of British nationality.

Level of Study: Postgraduate, Doctorate, Postdoctorate, Professional development.

Type: Scholarship.

No. of awards offered: Several.

Frequency: Annual.

Value: One major award of £9,000, and others at £6,000 each.

Length of Study: Minimum of six months.

Study Establishment: A Danish University or other approved institution.

Country of Study: Denmark.

Applications Procedure: Application forms are required to be completed. These are available between October 1st and December 31st from the Secretary, Mrs A-M Eastwood, 'Danewood', 4 Daleside, Gerrards Cross, Bucks, England, SL9 7JF. Please enclose a stamped addressed envelope or international reply coupon.

Closing Date: January 12th.

Additional Information: This scholarship program is running for ten years from 1996.

Scholarships

Subjects: Any subject.

Eligibility: Only open to British (UK) students wishing to study in Denmark, and only for Danish students wishing to study in the UK.

Level of Study: Postgraduate, Doctorate, Advanced student.

Purpose: To promote Anglo-Danish friendship.

Type: Scholarship.

No. of awards offered: Normally 6-8.

Frequency: Annual.

Value: One at £9,000; several at £6,000.

Length of Study: From six months.

Study Establishment: The universities of Copenhagen, Odense or Aarhus or at another approved institution.

Country of Study: Denmark.

Applications Procedure: Application form must be completed.

Closing Date: January 12th.

Additional Information: Successful applicants will be required to submit a report on work undertaken to the Society at the end of the study period. The Scholarships also provide for Danish students to attend UK universities for up to six months (value £175 per month).

For further information contact:
'Danewood', 4 Daleside, Gerrards Cross, Bucks, SL9 7JF, England
Tel: 01753 884846
Contact: Mrs A M Eastwood

ANGLO-GERMAN FOUNDATION FOR THE STUDY OF INDUSTRIAL SOCIETY

Anglo-German Foundation for the Study of Industrial Society, 17 Bloomsbury Square, London, WC1A 2LP, England
Tel: 0171 404 3137
Fax: 0171 405 2071

Research Grant

Subjects: Any aspect of industrial society, but especially economic and social policy. Current priority areas are: unemployment; the future of the welfare state; adjustment to European and global change.

Eligibility: Open to teams in the two countries who wish jointly to organize and carry out comparative research and conferences. Teams should submit a single application.

Level of Study: Applied research.

Purpose: To support bilateral research, seminars and conferences and to disseminate the resulting information; to cultivate and maintain better understanding and closer relations between the two countries; to establish practical and durable links between industry, academics, government and the media in the two countries.

Type: Research grant.

Frequency: Major grants (over £3,000): three times yearly; minor grants (up to £3,000): throughout the year.

Value: Up to £50,000.

Country of Study: Britain and Germany.

Applications Procedure: Application form must be completed.

Closing Date: Major projects: July, March, November.

ANGLO-ISRAEL ASSOCIATION

Anglo-Israel Association, 9 Bentinck Street, London, W1M 5RP, England
Tel: 0171 486 2300
Fax: 0171 935 4690
Email: aia@dircon.co.uk
Contact: H Stellman

Wyndham Deedes Travel Scholarships to Israel

Subjects: Intensive study of some aspect of life in Israel (sociological, scientific, cultural, economics, etc.) in the area in which the recipient is specially qualified or interested.

Eligibility: Open to UK citizens who have graduated from a British university or institute of higher education, or who are experienced and qualified in their field, and who intend to reside permanently in the UK.

Level of Study: Graduate.

Type: Scholarship.

No. of awards offered: Varies.

Frequency: Annual.

Value: Up to £2,000 to contribute towards the cost of direct travel to and from Israel, and residence.

Length of Study: A minimum period of six weeks.

Country of Study: Israel.

Applications Procedure: Application form must be completed; successful applicants will be invited for interview.

Closing Date: March 1st.

Additional Information: Recipients must undertake to submit a report of at least 5,000 words on their project within six months of their return. The Association has a right to publish these reports. A large self-addressed, stamped envelope should accompany all enquiries.

ANGLO-JEWISH ASSOCIATION

Anglo-Jewish Association, 5th Floor, Woburn House, Upper Woburn Place, London, WC1H OEP, England
Tel: 0171 387 5937
Contact: The Secretary

Anglo-Jewish Association

Subjects: Any subject.

Eligibility: Open to Jewish students of any nationality.

Purpose: To supplement students' financial aid.

Type: Bursary.

No. of awards offered: 100-120.

Frequency: Annual.

Value: Up to £500 per annum.

Country of Study: Great Britain.

Applications Procedure: Applicant must write formal letter of application in the first instance.

Closing Date: May 1st.

ANIMAL HEALTH TRUST

Animal Health Trust, P O Box 5, Newmarket, Suffolk, CB8 7DW, England
Tel: 01638 661111
Fax: 01638 665789
Contact: Head of Finance

A D and P A Allen Memorial Fund Project Award

Subjects: Farm animal welfare.

Eligibility: Open to veterinarians or scientists with postgraduate research experience. An interview in the UK will be required.

No. of awards offered: One.

Frequency: Annually, subject to funding.

Value: £10,000-£29,000 including project expenses.

Length of Study: 1-3 years.

Study Establishment: An approved institution.

Country of Study: UK.

Closing Date: March 31st.

Blount Memorial Trust Scholarship

Subjects: Veterinary and allied sciences.

Eligibility: Candidates should hold at least a good second class honours degree in science or veterinary medicine.

No. of awards offered: One.

Frequency: Annually; dependent on funds.

Value: £5,000 per annum including essential fees.

Length of Study: 1-3 years.

Study Establishment: An approved institution.

Country of Study: UK.

Closing Date: March 31st.

Livesey Memorial Fellowship

Subjects: Veterinary and allied sciences.

Eligibility: Candidates should be recently qualified veterinary surgeons. An interview in the UK will be required.

No. of awards offered: One.

Frequency: Annually, subject to funds.

Value: £5,000-£10,000 including essential fees, according to age and experience.

Length of Study: 1-3 years.

Study Establishment: An approved institution.

Country of Study: UK.

Closing Date: March 31st.

Wooldridge Farm Livestock Research Fellowship

Subjects: Major factors (including epidemiology) influencing health and productivity of cattle, sheep or pigs.

Eligibility: Candidates should be veterinarians or scientists with postgraduate research experience. An interview in the UK will be required.

Type: Fellowship.

Frequency: Annually, subject to funds available.

Value: £5,000-£9,000 per annum including essential fees, according to age and experience.

Length of Study: 1-3 years.

Study Establishment: An approved institution.

Country of Study: UK.

Closing Date: March 31st.

ANTI-CANCER FOUNDATION OF THE UNIVERSITIES OF SOUTH AUSTRALIA

Anti-Cancer Foundation, Universities of South Australia, PO Box 929, Unley, SA, 5061, Australia
Tel: 08 291 4111
Fax: 08 291 4122
Contact: Executive Director

*Research Grants

Subjects: Any scientific or medical field directly concerned with the cause, diagnosis, prevention or treatment of cancer.

Eligibility: Open to postgraduate research workers who have established themselves in the field of cancer research or show promise of doing so.

Level of Study: Postgraduate.

Type: Research Grant.

No. of awards offered: Approximately 30.

Frequency: Annual.

Value: Varies according to the needs of the proposed research project and available funds.

Length of Study: Up to 2 years.

Study Establishment: An appropriate establishment in South Australia.

Country of Study: Australia.

Closing Date: June.

THE APEX FOUNDATION FOR RESEARCH INTO INTELLECTUAL DISABILITY LTD

The Apex Foundation for Research into Intellectual Disability Ltd, PO Box 311, Mount Evelyn, Victoria, 3796, Australia
Tel: 03 973 61261
Contact: Mr Kevin Morrish

Annual Research Grants

Subjects: Disability research.

Eligibility: Open to suitably qualified researchers.

Level of Study: Unrestricted.

Purpose: To support research projects which are concerned with the causes, diagnosis, prevention or treatment of intellectual disability.

Type: Research grants.

No. of awards offered: Variable number.

Frequency: Annual.

Value: Varies (total annual funds around A$60,000).

Country of Study: Australia.

Applications Procedure: Application form to be completed.

Closing Date: July 31st.

APPRAISAL INSTITUTE EDUCATION TRUST

Appraisal Institute Education Trust, c/o Appraisal Institute, 875 North Michigan Avenue, Chicago, IL, 60611-1980, USA
Tel: 312 335 4136
Contact: Jennifer Shless, Project Coordinator

*Scholarships

Subjects: Real estate appraisal, land economics, real estate or allied fields.

Eligibility: Open to graduate students majoring in one of the designated fields who are US citizens.

Type: Scholarship.

No. of awards offered: Varies.

Frequency: Annual.

Value: US$3,000.

Country of Study: USA.

Applications Procedure: Applications should include a written statement from the Dean of the candidate's college recommending the application; a signed statement regarding the candidate's general activities and intellectual interests in college, college training (college attended, number of years, and degree secured or to be secured within the next year), activities and employment outside college for the past four years (or longer, if pertinent), contemplated line of study for a degree, and the career the candidate expects to follow after leaving college (this statement should not exceed 1,000 words); official copies of all collegiate grade records; the proposed study program, including a brief description of each course the candidate plans to pursue in working toward the degree indicated, and a certificate of approval of this program; letters from two individuals regarding the candidate's qualifications and character. Application forms are available from September.

Closing Date: March 15th.

THE ARCHAEOLOGICAL INSTITUTE OF AMERICA

656 Beacon Street, Boston, MA, 02215-2010, USA
Tel: 617 353 9361
Fax: 617 353 6550
Email: aia@bu.edu
Contact: The Secretary

Anna C and Oliver C Colburn Fellowship

Subjects: Archaeology.

Eligibility: Competition is open to United States or Canadian citizens or permanent residents. Current officers and members of the Governing Board of the Institute are not eligible for this award.

Level of Study: Postgraduate.

Type: Fellowship.

No. of awards offered: One.

Frequency: Annual.

Value: $11,000.

Length of Study: One year.

Applications Procedure: Contact the AIA for an application form.

Closing Date: February.

Additional Information: Other major fellowships may not be held during the requested tenure of the Colburn award.

Kenan T Erim Award

Subjects: Archaeology.

Eligibility: Open to scholars working on Aphrodisias material. Current officers and members of the Governing Board of the Institute are not eligible for this award.

Level of Study: Unrestricted.

No. of awards offered: One.

Frequency: Annual.

Value: $4,000.

Applications Procedure: Contact the AIA office for an application form.

Closing Date: November.

Additional Information: If the project involves work at Aphrodisias, candidates must submit written approval from the Field Director with their applications. Recipients of the Erim Award must submit a final report to the President of the AIA which will be forwarded to the President of the American Friends of Aphrodisias.

For further information contact:
The Archaeological Institute of America, 656 Beacon Street, Boston, MA, 02215-2010, USA
Tel: 617 353 9361
Fax: 617 353 6550
Email: aia@bu.edu

Olivia James Traveling Fellowship

Subjects: Classics, sculpture, architecture, archaeology and history.

Eligibility: Competition is open to citizens or permanent residents of the United States. Current officers and members of the Governing Board of the Institute are not eligible for this award.

Level of Study: Doctorate.

Type: Fellowship.

No. of awards offered: One.

Frequency: Annual.

Value: US$15,000.

Length of Study: At least six months.

Country of Study: Greece, the Aegean Islands, Sicily, Southern Italy, Asia Minor or Mesopotamia.

Applications Procedure: Contact the AIA office for an application form.

Closing Date: November.

Additional Information: Preference will be given to individuals engaged in dissertation research, or to recent recipients of the PhD. The award is not intended to support field excavation projects. Recipients may not hold other major fellowships during the requested tenure of the Olivia James award.

For further information contact:
The Archaeological Institute of America, 656 Beacon Street, Boston, MA, 02215-2010, USA
Tel: 617 353 9361
Fax: 617 353 6550
Email: aia@bu.edu
Contact: The Secretary

Harriet and Leon Pomerance Fellowship

Subjects: Archaeology.

Eligibility: Applicants must be residents of the United States or Canada. Current officers and members of the Governing Board of the Institute are not eligible for this award.

Level of Study: Unrestricted.

Purpose: To enable a person to work on an individual project of a scholarly nature related to Aegean Bronze Age Archaeology.

Type: Fellowship.

No. of awards offered: One.

Frequency: Annual.

Value: US$3,000.

Length of Study: One academic year.

Applications Procedure: Contact the AIA office for an application form.

Closing Date: November.

For further information contact:
The Archaeological Institute of America, 656 Beacon Street, Boston, MA, 02215-2010, USA
Tel: 617 353 9361
Fax: 617 353 6550
Email: aia@bu.edu

Helen M Woodruff Fellowship

Subjects: Archaeology and classical studies.

Eligibility: Competition is open to citizens or permanent residents of the United States. Current officers and members of the Governing Board of the Institute are not eligible for this award.

Level of Study: Doctorate, Postdoctorate.

Type: Fellowship.

No. of awards offered: One.

Frequency: Annual.

Study Establishment: The American Academy in Rome.

Country of Study: Italy.

Applications Procedure: Further information and application forms are available from The American Academy in Rome, 7 East 60th Street, New York, NY 10022.

Additional Information: At the conclusion of the Fellowship tenure, Woodruff recipients must submit a report to the President of the Institute and the President of the American Academy in Rome.

ARCHITECTURAL HISTORY FOUNDATION

Architectural History Foundation, 350 Madison Avenue, New York, NY, 10017, USA
Tel: 212 557 8441
Fax: 212 682 5969

Kress Fellowship in Architectural History

Subjects: Architectural history or a related field.

Eligibility: Open to individuals of any nationality.

Purpose: To allow a student to prepare a PhD dissertation for publication.

Type: Fellowship.

No. of awards offered: One.

Frequency: Annual.

Value: US$10,000.

Closing Date: January 31st.

THE ARC OF THE UNITED STATES

The Arc of the United States, 500 E. Border Street, Suite 300, Arlington, TX, 76010, USA
Tel: 817 261 6003
Fax: 817 277 3491
Email: http://TheArc.org/welcome.html
Telex: thearc@metronet.com
Contact: Ann Balson/Michael Wehmeyer, PhD

Research Grant

Eligibility: Open to US nationals only.

Purpose: To support research leading towards prevention, amelioration or cure of mental retardation.

Type: Research Grant.

No. of awards offered: 1-3.

Frequency: Annual.

Value: Various amounts up to $25,000.

Length of Study: One year, with the option of extension.

Country of Study: USA.

Applications Procedure: Applicants should submit project authorization form, budget form, project summary, maximum of 15 double-spaced pages for narrative, vitas of researchers and letters of support.

Closing Date: April 1st.

ARISTOTLE UNIVERSITY OF THESSALONIKI

Aristotle University of Thessaloniki, University Campus, Thessaloniki, 540 06, Greece
Tel: 30 31 991612/991651/996742/996743/996726/996727
Fax: 30 31 206138
Contact: Head, Public and International Relations Office

Scholarships

Subjects: Modern Greek language.

Eligibility: Open to foreign citizens as well as those of Greek origin, who hold at least a high school diploma.

Purpose: To encourage foreigners to learn the modern Greek language.

Type: A variable number of Scholarships.

Frequency: Annual.

Value: Dr75,000 in total.

Length of Study: One month.

Study Establishment: For intensive language instruction, accompanied by lectures on various academic and cultural topics, at the School of Modern Greek Language for the intensive summer course, for 1 month (mid-August to mid-September).

Country of Study: Greece.

Applications Procedure: Application form must be completed.

Closing Date: March 31st.

Additional Information: Application forms are available on request.

For further information contact:
Aristotle University of Thessaloniki, School of Modern Greek Language, GR-540 06 Thessaloniki, Greece
Tel: 01030 31 991380/991381
Fax: 01030 31 206138
Contact: Mrs Th Kaldi-Koulikidou, Secretary

ARTHRITIS FOUNDATION

Arthritis Foundation, Research Administration, 1314 Spring Street, NW, Atlanta, GA, 30309, USA
Tel: 1 404 872 7100
Fax: 1 404 872 8694
Email: dporter@arthritis.org
Contact: Research Department

The mission of the Arthritis Foundation is to encourage and support high quality, original clinical research on problems closely related to the diagnosis, prognosis, management, and health care delivery and epidemiology of adults and children with arthritis and related rheumatic diseases

Arthritis Investigator Award

Subjects: Research in a field broadly related to arthritis.

Eligibility: Open to US citizens and permanent residents. Applicants must have completed a minimum of three and maximum of seven years postdoctoral research experience as of the award date. The award is not an extended postdoctoral fellowship. Applicants must hold an MD, PhD or equivalent degree, and have demonstrated distinction and productivity in research. The applicant may not hold an NIH, RO1, NSF Grant, FIRST Award, Howard Hughes Award, Pew, Wellcome, Searle, VA Merit Award or equivalent at the time of application. If such an award is made subsequently, however, the individual may retain his/her Arthritis Foundation award. Holders of NIH Physician Scientist Awards, NIH Young Investigator Awards, VA Associate Clinical Investigatorships, and similar research training awards given by other agencies will be eligible. Individuals with tenured positions are ineligible to apply. If one establishes tenure after receiving an award, he/she may continue to receive the award for the remainder of the period under the conditions of the original award.

Level of Study: Postdoctorate.

Purpose: To provide support to physicians and scientists in research fields broadly related to arthritis for the period between completion of postdoctoral fellowship training and establishment as an independent investigator. The award may provide salary and/or research support.

Type: Investigator Award.

No. of awards offered: 25 new awards and 25 continuing awards.

Frequency: Annual.

Value: US$49,000 per annum for stipend only, stipend plus research, or research expenses only, plus a grant of US$1,000 to the sponsoring institution to cover health insurance, supplies, travel, publication costs, etc.

Length of Study: Two years; renewal is competitive.

Applications Procedure: Application form must be completed.

Closing Date: September 1st.

Additional Information: A senior scientist familiar with the applicant's area of research should be designated as the sponsor. The sponsor and the chairman of the relevant academic department are responsible for stating the role of the applicant within the department, promising protection of time for research activities related to the award, guaranteeing space for the investigative work, and outlining future opportunities for the applicant. Applications are rated on the basis of the applicant's background, training, evidence of productivity, and potential; the proposed research project, its scientific merit and relevance to arthritis; and the environment in which the program will be conducted, specifically, the sponsor, the academic department, the unit, available facilities, and potential for inter- and extra-departmental scientific and academic interactions. Each Arthritis Investigator is expected to devote 80% of his/her professional time to activities related to laboratory research. The Arthritis Foundation does not award part-time investigators. Supplementation from the sponsoring institution or other awards for salary and research expenses are permitted up to a level consistent with institutional policies. The extent of this supplementation must be stated on the application, and the Foundation must be notified of any subsequent support. All work involving human subjects must show documented compliance with NIH guidelines for human subjects, as provided by the sponsoring institution's committee for clinical investigation. All work involving animal experimentation should comply with NIH guidelines for care and use of laboratory animals.

Biomedical Science Grant

Subjects: Arthritis and related rheumatic diseases.

Eligibility: Open to individuals with doctoral degrees (MD, PhD, or equivalent) at the assistant professor level or higher at any US non-profit institution. Evidence of independence is required.

Level of Study: Postdoctorate.

Purpose: To encourage and support high quality, original biomedical research closely related to understanding the etiology, pathogenic mechanisms and control of arthritis and related rheumatic diseases in adults and children.

Type: Grant.

No. of awards offered: Varies.

Frequency: Annual.

Value: Up to US$75,000 per annum, paid quarterly to the investigator's institution.

Length of Study: 1-3.

Country of Study: USA.

Applications Procedure: Applicants should write for details.

Closing Date: September 1st.

Additional Information: Applications will be rated on the basis of originality, research design and the ability of the investigator(s) to carry out the proposed project. This criterion includes the past research record of the investigator(s), the involvement of critical collaborators, etc. and significance of the proposed project to the field of arthritis and rheumatic diseases. All work involving human subjects must show documented compliance with NIH guidelines as provided by the sponsoring institution's committee for clinical investigation. All work involving animal experimentation should comply with NIH guidelines for care and use of laboratory animals.

Clinical Science Grant

Subjects: Arthritis and related rheumatic diseases.

Eligibility: Open to physicians or non-physicians with doctoral degrees or equivalent who are associated with any US non-profit institution. Ordinarily, at least one physician with expertise in the disease area being studied should be closely associated with the project.

Level of Study: Postgraduate, Professional development.

Type: Grant.

No. of awards offered: Varies.

Frequency: Annual.

Value: Up to US$75,000 per annum, paid quarterly to the investigator's institution.

Length of Study: 1-3 years.

Closing Date: September 1st.

Additional Information: Applications are rated on the basis of potential impact on the diagnosis and management of arthritis and rheumatic diseases, research design, originality, and the researcher's background and experience as an investigator. Funds will not be provided for those aspects of studies which pharmaceutical or other commercial companies should support. All work involving human subjects must show documented compliance with NIH guidelines as provided by the sponsoring institution's committee for clinical investigation. All work involving animal experimentation should comply with NIH guidelines for care and use of laboratory animals.

Doctoral Dissertation Award

Subjects: The research project must be related to arthritis management and/or comprehensive patient care in rheumatology practice, research or education. Suitable studies include, but are not limited to, functional, behavioral, nutritional, occupational, or epidemiological aspects of patient care and management. Drug studies and laboratory in vitro studies are not appropriate.

Eligibility: Open to doctoral candidates entering the research phase of their programs. The doctoral chairman must approve the project. A dissertation project is preferred. A candidate must have membership or eligibility for membership in his/her professional organization.

Level of Study: Postgraduate, Doctorate.

Purpose: To advance the research training of men and women of promise in investigative or clinical teaching careers as they relate to the rheumatic diseases.

No. of awards offered: Varies.

Frequency: Annual.

Value: Up to US$10,000 per annum depending on the amount of time committed to research. Payments are made monthly.

Length of Study: One or two years.

Country of Study: USA.

Closing Date: September 1st.

Additional Information: Individuals must pursue their research under the direction of a supervisor who possesses recognized expertise in the candidate's specific field of study. Projects are rated on the basis of proposed research environment, background and potential of the researcher, and potential significance and relevance of the project to the rheumatic diseases. All work involving human subjects must show documented compliance with NIH guidelines as provided by the sponsoring institution's committee for clinical investigation. All work involving animal experimentation should comply with NIH guidelines for care and use of laboratory animals.

New Investigator Grant

Subjects: The research project must be related to arthritis management and/or comprehensive patient care in rheumatology practice, research or education. Suitable studies include, but are not limited to, functional, behavioral, nutritional, occupational, or epidemiological aspects of patient care and management. Drug studies and laboratory in vitro studies are not appropriate.

Eligibility: Open to holders of a PhD or equivalent doctoral degree and demonstrated research experience. These awards are meant to encourage investigators who have received a doctoral degree within the last five years. MDs are not eligible. A candidate must have membership or eligibility for membership in his/her professional organization.

Level of Study: Postdoctorate.

Purpose: To encourage PhD-level health professionals who have research expertise to design and carry out innovative research projects related to the rheumatic diseases. The grant is intended to provide support for the period between completion of doctorate work and establishment as an independent investigator.

Type: Grant.

No. of awards offered: Varies.

Frequency: Annual.

Value: US$25,000 per annum, paid quarterly to the investigator's institution.

Length of Study: One or two years (renewable for a third).

Country of Study: USA.

Closing Date: September 1st.

Additional Information: Approval of each application and research project is required from an academic institution. Endorsement of an application by the institution constitutes agreement to allow the necessary time for completion of the project within the alloted term. Principal investigators do not have to be associated with an arthritis unit. Individuals with limited research experience must apply in conjunction with a supervisor or co-investigator with demonstrated research expertise in the applicant's area of study. Projects are rated on the basis of design, originality, potential significance and relevance to the rheumatic diseases, and the principal investigator's background and experience as an investigator. All work involving human subjects must show documented compliance with NIH guidelines as provided by the sponsoring institution's committee for clinical investigation. All work involving animal experimentation should comply with NIH guidelines for care and use of laboratory animals.

Physician Scientist Development Award

Subjects: Fields related to arthritis.

Eligibility: Open to MD candidates with no research background or limited science background.

Level of Study: Postdoctorate, Professional development.

Purpose: To encourage qualified physicians without significant prior research experience to embark on careers in biomedical or clinical research related to the understanding of arthritis and the rheumatic diseases.

Type: Development Award.

No. of awards offered: Variable (six in 1993).

Value: US$27,000-US$32,000 per annum, plus a US$500 grant to the institution to cover health insurance, supplies, travel and publication costs.

Length of Study: Two years; renewable for a third year.

Country of Study: USA.

Applications Procedure: Application is required.

Closing Date: September 1st.

Additional Information: A candidate must plan to pursue a program under the supervision of a qualified supervisor. The written proposal may represent the joint effort of the applicant and the supervisor. Applications are rated on the basis of the environment in which the training program will be conducted, specifically, the qualifications of the supervisor as an investigator, the unit, the facilities available and the potential for inter- and extra-departmental interactions; the applicant's background, training and potential as a biomedical investigator; and the proposed research project, its scientific merit and broad relevance to arthritis. Each recipient is expected to devote 90% of his/her professional time to activities related to the fellowship program: laboratory research, clinical investigation, field studies, or training. The Arthritis Foundation does not award part-time fellowships. A recipient may receive salary supplementation from other sources to a total amount consistent with the ordinary institutional level for that individual's rank and position. The extent of this supplementation must be stated on the application, and the Foundation must be notified of subsequent support. All work involving human subjects must show documented compliance with NIH guidelines for human subjects, as provided by the sponsoring institution's committee for clinical investigation. All work involving animal experimentation should comply with NIH guidelines for care and use of laboratory animals.

Postdoctoral Fellowship

Subjects: Research in a field broadly related to the rheumatic diseases.

Eligibility: Open to persons with an MD, PhD or equivalent doctoral degree. MDs are not eligible after six years of laboratory training (or seven years in the case of a clinical training program which includes one year in the laboratory). PhDs are not eligible after four years of post-degree laboratory experience. Individuals at or above the Assistant Professor level, or those who have tenured positions, are ineligible to apply for the awards. If one is promoted or established tenure after receiving an award, he/she may continue to receive the award for the remainder of the Fellowship period under the conditions of the original award.

Level of Study: Postdoctorate.

Purpose: To encourage qualified physicians and scientists to embark on careers in research broadly related to the understanding of arthritis and the rheumatic diseases. A Fellowship provides the stipend support for the early years of the necessary training period.

Type: Fellowship.

No. of awards offered: Variable (25 in 1993).

Frequency: Annual.

Value: US$25,000-US$32,500 per annum, plus a grant of US$500 per annum to the sponsoring institution to cover health insurance, supplies, travel, publication costs, etc.

Length of Study: Two years; renewable for a third year; renewal is competitive.

Country of Study: USA.

Applications Procedure: Application package available.

Closing Date: September 1st.

Additional Information: A candidate must plan to pursue a program under the supervision of a qualified supervisor. The written proposal may represent the joint effort of the applicant and the supervisor. Applications are rated on the basis of the environment in which the training program will be conducted, specifically, the qualifications of the supervisor as an investigator, the unit, the facilities available and the potential for inter- and extra-departmental interactions; the applicant's background, training and potential as a biomedical investigator; and the proposed research project, its scientific merit and broad relevance to arthritis. Each Postdoctoral Fellow is expected to devote 90% of his/her professional time to activities related to the fellowship program: laboratory research, clinical investigation, field studies, or training. The Arthritis Foundation does not award part-time fellowships. A recipient of a Postdoctoral Fellowship may receive salary supplementation from other sources to a total amount consistent with the ordinary institutional level for that individual's rank and position. The extent of this supplementation must be stated on the application, and the Foundation must be notified of subsequent support. All work involving human subjects must show documented compliance with NIH guidelines for human subjects, as provided by the sponsoring institution's committee for clinical investigation. All work involving animal experimentation should comply with NIH guidelines for care and use of laboratory animals.

ARTHRITIS FOUNDATION OF AUSTRALIA

Arthritis Foundation of Australia, GPO Box 121, Sydney, NSW, 2001, Australia
Tel: 612 221 2456
Fax: 612 232 2538
Contact: National Executive Director

*AFA-ARA Heald Fellowship

Subjects: Clinical or laboratory research into the causes and treatment of rheumatic diseases.

Eligibility: Open to Australian citizens or permanent residents, no more than 35 years of age, who are either science graduates with several years' postdoctoral experience or medical graduates with at least six years' post-MBBS experience.

Type: Fellowship.

No. of awards offered: One.

Frequency: Annual.

Value: US$25,000 plus limited travel assistance.

Length of Study: One year; not renewable.

Country of Study: USA or Canada.

Closing Date: Last Friday in June.

Additional Information: A preliminary arrangement with the proposed place of work or unit with adequate facilities must have been made.

*APLAR Region Study Grant

Subjects: Clinical or research aspects of rheumatology.

Eligibility: Open to nationals of the Asian-Pacific area, no more than 40 years of age, who are medical graduates. Nationals of Australia, New Zealand and Japan and nationals of other countries already working or studying in Australia, New Zealand or Japan are ineligible.

No. of awards offered: One.

Frequency: Annual.

Value: A$6,000.

Length of Study: Not less than 3 months.

Country of Study: Australia.

Applications Procedure: Written evidence that the institution where candidates wish to work is able to accommodate them and that there is a suitable supervisor willing to oversee their programme, as well as the support of the head of the unit where they work at present and of their own national rheumatology society is required.

Closing Date: Last Friday in October.

*Benjamin Memorial Grant

Subjects: Clinical research into osteoporosis or, if no suitable application for this is received, into rheumatoid arthritis (with particular reference to Iatrogenic disease) or into histocompatibility antigens in rheumatic disease.

Eligibility: Open to suitably qualified researchers.

No. of awards offered: One.

Frequency: Annual.

Value: A$15,000 per annum.

Length of Study: One year; renewable for a second and possibly a third year upon reapplication.

Country of Study: Australia.

Closing Date: Last Friday in June.

*Bicentennial Fellowship

Subjects: Clinical or laboratory arthritis research.

Eligibility: Open to Australian citizens and permanent residents who are science graduates with several years' postdoctoral experience and medical graduates with at least six years post-MBBS experience.

Type: Fellowship.

No. of awards offered: One.

Frequency: Annual.

Value: A$30,000 per annum, plus A$5,000 conference and consumables allowances.

Length of Study: Two years.

Country of Study: Australia.

Closing Date: Last Friday in June.

Additional Information: Preliminary agreement with proposed place of work mandatory.

*Mary Paxton Gibson Scholarships

Subjects: Rheumatology.

Eligibility: Open to medical and science graduates with developed interests in, or working in units with, developed research lines. Applicants should be enrolled in studies leading to an MD or PhD degree.

Type: Scholarship.

No. of awards offered: Varies.

Frequency: Annual.

Value: A$20,000 per annum (medical graduates) or A$14,250 (science graduates), plus A$1,000 for consumables.

Length of Study: One year; renewable for a second year upon reapplication.

Country of Study: Australia.

Closing Date: Last Friday in June.

*Grants-in-Aid

Subjects: Rheumatology.

Eligibility: Open to medical, scientific or allied health professionals.

No. of awards offered: Varies.

Frequency: Annual.

Value: A$1,000-A$8,000.

Country of Study: Australia.

Closing Date: Last Friday in June.

*Michael Mason Fellowship

Subjects: Research or clinical studies in rheumatic diseases.

Eligibility: Open to Australian citizens or permanent residents, no more than 35 years of age, who are medically qualified trainees.

Type: Fellowship.

No. of awards offered: One.

Frequency: Annual.

Value: £15,000 plus limited travel assistance.

Length of Study: One year; not renewable.

Country of Study: UK.

Closing Date: Last Friday in June.

Additional Information: A preliminary arrangement with the proposed place of work or unit with adequate facilities must have been made.

*Special Project Grants

Subjects: Arthritis research: causes and management.

Eligibility: Open to Australian citizens and permanent residents.

Purpose: To help establish long-term research projects in the field of rheumatic diseases which may, if they progress well, attract other support.

No. of awards offered: Four.

Frequency: Annual.

Value: Up to A$10,000.

Length of Study: One year.

Country of Study: Australia.

Closing Date: Last Friday in June.

*Frank G Spurway Scholarship

Subjects: Rheumatology.

Eligibility: Open to medical and science graduates with developed interests in, or working in units with, developed research lines. Applicants should be enrolled in studies leading to an MD or PhD degree.

Type: Scholarship.

No. of awards offered: One.

Frequency: Annual.

Value: A$20,000 per annum (medical graduates) or A$11,000 (science graduates), plus A$1,000 for consumables.

Length of Study: One year; renewable for a second year upon reapplication.

Country of Study: Australia.

Closing Date: Last Friday in June.

*Eileen Urquhart Memorial Scholarship

Subjects: Arthritis research.

Eligibility: Open to Australian citizens and permanent residents.

Level of Study: Doctorate.

Purpose: To support medical or science graduates working in a unit with developed research lines, enrolled or prepared to enrol in studies leading to MD or PhD.

Type: Scholarship.

No. of awards offered: One.

Frequency: Biennially.

Value: A$15,000 per annum, plus A$1,000 per annum for consumables.

Length of Study: Two years.

Country of Study: Australia.

Closing Date: Last Friday in June.

THE ARTHRITIS & RHEUMATISM COUNCIL

The Arthritis & Rheumatism Council, Copeman House, St Mary's Court, St Mary's Gate, Chesterfield, S41 7TD, England
Tel: 01246 558033
Fax: 01246 558007
Contact: Research and Education Secretary

Clinical Research Fellowships

Subjects: Rheumatology.

Eligibility: Open to UK medical graduates at the registrar or senior registrar level.

Level of Study: Postgraduate.

Purpose: To encourage young physicians into a career in clinical rheumatology. Candidates will be expected to register for a higher degree (MD or PhD).

Type: Fellowship.

No. of awards offered: Varies.

Frequency: Twice yearly.

Value: Fellow's salary plus reasonable laboratory expenses.

Length of Study: 2-3 years.

Study Establishment: Any suitable centre.

Country of Study: UK.

Applications Procedure: Application forms and information regarding annual closing dates are available on request.

Closing Date: Around March and September each year.

Postdoctoral Research Fellowships

Subjects: Rheumatology or a related subject.

Eligibility: Open to UK and Commonwealth citizens. Candidates should normally be in their first or second postdoctoral appointment.

Level of Study: Postdoctorate.

Purpose: To attract and retain talented scientists in rheumatological research.

Type: Fellowship.

No. of awards offered: Varies.

Frequency: Twice yearly.

Value: Fellows' salary (usually within 1A or II range) plus reasonable running costs.

Length of Study: Up to five years; renewal subject to satisfactory review.

Study Establishment: A UK university department or similar research institute (preferably within a multidisciplinary research group).

Country of Study: UK.

Closing Date: Around April and November each year.

Project Grants

Subjects: Rheumatology.

Eligibility: Open to UK and Commonwealth citizens with previous experience of investigation and research.

Level of Study: Professional development.

Purpose: To further research into rheumatic diseases.

Type: Project grant.

Frequency: 4 times yearly.

Value: Varies.

Length of Study: Up to three years.

Study Establishment: Any suitable centre.

Country of Study: UK.

Applications Procedure: Application forms are available upon request.

Closing Date: January 27th, April 14th, August 4th and November 12th.

Additional Information: Grants are made in support of specific research projects.

Senior ARC Fellowships

Subjects: Rheumatology or a related subject.

Eligibility: Open to UK and Commonwealth citizens with previous experience of investigation and research. Candidates should have proven ability in establishing an independent research programme.

Level of Study: Professional development.

Purpose: To further research into rheumatic diseases and to attract high-flying medical or scientific researchers into rheumatology.

Type: Fellowship.

No. of awards offered: Varies.

Frequency: Annual.

Value: Fellow's salary with lecturer B/Senior lectureship scale, plus supporting technician, running costs and essential equipment.

Length of Study: Up to five years, with option to renew subject to satisfactory review.

Study Establishment: Any suitable centre.

Country of Study: UK.

Applications Procedure: Application forms are available on request.

Closing Date: Around February each year.

Travelling Fellowships

Subjects: Rheumatology.

Eligibility: Open to doctors up to and including senior registrar status.

Level of Study: Professional development.

Purpose: To provide training and experience for doctors committed to a career in clinical rheumatology.

Type: Fellowship.

No. of awards offered: Two.

Frequency: Annually/when advertised.

Value: Fellow's salary and travelling costs (APEX return).

Length of Study: One year.

Study Establishment: A centre of the Fellow's choice, subject to the Council's approval.

Closing Date: Varies.

THE ARTHRITIS SOCIETY

The Arthritis Society, 250 Bloor Street East, Suite 901, Toronto,
Ontario, M4W 3P2, Canada
Tel: 416 967 1414
Fax: 416 967 7171
Contact: Bonnie Thorn

Geoff Carr Lupus Fellowship

Subjects: Rheumatology.

Eligibility: Open to nationals of any country.

Level of Study: Postdoctorate.

Purpose: To provide advanced training to a rheumatologist specializing in lupus at an Ontario lupus clinic.

Type: Fellowship.

No. of awards offered: One.

Frequency: Annual.

Value: C$50,000.

Length of Study: One year.

Study Establishment: Approved Ontario lupus clinic.

Country of Study: Canada.

Applications Procedure: Application must be submitted with three letters of recommendation, a letter of acceptance from a proposed supervisor (to include an outline of proposed training program) and certified transcripts of undergraduate record.

Closing Date: November 15th.

Clinical Fellowships

Subjects: Rheumatology.

Eligibility: Open to Canadian citizens or landed immigrants who have completed three years of graduate training in internal medicine or paediatrics approved by the Royal College of Physicians and Surgeons (Canada) or the Corporation of Physicians and Surgeons (Quebec). One of these three years of training should be in rheumatology.

Level of Study: Postdoctorate.

Purpose: To augment arthritis residency training programmes and enhance research skills.

Type: Fellowships.

No. of awards offered: Varies; based on the number of ministry-funded positions available.

Frequency: Annual.

Value: Fellows training in Canadian medical schools are paid at the same rate as residents of their respective schools. Fellows training abroad are paid quarterly in advance in Canadian funds, the rates being the same as those paid by the Medical Research Council of Canada.

Length of Study: One year, usually commencing July 1st; renewable.

Study Establishment: Medical schools.

Country of Study: Canada or abroad.

Applications Procedure: Application must include: letters of recommendation from three sponsors, letter of acceptance from proposed supervisor to include outline of proposed training program, and a certified transcript of undergraduate record.

Closing Date: November 15th.

Additional Information: Clinical Fellowships are intended solely for the support of rheumatology trainees and are not awarded for the support of junior faculty. Fellowships are awarded by the Society on the advice of the Manpower Panel (MP). The Society reserves the right to approve or decline any application without stating its reasons. Applications must be signed by the applicant's supervisor and the Rheumatic Disease Unit Director.

Metro A Ogryzlo International Fellowship

Subjects: Clinical rheumatology.

Eligibility: The successful candidate will likely have completed his or her training in general medicine, and have a substantial prospect of returning to an academic position in his or her own country. Canadian citizens or landed immigrants are not eligible.

Level of Study: Postdoctorate.

Purpose: To provide advanced training.

Type: Fellowship.

No. of awards offered: One.

Frequency: Annual.

Value: Up to a maximum of C$31,000 per annum.

Length of Study: Twelve months; not renewable.

Study Establishment: A Rheumatic Disease Unit.

Country of Study: Canada.

Applications Procedure: Application must include: letters of recommendation from three sponsors, letter of acceptance from proposed supervisor to include outline of proposed training program, and a certified transcript of undergraduate record.

Closing Date: 15 November.

Additional Information: Fellows may not receive remuneration for any other work or hold a second major scholarship, except that, with the approval of their supervisors, they may engage in and accept remuneration for such departmental activities as are conducive to their development as clinicians, teachers or investigators. Ordinarily, a Fellow who is not a graduate of a medical school in the US, the UK, Republic of Ireland, Australia, New Zealand or South Africa must take the Medical Council of Canada evaluating examination to obtain the Medical Council of Canada certificate before an education license can be issued.

Research Fellowships

Subjects: Arthritis.

Eligibility: Preference is given to candidates who intend to embark on a research career in Canada. Candidates must hold a PhD, MD, DDS, DVM, PharmD (or the equivalent).

Level of Study: Postdoctorate.

Purpose: To provide support for highly qualified candidates to pursue full-time research.

Type: Fellowship.

No. of awards offered: Varies.

Frequency: Annual.

Value: Based on Medical Research Council scale.

Length of Study: One year, usually beginning July 1st; renewable.

Country of Study: Canada or abroad.

Applications Procedure: Application form must be completed and submitted with further documentation as outlined in the regulations.

Closing Date: November 15th.

Additional Information: Fellowships are awarded by the Society on the advice of the Manpower Panel (MP). The Society reserves the right to approve or decline any application without stating its reasons.

Research Grants

Subjects: Arthritis.

Eligibility: Open to investigators holding staff appointments at Canadian universities or other recognized Canadian institutions where the research is deemed relevant to the rheumatic diseases.

Level of Study: Postdoctorate.

Purpose: To search for the underlying causes and subsequent cures for arthritis while promoting the best possible care for the sufferer.

Type: Research Grant.

No. of awards offered: Varies.

Frequency: Annual.

Value: To cover research costs. Grant funds may not be used for the remuneration of Grantees. Current ceiling of C$60,000.

Length of Study: Usually three years; in some cases the Panel may request a progress report after one year.

Country of Study: Canada.

Applications Procedure: Application form and other documentation required - information can be found in regulations.

Closing Date: December 15th.

Research Scholarships

Subjects: Arthritis.

Eligibility: Open to applicants who have been guaranteed appropriate academic rank (minimum Assistant Professor) in the tenure track or equivalent career development stream by the Institute.

Level of Study: Postdoctorate.

Purpose: To provide support to newly appointed junior faculty members who are planning to pursue a career in basic or clinical research related to arthritis.

Type: Scholarship.

No. of awards offered: Varies.

Frequency: Annual.

Value: On a national salary scale, similar to other granting agencies.

Length of Study: Three years for junior scholarship, four years for senior scholarship; non-renewable.

Study Establishment: Canadian institutions.

Country of Study: Canada.

Applications Procedure: Completed application and other documentation as outlined in regulations.

Closing Date: December 15th.

Additional Information: Scholarships are awarded by the Society on the advice of the Manpower Panel and the Society reserves the right to approve or decline any application without stating reasons. Applications on behalf of candidates should be made to the Chairman of the

Department, in conjunction with the Rheumatic Disease Director, countersigned by the Dean. Scholars must report annually to the Society on their professional activities.

Research Scientist Awards

Subjects: Arthritis.

Eligibility: Open to applicants who have been guaranteed appropriate academic rank (minimum Associate Professor) in the tenure track or equivalent career development stream by their institution.

Level of Study: Postdoctorate.

Purpose: To provide support for individuals with a major interest in arthritis research and engaging in full-time academic careers in medical science, who have demonstrated their ability as independent research scientists.

Type: Research Grant.

No. of awards offered: Varies.

Frequency: Annual.

Value: On a national salary scale, similar to other granting agencies.

Length of Study: Three years; renewable subject to certain criteria.

Study Establishment: A Canadian institution.

Country of Study: Canada.

Applications Procedure: Completed application form plus other documentation as outlined in regulations.

Closing Date: December 15th.

Additional Information: Scientist awards are awarded by the Society on the advice of the Manpower Panel and the Society reserves the right to approve or decline any application without stating reasons. Applications on behalf of candidates should be made by the Chairman of the Department, in conjunction with the Rheumatic Disease Director, countersigned by the Dean. Scientists must report annually to the Society on their professional activities.

THE ARTS COUNCIL OF ENGLAND

The Arts Council of England, 14 Great Peter Street, London, SW1P 3NQ
Tel: 0171 973 6485
Fax: 0171 973 6590

The Arts Council is the national funding body for the performing and visual arts, touring and literature. It is an independent body operating at 'arms length' of Government to channel public funds to the arts and set an overall strategy for the funding and development of the arts. It works closely with other arts funding bodies in particular the ten Regional Arts Boards (RABs) for England. In 1994 the Scottish and Welsh Arts Councils, which were previously committees of the Arts Council of Great Britain, became autonomous and were funded directly by the Scottish Office and Welsh Office respectively. The Arts Council of Great Britain then became the Arts Council of England

*Artists Research and Development Fund

Subjects: All areas of music supported by the Arts Council.

Eligibility: Open to musicians of professional status resident in or performing regularly in England.

Purpose: To enable creative and performing musicians of professional status, working in all areas of music supported by the Arts Council, to research and prepare new or unusual repertoire, to explore new techniques, or to pursue a programme of work which will benefit their career in the music profession.

No. of awards offered: Varies.

Frequency: Annual.

Value: £500-£5,000.

Country of Study: Worldwide.

Closing Date: March.

For further information contact:
The Arts Council of England, 14 Great Peter Street, London, SW1P 3NQ, England
Tel: 0171 973 6496
Fax: 0171 973 6590
Contact: Music Department

Drama Grants

Subjects: Drama: writing or performance.

Eligibility: Open to playwrights and performers.

Value: Varies.

Applications Procedure: Write for application form.

Additional Information: Grants include new writing schemes for commissions, plus bursaries and residencies. Grants for specific projects are also available and subsidies of small scale touring.

For further information contact:
The Arts Council of England, 14 Great Peter Street, London, SW1P 3NQ, England
Tel: 0171 333 0100
Fax: 0171 973 6590
Contact: Drama Department

Independent Dance Project Grants

Subjects: Dance.

Eligibility: Open only to professional groups and soloists. Applications cannot be accepted for the following: a programme of work lasting 52 weeks; separate capital costs, e.g. vans or equipment; companies already receiving revenue subsidy from the Dance Department of the Arts Council. Applications for performances (and for projects initiated) in Scotland, Northern Ireland or Wales should be made to the Arts Councils of those countries. Priority will be given to companies planning to make and premiere new work outside London.

Level of Study: Professional development.

Purpose: To enable the making of innovative high quality performance work or research and development.

Type: Project Grant.

No. of awards offered: Varies.

Frequency: Twice yearly.

Value: Varies.

Country of Study: England.

For further information contact:
Dance Department, The Arts Council of England, 14 Great Peter Street, London, SW1P 3NQ
Tel: 0171 973 6485
Fax: 0171 973 6590
Contact: Janet Stephenson, Assistant Dance Officer

Music Grants

Subjects: Composition, commissioning, recording, music theatre development.

Eligibility: Open to suitably qualified musicians.

Level of Study: Unrestricted.

Purpose: To support artists undertaking projects in all music areas.

No. of awards offered: Approximately ten.

Frequency: Annual.

Closing Date: Varies - please contact the Arts Council office for individual deadlines.

Writer's Awards

Subjects: Poetry, fiction, literary autobiography and biography, writing for young people.

Eligibility: Open to writers resident in England and writing in English. The applicant must be a previously published author of a creative work, published in book form.

Level of Study: Professional development.

Purpose: To help published writers at a crucial stage of their career who need finance for a period of concentrated work on their next book.

Type: Bursary.

No. of awards offered: 15.

Frequency: Annual.

Value: £7,000.

Country of Study: England.

For further information contact:
The Arts Council of England, 14 Great Peter Street, London, SW1P 3NQ, England
Tel: 0171 333 0100
Fax: 0171 973 6590
Contact: Literature Department

ARTS COUNCIL OF IRELAND

The Arts Council, 70 Merrion Square, Dublin, 2, Republic of Ireland
Tel: 01 661 1840
Fax: 01 676 1320
Contact: Jennifer Traynor

The Arts Council awards grants in dance, drama, film and video, literature, music (opera as a separate section) and the visual arts. Write for 'Awards and Opportunities for Individuals' booklet

Artflight: Arts Council-Aer Lingus Travel Awards

Subjects: Creative arts, interpretative arts, arts administration.

Eligibility: Open to creative and interpretative artists in all fields, administrators, producers and directors of Irish birth or residence.

No. of awards offered: Varies.

Value: To cover the cost of the return fare to any destination on the Aer Lingus network.

Additional Information: Successful applicants must satisfy the Council that there is an artistic benefit to them and that their work as a whole will improve as a result of the travel award. In the case of an administrator, there must be a benefit to the applicant's employer or associated organization. Full details are given in a special brochure.

The Composers Commission Scheme

Subjects: Music composition.

Eligibility: Open to promoters of music events such as music societies, associations, festivals, established performing groups, instrumental ensembles and choral groups.

Purpose: To enable promoters of music events to commission work from a composer of their choice.

Frequency: As required.

Value: Varies.

The Macaulay Fellowship

Subjects: On a rotating basis: literature (1999); visual arts (1997); music (1998).

Eligibility: Open to applicants born in Ireland and under 30 years of age on 30 June in the year of application (or under 35 in exceptional circumstances).

Purpose: To further the liberal education of young creative artists.

Type: Fellowship.

No. of awards offered: One.

Frequency: Annual.

Value: Approximately IR£3,500.

Closing Date: April 15th.

The Marten Toonder Award

Subjects: On a rotating basis: visual arts (1999); music (1997); literature (1998).

Eligibility: Open to applicants of Irish birth or residence.

Purpose: To honour an artist of established reputation.

No. of awards offered: One.

Frequency: Annual.

Value: Approximately IR£3,500.

Closing Date: April 15th.

Additional Information: Applicants are required to complete an application form; available on request from the Council.

Travel Awards to Creative Artists

Subjects: Visual arts, writing, composition.

Eligibility: Open to applicants of Irish birth or residence.

Purpose: To assist professional development.

No. of awards offered: Varies.

Frequency: Quarterly.

Value: IR£750 maximum.

Length of Study: Normally for courses or projects of not more than 3 months duration.

Closing Date: 11 February, 13 May, 16 September, 11 November.

Additional Information: Travel awards are not intended for persons wishing to pursue degree or diploma courses in educational institutions.

ARTS COUNCIL OF NORTHERN IRELAND

Awards, Arts Council of Northern Ireland, 185 Stranmillis Road, Belfast, BT9 5DU, Northern Ireland
Tel: 01232 381591
Fax: 01232 661715

Arts Council of Northern Ireland Annual

Subjects: Any field of the arts.

Eligibility: Open to artists who contribute regularly to the artistic activities of the community, with residency in Northern Ireland of at least one year. Open to previous award holders. Registered students are not eligible to apply for visual arts awards. There are no stipulated age limits.

Level of Study: Professional development.

Purpose: To enable the artist to achieve objectives for specific projects or for the acquisition of equipment or materials. Awards may also be made for travel; for attending masterclasses; or for short-term training courses.

No. of awards offered: Variable.

Frequency: Annual.

Value: £500-£5,000 (for guidance only).

Closing Date: April.

Additional Information: Not intended for courses of vocational training leading to professional qualifications.

Arts Council Printmaker in Residence at Belfast Print Workshop

Subjects: Printmaking.

Eligibility: Open to a suitably qualified and experienced printmaker.

Level of Study: Professional development.

Purpose: To provide the opportunity for printmaker to pursue his or her printmaking at the print workshop situated in Arts Council of Northern Ireland premises, Stranmillis Road, Belfast.

Type: Fellowship.

No. of awards offered: One.

Frequency: Annual.

Value: £7,000 (under review), plus rent-free accommodation.

Length of Study: One year.

Study Establishment: The print workshop situated in Arts Council of Northern Ireland premises, Stranmillis Road, Belfast.

Country of Study: Ireland.

Closing Date: May.

Additional Information: Workshop has facilities for etching, screen-printing, stone lithography and relief printing as well as a small photographic darkroom.

For further information contact:
Arts Council of Northern Ireland, 185 Stranmillis Road, Belfast, BT9 5DU, Northern Ireland
Tel: 01232 381591
Fax: 01232 661715
Contact: Dorothy Stewart

or
Belfast Print Workshop, 185 Stranmillis Road, Belfast, BT9 5DU, Northern Ireland
Tel: 01232 381591
Fax: 01232 661715
Contact: James Allen

Bass Ireland Arts Awards

Subjects: Art.

Eligibility: Open to artists working in any field of the arts.

Level of Study: Professional development.

Purpose: To encourage the enrichment of the cultural scene in Northern Ireland.

No. of awards offered: Two.

Frequency: Annual.

Value: Major award £3,000; designated discipline award £1,500.

Length of Study: One year.

Closing Date: August.

Additional Information: Second Award for artist working in a nominated discipline. The Awards are part of Bass Ireland's commitment to supporting the arts.

For further information contact:
Arts Council of Northern Ireland, 185 Stranmillis Road, Belfast, BT9 5DU, Northern Ireland
Tel: 01232 381591
Fax: 01232 661715
Contact: Wilma Haines

British School at Rome

Subjects: Painting; sculpture.

Eligibility: Open to artists resident in Northern Ireland or the Republic of Ireland for a period of at least one year, or domiciled elsewhere but contributing regularly to the artistic activity of the community. There is no stipulated age limit.

Level of Study: Professional development.

Purpose: To provide working and living accommodation for visual arts scholars for the period of Fellowship in the British School at Rome.

Type: Fellowship.

No. of awards offered: One.

Frequency: Dependent on available studio space.

Value: £10,000 from the Arts Council to the British School to cover costs; £4,500 of this to the Fellow as stipend, and for materials allowance and travel expenses within Italy.

Length of Study: One year.

Study Establishment: The British School at Rome.

Country of Study: Italy.

Closing Date: April.

For further information contact:
Arts Council of Northern Ireland, 185 Stranmillis Road, Belfast, BT9 5DU, Northern Ireland
Tel: 01232 381591
Fax: 01232 661715
Contact: Dorothy Stewart

George Campbell Travel Award

Subjects: Visual arts.

Eligibility: Open to artists of Irish birth (no age limit). Particular attention is given to artists who wish to work on attachment to an art college, museum or organization.

Level of Study: Professional development.

Purpose: In memory of the painter, George Campbell. Instituted to celebrate his special relationship with both parts of Ireland and the strong cultural contact he developed with Spain.

Type: Travel Grant.

No. of awards offered: One.

Frequency: Annual.

Value: £1,000.

Country of Study: Spain.

Closing Date: April.

Additional Information: Awarded to Northern and Southern artists in alternate years.

For further information contact:
Arts Council of Northern Ireland, 185 Stranmillis Road, Belfast, BT9 5DU, Northern Ireland
Tel: 01232 381591
Fax: 01232 661715
Contact: Dorothy Stewart

Thomas Dammann Junior Memorial Trust

Subjects: Visual arts.

Eligibility: Open to students resident in Ireland, North and South, and registered for a postgraduate or undergraduate award at a third level institution. Also open to applicants pursuing serious academic research outside of normal educational institutions. Previous award winners may reapply.

Level of Study: Undergraduate, Postgraduate.

Purpose: To enable students to travel abroad to visit exhibitions, museums, galleries and buildings of architectural importance.

Type: Travel bursaries.

No. of awards offered: Twenty.

Frequency: Annual.

Value: Up to IR£2,000.

Country of Study: Any country.

Closing Date: March.

For further information contact:
Arts Council of Northern Ireland, 185 Stranmillis Road, Belfast, BT9 5DU, Northern Ireland
Tel: 01232 381591
Fax: 01232 661715
Contact: Dorothy Stewart

Tyrone Guthrie Centre at Annaghmakerrig

Subjects: All fields of the arts.

Eligibility: Open to all serious creative artists from both North and South of Ireland.

Level of Study: Professional development.

Purpose: For residential use by artists from all parts of Ireland.

Type: Residential centre for artists.

Frequency: All year round.

Value: Varies; Bursary covers costs of residential accommodation.

Length of Study: Usually for 2-5 weeks.

Study Establishment: Tyrone Guthrie Centre.

Country of Study: Ireland.

For further information contact:
Arts Council of Northern Ireland, 185 Stranmillis Road, Belfast, BT9 5DU, Northern Ireland
Tel: 01232 381591
Fax: 01232 661715

or
The Tyrone Guthrie Centre, Annaghmakerrig, Newbliss, Co Monaghan, Republic of Ireland
Contact: Resident Director

Alice Berger Hammerschlag Trust Award

Subjects: Visual arts.

Eligibility: Open to candidates normally resident in Northern Ireland or the Republic of Ireland who are practising in one of the visual or plastic arts.

Level of Study: Professional development.

Purpose: To assist young and unappreciated artists.

Type: Travel Award.

No. of awards offered: One.

Frequency: Annual.

Value: £1,000.

Country of Study: Any country.

Closing Date: April.

Additional Information: The Trust is a charity set up to honour the late Alice Berger Hammerschlag and to continue her work.

For further information contact:
Arts Council of Northern Ireland, 185 Stranmillis Road, Belfast, BT9 5DU, Northern Ireland
Tel: 01232 381591
Fax: 01232 661715
Contact: Dorothy Stewart

or
The Arts Council, 70 Merrion Square, Dublin, Eire

New York Fellowship

Subjects: Visual arts.

Eligibility: Open to artists resident in Northern Ireland or the Republic of Ireland for a period of at least one year, or domiciled elsewhere but contributing regularly to the artistic activity of the community. There is no stipulated age limit.

Level of Study: Professional development.

Purpose: To establish workspace for professional foreign artists in the US which, in turn, offers valuable exposure for these artists.

Type: Fellowship.

No. of awards offered: Two.

Frequency: Annual.

Value: To cover stipend, air fare and studio rent.

Length of Study: One year.

Country of Study: USA.

Closing Date: March.

Additional Information: Funded by Arts Councils and Ireland-America Arts Exchange.

For further information contact:
Arts Council of Northern Ireland, 185 Stranmillis Road, Belfast, BT9 5DU, Northern Ireland
Tel: 01232 381591
Fax: 01232 661715
Contact: Dorothy Stewart

or
The Arts Council, 70 Merrion Square, Dublin, 2, Eire

ARTS COUNCIL OF WALES

The Arts Council of Wales, Museum Place, Cardiff, CF1 3NX, Wales
Tel: 01222 394711
Fax: 01222 221447
Contact: Roy Bohana, Music Director

The Arts Council of Wales is the national organisation with specific responsibility for the funding and development of the arts in Wales. Most of its funds come from the Welsh Office, but it also receives funds from local authorities, the Crafts Council and other sources

Awards for Advanced Study in Music

Subjects: Instrumental and voice.

Eligibility: Open to singers and instrumentalists under 28 years of age on February 1st in the year of application, who were born and educated in Wales, or who have been permanently resident in Wales for at least two years.

Level of Study: Professional development.

Purpose: To provide opportunity for advanced study.

No. of awards offered: Limited.

Frequency: Annual.

Value: Varies.

Country of Study: UK and overseas.

Applications Procedure: Enquiries should be addressed to the Director of the Music Department.

Closing Date: February 1st.

For further information contact:
Arts Council of Wales, Museum Place, Cardiff, CF1 3NX, Wales
Tel: 01222 394711
Fax: 01222 221447
Contact: Roy Bohana, Music Director

Commissions to Composers

Subjects: Composition.

Eligibility: Commissions will be offered to composers of any nationality, providing the first performance will be in Wales.

Level of Study: Professional development.

Purpose: To commission new works.

Type: Commissions to composers.

No. of awards offered: Varies.

Frequency: Annual.

Value: Towards the cost of the Commission fee.

Applications Procedure: The Council will respond to applications from organizations and musicians who are able to guarantee the first performance of a new work. Enquiries should be addressed to the Director of the Music Department.

Closing Date: December 1st.

For further information contact:
Arts Council of Wales, Museum Place, Cardiff, CF1 3NX, Wales
Tel: 01222 394711
Fax: 01222 221447
Contact: Roy Bohana, Music Director

Grants to Dancers

Subjects: Dance projects.

Eligibility: Open to dancers and choreographers for projects taking place in Wales.

Purpose: To create new works of choreography and to commission new works of choreography.

Type: Grant.

No. of awards offered: Varies.

Frequency: Annual.

Value: Varies.

Country of Study: Wales.

Closing Date: November 30th.

For further information contact:
The Welsh Arts Council, 9 Museum Place, Cardiff, CF1 3NX, Wales
Tel: 01222 394711
Fax: 01222 221447
Contact: Maldwyn Pate, Dance Director

Masterclass/Industrial Experience Grants

Subjects: Visual arts.

Eligibility: Open to visual artists who live and/or work in Wales for at least nine months of the year, have been out of full-time education for at least two years and have previously sent details of themselves and their work to the Council's Slide Library.

Level of Study: Professional development.

Purpose: To enable artists to work for a period with another practitioner or to gain experience of using particular materials or processes.

Type: Grant.

No. of awards offered: Variable.

Frequency: Twice yearly.

Value: Varies.

Country of Study: No restrictions (worldwide).

Applications Procedure: Application form must be completed; expanded proposal submitted; and visual evidence of recent work must be shown.

Closing Date: April/May; September/October.

Additional Information: Enquiries should be addressed to the Director of the Visual Arts Department.

For further information contact:
Arts Council of Wales, Museum Place, Cardiff, CF1 3NX, Wales
Tel: 01222 394711
Fax: 01222 221447
Contact: Tessa Hartog, Executive Officer

Special Project Grants

Subjects: Crafts.

Eligibility: Open to craft societies, organizations and individuals.

Level of Study: Professional development.

Purpose: To assist projects specifically related to Wales.

Type: Grant.

No. of awards offered: Variable.

Frequency: Twice yearly.

Value: Varies according to project.

Country of Study: Wales.

Applications Procedure: Enquiries should be addressed to the Director of the Craft Department.

Closing Date: January 20th; April 20th.

For further information contact:
Arts Council of Wales, Museum Place, Cardiff, CF1 3NX, Wales
Tel: 01222 394711
Fax: 01222 221447
Contact: Roger Lefevre, Craft Director

Travel Grants

Subjects: Visual arts.

Eligibility: Open to visual artists who live and/or work in Wales for at least nine months of the year, have been out of full-time education for at least two years and have previously sent details of themselves and their work to the Council's Slide Library.

Level of Study: Professional development.

Purpose: To enable artists to spend periods of work and research abroad.

Type: Travel grant.

No. of awards offered: Variable.

Frequency: Twice yearly.

Value: Varies.

Country of Study: No restrictions.

Applications Procedure: Application form must be completed; expanded proposal submitted; and visual evidence of recent work must be shown.

Closing Date: April/May; September/October.

Additional Information: Enquiries should be addressed to the Director of the Visual Arts Department.

For further information contact:
Arts Council of Wales, Museum Place, Cardiff, CF1 3NX, Wales
Tel: 01222 394711
Fax: 01222 221447
Contact: Tessa Hartog, Executive Officer

Visual Arts Project Fund

Subjects: Fine and applied arts.

Eligibility: Open to artists living or working in Wales for at least nine months of the year.

Purpose: To support new one-off initiatives in the visual arts in Wales, including a wide range of activities.

Type: Grant.

No. of awards offered: Varies.

Frequency: Annual.

Applications Procedure: Application form must be supported by visual evidence of work and expanded proposal.

Closing Date: April 1st and September 1st.

For further information contact:
Arts Council of Wales, Museum Place, Cardiff, South Glamorgan, CF1 3NX, Wales
Tel: 01222 394711
Fax: 01222 221447
Contact: Tessa Hartog

Young Welsh Singers Competition

Subjects: Singing.

Eligibility: Open to singers at the beginning of their professional careers who were born and educated in Wales, or who have been permanently resident in Wales for at least two years.

Level of Study: Professional development.

Purpose: To assist young singers at the beginning of their professional careers.

Type: Competition.

No. of awards offered: Various.

Frequency: Every two years.

Value: First prize of £2,000.

For further information contact:
Arts Council of Wales, Museum Place, Cardiff, CF1 3NX, Wales
Tel: 01222 394711
Fax: 01222 221447
Contact: Roy Bohana, Music Director

THE ARTS FOUNDATION

The Arts Foundation, 40 Bucklersbury, London, EC4N 8BD, England
Tel: 0171 329 6775
Fax: 0171 329 6809
Contact: Prudence Skene

*Fellowships

Subjects: Six different art form categories are selected each year.

Eligibility: Open to British residents over the age of 25. Nominators are requested to nominate artists who have had at least five years' experience.

Purpose: To give annual Fellowships to creative artists.

No. of awards offered: 6.

Frequency: Throughout the year.

Value: £12,500.

Country of Study: Any country.

ARTS INTERNATIONAL

Arts International, 809 United Nations Plaza, 8th Floor, New York, NY, 10017-3580, USA
Tel: 212 984 5370
Fax: 212 984 5574
Email: ainternational@iie.org
Contact: Program Officer

Cintas Foundation

Subjects: Architecture, photography, visual arts, music composition and literature.

Eligibility: Open to creative artists of Cuban citizenship or descent, working in the above-mentioned fields, who are currently living outside Cuba.

Level of Study: Professional development.

Purpose: To provide grants of up to $10,000 to artists of Cuban citizenship or descent currently living outside Cuba.

Type: Fellowship.

No. of awards offered: 5-8.

Frequency: Annual.

Value: US$10,000.

Applications Procedure: Contact Arts International/IIE for an application form.

Closing Date: To be determined.

Additional Information: Cintas Fellowships are intended to acknowledge demonstrated creative accomplishments and to encourage the professional development of talented creative artists in the fields listed. The fellowships are not awarded towards the furtherance of academic study, research or writing, nor to performing artists.

THE ASCAP FOUNDATION

ASCAP Foundation, One Lincoln Plaza, New York, NY, 10023, USA
Tel: 212 621 6327
Fax: 212 721 0956
Email: frichard@ASCAP.com
www: ASCAP.COM
Contact: Frances Richard

Grants to Young Composers

Subjects: Music composition.

Eligibility: Open to US citizens or permanent residents who have not reached their 30th birthday by March 15th in the year of competition.

Level of Study: Unrestricted.

Purpose: To encourage composers, up to the age of 30; to provide recognition, appreciation and monetary awards to gifted, emerging talents.

Type: Cash award.

No. of awards offered: Varies from year to year.

Frequency: Annual.

Value: From US$250 to US$2,500.

Applications Procedure: Application required and reference letter encouraged.

Closing Date: March 15th.

ASHP FOUNDATION

ASHP Foundation, 7272 Wisconsin Avenue, Bethesda, MD, 20814, USA
Tel: 1 301 657 3000
Contact: Charles M King, Executive Vice President

*Anticoagulation Clinic Traineeship Program Grants

Subjects: Pharmacy administration.

Eligibility: Open to graduates of schools or colleges of pharmacy accredited by the American Council on Pharmaceutical Education who demonstrate basic knowledge and skills by citing academic courses completed or describing residency or work experience completed. The applicant will be employed at a general medical and surgical hospital or other organized health-care facility with resources for the provision of ambulatory care services. The pharmaceutical services department of the applicant's place of employment will meet the requirements of the ASHP Minimum Standard for Pharmacies in Institutions.

Purpose: To train pharmacy practitioners in the administrative aspects of establishing and maintaining outpatient clinics for patients who are receiving anticoagulation therapy.

No. of awards offered: Varies.

Frequency: Annual.

Value: Grant funds cover the cost of registration and all educational materials, as well as travel expenses.

Length of Study: Five days.

Study Establishment: Various sites throughout the USA.

Country of Study: USA.

Applications Procedure: Application forms are available from 15 June.

Closing Date: August 1st.

*Clinical Pharmacy Dialysis Service Traineeship Program

Subjects: Dialysis service training.

Eligibility: Open to pharmacists practising at a general medical and surgical hospital or other organized health-care facility. The applicant's organization will be a general medical and surgical hospital or other organized health-care facility with resources for the provision of inpatient and outpatient hemodialysis and peritoneal dialysis services.

Purpose: To prepare a pharmacist practitioner to establish and maintain a specialized service for the pharmacotherapeutic management of patients undergoing dialysis; to provide intensive, didactic, and experiential training for selected practising pharmacists; to offer the trainee an opportunity to observe and participate in the activities of an established clinical pharmacy dialysis service in an organized health-care setting.

Frequency: Annual.

Value: To cover the cost of registration and all educational materials, as well as travel expenses.

Length of Study: A combined 3-day didactic and 5-day experiential period (usually during the fall of each year).

Study Establishment: Various sites throughout the USA.

Country of Study: USA.

Applications Procedure: The applicant's employer, director of the pharmacy service, chief of the division of nephrology, or the director of the dialysis service, and the chief executive officer of the institution must confirm, in writing, support for the establishment of a clinical pharmacy dialysis service.

Closing Date: May 15th.

*Fellowships

Subjects: In categories, which may change annually, such as: oncology drug therapy, cardiovascular drug therapy, clinical pharmacokinetics, critical care drug therapy, drug information, geriatric drug therapy, infectious disease drug therapy, pharmacy nutritional support, and psychiatric drug therapy.

Eligibility: Open to graduates of schools or colleges of pharmacy accredited by the American Council on Pharmaceutical Education who hold a PharmD or advanced degree in pharmacy, have completed an ASHP-accredited residency program, or have equivalent postgraduate clinical experience, and are eligible for licensure to practise in the state where the Fellowship will be conducted.

Purpose: To develop competency in the scientific process, including conceptualizing, planning, conducting, and reporting research to prepare the participants to become independent researchers.

Type: Fellowship.

No. of awards offered: Varies.

Frequency: Annual.

Value: Stipend of US$24,600, plus an additional US$500 for travel and relocation expenses and US$2,000 benefit allowance to the institution.

Length of Study: Two years.

Applications Procedure: Additional qualifications for the fellowship site and preceptor are detailed in the application packet, available from 15 September.

Closing Date: January 15th.

*New Pharmacy Practice Researchers Grants

Subjects: Pharmacy; each year a research topic is selected by the funding sponsor.

Eligibility: Open to new pharmacy investigators who are within five years of having completed their most recent pharmacy degree, formal postgraduate training program or graduate education.

Purpose: To provide financial support to pharmacists who are beginning independent careers as practitioners, educators or researchers.

No. of awards offered: Varies.

Frequency: Annual.

Value: Up to US$6,000.

Length of Study: One year.

Country of Study: Territorial USA.

Applications Procedure: The sponsoring institution must approve the project proposal. Only one grant per individual will be awarded in any 12-month period, and concurrent grants to the same individual are not permissible.

Closing Date: June 1st.

*George P Provost Editorial Internship

Subjects: Pharmaceutical journalism.

Eligibility: Open to pharmacy graduates.

Purpose: To improve the quality of the published pharmaceutical literature; to train pharmacists for careers in pharmaceutical journalism; and to improve the writing and publishing skills of the intern.

Frequency: Annual.

Length of Study: Six months.

Study Establishment: ASHP headquarters.

Country of Study: USA.

*Research and Achievement Awards

Subjects: Hospital pharmacy.

Eligibility: The Award for Sustained Contributions to the Literature of Pharmacy Practice in Organized Health-Care Settings is offered to an individual for publishing in the hospital pharmacy literature, over several years, papers of consistently high quality and importance. Research Awards are offered for important contributions to the scientific pharmaceutical literature relating to either drug therapy in humans or pharmacy practice in organized health-care settings during the calendar year preceding the year in which the award is granted. (For this award, 'research' refers to the formalized testing of hypotheses using the scientific approach and includes, for example, methods improvement studies, drug stability studies, extemporaneous dosage from development, cost reduction studies, quality improvement studies, demonstration projects with built-in evaluation, behavioral science studies, problem-solving using research methods, and controlled clinical studies involving administrative or management techniques.) The Award for Achievement in the Professional Practice of Pharmacy in Organized Health-Care Settings is offered for the most noteworthy contribution to the literature in the professional practice of pharmacy in organized health-care settings in the calendar year preceding the year in which the award is granted. (For this award, 'professional practice' refers to all aspects of professional practice, including management, drug-use control, technological services, clinical services, and information processing.) The Student Research Award is offered to an undergraduate or graduate pharmacy student (BS, MS and PharmD programs are eligible) for a published or unpublished paper on a subject relevant to pharmacy in organized health-care settings prepared during the academic year preceding the ASHP Midyear Clinical Meeting in December, at which the award is presented.

Purpose: To honor noteworthy contributions to the literature of hospital pharmacy in organized health-care settings.

No. of awards offered: Varies.

Frequency: Annual.

Value: The Research and Achievement Awards each consist of a US$4,000 honorarium, a US$700 expense allowance to attend the ASHP Midyear Clinical Meeting for the awards presentation, and a plaque. The Student Award consists of a US$1,000 honorarium, a US$700 expense allowance to attend the ASHP Midyear Clinical Meeting for the awards presentation, and a plaque.

Closing Date: May 15th.

ASIAN CULTURAL COUNCIL

Asian Cultural Council, 1290 Avenue of the Americas, Room 3450, New York, NY, 10104, USA
Tel: 212 684 5450
Fax: 212 684 8075
Contact: Ralph Samuelson

*Fellowship Grants Program

Subjects: Visual and performing arts.

Eligibility: Open to individuals from East and Southeast Asia (Burma to Japan) and US citizens or permanent residents.

Level of Study: Unrestricted, but not undergraduate.

Purpose: To provide fellowship opportunities for research, training, travel and creative work.

Type: Fellowship.

No. of awards offered: Approximately 100 per year.

Frequency: Twice yearly.

Value: Varies.

Length of Study: One month to one year.

Country of Study: Asians to travel to the USA, Americans to travel to Asia.

Applications Procedure: Interested individuals and institutions should send a brief project description to the Council. If the proposal falls within the Council's guidelines, application forms will be forwarded to individual candidates or more detailed information will be requested from institutional applicants.

Closing Date: February 1st and August 1st.

Additional Information: Artists seeking aid for personal exhibitions or performances and students enrolled in undergraduate degree programs cannot be considered.

ASIAN PRODUCTIVITY ORGANIZATION

Asian Productivity Organization, 4-14 Akasaka 8-chome, Minato-ku, Tokyo, 107, Japan
Tel: 813 3408 7221
Fax: 813 3408 7220
Email: apo@gol.com
Telex: J26477
Contact: The Head, The Industry Division

*APO Productivity Fellowship

Subjects: Management systems and techniques.

Eligibility: Open to nationals of APO member countries: Bangladesh, Taiwan, Fiji, Hong Kong, India, Indonesia, Iran, Japan, Republic of Korea, Malaysia, Mongolia, Pakistan, Nepal, Philippines, Singapore, Sri Lanka, Thailand, Vietnam.

Level of Study: Postgraduate, Senior Consultants.

Purpose: To enable the fellows to develop the most suitable methods of adapting the management practices in Japan to their own environments, with the results thereof to be disseminated widely throughout the region.

Type: Fellowship.

No. of awards offered: Two.

Frequency: Annual.

Value: Airfare and accommodation.

Length of Study: 32 weeks.

Country of Study: Japan.

Closing Date: April 1997.

Additional Information: Applicants must have English and Japanese language proficiency.

THE ASPEN INSTITUTE'S NONPROFIT SECTOR RESEARCH FUND

The Aspen Institute's Nonprofit Sector Research Fund, 1333 New Hampshire Ave., NW, Suite 1070, Washington, DC, 20036, USA
Tel: 202 736 5831
Fax: 202 467 0790
Email: nsrfund1@aol.com
www: www.aspeninst.org
Contact: David Williams

Nonprofit Research Grants

Subjects: Social and Behavioural Sciences.

Level of Study: Doctorate, Postdoctorate.

Purpose: To support basic and applied research projects that address major policy and practice issues affecting nonprofit organizations.

Type: Research Grant.

Frequency: Semi-annual.

Value: Up to US$20,000 for doctoral research; up to US$50,000 for other projects.

Applications Procedure: Application guidelines and forms are available.

Closing Date: January 1st and June 1st.

ASSOCIATED BOARD OF THE ROYAL SCHOOLS OF MUSIC

Associated Board of the Royal Schools of Music, 14 Bedford Square, London, WC1B 3JG, England
Tel: 0171 636 5400
Fax: 0171 436 4520
Contact: Chief Executive

Music Scholarships

Subjects: Instrumental and vocal.

Eligibility: Open to students, normally between the ages of 17 and 24, except in certain circumstances, e.g. courses for singers and in-service teachers' courses.

Level of Study: Postgraduate, Professional development, Undergraduate.

Purpose: To enable exceptionally talented young musicians to study at one of the four Royal Schools of Music.

Type: Scholarship.

No. of awards offered: Varies.

Frequency: Annual.

Value: Full course fee, contribution to air travel and £3,000 per annum towards living expenses.

Length of Study: From one term to four years, according to designated course.

Study Establishment: Either the Royal Academy of Music, the Royal College of Music, the Royal Northern College of Music or the Royal Scottish Academy of Music and Drama.

Country of Study: UK.

Applications Procedure: Applicants must submit: application form, health certificate, exam marks, forms, testimonials, and an authenticated cassette tape of recent performance.

Closing Date: December 31st preceding year of entry.

Additional Information: Entries can be received from any of the 80 countries where the Associated Board organizes examinations. Candidates must have a good standard of general education and must normally have qualified by passing, with distinction, Grade 8 in a practical examination of the Board's, the Advanced Certificate or the LRSM diploma, plus one other practical examination of the Board's above Grade 5. Candidates should apply to the Board's representative in their own country or directly to the Board in London.

ASSOCIATION FOR LIBRARY AND INFORMATION SCIENCE EDUCATION

Association for Library and Information Science Education, 4101 Lake Boone Trail, Suite 201, Raleigh, NC, 27607, USA
Tel: 919 787 5181
Fax: 919 787 4916
Contact: Penney DePas, CAE, Executive Director

Doctoral Students' Dissertation Competition

Subjects: Dissertations in areas dealing with substantive issues in library and information science.

Eligibility: Open to recently graduated doctoral students. Applicants must submit evidence that the dissertation has or will be completed as of 31 December of the year prior to that in which the award is given.

No. of awards offered: Up to 2 honorariums.

Frequency: Annual.

Value: US$400 to defray travel expenses to the ALISE Annual Conference.

Closing Date: October 1st.

Research Grants Awards

Subjects: Research broadly related to education for library and information science.

Eligibility: Open to appropriately qualified candidates who are members of ALISE as of the application deadline.

Purpose: To support research.

Type: Grant.

No. of awards offered: One or more awards.

Frequency: Annual.

Value: A total of US$2,500.

Closing Date: October 1st.

Additional Information: Awards cannot be used to support a doctoral dissertation.

Research Paper Competition

Subjects: Any aspect of librarianship or information studies.

Eligibility: Open to suitably qualified candidates who are members of ALISE as of the application deadline, for previously unpublished research papers.

No. of awards offered: Up to 2 honorariums.

Frequency: Annual.

Value: US$500.

Closing Date: October 1st.

ASSOCIATION FOR SPINA BIFIDA AND HYDROCEPHALUS (ASBAH)

ASBAH House, 42 Park Road, Peterborough, Cambs, PE1 2UQ, England
Tel: 01733 555988
Fax: 01733 555985
Contact: Executive Director

ASBAH Bursary Fund

Subjects: Any course that will improve chances of employment of people with spina bifida and/or hydrocephalus.

Eligibility: Open to individuals with spina bifida and/or hydrocephalus resident in England, Wales and Northern Ireland.

Level of Study: Undergraduate, Postgraduate.

Purpose: To help with expenses of further education courses approved by, but not organized by, ASBAH.

Type: Bursary.

No. of awards offered: Varies.

Frequency: Varies; dependent on funds available.

Value: To cover course fees and other expenses.

Country of Study: UK.

Applications Procedure: Application forms are available from the Executive Director.

Closing Date: None.

Additional Information: Applicants are normally visited by an ASBAH fieldworker prior to award being considered.

Research Grant

Subjects: Medical sciences; natural sciences; education and teacher training; recreation, welfare, protective services.

Eligibility: Applicants must be resident in the UK.

Level of Study: Unrestricted.

Purpose: For research in an area directly related to spina bifida and/or hydrocephalus (the nature, causes, prevention and treatment); also ways of improving the quality of life for people with spina bifida and/or hydrocephalus, ie. medical, scientific, educational and social research.

Type: Research Grant.

No. of awards offered: Varies.

Frequency: Dependent on funds available.

Value: Varies.

Length of Study: Varies.

Study Establishment: Varies.

Country of Study: Varies, but usually UK.

Applications Procedure: In the first instance by letter to the Executive Director. If proposed research is considered to be interesting, the applicant will be asked to complete an application form.

Closing Date: February and September/October.

Additional Information: Applications should be made in good time for submission to the Committees which meet in February and September/October.

ASSOCIATION FOR WOMEN IN SCIENCE EDUCATIONAL FOUNDATION

Association for Women in Science Educational Foundation, 1522 K Street, NW, Suite 820, Washington, DC, 20005, USA
Tel: 202 408 0742
Fax: 202 408 8321
Email: awis@awis.org
www: http://www.awis.org/awis

Each spring, the Educational Foundation offers several awards of $500-$1,000, including the Luise Meyer-Schutzmeister Award, specifically designated for a graduate student in physics. At times, Honorable Mentions are awarded. Also, the Ruth Satter Memorial Award is open to women students who have interrupted their education for three years or more to raise a family

Predoctoral Awards

Subjects: Life, physical, behavioral or social science; engineering.

Eligibility: Open to female students enrolled in any physical, behavioral or social science or engineering program, leading to a PhD degree.

Level of Study: Predoctoral.

Type: Predoctoral Awards.

No. of awards offered: Varies.

Frequency: Annual.

Value: Varies, usually US$100-US$1,000.

Study Establishment: Institute of Higher Education.

Country of Study: US citizens: USA or abroad; non-US citizens: USA institutions.

Applications Procedure: Application includes a basic form, a 2-3 page summary of the candidate's dissertation research, two recommendation report forms, and official transcripts of all coursework conducted at post-secondary institutions.

Closing Date: Mid-January.

Additional Information: Winners are notified by mail in June and announced publicly in the July/August issue of the 'AWIS Magazine'.

ASSOCIATION OF AFRICAN UNIVERSITIES

Association of African Universities, PO Box 5744, Accra, Ghana
Tel: 233 21 774495
Fax: 233 21 774821
Email: JShabani@aau.org
Telex: 2284Adua GH
Contact: Juma Shabani, Deputy Secretary General

DAAD/AAU Graduate Education Scholarship

Subjects: All subjects except social sciences.

Eligibility: Applicants must be junior members of African universities, be less than 36 years old, and have a bachelor degree or equivalent.

Level of Study: Postgraduate, Doctorate.

Purpose: To contribute to the capacity building of African universities, by enabling junior staff members to undertake graduate education in African universities.

Type: Scholarship.

No. of awards offered: Ten each year.

Frequency: Annual.

Value: $3,000 to $10,000 per year.

Length of Study: 2-4 years.

Study Establishment: African universities.

Country of Study: Any African university.

Applications Procedure: Please submit application to the AAU Secretariat.

Closing Date: May 30th each year.

ASSOCIATION OF AMERICAN GEOGRAPHERS

Association of American Geographers, 1710 Sixteenth Street, NW, Washington, DC, 20009-3198, USA
Tel: 202 234 1450
Fax: 202 234 2744
Contact: Elizabeth Beetschen

AAG General Research Fund

Subjects: Geography.

Eligibility: Open to AAG members. The committee will not approve awards for masters or doctoral dissertation research.

Level of Study: Postdoctorate, Professional development.

Purpose: To support research and field work.

Type: Research fund.

No. of awards offered: Varies.

Frequency: Annual.

Value: Varies; grants can be used for direct expenses of research. Salary and overhead costs are not allowed.

Country of Study: USA.

Closing Date: December 31st.

Additional Information: No awards are made if funds are insufficient, or if proposals are not suitable. Guidelines are printed in the AAG Newsletter.

For further information contact:
Association of American Geographers, 1710 Sixteenth Street, NW, Washington, DC, 20009-3198, USA
Tel: 202 234 1450
Fax: 202 234 2744
Email: gaia@aag.org
Contact: Elizabeth Beetschen

Warren Nystrom Fund Awards

Subjects: Geography.

Eligibility: Open to young geographers who have received their doctorate within the last two years.

Level of Study: Doctorate, Postdoctorate.

No. of awards offered: Variable.

Frequency: Annual.

Value: Varies.

Closing Date: Mid-September for the following year.

Additional Information: The Awards are made for paper presented at the annual meeting of the Association; the paper submitted should be based on the students dissertation. The Association also offers the Robert D Hodgson/Paul P Vouras/Otis P Starkey Dissertation Research Grant which is awarded to AAG members only. Guidelines for individuals wishing to apply for Research Grants are printed in the AAG Newsletter.

THE ASSOCIATION OF ANAESTHETISTS OF GREAT BRITAIN AND IRELAND

Association of Anaesthetists of Great Britain and Ireland, 9 Bedford Square, London, WC1B 3RA, England
Tel: 0171 631 1650
Fax: 0171 631 4352
Email: 100567,3364
www: http://www.ncl.ac.uk/2nanaes/aagbi.html
Contact: Honorary Secretary

Baxter Travelling Fellowships, Research Grants, Travel Grants

Subjects: Anaesthesia or related fields: research or education.

Eligibility: Open to members in any category of the Association.

No. of awards offered: Varies.

Frequency: Varies, depending on funds available.

Value: Up to £2,500 (Baxter Travelling Fellowship); up to £5,000 (Research Grants); up to £500 (Travel Grants).

Length of Study: Unspecified duration.

Country of Study: Baxter Travelling Fellowship: any country; Research Grants: Great Britain and Ireland.

Applications Procedure: Application form is required.

Additional Information: There are also special Travel Grants to Third World Countries. Travel Grants are not awarded for attendance at a meeting of a learned society, but may be considered for extensions of such a journey. They may be given for study or for assistance in undertaking an approved teaching tour. Recipients of Travel Fellowships are expected to prepare a report.

ASSOCIATION OF COMMONWEALTH UNIVERSITIES

Association of Commonwealth Universities, John Foster House, 36 Gordon Square, London, WC1H 0PF, England
Tel: 0171 387 8572
Fax: 0171 387 2655
Contact: Awards Division

Commonwealth Fund for Technical Cooperation Third World Academic Exchange Fellowships

Subjects: Unrestricted.

Eligibility: Open to academic, administrative, professional or library staff at universities in developing countries of the Commonwealth.

Level of Study: Professional development.

Purpose: To enable the recipient to (i) obtain further experience at another university in a Commonwealth developing country; (ii) undertake a short study tour in at least one Commonwealth developing country; (iii)take part in specific exchanges between institutions in Commonwealth developing countries; (iv) support national/regional seminars at universities in Commonwealth developing countries and assist participants.

Type: Fellowship.

No. of awards offered: Up to 15.

Frequency: Annual.

Value: Varies according to the project and any supplementary funds available, but with a maximum value of £2,500.

Length of Study: Short periods, up to 3 months.

Study Establishment: Universities/institutions in Commonwealth countries.

Country of Study: Developing countries of the Commonwealth, other than the recipient's own country.

Applications Procedure: Applications should be made through the vice-chancellor's office of the home institution.

Closing Date: 31 May.

Development Fellowships

Subjects: Special preference for agriculture, forestry and food science (including fisheries, nutrition and processing); biotechnology, development strategies, earth and marine sciences (including mining engineering, mineral resource, oceanography); engineering, health and related social sciences, information technology (e.g. computing, computer-assisted learning); management for change; professional education and training (e.g. in accountancy, banking, business studies, insurance and law); social and cultural development; media studies; institutional management.

Eligibility: Open to Commonwealth citizens under 50 years of age. Candidates may be working in a university or in commerce, industry or the private sector; but must be nominated by the head of an institution which is a member of the ACU.

Level of Study: Professional development.

Purpose: To promote the development of human resource in subject areas in which the needs of developing countries are particularly great.

Type: Fellowship.

No. of awards offered: Initially 20-25 Fellowships, rising to 50.

Frequency: Annual.

Value: Determined by the ACU according to the scope and location of the programme, but up to a maximum of £5,000 covering fares, board and lodging, local travel and medical/travel insurance. There is no allowance for spouse or dependents.

Length of Study: Up to six months; not renewable.

Study Establishment: (For candidates working at ACU member university) another ACU member university or in industry, commerce or public service in another Commonwealth country other than that in which the applicant works, and (by candidates working in industry, commerce or public service) only at an ACU member university in another Commonwealth country.

Country of Study: Commonwealth countries.

Closing Date: May 31st.

Additional Information: Countries are invited on a biennial basis.

Times Higher Education Supplement Exchange Fellowship

Subjects: Unrestricted.

Eligibility: Open to academic, administrative, professional or library staff of ACU member universities in developing countries.

Level of Study: Professional development.

Purpose: To enable the recipient to (i) obtain further experience at another university in a Commonwealth developing country; (ii) undertake a short study tour of at least one Commonwealth developing country; (iii) visit another university in a Commonwealth developing country to realize a specific developmental objective.

Type: Fellowship.

No. of awards offered: One.

Frequency: Annual.

Value: Up to £3,000.

Length of Study: Up to 3 months.

Study Establishment: Universities in Commonwealth countries.

Country of Study: Developing countries of the Commonwealth, other than the Fellow's own country.

Applications Procedure: Applications should be made through the vice chancellor's office of the candidate's university.

Closing Date: End of May.

ASSOCIATION OF CONSULTING ENGINEERS AND THE WORSHIPFUL COMPANY OF ENGINEERS

Association of Consulting Engineers, Alliance House, 12 Caxton Street, London, SW1H 0QL, England
Tel: 0171 222 6557
Fax: 0171 222 0750
Contact: Mike Springett

Young Consulting Engineer of the Year

Subjects: Engineering projects, the profession.

Eligibility: Restricted to staff of member firms. Candidates must be under the age of 30.

Level of Study: Unrestricted.

Purpose: To encourage younger members of the profession in their work and to make them think about their role in society.

No. of awards offered: One.

Frequency: Annual.

Value: £500 plus a medal. Certificates for finalists.

Applications Procedure: Application form and other documentation required.

Closing Date: January 3rd.

For further information contact:
The Worshipful Company of Engineers, 1 Carlton House Terrace, London, SW1Y 5DB, England
Contact: The Clerk

ASSOCIATION OF INFORMATION, JAPAN

Association of Information, Japan, 4-5-29 Komaba, Meguro-ku, Tokyo, 153, Japan
Tel: 03 5454 5214
Fax: 03 5454 5234
Contact: AIEG

Short-term Student Exchange, Promotion Program for Foreign Students

Eligibility: Asia and Pacific region.

Level of Study: Student exchange.

Purpose: For students studying or interested in studying internationally.

No. of awards offered: Three.

Frequency: Dependent on funds available.

Value: YEN100,000 per month, Travel expenses, settling in allowances YEN50,000 per month.

Length of Study: One year or shorter.

Study Establishment: Universities which have (or will establish) international student exchange programs with ones that applicants are currently enrolled in.

Country of Study: Japan.

Applications Procedure: Students wishing to apply for the scholarship must submit the application to the host university through the university they are currently enrolled in.

Closing Date: Mid February, late June, late October.

ASSOCIATION OF INTERNATIONAL EDUCATION

Association of International Education, 4-5-29 Komaba, Meguro-ku, Tokyo, 153, Japan
Contact: Student Affairs Division

*Scholarships

Subjects: Any subject.

Eligibility: Open to self-supporting foreign students studying in a university graduate school in Japan who display excellence in their academic work and character and who are deemed to be in need of economic assistance during their stay in Japan.

Type: Scholarship.

Value: Y68,000 per month.

Length of Study: One year.

Study Establishment: A graduate school in Japan.

Country of Study: Japan.

Applications Procedure: Candidates should apply through their school in Japan.

Closing Date: Specified by each school.

ASSOCIATION OF MBAS (AMBA)

Association of MBAs, 15 Duncan Terrace, London, N1 8BZ, England
Tel: 0171 837 3375
Fax: 0171 278 3634
Contact: Peter Calladine

Business School Loan Scheme

Subjects: MBA only.

Eligibility: Open to UK residents (i.e. resident in the UK for at least three years immediately prior to study). Candidates must be graduates with a minimum of two years' relevant work experience, or, if not graduates, have at least five years' relevant work experience at an appropriate level of responsibility.

Level of Study: MBA.

Type: Loan.

No. of awards offered: Unlimited.

Value: Preferential bank loans to cover a maximum of two thirds of salary plus tuition fees for each year of study for full-time study; fees plus study equipment for part-time and distance learning.

Study Establishment: Specific courses at 33 UK and 12 continental European schools accredited by AMBA, AACSB-accredited schools in the USA, and a limited number of schools elsewhere.

Country of Study: Unrestricted.

Applications Procedure: Candidates may apply at any time providing a place has been secured.

ASSOCIATION OF RHODES SCHOLARS IN AUSTRALIA

Association of Rhodes Scholars in Australia, University of Melbourne, Parkville, Victoria, 3052, Australia
Tel: 61 3 9344 6937
Fax: 61 3 9347 6739
Email: glenn_swafford.research@muwayf.unimelb.edu.au
Contact: General Manager of Research

Postgraduate Scholarship

Subjects: Unrestricted.

Eligibility: Open to graduates of a Commonwealth university approved by the committee administering the Scholarship, who are currently enrolled as a research higher degree student at their home university. Applicants must be Commonwealth citizens and may not be graduates of an Australian or New Zealand university.

Purpose: To enable an overseas Commonwealth student to undertake research for six months at one or more universities in Australia.

Type: Scholarship.

No. of awards offered: One.

Frequency: Periodically, depending on funds available.

Value: Currently A$9,000 including travel expenses and monthly stipend.

Length of Study: Six months.

Study Establishment: A university.

Country of Study: Australia.

Closing Date: As advertised.

ASSOCIATION OF SURGEONS OF GREAT BRITAIN AND IRELAND

Association of Surgeons of Great Britain and Ireland, c/o The Royal College of Surgeons of England, 35-43 Lincoln's Inn Fields, London, WC2A 3PN, England
Tel: 0171 9730300
Fax: 0171 430 9235
Contact: Mrs Nechama Lewis

Moynihan Travelling Fellowship

Subjects: Surgery.

Eligibility: Open to Senior Registrars and recently appointed Consultants in surgery. Candidates must be residents of the United Kingdom or the Republic of Ireland but need not be either Fellows or Affiliate Fellows of the Association; they may be engaged in any surgical speciality.

Level of Study: Senior Registrars or Consultants.

Type: Fellowship.

No. of awards offered: One.

Frequency: Annual.

Value: £4,000.

Country of Study: Any country.

Applications Procedure: A full cv should be submitted giving details of past and present appointments and publications, together with a detailed account of the proposed programme of travel and the object to be achieved..

Closing Date: October.

Additional Information: Shortlisted candidates will be interviewed by the Council of the Association who will pay particular attention to originality, scope and practicability of the proposed journey. The successful candidate will be expected to act as an ambassador for British and Irish surgery and should be fully acquainted with the aims and objectives of the Association of Surgeons in its role in surgery. After the visit the Fellow will be asked to address the Association at its Annual General Meeting. A critical appraisal of the Centres visited should form the basis of the report.

THE ASSOCIATION OF TEACHERS AND LECTURERS (ATL)

The Association of Teachers and Lecturers, 7 Northumberland Street, London, WC2N 5DA, England
Tel: 0171 930 6441
Fax: 0171 930 1359
Contact: Miss G Evans

Walter Hines Page Scholarships

Subjects: Observation and study of teaching and the educational system in the USA.

Eligibility: Open to British teachers who are members of the Association and wish to visit the USA.

Level of Study: Professional development.

Type: Scholarship.

No. of awards offered: One.

Frequency: Annual.

Value: £1,200, plus full hospitality.

Length of Study: Three weeks.

Country of Study: USA.

Closing Date: November 30th.

Additional Information: These awards are given in conjunction with the English-Speaking Union of the Commonwealth.

ASSOCIATION OF UNIVERSITIES AND COLLEGES OF CANADA

International and Canadian Programs Division, Association of Universities and Colleges of Canada, 350 Albert Street, Suite 600, Ottawa, Ontario, K1R 1B1, Canada
Tel: 613 563 1236
Fax: 613 563 9745
Email: mleger@aucc.ca
Contact: Canadian Awards Program

Cable Telecommunications Research Fellowship

Subjects: Subjects directly related to the cable television industry in a degree program in a field of engineering or computer science.

Eligibility: Open to Canadian citizens or permanent residents who are eligible for enrolment in a graduate engineering program at a university in Canada, and who intend to use the Fellowship to assist them in completing a graduate degree which includes a thesis on a topic in the engineering of broadband communication systems. (In this context, a broadband system can be analogue or digital, or a combination, but must be capable of transporting upwards of ten video channels.).

Level of Study: Graduate.

Purpose: To encourage students at the master's or PhD level to tackle topics in the engineering of communications systems for video, voice and data signals or for computer applications to cable TV requirements.

Type: Fellowship.

No. of awards offered: Two.

Frequency: Annual.

Value: C$5,000.

Study Establishment: Any university which is a member, or affiliated to a member, of AUCC, for 1 year with the possibility of renewal.

Country of Study: Canada.

Applications Procedure: Selection is made by a committee of university faculty members chosen by the AUCC who will base their decision on academic achievement, suitability of the thesis project proposed and the interest expressed by the candidate in pursuing a career in the cable television industry.

Closing Date: February 1st (postmarked).

Additional Information: Fellows may not undertake paid employment during their academic term unless such employment is approved by the supervisor of studies, and conforms to university regulations. At the conclusion of the Fellowship, a thesis, or a reasonably detailed account of the work done, shall be admitted to AUCC. In addition, provided the university authorities concerned are in accord, the results of the investigations carried out under the Fellowship may be freely published. Specifically, a paper based on the work done shall be submitted for presentation to the annual convention of the Canadian Cable Television Association.

Department of National Defence Military and Strategic Studies Internship Program

Subjects: Strategic studies of relevance to current and future Canadian national security problems.

Eligibility: Open to Canadian citizens who hold a master's degree or its equivalent.

Level of Study: Postgraduate, Doctorate.

Purpose: To help recent graduates with a background in strategic studies to obtain work experience in that field by working for a year in a research or similarly valuable position in the private sector or in a non-governmental organization. University and government departments or agencies are excluded.

Type: Internship.

No. of awards offered: Approximately six.

Frequency: Annual.

Value: Up to C$16,000.

Length of Study: Up to twelve months; not renewable.

Study Establishment: In the private sector or non-governmental organizations.

Country of Study: Canada.

Applications Procedure: An independent committee of experts convened by the AUCC will evaluate all applications on the basis of academic merit. Successful applicants will then be judged by an independent Selection Committee of the Security and Defence Forum for relevance to issues of Canadian national security.

Closing Date: February 1st (postmarked).

Additional Information: On completion of the Award, a reasonably detailed account of the year's experience and of any research undertaken must be submitted to the AUCC, which will in turn forward a copy to the Department of National Defence. Normally a knowledge of both official languages is required. Referees will be asked to comment on the fluency of the candidate's second official language in reading, writing and speaking. A CV should be attached to each application.

Department of National Defence Military and Strategic Studies Language Program

Subjects: Any language which supports a PhD in the field of strategic studies relevant to current and future Canadian national security problems, including their political, international, historical, social, military, industrial and economic dimensions.

Eligibility: Open to Canadian citizens who hold an honours bachelor's degree. Normally a knowledge of both official languages is required.

Level of Study: Postgraduate.

Purpose: To provide PhD students with funding, and to facilitate the improvement of the students' capacity to research vital materials from primary sources.

Type: Scholarship.

No. of awards offered: Approximately two, depending on the availability of funds.

Frequency: Annual.

Value: Language scholarships are valued at up to C$16,000 for twelve months, pro-rated for shorter periods of time. Tuition fees of up to C$8,000 may also be covered.

Length of Study: A maximum of twelve months.

Study Establishment: A recognized institution.

Applications Procedure: An independent committee of experts convened by the AUCC will evaluate all applications on the basis of academic merit. Successful applications will then be judged by an independent Selection Committee of the Security and Defence Forum for relevance to issues of Canadian national security and defence.

Closing Date: February 1st (postmarked).

Additional Information: Selection decisions are final and are not open to appeal.

Department of National Defence Military and Strategic Studies Scholarship Program

Subjects: Strategic studies of relevance to current and future Canadian national security problems.

Eligibility: Open to Canadian citizens who hold an honours BA or equivalent.

Level of Study: Postgraduate, Doctorate.

Type: Scholarship.

No. of awards offered: Approximately eight PhD and eight MA scholarships, depending on the level of response and the quality of applications for these programs.

Frequency: Annual.

Value: PhD Scholarships: up to C$16,000; MA Scholarships: up to C$12,000.

Length of Study: At least one academic year, possibly renewable.

Study Establishment: Institutions in Canada.

Country of Study: Canada.

Applications Procedure: An independent committee of experts convened by the AUCC will evaluate all applications on the basis of academic merit. Successful applications will then be judged by an independent Selection Committee of the Security and Defence Forum for relevance to issues of Canadian national security.

Closing Date: February 1st (postmarked).

Additional Information: Award recipients may not concurrently hold any other awards whose cumulative value exceeds two-thirds of the value of the Scholarship accepted under this program.

Department of National Defence Security and Defence Forum R B Byers Postdoctoral Fellowship Program

Subjects: Strategic studies of relevance to current and future Canadian national security problems.

Eligibility: Open to Canadian citizens who hold a PhD or its equivalent. Individuals who hold a tenured or tenure-track appointment at any level are not eligible.

Level of Study: Postgraduate, Doctorate.

Type: Fellowship.

No. of awards offered: One.

Frequency: Annual.

Value: Up to C$27,000.

Length of Study: Twelve months.

Study Establishment: Educational institutions in Canada.

Country of Study: Canada.

Applications Procedure: An independent committee of experts convened by the AUCC will evaluate all applications on the basis of academic merit. Successful applications will then be judged by an independent

Selection Committee of the Security and Defence Forum for relevance to issues of Canadian national security.

Closing Date: February 1st (postmarked).

Additional Information: On completion of the Award, a reasonably detailed account of the research undertaken must be submitted to AUCC, which will in turn forward it to the Department of National Defence. Also, copies of all publications, including papers presented at conferences but not published, are to be submitted to the AUCC.

Emergency Preparedness Canada Research Fellowship in Honour of Stuart Nesbitt White

Subjects: All aspects of disaster and emergency studies as outlined in the EPC Annual Report, and especially urban and regional planning, economics, geography, risk analysis and management, systems science, social sciences, business and health administration.

Eligibility: Open to Canadian citizens or permanent residents. Preference is given to students who hold a master's degree and who would normally be pursuing doctoral studies. Candidates with a first degree will also be considered. Acceptance into a doctoral program is normally, but not necessarily, a prerequisite.

Level of Study: Doctorate.

Purpose: To encourage disaster research and emergency planning in Canada.

Type: Fellowship.

No. of awards offered: One.

Frequency: Annual.

Value: C$10,000.

Length of Study: The duration of the program, or to a maximum of four years, whichever occurs first, provided progress is satisfactory and continuation of the award is recommended by the supervisor.

Study Establishment: Normally, at any university in Canada. Since it is expected that studies would normally be based at a Canadian university, the applicant, if proposing otherwise, must include a supplementary statement identifying the foreign university; if possible, the sums involved in tuition and compulsory fees, the benefits deriving to the student from following the proposed study, and the benefits deriving to the emergency preparedness community in Canada.

Country of Study: Canada.

Closing Date: February 1st (postmarked).

Frank Knox Memorial Fellowships at Harvard University

Subjects: Arts and sciences (including engineering), business administration, dental medicine, design, divinity, education, law, medicine, dental medicine, public administration and public health.

Eligibility: Open to Canadian citizens or permanent residents who have recently graduated or are about to graduate from a university or college in Canada which is a member, or affiliated to a member, of AUCC. No application is considered from a student already in the USA, although applications will be considered from recent graduates who are working in the United States and will be applying to the MBA program.

Level of Study: Postgraduate, Undergraduate.

Type: Fellowship.

No. of awards offered: Up to two.

Frequency: Annual.

Value: US$13,500, plus tuition fees and student health insurance.

Length of Study: One academic year.

Study Establishment: Harvard University, Cambridge, Massachusetts.

Country of Study: USA.

Applications Procedure: Each candidate must apply directly to the graduate school of his or her choice. Candidates are responsible for gaining admission to Harvard University by the deadline set by the various faculties.

Closing Date: February 1st (postmarked).

Additional Information: Fellows may not accept any other grant for the award period unless approved by the Committee on General Scholarships and the Sheldon Fund of Harvard University. Candidates applying to the School of Business Administration are required to take the Admissions Test for Graduate Study in Business in October or January. This may be arranged by contacting the 'Educational Testing Service, Box 966, Princeton NJ 08540, USA'. Normally two months' notice should be given to ETS.

Petro-Canada Graduate Research Award Program

Subjects: Sciences, engineering, social sciences and business administration.

Eligibility: Open to Canadian citizens or permanent residents who are working towards a master's or doctoral degree in a subject related to the oil and gas industry. Awards are granted on the basis of academic standing and demonstrated potential for advanced study and research.

Level of Study: Postgraduate, Doctorate.

Purpose: To recognize academic excellence and to support and encourage graduate research in specialized fields of study relating to the petroleum industry.

Type: Research award.

No. of awards offered: Up to four.

Frequency: Annual.

Value: C$10,000.

Length of Study: One year; award holders may reapply.

Study Establishment: A university or college which is a member, or affiliated to a member, of AUCC.

Country of Study: Canada.

Applications Procedure: The selection is made by a committee of university faculty members chosen by the AUCC who will base their decision on academic achievement, suitability of the thesis project proposed, and the interest expressed by the candidate in pursuing his/her studies related to the oil and gas industry.

Closing Date: February 1st (postmarked).

Additional Information: There is no restriction on the number or value of other awards held concurrently by a student. However, recipients must be able to accept at least 75% of the Petro-Canada award in instances where restrictions apply to other awards received.

THE ASTHMA FOUNDATION OF VICTORIA

The Asthma Foundation of Australia, 101 Princess Street, Kew, VIC, 3101, Australia
Tel: 61 3 9853 5666
Fax: 61 3 9853 9196
Contact: Executive Director

Research Grants

Subjects: Medical or scientific research relating to increased knowledge of and improvements in asthma management, including development and evaluation of educational programs; ideally projects should have direct patient application.

Eligibility: Open to Australian citizens or permanent residents with appropriate qualifications and experience at various levels from honours graduates to postdoctoral.

Level of Study: Postgraduate, Doctorate, Postdoctorate.

Purpose: To encourage and assist asthma research in Victoria, Australia.

Type: Research Grant.

No. of awards offered: Dependent on funds available.

Frequency: Annually, depending on funds available.

Value: Up to A$30,000 to support research programmes or for salaries for research, technical and other assistants or cost of equipment, material or other necessary items.

Study Establishment: An approved institution within Victoria, Australia.

Country of Study: Australia.

Applications Procedure: Application forms are available from the Asthma Foundation.

Closing Date: September 30th for grants awarded for the following calendar year.

Additional Information: Specific purpose grants include: Dutton Paediatric Asthma Research Scholarship and Anna Jane Adolescent Asthma Scholarship.

Lilian Roxon Memorial Research Trust Travel Grant

Subjects: Research into the causes, prevention and treatment of asthma.

Eligibility: Open to Australian citizens or permanent residents with appropriate qualifications, currently engaged in asthma research. The travel grant may be held concurrently with other awards to cover total expenditure.

Level of Study: Postgraduate, Doctorate, Postdoctorate.

Purpose: To assist an asthma researcher to travel overseas to either continue research, or present their work at a recognized international meeting.

Type: Travel Grant.

No. of awards offered: One.

Frequency: Annually, subject to availability of funds.

Value: Up to A$2,000 towards travel expenses.

Country of Study: Any country outside Australia.

Applications Procedure: Application forms are available from the Asthma Foundation.

Closing Date: October 31st for grants awarded for the following calendar year.

For further information contact:
The Asthma Foundation of Australia, 101 Princess Street, Kew, 3101, Australia
Tel: 61 3 9853 5666
Fax: 61 3 9853 9196
Contact: Executive Director

ASTHMA FOUNDATION OF WESTERN AUSTRALIA

Asthma Foundation of Western Australia, 61 Heytesbury Road, Subiaco, WA, 6008, Australia
Tel: 09 382 1666
Fax: 09 388 1469
Contact: Matthew Tweedie

Asthma Foundation Research Grant

Subjects: Medical Sciences.

Level of Study: Unrestricted.

Purpose: To support local research into areas relevant to asthma.

Type: Research Grant.

No. of awards offered: Up to 5.

Frequency: Annual.

Value: Average A$30,000-A$40,000.

Length of Study: Usually 12-24 months.

Country of Study: Australia.

Applications Procedure: Application form must be completed.

Additional Information: Research must be locally based.

ASTHMA SOCIETY OF CANADA

Asthma Society of Canada, 130 Bridgeland Avenue, Suite 425,
Toronto, Ontario, M6A 1Z4, Canada
Tel: 416 787 4050
Fax: 416 787 5807
Contact: Dr Elizabeth Kovac, Executive Director

*Research Grants

Subjects: Clinical or basic research: problems related to asthma which have direct patient application; asthma education: development of educational programs and evaluation of the benefits of such programs.

Eligibility: Open to all researchers in asthma or related fields.

Purpose: To encourage and support asthma research.

No. of awards offered: Four.

Frequency: Annual.

Value: Up to a maximum of C$10,000.

Study Establishment: An appropriate institution.

Country of Study: Any country.

Closing Date: November 1st.

ATHENAEUM INTERNATIONAL CULTURAL CENTRE

Athenaeum International Cultural Centre, 8 Amerikis Street, Athens,
10671, Greece
Tel: 1 36 33 701/2
Fax: 1 36 35 957
Contact: The General Secretary and Founder

Maria Callas Grand Prix

Purpose: To recognize outstanding artists.

Applications Procedure: Application form must be completed and documentation submitted as in the prospectus of the Grand prix.

Closing Date: January 5th.

Maria Callas Grand Prix for Pianists

Subjects: Musical performance: piano.

Eligibility: Open to pianists of any nationality up to 30 years of age.

Level of Study: Unrestricted.

Purpose: To recognize outstanding pianists.

Type: Grand Prix.

No. of awards offered: One.

Frequency: Every two years.

Value: Drs 3,000,000 and a gold medal. Also offer silver medal and diploma.

Closing Date: January 5th.

Additional Information: Concert appearances are arranged for the winner.

For further information contact:
Athenaeum International Cultural Centre, 8 Amerikis Street, Athens,
10671, Greece
Tel: 1 36 33 701/2
Fax: 1 36 35 957

Maria Callas International Music Competition

Subjects: Musical performance: disciplines vary with each competition.

Eligibility: Open to musicians of all nationalities.

Level of Study: Unrestricted.

Type: Competition.

No. of awards offered: Varies, according to the discipline.

Frequency: Annual.

Value: Varies.

Applications Procedure: Full details of the categories and application procedures are available on request.

Closing Date: January 5th.

For further information contact:
Athenaeum International Cultural Centre, 8 Amerikis Street, Athens,
10671, Greece
Tel: 1 36 33 701/2
Fax: 1 36 35 957

Marie Callas Grand Prix for Opera and Oratorio-Lied

Subjects: Three categories: opera singers, female; opera singers, male; and Oratorio-Lied.

Eligibility: Open to singers of any nationality. Female singers should not be older than 30 years of age, and male singers not older than 32 years of age.

Level of Study: Unrestricted.

Purpose: To recognize outstanding singers.

Type: Grand Prix.

No. of awards offered: Three Grand Prix; one for each category.

Frequency: Every two years.

Value: Drs 1,500,000 and a gold medal. Drs 300,000 and a silver medal - Diploma.

Closing Date: January 5th.

Additional Information: Concert appearances are arranged for the winners. Next award 1997.

For further information contact:
Athenaeum International Cultural Centre, 8 Amerikis Street, Athens,
10671, Greece
Tel: 1 36 33 701/2
Fax: 1 36 35 957

ATLANTIC SALMON FEDERATION

Atlantic Salmon Federation, PO Box 429, St Andrews, New Brunswick,
EOG 2XO, Canada
Tel: 506 529 4581
Fax: 506 529 4438

Olin Fellowship

Subjects: Atlantic salmon biology, management or conservation.

Eligibility: Open to citizens and legal residents of the USA or Canada. Applicants need not be enrolled in a degree program.

Purpose: To support individuals seeking to improve their knowledge or skills in advanced fields while looking for solutions to current problems.

Type: Fellowship.

No. of awards offered: Varies.

Frequency: Annual.

Value: C$1,000 - C$3,000.

Study Establishment: Any accredited university or other research laboratory or in an active management program.

Country of Study: USA or Canada.

Applications Procedure: Application form must be completed.

Closing Date: March 15th for notification by May 15th.

Additional Information: Application forms are available on request.

For further information contact:
Atlantic Salmon Federation, PO Box 807, Calais, ME, 04619, USA
Tel: 506 529 4581
Fax: 506 529 4438

ATLANTIC SCHOOL OF THEOLOGY

Atlantic School of Theology, 640 Fracklyn Street, Halifax, Nova Scotia,
B3H 3B5, Canada
Tel: 902 423 6801
Fax: 902 492 4048
Email: theology@Pox.nstn.ca
Contact: The President

Evelyn Hilchie Betts Memorial Fellowship

Subjects: Any subject offered at the Atlantic School of Theology.

Eligibility: Open to ordained clergy male or female from developing countries, who are interested in theological education in an ecumenical atmosphere and are able to speak and write in the English language. Applicants must be interested in living and working in a Christian community and willing to share their work and experiences with the Canadian church.

Purpose: To enable ordained clergy from the Third World to study at the School and thereby to introduce persons from other Christian communities to the church and theological education in Canada.

Type: Fellowship.

No. of awards offered: One.

Frequency: Every four to five years.

Value: Approximately C$15,000. Pays transportation, tuition, room and board.

Length of Study: One academic year.

Study Establishment: The Atlantic School of Theology in Halifax, Nova Scotia.

Country of Study: Canada.

Applications Procedure: Application and letters of reference.

Closing Date: December 31st.

ATOMIC ENERGY OF CANADA LTD

Physical Division, Atomic Energy of Canada Limited , Chalk River Laboratories, Chalk River, Ontario, K0J 1JO, Canada
Tel: 613 584 3311
Fax: 613 584 1348
Telex: harveym@crl.aecl.ca
Contact: M Harvey

Research Associateships

Subjects: Physics and chemistry; heavy ion nuclear physics; condensed matter physics; astrophysical neutrino phsyics; theoretical physics; accelerator physics; physical chemistry; radiation applications research; and radiation chemistry.

Eligibility: In accordance with immigration requirements, the positions are directed in the first instance to Canadian citizens or permanent residents, but all qualified candidates will be considered.

Level of Study: Postdoctorate.

Purpose: To enable promising young scientists to avail themselves of the several unique facilities available at Chalk River Laboratories and Whiteshell Laboratories.

Type: Associateship.

No. of awards offered: Variable.

Frequency: Annually, subject to available funds.

Value: $42,000 per annum subject to review, plus an allowance toward relocation costs.

Length of Study: One year, renewable for one further year.

Study Establishment: Chalk River Laboratories, Chalk River, Ontario, and Whiteshell Laboratories, Pinawa, Manitoba.

Country of Study: Canada.

Applications Procedure: Application form must be completed, CV and at least three letters of reference must be submitted.

Closing Date: Varies.

Additional Information: AECL subscribes to the Canadian Government Employment Equity Policies.

AUCKLAND DIVISION CANCER SOCIETY OF NEW ZEALAND (ADCSNZ)

Auckland Division Cancer Society of New Zealand, PO Box 1724, Auckland, New Zealand
Tel: 09 524 0023
Fax: 09 520 0901
Contact: R G Williams, Chief Executive

*Bruce Cain Memorial Postdoctoral Fellowship

Subjects: Synthetic organic chemistry, pharmacology or tumour biology.

Eligibility: Open to individuals who hold a PhD in a relevant scientific discipline.

Level of Study: Postdoctorate.

Purpose: To provide an opportunity for postdoctoral research.

No. of awards offered: One.

Frequency: Triennially.

Value: NZ$35,000-NZ$43,000 per annum, according to experience.

Length of Study: Two years; renewable for one additional year.

Study Establishment: The ADCSNZ Cancer Research Laboratory, located at the University of Auckland Medical School.

Country of Study: New Zealand.

Closing Date: Varies; as advertised.

AUSTRALIAN ACADEMY OF THE HUMANITIES

Australian Academy of the Humanities, GPO Box 93, Canberra, ACT, 2601, Australia
Tel: 06 248 7744
Fax: 06 248 6287
Contact: The Secretariat

Travelling Fellowships

Subjects: Humanities.

Eligibility: Open to scholars resident in Australia working in the field of humanities.

Level of Study: Unrestricted.

Purpose: To enable short-term study abroad.

Type: Fellowship.

No. of awards offered: Variable.

Frequency: Annual.

Value: Varies, depending on project: up to A$3,000.

Length of Study: At least six weeks.

Study Establishment: An appropriate research centre.

Country of Study: Outside Australia.

Closing Date: July 30th.

Additional Information: Research projects should be near a state of completion.

AUSTRALIAN-AMERICAN EDUCATIONAL FOUNDATION

Australian-American Educational Foundation, GPO Box 1559,
Canberra City, ACT, 2601, Australia
Tel: 06 247 9331
Fax: 06 247 6554
Email: lindy@aaef.anu.edu.au
Contact: Program and Development Officer

Coral Sea Scholarship

Subjects: Business or industry.

Eligibility: Open to Australian citizens, resident in Australia, who hold a degree or diploma and are less than 35 years of age. Candidates should have relevant business or industry experience.

Level of Study: Professional development.

Purpose: To enable a student to investigate a problem or opportunity relevant to Australian business or industry in the USA.

Type: Scholarship.

No. of awards offered: One.

Frequency: Annual.

Value: Up to A$13,000.

Length of Study: Up to three months.

Country of Study: USA.

Applications Procedure: Requires application form to be completed; three referees' reports (included in application form), documentation of citizenship and qualifications to be submitted.

Closing Date: September 30th.

For further information contact:
Australian-American Educational Foundation, GPO Box 1559,
Canberra, ACT, 2601, Australia
Tel: 61 6 247 9331
Fax: 61 6 247 6554
Email: lindy@aaef.anu.edu.au
Contact: Program and Development Officer

Fulbright Awards

Subjects: Any subject.

Eligibility: Open to Australian postgraduate and postdoctoral students, senior scholars and professionals.

Level of Study: Postgraduate, Doctorate, Postdoctorate, Professional development.

No. of awards offered: Up to 15.

Frequency: Annual.

Value: Postgraduate students: up to A$30,850; postdoctoral fellows: up to A$34,050; senior scholars: up to A$22,350; professionals: up to A$17,150.

Length of Study: 3-12 months.

Country of Study: USA.

Applications Procedure: Application form must be completed, three referees' reports (included in the application form), documentation of citizenship and qualifications must be submitted.

Closing Date: September 30th.

For further information contact:
Australian-American Educational Foundation, GPO Box 1559,
Canberra, ACT, 2601, Australia
Tel: 61 6 247 9331
Fax: 61 6 247 6554
Email: lindy@aaef.anu.edu.au
Contact: Program and Development Officer

Fulbright Postdoctoral Fellowships

Subjects: Any subject.

Eligibility: Open to Australian citizens by birth or naturalization; naturalized citizens must provide a certificate of Australian citizenship with their application, and native-born Australians must provide a copy of their birth certificate. Applicants should have recently completed their PhD, normally less than three years prior to application, although those who have completed their PhD four to five years prior to application will be considered.

Level of Study: Postdoctorate.

Purpose: To enable those who have recently completed their PhD to conduct postdoctoral research, further their professional training or lecture at a university.

Type: Fellowship.

No. of awards offered: Up to two.

Frequency: Annual.

Value: Up to A$34,050`.

Length of Study: 3-12 months.

Study Establishment: A university, college, research establishment or reputable private practice.

Country of Study: USA.

Closing Date: September 30th.

For further information contact:
Australian-American Educational Foundation, GPO Box 1559,
Canberra, ACT, 2601, Australia
Tel: 61 6 247 9331
Fax: 61 6 247 6554
Email: lindy@aaef.anu.edu.au
Contact: Program and Development Officer

Fulbright Postgraduate Student Award for Aboriginal and Torres Strait Islander People

Subjects: All subjects.

Eligibility: Open to people of Aboriginal and Torres Strait Islander descent.

Purpose: To enable candidates to undertake an approved course of study for an American higher degree, or engage in research relevant to an Australian higher degree.

No. of awards offered: One.

Frequency: Dependent on funds available.

Value: Up to A$30,850.

Length of Study: 3-12 months funded; up to a further four years unfunded.

Study Establishment: An accredited institution.

Country of Study: USA.

Applications Procedure: Application form, three referees' reports (included in application form), documentation of citizenship and qualifications.

Closing Date: September 30th.

Fulbright Postgraduate Student Award for Engineering

Subjects: Engineering.

Eligibility: Open to Australian citizens.

Level of Study: Postgraduate, Doctorate.

Purpose: To enable candidates to undertake an approved course of study for an American higher degree, or engage in research relevant to an Australian higher degree.

No. of awards offered: One.

Frequency: Dependent on funds available.

Value: Up to A$30,850.

Length of Study: 3-12 months funded; up to a further four years unfunded.

Study Establishment: An accredited institution.

Country of Study: USA.

Applications Procedure: Application form, three referees' reports (forms included in application form), documentation of citizenship and qualifications.

Closing Date: September 30th.

Fulbright Postgraduate Student Award for Research relating to School-to-Work Transition

Subjects: Educational science.

Eligibility: Open to Australian citizens.

Level of Study: Postgraduate, Doctorate.

Purpose: For those enrolled in an Australian higher degree wishing to undertake research relating to school-to-work transition.

Type: Research award.

Frequency: Dependent on funds available.

Length of Study: Three to 12 months.

Country of Study: USA.

Applications Procedure: Application form, referees' reports (forms are available in application form), documentation of qualifications and citizenship.

Closing Date: September 30th.

Fulbright Postgraduate Student Award for the Visual and Performing Arts

Subjects: Fine and applied arts.

Eligibility: Open to Australian citizens.

Level of Study: Postgraduate, Doctorate, Professional development.

Purpose: To enable candidates to undertake a higher degree, research, or enter a program of training and professional development in the United States.

No. of awards offered: One.

Frequency: Dependent on funds available.

Value: Up to A$30,850.

Length of Study: 3-12 months funded; up to a further four years unfunded.

Country of Study: United States.

Applications Procedure: Application form, three referees' reports (forms included in application form), documentation of citizenship and qualifications.

Closing Date: September 30th.

For further information contact:
Australian--American Educational Foundation, GPO Box 1559, Canberra City, ACT, 2601, Australia
Tel: 06 247 9331
Fax: 06 247 6554
Email: lindy@aaef.anu.edu.au

Contact: Program and Development Officer

Fulbright Postgraduate Studentships

Subjects: Any subject.

Eligibility: Open to Australian citizens by birth or naturalization; naturalized citizens must provide a certificate of Australian citizenship with their application, and native-born Australians must provide a copy of their birth certificate. Applicants must be graduates.

Level of Study: Postgraduate, Doctorate, Professional development.

Purpose: To enable students to undertake an approved course of study for an American higher degree or its equivalent; to engage in research relevant to an Australian higher degree, or to undertake a program of training and professional development, in the visual and performing arts.

Type: Studentship.

No. of awards offered: Up to five.

Frequency: Annual.

Value: Up to A$30,850.

Length of Study: Three to twelve months, renewable for a maximum of five years, but without additional allowance.

Study Establishment: A university, college, research establishment or reputable private practice.

Country of Study: USA.

Applications Procedure: Application form must be completed, three referees' reports (included in the application form), and documentation of citizenship and qualifications must be submitted.

Closing Date: September 30th.

Additional Information: As the Award does not include any provision for maintenance payments, applicants must be able to demonstrate that they have sufficient financial resources to support themselves and any dependants during their stay in the USA.

For further information contact:
Australian-American Educational Foundation, GPO Box 1559, Canberra, ACT, 2601, Australia
Tel: 61 6 247 9331
Fax: 61 6 247 6554
Email: lindy@aaef.anu.edu.au
Contact: Program and Development Officer

Fulbright Professional Award

Subjects: Business management and industrial relations; or government and public policy.

Eligibility: Open to Australian citizens, resident in Australia, with a record of achievement in management or government and poised for advancement to a senior management or policy role.

Level of Study: Professional development.

Type: Fellowship.

No. of awards offered: One.

Frequency: Annual.

Value: Up to A$17,150.

Length of Study: One to four months between January and December; programs of longer duration may be proposed but without additional funding.

Country of Study: USA.

Applications Procedure: Application form must be completed, three referees' reports (included in the application form), and documentation of citizenship & qualifications must be submitted.

Closing Date: September 30th.

Additional Information: Programs should include an academic as well as a practical aspect.

For further information contact:
Australian-American Educational Foundation, GPO Box 1559, Canberra, ACT, 2601, Australia
Tel: 61 6 247 9331
Fax: 61 6 247 6554
Email: lindy@aaef.anu.edu.au
Contact: Program and Development Officer

Fulbright Professional Award for Vocational Education and Training

Subjects: Vocational education.

Eligibility: Open to Australian citizens.

Level of Study: Professional development.

Purpose: To visit institutions/organisations and people in the United States from their own field.

Frequency: Dependent on funds available.

Value: Up to A$30,850.

Length of Study: 3-12 months funded; up to a further four years unfunded.

Country of Study: USA.

Applications Procedure: Application form, three referees' reports (forms included in application form), documentation of citizenship and qualifications.

Closing Date: September 30th.

Fulbright Senior Awards

Subjects: Any subject.

Eligibility: Open to Australian citizens by birth or naturalization; naturalized citizens must provide a certificate of Australian citizenship with their application, and native-born Australians must provide a copy of their birth certificate. Applicants should be either scholars of established reputation working in an academic institution who intend to teach or research in the USA; leaders in the arts (e.g. music, drama, visual arts); or senior members of the academically based professions who are currently engaged in the private practice of their profession.

Level of Study: Professional development.

Purpose: To teach, undertake research, invited speaker, or visit institutions within their field.

No. of awards offered: Two.

Frequency: Annual.

Value: Up to A$22,200.

Length of Study: One to six months.

Study Establishment: A university, college, research establishment or reputable private organization.

Country of Study: USA.

Applications Procedure: Application form must be completed, three referees' reports (included in application form), and documentation of citizenship and qualifications must be submitted.

Closing Date: September 30th.

For further information contact:
Australian-American Educational Foundation, GPO Box 1559, Canberra, ACT, 2601, Australia
Tel: 61 6 247 9331
Fax: 61 6 247 6554
Email: lindy@aaef.anu.edu.au
Contact: Program and Development Officer

Fulbright Teacher Exchange Award in the Vocational Education and Training Sector

Subjects: Education.

Eligibility: Open to Australian citizens.

Level of Study: Teacher Exchange.

Purpose: To exchange with a teacher in the United States also working in the Vocational Education and Training Sector.

Type: Exchange Award.

Frequency: Dependent on funds available.

Value: Up to A$6,000.

Length of Study: One year.

Study Establishment: An accredited teaching institution.

Country of Study: USA.

Applications Procedure: Application form required, referees reports (included in application form), documentation of qualifications and citizenship.

Closing Date: September 30th.

AUSTRALIAN EARLY CHILDHOOD ASSOCIATION, INC

Australian Early Childhood Association, Inc, PO Box 105, Watson, ACT, 2602, Australia
Tel: 06 2416900
Fax: 06 2415547
Contact: National Director

*Alice Creswick and Sheila Kimpton Foundation Scholarship

Subjects: A wide range of areas of interest concerning policy, practice and research in the early childhood field.

Eligibility: Open to Australian citizens currently employed in positions which have a direct relationship with early childhood education and/or care and who have qualifications in early childhood or a related field.

Purpose: To provide the opportunity for travel, observation and/or major study in the early childhood field.

Type: Scholarship.

No. of awards offered: One.

Frequency: Annually, depending on funds available.

Value: A$15,000.

Country of Study: Within Australia or overseas.

Closing Date: October 19th.

Additional Information: The successful applicant will be required to undertake certain commitments including the preparation of a written report and speaking engagements as required by AECA.

THE AUSTRALIAN FEDERATION OF UNIVERSITY WOMEN, SOUTH AUSTRALIA, INC TRUST FUND

The Australian Federation of University Women, South Australia, Inc Trust Fund, GPO Box 634, Adelaide, South Australia, 5001, Australia
Contact: Fellowships Trustee

The AFUW-SA Inc Trust Fund Bursary

Subjects: Any subject.

Eligibility: Open to women enrolled for coursework Master's degrees at Australian universities.

Level of Study: Doctorate.

Purpose: To assist women to complete Master's degrees by coursework at Australian universities.

Type: Bursary.

No. of awards offered: One.

Frequency: Annual.

Value: Up to A$3,000.

Length of Study: One year, not renewable.

Country of Study: Australia.

Closing Date: March 1st.

Thenie Baddams Bursary; Jean Gilmore Bursary

Subjects: Any subject.

Eligibility: Open to women graduates who are enrolled at an Australian tertiary institution and have completed at least one year of postgraduate research.

Level of Study: Doctorate.

Purpose: To assist the recipient to complete a Master's (by research) or PhD degree at a recognized Australian higher education institution.

Type: Bursary.

No. of awards offered: Two.

Frequency: Annual.

Value: Up to A$6,000.

Length of Study: One year; not renewable.

Study Establishment: A recognized Australian higher education institution. The research or field trip assisted by the Bursary may be undertaken overseas as long as it is contributing to the postgraduate degree.

Country of Study: Open.

Closing Date: March 1st.

The Winifred E Preedy Postgraduate Bursary

Subjects: Dentistry or a related field.

Eligibility: Open to women who are past or present students of the Faculty of Dentistry at the University of Adelaide and who are enrolled as graduate students in dentistry or some allied field at the University of Adelaide or such other institution of tertiary education as the Trustees may approve. The applicant must have completed one year of her postgraduate degree.

Level of Study: Doctorate.

Purpose: To assist with study or research towards a Master's or higher degree.

Type: Bursary.

No. of awards offered: One.

Frequency: Annual.

Value: A$5,000.

Length of Study: One year; not renewable.

Country of Study: Any country if applicant is a past student of the Faculty of Dentistry at the University of Adelaide, South Australia, otherwise the applicant must currently be enrolled in the latter faculty.

Closing Date: March 1st.

AUSTRALIAN FEDERATION OF UNIVERSITY WOMEN - VICTORIA

Australian Federation of University Women - Victoria, Inc., PO Box 816, Mount Eliza, Victoria, 3930, Australia
Contact: Honorary Scholarship Secretary

Beatrice Fincher Scholarship, Lady Leitch Scholarship

Subjects: Any subject.

Eligibility: Open to women graduates who are members of the Australian Federation of University Women, or its international affiliates.

Level of Study: Postgraduate, Doctorate, Postdoctorate, Professional development.

Purpose: To assist advanced study or research.

Type: Scholarship.

No. of awards offered: Two.

Frequency: Annually - Beatrice Fincher; Biennially - Lady Leitch.

Value: A$5,000 each award.

Length of Study: One year.

Country of Study: Any country.

Applications Procedure: Application form must be completed, with documentation on university qualifications, names of three referees, and membership of AFUW or affiliate.

Closing Date: March 1st, annually.

For further information contact:
124 Overport Road, Frankston, 3199, Australia
Contact: Mrs M R Endersbee

THE AUSTRALIAN GOVERNMENT

Graduate Studies, Scholarships and Prizes, The University of Newcastle, Callaghan, NSW 2308, Australia
Tel: 049 21 6537
Fax: 049 21 6908

Australian Postgraduate Awards

Subjects: All academic disciplines.

Eligibility: Open to Australian citizens and permanent residents who have lived in Australia for 12 months prior to application. Applicants must have completed four years of full-time undergraduate study and gained a first class Honours, or equivalent award.

Level of Study: Postgraduate, Doctorate.

Purpose: To support students undertaking full-time higher research degree programs at Australian universities.

Type: Scholarship.

No. of awards offered: Approximately 30.

Frequency: Annually, depending on funds available.

Value: Living allowance of approximately $15,364 per annum tax exempt and index-linked, plus allowances for relocation and thesis production and exemption of HECS payments.

Length of Study: 2 years full-time study for research masters students, or 3 years full-time for doctoral degree students.

Country of Study: Australia.

Applications Procedure: Application form requires to be completed.

Closing Date: October 31st.

AUSTRALIAN INSTITUTE OF ABORIGINAL AND TORRES STRAIT ISLANDER STUDIES

Australian Institute of Aboriginal and Torres Strait Islander Studies, GPO Box 553, Canberra, ACT, 2601, Australia
Tel: 06 246 1157
Fax: 06 249 7714
Contact: Director of Research

Research Grants

Subjects: Health, human biology, social anthropology, linguistics, ethnomusicology, material culture, rock art, prehistory, ethnobotany, psychology, education and Aboriginal history including oral history.

Eligibility: Open to nationals of any country.

Level of Study: Unrestricted.

Purpose: To promote research into Aboriginal and Torres Strait Islander Studies.

Type: Research Grant.

No. of awards offered: Undetermined.

Frequency: Annual.

Value: No predetermined value.

Country of Study: Australia.

Applications Procedure: Application form must be completed.

Closing Date: June 30th.

Additional Information: Permission to conduct research project must be obtained from appropriate Aboriginal or Torres Strait Island community or organisation.

AUSTRALIAN INSTITUTE OF MEDICAL SCIENTISTS

Australian Institute of Medical Scientists, PO Box 450, Toowong, Queensland, 4066, Australia
Tel: 07 3371 3370
Fax: 07 3870 4857

Biomediq DPC/BioMerieux: AIMS Postgraduate Scholarship

Subjects: Medical laboratory science.

Eligibility: Open to members of AIMS only.

Level of Study: Postgraduate.

Purpose: To support postgraduate study.

Type: Scholarship.

No. of awards offered: One.

Frequency: Annually depending on funds available.

Value: A$3,000.

Study Establishment: Appropriate institutions.

Country of Study: Australia.

Closing Date: October 31st.

AUSTRALIAN INSTITUTE OF NUCLEAR SCIENCE AND ENGINEERING

Australian Institute of Nuclear Science and Engineering, Private Mail Bag, PO Menai, NSW, 2234, Australia
Tel: 61 2 717 3376
Fax: 61 2 717 9268
Email: ainse@ansto.gov.au
Contact: Executive Officer

AINSE Grants

Subjects: Fields associated with nuclear science and engineering.

Eligibility: Open to member organizations of AINSE which are undertaking projects in an appropriate field.

Type: Grant.

No. of awards offered: Varies.

Frequency: From time to time.

Value: Assistance is available mainly in the form of 'credits' enabling university researchers to meet costs associated with the use of facilities;

travel to and from Lucas Heights; and accommodation during periods of attachment. Direct grants for small items of equipment and materials may also be considered.

Length of Study: One year.

Country of Study: Australia.

Closing Date: September 30th.

AINSE Postgraduate Research Awards

Subjects: Applications of nuclear physics (neutron scattering and accelerator science); radiation biology, chemistry and physics; advanced materials, engineering and plasma science; environment science; biomedicine and health; and, in general, any field of research using nuclear techniques of analysis.

Eligibility: Open to postgraduate students whose research projects are associated with nuclear science and technology and require access to the unique national facilities at the Lucas Heights Laboratories. Candidates must be nominated by the Australian university where PhD enrolment is held or proposed.

Level of Study: Postgraduate.

Type: Research Grant.

Frequency: Annual.

Value: A$7,500 per annum (Research Supplements), plus A$2,500 for research expenses.

Length of Study: One year.

Study Establishment: Lucas Heights Research Laboratories, near Sydney, New South Wales.

Country of Study: Australia.

Closing Date: December 31st.

AUSTRALIAN KIDNEY FOUNDATION

Australian Kidney Foundation, GPO Box 2212, Canberra, ACT, 2601, Australia
Tel: 06 282 2913
Fax: 06 285 2060
Contact: Medical Director

Grants-in-Aid and Research Scholarships and Student Summer Vacation Scholarships

Subjects: The functions or diseases of the kidney, urinary tract and related organs, or relevant problems; dialysis, transplantation and organ donation; research.

Eligibility: Open to Australian citizens connected with Australian universities or medical centres with requisite research facilities.

Level of Study: Unrestricted.

Purpose: To promote research.

No. of awards offered: 30-35 Grants-in-Aid; up to 4 Scholarships; and up to 6 Student Summer Vacation Scholarships.

Frequency: Annual.

Value: Up to A$12,000 per annum for Grants-in-Aid; A$25,000 for Medical Research Scholarships; A$800 for Student Summer Vacation Scholarships.

Study Establishment: Any medical centre, university or research institute.

Country of Study: Australia.

Closing Date: June 15th for Grants-in-Aid; September 1st for Scholarships; September 15th for Student Summer Vacation Scholarships.

AUSTRALIAN MUSICAL FOUNDATION IN LONDON

The AMFL, 8 Salisbury Square, London, EC4Y 8BB, England
Tel: 0171 311 8370
Fax: 0171 311 8885
Contact: Christine McCrann

Award

Subjects: Any aspect of musical study chosen by the recipient.

Eligibility: Open to Australian singers and instrumentalists under 30 years of age who are resident in Australia or the UK.

Level of Study: Unrestricted.

No. of awards offered: One.

Frequency: Annual.

Value: £10,000, payable in two annual instalments of £5,000 each.

Length of Study: Two years; the second year is subject to assessment.

Country of Study: Europe.

Applications Procedure: Application forms and demo cassette need to be submitted before the end of April each year.

Closing Date: End of April.

Additional Information: Applications are considered in the first instance by the Foundation Committee, with a panel of adjudicators making the final choice. It is stressed that this award is intended for musicians of merit and ability. The Foundation will also take into account, how applicants (in the event of winning) propose to use the award to further their careers.

For further information contact:
c/o Grant Thornton, PO Locked Bag Q800, QVB Sydney, NSW, 2000, Australia
Tel: 02 284 6666
Fax: 02 267 4000
Contact: Ms Sheila Nicholson

AUSTRALIAN NATIONAL UNIVERSITY

Australian National University, Canberra, ACT, 0200, Australia
Tel: 06 249 2700
Fax: 06 248 0054
Email: administrator.HRC@anu.edu.au
Contact: Humanities Research Centre

Visiting Fellowships

Subjects: The humanities.

Eligibility: Open to candidates of any nationality who are at the post-doctoral level.

Level of Study: Postdoctorate.

Purpose: To provide scholars with time to pursue their own work in congenial and stimulating surroundings.

Type: Fellowship.

No. of awards offered: Up to twenty.

Frequency: Annual.

Value: Return economy airfare, plus a weekly stipend for a maximum of 3 months.

Length of Study: 3-12 months; not renewable.

Study Establishment: The Humanities Research Centre at the University.

Country of Study: Australia.

Closing Date: October 31st.

Additional Information: Fellows are required to spend at least three-quarters of their time in residence at the Centre.

AUSTRALIAN RESEARCH COUNCIL

Research Policy and Grants Branch, Department of Employment, Education and Training, GPO Box 9880, Canberra, ACT, 2601, Australia
Tel: 06 2767178
Fax: 06 2767188
Contact: The Director, Institutional Programs & Research Training Section

*Australian Postdoctoral Research Fellowships

Subjects: Sciences.

Eligibility: Open to applicants who have a PhD or equivalent qualification, an excellent academic record and a written agreement of the proposed Australian institution to accommodate the Fellow and host the project. Fellowships are awarded on merit. Preference will be given to Australian citizens.

Purpose: To encourage research by scientists of exceptional promise and/or proven capacity for original work.

Type: Fellowship.

No. of awards offered: Fifty.

Frequency: Annual.

Value: Salary within the range A$34,100-A$38,000. Commencing salary will be dependent on qualifications and experience. Necessary travel expenses to take up duty will be reimbursed and a supporting grant of A$3,500 will be provided to help cover research and development costs.

Length of Study: Up to three years.

Study Establishment: In industry, higher education institutions or government research organizations.

Country of Study: Australia.

Closing Date: March 1st.

Additional Information: Fellows are expected to accept within three months of notification. Fellows are strongly advised to apply for ARC or other appropriate project grants.

Australian Research Fellowships

Subjects: All fields except clinical medicine and dentistry.

Eligibility: Open to nationals of all countries.

Level of Study: Postdoctorate.

Purpose: To foster opportunities for the pursuit of independent research in all fields except clinical medicine and dentistry.

Type: 3-5 year fellowship.

No. of awards offered: Thirty.

Frequency: Annual.

Value: $42,198 - $50,111.

Length of Study: 3 to 5 years.

Study Establishment: Australian higher education institution.

Country of Study: Australia.

Applications Procedure: Application form must be completed.

Closing Date: March 30th, for award in next year.

For further information contact:
Research Branch, Department of Employment, Education and Training, Individual Grants Section, LOC 731, GPO Box 9880, Canberra, ACT, 2601, Australia
Tel: 06 240 9694
Fax: 06 240 9781
Email: RBFELLOW@DEET.GOV.AU
Contact: Mr S Tanzer

*Australian Senior Research Fellowships

Subjects: Sciences.

Eligibility: Open to applicants who have a PhD or equivalent qualification, international recognition as a leader in research and guaranteed funding for research project(s) for the duration of the Fellowship.

Purpose: To encourage outstanding international researchers who are proven leaders in their field to undertake innovative research of potential benefit to Australia.

Frequency: Annual.

Value: Salary within the range A$47,500-A$72,000. Commencing salary will be dependent on qualifications and experience. Necessary travel expenses will be reimbursed.

Length of Study: Five years; renewable subject to the competitive process.

Study Establishment: Higher education institutions or government research organizations in Australia.

Country of Study: Australia.

Closing Date: March 1st.

Additional Information: Fellows are expected to accept within three months of notification. Fellows are strongly advised to apply for ARC or other appropriate project grants.

Queen Elizabeth II Fellowships

Subjects: All fields except clinical medicine and dentistry.

Eligibility: Open to nationals of all countries.

Level of Study: Postdoctorate.

Purpose: To foster opportunities for the pursuit of independent research in all fields except clinical medicine and dentistry.

Type: 3 - 5 year fellowship.

No. of awards offered: Thirty.

Frequency: Annual.

Value: $42,198 - $50,111.

Length of Study: 3 to 5 years.

Study Establishment: Australian higher education institution.

Country of Study: Australia.

Applications Procedure: Application form must be completed.

Closing Date: March 30th, for award in next year.

For further information contact:
Research Branch, Department of Employment, Education and Training, Individual Grants Section, LOC 731, GPO Box 9880, Canberra, ACT, 2601, Australia
Tel: 06 240 9694
Fax: 06 240 9781
Email: RBFELLOW@DEET.GOV.AU
Contact: Mr S Tanzer

AUSTRALIAN WAR MEMORIAL

Australian War Memorial, GPO Box 345, Canberra, ACT, 2601, Australia
Tel: 06 243 4257
Fax: 06 243 4325
Email: peter.stanley@awm.gov.au
Contact: The Research Grants Officer

John Treloar Grants-in-Aid

Subjects: Australian military history, including the study of the experience of Australians in wartime, both at home and overseas, the effects of war on Australian society, the history of Australian armed forces in war and peace, and related research in areas such as biography, technology, literature, art or historiography.

Eligibility: Open to applications assessed on the following criteria: the quality of the applicant; the quality of the project; and the potential contribution to Australian military history.

Level of Study: Unrestricted.

Purpose: To assist research into Australian military history.

Type: Grants-in-Aid.

No. of awards offered: Up to ten.

Frequency: Annual.

Value: A$5,000 to help cover costs such as photocoyping, travel and accommodation, and oral history.

Length of Study: One year.

Country of Study: Any country.

Applications Procedure: Application form and attachments to be completed by late June in year before the grants are awarded.

Closing Date: June of the year prior to the award.

AUSTRIAN ACADEMY OF SCIENCES

Institute of Limnology, Austrian Academy of Sciences, Gaisberg 116, Mondsee, A-5310, Austria
Tel: 06232 4079/3125
Fax: 06232 3578
Contact: Course Secretariat

Institute of Limnology Postgraduate Training Fellowships

Subjects: Limnology.

Eligibility: Open to candidates from developing countries who are 25-35 years of age, have a good working knowledge of English, and have an academic degree in science, agriculture or veterinary medicine from a university or other recognized institution of higher education. Applicants should have practical experience within at least one special subject in their field of professional training.

Purpose: To give Fellows an overall insight into the various problems of limnology so that they may be better equipped to implement necessary research in their home countries in order to find solutions to their practical problems.

Type: Fellowship.

No. of awards offered: Twelve.

Frequency: Annual.

Value: 7,500 Schillings paid monthly to cover food, lodging and personal expenses, free tuition, health insurance, study material and equipment for laboratory and field work, plus travelling expenses to and from training sites within Austria.

Length of Study: Nine months.

Country of Study: Austria.

Closing Date: October 31st.

Additional Information: No provisions are provided for dependents. It is strongly advised that dependents do not accompany Fellows due to frequent moves during the course. Fellows must provide their own transportation to and from Austria. Participants originating from certain developing countries will be further assisted by the Austrian Government so that travel expenses will be fully covered. Application forms and further information may be obtained from the Austrian Diplomatic Mission, Cultural Attaché or Cultural Institute in the applicant's home country, or from the address below.

AUSTRIAN FEDERAL MINISTRY FOR SCIENCE AND RESEARCH

Embassy of Austria, 12 Talbot Street, Forrest, ACT, 2603, Australia

Tel: 06 295 1533
Fax: 06 239 6751

Austrian Government Scholarships

Subjects: Unrestricted in relation to Austria.

Eligibility: Open to Australian citizens who are postgraduates between 20 and 35 years of age. Candidates must be capable of undertaking tertiary studies in the German language. Only candidates will be considered who do not participate in another scholarship program offered by Austria, and are not capable of undertaking their research work on Austrian history or literature, or another field related to Austria, in their native country.

Level of Study: Postgraduate.

Type: Scholarship.

No. of awards offered: Limited.

Frequency: Annual.

Value: 7,500 schillings monthly (graduates) or 9,000 schillings monthly (lecturers), plus starting allowance of 2,500 schillings and a termly book allowance of 1,000 schillings.

Length of Study: Up to one academic year; not renewable.

Study Establishment: A university or research institution.

Country of Study: Austria.

Closing Date: March 15th.

For further information contact:
PO Box 3375, Manuka, ACT, 2603, Australia

AUSTRO-AMERICAN ASSOCIATION OF BOSTON

Austro - American Association of Boston, 480 Davis Ave, West Newton, MA, 02165, USA
Tel: 617 969 9324
Contact: Professor Harry Zohn

Scholarship

Eligibility: Unrestricted.

Level of Study: Unrestricted.

Purpose: To promote the appreciation and dissemination of Austrian culture.

No. of awards offered: One.

Frequency: Annual.

Value: US$500 or US$600.

Country of Study: Usually Austria or USA.

Applications Procedure: Submit a detailed description of the project, a CV, and two letters of recomendation from people familiar with the applicants achievement and potential.

Closing Date: April 15th.

Additional Information: The award is limited to individuals living or studying in the greater Boston area. Projects funded in the past have included the preparation of musical or dramatic performances, the facilitation of appropriate publications, and research trips to Austria. "Culture" is defined to include the humanities and the arts.

For further information contact:
Austro-American Association of Boston, 480 Davis Ave, West Newton, MA, 02165, USA
Tel: 617 969 9324
Contact: Prof. Harry Zohn

DR M AYLWIN COTTON FOUNDATION

Dr M Aylwin Cotton Foundation, c/o Albany Trustee Company Ltd, PO Box 232, Pollet House, St Peter Port, Guernsey, Channel Islands

Cotton Research Fellowships

Subjects: Archaeology, architecture, history, language and the arts of the Mediterranean.

Eligibility: Open to senior scholars.

Level of Study: Professional development.

Type: Fellowship.

No. of awards offered: Varies.

Frequency: Annual.

Value: Up to £7,500.

Applications Procedure: Application forms are available on request.

Closing Date: February 28th.

Additional Information: The Foundation also provides grants annually to finance the publication costs of a completed work or a work due for publication in the immediate future.

CHARLES BABBAGE INSTITUTE

Charles Babbage Institute, University of Minnesota, 103 Walter Library, 117 Pleasant Street, SE, Minneapolis, MN, 55455, USA
Tel: 612 624 5050
Fax: 612 624 2841
Email: cbi@vx.cis.umn.edu
www: www.itdean.umn.edu/cbi/welcome.htm

Adelle and Erwin Tomash Fellowship in the History of Information Processing

Subjects: History of information processing.

Eligibility: Open to graduate students whose dissertation deals with an historical aspect of information processing.

Level of Study: Doctorate.

Purpose: To advance the professional development of historians of information processing.

Type: Fellowship.

No. of awards offered: One.

Frequency: Annual.

Value: US$10,000 stipend, plus up to US$2,000 to be used for tuition, fees, travel and other research expenses.

Length of Study: One year.

Country of Study: Any country.

Closing Date: January 15th.

LEO BAECK INSTITUTE

Leo Baeck Institute, 129 E 73rd Street, New York, NY, 10021, USA
Tel: 212 744 6400
Fax: 212 988 1305
Email: BM.LBC@RLG.STANFORD.Edu
Contact: Carol Kahn Strauss, Executive Director

LBI Fellowships

Eligibility: US Citizenship plus a knowledge of German language.

Level of Study: Postgraduate, Doctorate.

Purpose: To assist research into German and German-Jewish history.

Type: Fellowship.

No. of awards offered: Five.

Frequency: Annual.

Value: Depending on requirement of project.

Length of Study: Six months to one year.

Study Establishment: Varies with the award.

Country of Study: USA or Germany.

Applications Procedure: Write for application form.

Closing Date: November 1st.

Additional Information: These awards are in conjunction with awards offered by the German Academic Exchange Service (DAAD) in New York, USA.

THE E A BAKER FOUNDATION FOR THE PREVENTION OF BLINDNESS

1929 Bayview Avenue, Toronto, Ontario, M4G 3E8, Canada
Tel: 416 480 7587
Fax: 416 480 7000
Contact: Glacia D'Cambre

E A Baker Fellowship/Grant

Subjects: Ophthalmology.

Eligibility: Open to Canadians for research or study in Canada or abroad if returning to practice in Canada, with priority given to university teaching.

Level of Study: Professional development.

Purpose: To further the prevention of blindness in Canada.

Type: Fellowships and grants.

No. of awards offered: Variable.

Frequency: Annual.

Value: C$40,000.

Length of Study: One year.

Country of Study: Canada or abroad.

Closing Date: December 1st.

JUNE BAKER TRUST

June Baker Trust, 16 Broughton Place, Edinburgh, EH1 3RX, Scotland
Tel: 0131 557 3587
Contact: Eric Robinson, Chairman

Awards

Subjects: Conservation of historic and artistic artefacts.

Eligibility: Open to individuals working in conservation in Scotland, or training with the intention of doing so.

Level of Study: Unrestricted.

No. of awards offered: One or two.

Frequency: Annual.

Value: Up to £500 towards travel, training, purchase of equipment, etc.

Country of Study: Any country.

Applications Procedure: No application form. Apply by letter with two references.

Closing Date: June.

Additional Information: The project need not be site specific.

THE BANFF CENTRE FOR THE ARTS

The Banff Centre, School of Fine Arts, Box 1020, Station 28, Banff, Alberta, T0L 0C0, Canada
Tel: 00 1 403 762 6180
Fax: 00 1 403 762 6345
Email: arts_info@banffcentre.ab.ca
www: http://www.banffcentre.ab.ca/
Contact: Office of the Registrar

The Banff Centre for the Arts is a year-round continuing education facility which offers committed artists a wide variety of opportunities for creative and technical development. Acceptance is based on adjudication of submitted materials and/or audition

Banff Centre Scholarships, Sir Mark Turner Memorial Scholarships, Edward Boyle Scholarships

Subjects: Studio art, photography, ceramics, performance art, video art, theatre production and design, stage management, opera, singing, dance, drama, music, writing, arts journalism, publishing, media arts, television and video, audio recording, computer applications and research.

Eligibility: Open to advanced students who have been accepted for a residency at the Banff Centre. UK residents only are eligible for the Sir Mark Turner and Edward Boyle Scholarships.

Level of Study: Postgraduate.

Purpose: To provide financial assistance to deserving artists for a residency at the Banff Centre.

Type: Scholarship.

No. of awards offered: A variable number of Banff Centre Scholarships; 3 Sir Mark Turner Scholarships; 3 Edward Boyle Scholarships.

Frequency: Annual.

Value: A major contribution towards tuition and living costs.

Length of Study: Courses of various lengths.

Study Establishment: The Banff Centre for the Arts.

Country of Study: Canada.

Applications Procedure: A completed application form must be submitted, accompanied by requested documentation.

Closing Date: Varies according to program.

THE BANK OF SWEDEN TERCENTENARY FOUNDATION

The Bank of Sweden Tercentenary Foundation, Box 5675, Stockholm, S-114 86, Sweden
Tel: 46 8 24 32 15
Fax: 46 8 10 30 76

Grants

Subjects: Scientific research.

Eligibility: Open to scientists of any nationality. Applicants from outside Sweden should describe a defined programme of cooperation with Swedish scholars or research institutes.

Level of Study: Postdoctorate.

Purpose: To support and promote research which has connections with Sweden. Priority is given to research which has fewer opportunities to receive grants. Large, long-range projects, and new fields of investigation requiring rapid, major supportive measures receive special attention.

Type: Grant.

No. of awards offered: Varies.

Frequency: Annual.

Value: A total of 85,400,000 Swedish crowns are expended annually.

Length of Study: 3-4 years.

Country of Study: Any country.

Applications Procedure: Applications should include a detailed description of the scientific publications and competence of the applicants, a full outline of the project, time required, expected results and methods the applicant will use in order to achieve them, and a detailed budget.

Closing Date: Mid March.

BEDDING PLANTS FOUNDATION, INC

Bedding Plants Foundation, Inc, PO Box 27241, Lansing, MI, 48909, USA

Contact: Scholarship Program

Harold Bettinger Memorial Scholarship

Subjects: Business and/or marketing related to horticulture.

Eligibility: Open to graduate or undergraduate students with a horticulture major with a business and/or marketing emphasis, or business and/or marketing major with a horticulture emphasis at an accredited college or university in either the USA or Canada during the complete next academic year. Citizens of any country may apply.

Level of Study: Postgraduate, Undergraduate.

Type: Scholarship.

No. of awards offered: One.

Frequency: Annual.

Value: US$1,000.

Study Establishment: An accredited college or university.

Country of Study: USA or Canada.

Applications Procedure: Application forms are available on request.

Closing Date: Postmark April 1st.

John Carew Memorial Scholarship

Subjects: Horticulture: specific interest in bedding or flowering potted plants.

Eligibility: Open to graduate students majoring in horticulture or a related field at an accredited university in either the USA or Canada during the complete next academic year. Citizens of any country may apply.

Level of Study: Postgraduate.

Type: Scholarship.

No. of awards offered: One.

Frequency: Annual.

Value: US$1,500.

Study Establishment: An accredited college or university.

Country of Study: USA or Canada.

Closing Date: Postmark April 1st.

Additional Information: Application forms are available on request.

Fran Johnson Scholarship for Non-Traditional Students

Subjects: Floriculture: specific interest in bedding or other floral crops.

Eligibility: Open to graduate or undergraduate students pursuing a degree in floriculture, who have been out of an academic setting for at least five years and who are now re-entering an academic program. Candidates must be enrolled in an accredited four-year college or university program in either the USA or Canada during the complete next academic year and be US or Canadian citizens or residents.

Level of Study: Postgraduate, Undergraduate.

Type: Scholarship.

No. of awards offered: One.

Frequency: Annual.

Study Establishment: An accredited college or university.

Country of Study: USA or Canada.

Closing Date: Postmark April 1st.

Additional Information: Application forms are available on request.

James K Rathmell Jr Memorial Scholarship to Work/Study Abroad

Subjects: Floriculture or horticulture.

Eligibility: Open to upper-level undergraduate and graduate students.

Level of Study: Postgraduate, Undergraduate.

Purpose: To allow students to pursue work or study abroad.

Type: Scholarship.

No. of awards offered: One.

Frequency: Annual.

Value: Up to US$2,000.

Closing Date: Postmark April 1st.

Additional Information: Applicants are urged to thoroughly research their proposed work/study program to formulate well-defined objectives. Library research, writing to organizations overseas and talking with faculty are strongly encouraged. The Scholarship Review Committee will consider the scholarship, character, integrity and maturity of the applicant as well as the work/study purpose and evidence of serious interest as indicated on the application. Also considered will be the promise of making continued contributions to the fields of floriculture, ornamental horticulture or landscape architecture. Preference will be given to those planning to work/study for six months or longer. Upon his or her return, each Scholarship recipient must submit a written report on his or her work/study experiences and impressions to the Bedding Plants Foundation. These reports will be used for the information of the bedding and container plant industry. Twenty percent of the scholarship money will be held back until receipt of this written report.

BEIT MEMORIAL FELLOWSHIPS

Beit Memorial Fellowships, c/o Molecular Immunology Group, Institute of Molecular Medicine, John Radcliffe Hospital, Headington, Oxford, OX3 9DU, England

Contact: Mrs M Goble, Administrative Secretary

Beit Memorial Fellowships

Subjects: Medical research.

Eligibility: Open to graduates of postdoctoral level or medically qualified of any faculty from an approved university in the UK or in any country which is or has been since 1910 a British Dominion, Protectorate or Mandated Territory.

Level of Study: Postdoctorate.

Purpose: To promote research into medicine and allied sciences.

Type: Fellowship.

No. of awards offered: Approximately five.

Frequency: Every two years (next in 1997).

Value: £14,396 - £18,855 per annum plus £2,134 London allowance if applicable.

Length of Study: Three years.

Study Establishment: An approved university, research institute or medical school.

Country of Study: UK or Republic of Ireland.

Closing Date: March 1st.

BEIT TRUST (ZIMBABWE, ZAMBIA & MALAWI)

Beit Trust Fellowships, PO Box 76, Chisipite, Harare, Zimbabwe
Tel: 496132
Fax: 494046
Contact: Secretary to the Advisory Board

Postgraduate Fellowships

Subjects: Unrestricted.

Eligibility: Open to persons under 30 years of age (35 in the case of medical doctors) who are university graduates domiciled in Zambia (4 Fellowships), Zimbabwe (4 Fellowships), or Malawi (2 Fellowships).

Level of Study: Postgraduate.

Purpose: To support postgraduate study or research.

Type: Fellowship.

No. of awards offered: Ten.

Frequency: Annual.

Value: Personal allowance and fees (variable); plus book, clothing, thesis and departure allowances.

Length of Study: Two years; possibly renewable for a further year.

Study Establishment: Approved universities and other institutions.

Country of Study: UK, Republic of Ireland or Southern Africa.

Applications Procedure: Application form must be completed.

Closing Date: September 30th.

BELGIAN-AMERICAN EDUCATIONAL FOUNDATION, INC

Belgian-American Educational Foundation, Inc, 195 Church Street, New Haven, CT, 06510, USA
Email: emile.boulpaep@yale.edu

Fellowships for Study in the USA

Subjects: Any subject.

Eligibility: Open to Belgian nationals. Applicants must have a good command of the English language.

Level of Study: Postgraduate.

Frequency: Annual.

Value: US$25,000.

Length of Study: One year.

Study Establishment: An American University.

Country of Study: United States.

Applications Procedure: Application form must be completed, and three to five letters of reference must be submitted.

Closing Date: October 31st.

Additional Information: The stipend consists of a fixed sum to cover living expenses, purchase of books etc. In addition, the Foundation pays for tuition and health insurance at the American university. Fellows are expected to stay in the USA for a full academic year.

For further information contact:
Belgian-American Educational Foundation, Inc, Egmonstraat 11 Rue d'Egmont, Brussels, 1050, Belgium
Tel: 02 513 59 55
Fax: 02 672 53 81
Contact: The Secretary

Graduate Fellowships for Study in Belgium

Subjects: Any subject.

Eligibility: Open to US citizens, preferably under 30 years of age, with a speaking and reading knowledge of Dutch, French or German. The candidate must have a master's or equivalent degree or be working towards a PhD or equivalent degree.

Level of Study: Postgraduate, Doctorate.

Type: Fellowship.

No. of awards offered: 10.

Frequency: Annual.

Value: US$12,000, which includes round-travel expenses, lodging and living expenses, as well as tuition and enrolment fees.

Length of Study: One academic year.

Study Establishment: A Belgian university or other academic institution of higher learning.

Country of Study: Belgium.

Applications Procedure: Application form must be completed.

Closing Date: January 31st.

Postgraduate Fellowships for study in the USA

Subjects: Any subject.

Eligibility: Open to Belgian nationals. Applicants must have a good command of the English language.

Level of Study: Postgraduate.

Frequency: Annual.

Value: US$10,000.

Length of Study: One year.

Study Establishment: An American university.

Country of Study: United States.

Applications Procedure: Application form must be completed, and three to five letters of reference must be submitted.

Closing Date: October 31st.

Additional Information: The stipend consists of a fixed sum to cover living expenses, purchase of books etc. In addition, the Foundation pays for health insurance at the American institution. Fellows are expected to stay in the USA for a full academic year.

For further information contact:
Belgian-American Educational Foundation, Inc, Egmontstraat 11 Rue d'Egmont, Brussels, 1050, Belgium
Tel: 02 513 59 55
Fax: 02 672 53 81
Contact: The Secretary

ALEXANDER GRAHAM BELL ASSOCIATION FOR THE DEAF

Alexander Graham Bell Association for the Deaf, 3417 Volta Place, NW, Washington, DC, 20007, USA
Tel: 202 337 5220
Contact: Scholarship Coordinator

Scholarships

Subjects: Any subject, although several awards give preference to science or engineering.

Eligibility: Open to auditory-oral students born with profound hearing loss (80 dB loss in the better ear, average), or a severe hearing loss (60 to 80 dB loss), who experienced such a loss before acquiring language. Candidates must use speech and residual hearing and/or speechreading as their preferred customary form of communication and demonstrate a potential for leadership. In addition, applicants must have applied to or already be enrolled full time in a regular college or university program for hearing students.

Purpose: To encourage severely or profoundly hearing-impaired students to attend regular hearing colleges.

Type: Scholarship.

No. of awards offered: 40-50.

Frequency: Annual.

Value: US$250-US$1,000.

Country of Study: USA.

Closing Date: April 1st.

Additional Information: One application is sufficient to be considered for all of the following awards: Lucile A Abt Scholarship Awards, Maude Winkler Scholarship Awards, Elsie Bell Grosvenor Scholarship Awards, Oral Hearing-Impaired Section Scholarship Awards, Herbert P Feibelman Jr Scholarship Award, Robert H Weitbrecht Scholarship Awards, Volta Scholarship Award, David von Hagen Scholarship Awards, Auxiliary of the National Rural Letter Carriers Association Scholarship Award, Allie Raney Hunt Memorial Scholarship Award, Second Century Fund Awards.

THE BERMUDA BIOLOGICAL STATION FOR RESEARCH, INC

The Bermuda Biological Station for Research, Inc, Ferry Reach, St Georges, GE 01, Bermuda
Tel: 441 297 1880
Fax: 441 297 8143
Email: education@bbsr.edu
www: http://www.bbsr.edu
Contact: Ms Helen Palfreman

Grant In Aid

Subjects: Oceanography.

Level of Study: Postgraduate.

Purpose: To provide financial assistance to help defray the costs of in-house charges for visiting scientists.

Type: Financial assistance.

No. of awards offered: Varies.

Frequency: Twice yearly.

Value: Varies.

Length of Study: As required.

Study Establishment: The Bermuda Biological Station.

Country of Study: Bermuda.

Applications Procedure: Grant proposals should be submitted with CV and budget. Proposals should be concise and contain an abstract, background, objectives, methods and significance of proposed research.

Closing Date: March 1st or October 1st for summer or winter projects respectively.

BERMUDA COLLEGE

Bermuda College, PO Box PG 297, Paget, PGBX, Bermuda
Tel: 809 236 9000
Fax: 809 236 8888
Contact: Director, Student Services

Government of Bermuda Scholarships in Hotel Studies

Subjects: Hotel and restaurant management (Associate Degree in Hospitality Management); front office reception (certificate); professional chefs (certificate).

Eligibility: Open to applicants, preferably over the age of 21. Associate in Hospitality Management applicants require five good GCE O-Level passes (or equivalent) including English language and maths. Certificate applicants require completion of a good level of general education at the secondary level.

Purpose: To provide training in hotel studies for candidates from areas in the Caribbean which do not themselves have such facilities.

Type: Scholarship.

No. of awards offered: Two.

Frequency: Every two years.

Value: Approximately BD$9,500.

Length of Study: Up to 3 years depending upon programme.

Study Establishment: Bermuda College.

Country of Study: Bermuda.

Closing Date: February 1st.

Additional Information: These Scholarships are awarded by the government of Bermuda in cooperation with the Commonwealth Fund for Technical Cooperation.

BETA PHI MU

School of Library and Information Studies, Florida State University, Tallahassee, FL, 32306-2048, USA
Tel: 904 644 3907
Fax: 904 644 6253
Email: Bata-Phi-Mu@Lis.Fsu.Edu
Contact: F William Summers, Executive Secretary

Harold Lancour Scholarship

Subjects: Library science.

Eligibility: Open to nationals of any country.

Level of Study: Unrestricted.

Purpose: To enable foreign study.

Type: Scholarship.

No. of awards offered: One.

Frequency: Annual.

Value: US$1,000.

Country of Study: Unrestricted.

Applications Procedure: Please write to Beta Phi Mu for further details.

Closing Date: March 15th.

Sarah Rebecca Award

Subjects: Library and information science.

Eligibility: Open to nationals of any country.

Level of Study: Postgraduate.

Purpose: To assist a student studying library and information science at an ALA-accredited school.

Type: Bursary.

No. of awards offered: One.

Frequency: Annual.

Value: US$1,500.

Study Establishment: ALA-accredited school.

Applications Procedure: Please request application from address shown.

Closing Date: March 15th.

Frank B Sessa Award

Subjects: Library science.

Eligibility: Open to nationals of any country.

Level of Study: Professional development.

Purpose: To enable continuing professional education.

Frequency: Annual.

Value: US$750.

Applications Procedure: Please request an application form from Beta Phi Mu.

BEVERLY HILLS THEATRE GUILD

Playwright Award Coordinator, Beverley Hills Theatre Guild, 2815 North Beechwood Drive, Los Angeles, CA, 90068, USA
Tel: 213 465 2703
Contact: Marcella Meharg

Julie Harris Playwright Award Competition

Subjects: Playwriting.

Eligibility: Open to US playwrights. The award is made for an original, unpublished full-length play. Musicals, one-act plays, adaptations, translations and plays that have previously been submitted, or have won other competitions are ineligible.

Level of Study: Unrestricted.

Purpose: To encourage and provide recognition to aspiring and/or established American playwrights.

Type: Competition.

No. of awards offered: Three.

Frequency: Annual.

Value: First award US$5,000; second award US$2,000 (Janet and Maxwell Salter Award); third award US$1,000 (Dr Henry and Lilian Nesburn Award).

Applications Procedure: Play entry must be submitted according to guidelines and with application form - both are available upon request.

Closing Date: August 1st to November 1st.

Additional Information: US$2,000 will be made available to a theatre company to help finance a showcase production of the first award winning play, provided it is produced in the Los Angeles area within one year after receipt of the award. All entries must be submitted with a signed application. Details of rules, submission procedures and applications are available upon request with SASE (business size) from the Guild.

BFWG CHARITABLE FOUNDATION (FORMERLY CROSBY HALL)

28 Great James Street, London, WC1N 3ES, England
Tel: 0171 404 6447
Fax: 0171 404 6505
Contact: The Secretary

BFWG Awards

Subjects: Any subject.

Eligibility: Open to graduate women who have completed their first year of graduate or doctoral study or research.

Level of Study: Postgraduate, Doctorate.

Purpose: Main Foundation Grants: to assist women graduates who have difficulty meeting their living expenses while studying/researching at approved institutions of higher education in Great Britain; Emergency grants: to assist graduate women facing a financial crisis which may prevent them completing an academic year's study.

Type: Grant.

No. of awards offered: Approximately 50-60 Foundation Grants. Approximately 50-60 Emergency Grants.

Frequency: Foundation Grants - annually; Emergency Grants - three times per year.

Value: Foundation Grants - will not exceed £2,500; Emergency Grants - no grant is likely to exceed £500.

Study Establishment: Approved institutions in Great Britain.

Country of Study: Great Britain.

Closing Date: Foundation Grants - January 31st; Emergency Grants - November 30th, March 31st and June 30th.

BICENTENNIAL SWEDISH-AMERICAN EXCHANGE FUND

Bicentennial Swedish-American Exchange Fund, Swedish Information Service, 1 Dag Hammarskjöld Plaza, 45th Floor, New York, NY, 10017-2201, USA
Tel: 212 751 5900 ext.3145
Fax: 212 752 4789
Email: swedinfo@ix.netcom.com
www: http://www.swedeninfo.com/sis

Travel Grants

Subjects: Politics, public administration, working life, human environment, mass media, business and industry, education, research and culture.

Eligibility: Open to nationals and permanent residents of the USA. Applicants should have the necessary experience and education for fulfilling the project. Applicants who have visited Sweden frequently will be considered only in exceptional cases.

Level of Study: Doctorate, Postdoctorate, Professional development.

Purpose: To provide opportunity for persons who are in a position to influence public opinion and contribute to the development of their society in areas of current concern to meet their professional counterparts.

Type: Travel Grant.

No. of awards offered: Approximately 12.

Frequency: Annual.

Value: 10,000-20,000 Swedish crowns.

Length of Study: A study visit of 3-6 weeks during the year following the award.

Country of Study: Sweden (US citizens); USA (Swedish citizens).

Applications Procedure: Candidates must submit a carefully defined project with a detailed plan for achieving specific goals. Current year application form must be completed and two letters of recommendation submitted. Please include a SASE.

Closing Date: First Friday in February.

Additional Information: Applications are processed by the Swedish Information Service, then sent to Sweden where a committee of experts reviews them. Applicants are notified during May. Study visits usually take place after 20 August. Acceptance of a grant carries with it the obligation to write a report within six months of return from Sweden.

BINATIONAL AGRICULTURAL RESEARCH & DEVELOPMENT FUND (BARD)

BARD, PO Box 6, Bet Dagan, 50250, Israel
Contact: Yoash Vaadia, Executive Director

BARD Research Grant

Subjects: Agriculture.

Eligibility: Open to public of non-profit research institutions that demonstrate the necessary research and development capabilities, and whose proposals meet the objectives and criteria set down.

Level of Study: Research.

Purpose: To support agricultural research projects of mutual interest to the USA and Israel. Projects cover any or all phases of research and development, including integrated research and development problems and basic/applied research.

Type: Research Grant.

No. of awards offered: Approximately 30 per year.

Frequency: Annual.

Value: US$300,000 paid over three years.

Length of Study: Usually three years.

Study Establishment: Non-profit research organization or university/government.

Country of Study: Israel and USA.

Applications Procedure: Proposals must be submitted by September 1st each year. Guidelines and application forms are available from either office and most eligible institutions.

Closing Date: September 1st each year.

For further information contact:
BARD-USDA-ARS-OIRP, Bldg 5 BARC West, Beltsville, MD, 20705, USA
Contact: Lynn Gipie

Postdoctoral Fellowship

Subjects: Agriculture.

Eligibility: Open to US or Israeli citizens who have completed a PhD in their home country within three years.

Level of Study: Postdoctorate.

Purpose: To enable young scientists to acquire new skills and techniques while becoming professionally-established in the agriculture community. Preference is given to innovative research topics relevant to agricultural issues.

Type: Fellowship.

No. of awards offered: 8-10.

Frequency: Annual.

Value: US$30,000.

Length of Study: One year; possibility of renewal.

Study Establishment: An appropriate host institution.

Country of Study: US citizens study in Israel; Israeli citizens study in USA.

Applications Procedure: Please submit written proposal and application forms by January 15th each year. Guidelines and forms are available from either office or most institutions.

Closing Date: January 15th.

THE BIOCHEMICAL SOCIETY

Personnel & Adminstration, The Biochemical Society, 59 Portland Place, London, W1N 3AJ, England
Tel: 0171 580 5530
Fax: 0171 637 7626
Contact: The Assistant Director

Krebs Memorial Scholarship

Subjects: Biochemistry and related areas.

Eligibility: Open to graduates in the top 5% of PhD candidates.

Level of Study: Doctorate, Postdoctorate.

Purpose: To encourage students whose careers were interrupted by very special circumstances and who are unlikely to qualify for support from public agencies to work toward an advanced degree (PhD only).

Type: Scholarship.

No. of awards offered: One.

Frequency: Usually biennially.

Value: Varies; covers all necessary fees.

Length of Study: One year; renewable possibly for a further two years.

Study Establishment: Any British university.

Country of Study: UK.

Applications Procedure: The application should be forwarded through the head of department concerned.

Closing Date: March 1st.

BIOTECHNOLOGY AND BIOLOGICAL SCIENCES RESEARCH COUNCIL

Biotechnology and Biological Sciences Research Council, Polaris House, North Star Avenue, Swindon, SN2 1UH, England
Tel: 01793 413345
Fax: 01793 413234
Contact: Secretariat and Liaison Group

The mission of the BBSRC is to promote and support basic, strategic applied research relating to the understanding and exploration of biological systems

Research Fellowships

Subjects: The Council's remit encompasses agriculture, food, pharmaceuticals, chemical and health care industries, biotechnology, biological sciences and related areas in the physical sciences and engineering.

Eligibility: Open to postdoctoral scientists.

Level of Study: Postdoctorate.

Purpose: To support outstanding research workers and to enable them to devote a significant period to full-time research and scholarship.

Type: Fellowship.

No. of awards offered: Varies.

Frequency: Annual.

Study Establishment: Fellowships can only be held at any appropriate UK higher education institution or BBSRC sponsored institute which is prepared to employ the fellow.

Country of Study: UK.

Applications Procedure: Application forms are available from the secretariat and liaison group.

Closing Date: Varies.

Additional Information: Full details of BBSRC's fellowship schemes and application procedures are available in the BBSRC publications: A guide to BBSRC research grants, studentships and fellowships; BBSRC postdoctoral research fellowships.

For further information contact:
Secretariat & Liaison Group, Biotechnology and Biological Sciences Research Council, Polaris House, North Star Avenue, Swindon, SN2 1UH, England
Tel: 01793 413345
Fax: 01793 413234
Email: Postdoc.fellowships@BBSRC.AC.UK
Contact: Avril Iles

Research Grants

Subjects: The purpose of the BBSRC is to advance fundamental and strategic scientific knowledge for agriculture, for food and other biologically based industries. The research programmes are multidisciplinary with emphasis on biological sciences, biotechnology and engineering.

Eligibility: Applicants should be resident in the UK. They must hold an academic position in a UK university, college or other similar higher education institution.

Level of Study: Postdoctorate.

Purpose: To support research in UK universities, colleges and other higher education institutions. BBSCR seeks to develop and sustain high quality research within its range of interest and to encourage links between university researchers and researchers at BBSRC sponsored institutes.

Type: Research Grant.

No. of awards offered: Varies.

Frequency: Ongoing.

Country of Study: UK.

Applications Procedure: Application forms and procedures are available from the secretariat and liaison group of the BBSRC.

Closing Date: April 1st, October 1st- committees; no closing dates - Directorates.

Additional Information: Full details are available in the publications: A guide to BBSRC research grants, studentships and fellowships; BBSRC research grants.

For further information contact:
Secretariat & Liaison Group, Biotechnology and Biological Sciences Research Council, Polaris House, North Star Avenue, Swindon, SN2 1UH, England
Tel: 01793 413271
Fax: 01793 413234
Email: Research-grant.application@BBSRC.AC.UK
Contact: Darren Pirt

Standard Research Studentships, Cooperative Studentships with Industry and Advanced Course Studentships

Subjects: The Council's remit encompasses the agriculture, food, pharmaceuticals, and health care industries, bioprocessing, chemical and other biotechnological related industry.

Eligibility: Open to candidates who have been ordinarily resident in Great Britain for the three years immediately preceding the date of application and have graduated with a first or upper second class honours degree. Students who are ordinarily resident in Northern Ireland, the Channel Isles or the Isle of Man should apply directly to their respective education authorities.

Level of Study: Postgraduate, Doctorate.

Purpose: To enable recently graduated scientists or engineers to study for a higher degree (primarily for a PhD).

Type: Studentship.

No. of awards offered: Approximately 600.

Frequency: Annual.

Value: A maintenance grant plus London Allowance if appropriate; dependants' and other allowances, if applicable. Approved tuition fees are payable directly to the institution.

Length of Study: Three years.

Study Establishment: British universities or other Higher Education Institutions and research institutes of the Biotechnology and Biological Sciences Research Council.

Country of Study: UK.

Applications Procedure: Intending candidates must apply in the first instance to the institution where they wish to carry out their studies. The Council does not accept applications direct from students.

Closing Date: Varies.

For further information contact:
Biotechnology and Biological Sciences Research Council, Polaris House, North Star Avenue, Swindon, SN2 1UH, England
Tel: 01793 414670/413380
Fax: 01793 413201
Email: nikki.tindall@bbsrc.ac.uk
www: http://bbsrc.ac.uk/
Contact: Human Resources Group

Underwood Fund

Subjects: Biotechnology and biological sciences.

Eligibility: Open to overseas research workers.

Purpose: To facilitate the exchange of scientific knowledge at international level. The Fund is used for the provision of grants to enable visits to be made to the UK by overseas scientists whose presence in the UK is likely to be of assistance to BBSRC-supported research in universities or BBSRC sponsored institutes.

Type: Grant.

No. of awards offered: Varies.

Value: To cover subsistence and travel expenses as approved by the BBSRC.

Length of Study: Up to one year.

Study Establishment: Universities and BBSRC sponsored institutes.

Country of Study: UK.

Applications Procedure: Applications should be submitted by the research institute or the holder of an BBSRC research grant and should include full details of the visitor, the scientific case for the collaboration, a break-down of funds being requested and an indication of the duration and timing of the stay.

Additional Information: Information on the BBSRC remit is available in the BBSRC publication 'a guide to BBSRC research grants, studentships and fellowships', available from secretariat and liaison group, BBSRC.

Wain Fund

Subjects: Biotechnology and biological sciences.

Eligibility: Open to the academic staff of British universities and similar research institutions (but not government or government-financed laboratories) and to scientists who are currently pursuing or have recently completed a course of research training leading to a higher degree and expect to enter a research career.

Purpose: To provide travel grants to UK university scientists wishing to spend a period abroad working in a laboratory on an agreed collaboration programme and/or to consult with others working in their fields of interest; and to provide Fellowships to enable younger research scientists to work or study abroad at a specified academic, industrial or agricultural institution for a period of up to three months.

Type: Travel Grant.

Frequency: Annual.

Value: To cover travel and subsistence expenses.

Study Establishment: Approved academic, industrial or agricultural institutions.

Country of Study: Overseas.

Applications Procedure: Application forms are available on request.

Closing Date: Contact the secretariat and liaison group for closing dates.

Additional Information: Full details of the BBSRC remit can be obtained in the BBSRC publication 'A guide to BBSRC research grants, studentships and fellowships'.

B H BLACKWELL LTD

c/o Office of Pro-Vice-Chancellor, Academic Services, Room 33, Forgan-Smith Building, University of Queensland, Queensland, 4072, Australia
Tel: 07 365 1603
Fax: 07 365 1604
Contact: F D O Fielding

*James Cook Bicentenary Scholarship

Subjects: Librarianship. The Selection Panel may nominate a specific purpose in any particular year.

Eligibility: Open to Australian or New Zealand citizens of at least 5 years' standing, aged not more than 45 years and eligible for professional membership of either the Australian Library and Information Association or the New Zealand Library Association. Candidates must be graduates of a recognized university.

Purpose: To provide an opportunity for middle-ranking Australian and New Zealand librarians to further their professional interests and to study specialized aspects of librarianship, either in a work situation or at an approved institution of higher education.

Type: Scholarship.

No. of awards offered: One.

Frequency: Biennially (even-numbered years).

Value: Up to A$25,000.

Study Establishment: As proposed by candidate and approved by the Selection Board.

Country of Study: UK, USA or Canada.

Closing Date: As advertised in ALIA and NZLA professional journals.

Additional Information: Occasional smaller grants are advertised for a project on a specific topic.

BLUES HEAVEN FOUNDATION, INC

Blues Heaven Foundation, Inc, 249 North Brand Boulevard #590, Glendale, CA, 91203, USA

Muddy Waters Scholarship

Subjects: Music, music education, Afro-American studies, folklore, performing arts, arts management, journalism, radio/TV/film.

Eligibility: Open to students with full-time enrolment status in a Chicago-area college or university. Students must be in at least their first year of undergraduate studies or graduate program.

Level of Study: Undergraduate, Graduate.

Type: Scholarship.

No. of awards offered: One.

Frequency: Annual.

Value: US$2,000.

Study Establishment: A Chicago-area college or university.

Country of Study: USA.

Closing Date: Applications are available beginning in February for the upcoming school year. The application deadline is March 31st for announcement May 15th. Funds are made available for the following fall semester, upon documentation of enrolment.

Additional Information: The Scholarship award shall be governed by the applicant's scholastic aptitude and extracurricular involvement, including grade point average, honors programs, memberships, etc. Eligibility will be based on projected expenses, student and family income. Special consideration will be given to applicants demonstrating need for financial assistance.

BOARD OF ARCHITECTS OF NEW SOUTH WALES

Board of Architects of New South Wales, 3 Manning Street, Potts Point, NSW, 2011, Australia
Tel: 61 2 356 4900
Fax: 61 2 357 4780
Contact: Registrar

Board of Architects Research Grant

Subjects: Any architectural topic approved by the Board.

Eligibility: Open to candidates who are registered as architects in New South Wales.

Level of Study: Professional development.

Purpose: To undertake research on a topic approved by the board to contribute to the advancement of architecture.

Type: Research grant.

No. of awards offered: One.

Frequency: Every two years.

Value: A$6,000 (in 1995).

Length of Study: One year.

Country of Study: Any country.

Closing Date: April 30th.

Additional Information: A report is to be submitted upon completion of tenure.

Byera Hadley Travelling Scholarship: Postgraduate Scholarship, Student Scholarship

Subjects: Architecture.

Eligibility: Open only to graduates or students, who are Australian citizens, of four accredited schools of architecture in New South Wales.

Level of Study: Postgraduate.

Purpose: To undertake a course of study or research or other activity approved by the Board as contributing to the advancement of architecture.

Type: Scholarship.

No. of awards offered: One grant in each category.

Frequency: Annual.

Value: Total value of combined awards: A$31,000 (in 1995).

Country of Study: Overseas.

Closing Date: Postgraduate Scholarship: August 30th; Student Scholarship: September 30th.

Additional Information: A report suitable for publication to be submitted within three years (maximum) of the date of the award.

BOARD OF TRUSTEES FOR THE AWARD OF THE HEINRICH WIELAND PRIZE

Board of Trustees for the Award of the Heinrich Wieland Prize, Gasstrasse 18, Haus 4, Hamburg, D-22761, Germany
Tel: 040 89 40 04
Fax: 040 89 40 06
Contact: Dr Ingo Witte

Heinrich Wieland Prize

Subjects: Medical Sciences.

Level of Study: Unrestricted.

Purpose: The prize is offered for work on the chemistry, biochemistry, and physiology of fats and lipids, as well as on their clinical importance and their significance in the physiology of nutrition.

Type: Prize. Monetary and a plaque.

No. of awards offered: One.

Frequency: Annual.

Value: DM50,000.

Closing Date: March 1st.

BOISE FOUNDATION

Boise Foundation, c/o Royal Academy of Music, Marylebone Road, London, NW1 5HT, England
Contact: Jean Shannon, Honorary Secretary

Scholarships

Subjects: Music practical.

Eligibility: Open to musical students of any nationality and under 30 years of age who are ordinarily resident in the UK or Republic of Ireland, or who are Commonwealth citizens temporarily resident in the UK for their musical education, or who are foreign nationals who have been resident in the UK for at least three years prior to commencing musical training.

Level of Study: Postgraduate.

Purpose: To enable vocalists or performing artists on any musical instrument to further their musical education.

Type: Scholarship.

No. of awards offered: 1 or 2.

Frequency: Biennially (next in 1997).

Value: Up to £5,000.

Study Establishment: Musical centres either in the UK or abroad, subject to the approval of the Scholar's plan of study by the Chairman of the Foundation Committee.

Country of Study: Any.

Applications Procedure: Application form must be completed and signed by nominator. Awards are made on the basis of a competitive audition for which candidates must be nominated; names of nominators are available on request from the Foundation Secretary.

Closing Date: Early March in the year of the award.

BOLOGNA CENTER OF THE JOHNS HOPKINS UNIVERSITY

The Registrar, Bologna Center of the Johns Hopkins University, Via Belmeloro 11, Bologna, BO, 1-40126, Italy
Tel: 39 51 23 21 85
Fax: 39 51 22 85 05
Email: uvlbolf7@cine88.cineca.it
Contact: (non-US students)

Paul H Nitze School of Advanced International Studies Financial Aid and Fellowships

Subjects: International relations, with emphasis on international economics and European studies (interdisciplinary program), with language studies; graduate study.

Eligibility: Open to students who have completed their first university degree. Students who are in the process of completing their first degree may apply providing they are awarded the degree prior to entry to the Bologna Center in the fall. Ideally, candidates should have some background knowledge in economics, history, political or other social sciences. All non-native English speaking students must have an excellent command, both written and spoken, of the English language, as the program is conducted entirely in English. Special fellowships administered by the Bologna Center on behalf of other donor organizations have certain restrictions, which vary depending upon the donor.

Level of Study: Postgraduate.

Type: Fellowship.

No. of awards offered: Varies, dependent on funds available.

Frequency: Annual.

Value: Varies; grants may cover partial or, occasionally, full tuition. Maintenance stipends are rarely provided.

Study Establishment: The Bologna Center of The Johns Hopkins University, Paul H Nitze School of Advanced International Studies.

Country of Study: Italy.

Applications Procedure: All candidates must submit an application form and a financial aid application. Certain donor organizations require a separate form.

Closing Date: US students, February 1st; non-US students, March 1st.

Additional Information: The Bologna Center is an integral part of the Paul H Nitze School of Advanced International Studies (SAIS) in Washington. Admission and financial aid for US citizens and permanent residents is administered by SAIS in Washington and all enquiries from US students should be addressed to the Admissions Office in Washington. Financial aid and admission of non-US students is administered in Bologna and all inquiries from non-US students should be addressed to the Registrar's Office in Bologna. Many of the Fellowships available to non-US students are provided by government ministries and other European organizations and are reserved for citizens of the country providing the Fellowship. Special Fellowships are available and reserved for citizens of the following countries: Austria, France, Germany, Italy, Turkey, and the UK. All Fellowships and financial aid awards are based on need as well as academic merit.

For further information contact:
The Admissions Office, Paul H Nitze SAIS, 1740 Massachusetts Avenue, NW, Washington, DC, 20036, USA
Tel: 202 663 5700
Fax: 202 663 5656
Contact: (US students/permanent residents)

ROBERT BOSCH FOUNDATION

Robert Bosch Foundation , c/o CDS International, Inc, 330 Seventh Avenue, New York, NY, 10001-5010, USA
Tel: 212 760 1400
Fax: 212 268 1288

Fellowship Program

Eligibility: Open to US nationals.

Level of Study: Postgraduate, Professional development.

Type: Fellowship.

No. of awards offered: 15.

Frequency: Annual.

Length of Study: Nine months (September to May).

Country of Study: Germany.

Closing Date: October 15th.

Internships

Subjects: Business administration; economics; public affairs; political science; law; journalism and mass communication.

Eligibility: Open to US citizens with a graduate or professional degree or equivalent work experience in the above subject areas. Candidates must provide evidence of outstanding professional or academic achievement and a strong knowledge of the German language. For those candidates who are outstanding in other areas but lack sufficient knowledge of German, the Foundation will provide language training prior to program participation.

Level of Study: Postgraduate, Professional development.

Purpose: To promote the advancement of American/German-European relations; to broaden the participants' professional competence and cultural horizons.

Type: Internship.

No. of awards offered: Fifteen.

Frequency: Annual.

Value: DM3,500 per month stipend, extra funding for family, language training and business travel.

Length of Study: Eight months, from September to May.

Country of Study: Germany.

Closing Date: October 15th.

Additional Information: Program participants receive internships in such German institutions as the Federal Parliament, private corporation headquarters, mass media, and other elements within the framework of government/commerce. Internships will be at a high level, closely related to senior officials. The program will follow the following schedule: an intensive course on German language; political, economic and cultural affairs; work experience; a visit to Berlin and the former East Germany, to the European Economic Community and NATO headquarters in Brussels; a group visit to France for an overview of the political, economic, and cultural perspective of another European country; final program evaluation in Stuttgart. All activities are conducted in German.

THE BOTANICAL SOCIETY OF SOUTH AFRICA

The Botanical Society of South Africa, Kirstenbosch, Claremont, Cape Province, 7735, South Africa
Tel: 21 797 2090
Fax: 21 797 2376
Contact: Conservation Officer

Flora Conservation Scholarships

Subjects: Botany.

Eligibility: Open to MSc and PhD students in Botany.

Level of Study: Doctorate, Postgraduate MSc.

Purpose: To support applied research in botany, relating to the conservation and wise utilization of the indigenous flora of southern Africa.

Type: Scholarship.

No. of awards offered: Two.

Frequency: Annual.

Value: R10,000 (South African Rands).

Length of Study: One year.

Study Establishment: Any South African University.

Country of Study: South Africa.

Applications Procedure: Write to conservation officer for an application form.

Closing Date: November 30th.

Additional Information: The area of study must fit in with research priorities of the Botanical Society. Students must be registered at a South African University. Students who are awarded the scholarship may reapply for a second year's funding.

BOYD ORR RESEARCH CENTRE

Boyd Orr Research Centre, Rowett Research Institute, Greenburn Road, Bucksburn, Aberdeen, AB2 9SB, Scotland
Tel: 01224 712751
Fax: 01224 715347
Email: c.cook@rri.sari.ac.uk
Contact: Christine Cook

PhD Studentships

Subjects: Agriculture and farm management, meat and poultry food science and production.

Eligibility: Eligible to nationals of any country.

Level of Study: Doctorate.

Type: Studentship.

No. of awards offered: 4-6.

Frequency: Annual.

Value: £6,450 per annum.

Length of Study: Three years.

Country of Study: Scotland.

Applications Procedure: Respond to advertisement, enclosing CV and references from two academic referees.

Closing Date: Advised in the advertisement.

BRADFORD CHAMBER OF COMMERCE

Bradford Chamber of Commerce, Park House, Cote Lane, Farsley, LS28 5XZ, England
Tel: 01274 363136
Fax: 01274 363128
Contact: Mrs L Cooper

John Speak Trust Scholarships

Subjects: Modern languages.

Eligibility: Open to British-born nationals intending to follow a career connected with the export trade of the UK, who are over 18 years of age. A sound, basic knowledge of a language is required.

Level of Study: Professional development.

Purpose: To promote British trade abroad by assisting people in perfecting a basic knowledge of a foreign language.

Type: Scholarship.

No. of awards offered: Approximately four.

Frequency: Annual.

Value: Approximately £1,800.

Length of Study: Abroad for six months, or three months if a candidate's knowledge of a language is advanced; not renewable.

Country of Study: Any non-English speaking country.

Closing Date: February 28th, May 31st, October 31st.

BRANDON UNIVERSITY

School of Music, Brandon University, Brandon, Manitoba, R7A 6A9, Canada
Tel: 204 727 9631
Fax: 204 726 4573
Contact: Professor Wayne Bowman, Chair, Graduate Music Programs

*Graduate Assistantships

Subjects: Music education, performance and literature (piano and strings).

Eligibility: Open to candidates with a bachelor's degree in music or music education with a minimum grade point average of 3.0 during the final year.

Purpose: To afford graduate students the opportunity to gain professional experience while studying, and to provide monetary assistance.

No. of awards offered: 4-8.

Frequency: Annual.

Value: C$6,000.

Length of Study: One year.

Study Establishment: School of Music, Brandon University.

Country of Study: Canada.

Closing Date: May 1st.

Additional Information: Candidates for the performance and literature major are also required to show, by audition, high potential as performers. For the music education major, candidates should have adequate related professional experience, preferably teaching.

BREAD LOAF WRITER'S CONFERENCE

Bread Loaf Writers' Conference, Middlebury College, Middlebury, VT, 05753, USA
Email: BLWC@mail.middlebury.edu
Contact: Mrs Carol Knauss

Fellowships and Scholarships

Subjects: Fiction; non-fiction; poetry.

Eligibility: Open to persons nominated by a publisher, editor, agent, established writer, or teacher of writing. Candidates for Fellowships are assumed to have published a book or to have had a book-length manuscript accepted for publication. Candidates for Scholarship assistance will have had articles published in periodicals. There are no restrictions regarding nationality or citizenship.

Purpose: To provide both recognition for established writers and writers who show unusual promise, and an atmosphere in which writing can be discussed and criticized intensively.

Type: Fellowships and scholarships.

No. of awards offered: Varies.

Value: Fellowships carry no cash value but cover all regular charges at the Conference. Scholarships cover full or partial tuition.

Length of Study: Two weeks.

Study Establishment: The Bread Loaf campus, Middlebury College, Vermont.

Country of Study: USA.

Applications Procedure: Application form must be completed.

Closing Date: March 1st.

THE BRITISH ACADEMY

The British Academy, 20-21 Cornwall Terrace, London, NW1 4QP, England
Tel: 0171 487 5966
Fax: 0171 224 3807
Contact: The Secretary

Archaeology Grants

Subjects: Archaeology.

Eligibility: Open to individuals and organizations based in the UK and undertaking academic archaeological research.

Level of Study: Unrestricted.

Purpose: To support all archaeological fieldwork, together with related general and scientific post-excavation work.

Type: Grant.

No. of awards offered: 96.

Frequency: Annual.

Value: Up to £10,000, although few exceed £7,000-£8,000 and in many cases the Academy may only be able to offer a token contribution.

Country of Study: Any country.

Closing Date: December 31st.

Elisabeth Barker Fund

Subjects: Recent European history.

Eligibility: Open to scholars of postdoctoral or equivalent status ordinarily resident in the UK. Applicants need not be British nationals.

Level of Study: Postdoctorate.

No. of awards offered: Up to six.

Frequency: Annual.

Value: Approximately £1,000.

Country of Study: Europe.

Closing Date: September 30th, December 31st, February 28th and April 30th.

British Conference Grants

Subjects: Humanities and social sciences.

Eligibility: Applicants must be UK citizens applying on behalf of an academic living outside the UK.

Purpose: To help meet the costs (mainly travel, but applications for maintenance will be considered) of overseas scholars contributing major papers at conferences held in Britain.

Value: No prescribed maximum amounts but awards rarely exceed £1,000 and are usually less than £750.

Country of Study: UK.

Applications Procedure: Applications to be submitted on prescribed form.

Closing Date: End of September, December, February, April.

Neil Ker Memorial Fund

Subjects: Western medieval manuscripts, particularly those of British interest.

Eligibility: Open to both younger and established scholars of any nationality.

Purpose: To promote the study of Western medieval manuscripts, in particular those of British interest.

No. of awards offered: Usually four awards, depending on funds available.

Frequency: Annual.

Value: Approximately £1,000.

Country of Study: Any country.

Closing Date: End of February.

Larger Research Grants at Postdoctoral Level

Subjects: Humanities: i.e. history in the widest sense (including the history of art, music, ideas, science, and of politics and economics); language and literature; law; philosophy; and religious studies.

Eligibility: Applicants must be resident in the UK.

Level of Study: Postdoctorate.

Purpose: To support research projects at postdoctoral level which are large in scale and extended in duration.

Type: Grant.

No. of awards offered: Varies.

Frequency: Annual.

Value: Normal upper limit of £17,500 in any one year.

Country of Study: Any.

Closing Date: September 30th.

Major International Conference Grant

Subjects: Humanities and social sciences.

Eligibility: Open to organizers of major international conferences in the UK.

Purpose: To help meet the costs of organizing major international congresses in Britain, but only where the congress is one of an established series, and where it is clearly the British turn to host the conference.

Type: Grant.

No. of awards offered: 4-5.

Frequency: Annual.

Value: Up to £2,000. Grants are for preliminary administration and general expenses only, not for the costs of invited overseas participants.

Country of Study: UK.

Applications Procedure: Applications to be submitted on prescribed form.

Closing Date: End of September and April.

Overseas Conference Grants

Subjects: Humanities and social sciences.

Eligibility: Open to scholars presenting an academic paper by invitation of the conference organizers.

Purpose: To help meet the costs of travel by British scholars to overseas conferences or similar gatherings. Awards will be contributions to travel expenses only.

Type: Grant.

No. of awards offered: Varies.

Frequency: Dependent on funds available.

Value: Usually restricted to a maximum of £650.

Country of Study: Any country.

Applications Procedure: Applications to be submitted on prescribed form.

Closing Date: End of September, December, February, April.

Small Personal Research Grants

Subjects: All arts and humanities, but not including accountancy, business and management studies, education studies or social work.

Eligibility: Applicants must be resident in the UK.

Level of Study: Postdoctorate.

Purpose: For original, creative research at postdoctoral level.

Type: Grant.

No. of awards offered: 229 made in 1994/5.

Frequency: Four times yearly.

Value: Maximum £5,000, but on average £2,500. Grants are personal to the applicant, and solely for the costs of the research itself; there is no element of salary or maintenance to the applicant.

Country of Study: Any country.

Closing Date: End of September, November, February and April.

Thank-Offering to Britain Fellowships

Subjects: Topics of an economic, industrial, social, political, literary or historical character relating to the British Isles. Preference will be given to projects in the modern period.

Eligibility: Open to persons ordinarily resident in the UK, and of post-doctoral status.

Level of Study: Postdoctorate.

Purpose: To fund a research fellowship.

Type: Fellowship.

No. of awards offered: One.

Frequency: Annual.

Value: Within the first two points of the Grade A university lecturers' scale.

Length of Study: Normally for two years.

Country of Study: UK.

Closing Date: February 28th.

Visiting Professorships for Overseas Scholars

Subjects: Humanities and social sciences.

Eligibility: Candidates for nomination must be either established scholars of distinction or younger people who show great promise and who would benefit from time to pursue their research in the UK.

Purpose: To enable distinguished scholars from overseas to spend time in the UK to pursue their personal research.

Type: Professorship.

No. of awards offered: Varies.

Frequency: Annual.

Value: Normally a maximum of £500 per week for visits of up to three weeks, and an overall maximum of £2,000 for visits of one month or more.

Country of Study: UK.

Applications Procedure: Applications to be submitted on the prescribed form, by the British sponsor. Sponsors must undertake to make all administrative arrangements on behalf of the visitor. Applications are considered in February, in respect of visits to take place during the following financial year. Applications directly from foreign scholars will not be accepted.

Closing Date: December 31st. It may be possible to entertain applications at other times of the year, but the Academy's aim is to allocate the available funds in one go.

BRITISH ASSOCIATION FOR AMERICAN STUDIES

British Association for American Studies, School of Humanities, De Montfort University, Leicester, LE1 9BH, England
Tel: 0116 257 7199
Fax: 0116 270 1254
Email: pjd@dmu.ac.uk
Contact: Mr P Davies, Secretary (STA)

Short Term Awards

Subjects: US culture and society.

Eligibility: Open to UK citizens. Preference is given to young scholars, particularly postgraduates.

Level of Study: Postgraduate, Doctorate, Postdoctorate, Professional development.

Purpose: To fund travel to the USA for research purposes.

No. of awards offered: 3-4.

Frequency: Annual.

Value: £400.

Study Establishment: Anywhere in the USA.

Country of Study: USA.

Applications Procedure: Application form must be completed; available from listed contacts.

Closing Date: September 30th.

For further information contact:
British Association for American Studies, School of Humanities, De Montfort University, Leicester, LE1 9BH, England
Tel: 0116 257 7199
Fax: 0116 270 1254
Email: pjd@dmu.ac.uk
Contact: Mr P Davies, Secretary (STA)

or
British Association for American Studies, School of English, University of Newcastle upon Tyne, Newcastle upon Tyne, NE1 7RU, England
Tel: 0191 222 7755
Contact: Professor J Newman, Chair, BAAS

BRITISH ASSOCIATION FOR CANADIAN STUDIES

British Association for Canadian Studies, 21 George Square,
Edinburgh, EH8 9LD, Scotland
Tel: 0131 662 1117
Fax: 0131 662 1118
Email: jrobson@afb1.ssc.ed.ac.uk
Contact: Jodie Robson

Foundation for Canadian Studies in the UK - Canada/UK Institutional Links Scheme

Subjects: Unrestricted; however the link is expected to contribute to the development of Canadian studies in the UK.

Eligibility: Open to institutions of higher education in the UK.

Level of Study: Postdoctorate.

Purpose: To support the development of an institutional link by the provision of 'seed corn' funding to visit a Canadian counterpart.

No. of awards offered: Five.

Frequency: Annual; under review.

Value: Up to £500 initially; the maximum grant for any one project is unlikely to exceed £1,000 within a period of 3 years.

Study Establishment: Universities or polytechnics.

Country of Study: Canada.

Applications Procedure: Applications must be supported by head of department/faculty, as appropriate, and demonstrate that contacts have already been established with the Canadian institution.

Closing Date: October 1st, February 1st and May 1st.

Ontario Bicentennial Award

Subjects: Canadian area and cultural studies.

Eligibility: Graduate students will normally only be considered in the final stages of their doctoral research.

Level of Study: Doctorate.

Purpose: To fund travel to Ontario to research topics concerned with that province in history and/or political science.

Type: Travel grant.

No. of awards offered: One.

Frequency: Dependent on funds available.

Value: £500 approximately.

Length of Study: Short visit.

Study Establishment: Univeristy/library.

Country of Study: Canada.

Applications Procedure: Application form, plus supporting letter, CV, and the names of two referees.

Closing Date: May 1st.

Additional Information: Administered by BACS on behalf of the Foundation for Canadian Studies in the UK.

Study Visit Awards

Subjects: Canadian studies: humanities; social sciences.

Eligibility: Open to academics from UK universities, polytechnics and colleges of higher education.

Level of Study: Postdoctorate.

Purpose: To encourage and fund visits to Canada directly related to applicants' actual or proposed teaching and/or research.

Type: Travel grant.

No. of awards offered: 3-5, depending on funds available.

Frequency: Annual.

Value: Up to £500.

Study Establishment: Universities or research institutions.

Country of Study: Canada.

Applications Procedure: Application form plus supporting letter, CV and names of two referees must be submitted.

Closing Date: October 1st, February 1st and May 1st.

Additional Information: The Awards are intended to increase contacts between academics and other scholars in Canada and the UK and to assist in the preparation of teaching about Canada. The BACS administers these Awards on behalf of the Foundation for Canadian Studies in the UK.

BRITISH ASSOCIATION OF PLASTIC SURGEONS

The British Association of Plastic Surgeons, The Royal College of Surgeons, 35-43 Lincoln's Inn Fields, London, WC2A 3PN, England
Tel: 0171 831 5161
Fax: 0171 831 4041
Contact: Honorary Secretary

BAPS Travelling Bursary

Subjects: Plastic surgery.

Eligibility: Open to members of the Association who are either senior registrars enrolled in a recognized training programme or consultant plastic surgeons of not more than three years' standing.

Level of Study: Professional development.

Purpose: To enable a plastic surgeon in the UK to study new techniques abroad.

Type: Bursary.

No. of awards offered: Two.

Frequency: Annual.

Value: £4,000 each.

Study Establishment: Approved centres.

Country of Study: Outside the UK.

Closing Date: September 1st.

European Travelling Scholarship

Subjects: Plastic surgery.

Eligibility: Open to members of the Association who are registrars or senior registrars enrolled in a recognized training programme.

Level of Study: Professional development.

Type: Scholarship.

No. of awards offered: Three.

Frequency: Annual.

Value: £1,000.

Study Establishment: Any plastic surgery centre.

Country of Study: Europe, not including the UK.

Closing Date: September 1st.

THE BRITISH COUNCIL AND THE CHINESE GOVERNMENT

Overseas Appointments Services, The British Council, Medlock Street, Manchester, M15 4AA, England
Tel: 0161 957 7383
Fax: 0161 957 7397

Postgraduate Scholarships to China

Subjects: Any subject of study will be considered but applications in the fields of law and governance, the environment, economics, human resource development and gender and development will be given priority. Candidates should also be aware of the possible sensitivities and restrictions which may exist on the part of the Chinese authorities.

Eligibility: Candidates for these awards should be British citizens with a full UK passport. A good working knowledge of Chinese is also required, unless a candidate can provide proof that their chosen institution is willing to accept them to work under the supervision of English speaking staff. Candidates for senior advanced awards should already hold a masters degree or be registered for a PhD.

Level of Study: Postgraduate, Doctorate.

Purpose: To deepen educational/cultural understanding between China and Britain.

Type: Scholarship.

No. of awards offered: To be confirmed.

Frequency: Annual.

Value: The Chinese government will provide tuition, accommodation and a small monthly stipend intended to cover living expenses. Successful candidates are likely to need additional funds of at least £1,100 for travel within China and other expenses during their stay in China. The British Council will provide a grant of £1,100 (subject to review) to cover the return airfare from London to Beijing, visa costs and medical tests and will arrange medical insurance which includes medical evaluation for the duration of the award (approximate value £580).

Length of Study: At least three months, and not more than ten months (appropriate to the research).

Country of Study: People's Republic of China.

Applications Procedure: Application form must be completed in duplicate, plus research/study proposal, documentary proof of qualifications, and confirmation of PhD registration (if applying for senior advanced status).

Closing Date: February.

Additional Information: Candidates should be aware that Chinese immigration rules require successful candidates to undergo a full medical examination which will include an HIV test.

BRITISH DENTAL ASSOCIATION

British Dental Association, 64 Wimpole Street, London, W1M 8AL, England

Tel: 0171 935 0875
Fax: 0171 487 5232
Contact: Leila Rutter

Dentsply Scholarship Fund

Subjects: Dentistry.

Eligibility: Open to British citizens studying in the UK or abroad, or citizens of any country studying in the UK.

Level of Study: Postgraduate, Undergraduate.

Purpose: To give financial assistance to undergraduate/postgraduate students of dentistry to enable them to undertake or continue studies in schools in the UK.

Type: Interest-free loans or grants.

No. of awards offered: Variable.

Frequency: Annual.

Value: A few hundred pounds.

Country of Study: UK.

Applications Procedure: Application forms must be completed and submitted by May 31st, along with an academic reference or supporting letter.

Closing Date: May 31st.

BRITISH DIABETIC ASSOCIATION

British Diabetic Association, 10 Queen Anne Street, London, W1M 0BD, England
Tel: 0171 323 1531
Fax: 0171 637 3644
Contact: Dr M Murphy

Diabetes Development Project

Subjects: Endocrinology.

Eligibility: Open to suitably qualified members of the medical or scientific professions, and health care professionals, who are resident in the UK.

Level of Study: Research/care.

Purpose: To benefit the diabetic community.

Type: Development project.

No. of awards offered: Varies.

Frequency: Twice per year.

Value: Not usually more than £30,000 per year.

Length of Study: 1-2 years.

Country of Study: UK.

Applications Procedure: Application form must be submitted.

Closing Date: Contact the BDA for dates; usually in March and October.

Equipment Grant

Subjects: Endocrinology.

Eligibility: Open to suitably qualified members of the medical or scientific professions, who are resident in the UK.

Level of Study: Research.

Purpose: To enable the purchase of equipment which is required only for a single project or programme which is solely concerned with diabetes research.

Type: Equipment grant.

No. of awards offered: Varies.

Frequency: Three times per year.

Value: A minimum of £5,000.

Country of Study: UK.

Applications Procedure: Application form must be submitted by the closing date, for assessment by the peer review.

Closing Date: May 1st, Septmeber 1st, December 1st.

Group Grant

Subjects: Endocrinology.

Eligibility: Open to suitably qualified members of the medical or scientific professions, who are resident in the UK.

Level of Study: Research.

Purpose: To provide funding to facilitate the development of new lines of research for which longer-term support may be required.

Type: Grant.

No. of awards offered: Varies.

Frequency: Three times per year.

Value: £62,000.

Length of Study: Five years.

Country of Study: UK.

Applications Procedure: Application by submission of detailed outline of research interests, which is assessed by peer review.

Closing Date: May 1st, September 1st, December 1st.

Project Grants

Subjects: Endocrinology.

Eligibility: Open to suitably qualified members of the medical or scientific professions, who are resident in the UK.

Level of Study: Research.

Purpose: To provide funding for a well-defined research proposal of timeliness and promise which, in terms of the application, may be expected to lead to a significant advance.

Type: Project grant.

No. of awards offered: Varies.

Frequency: Three times per year.

Value: Not usually more than £40,000 per year.

Length of Study: 1-3 years.

Country of Study: UK.

Applications Procedure: Application form submitted by closing dates will be assessed by peer review.

Closing Date: May 1st, September 1st, December 1st.

Research Fellowships

Subjects: Diabetes mellitus: research.

Eligibility: Open to suitably qualified members of the medical or scientific professions who are resident in the UK.

Level of Study: Postdoctorate.

Type: Varies.

Frequency: As advertised.

Value: Varies.

Length of Study: Two years.

Country of Study: UK.

Applications Procedure: Application form must be completed.

Closing Date: Advertised annually in October.

Additional Information: Availability is advertised annually in scientific/medical press.

Research Studentships

Subjects: Endocrinology.

Eligibility: Applications are invited from potential supervisors in single departments or in collaborative projects between departments, pre-clinical or clinical. Applicants must be resident in the UK.

Level of Study: Postgraduate.

Purpose: To train basic scientists in diabetes research.

Type: Studentship.

No. of awards offered: Varies.

Frequency: Annual.

Value: London: £11,500 maintenance and £4,500 expenses (lab); out of London: £10,500 maintenance and £4,500 expenses (lab).

Length of Study: Three years.

Country of Study: UK.

Applications Procedure: Application form must be submitted.

Closing Date: Advertised in scientific/medical press; December each year.

Small Grant Scheme

Subjects: Endocrinology.

Eligibility: Open to suitably qualified members of the medical or scientific professions who are resident in the UK.

Level of Study: Research.

Purpose: To enable research workers to progress new ideas in the field of diabetes.

Frequency: Throughout the year.

Value: Up to £5,000.

Length of Study: Usually one year.

Country of Study: UK.

Applications Procedure: Application form must be completed; will be assessed by the peer review within 6-8 weeks.

Closing Date: No defined date.

THE BRITISH DIGESTIVE FOUNDATION

The British Digestive Foundation, 3 St Andrew's Place, Regent's Park, London, NW1 4LB, England
Tel: 0171 486 0341
Fax: 0171 224 2012
Contact: The Administrator

Fellowships and Grants

Subjects: Gastroenterology.

Eligibility: Applicants must have been resident in the UK for a minimum of five years. Projects must contain an element of basic scientific training.

Level of Study: Postgraduate, Doctorate.

Purpose: To provide for gastroenterological research into the prevention and treatment of alimentary and liver disorders.

Type: Fellowships, research and travel grants.

No. of awards offered: Five.

Frequency: Awards are usually advertised in Nov/Dec and June/July.

Value: Up to £30,000 per year, paid quarterly in advance.

Length of Study: One year; renewable for a second year, subject to progress assessment.

Study Establishment: Recognized and established research centres.

Country of Study: Open.

Applications Procedure: An application form must be completed.

Closing Date: As advertised in 'The Lancet', and 'British Medical Journal'.

Additional Information: Conditions are advertised in the medical press.

BRITISH ECOLOGICAL SOCIETY

British Ecological Society, 26 Blades Court, Putney, London, SW15 2NU, England
Tel: 0181 871 9797
Fax: 0181 871 9779

Research Travel Grants

Subjects: Ecology.

Eligibility: Open to all ecologists provided that the work to be undertaken does not form part of that to be submitted for a degree. The awards will be granted according to the scientific merit of the application, taking into account not only the work to be done but also the experience and publication record of the applicant.

Level of Study: Professional development.

Purpose: To enable ecologists to travel from Great Britain or the Republic of Ireland to a third country, or vice versa, for the purposes of research when alternative sources of funding are inadequate.

Type: Travel grants.

Frequency: Twice yearly.

Value: To cover all, or part of, the cost of travel, subsistence and insurance, together with a contribution to a 'bench fee' charged by host institutions, but not for equipment, up to a maximum of £1,500 per applicant (or per party if two or more applicants travel together).

Applications Procedure: Applications may be made two years in advance of proposed travel. Every recipient shall furnish to the Awards Committee, within six months of the completion of the visit, a report of about 500 words on the work carried out, in a form suitable for possible publication in the Bulletin. Published papers containing results obtained with aid from this source should include an acknowledgement of that fact. The Awards Committee has power to attach to any grant such other conditions as it may deem desirable. The grants are regarded as personal to the recipients and intended to support a specific project to be carried out by the applicant personally. If the grant asked for will cover only a portion of the whole expense, this fact must be stated in the application, together with an indication of how the remainder has been, or is hoped to be, obtained. Referee's statements must arrive at the office on or before the closing date for application. This is the sole responsibility of the applicant and without both statements the application will not be considered. Recipients should note that money will be released only when satisfactory arrangements have been completed with the institution to be visited and when the visa and any necessary residence permits have been obtained. Any money left over must be returned to the BES. Application forms are available from the Executive Secretary.

Closing Date: March 1st, September 1st, for notification within around four weeks.

Small Ecological Project Grants

Subjects: Any aspect of ecological research and ecological survey.

Eligibility: Open to ecological researchers.

Level of Study: Professional development.

Purpose: To promote all aspects of ecological research and ecological survey.

Type: Project grant.

Frequency: Four times yearly.

Value: Up to £1,000 towards the cost of travel, for the employment of casual and short-term assistance, and for the purchase of small items of equipment (which will usually remain the property of the BES). Grants are not given to cover the salary or wages of the applicant, nor are they given for full-time students to undertake their research or project studies.

Applications Procedure: Application form must be completed.

Closing Date: January 1st, April 1st, July 1st, October 1st.

Additional Information: Support will not normally be given to projects forming part of an expedition proposal. Repeat applications, for essentially the same project, will be rejected. All recipients will be required to submit a report on the work undertaken. Information about the timing of reports will be given to successful applicants. Published papers, reports to other organizations, etc., should include an acknowledgement of the support from the BES. Other conditions, which may be deemed necessary by the Ecological Affairs Committee, may be attached to the award of a Small Ecological Project Grant. Application forms are available from the Secretary, Ecological Affairs Committee. Coalbourn Trust Grants: the Coalbourn Trust is an independent trust which looks to the British Ecological Society to nominate suitable projects for funding. Recommendations for funding will be made from among the applicants for Small Ecological Project Grants and the same overall rules will apply. All applicants for Small Ecological Project Grants will automatically be eligible for funding from the Coalbourn Trust, and separate applications are not required.

Visiting Lectureship

Subjects: Ecology.

Eligibility: Open to ecologists who are acknowledged experts in a particular field with a good publication record over the previous five to ten years. Applications should be made by a potential sponsor who must be prepared to coordinate the visit so that at least two centres (universities, research institutions, etc.) are visited.

Level of Study: Professional development.

Purpose: To support visits of distinguished ecologists from abroad to lecture in the United Kingdom or the Republic of Ireland, or vice versa.

Type: Lectureship.

Frequency: Twice yearly.

Value: Up to £1,000 to cover travel costs.

Applications Procedure: Applications should include: a letter stating reasons for inviting the visitor, a CV, and a statement in support from the centre(s) to be visited.

Closing Date: September 1st for visits in April to September; March 1st for visits in October to March.

Additional Information: Applications should normally be made by a closing date at least six months before the intended visit, and successful awards will be published in the Bulletin so that members are informed of the visit, and further institutions may be included in the programme.

BRITISH FEDERATION OF WOMEN GRADUATES

British Federation of Women Graduates, 4 Mandeville Courtyard, 142 Battersea Park Road, London, SW11 4NB, England
Tel: 0171 498 8037
Fax: 0171 498 8037
Contact: The Secretary

BFWG Scholarship Fund

Subjects: Any subject.

Eligibility: Open to UK nationals studying in the UK or overseas. UK nationals living outside the UK who plan to continue studying outside the UK are not eligible. It is a condition that, save in the case of a one-year course, the candidate will have completed at least one year of graduate research by the beginning of the academic year in which the award is made. Awards are not made for the first year's research towards a doctorate, a two-year master's degree or taught courses. The award can also be made for postdoctoral research.

Level of Study: Postgraduate, Doctorate, Postdoctorate.

Type: Scholarship; grant.

No. of awards offered: One or two scholarships; some grants.

Frequency: Annual.

Value: Scholarships of £1,000; grants of £500/£750.

Country of Study: UK.

Closing Date: Early September.

Additional Information: The recipient must submit a written report within six months of concluding the research.

Kathleen Hall Memorial Fund

Subjects: Any subject.

Eligibility: Open to UK nationals studying in the UK or overseas. UK nationals living outside the UK who plan to continue studying outside the UK are not eligible. It is a condition that, save in the case of a one-year course, the candidate will have completed at least one year of graduate research by the beginning of the academic year in which the award is made. Awards are not made for the first year's research towards a doctorate, a two-year master's degree or taught course. The award can also be made for postdoctoral research.

Level of Study: Postgraduate, Doctorate.

Type: Fellowship.

No. of awards offered: One or more.

Frequency: Annual.

Value: £1,000.

Country of Study: UK.

Closing Date: Early September.

Additional Information: The recipient must submit a written report within six months of concluding the research.

Joseph Prize

Subjects: Architecture or engineering.

Eligibility: It is a condition that, save in the case of a one-year course, the candidate will have completed at least one year of graduate research by the beginning of the academic year in which the award is made. Awards are not made for the first year's research towards a doctorate, a two-year master's degree or taught courses. The award can also be made for postdoctoral research.

Level of Study: Postdoctorate, Undergraduate.

Type: Prize.

No. of awards offered: One.

Frequency: Annual.

Value: £500.

Study Establishment: A university or institution of university status in England.

Country of Study: England.

Applications Procedure: Applicants should write for details.

Closing Date: Early September.

Additional Information: The recipient must submit a written report within six months of concluding the research.

Rose Sidgwick Memorial Fellowship

Subjects: Any subject. Preference will be given to applicants working to improve the lives of other women.

Eligibility: Open to members of BFWG who are UK nationals, for twelve months research in the USA. Preference is given to applicants under 30 years of age, working to improve the lives of other women. It is a condition that, save in the case of a one-year course, the candidate will have completed at least one year of graduate research by the beginning of the academic year in which the award is made. The award can also be made for postdoctoral research.

Level of Study: Postgraduate, Postdoctorate.

Type: Fellowship.

No. of awards offered: One.

Frequency: Annual.

Value: Approximately US$16,000. The Fellowship does not cover travel.

Length of Study: Twelve months.

Country of Study: USA.

Closing Date: Early September.

Additional Information: Recipients must submit a written report within six months of concluding the research.

Johnston and Florence Stony Fund

Subjects: Research in biological, geological, meteorological or radiological science.

Eligibility: Open to UK nationals studying in the UK or overseas. UK nationals living outside the UK who plan to continue studying outside the UK are not eligible. It is a condition that, save in the case of a one-year course, the candidate will have completed at least one year of graduate research by the beginning of the academic year in which the award is made. Awards are not normally made for the first year's research towards a doctorate, a two-year master's degree or taught courses . The award can also be made for postdoctoral research.

Level of Study: Postgraduate, Doctorate.

Type: Studentship.

No. of awards offered: One.

Frequency: Annual.

Value: £1,000.

Country of Study: Australia, New Zealand, South Africa.

Closing Date: Early September.

Additional Information: The recipient must submit a written report within six months of concluding the research.

BRITISH HEART FOUNDATION

British Heart Foundation, 14 Fitzharding Street, London, W1H 4DH, England
Tel: 0171 935 0185
Contact: Valerie Mason, Research Funds Manager

The British Heart Foundation exists to encourage research into the causes, diagnosis, prevention and advances of cardiovascular disease; to inform doctors throughout the country of advances in the diagnosis, cure and treatment of heart diseases; and to improve facilities for treatment of heart patients where the National Health Service is unable to help

Clinical Science Fellowships

Subjects: Research relevant to the cardiovascular system.

Eligibility: Open to British citizens and persons who have been resident in the UK for a minimum of three years at the time of application. Candidates should be clinicians (aged approximately 25-30 years).

Level of Study: Professional development.

Purpose: To enable clinicians who have demonstrated an interest in and potential for research to be trained.

Type: Fellowship.

No. of awards offered: Variable.

Frequency: Three times per year.

Value: The award reimburses for salary (commensurate with seniority within the health service) and carries a consumables allowance of up to £5,000 per annum.

Length of Study: Up to 7 years.

Study Establishment: The first 3 years are spent in a basic science department, preferably, but not necessarily, away from the sponsoring department.

Country of Study: Based in UK, but research training period can be spent overseas.

Applications Procedure: Application should be made by the proposed Fellow on the appropriate form and with the approval of the head of department. The application must include a full research protocol and/or training programme together with the curriculum vitae of the proposed Fellow. Shortlisted applicants will normally be required to attend for interview. Application forms and further information are available on request.

Closing Date: Available on request.

John Fyffe Memorial Fellowship

Subjects: Research in the field of collagen disease and, in particular, the causes, diagnosis, treatment including surgical techniques, and the eventual elimination of the disease known as Marfan's Syndrome.

Eligibility: Open to British citizens and persons who have been resident in the UK for a minimum of three years at the time of application.

Level of Study: Professional development.

Purpose: To enable researchers to visit other centres working in the field in order to acquire first-hand knowledge and techniques so that they may be applied to research being undertaken in the UK.

Type: Fellowship.

No. of awards offered: Variable.

Frequency: Three times yearly.

Value: Up to £3,000 per annum.

Country of Study: UK or overseas.

Closing Date: Available on request.

Additional Information: Application forms and further information are available on request.

Intermediate Research Fellowships

Subjects: Research projects in the field of basic or applied clinical cardiology.

Eligibility: Open to British citizens or those who have been resident in the UK for a minimum of three years at the time of application.

Level of Study: Professional development.

Purpose: To enable highly qualified independent researchers to pursue their research objectives.

Type: Fellowship.

No. of awards offered: Variable.

Frequency: Three times yearly.

Value: A salary commensurate with seniority within the university and health service at registrar/first-year senior registrar level (or academic equivalent), and up to £7,000 per annum may be applied for to cover running expenses which must be fully justified.

Length of Study: A maximum of three years.

Country of Study: UK.

Applications Procedure: Application may be made on the appropriate form by the proposed Fellows or the supervisor, with the approval of the head of department. The application must include a full research protocol, together with the curriculum vitae of the proposed Fellow.

Closing Date: Available on request.

Additional Information: These Fellowships are unlikely to be awarded to those who are unable to obtain advancement within the health services.

Junior Research Fellowships

Subjects: Research projects in the field of basic or applied clinical cardiology.

Eligibility: Open to postgraduates who wish to be trained in academic research under the direct supervision of senior and experienced research workers. Candidates must be British citizens or have been resident in the UK for a minimum of three years at the time of application.

Level of Study: Postgraduate.

Purpose: To enable postgraduates to be trained in academic research.

Type: Fellowship.

No. of awards offered: Variable.

Frequency: Three times yearly.

Value: A salary, not to be higher than the top of the registrar scale or equivalent, and up to £5,000 per annum to cover running expenses.

Length of Study: A total of two years, but Junior Research Fellows may proceed to the second year only after the head of department has submitted, and the Foundation has approved, a progress report on the first year's work.

Country of Study: UK.

Applications Procedure: Applications should be made on the approved form by the planned supervisor and with the approval of the head of department. The application must include a full research protocol together with the curriculum vitae of the proposed Fellow. The head of department must confirm that no additional financial support is necessary in order to carry out the project.

Closing Date: Available on request.

Overseas Visiting Fellowships

Subjects: Basic or applied clinical cardiology.

Eligibility: Open to established research workers of proven outstanding talent able to contribute to the work of the host department.

Level of Study: Professional development.

Purpose: To enable senior overseas research workers to undertake research in the UK.

Type: Fellowship.

No. of awards offered: Varies.

Frequency: Three times yearly.

Value: Funds to cover the Fellow's salary and up to £5,000 per annum as a contribution towards research expenses. The applicant must confirm that no additional financial support is necessary in order to carry out the project. Application may be made for funds to cover economy travel fares for the Fellow and one dependant (the latter only being eligible for travel funds if the Fellow is to be resident in the UK for one year or more).

Length of Study: Up to two years.

Study Establishment: A recognized research centre in the UK.

Country of Study: UK.

Applications Procedure: Application must be made by the head of department in the UK institution on behalf of the Fellow and should include a full research protocol. The role of the visiting Fellow in the research should be clearly stated. A curriculum vitae of the proposed Fellow and two letters of recommendation from the Fellow's country of origin should be included.

Closing Date: Available on request.

Additional Information: These Fellowships are not given for training.

PhD Studentships

Subjects: Basic or applied clinical cardiology.

Eligibility: Open to candidates who have obtained a minimum of an upper second class honours degree.

Level of Study: Doctorate.

Purpose: To enable graduates to proceed to a PhD degree.

Type: Studentship.

No. of awards offered: Varies.

Frequency: Three times yearly.

Value: The level of stipend is set by the British Heart Foundation. Applicants may apply for funds to cover university fees. Up to £5,000 per annum may also be applied for to cover research consumables.

Length of Study: Three years.

Study Establishment: An appropriate university.

Country of Study: UK.

Applications Procedure: Applications are actually made by heads of department and may be made for named or unnamed candidates, although priority will be given to named candidates. Application should be made on the appropriate form and should include a full research protocol and curriculum vitae of the candidate (if known).

Closing Date: Available on request.

Research Awards

Subjects: Cardiovascular research.

Level of Study: Postdoctorate.

Purpose: Research into cardiovascular disease (basic or clinical).

Type: Research awards.

No. of awards offered: Limited by funding.

Frequency: Varies according to committee.

Value: Varies.

Length of Study: Varies.

Study Establishment: Universities, medical schools.

Country of Study: United Kingdom.

Applications Procedure: Contact BHF.

Closing Date: Varies according to committee.

Additional Information: Annual report available upon request.

Senior Research Fellowships

Subjects: Research projects in the field of basic or applied clinical cardiology.

Eligibility: Open to British citizens or persons who have been resident in the UK for a minimum of three years at the time of application. The applicant should have been engaged in original research for at least two years and have published results, and should show outstanding ability both in original thought and practical application. This ability should already have been recognized outside the applicant's institution by invitations to talk to societies both at home and abroad. The applicant's career plans should be academic medicine and research. Senior Research Fellowships are awarded to those thought likely to gain high office in teaching and research institutions.

Level of Study: Professional development.

Purpose: To enable researchers with an international reputation of outstanding ability to pursue their research interests.

Type: Fellowship.

No. of awards offered: Varies.

Frequency: Annual.

Value: Salary commensurate with seniority within the university and health service up to consultant level. Up to £10,000 per annum may be applied for to cover running expenses which should be fully justified.

Length of Study: Three years initially; may be extended to five years after submission of a progress report which has been judged to be satisfactory by the Foundation.

Country of Study: UK.

Applications Procedure: Applications should be made by the proposed Fellow on the appropriate form and with the approval of the head of department. The application must include a full research protocol

together with the curriculum vitae of the proposed Fellow. Shortlisted applicants will be required to attend for interview.

Closing Date: Available on request.

Additional Information: A Senior Research Fellow may apply to the Committee for a second 5-year period by the end of which it would be expected that the Fellow would have secured a permanent and more senior position. In this case an interview will be required.

Travelling Fellowships

Subjects: Basic or applied clinical cardiology.

Eligibility: Open to established research workers who are UK citizens and who are of proven outstanding talent. At the time of application the proposed Fellow should hold a post in a research institution of university with tenure of not less than five years.

Level of Study: Professional development.

Purpose: To enable established research workers to undertake research abroad, or acquire special knowledge which would assist them in their research in the UK after their return.

Type: Fellowship.

No. of awards offered: Varies.

Frequency: Three times yearly.

Value: The proposed Fellow may apply for funds to cover the cost of economy travel and a reasonable subsistence allowance at the place of work. It is expected that the Fellow's salary would continue to be paid by the university or institution in the UK during his or her absence abroad.

Length of Study: A period of up to 6 months.

Country of Study: Any country outside the UK.

Applications Procedure: Application must be made on the appropriate form together with details of the purpose of the visit and what the Fellow expects to gain as a result of the visit. A curriculum vitae of the applicant and a letter of acceptance by the host institution must be included in the application.

Closing Date: Available on request.

BRITISH INSTITUTE IN EASTERN AFRICA

British Institute in Eastern Africa, PO Box 30710, Nairobi, Kenya
Tel: 43330/43721
Fax: 43365
Contact: Director

Research Studentships and Graduate Scholarships

Subjects: Pre-Colonial history and archaeology in East Africa: field research.

Eligibility: Open to citizens of East African countries, the UK and the Commonwealth who are over 21 years of age. Candidates must have a BA or equivalent degree and graduate or undergraduate training in African studies, archaeology or social anthropology.

Level of Study: Postgraduate.

Type: Studentship; scholarship.

No. of awards offered: Varies.

Value: Varies.

Country of Study: Kenya, Tanzania, Uganda and other Eastern African countries.

Closing Date: Normally May 1st.

Additional Information: Small grants and assistance may be offered on a discretionary basis to scholars of other nationalities. Archaeological students may be required to assist in excavation carried out by the Institute's staff. Details of awards are published in the 'Archaeology Abroad' bulletin.

BRITISH INSTITUTE IN PARIS

British Institute in Paris, University of London, Senate House, Malet Street, London, WC1E 7HU, England
Tel: 0171 636 8000 ext.3920
Fax: 0171 580 8486
Contact: London Secretary

Quinn, Nathan and Edmond Scholarships

Subjects: French studies.

Eligibility: Open to citizens of the UK, the Irish Republic, or Commonwealth countries, who are graduates and possess sufficient knowledge of French to pursue their proposed studies.

Level of Study: Postgraduate.

Purpose: To assist postgraduate research in France.

Type: Scholarship.

No. of awards offered: One to two.

Frequency: Annual.

Value: £450 per month.

Length of Study: One to nine months.

Study Establishment: In Paris.

Country of Study: France.

Applications Procedure: Applications should be accompanied by a written recommendation from the candidate's professor or tutor. The name of one other academic referee must be given.

Closing Date: March 15th.

BRITISH INSTITUTE OF ARCHAEOLOGY AT ANKARA

British Institute of Archaeology at Ankara, 31-34 Gordon Square, London, WC1H 0PY, England
Tel: 0171 388 2361
Fax: 0171 388 2361
Contact: Assistant Secretary

Research Grants

Subjects: Archaeology and related subjects.

Eligibility: Open to citizens of the UK or other Commonwealth countries, who are qualified to undertake advanced research. Preference is given to research projects in areas in which the Institute is already interested.

Level of Study: Postgraduate, Doctorate, Postdoctorate.

Purpose: To aid research into the archaeology of Turkey, of all periods.

Type: Grants-in-aid.

No. of awards offered: Varies.

Frequency: Annual.

Value: Determined individually in regard to the level of work involved, qualifications and seniority of the applicant, and any other relevant factors.

Length of Study: Determined individually.

Study Establishment: At the Ankara institute or at other centres.

Country of Study: Turkey.

Applications Procedure: Application form must be completed.

Closing Date: November 1st.

Additional Information: Application forms are obtainable from the Assistant Secretary.

Travel Grants

Subjects: Archaeology and related subjects.

Eligibility: Open to graduates or undergraduates who are nationals of the UK or a Commonwealth country.

Level of Study: Postgraduate, Doctorate, Undergraduate.

Purpose: To enable students of archaeology or other relevant subjects to travel to and from Turkey for the purpose of familiarizing themselves with its archaeology and geography, and to visit its sites and museums.

Type: Travel grant.

No. of awards offered: Varies.

Frequency: Annual.

Value: Up to £500 paid in one lump sum.

Country of Study: Turkey.

Applications Procedure: No application form; applicants must submit CV, itinerary, costing, and two references.

Closing Date: February 1st, but prospective candidates should check closing date for applications.

BRITISH INSTITUTE OF PERSIAN STUDIES

British Institute of Persian Studies, 63 Old Street, London, EC1V 9HX, England
Tel: 0171 490 4404
Fax: 0171 490 4404
Contact: Juliet Dryden, Assistant Secretary

Research Fellowships and Bursaries

Subjects: Iranian art, archaeology, history, literature, linguistics, religion, philosophy.

Eligibility: Open to undergraduate, postgraduate and postdoctoral students of the UK and the Commonwealth.

Level of Study: Postgraduate, Doctorate, Postdoctorate, Undergraduate.

Purpose: To enable the study of Iranian culture.

Type: Fellowships; bursaries.

No. of awards offered: Two or more fellowships and four bursaries.

Frequency: Annual.

Value: Travel grants up to £1,000; major research grants £3,000; undergraduate bursary grants £800.

Length of Study: One academic year.

Country of Study: Iran, except for periods when access is restricted; in this case, work will be permitted on original Iranian material in institutions outside Iran.

Applications Procedure: There is no application form for undergraduate applications, but postgraduates must submit a completed form.

Closing Date: April 21st.

Additional Information: The Selectors reserve the right to vary the amount of the awards in the event of there being two or more candidates of equal merit.

BRITISH INSTITUTE OF RADIOLOGY

British Institute of Radiology, 36 Portland Place, London, W1N 4AT, England
Tel: 0171 580 4085
Fax: 0171 255 3209
Contact: Chief Executive

Flude Memorial Prize

Subjects: Radiology.

Eligibility: Open to members of the Institute.

No. of awards offered: One.

Frequency: Annual.

Value: £250.

Closing Date: August 1st.

Nic McNally Memorial Prize

Subjects: Radiology.

Eligibility: Open to young scientists under 30 years of age at the time of application and employed in a scientific post. Applicants need not be members of the Institute.

Level of Study: Unrestricted.

Type: Travel Grant.

No. of awards offered: One.

Frequency: Annual.

Value: £250.

Study Establishment: Travel to either a scientific meeting or a laboratory.

Closing Date: August 1st.

Stanley Melville Memorial Award

Subjects: Radiology.

Eligibility: Open to members of the Institute who are under 35 years of age.

Purpose: To enable a member of the Institute to visit clinics and institutions abroad.

No. of awards offered: One.

Frequency: Triennially (1999).

Value: Approximately £250.

Country of Study: Any country.

Closing Date: December 31st of the year preceding the year of the award.

Additional Information: While the successful applicant will not be obliged to write a formal report on his or her visit, it is hoped that he or she will submit a description of the work seen during the visit in a form suitable for publication in the Journal.

Nycomed Scandinavian Scholarship

Subjects: Radiology: diagnostic or interventional procedures concerned with intravascular contrast media.

Eligibility: Open to diagnostic radiologists of senior registrar or junior consultant status. Preference is given to members of the Institute.

Purpose: To enable a diagnostic radiologist to gain in-depth experience abroad.

Type: Scholarship.

No. of awards offered: One.

Frequency: Annual.

Value: Up to £5,000.

Length of Study: Up to 2 months.

Study Establishment: One or more academic departments of radiology.

Country of Study: Scandinavian countries.

Closing Date: End August.

Additional Information: The successful Scholar will be required to produce a report of up to 1000 words for publication in the British Journal of Radiology bulletin.

Travel Bursary

Subjects: Radiology.

Eligibility: Open to members of the BIR who are under 35.

Purpose: To present a paper at a national or international forum.

No. of awards offered: One.

Frequency: Annual.

Value: Up to £500.

Closing Date: August 1st.

THE BRITISH LIBRARY

The British Library, 2 Sheraton Street, London, W1V 4BH, England
Tel: 0171 412 7044
Fax: 0171 412 7251
Email: bnbrf@bl.uk
www: http://www.portico.bl.uk:70/0/portico/servicesresearch/rddbnb.txt
Contact: BNB Research Fund Secretariat

BNB Research Fund

Subjects: The three areas of particular interest are the study of the relations between bookseller, librarian and publisher, the general theme of publications and their use within the community, and the impact of new technology on all aspects of the book world.

Eligibility: Applications open to all, but subject of research is restricted to UK and awards are only payable in UK.

Level of Study: Unrestricted.

Purpose: To support research into the book and information worlds in the UK.

No. of awards offered: Varies.

Frequency: Two or three times per year.

Value: Varies.

Country of Study: UK.

Applications Procedure: Booklet available; outline proposals welcomed.

Closing Date: Two or three per year, details available from the Secretary.

Additional Information: The Fund has limited resources and directs its efforts towards areas which do not qualify for research funding from other sources. Money cannot be allocated, however, for the preparation of historical bibliographies, nor to support students in undertaking graduate or postgraduate courses. The Fund is administered by a committee whose members represent the Library Association, Publishers' Association, Booksellers' Association, Book Trust, British Council, Royal Society, Aslib, the Joint Committee of the Five Copyright Libraries and the British Library.

BRITISH LUNG FOUNDATION

British Lung Foundation, New Garden House, 78 Hatton Garden, London, EC1N 8JR, England
Tel: 0171 831 5831
Fax: 0171 831 5832
Contact: Alex Mazzetta

Fellowships and Project/Equipment Grants

Subjects: Respiratory diseases.

Eligibility: Open to candidates wishing to carry out research in the UK.

Level of Study: Postgraduate, Postdoctorate, Professional development.

Purpose: To encourage the promotion of medical research into the prevention, treatment, alleviation and cure of chest and lung diseases.

No. of awards offered: Approximately 20 per year, split between fellowships/project/equipment grants.

Frequency: Twice yearly.

Value: Equipment grant maximum £5,000; Project grant (salary and running costs) maximum £85,000; Fellowship no maximum - salary plus 10% expenses.

Country of Study: UK.

Applications Procedure: Application forms are available from the BLF.

Closing Date: 1st week of March (first round), last week of August (second round).

BRITISH MEDICAL AND DENTAL STUDENTS' TRUST

British Medical and Dental Students' Trust, Mackintosh House, 120 Blythswood Street, Glasgow, G2 4EH, Scotland
Tel: 0141 221 5858
Fax: 0141 228 1208
Contact: Secretary

Scholarships and Travel Grants

Subjects: Medicine and dental medicine.

Eligibility: Open to clinical students from British medical and dental schools and hospitals of any nationality.

Purpose: To enable medical and dental students to study and travel outside the UK.

Type: Scholarship.

No. of awards offered: Approximately 160 scholarships and travel grants per annum.

Frequency: Twice yearly.

Value: £100-£500.

Length of Study: From 2 weeks to 3 months.

Country of Study: Any.

Applications Procedure: Application form, protocol for elective, confirmation of elective from hospital to be visited.

Closing Date: 31 January and 31 July.

BRITISH MEDICAL ASSOCIATION

Board of Science and Education, British Medical Association, Tavistock Square, London, WC1H 9JP, England
Tel: 383 6351
Fax: 383 6233
Contact: Ms H J Glanville

Brackenbury Research Award

Subjects: Research of immediate practical importance to public health, to a medico-political or medico-sociological problem, or to an educational question, whether general, medical or postgraduate.

Eligibility: Open to members of the BMA.

Level of Study: Postdoctorate.

Purpose: To assist research.

No. of awards offered: One.

Frequency: Triennially (1999).

Value: Approximately £1,000.

Length of Study: One year.

Applications Procedure: Application form must be completed; these are available in January of the award year.

Closing Date: End March.

John William Clark Research Award

Subjects: The causes of blindness.

Eligibility: Open to members of the BMA.

Level of Study: Postdoctorate.

Purpose: To assist research.

No. of awards offered: One.

Frequency: Annual.

Value: Approximately £6,000.

Length of Study: One year.

Applications Procedure: Application forms are available.

Closing Date: End March.

Additional Information: Advertised in January.

Joan Dawkins Fellowship

Subjects: Biomedicine.

Eligibility: Projects must relate to the UK only.

Level of Study: To be defined.

Purpose: To encourage, foster and maintain the highest possible standards in medical practice, medical learning and research.

Type: Fellowship.

No. of awards offered: To be defined.

Frequency: Annual.

Value: Approximately £50,000.

Length of Study: One year.

Country of Study: UK.

Applications Procedure: Application forms are available in January.

Closing Date: End of March.

Vera Down Research Award

Subjects: Disseminated sclerosis, muscular dystrophy and neurological disorders.

Eligibility: Open to registered medical practitioners.

Level of Study: Postdoctorate.

Purpose: To assist research.

No. of awards offered: One.

Frequency: Annual.

Value: Approximately £9,500.

Length of Study: One year.

Applications Procedure: Application forms are available in January.

Closing Date: End March.

Additional Information: Advertised in January.

T P Gunton Research Award

Subjects: Health education with special regard to the earlier diagnosis and treatment of cancer.

Eligibility: Open to both medical and non-medical scientists.

Level of Study: Unrestricted.

Purpose: To assist research.

No. of awards offered: One.

Frequency: Annual.

Value: Approximately £11,000.

Length of Study: One year.

Applications Procedure: Application forms are available in January.

Closing Date: End March.

Additional Information: Advertised in January.

Katherine Bishop Harman Research Award

Subjects: Research into the diminution and avoidance of risks to health and life in pregnancy and childbearing.

Eligibility: Open to medical practitioners registered in the UK or any country at any time forming part of the British Empire.

Level of Study: Postdoctorate.

Purpose: To assist research.

No. of awards offered: One.

Frequency: Biennially (1998).

Value: Approximately £600.

Length of Study: One year.

Applications Procedure: Application forms are available in January.

Closing Date: End March.

Additional Information: Advertised in January 1998.

Nathaniel Bishop Harman Research Award

Subjects: Hospital practice.

Eligibility: Open to registered medical practitioners on the staff of a hospital in GB or Northern Ireland who are not members of the staff of a recognized undergraduate or postgraduate medical school.

Level of Study: Postdoctorate.

Purpose: To assist research.

No. of awards offered: One.

Frequency: Biennially (1997).

Value: Approximately £600.

Length of Study: One year.

Applications Procedure: Application forms are available in January.

Closing Date: End March.

Additional Information: Advertised in January 1997.

Sir Charles Hastings and Charles Oliver Hawthorne Research Awards

Subjects: General practice; observation, research and record-keeping.

Eligibility: Open to members of the BMA engaged in general practice.

Level of Study: Postdoctorate.

Purpose: To assist research.

No. of awards offered: Two.

Frequency: Biennially (1998).

Value: Approximately £1,750 (Hastings Award); approximately £575 (Hawthorne Award).

Length of Study: One year.

Applications Procedure: Application forms are available in January.

Closing Date: End March.

Additional Information: Advertised in January 1998.

Doris Hillier Research Award

Subjects: Rheumatism, arthritis and/or Parkinson's disease.

Eligibility: Open to registered medical practitioners.

Level of Study: Postdoctorate.

Purpose: To assist research.

No. of awards offered: One.

Frequency: Annual.

Value: Approximately £14,000.

Length of Study: One year.

Applications Procedure: Application forms are available in January.

Closing Date: End March.

Additional Information: Advertised in January.

Geoffrey Holt, Ivy Powell and Edith Walsh Research Awards

Subjects: Cardiovascular and respiratory disease.

Eligibility: Open to members of the BMA.

Level of Study: Postdoctorate.

Purpose: To assist research.

No. of awards offered: Three.

Frequency: Annual.

Value: Approximately £1,500 (Holt and Walsh Awards); approximately £200 (Powell Award).

Length of Study: One year.

Applications Procedure: Application forms are available in January.

Closing Date: End March.

Additional Information: Advertised in January.

Insole Research Award

Subjects: The causation, prevention or treatment of disease.

Eligibility: Open to members of the BMA.

Level of Study: Postdoctorate.

Purpose: To assist research.

No. of awards offered: One.

Frequency: Biennially (1997).

Value: Approximately £500.

Length of Study: One year.

Applications Procedure: Application forms are available in January.

Closing Date: End March.

Additional Information: Advertised in January 1997.

T V James Research Fellowship

Subjects: The nature, causation, prevention or treatment of bronchial asthma.

Eligibility: Open to members of the BMA.

Level of Study: Postdoctorate.

Purpose: To assist research.

Type: Fellowship.

No. of awards offered: One.

Frequency: Annual.

Value: Approximately £20,000.

Length of Study: One year; renewable.

Applications Procedure: Application forms are available in January.

Closing Date: End March.

Additional Information: Advertised in January.

Albert McMaster and Helen Tomkinson Research Awards

Subjects: Cancer research, including health education.

Eligibility: Open to members of the BMA.

Level of Study: Postdoctorate.

Purpose: To assist research.

No. of awards offered: Two.

Frequency: Annual.

Value: Approximately £4,000 (McMaster Award); approximately £6,000 (Tomkinson Award).

Length of Study: One year.

Applications Procedure: Application forms are available in January.

Closing Date: End March.

Additional Information: Advertised in January.

Middlemore Research Award

Subjects: Any branch of ophthalmic medicine or surgery.

Eligibility: Open to all medical practitioners.

Level of Study: Postdoctorate.

Purpose: To assist research.

No. of awards offered: One.

Frequency: Triennially (1999).

Value: Approximately £1,000.

Length of Study: One year.

Applications Procedure: Application forms are available in January.

Closing Date: End March.

C H Milburn Research Award

Subjects: Medical jurisprudence and/or forensic medicine.

Eligibility: Open to registered medical practitioners.

Level of Study: Postdoctorate.

Purpose: To assist research.

No. of awards offered: One.

Frequency: Biennially (1998).

Value: Approximately £600.

Length of Study: One year.

Applications Procedure: Application forms are available in January.

Closing Date: End March.

Additional Information: Advertised in January 1998.

Doris Odlum Research Award

Subjects: Mental health.

Eligibility: Open to medical practitioners registered in the British Commonwealth or the Republic of Ireland.

Level of Study: Postdoctorate.

Purpose: To assist research.

No. of awards offered: One.

Frequency: Biennially (1998).

Value: Approximately £550.

Length of Study: One year.

Applications Procedure: Application forms are available in January.

Closing Date: End March.

Additional Information: Advertised in January 1998.

H C Roscoe Fellowship

Subjects: Elimination of the common cold and/or the diseases of the human respiratory system.

Eligibility: Open to members of the BMA and non-medical scientists working in association with a BMA member.

Purpose: To assist research.

Type: Fellowship.

No. of awards offered: One.

Frequency: Annual.

Value: Approximately £70,000.

Length of Study: 1 or 2 years.

Applications Procedure: Application forms are available in January.

Closing Date: End of March.

Additional Information: Advertised in January.

Margaret Temple Fellowship

Subjects: Psychiatry and mental health.

Eligibility: Projects must relate to the UK.

Level of Study: Unrestricted.

Purpose: For research into schizophrenia.

Type: Fellowship.

No. of awards offered: One.

Frequency: Annual.

Value: Approximately £24,000.

Length of Study: One year.

Applications Procedure: Application forms are available in January.

Closing Date: End of March each year.

Elizabeth Wherry Research Award

Subjects: Kidney treatment.

Eligibility: Open to registered medical practitioners.

Level of Study: Postdoctorate.

Purpose: To assist research.

No. of awards offered: One.

Frequency: Annual.

Value: Approximately £500.

Length of Study: One year.

Applications Procedure: Application forms are available in January.

Closing Date: End of March.

Additional Information: Advertised in January.

THE BRITISH NUTRITION FOUNDATION

The British Nutrition Foundation, High Holborn House, London, WC1V 6RQ, England
Tel: 0171 404 6504
Fax: 0171 404 6747
Contact: Fanny Griffin

The BNF/Nestle Bursary Scheme

Subjects: Nutritional problems associated with adults in apparent health and disease states, including special areas of maternal health and infant nutrition.

Eligibility: Open to medical students at UK medical schools.

Level of Study: Undergraduate.

Purpose: To help selected medical students to undertake an elective concerned with nutritional problems encountered in Third World countries.

Type: Bursary.

No. of awards offered: Up to twelve.

Frequency: Annual.

Value: Up to £500 to reimburse travel, accommodation, etc.

Country of Study: Third World countries.

Applications Procedure: Application form needs to be completed, with an outline of the proposed study and a reference from the medical school.

Closing Date: Normally January 31st.

Additional Information: Two copies of a detailed report of the study are required within five months of returning to the UK.

The Denis Burkitt Study Awards

Subjects: Public health and hygiene; social/preventive medicine; dietetics.

Eligibility: Open to UK and Irish nationals.

Level of Study: Postgraduate, Undergraduate.

Purpose: To help medical and nutrition science students, who wish to undertake elective or other studies in developing nations on food and nutrition, and their relationship to health and disease within any age group.

Type: Study Award.

No. of awards offered: Ten.

Frequency: Annual.

Value: £750.

Applications Procedure: Application form must be completed - details are sent to medical schools in the autumn. They can also be obtained from the British Nutrition Foundation at that time.

Closing Date: About January 20th - although it varies from year to year.

BRITISH PAEDIATRIC ASSOCIATION

British Paediatric Association, 5 St Andrew's Place, Regents Park, London, NW1 4LB, England
Tel: 0171 486 6151
Fax: 0171 486 6009
Contact: Ms B A Pettit, Fellowship Administrator

*Allen & Hanburys Research Award

Subjects: Paediatrics.

Eligibility: Open to UK residents who are paediatricians or research workers who are at least registrar/lecturer status up to those who are consultants/senior lecturers of not more than five years' standing.

Purpose: To encourage young paediatricians or research scientists working in the field of child health to travel to academic centres overseas to learn new research techniques, to establish collaborative research or to acquire new clinical skills.

No. of awards offered: Varies.

Frequency: Annual.

Value: Up to £3,000.

Country of Study: Anywhere outside the UK.

Closing Date: End September.

Heinz Fellowships (Types A and C)

Subjects: Paediatrics.

Eligibility: Type A Fellowships are open to paediatricians from any part of the Commonwealth who will benefit from meeting UK paediatricians and seeing something of their work; preference is given in general to applicants from developing countries who are not otherwise likely to visit the UK. Type C Fellowships are open to UK paediatricians in the early years of professional life.

Level of Study: Professional development.

Type: Fellowship.

No. of awards offered: Varies.

Frequency: Annual.

Value: To cover the cost of air fares and living expenses.

Length of Study: Up to 12 weeks (Type A); or for a short working visit to a centre for up to three months, teaching or conducting research that will benefit the Fellow and hosts (Type C).

Country of Study: UK (Type A) or a developing country (Type C).

Applications Procedure: Application form to be completed plus professional diplomas/certificates.

Closing Date: 31 January (Type A); 31 January and 31 July (Type C).

BRITISH SCHOOL AT ATHENS

British School at Athens, Odos Souedias 52, Athens, GR 106 76, Greece
Tel: 00 301 721 0974
Fax: 00 301 723 6560
Contact: Assistant Director

Hector and Elizabeth Catling Bursary

Subjects: Research in Greek studies: archaeology, art, history, language, literature, religion, ethnography, anthropology, geography of any period, and all branches of archaeological science.

Eligibility: Open to researchers of British, Irish or Commonwealth nationality.

Level of Study: Postgraduate, Doctorate, Postdoctorate.

Type: Bursary.

No. of awards offered: One.

Frequency: When funds permit, usually annual.

Value: Up to £500, to assist in travel and maintenance costs incurred in fieldwork, to pay for the use of scientific or other specialized equipment in or outside a laboratory in Greece or elsewhere, and to buy necessary supplies. The bursary is not intended for publication costs, nor can it be awarded to an excavation or field survey team.

Country of Study: Greece; Cyprus.

Applications Procedure: There are no application forms. Applicants should send a CV and state concisely the nature of the intended work, a breakdown of budget, the amount requested from the Fund, and how this will be spent. Applications should include two sealed letters of reference. Bursary holders must submit a short report to the Committee on completion of the project. Recipients cannot reapply to the Fund the following year.

Closing Date: December 15th for notification by end February.

Macmillan-Rodewald Studentship, School Studentship, Cary Studentship

Subjects: Research into the archaeology, architecture, art, history, language, literature, religion or topography of Greece in ancient, medieval or modern times.

Eligibility: Open to graduates of British, Irish or Commonwealth nationality.

Level of Study: Postgraduate, Doctorate, Postdoctorate.

Type: Studentship.

No. of awards offered: Three.

Frequency: Annual.

Value: Macmillan-Rodewald Studentship: 15% greater than the basic British Academy grant. School and Cary Studentships: 5% greater than the basic British Academy grant.

Length of Study: One year; renewable on reapplication.

Study Establishment: The School.

Country of Study: Greece.

Applications Procedure: Applicants should submit a CV and a statement of their proposed course of study with reasons for pursuing it in Greece. Applications should include the names of two referees.

Closing Date: May 1st.

Additional Information: The Student is required to spend a minimum of eight months in Greece, normally residing in the School when in Athens, and to undertake such duties in and for the School as the Director enjoins.

For further information contact:
British School at Athens, 31-34 Gordon Square, London, WC1H 0PY, England
Tel: 0171 387 8029
Fax: 0171 383 0781
Contact: The Secretary

THE BRITISH SCHOOL AT ROME

The British School at Rome, Piazzale W Churchill 5 (gia Via Gramsci 61), Rome, 00197, Italy
Tel: 00 39 6 3230743
Fax: 00 39 6 3221201
Contact: The Registrar

Abbey Scholarship in Painting

Subjects: Painting.

Eligibility: Open to UK, American or Commonwealth citizens of either sex.

Level of Study: Unrestricted.

Purpose: To give exceptionally promising emergent painters the opportunity to work in Rome.

Type: Scholarship.

No. of awards offered: One.

Frequency: Annual.

Value: £4,500, plus board and lodging at BSR.

Length of Study: Nine months.

Study Establishment: The British School at Rome.

Country of Study: Italy.

Applications Procedure: Application form must be completed.

Closing Date: Early December.

Archaeological Fieldwork Grants

Subjects: Archaeological excavation, post-excavation and research projects in Italy.

Eligibility: Open to individuals or teams from British and Commonwealth universities.

Level of Study: Postdoctorate.

Type: Grant.

No. of awards offered: Varies.

Frequency: Annual.

Value: Varies. Priority will be given to projects undertaken in collaboration with the School.

Country of Study: Italy.

Applications Procedure: Applicants should write to the Director with an outline of the proposed project and collaboration with the school.

Closing Date: Early January.

Balsdon Fellowship

Subjects: Arts and humanities; fine and applied arts.

Eligibility: Open to British and Commonwealth graduates.

Level of Study: Postdoctorate.

Purpose: To enable senior scholars engaged in research to spend a period in Rome for furtherance of their studies.

Type: Fellowship.

No. of awards offered: One.

Frequency: Annual.

Value: £650 plus board and lodging at BSR.

Length of Study: Three months.

Study Establishment: BSR.

Country of Study: Italy.

Applications Procedure: Application form must be completed.

Closing Date: Early January.

Hugh Last Award

Subjects: Classical antiquity: other things being equal, preference may be given to applications from scholars working in the field of the religious history of classical antiquity or the history of the Roman Republic.

Eligibility: Open to established individual scholars, who are graduates of a British or Commonwealth university.

Level of Study: Postdoctorate.

Purpose: To enable scholars to collect research material concerning classical antiquity.

No. of awards offered: Varies.

Frequency: Annual.

Value: £150 per month plus £180 travel plus board and lodging at the BSR.

Length of Study: One to four months.

Study Establishment: The BSR.

Country of Study: Italy.

Applications Procedure: Application form must be completed.

Closing Date: Early January.

Additional Information: The award may be used to cover the expenses of visits to Italy for the collection of material (but excludes any archaeological or other excavations or surveys and any work on Roman Britain).

Hugh Last Fellowship

Subjects: Ancient civilisations.

Eligibility: Open to British and Commonwealth graduates.

Level of Study: Postdoctorate.

Purpose: To enable senior scholars to collect research material concerning classical antiquity.

Type: Fellowship.

No. of awards offered: One.

Frequency: Annual.

Value: £650 plus board and lodging at BSR.

Length of Study: Three months.

Study Establishment: BSR.

Country of Study: Italy.

Applications Procedure: Application form must be completed.

Closing Date: Early January.

Rome Awards

Subjects: Archaeology; art history; history and literature of Italy.

Eligibility: Open to candidates of either sex who are of British or Commonwealth nationality.

Level of Study: Postgraduate, Doctorate, Postdoctorate.

Purpose: To enable persons engaged in research, either for a higher degree or at the postdoctoral level, to spend a period in Rome, in furtherance of their studies.

Type: Grant.

No. of awards offered: Varies.

Frequency: Annual.

Value: £150 per month plus £180 travel plus board and lodging at BSR.

Length of Study: 1-4 months.

Study Establishment: The BSR.

Country of Study: Italy.

Applications Procedure: Application form must be completed.

Closing Date: Early January.

Rome Scholarships in Ancient, Medieval & Later Italian Studies

Subjects: Archaeology; art history; history and literature of Italy.

Eligibility: Open to UK or Commonwealth citizens of either sex.

Level of Study: Postgraduate, Doctorate, Postdoctorate.

Purpose: To enable persons engaged in research, either for a higher degree or at the postdoctoral level, to spend a period in Rome in furtherance of their studies.

Type: Scholarship.

No. of awards offered: Usually not more than two.

Frequency: Annual.

Value: £4,000 (plus board and lodging at BSR).

Length of Study: Nine months.

Study Establishment: The British School at Rome.

Country of Study: Italy.

Applications Procedure: Application form must be completed.

Closing Date: Early January.

Rome Scholarships in the Fine Arts

Subjects: Painting, printmaking, sculpture, architecture and other suitable media.

Eligibility: Open to UK or Commonwealth citizens of either sex. Candidates for the architecture scholarship must have passed the RIBA Part II or its recognised equivalent.

Level of Study: Unrestricted.

Purpose: To give emergent and mid-career artists and architects the opportunity of working in Rome.

Type: Scholarship.

No. of awards offered: Varies.

Frequency: Annual.

Value: £4,500, plus board and lodging at BSR.

Length of Study: Three to nine months.

Study Establishment: The British School at Rome.

Country of Study: Italy.

Applications Procedure: Application form must be completed.

Closing Date: Early December.

Sargant Fellowship

Subjects: Sculpture; drawing and painting; architecture and town planning.

Eligibility: Open to British and Commonwealth students.

Level of Study: Unrestricted.

Purpose: To enable distinguished artists and architects to spend 3-9 months in Rome.

Type: Fellowship.

No. of awards offered: Varies.

Frequency: Annual.

Value: £1,000 per month plus £500 travel plus board and lodging at BSR.

Length of Study: 3-9 months.

Study Establishment: BSR.

Country of Study: Italy.

Applications Procedure: Please apply to BSR for precise procedure.

Closing Date: January.

BRITISH SCHOOL OF ARCHAEOLOGY IN IRAQ

British School of Archaeology in Iraq, 31-34 Gordon Square, London, WC1H 0PY, England
Tel: 0171 733 8912
Contact: Honorary Secretary

Grants and Travel Grants

Subjects: Archaeology, history and languages of Iraq from the earliest time to AD1700.

Eligibility: Open to UK or Commonwealth citizens who are undergraduates or postgraduates with a knowledge of Western-Asiatic archaeology.

Level of Study: Postgraduate, Postdoctorate.

Type: Grant; travel grant.

No. of awards offered: Varies.

Value: Usually between £770 and £3,350, depending on the nature of the research.

Length of Study: One academic year.

Country of Study: Iraq, when possible, for at least some of the period of tenure. Until work in Iraq can be resumed, grants are available for studying primary material outside Iraq, whether in the field or in museums.

Applications Procedure: No application form; written applications are not to exceed three pages, including CV.

Closing Date: April 30th.

Additional Information: Two references are required.

BRITISH SCHOOL OF ARCHAEOLOGY IN JERUSALEM

British School of Archaeology in Jerusalem, Top Flat, 21 Buccleuch Place, Edinburgh, EH8 9LN, Scotland
Tel: 0131 650 3975
Fax: 0131 650 3975
Contact: Dr L Maguire

Jerusalem Scholarship

Subjects: Levantine archaeology, history, architecture or epigraphy of any period from the Prehistoric to the Ottoman: research.

Eligibility: Applicants should be citizens of a Commonwealth country, and should normally be graduates of a Commonwealth university.

Level of Study: Postgraduate.

Purpose: To aid research into topics of Levantine archaeology, history, architecture or epigraphy, necessitating eight months residence in the area of postgraduate standard.

Type: Scholarship.

No. of awards offered: One.

Frequency: Annual.

Value: Varies depending on funds available (£6,000 in 1995).

Length of Study: At least eight months.

Study Establishment: British School of Archaeology in Jerusalem.

Country of Study: Israel.

Applications Procedure: Applicants are required to submit a summary of their proposed research, which should normally be of a postgraduate standard.

Closing Date: February 1st.

Additional Information: A report suitable for publication should be produced by the Scholar within two years of the conclusion of the period for which the award has been made.

Travel Grant

Subjects: Archaeology and related fields.

Eligibility: Applicants should be citizens of a Commonwealth country.

Purpose: To enable students to participate in the School's excavations or gain experience in a related field. Short-term projects will also be considered.

Type: Travel grant.

No. of awards offered: Several.

Frequency: Annual.

Value: Varies.

Country of Study: Israel and the area.

Closing Date: February 1st.

THE BRITISH SCHOOLS AND UNIVERSITIES FOUNDATION, INC

Hon UK Representative, 6 Windmill Hill, Hampstead, London, NW3 6RU, England
Tel: 0171 435 4648
Contact: Mrs S Wiltshire OBE BSc

Scholarships

Subjects: All subjects.

Eligibility: Scholarships are open to UK and US scholars and students.

Level of Study: Postgraduate, Doctorate, Professional development.

Purpose: To promote, foster and assist the education and academic work of British scholars and students at American educational institutions, and of American scholars and students at British educational institutions.

Type: Scholarship.

No. of awards offered: Four to six.

Frequency: Annual.

Value: US$10,000 maximum.

Study Establishment: USA educational institutions (UK candidates) or UK educational institutions (US candidates).

Country of Study: USA or UK.

Applications Procedure: Application form can be obtained from representative. Please enclose SAE with request.

Closing Date: March 1st, commencing the following September.

For further information contact:
British Schools and Universities Foundation, Inc, Suite 1006, 575 Madison Avenue, New York, NY, 10022, USA
Contact: Honorary Secretary

BRITISH SMALL ANIMAL VETERINARY ASSOCIATION CLINICAL STUDIES TRUST FUND LIMITED

British Small Animal Veterinary Association, Clinical Studies Trust Fund Ltd, 138 Kingston Road, Staines, Middlesex, TW18 1BL, England
Tel: 017844 52048
Fax: 017844 57232
Contact: Mr J J Oliver, BVet Med MRCVS

CSTF Award

Subjects: Small animal veterinary medicine and surgery.

Eligibility: Open to veterinary surgeons currently working in UK universities, centres of learning, or veterinary practices.

Level of Study: Professional development.

Purpose: To advance the science of small animal medicine and surgery, and further public education therein.

Type: Award.

No. of awards offered: Varies.

Frequency: Varies; dependent on funds available.

Value: Varies.

Length of Study: 1-3 years.

Country of Study: UK.

Applications Procedure: Applicants should write for details.

Additional Information: Projects must involve clinical cases only; no experimental animals.

BRITISH SOCIETY FOR THE STUDY OF ORTHODONTICS

BSSO Office, Eastman Dental Hospital, 256 Gray's Inn Road, London, WC1X 8LD, England
Tel: 0171 837 2193
Fax: 0171 837 2193
Contact: Honorary Secretary

*Chapman Prize

Subjects: An essay on orthodontics or an allied subject.

Eligibility: Open to members of BSSO holding a recognized orthodontic diploma or degree and within fifteen years of initial qualification.

Purpose: To promote research in orthodontics.

No. of awards offered: One.

Frequency: Annual.

Value: £750.

Closing Date: March 31st.

Additional Information: The essay shoud be no more than 8,000 words.

*Houston Research Scholarship

Subjects: Orthodontics.

Eligibility: Open to members of BSSO within fifteen years of initial dental qualification.

Purpose: To allow the scholar to pursue an academic or clinically based research project which will promote the specialty of orthodontics.

Type: Scholarship.

No. of awards offered: One.

Frequency: Annual.

Value: Up to £3,000.

Country of Study: UK or abroad as approved.

Closing Date: July 1st.

Additional Information: There may be a significant travel component to enable the scholar to study in another centre in the UK or overseas but the most significant factor will be the quality of the research proposed.

BRITISH SOCIOLOGICAL ASSOCIATION

British Sociological Association, Unit 3G, Mountjoy Research Centre, Stockton Road, Durham, DH1 3UR, England
Tel: 0191 383 0839
Fax: 0191 383 0782
Email: BSA.Admin@durham.ac.uk
Contact: Executive Secretary

BSA Support Fund

Subjects: Sociology.

Eligibility: Open to current paid-up members of the BSA, resident in the UK.

Level of Study: Unrestricted.

Purpose: To support BSA members who are on low incomes to pursue their research interests in sociology.

Type: Support fund.

No. of awards offered: Up to twenty per year.

Frequency: Throughout the year.

Value: Up to £120 per annum, to cover costs associated with research, but not tuition fees or text book purchase.

Country of Study: UK.

Applications Procedure: Applications should take the form of a letter stating: the purpose for which the grant is intended; an indication of the amount of the costs involved; a brief supporting statement, including a note of applicant's financial and work situation; and (for postgraduate applicants) a letter of support from their supervisor.

BRITISH TRAVEL EDUCATIONAL TRUST

c/o Career Concepts Ltd, 37 St Barnabas Street, London, SW1W 8QB, England
Tel: 0171 730 8253
Fax: 0171 730 7935
Contact: Julia Watson

*Travelling Bursaries

Subjects: Tourism.

Eligibility: Open to UK residents working in the tourism industry and educational establishments and to academic staff involved in teaching tourism studies. Not available to undergraduate or postgraduate students.

Purpose: To promote education in tourism. The Trust offers grants for research projects of practical value to the British tourism industry in the form of travelling bursaries.

Frequency: Dependent on funds available.

Value: Detailed costings should be submitted with each application and are considered by the Trustees.

Country of Study: Any country.

Closing Date: Proposals are considered in spring and autumn.

BRITISH VETERINARY ASSOCIATION

British Veterinary Association, 7 Mansfield Street, London, W1M 0AT, England
Tel: 0171 636 6541
Fax: 0171 637 0620
Contact: Mrs Helena Cotton

Harry Steele-Bodger Memorial Travelling Scholarship

Subjects: Veterinary science, agriculture.

Eligibility: Open to graduates of veterinary schools in the UK or the Republic of Ireland who have been qualified for not more than three years, and to penultimate or final year students at those schools.

Level of Study: Unrestricted.

Purpose: To further the aims and aspirations of the late Harry Steele-Bodger.

Type: Scholarship.

No. of awards offered: One.

Frequency: At least once every four years.

Value: Approximately £1,100.

Study Establishment: A veterinary or agricultural research institute or some other course of study approved by the Governing Committee.

Country of Study: Worldwide.

Applications Procedure: Application forms are available on request.

Closing Date: April.

Additional Information: Recipients must be prepared to submit a record of their study abroad.

BROADCAST EDUCATION ASSOCIATION

Broadcast Education Association, 343 Moore Hall, Central Michigan University, Mt Pleasant, MI, 78859, USA
Tel: 517 774 7279
Contact: Dr Peter B Orlik

BEA Scholarships

Eligibility: The applicant should be able to show substantial evidence of superior academic performance and potential to be an outstanding electronic media professional. There should be compelling evidence that the applicant possesses high integrity and a well articulated sense of personal and professional responsibility.

Level of Study: Postgraduate.

Type: Scholarship.

No. of awards offered: 14.

Frequency: Annual.

Value: Varies from US$1,250 to US$5,000 depending on the individual scholarship.

Applications Procedure: Send SASE for application (September 1st to December 15th) to; Scholarships, BEA, 1771 N Street NW, Washington DC, 20036, USA.

Closing Date: January 16th.

Additional Information: Application only available from the above address during the time specified.

THE BROADCASTING CORPORATIONS OF THE FEDERAL REPUBLIC OF GERMANY

International Music Competition, Bayerischer Rundfunk, München, D-80300, Germany
Tel: 89 5900 2471
Fax: 89 5900 3573
Contact: Secretariat

International Music Competition

Subjects: Music; categories vary annually.

Eligibility: Open to musicians of any nationality. Solo instrumentalists should be 17-30 years of age; female vocalists 20-30 years of age, male vocalists 20-32 years of age. Chamber music ensembles: duos should be 17-32 years of age; trios should be 17-32 years of age; string quartets should be 17-35 years of age, whereby the ages of the four musicians added together may not total more than 120; wind quintets should be 17-30 years of age, but two members can be 35.

Level of Study: Professional development.

Type: Competition.

No. of awards offered: Three per category.

Frequency: Annually (September).

Value: DM10,000-DM35,000.

Closing Date: May 1st.

Additional Information: There is an entry fee of DM150 per soloist; DM200 for duos; DM240 for trios; DM270 for quartets; DM300 for quintets.

BROADCAST MUSIC, INC

BMI Student Composer Awards, Broadcast Music Inc, 320 West 57th Street, New York, NY, 10019, USA
Tel: 212 830 9703
Contact: Ralph N Jackson, Director

*BMI Student Composer Awards

Subjects: Vocal, electronic or instrumental composition.

Eligibility: Open to citizens of countries within the Western Hemisphere who are either enrolled in an accredited public, private or parochial school, an accredited college or conservatory of music, or engaged in the private study of music with a recognized and established teacher other than a relative. Candidates must not have reached their 26th birthday by December 31st.

Purpose: To encourage the creation of concert music by student composers.

Frequency: Annual.

Value: Prizes totaling US$15,000 and ranging from US$500 to US$2,500 will be awarded at the discretion of the judges.

Closing Date: Early February.

Additional Information: Copies of the Official Rules and application forms are available on request. This is not a grant or college financial aid program. It is a competition for composers of serious contemporary music only.

BROOKINGS INSTITUTION

Brookings Institution, 1775 Massachusetts Avenue, NW, Washington, DC, 20036-2188, USA
Tel: 202 797 6000
Fax: 202 797 6181
www: www.brook.edu

Contact: Director of Economic/Governmental/Foreign Policy Studies

Research Fellowships

Subjects: Economics, government and foreign policy.

Eligibility: Open to doctoral candidates whose dissertation topics are directly related to public policy issues and thus to the major interests of the Institution. The recipients are scholars whose research will benefit from access to the data, opportunities for interviewing, and consultation with senior staff members afforded by the Institution and by residence in Washington, DC. Only candidates nominated by graduate departments of universities are considered. Candidates must have completed their preliminary examinations for the doctorate and be prepared to submit research plans leading to completion of their dissertations for the nominating university. Essential criteria are relevance of the topic to the appropriate Brookings research program and evidence that the research will be facilitated by access to the Institution's resources or to federal government agencies.

Level of Study: Doctorate.

Purpose: To support policy-oriented predoctoral research.

Type: Fellowships.

No. of awards offered: Varies.

Frequency: Annual.

Value: US$15,000, payable on a 12-month basis, for eleven months at the Brookings Institution and one month of vacation. Up to US$600 will be provided for typing and other essential research requirements, up to US$500 for some research-related travel, plus access to computer facilities.

Length of Study: 12 months, not renewable.

Study Establishment: The Brookings Institution.

Country of Study: USA.

Applications Procedure: Applicants are required to fill out a questionnaire and provide three reference statements (Brookings provides the forms).

Closing Date: December 15 for nominations; February 15 for applications.

Additional Information: Three of the fellowships are designated: the Arthur M Okun Memorial Fellowship, the Georges Lurcy Research Fellowship in Economics and the Leo Model Fellowship.

THE BROSS FOUNDATION, LAKE FOREST COLLEGE

The Bross Foundation, Lake Forest College, Religion Department, Lake Forest College, 555 North Sheridan, Lake Forest, IL, 60045, USA
Tel: 847 735 5175
Fax: 847 735 6291
Contact: Ron Miller

Bross Prize

Eligibility: There are no restrictions.

Level of Study: Unrestricted.

Purpose: To award the best unpublished manuscripts on the relation between any discipline and the Christian religion.

Type: Cash prizes.

No. of awards offered: Three.

Frequency: Every ten years.

Value: In 1990, US$15,000, US$,500, US$4,000.

Applications Procedure: Three copies of manuscript must be submitted.

Closing Date: September 2000.

Additional Information: Manuscript must be at least 50,000 words.

JOHN CARTER BROWN LIBRARY AT BROWN UNIVERSITY

John Carter Brown Library, Box 1894, Providence, RI, 02912, USA
Contact: Fellowship Coordinator

Jeannette D Black Memorial Fellowship

Subjects: Early history of the Americas from the late 15th century to 1830: research relating to materials at the Library regarding all aspects of the discovery, exploration, settlements and development of the New World.

Eligibility: Open to Americans and foreign nationals who are engaged in pre- or postdoctoral, or independent, research. Graduate students must have passed their preliminary or general examinations at the time of application.

Level of Study: Doctorate, Postdoctorate.

Purpose: To enable research into the history of cartography or a closely related area.

Type: Fellowship.

No. of awards offered: One.

Frequency: Annual.

Value: A stipend of US$1,000 monthly.

Length of Study: 2-4 months.

Country of Study: USA.

Closing Date: January 15th.

Center for New World Comparative Studies Fellowship

Subjects: Early history of the Americas from the late 15th century to 1830: research relating to materials at the Library regarding all aspects of the discovery, exploration, settlements and development of the New World.

Eligibility: Open to Americans and foreign nationals who are engaged in pre- or postdoctoral, or independent, research. Graduate students must have passed their preliminary or general examinations at the time of application.

Level of Study: Doctorate, Postdoctorate.

Purpose: To enable research with a definite comparative dimension.

Type: Fellowship.

No. of awards offered: Two.

Frequency: Annual.

Value: A stipend of US$1,000 monthly.

Length of Study: 2-4 months.

Country of Study: USA.

Closing Date: January 15th.

National Endowment for the Humanities Fellowship

Subjects: Early history of the Americas from the late 15th century to 1830: research relating to materials at the Library regarding all aspects of the discovery, exploration, settlements and development of the New World.

Eligibility: Open to American citizens and persons who have been resident in the USA for three years immediately preceding the term of the Fellowship. Graduate students are not eligible.

Type: Fellowship.

No. of awards offered: Three.

Frequency: Annual.

Value: US$15,000.

Length of Study: Six months.

Country of Study: USA.

Closing Date: January 15th.

Research Fellowships

Subjects: Early history of the Americas from the late 15th century to 1830: research relating to materials at the Library regarding all aspects of the discovery, exploration, settlement and development of the New World.

Eligibility: Open to Americans and foreign nationals who are engaged in pre- or postdoctoral, or independent, research. Graduate students must have passed their preliminary or general examinations at the time of application.

Level of Study: Doctorate, Postdoctorate.

Type: Fellowship.

No. of awards offered: Approximately seven.

Frequency: Annual.

Value: A stipend of US$1,000 monthly.

Length of Study: 2-4 months.

Country of Study: USA.

Closing Date: January 15th.

Additional Information: The following Fellowships are part of this program: Paul W McQuillen Memorial Fellowship, Charles H Watts Memorial Fellowship, Barbara S Mosbacher Fellowship, Library Associates Fellowship.

Touro National Heritage Trust

Subjects: Research on some aspect of the Jewish experience in the Western Hemisphere prior to c.1860.

Eligibility: Open to Americans and foreign nationals who are engaged in pre- or postdoctoral, or independent, research. Graduate students must have passed their preliminary or general examinations at the time of application.

Level of Study: Doctorate, Postdoctorate.

Type: Fellowship.

No. of awards offered: One.

Frequency: Annual.

Value: A stipend of US$1,000 monthly, plus a research travel reimbursement allowance of up to US$300.

Length of Study: 2-4 months.

Country of Study: USA.

Closing Date: February 1st.

Additional Information: The Touro Fellow will be selected by an academic committee consisting of representatives of Brown University, the American Jewish Historical Society, Brandeis University, the Newport Historical Society, and the John Carter Brown Library, as well as a representative of the Executive Committee of the Touro National Heritage Trust. The Touro Fellow must be prepared to participate in symposia or other academic activities organized by these institutions and may be called upon to deliver one or two public lectures.

Alexander O Vietor Memorial Fellowship

Subjects: Research in European and American maritime history between 1450 and 1800.

Eligibility: Open to Americans and foreign nationals who are engaged in pre- or postdoctoral, or independent, research. Graduate students must have passed their preliminary or general examinations at the time of application.

Level of Study: Doctorate, Postdoctorate.

Type: Fellowship.

No. of awards offered: One.

Frequency: Annual.

Value: A stipend of US$1,000 monthly.

Length of Study: 2-4 months.

Country of Study: USA.

Closing Date: January 15th.

BUDAPEST INTERNATIONAL MUSIC COMPETITION

Budapest International Music Competition, Interart Festivalcenter, PO Box 80, Budapest, H-1366, Hungary
Tel: 36 1 117 9838
Fax: 36 1 117 9910
Contact: Maria Liszkay, Secretary

Budapest International Music Competition

Subjects: Singing and composing.

Eligibility: Open to young artists of all nationalities under 32 years of age.

Frequency: Annual.

Value: Total of US$9,000.

Closing Date: April 30th.

BUNAC

BUNAC, 16 Bowling Green Lane, London, EC1R 0BD, England
Tel: 0171 251 3472
Fax: 0171 251 0215
Email: BUNAC@easynet.co.uk
Contact: Jill Tabuteau

BUNAC Educational Scholarship Trust (BEST)

Subjects: Any subject. Some awards are specifically for sports and geography-related courses.

Eligibility: Open to British citizens who have recently (within the last five years) graduated from a British university. Candidates must have a first degree.

Level of Study: Postgraduate.

Purpose: To help further Anglo-American understanding.

Type: Scholarship.

No. of awards offered: Ten.

Frequency: Annual.

Value: From a total of US$25,000. Usually approximately US$2,000.

Length of Study: From three months to three years.

Study Establishment: A North American university or college.

Country of Study: America or Canada.

Applications Procedure: Application forms are available on request.

Closing Date: March 25th.

THE BUNTING INSTITUTE OF RADCLIFFE COLLEGE

The Bunting Institute of Radcliffe College, 34 Concord Avenue, Cambridge, MA, 02138, USA
Tel: 617 495 8212
Fax: 617 495 8136
Contact: Fellowships Coordinator

Affiliation

Subjects: Any field, though visual artists must apply through the Bunting Fellowship.

Eligibility: Open to women scholars in any field, with receipt of a doctorate or appropriate terminal degree at least two years prior to appointment; women with a record of significant accomplishment.

Type: Affiliations.

No. of awards offered: Approximately 20.

Frequency: Annual.

Value: Appointment without stipend, includes office space and other resources available to all Fellows.

Length of Study: One semester or one academic year.

Country of Study: USA.

Closing Date: January 15th (usually).

Additional Information: The program seeks to support women of exceptional promise and demonstrated accomplishment. Applications are judged on the quality and significance of the proposed project, the applicant's record of accomplishment, and the difference the Fellowship might make in advancing the applicant's career. The Bunting Institute is a multidisciplinary program for women scholars, scientists, artists, and writers. Office or studio space, auditing privileges, and access to libraries and most other resources of Radcliffe and Harvard are provided. Residence in the Boston area is required during the Fellowship appointment. Fellows are expected to present their work in progress.

Berkshire Summer Fellowship

Subjects: Postdoctoral-level work in any field of history.

Eligibility: Open to women historians at the postdoctoral level working in any field of history. Preference is given to junior scholars and to those who do not normally have access to Boston-area resources.

Type: Fellowship.

No. of awards offered: One.

Frequency: Annual.

Value: US$3,000.

Length of Study: One summer.

Country of Study: USA.

Closing Date: January 15th (usually).

Additional Information: Applications are judged on the quality and significance of the proposed project, the applicant's record of achievement, and the difference the Fellowship might make in advancing the applicant's career. The Bunting Institute is a multidisciplinary program for women scholars, scientists, artists, and writers. Office or studio space, auditing privileges, and access to libraries and most other resources of Radcliffe and Harvard are provided. Residence in the Boston area is required during the Fellowship appointment. Fellows are expected to present their work in progress at public colloquia.

Bunting Fellowship

Subjects: Any discipline, including creative writing, visual and performing arts.

Eligibility: Open to women scholars in any field, with receipt of a doctorate or appropriate terminal degree at least two years prior to appointment; women creative writers, visual or performing artists with a record of significant accomplishment and equivalent professional experience.

Type: Fellowships.

No. of awards offered: Six to eight.

Frequency: Annual.

Value: US$30,000.

Length of Study: One year.

Country of Study: USA.

Closing Date: October 15th (usually).

Additional Information: The program seeks to support women of exceptional promise and demonstrated accomplishment. Applications are judged on the quality and significance of the proposed project, the applicant's record of accomplishment, and the difference the Fellowship might make in advancing the applicant's career. The Bunting Institute is a multidisciplinary program for women scholars, scientists, artists, and writers. Office or studio space, auditing privileges, and access to libraries and most other resources of Radcliffe and Harvard are provided. Residence in the Boston area is required during the Fellowship appointment. Fellows are expected to present their work in progress at public colloquia or in exhibitions.

Marian Cabot Putnam Fellowship

Subjects: Infant and child development within the framework of psychoanalysis.

Eligibility: Open to professional women in the field of infant and child development, conducting research within the framework of, or contributing to psychoanalysis.

Type: Fellowship.

No. of awards offered: One.

Frequency: Every 2-3 years.

Value: US$28,500.

Length of Study: One year.

Country of Study: USA.

Closing Date: October 15th (usually).

Additional Information: Applications are judged on the quality and significance of the proposed project in contributing to the field of infant and child development within the framework of psychoanalysis, as well as on the difference the Fellowship might make in the applicant's career. The Bunting Institute is a multidisciplinary program for women scholars, scientists, artists, and writers. Office or studio space, auditing privileges, and access to libraries and most other resources of Radcliffe and Harvard are provided. Residence in the Boston area is required during the Fellowship appointment. Fellows are expected to present their work in progress at public colloquia.

Peace Fellowship

Subjects: Peaceful solutions to conflict or potential conflict among groups or nations.

Eligibility: Open to women actively involved in finding peaceful solutions to conflict or potential conflict among groups or nations. Involvement with peace issues should be of an activist nature.

Type: Fellowship.

No. of awards offered: One.

Frequency: Annual.

Value: US$24,500.

Length of Study: One year.

Closing Date: January 15th (usually).

Additional Information: Applications are judged on the quality of the proposed project, the significance of the project in contributing to the peace movement or to peace studies, the applicant's capacity as an activist or public participant in peace-related organizations or actions, and the importance of the Fellowship at this time in the applicant's career. The Bunting Institute is a multidisciplinary program for women scholars, scientists, artists, and writers. Office or studio space, auditing privileges, and access to libraries and most other resources of Radcliffe and Harvard are provided. Residence in the Boston area is required during the Fellowship appointment. Fellows are expected to present their work in progress.

Science Scholars Fellowship

Subjects: Applications are accepted in the fields of astronomy, molecular and cellular biology, biochemistry, chemistry, cognitive and neural sciences, computer science, electrical engineering, aerospace/mechanical engineering, geology, materials science, physics, mathematics, naval architecture and ocean engineering, oceanography, and all fields that relate to the study.

Eligibility: Open to women scientists who are US citizens and have held the PhD for two years prior to appointment.

Purpose: To support women of exceptional promise and demonstrated accomplishment.

Type: Fellowships.

No. of awards offered: Eight.

Frequency: Annual.

Value: US$30,700 plus research expenses.

Length of Study: One year.

Country of Study: USA.

Closing Date: October 15th (usually).

Additional Information: Applications are judged on the quality and significance of the proposed project, the applicant's record of accomplishment, and the difference the Fellowship might make in advancing the applicant's career. The Bunting Institute is a multidisciplinary program for women scholars, scientists, artists, and writers. Office or studio space, auditing privileges, and access to libraries and most other resources of Radcliffe and Harvard are provided. Residence in the Boston area is required during the Fellowship appointment. Fellows are expected to present their work in progress at public colloquia or in exhibitions.

BURROUGHS WELLCOME FUND

Burroughs Wellcome Fund, 4709 Creekstone Drive, Suite 100, Durham, NC, 27703, USA
Tel: 919 991 5100
Fax: 919 941 5884
Email: info@bwfund.org
www: http://www.bwfund.org/bwfund
Contact: Carr Agyapong

Burroughs Wellcome Experimental Therapeutics Award

Subjects: Pharmacology, molecular biology, biochemistry, bioorganic chemistry, immunology, and genetics.

Eligibility: Open to medical schools and scientific institutions in the USA; to be used for the salary of full-time investigators who will direct their careers to some aspects of the entire spectrum of inquiry from the molecular mechanisms of drug action to the elucidation of drugs and their toxicity.

Level of Study: Doctorate.

Purpose: To identify and encourage the development of outstanding clinical scientists dedicated to improving the scientific basis of therapeutics.

No. of awards offered: At least two.

Frequency: Annual.

Value: US$400,000: the individual recipient receives US$60,000 salary per annum plus US$20,000 per annum for expenses.

Length of Study: Five years.

Study Establishment: An appropriate medical school.

Country of Study: USA.

Applications Procedure: Application must include a statement of purpose, CV, research plan, personal references and reprints.

Closing Date: November 1st.

Burroughs Wellcome Fund Life Sciences Research Fellowships

Subjects: Life sciences.

Eligibility: Open to US citizens holding MD or PhD degrees in the biological sciences.

Level of Study: Postdoctorate.

Purpose: To strengthen research and training.

Type: Fellowship.

No. of awards offered: Three.

Frequency: Annual.

Value: US$35,000 per annum.

Length of Study: Three years.

Study Establishment: Academic and non-profit research institutions.

Country of Study: USA.

Applications Procedure: Contact the Life Sciences Research Foundation for application materials.

Closing Date: October 1st.

For further information contact:
Life Sciences Research Foundation, 115 West University Parkway, Baltimore, MD, 21210, USA
Tel: 401 467 2597

Burroughs Wellcome OB/GYN Research Fellowship

Subjects: Obstetrics and gynecology.

Eligibility: Open to suitably qualified individuals who exhibit significant evidence of talent and dedication to a career in academic medicine.

Level of Study: Postdoctorate.

Purpose: To provide research training and experience to future leaders.

Type: Fellowship.

No. of awards offered: One.

Frequency: Annual.

Value: US$35,000 per annum.

Length of Study: Two years.

Country of Study: USA.

Closing Date: December 31st.

For further information contact:
The American Association of Obstetricians and Gynecologists Foundation, University of Texas at Houston, Department of Obstetrics and Gynecology, 6431 Fannin Street, Suite 3270, Houston, TX, 77030, USA
Tel: 713 798 4713

Burroughs Wellcome Toxicology Scholar Award

Subjects: Toxicology.

Eligibility: Open to individuals working in the field of toxicology.

Level of Study: Doctorate.

Purpose: To develop an increased number of toxicologists, well trained in understanding the interactions of chemicals with biological systems.

No. of awards offered: At least two.

Frequency: Annual.

Value: US$400,000 Award that provides a salary of US$60,000 per annum plus US$20,000 per annum for incidental research expenses, over five years.

Length of Study: Five years.

Study Establishment: A recognized school in the life sciences.

Country of Study: USA.

Closing Date: November 1st.

Additional Information: The Award is offered on behalf of the individual to the institution.

Career Awards in the Biomedical Sciences

Subjects: Biomedical science.

Eligibility: All candidates must have completed at least one year, and not more than four years, or postdoctoral research training at the time of application. All candidates must be citizens/permanent residents of Canada or USA.

Level of Study: Postdoctorate.

Purpose: To enhance the scientific development and productivity of outstanding young investigators at the postdoctoral level in the biomedical sciences.

Type: Career award.

No. of awards offered: 16.

Frequency: Annual.

Value: Up to US$484,000.

Length of Study: Up to 6 years.

Country of Study: UK and USA.

Applications Procedure: Please write for details.

Closing Date: October 2nd.

Hitchings-Elion Fellowships

Subjects: Clinical, biomedical and behavioral sciences.

Eligibility: Open to US citizens or permanent residents with a doctorate in the clinical, behavioral or biomedical sciences, who are within ten years of their last doctoral degree.

Level of Study: Doctorate.

Purpose: To provide a research experience in the biomedical and behavioral sciences in UK laboratories and to promote scientific collaboration between British and American scientists.

Type: Fellowship.

No. of awards offered: 15.

Frequency: Annual.

Value: Varies.

Length of Study: Three years: two years in the UK and the third year in the USA.

Country of Study: USA and UK.

Applications Procedure: Application must include completed form, CV, research proposal, letter of invitation from sponsor, letters of support and reprints of two research papers.

Additional Information: Scientists employed in US laboratories may apply. The third year of the Fellowship will not be given if it is spent in a government laboratory.

Molecular Parasitology Scholar Award

Subjects: The application of innovative methods of biochemistry and molecular biology to the problems of parasitic and tropical diseases.

Eligibility: Open to citizens or permanent residents of the USA and Canada.

Level of Study: Doctorate.

Purpose: To support investigators in molecular parasitology and encourage the development of novel approaches to the study of parasitic and tropical diseases.

No. of awards offered: At least one.

Frequency: Annual.

Value: US$400,000: US$80,000 per annum paid over 5 years.

Length of Study: Five years.

Country of Study: USA.

Applications Procedure: Application should include statement of purpose, CV, research plan, budget and personal references.

Closing Date: January 15th.

Additional Information: This Award is made on behalf of an individual who has demonstrated a commitment to bring innovative methods of biochemistry and molecular biology to bear upon the problems of parasitic and tropical diseases. Payment is made directly to the institution. Within the terms of the Award the Scholar may elect to undertake a period of study abroad. In that event up to US$5,000 additional funding may be provided. Seven copies of each application should be submitted.

New Initiatives in Malaria Research

Subjects: Malaria research.

Eligibility: Applicants must hold a doctorate degree and be US or Canadian citizens/permanent residents. They must also be affiliated with an accredited non-federal US or Canadian educational or education-affiliated institution.

Level of Study: Doctorate.

Purpose: To encourage new investigators to work on malaria and to enhance collaboration by supporting linkages between investigators at the same, or different, institutions.

No. of awards offered: Varies.

Frequency: Annual.

Value: US$400,000.

Length of Study: Four years.

Country of Study: USA or Canada.

Applications Procedure: Application should include a cover sheet, statement of purpose, CV, research plan, personal references and reprints.

Closing Date: January 15th.

New Investigator Awards in Basic Pharmacological Sciences

Subjects: Pharmacology.

Eligibility: Applicants must be US or Canadian citizens/permanent residents. They should be independent investigators appointed, within three years, to a tenure-track assistant professor (or equivalent).

Level of Study: Doctorate.

Purpose: To bring new approaches and novel thinking to this research area, through support of scientists early in their careers who are working on innovative solutions to pharmacological problems.

No. of awards offered: Four.

Frequency: Annual.

Value: US$195,000.

Length of Study: Three years.

Study Establishment: An accredited non-governmental US or Canadian educational or education-affiliated institution.

Country of Study: USA or Canada.

Applications Procedure: Application should include: cover sheet, sponsor's statement of purpose, CV, research plan, personal references and reprints.

Closing Date: November 1st.

Additional Information: Seven complete sets of application materials must be submitted.

Wellcome Research Travel Grants Program

Subjects: Health sciences.

Eligibility: Open to full-time, established research workers in institutions in the health sciences who are citizens or permanent residents of the USA.

Level of Study: Doctorate.

Purpose: To advance medical science by facilitating the rapid exchange of knowledge.

Type: Travel Grant.

No. of awards offered: Varies.

Frequency: Applications are reviewed continuously.

Value: Varies.

Length of Study: 2-12 weeks.

Country of Study: USA and UK.

Additional Information: The Grants are not awarded to predoctoral fellows or medical students or in support of long-term sabbatical leaves.

Wellcome Visiting Professorships

Subjects: Microbiological sciences and basic medical sciences.

Eligibility: Open to US institutions that wish to bring a distinguished professor to their campus to interact with students and faculty.

Level of Study: Doctorate.

Purpose: To introduce the newest ideas in clinical practice and research to undergraduates, graduates and faculty at US academic institutions.

No. of awards offered: 28 Professorships per year in the basic medical sciences and 5 Professorships in microbiological sciences.

Frequency: Annual.

Value: The Fund provides an award of US$5,000 to the US host institution for presentation to the Visiting Professor at the time of the Wellcome Lecture.

Country of Study: USA.

Closing Date: 1 March for basic medical sciences; 1 May for microbiological sciences.

Additional Information: Only eight researchers from abroad will be funded.

For further information contact:
American Society of Microbiology, 1325 Massachusetts Avenue, NW, Washington, DC, 20005, USA
Tel: 202 737 3600

THE BUSH FOUNDATION

The Bush Foundation, E-900 First National Bank Building, 332 Minnesota Street, St Paul, Minnesota, 55101, USA
Tel: 612 227 5222 or 1 800 605 7315

Bush Artists Fellowships

Eligibility: Must be at least 25 years old, be residents and have lived for at least 12 of the 36 months preceding the application deadlines in Minnesota, North Dakota, South Dakota or counties of northwestern Wisconsin.

Purpose: To allow artists of exemplary talent and demonstrated ability to spend periods of uninterrupted time working in their field.

Type: Stipend and expenses, Fellowship.

Frequency: Annual.

Value: Fellows recieve a stipend of US$26,000 for 12-18 months or US$2,166 per month for six to 11 months. An additional US$7,000 each is available for production and travel expenses.

Country of Study: USA.

Applications Procedure: Application form must be completed.

Closing Date: Literature and scriptworks October 21st ; Music composition October 28th; Visual Arts November 4th. Fellowships will be announced in late March.

Additional Information: Prefer written requests for applications.

BUSINESS AND PROFESSIONAL WOMEN'S FOUNDATION

Scholarships and Loans, Business and Professional Women's Foundation, 2012 Massachusetts Avenue, NW, Washington, DC, 20036, USA
Tel: 202 293 1200 ext.169

Avon Products Foundation Scholarship Program for Women in Business Studies

Subjects: Business studies.

Eligibility: Open to women who are US citizens, 25 years of age or older, who can demonstrate critical financial need, are officially accepted into a program of study at an accredited US institution and are graduating within 24 months of the time of application for a Scholarship. Candidates must be receiving a degree or certificate at the conclusion of their studies, be acquiring marketable skills that will increase their economic security and be entering the workforce after they receive their degree or certificate. Applicants should be women seeking the education necessary for a career in a business field.

Purpose: To assist women seeking the education necessary for entry or re-entry into the workforce, or career advancement in a business-related field.

Type: Scholarship.

No. of awards offered: Varies, approximately sixty.

Frequency: Annual.

Value: US$1,000.

Country of Study: USA.

Applications Procedure: Application forms are available from October 1st to April 1st. Please submit a business-size self-addressed, double-stamped envelope.

Closing Date: Postmark on or before April 15th.

BPW Career Advancement Scholarship Program

Subjects: Computer science, teacher education certification, paralegal studies, science, engineering or professional (JD, MD, DDS) degrees.

Eligibility: Open to women who are US citizens, 25 years of age or older, who can demonstrate critical financial need, are officially accepted into a program of study at an accredited US institution and are graduating within 24 months of the time of application for a Scholarship. Candidates must be receiving a degree or certificate at the conclusion of their studies, be acquiring marketable skills that will increase their economic security and be entering the workforce after they receive their degree or certificate. Applicants should be seeking the education necessary for re-entry or advancement within the workplace.

Purpose: To assist women seeking the education necessary for entry or re-entry into the workforce, or career advancement in a business-related field.

Type: Scholarship.

No. of awards offered: Varies; approximately fifty.

Frequency: Annual.

Value: Up to US$1,000.

Length of Study: One year.

Study Establishment: An accredited institution.

Country of Study: USA.

Applications Procedure: Application forms are available from October 1st to April 1st. Please submit a business-size, self-addressed, double-stamped envelope.

Closing Date: Postmark on or before April 15th.

BPW/Sears-Roebuck Loan Fund for Women in Graduate Business Studies and Engineering Studies

Subjects: Business studies or engineering studies.

Eligibility: Open to women who are US citizens and are able to demonstrate financial need. Candidates must have written notice of acceptance for enrollment at a school accredited by the American Assembly of Collegiate Schools of Business or by the Accreditation Board of Engineering and Technology, and academic and/or work experience records showing career motivation and ability to complete the course of study.

Purpose: To assist women seeking the education necessary for entry or re-entry into the workforce, or career advancement in a business-related field.

No. of awards offered: Varies.

Frequency: Annual.

Value: Loans of up to US$2,500 per academic year for business studies and up to US$5,000 for engineering studies.

Length of Study: One year.

Study Establishment: An accredited institution.

Country of Study: USA.

Applications Procedure: Application forms are available from October 1st to April 1st. Please submit a business-size self-addressed, double-stamped envelope.

Closing Date: Postmark on or before April 15th.

Additional Information: Interest of 7% per annum begins immediately after graduation. Loans are repaid in 20 equal installments commencing 12 months after graduation.

New York Life Foundation Scholarship for Women in the Health Professions Program

Subjects: Healthcare, including nursing in particular.

Eligibility: Open to women who are US citizens, 25 years of age or older, who can demonstrate critical financial need, are officially accepted into a program of study at an accredited US institution and are graduating within 24 months of the time of application for a Scholarship. Candidates must be receiving a degree or certificate at the conclusion of their studies, acquiring marketable skills that will increase their economic security and be entering the workforce after they receive their degree or certificate. Applicants should be women seeking the education necessary for a career in a healthcare field.

Purpose: To assist women seeking the education necessary for entry or re-entry into the workforce, or career advancement in a business-related field.

Type: Scholarship.

No. of awards offered: Varies; approximately fifty.

Frequency: Annual.

Value: US$500-US$1,000.

Length of Study: One year.

Study Establishment: An accredited institution.

Country of Study: USA.

Applications Procedure: Application forms are available from October 1st to April 1st. Please submit a business-size, self-addressed, double-stamped envelope.

Closing Date: Postmark on or before April 15th.

Wyeth-Ayerst Scholarship for Women in Graduate Medical and Health Business Programs

Subjects: Emerging health fields such as biomedical engineering, biomedical research, medical technology, pharmaceutical marketing, public health and public health policy.

Eligibility: Open to women who are US citizens, 25 years of age or older, who can demonstrate critical financial need, are officially accepted into a program of study at an accredited US institution and are graduating within 24 months of the time of application for a Scholarship. Candidates must be receiving a degree or certificate at the conclusion of their studies, be acquiring marketable skills that will increase their economic security and be entering the workforce after they receive their degree or certificate. Applicants should be women seeking the education necessary for a career in a healthcare field.

Purpose: To assist women in gaining entry into underrepresented and underutilized health-related occupations, especially in the medical and health business professions.

Type: Scholarship.

No. of awards offered: Varies.

Frequency: Annual.

Value: US$2,000.

Country of Study: USA.

Applications Procedure: Application forms are available from October 1st to April 1st. Please submit a business-size, self-addressed, double-stamped envelope.

Closing Date: Postmark on or before April 15th.

F BUSONI INTERNATIONAL PIANO COMPETITION

Concorso Pianistico Internazionale, 'F Busoni', Conservatorio Statale di Musica 'C Monteverdi', Piazza Domenicani 19, Bolzano, 39100, Italy
Tel: 471 976568
Fax: 471 973579
www: http://www.tqs.iunet.it/asteria/busoni.htm
Contact: La Segretaria

F Busoni International Piano Competition

Subjects: Piano performance.

Eligibility: Open to pianists of any nationality under 32 years of age.

Type: Prize.

No. of awards offered: Six.

Frequency: Annual.

Value: 1st prize 15,000,000 lire plus 60 important concert contracts; 2nd prize 9,000,000 lire; 3rd prize 7,000,000 lire; 4th prize 6,000,000 lire; 5th prize 5,000,000 lire; 6th prize 4,000,000 lire.

Country of Study: The competition is held in Bolzano, Italy.

Applications Procedure: Application form should be accompanied by birth certficate, reports or certificates of study, brief CV and documentation of any artistic activity, three recent photographs, entrance fee, and written evidence of prizes at international competitions, if any.

Closing Date: May 31st.

Additional Information: The competition is held in August and September each year.

CAIRO UNIVERSITY

Faculty of Archaeology, Cairo University, Conservation Department, 68 Khalil Sudek Street , Ainshanme Flat 4, Cairo, Egypt
Tel: 246 4705
Contact: Professor Fatma Mohamed Helmi

Study, restoration and conservation of archaeological materials

Level of Study: Professional development.

Purpose: Study, restoration and conservation of archaeological materials.

Frequency: Annual.

Length of Study: Six months.

Country of Study: Egypt.

THE CALEDONIAN RESEARCH FOUNDATION

The Carnegie Trust for the Universities of Scotland, Cameron House, Abbey Park Place, Dunfermline, Fife, KY12 7PZ, Scotland
Tel: 01383 622148

Fax: 01383 622149
Contact: The Secretary and Treasurer

Caledonian Scholarship

Subjects: All subjects in the university curriculum. At least one Scholarship each year is made in a non-scientific discipline.

Eligibility: Open to persons possessing a first class honours degree from a Scottish University.

Level of Study: Postgraduate.

Purpose: To support postgraduate research.

Type: Scholarship.

No. of awards offered: Two or three.

Frequency: Annual.

Value: £5,640 (in 1994/95) plus tuition fees and allowances.

Length of Study: A maximum of three years, subject to annual review.

Study Establishment: Any university in Scotland.

Country of Study: UK.

Closing Date: March 15th.

Additional Information: Considered along with Carnegie Scholarships.

CAMBRIDGE COMMONWEALTH TRUST

Cambridge Commonwealth Trust, PO Box 252, Cambridge, CB2 1TZ, England

Through the Cambridge Commonwealth Trust for Commonwealth countries, the Cambridge Overseas Trust for countries outside the Commonwealth, and associated Trusts, the University of Cambridge gives awards to enable overseas students of outstanding academic merit to study at Cambridge

Grants to Australians

Subjects: Research in a subject deemed relevant to Australia's needs and from time to time a Scholarship to read for the Master of Law (LLM) degree.

Eligibility: Open to citizens of Australia, graduates of Australian universities, who have, or expect to obtain before October, a first class honours degree or its equivalent and, for those wishing to pursue a course of research leading to the degree of PhD, who have been successful in winning an ORS award which pays the difference between the overseas and the home rate of the University Composition Fee.

Level of Study: Doctorate.

Purpose: To enable citizens of Australia to pursue a course of reearch leading to a PhD.

No. of awards offered: Varies.

Frequency: Annual.

Value: To cover the University Composition Fee at the home rate, approved College fees, a maintenance allowance sufficient for a single student and a contribution towards travel.

Length of Study: Up to three years.

Study Establishment: University of Cambridge.

Country of Study: UK.

Applications Procedure: Further details can be obtained from the Cambridge Commonwealth Trust.

Grants to Canadians

Subjects: Research leading to the degree of PhD.

Eligibility: Open to graduates who are citizens of Canada.

Level of Study: Doctorate.

Purpose: To enable citizens of Canada to pursue a course of research leading to a PhD at Cambridge.

Type: Scholarship.

No. of awards offered: Varies.

Frequency: Annual.

Value: To cover the University Composition Fee at the home rate and approved College fees.

Study Establishment: University of Cambridge.

Country of Study: UK.

Applications Procedure: Further details can be obtained from the Cambridge Commonwealth Trust.

Grants to New Zealanders

Subjects: Research leading to the degree of PhD.

Eligibility: Open to graduates who are citizens of New Zealand.

Level of Study: Doctorate.

Purpose: To enable citizens of New Zealand to pursue a course of research in Cambridge.

Type: Scholarship.

No. of awards offered: Five.

Frequency: Annual.

Value: To cover the University Composition Fee at the home rate, approved College fees, a maintenance allowance sufficient for a single student and a contribution towards travel.

Study Establishment: Cambridge University.

Country of Study: UK.

CAMBRIDGE LIVINGSTONE TRUST

Cambridge Livingstone Trust, PO Box 252, Cambridge, CB2 1TZ, England

*Scholarships

Subjects: Any subject.

Eligibility: Open to men and women graduates of recognized universities who are domiciled, resident, or normally resident in Botswana, Lesotho, Malawi, Namibia, South Africa, Swaziland, Zambia or Zimbabwe. Applications from those who would find it difficult to study at the University of Cambridge without financial assistance will be given preference.

Purpose: To enable applicants with outstanding academic qualifications to pursue either a taught postgraduate course of study or research leading to the degree of PhD at the University of Cambridge so that they may be better able to serve the development of their countries in Southern Africa.

No. of awards offered: Varies.

Frequency: Annual.

Value: To cover the University Composition Fee, approved College fees, a maintenance allowance sufficient for a single student, and a contribution towards travel.

Length of Study: Up to three years.

Study Establishment: University of Cambridge.

Country of Study: UK.

Closing Date: September 21st.

CAMBRIDGE UNIVERSITY LIBRARY

Cambridge University Library, West Road, Cambridge, CB3 9DR, England

Tel: 01223 333083
Fax: 01223 333160
Email: RWW@ULA.CAM.AC.UK
www: http://www.cam.ac.uk/libraries/
Contact: The Deputy Librarian

Munby Fellowship in Bibliography

Subjects: Historical bibliography, the history of the book trade and of book collecting. There is no restriction on choice of topic within these fields, which may concern printed or manuscript material, Western or Oriental, in any language.

Eligibility: Open to graduates of any university. Fellows may be of any nationality. Preference will be given to promising younger scholars already established in their careers.

Level of Study: Postgraduate.

Purpose: To sponsor bibliographical research based in the first instance on the collections of the libraries of Cambridge University.

Type: Fellowship.

No. of awards offered: One.

Frequency: Annual.

Value: £13,000, reviewed annually.

Length of Study: One year.

Study Establishment: Cambridge University Library.

Country of Study: UK.

Applications Procedure: Applications (no forms) consist of a CV, a statement outlining the research proposed, a list of publications, and names and addresses of two referees. There are no interviews. Selection takes place in October for the following October.

Closing Date: July 31st for October 1st the following year.

THE CANADA COUNCIL

The Canada Council, 350 Albert Street, PO Box 1047, Ottawa, Ontario, K1P 5V8, Canada
Tel: 613 566 4372
Fax: 613 566 4390
Contact: Arts Awards Service

*Arts Grants 'A'

Subjects: Art.

Eligibility: Open to Canadian citizens or permanent residents of Canada.

Purpose: To provide free time for personal creative activity for senior artists who have made a significant contribution over a number of years and are still active in their profession.

No. of awards offered: Varies.

Value: Up to C$31,000 to cover living expenses and project costs; travel expenses necessary to the project may also be provided. Artists in visual arts, video and performance art may receive up to C$39,000 if they expect to incur extraordinary materials costs.

Length of Study: 4-12 months; for dance artists, tenure may be from 2 weeks to 12 months.

Country of Study: Any country.

Additional Information: There are one or two competitions each year depending on the discipline. Interested individuals should request the Grants to Artists brochure for detailed information on the financial assistance offered by the Canada Council Arts Awards Service.

*Arts Grants 'B'

Subjects: Art.

Eligibility: Open to Canadian citizens or permanent residents of Canada who have finished their basic training in the arts and/or are recognized as professionals within their disciplines.

Purpose: To support personal creative activity or, in some fields, advanced training of professional Canadian artists.

No. of awards offered: Varies.

Value: Up to C$17,000 to cover living expenses, project costs and travel.

Length of Study: 4-12 months.

Country of Study: Any country.

Additional Information: There are one, two or three competitions each year depending on the form of art. Interested individuals shall request the Grants to Artists.

*Robert Fleming Award for Young Composers

Subjects: Composition.

Eligibility: Open to outstanding students of any age graduating in composition from a Canadian university, school of music or conservatoire, who are Canadian citizens or landed immigrants with at least one year's residence.

Purpose: To encourage young Canadian composers.

No. of awards offered: One.

Frequency: Annual.

Value: Varies (interest on an endowment).

Length of Study: Up to 12 months.

Country of Study: Canada or elsewhere if required.

Closing Date: April 1st.

Additional Information: Artists may not apply for this prize. All candidates in the Arts Grants 'B' competition for composers are considered automatically.

*Killam Research Fellowships

Subjects: Humanities, social sciences, natural sciences, health sciences, engineering, and studies linking any of the disciplines within these broad fields.

Eligibility: Open to Canadian citizens or permanent residents of Canada. Killam Research Fellowships are aimed at established scholars who have demonstrated outstanding ability through substantial publications in their fields over a period of several years.

Purpose: To support advanced research projects undertaken by permanent residents of Canada.

Type: Fellowship.

No. of awards offered: Varies.

Frequency: Annual.

Value: Killam Research Fellowships provide partial or full salary replacement, to a maximum of C$53,000, based on actual salary for the year before tenure of the award; the Council does not object if the Research Fellow's institution supplements the award during the year of tenure to reflect any salary increase.

Length of Study: Up to two years.

Country of Study: Canadians may hold the award in any country; permanent residents must use the award in Canada.

Applications Procedure: Requests must be submitted on the appropriate application forms which are available from the Canada Council Killam Program Section. The Killam Program brochure provides detailed information on the Killam Research Fellowships.

Closing Date: June 30th.

*Short-Term Grants

Subjects: Art.

Eligibility: Open to Canadian citizens or permanent residents of Canada who have finished their basic training in the arts and/or are recognized as professionals within their disciplines.

Purpose: To enable Canadian artists to pursue their creative work or artistic development, or to work on a specific project.

No. of awards offered: Varies.

Frequency: Annual.

Value: Up to C$4,000 to help defray living expenses and project costs, plus travel if applicable.

Length of Study: Up to 12 months.

Country of Study: Canada or elsewhere if required.

Additional Information: Interested individuals should request the Grants to Artists brochure for detailed information on the financial assistance offered by the Canada Council Arts Awards Service.

*Travel Grants

Subjects: Art.

Eligibility: Open to Canadian citizens or permanent residents of Canada who have finished their basic training in the arts and/or are recognized as professionals within their own disciplines.

Purpose: To enable Canadian artists to travel on occasions important to their professional careers.

Type: Travel Grant.

No. of awards offered: Varies.

Frequency: Annual.

Value: A maximum of C$2,800 to cover travel costs; may include an allowance of C$100 per day for up to five days to help defray living expenses.

Country of Study: Canada or elsewhere if required.

Additional Information: Interested individuals should request the Grants to Artists brochure for detailed information on the financial assistance offered by the Canada Council Arts Awards Service.

*J B C Watkins Award

Subjects: Architecture, music, dance, theatre.

Eligibility: Open to Canadian artists who are graduates of a Canadian university or post-secondary art institution or training school in the above subjects.

Purpose: To allow Canadian artists to pursue postgraduate study.

No. of awards offered: One.

Frequency: Annual.

Value: Up to C$17,000.

Country of Study: Preferably in Denmark, Norway, Sweden or Iceland, but applications are accepted for studies in all countries other than Canada.

Closing Date: April 1st (December 1st for performers of classical music).

Additional Information: Interested individuals should request the Grants to Artists brochure for detailed information on the financial assistance offered by the Canada Council Arts Awards Service.

CANADA MEMORIAL FOUNDATION

The Association of Commonwealth Universities, John Foster House,
36 Gordon Square, London, WC1H 0PF, England
Tel: 0171 387 8572
Fax: 0171 387 2655
Contact: Head, Awards Division

Scholarships

Subjects: Any subject: clinical medicine currently excluded.

Eligibility: Open to UK citizens who are permanently resident in the UK and hold, or expect to hold, an upper second class honours degree or equivalent qualification. Candidates should normally be under 30 years of age and must show convincing reasons why they wish to study in Canada.

Level of Study: Undergraduate, Postgraduate.

Purpose: To fund a student taking a research degree (12 months) or postgraduate course at a university or other appropriate institution in Canada. Not offered for study leading to PhD.

Type: Scholarship.

No. of awards offered: Two.

Frequency: Annual.

Value: Full cost; covers fees, maintenance, air fares. Other allowances for books, study travel, etc.

Length of Study: 12 months only. Candidates wishing to take a two-year course will be required to show they have funding to complete the course.

Study Establishment: A university or other appropriate institution.

Country of Study: Canada.

Applications Procedure: CVs not accepted; application form must be completed.

Closing Date: Last Friday in October.

Additional Information: Applications forms are not sent out in the week prior to closing date.

For further information contact:
c/o Alberta House, 1 Mount Street, London, W1Y 5AA, England
Contact: Canada Memorial Foundation

CANADIAN ACADEMIC INSTITUTE IN ATHENS/THE CANADIAN ARCHAEOLOGICAL INSTITUTE IN ATHENS

59 Queens Park Crescent, Toronto, Ontario, M5S 2C4, Canada

Thompson (Homer and Dorothy) Fellowship

Eligibility: Open to Canadian citizens or landed immigrants.

Level of Study: Postgraduate, Postdoctorate.

Purpose: The applicant must be pursuing graduate or postdoctorate studies and have a clear need to work in Greece.

Type: Fellowship.

Value: C$3,000, plus reduced rent in the CAIA hostel for the period of the fellowship.

Length of Study: One year.

Study Establishment: The Canadian Archaeological Institute at Athens.

Country of Study: Greece.

Applications Procedure: Write enclosing a curriculum vitae, outline proposed research and have three referees send letters to the Canadian address.

Closing Date: May 15th.

Additional Information: In addition to studies the Fellow assists the director of CAIA with office work (10 hours per week). Therefore some previous experience in Greece and some modern Greek is recommended. Greek address: Odos Aiginitou 7, Athens, Greece.

CANADIAN BAR ASSOCIATION

Canadian Bar Association, 50 O'Connor Suite 902, Ottawa, Ontario, K1P 6LZ, Canada
Tel: 613 237 2925
Fax: 613 237 0185
Email: info@cba.org
www: cba.org/abc
Contact: The Senior Director of Communications

Viscount Bennett Fellowship

Subjects: Law.

Eligibility: Open to Canadian citizens only.

Level of Study: Postgraduate.

Purpose: To encourage a high standard of legal education, training and ethics.

Type: Fellowship

No. of awards offered: One.

Frequency: Annual.

Value: C$20,000.

Length of Study: One year.

Study Establishment: An approved institution.

Country of Study: Canada, USA or abroad.

Applications Procedure: Please write for an application form.

Closing Date: November 15th.

CANADIAN BUREAU FOR INTERNATIONAL EDUCATION (CBIE)

Canadian Bureau for International Education, 220 Laurier Avenue West, Suite 1100, Ottawa, Ontario, K1P 5Z9, Canada
Tel: 613 237 4820 ext.234
Fax: 613 237 1073
Email: ctaha@cbie.ca

CIDA Awards for Canadians

Subjects: Fields related to international development.

Eligibility: Open to Canadian citizens who have completed a recognized undergraduate program of studies (degree or diploma) and have indicated, through their own education and experience, a definite commitment to and suitability for a career in international development work.

Level of Study: Postgraduate, Professional development.

Purpose: To develop a body of Canadians competent and expert in the field of international development.

No. of awards offered: Varies.

Frequency: Annual.

Value: Varies (maximum of C$15,000 in 1996).

Length of Study: Up to 12 months.

Country of Study: Canada.

Applications Procedure: Application form must be completed.

Closing Date: Contact CBIE for details.

Additional Information: Each applicant must develop a program of one of the three following types: a professional on-the-job training program involving extensive project-related fieldwork in one or more developing countries; a practical work/study assignment in a public or private (including non-government) organization or agency involved in international development work, with a substantial period of fieldwork in one or more developing countries; a development-oriented program combined with a substantial period of practical fieldwork in one or more developing countries. Research programs must have a practical orientation and should not be used exclusively for academic or theoretical studies. PhD programs will not be considered.

Commonwealth Scholarships

Subjects: Any subject.

Eligibility: Open to Canadian citizens, or permanent residents who are graduates of a Canadian university, of high intellectual promise who may be expected to make a significant contribution to Canada upon their return from study abroad.

Level of Study: Doctorate, Postgraduate.

Purpose: To enable Canadian university graduates to pursue full-time graduate training leading to either masters or PhD degrees in other Commonwealth countries.

Type: Scholarship.

No. of awards offered: Varies.

Frequency: Annual.

Value: Varies.

Length of Study: 1-3 years, depending on the country.

Country of Study: Commonwealth countries outside Canada.

Closing Date: October 31st.

CANADIAN CARBONIZATION RESEARCH ASSOCIATION

PO Box 85291, Brant Plaza, Burlington, Ontario, L7R 4K4, Canada
Tel: 905 637 0666
Fax: 905 637 9636
Contact: G A Chapman

J C Botham Scholarship

Subjects: Coal carbonization or related fields.

Eligibility: Open to Canadian citizens at graduate or undergraduate level in one of the Canadian universities listed above.

Level of Study: Unrestricted.

Purpose: To honour Mr Jack C Botham, one of the founding members of CCRA. The scholarship will be awarded to a graduate studying in the special area of coal carbonization or related R&D field.

Type: Scholarship.

No. of awards offered: One.

Frequency: At the Board's discretion.

Value: C$1,000.

Study Establishment: The University of British Columbia, the University of Regina, the University of Waterloo, McMaster University, Université de Sherbrooke, the Technical University of Nova Scotia, or the University of Western Ontario.

Country of Study: Canada.

Closing Date: November 15th.

CANADIAN COMMONWEALTH SCHOLARSHIP AND FELLOWSHIP PLAN

Association of Universities and Colleges of Canada, 151 Slater Street, Ottawa, Ontario, K1P 5N1, Canada
Tel: 613 563 1236
Fax: 613 563 9745
Contact: Awards Division

Commonwealth Scholarships

Subjects: Any subject.

Eligibility: Open to Canadian citizens, or those permanent residents who are graduates of a Canadian university, who have completed a university degree or expect to graduate prior to the tenure of the award. No age restriction pertains, but preference will be given to applicants who have obtained a university degree within the last five years.

No. of awards offered: Varies.

Frequency: Annual.

Value: Varies.

Country of Study: Australia, Ghana, Hong Kong, India, Jamaica, New Zealand, Nigeria, Sierra Leone, Sri Lanka, Trinidad and Tobago, or the UK.

Closing Date: Applications for Australia and New Zealand: 31 December; applications for other countries: 31 October.

Additional Information: The Canadian Commonwealth Scholarship and Fellowship Committee will select nominations to be forwarded to the awarding country. The number of nominations varies, but will be approximately double the number of awards expected to be made. The decision of the Canadian Committee is final and not open to appeal. The actual offer of a Scholarship will be made by the Commonwealth Scholarship Agency in the awarding country. In general, the Agency tries to place selected candidates in the institutions of their choice; however, where this is not possible, an alternative institution offering opportunities for the proposed course of study will be chosen.

*Research Fellowships

Subjects: Any subject.

Eligibility: Scholars from other Commonwealth countries may be nominated by the heads of Canadian universities. The host university should confirm that it is willing and able to extend the facilities necessary for the Fellow's work and should describe the contribution which the Fellow is expected to make to the work of the university. When considering the nominations, the Canadian Commonwealth Scholarship and Fellowship Committee will take into account demonstration of research ability, significance of the proposed research, and appropriateness of the proposed program.

Purpose: To bring to Canada, from universities and research centres of other countries of the Commonwealth, scholars of established reputation whose presence in Canadian universities is expected to benefit themselves, their home countries and Canada.

Type: Fellowship.

No. of awards offered: Up to three.

Frequency: Annual.

Value: Return air fare to Canada for the Fellow and spouse; a maintenance allowance of C$1,500 per month; a marriage allowance of C$250 per month; approved medical services for the Fellow and spouse; and payment of Canadian income tax as applicable.

Length of Study: One academic year.

Study Establishment: A university.

Country of Study: Canada.

Closing Date: October 31st.

*Visiting Fellowships

Subjects: Such topics as curriculum development, teaching methods, student/teacher evaluation, performance measures and administrative techniques applicable to the Fellow's discipline or field of study, or to their educational system more generally.

Eligibility: Individuals from other Commonwealth countries may be nominated by Canadian universities and other educational organizations and agencies. The Canadian Commonwealth Scholarship and Fellowship Committee will take into account the qualifications and experience of the nominee in relation to the proposed visit, the appropriateness and quality of the proposed visit, and the benefits of the proposed visit to Canada and the home country.

Purpose: To bring to Canada, from other countries of the Commonwealth, persons who are prominent in any educational institutions.

Type: Fellowship.

No. of awards offered: Up to five.

Frequency: Annual.

Value: Return fare to Canada; a maintenance allowance of C$1,500 per month; approved medical services; payment of Canadian income tax as applicable.

Length of Study: 2-4 months, although consideration will be given to programs of up to a maximum of 6 months.

Country of Study: Canada.

Closing Date: October 31st.

CANADIAN CRAFTS COUNCIL

Canadian Crafts Council, 189 Laurier Avenue E, Ottawa, Ontario, K1N 6P1, Canada
Tel: 613 235 8200
Fax: 613 235 7425

*Saidye Bronfman Award

Subjects: Any discipline within the crafts.

Eligibility: Open to Canadian citizens, or individuals who have had landed immigrant status for at least three years. The nominee must have made a significant contribution to the development of crafts in Canada over a significant period of time, usually more than ten years.

Purpose: To recognize excellence in the crafts. The award is made to a craftsperson judged to be an outstanding practitioner in their field, shown by their output over a working life, and their current level of achievement.

No. of awards offered: One.

Value: C$20,000.

Applications Procedure: Nominations are made through CCC member associations across Canada. Award recipients are selected by a committee of leading Canadian craftspersons, including the current President of the Canadian Crafts Council, a past recipient of the Award, a nominee of the Bronfman Foundation, a gallery or museum director, and a member of the CCC Board. Members are selected to represent all major disciplines and geographic areas of Canada.

Closing Date: October 15th.

CANADIAN CYSTIC FIBROSIS FOUNDATION

Canadian Cystic Fibrosis Foundation, 2221 Yonge Street 601, Toronto, Ontario, M4S 2B4, Canada
Tel: 416 485 9149
Fax: 416 485 0960

Fellowships

Subjects: Biomedical or behavioral science pertinent to cystic fibrosis.

Eligibility: Open to individuals who are graduates of a medical school or who hold a PhD degree. Medical graduates should have already completed their basic core years of residency training. Applications for a Fellowship in a clinical area must have a strong component of research in the proposed program; clinical, non-research 'residency-type' Fellowships will not be awarded. Canadian Fellowship applicants of exceptional quality requesting funding to study abroad will be considered; applications will be strengthened by an indication of intention to return to Canada.

Level of Study: Postgraduate, Doctorate.

Purpose: To encourage research training, basic research or clinical research.

Type: Fellowship.

No. of awards offered: Varies.

Frequency: Annual.

Value: Varies.

Length of Study: Two years; renewable for one further year.

Study Establishment: Any approved university, hospital or research institute.

Country of Study: Canada, USA or abroad.

Closing Date: October 1st, April 1st.

Scholarships for Research in Cystic Fibrosis

Subjects: Cystic fibrosis.

Eligibility: Open to holders of an MD or PhD degree who may recently have completed training or who are established investigators wishing to devote major research effort to cystic fibrosis. The beginning investigator should have demonstrated promise of ability to initiate and carry out independent research; the established investigator should have a published record of excellent scientific research.

Level of Study: Postgraduate, Doctorate.

Purpose: To allow investigators the opportunity to develop outstanding research programs unhampered by heavy teaching or clinical loads.

Type: Scholarship.

No. of awards offered: Varies.

Frequency: Annual.

Value: Salary support, dependent on the qualifications and experience of the Scholar and determined according to prevailing rates.

Length of Study: Three years; renewable for a further 2 years on receipt of a satisfactory progress report.

Study Establishment: Any approved university, hospital or research institute.

Country of Study: Canada.

Closing Date: October 1st.

CANADIAN FEDERATION OF UNIVERSITY WOMEN

Canadian Federation of University Women, 55 Parkdale Avenue, Ottawa, Ontario, K1Y 1E5, Canada
Tel: 613 722 8732
Contact: Fellowships Chair

*CFUW Memorial Award

Subjects: Science and technology.

Eligibility: Open to women who have a bachelor's degree or equivalent from a recognized university and who are Canadian citizens or have held landed immigrant status for at least one year prior to submission of application and have been accepted into the proposed programme of study.

Purpose: To assist with graduate study.

No. of awards offered: One.

Frequency: Annual.

Value: C$1,000.

Study Establishment: An appropriate institution.

Applications Procedure: Application forms are available from the Federation.

Closing Date: November 30th (postmark).

*The Dr Marion Elder Grant Fellowship

Subjects: Any subject.

Eligibility: Open to women who have a bachelor's degree or equivalent from a recognized university, who are Canadian citizens or have held landed immigrant status for at least one year prior to submission of application and who have been accepted into the proposed programme of study. All things being equal, preference will be given to the holder of an Acadia University degree.

Purpose: To provide partial funding for full-time graduate study.

Type: Fellowship.

No. of awards offered: One.

Frequency: Annual.

Value: C$8,000.

Study Establishment: An appropriate institution.

Country of Study: Canada.

Closing Date: November 30th.

*Beverley Jackson Fellowship

Subjects: Any subject.

Eligibility: Open to women over the age of 35 at the time of application who are enrolled in graduate work at an Ontario university; candidates should hold at least a bachelor's degree or equivalent from a recognized university and be Canadian citizens or have held landed immigrant status for at least one year prior to submission of application and must have been accepted into the proposed programme of study.

Purpose: To provide partial funding for graduate study.

Type: Fellowship.

No. of awards offered: One.

Frequency: Annual.

Value: C$3,500.

Country of Study: Canada.

Closing Date: November 30th.

Additional Information: The Fellowship is funded by UWC North York.

*Georgette Lemoyne Award

Subjects: Any subject.

Eligibility: Open to women who have a bachelor's degree or equivalent from a recognized university and who are Canadian citizens or have held landed immigrant status for at least one year prior to submission of application and who have been accepted into the proposed programme of study.

Purpose: To provide partial funding for graduate study.

No. of awards offered: One.

Frequency: Annual.

Value: C$1,000.

Study Establishment: A Canadian university where one language of administration and instruction is French.

Country of Study: Canada.

Applications Procedure: Application forms are available from the Federation.

Closing Date: November 30th (postmark).

*Margaret McWilliams Predoctoral Fellowship

Subjects: Any subject.

Eligibility: Open to women who are Canadian citizens or who have held landed immigrant status for at least one year prior to submission of application. A candidate should hold a bachelor's degree or its equivalent from a recognized university, not necessarily in Canada, and be a full-time student at an advanced stage (at least one year) in her doctoral programme.

Level of Study: Doctorate.

Purpose: To provide funding for doctoral study.

No. of awards offered: One.

Frequency: Annual.

Value: C$10,000 paid in two half-yearly instalments.

Country of Study: Any country.

Closing Date: November 30th (postmark).

Additional Information: The Fellowship is not renewable. Application forms are available from the Federation.

*Margaret Dale Philp Award

Subjects: The humanities or social sciences with special consideration given to candidates who wish to specialize in Canadian history.

Eligibility: Open to women who are Canadian citizens or who have held landed immigrant status for at least one year prior to submission of application. Candidates should hold a bachelor's degree or its equivalent from a recognized Canadian university, reside in Canada, and wish to embark on, or continue, a programme leading to an advanced degree and have been accepted into the proposed programme of study.

Purpose: To provide partial funding for graduate study.

No. of awards offered: One.

Frequency: Annual.

Value: C$1,000.

Study Establishment: An appropriate institution.

Country of Study: Canada.

Closing Date: November 30th (postmark).

*1989 Polytechnique Commemorative Award

Subjects: Any subject, with special consideration given to study of issues related to women.

Eligibility: Open to women who hold at least a bachelor's degree or equivalent from a recognized university, who are Canadian citizens or have held landed immigrant status for at least one year and who are able to justify the relevance of their work to women.

Purpose: To provide partial funding for graduate study.

No. of awards offered: One.

Frequency: Annual.

Value: C$1,400.

Study Establishment: An appropriate institution.

Country of Study: Canada.

Closing Date: November 30th.

*Professional Fellowship

Subjects: Any subject.

Eligibility: Open to women who are Canadian citizens or who have held landed immigrant status for at least one year prior to submitting application. Candidates should hold a bachelor's degree or its equivalent from a recognized Canadian university and wish to pursue graduate work below the PhD level. Acceptance into the proposed place of study or research must be shown at the time of application.

Purpose: To provide partial funding for graduate study below the PhD.

Type: Fellowship.

No. of awards offered: Two.

Frequency: Annual.

Value: C$5,000 paid in two half-yearly instalments.

Study Establishment: A recognized professional school.

Country of Study: Canada or elsewhere.

Closing Date: November 30th (postmark).

Additional Information: The Fellowship is not renewable. Application forms are available from the Federation.

Alice E Wilson Awards

Subjects: Any subject.

Eligibility: Open to women who are Canadian citizens or have held landed immigrant status for at least one year prior to submitting application. Candidates should have a bachelor's degree or its equivalent from a recognized university, not necessarily in Canada. Special consideration is given to candidates returning to study after a few years. Candidates must have been accepted into the proposed programme of study.

Purpose: To assist women who wish to do refresher work or specialized study in their chosen field, or retrain in new techniques applicable to their fields.

No. of awards offered: Varies.

Frequency. Annual.

Value: C$1,000.

Study Establishment: Appropriate institutions.

Country of Study: Canada or elsewhere.

Applications Procedure: Application forms are available from the Federation.

Closing Date: November 30th (postmark).

CANADIAN FITNESS AND LIFESTYLE RESEARCH INSTITUTE

Canadian Fitness and Lifestyle Research Institute, Suite 201, 185 Somerset St. West, Ottawa, Ontario, K2P 0J2, Canada
Tel: 613 233 5528
Fax: 613 233 5536
Email: cflri@hookup.net

Research Contributions Program

Subjects: Physical activity, physical fitness, and related lifestyles.

Eligibility: Open to any qualified researcher or group of researchers within Canada, provided the project does not constitute the doctoral or master's thesis of the principal investigator. Researchers from Canadian universities, colleges, national, provincial, territorial or municipal associations, agencies or institutions, research groups or individuals are eligible. In all cases, a qualified researcher must be designated as the principal investigator who will be responsible for the project. The principal investigator must be a Canadian citizen or landed immigrant. In addition, an agency acceptable to the Institute must be designated responsible for the financial administration of the project.

Purpose: To encourage investigations concerning physical activity, fitness, the inter-relationships between physical activity, fitness, lifestyle and health, and the use of this knowledge in the development of programs and services.

No. of awards offered: Varies.

Frequency: Annual.

Value: Varies.

Country of Study: Canada.

Closing Date: December 1st.

CANADIAN FORESTRY FOUNDATION

Canadian Forestry Foundation, 185 Somerset St. W, Suite 203, Ottawa, Ontario, K2P 0J2, Canada
Tel: 613 232 1815
Fax: 613 232 4210

Contact: Glen Blouin

The Canadian Forestry Foundation is a registered charity whose purpose is to support the educational programs of the Canadian Forestry Association in promoting understanding and co-operation in the wise use and environmentally sound sustainable development of Canada's forests

Forest Capital of Canada Award

Subjects: Forestry.

Eligibility: Open to forest communities in Canada which fulfil the terms of the purpose of the award.

Level of Study: Unrestricted.

Purpose: To recognize each year one community in Canada which is distinct because of its commitment to and dependence on, the forest (past, present and future) and the civic-minded recognition of the importance of the forest to the community.

No. of awards offered: Three.

Frequency: Annual.

Country of Study: Canada.

Closing Date: December 31st, three years prior to year of recognition.

Forest Education Scholarship

Subjects: Forest education and communication.

Eligibility: Eligible to Canadian citizens currently enrolled in the undergraduate or graduate forestry program at a recognized Canadian university. Applicants with backgrounds in communications or education who are registered in a forestry technical school may also be considered; likewise, students with a formal forestry background who are currently studying education at the university level may also apply.

Level of Study: Undergraduate, Postgraduate.

Purpose: To encourage students to consider a career in the education and communications side of forestry.

Type: Scholarship.

No. of awards offered: One.

Frequency: Annual.

Value: C$500.

Length of Study: One academic year.

Study Establishment: A recognized Canadian university or forestry technical school.

Country of Study: Canada.

Applications Procedure: Applications must be submitted in writing.

Closing Date: May 30th.

Trees and People (TAP) Award

Subjects: Forestry.

Eligibility: Open to extension forestry specialists.

Level of Study: Unrestricted.

Purpose: To recognize outstanding contribution to extension forestry. Some onsideration is given to contribution to previous Woodlot Extension Specialists' Seminars of CFA's National Tree Farm Committee.

No. of awards offered: One.

Frequency: Annual.

Country of Study: Canada.

CANADIAN FOUNDATION FOR PHARMACY

Canadian Foundation for Pharmacy, Suite 603, 123 Edward Street,
Toronto, Ontario, M59 1E2, Canada
Tel: 416 979 2024
Fax: 416 599 9244

*Clinical Practice Education Support Grant

Subjects: Clinical pharmacy.

Eligibility: Open to Canadian citizens or landed immigrants who hold a BSc degree in pharmacy and are enrolled full-time in an accredited PharmD degree program or can provide proof of admission into such a program.

Level of Study: Postgraduate.

Purpose: To encourage the entry of more individuals into clinical practice, where the training is expensive but critical.

No. of awards offered: Three.

Frequency: Annual.

Value: C$2,000 per award.

Closing Date: May 1st.

*Development Grants

Subjects: In assessing applications, priority will be given to projects devoted to the development of entry level education programs (curriculum development), post-entry level education programs as well as quality assurance programs for Canadian Pharmacy Education. The Foundation may, however, consider funding other types of projects.

Eligibility: Open to individuals or groups of investigators whose proposed project has received official approval by the sponsoring university.

Purpose: To provide financial support for developmental activities in education.

No. of awards offered: Varies.

Frequency: Annual.

Value: Up to C$10,000.

Length of Study: One year; renewable in certain cases.

Study Establishment: A Canadian faculty or School of Pharmacy.

Country of Study: Canada.

Closing Date: November 15th.

Additional Information: A project grant will be awarded to an individual or a group and the funds will be administered by the sponsoring university. Any individual or group will be limited to a single grant within a given 12-month period. The project Director must submit to the Foundation, within 60 days of the terminal date, a report on the accomplishments. An official financial report must be appended to the report. The Canadian Foundation for Pharmacy must receive appropriate acknowledgement in any publication or report based on the project. Applications will be screened on receipt for conformity with the objectives of this program, for completeness, and for compliance with the terms and conditions of the Foundation. Applications accepted for review will be assessed by a panel of experts selected by the Foundation. Final selection of grant recipients will be made by the Board of Directors based upon the recommendation of its Committee on Pharmaceutical Education and Research.

*Hospital Pharmacy Award

Subjects: Hospital pharmacy.

Eligibility: Open to Canadian citizens or landed immigrants who hold a BS degree in pharmacy, are enrolled or have been enrolled full-time in an accredited hospital pharmacy program in Canada during the year of application, and have successfully completed the bulk of their program requirements by the time of application.

Purpose: To recognize excellence of performance by students participating in an accredited hospital pharmacy program, and to encourage entry and continued progress of such individuals in the practice.

No. of awards offered: Two.

Frequency: Annual.

Value: C$1,000 and C$500 respectively.

Country of Study: Canada.

Closing Date: September 1st.

*Industrial Pharmacy Awards

Subjects: Industrial pharmacy.

Eligibility: Open to Canadian citizens or landed immigrants who are enrolled full-time in a bachelor of pharmacy program in Canada and have completed the PMAC Industrial Pharmacy Studentship Program during the summer immediately preceding the date of application.

Purpose: To honour distinguished performance of undergraduate pharmacy students participating in the PMAC Industrial Pharmacy Studentship Program.

No. of awards offered: Two.

Frequency: Annual.

Value: C$1,000 and C$500 respectively.

Country of Study: Canada.

Closing Date: October 1st.

*Lecture Grants

Subjects: Pharmacy.

Eligibility: Open to Canadian Faculties of Pharmacy.

Purpose: To assist Canadian Faculties of Pharmacy and the Association of Faculties of Pharmacy of Canada in bringing renowned speakers/educators to Faculties and to the AFPC Annual Education/Research Symposium.

Type: Grant.

No. of awards offered: Three.

Frequency: Annual.

Value: C$1,000.

Country of Study: Canada.

Additional Information: One grant is awarded annually to the Association of Faculties of Pharmacy of Canada; two grants are awarded on a rotational basis to Canadian Faculties of Pharmacy. Grants to Faculties of Pharmacy will be awarded only during the academic calendar year of eligibility for application. There are no official application forms. In the case of visiting educators, the Dean should supply a curriculum vitae and list of publications and research interests of the proposed candidate to the Foundation office. In addition, full details of the planned schedule of activities should be included.

*Pharmacy Administration Education Support Program

Subjects: Pharmacy administration with a clear orientation in healthcare administration and behavioural sciences.

Eligibility: Open to Canadian citizens or landed immigrants who hold a BS degree in pharmacy and are enrolled full-time in a program of study and research leading to a higher degree in pharmacy administration or can provide proof of admission into such a program.

Purpose: To assist in the provision of highly qualified manpower to universities, government and industry by providing financial support to excellent students working towards a higher degree.

No. of awards offered: One.

Frequency: Annual.

Value: C$5,000.

Country of Study: Canada.

Closing Date: December 1st.

Additional Information: The grant is renewable.

Pharmacy Research Awards Program

Subjects: Pharmacy.

Eligibility: Open to Canadian citizens or landed immigrants who are enrolled in a MSc or PhD program in a Canadian Faculty of Pharmacy.

Level of Study: Postgraduate, Doctorate.

Purpose: To give special recognition to deserving students pursuing graduate work.

No. of awards offered: Two.

Frequency: Annual.

Value: C$1,000.

Country of Study: Canada.

Closing Date: April 15th.

Additional Information: There are 2 award categories available within this program: Podium presentations and Poster presentations. Presentations must be made at the AFPC Annual Research Symposium and Conference. Selection will be based on form and content. Winners will be announced no later than June 30th.

Professional Practice Award

Subjects: Activities may be characterized as health services studies, demonstration projects, conferences and workshops, self-care strategies, innovative models for coping, aids or health care delivery services, etc.

Eligibility: Open to Canadian citizens or landed immigrants who are enrolled full-time in a bachelor of pharmacy program in Canada and have completed a project dealing with activities pertaining to the promotion, development, delivery or the evaluation of community health services.

Purpose: To support student initiatives designed to foster public health awareness.

No. of awards offered: Two.

Frequency: Annual.

Value: C$1,000 and C$500 respectively.

Country of Study: Canada.

Closing Date: September 15th.

Research Project Funding Support Grant

Subjects: In assessing applications, priority will be given to research projects in the areas of pharmacy practice and the development of novel teaching methods with emphasis on clinical practice, human relations and communications, geriatrics, economics and pharmacy management issues. The Foundation will, however, consider funding for other types of research.

Eligibility: Open to individuals or groups of investigators who have received official approval by the sponsoring institution (university, health-care facility, pharmacy, etc.).

Purpose: To provide financial support for innovative research activities.

No. of awards offered: Varies.

Frequency: Annual.

Value: Up to C$20,000.

Length of Study: One year; possibly renewable.

Country of Study: Canada.

Closing Date: November 15th.

Additional Information: Projects must be conducted in close cooperation with a Canadian Faculty or School of Pharmacy. A project grant will be awarded to an individual or group of investigators and the funds will be administered by the sponsoring university. An individual or group of investigators will be limited to a single grant within a given 12-month period. The project Director must submit to the Foundation, within 60 days of the terminal date, a report on the research accomplishments. The Canadian Foundation for Pharmacy must receive appropriate acknowledgement in any publication or report based on the project. Applications will be screened on receipt for conformity with the objectives of this program, for completeness, and for compliance with the terms and conditions of the Foundation. Applications accepted for review will be assessed by a panel of experts selected by the Foundation. Final selection of grant recipients will be made by the Board of Directors based upon the recommendation of its Committee on Pharmaceutical Education and Research. Details of requirements for the submission of applications are available from the Foundation.

CANADIAN FOUNDATION FOR THE STUDY OF INFANT DEATHS

Canadian Foundation for the Study of Infant Deaths, 586 Eglinton Avenue East, Suite 300, Toronto, Ontario, M4P 1P2, Canada
Tel: 416 488 3260
Fax: 416 488 3864
Email: sidscanada@inforamp.net
www: www.sidscanada.org/sids.html
Contact: Executive Director

Dr Sydney Segal Research Grants

Subjects: Any discipline (medical, psychological, nursing, biological, sociological, etc.) which is concerned with the causes, effects and/or prevention of Sudden Infant Death Syndrome.

Eligibility: Open to suitably qualified graduate students who are undertaking full-time training in research in the health sciences leading to an MSc or PhD or the equivalent (studentship level) and to suitably qualified persons who are undertaking higher-level training in research into Sudden Infant Death Syndrome (fellowship level).

Level of Study: Postgraduate, Doctorate, Postdoctorate.

Purpose: To enable students to pursue full-time higher degree studies researching into the possible causes, effects and/or prevention of Sudden Infant Death Syndrome.

Type: Research Grants.

No. of awards offered: Variable.

Frequency: Annual.

Value: In accordance with current MRC guidelines for studentships and fellowships.

Length of Study: Normally one year.

Study Establishment: A Canadian university.

Country of Study: Canada.

Applications Procedure: Applications required, including transcripts, budgets, references etc; application forms are available from the Foundation.

Closing Date: June 1st.

CANADIAN FRIENDS OF THE HEBREW UNIVERSITY

Canadian Friends of the Hebrew University, 3080 Yonge Street, Suite 5024, Toronto, Ontario, M4N 3P4, Canada
Tel: 416 485 8000
Fax: 416 485 8565
Contact: Academic Affairs Committee

Financial Assistance

Subjects: Any subject.

Eligibility: Open to Canadian citizens or landed immigrants.

Purpose: To enable Canadian students to attend the Hebrew University of Jerusalem.

Type: Bursary.

No. of awards offered: Varies.

Frequency: Annual.

Value: Approximately C$750-C$4,000, at the discretion of the Academic Affairs Committee.

Length of Study: One year.

Study Establishment: Hebrew University of Jerusalem.

Country of Study: Israel.

Closing Date: March 31st.

CANADIAN HOME ECONOMICS ASSOCIATION

Canadian Home Economics Association, 901-151 Slater Street, Ottawa, Ontario, K1P 5H3, Canada
Tel: 613 238 8817
Fax: 613 238 1677
Contact: M Martin

Ruth Binnie Scholarship

Subjects: Home economics or home economics education.

Eligibility: Open to Canadian citizens or landed immigrants who are holders of a professional teaching certificate and also members of the Canadian Home Economics Association. First consideration will be given to applicants proceeding towards a masters in education on a full-time basis. Second consideration will go to part-time students, and Scholarship monies will be pro-rated.

Level of Study: Postgraduate, Doctorate.

Type: Scholarship.

No. of awards offered: Two.

Frequency: Annual.

Value: C$5,000.

Study Establishment: An appropriate institution, for full-time graduate study.

Applications Procedure: Application form must be completed - these can be obtained through faculty offices or from CHEA.

Closing Date: Postmarked no later than January 15th.

Additional Information: The Awards are based on scholarship, personal qualities, contributions toward home economics education in junior or senior high school, and potential in the education field. All candidates should have a high commitment to the teaching profession and home economics education.

Mary A Clarke Memorial Scholarship, Silver Jubilee Scholarship and Fiftieth Anniversary Scholarship

Subjects: Home economics.

Eligibility: Open to Canadian citizens or landed immigrants who are graduates in home economics planning to undertake, or currently engaged in, graduate study leading to a higher degree. Candidates must be members of the Canadian Home Economics Association. The Fiftieth Anniversary Scholarship is for doctoral study.

Level of Study: Postgraduate, Doctorate.

Purpose: To promote skilled and imaginative inquiry.

Type: Scholarship.

No. of awards offered: Three.

Frequency: Annual.

Value: C$3,000-4,000.

Length of Study: One year.

Study Establishment: Any suitable location.

Applications Procedure: Application form must be completed - these can be obtained through faculty offices or the CHEA.

Closing Date: Postmarked no later than January 15th.

Additional Information: The Awards will be based on scholarship, personal qualities, past and/or potential contribution to the profession of home economics, and financial considerations.

Robin Hood Multifoods Scholarship

Subjects: Home economics.

Eligibility: Open to Canadian citizens or landed immigrants who are graduates in home economics and members of the Canadian Home Economics Association.

Level of Study: Postgraduate, Doctorate.

Type: Scholarship.

No. of awards offered: One.

Frequency: Annual.

Value: C$1,000.

Study Establishment: An appropriate institution for postgraduate study leading to an advanced degree.

Applications Procedure: Application form must be completed - these can be obtained through faculty offices or from CHEA.

Closing Date: Postmarked no later than January 15th.

Additional Information: The award is based on academic achievement, personal qualities, and past and/or potential contribution to the home economics profession. Preference is given to candidates planning a career in business, the consumer service (foods) field or food service management.

Nestlé Canada, Inc Scholarship

Subjects: Home economics.

Eligibility: Open to Canadian citizens or landed immigrants who have received a degree in home economics or a closely allied discipline. Candidates must be members of the Canadian Home Economics Association.

Level of Study: Postgraduate, Doctorate.

Type: Scholarship.

No. of awards offered: One.

Frequency: Annual.

Value: C$1,000.

Length of Study: One year.

Study Establishment: Any suitable location.

Applications Procedure: Application form must be completed - these can be obtained through faculty offices or CHEA.

Closing Date: Postmarked no later than January 15th.

Additional Information: Special consideration will be given to students undertaking postgraduate study in foods.

CANADIAN INSTITUTE FOR ADVANCED LEGAL STUDIES

Canadian Institute for Advanced Legal Studies, Suite 203, 4 Beechwood AVenue, Ottawa, Ontario, K1L 8L9, Canada
Tel: 613 744 6166
Fax: 613 744 5766
Contact: Mr Frank McArdle

Graduate Scholarships at Cambridge University

Subjects: Law.

Eligibility: Open to graduates of Canadian law schools, law students in their articling year at the time of application, and to students registered in a bar admission course at the time of application.

Level of Study: Postgraduate.

Purpose: To promote the study of law at Cambridge University by graduates of Canadian law schools.

Type: Fellowship.

No. of awards offered: Two.

Frequency: Annual.

Value: Approximately C$14,000 to cover tuition fee, a contribution towards living costs and return air fare.

Length of Study: One year.

Study Establishment: Cambridge University.

Country of Study: England.

Closing Date: December 31st.

Additional Information: The Scholarship may be held with another small award as approved by the Institute.

The Rt. Hon. Paul Martin Scholarship

Subjects: Law.

Eligibility: Open to graduates of Canadian Faculty of Law at the time of application; or law students in their articling year at the time of application; or to students registered in their Bar Admission course at the time of application.

Level of Study: Postgraduate.

Purpose: To study for an LL.M at the University of Cambridge.

Type: Scholarship.

No. of awards offered: Two.

Frequency: Annual.

Value: C$14,000.

Length of Study: One year.

Study Establishment: University of Cambridge.

Country of Study: England.

Applications Procedure: There is no application form. Application consists of: a letter of application, undergraduate and Faculty of Law transcripts, and no more than three letters of recommendation.

Closing Date: December 31st.

CANADIAN LIBRARY ASSOCIATION

Scholarships and Awards Committee, Canadian Library Association Membership Services, 200 Elgin Street, Suite 602, Ottawa, Ontario, K2P 1L5, Canada
Tel: 613 232 9625 ext.318
Fax: 613 563 9895

CLA Dafoe Scholarship

Subjects: Library science.

Eligibility: Open to Canadian citizens and landed immigrants.

Level of Study: Postgraduate.

Type: Scholarship.

No. of awards offered: One.

Frequency: Annual.

Value: C$1,750.

Length of Study: One year.

Study Establishment: An accredited library school.

Country of Study: Canada.

Applications Procedure: Application forms are available on request. Applicants must submit transcripts, reference and proof of admission to a library school.

Closing Date: May 1st.

Additional Information: Consideration is given to both academic standing and financial need.

CLA Research Grants

Subjects: Library and information science.

Eligibility: Open to Canadian citizens and landed immigrants who are personal members of the CLA.

Purpose: To support theoretical and applied research in Canada.

Type: Research Grant.

No. of awards offered: One or more.

Froquonoy: Annual.

Value: One or more grants totalling C$1,000.

Length of Study: One year.

Country of Study: Canada.

Applications Procedure: Application guidelines are available on request.

Additional Information: Consideration is given both to academic standing and financial need.

Howard V Phalin - World Book Graduate Scholarship in Library Science

Subjects: Library science.

Eligibility: Open to Canadian citizens or landed immigrants with a BLS or MLS degree. In exceptional circumstances the Scholarship may be given to an outstanding candidate with a degree in another discipline who wishes to obtain a BLS or MLS degree.

Level of Study: Postgraduate.

Type: Scholarship.

No. of awards offered: One.

Frequency: Annual.

Value: C$2,500.

Length of Study: One year.

Study Establishment: An accredited library school.

Country of Study: Canada or the USA.

Closing Date: May 1st.

Additional Information: Consideration is given to both academic standing and financial need. The Scholarship is given for study leading to a further library degree or related to library work in which the candidate is currently engaged, or to library work which will be undertaken upon completion of the studies.

H W Wilson Scholarship

Subjects: Library science.

Eligibility: Open to Canadian citizens or landed immigrants.

Level of Study: Postgraduate.

Type: Scholarship.

No. of awards offered: One.

Frequency: Annual.

Value: C$2,000.

Length of Study: One year.

Study Establishment: An accredited library school.

Country of Study: Canada.

Closing Date: May 1st.

Additional Information: Consideration is given to both academic standing and financial need.

CANADIAN LIVER FOUNDATION

Canadian Liver Foundation, 365 Bloor Street East, Suite 200, Toronto, Ontario, M4W 3L4, Canada
Tel: 416 964 1953
Fax: 416 964 0024
Contact: The Executive Director

Establishment Grants

Subjects: Hepatology.

Eligibility: Open to clinical investigators and basic scientists who hold an MD or PhD degree or equivalent and have a proven interest in the structure and function of the liver or its diseases. Applicants must have completed a minimum of two and preferably three years' formal research training (post-medical speciality training in the case of MDs) and have obtained additional research experience as a clinical investigator.

Level of Study: Postgraduate, Doctorate.

Purpose: To help young investigators to become established within three years of their first academic appointment with the clear intent for ongoing research in liver disorders.

Type: Grant.

Frequency: Annual.

Value: Up to C$60,000 per annum.

Length of Study: Two years.

Study Establishment: At the recipient's own laboratory in a Canadian university.

Country of Study: Canada.

Closing Date: 1 November.

Fellowships

Subjects: Hepatic function or disease.

Eligibility: Open to holders of an MD or PhD who are Canadian citizens normally resident in Canada or researchers resident in Canada at the time of application. Canadian citizens and landed immigrants will receive first consideration, others will be considered if the situation permits.

Level of Study: Postgraduate, Doctorate.

Purpose: To provide support for specialized clinical or experimental training for those who have already completed the basic graduate programme.

Type: Fellowship.

Frequency: Annual.

Value: Equivalent to current scales of other national Fellowship awards.

Length of Study: One year; renewable once.

Country of Study: Unrestricted.

Closing Date: 1 November.

Graduate Studentships

Subjects: Any discipline relevant to the objectives of the Canadian Liver Foundation.

Eligibility: Candidates must be accepted into a full-time university graduate science programme in a medically related discipline related to a Master's or Doctoral degree and hold a record of superior academic performance in studies relevant to the proposed training.

Level of Study: Postgraduate, Doctorate.

Purpose: To enable academically superior students to undertake full-time studies in a Canadian university.

Type: Studentship.

No. of awards offered: Up to four.

Frequency: Annual.

Value: A stipend equivalent to that awarded by a Medical Research Council of Canada studentship award.

Length of Study: One year; renewable up to three times.

Country of Study: Canada.

Closing Date: 15 February.

Additional Information: A student supported by the Foundation must not hold a current stipend award from another granting agency.

Operating Grant

Subjects: Hepatology.

Eligibility: Open to hepatobiliary research investigators who hold an academic appointment in a Canadian institution.

Purpose: To support research projects directed towards a defined objective.

Type: Grant.

Frequency: Dependent on funds available.

Value: C$60,000 per annum.

Country of Study: Canada.

Applications Procedure: Application plus supporting documentation.

Closing Date: December 15th.

CANADIAN NURSES FOUNDATION

Canadian Nurses Foundation, 50 Driveway, Ottawa, Ontario, K2P 1E2, Canada
Tel: 613 237 2133
Fax: 613 237 3520
Contact: Beverly Campbell, Executive Director

CNF Research Grants

Subjects: Nursing practice; nursing education; nursing administration.

Eligibility: Open to Canadian nurses who are members of the Canadian Nurses Foundation.

Purpose: To provide support for nursing research.

Type: Research grant.

No. of awards offered: Varies.

Frequency: Annual.

Value: C$5,000 for Small Research Grants; C$15,000 for Dr Dorothy J Kergin Research Grant in Primary Health Care; C$15,000 for Large Research Grants.

Study Establishment: An appropriate institution.

Country of Study: Any country.

Closing Date: 15 June.

Additional Information: The types of research to be funded are research proposals pertaining to nursing practice, education, or administration.

CNF Scholarships and Fellowships

Subjects: All nursing specialties; several awards are identified for neuro-surgical, oncology, community health nursing, epidemiology, gerontology, child/family health care, nursing administration, occupational health, northern nursing, dialysis nursing.

Eligibility: Open to Canadian nurses who are members of the Canadian Nurses Foundation.

Level of Study: Postgraduate, Doctorate, Baccalaureate.

Purpose: To assist Canadian nurses pursuing further education and research.

Type: Scholarship; fellowship.

No. of awards offered: Varies.

Frequency: Annual.

Value: C$3,000-C$3,500 for a master's program; C$4,500-C$6,000 for a doctoral program; C$1,500-C$2,000 for a baccalaureate program.

Length of Study: One year.

Country of Study: Any country.

Closing Date: 15 April.

Additional Information: In accepting an award from the Foundation, a recipient agrees to serve in a nursing position in Canada, for a period of one year for each year of financial assistance and to submit to CNF a copy of any thesis, study or major paper undertaken as part of the course.

CANADIAN POLITICAL SCIENCE ASSOCIATION

Canadian Political Science Association, 1 Stewart Street, Suite 205, University of Ottawa, Ottawa, Ontario, K1N 6H7, Canada
Tel: 613 564 4026
Fax: 613 230 2746
Contact: Program

*Parliamentary Internship Program

Subjects: Canadian parliamentary government.

Eligibility: Open to Canadian university graduates.

Purpose: To give university graduates an opportunity to supplement their theoretical knowledge of Parliament with practical experience of the day-to-day work of the Members of Parliament and to provide backbench Members with highly qualified assistants.

No. of awards offered: Ten.

Frequency: Annually, depending on funds available.

Value: A stipend of C$15,000, plus travel subsidies.

Length of Study: Ten months.

Country of Study: Canada.

Closing Date: Last Friday in January.

Additional Information: Interns will be assigned specific responsibilities with Members of the House of Commons and will be required to attend seminars and prepare a paper analysing an aspect of parliamentary government in Canada.

CANADIAN-SCANDINAVIAN FOUNDATION

Canadian-Scandinavian Foundation, c/o Department of Geography, McGill University, 805 Sherbrooke Street West, Montreal, Quebec, H3A 2K6, Canada
Tel: 514 398 4304
Fax: 514 398 7437
Email: LUNDGREN@FELIX.GEOG.MCGILL.CA
Contact: Dr Jan Lundgren

Brucebo Scholarship

Subjects: Fine arts.

Eligibility: Open to young Canadian painters, or other persons in the field of fine arts.

Level of Study: Unrestricted.

Purpose: To support two months' summer stay for a Canadian painter or artist.

Type: Scholarship.

No. of awards offered: One.

Frequency: Annual.

Value: Approximately C$4,000-C$5,000 (including transport costs and a food stipend).

Length of Study: Two months.

Study Establishment: At Brucebo on the Island of Gotland.

Country of Study: Sweden.

Applications Procedure: Please request application form.

Closing Date: January 31st.

Additional Information: The facility can accommodate a family member (or equivalent).

W B Bruce Fine Arts European Travel Scholarship

Subjects: Fine arts, preferably painting.

Eligibility: Open to Canadian residents and landed immigrants.

Level of Study: Unrestricted.

Purpose: To fund a European study visit, including visits to Nordic countries during fall or winter term (not peak season) for a talented, younger Canadian painter.

Type: Scholarship.

No. of awards offered: One.

Frequency: Annual.

Value: SEK25,000.

Study Establishment: Studios and other fine arts institutions.

Country of Study: Europe and Scandinavia.

Applications Procedure: Application form must be completed.

Closing Date: January 31st.

CSF Special Purpose Grants

Subjects: Any subject.

Eligibility: Open to qualified Canadians/landed immigrants.

Level of Study: Postgraduate.

Purpose: To provide travel support for shorter study or research visit to a Scandinavian or Nordic country destination.

Type: Grant.

No. of awards offered: Variable.

Frequency: Annual.

Value: Approximately C$500-C$800.

Length of Study: A short period of time.

Country of Study: Scandinavia.

Applications Procedure: Application form must be completed.

Closing Date: 31 January.

Swedish Institute Bursaries

Subjects: Academic studies at a postgraduate level, or other advanced studies or research.

Eligibility: Open to nationals of any country.

Level of Study: Postgraduate, Postdoctorate, Professional development.

Purpose: To support graduate and postgraduate studies or research in Sweden.

Type: Bursary.

No. of awards offered: Variable.

Frequency: Annual.

Value: C$8,000.

Length of Study: 3-8 months.

Study Establishment: An appropriate institution.

Country of Study: Sweden.

Applications Procedure: Please request application form from Swedish Institute, Stockholm.

Closing Date: December 1st, each year.

Additional Information: This is an international competition, with numbers of grants varying from one year to the next.

For further information contact:
The Swedish Institute, Scholarship Bureau, PO Box 7434, Stockholm, S-10391, Sweden
Tel: 46 8789 20 00
Fax: 46 820 72 48
Telex: 100 25 SWEDINS S

CANADIAN SOCIETY FOR CHEMICAL ENGINEERING

Canadian Society for Chemical Engineering, 130 Slater Street, Suite 550, Ottawa, Ontario, K1P 6E2, Canada
Tel: 613 232 6252
Fax: 613 232 5862
Email: cic_prog@fox.nstn.ca
Contact: Program Manager, Awards

J E Zajic Postgraduate Scholarship

Subjects: Biochemical engineering.

Eligibility: Open to postgraduate students registered in chemical engineering at a Canadian university and engaged in research of a biochemical nature.

Level of Study: Postgraduate.

Type: Scholarship.

No. of awards offered: One.

Frequency: Biennially (even-numbered years).

Value: Approximately C$1,000 per annum.

Length of Study: Two years.

Study Establishment: A Canadian University.

Country of Study: Canada.

Applications Procedure: Applications should include evidence of academic standing, a brief description of the work to be undertaken and letters of reference.

Closing Date: December 1st (even-numbered years) for selection by March 31st.

Additional Information: The Society is a constituent of the Chemical Institute of Canada.

CANADIAN SOCIETY FOR CHEMISTRY

Canadian Society for Chemistry, 130 Slater Street, Suite 550, Ottawa, Ontario, K1P 6E2, Canada
Tel: 613 232 6252
Fax: 613 232 5862
Email: cic_prog@fox.nstn.ca
Contact: Ms Diane Goltz, Awards Program Manager

Ichikizaki Fund for Young Chemists

Subjects: Synthetic organic chemistry.

Eligibility: Open to members of the Canadian Society for Chemistry who have not passed their 34th birthday as of 31 December of the year in which the application is submitted, who have a research specialty in synthetic organic chemistry and are scheduled to attend within one year

an international conference or symposium directly related to synthetic organic chemistry.

Purpose: To provide financial assistance to young chemists who are showing unique achievements in basic research by facilitating their participation in international conferences or symposia.

Frequency: Twice yearly.

Value: The maximum value of any one award is C$10,000. Successful applicants may, however, reapply in subsequent years, provided the cumulative total of all awards does not exceed C$15,000.

Closing Date: 30 June for conferences scheduled between 1 January and 30 June of the following year; 31 December for conferences scheduled between 1 July and 31 December of the following year.

Additional Information: The number of applicants to be recommended by the Society is limited to ten per year. Although the awards are intended primarily for established researchers, applications from postgraduate students and postdoctoral fellows will be considered. However, only one application per year from a graduate student can be recommended to the Fund. Applications should include a résumé, copies of recent research papers, the title and brief description of the conference the applicant wishes to attend, the title (and abstract, if available) of the research paper the applicant intends to present and a proposed budget. Applications from graduate students must be accompanied by a letter of reference from the research supervisor. The Society is a constituent of the Chemical Institute of Canada.

THE CANADIAN SOCIETY FOR CLINICAL INVESTIGATION

The Canadian Society for Clinical Investigation, 774 Echo Drive, Ottawa, Ontario, K1S 5N8, Canada
Tel: 613 730 6240
Fax: 613 730 8194
Contact: Dr J H Matthews, Secretary-Treasurer

Schering Travelling Fellowships

Subjects: Clinical investigation.

Eligibility: Open to clinical investigators who are members of the Society or are sponsored by members of the Society.

Purpose: To assist in the interchange of personnel involved in the field of clinical investigation.

Type: Fellowship.

No. of awards offered: Variable.

Value: Up to C$2,000.

Length of Study: Four weeks or more.

Study Establishment: Appropriate centres.

Country of Study: Canada and elsewhere.

Closing Date: April 1st.

Additional Information: The Fellowships are also available for invited visits to a medical faculty in Canada.

CANADIAN SOCIETY OF LABORATORY TECHNOLOGISTS

Canadian Society of Laboratory Technologists, PO 2830, LCDI, Hamilton, Ontario, L8N 3N8, Canada
Tel: 905 528 8642
Fax: 905 528 4968
www: http://www.cslt.com
Contact: Quebec CE Fund Committee

Quebec CE Fund Grants

Subjects: Medical technology.

Eligibility: Open to any person or group who is able to establish or coordinate the establishment of continuing education programs for francophone members of the CSLT. This would include individual CSLT members, an affiliated Society or Branch, the Ordre Professionnelle des Technologistes Médicaux du Québec (OPTMQ) and institutions which teach medical technology.

Purpose: To promote continuing education among medical laboratory technologists who are francophones.

Type: Grant.

No. of awards offered: Varies.

Value: Varies.

Country of Study: Canada.

Additional Information: It is CSLT policy that continuing education programs should normally be financially self-supporting through the fees charged for the program. However, there are some situations in which a program is needed in a particular location, but the program cannot be self-supporting without charging unacceptably high fees. There may also be a need to fund development costs for certain types of programs. All requests for the use of the Quebec CE funds shall be reviewed and approved or rejected by the Quebec CE Fund Committee and then considered for ratification at the next CSLT Board of Directors meeting. There is no standardized application form, but all applications must include the following documentation: the amount of the grant requested from the Quebec CE fund; an outline of the proposed program; a comprehensive budget including a breakdown of expenses; a statement of other support to be received or being applied for, e.g. a subsidy from a provincial Society; expected revenues; who will hold control of the program and the proposed method of administration; development times and the dates that progress reports will be submitted during development; evidence of the need for the program; and a signed statement declaring that CSLT members will be permitted to participate in the finished program at no increased differential fee.

CANADIAN WILDLIFE SERVICE

University Research Support Fund, Canadian Wildlife Service, Ottawa, Ontario, K1A 0H3, Canada
Tel: 819 953 1408
Fax: 819 953 6283
Contact: Program Integration Coordinator

*University Research Support Fund

Subjects: Wildlife (excluding fish and marine mammals).

Eligibility: Open to Canadian citizens or landed immigrants registered for postgraduate work at a Canadian university and assigned to the proposed project by the supervising professor. Winners are chosen on the basis of the quality of the research proposal, and relevance of the proposed research to Canadian Wildlife Service programs.

Purpose: To provide financial assistance to registered graduate students at Canadian universities.

No. of awards offered: Varies.

Frequency: Annual.

Value: Up to C$2,500.

Length of Study: One year; may be renewed for a second or third year upon reapplication.

Study Establishment: Any Canadian university.

Country of Study: Canada.

Applications Procedure: A three- to five- page research proposal written by the student must be submitted with the application. Applications submitted by students must have the approval of their supervising professor.

Closing Date: February 1st.

Additional Information: Awards are made in the form of a grant to the selected university, care of the professor responsible (grantee). The financial assistance provided is not intended to fully support a project, only to cover partial expenses. Eligible expenses include salaries for students and field assistants, field travel and laboratory expenses.

CANCER ASSOCIATION OF SOUTH AFRICA

Cancer Association of South Africa, PO Box 2000, Johannesburg, 2000, South Africa
Tel: 011 403 2825/8
Fax: 011 403 1946

*Lady Cade Memorial Fellowship

Subjects: Research into the causation, diagnosis and/or treatment of cancer.

Eligibility: Open to medical graduates of senior status who are resident in South Africa, or South African nationals who are domiciled in the British Commonwealth, or in some cases, elsewhere. Preference is given to those holding senior posts at approved universities or other institutions to which the Fellows will be expected to return within six months of the termination of the Fellowship and work there for a period of not less than two years.

Purpose: To encourage professional development in cancer research.

Type: Fellowship.

No. of awards offered: One.

Frequency: Occasionally; dependent on funds available.

Value: R80,000 plus return economy air fare to the UK for the Fellow and his family.

Length of Study: 1-3 years.

Country of Study: UK.

Closing Date: Approximately six months prior to commencement of the Fellowship.

Additional Information: South Africans in the UK may apply through Cancer Research Campaign, 2 Carlton House Terrace, London SW1Y 5AR.

*Research Grants

Subjects: All aspects of the cancer problem, particularly those aspects which have a South African significance and can be investigated locally.

Eligibility: Open to medical graduates, biochemists, graduates in social science, etc. who are in full-time employment and can show distinct evidence of a capacity for original research or, in the case of BSc graduates, have won distinctions during their undergraduate studies. Candidates should be resident in South Africa.

Purpose: To assist professional staff with major or specialized equipment, laboratory running expenses, skilled or unskilled laboratory or other assistants; also to assist with printing and/or publishing the results of all types of research which fall within the Association's scope.

Type: Research Grant.

No. of awards offered: Varies.

Frequency: Annual.

Value: Varies according to merit.

Length of Study: 1-3 calendar years.

Country of Study: South Africa.

Closing Date: May 31st.

Additional Information: All major equipment will remain the property of the Association. Specific details of the types of research which fall within the Association's scope and additional information are available from the Association.

*Travel and Subsistence (Study) Grants

Subjects: Cancer projects.

Eligibility: Open to suitably qualified applicants in some aspect of the cancer field who are in full-time employment.

Purpose: To assist workers in the cancer field in improving their academic and/or technical qualifications and experience for the furtherance of cancer research and education, and for the improvement of diagnostic and/or treatment services to cancer patients in South Africa.

No. of awards offered: Varies.

Frequency: Twice yearly; dependent on funds available.

Value: Not to exceed 50% of the minimum costs (on condition that the applicant, through his own institution or by other means, pays the balance of the minimum costs). Minimum costs are calculated on the basis of an economy class air fare to the furthest point of travel with such deviations as may be approved by the Association, plus a subsistence allowance appropriate to the geographical area concerned.

Country of Study: Local and overseas.

Closing Date: January 31st, July 31st.

Additional Information: Travel Grants are awarded to suitable applicants to enable them to attend national or international conferences in the cancer field. Study Grants are awarded to suitable applicants who, by study at specialized centres, will be able to increase their knowledge in the cancer field with a view to its subsequent application in South Africa. Grantees are required to return to South Africa wihin a period of six months after expiration of the period for which the Grant was awarded (an extension will be considered on application) and to continue for a period of two years in the service in which they were employed at the time of the award. Grants may not be used for the purpose of studying for or obtaining degrees or diplomas. The Association also offers support to certain foreign medical scientists in the cancer field who are invited to visit South Africa to participate in scientific meetings and congresses, or for particular purposes as the need may arise.

CANCER RESEARCH CAMPAIGN

Cancer Research Campaign, 10 Cambridge Terrace, London, NW1 4JL; England
Tel: 0171 224 1333
Fax: 0171 487 4302
Contact: Science Department

Research Grant

Subjects: Cancer research; the Campaign only considers research proposals which are cancer related and contain a definite research aspect.

Eligibility: Applications will be accepted from scientists, clinicians or healthcare workers who possess suitable academic qualifications, and have the support of the head of department in the proposed place of work. Grants are normally available to applicants who have been resident in the UK for at least three years.

Type: Research grants.

No. of awards offered: Varies; 50 new project grants were awarded in 1995.

Value: Salaries, running expenses and equipment.

Length of Study: Usually three years; renewable annually. Extensions are considered.

Study Establishment: Appropriate universities, medical schools, hospitals and some research institutions. The host institution is responsible for administering the grant.

Country of Study: UK.

Applications Procedure: Applications to be forwarded to the Scientific Department of the Cancer Research Campaign.

Closing Date: Project grant applications are considered in January, April, June and October. Contact the Project Grants Administrator for an application form and deadlines.

Additional Information: Funding is also available for cancer education and psychosocial research projects. Contact the Education Department for details. The Campaign also awards a limited number of Fellowships for clinicians wishing to undertake a period of research. These are advertised annually in October. Contact Dr F Hemsley for details.

CANCER RESEARCH FUND OF THE DAMON RUNYON-WALTER WINCHELL FOUNDATION

Fellowship Department, Cancer Research Fund of the Damon Runyon-Walter Winchell Foundation, 131 East 36th Street, New York, NY, 10016, USA
Tel: 212 532 3888
Fax: 212 779 2236
Email: BFONNER@aol.com
Contact: Clare M Cahill

Postdoctoral Research Fellowships for Basic Scientists

Subjects: All theoretical and experimental biology areas relevant to the study of cancer and the search for cancer causes, mechanisms, therapies and preventions.

Eligibility: Candidates must have completed at least one of the following degrees or its equivalent: MD, PhD, DDS or DVM; and have received their degrees not more than one year prior to the Scientific Advisory Committee meeting at which their applications are to be considered. Only candidates who are beginning their first full-time postdoctoral research fellowship are eligible.

Level of Study: Postdoctorate.

Purpose: To augment the training of scientists who have demonstrated the motivation and potential to conduct original research under the supervision of a sponsor, thus equipping the Fellow to become an independent investigator.

Type: Fellowship.

No. of awards offered: 15-20.

Frequency: Three times yearly.

Value: US$25,000 stipend for the first year, US$30,500 for the second year and US$34,000 for the third year. The amount of the Fellowship is paid monthly to the sponsoring institution for the support of the Fellow. In addition, US$2,000 is awarded annually to the laboratory in which the Fellow is working. This amount is to be used at the discretion of the sponsor for expenses incident to the scientific development of the Fellow. These funds may not be used for institutional overheads.

Length of Study: Three years; renewable annually.

Study Establishment: An approved institution under a sponsor.

Country of Study: Any country (US citizens only) or the USA (all candidates).

Applications Procedure: Application form must be completed.

Closing Date: August 15th, December 15th and March 15th.

Research Fellowships for Physician Scientists

Subjects: All theoretical and experimental research that is relevant to the study of cancer and the search for cancer causes, mechanisms, therapies and preventions.

Eligibility: Applicants must have completed at least one of the following degrees or its equivalent: MD, PhD, DDS, DVM; and have completed their residencies or clinical fellowship training within three years prior to the Scientific Advisory Committee meeting at which their applications are to be considered.

Level of Study: Postdoctorate.

Purpose: To augment the training of a physician scientist who has demonstrated the motivation and potential to conduct original research under the supervision of a sponsor, thus equipping the Fellow to become an independent investigator.

Type: Fellowship.

No. of awards offered: Up to fifteen.

Frequency: Three times yearly.

Value: US$46,500 stipend for the first year, US$47,500 for the second year and US$49,000 for the third year. In addition, US$2,000 expenses is awarded annually.

Length of Study: Three years; renewable annually.

Study Establishment: An approved institution under a sponsor.

Country of Study: Any country (US citizens only) or the USA (all candidates).

Applications Procedure: Application form must be completed.

Closing Date: March 15th, August 15th and December 15th.

THE CANCER RESEARCH SOCIETY, INC

The Cancer Research Society, Inc, 1 Place Ville Marie, Suite 2332, Montréal, Québec, H3B 3M5, Canada
Tel: 514 861 9227
Fax: 514 861 9220
Contact: Flora Caplan, President, or the Scientific Director

Postdoctoral Fellowships

Subjects: Basic medical sciences.

Eligibility: Open to holders of a PhD or MD degree, of any nationality.

Level of Study: Postdoctorate.

Purpose: To provide financial support to recent PhD and MDs to acquire a more complete formation in research.

Type: Fellowship.

No. of awards offered: Seven, including renewals.

Frequency: Annual.

Value: C$28,510.

Study Establishment: Canadian universities and their affiliated institutions.

Country of Study: Canada.

Closing Date: February 15th.

Predoctoral Fellowships

Subjects: Biology, physiology, biochemistry, molecular biology, genetics, microbiology and immunology, medical sciences.

Eligibility: Open to persons of any nationality. The candidate must be registered in a Canadian graduate school.

Level of Study: Postgraduate, Doctorate.

Purpose: To provide financial support for candidates registered in graduate programs leading to the MSc or PhD degrees.

Type: Fellowship.

No. of awards offered: Eighteen, including renewals.

Frequency: Annual.

Value: C$15,050.

Study Establishment: Canadian universities and their affiliated institutions, for MSc or PhD programs in a recognized Canadian graduate school.

Country of Study: Canada.

Closing Date: February 15th.

Research Grants

Subjects: Fundamental research on cancer.

Eligibility: Candidates must hold an academic position on the staff of a Canadian university.

Level of Study: Professional development.

Purpose: To provide support for new or continuing research activities by independent scientists or group of investigators in the field of cancer.

Type: Research grant.

No. of awards offered: 98.

Frequency: Annual.

Value: C$30,000-C$60,000 to cover the cost of research. No equipment or travel permitted.

Study Establishment: Canadian universities and their affiliated institutions.

Country of Study: Canada.

Closing Date: February 15th.

CANTERBURY HISTORICAL ASSOCIATION

Canterbury Historical Association, c/o History Department, University of Canterbury, Private Bag, Christchurch, New Zealand
Tel: 03 364 2283
Fax: 03 364 2003
Contact: Dr G W Rice, Secretary

J M Sherrard Award

Subjects: New Zealand regional and local history writing.

Level of Study: Unrestricted.

Purpose: To foster high standards of scholarship.

Type: Cash prize.

No. of awards offered: One.

Frequency: Biennially.

Value: NZ$1,000.

Country of Study: New Zealand.

Applications Procedure: Titles are selected from the New Zealand National Bibliography and are assessed by a panel of judges. No application is required.

Additional Information: The prize money is often divided among two or three finalists. A commendation list is also published.

CAPITAL RADIO

Capital Radio, PO Box 95.8, London, NW1 3DR, England
Tel: 0171 608 6193
Fax: 0171 608 6008
Contact: Kevin Appleby

Anna Instone Memorial Award

Subjects: Classical music.

Eligibility: Open to students of any nationality who are in their final year at one of the following colleges; London College, Royal Academy, Royal College of Music, Guildhall and Trinity.

Level of Study: Postgraduate.

Purpose: To enable a student at one of the five London colleges to undertake further studies in the UK or overseas.

No. of awards offered: One.

Frequency: Annual.

Value: £5,000.

Country of Study: Unrestricted.

Applications Procedure: No application form - candidates must be nominated by their colleges.

Closing Date: March 1st.

CARNEGIE TRUST FOR THE UNIVERSITIES OF SCOTLAND

Carnegie Trust for the Universities of Scotland, Cameron House, Abbey Park Place, Dunfermline, KY12 7PZ, Scotland
Tel: 01383 622148
Fax: 01383 622149
Contact: Secretary

Carnegie Grants

Subjects: Any subject in the University curriculum.

Eligibility: Open to graduates of a Scottish university, or full-time members of staff of a Scottish university.

Level of Study: Postgraduate, Professional development.

Purpose: To support personal research projects or aid in the publication of books in certain fields, where likely to benefit the universities of Scotland.

No. of awards offered: Variable.

Frequency: Throughout the year.

Value: Varies according to requests; candidates must provide a detailed estimate of anticipated costs, but the normal maximum is £1,000.

Country of Study: International.

Closing Date: 1 February, 1 June, 1 November, prior to Executive Committee meetings in those months.

Carnegie Scholarships

Subjects: Most subjects in the university curriculum (excluding, classics, philosophy and theology).

Eligibility: Open to persons possessing a first class honours degree from a Scottish university.

Level of Study: Postgraduate.

Purpose: To support postgraduate research.

Type: Scholarship.

No. of awards offered: Sixteen.

Frequency: Annual.

Value: £5,640 (in 1994/95) per annum, plus tuition fees and allowances.

Length of Study: A maximum of three years, subject to annual review.

Study Establishment: Any university in the UK.

Country of Study: UK.

Applications Procedure: Candidates should be nominated by a senior member of the staff of a Scottish university.

Closing Date: 15 March.

SIR ERNEST CASSEL EDUCATIONAL TRUST

Sir Ernest Cassel Educational Trust, 8 Malvern Terrace, Islington, London, N1 1HR, England
Tel: 0171 607 7879
Contact: Secretary

Mountbatten Memorial Grants to Commonwealth Students

Subjects: Unrestricted.

Eligibility: Open to Commonwealth students who are pursuing a course of study at undergraduate or postgraduate level at universities or other recognized institutions of higher education in the UK.

Level of Study: Postgraduate, Undergraduate.

Purpose: To assist overseas students from the Commonwealth who encounter unforeseen financial difficulties in their final year of study.

No. of awards offered: Varies.

Value: Up to £500.

Country of Study: UK.

Additional Information: Grants are administered and awarded, on the Trust's behalf, by a number of universities and other institutions of higher education. Applicants should consult their university or college student welfare officer for further information. The Trust does not sponsor or award scholarships.

Overseas Research Grants

Subjects: Language, literature or civilization of any country.

Eligibility: Open to the more junior teaching members of faculties of universities and other recognized institutions of higher education in the UK, regardless of country of birth.

Purpose: To help towards the expenses of approved research abroad.

Type: Research Grant.

No. of awards offered: Varies.

Value: £100-£500.

Country of Study: Outside the UK.

Applications Procedure: Candidates should write to the British Academy at 20-21 Cornwall Terrace, London NW1 4QP.

Closing Date: September 30th, December 31st, February 28th, April 30th.

Additional Information: These Grants are administered by the British Academy.

CATHOLIC LIBRARY ASSOCIATION

Catholic Library Association, St Joseph Central High School Library, 22 Maplewood Avenue, Pittsfield, MA, 01201, USA
Tel: 413 447 9121
Contact: Jean R Bostley

*The Rev Andrew L Bouwhuis Memorial Scholarship

Subjects: Library science.

Eligibility: Open to individuals who have been accepted into a graduate school program show promise of success based on collegiate record, and demonstrate need for financial help. Applicants must be members of the CLA.

Level of Study: Postgraduate.

Purpose: To encourage promising talent to enter librarianship and to foster advanced study in the library profession.

Type: Scholarship.

No. of awards offered: One.

Frequency: Annual.

Value: US$1,500.

Country of Study: USA.

Applications Procedure: Application forms are available on request.

Closing Date: February 1st.

*The World Book, Inc Grant

Subjects: Continuing education in school or children's librarianship.

Eligibility: Open to national members of the CLA.

No. of awards offered: One.

Frequency: Annual.

Value: US$1,500 to be divided among no more than three recipients.

Study Establishment: Special workshops, institutes, or seminars; summer sessions at institutions of higher learning.

Country of Study: Any country.

Closing Date: March 15th.

THE CATHOLIC UNIVERSITY OF LOUVAIN

Secrétariat à la Coopération Internationale, Halles Universitaires, Place de l'Université 1, Louvain-la-Neuve, 1348, Belgium
Tel: 32 10 47 30 93
Fax: 32 10 47 88 14
Email: baeyens@sco.ucl.ac.be
Contact: Mrs B Delcampe-Bal

Cooperation Fellowships

Subjects: Any subject relevant to third world development.

Eligibility: Open to nationals of developing countries, who hold all the requirements to be admitted at postgraduate level at UCL. Applicants should have an excellent academic background and some professional experience, they should demonstrate that their study programme is able to promote the development of their home country and they should have a good command of French.

Level of Study: Postgraduate, Doctorate.

Purpose: To promote economic, social, cultural and political progress in the developing countries by postgraduate training of graduates from these countries.

Type: Fellowship.

No. of awards offered: Up to twenty five.

Frequency: Annual.

Value: Tuition, living expenses, family allowance, medical insurance, transportation costs to home country at the end of studies.

Length of Study: A maximum of four years.

Study Establishment: The University of Louvain.

Country of Study: Belgium.

Applications Procedure: Application form must be completed; additional documentation is required.

Closing Date: October 31st.

Additional Information: Application forms available on request.

CDS INTERNATIONAL, INC

CDS International, Inc, 330 7th Avenue, New York, NY, 10001-5010, USA
Contact: Beate Witzler

Congress Bundestag Youth Exchange for Young Professionals

Subjects: Business, technical and vocational fields.

Eligibility: Open to US citizens aged 18-24 who are high school graduates, have well-defined career goals and related part or full-time work experience, who are able to communicate and work well with others and have maturity enabling them to adapt to new situations.

Level of Study: Graduate.

Purpose: To strengthen ties between the younger generations of Germany and the USA.

No. of awards offered: Approximately 64.

Frequency: Annually; subject to USIA funding.

Value: International air fare and partial domestic transportation, language training and study at a German professional school, seminars (including transportation, insurance).

Study Establishment: An appropriate institution.

Country of Study: Germany.

Closing Date: December 15th.

Additional Information: Participants must have US$350 pocket money per month. During their year American exchangees will have the opportunity to improve their skills through formal study and work experience. The program also includes intensive language instruction and housing with a host family or in a dormitory.

CENTER FOR ADVANCED STUDY IN THE BEHAVIORAL SCIENCES

Center for Advanced Study in the Behavioral Sciences, 202 Junipero Serra Boulevard, Stanford, CA 94305, CA, 94305, USA
Tel: 415 321 2052
Fax: 415 321 1192
Contact: Robert A Scott, Associate Director

Postdoctoral Residential Fellowships

Subjects: Behavioral sciences, biological sciences and the humanities.

Eligibility: There are no restrictions with regard to race or nationality.

Type: Fellowship.

No. of awards offered: Approximately 45.

Frequency: Annual.

Value: Equal to up to half of a nine-month university salary with an informal cap, plus travel allowance to and from the Center for recipients and their families.

Length of Study: 9-12 months.

Study Establishment: The Center.

Country of Study: USA.

Additional Information: Fellows should be nominated by academic officers or distinguished scholars and are expected to seek additional sources of support to share in Fellowship costs. All names submitted will be kept for reviews at two-year intervals. Persons authorized for Fellowships are invited to indicate the year which would best suit their program.

THE CENTER FOR FIELD RESEARCH

The Center for Field Research, Box 403, 680 Mount Auburn Street, Watertown, MA, 02272, USA
Tel: 617 926 8200
Fax: 617 926 8532
Email: cfr@earthwatch.org
Telex: 510 600 6452
Contact: Executive Director

Grants for Field Research

Subjects: Disciplines include, but are not limited to, anthropology, archaeology, biology, botany, cartography, conservation, ethnology, folklore, geography, geology, hydrology, marine sciences, meteorology, musicology, nutrition, ornithology, restoration, sociology, and sustainable development.

Eligibility: There are no residency requirements or nomination process. Preference is given to applicants who hold a PhD and have both field and teaching experience; however, support is also offered for outstanding projects by younger postdoctoral scholars and, in special cases, graduate students. Women and minority applicants are encouraged. Research teams must include qualified volunteers from Earthwatch.

Level of Study: Postgraduate, Doctorate, Postdoctorate.

Purpose: To provide grants for field research projects that can constructively utilize teams of non-specialist field assistants in accomplishing their research goals.

Type: Grant.

No. of awards offered: Approximately 150.

Frequency: Annual.

Value: Varies; grants are awarded on a per capita basis, depending upon the number of participants. Normal range of support is US$12,000-US$150,000.

Length of Study: 2-3 weeks.

Study Establishment: At research sites; approximately one-quarter of the research currently funded takes place within the USA. Teams are in the field for 2-3 weeks; longer-term support is available through multiple teams; renewals are encouraged.

Country of Study: Any country.

Applications Procedure: Preliminary proposal must be submitted 13 months prior to field dates.

CENTER FOR HELLENIC STUDIES

Center for Hellenic Studies, 3100 Whitehaven Street, NW, Washington, DC, 20008, USA
Tel: 202 234 3738
Fax: 202 797 3745
Email: DB159@umail.umd.edu KR44@umail.und.edu
Contact: The Directors

Junior Fellowships

Subjects: Ancient Greek studies (primarily literature), language, philosophy, history or religion, archeology, art history with restrictions.

Eligibility: Open to scholars and teachers of Ancient Greek studies with a PhD degree or equivalent qualification and some published work, in the early stages of their career.

Level of Study: Doctorate.

Purpose: To provide selected Classics scholars fairly early in their careers with an academic year free of other responsibilities to work on a publishable project.

Type: Fellowship.

No. of awards offered: Ten.

Frequency: Annual.

Value: Up to US$20,000, plus living quarters and a study at the Center building, limited funds for research expenses and research related travel.

Length of Study: Nine months from September to June; not renewable.

Study Establishment: At the Center, in Washington DC.

Country of Study: USA.

Applications Procedure: Application form, CV, description of research project, sample(s) of publications (up to 50pp), three letters of recommendation. Enquiries about eligibility and early applications are encouraged.

Closing Date: October 15th.

Additional Information: Residence at the Center is required.

CENTER FOR INDOOR AIR RESEARCH

Center for Indoor Air Research, 1099 Winterson Road, Suite 280, Linthicum, MD, 21090, USA
Tel: 410 684 3777
Fax: 410 684 3729
Email: ciarinc@aol.com

Postdoctoral Fellowships

Subjects: Indoor air research and related sciences.

Eligibility: Applicants must hold a PhD degree, an MD degree, or an equivalent degree at the time of the award, and have demonstrated an ability to conduct independent research.

Level of Study: Postdoctorate.

Purpose: To develop the scientific productivity of outstanding young people pursuing careers in indoor air research, and to stimulate interest in entering the field of indoor air research among individuals with strong backgrounds in related or allied sciences.

Type: Fellowship.

Frequency: Annual.

Value: The total budget each year is limited to US$25,000 for stipend and fringe benefits and up to US$5,000 for research supplies and other approved expenses.

Length of Study: One year; possibility of renewal for a further year.

Applications Procedure: Applicants should submit a three-page research proposal, applicant's CV, sponsoring investigator's CV, three letters of recommendation, and a letter of endorsement of the applicant by the sponsor indicating sources and level of research support for this project.

Closing Date: October 31st.

Additional Information: Following completion of the fellowship, the Center will request periodic updates of the fellow's academic accomplishments.

CENTRE FOR MENTAL HEALTH SERVICES

Center for Mental Health Services, American Psychiatric Association, 1400 K Street N W, Washington, DC, 20005, USA
Tel: 202 682 6096
Fax: 202 682 6352
Email: MKing@psych.org
Contact: Marilyn King

APA/CMHS Minority Fellowship Program

Subjects: Psychiatry and mental health.

Eligibility: Open to psychiatric residents in at least their PGY-2 of training. Applicants must be US citizens.

Level of Study: Postgraduate.

Purpose: Designed to provide recipients with enriching training experiences through particpation in APA's annual meeting and other component meetings.

Type: Stipend.

No. of awards offered: Varies.

Frequency: Dependent on funds available.

Value: Dependent on funds available.

Applications Procedure: Application form must be completed.

Closing Date: January 31st.

CENTER FOR THE STUDY OF WORLD RELIGIONS

Center for the Study of World Religions, Harvard University, 42 Francis Avenue, Cambridge, MA, 02138, USA
Tel: 1 617 495 4495
Fax: 1 617 496 5411
Contact: Tim Bryson, Administrator

*Dissertation Fellowship

Subjects: Religious studies: religious phenomena.

Eligibility: Open to doctoral candidates in any Harvard University program whose dissertation research involves a substantive study of religious phenomena. Preference goes to applicants who have not previously received support from the Center.

Level of Study: Doctorate.

Purpose: To foster excellence in the historical and comparative study of religion on the broadest scale and from many perspectives.

Type: Fellowship.

No. of awards offered: Two.

Frequency: Annual.

Value: US$10,000 and the option of residence at the Center.

Length of Study: One year.

Study Establishment: The Center, in Cambridge, Massachusetts.

Country of Study: USA.

Closing Date: January 15th.

*Fellows-in-Residence Program

Subjects: Religious studies: historical and comparative study of religions.

Eligibility: Open to doctoral candidates in any Harvard University program whose research focuses on the historical and comparative study of religions. Preference goes to applicants who have lived at the Center for less than two years.

Level of Study: Doctorate.

Purpose: To foster excellence in the historical and comparative study of religion on the broadest scale and from many perspectives.

No. of awards offered: Varies.

Frequency: Annual.

Value: To cover residence at the Center.

Length of Study: One year.

Study Establishment: The Center, in Cambridge, Massachusetts.

Country of Study: USA.

Closing Date: January 15th.

*Senior Fellowship

Subjects: Religious studies: historical and comparative study of religions.

Eligibility: Open to postdoctoral scholars whose research proposal is in the area of historical or comparative religion.

Level of Study: Postdoctorate.

Purpose: To foster excellence in the historical and comparative study of religion on the broadest scale and from many perspectives.

Type: Fellowship.

No. of awards offered: Varies.

Frequency: Annual.

Value: To cover residence at the Center, use of the Center and of other Harvard University resources.

Length of Study: One year.

Study Establishment: The Center, in Cambridge, Massachusetts.

Country of Study: USA.

Closing Date: January 15th.

CENTRAL QUEENSLAND UNIVERSITY

Central Queensland University, Research Services Office, Rockhampton, Queensland, 4702, Australia
Tel: 079 309 971
Fax: 079 361 361
Email: j.lock@cqu.edu.au
Contact: Research Higher Degrees Officer

University Postgraduate Research Award

Subjects: Agriculture, forestry and fishery, arts and humanities, business administration and management, engineering, education and teacher training, mass communication and information science, social and behavioural sciences.

Eligibility: Candidates must be eligible for admission for a research higher degree at CQU.

Level of Study: Postgraduate, Doctorate.

Purpose: To enable the scholar to proceed as a full-time student to a research masters or doctorate.

Type: Scholarship.

No. of awards offered: Five.

Frequency: Annual.

Value: $A15,364 living allowance, $A3,000 research support (per annum).

Length of Study: Two to three years.

Country of Study: Australia.

Applications Procedure: Application must be made on the prescribed proforma.

Closing Date: October 31st.

CENTRE DE RECHERCHE EN SCIENCES NEUROLOGIQUES

Centre de Recherche en Sciences Neurologiques, Faculté De Médecine, Université De Montréal, C.P. 6128, Succ. Centre-ville, Montréal, Québec, H3C 3J7, Canada
Tel: 514 343 6366
Fax: 514 343 613
Email: simardgi@ere.umontreal.ca
Contact: Postdoctoral Fellowship Committee

JP Cordeau Fellowship

Subjects: Neurology and neurosciences.

Eligibility: Open to Canadian citizens or permanent residents.

Level of Study: Postdoctorate.

Purpose: Offers the use of the exceptional research facilities of the Center for Research in Neurological Sciences of the Université De Montréal. Recipient works closely with the investigator of his/her choice within a large active group of neuroscientists who are members of the center.

Type: Fellowship.

No. of awards offered: One.

Frequency: Annual.

Value: C$25,000-C$30,000.

Length of Study: One year.

Study Establishment: Centre de Recherche en Sciences Neurologiques, Université de Montréal.

Country of Study: Canada.

Applications Procedure: A completed application form is required and can be obtained by writing to the Fellowship Committee.

Closing Date: December 31st.

Herbert H Jasper Fellowship

Subjects: Neurology, neurosciences.

Eligibility: Open to Canadian citizens or permanent residents.

Level of Study: Postdoctorate.

Purpose: Offers the use of the exceptional research facilities of the Center for Research in Neurological Sciences of the Université De Montréal. Recipient works closely with the investigator of his/her choice within a large active group of neuroscientists who are members of the center.

Type: Fellowship.

No. of awards offered: One.

Frequency: Annual.

Value: C$25,000 to C$30,000 per year.

Length of Study: One year.

Study Establishment: Centre de Recherche en Sciences Neurologiques, Université De Montréal.

Country of Study: Canada.

Applications Procedure: An application form is required and can be obtained by writing to the Fellowship Committee.

Closing Date: December 31st.

CENTRE FOR CONSERVATION STUDIES

Centre for Conservation Studies, Institute of Advanced Architectural Studies, University of York, The King's Manor, York, YO1 2EP, England
Tel: 01904 433963
Fax: 01904 433949
Contact: Director

Scholarships

Subjects: Conservation studies (two main options, building conservation and conservation of historic gardens and landscapes).

Eligibility: Open to persons who have been admitted to the MA course in conservation studies at the University of York, resident in countries of the EC.

Level of Study: Postgraduate.

Purpose: To provide assistance for citizens of EC countries reading for the MA.

Type: Scholarship.

Frequency: Annual.

Value: Varies.

Length of Study: One year.

Study Establishment: The Centre.

Country of Study: UK.

Additional Information: Applications should be made to the University of York.

CENTRE FOR INTERNATIONAL MOBILITY (CIMO)

The Centre for International Mobility (CIMO), PO Box 343, Hakaniemenkatu 2, Helsinki, SF-00531, Finland
Tel: 358 0 7747 7033
Fax: 358 0 7747 7064
Email: cimoinfo@oph.fi

Bilateral Scholarships

Subjects: Various subjects.

Eligibility: Open to applicants from: Australia, Austria, Belgium, Bulgaria, Canada, Cuba, Czech Republic, Denmark, Egypt, France, Germany, Great Britain, Greece, Hungary, Iceland, India, Ireland, Israel, Italy, Japan, Luxembourg, Mexico, Mongolia, the Netherlands, Norway, Poland, Portugal, Republic of Korea, Romania, Slovakia, Spain, Sweden, Switzerland, Turkey and the USA.

Level of Study: Postgraduate.

Type: Scholarship.

Value: The bilateral scholarships usually consist of a monthly allowance of FIM4,000 (in 1995-1996). For short-term visitors there is a daily allowance, the amount of which is determined annually (FIM154 in 1995) Accommodation is provided for short-term visitors. There are no travel grants to or from Finland.

Length of Study: Postgraduate research of three to nine months; study visits of one to two weeks.

Study Establishment: A Finnish university.

Country of Study: Finland.

Applications Procedure: Applications should be made to the appropriate authority in the applicant's country, who selects the candidates to be proposed to CIMO.

Closing Date: March 1st.

Nordic Scholarship Scheme for the Baltic Countries and Northwest Russia

Subjects: All subjects.

Level of Study: Postgraduate, Doctorate, Postdoctorate, Researchers/teachers/students.

Purpose: To promote collaboration between the five Nordic countries and the three Baltic Republics as well as areas in Northwest Russia within the fields of education and research.

Frequency: Twice a year.

Length of Study: 1-6 months.

Applications Procedure: Application form must be completed and can be obtained by writing to the Nordic Information offices of CIMO.

Closing Date: October 1st and March 1st.

Additional Information: Priority will be given to applications where contact or cooperation has been established.

Scholarships

Subjects: Teaching and research.

Eligibility: Open to foreign researchers not older than 35.

Level of Study: Postgraduate, Postdoctorate.

Purpose: To promote international cooperation in teaching and research.

Type: Scholarship.

Frequency: Annual.

Value: The monthly allowance (FIM3,000-6,000 in 1995-1996), which is intended to cover living expenses in Finland for a single person, may vary according to the academic qualifications of the recipient and to the support given by the receiving body. No additional allowance for housing is paid. Expenses due to international travel to and from Finland are not covered by CIMO.

Length of Study: 3-12 months.

Country of Study: Finland.

Scholarships for Advanced Finnish Studies and Research

Subjects: Finnish language, literature, Finno-Ugric linguistics, ethnology and folkloristics.

Eligibility: Open to nationals of all countries.

Level of Study: Postgraduate.

Purpose: For postgraduate research.

Type: Scholarship.

Value: Monthly allowance of FIM 4,000 (1995-1996). No travel grants are available to or from Finland.

Length of Study: 4-9 months.

Study Establishment: A Finnish university.

Country of Study: Finland.

Applications Procedure: Applications should be made, preferably in Finnish, on CIMO's application forms, which are available from Finnish embassies and consulates abroad.

Closing Date: Applications are considered at all times.

Scholarships for Young Researchers and University Teaching Staff

Subjects: All subjects.

Eligibility: Open to nationals of any county. The applicant should not be older than 35.

Level of Study: Postgraduate, Doctorate, Postdoctorate.

Purpose: To promote international cooperation in teaching and research.

Type: Scholarship.

Frequency: Every three months.

Value: FIM3,000-6,000 per month.

Length of Study: 3-12 months.

Study Establishment: University.

Country of Study: Finland.

Applications Procedure: Application form must be completed. The Finnish receiving university must apply for the grant.

Additional Information: Established contact with the receiving institute prior to application is required.

CENTRE FOR INTERNATIONAL STUDIES, UNIVERSITY OF MISSOURI

Centre for International Studies, University of Missouri - St Louis, St Louis, Missouri, 63121-4499, USA
Tel: 1 314 516 5753
Fax: 1 314 516 6757
Email: intlstud@umslvma.umsl.edu
www: http://www.umsl.edu
Contact: Dr Joel Glassman, Director

Theodore Lentz Postdoctoral Fellowship in Peace and Conflict Resolution

Subjects: International Relations.

Eligibility: Completed PhD required; preference is given to graduates of university programs in peace studies and conflict resolution; graduates of political science, international relations, and other social science pro-

grams who specialize in peace and conflict resolution are also invited to apply.

Level of Study: Postdoctorate.

Purpose: Recipient conducts own research projects in peace and conflict resolution and teaches an introductory peace studies course in the fall semester and one course in the spring semester (at University of Missouri - St Louis).

Type: Fellowship.

No. of awards offered: One.

Frequency: Annual.

Value: Approximately US$21,000 plus university benefits.

Length of Study: Nine months.

Study Establishment: University of Missouri-St Louis.

Country of Study: USA.

Applications Procedure: Applicants should send: curriculum vitae, letter of application, evidence of completion of PhD, three letters of recommendation, and a research proposal of approximately 750 words.

Closing Date: April 1st.

Additional Information: Supported in part by the Lentz Research Association.

CENTRE FOR SCIENCE DEVELOPMENT

Centre for Science Development, Private Bag X270, Pretoria, 0001, South Africa
Tel: 012 202 2742
Fax: 012 202 2892

Ad Hoc Grants for Self-Initiated Research in South Africa

Subjects: Humanities and social sciences.

Eligibility: Open to South African residents who can satisfy the Board of Trustees that the research problem justifies research and the project is practicable; that the methods to be used are scientific; and that the expenses are justified and are in respect of the necessary costs of the investigation.

Type: Grant.

No. of awards offered: Varies.

Frequency: Varies.

Value: According to budget submitted. Smaller grants may be used for feasibility studies or short projects.

Length of Study: A maximum of 2 years; renewable upon completion of previous research.

Country of Study: South Africa.

Applications Procedure: Applications must be accompanied by a detailed budget.

Closing Date: Large projects 30 June; smaller projects considered throughout the year.

Additional Information: Grants are made for the actual expenses in connection with the investigation and not for support of the applicant her/himself; however, subsistence and travel expenses at the current public service rates may be available while the candidate is away from her/his usual place of residence in connection with her/his research. Grants are not for degree purposes.

Bursaries for Honours Degree Studies at Universities in South Africa

Subjects: Humanities and social sciences.

Eligibility: Open to South African citizens with at least a 65% pass in the bachelor degree examination or in the subject in which they wish to specialize and wish to study full-time at a South African university for a bachelor honours degree or the equivalent advanced course in the field of humanities and social sciences.

Type: Bursary.

No. of awards offered: Varies.

Frequency: Annual.

Value: R5,000.

Length of Study: One year.

Study Establishment: An appropriate university.

Country of Study: South Africa.

Closing Date: January 15th.

Additional Information: A bursar must pass the honours degree examination within the prescribed time for which the bursary is awarded, otherwise the bursary must be refunded or the course repeated and successfully completed at the expense of the bursar.

Bursaries for Master's Degree Studies/Studies for Master's Diploma in Technology in South Africa

Subjects: Humanities and social sciences.

Eligibility: Open to South African citizens who have passed their previous degree examination with at least 65%.

Type: Bursary.

No. of awards offered: Varies.

Frequency: Annual.

Value: R5,500.

Length of Study: One year.

Study Establishment: An appropriate institution.

Country of Study: South Africa.

Applications Procedure: Applications should be submitted to the university on the prescribed form obtainable at the university.

Closing Date: January 15th.

Additional Information: Bursaries for part-time study are also available at the rate of R2,500.

Grants for Doctoral/Laureatus/Postdoctoral/Laureatus Studies Abroad

Subjects: Humanities and social sciences.

Eligibility: Open to South African citizens who hold at least a master's degree, and require specialized training as research workers in a field for which there are no, or inadequate, training facilities in South Africa.

Level of Study: Postgraduate.

Purpose: To enable researchers to achieve expertise in a particular research field in order to deliver the research output that will lead to their qualifying for grants for established researchers.

Type: Grant.

No. of awards offered: Varies.

Frequency: Annual.

Value: R36,000, plus a travel grant of R4,500.

Length of Study: Maximum of two years.

Study Establishment: Various universities abroad.

Country of Study: UK, Europe, USA, Canada, Australia or the Far East.

Closing Date: June 30th.

Additional Information: A scholarship holder must register for a degree and use the results of her/his research for obtaining such a degree. The bursary will be paid on production of proof that arrangements have been made for training at an approved institution.

Grants for Foreign Research Fellows

Subjects: Humanities and social sciences.

Eligibility: Open to distinguished researchers who are not South African citizens and are not resident in South Africa.

Purpose: To bring foreign researches of indisputable scientific status in the field of the human sciences to South Africa as Research Fellows to enable them to participate actively in research.

Type: A variable number of Fellowships.

Frequency: Varies.

Value: An economy return air ticket and a subsistence fee of R180 per day.

Length of Study: Not less than 2 weeks and not more than 4 weeks.

Country of Study: South Africa.

Applications Procedure: An application must be submitted on the prescribed form by the host institution and should include a detailed curriculum vitae of the prospective Research Fellow; particulars of the research programme of the host institution and a description of the role she/he will fulfil therein and a description of the manner in which other South African researchers may be exposed to the Fellow's expertise.

Closing Date: Four months prior to the visit.

Additional Information: A detailed report on the visit must be submitted to the CSD not later than one month after the conclusion of the visit.

Grants for the Attendance of International Conferences

Subjects: Humanities and social sciences.

Eligibility: Open to South African specialists, who are considered with due attention to the following: the status of the applicant in the particular field covered by the conference; that the applicant will read a paper at the conference; and the likelihood that research in South Africa will benefit through the participation of the applicant in the conference and that her/his position is such that the knowledge acquired will be easily disseminated on her/his return to South Africa. Preference will be given to applicants invited officially by the organizers of the conference, to read personally a paper, and whose work in the relative field justifies this.

Purpose: To provide South African specialists with the opportunity to participate in international conferences abroad.

Type: Grant.

No. of awards offered: Varies.

Frequency: Biennially.

Value: Not exceeding R4,500 for Europe, the British Isles and the Mediterranean area; R6,000 for the USA, Canada, South America, Australia, New Zealand, Japan and the Far East. These amounts represent approximately 50% of the normal total cost, and are provided only when the candidate's own institution contributes at least 30% of the total costs involved. Grantees already abroad may receive 50% of the travelling expenses from their base abroad to the conference centre, and a daily allowance of R300 with a maximum of six days for the duration of the conference, provided that the university or institution contributes 30% of the total cost.

Country of Study: Any country outside South Africa.

Applications Procedure: All applications should be accompanied by a complete list of the applicant's publications and a list of all conferences attended by her/him outside South Africa during the previous five years.

Closing Date: Four months prior to the conference date.

Additional Information: A report regarding attendance at the conference must be submitted to the CSD who may consider it for publication in Bulletin . Normally only one application for a particular conference will receive favourable consideration so as to ensure that available funds are distributed as widely as possible.

Prestige Scholarships for Doctoral/Laureatus Studies Abroad

Subjects: Humanities and social sciences.

Eligibility: Open to South African citizens who hold at least a master's degree, and require specialized training as research workers in a field for which there are no, or inadequate, training facilities in South Africa. These Scholarships are intended for oustanding achievers.

Frequency: Annual.

Value: R24,000, plus a travel grant of R4,500.

Length of Study: One academic year; may be renewed for an additional year.

Study Establishment: Various universities.

Country of Study: UK, Europe, USA, Canada, Australia or the Far East.

Closing Date: June 30th.

Additional Information: A Scholar must register for degree studies at a university abroad. The Scholarship will be paid on production of proof of registration. Annual reports must be submitted through the supervisor. On completion of their research abroad, candidates must return to South Africa for at least two years.

Publication Grants

Subjects: Humanities and social sciences.

Eligibility: Open to South African residents who can produce concisely and accurately presented work that is the result of original research, is of scientific value, and is mainly new material and not readily available to research workers. Short manuscripts which satisfy these requirements will receive priority.

Purpose: To publish work of outstanding quality which, owing to a limited sales potential or for other reasons, could not otherwise be published through the usual channels.

Frequency: As required.

Value: Partial or full cost of publication up to R9,000.

Country of Study: South Africa.

Applications Procedure: Applications for the publication of dissertations and doctoral theses will not normally be considered. Two copies of the manuscript must be presented to the Centre for Science Development in an edited form. The applicant must submit three quotations from well-known publishers with the condition of publication, format, type of paper, cost of illustrations and labour, etc., the guarantee required by the publisher, and the proposed selling price. Once notified that her or his application has been successful, the applicant must take steps to ensure, if possible, that publication takes place during the financial year in which the grant is made. Further information may be obtained from the registrars of any South African university as well as from the Centre itself.

Research Grants

Subjects: Humanities and social sciences.

Eligibility: Open to applicants who have already achieved recognition for academic achievements and earned a reputation as research leaders in the area concerned and hold a Doctor's degree.

Level of Study: Postdoctorate.

Purpose: To allow researchers of indisputable scientific status to undertake a demarcated and advanced research project locally or abroad.

Type: Varies, Grant.

Frequency: Varies.

Value: R36,000, plus a travel grant of R4,500.

Length of Study: 2-4 months; not renewable, local research has no time limit.

Study Establishment: A centre of high academic status outside South Africa, or locally.

Country of Study: Overseas or locally.

Closing Date: January 31st and June 30th.

Additional Information: A grant for overseas trips will be considered if the applicants have exhausted the research sources in the particular field in South Africa and have already determined that there are inadequate facilities in South Africa for the specific research. A grant will not

be considered if the research is to be undertaken for obtaining a further qualification.

Scholarships for Doctoral/Laureatus Studies at Universities and Technikons in South Africa

Subjects: Any subject.

Eligibility: Open to South African citizens who are registered at a South African university for doctoral/laureatus studies.

No. of awards offered: Varies.

Frequency: Twice yearly.

Value: R8,000.

Length of Study: One year; may be renewed for an additional year.

Study Establishment: An appropriate institution.

Country of Study: South Africa.

Applications Procedure: Applications should be submitted to the university on the prescribed form obtainable at the university.

Closing Date: 31 March and 30 June.

Additional Information: Bursaries for part-time study are also available at the rate of R2,500.

CENTRE FOR TROPICAL AGRONOMIC RESEARCH AND TRAINING (CATIE)

CATIE, Turrialba, Turrialba, 7170, Costa Rica
Tel: 506 556 1016
Fax: 506 556 0914
Email: pferreir@computo.catie.ac.cr
Contact: Pedro Ferreira

Scholarships

Subjects: Production systems, tropical woodlands, forestry and agroforestry, tropical crop protection, tropical crop improvement, integrated management of natural resources (protected areas, watershed management), environmental economics and sociology.

Eligibility: Open to citizens of Latin America and Caribbean countries. Priority is given to citizens of Central America and Caribbean countries.

Level of Study: Postgraduate, Doctorate, Postdoctorate.

Purpose: To improve human resources in tropical agriculture in the American tropics.

Type: Scholarship.

No. of awards offered: Thirty.

Frequency: Annual.

Value: Air fare, tuition and living expenses, thesis expenses.

Length of Study: One year of coursework and one year for a master's thesis.

Country of Study: Costa Rica.

Closing Date: April 30th.

CENTRO DE ESTUDIOS CONSTITUTIONALES

Centro de Estudios Constitucionales, Plaza de la Marina Espanola, 9, Madrid, 28043, Spain
Tel: 5415000
Fax: 5478549
Contact: Subdirreccion General

Grant

Subjects: Political science and constitutional law, theory of the study of law, contemporary history, public and European law.

Eligibility: Open to nationals of all countries with appropriate qualifications and a sound knowledge of Spanish.

Level of Study: Postgraduate.

No. of awards offered: One.

Frequency: Annual.

Value: 50,000 pesetas.

Country of Study: Spain.

Applications Procedure: Please submit certificates of educational qualifications.

CENTRO DE INVESTIGACION Y ESTUDIOS AVANZADOS DEL IPN

Centro De Investigacion Y Estudios Avanzados Del IPN, Departmento De Matematicas Del Cinvestav , Apartado Postal 14-740, Mexico City, 07000, Mexico
Tel: 525 747 7103
Fax: 525 747 7104
Email: matemat@math.cinvestav.mx
Contact: Dr Onesimo Hernandez-Lerma

Soloman Lefschetz Instructorships

Subjects: Mathematics, statistics.

Eligibility: Open to young mathematicians with a doctorate who show definite promise in research.

Level of Study: Postdoctorate.

Purpose: Research and teach a graduate course of speciality.

Type: Fellowship.

No. of awards offered: Two.

Frequency: Annual, dependent on funds available.

Length of Study: One year; possible renewal for an extra year.

Country of Study: Mexico.

Closing Date: December 31st.

Additional Information: Knowledge of Spanish is desirable.

FRANCIS CHAGRIN FUND

Francis Chagrin Fund, c/o Society for the Promotion of New Music, Francis House, Francis Street, London, SW1P 1DE, England
Tel: 0171 828 9696
Fax: 0171 931 9928
Contact: Elizabeth Webb

The Francis Chagrin Fund Awards

Subjects: Subjects relevant to musical compositions/electronic tapes awaiting their first performance.

Eligibility: Open to British composers or composers resident in the UK.

Level of Study: Unrestricted.

Purpose: To cover the costs of photocopying musical parts and scores for works awaiting their first performance.

No. of awards offered: Varies.

Frequency: Awards are considered once a month by committee.

Value: Amount available per year is limited to £3,000.

Country of Study: UK.

Applications Procedure: Application form is required plus CV, two references and relevant invoices.

Closing Date: There is no specific closing date; the committee meets once a month.

CHAMBER MUSIC AMERICA

Chamber Music America, 545 Eighth Avenue, New York, NY, 10018, USA
Tel: 212 244 2772
Fax: 212 244 2776
Contact: Dorothy Sassoer

Heidi Castleman Award for Excellence in Chamber Music Teaching

Subjects: Music, Education, Musical Instruments (performance).

Eligibility: Applicants must currently lead a chamber music education program for students aged between 6-18.

Level of Study: Professional development.

Purpose: To recognise the dedication and excellence of educators leading chamber music programs for students aged 6-18.

Type: Cash.

No. of awards offered: One.

Frequency: Annual.

Value: US$1,000.

Country of Study: USA.

Applications Procedure: Please submit completed application and tape of performance from program.

Closing Date: November each year; please call for details.

THE CHARTERED INSTITUTE OF MANAGEMENT ACCOUNTANTS

The Research Foundation, The Chartered Institute of Management Accountants, 63 Portland Place, London, W1N 4AB, England
Tel: 0171 637 2311
Fax: 0171 436 1582

Grants-in-Aid of Research

Subjects: Accountancy and related managerial disciplines.

Eligibility: Open to senior investigators.

Purpose: To promote and develop the science of management accountancy.

Type: Grant.

No. of awards offered: Variable.

Frequency: Throughout the year.

Value: Varies from practical assistance to approximately £50,000.

Study Establishment: Research in the UK or overseas (for UK researchers) or solely in the UK (for others).

Country of Study: UK or overseas.

Additional Information: The Institute does not provide assistance for research leading to higher degrees or fees for courses.

For further information contact:
CIMA Research Board Chairman, School of Management & Finance, University of Nottingham, University Park, Nottingham, NG7 2RD, England
Tel: 01159 515151
Fax: 01159 515262
Contact: Professor Bob Berry

CHARTERED INSTITUTE OF TRANSPORT

Chartered Institute of Transport, 80 Portland Place, London, W1N 4DP, England
Tel: 0171 636 9952
Fax: 0171 637 0511
Contact: Director of Education

Robert Bell Travelling Scholarship

Subjects: Overseas railway practice.

Eligibility: Open to persons engaged in railway transport in the UK.

Purpose: To assist a candidate to travel abroad.

Type: Scholarship.

No. of awards offered: One.

Frequency: Annual.

Value: Up to £500.

Country of Study: Outside the UK.

Sir William Chamberlain Awards

Subjects: Fields connected with road transport.

Eligibility: Open to persons engaged, or intending to be engaged, in road transport in the North West (defined as Cheshire, Clwyd, Cumbria, Derbyshire, Greater Manchester, Gwynedd, Merseyside or Lancashire).

Purpose: To encourage study and research.

No. of awards offered: Variable.

Frequency: Annual.

Value: Up to £1,350.

Study Establishment: A university, other recognized college, or a correspondence college.

Applications Procedure: Application forms are available from the Institute from January.

Closing Date: May 25th.

Additional Information: The money available can be awarded to one person or divided between more than one, according to the merit of the applications. The funds may be used for full-time study (fees, books, subsistence), part-time study (fees, books, non-local travelling expenses) or research (subsistence, clerical assistance and other expenses).

CMUA Road Transport Research Fellowship

Subjects: Road transport.

Eligibility: Open to British subjects over 30 years of age engaged in road transport in the UK.

Purpose: To enable the candidate to examine and report upon road transport arrangements abroad.

Type: Fellowship.

No. of awards offered: One.

Frequency: Annual.

Value: Up to £1,300.

Country of Study: Outside the UK.

Additional Information: The Fellowship is sponsored by the Commercial Motor Users' Association.

John Gilbraith Award

Subjects: Road freight transport.

Eligibility: Open to members of any grade in the Northern Region of the CIT in the UK who are directly engaged in road freight transport, logostics or distribution.

Purpose: To enable candidates to undertake research or travel to investigate practice and operation or to assist with studies.

No. of awards offered: Variable.

Frequency: Annual.

Value: £500.

Country of Study: UK or abroad.

Henry Spurrier Travelling Scholarship

Subjects: Fields connected with road transport, including traffic engineering.

Eligibility: Open to persons employed in, or in connection with road transport (administration, operation, engineering, staff, traffic, etc.).

Purpose: To encourage study and research in the sphere of road transport.

Type: Scholarship.

No. of awards offered: Variable.

Frequency: Annual.

Value: Approximately £2,000.

Study Establishment: A university, other recognized college, or an approved correspondence college.

Applications Procedure: Application forms are available from the Institute from January.

Closing Date: May 31st.

Additional Information: The money available can be awarded to one person or divided between more than one, according to the merit of the applications. The funds may be used for full-time study (fees, books, subsistence), part-time study (fees, books, non-local travelling expenses) or research (subsistence, clerical assistance and other expenses).

TTA Bursary Scheme

Subjects: Transport.

Eligibility: Open mainly to students who encounter financial problems in their country. UK candidates may be eligible where justified as special need.

Purpose: To assist people wishing to undertake distance-learning study for CIT qualifications.

Type: Bursary.

No. of awards offered: Variable.

Frequency: Annual.

Value: Up to £300 a year to cover study material, tuition and examination fees for Qualifying Examinations.

Length of Study: Up to three years.

Closing Date: May 31st.

For further information contact:
Chartered Institute of Transport, 80 Portland Place, London, W1N 4DP, England
Tel: 0171 636 9952
Fax: 0171 637 0511
Contact: Heather Miller, Examinations Officer

CHARTERED INSTITUTE OF TRANSPORT IN NEW ZEALAND

Chartered Institute of Transport in New Zealand, PO Box 13-635, Armagh, Christchurch, New Zealand
Tel: 01 64 3 365 4920
Fax: 01 64 3 379 4762
Contact: Peter J Goodwin, Executive Director

Scholarship and Sponsored Travel Award

Subjects: Research on a topic related to transport in New Zealand.

Eligibility: Open to any person who is a member, or an intending member of the Institute, with preference given to New Zealand residents and/or citizens.

Level of Study: Unrestricted.

Purpose: To assist the recipient with the preparation and the completion of a research project on a topic specified by the Trustees.

Type: Scholarship.

No. of awards offered: One or more provided that the total volume of all scholarships does not exceed NZ$15,000.

Frequency: Annual.

Value: Up to NZ$15,000.

Country of Study: Any country.

Applications Procedure: Applications and conditions are available from NZ polytechnics, universities or Executive Director of the institute. Applications must include full details of the intended project and a budget.

Closing Date: Applications are called for in October each year and close on February 28th following.

Additional Information: Projects are expected to be completed by the following October after announcement of the scholarship. A report is required to be presented to a suitable meeting of the Institute.

CHAUTAUQUA INSTITUTION

Chautauqua Institution, Box 1098, Dept 6, Schools Office, Chautauqua, NY, 14722, USA
Tel: 716 357 6233
Fax: 716 357 9014
Contact: Richard R Redington, Vice President

Pre-Season Awards

Subjects: Instrumental and vocal music; theatre; art and dance.

Eligibility: Open to candidates of any sex, nationality and age.

Purpose: To assist talented advanced students enrolled in the summer program.

Type: Awards.

No. of awards offered: Varies.

Frequency: Annual.

Value: US$200-US$2,000.

Length of Study: 7-8 weeks.

Study Establishment: The Chautauqua Institution.

Country of Study: USA.

Closing Date: Ten days before live audition (walk-ins accepted); 1st March for taped auditions; April 1st for art portfolio of slides.

Additional Information: Most scholarships are given in music. No travel grants are provided.

CHELYABINSK STATE TECHNICAL UNIVERSITY

Chelyabinsk State Technical University, 76 Lenin Avenue, Chelyabinsk, 454080, Russia
Tel: 7 3512 656 504
Fax: 7 3512 347 408
Email: dgsh@inter.tu-chel.ac.ru
Contact: Dimitry Sherbakov

CSTU Rector's Award

Subjects: Architecture and town planning; business administration and management; engineering; law; mathematics and computer science; transport and communications.

Eligibility: Open to citizens of any nationality. Applicants must be fluent in Russian.

Level of Study: Unrestricted.

Purpose: To give international students the opportunity to study in Chelyabinsk, Russia.

Type: Bursary.

No. of awards offered: Five.

Frequency: Annual.

Value: Two semesters of education at CSTU free of charge.

Length of Study: Two semesters.

Study Establishment: Chelyabinsk State Technical University.

Country of Study: Russia.

Applications Procedure: Application form must be completed. Available upon request.

Closing Date: March 1st.

CHEMICAL INDUSTRY INSTITUTE OF TOXICOLOGY

Chemical Industry Institute of Toxicology, PO Box 12137, Research Triangle Park, NC, 27709, USA
Tel: 919 541 2070
Fax: 919 541 9015
Contact: Human Resources Department

*Postdoctoral Fellowships

Subjects: Toxicology: genetic toxicology; biochemical toxicology; pathology; teratology; carcinogenesis; inhalation toxicology; risk assessment; molecular biology.

Eligibility: Open to those who hold a recently awarded PhD degree in a discipline related to toxicology, such as biochemistry, pharmacology, cell biology, genetics immunology, chemistry, medicinal chemistry. Applicants holding a recently awarded DVM or MD degree are expected to have substantial research experience.

Purpose: To support persons holding a recently earned PhD, MD or DVM degree during further training in toxicology at the Institute.

Type: Fellowship.

No. of awards offered: Varies.

Frequency: Varies.

Value: Varies; from US$26,000 depending upon the number of years of experience.

Length of Study: Two years.

Study Establishment: The Institute.

Country of Study: USA.

Closing Date: Applications are accepted at any time.

Additional Information: Fellowships are granted only for conduct of research at the Institute's facility in Research Triangle Park, NC.

*Postdoctoral Traineeships

Subjects: Fields related to toxicology.

Eligibility: Open to persons who have recently obtained the DVM or MD degree and who have been accepted into a course of advanced study in a subject related to toxicology by a degree-granting institution, and who agree to conduct their dissertation research at CIIT. The candidate must be enrolled in an accredited degree-granting institution for the duration of the program.

Level of Study: Postdoctorate.

Purpose: To support persons holding a DVM or MD degree who are currently enrolled in a program of study leading to the PhD degree. Trainees will pursue a PhD while conducting dissertation Research at CIIT.

No. of awards offered: Varies.

Frequency: Varies.

Value: Varies; from US$26,000 depending upon the number of years of experience.

Study Establishment: The Institute's facility in Research Triangle Park, NC.

Country of Study: USA.

Additional Information: These traineeships are only available for conduct of research at CIIT under the guidance of a CIIT staff scientist.

*Predoctoral Traineeships

Subjects: Fields related to toxicology: biochemistry; pharmacology; chemistry; zoology; biology, etc.

Eligibility: Open to persons who have recently obtained an undergraduate degree and who have been accepted into a course of graduate study in a subject related to toxicology by a degree-granting institution.

Purpose: To support persons enrolled in a program of study leading to a doctoral degree.

No. of awards offered: 4-6.

Frequency: Annual.

Value: US$8,000-US$12,000 per annum, plus tuition and fees.

Study Establishment: University of North Carolina at Chapel Hill, North Carolina State University or Duke University in the Research Triangle area, for the duration of the program.

Country of Study: USA.

Additional Information: Preference is given to individuals who wish to conduct their dissertation research at CIIT.

CHEMICAL INSTITUTE OF CANADA

The Chemical Institute of Canada, Suite 550, 130 Slater Street, Ottawa, Ontario, K1P 6E2, Canada
Tel: 613 232 6252
Fax: 613 232 5862
Contact: Diane Goltz

Pestcon Graduate Scholarship

Subjects: Any area of pesticide research including alternative pest control strategies.

Eligibility: Open to Canadian citizens (including landed immigrants), for graduate study.

Level of Study: Postgraduate.

Purpose: To support postgraduate work in pesticide research.

Type: Scholarship.

No. of awards offered: One.

Frequency: Annual.

Value: C$3,000.

Length of Study: One year.

Country of Study: Canada.

Applications Procedure: Written applications must include a CV and a brief description (500 words or less) of the research program undertaken and the program to date. Applications must be accompanied by an official transcript of the academic record of the candidate and the names of their supervisor and a second academic referee.

Closing Date: 1 March for notification by 1 June.

THE CHICAGO TRIBUNE

Tribune Books, The Chicago Tribune, 435 North Michigan Avenue, Chicago, IL, 60611, USA
Contact: Nelson Algren Awards

*Nelson Algren Awards

Subjects: Short fiction.

Eligibility: Open to US citizens.

No. of awards offered: Four.

Frequency: Annual.

Value: US$5,000 (1 award); US$1,000 (3 runner-up awards).

Closing Date: February 1st.

Additional Information: The work must be unpublished and 2,500-10,000 words in length.

CHILDREN'S MEDICAL RESEARCH INSTITUTE

Children's Medical Research Institute, Locked Bag 23, Wentworthville, NSW, 2145, Australia
Tel: 02 687 2800
Fax: 02 687 2120
Contact: Professor P B Rowe

Graduate Scholarships and Postgraduate Fellowships

Subjects: Muscle genetics: exploration of the role of genetic control systems in myogenesis and cytoarchitecture. Neurosciences: the study of the physical properties and genetic control of neuronal surface glycoproteins; Oncogenesis: the role of oncogenes in leukemogenesis and mechanisms of cellular immortalization; Teratology: the role of oncogenes in fetal development; Embryology: cell fate designation at gastrulation, gene imprinting.

Eligibility: Open to Australian residents with suitable qualifications (honours degree for postgraduate studies) in science or medicine.

Level of Study: Postgraduate, Postdoctorate.

Purpose: To undertake research leading to a PhD or MSc(Med) of the University of Sydney; and to undertake postgraduate research within one of the disciplines currently under study within the Institute.

Type: Scholarships and fellowships, Scholarship.

No. of awards offered: Up to three Postgraduate Scholarships and three Postdoctoral Fellowships.

Frequency: Annual.

Value: Award is based on National Health & Medical Research Council of Australia scale together with a Sydney loading.

Length of Study: Three to five years.

Country of Study: Australia.

Applications Procedure: No application form is required. Applicants must submit a letter outlining background, interests and referees.

Closing Date: None applicable: enrolment for PhD studies in January or August each year.

Additional Information: There are no course requirements; PhD candidates will be required to submit a dissertation.

JANE COFFIN CHILDS MEMORIAL FUND FOR MEDICAL RESEARCH

Jane Coffin Childs Memorial Fund for Medical Research, 333 Cedar Street, New Haven, CT, 06510, USA
Tel: 203 785 4612
Fax: 203 785 3301

Contact: Office of the Director

Fellowships

Subjects: Medical and related sciences relevant to the causes, origins and treatment of cancer: research.

Eligibility: Open to persons who possess an MD or PhD degree in the field in which they propose to work.

Level of Study: Postdoctorate, Doctorate.

Type: Fellowship.

No. of awards offered: 25.

Frequency: Annual.

Value: US$25,000 in the first year, US$26,000 in the second year, US$27,000 in the third year; plus dependant child allowance of US$750 each, and usually US$1,500 per annum departmental grant.

Length of Study: 2-3 years.

Study Establishment: Laboratories and other institutions where the candidate's proposed research is acceptable and where adequate facilities for work exist.

Country of Study: Any country (US citizens) or the USA only (non-US citizens).

Closing Date: February 1st.

CHINESE AMERICAN MEDICAL SOCIETY (CAMS)

Chinese American Medical Society, 281 Edgewood Avenue, Teaneck, NJ, 07666, USA
Tel: 201 833 1506
Fax: 201 833 8252
Email: HW5@COLUMBIA.EDU
Contact: H H Wang, MD, Executive Director

CAMS Scholarship

Subjects: Medical or dental studies.

Eligibility: Open to Chinese Americans, or Chinese residing in the USA. Applicants must be full-time medical or dental students in approved schools in the USA and be able to show academic proficiency and financial hardship.

Level of Study: Doctorate.

Purpose: To help defray the cost of study of the awardees.

Type: Scholarship.

No. of awards offered: Three to five.

Frequency: Annual.

Value: US$1,500.

Country of Study: USA.

Applications Procedure: Complete application form, send it together with letter for the Dean of Students verifying good standing, 2-3 letters of recommendation, personal statement and CV, financial statement.

Closing Date: March 31st.

WINSTON CHURCHILL FOUNDATION OF THE USA

Winston Churchill Foundation of the USA, PO Box 1240, Gracie Station, New York, NY, 10028, USA
Tel: 212 879 3480
Fax: 212 879 3480
Contact: Harold Epstein, Executive Director

Winston Churchill Scholarship

Eligibility: USA only, must be enrolled in one of 55 institutions participating in program.

Level of Study: Postgraduate.

Purpose: To encourage the development of American scientific and technological talent and foster Anglo-American ties.

Type: Scholarship.

No. of awards offered: 10.

Frequency: Annual.

Value: Approximately US$23,000.

Length of Study: One year.

Study Establishment: Churchill College, Cambridge University.

Country of Study: England.

Applications Procedure: Applications may be obtained from liaison person at institutions participating in program.

Closing Date: November 15th.

THE WINSTON CHURCHILL MEMORIAL TRUST (AUS)

The Winston Churchill Memorial Trust, 218 Northbourne Avenue, Braddon, ACT, 2612, Australia
Tel: 06 2478333
Contact: Chief Executive Officer

Churchill Fellowships

Subjects: Any subject.

Eligibility: Open to all Australian residents over the age of 18 years. There are no prescribed qualifications academic or otherwise for the award of most Churchill Fellowships. Merit is the primary test, whether based on past achievement or demonstrated ability for future achievements in any walk of life. Fellowships will not be awarded to enable the applicant to obtain higher academic or formal qualifications. The only criteria for the awarding of a Fellowship is that the applicant has gone as far as they can go in Australia and now needs to go overseas to obtain information not available in Australia.

Level of Study: Unrestricted.

Purpose: To enable Australians from all walks of life to undertake overseas study or an investigative project of a kind that is not fully available in Australia.

Type: Fellowship.

No. of awards offered: Approximately 90.

Frequency: Annual.

Value: Approximately A$15,000. Return economy air fare to country/countries to be visited. Living allowance plus fees if necessary.

Length of Study: Twelve weeks (but this may be longer or shorter depending upon the project).

Country of Study: No restrictions.

Applications Procedure: Application form must be completed.

Closing Date: Last day of February each year.

WINSTON CHURCHILL MEMORIAL TRUST (NZ)

Winston Churchill Memorial Trust, PO Box 10-345, Wellington, New Zealand
Tel: 495 9323
Fax: 495 7225
Contact: The Coordinator

Awards

Subjects: Unrestricted; however, awards are not made to assist purely academic study.

Eligibility: Open to New Zealand residents or persons normally resident in New Zealand. Applicants must have sufficient ability and experience to be regarded as able to make a contribution to New Zealand through their careers.

Level of Study: Unrestricted.

Purpose: To help provide assistance to some investigation or activity which will contribute to the advancement of the awardee's vocation, and will in some way be of general benefit to New Zealand or will aid the maintenance of the Commonwealth as a beneficial influence in world affairs.

No. of awards offered: Varies, depending on funds, but approximately 25 awards.

Frequency: Annual.

Value: Varies according to the needs of the successful applicants and their projects.

Country of Study: Any country outside New Zealand.

Applications Procedure: Application form must be completed and two references submitted.

Closing Date: July 31st.

Additional Information: Applicants must be able to contribute a portion of the actual costs. Applications must be made on the forms provided by the Secretariat. Awards are subject to conditions which are made known in an offer to the applicant and will include an obligation to publish a report within six months of return from the project.

WINSTON CHURCHILL MEMORIAL TRUST (UK)

Winston Churchill Memorial Trust, 15 Queen's Gate Terrace, London, SW7 5PR, England
Tel: 0171 584 9315
Fax: 0171 581 0410
Contact: Director General

Fellowships

Subjects: Approximately ten categories of occupation, which vary annually and are representative of culture, social and public service, technology, commerce and industry, agriculture and nature, recreation and adventure.

Eligibility: Open to British citizens, whose purposes must be covered by one of the categories chosen for the year.

Purpose: To enable men and women from all walks of life and all ages to travel abroad in pursuit of a worthwhile purpose and so to contribute more to their trade or profession, their community and their country.

Type: Travelling fellowship.

No. of awards offered: Approximately 100.

Frequency: Annual.

Value: By individual assessment, to cover all travel, living and equipment expenses; the average award is £4,750.

Length of Study: One to two months.

Country of Study: Outside the UK.

Applications Procedure: Application form must be completed.

Closing Date: Mid-October.

Additional Information: Fellows must undertake to disseminate the information they gain and to remain officially resident in the UK for three years following the termination of their Fellowship. Applications are accepted in September and October of every year, and awards are announced at the beginning of February. Travel expenses of short-listed candidates will be paid within the UK only.

THE CIBA FELLOWSHIP TRUST

The Ciba Fellowship Trust, Hulley Road, Macclesfield, Cheshire, SK10 2NX, England
Tel: 01625 421933
Fax: 01625 619637
Contact: The Secretary

Ciba Awards for Collaboration in Europe (ACE Awards)

Subjects: Chemistry, biochemistry, chemical technology, chemical engineering, biotechnology and biology.

Eligibility: Open to academic members of research groups at UK and Irish institutions.

Purpose: To encourage the development of cooperation between UK and Irish universities or comparable teaching institutions with collaborating research groups in Continental European institutions.

No. of awards offered: Six.

Frequency: Annual.

Value: £1,500 per annum.

Length of Study: Two years.

Study Establishment: Universities on the Continent of Europe.

Country of Study: Europe, excluding UK and Republic of Ireland.

Closing Date: November 1st.

Senior Ciba Fellowships

Subjects: Chemistry, biochemistry, chemical technology, chemical engineering, biotechnology and biology.

Eligibility: Open to lecturers, senior lecturers or readers who hold, and will return to, permanent teaching positions at universities or comparable teaching institutions in the UK or Republic of Ireland.

Purpose: To encourage the interchange of ideas between European scientists by providing opportunities for teaching staff of UK and Irish universities, polytechnics, or comparable teaching institutions to work on the European continent.

Type: Fellowship.

No. of awards offered: 4-6.

Frequency: Annual.

Value: £15,000 per annum, plus travel allowance.

Length of Study: Four-12 months.

Study Establishment: Universities on the continent of Europe.

Country of Study: Europe, excluding UK and Republic of Ireland.

Closing Date: November 1st.

CIBA FOUNDATION

Ciba Foundation, 41 Portland Place, London, W1N 4BN, England
Tel: 0171 636 9456
Fax: 0171 436 2840
Contact: The Director

Ciba Foundation Symposium Bursaries

Subjects: Biomedicine, chemistry and related topics.

Eligibility: Open to applicants (of any nationality), aged between 23 and 35 on the closing date for application, and actively engaged in research on the topic covered by the symposium of their choice.

Level of Study: Doctorate, Postdoctorate.

Purpose: To enable young scientists to attend Ciba Foundation symposia and immediately following the meeting, spend time in the laboratory of one of the symposium participants.

Type: Bursary.

No. of awards offered: Approximately eight.

Frequency: Twice yearly.

Value: Covers travel expenses, by the most economical means, bed and breakfast during the symposium and board and lodging while in the host's laboratory.

Length of Study: Up to a three-month period, which includes travel, attendance at a Ciba Foundation symposium and up to 12 weeks in the participant's laboratory or institution.

Country of Study: UK and worldwide.

Applications Procedure: Send full CV and statement of current research.

Additional Information: The availability of the Bursaries is advertised by circular to overseas members of the Ciba Foundation's Scientific Advisory Panel and invited symposiasts, and by an advertisement in 'Nature', or other journal if more appropriate. Bursaries are advertised every three to six months, and at least six months before the date of the relevant meetings. The Bursar is selected by the senior staff of the Foundation, usually at least four months before the symposium. Offers to host a Bursar are sought from symposiasts at the time of the invitation to the symposium. The successful Bursar is asked to select three names from the membership list of the symposium and every effort is made by the Ciba Foundation to accommodate the Bursar's choice. Successful candidates are expected to submit a short report following their return home.

CLEVELAND INSTITUTE OF MUSIC

Cleveland Institute of Music, 11201 East Boulevard, Cleveland, OH, 44106, USA
Tel: 216 791 5000
Fax: 216 791 3063
Contact: Office of Financial Aid

Scholarships; Accompanying Fellowships

Subjects: Music.

Eligibility: Open to US and foreign nationals. Candidates for the Teaching Fellowships should have a bachelor of music degree or equivalent and must be proficient in English.

Level of Study: Postgraduate.

No. of awards offered: Approximately 200 Scholarships; 3-10 Accompanying Fellowships.

Frequency: Annual.

Value: US$500-US$12,000 (Scholarships); US$375-US$1,500 (Accompanying Fellowships). No travel grants are provided.

Length of Study: One year (Scholarships) or from August to the following June (Accompanying Fellowships); Scholarships are renewable.

Study Establishment: The Institute.

Country of Study: USA.

Closing Date: March 1st.

COLLEGE OF EUROPE

College of Europe, Dijver 11, Brugge, B-8000, Belgium
Tel: 32 50 33 53 34
Fax: 32 50 34 31 58
Contact: Admissions Office

Scholarships

Subjects: European studies in public administration, economics, law, and human resources development.

Eligibility: Open to individuals holding a university degree in economics, law, political science or other social sciences, who possess a good active knowledge of both English and French.

Level of Study: Postgraduate.

Purpose: To fund postgraduate European studies (masters degree).

Type: Scholarship.

No. of awards offered: Approximately 240.

Frequency: Annual.

Value: BF400,000 for citizens of the 15 EU countries; BF600,000 for citizens of all other countries. These sums cover tuition as well as board and lodging in a student residence.

Length of Study: One academic year.

Study Establishment: The College.

Country of Study: Belgium.

Closing Date: March 15th.

COLLEGE OF OCCUPATIONAL THERAPISTS

College of Occupational Therapists, 6-8 Marshalsea Road, London, SE1 1HL, England
Contact: Education Department

Lord Byers Memorial Fund

Subjects: Occupational therapy.

Eligibility: Open to occupational therapists. Priority will be given to those undertaking postgraduate courses with a strong research element.

Level of Study: Postgraduate.

Purpose: To enable occupational therapists to undertake postgraduate degree courses.

No. of awards offered: Varies; two or three.

Frequency: Annual.

Value: Varies.

Applications Procedure: Application procedure is announced annually from July or August in OT News and BJOT.

Closing Date: End of November.

Margaret Dawson Fund

Subjects: Occupational therapy.

Eligibility: Open to occupational therapists in clinical practice.

Purpose: To provide travel bursaries for occupational therapists to travel abroad to observe the practice of occupational therapy or to attend relevant international conferences.

Frequency: Annual.

Country of Study: Outside the UK.

Additional Information: Applications should be made well in advance of the proposed travel and should be marked 'Private and Confidential'.

Farrer-Brown Professional Development Fund

Subjects: Occupational therapy, including awards for work-based projects, research or evaluation of aspects of occupational therapy, awards to enable the publication of relevant papers or for such other purposes of a like nature.

Eligibility: Open to occupational therapists.

Level of Study: Professional development.

Purpose: To encourage professional development of occupational therapy generally.

No. of awards offered: Varies; two or three.

Frequency: Annual.

Value: Varies.

Closing Date: End of November.

Agnes Storar/Constance Owens Fund

Subjects: Occupational therapy.

Eligibility: Open to occupational therapy teachers in recognized schools of occupational therapy.

Purpose: To provide travel bursaries for occupational therapists to travel abroad to observe the practice and teaching of occupational therapy or to attend relevant international conferences.

Frequency: Annual.

Country of Study: Outside the UK.

Additional Information: Applications should be made well in advance of the proposed travel and should be marked 'Private and Confidential'.

JOSEPH COLLINS FOUNDATION

Joseph Collins Foundation, 153 East 53rd Street, New York, NY, 10022, USA

Contact: Augusta L Packer, Secretary-Treasurer

Grants

Subjects: Medicine towards an M.D. degree.

Eligibility: Open to anyone attending an accredited medical school in the USA, located east of the Mississipi River, who intends to specialize in neurology, psychiatry or general practice. Applicants must have successfully completed their first year at an accredited medical school. No grants are available to students attending medical schools west of the Mississippi River.

Level of Study: Doctorate.

Purpose: To aid needy medical students with broad cultural interests who wish to receive an adequate medical education and obtain an MD degree without sacrificing other interests.

Type: Grant.

No. of awards offered: Varies.

Frequency: Annual.

Value: Varies; up to a maximum of US$5,000 annually. Average grants are usually substantially less than the maximum amount.

Length of Study: One year; renewable at the discretion of the Foundation.

Study Establishment: At any accredited medical school, located east of the Mississippi River.

Country of Study: USA.

Applications Procedure: Application form must be completed.

Closing Date: March 15th.

Additional Information: Consideration of all applicants will be based on financial need, scholastic record and demonstrated interest in arts and letters or other cultural pursuits or to outside the field of medicine. Preference is given to students who reside within 200 miles of the medical school they attend. Applications should be obtained through medical school authorities. Awards are not made to pre-medical or postgraduate medical students or to Chiropracter, Osteopathic, or to podiatry students.

COLOMBO PLAN

The Colombo Plan Bureau, 12 Melbourne Avenue, PO Box 596, Colombo, 4, Sri Lanka

Tel: 94 1 581813

Fax: 94 1 580754

Scholarships, Fellowships and Training Awards

Subjects: Colombo Plan awards are usually, but not necessarily, restricted to areas of study that are of significant interest to developing countries.

Eligibility: A request for an award usually originates from a recipient developing country on the basis of its priority needs, and the donor country to which the request is directed may grant it if training facilities and resources in the requested field are available. In some cases, however, offers of training originate from the donor countries themselves. Individuals wishing to apply for Colombo Plan Scholarships, etc. must be sponsored by their own governments.

No. of awards offered: Varies.

Value: Varies.

Country of Study: Colombo Plan member countries.

Additional Information: Please contact the Colombo Plan office for further details.

COLUMBIA UNIVERSITY

Columbia University, New York, NY, 10027, USA

Joseph H Bearns Prize in Music

Subjects: Musical composition.

Eligibility: Open to US citizens who are at least 18 and no more than 25 years of age on 1 January in the award year. A previous winner of the Bearns Prize may compete a second time, but not two years in succession.

Purpose: To encourage talented young people in the USA.

Type: Prizes.

No. of awards offered: Two.

Frequency: Annual.

Value: US$3,000 and US$2,000.

Country of Study: USA.

Closing Date: February 15th.

For further information contact:
703 Dodge Hall, Columbia University, New York, NY, 10027, USA

Contact: Bearns Prize Committee

Knight-Bagehot Fellowships in Economics and Business Journalism

Subjects: Economics and business journalism.

Eligibility: Open to professional journalists with at least four years of experience whose work appears regularly in the USA or Canada.

Level of Study: Postgraduate.

Purpose: To improve the quality of economics and business journalism through instruction to mid-career journalists.

Type: Fellowships.

No. of awards offered: Ten.

Frequency: Annual.

Value: A stipend to cover living expenses, plus tuition for the full academic year.

Length of Study: One academic year.

Study Establishment: The Graduate School of Journalism, Columbia University.

Country of Study: USA.

Applications Procedure: Completed application form, two 1,000 word essays, three letters of reference, and five work samples.

Closing Date: 1 March.

For further information contact:
Graduate School of Journalism, Columbia University, New York, NY, 10027, USA
Tel: 212 854 2711
Fax: 212 854 7837
Email: tat5@columbia.edu
Contact: Director

COMMITTEE ON SCHOLARLY COMMUNICATION WITH CHINA

1055 Thomas Jefferson Street, NW, Suite 2013, Washington, DC, 20007, USA
Tel: 202 337 1250
Fax: 202 337 3109
Email: China@NAS.edu
Contact: Committee on Scholarly Communication with China

Chinese Fellowships for Scholarly Development

Subjects: Social sciences and humanities.

Eligibility: Open to Chinese scholars with a master's or a doctorate from a Chinese institution. The Program does not support Chinese scholars enrolled in degree programs at the host institution, or Chinese scholars already resident in the USA.

Level of Study: Postgraduate.

Purpose: To support Chinese scholars in the social sciences and humanities with the MA/PhD or equivalent, from a Chinese institution to conduct research at a US institution.

Type: Fellowship.

No. of awards offered: Varies.

Frequency: Annual.

Value: Varies.

Length of Study: Five months.

Study Establishment: US institution.

Country of Study: USA.

Applications Procedure: American scholars must nominate Chinese candidates to the program.

Closing Date: November.

Graduate Program

Subjects: Social sciences or humanities.

Eligibility: Open to individuals enrolled in a graduate program.

Level of Study: Postgraduate.

Purpose: To promote open communication among US and Chinese scholars through encouragement of exchange visits and shared research.

No. of awards offered: Varies.

Frequency: Annual.

Length of Study: One academic year.

Study Establishment: A Chinese university.

Country of Study: China.

Closing Date: October.

Research Program

Subjects: Social sciences and humanities.

Eligibility: Open to holders of a PhD or equivalent at the time of application.

Level of Study: Postgraduate, Postdoctorate, Doctorate.

Purpose: To support individuals undertaking in-depth research on China, the Chinese portion of a comparative study, or an exploratory survey of an aspect of contemporary China.

No. of awards offered: Varies.

Frequency: Annual.

Value: Varies.

Length of Study: 2-12 months.

Country of Study: China.

Closing Date: October.

COMMITTEE ON SCIENCE AND TECHNOLOGY IN DEVELOPING COUNTRIES (COSTED)

Committee on Science and Technology in Developing Countries (COSTED), 24 Gandhi Mandap Road, Madras, 600025, India
Tel: 91 44 419 466/416 614
Fax: 91 44 491 543
Email: costed@sirnetm.ernet.in

COSTED Travel Fellowship

Eligibility: Open to scientists from developing Asian countries who have a good publication record.

Level of Study: Postdoctorate, Professional development.

Purpose: To provide international travel support to scientists from developing Asian countries to participate in training programmes and other scientific meetings.

Type: Travel support, Travel support.

No. of awards offered: About 25 per year.

Frequency: Dependent on funds available.

Value: Up to US$500 per award.

Length of Study: Maximum three months.

Applications Procedure: Application forms are available on request from The Scientific Secretary, COSTED.

Closing Date: At least three months prior to proposed meeting/training programme.

COMMONWEALTH FUND

The Commonwealth Fund, Harkness House, 1 East 75th Street, New York, NY, 10021-2692, USA
Tel: 212 535 0400
Fax: 212 249 1276

*Harkness Fellowships Program

Subjects: For UK Fellowships: promoting good health, human resources for the 21st century, people in cities and variations on these themes; varies for Australia and New Zealand.

Eligibility: Open to British, Australian and New Zealand citizens.

Purpose: To forward international understanding by providing opportunities for travel to young men and women of character and ability, thus exposing potential leaders from the UK, Australia and New Zealand to new ideas in the USA, enhancing their ability to bring about change at home and to build up enduring relationships of value to both.

Type: Fellowship.

No. of awards offered: Varies.

Frequency: Annual.

Value: Varies.

Study Establishment: A host institution, which is normally, but not exclusively, of an intellectual kind, such as a university graduate school, a research institute or a 'think tank'.

Country of Study: USA.

Closing Date: Varies.

For further information contact:
Harkness Fellowships, c/o Department of Transport and Communications, GPO Box 594, Canberra, ACT, 2601, Australia
Contact: Mr Roger D B Beale, Australian Representative

or

Department of Anatomy, School of Medicine, University of Auckland, Private Bag 92019, Park Road, Grafton, New Zealand
Contact: Professor R L M Faull, New Zealand Representative

THE COMMONWEALTH FUND OF NEW YORK

28 Bedford Square, London, WC1B 3EG, England
Tel: 0171 631 0411
Fax: 0171 580 5523

Harkness Fellowships

Subjects: Harkness Fellowship projects may address any subject which reflects the current priorities of The Commonwealth Fund.

Eligibility: Open to holders of a valid British citizen passport at time of application. There are no formal age limits, but successful candidates are likely to be between their late 20s and early 40s.

Level of Study: Unrestricted.

Purpose: To expose actual or potential leaders to new ideas, new approaches and new contacts in the USA; to enhance Fellows' ability to bring about change and improvement in the UK; and to build up enduring relationships offering reciprocal benefits to both countries.

Type: Fellowship.

No. of awards offered: Up to twelve.

Frequency: Annual.

Value: To cover basic expenses of travel, residence and study in the USA.

Length of Study: 7-12 months.

Study Establishment: An academic or other institution.

Country of Study: USA.

Applications Procedure: Application form must be completed.

Closing Date: Mid-October in the year preceding year of award.

Additional Information: Work leading to higher degrees, especially doctorates, is not encouraged. It is a condition of appointment that Fellows should leave North America for at least two years following their Fellowships. At the conclusion of the Fellowships, a written report must be submitted to the Fund.

COMMONWEALTH OF AUSTRALIA

Australian Biological Resources Study, GPO Box 636, Canberra, ACT, 2601, Australia
Tel: 062 509554
Fax: 062 509555
Email: lvisher@anca.gov.au
Contact: Ms L Visher, Grants Administration Secretary

Australian Biological Resources Study Participatory Program Grant

Subjects: Botany, zoology, taxonomy and biogeography.

Eligibility: Open to investigators of any nationality.

Purpose: To support research on the number and distribution of plant and animal species in Australia.

Type: Grant.

No. of awards offered: Dependent on funds. Usually about 60.

Frequency: Annual.

Value: Up to A$35,000.

Length of Study: One year, with potential for extension.

Country of Study: Australia.

Applications Procedure: Application forms and Guidelines for Research Grant Applicants are available from contact office.

Closing Date: April 10th of year prior to award.

Additional Information: The grant supports research leading to the publication of the Flora of Australia, Fauna of Australia, Zoological Catalogue, Fungi of Australia, and Algae of Australia.

COMMONWEALTH SCHOLARSHIP AND FELLOWSHIP PLAN

Commonwealth Scholarship Commission in the United Kingdom, c/o Association of Commonwealth Universities, John Foster House, 36 Gordon Square, London, WC1H 0PF, England
Tel: 0171 387 8572
Fax: 0171 387 2655
Contact: Executive Secretary

Commonwealth Scholarships, Fellowships and Academic Staff Scholarships

Subjects: In general arts, social studies, pure science, technology, medicine (largely tenable in the UK), dentistry, agriculture, forestry and veterinary science.

Eligibility: Commonwealth Scholarships are open to Commonwealth citizens under 35 years of age who are normally resident in some part of the Commonwealth other than the particular awarding country. Scholarships are intended for young graduates of high intellectual promise who may be expected to make a significant contribution to their own countries on their return from postgraduate study overseas. (Scholarships may also be awarded for undergraduate study in special circumstances.) Commonwealth Fellowships are intended for a few senior scholars of established reputation and achievement. The main emphasis is on awards to scholars in the academic (including technological) fields who play important roles in the life of their country.

Level of Study: Postgraduate.

Purpose: To enable Commonwealth students of high intellectual promise to pursue studies in Commonwealth countries other than their own so that on their return home they could make a distinctive contribution to life in their own countries and to mutual understanding in the Commonwealth. The following Commonwealth countries are at present offering Commonwealth Scholarships under the Plan: UK, Canada, Australia, New Zealand, India, Sri Lanka, Ghana, Brunei Darussalam, Malta, Nigeria, and Trinidad & Tobago. Professorships, Fellowships or awards for senior scholars and educational administrators have so far been instituted by the UK, Canada, Australia, New Zealand and India.

Type: Scholarship, Fellowship.

No. of awards offered: Over 1,000.

Frequency: Annual.

Value: Determined by each awarding country (i.e. the country in which the award is tenable). Generally, the emoluments for Scholarships include fares to and from the awarding country, payment of tuition fees, allowances for books, special clothing and local travel, and a personal maintenance allowance. In some countries a dependant's allowance is paid. Visiting Fellows will receive fares to and from the awarding country, a per diem expenses allowance, medical and hospital services and an allowance for travel within the awarding country.

Length of Study: 1-3 academic years (Scholarships), or for 3 months to 1 academic year (Fellowships).

Study Establishment: Universities; colleges; other educational institutions.

Country of Study: Commonwealth countries.

Applications Procedure: Applications for Scholarships should be made to the appropriate Scholarship agency in the candidate's country of normal residence. These agencies distribute prospectuses and application forms for the various awards and will, generally speaking, be the best local centres for information about the Plan. Academic Staff Scholarships and other awards for senior scholars are usually awarded by invitation only or through nomination by an individual's own university.

Closing Date: Varies according to the country in which the candidate applies; usually some 12-18 months before the period of study.

Additional Information: Award holders must undertake to return to their own countries on completion of their studies overseas. Please contact the London office for further contact details.

For further information contact:
Training Division, The Secretariat, The Valley, Anguilla, West Indies
Tel: 497 3522
Fax: 497 5873
Contact: The Director

or

Ministry of Education, Culture and Youth Affairs, PO Box 1264, Church Street, St John's, Antigua, West Indies
Tel: 462 4959
Fax: 462 4970
Contact: The Permanent Secretary

or

Secretary, Australian International Development Assistance Bureau, GPO Box 887, Canberra, ACT 2601, Australia
Contact: (for developing countries)

or

The Executive Director, Australian Vice-Chancellors' Committee, 1-5 Geils Court, Deakin, ACT 2600, Australia
Tel: 06 285 8200
Fax: 06 285 8211
Contact: (for developed countries)

or

Ministry of Education, Building No 6, 17th and 18th Floors, Bangladesh Secretariat, Dhaka 2, Bangladesh
Tel: 232 356
Contact: Secretary

or

Ministry of Education, Jemmotts Lane, St Michael, Barbados
Tel: 427 3272
Fax: 436 2411
Contact: Permanent Secretary

or

Ministry of the Public Service, Belmopan, Belize
Tel: 22204
Fax: 22206
Contact: Permanent Secretary

or

Ministry of Education, PO Box HM1185, Hamilton HM EX, Bermuda
Tel: 236 6904
Fax: 236 4006
Contact: Chief Education Officer

or

Bursaries Department, Ministry of Education, Private Bag 005, Gaborone, Botswana

Tel: 312954
Fax: 312891
Contact: First Secretary

or

Ministry of Health, Education and Welfare, Government of the British Virgin Islands, Road Town, Tortola Island, British Virgin Islands
Tel: 494 3701
Contact: Permanent Secretary

or

Ministry of Education, Bandar Seri Bagawan 1170, Brunei
Tel: 244233
Fax: 240250
Contact: Permanent Secretary

or

International Council for Canadian Studies, Commonwealth Scholarship Section, 325 Dalhousie Street, Suite 800, Ottawa, Ontario, K1N 7G2, Canada
Tel: 613 789 7828
Fax: 613 789 7830

or

Department of Education, PO Box 910, George Town, Grand Cayman, West Indies
Tel: 97999
Fax: 90372
Contact: Chief Education Officer

or

Ministry of Foreign Affairs, Nicosia, Cyprus
Contact: The Permanent Secretary

or

Office of the Prime Minister, Establishment and Personnel Department, Government Headquarters, Kennedy Avenue, Roseau, Dominica, Windward Islands
Tel: 82401
Fax: 85044
Contact: The Chief Establishment Officer

or

Falkland Islands Government Secretariat, Stanley, Falkland Islands, Southwest Atlantic
Tel: 27242
Fax: 27212
Contact: The Government Secretary

or

Ministry of Education, No 1 Bedford Place Building, Banjul, Gambia, West Africa
Contact: Permanent Secretary

or

Scholarships Secretariat, PO Box M75, Accra, Ghana
Tel: 662681
Contact: Registrar of Scholarships

or

Department of Education, 40 Town Range, Gibraltar
Tel: 77486
Fax: 71564
Contact: Director

or

Department of Personnel and Management Services (DPMS), Prime Minister's Ministry, Botanical Gardens, St George's, Grenada
Tel: 440 3767
Fax: 440 6609
Contact: Permanent Secretary

or

Public Service Ministry (Scholarships Administration Division), 65--67 High Street, Kingston, Georgetown, Guyana
Tel: 68732
Fax: 57899
Contact: Permanent Secretary

or

Ministry of Human Resource Development (Department of Education), External Scholarships Division, A1 W3, Curzon Road Barracks, Kasturba Gandhi Marg, New Delhi 110001, India
Tel: 384501
Fax: 381355
Contact: Deputy Secretary

or

Human Resource Planning Division, Ministry of Public Service, 50 Knutsford Boulevard, Kingston 5, Jamaica
Tel: 95470
Fax: 63579
Contact: Divisional Director

or

Ministry of Education, Jogoo House, Harambee Avenue, PO Box 30040, Nairobi, Kenya
Tel: 334411
Fax: 214287
Contact: Permanent Secretary

or

Ministry of Education, Science and Technology, PO Box 263, Bikenibeu, Tarawa, Kiribati Islands, West Pacific
Tel: 28091
Fax: 28222
Contact: Secretary

or

National Manpower Development Secretariat, PO Box 517, Maseru 100, Lesotho
Tel: 323842
Contact: Director

or

Department of Personnel Management and Training, PO Box 30227, Lilongwe 3, Malawi
Tel: 731766
Fax: 731675
Contact: Secretary for Personnel Management and Training

or

Public Services Department, Training and Career Development Division, 9th-11th Floors, Perkim Building, Jalan Ipoh, Kuala Lumpur 50510, Malaysia
Contact: Director-General of Public Service

or

External Resources Section, Ministry of Foreign Affairs, Male, Maldives, Indian Ocean
Tel: 323400
Fax: 323841
Contact: Director of External Resources

or

Ministry of Education and Human Resources, Floriana, Malta
Tel: 245389
Fax: 221634
Contact: Assistant Director of Education

or

Ministry of Education and Science, 2nd Floor, Sun Trust Building, Edith Cavell Street, Port Louis, Mauritius, Indian Ocean
Tel: 8411

Fax: 3783
Contact: Permanent Secretary

or

Department of Administration, Government Headquarters, PO Box 292, Plymouth, Montserrat, Leeward Islands, West Indies
Tel: 491 2444
Fax: 491 6234
Contact: Permanent Secretary

or

Ministry of Education and Culture, Bursaries and Scholarships Division, Private Bag 13186, Windhoek 9000, Namibia
Tel: 397 9111
Contact: The Permanent Secretary

or

Department of Education, Aiwo District, Republic of Nauru Islands, Central Pacific
Tel: 674 4095
Fax: 674 4170
Contact: Secretary for Health and Education

or

New Zealand Vice-Chancellors' Committee, PO Box 11-915, Manners Street, Wellington, New Zealand
Tel: 801 5091
Fax: 801 5089
Contact: Scholarships Officer

or

Federal Scholarship Board, Federal Ministry of Education, Block 353, Zone 6, Wuze, PMB 134, Abuja, Nigeria
Contact: The Secretary, Scholarship Board

or

International Cooperation Wing, Ministry of Education, Islamabad, Pakistan
Tel: 826714
Contact: The Deputy Educational Adviser (Scholarships)

or

Department of Personnel Management, PO Wards Strip, Waigani, National Capital District, Papua New Guinea
Contact: Secretary

or

Education Department, Government of St Helena, Jamestown, South Atlantic
Tel: 290 2710
Fax: 290 2461
Contact: Chief Education Officer

or

Establishment Division, Government Headquarters, Church Street, Basseterre, St Kitts, Leeward Islands, West Indies
Tel: 465 2521
Fax: 465 5202
Contact: Permanent Secretary

or

Ministry of Planning, Personnel, Establishment and Training, PO Box 709, Castries, St Lucia, Windward Islands
Tel: 452 1882
Fax: 452 5506
Contact: Permanent Secretary

or

Services Commissions Department, Kingstown, St Vincent and The Grenadines, Windward Islands
Tel: 456 1690
Fax: 456 2943

Contact: Chief Personnel Officer

or

Ministry of Education, Mont Fleuri, PO Box 48, Victoria, Mahe, Republic of Seychelles, Indian Ocean
Tel: 24777
Fax: 24859
Contact: The Principal Secretary

or

Ministry of Education, Youth and Sports, New England, Freetown, Sierra Leone
Contact: The Chief Education Officer

or

Ministry of Finance, Public Service Division, 8 Shenton Way, No 47--01 Treasury Building, Singapore 0106
Tel: 320 9288
Fax: 320 9932
Contact: Permanent Secretary

or

The National Training Unit, Ministry of Education Human Resources Development, PO Box G28, Honiara, Solomon Islands, West Pacific
Fax: 20485
Contact: The Chief Administrative Officer

or

Ministry of Higher Education, 18 Ward Place, Colombo 7, Sri Lanka
Tel: 693916
Contact: Secretary

or

Ministry of Labour and Public Service, PO Box 170, Mbabane, Swaziland
Tel: 43521
Fax: 45379
Contact: Principal Secretary

or

Ministry of Science, Technology and Higher Education, PO Box 2645, Dar-es-Salaam, Tanzania
Tel: 27701
Fax: 46167
Contact: Principal Secretary

or

Ministry of Education, PO Box 161, Nuku'alofa, Tonga Islands, SW Pacific
Tel: 24 122
Fax: 24 105
Contact: The Hon Minister

or

Scholarships and Advanced Training Section, AMBA Building, 55-57 St Vincent Street, Port-of-Spain, Trinidad and Tobago, West Indies
Tel: 625 9964
Fax: 624 2640
Contact: The Chief Personnel Officer, Personnel Department

or

Ministry of Education and Welfare, Grand Turk, Turks and Caicos Islands, West Indies
Tel: 62801
Fax: 62722
Contact: The Permanent Secretary

or

Ministry of Social Services, Funafuti Island, Tuvalu
Contact: Education Division

or

The Central Scholarships Committee (CSC), Ministry of Education and Sports, PO Box 7063, Kampala, Uganda
Tel: 234440
Fax: 230437
Contact: Permanent Secretary

or

Commonwealth Scholarship Commission in the United Kingdom, c/o Association of Commonwealth Universities, John Foster House, 36 Gordon Square, London, WC1H 0PF, UK
Tel: 0171 387 8572
Fax: 0171 387 2655
Contact: Executive Secretary

or

Training and Scholarships Coordination Unit, Public Service Department, Private Mail Bag 059, Port Vila, Vanuatu, South Pacific
Tel: 678 23708
Fax: 678 23142
Contact: Principal Training and Scholarships Officer

or

Ministry of Foreign Affairs, PO Box L1861, Apia, Western Samoa
Tel: 21500
Fax: 21504
Contact: Secretary

or

Bursaries Committee, Ministry of Higher Education, PO Box 50093, Lusaka, Zambia
Tel: 254720
Fax: 254242
Contact: Secretary

or

Office of the President and Cabinet, Department of National Scholarships, Private Bag 7763, Causeway, Harare, Zimbabwe
Contact: Secretary

COMMONWEALTH SCHOLARSHIP COMMISSION IN THE UNITED KINGDOM

Commonwealth Scholarship Commission in the United Kingdom, c/o Association of Commonwealth Universities, John Foster House, 36 Gordon Square, London, WC1H 0PF, England
Tel: 0171 387 8572
Fax: 0171 387 2655
Contact: Executive Secretary

Commonwealth Academic Staff Scholarships

Subjects: Unrestricted.

Eligibility: Open to Commonwealth citizens or British protected persons permanently resident in a developing country of the Commonwealth, who should hold, or be about to obtain, a degree or an equivalent qualification, and should already hold a teaching appointment in a university or similar institution or have the assurance of such an appointment on his or her return. Candidates should be under 35 years of age at the time the award is taken up; preference will be given to persons between 22-28 years of age. All candidates must have sufficient competence in English to profit by the proposed study.

Purpose: To help universities in the developing countries of the Commonwealth build up the numbers and enhance the experience of their locally born staff. The Scholarships are provided by the UK government and fall within the framework of the Commonwealth Scholarship and Fellowship plan. They are intended to enable promising staff members from universities and similar institutions in the developing

Commonwealth to obtain experience in a university or other appropriate institution in the UK. The Scholar's programme is devised by the Commission in conjunction with the candidate's own university and receiving institution (not necessarily the one proposed by the candidate) and will be related as closely as possible to the employment to which the Scholar will return. Scholarships are intended for those preparing for a postgraduate qualification.

Type: Scholarship.

No. of awards offered: 45-50.

Frequency: Annual.

Value: To cover cost of return air fare to the UK, approved tuition, laboratory and examination fees, personal maintenance allowance at the rate of £493 per month or £592 a month for those studying at institutions in the London Metropolitan area (1996 rates, reviewed annually), grant for books and equipment, and grant towards the expense of preparing a thesis or dissertation, where applicable, grant for approved travel within the UK, an initial clothing allowance in special cases, and in certain circumstances a marriage and child allowance. The emoluments are not subject to UK income tax.

Length of Study: 1-3 years.

Study Establishment: A university or comparable institution.

Country of Study: UK.

Applications Procedure: Candidates must be nominated by one of the following: (a) the vice-chancellor of a UK university, the vice-chancellor of the university on whose permanent staff the applicant serves or is to serve (heads of Indian universities should send their nominations to the University Grants Commission in New Delhi and heads of Bangladeshi universities to the University Grants Commission in Dhaka); (b) the Commonwealth Scholarship agency in the candidate's own country (for addresses, see the entry for the Commonwealth Scholarship and Fellowship Plan); (c) in special cases, the head of an autonomous non-university institution in the Commonwealth, or the vice-chancellor of a UK university.

Closing Date: December 31st.

Additional Information: Scholars are required to sign an undertaking to return to resume their academic post in their own country on completion of the Scholarships.

Commonwealth Fellowships

Subjects: Any academic discipline other than medicine.

Eligibility: Open to Commonwealth citizens and to British protected persons permanently resident in a developing Commonwealth country. Preference is given to candidates between 28-40 years of age. Candidates should normally hold a doctorate or other equivalent postgraduate qualification and should have had at least two years' experience as a staff member of a university or similar institution in their own country.

Purpose: To help universities in the developing countries of the Commonwealth build up the numbers and enhance the experience of their locally born staff. The Fellowships are provided by the UK government and fall within the framework of the Commonwealth Scholarship and Fellowship Plan [qv]. They are intended to enable promising staff members from universities and similar institutions in the developing Commonwealth to obtain experience in a university or other appropriate institution in the UK. The Fellow's programme is devised by the Commission in conjunction with the candidate's own university and receiving institution (not necessarily the one proposed by the candidate) and will be related as closely as possible to the employment to which the Fellow will return. Fellowships are not given for study for higher degrees.

Type: Fellowship.

No. of awards offered: Approximately 50.

Frequency: Annual.

Value: £705 per month or £846 for those studying at institutions in the London Metropolitan area (1995 rates, reviewed annually) plus approved air fares to and from the UK and in certain circumstances a marriage and child allowance. A grant for approved travel within the UK

and a book grant are also paid and, where recommended, an initial clothing allowance is offered. The emoluments are not subject to UK income tax.

Length of Study: Ten months; not renewable.

Study Establishment: A university or comparable institution.

Country of Study: UK.

Closing Date: December 31st.

Additional Information: Fellows are required to sign an undertaking to return to resume their academic post in their country on completion of the Fellowships. Candidates must be nominated by one of the following: (a) the vice-chancellor of a UK university, the vice-chancellor of the university on whose permanent staff the applicant serves or is to serve (heads of Indian universities should send their nominations to the University Grants Commission in New Delhi and heads of Bangladeshi universities to the University Grants Commission in Dhaka); (b) the Commonwealth Scholarship agency in the candidate's own country (for addresses, see the entry for the Commonwealth Scholarship and Fellowship Plan); (c) in special cases, the head of an autonomous non-university institution in the Commonwealth, or the vice-chancellor of a UK university. The Fellowship may not be held concurrently with other awards or with paid employment.

CONCORDIA UNIVERSITY

Concordia University, 1455 de Maisonneuve Boulevard West, Montreal, Quebec, H3G 1M8, Canada
Tel: 514 848 3801
Fax: 514 848 2812
Email: SGSCU@VAX2.Concordia.CA
Contact: Graduate Studies Office

David J Azrieli Graduate Fellowship

Subjects: Any subject.

Eligibility: Open to masters or doctoral students of any nationality.

Level of Study: Postgraduate, Doctorate.

Type: Fellowship.

No. of awards offered: One.

Frequency: Annual.

Value: TBA.

Length of Study: One year; non-renewable.

Study Establishment: The University.

Country of Study: Canada.

Applications Procedure: Completed application form; three letters of recommendation and official transcripts of all university studies must be received by the closing date.

Closing Date: February 1st.

Additional Information: Academic merit is the prime consideration in the granting of the award which is for full-time study in a graduate program leading to a masters or doctoral degree.

Bank of Montreal Pauline Varnier Fellowship

Subjects: Business administration.

Eligibility: Open to women with two years of cumulative business experience who are Canadian citizens or landed immigrants intending to pursue a full-time course of study for the MBA. This is an entrance Fellowship.

Level of Study: Postgraduate.

Type: Fellowship.

No. of awards offered: One.

Frequency: Annual.

Value: TBA.

Length of Study: Two years.

Study Establishment: The University.

Country of Study: Canada.

Applications Procedure: Completed application form; three letters of recommendation and official transcripts of all university studies must be received by the closing date.

Closing Date: April 30th.

Additional Information: Academic merit is the prime consideration in the granting of the awards.

Concordia University Graduate Fellowships

Subjects: Any subject.

Eligibility: Open to graduates of any nationality.

Level of Study: Postgraduate, Doctorate.

Type: Fellowship.

No. of awards offered: Varies.

Frequency: Annual.

Value: C$2,900 per term for masters level; C$3,600 per term for doctoral level.

Length of Study: A maximum of four terms at the masters level and nine terms at the doctoral level, calculated from the date of entry in the program.

Study Establishment: The University.

Country of Study: Canada.

Applications Procedure: Completed application form; three letters of recommendation and official transcripts of all university studies must be received by the closing date.

Closing Date: February 1st.

Additional Information: Academic merit is the prime consideration in the granting of the award.

Stanley G French Graduate Fellowship

Subjects: Any subject.

Eligibility: Open to graduates of any nationality.

Level of Study: Postgraduate, Doctorate.

Type: Fellowship.

No. of awards offered: One.

Frequency: Annual.

Value: C$3,300 per term for masters level; C$4,000 per term for doctoral level.

Length of Study: A maximum of three terms.

Study Establishment: The University.

Country of Study: Canada.

Applications Procedure: Completed application form; three letters of recommendation and official transcripts of all university studies must be submitted by the closing date.

Closing Date: February 1st.

Additional Information: Academic merit is the prime consideration in the granting of awards, which are for full-time study in a graduate program leading to a masters or doctoral degree.

J W McConnell Memorial Fellowships

Subjects: Any subject.

Eligibility: Open to Canadian citizens and permanent residents. Financial need is one of the criteria.

Level of Study: Postgraduate, Doctorate.

Type: Fellowship.

No. of awards offered: Variable.

Frequency: Annual.

Value: C$2,900 per term at the masters level; C$3,600 per term at the doctoral level.

Length of Study: A maximum of four terms at the masters level and nine terms at the doctoral level, calculated from the date of entry in the program.

Study Establishment: The University.

Country of Study: Canada.

Applications Procedure: Application form must be submitted; three letters of recommendation and official transcripts of all university studies must be submitted by the closing date.

Closing Date: February 1st.

Additional Information: Academic merit is the prime consideration in the granting of the Awards.

John W O'Brien Graduate Fellowship

Subjects: Any subject.

Eligibility: Open to full-time graduate students of any nationality.

Level of Study: Postgraduate, Doctorate.

Type: Fellowship.

No. of awards offered: One.

Frequency: Annual.

Value: C$3,300 per term at the masters level and C$4,000 per term at the doctoral level.

Length of Study: A maximum of three terms.

Study Establishment: The University.

Country of Study: Canada.

Applications Procedure: Application form must be completed; three letters of recommendation and official transcripts of all university studies must be submitted by closing date.

Closing Date: February 1st.

Additional Information: Academic merit is the prime consideration in the granting of awards which are for full-time study in a graduate program leading to a masters or doctoral degree.

CONFEDERATION OF BRITISH INDUSTRY

Confederation of British Industry, Centre Point, 103 New Oxford Street, London, WC1A 1DU, England
Tel: 0171 379 7400
Fax: 0171 240 1578
Contact: Manager, Overseas Scholarships

Overseas Scholarships

Subjects: Engineering work experience (not academic studies).

Eligibility: Open to graduate engineers from overseas countries, who hold a degree or diploma in engineering issued by a recognized university faculty, institute or school. Applicants should be able to profit from training in industrial (as distinct from academic surroundings); be medically fit; speak and write English well; possess good character, initiative and sense of responsibility; and undertake to return and follow their profession in their own country. Applicants should have had at least a year's postgraduate engineering experience in the field in question and are required to be in employment in their home country.

Level of Study: Postgraduate.

Purpose: To help promote business opportunities through increased awareness of British technology, products, services and standards and to provide technical assistance towards the development of overseas countries.

Type: Scholarship.

No. of awards offered: Approximately 80-90.

Frequency: Annual.

Value: £616 per month to cover basic cost of living. Scholars are required to pay their own air fare to the UK with CBI paying the homeward fare for scholarships of six months duration and over. Allowances are reviewed annually in September.

Length of Study: 6-12 months.

Country of Study: UK.

Applications Procedure: Candidates should apply through the British Embassy (Commercial Section), British High Commission, or British Council representatives in their own country.

Closing Date: As determined in individual countries by the CBI's representative.

Additional Information: Candidates are required to return to their own country upon completion of the scholarship.

CONSERVATION AND RESEARCH FOUNDATION

Conservation and Research Foundation, Box 5261 Connecticut College, New London, CT, 06320, USA

Grants

Subjects: Environmental studies and biological science.

Eligibility: There are no eligibility restrictions.

Level of Study: Postgraduate, Doctorate, Postdoctorate.

Purpose: To promote the conservation and enlightened use of renewable natural resources, to encourage related research in the biological sciences, and to deepen the understanding of the intricate relationships between people and the environment that supports them.

Frequency: Dependent on funds available.

Value: US$100 to US$5,000.

Length of Study: Unspecified.

Country of Study: Unrestricted.

Applications Procedure: The present policy of the Foundation is to invite the submission of proposals. Unsolicited applications will not be considered.

Closing Date: No deadlines.

Additional Information: The Foundation does not offer scholarships.

CONSORTIUM FOR GRADUATE STUDY IN MANAGEMENT

Consortium for Graduate Study in Management, 12855 North Outer 40 Drive, Suite 100, St Louis, MO, 63141-8635, USA
Tel: 314 935 5614

*Fellowships for Minorities

Subjects: Business administration.

Eligibility: Open to US citizens who are African-American, Hispanic American or Native American, and hold a bachelor's degree in any academic discipline.

Purpose: To hasten the entry of minority men and women into management positions in business by enabling them to obtain a master's degree.

Type: Fellowship.

No. of awards offered: Approximately 170.

Frequency: Annual.

Value: To cover full tuition, required fees, plus a US$5,000 stipend over two years of full-time MBA study. Additional financial aid may also be available.

Length of Study: Two years.

Study Establishment: Graduate schools of management at the following universities: Indiana University; University of Michigan; New York University; University of North Carolina; University of Rochester; University of Southern California; University of Texas at Austin; University of Virginia; Washington University; University of Wisconsin-Madison.

Country of Study: USA.

Closing Date: February 1st.

JAMES COOK UNIVERSITY OF NORTH QUEENSLAND

Academic Services Division, James Cook University of North Queensland, Townsville, Queensland, 4811, Australia
Tel: 077 81 4575
Fax: 077 81 5175
Contact: Scholarships Officer

W C Lacy Scholarship

Subjects: Economic geology.

Eligibility: Open to persons holding or expecting to hold an honours degree of at least 2A or its equivalent in geology or a related science.

Level of Study: Postgraduate.

Purpose: To encourage full-time postgraduate research leading to an MSc or PhD degree.

Type: Scholarship.

No. of awards offered: One.

Frequency: Annually, when funds are available.

Value: Up to equivalent value of Australian postgraduate award. The Award does not cover tuition fees for overseas students.

Length of Study: Three years (PhD); or two years (master's program).

Study Establishment: The Economic Geology Research Unit, James Cook University of North Queensland.

Country of Study: Australia.

Noel and Kate Monkman Postgraduate Award

Subjects: Marine biology.

Eligibility: Open to persons holding or expecting to hold an honours degree of at least 2A or its equivalent in marine biology or a related science. Applicants must be Australian citizens or have permanent resident status in Australia.

Level of Study: Postgraduate.

Purpose: To encourage full-time study towards a master of science or doctor of philosophy degree in marine biology.

Type: Scholarship.

No. of awards offered: One.

Frequency: Annually, when funds are available.

Value: To be determined.

Length of Study: Three years (PhD); or two years (master's degree).

Study Establishment: James Cook University.

Country of Study: Australia.

Postgraduate Research Scholarship Award

Subjects: Most subjects offered at the University.

Eligibility: Open to any student who has attained at least a bachelor's degree at honours level (Class 2A).

Level of Study: Postgraduate.

Purpose: To encourage full-time postgraduate research leading to a master's or PhD degree.

Type: Scholarship.

No. of awards offered: Up to four.

Frequency: Annual.

Value: A$15,364 per annum. The Award does not cover annual tuition fees for overseas students.

Length of Study: Three years with a possible additional six months in exceptional circumstances (PhD); or for two years (master's program).

Study Establishment: James Cook University.

Country of Study: Australia.

Closing Date: October 31st.

Postgraduate Research Scholarship in Electrical and Computer Engineering

Subjects: Any area relevant to the department of Electrical and Computer Engineering.

Eligibility: Open to any candidate eligible for entry to the degree of MEngSc (research) or PhD at James Cook University.

Level of Study: Postgraduate.

Purpose: To encourage full-time postgraduate research towards the master's degree or PhD.

Type: Scholarship.

No. of awards offered: One.

Frequency: Annually, when available.

Value: A$15,364per annum. The Award does not cover tuition fees for overseas students.

Length of Study: One year; may be extended if course of study exceeds one year.

Study Establishment: James Cook University.

Country of Study: Australia.

Closing Date: Varies.

COOLEY'S ANEMIA FOUNDATION

Cooley's Anemia Foundation , 129-09 26th Avenue, Flushing, NY, 11354, USA
Tel: 718 321 2873
Fax: 718 321 3340
Contact: Gina Cioffi, Esq

Cooley's Anemia Foundation Research Fellowship Grant

Level of Study: Postdoctorate.

Purpose: To promote an increased understanding of Cooley's anemia, develop improved treatment and acheive a final cure for this life threatening genetic blood disorder.

Frequency: Annual.

Length of Study: One year.

Applications Procedure: Application must be submitted to the national office.

Closing Date: March 11th.

COOPERATIVE INSTITUTE FOR RESEARCH IN ENVIRONMENTAL SCIENCES (CIRES)

CIRES Visiting Fellows Program, Campus Box 216, University of Colorado, Boulder, CO, 80309-0216, USA
Tel: 303 492 1143
Fax: 303 492 1149
Email: cires@cires.colorado.edu
www: http://cires.colorado.edu
Contact: Director

Visiting Fellowships

Subjects: Atmospheric chemistry; atmospheric dynamics; climate dynamics; environmental chemistry and biology; environmental measurements and instrumentation; global change; remote sensing.

Eligibility: Open to senior scientists including faculty on sabbatical leave, as well as recent PhD recipients. There are no nationality restrictions.

Level of Study: Postdoctorate.

Purpose: To advance scientific research collaboration in areas of interest to CIRES.

Type: Fellowship.

No. of awards offered: Five.

Frequency: Annual.

Value: Varies with experience; entry-level stipends average US$33,000 for one year.

Length of Study: One year; renewable depending on the availability of funding.

Study Establishment: University of Colorado at Boulder.

Country of Study: USA.

Applications Procedure: Applicants should submit CV, brief research proposal and three letters of recommendation.

Closing Date: Final deadline is December 15th.

Additional Information: Fellows will pursue their own research programs as well as participate in institute seminars. Selection is based in part on likelihood of interaction between the Visiting Fellow and the scientists at CIRES. The Fellowships are granted in conjunction with the University of Colorado and the National Oceanic and Atmospheric Administration.

CORNELL UNIVERSITY

Center for the Humanities, Cornell University, Andrew D White House, Ithaca, NY, 14853, USA
Tel: 1 607 255 9274
Email: as63@cornell.edu
Contact: Agnes Sirrine, Program Administrator

Mellon Postdoctoral Fellowships

Subjects: Arts and humanities.

Eligibility: Open to US and Canadian citizens and permanent residents who have completed requirements for the PhD within the last four or five years and before application deadline.

Level of Study: Postdoctorate, Doctorate.

Type: Fellowship.

No. of awards offered: 3-4.

Frequency: Annual.

Value: US$28,000.

Length of Study: Nine months (one academic year).

Study Establishment: The University.

Country of Study: USA.

Closing Date: Postmark January 4th.

Additional Information: While in residence at Cornell, postdoctoral fellows have department affiliation, limited teaching duties, and the opportunity for scholarly work. Areas of specialization change each year.

Society for the Humanities Postdoctoral Fellowships

Subjects: Humanities.

Eligibility: Open to holders of the PhD degree who have at least one or two years of teaching experience at the college level. Applicants should be scholars with interests that are not confined to a narrow humanistic specialty and whose research coincides with the 'focal theme' for the year. Fellows of the Society devote most of their time to research writing, but they are encouraged to offer a weekly seminar related to their special projects.

Level of Study: Postdoctorate, Doctorate.

Type: Fellowship.

No. of awards offered: 8-10.

Frequency: Annual.

Value: US$32,000.

Length of Study: 9 months (one academic year).

Study Establishment: The University.

Country of Study: USA.

Applications Procedure: Applicants must contact this office to receive information on the theme and application materials.

Closing Date: Postmark on or before October 21st.

Additional Information: Information about this year's theme is available on request.

THE CORPORATION OF YADDO

The Corporation of Yaddo, Box 395, Saratoga Springs, NY, 12866, USA
Tel: 518 584 0746
Fax: 518 584 1312
Contact: Candice Wait, Program Coordinator

Yaddo Residency

Subjects: Writing, photography, drawing, sculpture, music and drama.

Eligibility: Open to all who have achieved some professional standing by having work published, exhibited, or performed. Applications are welcomed from artists from the USA and abroad. Open to visual artists, writers, composers, and artists working in film/video and choreography performance.

Level of Study: Professional development.

Purpose: To provide uninterrupted time and space for creative artists to think, experiment and create.

Type: Residency.

No. of awards offered: Approximately 120.

Value: Room, board and studio space. No stipend.

Length of Study: From two weeks to two months.

Study Establishment: Yaddo.

Country of Study: USA.

Applications Procedure: Write to Corporation of Yaddo, Box 395, Saratoga Springs, NY 12866; Attn: Admissions. Requirements include: completed application form, letters from two sponsors, copies of professional resume, work samples, and US$20 application fee.

Closing Date: January 15th, August 1st.

THE COSTUME SOCIETY OF AMERICA

The Costume Society of America, 55 Edgewater Drive, PO Box 73, Earleville, MD, 21919, USA
Tel: 410 275 2329/1 800 CSA 9447
Fax: 410 275 8936
Email: 71554.3201@compuserve.com

Stella Blum Research Grant

Subjects: North American costume.

Eligibility: Open to students who are matriculating in a degree program at an accredited institution and who are members of the Society.

Level of Study: Unrestricted.

Purpose: To assist students with research expenses.

Type: Grant.

No. of awards offered: One.

Frequency: Annual.

Value: Up to US$3,000. Allowable costs include: transportation to and from the research site; living expenses at the research site; supplies such as film, photographic reproductions, books, paper, computer disks; postage and telephone; services such as typing, computer searches, graphics.

Study Establishment: An accredited institution.

Country of Study: USA.

Applications Procedure: Applicants must complete an application form; these are available upon request.

Closing Date: February 1st.

Additional Information: The award will be given based on merit rather than need. Judging criteria will include: creativity and innovation, specific awareness of and attention to costume matters, impact on the broad field of costume, awareness of interdisciplinarity of the field, ability to successfully implement the proposed project in a timely manner, and faculty advisor recommendation.

CSA Travel Research Award

Eligibility: Applicants must be current CSA members, and have held membership two years or more. They must give proof of work in progress, and indicate why the particular collection is important to the project.

Level of Study: Professional development.

Purpose: To aid any individual non-student CSA member in travelling to collections for research purposes.

Frequency: Annual.

Value: US$500.

Applications Procedure: Contact the CSA National Office (1 800 CSA 9447).

Closing Date: September 1st.

Adele Filene Purse Student Travel Award

Eligibility: Open to currently enrolled students with CSA membership who have been accepted for presentation of a juried paper or poster. Accompanied by a letter of support by major advisor and two additional letters from persons knowledgable of past or present work.

Level of Study: Unrestricted.

Purpose: To assist CSA members currently enrolled as students in their travel to CSA national symposia to present either a juried paper or a poster.

No. of awards offered: 1-3.

Frequency: Annual.

Value: Up to US$500.

Country of Study: USA.

Applications Procedure: Send three letters of support with the following: a copy of the juried abstract and a one-page letter of application.

Closing Date: Varies.

COUNCIL FOR BRITISH ARCHAEOLOGY

Council for British Archaeology, Bowes Morrell House, 111 Walmgate, York, YO1 2UA, England
Tel: 01904 671417
Fax: 01904 671384
Email: 100271.456@compuserve.com
Contact: Finance Officer

British Archaeological Research Trust Grants

Subjects: Archaeology.

Eligibility: Open to UK residents; academic qualifications are not required.

Level of Study: Unrestricted.

Purpose: To support personal archaeological research, particularly that which is innovative and extends the range of techniques available to archaeologists.

Type: Research Grant.

No. of awards offered: 2-3.

Frequency: Annual.

Value: Approximately £1,000.

Study Establishment: An approved location.

Country of Study: UK.

Closing Date: June 30th.

Additional Information: Grants may be held concurrently with other income.

CBA Grant for Publication

Subjects: British archaeology.

Eligibility: Open to all members of the council, except those already in receipt of a direct government grant.

Type: Grant.

No. of awards offered: 5-10.

Frequency: Annual.

Value: Up to £1,500.

Country of Study: UK.

Closing Date: March 31st.

Additional Information: Grants will be made available for publications which contribute substantially to research on problems of national or special regional significance. No grant will be made for the publication of records or of publications based exclusively on records, or for the publication of excavation reports where the excavation has been financed by government agencies. Grants will not normally be given to finance other than final excavation reports.

COUNCIL FOR EUROPEAN STUDIES

Council for European Studies, 808-809 International Affairs Building, Columbia University, New York, NY, 10027, USA
Tel: 212 854 4172
Fax: 212 854 4703
Email: ces@columbia.edu
Contact: Pre-Dissertation Fellowship Program

Pre-Dissertation Fellowships

Subjects: Anthropology (excluding archaeology), economics, post-1750 history, geography, political science, sociology, social psychology, urban planning.

Eligibility: Open to citizens or permanent residents of the USA and citizens or landed immigrants of Canada who are enrolled in a doctoral program at an American or Canadian university and have completed the equivalent of at least two years of full-time graduate study prior to the commencement of their proposed research.

Level of Study: Doctorate.

Purpose: To enable students in the social science disciplines to pursue short-term, exploratory research in order to determine the viability and to better define the scope of their proposed dissertation.

Type: Fellowship.

No. of awards offered: 12-15.

Frequency: Annual.

Value: US$3,000.

Length of Study: Two or three months.

Country of Study: Western or Southern Europe or East-West comparative studies (including one Eastern European country).

Applications Procedure: Applications may be requested from the Council. Documentation must include a narrative, three reference letters and a language evaluation.

Closing Date: February 1st.

Pre-Dissertation Fellowships for Topics Related to the European Community

Subjects: Proposed topics may address any aspect or the process of European integration, including subjects related to the Treaties of Paris and Rome as well as the Single European Act.

Eligibility: Open to citizens of the USA only, who are enrolled in a doctoral program in economics, history, political science or sociology at an American university and have completed at least two years of full-time graduate study prior to the commencement of their proposed research.

Purpose: To enable students to pursue short-term, exploratory research in order to determine the viability and to better define the scope of their proposed dissertation.

Type: Fellowship.

No. of awards offered: Approximately three.

Frequency: Annual.

Value: US$3,000.

Length of Study: For two or three months.

Country of Study: EC countries.

Closing Date: February 1st.

Additional Information: Fellowship recipients are required to submit a written report to the Council upon their return. In the report, students are requested to outline their research in specific archives or libraries, their contacts with European scholars in their field, any problems which they may have encountered in the course of their research and the ways in which their experience has reshaped their dissertation project. The Council is part of Columbia University.

Research Planning Group Grants

Subjects: Social sciences, modern history, including comparative studies.

Eligibility: Open only to scholars based in North America and Europe (East and West).

Level of Study: Postdoctorate, Professional development.

Purpose: To establish an international working committee whose members have agreed to coordinate their research around a major topic.

Type: Grant.

No. of awards offered: Two to four.

Frequency: Annual.

Value: US$15,000. The grant pays only for travel to meetings of the Research Planning Group.

Country of Study: Europe or European-North American comparative.

Applications Procedure: Letter of enquiry, followed by a draft proposal, followed by a final project proposal.

Closing Date: January 15th.

Additional Information: List of publications resulting from the program are available from the Council; project descriptions are published in the European Studies Newsletter, and sample copies are available upon request.

COUNCIL FOR INTERNATIONAL EXCHANGE OF SCHOLARS

Council for International Exchange of Scholars, 3007 Tilden Street, NW, Suite 5M, Washington, DC, 20008-3009, USA
Tel: 202 686 7877
Fax: 202 686 7877
Email: cies1@ciesnet.cies.org
www: http://www.cies.org/

Fulbright Scholar Awards for Research and Lecturing Abroad

Subjects: All academic disciplines and some professional fields.

Eligibility: Open to US citizens with a PhD or comparable professional qualification. University or college teaching experience is normally expected for lecturing awards. For selected assignments, proficiency in a foreign language may be required.

Level of Study: Postdoctorate.

Purpose: To increase mutual understanding between the people of the USA and the people of other nations, strengthen the ties which unite the USA with other nations and promote international cooperation for educational and cultural advancement.

Type: Research and/or lecturing.

No. of awards offered: In excess of 800.

Frequency: Annual.

Value: Varies by country.

Length of Study: 2 months to one academic year.

Country of Study: 135 countries in the world.

Applications Procedure: Applications are available from CIES.

Closing Date: August 1st.

Additional Information: Individual countries' programs are described in the Council's publication .

NATO Advanced Research Fellowships and Institutional Grants

Subjects: Social sciences and related fields: NATO political, economic, and defense security issues; functioning of democratic institutions in Europe.

Eligibility: Open to US citizens with the PhD or equivalent professional status. Fellowships are intended for scholars of established reputation.

Level of Study: Postdoctorate.

Purpose: To promote research on political, security, and economic issues directly affecting the health of the NATO Alliance. Institutional research grants are also available.

Type: Research awards, fellowships, and institutional grants.

No. of awards offered: Up to five.

Frequency: Annual.

Value: Fellowships of 240,000 Belgian francs; institutional grants of 250,000 francs. All awards are fixed-sum grants, inclusive of travel costs.

Length of Study: Variable, must be completed by June 30th, 1998.

Study Establishment: Research to be conducted in one or more of the European member countries with time spent at NATO headquarters.

Country of Study: NATO member countries/NATO Alliance.

Applications Procedure: Application form must be completed.

Closing Date: January 1st.

Additional Information: Application forms are available at the beginning of September.

For further information contact:
Council for International Exchange of Scholars, 3007 Tilden Street, NW, Suite 5M, Washington, DC, 20008-3009, USA
Tel: 202 686 6244
Fax: 202 362 3442
www: http://www.cies.org/

COUNCIL FOR THE ADVANCEMENT OF SCIENCE WRITING, INC

Council For The Advancement Of Science Writing, Inc, PO Box 404, Greenlawn, New York, 11740, USA
Tel: 516 757 5664
Contact: Diane McGusgan

Taylor/Blakeslee Fellowships for Graduate Study in Science Writing

Eligibility: Students must have undergraduate degrees in science or journalism and must convince the CASW selection committee of their ability to pursue a career in writing science for the general public.

Level of Study: Postgraduate.

Purpose: Graduate study in science writing.

Type: Fellowship/Grant, Fellowship.

No. of awards offered: Two to four.

Frequency: Annual.

Value: Up to US$2,000.

Length of Study: One year.

Country of Study: USA.

Applications Procedure: Applicants should submit four collated sets of the following: a completed application form; a resume; transcript of undergraduate studies (if student); three faculty or employer recommendations; three samples of writing (on 8-1/2 * 11-inch sheets only); short statement of career goals.

Closing Date: June 15th.

Additional Information: Science writng is here defined as writing about science, medicine, health, technology, and the environment for the general public via the mass media.

COUNCIL OF EUROPE

CDCC Teacher Bursaries Scheme, Council of Europe In-Service Training Programme for Teachers, School and Out-of-School Education Section, Council of Europe, Strasbourg, Cedex, F-67075, France
Tel: 33 88 41 26 21
Fax: 33 88 41 27 88
Contact: Mrs C Parvé-Puydarrieux

CDCC Teacher Bursaries Scheme

Subjects: All subjects related to general, technical and vocational education.

Eligibility: Open to inspectors, head teachers and teachers of member states.

Level of Study: Professional development.

Purpose: To enable educationalists (inspectors, head teachers and teachers) from member states of the Council for Cultural Cooperation (CDCC) to attend short national in-service training courses organized in these countries.

Type: Bursary.

No. of awards offered: Variable.

Value: Subsistence expenses and enrolment fees are borne by the host country. Travel expenses are covered by the Cultural Fund of the Council of Europe and, in most cases, by voluntary contributions from the majority of these countries to this Fund.

Country of Study: The member states of the CDCC are: Austria, Belgium, Cyprus, Denmark, Finland, France, Germany, Greece, Holy See, Hungary, Iceland, Ireland, Italy, Liechtenstein, Netherlands, Norway, Poland, Portugal, San Marino, Spain, Sweden, Switzerland, Turkey, the UK (England, Wales and Scotland), Bulgaria, Luxembourg, Malta, Albania, Croatia, the Czech Republic, Estonia, Latvia, Lithuania, Romania, the Russian Federation, the Slovak Republic, Slovenia, Andorra, Moldova, Ukraine, Belarus, Monaco, Bosnia-Herzegovina, the former Yugoslav Republic of Macedonia.

Applications Procedure: Course programmes and application forms are distributed by the Council of Europe Secretariat to a network of national liaison officers of ministries of education in the CDCC member states.

Additional Information: Good knowledge of the working language of the course is required.

COUNCIL ON FOREIGN RELATIONS

Membership and Fellowship Affairs, Council on Foreign Relations, 58 East 68th Street, New York, NY, 10021, USA
Tel: 212 734 0400
Fax: 212 861 2701
Email: SSTONECIPHER@email.CFR.ORG
Contact: Elise Carlson Lewis, Director

International Affairs Fellowships

Subjects: Important problems in international affairs and their implications for the interests and policies of the USA, foreign states or international organizations.

Eligibility: Open to US citizens (or permanent residents who have applied to become citizens), between 27 and 35 years of age, with demonstrated intellectual ability and promise who come from academic, government, business and professional communities. The PhD degree or its equivalent is not a firm requirement.

Level of Study: Postdoctorate, Professional development.

Purpose: To bridge the gap between theory and practice in international relations and to encourage the better use of scholarly reflective wisdom in the making of decisions on international problems.

Type: Fellowship.

No. of awards offered: 10-15.

Frequency: Annual.

Value: Varies according to need, with a maximum of US$40,000 per annum. The Fellowship stipend does not normally exceed the salary relinquished during the Fellowship period.

Length of Study: A period not exceeding 12 months.

Study Establishment: Usually the Fellow is not permitted to remain at his or her home institution during the Fellowship period.

Country of Study: Any country.

Applications Procedure: Application must include references and a five-page proposal.

Closing Date: September 15th for nomination; October 31st for application.

Additional Information: Application is primarily by invitation. However, people who apply directly and who meet preliminary requirements may also be invited to apply without formal nomination. Fellowships will not be awarded to support writing, dissertations or research towards the PhD, and the programme is not intended to support research of which the results will be of primary interest only to scholars or theoreticians. While the Fellow is not required to produce a book, article or report, it is hoped that some written output will result.

Edward R Murrow Fellowship for Foreign Correspondents

Subjects: Issues in international affairs and their implications for the interests and policies of the US, foreign states or international organizations.

Eligibility: Open to any US citizen who is a correspondent, editor, or producer for radio, television, a newspaper, or a magazine widely available in the USA, and who is either now serving abroad or, having recently served abroad, plans to return to foreign posts.

Level of Study: Professional development.

Purpose: To help the Fellow increase his or her competence in reporting and interpreting events abroad and to give him or her a period of nearly a year for sustained analysis and writing, free from the daily pressures that characterize journalistic life.

Type: Fellowship.

No. of awards offered: One.

Frequency: Annual.

Value: A stipend equivalent to the salary relinquished, not to exceed US$60,000 per annum.

Length of Study: Normally a period of nine months, not to exceed 12 months.

Study Establishment: The Fellow is expected to remain in residence at the Council headquarters in New York City for the duration of his/her tenure.

Applications Procedure: Application form must be completed.

Closing Date: November 15th for nomination; February 1st for application.

Additional Information: Application forms and further details are available on request.

COUNCIL ON LIBRARY RESOURCES

Council on Library Resources, 1400 16th Street NW, Suite 510, Washington, DC, 20036-2217, USA
Tel: 1 202 483 7474
Fax: 1 202 483 6410
Contact: Julia Blixrud, Program Officer

*CLR Fellows Program

Subjects: Research or analytical studies pertinent to library and information services or other professional projects of importance to such operations. Topics to be examined should be in the Council's program areas of human resources, economics, infrastructure, or access and processing.

Eligibility: Applicants must be librarians or other professionals working directly with libraries or related information systems and services. They must be citizens of the USA or Canada or have permanent resident status in either country. There must be evidence of institutional support for the Fellow's study, including provision of leave with pay for at least a portion of the Fellowship period.

Type: Fellowship.

No. of awards offered: Varies.

Frequency: Twice yearly.

Value: Varies.

Length of Study: 4-12 months.

Country of Study: USA or Canada.

Closing Date: March 1st, October 1st.

*Faculty/Librarian Cooperative Research Grants

Subjects: The program areas of the Council: human resources, economics, infrastructure, or access and processing.

Eligibility: Open to staff members of academic or research libraries and teaching faculties.

Purpose: To support cooperative research projects jointly proposed by librarians and members of university or college teaching faculties (usually library science faculties).

Type: Research Grant.

No. of awards offered: Varies.

Frequency: Twice yearly.

Value: Up to US$4,000 to cover all costs, excluding the salaries of the principals.

Length of Study: An unspecified time frame, but usually projects last no more than 12 months.

Country of Study: USA or Canada.

Closing Date: April 1st, November 1st.

COUNCIL ON SOCIAL WORK EDUCATION

Council on Social Work Education, 1600 Duke Street, Ste 300,
Alexandria, VA, 22314, USA
Tel: 703 683 8080
Fax: 703 683 8099
Email: CSWE@access.digex.net
Contact: Dr E Aracelis Francis

CSWE Minority Fellowship Program

Eligibility: Must have masters degree in social work.

Level of Study: Postgraduate.

Purpose: This program is designed to equip ethnic minority individuals for the provision of leadership, teaching, consultation, training, policy, development, and administration in mental health and/or substance abuse programs and to enhance the development and dissemination of knowledge requisite for the provision of relevant clinical and social services to ethnic minority individuals and communities.

Type: Fellowship.

No. of awards offered: 20.

Frequency: Annual, dependant on funds available.

Value: US$10,008 per annum, may receive US$1,800 towards tuition costs.

Length of Study: Renewal up to three years.

Study Establishment: Doctoral programs in Schools of social work.

Country of Study: USA.

Applications Procedure: Applicants must request application materials.

Closing Date: February 28th.

THE COUNTESS OF MUNSTER MUSICAL TRUST

Countess of Munster Musical Trust, Wormley Hill, Godalming, Surrey,
GU8 5SG, England
Tel: 01428 685427
Fax: 01428 685064
Contact: The Secretary

Awards

Subjects: Musical studies.

Eligibility: Open to UK or British Commonwealth citizens, who are under 18 years of age for female singers and under 28 years of age for male singers; and under 25 years of age for instrumentalists and composers, who show outstanding musical ability and potential.

Level of Study: Postgraduate, Doctorate.

Purpose: To enable students, selected after interview and audition, to pursue a course of specialist or advanced studies.

No. of awards offered: Approximately 80.

Frequency: Annual.

Value: By individual assessment to meet tuition fees and maintenance according to need (£500-£5,000).

Length of Study: One year, with the possibility of renewal.

Country of Study: UK or overseas.

Applications Procedure: Application form must be completed and submitted between November 1st and January 31st for awards to be applied from the following September.

Closing Date: January 31st.

Additional Information: Awards are made to selected applicants following audition and interview.

CRIMINOLOGY RESEARCH COUNCIL

Criminology Research Council, GPO Box 2944, Canberra, ACT, 2601,
Australia
Tel: 06 2609200
Fax: 06 2609201
Email: lizr@aic.gov.au
Contact: Administrator

Awards

Subjects: Criminological research.

Eligibility: Open to Australian residents or visitors (actual or intending) who are pursuing or intend to pursue studies of consequence to the furtherance of criminological research in Australia. Grants are not likely to be given for assistance with research leading to the award of postgraduate degrees.

No. of awards offered: Approximately six.

Frequency: Annual.

Value: On average A$25,000, paid in three instalments.

Length of Study: Generally twelve months; extendable for up to three years.

Country of Study: Australia.

Applications Procedure: Application form must be completed; forms can be obtained from CRC or any Australian university.

Closing Date: Early March, June and October each year.

Additional Information: The Council does not ordinarily consider applications involving travelling expenses outside of Australia. Applications are considered three times a year. Research in the areas of sociology, psychology, law, statistics, police, judiciary, corrections etc; but not for postgraduate degrees. From time to time the Council will call for research in specific areas.

THE CROHN'S & COLITIS FOUNDATION OF AMERICA, INC

Director of Research and Education, Crohn's & Colitis Foundation of America, Inc, 386 Park Avenue South, 17th Floor, New York, NY, 10016-8804, USA
Tel: 212 685 3440/800 932 2423
Fax: 212 779 4098
Contact: James V Romano, PhD

*Career Development Awards

Subjects: Crohn's disease; ulcerative colitis.

Eligibility: Open to candidates working in US laboratories who have at least five years of postdoctoral experience, two years of which must be research relevant to inflammatory bowel disease, prior to the beginning date of the award and not in excess of ten years beyond the attainment of the doctoral degree. Research projects must be in the field of inflammatory bowel disease and individuals who are already well established in the field are not eligible.

Purpose: To encourage the development of young outstanding scientists with research potential to help them prepare for careers of independent research in inflammatory bowel disease.

No. of awards offered: Varies.

Frequency: Biennially.

Value: Up to US$40,000 salary and US$20,000 for supplies etc.

Length of Study: Two years.

Study Establishment: Approved research institutions.

Country of Study: USA.

Closing Date: January 1st, July 1st.

Additional Information: The awards are made to eligible institutions on behalf of qualified candidates, and each awardee is directly responsible to the institution to which the award is made. Application material is available from the Foundation.

*Research Fellowship Awards

Subjects: Crohn's disease; ulcerative colitis.

Eligibility: Open to candidates working in US laboratories who have had at least two years of postdoctoral experience, one year of which must be research relevant to inflammatory bowel disease, prior to the beginning date of the award and who have demonstrated an interest and capability in research. Research projects must be in the field of inflammatory bowel disease and individuals who are already well established in the field are not eligible.

Purpose: To encourage the development of young outstanding scientists with research potential to help them prepare for careers of independent research in inflammatory bowel disease.

No. of awards offered: Varies.

Frequency: Biennially.

Value: US$30,000 per annum for salary only.

Length of Study: 1-3 years.

Study Establishment: Approved research institutions.

Country of Study: USA.

Closing Date: January 1st, July 1st.

*Research Grant Program

Subjects: Inflammatory bowel disease: cause, pathogenesis or treatment.

Eligibility: Open to qualified investigators in the USA and abroad.

Purpose: To provide financial support for innovative basic and clinical research in inflammatory bowel disease.

Type: Research Grant.

No. of awards offered: Varies.

Frequency: Biennially.

Value: Up to US$80,000 for direct costs for two years. Requests for purchases of major equipment totalling more than US$5,000 are not generally considered. The maximum amount allowed for overhead is 15% of total direct costs.

Length of Study: Two years; possibly renewable for a third.

Closing Date: January 1st, July 1st.

THE CROMBIE SCHOLARSHIP TRUST

51 Irvine Crescent, St Andrews, Fife, KY16 8LG, Scotland
Contact: Professor William McKane

*Crombie Scholarship

Subjects: Hebrew and Greek.

Eligibility: Open to students matriculated at one of four Scottish universities who have taken a university course in Greek (Classical or Hellenistic but not modern) and Hebrew for at least two academic years at a level more advanced than the course prescribed for the first year of study and whose performance merits an award. The candidates will be nominated annually to the Trustees by the Deans of Divinity of the Universities of St Andrews, Glasgow, Aberdeen and Edinburgh.

Purpose: To further the study of Biblical Hebrew and Classical or Hellenistic Greek (including New Testament Greek).

Type: Scholarship.

No. of awards offered: 4 Scholarships (1 to a student from each of the Universities of Glasgow, St Andrews, Aberdeen and Edinburgh).

Frequency: Annual.

Value: £150.

Country of Study: Scotland.

CROSS-CULTURAL DANCE RESOURCES, INC

Cross-Cultural Dance Resources, Inc, 518 South Agassiz Street, Flagstaff, AZ, 86001, USA
Tel: 602 774 8108
Fax: 602 774 8108
Contact: Kathleen Stemmler or Joann Kealiinohomoku

*Halla K Kealiinohomoku Memorial Research-Choreography Residency

Subjects: Choreography/research.

Eligibility: Open to any career choreographer who completes the application requirements and is selected by a board of adjudicators.

Purpose: To allow a career choreographer opportunity to pursue research that is needed in order to make or complete a choreographic work.

No. of awards offered: One.

Frequency: Annual.

Value: Housing provided, research facilities available, bread-and-butter stipend of four monthly increments of US$250 (total US$1,000).

Length of Study: 4 months.

Country of Study: USA (Arizona).

Closing Date: July 31st.

Additional Information: Cross-Cultural Dance Resources is a 501(C)(3) non-profit organization established in 1981 to promote research, consultation and performance of dance. It is not affiliated, but collaborates with Northern Arizona University.

THE CROSS TRUST

The Cross Trust, McCash & Hunter, PO Box 17, 25 South Methven Street, Perth, PH1 5ES, Scotland
Tel: 01738 20451
Fax: 01738 31155
Contact: Secretaries

*Scholarships and Grants

Subjects: Any approved subject.

Eligibility: Open to graduates or undergraduates of Scottish universities or of Central Institutions in Scotland and to Scottish secondary school pupils. Applicants must be of Scottish birth or parentage.

Purpose: To enable young Scottish people to extend the boundaries of their knowledge through monetary awards that will promote a love of nature or Scottish scenery, allow travel to extend experience, or encourage performance and participation in drama or opera. The Trust may support the pursuit of studies or research and provide opportunities for participation in appropriate life and activities.

Type: Varies.

Value: Varies.

Study Establishment: Anywhere as approved.

Additional Information: At the discretion of the Trustees aid may be given to organizations which have as their aim the promotion of outdoor activities and projects within Scotland.

CROUCHER FOUNDATION

Croucher Foundation, Suite 534, Star House, 2 Salisbury Road, Kowloon, Hong Kong
Tel: 27366337
Fax: 27300742
Contact: Administrative Officer

Fellowships and Scholarships

Subjects: Natural science, medicine or technology.

Eligibility: Open to permanent residents of Hong Kong. Fellowships are intended for those at postdoctoral or equivalent level. Scholarships are intended for holders of a Master's degree or those in the process of completing an MPhil or PhD programme. In exceptional circumstances a holder of a first degree may apply, but at the time of making the application he or she must hold a first class honours degree.

Level of Study: Postgraduate, Doctorate, Postdoctorate.

Purpose: To enable selected students of outstanding promise to devote themselves to full-time postgraduate study or research.

Type: Scholarship; fellowship.

No. of awards offered: About 20-25.

Frequency: Annual.

Value: £12,500 (fellowships) and £6,000 (scholarships) maintenance allowance, assistance towards air fare, plus tuition fees. Married Fellows/Scholars will be given a special spouse allowance of £2,500 per annum including assistance towards air fare if he or she is dependent and accompanying the holder of the award. In addition, children allowance (first child: £336 per annum; second child: £289 per annum) will also be provided if they are residing with the Fellow/Scholar. If the successful applicant is on paid study leave during the tenure of the award the maintenance allowance may be modified. A one-off grant of £500 for books/apparatus and clothing will be given during the first year of tenure. A London Weighting Allowance of £1,500 per annum will be given to candidates who are studying in the London area. An allowance of up to £250 for thesis expenses will be given to final year PhD students on application, against receipts. Fellows and Scholars will be expected to devote their whole time to the objects of their award. Fellows and Scholars will not be debarred from holding another position of emolument but if at the date of application they hold or at a later date are appointed to such a position, they must notify the Trustees and must obtain prior approval from them, who may at their discretion modify the value of the Fellowship or Scholarship.

Length of Study: 1-2 years (fellowships); 1-3 years (scholarships).

Country of Study: UK, Hong Kong or other country in the Commonwealth.

Applications Procedure: Application form can be obtained from the Foundation on production of a study/research proposal and academic qualifications.

Closing Date: Mid November.

CYSTIC FIBROSIS FOUNDATION

Office of Grants Management, Cystic Fibrosis Foundation, 6931 Arlington Road, Bethesda, MD, 20814, USA
Tel: 1 800 FIGHT CF
Contact: Kathleen Curley, Grants Manager

CFF Research Programs in Cystic Fibrosis

Level of Study: Doctorate, Professional development.

Purpose: Competitive awards for research related to cystic fibrosis.

Type: Research Grant.

No. of awards offered: Six.

Frequency: Annual.

Value: Depending on the award from US$25,000 to US$75,000.

Applications Procedure: Write for application form.

Closing Date: Varies with each award.

Training Programs in Cystic Fibrosis

Level of Study: Doctorate, Professional development.

Purpose: Research into Cystic Fibrosis.

Type: Fellowships and Scholarships.

Frequency: Annual.

Value: Depending on the award from US$300 to US$45,000.

Applications Procedure: Write for application form.

Closing Date: Varies with the award.

CYSTIC FIBROSIS RESEARCH TRUST

Cystic Fibrosis Research Trust, Alexandra House, 5 Blyth Road, Bromley, Kent, BR1 3RS, England
Tel: 0181 464 7211
Fax: 0181 313 0472
Contact: The Medical and Scientific Administration

Research Grants

Subjects: Medical and scientific research related to cystic fibrosis.

Eligibility: Open to suitably qualified persons.

Level of Study: Doctorate, Postgraduate.

Purpose: To find a cure for cystic fibrosis and also to improve the management, care and treatment of those with cystic fibrosis.

Type: Research Grant.

No. of awards offered: Varies.

Frequency: Twice yearly.

Value: From a total fund of £1m per annum; grants are made to cover such matters as salaries, expenses and equipment.

Length of Study: Up to three years, subject to annual renewal.

Country of Study: UK.

Applications Procedure: Application by CF Trust form plus justification of support requested.

Closing Date: Available on application to the Trust.

J W DAFOE FOUNDATION

Faculty of Graduate Studies, 500 University Centre, University of Manitoba, Winnipeg, Manitoba, R3T 2N2, Canada
Tel: 204 474 9836
Fax: 204 275 6488
Email: IKRENTZ@BLDGUMSU.LANI.UMANITOBA.CA
www: http://www.umanitoba.ca/gradstud/gradstud.htm/
Contact: Ms Ilse Krentz, Awards Officer

J W Dafoe Graduate Fellowship

Subjects: International relations.

Eligibility: Open to graduates with first class averages of any recognized university who possess the honours BA degree or equivalent and who intend to work for a higher degree in the field of international studies at the University of Manitoba in the departments of economics, political studies, or history.

Level of Study: Postgraduate.

Purpose: To encourage graduate study and to further international understanding.

Type: Fellowship.

No. of awards offered: One or two.

Frequency: Annual.

Value: One @ C$10,000 or two @ C$5,000; non renewable.

Study Establishment: Departments of political science, economics or history at the University of Manitoba.

Country of Study: Canada.

Applications Procedure: Letter of application must accompany official transcripts of all universities attended.

Closing Date: February 15th.

DAIRY MANAGEMENT INC.(DMI)

Nutrition and Health Research Program, National Dairy Council, 10255 West Higgins Road, Suite 900, Rosemont, IL, 60018-5616, USA
Tel: 708 803 2000
Fax: 708 803 2077
Contact: Douglas B Dirienzo, PhD, Director

Nutrition Research Projects

Subjects: Nutrition research.

Eligibility: Open to qualified investigators associated with accredited institutions of higher learning in the USA who hold a PhD, MD, DDS, DVM or equivalent degree.

Purpose: To support nutrition research which will identify and clarify nutritional attributes of dairy foods which offer product positioning and/or promotion opportunities or to resolve or put into perspective nutrition/health-related concerns which consumers or health professionals may have about dairy foods.

Type: Grant.

No. of awards offered: Varies.

Frequency: Twice yearly.

Value: Average approximately US$40,000-US$60,000 per annum. Funds are not available for alteration of facilities or purchase of permanent equipment.

Length of Study: Projects are funded on a yearly basis, up to three years.

Country of Study: USA.

Closing Date: February 12th and September 1st for support to commence June 1st and January 1st.

Additional Information: As a unit of DMI, National Dairy Council will be responsible for the review process for nutrition and health applications and management of nutrition research projects funded through DMI.

DALHOUSIE UNIVERSITY

Dalhousie University, Department of Mathematics, Statistics and Computing Science, Halifax, Nova Scotia, B3H 3J5, Canada
Tel: 902 494 3568
Fax: 902 494 5130
Email: hamilton@cs.dal.ca
Contact: Dr David C Hamilton

Pierre Robillard Award

Subjects: Maths, statistics and computer science.

Level of Study: Doctorate.

Purpose: To recognise the best PhD thesis defended at a Canadian university and written in a field covered by The Canadian Journal of Statistics.

Type: Certificate, monetary prize, and one year membership in the Statistical Society of Canada.

No. of awards offered: Varies.

Frequency: Annual.

Value: Varies.

Applications Procedure: Please submit four copies of the thesis together with a covering letter from the thesis supervisor.

Closing Date: February 15th.

DATATEL SCHOLARS FOUNDATION

Datatel Scholars Foundation, 4375 Fair Lakes Court, Fairfax, VA, 22033, USA
Tel: 703 968 9000
Fax: 703 968 4573
Email: scholars@datatel.com
Contact: Elizabeth Early/Jane Roth

Scholarship

Subjects: Unrestricted.

Eligibility: Open to students attending a higher learning institution selected from Datatel, Inc.'s more than 300 college, university and non-profit client sites.

Level of Study: Postgraduate, Doctorate, Undergraduate.

Purpose: To award scholarships to eligible students to attend a higher learning institution selected from Datatel's more than 300 college, university and non-profit client sites.

Type: Scholarship.

No. of awards offered: Determined yearly.

Frequency: Annual.

Value: US$700 to US$2,000 depending on tuition amount.

Length of Study: One year.

Study Establishment: Datatel client site institution.

Applications Procedure: Applications must be completed and forwarded by the institution's Office of Financial Aid. The Foundation does not accept applications directly from students.

Closing Date: February 28th of each year.

Additional Information: If requesting applications from the Foundation, please mention the name of your college or university so we can determine if the institution qualifies.

RYAN DAVIES MEMORIAL FUND

Ryan Davies Memorial Fund, Dinefwr House, Llandeilo, Dyfed, SA19 6RT, Wales
Tel: 01558 823864
Fax: 01558 823867
Contact: Michael D Evans, Secretary

Scholarship Grants

Subjects: Music and drama.

Eligibility: Open to Welsh artists only.

Purpose: To enable Welsh artists to continue studies following their formal training.

Type: Grant.

No. of awards offered: Ten.

Frequency: Annual.

Value: Up to £2,500 each.

Country of Study: Worldwide.

Applications Procedure: Applications are made by forwarding all relevant information (reason for application, qualifications, referees and any further background information) to the Secretary.

Closing Date: 30 April for notification by 31 July.

LADY DAVIS FELLOWSHIP TRUST

Lady Davis Fellowship Trust, PO Box 1255, Jerusalem, 91904, Israel
Tel: 02 663 848
Fax: 02 663 848
Contact: M Mark Sopher, Executive Secretary

Graduate and Postdoctoral Fellowships: Visiting Professorships

Subjects: Unrestricted.

Eligibility: There are no restrictions of age, sex, citizenship or residency. Individuals are selected on the basis of demonstrated excellence in their studies, promise of distinction in chosen fields of specialization, as well as on qualities of mind, intellect and character which would enable the recipient to benefit from the opportunity for study in Israel. Postdoctoral fellows must have completed their doctoral thesis three years before arrival in Israel. Graduate fellowships at the Hebrew University are intended for students enrolled in a Doctoral program abroad who wish to study or use library facilities in Israel.

Purpose: To advance the interests of international scholarship and Israeli higher education.

Type: Varies.

Frequency: Annual.

Value: Awards are intended to defray transportation, tuition and maintenance expenses; payments are made on a monthly basis.

Length of Study: For one year; renewable.

Study Establishment: The Hebrew University, Jerusalem, or at the Technion, Israel Institute of Technology, Haifa.

Closing Date: December 1st.

Additional Information: Similar awards are available to promising students of the Hebrew University or the Technion to study or undertake research in outstanding institutions abroad.

DEAFNESS RESEARCH FOUNDATION

Deafness Research Foundation, 15 West 39th Street, New York,, NY, 10018-3806, USA
Tel: 212 768 1181
Fax: 212 768 1782
Contact: Medical Director

Otological Research Fellowship

Subjects: Otological research.

Eligibility: Open to third year medical students sponsored by a Department of Otolaryngology conducting otological research.

Level of Study: 3rd year medical student.

Purpose: To increase the number of physicians involved in otological research.

Type: Fellowship.

No. of awards offered: Varies.

Frequency: Annual.

Value: US$10,000 (plus up to US$3,500 for animals and consumable supplies).

Length of Study: One year.

Country of Study: USA.

Applications Procedure: A letter from the Dean and three letters of recommendation are required.

Closing Date: March 15th.

Additional Information: The Fellowship would be scheduled as a one-year block of time at the end of the third year of medical school, thus requiring a one-year leave of absence from the medical school curriculum.

*Research Grants

Subjects: Research into the function, physiology, genetics, anatomy or pathology of the ear.

Eligibility: Open to investigators on the staff of universities, hospitals and other non-profit, tax-exempt institutions, public or private, in the USA or Canada.

Purpose: To encourage research into the causes, treatment and prevention of hearing loss and related ear disorders.

Type: Research Grant.

No. of awards offered: Varies.

Frequency: Annual.

Value: Up to US$15,000.

Length of Study: One year; renewable for 1 or 2 further years.

Country of Study: USA or Canada.

Closing Date: July 15th (new applications); August 15th (renewal applications).

GLADYS KRIEBLE DELMAS FOUNDATION

Gladys Krieble Delmas Foundation, 521 Fifth Avenue, Suite 1612, New York, NY, 10175-1699, USA
Tel: 212 687 0011
Fax: 212 687 8877
Email: delmasfotn@aol.com

Grants

Subjects: The history of Venice and the former Venetian empire in its various aspects: art; architecture; archaeology; theatre; music; literature; political science; economics and law.

Eligibility: Open to US citizens and permanent residents of the USA who have some experience in advanced research. Graduate students must have fulfilled all doctoral requirements except for completion of the dissertation at the time of application.

Level of Study: Postgraduate, Doctorate.

Purpose: To promote research in Venice and the Veneto.

Type: Grant.

No. of awards offered: Usually 15-25.

Frequency: Annual.

Value: From US$500 up to a maximum of US$12,500 for a full academic year. At the discretion of the trustees and advisory board of the Foundation, funds may be made available for aid in publication of results.

Length of Study: Up to one academic year.

Country of Study: Italy.

Applications Procedure: Candidates should obtain the Foundation's instruction sheet and application forms for application.

Closing Date: December 15th.

DEL PICHINCHA BANK

Culture Department, Del Pichincha Bank, U.T.E Borgeois 210 y Rumipamba, Quito, Ecuador
Tel: 446 233
Telex: 17-01-2764
Contact: Dr Gonzalo Peñaherrera, Culture Director

First Universitarian National Contest

Eligibility: The award is open to students, professors and university employees with no other limitation. All the universities are being called to participate.

Purpose: To promote the culture at a national level, among the universities, in order to give them the possibility of being integrated into all the aspects of culture, not only the technical ones.

No. of awards offered: Two.

Frequency: Annual.

Value: Novel $1,017, Stories $678.

Country of Study: Ecuador.

THE DENMARK-AMERICA FOUNDATION

Denmark-America Foundation, Fiolstraede 24, 3rd Floor, Copenhagen, 1171, Denmark
Tel: 45 33128323
Fax: 45 33325323
Email: fulbdk@unidhp.uni-c.dk

Danmark-Amerika Fondet

Subjects: All subjects.

Eligibility: Open to Danes only.

Level of Study: Graduate.

Purpose: To further understanding between Denmark and the USA.

Type: Bursary.

No. of awards offered: Varies.

Frequency: Several times per year - to be announced.

Value: Varies.

Length of Study: Between 3 months and one year.

Country of Study: USA.

Applications Procedure: Special application form must be completed - please contact the Secretariat.

Closing Date: To be announced each year.

DENTAL ASSOCIATION OF SOUTH AFRICA

Dental Association of South Africa, Private Bag 1, Houghton, 2041, South Africa
Tel: 27 11 642 4687
Fax: 27 11 642 5718
Contact: Dr Helmut Heydt

Lever Pond's Postgraduate Fellowship

Subjects: Any biological field related to dentistry.

Eligibility: Open to South African nationals, normally resident in South Africa, who are either dentists registered with the South African Medical and Dental Council wishing to qualify themselves further or to equip themselves for research by taking an additional degree, or who are suitably qualified persons wishing to concentrate on dental research.

Purpose: To promote dental research and ensure its continuation in South Africa.

Type: Fellowship.

No. of awards offered: One.

Frequency: Annual.

Value: Up to R17,000.

Length of Study: One year; renewable in special circumstances.

Country of Study: South Africa unless facilities are not available.

Applications Procedure: Applications must be made on an official application form and must be supported by and submitted through a university or other such institution. An award may be made for research overseas, provided that the application is accompanied by a statement from the sponsoring institution that the proposed project can best be carried out in another country.

Closing Date: July 31st.

Additional Information: A Fellow working overseas must undertake to return to South Africa for a minimum period of two years after completing his project under the award, or refund to the Fellowship Fund any money he/she has received.

Julius Staz Scholarship

Subjects: Dentistry.

Eligibility: Open to individuals with a proven record of research or who are sponsored by such an individual. The applicant must undertake to live and work in South Africa for at least two years after the tenure of the scholarship, or to refund the monies.

Purpose: To enable a qualified person to spend time in a laboratory to study a research technique.

Type: Scholarship.

No. of awards offered: One.

Frequency: Annual.

Value: R8,000.

Length of Study: At least one month; the Scholarship must be held during the year it is awarded.

Country of Study: South Africa or elsewhere.

Closing Date: July 31st.

Additional Information: This award does not render itself solely to the specific support of research nor to the study of research techniques.

DENTISTRY CANADA FUND/FONDS DENTAIRE CANADIEN

Dentistry Canada Fund/Fonds Dentaire Canadien, 205-1815 Alta Vista Drive, Ottawa, ON, K1G 3Y6, Canada
Tel: 613 731 0493
Fax: 613 523 7489
Email: dcfsjw@magi.com
Contact: James Wegg

Biennial Research Award

Subjects: Dentistry.

Eligibility: Open to graduate or postgraduate students who have conducted their research in association with a Canadian Dental faculty.

Level of Study: Graduate, Postgraduate.

Purpose: To encourage research related to dentistry conducted by graduate or postgraduate students in Canada.

Type: Research Grant.

No. of awards offered: One.

Frequency: Every two years.

Value: C$2,000 plus a commemorative plaque.

Applications Procedure: Applicants should submit one typewritten, double-spaced copy and four copies of an original research project in the form of a paper. The manuscript should not exceed 25 pages; or, a previously published paper of the applicant's graduate work either currently in press or already published in a scientific journal provided the date of publication is not more than two years from the date of application and provided the applicant is demonstrably the senior author.

Closing Date: December 1st biennially (next 1998).

Additional Information: Each entry will be reviewed by three referees appointed by the CDA Committee on Dental Materials and Devices. The decision of the Committee is final.

DCF/Wrigley Dental Student Research Awards

Subjects: Oral biology.

Eligibility: Open to students enrolled in Canadian dental schools.

Purpose: To enable applicants to undertake research projects in oral biology.

Type: Research Grant.

No. of awards offered: Up to three.

Frequency: Annual.

Value: C$3,000.

Applications Procedure: Each application must include the background on the subject matter, the research objectives, the proposed hypothesis, the research approach and the project's timetable and budget.

Closing Date: March 1st.

Fellowships for Teacher/Researcher Training

Subjects: Dentistry.

Eligibility: Applicants must be Canadian citizens or permanent residents who have completed an undergraduate course in dentistry, a dental hygiene program, or a program in science and who are also eligible for admission to a graduate or other advanced education program.

Level of Study: Graduate.

Purpose: To provide financial assistance to students who wish to pursue a career in dentistry research and/or teaching at graduate level.

Type: Fellowship.

Applications Procedure: First-time applications must include official transcripts of previous post-secondary education and letters of recommendation from a faculty member of the applicant's post-secondary insti-

tution and from the Administrative Head of the Institution and Department where he/she expects to be employed. All applications must include a CV.

Closing Date: March 1st each year.

DEPARTMENT OF EDUCATION FOR NORTHERN IRELAND

Student Support Branch, Department of Education, Rathgael House, Balloo Road, Bangor, Co Down, BT19 7PR, Northern Ireland
Tel: 01247 279279
Fax: 01247 279100
Contact: Miss R Duffy

Postgraduate Studentships and Bursaries for Northern Ireland Students

Subjects: Science and technology, social sciences and humanities.

Eligibility: Open to UK and EC resident students only. Applicants must have at least an Upper Second degree.

Level of Study: Postgraduate.

Purpose: To provide students ordinarily resident in Northern Ireland with assistance similar to that given by the Department for Education (England and Wales), the British Academy, the Science and Engineering Council, the Economic and Social Research Council and the Natural Environment Research Council for attendance at courses in Northern Ireland or the Republic of Ireland.

No. of awards offered: Varies, but is proportional to the number available in the rest of the UK.

Frequency: Annual.

Value: In line with the other UK awarding bodies.

Study Establishment: Institutions in Northern Ireland or the Republic of Ireland.

Country of Study: Northern Ireland or the Republic of Ireland.

Applications Procedure: Application form must be completed and can be obtained from DENI or most universities.

Closing Date: June 30th (for awards tenable at institutions in the Repubic of Ireland), or as determined by the institution concerned (for awards tenable at institutions in Northern Ireland).

DEPARTMENT OF EDUCATION (IRELAND)

International Section, Department of Education, Floor 6, Apollo House, Tara Street, Dublin, 2, Republic of Ireland
Tel: 01 8734700 ext.2435
Fax: 01 6791315
Contact: Mary Kelleher or Andrea Hudson

Exchange Scholarships and Postgraduate Scholarships Exchange Scheme

Subjects: Any subject.

Eligibility: Open to Australian, Austrian, Belgian, Chinese, Finnish, German, Greek, Italian, Japanese, Netherlands, Norwegian, Russian Federation, Spanish and Swiss nationals, who are university graduates or advanced undergraduates who have completed at least three years of academic study. A good knowledge of English and/or Irish is necessary, depending on the course taken.

Level of Study: Postgraduate.

Purpose: To assist students to pursue study or research in Ireland.

Type: Scholarships.

No. of awards offered: 30.

Frequency: Annual.

Value: IR£2,912.

Length of Study: Eight months.

Study Establishment: An Irish university: University College Dublin, University College Cork, University College Galway, Trinity College Dublin, Dublin City University, University of Limerick, St Patrick's College Maynooth or other similar institution of higher learning.

Country of Study: Republic of Ireland.

Applications Procedure: Candidates should apply to the appropriate institution in their home country, as follows: Austria - the Federal Ministry for Science and Research, Vienna; Australia - the Ministry of Education, Canberra; Belgium - the Ministry of Education for the Flemish Community, Brussels; China - the Ministries of Foreign Affairs and Education, Beijing; Finland - Finnish Centre for International Mobility (Cimo), Helsinki; France - the Foreign Ministry, Paris; Germany - the German Academic Exchange Board (Deutscher Akademischer Austauschdienst--DAAD), Bonn; Greece - the Ministries of Foreign Affairs and Education, Athens; Italy - the Ministry of Foreign Affairs, Rome; Japan - the Ministries of Foreign Affairs and Education, Tokyo; Netherlands - Netherlands Organisation for International Cooperation in Higher Education (NUFFIC), The Hague; Norway - the Ministry of Foreign Affairs, Office of Cultural Relations, Oslo; Russian Federation - the Ministry of Education of the Russian Federation; Spain - the Ministry of Foreign Affairs, Madrid; Switzerland - Swiss University Authorities, Berne. Five scholarships are offered to students from the United Kingdom to pursue postgraduate studies in Ireland. The value of each scholarship is £6,000. Applications should be made to the Irish Embassy, London.

Closing Date: April 30th.

Irish Government Scholarship

Subjects: Unrestricted.

Eligibility: Open to Australian postgraduate students. The Scholar is required to return to Australia on the completion of the Scholarship program or on the completion of further studies leading on from the initial Scholarship program.

Level of Study: Postgraduate.

Type: Scholarship.

No. of awards offered: One.

Frequency: Annual.

Value: IR£2,912 payable in 8 monthly instalments, plus university or college registration and tuition fees.

Length of Study: One academic year.

Study Establishment: University or institute of higher learning.

Country of Study: Republic of Ireland.

Closing Date: March.

For further information contact:
Embassy of Ireland, 20 Arkana Street, Yarralumla, ACT, 2600, Australia
Tel: 06 273 3022
Fax: 06 273 3741

Summer School Exchange Scholarships

Subjects: Any subject.

Eligibility: Open to Belgian, French, Finnish, German, Hungarian, Italian, Netherlands, Russian Federation and Spanish nationals who are university graduates or advanced undergraduates. A good knowledge of English and/or Irish is necessary, depending on the course taken.

Level of Study: Postgraduate.

Purpose: To assist European students to attend a summer school in Ireland.

Type: Scholarships.

No. of awards offered: 33.

Frequency: Annual.

Value: IR£650. Exception - IR£875 for Hungarian and Russian Federation nationals.

Length of Study: From two weeks to one month.

Study Establishment: Summer schools at University College Dublin, University College Galway or University College Cork.

Country of Study: Republic of Ireland.

Applications Procedure: Candidates should apply to the appropriate institution in their home country, as follows: Belgium - the Ministry of Education for the Flemish Community, Brussels; France - the Foreign Ministry, Paris; Finland - Finish Centre for International Mobility (Cimo), Helsinki; Germany - the German Academic Exchange Board (Deutscher Akademischer Austauschdienst--DAAD), Bonn; Hungary - the Ministry of Culture and Education, Budapest; Italy - the Ministry of Foreign Affairs, Rome; Netherlands - Netherlands Organisation for International Cooperation in Higher Education (NUFFIC), The Hague; Russian Federation - the Ministry of Education of the Russian Federation; Spain - the Ministry of Foreign Affairs, Madrid.

Closing Date: April 30th.

DEPARTMENT OF EMPLOYMENT, EDUCATION AND TRAINING (AUS)

Australian Vice Chancellors' Committee, GPO Box 1142, Canberra, ACT, 2601, Australia
Tel: 06 285 8200
Fax: 06 285 8211

National Asian Languages Scholarship Scheme (NALSS)

Subjects: Asian language.

Eligibility: Open to Australian citizens or permanent residents who have completed two years' tertiary study of a relevant language; students who will undertake either one or two semesters of formal language study in Asia, which is fully accredited by their enrolling Austrlian tertiary institution, as part of their undergraduate studies.

Level of Study: Non formal program.

Purpose: To enable Australian teachers of an Asian language to study advanced language while experiencing cultural immersion.

Type: Scholarship.

No. of awards offered: Sixty.

Frequency: Annual.

Value: Return air fare, tuition fees and contribution to living costs.

Length of Study: One or two semesters.

Study Establishment: A recognized language institution in the country of study.

Country of Study: Any Asian country where the language is spoken.

Applications Procedure: Application forms are available from Australian universities or the Australian Vice Chancellor's Committee.

Closing Date: June 30th in preceding year.

Additional Information: Preference is given to teachers of Asian language in Australia.

For further information contact:
Australian Vice Chancellors' Committee, GPO Box 1142, Canberra, ACT, 2601, Australia
Tel: 06 285 8200
Fax: 06 285 8211
Contact: The Manager (NALSS)

Visiting Fellowships

Subjects: Any subject.

Eligibility: Nominees should be citizens of Commonwealth or European countries or Greece or have been resident in one of those countries for the last five years. Submissions are invited from Australian educational institutions and organizations seeking to nominate eminent scholars and other distinguished people to visit Australia.

Level of Study: Professional development.

Purpose: To enable visitors to meet Australians who are working in the same fields of expertise and to exchange views and information.

Type: Fellowship.

No. of awards offered: Eight.

Frequency: Annual.

Value: Return air fare; necessary internal travel; an establishment allowance paid on arrival; and a daily allowance.

Length of Study: 1-3 months.

Study Establishment: Educational institutions and organizations.

Country of Study: Australia.

Applications Procedure: Application form is available from the Australian Vice Chancellor's Committee.

Closing Date: Mid-September.

Additional Information: These Fellowships are made available under the Commonwealth Scholarship and Fellowship Plan, the Australian-European Awards Program and the Australian-Greek Awards Program.

For further information contact:
Australian Vice Chancellors' Committee, GPO Box 1142, Canberra, ACT, 2601, Australia
Tel: 06 285 8200
Fax: 06 285 8211
Contact: The Manager (Visiting Fellow)

DEPARTMENT OF INDIAN AND NORTHERN AFFAIRS

Department of Indian and Northern Affairs, 20th Floor, North Tower, Les Terrasses de la Chaudière, Ottawa, Ontario, K1A 0H4, Canada
Tel: 819 994 3101
Fax: 819 953 3851
Contact: Indian Programming & Funding Allocations Directorate

Inuit Cultural Grants Program

Subjects: Inuit literature, music and art, cross-cultural crafts and cultural exchange.

Eligibility: Open to Canadian Inuit whose applications meet the purpose of the programme.

Purpose: To promote and preserve Inuit culture and language.

No. of awards offered: Approximately 15.

Frequency: Annual.

Value: Averaging C$2,000 and not to exceed C$5,000 per award.

Country of Study: Any country.

Closing Date: Applications are accepted throughout the year.

DEPARTMENT OF INTERNAL AFFAIRS

New Zealand ANZAC Fellowship Selection Committee, c/o Department of Internal Affairs, Box 805, Wellington, New Zealand
Tel: 04 495 7200
Fax: 04 499 1865
Contact: Secretary

ANZAC Fellowships

Subjects: Such fields as primary and secondary industry, commerce,

education, the arts or public service. Projects should not be totally academic in nature.

Eligibility: Open to New Zealand citizens who are of high standing in their occupation. The Fellowships will be directed towards persons who are likely to benefit both themselves and the New Zealand community by a period in Australia.

Purpose: To enable New Zealanders who have shown outstanding ability and achievement in their fields to spend up to one year studying or gaining practical experience in Australia.

No. of awards offered: 4-10.

Frequency: Annual.

Value: A daily allowance of A$50 (A$18,250 per annum), a marriage allowance of A$1,160 per annum, and a dependant child allowance at the rate of A$460 per annum. Payment is at a special rate of A$61.30 per diem where the Fellow does not establish a permanent base. Fellowships include provision for return air fares to Australia, approved internal travel costs and approved tuition or other fees and payment of a medical insurance premium for the Fellow only.

Length of Study: Up to 12 months.

Country of Study: Australia.

Closing Date: March 31st.

Additional Information: The New Zealand selection committee will make nominations to the Australian selection committee which in turn will make appropriate arrangements with the institutions or organizations concerned and will make the final selection of candidates. These ANZAC Fellowships are offered by the Australian government. The New Zealand government also participates in the scheme by making similar awards available annually to Australians.

DEPARTMENT OF NATIONAL HEALTH AND WELFARE

Extramural Research Programs Directorate, Health Programs & Services Branch, Health Canada, Ottawa, Ontario, K1A 1B4, Canada
Tel: 613 954 8549
Fax: 613 954 7363
Contact: Information & Resource Officer

National Health Research Scholar Awards

Subjects: Public health and related areas.

Eligibility: Open to Canadian citizens or landed immigrants who have completed all formal academic training and have not less than two and not more than six years of proven research experience in an established health research setting.

Purpose: To facilitate the development of a high level of health science research activity in Canada.

No. of awards offered: Varies.

Frequency: Annual.

Value: Based on candidate's qualifications and experience.

Study Establishment: A university, hospital, provincial health department or institution with appropriate research facilities.

Country of Study: Canada.

Applications Procedure: Prior to application candidates should obtain a copy of the Career Awards Guide.

Closing Date: July 31st.

National Health Scientist Award

Subjects: Public health and related areas.

Eligibility: Open to Canadian citizens or landed immigrants who have demonstrated a strong commitment to population-based health research for a minimum of ten years following completion of all formal academic training, including at least seven years of independent and/or collaborative research.

Purpose: To foster a high level of health research activity in Canada by providing acknowledged leaders in population health inquiry the opportunity to pursue a full-time research career.

No. of awards offered: Varies.

Frequency: Annual.

Value: Based on candidate's qualifications and experience.

Study Establishment: A university, hospital, provincial health department or other institution which can provide a research environment and resources essential to the conduct of population-health research.

Country of Study: Canada.

Applications Procedure: Prior to application the candidate should obtain a copy of the Career Awards Guide.

Closing Date: July 31st.

*Postdoctoral Fellowships

Subjects: Public health and related areas.

Eligibility: Open to Canadian citizens or landed immigrants who have completed all formal academic training.

Level of Study: Postdoctorate.

Purpose: To provide support to highly qualified candidates who have recently completed their formal research training and wish to acquire further experience in an established health research setting.

Type: Fellowship.

No. of awards offered: Varies.

Frequency: Annual.

Value: Based upon the candidate's qualifications and experience.

Study Establishment: Canadian centres with established health research programs.

Country of Study: Normally Canada.

Applications Procedure: Prior to application, candidates should obtain a copy of the Career Awards Guide.

Closing Date: July 31st.

*Visiting National Health Scientist Awards

Subjects: Independent or collaborative health research with particular emphasis on public health.

Eligibility: Open to Canadians and foreign nationals who can demonstrate high aptitude for the proposed research. Candidates should seek nomination by Canadian universities or research institutions.

Purpose: To keep Canadian health research centres abreast of developments in the international and domestic population-health research scene so as to facilitate the pursuit of research relevant to the missions of the NHRDP.

No. of awards offered: Varies.

Frequency: Annual.

Value: A stipend of up to C$24,000 per annum.

Length of Study: Periods from 3 months to 2 years, while on sabbatical leave; not renewable.

Study Establishment: An appropriate institution.

Country of Study: Canada or abroad for Canadians: Canada for non-Canadians.

Applications Procedure: Prior to application, candidates should obtain a copy of the Career Awards Guide.

Closing Date: July 31st.

Additional Information: The awards are offered as part of the National Health Research and Development Program.

DEPARTMENT OF TRANSPORTATION - NATIONAL HIGHWAY INSTITUTE

Department of Transportation - National Highway Institute, 901 N. Stuart Street, Suite 301, Arlington, VA, 22203, USA
Tel: 703 235 0538
Fax: 703 235 0593
Contact: Dr Ilene D. Payne

Dwight David Eisenhower Transportation Fellowship Program

Eligibility: Open to full-time students who are US citizens, or in the process of becoming US citizens.

Level of Study: Postgraduate, Doctorate, Postdoctorate.

Purpose: The objectives of the overall program are to attract the Nation's brightest minds to the field of transportation, to enhance the careers of transportation professionals by encouraging them to seek advanced degrees, and to retain top talent in the transportation community. This program is intended to upgrade the total transportation community in the United States and encompasses all areas of transportation.

Type: Fellowship.

No. of awards offered: Approximately 115.

Frequency: Annual.

Length of Study: Varies.

Study Establishment: Varies.

Country of Study: United States.

Applications Procedure: Completed application, letters of recommendation, transcripts.

Closing Date: February 15th.

DESCENDANTS OF THE SIGNERS OF THE DECLARATION OF INDEPENDENCE

DSDI Scholarship Committee, PO Box 224, Suncook, NH, 03275-0224, USA
Contact: Mrs Phillip F Kennedy

*Scholarship

Subjects: Any subject.

Eligibility: Open to proven direct lineal descendants of a signer of the Declaration of Independence (proof must be established before an application is sent). Applicants must give the name of their ancestor signer in their first communication or they will not receive a reply. Applicants must be attending an accredited four-year college or university course full-time, in graduate or undergraduate study.

Purpose: Financially to assist Descendants of the Signers of the Declaration of Independence (those who prove eligibility and become members of this Society) to pursue their goals in higher education.

Type: Scholarship.

No. of awards offered: 5-6.

Frequency: Annual.

Value: US$1,200-US$2,000, paid directly to the institution. Funds may be applied toward any costs chargeable to the students college account, i.e. room, board, books, fees, tuition.

Country of Study: USA.

Closing Date: March 15th.

Additional Information: Only those with proven descent (a Society member number) will receive an application. Competition among eligible applicants is based on merit, need, and length of time to graduation.

THE DIRKSEN CONGRESSIONAL CENTER

The Dirksen Congressional Center, 301 South 4th Street, Suite A, Pekin, Illinois, 61554, USA
Tel: 309 347 7113
Fax: 309 347 6432
Email: dirksenctr@aol.com
Contact: Frank H. Mackaman

Congressional Research Grants Program

Subjects: Political science and government.
Eligibility: Open to nationals of any country.
Level of Study: Unrestricted.
Purpose: To fund the study of the US Congress and its leaders.
Type: Research Grant.
No. of awards offered: Six to ten.
Frequency: Annual.
Value: Up to US$3,000.
Length of Study: Not defined.
Study Establishment: Unrestricted.
Country of Study: USA.
Applications Procedure: The awards brochure describes application procedure.
Closing Date: April 30th.

DOW JONES NEWSPAPER FUND, INC

Dow Jones Newspaper Fund, Inc, PO Box 300, Princeton, NJ, 08543-0300, USA
Tel: 800 DOW FUND
Fax: 609 520 5804
Email: newsfund@plink.geis.com

Editing Intern Program

Eligibility: Open only to US citizens.
Level of Study: College Senior, Postgraduate.
Purpose: To encourage careers in copy editing.
Type: Internship, Scholarship.
No. of awards offered: Up to 80.
Frequency: Annual.
Length of Study: Summer program.
Country of Study: USA.
Applications Procedure: Please submit formal application, resume, list of grades/courses, essay and test. No-one will be considered unless an application form is sent with other materials.
Closing Date: Applications available August 15th and November 1st. All materials must be postmarked by November 15th.
Additional Information: This is a national competition for college juniors, seniors and graduate students. All students selected will attend a one or two week pre-internship training course. All internships take place at daily newspapers, on line newspapers or real-time news services. All internships are paid and take place during the summer. Interns returning to school at the end of the summer receive a US$1,000 scholarship.

Teacher Fellowship Program

Subjects: Journalism: basic courses, including reporting, layout and design, newspaper publication workshops, desktop publishing, staff diversity, and the first amendment.

Eligibility: Open to US high school teachers who teach journalism and/or have advised the student newspaper.
Purpose: To provide education for high school journalism teachers.
Type: Fellowship.
Frequency: Annual.
Value: US$500 to be used for tuition, books, fees and transportation.
Study Establishment: In a department of journalism in a college or university approved by the Fund.
Country of Study: USA.
Additional Information: Grants will be awarded to colleges, universities and journalism organizations offering summer workshops and courses on specific topics. Directors of the workshops will select the Fellowship recipients based on eligibility requirements along with additional restrictions based on the workshop. Interested teachers should request a list of workshops between 1 March and 1 June.

DUBLIN INSTITUTE FOR ADVANCED STUDIES

Dublin Institute for Advanced Studies, 10 Burlington Road, Dublin, 4, Republic of Ireland
Tel: 668 0748
Fax: 668 0561
Email: registrar@admin.dias.ie
Contact: J Duggan, Registrar

Scholarship

Subjects: Celtic studies, futurology, anthropology.
Eligibility: Open to nationals of any country.
Level of Study: Postgraduate, Doctorate, Postdoctorate.
Purpose: To enable training in advanced research methods in the fields of Celtic studies, theoretical physics and cosmic physics.
Type: Scholarship.
No. of awards offered: Approximately 8 in each school.
Frequency: Annual.
Value: IR£4,400-5,800 (masters); IR£6,468-6,992 (doctoral).
Length of Study: One year.
Study Establishment: The Institute.
Country of Study: Republic of Ireland.
Applications Procedure: Application forms are available upon request.
Closing Date: March 11th (theoretical physics); no fixed date for the other schools.

DUKE UNIVERSITY CENTER

Duke University Center, Box 29008, Durham, NC, 27710, USA
Tel: 919 681 8777
Fax: 919 681 8744
Email: grm@acpub.duke.edu
Contact: Gail R Marsh

Postdoctoral Training in Ageing Research

Subjects: Histology.
Eligibility: Open to US citizens and permanent residents.
Level of Study: Postgraduate.
Purpose: To train research scientists in the methods used in research on ageing in any scientific field.
Type: Training award.
No. of awards offered: About four.

Frequency: Annual.

Value: US$19,608 up to US$32,300 depending on experience.

Length of Study: Two years.

Study Establishment: Duke University.

Country of Study: USA.

Applications Procedure: Applicants should send CV and letter requesting further application materials. Applicant should also supply a project description, three letters of reference, a training plan, a career plan and graduate transcripts.

Closing Date: April 1, 1997.

DUMBARTON OAKS: TRUSTEES FOR HARVARD UNIVERSITY

Dumbarton Oaks, 1703 32nd Street, NW, Washington, DC, 20007, USA
Tel: 202 339 6410
Contact: Assistant Director

Dumbarton Oaks Fellowships and Junior Fellowships

Subjects: Byzantine civilization in all its aspects, including the late Roman and Early Christian period, and the Middle Ages generally; studies of Byzantine cultural exchanges with the Latin West, Slavic and Near Eastern Countries; pre-Columbian studies; studies in landscape architecture.

Eligibility: Junior Fellowships are open to persons of any nationality who have passed all preliminary examinations for a higher degree and are writing a dissertation. Candidates must have a working knowledge of any languages required for research, Fellowships are open to scholars of any nationality holding a PhD or relevant advanced degree and wishing to pursue research on a project of their own at Dumbarton Oaks.

Purpose: To promote study and research or to support writing of doctoral dissertations in Byzantine studies, Pre-Columbian studies and studies in landscape architecture.

No. of awards offered: 10-11 Fellowships in Byzantine studies; three to four in each of the other fields.

Frequency: Annual.

Value: US$12,000 per annum (Junior Fellowships); US$21,000 per annum (Fellowships). Both Junior and Regular Fellows receive furnished accommodation or a housing allowance of US$1,700, if needed, to assist with the cost of bringing and maintaining dependants in Washington, and an expense account of US$800 for approved research expenditure during the academic year. Fellows who reside outside North America may be provided with travel assistance.

Length of Study: Up to one year full-time study non-renewable.

Study Establishment: For full-time resident work at Dumbarton Oaks.

Country of Study: USA.

Closing Date: November 1st of the academic year preceding that for which the Fellowship is required.

Additional Information: Dumbarton Oaks also awards a limited number of Summer Fellowships.

DUQUESNE UNIVERSITY

Graduate Program, Department of Philosophy, Duquesne University, Pittsburgh, PA, 15282, USA
Tel: 412 396 6500
Fax: 412 396 5197
Email: thompson@duq.cc.duq.edu
Contact: Joan Thompson, Senior Secretary

Graduate Assistantships

Subjects: Philosophy.

Eligibility: Open to holders of a BA in philosophy, or its equivalent, who have a QPA of at least 3.7 and an excellent GRE. Candidates should have knowledge of a second language.

Level of Study: Doctorate.

Purpose: To provide a stipend to enable students to obtain a PhD in philosophy.

Type: Graduate Assistantships.

No. of awards offered: 12 new each year.

Frequency: Annual.

Value: A stipend of approximately US$9,000, plus all tuition for coursework.

Length of Study: Four years.

Country of Study: USA.

Closing Date: February 15th before the fall term.

Additional Information: Applications should include a statement of intent and three letters of recommendation, GREs and application form, TOEFL.

A J DYER OBSERVATORY

A J Dyer Observatory, Box 1803, Station B, Vanderbilt University, Nashville, TN, 37235, USA
Tel: 615 373 4897
Fax: 615 343 7263
Telex: 554323
Contact: Director

Research Assistantship

Subjects: Observational optical astronomy.

Eligibility: Open to persons holding a bachelor's degree who are acceptable to the Graduate School of Vanderbilt University.

Level of Study: Postgraduate, Doctorate.

Purpose: To provide assistance in research programs of the Dyer Observatory.

No. of awards offered: One.

Frequency: Annual.

Value: US$23,500 paid monthly.

Length of Study: One year.

Study Establishment: The Dyer Observatory, Vanderbilt University.

Country of Study: USA.

Applications Procedure: Contact the Observatory Director to request application materials.

Closing Date: February 15th.

EARLY AMERICAN INDUSTRIES ASSOCIATION

Early American Industries Association, Inc, 1324 Shallcross Avenue, Wilmington, DE, 19806, USA
Tel: 302 652 7297
Contact: Justine J Mataleno, Coordinator, Grants-in-Aid Committee

Grants-in-Aid

Subjects: Early American industrial development.

Eligibility: Open to US citizens or permanent residents; individuals may be sponsored by an institution or be engaged in self-directed projects.

Level of Study: Postgraduate.

Purpose: To encourage graduate or postgraduate research or publication and the preservation and classification of obsolete tools and mechanical devices.

Type: Grant.

No. of awards offered: Three to five.

Frequency: Annual.

Value: US$1,000.

Length of Study: One year; not renewable.

Country of Study: USA.

Applications Procedure: Application plus three letters of recommendation.

Closing Date: March 15th.

Additional Information: Awards may be used to supplement existing financial awards. Successful applicants are required to file a project report on forms supplied by the Association. These are not scholarship funds.

THE EASTER SEAL RESEARCH INSTITUTE

Easter Seal Research Institute, 250 Ferrand Drive, Suite 200, Don Mills, ON, M3C 3P2, Canada
Tel: 416 421 8377
Fax: 416 696 1035
Email: info@easterseals.org
www: http://www.cyberplex.com/CyberPlex/Easterseals.html
Contact: The Administrator

Research Grants; Fellowships; Training Grants; Summer Fellowships

Subjects: Treatment techniques.

Eligibility: Funding is limited to Canadian citizens or landed immigrants in the province of Ontario only.

Level of Study: Doctorate, Postdoctorate, Professional development.

Purpose: To support research, development and professional training concerned with the prevention, treatment and management of physical disabilities in children and young adults in the province of Ontario.

Frequency: Annual.

Value: C$3,000-C$30,000.

Length of Study: 1-2 years.

Country of Study: Canada.

Applications Procedure: Application form must be completed.

Closing Date: March 1st and April 15th.

Additional Information: Grants are not made for special projects, operating funds, building funds, emergency funds, conferences and seminars, deficit financing, endowment funds, equipment funds, matching funds, and seed money.

EASTMAN DENTAL CENTER

Eastman Dental Center, 625 Elmwood Avenue, Rochester, NY, 14620, USA
Tel: 716 275 8315
Fax: 716 256 3153
Contact: Registrar

Clinical Dental Fellowships

Subjects: Dental medicine.

Eligibility: Open to recent dental graduates who have a DDS degree or

equivalent qualification. Candidates from overseas must show evidence of high academic achievement and of their intention to follow an academic or research career.

Level of Study: Postdoctorate.

Purpose: To enable suitably qualified dental graduates to undertake training and/or research at the Center.

Type: Fellowship.

No. of awards offered: Approximately ten.

Frequency: Annual.

Value: Approximately US$14,000 per annum.

Length of Study: One academic year; renewable.

Study Establishment: At the Center.

Country of Study: USA.

Applications Procedure: Please submit application form, CV, dental transcripts, undergraduate transcripts and three letters of recommendation from dental professors and Dean of Dental School.

Closing Date: October 31st.

FRIEDRICH EBERT FOUNDATION

Friedrich Ebert Foundation, Godesberger Allee 149, Bonn, D-53175, Germany
Tel: 0228 883 634
Fax: 0228 883 697
Telex: 885479 fest d
Contact: Scholarship Department

Fellowship Program

Subjects: Any subject in the social sciences and related disciplines.

Eligibility: Open to highly qualified applicants with a good knowledge of German.

Level of Study: Postgraduate, Doctorate.

Purpose: To offer study and research fellowships.

Type: Fellowship.

Frequency: Monthly.

Value: Between 1,150DM and 1,290DM per month.

Length of Study: 5-12 months.

Country of Study: Germany.

Applications Procedure: Application form must be completed and submitted with CV and short description of research program.

Additional Information: The Friedrich-Ebert-Stiftung (FES) is the first and earliest German foundation with a socio-economic and political background. Its constitution of 15 April 1925 was based upon the political legacy of Friedrich Ebert, the first President of the Weimar Republic.

ECONOMIC AND SOCIAL RESEARCH COUNCIL

Economic and Social Research Council, Polaris House, North Star Avenue, Swindon, SN2 1UJ, England
Tel: 01793 413000
Fax: 01793 413001
Contact: Postgraduate Training Division

Research and Advanced Course Studentships

Subjects: Social sciences.

Eligibility: Open to persons with a first or upper second class honours degree in any subject from a UK university or the CNAA; a masters degree from a UK university or the CNAA; a degree from a UK university or the CNAA or a UK professional qualification acceptable to the

ESRC as of degree standard plus at least one academic year, having been satisfactorily completed of full-time study, or its part-time equivalent, towards a UK higher degree; or a UK professional qualification acceptable to the ESRC as of degree standard plus three years' subsequent full-time relevant professional work experience. Candidates must have been ordinarily resident in Great Britain throughout the three-year period preceding the date of application and not have been so resident during any part of that three-year period wholly or mainly for the purpose of receiving full-time education.

Purpose: To promote social science research and postgraduate training. The ESRC aims to provide funding for high quality postgraduate training and research on issues of importance to business, the public sector and government.

Type: Standard Research Studentships (363 in 1995-96). Standard Advanced Course Studentships (90 Competition and 521 Quota in 1995-96). Case, including Innovation and Industrial Awards (112 in 1995-96). Standard Joint Panel Research (21 in 1995-96). Joint Panel Course (71 in 1995-96). Housing Management (98 in 1995-96).

No. of awards offered: Varies.

Frequency: Annual.

Value: ESRC studentship awards can cover fees, maintenance, dependants' allowances and travel expenses, depending on the student's situation, circumstances and the type of award.

Length of Study: Up to three years.

Study Establishment: Institutions which have been given recognition by ESRC.

Country of Study: UK.

Applications Procedure: Application forms and information sheets are available from February and should be collected from the Academic Registrar's Office of any university or Institute of Higher Education at that time.

Closing Date: May 1st (complete applications), June 1st (quota nominations), July 31st (joint panel applications).

Additional Information: Guidance notes are available from recognised departments or course organiser, and university careers service from the middle of February.

ECONOMIC EDUCATION FOR CLERGY, INC

Economic Education for Clergy,Inc, PO Box 501908, Indianapolis, IN, 46250, USA
Tel: 317 841 0881
Fax: 317 841 0881
Email: Guido@aol.com
Contact: Guido L Burgis, Executive Director

Economics and Ethics Grant Program for Clergy

Eligibility: There are no eligibility restrictions.

Level of Study: Professional development.

Purpose: To provide clergy with the opportunity to better understand economic and ethical issues at the national, regional and local levels.

Type: Workshop support.

No. of awards offered: Five.

Frequency: Dependent on funds available.

Value: US$2,000-US$5,000.

Country of Study: USA.

Applications Procedure: Please submit a proposal with budget.

Closing Date: Evaluated monthly.

EDUCATIONAL COMMISSION FOR FOREIGN MEDICAL GRADUATES

Educational Commission for Foreign Medical Graduates, 2401 Pennsylvania Avenue, NW, Suite 475, Washington, DC, 20037, USA
Tel: 202 293 9320
Fax: 202 457 0751
Contact: Magdalena Miranda, MS

Foreign Faculty Fellowship Program in the Basic Medical Sciences

Subjects: Basic medical sciences: anatomy, biochemistry, biophysics, cell biology, genetics, immunology, microbiology, molecular biology, pathology, pharmacology, and physiology and medical education especially teaching.

Eligibility: Open to foreign nationals who work and reside in their home country at the time of application. Candidates must have a graduate or professional degree (MSc minimum); not less than three years of teaching experience; endorsement of the home country medical school; and be a full-time faculty member actively involved in teaching a basic medical science, or a clinician who has taught basic science. Must document English language competence, both written and oral.

Level of Study: Professional development, Postgraduate.

Purpose: To strengthen basic science departments in foreign medical schools by providing selected faculty members with an opportunity to enhance their knowledge and teaching skills in the basic medical sciences; to support the international exchange of information in science and technology; to contribute to the promotion of cultural understanding among medical educators.

Type: Fellowship.

No. of awards offered: 12-15.

Frequency: Biennially.

Value: US$2,000 monthly stipend, plus US$1,000 for instruments/supplies, US$500 for books, US$2,000 for the sponsoring department, US$2,500 for foreign medical school, round-trip air fare, health insurance.

Country of Study: USA.

Applications Procedure: Must request and complete an application form and submit two reference reports.

Closing Date: July 13th (partial), December 15th (complete).

Additional Information: Teaching of undergraduate medical students must comprise 70% of the educational program. No awards for research or degree granting programs.

International Medical Scholars Program

Eligibility: Open to citizens of all countries except the United States and Canada. Candidates must document English language competence, both written and oral. Candidates must have a graduate or professional degree that relates to the proposed area of study. They must have two years of work experience in their chosen field following completion of their formal academic and clinical training.

Level of Study: Postgraduate, Postdoctorate, Professional development.

Purpose: To facilitate placement of foreign scholars in the US academic institutions able to provide educational opportunities of high quality; to match educational opportunities in the USA with the determined needs of nations and health care institutions abroad.

Type: Fellowship.

No. of awards offered: 15-20.

Frequency: Every two years.

Value: US$30,000 per year.

Length of Study: Three months to one year.

Study Establishment: US medical institution.

Country of Study: USA.

Applications Procedure: Application forms must be requested and completed. Two reference reports must be submitted.

Closing Date: August 15th.

Additional Information: Candidates must reside and work in their home countries at the time of application. Awards are not given for progams in research or for degree granting educational programs.

EDUCATIONAL FOUNDATION OF THE NATIONAL RESTAURANT ASSOCIATION

The Educational Foundation of the National Restaurant Association, 250 South Wacker Drive, Suite 1400, Chicago, IL, 60606-5834, USA
Tel: 312 715 1010
Fax: 312 715 0807
Contact: Scholarship Department

*H J Heinz Fellowship Program

Subjects: Food service/hospitality and education.

Eligibility: Open to US applicants who are or have been full-time educators or administrators of a food service/hospitality-related program. Applicants must be enrolled in a program.

Purpose: To assist educators and administrators in the food service/hospitality industry in their pursuit of postgraduate degrees.

Type: Fellowship.

No. of awards offered: 7.

Frequency: Annual.

Value: One at US$2,000, one at US$1,200 and five at US$1,000.

Study Establishment: An appropriate institution.

Country of Study: USA.

Applications Procedure: Call or write to request applications.

Closing Date: March 15th.

Teacher Work-Study Gants

Subjects: Hotel, restaurant and institutional management; food service; culinary arts; commercial foods.

Eligibility: Open to US citizens who are full-time teachers or administrators at an educational institution at the high school or college level who will continue to be full-time teachers/administrators in a food service/hospitality-oriented program, or who will be full-time students pursuing an advanced degree during the next academic year.

Purpose: To provide the opportunity for educators in the food service/hospitality industry to gain hands-on work experience during the summer.

Type: Grant.

No. of awards offered: Eight.

Frequency: Annual.

Value: US$3,000.

Study Establishment: An appropriate institution.

Country of Study: USA.

Applications Procedure: Applications available from November 1st.

Closing Date: February.

Additional Information: Applicants must arrange for 320 hours of full-time employment in the food service/hospitality industry in a line or staff position and at a pay commensurate with the position.

EDUCATIONAL TESTING SERVICE

Educational Testing Service, Mail Stop 16-T, Princeton, NJ, 08541-0001, USA
Tel: 609 734 1806
Email: ldelauro@ets.org
Contact: Linda J DeLauro

Postdoctoral Fellowships

Subjects: Psychology, education, sociology of education, psychometrics, statistics, computer science, linguistics.

Eligibility: Open to any individuals with a doctorate in a relevant discipline.

Level of Study: Postdoctorate.

Purpose: To provide research opportunities to individuals, and to increase the number of women and minority professionals in educational measurement and related fields.

Type: Fellowship.

No. of awards offered: Up to three.

Value: US$35,000.

Length of Study: 12 months, including one month vacation.

Country of Study: USA.

Applications Procedure: There is no formal application form. Please call for a Research Division description. Applicants should submit: a resume, research proposal, officials transcripts of previous studies and three letters of recommendation from people who are familiar with the applicant's work.

Additional Information: Affirmative action goals will also be considered in the selection process.

Summer Internships in Program Direction

Subjects: Measurement and evaluation.

Eligibility: Applicants must have completed a master's level graduate program; those in predoctoral studies are especially welcome. More specific criteria will be enclosed with application materials.

Level of Study: Postgraduate, Doctorate.

Purpose: To provide opportunities, especially for women and minority professionals, for a work and learning experience that will assist the participants in exploring career alternatives in the field of measurement and evaluation.

Type: Internship.

Value: Each participant will receive US$2,500 for the eight week period, with a supplemental living allowance for an accompanying spouse or child (US$350), or for a spouse and children (US$500). Reasonable round-trip expenses will be reimbursed upom presentation of receipts.

Length of Study: Eight weeks.

Study Establishment: ETS headquarters in Princeton.

Country of Study: USA.

Applications Procedure: Application should include references and transcripts.

Closing Date: February.

Additional Information: A background in psychology, teaching/administration in secondary or higher education, or business management would be helpful for potential interns in Program Direction.

Summer Program in Research for Graduate Students

Subjects: Educational measurement. Psychology, sociology of education, statistics, computer science and testing issues.

Eligibility: Open to graduate students who are pursuing a doctorate in a relevant discipline and who provide evidence of prior research.

Level of Study: Doctorate.

Purpose: To increase the number of women and minority professionals in educational measurement and related fields.

No. of awards offered: Up to 12.

Value: US$2,500 for the eight week period with a supplementary living allowance for participants who bring either their spouse or child (US$350), or spouse and child (US$500). Reasonable round-trip travel expenses will be reimbursed upon presentation of receipts.

Length of Study: Eight weeks.

Country of Study: USA.

Applications Procedure: Application should include a resume, two letters of reference and official transcripts.

Closing Date: February.

Additional Information: Affirmative action goals will also be considered in the selection process.

TOEFL Postdoctoral Fellowship Program

Eligibility: Applicants should have a doctorate in second-language testing or a related field.

Level of Study: Postdoctorate.

Purpose: To enable a suitable candidate to conduct research and development with ETS staff on the TOEFL 2000 project.

Type: Fellowship.

No. of awards offered: One.

Value: US$35,000. Limited relocation expenses, consistent with ETS guidelines, will be reimbursed upon presentation of receipts.

Length of Study: One year, with the possibility of renewal for a further year.

Study Establishment: ETS, Princeton.

Country of Study: USA.

Applications Procedure: There is no formal application form. Applicants should submit: a resume, publications and other relevant documents, official transcripts and three letters of recommendation.

Closing Date: March.

Visiting Scholar Program

Subjects: Educational policy.

Eligibility: Applicants should hold a doctorate in a related discipline and provide evidence of scholarship.

Level of Study: Doctorate.

Purpose: To provide research opportunities for scholars, encourage secondary analyses of NAEP data, and increase the number of minority professionals in educational measurement and related fields.

No. of awards offered: One.

Value: The award will be comparable to that of an ETS researcher who possesses similar training and experience. Scholars will be reimbursed for relocation expenses, concurrent with ETS guidelines, upon presentation of receipts.

Length of Study: Ten months.

Country of Study: USA.

Applications Procedure: There is no formal application form. Applicants should submit a resume, research proposal, and three references.

Closing Date: January.

Additional Information: Studies focused on issues concerning the education of minority students are especially encouraged.

ELECTRICAL WOMEN'S ROUND TABLE, INC

Electrical Women's Round Table, Inc, PO Box 292793, Nashville, TN, 37229-2793, USA

Tel: 615 890 1272
Fax: 615 890 1272
Contact: Ann Cox

Julia Kiene Fellowship and Lyle Mamer Fellowship

Subjects: Fields related to electrical energy, for example: advertising; education; electric utilities; electrical engineering; electric home equipment manufacturers; extension; housing; journalism; radio-television; research.

Eligibility: Open to female graduating seniors or those who hold a degree from an accredited institution.

Level of Study: Postgraduate.

Purpose: To promote the efficient use of electricity by encouraging high calibre women college graduates to study towards advanced degrees as preparation for leadership.

Type: Fellowship.

No. of awards offered: Two.

Frequency: Annual.

Value: US$2,000 (Kiene Fellowship); US$1,000 (Mamer Fellowship).

Study Establishment: Any college or university accredited and approved by the EWRT Fellowship Committee.

Applications Procedure: Applications are judged on the basis of scholarship, character, financial need, and professional interest in electrical energy. Applicants must submit transcripts and four references.

Closing Date: March 1st.

THE ELECTROCHEMICAL SOCIETY, INC

The Electrochemical Society, 10 South Main Street, Pennington, NJ, 08534, USA
Tel: 609 737 1902
Fax: 609 737 2743
Email: ecs@electrochem.org
www: http://www.electrochem.org
Contact: John R Stanley

F M Becket Memorial Award

Subjects: Electrochemical and Solid State Science.

Eligibility: Open to nationals of any country.

Level of Study: Unrestricted.

Purpose: To support overseas summer study.

Type: Fellowship.

No. of awards offered: One.

Frequency: Every two years.

Value: US$3,500.

Length of Study: Three months.

Study Establishment: An overseas university.

Country of Study: Must meet with the approval of the honors and awards committee.

Applications Procedure: Applicants are required to complete application form and submit with supporting documents.

Closing Date: January 1st of odd years.

Energy Research Summer Fellowships

Subjects: Electrochemical and Solid State Science.

Eligibility: Open to nationals of any country.

Level of Study: Unrestricted.

Purpose: To fund a student's research through the summer months.

Type: Fellowship.

No. of awards offered: Five.

Frequency: Annual.

Value: US$3,000.

Length of Study: Three months (one summer).

Study Establishment: Any US or Canadian university.

Country of Study: USA or Canada.

Applications Procedure: Application and supporting materials must be submitted.

Closing Date: January 1st each year.

Summer Fellowships

Subjects: Electrochemical and Solid State Science.

Eligibility: Open to nationals of any country.

Level of Study: Unrestricted.

Purpose: To fund a student's research through the summer months.

Type: Fellowship.

No. of awards offered: Three.

Frequency: Annual.

Value: US$3,000.

Length of Study: Three months (one summer).

Study Establishment: Any USA or Canadian university.

Country of Study: USA or Canada.

Applications Procedure: Application and supporting materials must be submitted.

Closing Date: January 1st each year.

BESSY EMANUEL EDUCATION TRUST

Academic Study Group, PO Box 7545, London, NW2 2Q2, England
Tel: 0171 435 6803
Fax: 0171 794 0291
Contact: John D A Levy

Bessy Emanuel Travel Scholarships

Subjects: Studies relevant to Israel.

Eligibility: Open to any UK student in a British institution of higher education. In exceptional cases students intending to enter higher education as well as graduates will be considered.

Level of Study: Postgraduate, Unrestricted.

Type: Scholarship.

No. of awards offered: 1 or 2.

Frequency: Annual.

Value: £500.

Length of Study: Four to six weeks.

Study Establishment: A small independent research project.

Country of Study: Israel.

Applications Procedure: Application form required.

Closing Date: February 1st.

Additional Information: There have been one or two awards annually for the past fifteen years.

EMBLEM CLUB SCHOLARSHIP FOUNDATION

Emblem Club Scholarship Foundation, PO Box 712, San Luis Rey, CA, 92068, USA

Tel: 619 757 0619
Contact: Shirley Perkins, Administrative Secretary

Grant

Eligibility: Applicants must be US citizens of no more than fifty years of age, and must agree to teach within the USA; otherwise no restrictions as to minority, religion, language.

Level of Study: Postgraduate.

Purpose: These grants are made to those teachers who are working towards their Master's Degree and Accreditation in order to teach the deaf and hearing impaired. This does not include Audiology.

Type: Grant.

No. of awards offered: 40.

Frequency: Quarterly, dependent on funds available.

Value: Varies, US$1,000-US$5,000.

Country of Study: USA.

Applications Procedure: Apply to the schools concerned.

Closing Date: March 1st, June 1st, September 1st, January 1st.

EMIGRÉ MEMORIAL GERMAN INTERNSHIPS PROGRAM

Emigré Memorial German Internships Program (EMGIP), PO Box 345, Durham, NH, 03824, USA

Emigré Memorial German Internships Program

Subjects: Government service, social studies.

Eligibility: Open to advanced undergraduate and graduate students who are not German citizens. Fluency in German is required.

Purpose: To promote professional work on German government and society.

Type: Grant.

No. of awards offered: 12-13.

Frequency: Annual.

Value: Up to DM6,000.

Length of Study: Up to three months.

Study Establishment: Work-study programs in government offices.

Country of Study: Germany.

Applications Procedure: Application form must be completed.

Closing Date: January 17th.

ENERGY RESEARCH AND DEVELOPMENT CORPORATION

Energy Research and Development Corporation, PO Box 629, Canberra, ACT, 2601, Australia
Tel: 61 6 2744800
Fax: 61 6 2744801
Email: michelle@erdc.com.au
Contact: Managing Director

ERDC Postgraduate Award 1997

Subjects: Energy-related research.

Eligibility: Only available to Australian citizens or persons with permanent resident status in Australia at the time of their application.

Level of Study: Postgraduate.

Frequency: Annual.

Value: A$60,000.

Length of Study: Three years.

Study Establishment: A suitable Australian institution.

Country of Study: Australia.

Applications Procedure: Applicants must provide details of the proposed research project, a copy of their academic record (full transcript), and any prior research experience of other relevant experience.

Closing Date: September 27th.

ENGINEERING AND PHYSICAL SCIENCES RESEARCH COUNCIL

Engineering and Physical Sciences Research Council, Polaris House, North Star Avenue, Swindon, SN2 1ET, England
Tel: 01793 444308
Fax: 01793 444012
Contact: Postgraduate Training

Advanced Fellowships

Subjects: Engineering, physics, chemistry and mathematics.

Eligibility: Open to research workers normally under 35 years of age. Candidates must hold a PhD or be of equivalent standing in their profession and have at least two years of research experience at postdoctoral level when the application is made.

Purpose: To support a small number of outstanding young research workers.

Type: Fellowship.

No. of awards offered: 25.

Frequency: Annual.

Value: Awards are made based on age, according to the first 14 points on the UFC scale for non-clinical academic and related staff in UK universities.

Length of Study: Up to five years.

Study Establishment: Any academic institution acceptable to the Council.

Country of Study: UK.

Closing Date: September 30th.

Cooperative Awards in Science and Engineering

Subjects: Science and technology outside the fields of: agriculture (including horticulture), agricultural economics, agricultural engineering, and the more applied aspects of agricultural science; natural environment sciences, which may be defined broadly as geology and geophysics (including seismology and geomagnetism), meteorology, hydrology, oceanography, marine and freshwater biology, and terrestrial ecology; medicine; food science; social science, biological sciences, particle physics, astronomy.

Eligibility: Open to persons who have been ordinarily resident in Great Britain for a period of three years prior to the date of application and have devoted no part of those three years to full-time education, hold a good honours degree from a UK university (i.e. first or upper second class honours) or alternatively a qualification or combination of qualifications and experience acceptable to the Council as demonstrating equivalent ability and who are nominated by the authorities of the institution of tenure.

Level of Study: Postgraduate.

Purpose: To encourage collaboration between academic institutions and outside bodies (i.e. industry and the public sector); also to provide an opportunity for graduates to broaden their research training by gaining first-hand experience of work outside the academic environment.

No. of awards offered: Varies.

Frequency: Annual.

Value: Varies; at least £2,500 per annum more than Standard Research Studentships.

Length of Study: Up to three years.

Study Establishment: The student normally spends at least one month per year working at the premises of the cooperating body during tenure of the award.

Country of Study: UK.

Applications Procedure: Nominations for CASE Studentships should be submitted through heads of the chosen departments.

Closing Date: July 31st.

Additional Information: The basis of the CASE scheme is a research project, jointly set up between an academic department and a collaborating body, approved by EPSRC for the tenure of these awards. Students are allowed to receive a payment from the cooperating body and may participate in patent agreements together with the academic supervisor and the cooperating body.

Senior Fellowships

Subjects: Engineering, physics, chemistry and mathematics.

Eligibility: Open to scientists who are already established in their careers, having proved their exceptional research and interpretative ability. Applicants must be members of permanent staff of UK universities, technical colleges or similar institutions. Fellows are expected to return to their normal employment at the termination of the Fellowship.

Purpose: To enable a small number of outstanding scientists at the peak of their capabilities to devote themselves to full-time research free of the restrictions imposed by their normal employment.

Type: Fellowship.

No. of awards offered: Three.

Frequency: Annual.

Value: The Council will pay the salary, but not the superannuation or NI contributions, as if the Fellow were continuing in his/her normal employment at his/her home institution.

Study Establishment: Any institution which has a firm working link with a university or similar academic establishment.

Country of Study: UK.

Closing Date: September 30th.

Additional Information: Fellowships are not intended to replace sabbatical leave.

Research Studentships; Cooperative Awards in Science & Engineering; Advanced Course Studentships

Subjects: Engineering and the physical sciences (physics, chemistry and mathematics).

Eligibility: Open to nationals of EC countries and the UK.

Level of Study: Postgraduate.

Purpose: To enable training in the methods of research and vocational training at master's level.

Type: Studentship.

No. of awards offered: About 2,000.

Frequency: Annual.

Value: At least £5,050 per year.

Length of Study: Usually one year.

Study Establishment: Higher education institution.

Country of Study: The United Kingdom (excluding Northern Ireland).

Applications Procedure: Nomination by departments of higher education institutions.

Closing Date: July 31st.

Royal Society-EPSRC Industrial Fellowships

Subjects: Science and technology outside the fields of: a) agriculture (including horticulture), agricultural economics, agricultural engineering, and the more applied aspects of agricultural science; b) natural environment sciences, which may be defined broadly as geology and geophysics (including seismology and geomagnetism), meteorology, hydrology, oceanography, marine and freshwater biology, and terrestrial ecology; c) medicine; d) food science; e) social science; except for awards made by the Joint Research Councils Committee, and including those aspects of psychology which are closely related to fundamental biology and to the engineering and biological aspects of ergonomics and cybernetics.

Eligibility: Open to individuals ordinarily resident in the UK, Channel Islands or the Isle of Man. Candidates should be of PhD status or equivalent, normally holding a tenured post in a university, or employed as a scientist, mathematician or engineer in industry, an industrial research organization or an organization in the public service. Candidates should preferably be 30-50 years of age. Additional consideration may be shown to applicants who have already had previous contact with or interest in the opposite sector of employment.

Level of Study: Doctorate.

Purpose: To enhance communication between those in industry and those in institutions of higher learning to the benefit of UK firms or higher education institutions or both. To this end the scheme aims to provide opportunities for academic scientists, mathematicians and engineers to hold a job in an industrial environment and undertake a project at any stage in the chain from fundamental science to industrial innovation, and, conversely, for industrial scientists, mathematicians and engineers to undertake research or course-development work in a university.

Type: Fellowship.

No. of awards offered: Varies.

Value: Varies.

Length of Study: Normally for periods of 6 months to 2 years.

Country of Study: UK, although proposals to hold Fellowships overseas will be considered.

Closing Date: March 31st, October 31st.

Standard Research Studentships and Advanced Course Studentship

Subjects: Science and technology outside the fields of: agriculture (including horticulture), agricultural economics, agricultural engineering, and the more applied aspects of agricultural science; natural environment sciences, which may be defined broadly as geology and geophysics (including seismology and geomagnetism), meteorology, hydrology, oceanography, marine and freshwater biology, and terrestrial ecology; medicine; food science; social science, biological sciences, particle physics,astronomy. Applications are also considered for awards for certain courses in business and industrial administration or management, and from candidates with some industrial experience who wish to be trained in the investigation of problems of industrial productivity and organization.

Eligibility: Open to persons who have been ordinarily resident in Great Britain for a period of three years prior to the date of application and have devoted no part of those three years to full-time education, hold a good honours degree from a UK university (i.e. first or upper second class honours for a Research Studentship, first or second class honours for an Advanced Course Studentship) or alternatively a qualification or combination of qualifications and experience acceptable to the Council as demonstrating equivalent ability and who are nominated by the authorities of the institution of tenure.

Level of Study: Postgraduate.

Purpose: To enable training in the methods of research (PhD) and vocational training at masters level.

Type: Studentships.

No. of awards offered: Varies.

Frequency: Annual.

Value: £6,540 for students in London; £5,050 for students elsewhere (1995/96 rates). Values are reviewed annually. In addition, allowances for dependants and experience are payable under certain conditions. Approved tuition fees are paid directly to the institution.

Length of Study: For up to three years (PhD Research Studentships) or for one year (Master's Advanced Course Studentships).

Study Establishment: Wholly or partly at universities, research laboratories or other suitable research institutions sponsoring the candidate's application.

Country of Study: UK (except Northern Ireland).

Closing Date: July 31st.

Additional Information: Nominations should be submitted by the heads of the chosen departments. Applications on behalf of students from the following locations should be directed to the addresses below: Isle of Man: Isle of Man Education Authority, Strand Street, Douglas, Isle of Man; Channel Islands: Jersey Education Committee, St Helier, Jersey or Guernsey Education Council, St Peter Port, Guernsey. Full information concerning EPSRC Studentships is given in the booklet EPSRC Studentships available at academic institutions or from EPSRC.

ENGINEERING FOUNDATION

Engineering Foundation, 345 East 47 Street (Suite 303), New York, NY, 10017, USA
Tel: 212 705 7837
Fax: 212 705 7441
Email: engfnd@aol.com
www: http://www.engfnd.org/engfnd
Contact: Dr Charles Freiman, Director

Grants for Exploratory Research

Purpose: To provide seed funding for significant areas of engineering research with results to be in the public domain.

Type: Research Grant.

No. of awards offered: Up to five.

Frequency: Annual.

Value: Up to US$25,000 with one renewal possible.

Country of Study: North America.

Applications Procedure: Two to three page preliminary proposal.

Closing Date: January each year for award to be made the following year.

Additional Information: Interdisciplinary projects are encouraged. Projects should fall outside the scope of conventional funding sources. For example they may be extremely novel or cross organizational boundaries.

Grants for the Advancement of Engineering

Eligibility: Open to nationals of any country.

Purpose: To provide start-up funding for promising endeavors and incremental funding for signififcant opportunities in areas such as: precollegiate technical programs, professional planning information, public image of the engineer.

Type: Grant.

No. of awards offered: Two to five.

Frequency: Annual.

Country of Study: North America.

Applications Procedure: Two to three page preliminary proposal.

Closing Date: January each year for the award to be made in the following year.

Additional Information: Preference to inter-engineering programs which are national in scope.

THE ENGINEERING INSTITUTE OF CANADA

The Engineering Institute of Canada, 280 Albert Street, Suite 202, Ottawa, Ontario, K1P 5G3, Canada
Tel: 613 232 4211
Fax: 613 232 0390
Contact: Roger Blais

*The Canadian Pacific Railway Engineer Medal

Eligibility: Open to corporate members of the member societies of the EIC Federation.

Purpose: To recognize service at the regional, branch and section levels of engineering.

Type: Medal.

No. of awards offered: Two.

Frequency: Annual.

Closing Date: November 20th.

*Fellowship Award

Subjects: Engineering.

Eligibility: Open to corporate members in good standing of a member or associate member society of the EIC Federation for a consecutive period of not less than five years prior to being nominated and to members in good standing of a Canadian professional engineering association or the Order of Engineers of Quebec for a consecutive period of not less than five years prior to being nominated. Candidates must be at least 45 years of age.

Purpose: To recognize excellence in engineering practice and exceptional contributions to the well-being of the profession and to the good of society.

Type: Fellowship.

No. of awards offered: 15.

Frequency: Annual.

Closing Date: November 20th.

THE ENGLISH ASSOCIATION, SOUTH AFRICAN BRANCH

The English Association, South African Branch, PO Box 32330, Camps Bay, Cape Town, 8040, South Africa
Contact: The Secretary

English Association Literary Competition

Subjects: Works of various literary genres, including radio plays, essays, profiles of writers, narrative poems, sonnets, short stories, novels, anthologies of short poems, children's stories. A specific topic is selected by the Association's Committee in its final meeting of the year preceding the award of prizes.

Eligibility: Open to residents of South Africa of any age.

Purpose: To promote and uphold the standards of English writing and speech.

No. of awards offered: 3.

Frequency: Annually or every 18 months.

Value: R1,400-R2,000.

Closing Date: Late July for notification in late November. The closing date may vary (see press advertisements).

Additional Information: Winners retain copyright, but acknowledgement must be made to the Association should the work be published or produced. The Association reserves the right to publish any prize-winning entry in its circulars or to present it at any of its meetings. The Selection Committee will not be obliged to award any prize should the standard not be considered high enough.

For further information contact:
The English Association, South African Branch, B204 Devonshire Hill, Grotto Road, Rondebosch, Cape Town, 7700, South Africa
Contact: Miss O M Edmonds, Secretary

EMILY ENGLISH TRUST

Emily English Trust, 16 Ogle Street, London, W1P 7LG, England
Tel: 0171 636 4481
Fax: 0171 637 4307
Contact: Valerie Beale, Administrator

*Emily English Award

Subjects: Musical performance: violin.

Eligibility: Open to violinists under the age of 24 years of any nationality who have been resident in the UK for three years.

Purpose: To assist the studies of a talented young violinist.

No. of awards offered: One.

Frequency: Annual.

Value: £5,000.

Country of Study: Unrestricted.

Closing Date: Mid-February.

Additional Information: Selected students will be asked to audition.

ENGLISH-SPEAKING UNION

English-Speaking Union, Dartmouth House, 37 Charles Street, London, W1X 8AB, England
Tel: 0171 493 3328
Fax: 0171 495 6108
Contact: Director of Education

Chautauqua Scholarships; Rebecca Richmond Memorial Scholarships

Subjects: Art (painting, ceramics and sculpture), music education, literature and international relations.

Eligibility: Open to British teachers, 25-35 years of age, with particular interest in the arts.

Level of Study: Professional development.

Purpose: To enable British teachers to study at the Chautauqua Summer School organized by the University of Syracuse.

Type: Scholarship.

No. of awards offered: Two.

Frequency: Annual.

Value: £850 plus board, room, tuition and lecture sessions at the Summer School.

Length of Study: Six weeks.

Study Establishment: Chautauqua Institution's Summer School, Chautauqua, New York.

Country of Study: USA.

Closing Date: November 30th.

Horticulture Scholarships

Subjects: Horticulture.

Eligibility: Applicants should have gained horticultural qualification and be in the early stages of their career.

Level of Study: Postgraduate.

Type: Scholarship.

No. of awards offered: Four.

Frequency: Annual.

Study Establishment: University.

Applications Procedure: Application form must be completed - these are available from the Director of Cultural Affairs.

Additional Information: The European Gardens Scholarship is a study tour of the UK by Europeans and a study tour of Europe by UK applicants. The Martin Mclaren Horticultural Scholarship/Garden Club of America Interchange Fellowship is one year spent in UK/US university.

Music Scholarships

Subjects: Music.

Eligibility: Candidates must be aged 28 or under and be from Britain or the Commonwealth and be students or graduates from music colleges and other equivalent institutions.

Level of Study: Professional development.

Purpose: To enable musicians of outstanding ability to study at summer schools in North America, Canada, France and the UK.

Type: Scholarship.

No. of awards offered: Nine.

Frequency: Annual.

Value: Covers the cost of tuition, board and lodging and relevant flight costs.

Length of Study: From three to nine weeks, depending on particular scholarship.

Study Establishment: Summer school.

Country of Study: USA.

Applications Procedure: Candidates must be nominated by the relevant college heads of department and supported by a teacher's reference.

Closing Date: November.

ESU Travelling Librarian Award

Subjects: Library science.

Eligibility: Open to professionally qualified UK librarians aged 25-39.

Level of Study: Professional development.

Purpose: To encourage US/UK contacts in the library world and establish links between pairs of libraries. The successful candidate should be prepared to act as an ambassador for the ESU and undertake occasional speaking engagements at the ESU branches.

Type: Travel Grant.

No. of awards offered: One.

Frequency: Twice a year.

Value: Cover board and lodging and relevant flight costs.

Length of Study: A minimum of two weeks.

Country of Study: USA.

Applications Procedure: Candidates should submit a CV and covering letter explaining how they propose to use the award if successful.

Closing Date: Early 1997.

Nellie Gwendolyn Lewis Scholarship

Subjects: Business administration.

Eligibility: Candidates must have been born and educated in Wales, born in Wales but educated outside Wales, or educated in Wales but born in another part of the UK. Candidates should be qualified for admission to Indiana University's MBA programme.

Level of Study: Professional development.

Type: Scholarship.

No. of awards offered: One.

Frequency: Biennially (next in 1997).

Value: To cover most expenses.

Length of Study: One year; renewable for a second year subject to satisfactory academic progress.

Study Establishment: Indiana University.

Country of Study: USA.

Closing Date: November 6th.

Lindemann Trust Fellowships

Subjects: Astronomy, chemistry, engineering, geology, geophysics, mathematics and physics.

Eligibility: Open to UK and Commonwealth citizens who are graduates of a UK university and to UK and Commonwealth citizens who are pursuing postgraduate research at a UK University although not graduates of that Institution. Preference is given to those who have demonstrated their capacity for original research and who will be under 30 years of age on 1 September of the Fellowship year, but candidates up to 35 years of age are not debarred.

Level of Study: Postgraduate.

Type: Fellowship.

No. of awards offered: Four.

Frequency: Annual.

Value: A stipend of US$28,000; round-trip travel expenses; and, where appropriate, a dependants allowance.

Length of Study: One year.

Study Establishment: A university.

Country of Study: USA.

Closing Date: November 1st.

Additional Information: Fellows are not required to work for an American degree but are expected to be attached to a university, college or seat of advanced learning and technical repute in the USA. The place of study and research programme must be approved by the Committee. A limited amount of teaching as an adjunct to research activities is not excluded.

Senior Page Scholarship

Subjects: US education.

Eligibility: Open to British teachers, normally 25-55 years of age.

Level of Study: Professional development.

Purpose: To enable British teachers to visit the USA to study a particular aspect of American education in which they are interested.

Type: Scholarship.

No. of awards offered: One.

Frequency: Annual.

Value: £1,200 plus full hospitality.

Length of Study: Six weeks.

Country of Study: USA.

Closing Date: November 30th.

Additional Information: A visit to the West Coast of the USA must be included. Hospitality is provided by the American members of the English-Speaking Union. Scholarships must be taken up during the American academic year while educational institutions are in session.

EPILEPSY FOUNDATION OF AMERICA

Epilepsy Foundation of America, 4351 Garden City Drive, Landover, MD, 20785, USA

Tel: 301 459 3700
Fax: 301 577 2684
Contact: Ruby Gerald

*Behavioral Sciences Research Training Fellowship

Subjects: Epilepsy research relative to the behavioral sciences; appropriate fields of study include sociology, social work, psychology, anthropology, nursing, political science, and others relevant to epilepsy research and practice.

Eligibility: Open to individuals who have received their doctoral degree in a field of the behavioral sciences by the time the Fellowship commences and desire additional postdoctoral research experience in epilepsy. Applications from women and minorities are encouraged.

Purpose: To offer qualified individuals the opportunity to develop expertise in epilepsy research through a training experience or involvement in an epilepsy research project.

Type: Fellowship.

No. of awards offered: One.

Frequency: Annual.

Value: A stipend of up to US$30,000, depending on the experience and qualifications of the applicant and the scope and duration of the proposed project.

Length of Study: One year.

Study Establishment: An approved facility.

Country of Study: USA or Canada.

Applications Procedure: Application forms and guidelines are available from the Foundation on request.

Closing Date: September 1st.

*International Clinical Research Fellowship

Subjects: Epilepsy.

Eligibility: Applicants must have received their MD (or foreign equivalent) and completed residency training. Either the Fellow or the host institution must be from the USA.

Purpose: To provide an individual with the opportunity to develop expertise in clinical epilepsy and research through a one-year training experience to promote the exchange of medical and scientific information and expertise on epilepsy between the USA and other countries.

Type: Fellowship.

No. of awards offered: One.

Frequency: Annual.

Value: US$30,000 stipend only.

Length of Study: One year.

Study Establishment: An approved facility where there is an ongoing epilepsy research program.

Country of Study: USA or abroad.

Closing Date: September 1st.

*International Visiting Professorship

Subjects: Epilepsy.

Eligibility: Either the visitor or the host institution must be from the USA.

Purpose: To provide an opportunity for a visiting professor to spend time at a host institution to promote the exchange of medical and scientific information and expertise on epilepsy between the USA and other countries.

No. of awards offered: Up to ten, depending on funds available.

Frequency: Throughout the year.

Value: To cover travel expenses and minor incidental expenses.

Length of Study: 3-6 weeks.

Study Establishment: An approved facility.

Country of Study: USA or abroad.

*Research/Clinical Training Fellowships

Subjects: Basic or clinical epilepsy research, with an equal emphasis on clinical training and clinical epileptology.

Eligibility: Open to individuals who have received their MD degree and completed residency training. Applications from women and minorities are encouraged.

Purpose: To offer qualified individuals the opportunity to develop expertise in epilepsy research through a training experience and involvement in an epilepsy research project.

Type: Fellowship.

No. of awards offered: Varies.

Frequency: Annual.

Value: A stipend of US$30,000.

Length of Study: One year.

Study Establishment: A facility where there is an ongoing epilepsy research program.

Closing Date: September 1st.

Additional Information: These Fellowships include the Merrit-Putnam Fellowship.

*Research Grants

Subjects: Basic biomedical, behavioral and social sciences; particular encouragement is given to applications in the behavioral sciences.

Eligibility: Open to US researchers; priority is given to beginning investigators just entering the field of epilepsy, to new or innovative projects, and to investigators whose research is relevant to developmental or pediatric aspects of epilepsy. Applications from women and minorities are encouraged; applications from established investigators with other sources of support are discouraged, and Research Grants are not intended to provide support for postdoctoral fellows.

Purpose: To support basic and clinical research which will advance the understanding, treatment and prevention of epilepsy.

Type: Research Grant.

No. of awards offered: Varies.

Frequency: Annual.

Value: Varies; support is limited to US$30,000.

Length of Study: One year.

Country of Study: USA.

Applications Procedure: Application forms and guidelines are available from the Foundation on request.

Closing Date: September 1st.

*Research Training Fellowships

Subjects: Basic or clinical epilepsy research, which must address a question of fundamental importance; a clinical training component is not required.

Eligibility: Open to physicians and PhD neuroscientists who desire postdoctoral research experience; preference is given to applicants whose proposals have a pediatric or developmental emphasis. Applications from women and minorities are encouraged.

Purpose: To offer qualified individuals the opportunity to develop expertise in epilepsy research through involvement in an epilepsy research project.

Type: Fellowship.

No. of awards offered: Varies.

Frequency: Annual.

Value: A stipend of US$30,000.

Length of Study: One year.

Study Establishment: A facility where there is an ongoing epilepsy research program.

Country of Study: USA.

Applications Procedure: Application forms and guidelines are available from the Foundation upon request.

Closing Date: September 1st.

EPISCOPAL CHURCH FOUNDATION

Episcopal Church Foundation, 815 Second Avenue , Room 400, New York, NY, 10017, USA
Tel: 212 697 2858
Fax: 212 297 0142
Contact: Jennifer R Burlington

Graduate Fellowship Program

Subjects: Religious studies.

Eligibility: Open to graduates of an accredited seminary of the Episcopal Church or of another recognized US seminary as an Episcopal candidate and members of the senior class. Applicants must be recommended by the deans of their theological seminaries.

Level of Study: Doctorate.

Purpose: To encourage doctoral study by recent seminary graduates to qualify themselves for the teaching ministry of the Episcopal Church.

Type: Fellowship.

No. of awards offered: Three.

Frequency: Annual.

Value: Dependent on individual circumstances.

Length of Study: One year; renewable for up to two additional years.

Study Establishment: At accredited institutions in the USA and abroad.

Country of Study: Unrestricted.

Applications Procedure: Application materials are available from the Dean's office at any of the eleven accredited episcopal seminaries as well as Harvard Divinity and the Union Theological Seminary.

Closing Date: November 1st.

THE EPPLEY FOUNDATION FOR RESEARCH, INC

The Eppley Foundation for Research, Inc, 575 Lexington Avenue, New York, NY, 10022, USA
Contact: Huyler C Hold, Secretary

Eppley Foundation Postdoctoral Grants

Subjects: Biological and physical sciences.

Eligibility: Open to individuals who have had several years of postdoctoral research experience in the biological and physical sciences.

Level of Study: Postdoctorate.

Type: Grant.

No. of awards offered: 10.

Frequency: Annual.

Value: Grants do not usually exceed US$30,000.

Country of Study: USA.

Closing Date: February 1st, May 1st, August 1st, November 1st.

EUROPEAN DEVELOPMENT FUND OF THE EUROPEAN COMMUNITY

c/o Information Department, NUFFIC, PO Box 29777, The Hague, 2502 LT, The Netherlands
Tel: 070 4260 260
Fax: 070 4260 229
www: http://www.nufficcs.nl
Contact: European Development Fund of the EC

Awards for Citizens of ACP Countries

Subjects: Any subject.

Eligibility: Open to citizens of the African, Caribbean and Pacific countries associated with the EC.

No. of awards offered: Varies.

Value: Course fee, books and field trips, international travel expenses, insurance, monthly allowance, and stipend to cover initial expenses of getting established.

Length of Study: For the duration of the course.

Country of Study: States associated with the European Community, ACP countries.

Applications Procedure: Information and application forms must be obtained from the EC diplomatic representative in the candidate's own country. The application is submitted through the candidate's employer and government.

Additional Information: Scholarships are always associated with development projects funded by the EC.

THE EUROPEAN INSTITUTE FOR BUSINESS ADMINISTRATION (INSEAD)

MBA Admissions Office, The European Institute for Business Administration, Boulevard de Constance, Fontainebleau Cedex, 77305, France
Tel: 1 60 72 42 73
Fax: 1 60 74 55 30
Email: admissions@insead.fr

Postgraduate Scholarships

Subjects: Business administration.

Eligibility: Open to young professionals who hold a university degree, have some experience in business or other organisations, and are 24-34 years of age. Candidates should be fluent in English. A working knowledge of French must be demonstrated on entry and knowledge of a third language is required for graduation.

Level of Study: Postgraduate.

Purpose: To enable postgraduate students to participate in the International MBA Programme.

Type: Scholarship.

No. of awards offered: Approximately 30 Scholarships which are offered by specific organizations in different countries.

Frequency: Annual.

Value: Up to the equivalent of FF140,000 per annum. Full fees and accommodation.

Length of Study: One academic year. The MBA programme is offered as follows: August, graduating in July of the following year; January, graduating in December of the same year.

Study Establishment: INSEAD, Fontainebleau.

Country of Study: France.

Applications Procedure: Application must be submitted with two recommendations, GMAT and TOEFL scores (for non-native English speakers), and grade transcripts.

Closing Date: April and August.

Additional Information: Scholarships available to nationals of particular countries include the following: Australia: Macquarie/Hill Samuel Graduate Management Scholarship-apply to Hill Samuel Graduate Education Foundation, PO Box H68, Australia Square, Sydney NSW 2000. Canada: Canadian Foundation of International Management-apply to MBA Scholarship, Box 816, Tour de la Bourse, Montréal, Québec H4Z 1K1. UK: Louis Franck Scholarships (up to 10 annually, generally £5,000 each)-apply to INSEAD, Admissions Office; Kitchener European Scholarships (up to 4 annually, £1,800 each)-apply to INSEAD, Admissions Office; London Chamber of Commerce and Industry Scholarships; Charles R E Bell Fund Scholarship-apply through the London Chamber of Commerce and Industry, Marlowe House, Station Road, Sidcup, Kent DA15 7BJ; Rotary International Scholarships-apply through local Rotary branch one year in advance. There are also various sources of support available for Jewish candidates in the UK-apply to Alan Philipp, 9 Courtleigh Gardens, London NW11 9JK; Sainsbury Management Fellowships for Engineers-apply to the Royal Academy of Engineering, 2 Little Smith Street, London SW1P 3DW. This list is not exhaustive. INSEAD can also provide information on preferential loan programmes.

EUROPEAN MOLECULAR BIOLOGY ORGANIZATION

European Molecular Biology Organization, Postfach 1022.40, Heidelberg, D-69012, Germany
Tel: 6221 383031
Fax: 6221 384879
Email: embo@embl-Heidelberg.de
www: http://www.embl-heidelberg.de/extemalInfo/embo/
Contact: Dr F Gannon, Executive Secretary

Long-Term Fellowships in Molecular Biology

Subjects: Molecular biology.

Eligibility: Open to holders of a doctorate degree.

Level of Study: Postdoctorate.

Purpose: To promote the development of molecular biology and allied research in Europe and Israel.

Type: Fellowship.

No. of awards offered: Varies.

Frequency: Twice yearly.

Value: Return travel allowance for the Fellow and any dependants, and a stipend and dependants' allowance.

Length of Study: For one year, renewable for a second year; or in the case of exceptional scientific merit, for two years.

Study Establishment: At a laboratory anywhere. EMBO Fellowships are not awarded for exchanges between laboratories within any one country.

Country of Study: Worldwide.

Applications Procedure: Enquiries should be accompanied by a self-addressed adhesive label.

Closing Date: February 15th, August 15th.

EUROPEAN ORGANIZATION FOR NUCLEAR RESEARCH

CERN-Personnel Division, Geneva, CH-1211, Switzerland

Fellowships

Subjects: Theoretical physics, applied science, computing and engineering.

Eligibility: Applicants must be nationals of member states of CERN.

Level of Study: Postgraduate, Doctorate.

Purpose: To support research in theoretical particle physics and development work in applied science, computing and engineering.

Type: Fellowship.

No. of awards offered: Approximately 70 per year.

Frequency: Annual.

Length of Study: One year, normally extended for a second year.

Applications Procedure: Write for details.

Technical Student Programme

Subjects: Physics, electrical, electronic or mechanical engineering, mathematics and computing.

Eligibility: Applicants must be nationals of the member states of CERN. Please check for details.

Level of Study: Doctorate.

Purpose: To assist students who are preparing a thesis at the doctoral level.

No. of awards offered: Varies.

Frequency: Annual.

Length of Study: 12 months initially, normally renewable for a further year.

Study Establishment: CERN.

Country of Study: Switzerland.

Applications Procedure: Application form must be completed and two references submitted.

Closing Date: Varies.

EUROPEAN UNIVERSITY INSTITUTE

European University Institute, Badia Fiesolana, Via Badia dei Roccettini 9, 50016 San Domenico di Fiesole, Florence, Italy
Tel: 055 50 921
Fax: 055 59 98 87
Contact: Academic Service

*Jean Monnet Fellowships

Subjects: All areas of the humanities and social sciences, with special attention to problems related to the European Community and to the development of Europe's cultural and academic heritage.

Eligibility: Open mainly to candidates with a doctoral degree at an early stage of their academic career. Established academics on leave are also eligible.

Level of Study: Postdoctorate.

Purpose: To encourage postdoctoral research.

Type: Fellowship.

No. of awards offered: 20.

Frequency: Annual.

Value: 24,000,000-36,500,000 lire per annum, depending on age, plus allowances for dependants, travel and medical insurance.

Study Establishment: European University Institute, Florence.

Country of Study: Italy.

Closing Date: November 10th.

*Postgraduate Scholarships

Subjects: History and civilization, economics, law or political and social sciences.

Eligibility: Open to nationals of the 12 EC member states. Candidates must possess a good honours degree or its equivalent, and have full written and spoken command of at least two of the Institute's official languages. Under certain conditions, nationals of countries other than the EC may also be admitted to the Institute and be eligible for a Scholarship.

Level of Study: Postgraduate, Doctorate.

Purpose: To provide the opportunity for study leading to the doctorate degree from the Institute.

Type: Scholarship.

No. of awards offered: c.160.

Frequency: Annual.

Value: Varies.

Length of Study: 12 months; renewable for up to an additional 2 years.

Study Establishment: The Institute, in Florence.

Country of Study: Italy.

Applications Procedure: Application forms are available from the Institute.

Closing Date: January 31st.

Additional Information: The Scholarships are granted by the governments of the 12 EC member states to nationals of their own countries, currently distributed as follows: Federal Republic of Germany 25; France 25; Italy 29; UK 26; Spain 24; Netherlands 15; Denmark 9; Belgium 8; Republic of Ireland 6; Greece 9; Luxembourg 3; Portugal 9.

EUROTOX

Eurotox, RIKILT-DLO, PO Box 230, Wageningen, NL-6700AE, The Netherlands
Tel: 31 317 475 453
Fax: 31 317 417 717
Contact: Dr A J Baars, The Secretary General

Eurotox Merit Award

Eligibility: The award is presented to a European Toxicologist.

Purpose: The Eurotox Merit Award aims at recognising a distinguished career in European toxicology.

No. of awards offered: One.

Frequency: Annual.

Applications Procedure: Nominations must be submitted in writing by National Society Eurotox members, by Eurotox specialty sections, or by at least ten individual Eurotox members. Nominations have to be motivated, including a short CV and a list of five to ten key publications, and must reach the Secretary General before November 30th preceding the year for consideration.

Closing Date: November 30th.

Additional Information: The awardee is invited to the congress where he/she will be presented with a diploma. The registration fee for the awardee will be waived.

Young Scientist's Poster Award

Subjects: Toxicology, clinical or experimental.

Eligibility: Open to scientists no more than 35 years of age on 31 December of the year of the Congress and living in Europe.

Purpose: To encourage young scientists to do research and to present high quality posters at Eurotox Congresses.

Type: Award.

No. of awards offered: One.

Frequency: Annual.

Value: DFL1,000, plus certificate.

Closing Date: To be determined at Eurotox Congress.

Gerhard Zbinden Memorial Lecture

Eligibility: Open to scientists who have made recent outstanding research contributions to this field.

Purpose: The Gerhard Zbinden Memorial Lecture aims at recognising scientific excellence in the area of drug and chemical safety.

Type: Diploma.

Applications Procedure: Nominations must be submitted in writing by National Society Eurotox members, by Eurotox specialty sections, or by at least ten individual members. Nominations have to be motivated including a short CV and a list of five to ten key publications.

Closing Date: November 30th preceding the year for consideration.

EVANGELICAL LUTHERAN CHURCH IN AMERICA (ELCA)

Evangelical Lutheran Church in America (ELCA), Division for Ministry, 8765 West Higgins Road, Chicago, IL, 60631-4195, USA
Tel: 312 380 2885
Fax: 312 380 1465
Contact: Dr Phyllis Anderson

Educational Grant Program

Subjects: Theological studies.

Eligibility: Restricted to members of the Evangelical Lutheran Church in America who are pursuing advanced degree programs (PhD/ThD) in theological education and intend to teach in that field.

Level of Study: Doctorate.

Purpose: To provide funding for students in advanced degree track in theological education who intend to teach.

Type: Grant.

No. of awards offered: Approximately 40.

Frequency: Annual.

Value: US$500-US$3,000.

Length of Study: Four years.

Country of Study: USA.

Applications Procedure: Application forms are available through the Department for Theological Education in the Division for Ministry. Forms are available in January, and must be returned by March 15th with two references.

Closing Date: March 15th.

EXETER COLLEGE

Exeter College, Oxford, OX1 3DP, England
Tel: 865 279 648
Fax: 865 279 630

Monsanto Senior Research Fellowship

Purpose: For research in Molecular or Cellular Biology or in Biochemistry.

Type: Fellowship.

Frequency: Every fifth year.

Value: Stipend between £13,941 and £19,326 p.a. as at October 1st 1994. Entitled to free lunch and dinner, free rooms in college if unmarried, and housing allowance (£2,422 p.a. as at October 1st 1994) if not resident in college.

Length of Study: Three to five years.

Study Establishment: Exeter College.

Country of Study: United Kingdom.

Applications Procedure: Enquires addressed to the Tutor for Graduates.

Closing Date: Not available until 1999.

Queen Sofia Research Fellowship

Eligibility: Applicants should be close to completing doctoral work, or postdoctoral and must be under 31 at the time of taking up the fellowship.

Level of Study: Postdoctorate.

Purpose: For research into modern and contemporary Spanish literature.

Type: Fellowship.

Frequency: Every three or four years.

Value: Entitled to free lunch and dinner, free rooms in college if unmarried, and housing allowance (£2,422 p.a. as at October 1st 1994) if not resident in the college.

Length of Study: Two to three years.

Study Establishment: Exeter College, University of Oxford.

Country of Study: United Kingdom.

Applications Procedure: Enquiries may be addressed to the Tutor for Graduates.

Closing Date: Not available until 1997; please write for details.

Senior Scholarship in Theology

Eligibility: Applicants must hold by the time of admission at least a second class honours degree in a suject other than theology.

Level of Study: Postgraduate.

Purpose: To read for the Final Honour School of Theology or of Philosophy and Theology.

Type: Scholarship.

Frequency: Every two years.

Value: Minimum value £200 may be supplemented up to a maximum of all college fees, university fees to the amount charged to home and EU students, and maintenance to the current maximum Local Education Authority maintenance grant.

Length of Study: One to two years.

Study Establishment: Exeter College, University of Oxford.

Country of Study: United Kingdom.

Applications Procedure: Enquiries addressed to the Tutor for Graduates.

Closing Date: Not available until 1997.

Staines Medical Research Fellowship

Eligibility: Applicants should be close to completing doctoral work, or postdoctoral and must be under 31 at the time of taking up the fellowship.

Level of Study: Doctorate, Postdoctorate.

Purpose: For research into medical science.

Type: Fellowship.

Frequency: Every third year.

Value: Stipend between £300 and £9,228 p.a. as at October 1st 1994. Entitled to free lunch and dinner, free rooms in college if unmarried, and housing allowance (£2,422 p.a. as at October 1st 1994) if not resident in college.

Length of Study: Two to three years.

Study Establishment: Exeter College.

Country of Study: United Kingdom.

Applications Procedure: Enquiries should be addressed to the Tutor for Graduates.

Closing Date: This award is not available until 1998.

FACULTY OF AGRONOMICAL SCIENCES, GEMBLOUX

Faculty of Agronomical Sciences, Gembloux, 5030, Belgium
Tel: 32 81 62 22 66
Fax: 32 81 61 45 44

*Scholarships

Subjects: Agronomical sciences.

Eligibility: Open to nationals of developing countries. Candidates must have a suitable qualification in agriculture, chemistry or industrial agriculture.

Type: Scholarship.

No. of awards offered: One.

Frequency: Annual.

Value: BF120,000.

Length of Study: One year; renewable.

Study Establishment: Faculty of Agronomical Sciences.

Country of Study: Belgium.

Closing Date: May 1st.

FARGO-MOORHEAD SYMPHONY ORCHESTRAL ASSOCIATION

Fargo-Moorhead Symphony Orchestral Association, PO Box 1753, Fargo, ND, 58107-1753, USA
Tel: 218 233 8397
Fax: 218 236 1845
Contact: Executive Director

Sigvald Thompson Composition Award Competition

Subjects: Musical composition.

Eligibility: Open to any composer who is a US citizen.

Purpose: To stimulate and encourage the writing and performance of new works by American composers.

No. of awards offered: One.

Frequency: Biennially (1998).

Value: US$2,500 plus the premiere performance of the work by the Fargo-Moorhead Symphony Orchestra.

Closing Date: September 30th.

Additional Information: Compositions should be of medium length and scoring should not include soloists. Only manuscripts written or completed during the two years prior to the Competition and which have not been performed publicly will be considered.

THE FELLOWSHIP PROGRAM IN ACADEMIC MEDICINE

National Medical Fellowship, Inc, 254 West 31st Street, New York, NY, 10001, USA

*Fellowships for Minority Students

Subjects: Academic medicine and biomedical research.

Eligibility: Preference is given to Blacks, American Indians, mainland Puerto Ricans and Mexican Americans who are US citizens and are second- or third-year medical students at MD degree-granting medical schools in the USA accredited by the Liaison Committee on Medical Education of the Association of American Medical Colleges, or third-year students in DO degree-granting programs at colleges of osteopathic medicine in the USA accredited by the Bureau of Professional Education in the American Osteopathic Association.

Purpose: To help academically gifted minority medical students prepare for and begin careers and thus over time increase minority representation among the leaders in America.

Type: Fellowship.

No. of awards offered: At least 35.

Frequency: Annual.

Value: US$6,000. Up to US$2,000 is earmarked for the mentor to offset expenses incurred during the research period.

Length of Study: 8-12 weeks.

Country of Study: USA.

Closing Date: November 15th for announcement March 15th.

Additional Information: The program fosters mentor relationships between minority medical students and prominent biomedical scientists, who will take personal responsibility for guiding the students towards academic careers. Candidates should have demonstrated academic excellence and motivation to pursue a career in academic medicine and biomedical research. The advisory committee will seek to select students who provide evidence of a strong student-mentor relationship. A dean of a medical college may nominate up to three candidates. For each nominee, the dean should also nominate a mentor, who can be a member of the faculty of the same or another school. Details of application and nomination procedure are available on request. The program is managed by National Medical Fellowships, Inc.

FIGHT FOR SIGHT, INC

Fight for Sight, Inc, Research Division of Prevent Blindness America, 500 East Remington Road, Schaumburg, IL, 06173, USA
Tel: 708 843 2020
Contact: Research Awards Coordinator

Grants-in-Aid

Subjects: Ophthalmology, vision and related sciences.

Eligibility: Open to young or mature investigators. The policy regarding non-US applications is set out in the brochure available from Fight for Sight.

Type: Grant.

No. of awards offered: 20.

Frequency: Annual.

Value: By individual assessment, US$1,000-US$12,000 maximum; to help defray the cost of personnel, equipment and supplies needed for a specific research investigation.

Length of Study: One year, support may be renewed.

Study Establishment: Any institution in the USA or Canada which offers research facilities suitable to the research project in question.

Country of Study: USA or Canada.

Closing Date: March 1st.

Additional Information: It is the responsibility of candidates to make arrangements with the institutions of their choice in the USA or Canada. Applications for support of pilot projects are welcome.

Postdoctoral Research Fellowships

Subjects: Ophthalmology, vision and related sciences: basic or clinical research.

Eligibility: Open to physicians and other scientists with doctoral degrees who are interested in academic careers, whose proposed projects are original, and whose background and interests are likely to contribute to the project undertaken. Applications from foreign nationals for work outside the USA must be deemed particularly significant, or where the circumstances are such to provide unusual opportunities for the proposed research study. Foreign investigators seeking Fellowships at USA institutions must show that they will be able to continue to apply their research interests in their home countries and that the tenure within the USA may contribute significantly to the total research effort. The candidate's knowledge of the English language will also be a consideration.

Type: Fellowship.

No. of awards offered: 15.

Frequency: Annual.

Value: US$5,000-US$14,000 per annum. Recipients may supplement this stipend with institutional funds from another source, not to exceed US$28,000 per annum.

Length of Study: For one year; possibly renewable.

Study Establishment: At any approved institution in the USA or Canada.

Country of Study: USA or Canada.

Closing Date: March 1st.

Additional Information: It is the responsibility of candidates to make arrangements with the institutions of their choice in the USA or Canada.

Student Fellowships

Subjects: Ophthalmology, vision and related sciences.

Eligibility: Open to undergraduate students of medicine and graduate students who are interested in eye-related clinical or basic research. Student Fellowships are not offered to Americans who wish to study abroad.

Type: Fellowship.

No. of awards offered: 15.

Frequency: Annual.

Value: US$500 per month.

Length of Study: Two to three months, usually during the summer holidays.

Study Establishment: For full-time vacation work at approved institutions.

Country of Study: USA or Canada.

Closing Date: March 1st.

Additional Information: It is the responsibility of candidates to make arrangements with the institutions of their choice in the USA or Canada.

FINE ARTS WORK CENTER IN PROVINCETOWN, INC

Fine Arts Work Center, Box 565, Provincetown, MA, 02657, USA
Tel: 508 487 9960
Fax: 508 487 8873
Contact: Michael Wilkerson, Executive Director

Fellowships

Subjects: Visual arts and creative writing.

Eligibility: Open to all, but preference is given to emerging artists of outstanding promise; applicants are accepted on the basis of work submitted.

Level of Study: Unrestricted.

Purpose: To give artists the opportunity to work at the Center in a congenial and stimulating environment and to devote most of their time to their art.

Type: Fellowship.

No. of awards offered: 20 (10 for the visual arts, 10 for writing).

Frequency: Annual.

Value: US$300-US$480 per month, plus housing and studio space.

Length of Study: Seven months.

Study Establishment: Provincetown, Massachusetts.

Country of Study: USA.

Applications Procedure: Send SASE for application, fee US$35.

Closing Date: February 1st.

Additional Information: The Center is a working community, not a school.

Munro Moore Award for Emerging Playwrights

Subjects: Drama.

Level of Study: Unrestricted.

Purpose: To provide an emerging playwright with seven months of time to pursue his or her work at the Fine Arts Work Center among a community of peers.

Type: Fellowship.

No. of awards offered: One.

Frequency: Annual.

Value: US$2,626 plus housing for seven months, plus utilities.

Length of Study: Seven months.

Study Establishment: Artists Residency.

Country of Study: USA.

Applications Procedure: Send SASE for application.

Closing Date: February.

For further information contact:
Fine Arts Work Center, 24 Pearl Street, Provincetown, MA, 02657, USA
Tel: 508 487 8873
Fax: 508 487 8873
Contact: Sara London

IAN FLEMING CHARITABLE TRUST

Fleming Awards, 16 Ogle Street, London, W1P 7LG, England
Tel: 0171 636 4481
Fax: 0171 637 4307
Contact: Valerie Beale, Administrator

*Music Education Awards

Subjects: Musical performance.

Eligibility: Open to singers and instrumentalists possessing the potential to become first-class performers who have been resident in the UK for three years and are no more than 26 years of age (30 years for singers). The awards are intended to benefit those in financial need.

Purpose: To help exceptionally talented young musicians.

No. of awards offered: Approximately 20.

Frequency: Annual.

Value: Varies; to cover tuition, maintenance and the purchase of instruments.

Country of Study: Unrestricted.

Closing Date: Mid-February.

Additional Information: Selected applicants will be asked to audition

in April.

DONATELLA FLICK ASSOCIAZIONE

Donatella Flick Associazione, 47 Brunswick Gardens, London, W8 4AW, England
Tel: 0171 792 2885
Fax: 0171 792 2574
Contact: Judy Strang

Donatella Flick Conducting Competition

Subjects: Conducting.

Eligibility: Open to conductors who are citizens of member states of the EC and aged under 35.

Level of Study: Professional development.

Purpose: To assist a young conductor to establish an international conducting career. Prize offers funding for further study and conducting engagements and post of assistant conductor with London Symphony Orchestra for one year.

Type: Prize.

No. of awards offered: One.

Frequency: Biennially 1998/2000.

Value: £15,000.

Applications Procedure: Application form to be submitted with references and video.

Closing Date: January 1998.

Additional Information: Entry is by recommendation, documentation and supporting video; finalists are selected for audition. Three finalists conduct a public concert. The course of study of entrants must be approved by the organizing committee.

JOHN E FOGARTY INTERNATIONAL CENTER FOR ADVANCED STUDY IN THE HEALTH SCIENCES

International Research and Awards Branch, Building 31, Room B2C39, Fogarty International Center, Bethesda, MD, 20892, USA
Tel: 301 496 1653
Fax: 301 402 0779

The John E Fogarty International Center (FIC) for Advanced Study in the Health Sciences, a component of the National Institutes of Health (NIH), promotes international cooperation in the biomedical and behavioral sciences. This is accomplished primarily through long- and short-term fellowships, scientists exchanges and small grants. This compendium of international opportunities is prepared by the FIC with the hope that it will stimulate scientists to seek research-enhancing experiences abroad

*AIDS Fellowship Program (Institutional)

Subjects: AIDS research: biomedical and behavioral.

Eligibility: Open to AIDS researchers from any country and at all career levels, although priority will be given to AIDS researchers from developing countries.

Level of Study: Doctorate.

Purpose: To support collaborative postdoctoral research and training for US and foreign scientists who want to expand their capabilities in the epidemiology, diagnosis, prevention and treatment of AIDS.

Type: Fellowship.

Frequency: Annual.

Country of Study: USA and overseas.

Applications Procedure: Interested researchers must apply for training through FIC-supported institutions.

*Biomedical Research Exchanges

Subjects: Biomedical sciences.

Eligibility: Open to US researchers. Similar provisions are made for scientists from Austria and Bulgaria.

Purpose: To fund collaborative research.

Frequency: Annual.

Value: To include the cost of lodging, a living allowance, international and in-country travel costs and health insurance for participants and accompanying dependants.

Length of Study: 2-12 weeks (short-term) or for 3-6 months (long-term).

Country of Study: Austria, Bulgaria.

Fogarty International Research Collaboration Award (FIRCA)

Subjects: Biomedical and behavioral sciences.

Eligibility: Principal Investigators of currently funded NIH grants are eligible to apply for a FIRCA so as to include a foreign collaborator on an aspect of the research not already supported by the parent research grant.

Purpose: These small grants were established, under the auspices of the FIC's Central and Eastern European and Latin American and Caribbean Initiatives, to facilitate collaborative research between US scientists and scientists from Central and Eastern Europe (Bulgaria, the Czech and Slovak Federal Republic, Hungary, Poland, Romania, the USSR, and Yugoslavia), Latin America, and the non-US Caribbean.

Frequency: Three times yearly.

Value: Up to US$20,000 per annum to the US institution. Funds may be used for travel for the US Principal Investigator, the foreign collaborator, and/or their research associates, as required to conduct the research; supplies and equipment (for the foreign collaborator's lab only), which are necessary to the collaboration.

Length of Study: One to three years; non-renewable.

Applications Procedure: Applications must be submitted on the grant application form PHS 398 (rev 10/88), which is available in most institutional business offices and from the Office of Grants Inquiries, Division of Research Grants, Westwood Building, Room 4, NIH, Bethesda, MD 20892; Tel: 301 496 7441. Special instructions are required for this program and are available from FIC.

Closing Date: October 1st, February 1st, June 1st.

Additional Information: FIRCA grants are awarded to US institutions to provide funds for equipment and supplies for the foreign collaborator at his/her home institution to enable the foreign scientist to continue the collaborative research project at the home institution. The NIH awarding unit need not continue its support of the foreign component when the parent grant next competes for funding..

Foreign-Funded Fellowship Programs

Subjects: Biomedical and behavioral sciences.

Eligibility: Open to scientists who are US citizens or permanent residents invited by foreign host scientists to participate in research projects of mutual interest.

Purpose: To allow US scientists to conduct collaborative research abroad.

Frequency: Some are awarded annually, others throughout the year.

Value: To cover the visiting scientist's individual expenses abroad.

Length of Study: Generally for up to 12 months (UK up to two years, plus a third year in the USA); extensions are possible in some countries.

Country of Study: Finland, France, Germany, Ireland, Israel, Japan, Norway, Sweden, Switzerland, the UK or Taiwan.

Closing Date: Varies according to the country visited, but generally May 10th.

Additional Information: Because fellowships are intended to support an individual's expenses abroad, the foreign host is expected to have the resources to support the research project. Types of activities in which Fellows engage include collaboration in basic or clinical research and familiarization with or utilization of special techniques and equipment not otherwise available to the applicant. The programs do not provide support for activities which have as their principal purpose conducting brief observational visits; attending scientific meetings or formal training courses; or providing full-time clinical, technical or teaching services. Funding is provided by the Alexander von Humboldt Foundation (Germany), the Academy of Finland, the Institut National de la Santé et de la Recherche Médicale (INSERM) (France), the Centre National de la Recherche Scientifique (France), the Health Research Board (Ireland), the Israeli Ministry of Health, the Japan Society for the Promotion of Science, the Japan Science and Technology Agency, the Norwegian Research Council for Science and the Humanities, the Swedish Medical Research Council, the Swiss National Science Foundation, the Wellcome Trust (UK), the Burroughs Wellcome Fund (UK) (through the Hitchings-Elion Fellowships) and the National Science Council of Taiwan. Candidates may apply to only one of these programs during any given year.

*Health Scientist Exchanges

Subjects: The programs address health and biomedical problems that are of mutual interest to scientists from different countries and benefit from a cooperative approach.

Eligibility: Open to holders of an advanced degree (normally a doctoral degree) in one of the biomedical, behavioral, or clinical sciences who have professional experience in the appropriate field and are affiliated with a US public or private not-for-profit educational, research, or clinical institution. Similar provisions are made for scientists from the foreign country to visit a laboratory in the United States.

Purpose: To foster, through bilateral exchange programs, collaborative activities between health professionals and biomedical scientists in the USA and participating countries.

Value: The conditions of the bilateral exchanges require that the sending side pay all international transportation costs to the port of entry and that the receiving side pay a living allowance, in-country travel, laboratory costs, and health insurance.

Length of Study: 2-12 weeks.

Country of Study: Hungary, Poland, Romania, the former USSR, or the former Yugoslavia.

Additional Information: Individuals from each country are supported for varying periods of work in other countries. Activities may include research collaboration or consultation on individually conducted research in either country. Those selected to work in the host country must pursue activities that will benefit the United States and the participating country, and lead to future continuing collaborative ties. The programs do not provide support for formal, academic, clinical, or research training, or for the primary purpose of attendance at scientific meetings. Working knowledge of the host country language is highly desirable. Long-term participants are encouraged to study the language intensively in preparation for the visits.

*International Neurosciences Fellowship Program

Subjects: Emphasis is on research and research training in epilepsy and stroke.

Eligibility: Preference is given to applicants from developing countries who are currently working or planning careers in health agencies or health-profession schools.

Level of Study: Postdoctorate.

Purpose: To provide opportunities for junior or mid-career health professionals and scientists in the neurosciences to enhance their research skills in a laboratory in the USA.

Type: Fellowship.

Value: The level of stipend (US$19,000-US$23,000 per annum) depends on the number of years of professional or other relevant post-doctoral experience of the awardee. The host institution receives a modest allowance to cover such costs as health insurance, supplies, and equipment. The home institution of a successful applicant provides round-trip transportation to the US host institution.

Length of Study: 6-12 months.

International Research Fellowship Program

Subjects: Biomedical and behavioral sciences.

Eligibility: Open to foreign scientists who have been selected by the Nominating Committee in their country; have a doctoral degree; have ten years or less of postdoctoral experience; have demonstrated the ability to engage in independent basic or clinical research; have been invited by a scientist employed in a US non-profit institution; have assurance from a non-profit institution in the home country of a position after completion of the Fellowship; and are proficient in spoken and written English.

Purpose: To allow foreign scientists to extend their research experiences in US laboratories.

Value: A stipend of US$20,000-US$33,100 per annum (the level is determined by the number of years since receipt of the doctoral degree); and round-trip air travel expenses for the Fellow only. The US host institution receives an allowance to cover mandatory health insurance for the Fellow and accompanying family members, trips to domestic scientific meetings, and incidental research expenses.

Length of Study: 12-24 months.

Country of Study: USA.

Additional Information: More than 60 countries participate in this program. Countries and areas with Nominating Committees are: Argentina, Australia, Austria, Belgium, Bolivia, Brazil, Bulgaria, the Cameroon, Canada, Chile, China, Colombia, Costa Rica, the Czech and Slovak Federal Republics, Denmark, Egypt, Ethiopia, Finland, France, the Federal Republic of Germany, Ghana, Greece, Hong Kong, Hungary, Iceland, India, Ireland, Israel, Italy, Japan, Kenya, the Republic of Korea, Lebanon, Mexico, Mongolia, the Netherlands, New Zealand, Nigeria, Norway, Peru, the Philippines, Poland, Romania, Singapore, Spain, Sudan, Sweden, Switzerland, Tanzania, Thailand, the UK, Uruguay, the former USSR, Venezuela, former Yugoslavia, Zimbabwe, and Taiwan. Regional committees are located in Africa, the Caribbean, and Central/South America. Nominating Committees are being formed in other regions; candidates should enquire if their country of interest is not listed.

*International Training Grants in Epidemiology Related to AIDS (Institutional)

Subjects: AIDS: epidemiological research.

Eligibility: Open to foreign scientists.

Purpose: To increase scientists' capability to conduct epidemiological research related to AIDS and to use epidemiology in clinical trials and prevention research.

Applications Procedure: Interested applicants must apply to the grantee institution.

Additional Information: The following types of training for foreign scientists (especially those from developing countries), are available though this program: training in epidemiological concepts, methods, field studies, and research related to AIDS that will lead to the MS or PhD degree for individuals with previous field research experience; training in epidemiological field studies and research related to AIDS that will lead to the MS degree for individuals without prior field research experience; short-term comprehensive courses in epidemiology with an emphasis on AIDS for health professionals; training in laboratory procedures and research techniques related to AIDS for individuals with either the MS or PhD degree; practical and applied short-term training related to AIDS conducted in the foreign country for professionals, technicians, and

allied health professionals. Program Directors in charge of the training programs have developed collaborative activities with the following countries: Argentina, Brazil, the Caribbean, China, Colombia, Cote D'Ivoire, the Dominican Republic, Ecuador, Haiti, Honduras, Kenya, Malawi, Mexico, Mozambique, Peru, the Philippines, Rwanda, Senegal, Singapore, Thailand, Uganda, Zaire, Zimbabwe, and Taiwan. The collaborative programs have been recently expanded to include Eastern Europe and the former Soviet Union. Further information about whom to contact, the epidemiology training programs, necessary qualifications, and application procedures is available on request.

National Research Service Awards: Individual Fellowships

Subjects: Biomedical and behavioral sciences.

Eligibility: Open to postdoctoral researchers who are US citizens or permanent residents.

Type: Fellowship.

Frequency: Annual.

Study Establishment: A laboratory or institution outside the USA.

Additional Information: The FIC is part of the Federal Public Health Service (PHS) and serves as its focus for providing scientists with opportunities to study abroad. However, all of the Institutes of the NIH make international research and training available through judicious use of mechanisms which allow foreign research as a special, justified condition. In such cases, there must be a clear scientific reason for seeking an assignment abroad. The research and training assignment or request must describe the advantages of the facilities and/or research opportunities at the foreign site. Institute program staff should be consulted whenever special assignments are to be made to foreign laboratories or institutions. The Principal Investigator must acquire approval from the Institute prior to leaving for an absence of more than three months.

National Research Service Awards: Senior Faculty Fellowships

Subjects: Biomedical or behavioral sciences.

Eligibility: Open to experienced US scientists and permanent residents who are supported by the NIH.

Purpose: To allow experienced scientists to broaden their scientific background, acquire new reserch capabilities, make major changes in the direction of their research careers, learn new techniques, or participate in opportunities inherent in a research activity at a foreign institution and/or laboratory.

Frequency: Annual.

Country of Study: Outside the USA.

Additional Information: The FIC is part of the Federal Public Health Service (PHS) and serves as its focus for providing scientists with opportunities to study abroad. However, all of the Institutes of the NIH make international research and training available through judicious use of mechanisms which allow foreign research as a special, justified condition. In such cases, there must be a clear scientific reason for seeking an assignment abroad. The research and training assignment or request must describe the advantages of the facilities and/or research opportunities at the foreign site. Institute program staff should be consulted whenever special assignments are to be made to foreign laboratories or institutions. The Principal Investigator must acquire approval from the Institute prior to leaving for an absence of more than three months.

*NIH International Medical Scholars Program

Subjects: Basic and clinical biomedical research training.

Eligibility: Open to foreign medical graduates.

Purpose: To assist foreign medical graduates in obtaining placement in the advanced basic and clinical research training programs at the NIH.

Country of Study: USA.

NIH Visiting Program

Subjects: Biomedical research.

Eligibility: Open to talented foreign scientists throughout the world. An appointment or award to the Visiting Program must be requested by a senior investigator in an NIH laboratory.

Purpose: To provide talented foreign scientists throughout the world with the opportunity to share in the varied resources of the NIH. Through this program, scientists at all levels of their careers are invited to the NIH for further experience and to conduct collaborative research in their biomedical specialties.

Country of Study: USA.

Additional Information: Each participant works closely with a senior NIH investigator, who serves as a sponsor or supervisor during the period of award or appointment. Anyone interested in a Visiting Program fellowship appointment or award should send a résumé and brief description of research interests to individual NIH senior staff scientists working in those fields. These investigators are listed in the 'Scientific Director and Annual Bibliography', which is published each year by the NIH and is available in many libraries throughout the world. Also, the 'Postdoctoral Research Fellowship Opportunities Catalog' describes research being conducted in laboratories at the NIH and is available on request.

*Research Project, Program Project and Center Grant Mechanisms

Subjects: Biomedical and behavioral sciences.

Eligibility: Open to US scientists and permanent residents.

Purpose: When it is germane to the conduct of the research supported by the grant, the domestic awardee institution under an NIH grant may permit the Principal Investigator, Program Director, or a participating scientist to work in a laboratory outside the United States.

Value: The awardee institutions may continue to pay the appropriate portion of the investigator's salary and make funds available for travel (following the NIH guidelines for foreign travel) and supplies to be used in conducting the work at the host laboratory.

Additional Information: The FIC is part of the Federal Public Health Service (PHS) and serves as its focus for providing scientists with opportunities to study abroad. However, all of the Institutes of the NIH make international research and training available through judicious use of mechanisms which allow foreign research as a special, justified condition. In such cases, there must be a clear scientific reason for seeking an assignment abroad. The research and training assignment or request must describe the advantages of the facilities and/or research opportunities at the foreign site. Institute program staff should be consulted whenever special assignments are to be made to foreign laboratories or institutions. The Principal Investigator must acquire approval from the Intitute prior to leaving for an absence of more than three months. The awardee institution is responsible for assuring that the research is carried out in a responsible and accountable fashion, and the Principal Investigator is responsible for the scientific conduct of the research.

Senior International Fellowship Program

Subjects: Biomedical and behavioral sciences.

Eligibility: Open to scientists who are US citizens or permanent residents invited by foreign host scientists to participate in research projects of mutual interest. Candidates should hold a doctoral degree in one of the biomedical, behavioral, or health sciences; have five years or more of postdoctoral experience; have professional experience in one of the biomedical, behavioral, or health sciences for at least two of the last four years; hold a full-time appointment on the staff of a public or private not-for-profit research, clinical or educational institution; be invited by a not-for-profit foreign institution; and not have received more than one Senior International Fellowship previously.

Purpose: To provide opportunities for research experience and the exchange of information.

Frequency: Throughout the year.

Value: A stipend of US$1,250 per month (or a maximum of US$15,000 per annum); a foreign living allowance of US$2,000 per month (or a maximum of US$24,000 per annum); economy class round-trip air travel for the Fellow only on a US air carrier between the US city and the host city abroad; and a host institutional allowance of up to US$6,000 per annum or a pro-rated allowance for a shorter time. (US home institutions use these funds to help defray the costs of research supplies and equipment that are required at the foreign host institutions.).

Length of Study: From 3-12 months. The award may be divided into as many as three terms, utilized over a three-year period, with a minimum term of three months.

Additional Information: The stipend plus the home institution salary during the tenure of the fellowship cannot exceed the awardee's annual salary. No stipend will be provided if the awardee receives salary from other federal sources. Because fellowships are intended to support an individual's expenses abroad, the foreign host is expected to have the resources to support the research project. Types of activities in which fellows engage include collaboration in basic or clinical research and familiarization with or utilization of special techniques and equipment not otherwise available to the applicant. The programs do not provide support for activities which have as their principal purpose conducting brief observational visits; attending scientific meetings or formal training courses; or providing full-time clinical, technical or teaching services.

FOOD AND AGRICULTURE ORGANIZATION OF THE UNITED NATIONS (FAO)

Food and Agriculture Organization of the United Nations, Via delle Terme di Caracalla, Rome, 00100, Italy
Tel: 57971
Fax: 6799563
Contact: Senior Fellowship Officer

*Fellowships and Scholarships

Subjects: Agriculture, fisheries, forestry, nutrition, agricultural economics and statistics, rural institutions and services, and related areas.

Eligibility: Open to nationals of countries in which FAO carries out projects of technical assistance, provided they are working or destined to work on these projects. Candidates must have adequate basic and technical education and practical experience in the field of study.

Purpose: To develop the skills of counterparts working in FAO projects through short-term, mainly practical, training.

No. of awards offered: Varies.

Frequency: Annual.

Value: At least US$1,000 per month, plus training fees, costs of approved travel to, from and within the country of study, and a book allowance.

Length of Study: 2-5 months.

Country of Study: Any country.

Applications Procedure: Applications must be made to the relevant government department in the candidate's own country. Individual requests are not considered.

Additional Information: These Fellowships are offered under projects within the United Nations Development Programme, and projects jointly operated by FAO and other UN agencies, individual governments or funds in trust arrangements.

FORT COLLINS SYMPHONY ASSOCIATION

Young Artist Competition, PO Box 1963, Fort Collins, CO, 80522, USA
Tel: 970 482 4823

Fax: 970 482 4858

Contact: Fort Collins Symphony Orchestra

Adeline Rosenberg Memorial Prize

Subjects: Music performance.

Eligibility: Senior division: open to musicians 25 years of age or under; Junior division: open to all musicians 18 years of age or under.

Level of Study: Unrestricted.

Purpose: To foster excellence in young performers of classical music.

No. of awards offered: Senior division: three prizes; Junior division: four prizes.

Frequency: Annual.

Value: Senior division: 1st prize US$2,000, 2nd prize US$1,000, third prize US$500; Junior division: 1st prize US$250, 2nd prize US$100.

Applications Procedure: Application form, plus application fee: seniors-US$35, juniors-US$25.

Closing Date: January 20th.

Additional Information: The Senior Division alternates between orchestral instruments and piano and winning contestants are invited to perform with the Fort Collins Symphony Orchestra. Junior Division encompasses both instrumental and piano categories every year and 1st prize Junior winners may be offered a performance with the Symphony (depending on available concert).

FOULKES FOUNDATION FELLOWSHIP

Foulkes Foundation Fellowship, 37 Ringwood Avenue, London, N2 9NT, England
Tel: 0181 444 2526
Fax: 0181 444 2526
Contact: The Registrar

Foulkes Foundation Fellowship

Subjects: All aspects of medical research, especially in the areas of molecular biology and biological sciences.

Eligibility: Open to recently qualified scientists and medical graduates who have a PhD or equivalent degree or proven research ability and who intend to contribute to medical research. Applicant must study in the USA.

Level of Study: Postdoctorate.

Purpose: To promote medical research by providing financial support for science graduates needing a medical degree before they can undertake medical research, and for medical graduates in need of a science degree.

Type: Varies.

Frequency: Annual.

Value: Varies. The amount of the Fellowship depends on individual need, but the scale for the basic SRC Studentship is used as a guideline. Fellowships do not cover fees.

Length of Study: Up to three years.

Country of Study: UK.

Applications Procedure: A stamped self-addressed envelope should be sent to the Foundation for additional information and application form.

Closing Date: March 15th.

FOUNDATION FOR EUROPEAN LANGUAGE AND EDUCATIONAL CENTRES (EUROCENTRES)

Foundation for European Language and Educational Centres, Seestrasse 247, Zurich, CH-8938, Switzerland
Tel: 01 485 52 51
Fax: 01 482 50 54
Contact: Eric Steenbergen

Scholarship

Subjects: Languages: English, French, Italian, Spanish and German.

Eligibility: Open to applicants between 18 and 30 years of age who are able to submit proof of satisfactory scholastic and professional (practical experience) records and who have good previous knowledge of the language to be studied.

Purpose: To assist people to attend a language course or learn a language.

Type: Scholarship.

No. of awards offered: Varies.

Frequency: Varies.

Value: Between US$250 and US$750 per grant; to cover part of the tuition fees but not the cost of travel accommodation, personal expenses, etc.

Study Establishment: For one of the various courses organized by the Foundation.

Country of Study: Various countries in Europe; and the USA.

Closing Date: October 15th for courses beginning in January; January 15th for courses beginning in April; March 31st for courses beginning in July; June 15th for courses beginning in September/October.

Additional Information: The Scholarships should assist those people with a special aptitude for learning. Candidates must also show that further language study is an essential element of their work career.

FOUNDATION FOR PHYSICAL THERAPY

Foundation for Physical Therapy, 1055 North Fairax Street, Suite 350, Alexandria, VA, 22314, USA
Tel: 703 684 5984
Fax: 703 684 3218
Contact: Grants Administrator

Doctoral Research Award

Subjects: Rehabilitation medicine and therapy.

Eligibility: Open to permanent residents of the USA who are eligible for licensure as physical therapists.

Level of Study: Doctorate.

Purpose: To fund doctoral research for students who are physical therapists who have reached candidate status, or who have an approved research plan.

No. of awards offered: One.

Frequency: Annual.

Value: Up to US$15,000 per year.

Country of Study: USA.

Applications Procedure: Please contact the Foundation for an application form.

Closing Date: March 1st.

Research Grant

Subjects: Rehabilitation medicine and therapy.

Eligibility: Open to individuals or groups of investigators independently or through a sponsoring institution/organization with which they are affiliated. This person must be eligible for licensure as a physical therapist and must be a permanent resident of the USA.

Purpose: To fund the highest quality scientifically based/clinically relevant research with priority given to projects having practical application.

Type: Research Grant.

No. of awards offered: 2-4.

Frequency: Annual.

Value: Up to US$30,000 per annum.

Country of Study: USA.

Applications Procedure: Please contact the Foundation for an application form.

Closing Date: February 1st.

Additional Information: Proposed studies should add or refine the body of theoretical, scientific and clinical knowledge on which physical therapy practice is based, using any of a variety of recognized investigative methods, such as experimental, descriptive or correlational.

FOUNDATION FOR RESEARCH DEVELOPMENT (FRD)

Foundation for Research Development, PO Box 2600, Pretoria, 0001, South Africa
Tel: 012 481 4102
Fax: 012 481 4010
Email: rose@frd.ac.za
Contact: Mrs Rose Robertson

Bursaries for Honours Study

Subjects: Natural and applied sciences, engineering and technology.

Eligibility: Restricted to South African citizens who have obtained a bachelors degree, and are registered for full-time study at a South African university.

Level of Study: Postgraduate.

Purpose: To foster studies in the fields of science, engineering and technology.

Type: Bursary.

No. of awards offered: 200.

Frequency: Annual.

Value: Registration and tuition fees.

Length of Study: One year; not renewable.

Study Establishment: Any South African university for full-time study.

Country of Study: South Africa.

Applications Procedure: Application form must be completed and submitted with full academic record.

Closing Date: October 31st of the preceding year.

Additional Information: The award of a bursary does not bind the candidate to enter the Foundation's service.

For further information contact:
Foundation for Research Development, PO Box 2600, Pretoria, 0001, South Africa
Tel: 012 481 4037
Fax: 012 481 4037
Email: dlamini@frd.ac.za
Contact: Mr S Dlamini

*Fellowships

Subjects: Natural and applied sciences, engineering and technology.

Eligibility: Open to senior scientists.

Purpose: To strengthen areas of expertise needed in South Africa.

Type: Fellowship.

No. of awards offered: Varies.

Frequency: Annually, depending on the availability of funds.

Value: To cover air fares and accommodation.

Length of Study: Up to 3 months.

Study Establishment: Any South African university, technikon, museum or scientific society.

Country of Study: South Africa.

Applications Procedure: Applications should be submitted by a South African counterpart attached to a South African university, technikon, museum or scientific society.

Closing Date: Three months before the visit.

Fellowships for Postdoctoral Research

Subjects: Natural and applied sciences, engineering and technology.

Eligibility: Open to South African citizens or holders of permanent residence permits who have recently received their PhD degrees (ie in last five years).

Level of Study: Postgraduate.

Purpose: To foster postgraduate research in science, engineering and technology.

Type: Fellowship.

No. of awards offered: 20.

Frequency: Three times yearly.

Value: Up to R40,000.

Length of Study: Up to two years.

Study Establishment: Any South African university or research institution for full-time research.

Country of Study: South Africa.

Applications Procedure: Application forms need to be completed and submitted together with full academic record.

Closing Date: March 31st, July 31st, November 30th.

Additional Information: A limited number of postdoctoral bursaries are also available for outstanding foreign candidates for full-time research in South Africa.

Initiative for Developing Enterprising Activities (IDEA)

Subjects: Science, engineering and technology.

Eligibility: Open to South African graduates and diplomates whose products/projects have been evaluated and are deemed to have commercial potential.

Purpose: To enable entrepreneurial students in higher education with a scientific, engineering or technological background to establish wealth and job creating enterprizes based on technology.

Frequency: Annually by announcement.

Value: Varies: development and research costs only. Funds are provided to enable recipients to improve their skills and expertise to further develop their product/project.

Country of Study: South Africa.

Additional Information: Support is restricted to the manufacturing industry.

For further information contact:
Foundation for Research Development, PO Box 2600, Pretoria, 0001, South Africa
Tel: 012 481 4043
Fax: 012 481 4076

321

Contact: Mr Sieg Erdmann

Research Equipment Grants

Subjects: Natural and applied sciences, engineering and technology.

Eligibility: Open to research teams with a proven track record, or strong potential, in using equipment. South African researchers.

Level of Study: Postgraduate, Doctorate, Postdoctorate, Professional development.

Purpose: The acquisition of capital research equipment where only one or a limited number of items are required for the national or regional science engineering and technology research development effort.

Type: A variable number of grants.

Frequency: Annual.

Value: From a total of R2-R4 million per annum variable.

Study Establishment: Any South African university, technikon or museum.

Applications Procedure: Contact FRD for information.

Closing Date: Announced by FRD.

Additional Information: Equipment must be made available on a multi-user basis. Research capacity building is a strong motivation.

For further information contact:
Foundation for Research Development, PO Box 2600, Pretoria, 0001, South Africa
Tel: 012 481 4024
Fax: 012 349 1179
Email: paulo@frd.ac.za
www: http://www.frd.ac.za
Contact: Dr Anthon Botha

Scholarships for Doctoral and Postdoctoral Fellowships for Study Abroad

Subjects: Natural and applied sciences, engineering and technology.

Eligibility: Open to South African citizens who have obtained their masters or doctoral degree.

Level of Study: Postgraduate.

Purpose: To foster postgraduate studies and research in science, engineering and technology.

No. of awards offered: 20.

Frequency: Scholarships annually, Fellowships three times yearly.

Value: Postdoctoral up to $14,000; Scholarships still to be determined.

Length of Study: Up to 3 years (doctoral study), or for up to 2 years (postdoctoral research).

Study Establishment: Approved institutions abroad for full-time study or research.

Country of Study: Outside South Africa.

Applications Procedure: Application form must be completed and submitted with full academic record.

Closing Date: Scholarships: 31 July of preceding year, Fellowships 30 November, 31 March, 31 July.

Additional Information: Candidates should motivate their choice of overseas institution and supervisor of research.

Scholarships for Doctoral Study

Subjects: Natural and applied sciences, engineering and technology.

Eligibility: Open to South African citizens who are accepted as full-time doctoral students at South African universities.

Level of Study: Postgraduate.

Purpose: To foster postgraduate studies in science, engineering and technology.

Type: Scholarship.

No. of awards offered: 30.

Frequency: Annual.

Value: Still to be determined.

Length of Study: Up to three years.

Study Establishment: Any South African university for full-time study.

Country of Study: South Africa.

Applications Procedure: Application forms to be completed and submitted with academic record.

Closing Date: July 31st of preceding year.

Additional Information: The award of a bursary does not bind the candidate to enter the Foundation's service, however, candidates are expected to obtain the degree for which the award was made.

Scholarships for Masters Study

Subjects: Natural and applied sciences, engineering and technology.

Eligibility: Open to South African citizens who are accepted as full-time masters students at South African universities.

Purpose: To foster studies in the fields of applied and natural sciences, engineering and technology.

Type: Fellowship.

No. of awards offered: 50.

Frequency: Annual.

Value: Still to be determined.

Length of Study: Two years. Where masters registration is upgraded to PhD the maximum period of support for masters and doctoral study will be four years in total.

Study Establishment: Any South African University for full-time study.

Country of Study: South Africa.

Applications Procedure: Application forms need to be completed and submitted together with full academic record.

Closing Date: July of preceding year.

Additional Information: The award of a bursary does not bind the candidate to enter the Foundation's service, however, candidates are expected to obtain the degree for which the award was made.

Targeted Research Awards: Competitive Industry Theme

Subjects: Natural and applied sciences, engineering and technology.

Eligibility: Open to South African citizens only, who qualify for postgraduate support. Postdoctorate support is available for any nationality.

Level of Study: Postgraduate, Doctorate, Postdoctorate.

Purpose: To support research in priority areas where expertise is lacking.

No. of awards offered: Approximately 200.

Value: From a total of approximately R20 million per annum.

Length of Study: Any tertiary educational institution in South Africa.

Country of Study: South Africa, or abroad in the case of multi-national teams.

Applications Procedure: Application form FRD 2 must be completed.

Closing Date: Open, usually mid-year.

Additional Information: Joint ventures and collaboration with industry are strongly encouraged.

FOUNDATION FOR SCIENCE AND DISABILITY, INC

Foundation for Science and Disability, Inc, 503 NW 89 Street, Gainsville, FL, 32607, USA
Tel: 352 374 5774
Fax: 352 374 5781

Email: mankin@nervm.nerdc.ufl.edu
Contact: Dr Richard Mankin

Science Student Grant Fund

Subjects: Engineering, mathematics, medicine and natural sciences.

Level of Study: Postgraduate, Doctorate, Postdoctorate.

Purpose: To increase opportunities in science for physically disabled students at the graduate or professional level.

Type: Grant.

No. of awards offered: 1-3.

Frequency: Annual.

Value: US$1,000.

Country of Study: Unrestricted.

Applications Procedure: Please submit a completed application form, copies of official college transcripts, a letter from research or academic supervisor in support of request, and a second letter from another faculty mombor.

Closing Date: December 1st.

Additional Information: The award may be used for an assistive device or instrument, or as financial support to work with a professor, or on an individual research project, or for some other special need.

FOUNDATION FOR THE STUDY OF INFANT DEATHS

The Foundation for the Study of Infant Deaths, 14 Halkin Street, London, SW1X 7DP, England
Tel: 0171 235 0965
Fax: 0171 823 1986
Contact: Dr S Chantler

Research Grant Award

Subjects: The Foundation is concerned with the problem of sudden death in infancy and particularly that aspect of the problem which relates to unexplained sudden infant deaths. The Foundation is currently supporting a wide range of research programmes into related topics. These include the fields of epidemiology, developmental physiology, metabolism, immunology, pathology, infection, psycho-social science, infant care practices and statistics.

Eligibility: Open to any graduate research worker linked to academic/medical institution within the UK.

Level of Study: Unrestricted.

Purpose: To promote and support relevant research, to further the welfare of those affected by sudden death in infancy, and to raise funds for these purposes.

No. of awards offered: Dependent on funds available.

Frequency: Twice yearly.

Value: The Foundation's policy is that it prefers to make several smaller grants rather than a few very large grants. While there is no fixed upper limit, applications are unlikely to succeed if recurrent expenditure is much more than £30,000 per annum and total expenditure in any one year exceeds £50,000.

Length of Study: For the duration of the project, normally up to a maximum of 3 years; extensions beyond this will be approved only after special review.

Country of Study: Restricted to UK based research.

Applications Procedure: Application form (10 copies) to be completed.

Closing Date: Early February and Mid July.

Short Term Training Fellowship

Subjects: Paediatrics.

Eligibility: Open to graduate research workers linked to academic/medical institutions within the UK.

Level of Study: Unrestricted.

Purpose: To allow research workers in the field of sudden infant death to visit and work in specialist labs for short periods to acquire new technical skills, apply new methods of data analysis or establish collaborative research.

Frequency: Dependent on funds available.

Value: Uaually up to £2,500, maximum £5,000.

Length of Study: Six to 26 weeks.

Country of Study: UK.

Applications Procedure: Application form to be completed.

Closing Date: None.

FOUNDATION OF THE AMERICAN COLLEGE OF HEALTHCARE EXECUTIVES

Foundation of the American College of Healthcare Executives, 840 North Lake Shore Drive, Chicago, IL, 60611, USA

*Albert W Dent Student Scholarships

Subjects: Healthcare management.

Eligibility: Open to US and Canadian citizens who are Student Associates of the American College of Healthcare Executives in good standing; minority or handicapped undergraduate students who have been accepted for full-time study for the fall term in a healthcare management graduate program accredited by the Accrediting Commission on Education for Health Services Administration or who are enrolled full time and in good academic standing in an ACEHSA-accredited graduate program in healthcare management; and are able to demonstrate financial need. Candidates may not be previous recipients.

Purpose: To provide financial aid and increase the enrolment of minority and handicapped students in healthcare management graduate programs, and to encourage students (through structured, formalized study) to obtain positions in middle and upper levels of healthcare management.

No. of awards offered: Varies.

Frequency: Annual.

Value: US$3,000.

Applications Procedure: Applications are accepted between 1 January and 31 March and candidates are selected by the Foundation's Scholarship Committee shortly after the deadline date. Candidates should request an application from their program director or from the Foundation.

*Foster G McGaw Student Scholarships

Subjects: Healthcare management.

Eligibility: Open to US and Canadian citizens who are Student Associates of the American College of Healthcare Executives in good standing; who are enrolled full time and are in good academic standing in a graduate program in healthcare management that is accredited by the Accrediting Commission on Education for Health Services Administration; and who can demonstrate financial need. Candidates may not be previous recipients.

Purpose: To assist financially worthy persons to better prepare themselves for healthcare management, thereby contributing to improvements in the field.

Type: Scholarship.

No. of awards offered: Varies.

Frequency: Annual.

Value: US$3,000.

Applications Procedure: Because the Foundation receives more applications for Scholarships than it can honor, it has instructed the director of each graduate program to recommend students with the greatest financial need. To apply, candidates should obtain an application from their program director. The Foundation accepts applications for Scholarships each year between 1 January and 31 March. Students selected to receive Scholarships are announced soon after the deadline date.

FRANCIS FAMILIES FOUNDATION

Department of Medicine, Division of Pulmonary and Critical Care Medicine, 37-131 CHS, UCLA, 10833 Le Conte Avenue, Los Angeles, CA, 90095-1690, USA
Tel: 310 206 7066
Fax: 310 206 8622
Email: SOISHI@medicine.medsch.ucla.edu
Contact: Donald F Tierney, MD, Director

Parker B Francis Fellowship Program

Subjects: Pulmonary research.

Eligibility: The director of any training program, or pulmonary divison, or research laboratory, may apply on behalf of a candidate for Fellowship. Awards are limited to institutions located in the USA and Canada. Each department may submit only one application annually and is limited to a maximum of two active Fellowships at any one time. Parker B Francis Fellowship grants are awarded to institutions for the purpose of providing stipends and modest incidental expenses in support of qualified postdoctoral candidates who will thereby be enabled to devote the major part of their professional effort to research related to pulmonary disease. Candidates may hold either the MD or PhD degree, but it is essential there be evidence of aptitude and proficiency in research. Sponsorship of the Fellow by an established investigator is required. Open to foreign nationals who are in the process of becoming permanent residents of the USA or Canada.

Level of Study: Postdoctorate.

Type: Fellowship.

No. of awards offered: Fifteen.

Frequency: Annual.

Value: The total budget is limited to US$34,000 for the first, US$36,000 for the second, and US$38,000 for the third year. These totals are to include stipend plus fringe benefits and may include travel to a maximum of US$1,000. Direct research project costs and indirect costs are not allowed. These expenses ought to be supported by research project grants which are an essential part of the application in documenting the availability of sufficient research project support to make possible fulfilment of the Fellow's research aims.

Length of Study: One to three years (usually three).

Country of Study: USA or Canada.

Applications Procedure: Application packet with copies of any applicable publications. Full application details are available on request.

Closing Date: October 11th for notification in February.

Additional Information: It is permissible, indeed encouraged, for a grant to span a period during which the awardee graduates from fellowship to faculty status. Awards are made to institutions on behalf of the fellows and can be transferred to other institutions only under special circumstances with prior approval. Fellows supported by the Fellowships must be assured of at least 75% of their time available for research.

FRANK EDUCATIONAL FUND

Frank Educational Fund, 1506 Pennsylvania Avenue, SE, Washington, DC, 20003, USA

Postgraduate Scholarships

Subjects: Federalism, sovereignty, and international integration.

Eligibility: Fifty percent of the scholarships are designated for US citizens, and the remaining scholarships are open to applicants of any nationality. Applicants must be engaged in a course, independent study, or completion of a paper, thesis, dissertation, or innovative project dealing in major part with the issues of federalism.

Level of Study: Postgraduate.

Purpose: To support postgraduate students in furthering their education in application of the 'federal principle' and its best use to promote freedom and peace.

Type: Scholarship.

Frequency: Semi-annual.

Value: Between US$500 and US$2,000 per scholarship.

Closing Date: April 1st for Fall, and October 1st for Spring.

FRENCH-AMERICAN FOUNDATION

French-American Foundation, 41 East 72nd Street, New York, NY, 10021, USA
Tel: 212 744 3433
Fax: 212 288 4769
Contact: Ellen F Pope, Programs Associate

Bicentennial Fellowships

Subjects: French society, civilization and culture, including interdisciplinary research.

Eligibility: Open to outstanding scholars in history, political science, literature, art history, anthropology, and sociology, whose dissertation necessitates extensive archival research in France. Candidates must be US doctoral students who have completed their doctoral examinations, and who expect to pursue a career teaching French civilization and culture. Applicants must be US citizens or permanent residents.

Level of Study: Doctorate.

Frequency: Annual.

Value: US$1,750 per month, plus a travel allowance of up to US$500.

Length of Study: Ten months.

Study Establishment: An officially recognized institution of higher learning.

Country of Study: France.

Applications Procedure: Application form, three letters of recommendation, official transcripts, proposal.

Closing Date: March 1st for notification by April 30th.

Additional Information: The Bicentennial Fellowships are made possible by a grant from the American Committee on the Bicentennial of the French Revolution and by the French Ministry of Foreign Affairs.

*Journalists Program

Subjects: Journalism.

Eligibility: Open to US journalists who are not more than 35 years of age and have a minimum of three to five years' professional experience, including some international reporting experience.

Purpose: To enable American journalists to gain firsthand knowledge of the French political system and media organizations.

Frequency: Annual.

Value: A stipend of US$4,000 to be used for round-trip international air fare and toward the costs of meals, lodging and travel in France and Europe. The Foundation will assist in providing some meals and lodging wherever possible. While this stipend is intended to be sufficient for the duration of the exchange, some out-of-pocket expenses may be incurred by the participants.

Length of Study: 8 weeks.

Country of Study: France.

Closing Date: May 1st for notification by July 1st.

Additional Information: During the program, awardees will spend two weeks in Paris learning about and visiting major French institutions and media organizations. The Paris office of the French-American Foundation will also arrange orientation visits to Strasbourg, Luxembourg and Brussels for a broader view of France within Europe. The remainder of the exchange program will be spent working at the offices of an important regional news organization outside Paris. The Foundation also provides an exchange program for French journalists to work for two months at regional news organizations in the USA. The French and American Journalist Program participants will meet for a one-day program orientation session immediately prior to the exchange program. Immediately following the exchange, participating journalists are to submit a complete report to the French-American Foundation. Copies of articles written during the exchange for either the French host news organization or the journalist's home news organization are requested upon completion of the program. This program is supported in part through funding from the German Marshall Fund of the United States and the Hillsdale Fund, Inc.

FRIENDS OF AMERICAN WRITERS

Friends of American Writers, 6101 N. Sheridan Road East, Chicago, IL, 60660, USA
Tel: 312 743 7323

Adult Literature Award, Juvenile Literary Award

Subjects: Fiction and non-fiction.

Eligibility: Open to residents of, or those who have lived for at least five years in, Arkansas, Illinois, Indiana, Iowa, Kansas, Michigan, Minnesota, Missouri, North Dakota, South Dakota, Nebraska, Ohio or Wisconsin, and to books set in those regions. Candidates may not have published more than three books.

Purpose: To encourage the study of American literature and to encourage emerging American writers.

Type: Prize.

No. of awards offered: Two Adult Literature Awards; two Juvenile Literary Awards.

Frequency: Annual.

Value: Adult Literature Awards: first prize US$1,600; second prize US$1,000. Juvenile Literary Awards: first prize US$1,000; second prize US$600.

Applications Procedure: No applications are necessary, but candidates should send two copies of each book as early as possible along with biographical material regarding the author.

Closing Date: December 1st for notification in April.

For further information contact:

Adult Literature Award, Friends of American Writers, 6101 N. Sheridan Road East, Chicago, IL, 60660, USA
Tel: 312 743 7323
Contact: Pearl Robbins

or

Juvenile Literary Award, Friends of American Writers, 15237 W.Redwood Lane, Libertyville, IL, 60048, USA
Tel: 847 362 3762
Contact: Kay O'Connor

FRIENDS OF ISRAEL EDUCATIONAL TRUST

Academic Study Group, Friends of Israel Educational Trust, PO Box 7545, London, NW2 2OZ, England
Tel: 0171 435 6803
Fax: 0171 794 0291
Contact: John Levy

Academic Study Bursary

Subjects: Any subject.

Eligibility: Open to research or teaching postgraduates.

Level of Study: Postdoctorate.

Purpose: To provide funding for British academics planning to pay a first research/study visit to Israel.

Type: Bursary.

No. of awards offered: 15.

Frequency: Annual.

Value: £300 per person.

Study Establishment: The Academic Study Group will only consider proposals from British academics who have already linked up with professional counterparts in Israel and agreed terms of reference for an initial visit.

Country of Study: Israel.

Applications Procedure: There is no application form.

Closing Date: November 15th and March 15th each year.

Jerusalem Botanical Gardens Scholarship

Subjects: Botany, horticulture.

Eligibility: Open to UK graduates of recognized colleges and universities who hold a degree in a relevant subject.

Level of Study: Postgraduate, Professional development.

Purpose: To provide opportunities for botanists and horticulturists to work at the Jerusalem Botanical Gardens.

Type: Scholarship.

No. of awards offered: Several.

Frequency: Annual.

Value: To cover round-trip air fare and accommodation.

Study Establishment: The Jerusalem Botanical Gardens.

Country of Study: Israel.

Applications Procedure: There is no application form.

Closing Date: March 31st.

Young Artist Award

Subjects: Fine arts.

Eligibility: Open to promising young British painters and illustrators.

Level of Study: Postgraduate, Professional development.

Purpose: To enable a promising British painter to pay a working visit to Israel and prepare work for an exhibition on Israeli themes, in the UK.

No. of awards offered: One or two awards.

Frequency: Annual.

Value: To cover air fare, accommodation and keep.

Length of Study: Minimum of two months.

Study Establishment: A kibbutz.

Country of Study: Israel.

Closing Date: Mid-April.

FROMM MUSIC FOUNDATION

c/o Department of Music , Harvard University, Cambridge, MA, 02138, USA
Tel: 617 495 2791
Fax: 617 496 8081
Contact: Ms Ann Stevernagel

Fromm Foundation Commission

Subjects: Music (composition only).

Level of Study: Postdoctorate.

Purpose: To support composition by young and lesser well known composers. Includes a stipend for premiere performance of commissioned work.

No. of awards offered: Up to ten.

Frequency: Annual.

Applications Procedure: Obtain guidelines from Fromm Music Foundation.

Closing Date: June 1st.

FULBRIGHT COMMISSION (ARGENTINA)

Fulbright Commission (Argentina), Viamonte 1653 2 Piso, 1055 Cap Fed, Buenos Aires, 1055, Argentina
Tel: 541 814 3561/2
Fax: 541 814 1377
Email: GC@FULB-BA.SATLINK.NET
Contact: Gabriela Cosentino, Program Officer

Awards for US Lecturers and Researchers

Subjects: All subjects except medical science.

Eligibility: Open to US researchers and lecturers. Applicants must be proficient in spoken Spanish.

Level of Study: Professional development.

Purpose: To enable US lecturers to teach at an Argentine university for one semester, and to enable US researchers to conduct research at an Argentine institution for six months.

No. of awards offered: 8-10.

Frequency: Annual.

Value: Varies according to professional experience.

Length of Study: 3-6 months.

Country of Study: Argentina.

Applications Procedure: For further details please contact Ralph Blessing at CIES, Washington DC.

Closing Date: August 1st.

US Students Research Grant

Subjects: All subjects except medical science.

Eligibility: Open to US citizens who hold a bachelor's degree, are writing a master's thesis or PhD dissertation and are proficient in Spanish.

Level of Study: Postgraduate, Doctorate.

Purpose: To enable US students to study in Argentina.

Type: Research Grant.

No. of awards offered: 10-12.

Frequency: Annual.

Value: Approximately US$17,350 for eight months.

Length of Study: 8 months.

Country of Study: Argentina.

Applications Procedure: Application form must be completed - for further details please contact Mary Fedorko at IIE, New York.

FULBRIGHT FOUNDATION

Fulbright Foundation, Fulbright House, 62 Doughty Street, London, WC1N 2LS, England
Tel: 0171 404 6880
Fax: 0171 404 6834

*British-American Chamber of Commerce Awards

Eligibility: Open to graduates.

Purpose: To fund postgraduate education between Britain and America.

No. of awards offered: 1-3.

Frequency: Annually, subject to funds.

Value: £8,000.

Country of Study: USA.

FULBRIGHT SCHOLAR PROGRAM

Council for International Exchange of Scholars, Suite 5M, 3007 Tilden Street, NW, Washington, DC, 20008-3009, USA
Tel: 202 686 8664
Fax: 202 362 3442
Email: cies1@ciesnet.cies.org
www: http://www.cies.org/

Postdoctoral Research and Lecturing Awards for Non-US Citizens

Subjects: Any subject.

Eligibility: Open to nationals of countries and territories having US diplomatic or consular posts, who have a doctoral degree or equivalent qualification. Preference is given to those persons who have not had extensive previous experience in the USA.

Level of Study: Postdoctorate.

No. of awards offered: Varies, approximately 800 are granted each year.

Frequency: Annual.

Value: A maintenance allowance and international travel expenses.

Length of Study: 3 months to one academic year.

Country of Study: USA.

Applications Procedure: Applications must be made to the binational educational commission or the US embassy or consulate in the candidate's home country.

Closing Date: Varies by country.

FUND FOR EDUCATION AND TRAINING

1830 Connecticut Avenue NW, Washington, DC, 20009-5732, USA
Tel: 202 483 1242
Fax: 202 483 1246
Email: nisbco@igc.apc.org
Contact: John David Thacker

FEAT Loan

Subjects: Any subject.

Eligibility: FEAT loans are a last resort for those who are denied government aid because they have refused to register for the draft (this presently pertains only to men).

Level of Study: Unrestricted.

Purpose: To assist young people who believe it is wrong to comply with the law enforcing registration for the draft.

Type: Loan.

No. of awards offered: Varies.

Frequency: Annual.

Value: Varies.

Country of Study: USA.

FUND FOR INVESTIGATIVE JOURNALISM

Fund for Investigative Journalism, Inc, Room 324, 1755 Massachusetts Avenue, NW, Washington, DC, 20030, USA
Tel: 202 462 1844
Contact: Executive Director

Grants

Subjects: Investigative journalism; the subjects of Fund grants have covered a broad spectrum including environmental hazards, political corruption, invasion of privacy, organized crime, threats to civil rights, and abuses of corporate and union authority.

Eligibility: Open to writers. The Fund encourages aspirants to investigative journalism so persons without a 'track record' should not hesitate to apply.

Purpose: To increase public knowledge about the concealed, obscure or complex aspects of matters significantly affecting the public; to enable writers to probe abuses of authority or the malfunctioning of institutions and systems which harm the public.

No. of awards offered: Varies.

Frequency: Three times yearly.

Value: Individually assessed.

Study Establishment: For the preparation and writing of reports (factual as distinguished from ideological or philosophical) to be published in newspapers, magazines, as books or broadcast.

Additional Information: Applicants should write to the Executive Director describing the subject of the proposed investigation, its significance, the proof in hand, further evidence needed and how the project will be completed; and providing an itemized budget, résumé, samples of published work, and a statement of intent to publish from a suitable outlet, or the first and last pages of a book contract. The Fund is not endowed and depends for its support entirely on private donations, which are tax-exempt. The Fund provides grants for news media criticism through the Albert C Kihn Memorial Fund. Grants are not awarded for study.

Grants for Investigative Journalism

Level of Study: Professional development.

Purpose: To aid in the uncovering of facts or situations of an obscure or complex nature, showing institutional or individual abuses of power.

Type: Cash.

No. of awards offered: 20-30.

Frequency: Dependent on funds available.

Value: US$1,500 to US$3,000.

Applications Procedure: Letter, resume, writing samples, letter of commitment from publisher, editor or broadcast outlet.

Closing Date: None.

FUND FOR THEOLOGICAL EDUCATION, INC

The Fund for Theological Education, Inc, 475 Riverside Drive, Suite 832, New York, NY, 10115-0008, USA
Tel: 212 870 2058

*Black North American Doctoral Scholarships for the Study of Religion

Subjects: Religious studies.

Eligibility: Open to Black citizens of the USA or Canada who are studying for a PhD, ThD or EdD degree in a field of religious study. Candidates must have completed one year of coursework toward the PhD, ThD or EdD and must be members of a Christian church. A person is selected as a Scholar of the Fund for Theological Education on the basis of academic competence and promise for scholarship and teaching effectiveness.

Level of Study: Doctorate.

Purpose: To strengthen Christian theological education in the USA and Canada by supporting Black North Americans who demonstrate high promise for academic excellence and teaching effectiveness.

No. of awards offered: Varies.

Frequency: Annual.

Value: The amount of the award will vary according to individual need. Awards may be supplemented with other scholarships or financial aid.

Applications Procedure: Direct applications are not accepted. Each candidate must be nominated by a faculty member of a college, seminary or university who holds a PhD, ThD, or EdD degree. The nominator must have taught the student and known him/her for at least one year. No more than two nominations may be made by the same nominator. Each nomination should be in the form of a letter which identifies the qualities the nominee exemplifies for the vocation of teaching.

Closing Date: 10 February for nominations; 15 March for applications.

*Dissertation Year Scholarships for Doctoral Study of Religion for Black North Americans

Subjects: Religious studies.

Eligibility: Open to Black citizens of the USA or Canada who are members of a Christian church and have a prospectus or dissertation proposal approved by the appropriate faculty committee by the time they are interviewed by the final selection committee of the FTE. A person is selected as a Doctoral Scholar of the Fund for Theological Education on the basis of academic excellence and promise for scholarship and teaching effectiveness.

Level of Study: Doctorate.

Purpose: To strengthen Christian theological education in the USA and Canada by supporting Black North American women and men who demonstrate high promise for academic excellence and teaching effectiveness; to enable Black North American graduate students within the fields of religious studies to complete their PhD, ThD, or EdD dissertation.

Type: Scholarship.

No. of awards offered: Varies.

Frequency: Annual.

Value: The amount of the Scholarship will vary according to individual need. Scholarships may be supplemented with financial aid.

Length of Study: One year.

Applications Procedure: Direct applications are not accepted. Candidates must be nominated by a faculty member of a college, seminary or university who holds a PhD, ThD, or EdD degree. The nominator must have taught the student and known him/her for at least one year. No more than two nominations may be made by the same nominator. Each nomination should be in the form of a letter which identifies the qualities the nominee exemplifies for the vocation of teaching.

Closing Date: 10 February for nominations; 15 March for applications.

*Hispanic American Dissertation Year Scholarships

Subjects: Religious studies.

Eligibility: Open to Hispanic American women and men who have a prospectus or dissertation proposal approved by the appropriate faculty committee by the time the candidate is interviewed by the final selection committee of the FTE and have demonstrated identification with the Hispanic communities and commitment to theological scholarship and teaching in the USA, Canada or Puerto Rico. Candidates must be members of a Christian church and be PhD, ThD or EdD students. A person is selected as a Scholar of the Fund for Theological Education on the basis of academic competence and promise for scholarship and teaching effectiveness. It is expected that the dissertation will be completed by the end of the award year.

Purpose: To strengthen Christian theological education in the USA, Canada and Puerto Rico by supporting Hispanic American women and men who demonstrate high promise for academic excellence and teaching effectiveness; to enable Hispanic American graduate students within the field of religious studies to complete their PhD, ThD or EdD dissertation.

No. of awards offered: Varies.

Frequency: Annual.

Value: The amount of the award will vary according to individual need. Awards may be supplemented with other scholarships or financial aid.

Length of Study: One year.

Applications Procedure: Direct applications are not accepted. Each candidate must be nominated by a faculty member of a college, seminary or university who holds a PhD, ThD, or EdD degree. The nominator must have taught the student and known him/her for at least one year. No more than two nominations may be made by the same nominator. Each nomination should be in the form of a letter which identifies the qualities the nominee exemplifies for the vocation of teaching.

Closing Date: 10 February for nominations; 15 March for applications.

*Hispanic American Doctoral Scholarships for the Study of Religion

Subjects: Religious studies.

Eligibility: Open to Hispanic American women and men who are at least graduating seniors in an accredited college, university or seminary degree program and who are applying to a PhD, ThD or EdD program in a field of religious study. Candidates must have completed no more than one year of coursework toward the PhD, ThD or EdD; have demonstrated identification with the Hispanic communities and commitment to theological scholarship and teaching in the US, Canada or Puerto Rico and be members of a Christian church. A person is selected as a Scholar of the Fund for Theological Education on the basis of academic competence and promise for scholarship and teaching effectiveness.

Purpose: To strengthen Christian theological education in the USA, Canada and Puerto Rico by supporting Hispanic American women and men who demonstrate high promise for academic excellence and teaching effectiveness.

Type: Scholarship.

No. of awards offered: Varies.

Frequency: Annual.

Value: The amount of the award will vary according to individual need. Awards may be supplemented with other scholarships or financial aid.

Applications Procedure: Direct applications are not accepted. Each candidate must be nominated by a faculty member of a college, seminary or university who holds a PhD, ThD, or EdD degree. The nominator must have taught the student and known him/her for at least one year. No more than two nominations may be made by the same nominator. Each nomination should be in the form of a letter which identifies the qualities the nominee exemplifies for the vocation of teaching.

Closing Date: 10 February for nominations; 15 March for applications.

*Hispanic American Scholarships for Ministry

Subjects: Divinity.

Eligibility: Open to Hispanic American women and men who have demonstrated identification with and commitment to the practice of ministry in Spanish-speaking communities in the USA, Canada or Puerto Rico; are graduates of an accredited college or university; are ordained or are official candidates for ordination and are enrolled or prepared to enrol full time in a master of divinity program at a fully accredited theological school. A person is selected as a Scholar of the Fund for Theological Education on the basis of academic competence and promise for ministry.

Purpose: To support Hispanic Americans who hold high promise for effectiveness in the ministries of the Christian churches; to recruit women and men from the Hispanic communities in the USA, Canada and Puerto Rico who are committed to the ordained ministry.

Type: Scholarship.

No. of awards offered: Varies.

Frequency: Annual.

Value: The amount of the award will vary according to individual need. The award is not intended to replace financial aid normally offered by the student's church or school.

Applications Procedure: Candidates must be nominated by a minister, member of faculty or administration, or FTE alumni. The letter of nomination should provide the person's name, address and indication of the qualities for ministry which the person exemplifies.

Closing Date: 10 November for nominations; 15 December for applications.

*Hispanic American Scholarships for Ministry for Part-Time Students

Subjects: Divinity.

Eligibility: Open to Hispanic men and women who have demonstrated gifts for and commitment to the practice of ministry in Spanish-speaking communities in the USA, Canada or Puerto Rico; have circumstances, either professional and/or personal, which preclude full-time theological education and who are enrolled or prepared to be enrolled in a master of divinity program at a theological school fully accredited by the Association of Theological Schools. Consideration will be given to persons pursuing other 'first-level' seminary degrees, such as the MRE and the MAR. A person is selected as a Fellow of the Fund for Theological Education on the basis of academic competence, and continued employment in ministry.

Purpose: To identify and support Hispanic women and men who demonstrate effectiveness in Christian ministry and intend to complete the master of divinity degree on a part-time basis.

Type: Scholarship.

No. of awards offered: Varies.

Frequency: Annual.

Value: The amount of the award will vary according to the individual's educational expenses. The award is intended to defray an individual's educational expenses. The award is not intended to replace financial aid normally offered by the student's church or school.

Applications Procedure: Candidates must be nominated by a minister, member of faculty or administration, or FTE alumni. The letter of nomination should provide the person's name, address, and indication of the qualities for ministry and preparedness to engage in graduate professional studies.

Closing Date: 10 November for nominations; 15 December for applications.

*The Benjamin E Mays Scholarships for Ministry

Subjects: Divinity.

Eligibility: Open to Black citizens of the USA or Canada who are graduates of an accredited college or university. A candidate must be ordained, or an official candidate for ordination, and be enrolled or be prepared to enrol full-time in a master of divinity program at a fully accredited theological school. A person is selected as a Fellow of the Fund for Theological Education on the basis of academic competence and promise for ministry.

Purpose: To support Black North Americans who hold high promise for effectiveness in the ministries of the Christian churches; to recruit women and men in the USA and Canada who are committed to the ordained ministry.

Type: Scholarship.

No. of awards offered: Varies.

Frequency: Annual.

Value: The amount of the award will vary according to individual need. The award is not intended to replace financial aid normally offered by the student's church or school.

Length of Study: One academic year; renewable for up to a further 2 years subject to the fellow maintaining a high academic record as well as other evidence of promise for ministerial effectiveness.

Study Establishment: Any theological school fully accredited by The Association of Theological Schools.

Country of Study: USA or Canada.

Applications Procedure: Candidates must be nominated by a minister, member of faculty or administration, or FTE alumni. The letter of nomination should provide the person's name, address, and indication of the qualities for ministry which the person exemplifies.

Closing Date: 10 November for nominations; 15 December for applications.

*The Benjamin E Mays Scholarships for Ministry for Part-Time Students

Subjects: Divinity.

Eligibility: Open to Black citizens of the USA or Canada who are graduates of an accredited college or university, have circumstances, either professional and/or personal which preclude full-time theological education and are enrolled or prepared to enroll in a master of divinity program at a theological school fully accredited by the Association of Theological Schools. Considerations will be given to persons pursuing other 'first-level' seminary degrees (such as the MRE and the MAR). Candidates must be ordained or be official candidates for ordination. A person is selected as a Scholar of the Fund For Theological Education on the basis of academic competence and promise for ministry.

Purpose: To identify and support Black North American women and men who are already in Christian ministry, have demonstrated effectiveness and intend to complete the master of divinity degree on a part-time basis.

Type: Scholarship.

No. of awards offered: Varies.

Frequency: Annual.

Value: The amount of the Scholarship will vary according to individual need. The Scholarship is not intended to replace financial aid normally offered by the student's church or school.

Applications Procedure: A person must be nominated by a church administrator, minister, faculty member or administrator or FTE alumni. The letter of nomination must provide the person's name, address, indication of the ministry in which they are involved and some of the qualities for ministry which the person exemplifies.

Closing Date: 10 November for nominations; 15 December for applications.

FUND FOR UFO RESEARCH, INC

Fund for UFO Research, PO Box 277, Mt Rainier, MD, 20712, USA
Tel: 703 684 6032
Fax: 703 684 6032

Contact: Richard Hall, Chairman

Research Grants

Subjects: Possible topics for research include analysis of sighting reports, physical trace and photographic cases, government involvement in UFOs, and 'abduction' cases.

Eligibility: Open to anyone wishing to undertake scientific research or public education projects related to UFOs. There are no restrictions, except that reports must be written in English.

Level of Study: Unrestricted.

Purpose: To provide financial assistance for scientific research and public education projects relating to the phenomenon of unidentified flying objects.

Type: Research grants.

Frequency: Varies.

Value: Generally to cover out-of-pocket expenses only.

Applications Procedure: Application form must be completed.

Additional Information: Application forms are available on request.

GENERAL BOARD OF HIGHER EDUCATION AND MINISTRY

PO Box 891, Nashville, TN, 37202-0871, USA
Tel: 415 340 7388
Fax: 615 340 7048
Contact: John E Harnish

Dempster Fellowship

Subjects: Theology.

Eligibility: Open to members of the United Methodist Church who are teaching or plan to teach in seminaries, or to teach religion or related subjects in universities or colleges. Applicants must have received a MDiv from one of the member seminaries at the Association of United Methodist Schools.

Level of Study: Doctorate.

Purpose: To support research in the field of theology.

Type: Fellowship.

No. of awards offered: Five.

Frequency: Annual.

Value: US$10,000 per year.

Closing Date: February 1st.

GEOLOGICAL SOCIETY OF AMERICA

Geological Society of America, 3300 Penrose Place, PO Box 9140, Boulder, CO, 80301, USA
Tel: 303 447 2020 ext.137
Fax: 303 447 1133
Contact: June R Forstrom, Research Grants Administrator

Gladys W Cole Memorial Research Award

Subjects: Semi-arid terrains in the USA and Mexico.

Eligibility: Open to a GSA Member or Fellow between 30 and 65 years of age.

Purpose: To provide financial support for research.

Type: Research Award.

No. of awards offered: One.

Frequency: Annual.

Value: Minimum US$12,000.

Country of Study: USA and Mexico.

Applications Procedure: Application form must be completed.

Closing Date: February 15th.

Additional Information: Funds cannot be used to pay for work already accomplished, but recipients of a previous Award may reapply if additional support is needed to complete their work.

Penrose Research Grants

Subjects: Geology and closely related fields.

Eligibility: Open to citizens of countries within North America. Candidates need not necessarily be members of the Society.

Purpose: To aid a research project.

Type: Research Grant.

No. of awards offered: Varies; approximately 240.

Frequency: Annual.

Value: US$200-US$2,000.

Length of Study: One year; renewable.

Country of Study: North America, occasionally abroad.

Applications Procedure: Application form must be completed.

Closing Date: February 15th.

Additional Information: Grants are awarded on the basis of the scientific merits of the problem, the capability of the investigator and reasonableness of the budget; they may be used in support of research on thesis projects but not undergraduate research projects. Grants are awarded as an aid to a research project and not to sustain the entire cost; preference is given to smaller projects.

GEORGIA LIBRARY ASSOCIATION

Georgia Library Association, PO Box 39, Young Harris, GA, 30582, USA

Hubbard Scholarship

Subjects: Library science.

Eligibility: Open to US citizens accepted for admission to a masters program at an ALA-accredited library school, who intend to complete the course of study within two years.

Level of Study: Postgraduate.

Purpose: To provide financial aid to a qualified candidate completing a masters.

Type: Scholarship.

No. of awards offered: One.

Frequency: Annual.

Value: US$3,000, paid in equal instalments at the beginning of each term, semester or quarter.

Length of Study: Two years.

Study Establishment: An American Library Association-accredited school.

Country of Study: USA.

Applications Procedure: Please write for details.

Closing Date: May 1st.

Additional Information: The Scholar is required to work in a library or library-related capacity in Georgia for one year following completion of the program, or agree to pay back a pro-rated amount of the Scholarship plus interest within a two-year period.

GERMAN ACADEMIC EXCHANGE SERVICE (DAAD)

German Academic Exchange Service (DAAD), Suite 350, 11 Dupont Circle, NW, Washington, DC, 20036, USA
Tel: 202 332 9312

*DAAD-AICGS Grant

Subjects: Topics dealing with postwar Germany.

Eligibility: Open to PhD candidates, recent PhDs and junior faculty members.

Level of Study: Doctorate, Postdoctorate.

Type: Fellowship.

No. of awards offered: One.

Frequency: Annual.

Study Establishment: The American Institute for Contemporary German Studies (AICGS).

Country of Study: USA.

Closing Date: April 15th.

DAAD-ALCS Collaborative Research Grants

Subjects: Social sciences and humanities.

Eligibility: Open to scholars at US universities who wish to carry out joint research projects with German researchers.

Type: Research Grant.

No. of awards offered: Varies.

Value: Support for travel and living expenses.

Country of Study: Germany.

Closing Date: November 1st.

Additional Information: Administered jointly with the American Council of Learned Societies.

DAAD-Bourses Québec-RFA

Subjects: Any subject.

Eligibility: Open to Canadian citizens between 18 and 32 years of age who are residents of Québec and who have a very good command of German.

No. of awards offered: Varies.

Frequency: Annual.

Value: Varies.

Length of Study: One academic year.

Country of Study: Germany.

Closing Date: October 12th.

DAAD-Canadian Government Grants

Subjects: Any subject.

Eligibility: Open to Canadian citizens between 18 and 32 years of age who have a good command of German.

Level of Study: Postgraduate.

Type: Grant.

No. of awards offered: Varies.

Frequency: Annual.

Value: Varies.

Length of Study: One academic year.

Country of Study: Germany.

Applications Procedure: Forms to be obtained from Canadian university or ICCS.

Closing Date: October 15th.

For further information contact:
International Council for Canadian Studies, 325 Dalhousie, S-800, Ottawa, Ontario, K1N 7G2, Canada
Tel: 613 789 7834
Email: DAADNY@DAAD.ORG
www: http://wwwDAAD.ORG
Contact: Program Officer

*DAAD-Center for Contemporary German Literature Grant

Subjects: Research in contemporary German literature.

Eligibility: Open to suitably qualified scholars.

No. of awards offered: One.

Frequency: Annual.

Value: US$3,000.

Length of Study: 3 months.

Study Establishment: The Center for Contemporary German Literature.

Country of Study: USA.

For further information contact:
Center for Contemporary German Literature, Campus Box 1104, Washington University, St Louis, MO, 63130, USA
Contact: Professor Paul Michael Luetzeler, Director

DAAD- Fulbright Grants

Subjects: Any subject.

Eligibility: Open to US citizens between 18 and 32 years of age who have a good command of German. Must have been enrolled at a US university for at least one year at time of application.

Level of Study: Postgraduate.

Type: Grant.

No. of awards offered: Varies.

Frequency: Annual.

Value: Varies.

Length of Study: One academic year.

Country of Study: Germany.

Applications Procedure: Forms may be obtained from campus Fulbright advisor.

Closing Date: October 31st.

For further information contact:
Institute of International Education, 809 United Nations Plaza, New York, NY, 10017, USA
Tel: 212 883 8200

(DAAD) Information Visits

Subjects: All fields.

Eligibility: Applicants must have been enrolled at a US university for at least one year at time of application.

Level of Study: Unrestricted.

Purpose: To increase knowledge of specific German subjects and institutions within the framework of an academic study tour homogenous group of 15-25 students.

Frequency: Annual.

Length of Study: 7 to 21 days.

Country of Study: Germany.

Applications Procedure: Forms may be obtained from the DAAD New York office or downloaded from the internet.

Closing Date: At least six months before the intended visit.

DAAD-Leo Baeck Institute Grants

Subjects: The social, communal and intellectual history of German-speaking Jewry.

Eligibility: Open to doctoral students and recent PhDs.

Level of Study: Doctorate.

Type: Fellowship.

No. of awards offered: Six.

Frequency: Annual.

Value: Varies.

Study Establishment: The Leo Baeck Institute in New York or in Germany.

Country of Study: USA and Germany.

Closing Date: November 1st.

For further information contact:
The Leo Baeck Institute, 129 East 73rd Street, New York, NY, 10021, USA
Tel: 212 744 6400
Fax: 212 988 1305
Email: BM.LBC@RLG.STANFORD.Edu
Contact: Carol Kahn Strauss

or

German Academic Exchange Service, 950 Third Avenue, 19th Floor, New York, NY, 10022, USA
Tel: 212 758 3223
Fax: 212 755 5780
Contact: New York Office

DAAD Prizes for Best Syllabi in German Studies

Subjects: Innovative interdisciplinary or comparative approaches to the teaching of German studies (including language, politics, history, literature, cinema, anthropology, culture, art, music, women's studies, Jewish studies, etc.).

Eligibility: Open to suitably qualified scholars.

Frequency: Annual.

Value: US$1,000.

Closing Date: March 1st.

Additional Information: All syllabi submitted for the competition will be included in an on-line, multi-year data base of teaching materials for German studies. Complete and detailed syllabi, including detailed references, sources, and pedagogical goals, should be submitted as hard copy and on computer disk clearly labeled to indicate computer (PC/Mac), author, and software.

For further information contact:
DAAD Syllabi Prize, AICGS, 1400 16th Street, NW, Suite 420, Washington, DC, 02236-2217, USA
Tel: 202 332 9312
Contact: Professor Sander L Gilman

Deutschlandkundlicher Sommerkurs at the University of Regensburg

Subjects: Various fields in the social sciences and humanities.

Eligibility: Applicants must have been enrolled for at least one year at a US or Canadian university at the time of application.

Purpose: To provide language instruction and courses on historical, cultural and economic aspects of contemporary Germany.

Frequency: Annual.

Length of Study: Six weeks.

Study Establishment: German universities.

Country of Study: Germany.

Applications Procedure: Forms may be obtained from the New York

DAAD office or downloaded from the internet.

Closing Date: January 31st.

Hochschulsommersprachkurse at German Universities

Subjects: All fields.

Eligibility: At least one year enrolment at US or Canadian university.

Purpose: German Studies and Language courses.

Frequency: Annual.

Length of Study: Three to four weeks.

Study Establishment: German universities.

Country of Study: Germany.

Applications Procedure: Forms may be obtained from the DAAD office New York or downloaded from the internet.

Closing Date: January 31st.

For further information contact:
German Academic Exchange Service (DAAD), 950 Third Avenue, 19th Floor, New York, New York, 10022, USA
Tel: 212 758 3223
Fax: 212 755 5780
Email: DAADNY@DAAD.ORG
www: http://www.daad,org
Contact: Barbara Motyka

Learn 'German in Germany' for Faculty

Subjects: All fields but in English and German.

Eligibility: Open to faculty of US universities.

Level of Study: Faculty.

Purpose: To enable recipients to attend intensive language courses at the Goethe Institutes.

Frequency: Annual.

Length of Study: Four and eight weeks.

Study Establishment: Goethe Institutes.

Country of Study: Germany.

Applications Procedure: Forms may be obtained from the DAAD office in New York or downloaded from the internet.

Closing Date: January 31st.

Research Grants for Recent PhDs and PhD Candidates

Subjects: Any subject.

Eligibility: Open to recent PhDs (up to two years after the degree) of no more than 35 years of age and PhD candidates of no more than 32 years of age. Must have been enrolled at a US university for at least one year at time of application.

Level of Study: Doctorate, Postdoctorate.

Type: Grant.

No. of awards offered: Varies.

Frequency: Annual.

Value: A monthly maintenance allowance, international travel subsidy, and health insurance.

Length of Study: 2-6 months.

Country of Study: Germany.

Applications Procedure: Request forms from the DAAD or download from the internet.

Closing Date: November 1st.

Study Visit Research Grants for Faculty

Subjects: Any subject.

Eligibility: Open to individuals with at least two years of teaching and/or research experience after the PhD or equivalent and a research record in the proposed field.

Level of Study: Faculty.

Purpose: To allow scholars to pursue research at universities and other institutions in Germany.

Type: Grant.

No. of awards offered: Varies.

Frequency: Annual.

Value: A monthly maintenance allowance.

Study Establishment: For specific research projects, for one to three months. Grants cannot be used for travel only, attendance at conferences or conventions, editorial meetings, lecture tours or extended guest-professorships.

Country of Study: Germany.

Applications Procedure: Forms may be obtained from the New York office or downloaded from the internet.

Closing Date: November 1st.

Summer Language Course at the University of Leipzig

Subjects: All fields - but students in the fields of English, German or any other modern language are not eliglble.

Eligibility: Applicants must have been enrolled at a US university for at least one year at time of application.

Level of Study: Postgraduate, Undergraduate.

Purpose: To support intensive language course, lectures, discussions on contemporary issues, independent project work, and excursions.

Frequency: Annual.

Length of Study: Eight weeks.

Study Establishment: University of Leipzig.

Country of Study: Germany.

Applications Procedure: Forms may be obtained from the DAAD New York office or downloaded from the internet.

Closing Date: January 31st.

Summer Language Courses at Goethe Institutes

Subjects: All fields but English and German.

Eligibility: Applicants must be enrolled at a US university at time of application.

Purpose: To offer intensive eight week language courses.

Frequency: Annual.

Length of Study: Eight weeks.

Study Establishment: Goethe Institutes.

Country of Study: Germany.

Applications Procedure: Forms may be obtained from the New York office or downloaded from the internet.

Closing Date: January 31st.

*Alexander von Humboldt 'Bundeskanzler' Scholarships

Subjects: Unrestricted, but a background in the humanities, social sciences, law or economics is preferred.

Eligibility: Candidates with demonstrated leadership qualities and excellence in their field should be nominated by US university presidents. Nominees must be US citizens and no more than 30 years of age.

Purpose: To enable highly qualified young Americans in academia, business or politics to gain substantial insight into German political, economic, social and cultural life in the course of an extended, self-structured stay.

Type: Scholarship.

No. of awards offered: Up to 10.

Frequency: Annual.

Value: Varies.

Country of Study: Germany.

Closing Date: October 13th.

For further information contact:
Alexander von Humboldt Foundation, North America Office, Suite 903, Connecticut Avenue, NW, Washington, DC, 20036, USA
Tel: 202 296 2990
Fax: 202 833 8514

or

German Academic Exchange Service, 950 Third Avenue, 19th Floor, New York, NY, 10022, USA
Tel: 212 758 3223
Fax: 212 755 5780
Contact: New York Office

*Alexander von Humboldt Research Fellowships

Subjects: Any subject.

Eligibility: Open to highly qualified scholars and scientists of any nationality, who hold a PhD or equivalent and are not yet 40 years of age.

Type: Fellowship.

No. of awards offered: Varies.

Frequency: Annual.

Value: Varies.

Country of Study: Germany.

Young Lawyers Program

Subjects: Law.

Eligibility: Open to candidates who hold a JD and the bar exam. A good command of German is required. The age limit is 32.

Level of Study: Postgraduate.

Purpose: To provide an opportunity to gain unique insight into the structure and function of German law.

Type: Grant.

No. of awards offered: Varies.

Value: Tuition/fees, monthly allowance, travel subsidy and health insurance.

Length of Study: For a total of 10 months between November and August, comprising a two month course in legal terminology at a German university, followed by a five-month course offered by the North Rhine-Westphalian Ministry of Justice, and a three-month internship.

Country of Study: Germany.

Applications Procedure: Forms may be obtained form the New York office of DAAD (or downloaded form the internet).

Closing Date: March 15th.

For further information contact:
German Academic Exchange Service, 950 Third Avenue, 19th Floor, New York, NY, 10022, USA
Tel: 212 758 3223
Fax: 212 755 5780
Email: DAADNY@DAAD.ORG
www: http://www.DAAD.ORG
Contact: New York Office

GERMAN HISTORICAL INSTITUTE

German Historical Institute, 1607 New Hampshire Avenue, NW, Washington, DC, 20009, USA
Tel: 202 387 3355
Fax: 202 483 3430

Dissertation Scholarships

Subjects: Humanities and social sciences: comparative studies in social, cultural and political history, studies of German-American relations, transatlantic studies.

Eligibility: Open to German and American doctoral students. Applications from women and minorities are especially encouraged.

Purpose: To give support to German and American doctoral students working on topics related to the Institute's general scope of interest.

Type: Scholarship.

No. of awards offered: 12.

Frequency: Annually; dependent on funds available.

Value: US$1,000 per month.

Length of Study: Up to six months.

Country of Study: USA.

Closing Date: May 31st.

Additional Information: The American candidates are expected to evaluate source material in the United States which is important for their research on German history. At the end of the scholarship they are required to report on their findings.

Volkswagen Research Fellowship

Subjects: History, social sciences.

Eligibility: Open to postdoctoral scholars at the junior or senior level. Applications from women and minorities are especially encouraged.

Purpose: To promote the research of young scholars in the areas of post-World War II Germany and German-American relations.

Type: Fellowships.

No. of awards offered: Three.

Frequency: Annually; dependent on funds available.

Value: US$25,000-US$40,000.

Country of Study: USA.

Closing Date: January 1st.

Additional Information: The candidates should pursue their own research projects using archival resources of the Washington area, conduct seminars and colloquia, deliver lectures at both the German Historical Institute and the American Institute for Contemporary German Studies. Fellows must be in residence.

For further information contact:
American Institute for Contemporary German Studies at the John Hopkins University, 11 Dupont Circle, NW, Suite 350, Washington, DC, 20036, USA

GERMANISTIC SOCIETY OF AMERICA

Germanistic Society of America, Institute of International Education, 809 United Nations Plaza, New York, NY, 10017, USA
Tel: 212 984 5330
Contact: US Student Programs

Fellowships

Subjects: Primarily in the fields of German language, literature, philosophy, history, art history, political science, economics and banking, international law and public affairs.

Eligibility: Open to US citizens who have a good academic record, capacity for independent study, and preferably a master's degree.

Level of Study: Postgraduate.

Type: Fellowship.

No. of awards offered: Six.

Frequency: Annual.

Value: US$10,000 per annum.

Length of Study: One academic year (nine months).

Country of Study: Germany.

Closing Date: October 31st.

Additional Information: Preference is given to prospective teachers of German.

GERMAN MARSHALL FUND OF THE UNITED STATES

German Marshall Fund of the United States, 11 Dupont Circle, NW, Suite 750, Washington, DC, 20036, USA
Tel: 202 745 3950
Fax: 202 265 1662
Email: gmfus@cais.com
Contact: Peter R Weitz, Director of Programs

GMF Research Fellowships

Subjects: Projects may focus on either comparative domestic or international issues.

Eligibility: Open to US citizens or permanent residents who are scholars in various stages of their careers in the social sciences. Applicants must have completed all degree requirements by the time of application. Awards are made to applicants who will devote themselves full-time to their projects. The program will not support preparation for any degree.

Purpose: To support research projects that seek to improve the understanding of significant contemporary economic, political and social developments involving the USA and Europe.

No. of awards offered: Approximately 12.

Frequency: Annual.

Value: Up to US$30,000 per annum. To maximize the Fund's resources, each applicant for financial assistance will be expected to apply for any available leave, sabbatical or other funding from his or her home institution, for the Fellow's support during the period of appointment, and then, when feasible, to explore other possible outside sources of funding. Thereafter it is the Fund's policy to attempt to meet, but not exceed, his or her current income. Certain travel expenses necessary to the proposed work may also be sought.

Study Establishment: There is no restriction on place of tenure.

Country of Study: USA and Europe.

Closing Date: November 15th.

Additional Information: Projects should establish the significance of their findings either by comparative analysis of a specific issue in more than one country, or by an exploration of that issue in a single country in ways that can be expected to have relevance for other countries.

GETTY GRANT PROGRAM

Getty Grant Program, 401 Wilshire Boulevard, Suite 1000, Santa Monica, CA, 90401-1455, USA
Tel: 310 393 4244
Fax: 310 395 8642
Contact: Joan Weinstein, Program Officer

Central and Eastern European Fellowships in the History of Art and the Humanities

Eligibility: These fellowships are designated specifially for scholars from this region (Central and Eastern Europe) who are at or beyond the postdoctorate level in art history and related fields. Preference is given to scholars in the early stages of their careers and to those who have not had significant opportunities for travel and research outside their home countries.

Level of Study: Postdoctorate.

Purpose: The fellowships are intended to enable scholars from Central and Eastern Europe to pursue Art-Historical research outside their home countries and to enhance opportunities for scholarly access and cultural exchange.

Type: Fellowship.

No. of awards offered: Varies.

Frequency: Annual.

Value: US$10,000.

Length of Study: Four months.

Country of Study: Any.

Applications Procedure: Application forms, detailed instructions, and additional information are available form the Grant Program Office.

Closing Date: January 11th.

The J Paul Getty Postdoctoral Fellowships in the History of Art and Humanities

Eligibility: Fellowships are open to scholars of all nationalities who have earned a doctoral degree within the past six years.

Level of Study: Postdoctorate.

Purpose: To provide support for outstanding scholars in the early stages of their careers to pursue interpretive research projects that make a substantial and original contribution to the understanding of art and its history.

Type: Fellowship.

No. of awards offered: 30.

Frequency: Annual.

Value: US$30,000.

Length of Study: 12 months.

Country of Study: Any.

Applications Procedure: Applicants must submit one original and seven full copies of the completed application as well as two letters from the applicant's recommenders.

Closing Date: November 1st.

Getty Program Senior Research Grants

Eligibility: Open to teams of scholars to pursue collaborative research projects that offer new explanations of art and its history. Collaborations that foster a crossfertilisation of ideas and methodologies are particularly encouraged. Teams may consist or two or more art historians or museum curators, or of an art historian and one or more scholars from other disciplines.

Purpose: To provide opportunities for teams of scholars to pursue interpretive research projects that offer new explanations of art and its history.

Type: Research Grant.

No. of awards offered: Varies.

Frequency: Annual.

Value: Varies according to the needs of the various projects.

Length of Study: One to two years.

Country of Study: Any.

Applications Procedure: Application forms, detailed instructions, and additional information are available from the Grant Program Office.

Closing Date: January 1st.

GILCHRIST EDUCATIONAL TRUST

Gilchrist Educational Trust, Mary Trevelyan Hall, 10 York Terrace East, London, NW1 4PT, England
Tel: 0171 631 8300 ext.773
Contact: Mrs Everidge, Secretary

GET Grants

Subjects: Any subject.

Eligibility: Open to students in the UK who are within sight of the end of a course and are facing "unexpected" financial difficulties which may prevent completion of their studies; students in the UK who are required to spend a short period studying abroad as part of their course; recognized British university expeditions; pioneer educational establishments.

Level of Study: Postgraduate, Doctorate.

Purpose: To promote the advancement of education and learning in every part of the world.

No. of awards offered: Varies.

Value: Modest.

Country of Study: Unrestricted.

Applications Procedure: University expeditions are required to complete an application form. Eligible individuals are sent a list of information required.

Closing Date: For University Expeditions: 20 February. All other categories: at any time.

Gilchrist Expedition Award

Subjects: Any subject.

Eligibility: Open to teams of not more than ten members, most of them British, with the majority holding established positions in research departments at universities or similar establishments, wishing to undertake a field season of over six weeks in relation to one or more scientific objectives. The proposed research must be original and challenging, achievable within the timetable and preferably of benefit to the host country or region.

Purpose: To fund an intermediate-sized expedition by established scientists or academics.

Type: Grant.

No. of awards offered: One.

Frequency: Biennially (even-numbered years).

Value: £10,000.

Country of Study: Unrestricted.

Closing Date: January 31st.

Additional Information: The Award is competitive.

WILLIAM HONYMAN GILLESPIE SCHOLARSHIP TRUST

William Honyman Gillespie Scholarship Trust, Messrs Tod Murray WS, 66 Queen Street, Edinburgh, EH2 4NE, Scotland
Tel: 0131 226 4771
Fax: 0131 225 3676

*Scholarships

Subjects: Theology.

Eligibility: Open to graduates in theology of any Scottish university.

Purpose: To support theological research or study in Scotland.

Type: Scholarship.

No. of awards offered: One.

Frequency: Biennially.

Value: £1,000 per annum.

Length of Study: Two years.

Study Establishment: An approved university or similar institution.

Country of Study: Scotland or overseas.

Applications Procedure: Application guidelines are available from the Trust or the candidate's university department. Applications should be submitted through the Principal of the theological college of the Scottish university of which the applicant is a graduate.

Closing Date: May 15th.

RUTH ESTRIN GOLDBERG MEMORIAL FOR CANCER RESEARCH

Ruth Estrin Goldberg Memorial for Cancer Research, 885 Gloucester Road, Union, New Jersey, 07083, USA
Tel: 908 688 1725
Contact: Myra Abramson

Ruth Estrin Goldberg Memorial for Cancer Research

Eligibility: Eastern USA.

Level of Study: Unrestricted.

Purpose: Cancer Research.

No. of awards offered: Two.

Frequency: Dependent on funds available, annual.

Value: US$10,000 to US$15,000.

Country of Study: USA.

Applications Procedure: Please contact by mail for application and guidelines.

Closing Date: February 28th.

Additional Information: We are an organization of volunteers and not too many active workers. We try to draw our applicants from the eastern part of the country, preferably from around New Jersey, New York, Pennsylvania and Massachusetts area.

THE GOLDSMITHS' COMPANY

The Goldsmith's Company, Goldsmiths' Hall, Foster Lane, London, EC2V 6BN, England
Tel: 0171 606 7010
Fax: 0171 606 1511
Contact: The Clerk

Science for Society Courses

Subjects: Medical physics.

Eligibility: Open to UK science teachers of secondary age children, but other disciplines are accepted.

Level of Study: Professional development.

Purpose: To provide teachers of A levels, first hand practical experience of the theory which they teach.

No. of awards offered: Approximately 80 vacancies per annum.

Frequency: Annual.

Value: Free accommodation and travel after joining.

Length of Study: For 1 week in July.

Study Establishment: Various locations around the UK.

Country of Study: UK.

Closing Date: Vacancies are on a first come, first served basis.

*Travelling Grants for Schoolmasters and Schoolmistresses

Subjects: Refreshment study in a field different from their professional expertise.

Eligibility: Open to candidates who are teachers in schools whose pupils are of secondary age, in both the private and maintained sectors. They should have had at least 10 years teaching experience and should not normally be over 55 years of age.

Purpose: To enable schoolmasters and schoolmistresses to undertake refreshment study during periods of sabbatical leave from their schools.

Type: Travel Grant.

No. of awards offered: Up to ten.

Frequency: Annual.

Value: Up to £6,250 to the school, towards the salary of a substitute for the candidate granted leave who is expected to receive his or her normal salary during absence; a payment, not normally exceeding £3,500, direct to the individual, towards travel and incidental expenses. The Company will take into account the candidate's salary, financial commitments and other estimated expenses when determining the amount of this award.

Length of Study: 2-6 months.

Country of Study: Unrestricted.

Applications Procedure: The applicant should complete the application form (available from the Company) with his/her personal details, education, qualifications and teaching experience; provide a letter of application setting out, on not more than three sides but with as much detail as possible, the proposal for the period of leave, outline itinerary and estimate of expenses; and forward the application to his/her Head. The Head should complete the appropriate part of the application form with an assessment of the merit of the application and a recommendation of the candidate. The Employer (who may be the Head acting on behalf of the Governors or Local Education Authority) should complete the statement on the application form agreeing to the candidate's leave of absence, indicating whether or not the candidate will be paid on full salary during his/her leave of absence, and should then ensure that the letter of application is attached to the application form and forward both to the Clerk of the Goldsmiths' Company at the address shown.

Closing Date: January 1st.

ADOLPH AND ESTHER GOTTLIEB FOUNDATION, INC

Adolph and Esther Gottlieb Foundation, 380 West Broadway, New York, NY, 10012, USA
Tel: 212 226 0581
Fax: 212 226 0584
Contact: Jenny Gillis, Grants Manager

Emergency Assistance Grants

Subjects: Painting, sculpture, printmaking only.

Eligibility: Open to artists who can demonstrate a minimum of 10 years' involvement in a mature phase of their work and who do not have the resources to meet the costs incurred by the catastrophic event.

Purpose: To provide interim financial assistance to creative visual artists (painters, sculptors and printmakers) whose need is the result of unforeseen catastrophic events, e.g. fire, flood or emergency medical expenses.

Type: Grant.

No. of awards offered: Varies.

Frequency: Varies, depending on funds available.

Value: Up to US$10,000; US$5,000 is typical, on a one-time basis only.

Country of Study: Unrestricted.

Applications Procedure: Application form must be completed and submitted with documentation of situation (such as bills) and professional references.

Additional Information: The disciplines of film, photography, or related forms are not eligible unless the work involves directly, or can be interpreted as, painting or sculpture. 'Maturity' is based on the level of technical, intellectual and creative development of the artist. The program does not cover general indebtedness, unemployment, capital improvements, long-term disabilities, or project funding.

Individual Support Grants

Subjects: Painting; sculpting; printmaking.

Eligibility: Open to creative painters, sculptors, and printmakers who have been in a mature phase of their work for at least 20 years and require financial assistance to continue this work. US residency is not required.

Purpose: To recognize and support serious, fully committed artists who have been working in a mature phase of their art for at least 20 years and are in financial need.

Type: Grant.

No. of awards offered: Ten.

Frequency: Annual.

Value: Varies (US$20,000 each in 1996).

Country of Study: Unrestricted.

Applications Procedure: Application form must be completed and submitted with slides to document twenty years of mature work, narrative statement and financial information.

Closing Date: December 15th. Awards are distributed the following March.

Additional Information: Artists who have been awarded a Grant must allow one year to elapse before reapplication. Only first-person written requests for application forms will be honored.

GRADUATE INSTITUTE OF INTERNATIONAL STUDIES

Institut Universitaire de Hautes Études Internationales, Case Postale 36, 132 rue de Lausanne, Genève 21, CH-1211, Switzerland
Tel: 731 17 30
Fax: 738 43 06
Telex: 412 151 Pax Ch
Contact: Secretary General

Scholarships

Subjects: History and international politics, international economics, international law, political science.

Eligibility: Open to any person who can give evidence of a sound knowledge of the French language and of sufficient prior study in political science, economics, law or modern history, by the presentation of a college or university degree.

Level of Study: Doctorate, Postgraduate, Professional development.

Type: Scholarship.

No. of awards offered: Twenty.

Frequency: Annual.

Value: SwFr1,000 per month.

Length of Study: One year; possibly renewable.

Study Establishment: Intensive research and study towards a doctorate at the Graduate Institute of International Studies, Geneva.

Country of Study: Switzerland.

Closing Date: March 1st.

Additional Information: Scholarships are normally awarded to more advanced students of the Institute. As a general rule, they are not granted during the first year of studies. Scholars are exempted from Institute fees, but not from the obligatory fees of the University of Geneva which confers the doctorate (doctorat en relations internationales).

GRAHAM FOUNDATION FOR ADVANCED STUDIES IN THE FINE ARTS

Graham Foundation for Advanced Studies in the Fine Arts, 4 West Burton Place, Chicago, IL, 60610, USA
Tel: 312 787 4071
Contact: Patricia M Snyder, Administrator

Grants

Subjects: Architecture and fine arts only as they relate to architecture.

Eligibility: Open to recognized educational or cultural institutions as well as individuals who demonstrate creative talent and who have specific project objectives.

Level of Study: Postdoctorate, Professional development.

Type: Grant.

No. of awards offered: 50-60.

Frequency: Twice yearly.

Value: Up to US$10,000.

Applications Procedure: No special application forms are required. A proposal describing the project, the people involved, and the amount sought, must be submitted. A supporting budget is required. No direct scholarship aid is offered.

Closing Date: January 15th and July 15th.

GRAINS RESEARCH AND DEVELOPMENT CORPORATION

Grains Research and Development Corporation, PO Box E6, Queen Victoria Terrace, Canberra, ACT, 2600, Australia
Tel: 06 272 5525
Fax: 06 271 6430
Contact: Ms Cathy Stewart

Industry Development Awards

Subjects: Grains research and development.

Eligibility: Open to permanent Australian residents who are experienced growers, processors or other contributors to the work of the Corporation who are not engaged in research and development activity.

Purpose: To fund study tours or for other purposes approved by the Corporation.

Type: Development award.

No. of awards offered: Up to two.

Frequency: Annual.

Value: Up to a total of A$15,000 towards personal travel costs, including economy class air fares and contribution to living expenses.

Country of Study: Australia or overseas.

Applications Procedure: Applications should include five copies of the following documentation: the nominee's CV; details of the proposed programme; the names, positions and locations of the proposed collaborators; approximate dates for the programme; details of any internal travel directly related to the proposed programme; a proposed budget, including the cost of international and internal travel, and expected accommodation and living expenses; an indication of other forms of support available to the nominee; evidence that the proposed collaborators are agreeable to the programme; supporting comments from two referees; and a covering letter.

Closing Date: End of November for the following year.

Additional Information: On completion of the award, a report must be furnished to the Board. Preference may be given to applicants who have access to matching funds.

In-Service Training

Subjects: Grains research and development.

Eligibility: Open to permanent Australian residents.

Purpose: To support training on an industry-wide basis by funding younger scientists, technical staff or other persons engaged in work relevant to the Corporation's objectives who may not be competitive for other forms of support. Funds may be provided for travel, secondment or interchange between institutions.

Type: Training.

Frequency: Annual.

Value: To cover personal travel costs, including economy class air fares and contribution to living expenses.

Length of Study: Up to six months.

Applications Procedure: Applications should include ten copies of the following documentation: a CV; details of the proposed in-service training; the names, positions and locations of the proposed collaborators and training venue; approximate dates for the programme, which must fall within the appropriate funding year; details of any travel directly related to the proposed programme; a proposed budget, including the cost of travel, and expected accommodation and living expenses; an indication of other forms of support available to the applicant; evidence that the proposed collaborators are agreeable to the training programme; supporting comments from two referees; and a covering letter.

Closing Date: November for the following year.

Additional Information: On completion of their award, trainees must furnish a report to the Board.

Junior Research Fellowships

Subjects: Postgraduate training to a PhD level in fields of high priority to the grains industry. The Corporation's Five-Year Research and Development Plan outlines the objectives and programs to be covered. Copies of the plan may be obtained from the Secretariat.

Eligibility: Open to permanent Australian residents who hold academic qualifications equivalent to a first-class honours degree or have otherwise demonstrated a high level of postgraduate achievement in research, teaching or extension activities.

Level of Study: Postgraduate, Doctorate.

Type: Fellowship.

No. of awards offered: Up to six.

Frequency: Annual.

Value: Tax-free stipend of A$21,000 with no allowances for dependants. An additional grant of up to A$3,000 per annum may be provided to the host organization to support the work.

Length of Study: Up to three years.

Study Establishment: Any Australian university with a record of achievement in the subject area, for full-time research leading to a DPhil.

Country of Study: Australia.

Applications Procedure: Application forms are available on request. Applications (ten copies) should include the CV of the applicant and the report of at least two referees. Evidence that the university and collaborating organizations will provide facilities and supervision of the project must also be supplied.

Closing Date: November for the following year.

Senior Fellowships

Subjects: Grains research and development.

Eligibility: Open to permanent Australian residents.

Purpose: To allow experienced research and development personnel to enhance their experience and their potential to contribute to the work of the Corporation by working at an institution in Australia or overseas.

Type: Fellowship.

Frequency: Annual.

Value: Up to a total of A$50,000 towards personal travel costs, including economy class air fares and contribution to living expenses.

Length of Study: Up to 12 months.

Country of Study: Australia or overseas.

Applications Procedure: Applications should include ten copies of the following documentation: the nominee's CV, including a list of publications; details of the nominee's research project and its relationship to the host institution's programme of research (this should include evidence that the host institution already has an interest and competence in the area of research proposed by the applicant and that it is relevant to the Corporation's objectives); the names, positions and major publications of the proposed collaborators, together with a letter of invitation from the Head of the host institution; approximate dates for the programme, which must fall within the appropriate funding year; details of any internal travel directly related to the proposed programme; a proposed budget, including the cost of international and internal travel, and expected accommodation and living expenses; an indication of other forms of support available to the applicant; evidence that the host institution has available the necessary facilities and is willing to accept the Fellow; supporting comments from two referees; and a covering letter. On completion of their award Fellows must furnish a report to the Board. Preference may be given to applicants who have access to matching funds.

Closing Date: November for the following year.

Visiting Fellowships and Industry Awards

Subjects: Grains research and development.

Eligibility: Nominations may be made on behalf of potential visitors or by the visitors themselves.

Purpose: To give support and stimulus to research programmes supported by the Corporation by funding visits by overseas personnel who could enhance those programmes.

Type: Fellowship.

Frequency: Annual.

Value: The Corporation will consider paying the nominee's personal travel costs, contributing to living expenses and providing some support to the host institution or company. The maximum total level of support will normally be A$17,500.

Length of Study: Up to 12 months.

Country of Study: Australia.

Applications Procedure: Applications should include ten copies of the following documentation: the nominee's CV; details of the nominee's research project or itinerary for study and its relationship to the host institution's or company's programme of research, development or other industry contribution; the name, position and industry contributions of the person proposing the nominee, together with a letter of support from the Head of the host institution or company, where appropriate; the names, positions and institutions of collaborators of the proposed project or study tour; approximate dates for the programme, which must fall within the appropriate funding year; details of any travel directly related to the proposed programme; a proposed budget, including the cost of international and internal travel, and expected accommodation and living expenses; an indication of other forms of support available to the nominee, including those from the home institution or company; evidence that the host institution or company has accepted the nomination; supporting comments from two referees; and a covering letter.

Closing Date: November for the following year.

Additional Information: Preference may be given to nominees who have access to matching funds. On completion of their visit nominees must furnish a report to the Board, via their host institution and/or collaborators.

GRAND PRIX INTERNATIONAL DU SALON DE LA RECHERCHE PHOTOGRAPHIQUE

SIRP-Animation Royan, Palais des Congres, BP 102, Royan Cedex, 17201, France
Tel: 46 38 65 11 or 46 23 95 91
Fax: 46 38 52 01

*Grand Prix International du Salon de la Recherche Photographique

Subjects: Photography.

Eligibility: Open to amateurs and professionals from all over the world.

No. of awards offered: Two.

Frequency: Annual.

Value: 1st prize FF15,000; 2nd prize FF10,000.

Closing Date: April 4th.

ELIZABETH GREENSHIELDS FOUNDATION

Elizabeth Greenshields Foundation, 1814 Sherbrooke Street West, Montréal, Québec, H3H 1E4, Canada
Tel: 514 937 9225
Contact: Micheline Leduc, Administrator

Grants

Subjects: Painting, drawing, printmaking, sculpture.

Eligibility: Open to nationals of any country, there is no age limit.

Level of Study: Unrestricted.

Purpose: To assist talented young artists in the early stages of their career.

No. of awards offered: Varies.

Value: Varies; C$10,000 in 1995.

Applications Procedure: Requests for application are made in writing (return postage paid). Applications are submitted along with six slides (12 for sculptors).

Closing Date: Grants are awarded throughout the year.

Additional Information: Applicant's work must be representational (the Foundation's charter precludes abstract art). Application forms are sent upon request to individuals only.

GRIFFITH UNIVERSITY

Office for Research and International Projects, Griffith University, Nathan, Queensland, 4111, Australia
Tel: 61 7 3875 6596
Fax: 617 3875 7994
Email: M.Brown@or.gu.edu.au
Contact: Ms Maxine Brown, Postgraduate Scholarships Officer

Jackson Memorial Fellowship

Subjects: Fellowship is to be taken up within a faculty of Griffith University. Preference will be given to those with an interest in the application of the social, political, economic, environmental or technological sciences to the analysis and resolution of substantial policy issues at the national or regional levels.

Eligibility: Senior member of faculty staff of Association of the Southeast Asian Institutions of Higher Learning (ASAIHL) member institutions.

Level of Study: Research and Teaching.

Purpose: To consolidate links with a variety of institutions in Southeast Asia and to provide funding to facilitate visits to Griffith University by faculty staff of Association of Southeast Asian Institution of Higher Learning (ASAIHL) member institutions.

Type: Fellowship.

No. of awards offered: One.

Frequency: Annual.

Value: A$2,500 to assist with travel to and from Australia; A$350 stipend per week during period of residence; accommodation expenses; travel assistance to other tertiary institutions in Australia up to a total of A$1,200.

Length of Study: 1-3 months (during a teaching semester; Feb to Jun; July to Oct).

Study Establishment: University.

Country of Study: Australia.

Applications Procedure: Candidates should apply through the heads of their employing institutions.

Closing Date: September 1st of the year preceding that in which the award is offered.

For further information contact:
Griffith University, Queensland, 4111, Australia
Tel: 61 7 3875 7931
Contact: Ms Donna Hannan

Postgraduate Research Scholarships

Subjects: Any subject.

Eligibility: Open to any person, irrespective of nationality, holding or expecting to hold an upper IIA honours degree or equivalent from a recognized institution.

Level of Study: Postgraduate.

Purpose: To provide financial support for candidates undertaking full-time research leading to the award of the degree of Doctor of Philosophy or Master of Philosophy.

Type: Scholarship.

No. of awards offered: Varies.

Frequency: Annual.

Value: A$15,364 per annum (tax exempt), plus a dependent child allowance of A$1,500 per annum (tax exempt) for some overseas students, limited travel allowance and a thesis production allowance.

Length of Study: Up to two years for MPhil, and up to three years for PhD (with possible extension of up to six months for PhD), subject to satisfactory progress.

Study Establishment: Griffith University.

Country of Study: Australia.

Applications Procedure: Application form to be received by October 30th in the year preceding the commencement of study.

Closing Date: October 30th for commencement by March 30th the following year.

Additional Information: The Scholarship does not cover the cost of tuition fees which range between A$12,000 and A$14,000 per annum. Applicants must demonstrate proficiency in the English language by scoring an overall score of 6.0 in an International English Language Testing System (IELTS) test, or test score of 580 on the Test of English as a Foreign Language (TOEFL) including the Test of Written English score of no less than 5.0.

The Sir Allan Sewell Visiting Fellowship

Subjects: Available for all faculties of Griffith University.

Level of Study: Research and Teaching.

Purpose: To commemorate the distinguished service of Sir Allan Sewell to Griffith University by offering awards to enable visits by distinguished

scholars engaged in academic work who can contribute to the research and teaching in one or more areas of interest to a faculty or college of the university.

Type: Fellowship.

No. of awards offered: Four.

Frequency: Annual.

Value: Up to A$6,000.

Length of Study: Minimum of eight weeks.

Study Establishment: University.

Country of Study: Australia.

Applications Procedure: Fellows must be invited by faculties/colleges of the University to apply.

Closing Date: July 1st of the year preceding that in which the award is offered.

GRIMSBY INTERNATIONAL SINGERS COMPETITION

Grimsby International Singers Competition, 23 Enfield Avenue, New Waltham, Grimsby, DN36 5RD, England
Tel: 01472 812 113
Fax: 01472 821 114
Contact: Dr Anne Holmes

Alec Redshaw Memorial Awards

Subjects: Vocal performance: oratorio, concert and operatic repertoire; Lieder and early music; contemporary and French melodie.

Eligibility: Open to males and females of any nationality, between the ages of 20 and 30 years (singers), 20 and 27 years (accompanists).

Purpose: To give young professional singers a platform, and possibly engagements. All rounds are open to the public. Music society secretaries are invited, also agents.

Type: Competition.

No. of awards offered: 17 prizes, 16 for singers and 1 for an accompanist.

Frequency: Triennially.

Value: 4 Prizes of £2,000; 4 Prizes of £1,000; 4 Prizes of £750; new prizes of £250 each for best Italian aria, German Lied, French melodie, English song; and £600 for accompanist.

Applications Procedure: Application form plus two references; entry fee of £45.00, copy of birth certificate, and two passport size photographs.

Closing Date: March 31st 1998.

Additional Information: The competition is held in the Town Hall, Grimsby, next 4-8 October 1998. Winners concert: October 10th 1998.

HARRY FRANK GUGGENHEIM FOUNDATION

Harry Frank Guggenheim Foundation, 527 Madison Avenue, New York, NY, 10022-4301, USA
Tel: 212 644 4907
Fax: 212 644 5110

Dissertation Fellowship

Subjects: Any discipline which includes the study of dominance, aggression and violence.

Eligibility: Open to PhD candidates of any nationality.

Level of Study: Doctorate.

Purpose: To support a PhD candidate in the write-up phase of a dissertation. Work must be relevant to HFG program interests.

Type: Fellowship.

No. of awards offered: Ten.

Frequency: Annual.

Value: US$10,000.

Length of Study: One year.

Country of Study: Any country.

Applications Procedure: Application form, research proposal and letter from advisor.

Closing Date: February 1st.

Additional Information: A final report to the Foundation is mandatory. Recipients of Dissertation Fellowships must submit a copy of the dissertation, approved and accepted by the home university or college, within six months after the end of the award year. The award is only available in circumstances where all research has been done and the dissertation will be complete within one year.

Research Program

Subjects: Support is provided mainly for basic research in the social, behavioral and biological sciences, but research which is related to the Foundation's program will be considered regardless of the disciplines involved.

Eligibility: Open to individuals or institutions in any country.

Level of Study: Postgraduate, Postdoctorate.

Purpose: To promote understanding of the human social condition through the study of the causes and consequences of dominance, aggression and violence.

Type: Research Grant.

No. of awards offered: A variable number.

Frequency: Annual.

Value: Approximately US$25,000 per annum; applications for a greater or lesser sum will be judged on their merits.

Length of Study: A one year period; two and three year projects may be considered.

Country of Study: Any country.

Applications Procedure: Application form and research proposal along with CV and budget request.

Closing Date: August 1st.

Additional Information: The Foundation operates a program of specific and innovative study and research. Proposals should be for a specific project and should describe well-defined aims and methods; they should not be for general institutional support. Grants will be considered for salaries, employee benefits, research assistantships, computer time, supplies and equipment, field work, reasonable secretarial and technical help, and other items necessary to the successful completion of a project. The Foundation cannot supply funds for overhead costs of institutions, travel to professional meetings, publication subsidies, self-education or elaborate fixed equipment.

Guggenheim Fellowships to Assist Research and Artistic Creation (Latin America and the Caribbean)

Subjects: Creative (but not performing) arts.

Eligibility: Open to citizens and permanent residents of countries of Latin America and the Caribbean who have demonstrated an exceptional capacity for productive scholarship or exceptional creative ability in the arts.

Level of Study: Postdoctorate, Professional development.

Purpose: To further the development of scholars and artists by assisting them to engage in research in any field of knowledge and creation in any of the arts, under the freest possible conditions and irrespective of race, color or creed.

Type: Fellowship.

No. of awards offered: Approximately 27.

Frequency: Annual.

Value: Grants will be adjusted to the needs of Fellows, considering their other resources and the purpose and scope of their plans.

Length of Study: Ordinarily for one year, but in no instance for a period shorter than six consecutive months.

Applications Procedure: Application form is required to be completed.

Closing Date: December 1st.

Additional Information: Members of the teaching profession receiving sabbatical leave on full or part salary are eligible for appointment, as are holders of other Fellowships and of appointments at research centers. The Fellowships are awarded by the Trustees upon nominations made by a committee of selection.

Guggenheim Fellowships to Assist Research and Artistic Creation (US and Canada)

Subjects: Creative (but not performing) arts.

Eligibility: Open to citizens and permanent residents of the USA and Canada who have demonstrated an exceptional capacity for productive scholarship or exceptional creative ability in the arts.

Level of Study: Postdoctorate, Professional development.

Purpose: To further the development of scholars and artists by assisting them to engage in research in any field of knowledge and creation in any of the arts, under the freest possible conditions and irrespective of race, color or creed.

Type: Fellowship.

No. of awards offered: 152.

Frequency: Annual.

Value: Grants will be adjusted to the needs of the Fellows, considering their other resources and the purpose and scope of their plans.

Length of Study: Ordinarily for one year, but in no instance for a period shorter than six consecutive months.

Applications Procedure: Application form is required to be completed.

Closing Date: October 1st.

Additional Information: Members of the teaching profession receiving sabbatical leave on full or part salary are eligible for appointment, as are holders of other Fellowships and of appointments at research centers. Fellowships are awarded by the Trustees upon nominations made by a committee of selection.

JOHN SIMON GUGGENHEIM MEMORIAL FOUNDATION

John Simon Guggenheim Memorial Foundation, 90 Park Avenue, New York, NY, 10016, USA
Tel: 212 687 4470
Fax: 212 697 3248
Email: fellowships@gf.org
www: http://www.gf.org

CALOUSTE GULBENKIAN FOUNDATION (INTERNATIONAL DEPARTMENT)

Calouste Gulbenkian Foundation (International Department), Av. de Berna, 45, Lisbon, A-1093, Portugal
Tel: 793 51 31
Fax: 793 51 39

Telex: 63768 GULBEN P
Contact: The Director

Research Fellowships

Subjects: Humanities.

Eligibility: Open to postgraduates of foreign nationality.

Level of Study: Postgraduate.

Purpose: To stimulate research and specialisation on themes relating to Portuguese culture, namely in the field of humanities.

Type: Fellowship.

No. of awards offered: Limited.

Frequency: Annual.

Value: Varies.

Length of Study: A maximum of twelve months.

Country of Study: Portugal.

Applications Procedure: Application form must be completed.

Closing Date: October 31st.

Additional Information: In the selection of applications, the Foundation will bear in mind the importance and originality of the work proposed to promote Portuguese culture, or cultural exchange between the candidate's country of origin and Portugal.

CALOUSTE GULBENKIAN FOUNDATION (LISBON) UNITED KINGDOM BRANCH

Calouste Gulbenkian Foundation (Lisbon) United Kingdom Branch, 98 Portland Place, London, W1N 4ET, England
Tel: 0171 636 5313/7
Fax: 0171 636 3421
Contact: Assistant Director, Arts

Anglo-Portuguese Cultural Relations Programme

Subjects: Activities in the UK and Republic of Ireland concerned with Portugal: its language, culture and people, past and present, cultural and educational interaction between British or Irish and Portuguese people; the educational, cultural and social needs of the Portuguese immigrant communities (not individual Portuguese immigrants or visitors) in the UK or the Republic of Ireland.

Eligibility: Open, in most cases, to organizations, and occasionally to individuals, who should present proposals of a charitable nature to the Foundation.

Purpose: To help Portuguese cultural projects in the UK and Ireland. 'Cultural relations' are taken to include social welfare, as well as activities in the arts, crafts and education.

Type: Grant.

No. of awards offered: Varies.

Value: Varies; up to £10,000.

Country of Study: UK and the Republic of Ireland.

Arts Programme

Subjects: Practical Research and Development: support will be available for groups of professional artists to devise and experiment before they perfect a project. Priority will be given to applications which demonstrate some genuine ground-breaking development for the art-form as a whole, as well as being challenging for the artists involved; Creative use of new technologies: applications are invited from arts organisations for projects which demonstrate a practical application of new multimedia technology in developing their art (applications for the use of new technology in arts administration will not be eligible); Cultural equity: the

Foundation is interested in encouraging projects which help to establish equity in the arts for people from Britain's diverse ethnic groups and disabled people, whether as artists or audiences.

Eligibility: Open, in most cases, to organizations who should present proposals of a charitable kind to the Foundation.

Level of Study: Professional development.

Type: Grant.

No. of awards offered: Varies.

Value: Varies; up to £10,000.

Country of Study: UK or the Republic of Ireland.

Education Programme

Subjects: Arts for young people (up to the age of 25): support for the arts in schools and for the arts 'out of school'; educational innovations and developments - the ethos of the school, parental involvement in schools, projects which prepare young people for parenthood, democracy in schools.

Eligibility: Open, in most cases, to organizations, and occasionally to individuals, who should present proposals of a charitable nature to the Foundation.

Type: Grant.

No. of awards offered: Varies.

Value: Varies; up to £10,000.

Country of Study: UK and the Republic of Ireland.

For further information contact:
Calouste Gulbenkian Foundation (Lisbon) United Kingdom Branch, 98 Portland Place, London, W1N 4ET, England
Tel: 0171 636 5313/7
Fax: 0171 636 3421
Contact: Assistant Director, Education

Social Welfare Programme

Subjects: Needs and rights of children and young people; parent education and support.

Eligibility: Open, in most cases, to organizations who should present proposals of a charitable nature to the Foundation.

Type: Grant.

No. of awards offered: Varies.

Value: Varies; up to £10,000.

Country of Study: UK and the Republic of Ireland.

DR HADWEN TRUST FOR HUMANE RESEARCH

Dr Hadwen Trust for Humane Research, 22 Bancroft, Hitchin, Herts, SG5 1JW, England
Tel: 01462 436819
Fax: 01462 436819
Contact: Dr G Langley

Grants

Subjects: Scientific research to develop humane alternative methods to the use of living animals in biomedical research and testing.

Eligibility: Applications may be made by any postgraduate in a university, medical school, hospital or other scientific institution. Exceptionally, applications may be considered from postgraduates not attached to an institution, or from more junior scientists. Applicants must be based in the UK.

Level of Study: Postgraduate.

Purpose: To advance medical progress and relieve animal suffering.

No. of awards offered: Varies.

Frequency: Dependent on funds available.

Value: Varies according to need and to funds available. Payments are usually made quarterly, and may be used as salary for the researcher, for technical assistance, for expenses incurred during the research, purchase of equipment or attendance at meetings.

Length of Study: For a maximum of three years; interim progress reports are required. Renewal past three years is awarded only in exceptional circumstances.

Country of Study: UK.

Applications Procedure: Official application form must be completed.

Additional Information: Recipients are required to sign an agreement not to use Trust funds for any procedure using living animals or animal tissues. Applications must be signed by the candidate's head of department and administrative authority. Applications may be submitted at any time on official application forms.

HAGLEY MUSEUM AND LIBRARY

Hagley Museum and Library, PO Box 3630, Wilmington, DE, 19807, USA
Tel: 302 658 2400 ext.243
Fax: 302 655 3188
Email: Cvl@strauss.udel.edu
Contact: Dr Philip B Scranton

Henry Bellin du Pont Fellowship

Subjects: Areas of study relevant to the Library's archival and artefact collections.

Eligibility: Open to persons who have already completed their formal professional training. Consequently, degree candidates and persons seeking support for degree work are not eligible to apply. Applicants must be from out of state and preference will be given to those whose travel costs to Hagley will be higher.

Level of Study: Doctorate, Postdoctorate.

Purpose: To support access to and use of Hagley's research collections; to enable individual out-of-state scholars to pursue their own research and to participate in the interchange of ideas among the Center's scholars.

Type: Fellowships.

No. of awards offered: Varies.

Frequency: Annual.

Value: A stipend of US$1,500 per month.

Length of Study: Two to six months.

Study Establishment: The Library.

Country of Study: USA.

Applications Procedure: Application and proposal of five pages.

Closing Date: March 31st, June 30th, October 31st.

Additional Information: Fellows must devote their full time to their studies and may not accept teaching assignments or undertake any other major activities during the tenure of their Fellowships. Tenure must be continuous and last from two to six months. At the end of their tenure, Fellows must submit a final report on their activities and accomplishments. As a center for advanced study in the humanities, Hagley is a focal point of a community of scholars. Fellows are expected to participate in seminars which meet periodically, as well as attend noon-time colloquia, lectures, concerts, exhibits, and other public programs offered during their tenure. Research fellowships are to be used in the Hagley Library only. Not as scholarships for college.

Grants-in-Aid of Research

Subjects: American economic and technological history, and French eighteenth-century history.

Eligibility: Open to degree candidates and advanced scholars of any nationality.

Level of Study: Doctorate, Postdoctorate.

Purpose: To support travel to the Hagley Library for scholarly research in the collections.

No. of awards offered: 25 grants-in-aid each year.

Frequency: Quarterly.

Value: Up to US$1,000 per month.

Length of Study: Two to eight weeks.

Study Establishment: The Hagley Library.

Country of Study: USA.

Applications Procedure: Application and five pages of proposal.

Closing Date: March 31st, June 30th, September 30th.

Additional Information: Candidates may apply for research in the imprint, manuscript, pictorial and artefact collections of the Hagley Museum and Library. In addition the resources of the 125 Libraries in the greater Philadelphia area will be at the disposal of the visiting Scholar. The research fellowship is to be used only in the Hagley Library.

Hagley/Winterthur Arts & Industries Fellowship

Subjects: Business and economics, design, architecture, crafts, fine arts, technology and industrial history.

Eligibility: Open to advanced scholars, graduate students and independent researchers.

Level of Study: Doctorate, Postdoctorate.

Purpose: To support scholarly research at Hagley and Wintherthur Libraries on historical and cultural relationships between economic life and the arts.

Type: Fellowship.

No. of awards offered: Six.

Frequency: Annual.

Value: US$1,000 per month.

Length of Study: Maximum of three months.

Country of Study: USA.

Applications Procedure: Please submit application and proposal (five pages), and two recommendations.

Closing Date: December 1st.

Additional Information: The award is a residential travel grant; the scholar must travel to Delaware to use the Collections at the Hagley and Winterthur libraries.

THE HAGUE ACADEMY OF INTERNATIONAL LAW

The Hague Academy of International Law, Peace Palace, Carnegieplein 2, Den Haag, 2517 K J, The Netherlands
Tel: 31 70 302 4242
Contact: Secretariat

Doctoral Scholarships

Subjects: International law.

Eligibility: Open to doctoral candidates from developing countries and the former east block who reside in their home country and who do not have access to scientific sources.

Purpose: To aid doctoral candidates with the completion of their theses through the assistance of the Academy.

Type: Scholarships.

No. of awards offered: Four.

Frequency: Annual.

Value: 75 Dutch florins per diem with a contribution towards travelling expenses.

Length of Study: Two months from July 1st.

Study Establishment: The Hague Academy of International Law.

Country of Study: The Netherlands.

Applications Procedure: Applications should be accompanied by a letter of recommendation from the professor under whose direction the thesis is being written. The thesis may be concerned with either private or public international law.

Closing Date: March 1st.

Scholarships for Sessions or Courses

Subjects: International law.

Eligibility: Open to persons no more than 40 years of age who have not received an Academy Scholarship before.

Level of Study: Doctorate.

Purpose: To assist students with living expenses during summer courses.

Type: Scholarship.

No. of awards offered: Varies.

Frequency: Annual.

Value: 1,600 Dutch Florins to cover expenses for the period of tenure. Scholars are exempt from registration and examination fees. Travelling expenses will not be refunded.

Length of Study: The three weeks of the course period.

Study Establishment: The Academy.

Country of Study: The Netherlands.

Applications Procedure: Applications should be made by the applicant personally and submitted with a curriculum vitae, a photograph and a statement of the evidence which he/she considers to be of value in support of the candidature. Every application must be typed and accompanied by a recommendation from a professor of international law. Candidates should, if possible, attach copies of any scientific publications. As documents forwarded by applicants are not returned, university certificates or other documents must be submitted in the form of copies duly verified by a competent authority. The teaching period for which the candidate wants to be registered should be clearly stated.

Closing Date: March 1st.

THE HAMBIDGE CENTER

The Hambidge Center, PO Box 339, Rabun Gap, GA, 30568, USA
Tel: 706 746 5718
Fax: 706 746 9933

Residency Program

Subjects: Any field or discipline of creative work.

Eligibility: Open to qualified applicants in all disciplines who can demonstrate seriousness, dedication and professionalism. International residents are welcome.

Level of Study: Unrestricted.

Purpose: To provide an environment for creative work.

Type: Residency.

No. of awards offered: 70-80.

Frequency: Throughout the year.

Value: Cost to residents is US$125 per week and includes all linens plus evening meals Monday to Friday for the May to October season. No meals are available November to April.

Length of Study: Two weeks to two months.

Study Establishment: The Center.

Country of Study: USA.

Applications Procedure: Application form provided with SASE sent to center for the attention of the Residency Program. (Form requests, examples of work, resume, publicity, references etc...).

Closing Date: Applications are accepted and reviewed periodically throughout the year. January 31st is the deadline for major review; the Schedule is set in March for the May to October season.

Additional Information: The Hambidge Center, located in Northeast Georgia, is set in 600 acres of mountain/valley terrain, with waterfalls and nature trails.

HARBOR BRANCH INSTITUTION

Harbor Branch Institution, Harbor Branch Oceanographic Institution, 5600 US #1 North, Fort Pierce, FL, 34946, USA
Tel: 407 465 2400 ext.500
Fax: 407 465 5743
Email: EDUCATION@HBOI.edu
www: wwwhboi.edu
Contact: Dr Susan Cook; Mrs Beverley Heuna

Postdoctoral Fellowships

Subjects: Oceanography, Marine Biology, Aquaculture, Marine Engineering.

Eligibility: PhD must be recieved before award begins. Applicants must have received the PhD within five years of the start date of the fellowship.

Level of Study: Postdoctorate.

Purpose: Advanced training in Marine Science, Ocean Engineering, Aquaculture, Biomedical Marine Research, Environmental Analysis Monitoring.

Type: Fellowship.

No. of awards offered: 6-8.

Frequency: Every two years.

Value: US$25,000 per year.

Length of Study: 18 months.

Country of Study: USA.

Applications Procedure: Submit form; essay proposal; transcripts of graduate work; and three letters of reference.

Additional Information: Award includes a small supply and travel budget; health insurance cover is also available.

THE J B HARLEY RESEARCH FELLOWSHIPS TRUST

The J B Harley Research Fellowships Trust, c/o British Library Map Library, Great Russell Street, London, WC1B 3DG, England
Tel: 0171 412 7525
Fax: 0171 412 7780
Email: tony.campbell@bl.uk
Contact: Tony Campbell

The J B Harley Research Fellowships in the History of Cartography

Subjects: History of Cartography.

Eligibility: Excluding London commuters.

Level of Study: Doctorate, Postdoctorate, Professional development.

Purpose: To promote the use of the great wealth of historical cartographical material available in London.

Type: Maintenance grant, Grant.

No. of awards offered: Two.

Frequency: Annual.

Value: £400 - £800.

Length of Study: Two to four weeks.

Study Establishment: London libraries.

Country of Study: United Kingdom.

Applications Procedure: Outline research proposal and CV. Details in leaflet on request.

Closing Date: November 1st.

HARVARD BUSINESS SCHOOL

Harvard Business School, Morgan 297, Soldiers Field, Boston, MA, 02163, USA
Tel: 617 495 6354
Fax: 617 496 5985
Contact: Professor Thomas K McCraw

Alfred D Chandler Jr Traveling Fellowships in Business History and Institutional Economic History

Subjects: Business history, institutional economic history; topics such as labor relations and government regulation will also be considered if the approach is primarily institutional.

Eligibility: Open to Harvard University graduate students in history, economics, business administration, or a related discipline such as sociology, government, or law, whose research requires travel to distant archives or repositories; graduate students or non-tenured faculty in those fields from other North American universities, whose research requires travel to the Boston-Cambridge area (to study, for example, in the collections at the Baker, Widener, McKay, Law, Kress, or Houghton libraries); and Harvard College undergraduates writing senior theses in those fields, whose research requires similar travel.

Level of Study: Postgraduate.

Purpose: To facilitate library and archival research in business history or institutional economic history, broadly defined.

Type: Fellowship.

No. of awards offered: Varies.

Frequency: Annual.

Value: US$1,000-US$3,000 from a total of approximately US$10,000.

Closing Date: December 1st.

Additional Information: Application forms are available on request.

Harvard-Newcomen Fellowship in Business History

Subjects: Any research project connected with economic and business history.

Eligibility: Open to applicants who have received a PhD within the ten years preceding the start of the Fellowship (i.e. 1 July or 1 September). The award is for 12 months' study. Harvard University is an equal employment, equal opportunity, affirmative action employer.

Level of Study: Postdoctorate.

Purpose: To assist young scholars in improving their professional acquaintance with business and economic history and to engage in research that will benefit from the resources of the Harvard Business School and the Boston-Cambridge scholarly community.

Type: Fellowship.

No. of awards offered: One.

Frequency: Annual.

Value: US$45,000.

Study Establishment: Harvard Business School for one year, including participation in the business history course and seminar (one semester each) plus other courses the applicant wishes to audit.

Country of Study: USA.

Closing Date: November 1st.

Additional Information: Application forms are available on request.

HARVARD LAW SCHOOL

ILS 331, Harvard Law School, 1557 Massachusetts Avenue, Cambridge, MA, 02138, USA
Contact: Professor Lewis Sargentich

Liberal Arts Fellowship

Subjects: Law.

Eligibility: Open to college and university teachers in the arts and sciences. There are no further eligibility restrictions.

Level of Study: Professional development.

Purpose: To enable teachers in the social sciences or humanities to study fundamental techniques, concepts, and aims of law, so that in their teaching and research they will be better able to use legal materials and legal insights which are relevant to their own disciplines.

Type: Fellowships.

No. of awards offered: 4-5.

Frequency: Annual.

Value: The Fellowship grant covers tuition and health fees only, as well as provision of office space.

Length of Study: One year.

Country of Study: USA.

Applications Procedure: Applications should include a biological resume (including academic record and list of publications), a statement explaining what the applicant hopes to achieve through the year of study, and two letters of recommendation (mailed to the Chair directly from the referees). There is no special application form.

Closing Date: January 15th.

HARVARD UNIVERSITY

The Center for International Affairs, Harvard University, 1737 Cambridge Street, Cambridge, MA, 02138, USA
Tel: 617 495 3671
Fax: 617 495 8292
Contact: CFIA Fellowship Office

*The Academy Scholars Program

Subjects: Area studies.

Eligibility: Open to both doctoral candidates (PhD or comparable professional school degree) and recent recipients of these degrees who already hold teaching or research positions. Those who are still candidates for advanced degrees should have completed all coursework and general examinations by the beginning of the academic year for which they seek support. Applicants are welcome from any accredited university without regard to nationality.

Level of Study: Doctorate, Postdoctorate.

Purpose: To assist those who, having developed significant expertise in a given geographical area, require further training in an established discipline; or those who, having achieved a high level of competence in a discipline, wish to gain further mastery of a given geographical area.

No. of awards offered: 4-6.

Frequency: Annual.

Value: The stipend will depend on the situation of the individual. Predoctoral students will be provided with a stipend of US$20,000-US$22,000 per annum. Postdoctoral recipients will be provided with a stipend of US$30,000-US$35,000.

Length of Study: Two years.

Country of Study: Any country.

Closing Date: October 14th for awards commencing the following academic year.

Additional Information: Language proficiency is important and successful candidates who require further training will be expected to take courses necessary to achieve fluency.

Harvard Academy for International and Area Studies Predoctoral and Postdoctoral Fellowships

Subjects: The program focuses on training social scientists in area studies, especially those areas of the world that require the use of difficult languages, or conversely, assisting area specialists in developing expertise in an established discipline.

Eligibility: Open to predoctoral applicants who have completed all course work and general examinations by the beginning of the first year for which they seek support; and to postdoctoral scholars.

Level of Study: Doctorate, Postdoctorate.

Purpose: To assist young scholars who are preparing for an academic career involving both a social science discipline and a particular area of the world.

Type: Scholarship.

No. of awards offered: Variable.

Value: Predoctoral: US$20,000-US$25,000, plus university facilities fees and health insurance; postdoctoral: US$30,000-US$35,000, plus health insurance.

Study Establishment: The Center for International Affairs (CFIA), Harvard University.

Country of Study: USA.

Applications Procedure: Program details and application guidelines are available in July for the following academic year.

Closing Date: October.

Mellon Foundation Fellowships

Subjects: The program focuses on institutional structure, the changing nature of politics, global influences, economic and social structure, culture and public ethics, and social capital as they effect the performance of democracies.

Eligibility: Predoctoral applicants must have completed all course work and general examinations by the beginning of the first year for which they seek support.

Level of Study: Doctorate, Postdoctorate.

Purpose: To assist young scholars and form an interdisciplinary group studying the performance of democracies.

Type: Fellowship.

Value: Predoctorate: US$12,500; postdoctorate: US$26,000.

Study Establishment: CFIA, Harvard University.

Country of Study: USA.

Applications Procedure: Program details and application guidelines are available from the CFIA Fellowships Office; please contact Clare Putnam.

Closing Date: February.

John M Olin Institute for Strategic Studies Predoctoral and Postdoctoral Fellowships

Subjects: The causes and conduct of war, military strategy and history, defense policy and institutions; economic security, defense economics, the defense industrial base.

Eligibility: Open to predoctoral candidates who have completed all course work and general examinations by the beginning of the year for which they seek support; and to postdoctoral scholars.

Purpose: To support young scholars conducting basic research in the broad area of security and strategic affairs, including the economics of these issues.

Type: Fellowship.

No. of awards offered: Varies.

Frequency: Annual.

Value: Predoctoral: up to US$16,500, plus university facilities fees and health insurance; postdoctoral: up to US$28,000, plus health insurance.

Study Establishment: Center for International Affairs (CFIA), Harvard University.

Country of Study: USA.

Applications Procedure: Program details and application guidelines are available in October.

Closing Date: February 1st.

Postdoctoral Fellowship on International Conflict Resolution

Subjects: Projects which focus on the integration of research, practice, and education in the field of conflict resolution.

Eligibility: Applicants must be in residence at the CFIA.

Level of Study: Postdoctorate.

Type: Fellowship.

Value: Non-stipendary award.

Study Establishment: CFIA, Harvard University.

Country of Study: USA.

Applications Procedure: Program details and application guidelines are available from the Program in International Conflict Analysis and Resolution (PICAR).

Closing Date: Rolling applications.

For further information contact:
The Center for International Affairs, Harvard University, 1737 Cambridge Street, Cambridge, MA, 02138, USA

Tel: 617 496 0680

Fax: 617 495 8292

Email: picar@CFIA.harvard.edu

Contact: Donna Hicks

*Program on Non-Violent Sanctions Predoctoral and Postdoctoral Fellowships and Visiting Scholar Affiliations

Subjects: Development of theory and data collection protocols, comparative and case study analyses.

Eligibility: Open to suitably qualified scholars.

Level of Study: Doctorate, Postdoctorate.

Purpose: To support research on the degree to which, and how, non-violent direct action provides an alternative to violence in resolving the problems of totalitarian rule, war, genocide, and oppression.

Type: Fellowship.

No. of awards offered: Varies.

Frequency: Annual.

Value: Varies.

Study Establishment: Center for International Affairs (CFIA), Harvard University.

Country of Study: USA.

Applications Procedure: Applicants should contact the program director to discuss the research project before compiling an application. Program details and application guidelines are available in July.

Closing Date: January.

Program on US-Japan Relations Advanced Research Fellowships

Subjects: Issues or problems in contemporary US-Japan relations, Japan's international relations, other studies of Japan that contribute to the understanding of Japan's international behaviour.

Eligibility: Preference is given to US citizens, but others, especially from Pacific Rim countries, may apply.

Level of Study: Postdoctorate.

Purpose: To support the work of scholars engaged in the study of contemporary Japan and/or US-Japan relations.

Type: Fellowship.

No. of awards offered: Variable.

Frequency: Annual.

Value: Up to US$27,000.

Study Establishment: The Center for International Affairs (CFIA), Harvard University.

Country of Study: USA.

Applications Procedure: Program details and guidelines are available from the CFIA in October.

Closing Date: March.

Villa I Tatti Fellowships

Eligibility: Open to candidates of any nationality.

Level of Study: Postdoctorate.

Purpose: Italian Renaissance Studies.

Type: Fellowship.

No. of awards offered: Up to fifteen.

Frequency: Annual.

Value: The maximum grant will be no higher than US$30,000; most grants will be considerably less.

Length of Study: Up to one year.

Study Establishment: With Professor Walter Kaiser, Director at Villa I Tatti, Via di Vincigliata 26, 50135, Florence Italy Tel: 39 55 603 251/608 909.

Country of Study: Italy.

Applications Procedure: Applicants should provide 1) a fellowship application form 2) a curriculum vitae 3) a statement of proposal of no more than ten pages 4) three confidential letters of recommendation to be mailed by the authors. Provided in duplicate, one set mailed to each address.

Closing Date: October 15th.

Additional Information: Applications by fax not accepted.

For further information contact:
The Harvard University Centre for Italian Renaissance Studies, Villa I Tatti, University Place, 124 Mt. Auburn Street, Cambridge, MA, 02138-5762, USA
Tel: 617 495 8042

Visiting Scholar Affiliations

Subjects: Political economy of reform, ethnicity and nationalism, performance of democratic institutions, conflict analysis and resolution, nonviolent sanctions, US-Japan relations, and security issues, including transnational security.

Eligibility: Applicants must be in residence at the CFIA during the period of research.

Purpose: To facilitate and supplement the independent research of scholars on leave from their parent universities or research institutions where that research is related to the Center's current research programs.

Value: Non-stipendary award.

Study Establishment: CFIA, Harvard University.

Country of Study: USA.

Applications Procedure: Send a four-page description of research, a statement indicating the aplicant's source of funding, and three references to the CFIA.

Closing Date: Rolling applications.

For further information contact:
Center for International Affairs, Harvard University, 1737 Cambridge Street, Cambridge, MA, 02138, USA
Tel: 617 495 9899
Fax: 617 495 8292
Contact: Anne Emerson

CLARA HASKIL ASSOCIATION

Clara Haskil Association, rue du Simplon 40, Case postale 234, Vevey 1, 1800, Switzerland
Tel: 021 922 67 04
Fax: 021 922 67 34
Contact: Patrick Peikert, Director

Clara Haskil Competition

Subjects: Piano.

Eligibility: Open to pianists of any nationality and either sex, who are no more than 30 years of age.

Type: Prize.

No. of awards offered: One.

Frequency: Biennially (1997, 1999).

Value: SwFr20,000.

Closing Date: July 5th of the Competition year.

Additional Information: The Competition is usually held during the last week of August. There is an entry fee of SwFr250.

THE HASTINGS CENTER

The Hastings Center, 255 Elm Road, Briarcliff Manor, NY, 10510, USA
Tel: 914 762 8500
Fax: 914 762 2124
Contact: Strachan Donnelley PhD, Director of Education

*Eastern European Program

Subjects: Ethical issues in medicine, the life sciences and the professions.

Eligibility: Open to Eastern European scholars conducting significant work in biomedical ethics.

Purpose: To support independent research or study by Eastern European scholars.

Type: Scholarship.

No. of awards offered: 7-10.

Frequency: Annual.

Value: US$1,500-US$3,000 depending on length of stay.

Length of Study: 1-3 months.

Study Establishment: Hastings Center and the Centre for Philosophy and Health Care, Swansea, Wales.

Country of Study: USA and UK.

Closing Date: Four months prior to proposed stay.

International Scholars Program

Subjects: Ethical issues in medicine, the life sciences and the professions.

Eligibility: Open to foreign scholars conducting significant work in biomedical ethics.

Level of Study: Doctorate, Postdoctorate.

Purpose: To support independent research or study by foreign scholars.

Type: Scholarship.

No. of awards offered: 12-15.

Frequency: Annual.

Value: US$500-US$1,000 depending on need.

Length of Study: 2-6 weeks.

Study Establishment: The Hastings Center.

Country of Study: USA.

Applications Procedure: Write for application.

Closing Date: Two months prior to proposed stay.

HATTORI FOUNDATION

72D Leopold Road, London, SW19 7JQ, England
Tel: 0181 944 5319
Fax: 0181 946 0581
Contact: Mrs Noel L Masters, Administrator

Awards

Subjects: Solo performance (instrumental); chamber music (trio, quartet or quintet).

Eligibility: Open to British or foreign nationals studying full-time in the UK. Foreign applicants must have won a major prize in an international competition or won a national one. Candidates should be of postgraduate performance status.

Level of Study: Postgraduate, Professional development.

Purpose: To assist young instrumentalists of exceptional talent in establishing a soloist (or chamber music) career at international level.

Type: Individual project assistance.

No. of awards offered: Varies.

Frequency: Annual.

Value: No pre-determined amounts. The grant is based on the requirements of the approved project.

Length of Study: Variable, but one year limit.

Country of Study: British nationals: any country; foreign nationals: UK only.

Applications Procedure: Please submit application and reference forms, plus 30 minute performance (recital) on cassette tape.

Closing Date: May 1st.

Additional Information: Grants may be made for study, concert experience, international competitions, etc. Projects must be submitted for approval and discussion with the Director of Music and the trustees. Auditions take place in June and are in two stages.

HAYSTACK MOUNTAIN SCHOOL OF CRAFTS

Haystack Mountain School of Crafts, PO Box 518, Deer Isle, ME, 04627, USA
Tel: 207 348 2306
Fax: 207 348 2307
Contact: Stuart Kestenbaum

Haystack Scholarship

Subjects: Handicrafts.

Eligibility: Open to nationals of any country.

Level of Study: All skill levels.

Purpose: To allow craftspeople of all skill levels to study at Haystack sessions for two or three week periods. Technical Assistant and Work Study positions.

Type: Scholarship.

No. of awards offered: 90.

Frequency: Annual.

Value: US$480 to US$630.

Length of Study: Two to three weeks.

Applications Procedure: Application including references and supporting materials are required.

Closing Date: March 25, 1997.

HEALTH AND WELFARE CANADA NATIONAL HEALTH RESEARCH AND DEVELOPMENT PROGRAM (NHRDP)

Extramural Research Programs Directorate, Health Program & Services Branch, Health Canada, Ottawa, Ontario, K1A 1B4, Canada
Tel: 613 954 8545
Fax: 613 954 7363
Contact: Lucille Poirier

MSc Fellowship

Subjects: From a variety of research fields closely associated with population health enquiry, e.g. epidemiology, bio-statistics, health economics.

Eligibility: Open to Canadian citizens or legally landed immigrants, who hold an honours bachelors degree or equivalent or a health professional degree or are engaged in a masters program.

Purpose: To support individuals who wish to undertake full-time training leading to MSc degree or equivalent.

Type: Fellowship.

No. of awards offered: Varies.

Frequency: Annual.

Value: A stipend, tuition costs and research and travel allowances.

Study Establishment: Universities offering suitable programs.

Country of Study: Canada; in exceptional cases, i.e. if there is no equivalent Canadian program, outside Canada.

Closing Date: February.

National Health Research Scholarships

Subjects: Health care, public health and health services research.

Eligibility: Open to Canadian citizens or legally landed immigrants who hold a PhD in a research field associated with public health, or health services, or an MD, DDS and a masters degree in an appropriate health research field. Highest earned research qualifications will have been conferred not less than two and not more than six years prior to due date for receipt of applications.

Purpose: To afford exceptionally promising investigators with proven research abilities the freedom to pursue research relevant to the National Health Research and Development Program missions on a full-time basis.

Type: Scholarship.

No. of awards offered: Varies.

Frequency: Annual.

Value: Stipend plus research and travel allowances.

Study Establishment: Centres with established health research programs but not in the same institution in which the candidate's highest research qualification was earned and where the postdoctoral research experience was acquired.

Country of Study: Canada.

Closing Date: July 31st.

*PhD Fellowship

Subjects: From a variety of research fields closely associated with population health enquiry, e.g. epidemiology, bio-statistics, health economics.

Eligibility: Open to Canadian citizens or legally landed immigrants, who hold an honours bachelors degree or equivalent or a health professional degree or are already engaged in a PhD program.

Level of Study: Doctorate.

Purpose: To support individuals who wish to undertake full-time training leading to a masters degree or equivalent.

Type: Fellowship.

No. of awards offered: Varies.

Frequency: Annual.

Value: A stipend, tuition costs and research and travel allowances.

Study Establishment: Universities offering suitable programs.

Country of Study: Canada; in exceptional cases, i.e. if there is no equivalent Canadian program, outside Canada.

Closing Date: February.

*Postdoctoral Fellowships

Subjects: Health care, public health, health services research.

Eligibility: Open to Canadian citizens or legally landed immigrants who hold a PhD in a research field associated with public health, or health services, or an MD, DDS and a masters degree in an appropriate health research field.

Level of Study: Postdoctorate.

Purpose: To enable recipients to acquire up to two years' supervised research experience in an established health research setting.

Type: Fellowship.

No. of awards offered: Varies.

Frequency: Annual.

Value: An annual stipend, plus research and travel allowances.

Study Establishment: Centres with established health research programs.

Country of Study: Canada; in exceptional cases, i.e. if there is no equivalent Canadian program, outside Canada.

Applications Procedure: Prior to application, candidates should obtain a copy of the Career Awards Guide.

Closing Date: July 31st.

HEALTHCARE INFORMATION AND MANAGEMENT SYSTEMS SOCIETY FOUNDATION

Healthcare Information and Management Systems Society Foundation, 230 East Ohio Street, Suite 600, Chicago, IL, 60611, USA
Tel: 312 664 4467
Fax: 312 664 6143
www: http://www.himss.org
Contact: Executive Director

Richard P Covert Scholarship

Subjects: Industrial engineering, computer science, hospital administration or telecommunications management.

Eligibility: Open only to full-time junior, senior or graduate students who are student members of the Society.

Level of Study: Graduate.

Purpose: To assist graduate and undergraduate students who are interested in healthcare information management.

Type: Scholarship.

No. of awards offered: Two.

Frequency: Annual.

Value: US$1,000, plus full expenses to attend the annual conference to receive the award.

Country of Study: Any country.

Applications Procedure: Application is required; essay/paper required for graduate award.

Closing Date: October 15th.

HEALTH RESEARCH BOARD

Health Research Board, 73 Lower Baggot Street, Dublin, 2, Republic of Ireland
Tel: 01 6761176
Fax: 01 6611856
Email: HRB@HRB.ie
Contact: Secretary

Fellowships; Training Grants; Grants-in-Aid; Student Grants; Postgraduate Student Scholarships; Summer Research Projects

Subjects: Medical, epidemiological, health and health services research.

Eligibility: The general academic requirement for the awarding of any Grant is the possession of a medical, science, dental, or related biomedical science degree. There are no requirements regarding citizenship or age. However, Grants in general are normally available only to workers carrying out research in the Republic of Ireland, and training Grants are confined to recent graduates who are working towards a higher degree.

Level of Study: Postgraduate.

Type: Varies.

Frequency: Annual.

Value: Varies.

Country of Study: Usually Republic of Ireland.

Applications Procedure: Application form must be completed.

Closing Date: Normally March 1st.

HEBREW IMMIGRANT AID SOCIETY (HIAS)

Hebrew Immigrant Aid Society (HIAS), 333 Seventh Avenue, New York, NY, 10001, USA
Tel: 212 967 4100
Fax: 212 967 4483
Contact: Sally Hespe, Membership Associate

HIAS Scholarship Awards

Subjects: All subjects.

Eligibility: Open to HIAS-assisted refugees and their children who arrived in the USA 1985 or later. Must have completed one year (two semesters) at a USA high school, college, or graduate school.

Level of Study: Postgraduate, Doctorate.

Purpose: To assist HIAS-assisted refugees and their children.

Type: One-time grant.

No. of awards offered: 50-60.

Frequency: Annual.

Value: Average award: US$1,000.

Length of Study: One year must be completed.

Country of Study: USA.

Applications Procedure: Requests for application must be in writing and must include a self-addressed stamped envelope. Applications are judged on financial need, academic scholarship and community service.

Closing Date: April 19th.

HEBREW UNIVERSITY OF JERUSALEM

Institute of Jewish Studies, Hebrew University of Jerusalem, Mt Scopus Campus, Jerusalem, Israel
Tel: 02 883506/4/2
Fax: 02 322545

Moritz and Charlotte Warburg Prizes

Subjects: Jewish studies.

Eligibility: Open to nationals of all countries. Candidates for PhD degrees should be 35 years of age or younger; postdoctoral candidates may be up to 40 years of age.

Level of Study: Postgraduate, Doctorate.

Type: Prize.

No. of awards offered: Eight.

Frequency: Annual.

Value: US$5,000-US$7,000 per annum.

Length of Study: One year; renewable.

Study Establishment: The Institute of Jewish Studies.

Country of Study: Israel.

Closing Date: End of December.

HEED OPHTHALMIC FOUNDATION

Cleveland Clinic Foundation, 9500 Euclid Avenue, Cleveland, OH, 44195-5024, USA
Tel: 216 445 8145
Fax: 216 444 9137
Contact: F A Gutman, MD

*Heed Award

Subjects: Diseases and surgery of the eye and/or research in ophthalmology.

Eligibility: Open to US citizens who are graduates of an institution approved by the AMA.

Purpose: To provide assistance to men and women who desire to further their education or to do research.

Type: Fellowship.

No. of awards offered: Approximately 25.

Frequency: Annual.

Value: US$800 per month for up to one year.

Length of Study: One year; not renewable.

Country of Study: USA.

Closing Date: January 15th of the year in which the Fellowship starts.

ROSE HELLABY MEDICAL SCHOLARSHIPS TRUST

c/o NZ Guardian Trust, 105 Queen Street, PO Box 1934, Auckland, New Zealand
Tel: 09 377 7209
Fax: 09 377 7420
Contact: Lorraine Adams

Scholarships

Subjects: Rheumatic disease, physical medicine and manipulative treatment.

Eligibility: Open to persons who are registered or eligible to be registered as medical practitioners under the Medical Practitioners Act 1950.

Level of Study: Postgraduate.

Purpose: To enable the Scholar to pursue research or postgraduate training and experience overseas.

Type: Scholarship.

No. of awards offered: Varies.

Frequency: Dependent on funds available.

Value: Up to NZ$30,000 or equivalent in other foreign currency.

Length of Study: Up to two years.

Study Establishment: An approved medical school or other institution overseas for a program of study approved by the Trust's Board of Governors.

Country of Study: Any, except New Zealand.

Applications Procedure: Applications are available from the Trust Secretary.

Closing Date: March 31st and September 30th.

Additional Information: The Scholar must undertake to return to New Zealand upon the termination of the Scholarship and to engage in the practice of his or her profession in New Zealand for a period of at least three years.

CHARLES AND JULIA HENRY FUND

Charles and Julia Henry Fund, University Registry, The Old Schools, Cambridge, CB2 1TN, England
Contact: Secretary of the Trustees

Henry Fellowships (Harvard and Yale)

Subjects: Unrestricted, but subject to approval and feasibility.

Eligibility: Open to unmarried citizens, under 26 years of age, of the UK and commonwealth. They should be undergraduates of a UK university who have completed six terms of residence by January 1st preceding the Fellowship, or graduates of a UK university who are in their first year of postgraduate study at a UK university.

Purpose: To strengthen bonds between Britain and the USA.

Type: Fellowships.

No. of awards offered: Two.

Frequency: Annual.

Value: US$14,000 plus a travel grant of £1,100,(reviewed annually), tuition fees and health insurance.

Length of Study: One year only.

Study Establishment: Harvard University, Cambridge, Massachusetts, or Yale University, New Haven, Connecticut.

Country of Study: USA.

Closing Date: Early December.

Additional Information: Applicants must produce evidence of intellectual ability and must also submit a scheme of study or research not consisting of a degree course. The Fellowships are awarded in conjunction with other awards to finance a continuing course of study and are not tenable for degree courses. Fellows must undertake to return to the British Isles or some other part of the Commonwealth on the expiration of their term of tenure. The Fellowship must be vacated if the Fellow marries.

THE HERB SOCIETY OF AMERICA

The Herb Society of America, 9019 Kirtland Chardon Road, Kirtland, OH, 44094, USA
Tel: 216 256 0514
Fax: 216 256 0541
Contact: Research Grant

Research Grant

Subjects: Research on herbal projects.

Eligibility: Open to persons with a proposed program of scientific, academic or artistic investigation of herbal plants.

Purpose: To further the knowledge and use of herbs and contribute the results of the study and research to the records of horticulture, science, literature, history, art or economics.

Type: Research Grant.

Frequency: Annual.

Value: Up to US$5,000.

Length of Study: Up to one year.

Country of Study: Unrestricted.

Applications Procedure: Application should include proposal and expected budget.

Closing Date: January 31st.

Additional Information: Finalists will be interviewed.

FANNIE AND JOHN HERTZ FOUNDATION

Fannie and John Hertz Foundation, Box 5032, Livermore, CA, 94551-5032, USA
Tel: 510 373 1642
Contact: Dr Wilson K Talley

Fellowships

Subjects: Applied physical sciences.

Eligibility: Open to US citizens or permanent residents who have received a bachelors degree by the start of tenure and propose to complete a program of graduate study leading to an advanced degree. Students who have already commenced graduate study are also eligible.

Level of Study: Doctorate.

Purpose: To promote the education and enhancement of the defense potential and technological stature of the United States, by aiding in the education of the most capable students, particularly with respect to the applied physical sciences.

Type: Fellowship.

No. of awards offered: 25-30.

Frequency: Annual.

Value: US$17,000 per nine-month academic year, plus up to US$12,000 toward cost of tuition.

Length of Study: One academic year; may be renewed annually.

Study Establishment: Certain universities.

Country of Study: USA.

Applications Procedure: Hertz application form must be completed (in

duplicate), four reference reports (forms are provided) and official transcripts of all college work must be submitted.

Closing Date: Second to last Friday in October each year.

Additional Information: A full list of approved universities and institutes can be obtained from the Foundation. The Foundation does not support candidates pursuing joint PhD/professional degree programs.

MYRA HESS TRUST

Myra Hess Trust, 16 Ogle Street, London, W1P 7LG, England
Tel: 0171 636 4481
Fax: 0171 637 4307
Contact: Administrator

*Awards for Instrumentalists

Subjects: Musical performance.

Eligibility: Open to outstanding young instrumentalists between 18 and 30 years of age; preference is given to those entering upon a professional career. Singers, organists, harpists, harpsichordists and those playing percussion, brass or baroque instruments are ineligible.

Purpose: To give assistance for the purchase of instruments, for tuition and maintenance, and towards the cost of first recitals.

No. of awards offered: 5-10.

Frequency: Twice yearly.

Value: Up to £1,500.

Country of Study: Unrestricted.

Applications Procedure: Selected applicants are asked to audition in January or June/July.

Closing Date: 1 December, 1 June.

HEWLETT PACKARD COMPANY AND AMERICAN ASSOCIATION OF CRITICAL CARE NURSES

Hewlett Packard Company, 3000 Minuteman Road MS210, Andover, MA, 01810, USA
Tel: 508 659 2128
Contact: Michael Chase

HP/AACN Critical Care Nursing Research Grant

Subjects: Nursing.

Eligibility: AACN members may apply, (current registered nurse members only). Research must be undertaken in the USA only.

Level of Study: Postgraduate.

Purpose: To support research in critical care nursing. Preferred topics will address information technology requirements of patient management in critical care.

Type: Cash and equipment.

No. of awards offered: One.

Frequency: Annual.

Value: US$37,000.

Length of Study: One year.

Study Establishment: Hospital.

Country of Study: USA.

Applications Procedure: Potential applicants may write to Hewlett Packard address for applications.

Additional Information: Questions about suitability of research topics should be addressed to: AACN Research Department, 101 Columbia, Aliso Vicjo, CA 92656, USA. Tel: 1 800 394 5995.

HILGENFELD FOUNDATION FOR MORTUARY EDUCATION

Hilgenfeld Foundation for Mortuary Education, PO Box 4311, Fullerton, CA, 92634, USA
Contact: The Secretary

Hilgenfeld Foundation Grant

Subjects: Mortuary science education.

Eligibility: Eligible to nationals of the United States.

Level of Study: Postgraduate, Professional development, Undergraduate.

Purpose: To support mortuary science education through scholarships and research.

Type: Scholarship and research grant.

No. of awards offered: 20+.

Frequency: Dependent on funds available.

Length of Study: Varies.

Study Establishment: Applicants must be enrolled in a funeral service program, or be employed in the funeral service industry.

Country of Study: USA.

Applications Procedure: Application to be submitted on forms provided by the Hilgenfeld Foundation.

Closing Date: None.

THE HINRICHSEN FOUNDATION

The Hinrichsen Foundation, 10-12 Baches Street, London, N1 6DN, England
Contact: The Secretary

Awards

Subjects: Contemporary music composition, performance and research.

Eligibility: Preference will be given to UK applicants and/or projects taking place in the UK.

Level of Study: Unrestricted.

Purpose: To promote the written areas of music by assisting contemporary composition and its performance, and musical research.

No. of awards offered: Varies.

Frequency: Dependent on funds available.

Value: Varies.

Applications Procedure: Application form and two references are required.

Closing Date: Applications are accepted throughout the year.

Additional Information: Grants are not given for recordings, for the funding of commissions, for degree or other study courses or for the purchase of instruments or equipment.

HISTORIC NEW ORLEANS COLLECTION

Historic New Orleans Collection, 533 Royal Street, New Orleans, LA, 70130, USA
Tel: 523 4662
Fax: 598 7108
Contact: Dr Jon Kukla

L Kempa Williams Prizes

Subjects: History.

Eligibility: There are no eligibility restrictions.

Level of Study: Unrestricted.

Purpose: To honor best contributions to historical scholarship about Louisiana.

Type: Cash and plaque.

No. of awards offered: Two.

Frequency: Annual.

Value: US$1,000 published work; US$500 manuscript.

Applications Procedure: Please submit three copies of work and three copies of the application form.

Closing Date: February 1st each year.

Additional Information: The administration of these prizes is determined by a committee of scholars chosen by the Louisiana Historical Association. Funding is provided by the Historic New Orleans Collection.

HISTORY OF SCIENCE SOCIETY

History of Science Society, HSS Executive Office, Box 351330, University of Washington, Seattle, WA, 98195, USA
Tel: 206 543 9366
Fax: 206 685 9544
Email: hssexec@u.washington.edu
Contact: Keith R. Benson

HSS Travel Grant

Subjects: History; history of science (ancient to modern).

Eligibility: No restrictions.

Level of Study: Postgraduate, Doctorate.

Purpose: For travel to the annual HSS meeting.

Type: Travel Grant.

No. of awards offered: Approximately 50.

Frequency: Annual.

Value: US$350-US$500.

Country of Study: USA.

Applications Procedure: Application to HSS Executive Office (April newsletter - form).

Closing Date: June 1st.

CHARLES H HOOD FOUNDATION

Charles H Hood Foundation, 95 Berkeley Street, Suite 201, Boston, MA, 02116, USA
Tel: 617 695 9439
Fax: 617 423 4619
Contact: Raymond Considine

Child Health Research Grant

Subjects: Emphasis is on the initiation and furtherance of medical research which will help to diminish health problems affecting large numbers of children.

Eligibility: Funds may only be paid to a New England (6-states) medical or academic institution.

Level of Study: Doctorate.

Purpose: Designed for junior faculty who are initiating independent research in new areas of inquiry, and have limited federal grant experience.

Type: Research Grant.

No. of awards offered: 10-12 per year.

Frequency: Annual.

Length of Study: One year.

Applications Procedure: Write for application forms. These must be completed and submitted along with letters of recommendation, curriculum vitae, non-technical summary, scientific summary and itemized budget.

Closing Date: Exact date varies each year, but in April and October.

Child Health Research Grant (2)

Subjects: Biomedicine, paediatrics.

Eligibility: Open to nationals of any country.

Level of Study: Professional development.

Purpose: To promote independent medical research to benefit children. Undertaken by junior faculty who wish to establish an independent research career.

Type: Research Grant.

No. of awards offered: 12.

Frequency: Twice a year.

Value: US$50,000 per grant.

Length of Study: One year.

Country of Study: USA, New England states only.

Applications Procedure: Write for application forms. These must be completed and submitted with letters of recommendation, CV, non-technical summary, scientific summary and itemized budget.

Closing Date: April and October (dates vary each year).

HERBERT HOOVER PRESIDENTIAL LIBRARY ASSOCIATION

Herbert Hoover Presidential Library Association, PO Box 696, West Branch, IA, 52358, USA
Tel: 319 643 5327
Fax: 319 643 2391
Email: pachand@aol.com
Contact: Patricia A Hand

Travel Grants

Subjects: American history, journalism, political science.

Eligibility: Open to current graduate students, postdoctoral students, and qualified non-academic researchers. Priority is given to well-developed proposals that utilize the resources of the Hoover Presidential Library and which have the greatest likelihood of publication and subsequent use by educators, students and policy-makers.

Level of Study: Postgraduate, Postdoctorate.

Purpose: To encourage scholarly use of the holdings, and to promote the study of subjects of interest and concern to Herbert Hoover, Lou Henry Hoover and other public figures.

Type: Travel Grant.

No. of awards offered: Varies.

Frequency: Annual.

Value: Usually US$500-US$1,200 to cover the cost of a trip to the Library, but requests will be considered for longer research stays.

Study Establishment: The Library.

Country of Study: USA.

Applications Procedure: Please submit application form, project proposal of not more than 1200 words, and three letters of reference mailed separately.

Closing Date: March 1st.

Additional Information: For archival holdings information, call 319

643 5301.

JOHNS HOPKINS CENTER FOR ALTERNATIVES TO ANIMAL TESTING

Johns Hopkins Center for Alternatives to Animal Testing, 111 Market Place, Suite 840, Baltimore, Maryland, 21202-6709, USA
Tel: 410 223 1693
Fax: 410 223 1603
Email: caat@caat.spharbor.thu.edu
www: http://infonet.welch.jhu.edu/~caat/
Contact: Ann P Kerr

CAAT Research Grants

Subjects: Alternatives to current testing methods to replace or refine the use of animals.

Level of Study: Unrestricted.

Purpose: Starter Grants.

Type: Research Grant.

No. of awards offered: Up to 10.

Frequency: Annual.

Value: US$20,000 to US$30,000 maximum.

Country of Study: USA.

Applications Procedure: A one page proposal is submitted. After review, those which are applicable are invited to submit a full application.

HORSERACE BETTING LEVY BOARD

Horserace Betting Levy Board, 52 Grosvenor Gardens, London, SW1W 0AU, England
Tel: 0171 333 0043
Fax: 0171 333 0041
Contact: Ms E Tucker or Mrs Louise Giles, Assistant

Residencies in Equine Studies

Subjects: Postgraduate clinical training in equine studies with emphasis on the thoroughbred.

Eligibility: Open to holders of degrees, registerable with the RCVS, in veterinary science/medicine who have had at least one year's practical experience following graduation and who wish to undertake specialized higher clinical training in the equine veterinary field.

Level of Study: Postgraduate.

No. of awards offered: Up to eight residencies at any one time.

Frequency: Annual.

Value: Salary is based on the age-related non-medical university lecturer scale. Maximum award £22,800 per annum (reviewed annually), including a small allowance for travel and other expenses.

Length of Study: Up to three years subject to satisfactory progress.

Study Establishment: At any of the six veterinary schools, or at any appropriate university department or research institute or veterinary practice in the UK.

Country of Study: UK.

Applications Procedure: Applications on appropriate forms must be submitted.

Closing Date: April 1st.

Additional Information: Awards normally commence on October 1st.

Veterinary Research Training Scholarship

Subjects: Postgraduate training in equine veterinary medicine or science, with emphasis on the thoroughbred.

Eligibility: Open to holders of a degree, registerable with the RCVS, in veterinary medicine/science who wish to undertake full-time training in research in the equine veterinary field leading to a PhD.

Level of Study: Postgraduate.

No. of awards offered: Up to thirteen at any one time.

Frequency: Annual.

Value: Salary to the holder £11,000 (year one) with increments for years two and three. £2,780 (accountable) per annum for fees and expenses, and £1,850 (unaccountable) per annum to the department in which the holder works. Scales are reviewed annually.

Length of Study: Up to three years (subject to satisfactory progress).

Study Establishment: Any of the six veterinary schools or at any appropriate university department, research institute or veterinary practice in the UK.

Country of Study: UK.

Applications Procedure: Applications on appropriate forms.

Closing Date: April 1st.

Additional Information: Candidates must be nominated by a professor, lecturer, director or head of department of an eligible institution. Candidates will be interviewed by the boards veterinary advisory committee. Awards normally commence on October 1st.

HORTICULTURAL RESEARCH INSTITUTE

Horticultural Research Institute, Suite 500, 1250 I Street, NW, Washington, DC, 20005, USA
Tel: 202 789 2900
Fax: 202 789 1893
Contact: Ashby P Ruden, Director of Horticultural Research

Grants

Subjects: Nursery and landscape industry, especially concerning woody and perennial landscape plants, their production, marketing, landscape, water management and the environment.

Eligibility: Open to any researcher submitting an appropriate project which the Institute feels is deserving of support.

Purpose: To support necessary research for the advancement of the nursery, greenhouse and landscape industry.

Type: Grant.

No. of awards offered: 30+.

Frequency: Annual.

Value: Varies. A total of US$250,000 was awarded in 1996.

Length of Study: One year; occasionally renewable by reapplication.

Study Establishment: At state/federal research laboratories, land-grant universities, forest research stations, botanical gardens and arboreta, etc.

Country of Study: USA.

Closing Date: May 1st.

HORTICULTURAL RESEARCH INTERNATIONAL

Horticultural Research International, West Malling, Kent, ME19 6BJ, England
Tel: 01732 843833
Fax: 01732 847117
Contact: Personnel Officer

Agricultural and Food Research Council Scholarships

Subjects: Any area of science relevant to horticulture, in particular: crop production, of annual and perennial crops; hops; soil science; storage and market quality; plant pathology; entomology and insect pathology; ecology and control of weeds; breeding and genetics; microbiology; biochemistry and molecular biology; physiology; statistics.

Eligibility: Open to UK honours graduates and those who are shortly to graduate.

Purpose: To enable a Scholar to pursue further studies and obtain training.

Type: Varies.

Value: £7,200 per annum, plus university fees for a higher degree.

Length of Study: Three years.

Study Establishment: One of the company's sites: East Malling, Kent; Wye, Kent; Littlehampton, Sussex; Wellesbourne, Warwickshire.

Country of Study: UK.

Closing Date: 28 February for commencement in October.

British Society for Horticultural Research Blackman Studentship

Subjects: Fields relating to horticulture.

Eligibility: Open to British subjects usually resident in the UK who have a first or upper second class honours degree in a relevant scientific subject from a British Commonwealth university.

Level of Study: Postgraduate.

Purpose: To assist postgraduate study.

Type: Studentship.

No. of awards offered: One.

Frequency: Periodically.

Value: A basic tax-free maintenance allowance similar in amount to government studentships; paid quarterly.

Length of Study: Three years.

Study Establishment: The Institute.

Country of Study: UK.

Additional Information: When a studentship is available, an advertisement would appear in Nature or New Scientist. Applicants should respond to the advertisement.

HOSEI UNIVERSITY

Hosei University, 17-1 Fujimi 2 chome, Chiyoda-ku, Tokyo, 102, Japan
Tel: 3 3264 9662
Fax: 3 3239 9873
Contact: Toshio Yamazaki, Director, International Center

Hosei International Fund Foreign Scholars Fellowship

Subjects: Humanities, social and natural sciences, and engineering.

Eligibility: Open to foreign citizens who have sufficient knowledge and fluency in either English or Japanese, hold advanced academic degree(s) (master's or doctorate) or the equivalent, and are not more than 35 years of age as of April 1st the year he/she starts his/her research.

Purpose: To enable young foreign scholars to undertake non-degree research through a specific research project.

Type: Fellowship.

No. of awards offered: Three.

Frequency: Annual.

Value: Y210,000 per month, Y300,000 maximum for travelling expenses.

Length of Study: Six to 12 months.

Study Establishment: Hosei University.

Country of Study: Japan.

Closing Date: May 31st every year.

Additional Information: The study undertaken at the University on this program is non-degree; the participants will receive no course credits.

THE HOSPITAL FOR SICK CHILDREN FOUNDATION

Grants and Fellowships, The Hospital for Sick Children Foundation, 555 University Avenue, Toronto, Ontario, M5G 1X8, Canada
Tel: 416 813 5437
Fax: 416 813 7310
Contact: Natalia Jascolt, Director

External Grants

Subjects: All areas of child health: research, special programs, film productions, conference support, and/or health education programs.

Eligibility: Open to researchers in Canada.

Purpose: To support research and innovative programs in child health across Canada.

Type: Grant.

No. of awards offered: Approximately 40.

Frequency: Annual.

Value: From C$1,000 per project; not to exceed C$65,000 per year.

Length of Study: One to two years.

Country of Study: Canada.

Applications Procedure: Applications should be made through the institution or organization under whose auspices the project will be carried out.

Closing Date: October 1st, April 1st.

Additional Information: Grants will not be made to support annual campaigns, operating expenses, new undertakings (except temporarily), operating deficits, general endowment or sustaining funds, projects which might result in gain or profit to the organization, or building construction or improvement.

Duncan L Gordon Fellowships

Subjects: Paediatric health care.

Eligibility: Open to physicians and scientists wishing to obtain postdoctoral training, who are Canadian citizens or landed immigrants, are of outstanding academic achievement, and can provide evidence of special aptitude for teaching, research and administration.

Level of Study: Postdoctorate.

Purpose: To provide postdoctoral training.

Type: Fellowship.

No. of awards offered: Up to four.

Frequency: Annual.

Value: C$42,500 per year.

Length of Study: One or two years.

Study Establishment: Any agreed institution.

Country of Study: Any country.

Applications Procedure: Candidates should be nominated by the head of the department in which they are employed or in which they will be employed upon completion of the Fellowship.

Closing Date: October 1st.

Additional Information: Nominating institutions must affirm their intention to employ the Fellow upon completion of studies and to continue or establish a program in the field concerned. Processing of applications normally takes three months.

HOSPITAL FOR SICK CHILDREN RESEARCH TRAINING COMMITTEE (RESTRACOM)

Hospital for Sick Children Foundation, 555 University Avenue, Toronto, Ontario, M5G 1X8, Canada
Tel: 416 813 4992
Contact: Dr J Rovet

*Foreign Research Fellowship

Subjects: Paediatric research.

Eligibility: Open to those nominated by the active senior staff of the Research Institute of the Hospital for Sick Children.

Level of Study: Postgraduate.

Purpose: To provide funds to postgraduate foreign students seeking training.

Type: Fellowship.

No. of awards offered: 10-12.

Frequency: Annual.

Value: Up to C$26,320 per annum.

Length of Study: One year.

Study Establishment: The Hospital for Sick Children, in Toronto.

Country of Study: Canada.

Applications Procedure: The application is entered into a competition with other candidates.

Closing Date: Applications are accepted in mid-April and mid-October.

HOUBLON-NORMAN FUND

Houblon-Norman Fund, Secretary's Department HO-1, c/o Bank of England, Threadneedle Street, London, EC2R 8AH, England
Tel: 0171 601 4751
Fax: 0171 601 5460
Contact: Secretary

Fellowships

Subjects: Economics and finance.

Eligibility: Senior fellowships and fellowships are open to distinguished research workers as well as younger postdoctoral or equivalent applicants of any nationality. Preference will be shown to British and EC nationals for Fellowships.

Level of Study: Postdoctorate.

Purpose: To promote research into and disseminate knowledge and understanding of the working, interaction and function of financial and business institutions in Great Britain and elsewhere, and the economic conditions affecting them.

Type: Fellowship.

No. of awards offered: Varies.

Frequency: Annual.

Value: The value of a Fellowship depends on the candidate's circumstances, and will be of such amount as seems necessary for undertaking the work. It might take the form of payment to the individual's employer.

Length of Study: From one month to one year.

Study Establishment: The Bank of England.

Country of Study: UK.

Applications Procedure: Application form needs to be completed.

Closing Date: As advertised in the press.

HOUSE OF HUMOUR AND SATIRE

House of Humour and Satire, PO Box 104, Gabrovo, 5300, Bulgaria
Tel: 359 66 27229
Fax: 359 66 26989
Telex: 67413
Contact: Tatyana Tsankova, Director

Prizes

Subjects: Drawing and painting.

Eligibility: Open to nationals of any country.

Level of Study: Unrestricted.

Purpose: To stimulate the creation of humour art.

Type: Cash prize.

No. of awards offered: Four.

Frequency: Every two years.

Valuo: From US$700 to US$1,100.

Applications Procedure: Application form must be completed.

Closing Date: March 1st, every odd year.

Additional Information: There are four categories: best cartoon, best sculpture, best painting, and best humorous drawing/graphic work.

GEORGE A AND ELIZA GARDNER HOWARD FOUNDATION

Howard Foundation, Brown University, Box 1956, 42 Charlesfield Street, Providence, RI, 02912, USA
Tel: 401 863 2640
Fax: 401 863 7341
Email: Howard-Foundation@brown.edu
Contact: Administrative Director

Howard Foundation Fellowships

Subjects: The Foundation awards a limited number of fellowships each year for independent projects in fields selected on a rotational basis. Seven fellowships will be offered for the 1997-98 fellowship year to support persons engaged in independent projects in the fields of: history, history of science, archeology, and political science.

Eligibility: Nominees should normally have the rank of assistant or associate professor or their non-academic equivalents. Support is intended to augment paid sabbatical leaves, making it financially possible for grantees to have an entire year in which to pursue their projects, free of any other professional responsibilities. Accepted nominees should therefore be eligible for sabbaticals or other leave with guaranteed additional support. Candidates regardless of their country of citizenship, must be professionally based in the USA either by affiliation with an institution or by residence.

Purpose: To assist individuals in the middle stages of their careers.

Type: Fellowship.

No. of awards offered: Seven.

Frequency: Annual.

Value: US$18,000.

Length of Study: One year.

Country of Study: Unrestricted.

Applications Procedure: Applications are accepted only upon nomination. Details of the nomination procedure are available from the Foundation. Fellowships are not available for work leading to any academic degree.

Closing Date: October 15th for nominations; November 30th for completed applications. Fellowships will be announced May 1st, for commencement of tenure July 1st.

HUDSON INSTITUTE, INC

Hudson Institute, Inc, PO Box 26919, Indianapolis, IN, 46226-0919, USA
Tel: 317 545 1000
Fax: 317 545 9639
Contact: Neil C Pickett, Director of Program Management

*Herman Kahn Fellowship

Subjects: Educational policy; domestic and international political economy; national security studies; technology policy; and political theory and institutions.

Eligibility: Open to graduate students who have completed all PhD coursework within the last five years and can provide evidence that they have been formally admitted to candidacy for the PhD. Consideration will be given only to applicants with an outstanding academic record, who are strongly recommended by faculty members and have demonstrated interest in, and capability for, policy-oriented research.

Level of Study: Doctorate.

Purpose: To support PhD candidates who have completed their course work and have only their dissertation remaining.

Type: Fellowship.

No. of awards offered: Up to 3.

Frequency: Annual.

Value: US$18,000, plus certain travel expenses.

Length of Study: One academic year.

Study Establishment: Indianapolis, Indiana, or in Washington, DC.

Country of Study: USA.

Closing Date: 30 April for notification by 15 June.

Additional Information: The Fellow's time will be divided equally between dissertation work and policy research assigned by the Institute. Application requirements are available on request. Selected candidates will be interviewed in Indianapolis.

S S HUEBNER FOUNDATION FOR INSURANCE EDUCATION

S S Huebner Foundation for Insurance Education, 430 Vance Hall, Philadelphia, PA, 19104-6301, USA
Tel: 215 898 9631
Fax: 215 573 2218
Contact: J David Cummins, Executive Director

Postdoctoral Fellowships

Subjects: Insurance and risk.

Eligibility: Open to citizens of the USA and Canada who hold a PhD or other terminal degree from an accredited university and intend to follow an insurance teaching career.

Level of Study: Postdoctorate.

Purpose: To increase the supply of qualified teachers.

Type: Fellowship.

No. of awards offered: Varies.

Frequency: Annual.

Value: US$14,000 for 9 months.

Length of Study: One year.

Study Establishment: University of Pennsylvania.

Country of Study: USA.

Closing Date: February 15th.

Predoctoral Fellowships

Subjects: Insurance: study towards a PhD in business and applied economics.

Eligibility: Open to citizens of the USA and Canada who hold a bachelor's degree from an accredited US or Canadian university or college and intend to follow an insurance teaching career.

Level of Study: Predoctorate.

Purpose: To increase the supply of qualified teachers.

Type: Fellowship.

No. of awards offered: Varies.

Value: Approximately US$34,000 per annum, consisting of full tuition and fees plus a monthly living stipend of US$14,000 per year.

Study Establishment: Wharton School of the University of Pennsylvania.

Country of Study: USA.

Closing Date: February 1st.

Additional Information: Candidates are required to certify that it is their intention to follow an insurance teaching career and that they will major in risk and insurance for a graduate degree. Candidates must take the Admission Test for Graduate Study in Business. For information concerning these examinations, candidates should write directly to the Educational Testing Service, 20 Nassau Street, Princeton, New Jersey 08540, USA.

HOWARD HUGHES MEDICAL INSTITUTE

Howard Hughes Medical Institute, National Research Council, 2101 Constitution Avenue, Washington, DC, 20418, USA
Tel: 202 334 2872
Fax: 202 334 3419
Email: infofell@nas.edu
www: http://www.hhmi.org
Contact: The Fellowship Office

Postdoctoral Research Fellowships for Physicians

Subjects: Biological processes.

Eligibility: Applicants must have gained their first degree within the last ten years, and must have had two years of postgraduate clinical training, and no more than two years of postdoctoral training in fundamental research.

Level of Study: Postdoctorate.

Purpose: To help increase the supply of well-trained physician-scientists, through fellowships for three years of training in fundamental research (basic biological processes or disease mechanisms).

Type: Fellowship.

No. of awards offered: Thirty.

Frequency: Annual.

Value: US$69,000-US$86,500 per year.

Length of Study: Three years.

Study Establishment: Academic or non-profit research institution.

Country of Study: USA.

Applications Procedure: Application forms and instructions should be obtained from the address shown. Panels of scientists review applications, and the Institute makes the final selection.

Closing Date: Late December. Awards are announced in June.

Additional Information: Fellows must engage in research full-time. During the fellowship term, they may not be enrolled in a graduate degree program, nor hold a faculty appointment. The applicant is responsible for selecting a research mentor and making arrangements to work in that person's laboratory.

For further information contact:
Howard Hughes Medical Institute, 4000 Jones Bridge Road, Chevy Chase, MD, 20815-6789, USA
Tel: 301 215 8889
Fax: 301 215 8888
Email: fellows@hq.hhmi.org
www: http://www.hhmi.org
Contact: Barbara Filner

Predoctoral Fellowships in Biological Sciences

Subjects: Biological sciences.

Eligibility: Awards go to students at or near the beginning of their graduate study towards a PhD or ScD in any field of biological science.

Level of Study: Doctorate.

Purpose: To promote excellence in biomedical research by helping prospective researchers with exceptional promise to obtain high-quality graduate education.

Type: Fellowship.

No. of awards offered: 80.

Frequency: Annual.

Value: US$28,500 (includes US$14,500 stipend and US$14,000 cost-of-education allowance).

Length of Study: Up to five years.

Study Establishment: Institution of higher education.

Country of Study: USA.

Applications Procedure: Application forms and instructions should be obtained from the address shown. The Institute makes awards to those who, in the judgement of the review panels, have demonstrated superior scholarship and show greatest promise for achievement in biomedical research.

Closing Date: Early November. Awards are announced in April.

HUMANE RESEARCH TRUST

Humane Research Trust, Brook House, 29 Bramhall Lane South, Bramhall, Stockport, Cheshire, SK7 2DN, England
Tel: 0161 439 8041
Fax: 0161 439 3713
Contact: Margaret Pritchard, Trust Secretary

Prize

Subjects: Humane research.

Eligibility: Open to established scientific workers engaged in productive research.

Level of Study: Unrestricted.

Purpose: To encourage scientific programmes where the use of animals is replaced by other methods.

Type: Prize.

No. of awards offered: Varies.

Value: Varies.

Country of Study: Any country.

Applications Procedure: Application form must be completed.

Closing Date: Varies; the Trustees meet every three to four months.

Additional Information: The Trust is a registered charity and donations are encouraged.

HUMANITARIAN TRUST

Humanitarian Trust, 64 Aberdale Gardens, London, NW6 3QD, England

Contact: Mrs M Myers, Secretary of Trustees

Research Awards

Subjects: Unrestricted; subject to the discretion of the Trustees. Awards are not made for journalism, theatre, music or any arts subjects. Candidates are only considered when studying 'academic' subjects.

Eligibility: Open to persons already holding an original grant.

Level of Study: Postgraduate, Undergraduate.

Purpose: General charitable purposes beneficial to the community.

No. of awards offered: Varies according to the availability of funds.

Frequency: Twice yearly.

Value: Approximately £200-£300.

Length of Study: One year; not renewable.

Study Establishment: Any approved institution.

Country of Study: UK.

Applications Procedure: Write in. Submit two references, preferably from tutors or heads of department, and a breakdown of anticipated income and expenditure.

Additional Information: Awards are not made for travel. They are intended only as supplementary assistance and are to be held concurrently with other awards.

HUNGARIAN TELEVISION

Interart Festivalcenter, PO Box 80, Budapest, H-1366, Hungary
Tel: 36 1 1179 838
Fax: 36 1 1179 910

*International Conductors Competition

Subjects: Conducting.

Eligibility: Open to conductors of all nationalities.

No. of awards offered: Four.

Frequency: Triennially.

THE HUNTINGTON

Committee on Awards, The Huntington , 1151 Oxford Road, San Marino, CA, 91108, USA
Tel: 818 405 2194
Fax: 818 449 5703
Contact: Robert C Ritchie, Chairman

The W M Keck Foundation Fellowship for Young Scholars

Subjects: British and American history, literature and art.

Eligibility: There are no restrictions on age, nationality, or citizenship.

Purpose: To encourage outstanding young scholars to pursue their own lines of inquiry (completing dissertation research or beginning a new project) in the fields of British and American history, literature and art.

Type: Fellowship.

No. of awards offered: Varies.

Frequency: Annual.

Value: US$2,300 per month.

Length of Study: One to three months.

Study Establishment: The Huntington.

Country of Study: USA.

Closing Date: Applications are welcome between October 1st and December 15th.

Short-Term Fellowships

Subjects: English or American history, literature, history of science and of art.

Eligibility: Open to nationals of any country who have demonstrated, to a degree commensurate with their age and experience, unusual abilities as scholars through publications of a high order of merit. Attention is paid to the value of the candidate's project and the degree to which the special strengths of the Library and Gallery will be used.

Purpose: To enable outstanding scholars to carry out significant research in the collections of the Library and Gallery by assisting in balancing budgets of such persons on leave at reduced pay and living away from home.

Type: Fellowship.

No. of awards offered: Approximately 90 Fellowships, depending on funds available.

Frequency: Annual.

Value: US$1,800 per month.

Length of Study: One to five months.

Study Establishment: The Huntington.

Country of Study: USA.

Closing Date: Applications are welcome between October 1st and December 15th for commencement June 1st.

Additional Information: Fellowships are available for work towards doctoral dissertations.

Barbara Thom Postdoctoral Fellowship

Subjects: English, medieval history, modern history, fine and applied arts.

Eligibility: Preference will be given to scholars who are four or five years beyond the award of PhD.

Level of Study: Postdoctorate.

Purpose: To support a non-tenured faculty member while revising a manuscript for publication.

Type: Fellowship.

No. of awards offered: One per year.

Frequency: Annual.

Value: US$25,000.

Length of Study: One year.

Study Establishment: The Huntington.

Country of Study: USA.

Applications Procedure: For application information please contact the Chair-Committee on Awards at the address given.

Closing Date: Applications are accepted between October 1st and December 15th each year.

HUNTINGTON'S DISEASE ASSOCIATION

Huntington's Disease Association, 108 Battersea High Street, London, SW11 3HP, England
Tel: 0171 223 7000/01455 239570
Fax: 0171 223 9489
Contact: Fred A Tozer

Research Grant

Subjects: Any medical or social research project associated with Huntington's disease.

Eligibility: Open to suitably qualified researchers.

Type: Research Grant.

No. of awards offered: A variable number, depending on the annual budget.

Frequency: Throughout the year.

Country of Study: UK.

Closing Date: Reviewed every two months.

HUNTINGTON'S DISEASE SOCIETY OF AMERICA (HDSA)

HDSA, 140 West 22nd Street, New York, NY, 10011-2420, USA
Tel: 212 242 1968
Fax: 212 243 2443
Contact: Claudia Archimede

Research Grants and Fellowships

Subjects: Cure and treatment of Huntington's Disease at the basic and clinical level.

Eligibility: Open to MDs or PhDs from accredited medical schools and universities.

Level of Study: Postdoctorate.

Type: Grants and fellowships.

No. of awards offered: Varies.

Frequency: Annual.

Value: Up to US$35,000 for Grants; up to US$30,000 for Fellowships.

Country of Study: Any country.

Applications Procedure: Application form must be completed.

Closing Date: January 5th.

Additional Information: Call for an application form.

EDMUND NILES HUYCK PRESERVE, INC

Edmund Niles Huyck Preserve, Inc, PO Box 189, Rensselaerville, NY, 12147, USA

Graduate and Postgraduate Grants

Subjects: Any research involving the ecology, behaviour, evolution and natural resources of the area, and conservation biology.

Eligibility: Awards are made without regard to sex, colour, religion, ethnic origin or academic affiliation of the applicant. Support is based solely on the quality of the proposed research and its appropriateness to the natural resources and facilities of the Preserve.

Level of Study: Postgraduate, Doctorate, Graduate.

Purpose: To promote scientific research on the flora and fauna of the Huyck Preserve and vicinity.

Type: Grant.

No. of awards offered: Ten.

Frequency: Annual.

Value: Up to US$2,500, plus laboratory space and lodging.

Length of Study: Varies; renewable.

Study Establishment: At the Preserve.

Country of Study: USA.

Applications Procedure: Send for application.

Closing Date: February 1st.

IMPERIAL CANCER RESEARCH FUND

Imperial Cancer Research Fund, PO Box 123, Lincoln's Inn Fields, London, WC2A 3PX, England
Tel: 0171 269 3328
Fax: 0171 269 3585
www: http://www.icnet.uk
Contact: Dr M C Swain, Assistant Director (Scientific Liaison)

Clinical Research Fellowships

Subjects: All areas of cancer research.

Eligibility: Open to medical graduates of registrar or senior registrar status having obtained MRCP, FRCS, or other higher medical qualifications.

Level of Study: Postdoctorate, Doctorate.

Purpose: To enable research training.

Type: Fellowship.

No. of awards offered: Approximately 10.

Frequency: Annual.

Value: Remuneration is based on current NHS salary scales.

Length of Study: Up to four years.

Study Establishment: Imperial Cancer Research Fund Laboratories and Clinical Units. Fellows based in the Research Laboratories are expected to register for a PhD degree; fellows based in the Clinical Units will submit their work for either a PhD or MD.

Country of Study: UK.

Applications Procedure: As detailed in advertisements.

Additional Information: Fellowships are advertised in scientific and medical journals.

For further information contact:
Imperial Cancer Research Fund, PO Box 123, Lincoln's Inn Fields, London, WC2A 3PX, England
Tel: 0171 269 3230
Fax: 0171 269 3313
Contact: Mr W House, Deputy Director (Clinical Research)

Graduate Studentships

Subjects: All areas of cancer research.

Eligibility: Candidates should normally have been resident in the UK for at least three years, and have, or be about to obtain, a first or upper class degree in science, and not be over 25 years of age. Non-residents are not excluded from consideration.

Level of Study: Doctorate.

Purpose: To enable research training.

No. of awards offered: Approximately 30.

Frequency: Annual.

Value: Approximately £8,746-£11,446 (taxable) per annum, depending on location, plus additional allowances in some cases.

Length of Study: Three years.

Study Establishment: Imperial Cancer Research Fund Laboratories and Clinical Units.

Country of Study: UK.

Applications Procedure: As detailed in advertisements.

For further information contact:
Laboratory Research Directorate, Imperial Cancer Research Fund, PO Box 123, Lincoln's Inn Fields, London, WC2A 3PX, England
Tel: 0171 269 3090
Fax: 0171 269 3585
Contact: Dr Lilian Gann

Research Fellowships

Subjects: All areas of cancer research.

Eligibility: Applicants must have been awarded a PhD or equivalent, or show written proof of submission of their thesis.

Level of Study: Postdoctorate.

Purpose: To assist postdoctoral research.

Type: Fellowship.

No. of awards offered: Approximately 30.

Frequency: Annual.

Value: Approximate starting salary of £17,400-£23,647 per annum, depending on experience.

Length of Study: Up to three years.

Study Establishment: Imperial Cancer Research Fund Laboratories and Clinical Units.

Country of Study: UK.

Applications Procedure: As detailed in advertisements.

IMPERIAL COLLEGE OF SCIENCE, TECHNOLOGY AND MEDICINE

Imperial College, London, SW7 2AZ, England
Fax: 0171 594 8004
Email: d.atkins@ic.ac.uk
Contact: Assistant Registrar (Admissions)

Beit Fellowship For Scientific Research

Subjects: Sciences, engineering and technology.

Eligibility: Candidates must hold a first clas honours degree awarded by a recognized university in a territory which is currently part of the British Commonwealth (or formed part of the British Empire on 20 September 1913).

Level of Study: Doctorate.

Purpose: To enable a student of outstanding research ability to undertake research in a scientific or technological field to be conducted at Imperial College.

Type: Fellowship.

No. of awards offered: One.

Frequency: Annual.

Value: £6,600 per annum plus college fees.

Length of Study: One year, renewable for up to two additional years.

Study Establishment: Imperial College, for research leading to the PhD degree of the University of London.

Country of Study: UK.

Applications Procedure: Application form must be completed and submitted with two references. Transcript and academic record required from non-UK applicants.

Closing Date: April 30th.

Additional Information: Enquirers should state desired subject of study. Research in medicine is not included in this fellowship.

Concrete Structures Bursaries

Subjects: Concrete Structures.

Eligibility: Open to candidates who have a good first degree and approximately 3 years' practical experience.

Level of Study: Postgraduate.

Purpose: To assist outstanding candidates for the MSc/DIC course.

Type: Bursary.

No. of awards offered: 1 or 2.

Frequency: Annual.

Value: Up to £2,000.

Length of Study: One year.

Study Establishment: Department of Civil Engineering at Imperial College.

Country of Study: UK.

Applications Procedure: Application form must be completed and submitted with two references. Transcript and academic record required for non-UK applicants.

Closing Date: March 31st.

Additional Information: The award is intended as a supplement to other finance or own funds.

Stephen and Anna Hui Fellowship

Subjects: The fields of earth sciences, defined as geology, extraction metallurgy, minerals, and mining and petroleum engineering.

Eligibility: Open to students with a first or upper second honours degree from universities in Hong Kong, People's Republic of China or the Republic of China.

Level of Study: Postgraduate, Doctorate.

Purpose: To facilitate postgraduate study or research.

Type: Fellowship.

No. of awards offered: One.

Frequency: Every 2-3 years.

Value: To cover fees, plus a maintenance allowance based on Research Council Studentship rates.

Length of Study: One year; renewable for up to 2 additional years.

Study Establishment: Imperial College.

Country of Study: UK.

Applications Procedure: Application form must be completed and submitted with two references and a transcript of academic record.

Closing Date: January 31st.

Additional Information: This award is not offered every year.

Rees Jeffreys Road Fund Bursaries

Subjects: Transport.

Eligibility: Open to UK citizens who hold at least an upper second class honours degree.

Level of Study: Postgraduate.

Purpose: To facilitate postgraduate study or research.

Type: Bursary.

No. of awards offered: Two (at the discretion of the Trustees).

Frequency: Annual.

Value: To cover fees and maintenance at the Research Council Studentship basic rates.

Study Establishment: Department of Civil Engineering at Imperial College.

Country of Study: UK.

Applications Procedure: Application form plus two references required.

Closing Date: June 20th.

RTZ Advanced Course Bursary

Subjects: Engineering rock mechanics, petroleum geoscience, mineral deposit evaluation, advanced chemical engineering, environmental technology.

Eligibility: Open to candidates with at least an Upper Second class honours degree in a relevant subject.

Level of Study: Postgraduate.

359

Purpose: To facilitate study on specified postgraduate MSc course.

Type: Bursary.

No. of awards offered: One.

Frequency: Annual.

Value: Varies. Covers fees plus a maintenance allowance of at least Research Council rates.

Length of Study: One year.

Study Establishment: Imperial College.

Country of Study: UK.

Applications Procedure: Application form must be completed and submitted with two references. Transcript of academic record is required from non-UK candidates.

Closing Date: May 15th.

Additional Information: Preference will be given to those with appropriate postgraduate industrial experience.

THE INCORPORATED EWIN AUSTIN ABBEY MEMORIAL SCHOLARSHIPS

The Incorporated Ewin Austin Abbey Memorial Scholarships, PO Box 5, Rhayadar, Powys, LD6 5WA, United Kingdom
Tel: 01597 810 704
Contact: Faith Clark

Abbey Awards in Painting

Eligibility: No age restriction.

Level of Study: Professional development.

Purpose: To allow mid-career painters to pursue their artistic studies.

Frequency: Annual, dependent on funds available.

Value: Depends.

Length of Study: Two to three months.

Study Establishment: British School at Rome.

Country of Study: Italy.

Applications Procedure: Awards are advertised. Application forms sent in response to letters.

Closing Date: January 31st.

Additional Information: Awards are for painters only.

Abbey Scholarship in Painting

Level of Study: Postgraduate.

Purpose: To spend one academic year at the British School at Rome in order to pursue artistic studies.

Type: Scholarship.

No. of awards offered: One.

Frequency: Annual.

Value: Depends.

Length of Study: One year (academic).

Study Establishment: British School at Rome.

Country of Study: Italy.

Applications Procedure: Scholarship is advertised and administered through the British School at Rome.

Closing Date: Depends.

Additional Information: All enquiries and requests for forms to The British School at Rome.

INDIAN COUNCIL FOR CULTURAL RELATIONS

Indian Council for Cultural Relations, c/o High Commission of India, 3-5 Moonah Place, Yarralumla, ACT, 2600, Australia
Tel: 273 3999
Fax: 273 3328

*Commonwealth Scholarship and Fellowship Plan

Subjects: Unrestricted (except MBBS, BDS, BPharma).

Eligibility: Open to Australian citizens who are resident in Australia.

Level of Study: Postgraduate, Doctorate, Postdoctorate.

No. of awards offered: c.2.

Frequency: Annual.

Value: A monthly maintenance allowance of RS1,500 for students up to postgraduate level, RS2,000 for PhD students and RS2,500 for post-doctoral students; an annual contingency allowance of RS3,000 for students up to postgraduate level, RS5,000 for PhD humanities students and RS7,500 for PhD students of science, engineering and technology. Tuition and examination fees are paid by the Council directly to the university; medical expenses and accommodation are paid by the Council. Airfare is not covered by the awards.

Study Establishment: University.

Country of Study: India.

Applications Procedure: Application forms and information are available on request.

Closing Date: March 31st.

*Indo-Australian Cultural Exchange Programme

Subjects: Unrestricted (except MBBS, BDS, BPharma).

Eligibility: Open to Australian citizens who are resident in Australia.

Level of Study: Postgraduate.

No. of awards offered: c.5.

Frequency: Annual.

Value: A monthly maintenance allowance of RS1,500 for students up to postgraduate level, RS2,000 for PhD students and RS2,500 for post-doctoral students; an annual contingency allowance of RS3,000 for students up to postgraduate level, RS5,000 for PhD humanities students and RS7,500 for PhD students of science, engineering and technology. Tuition and examination fees are paid by the Council directly to the university; medical expenses and accommodation are paid by the Council. Airfare is not covered by the awards.

Study Establishment: University.

Country of Study: India.

Applications Procedure: Application forms and information are available on request.

Closing Date: March 31st.

INDIAN COUNCIL OF SOCIAL SCIENCE RESEARCH

Indian Council of Social Science Research, 35 Ferozeshah Road, New Delhi, 110001, India
Tel: 91 11 384734
Fax: 91 11 388037
Contact: Member Secretary

*General Fellowships

Subjects: All social sciences and social science aspects of other sciences: economics, commerce, education, management, business administration, psychology, political science, international relations, public administration, sociology, social work, criminology, social science aspects of anthropology, demography, geography, history, law, linguistics.

Eligibility: Open to scholars holding a PhD and to outstanding scholars with equivalent research work of merit.

Level of Study: Postdoctorate.

Purpose: To enable scholars to devote their full time to research in their area of interest.

Type: Fellowship.

No. of awards offered: Varies.

Frequency: Quarterly.

Value: 2,500 rupees per month, plus contingency 7,500 rupees per annum in the case of scholars who are not in employment. The salary of scholars in a regular job in India is protected, plus the contingency.

Length of Study: Two years.

Country of Study: India.

Applications Procedure: Four copies each of detailed self-contained research proposal and bio-data must be submitted.

*Senior Fellowships

Subjects: All social sciences and social science aspects of other sciences: economics, commerce, education, management, business administration, psychology, political science, international relations, public administration, sociology, social work, criminology, social science aspects of anthropology, demography, geography, history, law, linguistics.

Eligibility: Open to professional social scientists having significant publications including a book and/or papers in professional journals to their credit. Scholars from neighbouring countries are preferred.

Purpose: To enable scholars to devote themselves full time to research on their area of interest.

Type: Fellowship.

No. of awards offered: Varies.

Frequency: Quarterly.

Value: 3,000-4,000 rupees per month, plus contingency 7,500 rupees per annum. In the case of scholars in India with permanent employment salary is protected, plus contingency.

Length of Study: Two years.

Country of Study: India.

Applications Procedure: Four copies each of detailed self-contained research proposal and bio-data must be submitted.

INDUSTRIAL MARKETING COUNCIL

Industrial Marketing Council, 18 St Peters Steps, Brixham, Devon, England
Contact: Philip Allen

*Training Grant

Subjects: Industrial marketing research, business to business research, marketing intelligence, international marketing.

Eligibility: Open to UK residents over 21 years of age who hold a first degree or equivalent.

Purpose: To assist participants attending training courses in industrial marketing research, marketing intelligence and international marketing held by the European College of Marketing and Marketing Research.

No. of awards offered: 10.

Frequency: Twice yearly.

Value: Reimbursement of 30% of fees.

Study Establishment: European College of Marketing and Marketing Research.

Country of Study: UK.

INSTITUTE FOR ADVANCED STUDIES IN THE HUMANITIES

Institute for Advanced Studies in the Humanities, University of Edinburgh, Hope Park Square, Edinburgh, EH8 9NW, Scotland
Tel: 0131 650 4671
Fax: 0131 668 2252
Email: IASH@ed.ac.uk
www: http://www.ed.ac.uk/~iash/home_page.html
Contact: Professor Peter Jones, Director

European Enlightenment Project Fellowships

Eligibility: Open to postdoctoral candidates; degree candidates are not eligible. Fellows must be able to speak English.

Level of Study: Postdoctorate.

Purpose: Fellowships for leading scholars, from any discipline, whose work concerns the European Enlightenment (C.1720-1800), to take part in the institutes five year project on the Enlightenment.

Type: Non stipendiary Fellowships.

No. of awards offered: 100 over five years.

Frequency: Annual.

Length of Study: Three to six months.

Study Establishment: The Institute.

Country of Study: Scotland.

Applications Procedure: Application forms are available from the Institute.

Closing Date: December 1st.

Andrew W Mellon Foundation Fellowships in the Humanities

Eligibility: Restricted to Czech, Hungarian, Polish and Slovak scholars. Fellows must be able to speak English.

Level of Study: Postgraduate.

Purpose: To promote advanced research within the field of humanities, broadly understood, and to sponsor inter-disciplinary research.

Type: Stipendiary.

No. of awards offered: Three.

Frequency: Annual.

Length of Study: Three months.

Study Establishment: At the Institute.

Country of Study: Scotland.

Applications Procedure: Application forms are available from the Institute.

Closing Date: March 31st.

Visiting Research Fellowships

Subjects: Archaeology, history of art, classics, English literature, history, European and oriental languages and literature, linguistics, philosophy, Scottish studies, history of science, law, divinity, music and the social sciences.

Eligibility: Open to scholars of any nationality holding a doctorate or offering equivalent evidence of aptitude for advanced studies. Degree candidates are ineligible.

Purpose: To promote advanced research within the field of the humanities, broadly understood, and also to sponsor inter-disciplinary research.

Type: Fellowship.

No. of awards offered: 25.

361

Frequency: Annual.

Value: Most Fellowships are honorary, but stipends of up to £500 are occasionally available.

Length of Study: Two to six months.

Study Establishment: At the Institute.

Country of Study: UK.

Closing Date: December 1st.

Additional Information: Fellows have the use of study-rooms at the Institute, near the University library and within easy reach of the National Library of Scotland, the Central City Library, the National Galleries and Museums, the Library of the Society of Antiquaries in Scotland, and the Scottish Record Office. Candidates should advise their referees to write on their behalf direct to the Institute and to ensure that references are received in Edinburgh before 7 January.

INSTITUTE FOR ADVANCED STUDY

Institute for Advanced Study, Olden Lane, Princeton, NJ, 08540, USA
Tel: 609 734 8000
Fax: 609 924 8399
Email: mcnatt@IAS.EDU
www: http://www.ias.edu
Contact: Norman McNatt

Postdoctoral Residential Fellowships

Subjects: Social science, history, astronomy, theoretical physics and mathematics.

Eligibility: There are no restrictions on eligibility.

Level of Study: Postdoctorate.

Purpose: To support advanced study.

Type: Stipend.

No. of awards offered: 160.

Frequency: Annual.

Value: US$25,000-US$35,000.

Length of Study: Average: one year.

Country of Study: USA.

Applications Procedure: Application materials are available from the School administrative officers.

Closing Date: Varies: November 15th - December 15th.

INSTITUTE FOR ECUMENICAL AND CULTURAL RESEARCH

Institute for Ecumenical and Cultural Research, PO Box 6188, Collegeville, MN, 53621-6188, USA
Tel: 320 363 3366
Fax: 320 363 3313
Email: iecr@csbsju.edu
www: http://www.csbsju.edu/iecr
Contact: Patrick Henry, Executive Director

Bishop Thomas Hoyt Junior Fellowship

Eligibility: Open to a North American person of color writing a doctoral dissertation within the general area of the Institute's concern.

Purpose: To provide the Institute's residency fee to a North American person of color writing a doctoral dissertation, in order to help the churches to increase the number of their persons of color in fields of scholarship.

Type: Residency fee.

No. of awards offered: One per year (or two if for semesters).

Frequency: Annual, or semester.

Value: US$2,500.

Length of Study: Academic year or semester.

Study Establishment: The Institute.

Country of Study: USA.

Applications Procedure: A candidate will apply in the usual way to the Resident Scholars Program (see separate listing). If invited by the admissions committee to be a Resident Scholar, the person will then be eligible for consideration for the Hoyt Fellowship.

Closing Date: January 15th prior to intended period of stay.

Resident Scholars Program

Eligibility: The normal prerequisite is possession of the academic doctorate, but the admission committee will on occasion consider candidates with some other preparation, or those writing a dissertation.

Level of Study: Postdoctorate.

Purpose: To encourage constructive and creative thought, in a community setting, not only in theology and religious studies, but also more generally in scholarly research as it relates to the Christian tradition, including the interplay of Christianity and culture. The Institute also welcomes persons from other religious traditions.

No. of awards offered: 9-18 (depending on year/semester).

Frequency: Annual, or semester.

Value: The Institute charges a residency fee (US$2,500, per year; US$1,100 fall and US$1,400, spring), considerably less than the value of the housing (incl. utilities), library study, and Institute program provided.

Length of Study: Academic year or semester.

Study Establishment: The Institute.

Country of Study: USA.

Applications Procedure: Applications on the form provided.

Closing Date: January 15th prior to intended period of stay.

INSTITUTE FOR HOUSING AND URBAN DEVELOPMENT STUDIES

Institute for Housing and Urban Development Studies, PO Box 1935, Rotterdam, 3000 BX, The Netherlands
Tel: 0110 4021540
Fax: 0110 4045671
Contact: Mrs Carolien Bos, Registrar

Fellowships for Courses

Subjects: International course on housing planning and building.

Eligibility: Open to participants from any country who have relevant professional experience and are engaged in work related to urban development, are proficient in English (the language of the course) and have an undergraduate level degree from a university or similar institution.

Level of Study: Postgraduate.

Type: Fellowship.

No. of awards offered: Varies.

Frequency: Four times yearly.

Value: Varies.

Length of Study: Usually for three or five months.

Study Establishment: IHS.

Country of Study: The Netherlands.

Applications Procedure: Applications should be initiated at national government level.

Additional Information: Technical assistance agencies include: the Fellowships Programme of the Netherlands Government-application forms can be obtained from the Dutch Embassy in the applicant's home country, and should be submitted to the Fellowships Programme through the national governments; the European Union-candidates from countries associated with the EU through the Lomé Convention may apply for a Fellowship through their national government to the EU Resident Representative in their own country; the United Nations-details of Fellowships and procedures to be followed are obtainable from the Resident Representative, UN Development Programme in the applicant's home country. In addition, international financing agencies, such as World Bank, may award Fellowships to local personnel involved in their project activities.

INSTITUTE FOR HUMANE STUDIES

Institute for Humane Studies, 4084 University Drive, Suite 101, Fairfax, VA, 22030, USA
Tel: 703 934 6920
Fax: 703 352 7535
Email: ihs@gmu.edu
www: http://osf1.gmu.edu/~ihs

Humane Studies Fellowships

Subjects: Social sciences, law, humanities, literature, communications or journalism.

Eligibility: Open to graduate students/undergraduates with junior or senior standing in the next academic year at accredited colleges and universities.

Level of Study: Postgraduate, Doctorate, Undergraduate.

Purpose: To support outstanding students with a demonstrated interest in the classical liberal tradition intent on pursuing an intellectual/scholarly career.

Type: Fellowship.

Frequency: Annual.

Value: Up to US$18,500.

Applications Procedure: Application form must be completed and submitted with three completed evaluations, three essays, official test scores, official transcripts and term paper/writing sample.

Closing Date: December 31st.

Summer Graduate Research Fellowship

Subjects: Research within the humane sciences: history, political and moral philosophy, political economy, economic history, legal and social theory.

Eligibility: Open to graduate students in the humanities, social sciences and law, who intend academic careers and are pursuing research in the classical liberal tradition.

Level of Study: Postgraduate, Doctorate.

Purpose: To encourage interdisciplinary studies in classical liberal/libertarian thought.

Type: Fellowship.

No. of awards offered: 8-10.

Frequency: Annual.

Value: US$5,000.

Study Establishment: George Mason University.

Country of Study: USA.

Applications Procedure: Please submit proposal, current CV, a copy of GRE or LSAT scores and transcripts, a writing sample, and reference details.

Closing Date: February 15th.

Young Communicators Fellowship

Subjects: Journalism, film, writing (fiction or non-fiction), publishing or free-market-oriented public policy.

Eligibility: Open to advanced students and recent graduates who have a clearly demonstrated interest in the classical liberal tradition of individual rights and market economies.

Level of Study: Professional development.

Purpose: To help place Fellows in strategic positions that can enhance their abilities and credentials to pursue targeted careers.

Type: Fellowship.

No. of awards offered: Varies.

Frequency: Annual.

Value: US$5,000, to include stipend, housing and travel.

Applications Procedure: Candidates should submit a proposal of 500-1,000 words explaining what specific summer position, similar short-term position, or training program could be pursued if supported by a Fellowship; how the proposed opportunity would enhance the applicant's career prospects; and how the proposed opportunity could contribute to the applicant's understanding of classical liberal principles and their application to today's issues; as well as a current résumé listing educational background, including major field and any academic honors received; current educational status; work experience, including summer positions and internships; and citations of any publications. Candidates should also submit a writing sample or other sample of work appropriate to the intended career and provide the name, address, and phone number of an academic and/or professional reference.

Closing Date: March 15th for summer positions; ten weeks prior to the start of other positions.

INSTITUTE FOR THE STUDY OF MAN IN AFRICA

Room 2B17, Medical School, University of the Witwatersrand, York Road, Parktown, Johannesburg, 2193, South Africa
Tel: 647 2203
Fax: 643 4318
Contact: The Secretary

Research Grant

Subjects: Physical and social anthropology, archaeology, sociology, history, linguistics, literature of Africa.

Eligibility: Open to persons at the graduate and postgraduate level.

Level of Study: Postgraduate.

Purpose: To encourage research relating to any aspect of man in Africa, past and present.

Type: Grant.

No. of awards offered: One.

Frequency: Annual.

Value: Approximately R500.

Country of Study: Africa, preferably South Africa.

Applications Procedure: Applications should contain an outline of the proposed project and its aim, details of present work or related work in progress, details of the applicant's past experience, the estimated cost of the project, details of any other financial assistance applied for or received and the name of one or more referees.

Additional Information: After the recipient has done field work in his chosen subject, he/she may be asked to present their findings at one of the Institute's monthly meetings or submit a paper for publication. The Institute also offers a prize of US$1,000 in the annual 'Phillip V Tobias Essay Competition'. Essays of no more than 6,000 words should present the results of original research on man in Africa, past and present. A different essay title is set each year. The Institute will seek to facilitate the publication of the prizewinning essay in the appropriate journal. The Institute reserves the right to withhold the award should no entry be adjudged to be of sufficient merit.

THE INSTITUTE OF ACTUARIES

Institute of Actuaries, Napier House, 4 Worcester Street, Oxford, OX1 2AW, England
Tel: 01865 794144
Fax: 01865 794094
Email: 100316.3313@compuserve.com
Contact: Paul King

Memorial Education and Research Fund

Subjects: Actuarial science and related subjects.

Eligibility: Open to actuaries or to persons intending to become actuaries.

Level of Study: Unrestricted.

Purpose: The promotion for educational purposes of research, and the publication of the results of such research; the advancement of education in actuarial science and related subjects; or study by actuaries or by persons intending to become actuaries at any educational establishment approved by the Institute; or for the purpose of obtaining professional training.

Type: Grant.

No. of awards offered: Varies.

Frequency: Throughout the year.

Value: Varies.

Country of Study: UK.

Additional Information: The Institute also administers the 'Memorial Prize Fund' which gives prizes for meritorious contributions to actuarial science, for special merit in passing Institute examinations, and for papers presented to the Institute.

INSTITUTE OF ADVANCED LEGAL STUDIES (IALS)

Institute of Advanced Legal Studies (IALS), 17 Russell Square, London, WC1R 5DR, England
Tel: 0171 637 1731
Fax: 0171 580 9613
Email: dphillip@sas.ac.uk
Contact: Mr D E Phillips

Howard Drake Memorial Fund

Subjects: Law; library science.

Level of Study: Professional development.

Purpose: To encourage collaboration and exchanges between legal scholars and law librarians, especially between those of different countries, and to promote the study of law librarianship and the training of law librarians.

Type: Grant.

No. of awards offered: One or two per year.

Frequency: Dependent on funds available.

Value: Up to approximately £800 per grant.

Study Establishment: IALS.

Country of Study: UK.

Applications Procedure: Application (no form) to be made to the administrative secretary.

IALS Visiting Fellowships

Subjects: Law.

Eligibility: Open to nationals of any country.

Level of Study: Unrestricted.

Purpose: To enable established legal scholars, who are undertaking research in appropriate fields, to relate their work with the institute's own research programmes.

Type: Non-stipendary fellowship.

No. of awards offered: Up to six per year.

Frequency: Annual.

Value: Non-stipendary.

Length of Study: Minimum of three months, maximum of 12 months.

Study Establishment: IALS.

Country of Study: UK.

Applications Procedure: Applicants must submit to the administrative secretary: a full CV; names, addresses and telephone numbers of two referees; plus a brief statement of the research programme to be undertaken.

Closing Date: January 31st in respect of the following academic year (Oct-Sept).

Additional Information: This award is not available for postgraduate research.

Inns of Court Fellowship

Subjects: Law.

Level of Study: Unrestricted.

Purpose: To enable established legal scholars, who are undertaking research in appropriate fields, to relate their work with the institute's own research programmes.

Type: Fellowship.

No. of awards offered: Up to three per year.

Frequency: Annual.

Length of Study: Minimum of three months; maximum of twelve months.

Study Establishment: IALS.

Country of Study: UK.

Applications Procedure: Applicants must submit to the administrative secretary: a full CV; names, addresses and telephone numbers of two referees; plus a brief statement of the research programme to be undertaken.

Closing Date: January 31st in respect of the following academic year (Oct-Sept).

INSTITUTE OF BIOLOGY

Institute of Biology, 20-22 Queensberry Place, London, SW7 2DZ, England
Tel: 0171 581 8333
Fax: 0171 823 9409
Contact: Mrs R Sandford

Student Expeditions Overseas

Subjects: Biological sciences.

Eligibility: Open to undergraduate and postgraduate students in the biological sciences.

Level of Study: Postgraduate.

Purpose: To fund student expeditions overseas with a specific biological aim or where there is a clearly defined biological component in a multidisciplinary approach.

Type: Sponsorship award.

No. of awards offered: Varies.

Frequency: Annual.

Value: Up to £250; dependent on funds available.

Country of Study: Outside the UK.

Closing Date: Mid-January.

Additional Information: The funds are to be expended in the support or travel expenses of undergraduate or postgraduate students in the biological sciences. A statement of general approval of the aims, proposed methods and planning of the expedition is required from the head of the applicant's department. Applicants receiving awards will be expected to provide the institute with a report of their expedition within six months of its end.

THE INSTITUTE OF CANCER RESEARCH

The Institute of Cancer Research, McElwain Laboratories, 15 Cotswold Road, Sutton, Surrey, SM2 5NG, England
Tel: 0181 643 8901 ext. 4643
Fax: 0181 643 3216
Email: lindy_s@icr.ac.uk
Contact: The Deans Office

Research Studentships

Subjects: Cancer research.

Eligibility: No restrictions.

Level of Study: Postgraduate.

Purpose: To encourage research into the causes, prevention and treatment of cancer.

Type: Studentships.

No. of awards offered: 10-15.

Frequency: Annual.

Value: Equivalent to MRC Studentship rates.

Length of Study: Up to three years.

Study Establishment: The Institute.

Country of Study: UK.

Applications Procedure: Apply on application form; attendance at interview compulsory.

Additional Information: A limited number of Postdoctoral Fellowships are offered from time to time as vacancies occur.

INSTITUTE OF CLASSICAL STUDIES

Institute of Classical Studies, 31-34 Gordon Square, London, WC1H 0PY, England
Tel: 0171 387 7696
Contact: Chairman

Michael Ventris Memorial Award

Subjects: Mycenaean studies, architecture.

Eligibility: Open to applicants from all countries who are postgraduate students or young scholars who have obtained a doctorate in the last eight years.

Level of Study: Postgraduate, Postdoctorate.

Purpose: To promote the study of Mycenaean civilization.

No. of awards offered: One.

Frequency: Annual.

Value: £1,000.

Applications Procedure: Please send typewritten letter with two references.

Closing Date: April 30th.

Additional Information: A second Michael Ventris Award is made annually for Architecture and is administered by the Architectural Association.

INSTITUTE OF CURRENT WORLD AFFAIRS

Institute of Current World Affairs, 4 West Wheelock Street, Hanover, NH, 03755, USA
Tel: 603 643 5548
Fax: 603 643 9599
Email: ICWA@VALLEY.NET
Contact: Peter B Martin or Gary L Hansen

Fellowships

Subjects: International affairs.

Eligibility: Open to individuals in their 20s or early 30s who have finished their formal education. Applicants must have a good command of spoken and written English.

Level of Study: Unrestricted.

Purpose: To enable recipients to gain experience overseas and to create a corps of international generalists well versed in world affairs through a process of immersion in them. The Institute identifies an area or issue of the world outside the USA in need of in-depth understanding, and then selects a young person of outstanding promise and character to study and write about that area or issue.

Type: Fellowship.

No. of awards offered: 2 or 3.

Frequency: Annual.

Value: Full support.

Length of Study: Minimum of two years.

Country of Study: Outside the USA.

Applications Procedure: Candidates are invited to write to the executive director, explaining briefly the personal background and professional experience that would qualify them in the Institute's current areas of concern, details of which are available upon request.

Closing Date: Varies.

Additional Information: Fellowships are not awarded to support work toward academic degrees nor to underwrite specific studies or research projects. In selecting Fellows the Institute takes into account the candidates' previous experience, training, interest, self-discipline, writing ability, powers of analysis, language facility and other attributes. It is hoped that the Fellows' experience will enhance useful careers in academic, government, foundation administration, writing, corporate management, law, medicine, and other fields. The Institute is also known as the Crane-Rogers Foundation.

INSTITUTE OF ELECTRICAL AND ELECTRONICS ENGINEERS, INC

IEEE Center for the History of Electrical Engineering, Rutgers - The State University of New Jersey, 39 Union Street, PO Box 5062, New Brunswick, NJ, 08903-5062, USA
Tel: 908 932 1066
Fax: 908 932 1193
Email: history@ieee.org
www: http://www.iee.org/history_center
Contact: Director

*Charles LeGeyt Fortescue Fellowship

Subjects: Electrical engineering.

Eligibility: Open to graduates in electrical engineering from an engineering college or university of recognized standing. Candidates need not be US citizens. Candidates should be about to begin their first year of graduate work.

Type: Fellowship.

No. of awards offered: One.

Frequency: Annual.

Value: US$24,000 per annum.

Length of Study: One year.

Study Establishment: An engineering school of recognized standing.

Country of Study: USA or Canada.

Closing Date: January 15th.

Additional Information: The Institute also offers many prize awards (service awards, field awards, and prize paper awards), and a number of medals.

For further information contact:
Department of Awards and Recognition, Institute of Electrical and Electronics Engineers, Inc, 445 Hoes Lane, Piscataway, NY, 08855-1331, USA
Tel: 908 562 3839
Fax: 908 981 9515
Contact: Secretary

IEEE Fellowship in Electrical History

Subjects: History of electrical engineering and technology.

Eligibility: Open to suitably qualified graduate students.

Level of Study: Postgraduate.

Purpose: To support graduate work in the history of electrical engineering.

Type: Fellowship.

No. of awards offered: One.

Frequency: Annual.

Value: US$14,000.

Length of Study: One year.

Study Establishment: A college or university of recognized standing.

Applications Procedure: Completed application, transcripts, three letters of recommendation and research proposal must be submitted for consideration.

Closing Date: February 1st.

Additional Information: The Fellowship is made possible by a grant from the IEEE Life Member Fund and is awarded by the IEEE History Committee. Application materials become available in October. Materials may be requested from the Center directly.

INSTITUTE OF EUROPEAN HISTORY

Institut für Europäische Geschichte, Alte Universitätsstrasse 19, Mainz, D-55116, Germany
Tel: 0 61 31 39 93 60
Fax: 0 61 31 23 79 88

Fellowships

Subjects: Scientific research on Western religious history and on European history generally.

Eligibility: Open to holders of a bachelors degree; and to Fellows in the advanced stages of graduate work, i.e. at least two years after admission to doctoral candidacy, and who have successfully completed their comprehensive examinations (orals).

Level of Study: Postgraduate.

Type: Fellowship.

Frequency: Three times yearly.

Value: In line with the guidelines of the German Academic Exchange Service (DAAD): a monthly stipend, a family allowance, health insurance and a travel allowance.

Study Establishment: The Institute.

Country of Study: Germany.

Closing Date: February, June, October.

INSTITUTE OF FOOD TECHNOLOGISTS

Institute of Food Technologists, 221 North LaSalle Street, Chicago, IL, 60601, USA
Tel: 312 782 8424
Fax: 312 782 8348
Contact: Scholarship Department

Freshman/Sophomore Scholarships

Subjects: Food technology, food science.

Eligibility: Freshman Scholarships: open to high school seniors who expect to graduate by the effective date of the scholarship, and to previous graduates entering college for the first time, who are enrolled in an approved program in food science or technology. Sophomore Scholarships: open to freshmen who are, or will be, enrolled in an approved program at the time the scholarship becomes effective.

No. of awards offered: 15 Freshman Scholarships and 14 Sophomore Scholarships.

Frequency: Annual.

Value: Freshman Scholarships: 1 at US$1,000, 14 at US$750; Sophomore Scholarships: 14 at US$750.

Study Establishment: An approved educational institution.

Country of Study: USA or Canada.

Applications Procedure: Applications should be submitted to the candidate's department head.

Closing Date: Freshman Scholarships: 15 February; Sophomore Scholarships: 1 March.

Graduate Fellowships

Subjects: Food science and technology.

Eligibility: Open to final year students who will be enrolled in graduate studies at the time the Fellowship becomes effective and to current graduates pursuing a course of study leading to an MS and/or PhD degree. Candidates must possess an above-average interest in research together with demonstrated scientific aptitude.

Level of Study: Graduate, Postgraduate, Doctorate.

Purpose: To encourage and support outstanding research in food science/technology.

Type: Fellowship.

No. of awards offered: 27.

Frequency: Annual.

Value: 6 at US$10,000; 4 at US$5,000; 5 at US$2,500; 6 at US$2,000; 2 at US$1,250; 3 at US$1,000; and 1 at US$3,000.

Study Establishment: An approved institution.

Country of Study: USA or Canada.

Closing Date: February 1st.

INSTITUTE OF HISTORICAL RESEARCH

Institute of Historical Research, Senate House, Malet Street, London, WC1E 7HU, England
Tel: 0171 636 0272
Fax: 0171 436 2183
Email: ihrdir@sas.ac.uk
www: http://ihr.sas.ac.uk:8080/
Contact: The Director

Royal History Society Fellowship

Subjects: Arts and humanities: medieval history; modern history; contemporary history.

Eligibility: Open to nationals of any country.

Level of Study: Doctorate.

Purpose: To help candidates at an advanced stage of a PhD to complete their doctorates.

Type: Fellowship.

No. of awards offered: One.

Frequency: Annual.

Value: c. £6,000.

Length of Study: One year.

Study Establishment: IHR.

Country of Study: UK.

Applications Procedure: Application forms are available from the Director in early January.

Closing Date: Around mid-February.

Scouloudi Fellowships

Subjects: Arts and humanities; medieval history; modern history; contemporary history.

Eligibility: Only open to UK citizens or to candidates with a first degree from a UK university.

Level of Study: Doctorate.

Purpose: To help candidates at an advanced stage of a PhD to complete their doctorates.

Type: Fellowship.

No. of awards offered: Seven.

Frequency: Annual.

Value: c. £6,000.

Length of Study: One year.

Study Establishment: IHR.

Country of Study: UK.

Applications Procedure: Application forms are available from the Director in early January.

Closing Date: Around mid-February.

Isobel Thornley Research Fellowship

Subjects: Arts and humanities; medieval history; modern history; contemporary history.

Eligibility: Open to candidates without regard to nationality, but only to those registered for a PhD at London University.

Level of Study: Doctorate.

Purpose: To help candidates at an advanced stage of a PhD to complete their doctorate.

Type: Fellowship.

No. of awards offered: Two.

Frequency: Dependent on funds available.

Value: £6,000.

Length of Study: One year.

Study Establishment: IHR.

Country of Study: UK.

Applications Procedure: Application forms are available from the Director in early January.

Closing Date: Around mid-February.

Yorkist History Trust Fellowship

Subjects: Arts and humanities; medieval history.

Eligibility: Open to candidates without regard to nationality, but only to those researching British history or topics relevant to British history from the late 14th to early 16th century.

Level of Study: Doctorate.

Purpose: To help candidates at an advanced stage of a PhD to complete their doctorates.

Type: Fellowship.

No. of awards offered: One.

Frequency: Dependent on funds available.

Value: c. £6,000.

Length of Study: One year.

Study Establishment: IHR.

Country of Study: UK.

Applications Procedure: Application forms are available from the Director in early January.

Closing Date: Around mid-February.

INSTITUTE OF HUMAN PALAEONTOLOGY

Institut de Paléontologie Humaine, 1 rue René Panhard, Paris, 75013, France
Tel: 43 31 62 91
Fax: 43 31 22 79
Contact: Professor H de Lumley, Director

Prince Rainier III Bursary

Subjects: Field work or laboratory research in the fields of prehistory, human palaeontology or quaternary geology.

Eligibility: Open to young researchers of any nationality.

Type: Bursary.

No. of awards offered: One.

Frequency: Biennially.

Value: FF20,000.

Country of Study: Unrestricted.

Applications Procedure: Applications should include a CV and a three-page outline of the proposed research.

Closing Date: January 1st.

INSTITUTE OF IRISH STUDIES

Institute of Irish Studies, Queen's University, 8 Fitzwilliam Street, Belfast, BT9 6AW, Northern Ireland
Tel: 01232 245133 ext.3386
Fax: 01232 439238
Email: IRISH.STUDIES@QUB.AC.UK
Contact: Dr B M Walker, Director

Research Fellowships

Subjects: Any academic discipline relating to Ireland.

Eligibility: Open to all.

Level of Study: Postdoctorate.

Purpose: To promote research.

Type: Fellowship.

No. of awards offered: Up to three.

Frequency: Annual.

Value: £12,500.

Length of Study: One year.

Study Establishment: The Institute of Irish Studies.

Country of Study: Northern Ireland.

Applications Procedure: Applicants must complete application form.

Closing Date: January 14th.

Senior Visiting Research Fellowship

Subjects: Any academic discipline relating to Ireland.

Eligibility: Open to senior academics of at least ten years standing with a strong publication record.

Level of Study: Postdoctorate.

Purpose: To promote research.

Type: Fellowship.

No. of awards offered: Two.

Frequency: Annual.

Value: £16,500.

Length of Study: One year.

Study Establishment: The Institute of Irish Studies.

Country of Study: Northern Ireland.

Applications Procedure: Application form must be completed.

Closing Date: January 14th.

THE INSTITUTE OF SPORTS MEDICINE

The Institute of Sports Medicine, Burlington House, Piccadilly, London, W1V OLQ, England
Tel: 0171 287 5269
Contact: The Honorary Secretary

The Robert Atkins Award

Subjects: Sports medicine.

Eligibility: Open to medical practitioners in the UK.

Level of Study: Postgraduate.

Purpose: To increase medical support for and active involvement in sports medicine and to recognize a doctor who has provided, for not less than five years, the most consistently valuable medical (clinical/preventive) service to a national sporting organization or sport in general.

No. of awards offered: One.

Frequency: Anually.

Value: Varies; a substantial cash prize.

Country of Study: UK.

Applications Procedure: Applicants should write for an entry/nomination form in the first instance.

Closing Date: Varies annually.

Duke of Edinburgh Prize for Sports Medicine

Subjects: Clinical and/or research work in the field of sports medicine in the community, with particular reference to the disabled.

Eligibility: Open to medical practitioners in the UK.

Level of Study: Postgraduate.

Purpose: To promote postgraduate work and to signify standards of excellence amongst medical practitioners in the UK.

No. of awards offered: One.

Frequency: Annual.

Value: Varies; a substantial cash prize.

Country of Study: UK.

Applications Procedure: Applicants should write for an entry/nomination form in the first instance.

Closing Date: Varies annually. Specified in conditions of entry.

INSTITUT FRANÇAIS DE WASHINGTON

Institut Français de Washington, University of North Carolina, CB 3170, Department of Romance Languages, Chapel Hill, NC, 27599-3170, USA
Tel: 919 962 0154
Fax: 919 962 5457
Email: cmaley@email.unc.edu
Contact: Dr Catherine A Maley, President

Gilbert Chinard Fellowships

Subjects: French history, literature, art and music.

Eligibility: Final stage PhD dissertation, or PhD held no longer than six years before application deadline.

Level of Study: Doctorate, Postdoctorate.

Type: Fellowship.

No. of awards offered: Three.

Frequency: Annual.

Value: US$1,000.

Length of Study: Two months.

Country of Study: France.

Applications Procedure: No application form; applicants write two pages maximum describing research project and planned trip and giving curriculum vitae. A letter of recommendation from dissertation director is also required.

Closing Date: January 15th.

Additional Information: Awards are for maintenance (not travel) during research in France for a period of at least two months.

Sir Edouard Morot Fellowship

Subjects: French history, literature, arts and music.

Eligibility: Final stage PhD dissertation, or PhD held no longer than six years before application deadline.

Level of Study: Doctorate, Postdoctorate.

Frequency: Annual.

Value: US$1,000.

Country of Study: France.

Applications Procedure: No application form; applicants write two pages maximum describing research project and planned trip and giving curriculum vitae. A letter of recommendation from dissertation director is also required.

Closing Date: January 15th.

Additional Information: Awards are for maintenance (not travel) during research in France for a period of at least two months.

THE INSTITUTION OF CIVIL ENGINEERS

The Institution of Civil Engineers, 1-7 Great George Street, Westminster, London, SW1P 3AA, England
Tel: 0171 222 7722
Fax: 0171 233 0515
Contact: Education Officer

Continuing Education Award

Subjects: Civil engineering.

Eligibility: Open to graduates of any nationality who hold an accredited first degree in civil engineering and have been members of the Institution (any grade) for not less than two years.

Level of Study: Postgraduate.

Purpose: To enable approved persons to undertake MSc courses, either on completion of an accredited first degree, or after some years' industrial experience.

No. of awards offered: 10-15.

Frequency: Annual.

Value: Up to £2,000.

Country of Study: UK.

Applications Procedure: Application forms to be completed.

Closing Date: End of February.

Overseas Travel Awards

Subjects: Civil engineering, environmental engineering, transportation and agricultural engineering.

Eligibility: Open to institution members, preference being given to postgraduate applicants proposing individual overseas projects or requiring mid-career support.

Level of Study: Postgraduate.

Purpose: To support overseas travel by Institution Members to overseas universities, specific overseas projects and mid-career support and development.

No. of awards offered: Approximately 15.

Frequency: Annual.

Value: Up to £2,000.

Length of Study: 3-12 months.

Study Establishment: Exchange visits with overseas universities, specific overseas projects proposed by individual applicants, or mid-career support and development.

Country of Study: International.

Applications Procedure: Application form must be completed.

Closing Date: End of February.

Additional Information: Applications are not necessarily restricted to technical developments, but may be concerned with organizational, managerial or financial aspects of civil engineering. Awards will be judged on merit.

C H Roberts Bequest

Subjects: Civil engineering.

Eligibility: Open to members or associate members of the Institution; British candidates must be members of the Institution of Civil Engineers.

Level of Study: Postgraduate.

Purpose: To promote the exchange of engineering graduates between the UK and Spain for the purpose of furthering their academic studies

and engineering training.

Type: Bursary.

No. of awards offered: Two.

Frequency: Annually (alternately to each country).

Value: Approximately £2,000.

Length of Study: 6-9 months.

Country of Study: Spain (UK candidates) or the UK (Spanish candidates).

Applications Procedure: Application form must be completed.

Closing Date: End of February.

Additional Information: Successful applicants are encouraged under the terms of the bequest to learn the language of the other country (some prior knowledge is essential) and to acquire a knowledge of its people by residence, study and engineering experience. They will be required to further their knowledge of the language by spending one to two hours weekly on additional language study with an approved institute or teacher, whose fees will be covered by the award. Practical experience gained in Spain under the award will be accepted towards the experience required for permission to take the professional examination.

THE INSTITUTION OF ELECTRICAL ENGINEERS

Qualifications Department ref Q (SP), The Institution of Electrical Engineers, Savoy Place, London, WC2R 0BL, England
Tel: 0171 240 1871
Fax: 0171 497 3633
Email: twatter@iee.org.uk

IEE Bursaries for IEE Vacation Schools, Technical Seminars and Workshops

Subjects: Electrical, electronic, manufacturing or related engineering.

Eligibility: Open to IEE members working in small companies or in the academic field who cannot readily find an alternative source of finance.

Level of Study: Professional development.

Purpose: To assist IEE members to update/broaden their professional and educational experience.

No. of awards offered: 2 bursaries per event.

Value: Total cost of course and residential fees.

Study Establishment: IEE vacation schools, technical seminars and workshops.

Country of Study: UK.

Applications Procedure: Application form must be completed.

Closing Date: Two months prior to the commencement of the event.

Additional Information: Bursaries are available to candidates whose needs and merits are assessed as being the most deserving. The candidate must be nominated by a corporate member of the IEE who can speak from first-hand knowledge of the candidate's present educational background, attainments and the likelihood of benefit attendance at the event would have in furthering his/her professional and educational experience.

IEE Conference Overseas Bursary

Subjects: Electrical, electronic and related engineering.

Eligibility: Open to members and non-members of the IEE who are not citizens of the UK and not living and working in the UK, who have had papers accepted for presentation at an IEE conference. Candidates must be able to show that funds are not available from any source to meet their conference registration fees and accommodation costs. Full-time students are not eligible for a bursary.

Type: Bursary.

No. of awards offered: Varies.

Frequency: Annual.

Value: The registration fee for full-time attendance at the conference plus reasonable bed and breakfast accommodation for the period of the conference. Applicants will not be eligible for any other form of grant or financial assistance from the IEE, and accommodation will be selected and booked by the Secretariat. Travel expenses and other meals will not be covered.

Study Establishment: IEE conferences.

Country of Study: UK.

Applications Procedure: Applications must be made at the time of submitting a synopsis to the conference, and must be accompanied by an appropriate reference, preferably from an IEE member.

For further information contact:
Conference Services Department, The Institution of Electrical Engineers, Savoy Place, London, WC2R 0BL, England
Tel: 0171 240 1871
Fax: 0171 497 3633
Contact: Miss S J Hall

IEE Hudswell Bequest; Travelling Fellowships

Subjects: Electrical and electronics science and engineering.

Eligibility: Open to candidates with any class of IEE membership who are registered as research students in the UK.

Purpose: To assist IEE members with travel undertaken to further their research.

Type: Fellowship.

No. of awards offered: Four.

Frequency: Annual.

Value: Up to £1,000.

Applications Procedure: Application form must be completed.

Closing Date: April 30th.

IEE J R Beard Travelling Fund Awards

Subjects: Electrical, electronic, manufacturing and related engineering.

Eligibility: The Scholarship is open to IEE members intending to expand their experience in the field of manufacturing techniques conducted overseas. Grants are available to assist, in particular, younger IEE members to broaden their professional experience through overseas travel. Applicants must be studying in the UK.

Level of Study: Unrestricted.

Purpose: To enable members of the Institution to travel overseas to study developments in electrical or electronics technology, or to present a paper outside the UK.

No. of awards offered: 2 Grants and 1 Scholarship.

Frequency: Annual.

Value: Up to £1,000.

Applications Procedure: Application form must be completed.

Closing Date: April 30th.

IEE Management Scholarship

Eligibility: Open to Corporate Members of the IEE.

Level of Study: Postgraduate.

Purpose: To encourage IEE members to undertake formal management training leading to the award of an MBA or similar qualification.

Type: Scholarship.

No. of awards offered: One.

Frequency: Annual.

Value: £1,000 per year.

Length of Study: Maximum period of 2 years.

Applications Procedure: Application form must be completed.

Closing Date: April 30th.

IEE Postgraduate Scholarships and Grants

Subjects: Electrical, electronic, manufacturing or related engineering.

Eligibility: Open to students undertaking advanced study or research degree in the field of electrical/electronic science or manufacturing engineering. Applicants must be resident in the UK and have satisfied the educational requirements for corporate membership of the Institution.

Level of Study: Postgraduate.

Purpose: To enable research students to undertake postgraduate work on a course approved by the IEE.

Type: Scholarship.

No. of awards offered: Up to three.

Frequency: Annual.

Value: Up to £1,200, payable in instalments.

Length of Study: One year.

Country of Study: UK.

Applications Procedure: Application form must be completed.

Closing Date: April 30th.

Leslie H Paddle Scholarships

Subjects: Any subject relevant to electronic or radio engineering.

Eligibility: Open to graduates in a relevant discipline.

Level of Study: Postgraduate.

Purpose: For postgraduate research which will further the art, science or practice of electronic engineering or radio engineering.

Type: Scholarship.

No. of awards offered: Two.

Frequency: Annual.

Value: £1,250 per annum, payable in instalments.

Length of Study: Two years; with discretion for extension for a third year.

Study Establishment: UK university.

Country of Study: UK.

Applications Procedure: Application form must be completed.

Closing Date: April 30th.

INSTITUTION OF FIRE ENGINEERS

Institution of Fire Engineers, 148 New Walk, Leicester, LE1 7QB, England
Tel: 0116 255 3654
Fax: 0116 247 1231
Contact: General Secretary

Scholarships

Subjects: Firefighting, fire engineering, fire protection or fire research.

Eligibility: UK Scholarships are open to any candidates from the UK.

Purpose: To assist men and women in the profession of fire engineering who wish to carry out research or further their studies in some particular aspect of the field.

Type: Scholarship.

No. of awards offered: One UK, and one European Scholarship.

Frequency: Annual.

Value: Approximately £1,000 for UK Scholarships; approximately £2,000 for European Scholarships.

Length of Study: About one month.

Country of Study: UK or immediately adjacent countries (UK and European Scholarships).

Closing Date: Notified in Fire Engineers Journal.

Additional Information: Selection for both Scholarships will be made on the merit of the project and its relevance and value to firefighting, fire engineering, fire protection, or fire research.

THE INSTITUTION OF GAS ENGINEERS

The Institution of Gas Engineers, 21 Portland Place, London, W1N 3AF, England
Tel: 44 71 245 9811
Fax: 44 71 245 1229
Contact: Jim Gould

W H Bennett Travelling Fellowship

Subjects: Gas engineering.

Eligibility: Open to qualified engineers or technologists within the age group of 25-35 years.

Purpose: To enable the holder to study, either in the UK or overseas, technical developments of interest to the gas industry.

Type: Fellowship.

No. of awards offered: One.

Frequency: From time to time.

Value: To assist with costs of travel.

Country of Study: UK or overseas.

Celette Prize

Subjects: Gas engineering.

Eligibility: Open to non-Corporate Members of the Institution who are no more than 35 years of age.

Purpose: To further the education of a non-Corporate Member of the Institution.

Type: Prize.

No. of awards offered: One.

Frequency: Annual.

Value: Varies.

Country of Study: UK or overseas.

Clark Travelling Fellowship

Subjects: Gas engineering.

Eligibility: Open to members of the Institution who are no more than 35 years of age, and are qualified academically in an engineering or technical subject.

Purpose: To enable the holder to study technical developments overseas in areas of interest to the gas industry.

Type: Fellowship.

No. of awards offered: One.

Frequency: From time to time.

Value: To assist with costs of travel.

Country of Study: Outside the UK.

Dempster Travelling Fellowship

Subjects: Gas engineering.

Eligibility: Open to candidates who are no more than 30 years of age.

Purpose: To enable the holder to study, either in the UK or overseas, technical developments of interest to the gas industry.

Type: Fellowship.

No. of awards offered: One.

Frequency: From time to time.

Value: To assist with costs of travel.

Country of Study: UK or overseas.

T V Garrud Fellowship

Subjects: Gas industry.

Eligibility: Open to candidates under 30 years of age who have been members of a Gas Association for at least 12 months.

Purpose: To enable the holder to develop his/her experience in matters relating to the gas industry.

Type: Fellowship.

No. of awards offered: One.

Frequency: From time to time.

Value: Varies.

Country of Study: UK.

Corbet and Henry Woodall-William Cartwright Holmes Postgraduate Award

Subjects: Gas engineering.

Eligibility: Open to suitably qualified postgraduates.

Level of Study: Postgraduate.

Purpose: To encourage postgraduate education and research.

No. of awards offered: One.

Frequency: From time to time.

Value: Varies.

Study Establishment: University of Leeds.

Country of Study: UK.

INSTITUTION OF MECHANICAL ENGINEERS

Institution of Mechanical Engineers, 1 Birdcage Walk, London, SW1H 9JJ, England
Tel: 0171 222 7899
Fax: 0171 222 4557
Contact: Council Officer

Joseph Bramah Scholarship

Subjects: Mechanical engineering; hydraulic mechanisms, particularly hydrostatic transmissions and servomechanisms.

Eligibility: Candidates must be members of the Institution and must satisfy or be making adequate progress towards satisfying the academic requirements for graduate membership, and preferably have had two years or more of acceptable professional training.

Level of Study: Postgraduate.

Purpose: To encourage engineers to study or to obtain special experience.

Type: Scholarship.

No. of awards offered: One.

Frequency: Annual.

Value: Up to £1,100.

Length of Study: One year; with the possibility of an extension to a maximum of two years. Shorter periods of study will also be considered.

Study Establishment: An approved centre or laboratory.

Country of Study: UK.

Applications Procedure: Application form must be completed and submitted with three references.

Closing Date: 31 January (31 December for overseas candidates).

Additional Information: At the completion of a Scholarship, or at the end of each 12 months, a report of work must be submitted. It is one of the major objectives of the Institution to publish new or original work. The Institution has the copyright in and the right to publish any report made by a Scholar. Application forms are available on request.

Clayton Grants

Subjects: Mechanical engineering.

Eligibility: Open to Institution members over 23 years of age who hold an accredited engineering degree, or have satisfied the academic requirements for Institution membership by other means, and have had not less than two years' acceptable training in mechanical engineering.

Level of Study: Postgraduate.

Purpose: To enable the recipient to obtain special experience or training, or to supplement previous experience or training.

No. of awards offered: Varies.

Frequency: Annual.

Value: Up to £1,000.

Study Establishment: An approved centre.

Country of Study: Normally UK.

Applications Procedure: Application form must be completed and submitted with three references.

Closing Date: 31 January (31 December for overseas candidates).

Additional Information: A report is required within three months of completion of the project.

For further information contact:
Institution of Mechanical Engineers, Northgate Avenue, Bury St Edmunds, Suffolk, IP32 6BN, England
Tel: 01284 763277 ext.492
Fax: 01284 704006
Contact: Awards Assistant

Clayton Grants for Postgraduate Studies

Subjects: Mechanical engineering.

Eligibility: Open to candidates who have completed a degree course in mechanical engineering accredited by IMechE and have gained graduate membership of IMechE.

Level of Study: Postgraduate.

Purpose: To assist outstanding postgraduates who experience hardship while undertaking courses of advanced study, training or research work on a course approved by the Institution.

Type: Grant.

No. of awards offered: Up to three.

Frequency: Annual.

Value: £1,000.

Length of Study: One year.

Applications Procedure: Application form must be completed and submitted with three references.

Closing Date: March 31st.

Additional Information: A report will be required three months after the activity has been completed.

Thomas Andrew Common Grants

Subjects: Areas related to mechanical engineering.

Eligibility: Open to members under the age of 40 who have been invited to contribute in some way to a conference or who could be expected to make a significant contribution to the aims of a conference by attending.

Level of Study: Postgraduate, Professional development.

Purpose: To provide assistance for attending conferences.

Type: Grant.

No. of awards offered: Varies.

Frequency: Varies.

Value: By individual assessment.

Study Establishment: Approved conferences.

Country of Study: Normally overseas.

Applications Procedure: Application form must be completed and submitted with three references.

Closing Date: At least three months prior to the date by which a decision is required.

Additional Information: Application forms are available on request. A report is required within three months of return from the conference.

Bryan Donkin Award

Subjects: The science or practice of mechanical engineering.

Eligibility: Open to British-born members of the Institution.

Level of Study: Postgraduate, Doctorate, Postdoctorate.

Purpose: To assist members of the Institution to carry out original research.

No. of awards offered: One.

Frequency: Annual.

Value: Up to £1,500.

Applications Procedure: Application form must be completed and can be obtained from the Educational Services Department. Three references are also required.

Closing Date: January 31st.

Additional Information: Application forms are available on request. The award may be made to supplement grants from other sources. A report of the work must be submitted.

Hinton Fellowship

Subjects: Mechanical engineering (but not exclusively).

Eligibility: Open to candidates who have completed the academic and practical training requirements of a Chartered Engineer. No age limit is imposed but it is expected that the Fellowship will be more appropriate to a younger engineer. Likely candidates will be qualified in mechanical engineering although all disciplines are eligible. Candidates are expected to be normally resident in the UK.

Purpose: To support a Hinton Fellow to undertake a study on some specific topic aimed at promoting excellence in engineering.

Type: Fellowship.

No. of awards offered: One.

Frequency: Triennially.

Value: Up to £30,000 per annum, by individual assessment.

Study Establishment: In industry at a university, other educational establishment or research body.

Country of Study: UK.

Closing Date: July 31st.

Additional Information: The Fellowship is jointly administered by the Institution and the Royal Academy of Engineering. Application forms are available on request. Reports of work progress will be required at regular intervals.

Labrow Grants

Subjects: Mechanical engineering.

Eligibility: Open to members of the IMechE.

Level of Study: Unrestricted.

Purpose: To assist research.

No. of awards offered: Varies.

Frequency: Varies.

Value: Up to £4,000.

Applications Procedure: Application form must be completed; forms are available from the Educational Services Department. References must also be submitted.

Additional Information: A report will be required three months after the activity.

For further information contact:
Institution of Mechanical Engineers, Northgate Avenue, Bury St Edmunds, Suffolk, IP32 6BN, England
Tel: 01284 763277 ext.492
Fax: 01284 704006
Contact: Awards Assistant

Raymond Coleman Prescott Scholarship

Subjects: Mechanical engineering or related science.

Eligibility: Open to members who hold an approved engineering qualification and have had two years' acceptable professional training.

Level of Study: Postgraduate, Professional development.

Purpose: To enable Scholars to study for a first degree after having obtained an outstanding HNC or other technical or non-professional qualification; or to obtain special experience which might include a study period abroad; or to pursue advanced studies of a postgraduate character; or to pursue an approved programme of research.

Type: Scholarship.

No. of awards offered: One.

Frequency: Annual.

Value: Up to £500.

Length of Study: One year, with the possibility of an extension. Applications for shorter periods will also be considered.

Country of Study: Any country.

Applications Procedure: The application must be supported by the names and addresses of three referees. At the completion of a Scholarship, or at the end of each 12 months, a report of work must be submitted. It is one of the major objectives of the Institution to publish new or original work. The Institution has the copyright in and the right to publish any report made by the Scholar. Application forms are available on request.

Closing Date: 31 January (31 December for overseas candidates).

Senior Engineer Conference Grants

Subjects: Mechanical engineering.

Eligibility: Open to Senior Engineers over 40 years of age. The grants are intended for members who have been invited to contribute in some way to the conference or who could be expected to make a significant contribution to the aims of the conference by their attendance.

Level of Study: Professional development.

Type: Grant.

No. of awards offered: Varies.

Value: Varies.

Study Establishment: Conferences.

Applications Procedure: Application form must be completed and submitted with three references.

Additional Information: A report will be required three months after the conference.

Neil Watson Grants

Subjects: Mechanical engineering, power generation, internal combustion engines.

Eligibility: Open to non-corporate members of the IMechE under the age of 30.

Purpose: To enable young engineers to attend conferences and seminars and travel abroad to study engineering practices overseas.

Type: Grant.

No. of awards offered: Varies.

Frequency: Annual.

Value: £500.

Applications Procedure: Application form must be completed and submitted with three references.

Additional Information: A report will be required three months after the conference, seminar etc.

THE INSTITUTION OF MINING AND METALLURGY

The Institution of Mining and Metallurgy, 44 Portland Place, London, W1N 4BR, England
Tel: 0171 580 3802
Fax: 0171 436 5388
Contact: The Secretary

Bosworth Smith Trust Fund

Subjects: Metal mining, non-ferrous extraction metallurgy or mineral dressing.

Eligibility: Open to persons who possess a degree in a relevant subject.

Purpose: To assist postgraduate research.

No. of awards offered: Varies.

Frequency: Annual.

Value: Approximately £4,500 is available for grants towards working expenses, the costs of visits to mines and plants in connection with such research, and purchase of apparatus.

Length of Study: One year.

Study Establishment: An approved university.

Country of Study: UK.

Closing Date: March 15th.

Additional Information: Application forms are available on request.

Stanley Elmore Fellowships

Subjects: Research into all branches of extractive metallurgy and mineral processing.

Eligibility: Open to persons who are fully qualified to undertake postdoctoral research. In general, preference will be given to applicants who are members of the Institution.

Level of Study: Postdoctorate.

Type: Fellowship.

No. of awards offered: 1-2.

Frequency: Annual.

Value: £11,000.

Length of Study: One year; with possible renewal to a maximum of three years.

Study Establishment: An approved UK university.

Country of Study: UK.

Closing Date: March 15th.

Additional Information: Application forms are available on request.

G Vernon Hobson Bequest

Subjects: Mining geology.

Eligibility: Open to members of university staffs in the UK.

Purpose: To advance the teaching and practice of geology as applied to mining.

No. of awards offered: At least one.

Frequency: Annual.

Value: From a total of approximately £1,500, for travel, research or other objects in accordance with the terms of the Bequest.

Country of Study: UK.

Closing Date: March 15th.

Additional Information: Application forms are available on request.

Mining Club Award

Subjects: Mineral industry operations.

Eligibility: Open to British citizens between the ages of 21 and 35 who are actively engaged (in full- or part-time postgraduate study or in employment) in the minerals industry.

Level of Study: Postgraduate, Professional development.

Purpose: To enable candidates to study mineral industry operations in the UK or overseas, to present a paper at an international minerals industry conference; or to assist the candidate in attending a full-time course of study related to the minerals industry outside the UK.

Type: Award.

No. of awards offered: Varies.

Value: Approximately £1,000.

Country of Study: Any country.

Applications Procedure: Application form may be obtained from the Secretary.

Closing Date: March 15th.

Edgar Pam Fellowship

Subjects: All subjects within the Institution's fields of interest, which range from exploration geology to extractive metallurgy.

Eligibility: Open to young graduates domiciled in Australia, Canada, New Zealand, South Africa, and the UK who wish to undertake advanced study or research in the UK.

Level of Study: Postgraduate.

Type: Fellowship.

No. of awards offered: One.

Frequency: Biennially (even-numbered years).

Value: £2,250.

Length of Study: One year.

Study Establishment: Approved universities in the UK.

Country of Study: UK.

Closing Date: March 15th.

INSTITUTO NACIONAL DE CANCEROLOGIA

Instituto Nacional de Cancerologia, Calle 1 #9-85 Seccion Educacion Medica, Santafé de Bogota, Cundinamarca, Colombia
Tel: 2338957
Fax: 2893287
Contact: Chief of Medical Education

Postgraduate Training in Oncologic Topics

Subjects: Oncology.

Eligibility: Candidates must be medical doctors with a postgraduate degree.

Level of Study: Postgraduate.

Purpose: To train medical specialists in a subspecialization in a specific oncologic topic, ie. surgical oncology, gynaecological oncology, haemato-oncology etc;.

Type: Bursary.

No. of awards offered: 30 per year.

Frequency: Annual.

Value: US$250 per month.

Length of Study: One to two years.

Study Establishment: Hospital.

Country of Study: Colombia.

Applications Procedure: Candidates must submit a letter requesting the specific area, a letter from the home institution with a guarantee that the candidate will be received when s/he goes back, in addition to attending an interview with the chairman of the program.

Closing Date: October and March.

INSTITUTO NACIONAL DE METEOROLOGIA (INM)

Instituto Nacional de Meteorologia (INM), Camino de las Moreras, S/N - Ciudad Universitaria, Madrid, 28040, Spain
Tel: 34 1 5819860
Fax: 34 1 5819892
Email: Carlos.Legaz@inm.es
Telex: 2247 LEMMC
Contact: Dr Carlos Garcia-Legaz Martinez

Fellowship for 'Curso Internacional de Meteorologia Clase II OMM'

Subjects: Atmospheric sciences and meteorology.

Eligibility: Candidates should have a background of training/professional experience in sciences, engineering or meteorology. A good knowledge of Spanish language is required.

Level of Study: Professional development.

Type: Fellowship.

No. of awards offered: 20-25.

Frequency: Every two years.

Value: 2,200,000 pesetas.

Length of Study: 22 months.

Study Establishment: INM training centre.

Country of Study: Spain.

Applications Procedure: Application forms are distributed by the INM. Candidates should be supported by a meteorological or academic authority.

Closing Date: July 1997.

Additional Information: Applications can also be submitted through the WMO in Geneva.

Short-term Fellowship

Subjects: Atmospheric sciences and meteorology.

Eligibility: Candidates must be staff of the meteorological service in their country. A good knowledge of English or Spanish language is required.

Level of Study: Professional development.

Purpose: To support on-the-job training in different departments of the INM.

Type: Fellowship.

No. of awards offered: 20-25.

Frequency: Annual.

Value: 100,000 pesetas monthly plus 40,000 for travel allowance.

Length of Study: 15-60 days.

Study Establishment: INM technical departments.

Country of Study: Spain.

Applications Procedure: Applications (no form required) must be submitted through the permanent representatives of their countries with WMO expressing their support of the candidate.

Closing Date: Beginning of February for fellowships to be initiated in the first semester; beginning of June for fellowships to be initiated in the second semester.

INTER-AMERICAN FOUNDATION

Inter-American Foundation, 901 North Stuart Street, 10th Floor,
Dept 555, Arlington, VA, 22203, USA
Contact: The Administrator

The Inter-American Foundation, as an independent agency of the US government, receives annual funding from Congressional appropriations and from the Social Progress Trust Fund. Foundation fellowship programs are budgeted annually. The Foundation was established in 1969 to fund the self-help efforts of the poor of Latin America and the Caribbean

Dante B. Fascell Inter-American Fellowship

Eligibility: Open to distinguished Latin American and Caribbean leaders.

Level of Study: Professional development.

Purpose: To support grassroots development dissemination by distinguished Latin American and Caribbean leaders.

Type: Fellowship.

Value: Each fellowship provides financial support up to US$50,000 for a period not exceeding 12 months. Some dissemination projects may cost more than US$50,000, and each Fellow is encouraged to obtain additional funds from other sources. Fellows may use funds for salary and benefits, domestic and international travel, limited administrative support, and direct dissemination activities.

Length of Study: No more than 12 months.

Country of Study: The Western Hemisphere.

Applications Procedure: Applicants must complete an IAF-printed 'Candidate Information Form' which summarizes the applicant's career highlights, career dissemination achievements, awards and honors, and dissemination budget; a 'Fellowship Proposal' which describes the applicant's qualifications, explains proposed dissemination activities, and addresses the four selection criteria (commitment to grassroots development, past achievements, proposed contributions, and ability to communicate); letters of recommendation for each nominee (2 letters only) and each self-applicant (3 letters ony) from Latin American and Caribbean citizens who are development specialists.

Field Research Program at the Master's Level

Eligibility: Applicants must be enrolled in US universities in a Master's or equivalent-level program during and after field research. This program also covers law and pre-dissertation field research. Applicants must be able to write and speak the local language.

Level of Study: Master's.

Purpose: To support field research in Latin America and the Caribbean on grassroots level development topics by graduate students enrolled in US universities in Master's or equivalent-level programs (including law and PhD programs at the pre-dissertation level).

Type: Fellowship.

No. of awards offered: 15.

Frequency: Annual.

Value: Monthly living stipend, adequate health insurance, and round-trip international transportation to the field research site. Financial support for the researcher only. IAF awards usually average between US$2,000-US$3,000.

Country of Study: Independent Latin American and Caribbean countries.

Applications Procedure: Applicants must complete an IAF-printed application form, a 'Personal Statement' which addresses the applicant's: a) personal history; b) special interests and abilities; c) career plans; and d) reasons for interest in Latin American and Caribbean development issues, a Prospectus of not more than 750 words, a 200 word extract, two letters of reference, and a two-page 'Foreign Language Report' in which a professional language teacher evaluates the applicant's language capability.

Field Research Program at the Doctoral Level

Subjects: Social and Behavioural Sciences.

Eligibility: All applicants must be enrolled in US universities. Applicants must be able to write and speak the local language. Approximately 30% of Field Research Fellows each year are Latin American and Caribbean citizens.

Level of Study: Doctorate.

Purpose: To support dissertation field research in Latin America and the Caribbean on grassroots development topics by doctoral students enrolled at USA universities.

Type: Fellowship.

No. of awards offered: 15.

Frequency: Annual.

Value: Monthly living stipend, adequate health insurance, and round-trip transportation to the field research site. IAF awards usually average between US$14,000-US$16,000.

Country of Study: Independent Latin American and Caribbean countries.

Applications Procedure: Applicants must complete an IAF-printed application form, a 'Personal Statement' which addresses the candidate's: a) personal history; b) special interests and abilities; c) career plans; and d) reasons for interest in Latin American and Caribbean development issues, a prospectus of not more than 1,500 words, and a 200 word abstract.

Closing Date: November 21st.

Additional Information: Candidates should demonstrate a commitment to an interdisciplinary approach, while showing promise of excellence in their research products or future careers. Candidates must complete all course requirements for the doctoral degree before initiating IAF-funded field research.

US Graduate Study Program for Latin American and Caribbean Citizens

Eligibility: Open to development practitioners and applied researchers who are citizens of independent Latin American and Caribbean countries (except Cuba), and whose work in grassroots development would benefit from advanced academic experience in the US on grassroots models for self-help and economic progress.

Level of Study: Doctorate, Masters.

Purpose: To assist development practitioners and applied researchers from these regions to pursue graduate studies in the United States.

Type: Fellowship.

No. of awards offered: 15.

Value: IAF awards usually average between US$18,000-US$22,000. Possible budget items may include tuition as well as those costs of the Fellow and accompanying dependants for a modest living stipend, health insurance, and round-trip international transportation to the Fellow's university.

Length of Study: Maximum of 24 months.

Country of Study: United States.

Applications Procedure: Applicants must complete an IAF-printed application form; a 'Personal Statement'; a 'Plan of Study'; one letter of nomination from a supervisor at the institution where the applicant is currently employed and plans to return on completion of US graduate study; two letters of recommendation from persons knowledgeable about the applicant's experience and academic potential; university transcripts; and photocopies of two publications.

Closing Date: To be announced.

Additional Information: The Foundation dedicates approximately 60% of fellowship financial resources to the US Graduate Study Program.

INTER-AMERICAN PRESS ASSOCIATION

IAPA Scholarship Fund, Inc, 2911 39th Street, NW, Miami, FL, 33142, USA

*IAPA Scholarship Fund, Inc

Subjects: Journalism.

Eligibility: Open to residents of North America, Latin America and the West Indies who are between 21 and 35 years of age and are either professional journalists with at least three years' experience, or graduates of a school of journalism.

Purpose: To help develop more rounded journalists through cultural exposure and study in a foreign country.

Type: Scholarship.

No. of awards offered: Varies.

Frequency: Annual.

Value: US$10,000.

Length of Study: One year.

Study Establishment: US or Canadian university school of journalism approved by the Fund (Latin American and West Indian candidates); or an approved university or field work in a Latin American country (US and Canadian candidates).

Country of Study: USA or Canada, or Latin American countries.

Closing Date: August 1st.

Additional Information: Candidates should have good command of the language of the country they intend to visit. US and Canadian Scholars must take a minimum of three university courses, participate in the Fund's Reporting Program, and undertake a major research project. The Association also gives IAPA awards of US$500-US$1,000 and a scroll or plaque to Latin American and American journalists.

INTERNATIONAL SOCIETY OF ABORICULTURE RESEARCH TRUST

International Society of Aboriculture Research Trust, PO Box GG, Savoy, IL, 61874, USA
Tel: 217 355 9411
Fax: 217 355 9516

The John Z Duling Grant Program

Level of Study: Unrestricted.

Purpose: To provide seed money to support research projects that address topics to benefit the work of Aborists.

Type: Research Grant.

Frequency: Annual.

Value: Maximum of US$5,000.

Applications Procedure: For details write to the ISA Research Trust.

Closing Date: November 1st.

The Hyland R Johns Grant Program

Level of Study: Unrestricted.

Purpose: Provides funds to qualified researchers for projects of interest to the aboricultural industry.

Type: Research Grant.

Frequency: Annual.

Value: In excess of US$5,000.

Country of Study: USA.

Applications Procedure: Write to the ISA Research Trust for details.

Closing Date: May 1st.

The Sponsored Grant Program

Eligibility: Dependent on the individual project.

Level of Study: Unrestricted.

Purpose: Funded by a sponsor or donor for a specific project or topic.

Frequency: Annual.

Country of Study: USA.

Applications Procedure: Must be on "Request for Proposal" mailing list. Send your name and address to the Society.

INTERNATIONAL AGENCY FOR RESEARCH ON CANCER

Cancer Research Fellowship Programme, 150 cours Albert Thomas, Lyon Cedex 08, 69372, France
Tel: 72 73 84 85
Fax: 72 73 85 75
Email: elakroud@IARC.FR
www: http://www.iarc.fr/
Telex: 380 023

Fellowships for Research Training in Cancer

Subjects: Environmental carcinogenesis: biostatistics and epidemiology of cancer and all aspects of chemical and viral carcinogenesis and mechanisms of carcinogenesis. Applications are encouraged from epidemiologists and laboratory scientists for interdisciplinary training that will facilitate the conduct of genetic and molecular epidemiological research.

Eligibility: Open to persons who have had some postdoctoral experience in medicine or the natural sciences. Applicants requiring basic training in cancer epidemiology will also be considered. Applications can not be accepted from people who are receiving, or have received postdoctoral training abroad.

Level of Study: Postdoctorate.

Purpose: To assist junior scientists who are actively engaged in research in medical or allied sciences, and wish to pursue a career in cancer research.

Type: Fellowship.

No. of awards offered: Approximately 15.

Frequency: Annual.

Value: Travel for the Fellow and for one dependant if accompanying the Fellow for at least eight months. Stipends in accordance with UN scales. Family allowances of US$400 for spouse and US$450 for each dependant, paid annually.

Length of Study: One year.

Study Establishment: The Agency in Lyon or in any country and institution where suitable research facilities and material exist.

Country of Study: Any country.

Applications Procedure: Application form must be completed.

Closing Date: December 31st.

Additional Information: Applicants should provide reasonable assurance that they will return to a post in their own country at the end of the Fellowship.

INTERNATIONAL AGRICULTURAL CENTRE

Internationaal Agrarisch Centrum, PO Box 88, Wageningen, 6700 AB, The Netherlands
Tel: 0 317 490111
Fax: 0 317 418552
Email: IAC@IAC.AGRO.NL

Fellowships

Subjects: Agricultural sciences.

Eligibility: Open to postgraduates who have experience in the field of study.

Purpose: To offer postgraduate specialization, through individual study programs, to nationals of industrial countries.

Type: Fellowship.

Value: DFL540 per month, plus free board and lodging in WIR-IAC hostel, insurance, a book allowance, allowance for study tours in the Netherlands. International travel costs from, and to, the home country are not paid.

Length of Study: 6 months; renewable for a further 6 months in some cases.

Country of Study: The Netherlands.

Applications Procedure: Application form must be completed.

Closing Date: July 31st of the year preceding the award.

INTERNATIONAL ASSOCIATION FOR THE STUDY OF INSURANCE ECONOMICS

International Association for the Study of Insurance Economics, 18 chemin Rieu, Geneva, 1208, Switzerland
Tel: 41 22 347 0938
Fax: 41 22 347 2078
Contact: Prof Orio Giarini

Ernst Meyer Prize

Subjects: University research work which makes a significant and original contribution to the study of risk and insurance economics.

Eligibility: Open to professors, researchers or students of economics.

Type: Prize.

No. of awards offered: One.

Frequency: Annual.

Value: SwFr10,000.

Closing Date: March 31st.

Research Grants

Subjects: Risk and insurance economics.

Eligibility: Open to graduates involved in research for a thesis leading to a doctor's degree in economics.

Level of Study: Postgraduate.

Purpose: To promote economic research.

Type: Research Grant.

No. of awards offered: Two.

Frequency: Annual.

Value: SwFr8,000.

Length of Study: 10 months.

Closing Date: March 31st.

Additional Information: The Association reserves the right to support research on other subjects which may be submitted. Applications must be accompanied by a personal history, a description of the research undertaken and a letter of recommendation from a professor of economics. The Association also grants authors of university theses already submitted, dealing in depth with a subject in the field of risk and insurance economics, a subsidy of up to SwFr2,000 towards printing costs.

INTERNATIONAL ASSOCIATION OF FIRE CHIEFS FOUNDATION

International Association of Fire Chiefs Foundation, 1257 Wiltshire Rd, York, PA, 17403, USA
Tel: 1 717 846 9705/854 9083
Contact: Sue Hawkins

Each year the IAFC Foundation coordinates a scholarship program made possible through the generosity of corporations throughout the United States, as well as donations from individuals and persons sponsoring a scholarship as a memorial to a friend or colleague

IAFC Foundation Scholarship

Subjects: Fire sciences.

Eligibility: Open to any person who is an active member of a state, county, provincial, municipal, community, industrial, or federal fire department, who has demonstrated proficiency as a member. Dependants of members are NOT eligible.

Level of Study: Undergraduate, Professional development.

Purpose: To assist fire service personnel towards college degrees.

Type: Scholarship.

No. of awards offered: Thirty.

Frequency: Dependent on funds available.

Value: US$250-US$4,000.

Country of Study: Any country.

Applications Procedure: Application from must be completed. This includes a 250 word statement outlining reasons for applying for assistance and an explanation why the candidate thinks that the course will be useful in their chosen field.

Closing Date: August 1st.

Additional Information: In evaluating the applications, preference will be given to those demonstrating need, desire and initiative.

INTERNATIONAL ASTRONOMICAL UNION

98 bis, boulevard Arago, Paris, 75014, France
Contact: IAU-UAI Secretariat

*Travel Grants

Subjects: Astronomy.

Eligibility: Open to faculty/staff members, postdoctoral fellows, or graduate students at any recognized educational/research institution or observatory. All candidates must have an excellent record of research and must have made permanent and professional commitments to astronomy. The programme is designed to support both the work of young astronomers and established astronomers whose visits may benefit the country or institution visited. It is emphasized that all recipients should return to their home institutions or home countries upon the completion of their visits.

Purpose: To enable astronomers to undertake research or study at observatories and universities abroad.

No. of awards offered: Varies.

Frequency: Varies, according to funds available.

Value: Travel expenses only.

Length of Study: Varies.

Study Establishment: Approved observatories.

Country of Study: Any country.

INTERNATIONAL BEETHOVEN PIANO COMPETITION

Lothringerstrasse 18, Wien, A-1030, Austria
Tel: 00 43 1 58 806 171
Fax: 00 43 1 58 72897
Contact: Mag Elga Ponzer, Secretary General

International Beethoven Piano Competition

Subjects: Piano.

Eligibility: Open to pianists of all nationalities born between 1 January 1965 and 31 December 1980.

Purpose: To encourage the artistic development of young pianists.

No. of awards offered: 6.

Frequency: Every four years.

Value: 1st prize: Sch80,000 and a Bosendorfer Model 200 piano; 2nd Prize: Sch60,000; 3rd Prize: Sch50,000; plus three further prizes of Sch20,000.

Country of Study: Austria.

Additional Information: The Tenth International Beethoven Piano Competition in Vienna will take place in 1997.

INTERNATIONAL BRAIN RESEARCH ORGANIZATION

IBRO Fellowship Committee, 51 boulevard de Montmorency, Paris, 75106, France
Contact: Dr S H Barondes

IBRO/UNESCO Research Fellowships

Subjects: Neuroanatomy, neurochemistry, neuroendocrinology, neuropharmacology, neurophysiology, behavioural sciences (specifically confined to the relationships of brain and behaviour), neurocommunication and biophysics, and brain pathology.

Eligibility: Open to young scientists, especially from developing countries wishing to acquire new techniques in a discipline other than their primary field of research. Candidates must have established competence in one of the subject areas listed.

Purpose: To stimulate and facilitate international interdisciplinary advanced research in neurosciences.

Type: Fellowship.

No. of awards offered: Varies.

Length of Study: 6-24 months.

Country of Study: Czech Republic or Hungary.

Closing Date: December 1st.

INTERNATIONAL BUREAU OF WEIGHTS AND MEASURES

Bureau International des Poids et Mesures, Pavillon de Breteuil, Sèvres Cedex, F-92312, France
Tel: 33 1 45 07 70 70
Fax: 33 1 45 34 20 21
Contact: The Director

Training Opportunities

Subjects: Metrology; study of high-precision standards of measurement.

Eligibility: Open to persons who possess at least a BSc degree in the physical sciences and have a good knowledge of English or French. A candidate must show the possibility of exchange of profitable scientific information between himself and the physicists of the Bureau.

Purpose: To encourage the exchange of experience between physicists from the national laboratories of the member countries of the Convention du Mitre.

Frequency: As the opportunity arises.

Value: No financial assistance.

Length of Study: From a few days to a few months.

Study Establishment: At the Bureau.

Country of Study: France.

Applications Procedure: Applications should be made through the agency of a laboratory or an official metrological service.

Closing Date: At least four months before the desired period of study.

INTERNATIONAL CELLO FESTIVAL

International Cello Festival, PO Box 782, 00101, Helsinki, 00101, Finland
Tel: 358 0 405 4690
Fax: 358 0 400 3110
Contact: Minna Pitkänen, Competition Secretary

International Paulo Cello Competition

Subjects: Cello.

Eligibility: Open to cellists born between 1963 and 1980 inclusive.

Type: Competition.

No. of awards offered: Six prizes.

Frequency: Every five years (next in 2001).

Value: Prizes as follows; 1) 70,000 FIM 2) 40,000 FIM 3) 25,000 FIM 4) 10,000 FIM 5) 10,000 FIM 6) 10,000 FIM.

Country of Study: Finland.

Applications Procedure: Send for brochure containing details of application and audition pieces.

INTERNATIONAL CENTRE OF HYDROLOGY 'DINO TONINI'

International Centre of Hydrology 'Dino Tonini', Villa Duodo, Via Sette Chiese, Monselice (Padova), 35043, Italy
Tel: 0429 782152
Fax: 0429 781960
Contact: Professor Andrea Rinaldo

Scholarships for International Postgraduate Courses in Hydrology

Subjects: Hydrology, especially hydrometeorology and the application of hydraulic construction techniques.

Eligibility: Open to civil engineers, particularly from developing countries, who are not over 35 years of age and who specialize in hydrology.

Purpose: To enable civil engineering graduates to complete their training.

No. of awards offered: Varies.

Frequency: Annual.

Value: Monthly living expenses, allowance, round-trip travel costs and tuition fees.

Length of Study: 6 months (January to July).

Study Establishment: The Centre.

Country of Study: Italy.

Closing Date: Mid-October.

Additional Information: Instruction on the course is in English. The course is organized by the Centre at the University of Padua under the auspices of the Italian National Research Council, the Italian Ministry of Foreign Affairs and Unesco.

INTERNATIONAL CHAMBER MUSIC COMPETITION

International Chamber Music Competition, UFAM, 10 rue du Dôme, Paris, 75116, France
Tel: 1 47047638
Fax: 1 47273503
Contact: Ms C de Bayser, President

International Chamber Music Competition

Subjects: Groups of wind instruments, with or without piano, harp, guitar or percussion instruments. String instruments accompanying wind instruments are also permitted.

Eligibility: Open to groups of musicians of any nationality, who are no more than 36 years of age; the average age of the group should not exceed 34 years.

No. of awards offered: Varies.

Frequency: Biennially (1998).

Value: From a total fund of FF110,000. Winners are also offered important performance engagements.

Closing Date: September 20th in the year of the Competition.

Additional Information: The Competition includes various sections for groups of various sizes, who may perform with or without piano accompaniment.

INTERNATIONAL COLLEGE OF SURGEONS

International College of Surgeons, 1516 North Lake Shore Drive, Chicago, IL, 60610-1694, USA
Tel: 312 642 3555
Fax: 312 787 1624

ICS Scholarship

Eligibility: Typically given to physicians from third world countries traveling to developed nations to further their education.

Level of Study: Postgraduate, Postdoctorate, Doctorate, Professional development.

Purpose: Education and research out of home country with sponsored program.

Type: Scholarship.

No. of awards offered: Varies.

Frequency: Dependent on funds available.

Value: US$500, to US$1,500.

Length of Study: One week to one year.

Country of Study: USA.

Applications Procedure: Send request to ICS HQ.

INTERNATIONAL COUNCIL FOR BUILDING RESEARCH STUDIES AND DOCUMENTATION (CIB)

CIB, PO Box 1837, 3000 BV Rotterdam, The Netherlands
Tel: 31 10 411 0240
Fax: 31 10 433 4372
Email: secretariat@cibworld.nl
www: http://bcn.arch.ufl.edu/cib.html
Contact: The Secretary General

CIB Developing Countries Fund

Subjects: All aspects of building research.

Eligibility: Candidates must be a staff member of a CIB member institute in a developing country and must themselves be nationals of developing countries.

Purpose: To enable staff members of CIB member institutes in developing countries to participate in events of professional benefit.

Type: Fellowship.

Frequency: No limit on frequency but dependent on funds available.

Value: Total or partial reimbursement of fees, travel and subsistence costs.

Country of Study: International.

Closing Date: No closing date but at least two months before date of commencement of event.

INTERNATIONAL COUNCIL FOR CANADIAN STUDIES

International Council for Canadian Studies, 325 Dalhousie S 800, Ottawa, Ontario, K1N 7G2, Canada
Tel: 613 789 7828
Fax: 613 7897830
Contact: Program Officer

Commonwealth Scholarships

Subjects: Any subjects except medicine, and introduction to languages.

Eligibility: Open to Canadian citizens and certain permanent residents of Canada. Applicants must have completed a university degree or expect to graduate prior to the commencement of the award.

Level of Study: Postgraduate, Doctorate.

Purpose: To provide opportunities for students to pursue advanced studies in Canada.

Type: Scholarship.

No. of awards offered: Varies.

Frequency: Annual.

Length of Study: Maximum of three years.

Country of Study: Australia; India; New Zealand; United Kingdom;

Ghana; Jamaica; Nigeria; Sierra Leone; Sri Lanka; Trinidad and Tobago.

Applications Procedure: The Canadian Commonwealth Scholarship and Fellowship Committee will select the nominations to be forwarded to the awarding country. the actual offer of a scholarship will be made by the Commonwealth Scholarship Agency in the awarding country.

Closing Date: October 31st for all awarding countries except Australia and New Zealand; December 31st for Australia and New Zealand.

Additional Information: Commonwealth scholars cannot normally hold any other scholarships or awards. They may not, without the written consent of the awarding agency, undertake paid employment during the tenure of the award or serve on the staff of the Canadian High Commission in the awarding country.

Foreign Government Awards

Subjects: Any subject, except medicine or introduction to language.

Eligibility: Open to Canadian citizens with a working knowledge of the host country's language and a bachelor's degree (or PhD for postdoctoral fellowships), completed before the beginning of the award term.

Level of Study: Postgraduate, Doctorate.

Purpose: To assist Canadians to study or conduct research abroad at the masters, doctoral or postdoctoral level.

No. of awards offered: Varies.

Frequency: Annual.

Value: Generally to cover tuition fees, books, a living allowance, transportation and miscellaneous expenses.

Country of Study: Colombia, Finland, France, Germany, Mexico and Poland.

Applications Procedure: Applications are initially evaluated by a 'preselection committee' of Canadian academics. The committee submits a list of recommended candidates and alternates to each host country, where award recipients are chosen. A list of participating countries is available on request.

Closing Date: October 15th.

INTERNATIONAL CROPS RESEARCH INSTITUTE FOR THE SEMI-ARID TROPICS

International Crops Research Institute for the Semi-Arid Tropics, Patancheru, PO 502 324, Andhra Pradesh, India
Tel: 91 40 596161
Fax: 91 40 241239
Email: icrisat@cgnet.com
Telex: 402 203 ICRI IN
Contact: Training & Fellowships Program

Postdoctoral Fellowships; Research Fellowships

Subjects: Agronomy, plant breeding, genetics, genetic resources, physiology, entomology, pathology, microbiology, soil physics, economics and statistics related to sorghum, pearl millet, groundnut, pigeonpea, chickpea, and rain-fed semi-arid tropical resource management, cellular and molecular biology.

Eligibility: There are no nationality restrictions. Applicants holding a PhD or equivalent degree in agriculture or related science compete on an international basis in specific research areas. Sponsoring agency or employer recommendations are requested.

Level of Study: Postgraduate, Doctorate.

Purpose: To provide opportunities for scientists with a PhD qualification to work with senior research scientists on research problems of the semi-arid tropics with ICRISATS' mandate.

Type: Fellowship.

No. of awards offered: Approximately 10.

Frequency: Annual.

Value: Competitive stipend on an international basis.

Length of Study: One year; possibly extendable for one additional year.

Study Establishment: The Institute.

Country of Study: India.

Applications Procedure: Application form can be obtained from the Institute.

Closing Date: Open.

Research Scholarships

Subjects: Agronomy, plant breeding, genetics, genetic resources, physiology, entomology, pathology, microbiology, biochemistry, cellular and molecular biology, soil physics, economics and statistics related to sorghum, pearl millet, groundnut, pigeonpea and chickpea, and rain-fed semi-arid tropical resource management.

Eligibility: There are no nationality restrictions. Applicants must have completed all coursework and preliminary examinations for an MSc or PhD in agricultural or related sciences. The Scholar's university must accept the Institute's research guide.

Level of Study: Postgraduate, Doctorate, Postdoctorate, Professional development.

Purpose: To provide an opportunity for students to conduct research for an MSc or PhD thesis.

No. of awards offered: 15-20.

Frequency: Annual.

Value: Varies; stipends are intended to meet the Scholar's expenses. Scholarships include a university committee guide's visit to the Institute.

Length of Study: 18-36 months.

Study Establishment: The Institute.

Country of Study: India.

Applications Procedure: Application form can be obtained from the Institute.

Closing Date: 30 March, 31 July and 30 November.

INTERNATIONALER ROBERT-SCHUMANN-WETTBEWERB ZWICKAU

Internationaler Robert-Schumann-Wettbewerb Zwickau, Kulturbüro, Münzstrsse 12, Zwickau, D 08056, Germany
Tel: 0049 375 212 636
Fax: 0049 375 834 730

International Robert Schumann Competitions

Subjects: Piano performance, individual singing, and choral singing.

Eligibility: Open to pianists up to the age of 30 and to individual singers up to the age of 32. There is no age restriction for members of choirs, which may be all male, all female or mixed. Choirs which include professional singers are eligible.

Frequency: Every three to four years.

Country of Study: Germany.

Applications Procedure: Write for further information.

INTERNATIONAL EYE FOUNDATION

Tv 21 No 100-20 Piso 7, Bogotá, Colombia
Tel: 6 11 17 11
Fax: 6 17 09 02
Contact: Eduardo Arenas A, MD

Fellowship

Subjects: Anterior segment surgery.

Eligibility: Open to ophthalmologists from any country.

Level of Study: Postdoctorate.

Purpose: To bring ophthalmologists up to date with advances in procedures of cornea, glaucoma and cataract.

Type: Fellowship.

Frequency: Every six months.

Value: US$125 monthly.

Length of Study: Six months.

Study Establishment: Santa Fe de Bogotá Foundation.

Country of Study: Colombia.

INTERNATIONAL FEDERATION OF UNIVERSITY WOMEN

c/o The British Federation of Women Graduates, 4 Mandeville Court,
142 Battersea Park Road, London, SW11 4NB, England
Tel: 0171 498 8037
Fax: 0171 498 8037

The British Federation Crosby Hall Fellowship

Subjects: Any subject.

Eligibility: Women applicants for all awards must be either a member of one of IFUW's national federations or associations or, in the case of women graduates living in countries where there is not yet a national affiliate, an independent member of IFUW.

Level of Study: Postgraduate.

Purpose: To assist with living expenses.

Type: Fellowship.

No. of awards offered: One.

Frequency: Every two years.

Value: £2,500, of which the first £1,000 will be paid at the beginning of the academic year on proof of registration.

Study Establishment: An approved institution of higher education.

Country of Study: Great Britain.

Applications Procedure: Applicants MUST apply through their respective Federation or Association, and members of BFWG may apply for consideration by IFUW for one of the awards. A list of IFUW national federations can be sent upon request.

Closing Date: November 1st of year preceding competition.

Winifred Cullis and Dorothy Leet Grants

Subjects: Humanities, social sciences, natural sciences.

Eligibility: Open to IFUW members. Dorothy Leet Grants are reserved for candidates from developing countries or women planning to work in those countries.

Purpose: To enable recipients to carry out research, obtain specialized training essential to research, or training in new techniques.

No. of awards offered: Varies.

Frequency: Biennially.

Value: Varies; SwFr3,000-SwFr6,000.

Length of Study: 2-3 months.

Country of Study: International.

Applications Procedure: Members of a national federation or association affiliated to the IFUW must apply through their national affiliate. IFUW Independent Members may apply direct to IFUW headquarters. Application forms are available on request.

Closing Date: Normally November 1st of the year preceding the award.

For further information contact:
IFUW Fellowships Programme, 8 rue de l'Ancien Port, 1201 Geneva, Switzerland

Ida Smedley Maclean, CFUW/A Vibert Douglas and SAAP Fellowships

Subjects: Humanities, social sciences, natural sciences.

Eligibility: Open to IFUW members who are well started on a research programme and have completed at least one year of graduate work.

Purpose: To encourage advanced scholarship and original research.

No. of awards offered: One of each Fellowship.

Frequency: Biennially.

Value: Maclean Fellowship: SwFr8,000-10,000; Douglas Fellowship: C$6,000, Queensland Fellowship. A$12,000, SAAP Fellowship. SwFr8,000-10,000.

Length of Study: At least eight months.

Country of Study: International.

Closing Date: Normally November 1st of the year preceding the award.

INTERNATIONAL FOUNDATION FOR ETHICAL RESEARCH

International Foundation for Ethical Research, 53 West Jackson
Boulevard, Suite 1552, Chicago, IL, 60604, USA
Tel: 312 427 6025
Fax: 312 427 6524
Contact: John R Hughes, Executive Director

*Grants

Subjects: Tissue cultures, cell cultures, organ cultures, gas chrometography, mathematical and computer models, clinical and epidemiologic surveys are examples of some of the research areas previously awarded grants.

Eligibility: Open to qualified educators and/or researchers who seek to provide alternatives to the use of live animals in research, testing and education.

Purpose: To develop, validate and disseminate alternatives to the use of live animals in research, education and product testing. Alternatives are defined as methods which replace, refine or reduce the number of animals traditionally used.

No. of awards offered: 2-4.

Frequency: Annual.

Value: Total amount awarded is approximately US$75,000-US$100,000 annually among 2-4 projects.

Country of Study: Unrestricted.

Closing Date: 1 August for pre-proposals; 1 December for full proposals.

INTERNATIONAL FOUNDATION FOR SCIENCE

International Foundation for Science, Grev Turegatan 19, Stockholm,
11438, Sweden
Tel: 8 791 2900
Fax: 8 660 2618
Contact: Judith Furberg

*IFS Grant

Subjects: Research projects in the fields of biological and agricultural sciences and the chemistry of natural resources. The IFS areas are aquatic resources, animal production, crop science, forestry/agroforestry, food science, and natural producers.

Eligibility: Open to scientists who are native to a developing country, in possession of an academic degree (not less than an MSc or the equivalent), currently employed at a university or research institution in a developing country, young (normally under 40 at the time of first application for a grant) and at the beginning of their research careers.

Purpose: To help reverse the brain-drain of developing country scientists. A complementary goal is to contribute to the strengthening of scientific and intellectual human resources, viz. capacity building, in developing countries.

Value: Awards are limited to US$12,000 per research period and may be renewed twice. IFS also gives other support to help grantees further their research. IFS funding is not intended for travel or study, but should be used for purchasing the basic tools of research: equipment, expendable supplies, and literature.

Additional Information: Research proposed by applicants shall be conducted in a developing country and relevant to the needs of a developing country. Application forms (in English or French) are available on request. Regular financing comes from 13 countries: Belgium, China, Denmark, Finland, France, Germany, Japan, the Netherlands, Nigeria, Norway, Sweden, Switzerland, and the USA. A number of national and international development agencies contribute to the IFS granting and supporting programmes.

INTERNATIONAL FOUNDATION OF EMPLOYEE BENEFIT PLANS

International Foundation of Employee Benefit Plans, 18700 West Bluemound Road, PO Box 69, Brookfield, WI, 53008-0069, USA
Tel: 414 786 6710 ext.8440
Fax: 414 786 8670
Email: research@ifebp.org
www: http://www.ifebp.org
Contact: Ellen Mlada

Grants for Research

Subjects: Original research on employee benefit topics: including health care benefits, retirement and income security, and other aspects of employee benefits systems. Special consideration may be given to proposals on particular topics according to the year of application.

Eligibility: Open to citizens of the United States or Canada who are pursuing a graduate or postgraduate degree from an accredited college or university, or who hold a terminal degree from an accredited institution and are employed by a non-profit educational or research institution. The following academic disciplines are examples of appropriate backgrounds for grant applicants: business and finance, labor and industrial relations, economics, law, social/health sciences.

Level of Study: Postgraduate, Postdoctorate, Professional development.

Type: Grant.

Frequency: Throughout the year.

Value: Up to US$5,000 (Graduate) and US$10,000 (postdoctoral), paid in three equal disbursements.

Applications Procedure: No application form; must submit proposal.

Additional Information: Interested individuals may apply by submitting a proposal and current curriculum vitae. Proposals should address the following within 20 typed, single-spaced pages: the intended topic and its potential significance to the employee benefits industry; proposed methodology; itemized cost of doing the study; and the expected timetable for completion. Applications are reviewed by the Director of Research and evaluated on the relevance of the proposed research for

the Grants for Research program and the potential for successful completion of the project. Applications will be reviewed within 60 days of receipt. Grants for Research recipients are expected to adhere to their proposals once grants are awarded. After an award is made, any changes in the proposed topic or methodology must be approved, in advance, by the Director of Research. Grant recipients must submit a final report upon completion of the project. Dot-matrix copies will not be accepted. Grantees assign all copyrights for publication and distribution of their final reports to the International Foundation. However, grant recipients are encouraged to publish articles for professional journals based on their research.

INTERNATIONAL FREDERIC CHOPIN COMPETITION

International Frederic Chopin Competition, Frederic Chopin Society in Warsaw, Ostrogski Castle, ul Okolnik 1, Warsaw, 00-368, Poland
Tel: 27 54 71
Fax: 27 95 99
Contact: The Jury

International Frederic Chopin Competition

Subjects: Piano performance of Chopin music.

Eligibility: Open to pianists of any nationality, between 18 and 30 years of age.

Purpose: To recognize the best artistic interpretation of Chopin's music and to encourage professional development.

Type: Prize.

No. of awards offered: Six to eight prizes.

Frequency: Every five years; next in 2000.

Value: First prize 150,000,000 zlotys and a gold medal; second prize 100,000,000 zlotys and a silver medal; third prize 75,000,000 zlotys and a bronze medal; fourth prize 50,000,000 zlotys; fifth prize 40,000,000 zlotys; sixth prize 30,000,000 zlotys.

Closing Date: Please contact the Society for details.

Additional Information: Apart from the prizes specified above, the following special awards shall be granted by: the Frederic Chopin Society for the best performance of a polonaise 20,000,000 zlotys; the Polish Radio for the best performance of mazurkas 20,000,000 zlotys; the National Philharmonic for the best performance of a concerto 20,000,000 zlotys.

INTERNATIONAL HARP CONTEST IN ISRAEL

International Harp Contest in Israel, 4 Aharonowitz Street, Tel Aviv, 63 566, Israel
Tel: 972 3 528 0233
Fax: 972 3 629 9524
Contact: Secretariat

International Harp Contest

Subjects: Harp.

Eligibility: Open to harpists of any nationality who are no more than 35 years of age.

Level of Study: Postgraduate, Professional development.

Purpose: To encourage excellence in harp playing.

Type: Prize.

Frequency: Triennially (next in 1998).

Value: 1st prize: a grand concert harp from the House of Lyon & Healy, Chicago; 2nd prize: US$5,000; 3rd prize: US$3,000; Gulbenkian Prize:

US$2,500; Propes Prize: US$1,500.

Country of Study: Any country.

Applications Procedure: Application form needs to be completed and submitted with recommendations and record of concert experience.

Closing Date: 1 July 1997.

Additional Information: Board and lodging is provided by the Contest Committee. There is a registration fee of US$150.

INTERNATIONAL INSTITUTE FOR POPULATION SCIENCES

International Institute for Population Sciences, Govandi Station Road, Deonar, Mumbai, Maharashtra, 400 088, India
Tel: 91 22 5563254/55/56
Fax: 91 22 5563257
Email: iips.nfhs@axcess.net.in
Contact: Dr K B Pathak

Diploma in Population Studies

Subjects: Population studies.

Eligibility: Open to ESCAP and Pacific Region nationals who are already working in the fields of population and health.

Level of Study: Professional development.

Purpose: To train the recipient in obtaining basic knowledge in the field of population.

Type: Diploma course.

No. of awards offered: Thirty.

Frequency: Dependent on funds available.

Value: Return air ticket plus US$6,875 per student per year.

Length of Study: One year.

Country of Study: India.

Applications Procedure: Application must be made through UNFPA country Directors/representatives in the applicant's own country.

Closing Date: April 15th every year.

INTERNATIONAL INSTITUTE OF TROPICAL AGRICULTURE

International Institute of Tropical Agriculture, c/o L W Lambourn and Company, Carolyne House, Dingwall Road, Croydon, CR9 3EE, England
Tel: 181 681 8583
Fax: 874 177 2276
Email: IITA@CGNET.COM
Telex: 31417 TROPIB NG
Contact: Program Leader

Research Fellowships

Subjects: Agricultural economics, agroclimatology, agronomy, biotechnology, biological control, crop production, entomology, plant breeding, plant pathology, plant physiology, soil chemistry, soil physics, soil microbiology, and weed sciences.

Eligibility: Candidates should be residents of Sub-Saharan Africa and be registered for a postgraduate degree at a university in Africa or abroad (generally a faculty of agriculture).

Level of Study: Postgraduate, Doctorate.

Purpose: To enable African postgraduate degree candidates to conduct research at the Institute or one of its satellites.

Type: Fellowship.

No. of awards offered: Approximately 10.

Frequency: Twice yearly.

Value: Up to US$12,000 per annum; includes board and lodging, various allowances for personal and other expenses, travel to and from the Institute, medical accident insurance, and all research costs. It also includes one trip for the student's university supervisor to IITA for PhD students.

Length of Study: Six months to one year (MSc degree) or for 1-2 years (PhD degree).

Study Establishment: The Institute.

Country of Study: Nigeria, Cameroon and Benin.

Applications Procedure: Application form must be completed and submitted with a research proposal and references.

Closing Date: March, September.

Additional Information: Applications for admission to the Institute's training program may be submitted by individuals. However, it is preferred that all applications be made through the university and supported by a letter from the candidate's adviser. Candidate, adviser and university must agree to accept a scientist from the Institute as supervisor of research while the Fellow is at the IITA.

For further information contact:
International Institute of Tropical Agriculture, Oyo Road, PMB 5320, Ibadan, Nigeria
Tel: 234 2 241 2626
Fax: 234 2 241 2221
Contact: Program Leader

INTERNATIONAL LEAD ZINC RESEARCH ORGANIZATION, INC

International Lead Zinc Research Organization, Inc, 2525 Meridian Parkway, PO Box 12036, Research Triangle Park, NC, 27709, USA
Tel: 919 361 4647
Fax: 919 361 1957
Contact: Dr Jerome F Cole, President, or Dr Frank E Goodwin, VP Metals Sciences

Postgraduate, Predoctoral, Postdoctoral Research and Project Fellowships

Subjects: Zinc die casting; process improvement; finishing; cadmium; lead and zinc chemicals; paints and pigments; ceramics; batteries; cable sheathing; composites.

Eligibility: There are no restrictions except for academic qualifications in the chosen area.

Purpose: To develop new products and processes employing lead, zinc, and cadmium.

No. of awards offered: 6-10.

Frequency: As vacancies occur or as the opportunity arises.

Value: Usually US$17,000-US$30,000 per annum, paid either quarterly or in full in advance.

Length of Study: 2-3 years.

Study Establishment: Various universities.

Country of Study: Any country.

Closing Date: 1 June for Fellowships commencing the following year.

INTERNATIONAL MATHEMATICAL UNION

International Mathematical Union, Estrada Dona Castorina, 110, Jardim Botanico, Rio De Janeiro, RJ, 22460, Brazil
Tel: 55 21 294 9032
Fax: 55 21 512 4112

Contact: Jacob Palis Jr

Fellowship

Subjects: Mathematics.

Eligibility: Open to active mathematicians at the PhD level. The Fellowship is mainly intended for mathematicians in developing countries.

Purpose: To promote mathematical research in third world countries.

Type: Fellowship.

No. of awards offered: One.

Frequency: Annual.

Value: Varies.

Length of Study: At least 2 months.

Study Establishment: A well-known university or institute.

Closing Date: Six months prior to the research visit.

Fields Medals

Subjects: Mathematics.

Eligibility: Open to young mathematicians (up to 40 years old) of any nationality.

Purpose: To reward outstanding achievements.

Type: Medal.

No. of awards offered: 2-4.

Frequency: Every four years.

Value: CHF15,000.

Rolf Nevanlinna Prize

Subjects: Mathematical aspects of information science.

Eligibility: Open to young mathematicians (up to 40 years old) of any nationality.

Type: Prize.

No. of awards offered: One.

Frequency: Every four years.

Value: CHF5,000.

Visiting Mathematician Programme

Subjects: Core of mathematics (pure and applied).

Eligibility: Open to active mathematicians at PhD level with strong research possibilities. The programme is mainly intended for mathematicians working in a developing country to make an extended research visit to an advanced mathematical centre.

Level of Study: Postdoctorate, Professional development.

Purpose: To provide partial travel support for extended research visits in an advanced mathematical centre.

Type: Travel Grant.

No. of awards offered: Varies.

Frequency: Annually, depending on funds available.

Value: Dependent on travel costs and duration of visit: local support.

Length of Study: Two months.

Study Establishment: At an advanced mathematical research centre.

Applications Procedure: Bio-data, list of publications, research program, invitation letter from host lab confirming it will cover local expenses.

Closing Date: Six months prior to visit.

Additional Information: The host center must commit itself to supporting local expenses.

For further information contact:
Commission on Development and Exchanges, Secretariat, Institut Fourier, Université Grenoble 1, BP 74, 38402 St-Martin d'Hères Cedex, France
Tel: 33 76 51 49 80
Fax: 33 76 51 44 78
Email: pierre.berard@ujf-grendde.fr
Contact: Professor P Bérard

INTERNATIONAL M LONG-J THIBAUD COMPETITION

International M Long-J Thibaud Competition, 32 Avenue Matignon, Paris, 75008, France
Tel: 1 42 66 66 80
Fax: 1 42 66 06 43
Contact: Claude Perin

Premier Grand Prix Marguerite Long, Premier Grand Prix Jacques Thibaud

Subjects: Piano (Prix Marguerite Long) and violin (Prix Jacques Thibaud).

Eligibility: Open to young musicians between 16 and 30 years of age, of all nationalities.

Level of Study: Professional development.

Type: 6 prizes and special prizes.

Frequency: Triennially.

Value: FF150,000, plus 30 concert engagements and a tour of Asia and America South and North.

Country of Study: France.

Applications Procedure: Registration form to be completed and copies of Diplomas submitted.

Closing Date: September 1st.

Additional Information: Full particulars are given on the application form, available on request. There is a registration fee of FF500.

INTERNATIONAL ORGAN COMPETITION 'GRAND PRIX DE CHARTRES'

Grand Prix de Chartres, Concours international d'orgue, 75 rue de Grenelle, Paris, 75007, France
Tel: 33 1 45 48 31 74
Fax: 33 1 45 49 14 34
Contact: Secretariat

International Organ Competition 'Grand Prix de Chartres'

Subjects: Organ performance, in two categories: interpretation and improvization.

Eligibility: Open to organists of any nationality who are 35 years of age or under in the year of the Competition.

Type: Prize plus concerts in France and other countries.

No. of awards offered: Two.

Frequency: Biennially.

Value: First prize FF30,000; second prize FF10,000.

Country of Study: France.

Closing Date: April 15th.

INTERNATIONAL READING ASSOCIATION

International Reading Association, 800 Barksdale Road, PO Box 8139, Newark, Delaware, 19714-8139, USA
Tel: 302 731 1600 ext.226
Fax: 302 731 1057
Email: 73314.1411@compuserve.com
Contact: Gail Keating

Developing Country Literacy Project Support Fund Grant

Subjects: Curriculum.

Eligibility: Applicant must be a member of the International Reading Association.

Level of Study: Professional development.

Purpose: To assist with the funding of literacy projects and with the professional development of literacy educators in developing countries (using the World Bank definition).

Type: Grant.

No. of awards offered: Not determined.

Frequency: Dependent on funds available.

Value: Up to US$2,000.

Length of Study: Two years.

Country of Study: Any developing country (using the World Bank definition).

Applications Procedure: Completion and submission of application is required. Committee of international reviewers selects nominee for the Board of Directors to approve.

Closing Date: November 15th.

Albert J Harris Award

Eligibility: Publications that have appeared in a refereed professional journal or monograph.

Level of Study: Postgraduate.

Purpose: For outstanding contribution to the prevention and/or assessment of reading or learning disabilities. Publications that have appeared in a professional journal between June 1st, 1995 and June 1st, 1996 are eligible and may be submitted by the author or anyone else.

Type: Literacy publication.

No. of awards offered: One.

Frequency: Annual.

Value: US$500.

Country of Study: Open.

Closing Date: October.

Elva Knight Research Grant

Subjects: Literacy education; education research.

Eligibility: Applicants must be members of the International Reading Association.

Level of Study: Postgraduate.

Purpose: To assist research in reading and literacy. Research is defined as that which addresses significant questions for the disciplines of literacy research and practice.

Type: Research Grant.

No. of awards offered: Up to seven annually.

Frequency: Annual.

Value: Maximum of US$5,000.

Length of Study: Two years.

Country of Study: Any country.

Applications Procedure: Please write for guidelines and forms.

Closing Date: October 15th.

Constance McCulloch Award

Subjects: Teaching and learning.

Eligibility: Applicants must be members of the International Reading Association; activity must be carried out in country outside North America.

Level of Study: Professional development.

Purpose: To encourage international professional development activities that are carried out in countries outside North America, with focus on reading-related problems.

Type: Award.

No. of awards offered: One.

Frequency: Annual.

Value: US$5,000.

Length of Study: Up to two years.

Country of Study: Any country outside North America.

Applications Procedure: Completion and submission of application is required. Committee of international reviewers selects nominee for the Board of Directors to approve.

Closing Date: Postmarked October 1st; must be received by October 10th.

For further information contact:
International Reading Association, 800 Barksdale Road, PO Box 8139, Newark, Delaware, 19714-8139, USA
Tel: 302 731 1600
Fax: 302 731 1057
Email: 102556.1076@compuserve.com
Contact: Gerald Casey

Outstanding Dissertation of the Year Award

Eligibility: Must be a member of International Reading Association.

Level of Study: Doctorate.

Purpose: To recognise completed dissertations in the field of reading and literacy.

No. of awards offered: One.

Frequency: Annual.

Value: US$1,000.

Country of Study: Open.

Applications Procedure: Write for guidelines and forms.

Reading/Literacy Research Fellowship

Subjects: Literacy education; educational research.

Eligibility: Open to any IRA member outside the United States or Canada.

Level of Study: Postdoctorate.

Purpose: To assist a researcher outside the United States or Canada, who has shown exceptional promise in reading/literacy research.

Type: Fellowship.

No. of awards offered: One.

Frequency: Annual.

Value: US$1,000.

Country of Study: Outside the United States and Canada.

Applications Procedure: Applicants must write for guidelines with specific forms.

Closing Date: October 15th.

Helen M. Robinson Award

Subjects: Literacy education.

Eligibility: Applicant must be a member of the International Reading Association and in a doctoral program.

Level of Study: Postgraduate.

Purpose: To support International Reading Association members who are doctoral students at the early stages of their dissertation research in the area of reading and literacy.

Type: Dissertation award.

No. of awards offered: One.

Frequency: Annual.

Value: US$500.

Country of Study: Any country.

Applications Procedure: Please write for guidelines and forms.

Closing Date: June 15th.

Gertrude Whipple Professional Development Grant

Subjects: Teaching and learning.

Eligibility: Applicants must be members of the International Reading Association.

Level of Study: Professional development.

Purpose: To assist with the planning and creation of professional development projects, with the production of high quality materials, with the marketing and scheduling of meetings and workshops, and with the logistic support for conducting them.

Type: Grant.

No. of awards offered: One or more.

Frequency: Annual.

Value: Up to US$5,000.

Length of Study: Two years.

Country of Study: Not specified.

Applications Procedure: Completion and submission of application is required. Committee of reviewers selects nominee for the Board of Directors to approve.

Closing Date: January 2nd.

INTERNATIONAL RESEARCH AND EXCHANGES BOARD

International Research and Exchanges Board, 126 Alexander Street, Princeton, NJ, 08540-7102, USA
Tel: 609 683 9500
Fax: 609 683 1511
Contact: Stan Zylowski

*Developmental Fellowships

Subjects: Fields outside former Soviet and East European studies, such as archaeology, anthropology, business, economics, geography, demography, law, musicology, political science, psychology, and sociology.

Eligibility: Open to US citizens who are planning doctoral or postdoctoral research that will require subsequent field access to the former USSR or East Europe. Applicants must be faculty members, postdoctoral researchers or PhD candidates.

Purpose: To prepare scholars for eventual field research in the former USSR or East Europe.

Type: Fellowship.

No. of awards offered: Varies.

Frequency: Annual.

Value: Academic tuition, language training or tutoring, stipend, and research allowance.

Study Establishment: Training in language and area studies background.

Country of Study: USA.

Closing Date: February 15th.

*Individual Advanced Research Exchanges: Former USSR

Subjects: Any subject.

Eligibility: Open to US citizens who should normally have a full-time affiliation with a North American college or university and be faculty members or advanced doctoral candidates who will have completed all requirements for the PhD (or equivalent professional degree) except the thesis by the time of application. However, many scholars not academically employed and candidates for the MA degree may also be qualified if they are proposing professional-level, independent research projects.

Type: Exchanges.

No. of awards offered: Varies.

Frequency: Annual.

Value: Travel, housing, medical and dental care, monthly ruble allowance, plus an allowance or stipend from IREX.

Length of Study: One semester to one academic year.

Study Establishment: Institutions under the jurisdiction of the State Committee.

Country of Study: Former USSR.

Closing Date: October 15th.

Additional Information: IREX will award Distinguished Fellowships in International Relations to the most outstanding doctoral candidates in international relations among the applicants to the Long-Term Research Exchange program. Fellows will be identified by the selection committee and notified after the competition. The award provides for placement at institutes under the division of international relations of the USSR Academy of Sciences and an enhanced stipend. Fellows are also offered opportunities to participate in occasional meetings of young Soviet and American scholars in international relations and other special activities. These Distinguished Fellowships are made possible by the Fund for Peace and the Soviet Peace Fund.

For further information contact:
Department of Foreign Relations, State Committee for Public Education, ul Shabolovka 33, Moscow, 113162, Russia

*Individual Research Exchanges: East Europe

Subjects: Any subject.

Eligibility: Open to US citizens who should normally have a full-time affiliation with a North American college or university and be faculty members or advanced doctoral candidates who will have completed all requirements for the PhD (or equivalent professional degree) except the thesis by the time of application. However, many scholars not academically employed and candidates for the MA degree may also be qualified if they are proposing professional-level, independent research projects.

Type: Exchanges.

No. of awards offered: Varies.

Frequency: Annual.

Value: Travel and travel-related expenses, medical and dental care, housing, certain other expenses, stipend or allowance.

Length of Study: Two months.

Country of Study: Bulgaria, Czech Republic, Hungary, Poland, Romania.

Closing Date: October 15th.

Individual Research Exchanges: Mongolian People's Republic

Subjects: Any subject.

Eligibility: Open to US citizens who should normally have a full-time affiliation with a North American college or university and be faculty members or advanced doctoral candidates who will have completed all requirements for the PhD (or equivalent professional degree) except the thesis by the time of application. However, many scholars not academically employed and candidates for the MA degree may also be qualified if they are proposing professional-level, independent research projects.

No. of awards offered: Up to 10 exchanges.

Frequency: Annual.

Value: Travel, housing, medical care, monthly tugrig allowance, plus an allowance or stipend from IREX.

Length of Study: For a total of 20 months.

Country of Study: Mongolian People's Republic.

Closing Date: October 15th.

Additional Information: Preference will be given to established scholars who have demonstrated interest in Inner Asia.

For further information contact:
Department of Foreign Relations, Academy of Sciences of the MPR, 2 Lenin Street, Ulaanbaatar, Mongolia

Short-Term Travel Grants

Subjects: Humanities or social sciences.

Eligibility: Open to US citizens who have the PhD or equivalent prefessional degree and need project support.

Type: Travel Grant.

No. of awards offered: Varies.

Frequency: Three times yearly.

Value: Travel expenses.

Length of Study: One to two weeks.

Country of Study: Former USSR, East Europe, or the Mongolian People's Republic.

Closing Date: October 1st, February 1st.

Additional Information: In order to encourage wider participation in East-West scholarly contacts, grants may be awarded to US scholars outside the field of Soviet and East European studies. The programs are designed to facilitate collaborative projects with CIS, East European or Mongolian colleagues; lectures or seminars in the former USSR, East Europe or the Mongolian People's Republic; or individual research in the former USSR, East Europe or the Mongolian People's Republic. Grant recipients are responsible for their own visa, travel and academic arrangements.

THE INTERNATIONAL RICE RESEARCH INSTITUTE

Training Center, PO Box 933, Los Banos, Manila, Laguna, 1099, Phillipines
Tel: 63 2 818 1926
Fax: 63 2 981 1292
Email: rraab@IRRI.cgnet.com
Telex: 40890 RICE PM
Contact: The Head

IRRI Degree Scholarships

Subjects: Agriculture, fisheries and food; engineering; social and behavioural studies; natural sciences; environmental studies.

Eligibility: Open to scientists in the national agricultural research systems of rice-producing and rice-eating nations, between the ages of 25 and 45.

Level of Study: Postgraduate, Doctorate.

Purpose: To provide rice scientists from national agricultural research systems with formal postgraduate training to increase their capability for research leadership in their specific fields of specialization.

Type: Scholarship.

No. of awards offered: 11 PhD and 13 MSc.

Frequency: Dependent on funds available.

Value: US$16, 470 per year for the PhD scholarship; US$16,201 per year for the MSc scholarship.

Length of Study: Between 2 and 3 years.

Study Establishment: Academic courses in college/university; thesis at IRRI.

Country of Study: Home country and Phillipines.

Applications Procedure: Please submit application form, endorsements from nominating/sponsoring institution and medical report.

Closing Date: March/July.

IRRI Postdegree On-the-Job Training Fellowship

Subjects: Agriculture, fisheries and food; engineering; natural sciences; social and behavioural sciences; environmental studies.

Eligibility: Open to scientists in the national agricultural research systems of a rice-producing and rice-eating nation. Applicants must be between the ages of 25 and 45, hold a BSc or MSc degree and be involved in rice-based systems research.

Level of Study: Professional development.

Purpose: To update the skills of midcareer rice scientists in the IRRI research environment, and to expose them to new developments in their fields of specialization.

Type: Fellowship.

No. of awards offered: 24.

Frequency: Dependent on funds available.

Value: Post BSc: US$15,157 per year; and post MSc: US$15,476 per year.

Length of Study: 1-3 months.

Study Establishment: Academic course in college/university; thesis at IRRI.

Country of Study: Phillipines.

Applications Procedure: Application form must be completed and submitted with endorsement from nominating/sponsoring institution and a medical report. Candidates must be proficient in the English language.

Closing Date: Two months prior to commencement.

INTERNATIONAL ROAD EDUCATIONAL FOUNDATION

International Road Educational Foundation, 2600 Virginia Ave, NW, Suite 208, Washington, DC, 20037, USA
Fax: 202 338 4641
Email: http://irfnet.org
Contact: Wayne McDaniel

IREF Fellowship

Subjects: Engineering and management.

Eligibility: Each year a specific list of countries is identified and the fellowship is offered to organizations within those countries.

Level of Study: Postgraduate.

Purpose: To support technology transfer in selected countries.

Type: Fellowship.

Frequency: Annual.

Value: US$13,500.

Length of Study: Minimum of one year.

Study Establishment: Unrestricted.

Country of Study: Unrestricted.

Applications Procedure: Applicants secure form from organization (either road association or government agency) within country.

Closing Date: January 30th.

INTERNATIONAL SCHOOL OF CRYSTALLOGRAPHY, E MAJORANA CENTRE

c/o Dip to Scienze Mineralogiche, Pza Porta San Donato 1, Bologna, 40126, Italy
Tel: 39 51 243556
Fax: 39 51 243336
Contact: Professor L Riva Di Sanseverino

Grants

Subjects: Frontier topics in crystallography.

Eligibility: Open to all who have knowledge of the English language and scientific interests related to the topic chosen each year.

Level of Study: Postgraduate, Doctorate, Postdoctorate.

Purpose: To enable postgraduates to attend yearly courses at Erice.

Type: Grant.

No. of awards offered: 15-20.

Frequency: Annual.

Value: Fees, board and lodging during the course.

Length of Study: 8-12 days.

Study Establishment: E Majorana Centre, Erice.

Country of Study: Italy.

Applications Procedure: Please submit letter of recommendation, personal data, and details of scientific interests.

Closing Date: End of November each year.

For further information contact:
Department of Organic Chemistry, Via Marzolo 1, 35131 Padova, Italy
Tel: 39 49 8275275
Fax: 39 49 8275239
Email: paola@choroo.unipd.it
Contact: Dr Paola Spadon

INTERNATIONAL SCHOOL OF GEOTHERMICS

Scuola Internazionale di Geotermia, Istituto Internazionale per le Ricerche Geotermiche, 2 Piazza Solferino, Pisa, 56126, Italy
Tel: 50 41503/46069/41327
Fax: 50 47055
Contact: Mrs Mary H Dickson

Scholarships for Courses in Geothermics

Subjects: Geothermics.

Eligibility: Open to geologists, geophysicists and chemists who possess a university degree or the equivalent and wish to undertake advanced training in geothermics. The course is open to all member countries of Unesco. The Scholarships are available only for participants from non-industrialized countries. Instruction is in English.

Purpose: To train experts in geothermal research and development.

No. of awards offered: Approximately 15 places for each course.

Frequency: Annual.

Value: 1,200,000 lire per month, plus return travel costs.

Length of Study: From November to June.

Study Establishment: The Institute.

Country of Study: Italy.

Closing Date: August 31st.

Additional Information: Applications must be submitted to the Italian embassy in the candidate's home country. The course is organized by the Institute under the auspices of the Italian National Research Council, the Italian Ministry for Foreign Affairs, and Unesco.

INTERNATIONAL SOCIETY FOR OPTICAL ENGINEERING

SPIE Scholarship Committee, PO Box 10, Bellingham, WA, 98227-0010, USA
Tel: 360 676 3290
Fax: 360 647 1445
Contact: Mr Alson E Hatheway, Chairman

SPIE Educational Scholarships and Grants in Optical Engineering

Subjects: Optical or optoelectronic applied science or engineering.

Eligibility: Open to graduate and undergraduate students. Applications are judged on the basis of the long-range contribution which the granting of the award would make to optics and optical engineering. Awards are not made on the basis of need.

Level of Study: Graduate.

No. of awards offered: Varies.

Frequency: Annual.

Value: Scholarships: US$500-US$5,000.

Study Establishment: Society's headquarters in Bellingham, Washington.

Closing Date: April 5th.

Additional Information: The Society also offers grants to educational institutions and makes a number of awards for achievement in the field of optical engineering.

INTERNATIONAL SOCIETY OF ARBORICULTURE

Research Committee Chairman, Department of Botany and Microbiology, Ohio Wesleyan University, Delaware, OH, 43015, USA
Tel: 614 368 3508
Fax: 614 368 3999
Contact: Dr Bruce R Roberts

Grants

Subjects: Arboriculture.

Eligibility: Open to horticulturalists, plant pathologists, plant physiologists, entomologists, soil scientists and other qualified scientists. There are no restrictions on the basis of religion, race, sex, age or nationality.

Purpose: To encourage scientific or educational research relating to shade and landscape trees.

Type: Grant.

No. of awards offered: Currently 10.

Frequency: Annual.

Value: Currently up to US$5,000 to help buy supplies or equipment and hire technical or student help. Administrative overheads are not to be deducted from the grant.

Length of Study: One year.

Country of Study: Any country.

Applications Procedure: Candidates should complete a two-page application form available from the ISA office at PO Box GG, Savoy, IL 61874-9902, USA.

Closing Date: November 1st.

Additional Information: Recipients will ultimately be asked to publish their results in ISA's 'Journal of Arboriculture'. Proposals most likely to be selected are those whose results appear most likely to help arborists earn their living by daily tree-care work.

INTERNATIONAL STRING QUARTET COMPETITION

London International String Quartet Competition, 62 High Street, Fareham, Hants, PO16 7BG, England
Tel: 01329 283603
Fax: 01705 281969
Contact: Mr Dennis Sayer, Administrator

International String Quartet Competition

Eligibility: No restrictions except age. Quartets must not exceed an aggregate age of 30 years on 15 April 1997.

Level of Study: Unrestricted.

Purpose: To encourage young string quartets to participate in an international competition.

No. of awards offered: 6 major monetary prizes with concerts organized for the 1st prizewinner.

Frequency: Triennially - next in April 1997.

Value: 1st £8,000 plus The Amadeus Trophy; 2nd £5,600; 3rd £4,000; 4th £2,800; 5th £2,000; Menuhin Prize £1,000; Audience Prize £1,000; Sidney Griller Award: £1,000 plus trophy.

Applications Procedure: Application form must be completed.

Closing Date: December 1st.

INTERNATIONAL UNION AGAINST CANCER

Fellowships Department, International Union Against Cancer, 3 rue de Conseil-Général, Geneva, 1205, Switzerland
Tel: 41 22 320 18 11
Fax: 41 22 320 18 10
Email: BBAKER@atge.automail.com
Contact: Brita M Baker, Head

American Cancer Society International Cancer Research Fellowships

Subjects: Cancer research.

Eligibility: Open to highly qualified and recognized senior investigators from any country who have been actively engaged in cancer research for at least five years.

Purpose: To fund original research by recognized senior investigators.

Type: Fellowship.

No. of awards offered: 15.

Frequency: Annual.

Value: The average stipend is US$30,000.

Length of Study: Six to 12 months; may be extended.

Closing Date: October 1st for notification by mid-April.

Additional Information: The Fellowships are funded by the American Cancer Society.

International Cancer Research Technology Transfer Project (ICRETT)

Subjects: Cancer research.

Eligibility: Open to qualified investigators and experienced clinicians.

Purpose: To enable recipients to learn or teach up-to-date research techniques, transfer appropriate technology, or acquire advanced clinical management, diagnostic and therapeutic skills.

Type: Fellowship.

No. of awards offered: 120.

Frequency: Annual.

Value: The average stipend is US$2,800.

Length of Study: Up to 3 months (with stipend support for 1 month).

Applications Procedure: Applications may be submitted at any time. Awards are normally notified within 60 days of registration of a complete application.

Closing Date: There is no deadline.

Additional Information: The Fellowships are funded by a group of North American and European cancer institutes and societies.

International Oncology Nursing Fellowships

Subjects: Cancer nursing training.

Eligibility: Open to English-speaking nurses who are actively engaged in the care of cancer patients in their home institutes and who come from developing or Eastern European countries where specialist cancer nursing training is not yet widely available.

Type: Fellowship.

No. of awards offered: Five.

Frequency: Annual.

Value: The average stipend is US$2,800.

Length of Study: One to three months (with stipend support for 1 month).

Closing Date: November 15th for notification mid-February.

Additional Information: The Fellowships are funded by the Oncology Nursing Society.

Yamagiwa-Yoshida Memorial International Cancer Study Grants

Subjects: Cancer research.

Eligibility: Open to appropriately qualified investigators from any country who are actively engaged in cancer research.

Purpose: To establish bilateral research projects which exploit complementary materials or skills, including advanced training in experimental methods.

Type: Grant.

No. of awards offered: 15.

Frequency: Twice yearly.

Value: The average stipend is US$8,000.

Length of Study: One to three months.

Closing Date: January 1st for notification by mid-April; July 1st for notification by mid-October.

Additional Information: These Grants are funded by the Japanese National Committee for UICC and the Olympus Optical Company in Tokyo.

INTERNATIONAL UNION FOR THE SCIENTIFIC STUDY OF POPULATION

International Union for the Scientific Study of Population, rue des Augustins 34, Liège, 4000, Belgium
Tel: 41 224080
Fax: 41 223847
Contact: M Lebrun, Deputy Director

*Grants for Junior Demographers

Subjects: Demography.

Eligibility: Open to members and non-members who are junior in demography and hold an MA or PhD degree in demography.

Purpose: To promote the participation of junior demographers in the activities of the Union by enabling the successful candidate to attend a seminar organized or co-sponsored by the Union.

Type: Grant.

No. of awards offered: One.

Frequency: Annual.

Value: Full travel and per diem allowance.

Country of Study: Belgium.

Additional Information: Applicants must be sponsored by two Union members.

INTERNATIONAL UNION FOR VACUUM SCIENCE, TECHNIQUE AND APPLICATIONS

International Union for Vacuum Science, Technique and Applications, Advanced Technology Laboratory, BNR, Box 3511, Station C, Ottawa, Ontario, K1Y 4H7, Canada
Tel: 613 763 3248
Fax: 613 763 2404
Email: bill_westwood@vacuum.org
Contact: Dr W D Westwood

Welch Foundation Scholarship

Subjects: Vacuum science.

Eligibility: Open to applicants of any nationality who hold at least a bachelor's degree, although a doctor's degree is preferred.

Level of Study: Postdoctorate, Doctorate, Postgraduate.

Purpose: To encourage promising scholars who wish to contribute to the study of vacuum science techniques or their application in any field.

Type: Scholarship.

No. of awards offered: One.

Frequency: Annual.

Value: US$12,500.

Length of Study: One year.

Study Establishment: An appropriate laboratory overseas.

Country of Study: Unrestricted.

Applications Procedure: Application form must be completed and submitted with research proposal, CV and two letters of reference.

Closing Date: April 15th.

IREX (INTERNATIONAL RESEARCH AND EXCHANGES BOARD)

IREX , 1616 H Street NW, Washington, DC, 20006, USA
Tel: 202 628 8188
Fax: 202 628 8189
Email: irex@info.irex.org
www: http://www.irex.org

Grant Opportunities for US Scholars

Eligibility: Open to US citizens/permanent residents. Applicants must have a good command of host country language.

Level of Study: Doctorate, Professional development.

Purpose: Founded in 1968, IREX provides field access for US specialists to scholars, policymakers, and research resources of the NIS.

Type: Grant.

No. of awards offered: Varies.

Value: Varies.

Length of Study: Varies depending on program.

Applications Procedure: Contact IREX for application forms and booklets on current programs.

Closing Date: Varies.

Additional Information: Includes host opportunities for US universities. Grant opportunities for international scholars may soon be available; contact IREX for further information.

IRIS FUND FOR PREVENTION OF BLINDNESS

Iris Fund for Prevention of Blindness, Ground Floor, York House, 199 Westminster Bridge Road, London, SE1 7UT, England
Tel: 0171 928 7743
Fax: 0171 928 7919
Contact: The Director

Grants for Research and Equipment (Ophthalmology)

Subjects: Ophthalmology.

Eligibility: Open to suitably qualified individuals. Applications must be submitted by qualified Consultant Ophthalmologists or equivalent for research under his/her supervision. Research projects can only take place in the UK.

Level of Study: Unrestricted.

Purpose: To prevent and cure blindness and serious eye disorders.

Type: Grant.

No. of awards offered: Varies.

Frequency: Quarterly, depending on funds available.

Value: As funds become available.

Length of Study: Usually for a maximum of three years.

Country of Study: UK.

Applications Procedure: Application form with four copies, including supporting paperwork required.

Additional Information: No London hospitals other than St Thomas' and the Hospital for Sick Children, Great Ormond Street.

Iris Fund Award

Subjects: Ophthalmology.

Eligibility: Open to UK citizens only, under the age of forty.

Level of Study: Professional development.

Purpose: In recognition of distinction either in training or in the chosen area of ophthalmic research.

No. of awards offered: One.

Frequency: Every two years.

Value: £5,000.

Country of Study: United Kingdom.

Applications Procedure: Application form must be completed with four copies of supporting paperwork.

Closing Date: To be announced.

IRISH-AMERICAN CULTURAL INSTITUTE

Irish-American Cultural Institute, 2115 Summit Avenue, University of St Thomas 5026, St Paul, MN, 55105, USA
Tel: 612 962 6040
Fax: 612 962 6043

*Irish Research Funds

Subjects: Any subject. Historical research has predominated, but other areas of research will be considered equally.

Eligibility: Open to individuals of any nationality. Media production costs and journal subventions will not be considered for funding.

Purpose: To promote scholarly inquiry and publication regarding the Irish-American experience.

Type: Grant.

No. of awards offered: Varies.

Frequency: Annual.

Value: US$1,000-US$5,000.

Country of Study: Any country.

Closing Date: Usually August 1st.

*Visiting Fellowship in Irish Studies at University College Galway

Subjects: Irish studies.

Eligibility: Open to scholars normally resident in the USA whose work relates to any aspect of Irish studies.

Type: Fellowship.

No. of awards offered: One.

Frequency: Annual.

Value: Stipend of US$13,000, plus transatlantic transportation.

Length of Study: For a period of not less than four months.

Country of Study: Ireland.

Closing Date: December 31st for the forthcoming academic year.

Additional Information: The holder of the Fellowship will be provided with services appropriate to a visiting faculty member during his or her time at UCG. There are certain relatively minor departmental responsibilities expected of the holder during his or her time at UCG, and certain other expectations regarding publication, etc., upon completion of the Fellowship. The application form is brief, and requests a current CV and list of publications. Applications must be received on a form which is available on request. The Fellowship is jointly funded with University College Galway.

RICHARD D IRWIN FOUNDATION

Richard D Irwin Foundation, 1333 Burr Ridge Parkway, Burr Ridge, Cook, IL, 60521, USA
Tel: 708 789 4000
Fax: 708 789 6942
Contact: Gail V. Ryba

Richard D Irwin Postdoctoral Fellowship

Eligibility: Candidates will be limited to persons who have been admitted to candidacy for the doctorate degree and have completed all work in connection therewith except writing the dissertation and passing final orals. Will also consider those already working on their dissertation and who may need assistance to complete.

Level of Study: Postdoctorate.

Purpose: To help in the development of qualified teachers in the area of business and economics. The Foundation will make available a limited number of fellowships to assist prospective teachers in these fields toward the completion of their dissertation.

Type: Fellowship.

No. of awards offered: 10-20.

Frequency: Annual.

Value: US$2,000-US$2,500.

Country of Study: USA or Canada.

Applications Procedure: A candidate must be nominated by the business school Dean who has been invited to submit a nomination. The Dean will also request supporting recommendations from the chairperson of the applicant's dissertation committee and the director of the doctoral program or other individuals who may be in a position to supply helpful information to the selection committee as to the candidate's promise as a university teacher. The Deans of the School of Business are considered the Deans who nominate and submit applications from the area of business and economics.

Closing Date: February 15th.

Additional Information: Direct applications from candidates are not accepted. Successful candidates will be notified early in April.

ITALIAN INSTITUTE FOR HISTORICAL STUDIES

Italian Institute for Historical Studies, Via Benedetto Croce 12, Naples, 80134, Italy
Tel: 39 81 5517159
Fax: 39 81 5512390
Contact: Marta Herling, Secretary

Frederico Chabod Scholarship

Subjects: History and philosophy. the study of history is seen in connection with the disciplines of philosophy, the arts, economics and literature.

Eligibility: Open to nationals of all countries; applicants must possess a BA degree.

Level of Study: Postgraduate.

Purpose: To allow students to participate in life at the Institute, while completing a personal research project with the assistance of its staff.

Type: Scholarship.

No. of awards offered: One.

Frequency: Annual.

Value: 12,000,000 lire.

Length of Study: Eight months.

Study Establishment: Italian Institute for Historical Studies.

Country of Study: Italy.

Applications Procedure: Applications must include birth certificate, proof of citizenship, university diploma, scholarly work, curriculum, program of research, letters of reference, and copies of publications.

Closing Date: September 15th.

Adolfo Omodeo Scholarship

Subjects: History and philosophy. The study of history is seen in connection with the disciplines of philosophy, the arts, economics and literature.

Eligibility: Open to nationals of all countries.

Level of Study: Postgraduate.

Purpose: To allow students to participate in life at the Institute while completing a personal research project with the assistance of its staff.

Type: Scholarship.

No. of awards offered: One.

Frequency: Annual.

Value: 12,000,000 lire.

Length of Study: Eight months.

Study Establishment: Italian Institute for Historical Studies.

Country of Study: Italy.

Applications Procedure: Application must include: birth certificate, proof of citizenship, university diploma, scholarly work, curriculum, program of research, letters of reference, and copies of publications.

Closing Date: September 15th.

JACOB'S PILLOW DANCE FESTIVAL, INC

Jacob's Pillow Dance Festival, Inc, Box 287, Lee, MA, 01238, USA
Tel: 413 637 1322
Fax: 413 243 4744
Contact: Wende Garton

*Dance Scholarships

Subjects: Dance.

Eligibility: Open to US and foreign nationals who are over 16 years of age and have experience in the field of dance.

Purpose: To allow high-level dancers an opportunity to participate in summer dance workshops.

Type: Scholarship.

No. of awards offered: Varies.

Frequency: Annual.

Value: Room, board and tuition, or tuition only. There is no travel allowance for foreign nationals.

Study Establishment: Summer study at the Jacob's Pillow Dance Festival School.

Country of Study: USA.

Applications Procedure: Information on audition requirements is available from the school.

Closing Date: March 31st.

CATHERINE AND LADY GRACE JAMES FOUNDATION

Catherine and Lady Grace James Foundation, Pantyfedwen, 9 Market Street, Aberystwyth, Dyfed, SY23 1DL, Wales
Tel: 01970 612806
Contact: Executive Secretary

Grants and Loans

Subjects: Any subject.

Eligibility: Open to Welsh persons, especially those who wish to train to become ministers of religion of any denomination.

Purpose: To promote mainly postgraduate research.

No. of awards offered: Varies.

Value: Varies.

Country of Study: Usually UK.

Applications Procedure: Applications are accepted on an ongoing basis and should be made on the appropriate forms.

Closing Date: July 31st in any year.

JANSON JOHAN HELMICH OG MARCIA JANSONS LEGAT

Janson Johan Helmich Og Marcia Jansons Legat, Blommeseter, Norderhov, Hönefoss, N-3500, Norway
Tel: 32 13 54 65
Fax: 32 13 56 26
Contact: Reidun Haugen

Scholarships and Travel Grants

Eligibility: Open to qualified Norwegian postgraduate students with practical experience, for advanced study abroad.

Level of Study: Postgraduate, Doctorate, Professional development.

Purpose: Practical or academic training.

Type: Scholarships and Travel Grants.

No. of awards offered: 30.

Frequency: Annual.

Value: Maximum NOK50,000.

Country of Study: Any country.

Applications Procedure: Application form must be completed.

Closing Date: March 15th.

JAPAN-AMERICA SOCIETY OF WASHINGTON, DC

Japan-America Society of Washington, DC, 606 18th Street, NW, Washington, DC, 20006, USA
Tel: 202 289 8290
Fax: 202 789 8265
Contact: Patricia Kearns

*Japan-America Society's Scholarships for Study in Japan

Subjects: Japanese language and culture.

Eligibility: Open to US citizens who are college students studying at accredited colleges in Virginia, Maryland, Washington, DC, or West Virginia. Students must be enrolled full-time in a program of Japanese language and area studies.

Type: Scholarship.

No. of awards offered: One or more.

Frequency: Annual.

Value: US$1,500-US$6,000 and/or round-trip ticket to Japan.

Study Establishment: Full-time study at a college or university in Japan.

Country of Study: Japan.

Applications Procedure: Application should incude three letters of recommendation, transcripts, a statement of purpose and status of financial support.

Closing Date: March 1st.

THE JAPAN FOUNDATION

The Japan Foundation (London Office), 17 Old Park Lane, London, W1Y 3LG, England

Tel: 0171 499 4726
Fax: 0171 495 1133

The Japan Foundation is a semi-governmental organization designed to promote Japanese studies, language, arts and cultural exchange overseas

Fellowship Program: Artists

Subjects: Fine arts, performing arts, music and creative writing.

Eligibility: Open to individuals who hold citizenship or permanent residency status in any country that has diplomatic relations with Japan. Candidates must be artists specializing in the fields offered. Applicants must be in good health and have sufficient ability in Japanese and/or English to conduct research in Japan.

Purpose: To provide individuals with opportunities both to learn more about Japan and its people and to conduct research or pursue creative projects in Japan, and thereby to promote cultural exchange and mutual understanding.

Frequency: Annual.

Value: A monthly stipend of Y370,000 or Y430,000, according to the level of the grantee's professional career; plus further allowances, including one round-trip, business-class air ticket to and from Japan. (Grantees already in Japan will receive tickets for their return home only.).

Length of Study: Two to six months; the award cannot be extended beyond the period specified in the award.

Closing Date: Postmarked November 1st.

Additional Information: Former Japan Foundation Fellowship recipients are eligible to reapply to this program only when three years have elapsed since the termination of their most recent grants. Applicants whose research projects require the cooperation of Japanese professionals or institutions are requested to make the necessary arrangements for affiliation before submitting their applications. Fellows must also find their own long-term accommodation. Applications in the natural sciences, medicine and engineering cannot be considered. Also, undergraduate students and those who intend to enhance their Japanese language ability are not eligible. Grantees may not hold another grant concurrently; nor may they alter the start date or the duration of the grants period in order to be able to accept another award.

Fellowship Program: Cultural Administrators

Subjects: Skills development in cultural administration.

Eligibility: Open to individuals who hold citizenship or permanent residency status in any developing country that has diplomatic relations with Japan. Candidates must be specialists involved in professional management, the planning of cultural enterprises or the administration of cultural activities. Applicants must be in good health and have sufficient ability in Japanese and/or English to conduct research in Japan.

Purpose: To provide individuals with opportunities both to learn more about Japan and its people and to conduct research or pursue creative projects in Japan, and thereby to promote cultural exchange and mutual understanding.

Frequency: Annual.

Value: A monthly stipend of Y370,000 or Y430,000, according to the level of the grantee's professional career; plus further allowances, including one round-trip, business-class air ticket to and from Japan. (Grantees already in Japan will receive tickets for their return home only.).

Length of Study: Two to six months; the award cannot be extended beyond the period specified in the award.

Closing Date: Postmarked November 1st.

Additional Information: Former Japan Foundation Fellowship recipients are eligible to reapply to this program only when three years have elapsed since the termination of their most recent grants. Applicants whose research projects require the cooperation of Japanese professionals or institutions are requested to make the necessary arrange-

ments for affiliation before submitting their applications. Fellows must also find their own long-term accommodation. Applications in the natural sciences, medicine and engineering cannot be considered. Also, undergraduate students and those who intend to enhance their Japanese language ability are not eligible. Grantees may not hold another grant concurrently; nor may they alter the start date or the duration of the grants period in order to be able to accept another award.

Fellowship Program: Cultural Properties Specialists

Subjects: Research or skills training in the preservation and restoration of cultural properties.

Eligibility: Open to individuals who hold citizenship or permanent residency status in any country that has diplomatic relations with Japan. Candidates must be specialists in their field. Applicants must be in good health and have sufficient ability in Japanese and/or English to conduct research in Japan.

Purpose: To provide individuals with opportunities both to learn more about Japan and its people and to conduct research or pursue creative projects in Japan, and thereby to promote cultural exchange and mutual understanding.

Frequency: Annual.

Value: A monthly stipend of Y370,000 or Y430,000, according to the level of the grantee's professional career; plus further allowances, including one round-trip, business-class air ticket to and from Japan. (Grantees already in Japan will receive tickets for their return home only.).

Length of Study: Two to six months; the award cannot be extended beyond the period specified in the award.

Closing Date: Postmarked November 1st.

Additional Information: Former Japan Foundation Fellowship recipients are eligible to reapply to this program only when three years have elapsed since the termination of their most recent grants. Applicants whose research projects require the cooperation of Japanese professionals or institutions are requested to make the necessary arrangements for affiliation before submitting their applications. Fellows must also find their own long-term accommodation. Applications in the natural sciences, medicine and engineering cannot be considered. Also, undergraduate students and those who intend to enhance their Japanese language ability are not eligible. Grantees may not hold another grant concurrently; nor may they alter the start date or the duration of the grants period in order to be able to accept another award.

Fellowship Program: Doctoral Candidates

Subjects: Dissertation research in the fields of the humanities and the social sciences. Proposals must be related in substantial part to Japan; comparative research is also acceptable.

Eligibility: Open to individuals who hold citizenship or permanent residency status in any country that has diplomatic relations with Japan. Candidates must have completed all academic requirements except the dissertation and be eligible for the submission of their thesis when they begin the Fellowship. Applicants must be in good health and have sufficient ability in Japanese and/or English to conduct research in Japan.

Level of Study: Doctorate.

Purpose: To provide individuals with opportunities both to learn more about Japan and its people and to conduct research or pursue creative projects in Japan, and thereby to promote cultural exchange and mutual understanding.

Frequency: Annual.

Value: A monthly stipend of Y310,000; plus further allowances, including one round-trip, business-class air ticket to and from Japan. (Grantees already in Japan will receive tickets for their return home only.).

Length of Study: Two to fourteen months; the award cannot be extended beyond the period specified in the award.

Closing Date: Postmarked November 1st.

Additional Information: Former Japan Foundation Fellowship recipients are eligible to reapply to this program only when three years have elapsed since the termination of their most recent grants. Applicants whose research projects require the cooperation of Japanese professionals or institutions are requested to make the necessary arrangements for affiliation before submitting their applications. Fellows must also find their own long-term accommodation. Applications in the natural sciences, medicine and engineering cannot be considered. Also, undergraduate students and those who intend to enhance their Japanese language ability are not eligible. Grantees may not hold another grant concurrently; nor may they alter the start date or the duration of the grants period in order to be able to accept another award.

*Fellowship Program: Scholars and Researchers

Subjects: Research in the fields of the humanities and the social sciences. Proposals must be related in substantial part to Japan; comparative research is also acceptable.

Eligibility: Open to individuals who hold citizenship or permanent residency status in any country that has diplomatic relations with Japan. Candidates must be scholars or researchers in the humanities and the social sciences affiliated with research or tertiary educational establishments. Applicants must be in good health and have sufficient ability in Japanese and/or English to conduct research in Japan.

Purpose: To provide individuals with opportunities both to learn more about Japan and its people and to conduct research or pursue creative projects in Japan, and thereby to promote cultural exchange and mutual understanding.

Frequency: Annual.

Value: A monthly stipend of Y370,000 or Y430,000, according to the level of the grantee's professional career; plus further allowances, including one round-trip, business-class air ticket to and from Japan. (Grantees already in Japan will receive tickets for their return home only.).

Length of Study: Two to twelve months; the award cannot be extended beyond the period specified in the award.

Closing Date: Postmarked November 1st.

Additional Information: Former Japan Foundation Fellowship recipients are eligible to reapply to this program only when three years have elapsed since the termination of their most recent grants. Applicants whose research projects require the cooperation of Japanese professionals or institutions are requested to make the necessary arrangements for affiliation before submitting their applications. Fellows must also find their own long-term accommodation. Applications in the natural sciences, medicine and engineering cannot be considered. Also, undergraduate students and those who intend to enhance their Japanese language ability are not eligible. Grantees may not hold another grant concurrently; nor may they alter the start date or the duration of the grants period in order to be able to accept another award.

*Fellowship Program: Young Researchers from Eastern Europe and the Former USSR (Special Fellowships)

Subjects: Research in the field of social sciences relevant to the democratization and liberalization of Eastern European countries and the countries of the former USSR.

Eligibility: Open to individuals who hold citizenship or permanent residency status in any Eastern European country or a country of the former USSR that has diplomatic relations with Japan. Candidates must be already involved in relevant projects in their own country. Applicants must be in good health and have sufficient ability in Japanese and/or English to conduct research in Japan.

Purpose: To provide individuals with opportunities both to learn more about Japan and its people and to conduct research or pursue creative projects in Japan, and thereby to promote cultural exchange and mutual understanding.

Type: Fellowship.

Frequency: Annual.

Value: A monthly stipend of Y370,000 or Y430,000, according to the level of the grantee's professional career; plus further allowances, including one round-trip, business-class air ticket to and from Japan. (Grantees already in Japan will receive tickets for their return home only.).

Length of Study: Two to twelve months; the award cannot be extended beyond the period specified in the award.

Closing Date: Postmarked November 1st.

Additional Information: Former Japan Foundation Fellowship recipients are eligible to reapply to this program only when three years have elapsed since the termination of their most recent grants. Applicants whose research projects require the cooperation of Japanese professionals or institutions are requested to make the necessary arrangements for affiliation before submitting their applications. Fellows must also find their own long-term accommodation. Applications in the natural sciences, medicine and engineering cannot be considered. Also, undergraduate students and those who intend to enhance their Japanese language ability are not eligible. Grantees may not hold another grant concurrently; nor may they alter the start date or the duration of the grants period in order to be able to accept another award.

*Film Production Support Program

Subjects: Film-making.

Eligibility: Open to film-makers.

Purpose: To provide financial support for the production of films, TV programs, and other audio-visual materials that serve to promote an understanding of Japan and Japanese culture abroad.

Type: Grant.

No. of awards offered: Varies.

Value: Assistance will, in principle, take the form of subsidies for production costs, to a maximum of Y5 million. Awards will not, however, exceed one-half of the total cost of the production.

REES JEFFREYS ROAD FUND

Rees Jeffreys Road Fund, 13 The Avenue, Chichester, West Sussex, PO19 4PH, England
Tel: 01243 787013
Fax: 01243 787013
Contact: B Fieldhouse, CPFA

Bursaries

Subjects: Transport.

Eligibility: Open to candidates who hold at least an upper second class honours degree.

Level of Study: Postgraduate, Doctorate.

Purpose: To facilitate postgraduate study or research into transport.

Type: Bursary.

No. of awards offered: Approximately ten.

Frequency: Annually, dependent on funds available.

Value: To cover fees and equivalent of SERC maintenance.

Study Establishment: UK universities.

Country of Study: UK.

Applications Procedure: A recommendation from the intended institution of study is required.

Closing Date: July 10th for study courses.

JEUNESSES MUSICALES OF SERBIA

Jeunesses Musicales of Serbia, Terazije 26/11, Belgrade, 11000, Yugoslavia
Tel: 38 11 686 380

Fax: 38 11 23 51 51 7
Contact: Mrs Biljana Zdravkovic, Executive Secretary

International Jeunesses Musicales Competition

Eligibility: Open to young musicians ready for international appearances.

Purpose: The competition is dedicated to the most promising young musicians at the beginning of their international careers.

Frequency: Annual.

Value: Cash prizes in YU Dinars, special prizes, concert engagements.

Applications Procedure: Please submit application form, recommendations, photo, and curriculum vitae.

Closing Date: December 31st.

Additional Information: This competition has been organised for 25 years.

JEWISH COMMUNITY CENTERS ASSOCIATION

JCC Association, 15 East 26th Street, New York, NY, 10010, USA
Tel: 212 532 4949
Contact: Scholarship Coordinator

*JCC Association Scholarships

Subjects: Social work; Jewish education; health; physical education and recreation; education; non-profit business administration.

Eligibility: Open to applicants who have a BA with at least a 3.0 grade point average and a strong commitment to the Jewish Community Center movement. It is preferred that applicants have knowledge of Jewish community practices, customs, rituals and organization. The recipients must make the commitment of working at a JCC following completion of graduate work.

Purpose: To provide Scholarships for graduate study at the masters level in areas leading to full-time professional employment at a Jewish Community Center.

Type: Scholarship.

No. of awards offered: Eight to ten.

Frequency: Annual.

Value: Up to US$7,500 for tuition costs.

Length of Study: One year; renewable for one more year based on satisfactory academic performance.

Country of Study: USA or Canada.

Closing Date: January 31st.

JEWISH FOUNDATION FOR EDUCATION OF WOMEN

Jewish Foundation for Education of Women, 330 West 58th Street, Suite 509, New York, NY, 10019, USA
Contact: Florence Wallach, Executive Director

Jewish Foundation for Education of Women

Purpose: Awards are made to women of all ages who are enrolled in full time academic programs.

Type: Grant.

No. of awards offered: 200-250.

Frequency: Annual.

Value: US$2,000-US$4,000.

Length of Study: One to four years.

Country of Study: USA.

Applications Procedure: Apply in writing between September 15th and November 15th for the following school year.

JILA (FORMERLY JOINT INSTITUTE FOR LABORATORY ASTROPHYSICS)

JILA , CB 440 , University of Colorado, Boulder, CO, 80309-0440, USA
Tel: 303 492 7789
Fax: 303 492 5235
Email: Various
www: http://www.boulder.nist.gov/jila/jilahome.html
Contact: D J Nesbitt, Visiting Scientists Secretary

Postdoctoral Research Associateship and Visiting Fellowships

Subjects: Natural sciences.

Eligibility: No restriction other than those which might be required by the grant which supports the research.

Level of Study: Postdoctorate, Professional development.

Purpose: Postdoctoral: additional training beyond the PhD. Visiting Fellowship: sabbatical research.

Type: Fellowship.

No. of awards offered: Varies.

Frequency: Annual, dependent on funds available.

Value: Varies.

Length of Study: VF 4-12 months; Postdoctorate - one year.

Country of Study: USA.

Applications Procedure: Application forms can be obtained by writing to The Secretary, Visiting Scientists Program, JILA, CB 440, University of Colorado, Boulder, CO 80309-0440, USA.

Closing Date: November 1st each year for visiting fellowships. No closing date for Postdoctorate applications.

THE LYNDON BAINES JOHNSON FOUNDATION

The Lyndon Baines Johnson Foundation, 2313 Red River, Austin, TX, 78705, USA
Tel: 512 478 7829
Fax: 512 478 9104
Contact: Executive Director

Grants-in-Aid of Research

Subjects: Any subject relevant to the Library's collections.

Eligibility: There are no restrictions in regard to age, sex, academic background, citizenship or residency.

Level of Study: Unrestricted.

Purpose: To defray living and travel expenses incurred through conducting research while at the Johnson Library.

Type: Research Grant.

No. of awards offered: Varies.

Frequency: Twice yearly.

Value: Calculated on the basis of US$75 per day, plus actual travel costs. Air travel should be by the least expensive route.

Length of Study: One year; not renewable.

Study Establishment: The Johnson Library.

Country of Study: USA.

Applications Procedure: Application form must be completed.

Closing Date: January 31st, July 31st.

Additional Information: It should be agreed that the product of the research, made possible through the grant, will not be used for any political purposes. A copy of any publication, article or book resulting from this grant-in-aid will be presented to the chief archivist of the Library. Funds are not awarded for reproduction expenses, secretarial or research assistance, etc. Prior to submitting a grant proposal, applicants are recommended to write to the Chief Archivist at the Foundation to obtain information on the materials available.

JOURNALISTS IN EUROPE

Journalists in Europe, 33 rue de Louvre, Paris, 75002, France
Tel: 44 82 20 00
Fax: 45 08 42 32

Study Program on European Affairs

Subjects: Journalism.

Eligibility: Open to working journalists between the ages of 25 and 35. Applicants must have a minimum of four years' full-time experience as a journalist, and must speak both English and French.

Level of Study: Professional development.

Purpose: To combine lectures, seminars, workshops and reporting assignments in the field of journalism.

Frequency: Dependent on funds available.

Length of Study: 8 months.

Study Establishment: Journalists in Europe.

Country of Study: France.

Applications Procedure: Application form must be completed and submitted with CV, samples of work, copies of diplomas and three letters of reference.

Closing Date: January 15th.

JUVENILE DIABETES FOUNDATION INTERNATIONAL

Juvenile Diabetes Foundation International, 432 Park Avenue South, New York, NY, 10016-8013, USA
Tel: 212 889 7575
Fax: 212 532 8791/212 725 7259
Contact: Grants Administrator

Career Development Award

Subjects: Diabetes and its complications.

Eligibility: Candidates should have a doctoral degree or the equivalent from an accredited institution with between three and seven years of total professional postdoctoral clinical and/or research experience by the projected start of the Award. In exceptional circumstances, individuals with less than three and more than seven years of such experience may apply, but must justify those special circumstances (e.g. time in service). Individuals holding the academic position of associate professor or professor at the time of award are not eligible for this Award. Candidates should have broad training, should demonstrate individual competence in clinical and/or research activities, and should show research potential in the chosen area of interest. Candidates should provide evidence of serious intent for an academic career related to that area. The grantee institution must be a university, medical school, or comparable institution with strong, well-established research and training programs in the chosen area, adequate members of highly trained faculty in clinical and basic departments relevant to the chosen area, and interest and capability to provide guidance to clinically trained individuals in the development of research independence.

Purpose: To provide the opportunity for promising young investigators with demonstrated aptitude to develop into independent investigators.

No. of awards offered: Varies.

Frequency: Annual.

Value: Salary support not to exceed US$40,000 annually. The actual salary must be consistent with the established salary structure of the institution for persons of equivalent qualifications, experience and rank. Up to a total of US$5,000 annually is provided for necessary items such as supplies, travel, etc.

Length of Study: One year; CDA recipients may apply for second and third years of funding, subject to a satisfactory progress report.

Study Establishment: Appropriate institutions.

Country of Study: Any country.

Closing Date: September 15th, first two pages of application; October 1st, original and 15 copies, bound and signed.

Additional Information: The Award, made to the institution, is designed to enable such individuals to investigate a well-defined problem with a sponsor competent to provide guidance in the chosen problem and to foster growth toward independent research. It is anticipated that this Award may provide the transition between fellowship or traineeship experience and a career in independent investigation and that it will also provide future faculty for health professional institutions. The applicant is expected to spend a minimum of 75% of time in research. An appropriate sponsor must assume responsibility and provide guidance for the research development in the chosen area.

Fellowships

Subjects: Diabetes and its complications.

Eligibility: Open to applicants who, by the beginning of the period of support, have a doctoral degree or the equivalent from an accredited institution. Fellows may not simultaneously hold an internship or residency appointment. Each application should be sponsored by a scientist affiliated full-time with an accredited institution who agrees to supervise the Fellow's training. The institution must have adequate staff and facilities to support the proposed training.

Purpose: To attract qualified and promising scientists, entering on their professional career into fields of research which can reasonably be expected to bear directly on future discoveries of cause, treatment, cure and prevention in this field.

Type: Fellowship.

No. of awards offered: Varies.

Frequency: Annual.

Value: A stipend of US$17,000-US$29,000 depending on years of relevant experience. In addition, a US$3,000 research allowance is awarded to cover research support and fringe benefits. Payments are made quarterly.

Length of Study: One year; Fellows may apply for a second year of funding subject to a satisfactory progress report.

Study Establishment: Appropriate institutions.

Country of Study: Any country.

Closing Date: September 15th, first two pages of application; October 1st, original and 15 copies, bound and signed.

Research Grants

Subjects: Diabetes and its complications.

Eligibility: Open to suitably qualified (MD, PhD or equivalent) investigators.

Purpose: To support biomedical diabetes research projects.

Type: Research Grant.

No. of awards offered: Varies.

Frequency: Annual.

Value: Up to US$50,000, usually made to cover the cost of such items as salaries for technical assistance, special equipment, animals, consumable supplies and other miscellaneous supplies required to conduct the proposed research.

Length of Study: One year; renewable for a second year subject to a satisfactory progress report.

Country of Study: Any country.

Closing Date: February 15th, first two pages of application; March 1st, original and 15 copies, bound and signed.

Additional Information: Grant funds are not awarded to discharge an institution's obligation for a tenure position, except under special circumstances.

*Summer Student Program

Subjects: Diabetes research.

Eligibility: Open to undergraduates, graduate students or medical students. Applications, however, may only be submitted by institutions, not by individual students.

Purpose: To allow colleges, universities, medical schools and other accredited research facilities to support student work.

No. of awards offered: Varies; dependent on funds available.

Frequency: Annual.

Value: Each sponsoring institution will provide each summer student with a US$2,500 stipend for the period of the Award. Indirect costs will not be awarded. The funds will be made available on or about July 1st.

Length of Study: Eight weeks (the program must begin no earlier than June 15th and conclude no later than September 15th).

Study Establishment: Appropriate institutions.

Country of Study: Any country.

Closing Date: October 15th.

Additional Information: The sponsoring institution must place each student supported through this program in a laboratory or series of laboratories conducting research projects related to the cause, cure, treatment and/or prevention of diabetes or its complications. The actual research project that the student will participate in must be diabetes-related. The sponsoring institution must recruit eight students to participate in the program. Three or four students should be enrolled at other academic institutions. It is the responsibility of the sponsoring institution to develop a didactic program for the students supported through this mechanism.

KAUNAS MEDICAL ACADEMY SENATE

Kaunas Medical Academy, Laboratory of Neurophysiology, 9 Mickevivaus Street, Kaunas, LT 3000, Lithuania
Tel: 370 7 204536
Fax: 370 7 229733
Email: arbagi@kma.lt
Telex: RASA 269268
Contact: Aron Gutman

Postdoctoral Fellowship in Physiology of Vision and Neuroscience

Subjects: Experimental and theoretical studies of visual object perception in humans, neurophysiological and mathematical modelling of cortical neuron networks.

Eligibility: Open to graduates or those with a PhD in sensory physiology, neurophysiology, or applied mathematics, who are fluent in English, Russian, or Lithuanian.

Level of Study: Postgraduate, Doctorate, Postdoctorate.

Type: Fellowship.

No. of awards offered: One.

Frequency: Every two years.

Value: Salary of an associate professor in Lithuania.

Length of Study: Four months.

Study Establishment: Vision Research Group, Dept. of Biology, Kaunas Medical Academy.

Country of Study: Lithuania.

Applications Procedure: Application must include: a CV, university certification, reprints of publications, and two recommendations from the university authorities.

Postdoctoral Fellowship in Theoretical Biophysics and Neuroscience

Subjects: Theoretical investigations in neurone electrophysiology, calculations of reconstructed nerve cell, and search for electronic measurement methods.

Eligibility: Applicants must be English, Lithuanian or Russian speaking; graduates/PhD in biophysics, theoretical physics or applied mathematics; skilled in numerical calculations.

Level of Study: Postgraduate, Doctorate, Postdoctorate.

Type: Fellowship.

No. of awards offered: One.

Frequency: Every two years.

Value: Salary of associate professor (docent) in Lithuania.

Length of Study: Four months.

Study Establishment: Laboratory of Neurophysiology, Kaunas Medical Academy.

Country of Study: Lithuania.

Applications Procedure: Application must include a CV, university certifications, reprints of publications, two letters of recommendation from the university teachers or supervisors.

KAZAN STATE TECHNICAL UNIVERSITY (KSTU)

Kazan State Technical University (KSTU), K. Marx str. 10, Kazan, Tatarstan, 420111, Russia
Tel: 7 8432 38 41 10
Fax: 7 8432 36 60 32
Email: agishev@kaiadm.kazan.su
Contact: Professor Ravil R. Agishev

Rector's Grant

Subjects: Scientific research.

Eligibility: Applicants must be proficient in Russian, have a PhD or DSc and not be more than 45 years of age.

Level of Study: Postdoctorate, Professional development.

Purpose: To support joint research on scientific and technical issues, and to invite eligible applicants to deliver lectures on new scientific branches of mutual interest.

Type: Research Grant.

No. of awards offered: Two.

Frequency: Annual.

Value: US$1,500 plus the monthly loan of Professor or Associate Professor of the KSTU accordingly.

Length of Study: Three to six months.

Study Establishment: KSTU.

Country of Study: Russia.

Applications Procedure: Application form must be completed, abstract must be submitted (four pages of resume with aim and ground), and recommendations from three professors.

Closing Date: August 31st.

KENNEDY MEMORIAL TRUST

Kennedy Memorial Trust, 16 Great College Street, London, SW1P 3RX, England
Tel: 0171 222 1151
Fax: 0171 222 8550
Contact: Anna Mason, Secretary

Kennedy Scholarships

Subjects: All fields of arts, science, social science and political studies.

Eligibility: Open to UK citizens who are resident in the UK, or who have been wholly or mainly educated in the UK. At the time of application, candidates must have spent at least two of the last five years at a UK university or university college, and must have graduated by the start of tenure in the following year; or have graduated not more than three years prior to the commencement of studies.

Level of Study: Postgraduate.

Purpose: As part of the British National Memorial to President Kennedy to enable students to undertake a course of postgraduate study in the US.

Type: Scholarship.

No. of awards offered: 12.

Frequency: Annual.

Value: US$14,500 to cover support costs, special equipment and some travel in the USA, plus tuition fees and travelling expenses to and from the USA.

Length of Study: One year.

Study Establishment: At Harvard University and the Massachusetts Institute of Technology, Cambridge.

Country of Study: USA.

Applications Procedure: Form, statement of purpose, references, and letter of endorsement from applicant's British university. Applications should come via the applicant's UK university.

Closing Date: November 8th.

Additional Information: No application will be considered from persons already in the USA. Scholarships for the study of business administration and management will only be granted in exceptional circumstances, and candidates must have completed two years' employment in business or public service since graduation. An independent application to Harvard or MIT is necessary. Scholars are not required to study for a degree in the USA but are encouraged to do so if they are eligible and able to complete the requirements for it.

SISTER KENNY INSTITUTE

Sister Kenny Institute, Abbott Northwestern Hospital, 800 East 28th Street, Minneapolis, MN, 55407, USA
Tel: 612 863 4630
Fax: 612 863 3299
Contact: Linda Frederickson

International Art Show by Artists with Disabilities

Subjects: Original art work in mediums including oils, acrylics, watercolors, pen and ink, pastels, sculpture and photography.

Eligibility: Open to individuals having a physical or mental impairment which substantially limits one or more major life activity (such as caring for oneself, performing manual tasks, walking, seeing, hearing, breathing, learning and working).

Level of Study: Unrestricted.

Purpose: To provide an Art Selling forum for the creative talents of persons with disabilities; to give disabled artists an outlet to sell their work on a competitive basis; to create an awareness and appreciation of the talents of disabled artists.

No. of awards offered: 26 plus.

Frequency: Mid April to mid May.

Value: US$50-US$500; awards of US$5,000 and sales of about US$12,000.

Country of Study: Any country.

Applications Procedure: Application registration form accompanies artwork; please call 612 863 4630 for form.

Closing Date: March 22nd.

Additional Information: Artists may submit up to two pieces of art not exceeding 36 inches in length or width, including frame. The show is held for one month, form April to mid May.

THE KIDNEY FOUNDATION OF CANADA

The Kidney Foundation of Canada, 5160 Decarie Blvd, Suite 780, Montreal, Quebec, H3X 2H9, Canada
Tel: 514 369 4806
Fax: 514 369 2472
Contact: C Serge, Research Grants Coordinator

Allied Health Fellowship

Subjects: Social/preventive medicine; dietetics; nephrology; urology; nursing.

Eligibility: Open to Canadian citizens.

Level of Study: Doctorate.

Purpose: To provide for full-time academic and research preparation at the doctoral level; to promote development of allied health investigators.

Type: Fellowship.

Frequency: Annual.

Value: Up to C$31,000.

Length of Study: Up to four years.

Applications Procedure: Application forms and guidelines are available.

Closing Date: February 15th.

Allied Health Operating Grant

Subjects: Social/preventive medicine; dietetics; nephrology; urology; nursing.

Eligibility: Open to Canadian citizens.

Level of Study: Allied health professional.

Purpose: To foster research relevant to clinical practice in the area of nephrology and urology by allied health professionals.

Type: Grant.

Frequency: Annual.

Value: Up to C$40,000.

Length of Study: Two years.

Country of Study: Canada.

Applications Procedure: Application forms and guidelines are available.

Closing Date: February 15th.

Allied Health Scholarship

Subjects: Social/preventive medicine; dietetics; nephrology; urology; nursing.

Eligibility: Open to Canadian citizens.

Level of Study: Professional development.

Purpose: To assist the student in pursuing education at the masters or doctoral level.

Type: Scholarship.

Frequency: Annual.

Value: Up to C$3,500.

Length of Study: Up to four years.

Applications Procedure: Application forms and guidelines are available.

Closing Date: February 15th.

Fellowship

Subjects: Nephrology; urology.

Eligibility: Open to Canadian citizens.

Level of Study: Postdoctorate.

Purpose: To provide for full-time postdoctoral research training.

Type: Fellowship.

Frequency: Annual.

Value: Up to C$42,505.

Length of Study: Up to four years.

Applications Procedure: Application forms and guidelines are available.

Closing Date: November 1st.

Medical Operating Grant

Subjects: Nephrology; urology.

Eligibility: Open to Canadian citizens.

Level of Study: Postdoctorate.

Purpose: To assist in defraying the cost of research.

Type: Grant.

Frequency: Annual.

Value: C$40,000 per year.

Length of Study: Two years.

Country of Study: Canada.

Applications Procedure: Application form and guidelines are available.

Closing Date: October 15th.

Scholarship

Subjects: Nephrology; urology.

Eligibility: Open to Canadian citizens.

Level of Study: Postdoctorate.

Purpose: To provide salary support for two years of an initial faculty appointment at an approved medical school.

Type: Scholarship.

Frequency: Annual.

Value: C$45,000 per year.

Length of Study: Two years.

Study Establishment: An approved medical school.

Country of Study: Canada.

Applications Procedure: Application forms and guidelines are available.

Closing Date: November 1st.

KING EDWARD VII BRITISH-GERMAN FOUNDATION

King Edward VII British-German Foundation, 3 The Courtyard, Gowan Avenue, London, SW6 6RH, England
Contact: Secretary

Scholarships

Subjects: Any subject.

Eligibility: Open to British nationals who are graduate students at British universities, are under 30 years of age and have a working knowledge of German.

Level of Study: Postgraduate.

Type: Scholarship.

No. of awards offered: One to two.

Frequency: Annual.

Value: DM800 per month, a book grant of DM150, exemption from tuition fees, plus travelling expenses between a Scholar's home in the UK and his/her place of study in Germany.

Length of Study: Ten months.

Study Establishment: A university or other institution of higher education.

Country of Study: Germany.

Applications Procedure: Write for application form, enclose CV and two references.

Closing Date: December 31st.

THE NORMAN KIRK MEMORIAL TRUST

The Norman Kirk Memorial Trust, PO Box 10-345, Wellington, New Zealand
Tel: 04 495 9323
Fax: 04 495 7225
Contact: The Co-ordinator

Grants

Subjects: Education.

Eligibility: Open to citizens of New Zealand and the South Pacific.

Level of Study: Unrestricted.

Purpose: To assist the welfare and progress of the people of New Zealand and the South Pacific.

Type: Grant.

No. of awards offered: Varies.

Frequency: Annual.

Value: Up to NZ$3,000.

Country of Study: New Zealand and the South Pacific.

Applications Procedure: Please submit completed application form plus one reference.

Closing Date: August 31st.

ESTHER A AND JOSEPH KLINGENSTEIN CENTER FOR INDEPENDENT EDUCATION

Klingenstein Center, Box 125, Teachers College, Columbia University, New York, NY, 10027, USA
Tel: 212 678 3449
Fax: 212 678 4048

Klingenstein Summer Institute

Subjects: Secondary education.

Eligibility: Restricted to teachers currently employed in independent secondary schools with 2-5 years' experience.

Level of Study: Professional development.

Purpose: Professional development for teachers in independent secondary schools with 2-5 years' experience.

Type: Fellowship.

No. of awards offered: Fifty.

Frequency: Annual.

Value: Room and board plus four graduate credits from Teachers College. Approximately US$2,000.

Length of Study: Three weeks.

Country of Study: USA.

Applications Procedure: Call for application materials.

Closing Date: January 15th.

Esther A and Joseph Klingenstein Fellowship Awards

Subjects: Education: administrative or academic disciplines.

Eligibility: Open to qualified applicants having at least five years' teaching experience in grades 5-12 in an independent school and who plan to return to their home school following the Fellowship year.

Level of Study: Doctorate, Professional development.

Purpose: To foster educational leadership skills.

Type: Fellowship.

No. of awards offered: Twelve.

Frequency: Annual.

Value: US$13,000 tuition allowance, a US$23,000 stipend and other benefits.

Length of Study: One academic year.

Study Establishment: The Klingenstein Center, Teachers College, Columbia University.

Country of Study: USA.

Applications Procedure: Application form must be completed.

Closing Date: January 15th.

FRANK KNOX MEMORIAL FELLOWSHIPS

Frank Knox Memorial Fellowships, 16 Great College Street, London, SW1P 3RX, England
Tel: 0171 222 2096
Fax: 0171 222 8550
Contact: M M Watson, Secretary

Frank Knox Fellowships at Harvard University

Subjects: Arts; sciences (including engineering and medical sciences); business administration; design; divinity; education; law; public administration; public health.

Eligibility: Open to UK citizens normally resident in the UK who, at the time of application, have spent at least two of the last four years at a UK university or university college and will have graduated by the start of tenure.

Type: Fellowship.

No. of awards offered: Four.

Frequency: Annual.

Value: US$13,500 plus tuition fees. Unmarried Fellows may be accommodated in one of the university dormitories or halls.

Length of Study: One academic year. Depending on the availability of sufficient funds the Fellowships may be renewed for Fellow's registered for a degree programme of more than one year's duration.

Study Establishment: Harvard University, Cambridge, Massachusetts.

Country of Study: USA.

Applications Procedure: Harvard University will try to arrange a suitable course for each individual. Fellowships are not awarded for postdoctoral study, and no application will be considered from persons already in the USA. Candidates must file an 'Admissions Application' directly with the graduate school of their choice at an early date; admission to a school is a prior condition of the award of a Fellowship. Candidates wishing to study business administration should apply by November 9th. A period of full-time work since graduation is necessary prior to embarking on the MBA programme. Travel grants are not awarded, although in cases of extreme hardship applications can be made to Harvard University for travel cost assistance.

Closing Date: November 1st.

KOSCIUSZKO FOUNDATION

Kosciuszko Foundation, 15 East 65th Street, New York, NY, 10021-6595, USA
Tel: 212 734 2130
Email: The KF@aol.com
Contact: Grants Office

Chopin Piano Competition

Subjects: Piano performance of Chopin.

Eligibility: Open to citizens and permanent residents of the USA, and to international full-time students with valid student visas. Applicants must be 16-22 years of age as of the opening date of the Competition.

Purpose: To encourage highly talented students of piano to study and play works of Chopin.

Type: Prizes.

No. of awards offered: Three.

Frequency: Annual.

Value: 1st prize of US$2,500; 2nd prize of US$1,500; 3rd prize of US$1,000. Scholarships may be awarded in the form of shared prizes.

Country of Study: USA.

Applications Procedure: Write for application form and listing of other requirements.

Closing Date: April 15th.

Additional Information: The Competition is held on three consecutive days in mid-May. Applications should be marked 'Chopin Piano Competition'.

*Domestic Scholarships

Subjects: Polish-American-related issues and activities.

Eligibility: Open to full-time graduate and junior and senior undergraduate level college students who are pursuing a degree in the USA. Candidates must be US citizens of Polish descent, Poles who are permanent residents of the USA, or Americans who are pursuing a course of Polish subjects.

Type: Scholarship.

No. of awards offered: Varies.

Frequency: Annual.

Value: Varies.

Length of Study: One academic year; renewable for one additional academic year in exceptional cases.

Country of Study: USA.

Closing Date: January 15th.

*Graduate and Postgraduate Studies and Research in Poland Program

Subjects: Any subject.

Eligibility: Open to US graduate and postgraduate students who wish to pursue a course of graduate or postgraduate study and/or research at institutions of higher learning in Poland. Also eligible are university faculty who wish to spend a sabbatical pursuing research in Poland.

Purpose: To enable Americans to continue their graduate and postgraduate studies in Poland.

Type: Grant.

No. of awards offered: Varies.

Frequency: Annual.

Value: Tuition and housing, plus a monthly stipend in Polish currency for living expenses.

Country of Study: Poland.

Closing Date: January 15th.

Additional Information: Applicants must have a working knowledge of the Polish language and are reviewed based on academic background, motiviation for pursuing graduate studies and/or research in Poland, and a proposal of studies and research in Poland.

*Year Abroad Program at the Jagiellonian University in Krakow

Subjects: Polish language.

Eligibility: Open to US citizens of Polish background. Students may participate in this program during their junior or senior year of college. Although it is an undergraduate program, students in a MA or PhD program (but not at the dissertation level) can also apply.

Purpose: To enable American students to study in Poland.

Type: Travel Grant.

No. of awards offered: Varies.

Frequency: Annual.

Value: Tuition and housing, plus a monthly stipend in Polish currency for living expenses.

Length of Study: One year.

Country of Study: Poland.

Closing Date: January 15th.

KPMG/MARTIN MUSICAL SCHOLARSHIP FUND

KPMG/Martin Music Scholarship Fund, 76 Great Portland Street,
London, W1N 6HA, England
Tel: 0171 580 9961
Fax: 0171 436 5517
Contact: Vivienne Dimant, Administrator

Pierre Fournier Award

Subjects: Music performance (cello).

Eligibility: Open to UK citizens or persons who have been resident in the UK for some time, who are no more than 28 years of age.

Level of Study: Professional development.

Purpose: To assist exceptional talent with a debut recital.

No. of awards offered: One.

Frequency: Biennially.

Value: Varies - covers the cost of debut recital.

Country of Study: UK.

Applications Procedure: Application form must be completed.

Closing Date: Applicants should write for full details.

Additional Information: Selection of candidates is by audition. Candidates must have a complete recital prepared including one contemporary work written since 1940 and this programme must be submitted with the application. The first audition will be of 15 minutes dura-

tion and will consist of a piece or pieces from the candidate's repertoire chosen by the panel. The final round should consist of the entire recital programme. Written references need not accompany the application but the names and addresses of two referees are required.

KPMG Scholarship

Subjects: Musical performance.

Eligibility: Open to nationals of any country.

Level of Study: Unrestricted.

Purpose: To assist with tuition fees and/or maintenance whilst studying.

Type: Fees/maintenance.

No. of awards offered: One.

Frequency: Annual.

Value: £2,000.

Country of Study: Worldwide.

Applications Procedure: Application form must be completed.

Closing Date: October 1st each year.

Martin Musical Scholarships

Subjects: Music performance.

Eligibility: Open to practising musicians as well as students who are instrumental performers (including pianists) preparing for a career on the concert platform either as a soloist or orchestral player, and no more than 25 years of age. Preference is given to UK citizens.

Level of Study: Postgraduate.

Purpose: To assist exceptional musical talent with specialist and advanced study and to help in bridging the gap between study and fully professional status.

Type: Scholarship.

No. of awards offered: Varies.

Frequency: Annual.

Value: Varies.

Length of Study: Two years; renewable.

Country of Study: UK, Europe and USA.

Applications Procedure: Application form must be completed.

Closing Date: October 1st.

Additional Information: It is not the present policy of the Fund to support organists, singers, conductors, composers, academic students or piano accompanists.

Sidney Perry Scholarship

Subjects: Musical performance.

Eligibility: Open to nationals of any country.

Level of Study: Postgraduate.

Purpose: For postgraduate study.

Type: Scholarship.

No. of awards offered: Varies.

Frequency: Annual.

Value: Varies.

Length of Study: Up to two years.

Country of Study: Worldwide.

Applications Procedure: Application form must be completed.

Closing Date: October 1st each year.

Trevor Snoad Memorial Trust

Subjects: Music performance (viola).

Eligibility: Open to outstanding viola players.

Level of Study: Postgraduate.

No. of awards offered: One.

Frequency: Annual.

Value: £500.

Applications Procedure: Application form must be completed.

Closing Date: October 1st each year.

Additional Information: An award is valid for two years and must be taken up within that time. There is no limit to the number of times an unsuccessful candidate may apply. Each candidate is eligible to apply for two awards. Selection of candidates is by audition; preliminary auditions are held in the autumn with final auditions in the spring.

KRASNOYARSK STATE ACADEMY OF TECHNOLOGY

Office 2-326, Mir Avenue 82, Krasnoyarsk, 3912, Russia
Tel: 3912 27 6382
Fax: 3912 27 4440
Contact: Dr Viktorova

Scholarship

Subjects: Forestry, landscape architecture, town planning, business management, computer engineering, control engineering, computer science, biotechnology, analytical chemistry, ecology, economics, sociology and psychology.

Eligibility: There are no restrictions on eligibility.

Level of Study: Postgraduate, Professional development.

Type: Scholarship.

No. of awards offered: Varies.

Frequency: Annual.

Length of Study: 2-5 years.

Study Establishment: KSAT.

Country of Study: Russia.

Applications Procedure: Please submit application form and certificates from secondary education.

Closing Date: Spring each year.

SAMUEL H KRESS FOUNDATION

Samuel H Kress Foundation, 174 East 80th Street, New York, NY, 10021, USA
Tel: 212 861 4993
Contact: Raissa Fitzgerald

Dissertation Fellowships

Subjects: Art history.

Eligibility: Open to predoctoral candidates at American universities.

Level of Study: Predoctoral.

Purpose: To assist final preparation of the doctoral dissertation.

Type: Fellowship.

No. of awards offered: Ten.

Frequency: Annual.

Value: US$10,000.

Applications Procedure: Applicants must be nominated by their art history department. Limit of one applicant per department.

Closing Date: March 31st.

402

Fellowships for Advanced Training in Fine Arts Conservation

Subjects: Specific areas of fine arts conservation.

Eligibility: Open to US nationals, or students matriculated at US institutions, who have completed their initial training in conservation.

Purpose: To enable young American conservators to receive advanced training.

Type: Fellowship.

No. of awards offered: Varies.

Frequency: Annual.

Value: US$1,000-US$12,000.

Study Establishment: Appropriate institutions.

Country of Study: USA.

Closing Date: February 28th.

Additional Information: Emphasis is on hands-on training. These grants are not for completion of degree programs.

For further information contact:
Samuel H Kress Foundation, 174 East 80th Street, New York, NY, 10021, USA
Tel: 212 861 4993
Contact: Lisa M Ackerman

Kress Fellowships for Field Archaeology

Subjects: Art history, archaeology, classical studies, conservation.

Eligibility: Limited to US citizens accepted to US sponsored excavations abroad.

Level of Study: Doctorate.

Purpose: To enable advanced training for PhD candidates.

Type: Fellowship.

No. of awards offered: Varies.

Value: Varies; US$500-US$1500.

Applications Procedure: Site coordinator should apply on behalf of student(s).

Closing Date: February 28th.

Additional Information: Sites must have a strong art historical component and must focus on Greco-Roman traditions, the ancient Near East or the Biblical lands.

For further information contact:
Samuel H Kress Foundation, 174 East 80 Street, New York, NY, 10021, USA
Tel: 212 861 4993
Contact: Fellowship Administrator

Travel Fellowships

Subjects: Art history.

Eligibility: Open to predoctoral candidates at American universities.

Level of Study: Predoctoral.

Purpose: To facilitate travel to view materials essential for the completion of dissertation research.

Type: Fellowship.

No. of awards offered: 15-20.

Frequency: Annual.

Value: Varies (US$1,000-US$12,000).

Country of Study: Unrestricted.

Applications Procedure: Applicants must be nominated by their art history department. Limit of two applicants per department.

Closing Date: November 30th.

Two-Year Research Fellowships at Foreign Institutions

Subjects: Art history.

Eligibility: Open to predoctoral candidates at American universities.

Level of Study: Predoctoral.

Purpose: To facilitate advanced dissertation research in association with a selected art historical institute in Florence, Jerusalem, Leiden, London, Munich, Nicosia, Paris, Rome or Zurich.

Type: Fellowship.

No. of awards offered: Four.

Frequency: Annual.

Value: US$15,000 per annum.

Length of Study: Two years.

Study Establishment: One of a number of art historical institutes in Florence, Jerusalem, Leiden, London, Munich, Nicosia, Paris, Rome or Zurich.

Country of Study: Various countries outside the USA.

Applications Procedure: Applicants must be nominated by their art history department. Limit of one applicant per department.

Closing Date: November 30th.

For further information contact:
Samuel H Kress Foundation, 174 East 80th Street, New York, NY, 10021, USA
Tel: 212 861 4993
Contact: Lisa Ackerman

THE LALOR FOUNDATION

Lalor Foundation, PO Box 2493, Providence, RI, 02906, USA
Tel: 401 272 1973

Postdoctoral Fellowships

Subjects: Basic postdoctoral research in reproductive biology as related to the regulation of fertility.

Eligibility: Open to tax-exempt institutions within or outside the USA. Candidates should apply for details. The individual nominated by the applicant institution for the Postdoctoral Fellowship for conduct of the work may be a citizen of any country and should have training and experience at least equal to the PhD or MD level. People who have held the doctoral degree for less than five years are preferred. The applicant institution may make its nomination of a Fellow from among its own personnel or elsewhere, but, qualifications being equal, candidates from other than the proposing institution itself may carry modest preference. The application must name the institution's nominee for Fellowship and include his or her performance record.

Level of Study: Postdoctorate.

Purpose: To promote intensive research and to assist and encourage able young investigators in academic positions to follow research careers in reproductive physiology.

Type: Fellowship.

No. of awards offered: Fifteen.

Frequency: Annual.

Value: Up to US$20,000 per annum to cover fellowship stipend, institutional overhead and miscellaneous expenses.

Study Establishment: An institution which is tax-exempt.

Country of Study: Any country.

Applications Procedure: Application forms are available on request.

Closing Date: January 15th.

LAND AND WATER RESOURCES RESEARCH AND DEVELOPMENT CORPORATION

Land and Water Resources Research and Development Corporation, GPO Box 2182, Canberra, ACT, 2601, Australia
Tel: 06 257 3379
Fax: 06 257 3420
Email: public@lwrrdc.iwdc.gov.av
Contact: Executive Director

LWRRDC Postgraduate Scholarship

Level of Study: Postgraduate.

Purpose: To build up the pool of scientific expertise in Australia in the field of natural resources management (land, water, and vegetation).

Type: Scholarship.

No. of awards offered: Minimum of four.

Frequency: Annual, dependent on funds available.

Value: About A$25,000 annually for three years (A$75,000 total) dependent on funds available/number of awards made.

Length of Study: Three years.

Country of Study: Australia.

Applications Procedure: Two page preliminary application form.

Closing Date: September.

*Postgraduate Research and Development Scholarship

Subjects: Scientific, social, economic or management studies related to Australian land, water and vegetation resources. Fields of study should be consistent with the R&D priorities identified by the Corporation from time to time.

Eligibility: Generally candidates must be Australian citizens enrolled in an approved program leading to the award of either doctoral or master's degree by research and thesis.

Purpose: To assist in the development of greater research capacity in scientific fields covering land, water and vegetation resources.

Type: Scholarship.

No. of awards offered: Up to four.

Frequency: Annual.

Value: Stipend of A$20,000 per annum tax free, plus A$5,000 per annum for the holder's expenses.

Length of Study: Three years for doctoral scholarships or two years for master's scholarships.

Country of Study: Australia.

Applications Procedure: Calls for applications usually occur in early June and applicants are required to use a two-page preliminary application form available from the Corporation.

Closing Date: End of July.

Research and Development Grants

Subjects: Scientific, social, economic or management studies related to Australian land, water and vegetation resources. Applications should be consistent with R&D priorities identified by the Corporation from time to time.

Eligibility: Generally, applicants must be Australian citizens or residents.

Level of Study: Postgraduate.

Purpose: To fund R&D activities which will enhance the sustainable use, productivity and conservation of Australia's land, water and vegetation resources.

Type: Grant.

No. of awards offered: Minimum of four.

Frequency: Annual.

Value: A\$75,000 over three years dependent on the total number of grants approved and funds available.

Length of Study: About three years.

Country of Study: Australia.

Applications Procedure: A call for applications is made in early September, closing October, and Applicants are required to use a two-page preliminary application form available from the Corporation. Successful applicants are advised in December.

Closing Date: End July.

LANDSCAPE ARCHITECTURE FOUNDATION

Landscape Architecture Foundation, 4401 Connecticut Avenue, NW #500, Washington, DC, 20008, USA
Tel: 202 686 8306
Fax: 202 686 1001
Contact: Kathy Shields, Scholarship Coordinator

AILA/Yamagani/Hope Fellowship

Subjects: Landscape architecture.

Eligibility: The applicant must have a bachelors or master's degree in landscape architecture.

Level of Study: Professional development, Postgraduate.

Purpose: The fellowship may be used to support credit or non credit courses, seminars or workshops; for travel or related expenses in support of an independent research project; or for development of post-secondary educational materials or curriculum plans.

Type: Fellowship.

No. of awards offered: One.

Frequency: Annual.

Value: US\$1,000.

Applications Procedure: Applicants should submit a 500 word essay, a 100 word statement of intent, two letters of recommendation, and a completed application form.

Closing Date: August.

Ralph Hudson Environmental Fellowship

Subjects: Landscape architecture.

Eligibility: Application is open to a full-time individual professor in landscape architecture. Resident of the USA, Canada or Mexico.

Level of Study: Professional development.

Purpose: In order for landscape architecture to make its full contribution as a profession and a discipline, the knowledge base on which it rests must be systematically examined, tested, refined and extended through providing a high level of university education. This award is intended to advance the educational profession and academic community through reearch in areas relating to open space, parks and recreation.

Type: Fellowship.

No. of awards offered: One.

Frequency: Annual.

Value: US\$3,000.

Applications Procedure: Application form must be completed.

Closing Date: August.

LANDCADD, Inc. Scholarship

Subjects: Landscape architecture.

Eligibility: Open to landscape architecture students.

Level of Study: Undergraduate, Postgraduate.

Purpose: To enable an undergraduate or graduate student of landscape architecture to utilize technological advancements such as computer aided design, video imaging, or telecommunications in his/her career.

Type: Scholarship.

Frequency: Annual.

Value: US\$500, accompanied by a gift of US\$500 in LANDCADD software to the recipient's department.

Applications Procedure: Applicants should submit a typed 500 word essay, two recommendation letters, and a completed application form.

Raymond E Page Scholarship

Subjects: Landscape architecture.

Eligibility: Open to students of landscape architecture.

Level of Study: Postgraduate, Undergraduate.

Purpose: To further the profession through the development of parks and other public facilities.

Type: Scholarship.

No. of awards offered: Two.

Frequency: Annual.

Value: US\$500.

Applications Procedure: Applicants should submit a two page essay, describing how the award is to be used, a letter of recommendation from a previous professor, and a completed application form.

David T Woolsey Scholarship

Subjects: Landscape architecture.

Eligibility: Open to students from Hawaii.

Level of Study: Postgraduate, Undergraduate.

Purpose: The award provides funds for a third, fourth, or fifth year or graduate student of landscape architecture from Hawaii.

Type: Scholarship.

No. of awards offered: One.

Frequency: Annual.

Value: US\$1,000.

Applications Procedure: Applicants should submit: a typed autobiography and personal statement of 500 words maximum, three photographic samples of their work, two letters of recommendation, completed application forms, and a financial aid form.

Closing Date: April.

LA TROBE UNIVERSITY

Research & Graduate Studies, La Trobe University, Bundoora Campus, Melbourne, Victoria, 3083, Australia
Tel: 03 479 2043
Fax: 03 479 1994
Contact: Dr Stewart J Sharlow

*Postdoctoral Research Fellowship

Subjects: Unrestricted.

Eligibility: Open to students who have been awarded their doctorates within the last five years. Applicants must hold a doctoral degree or equivalent at the closing date of applications. The University may also take into account the proposed area of research having regard to the University's research promotion and management strategy policies.

Purpose: To advance research activities on the various campuses of the University by bringing to or retaining in Australia promising scholars.

Type: Fellowship.

No. of awards offered: One.

Frequency: Annual.

Value: A$28,700-A$38,950 per annum, plus air fares and a resettlement allowance.

Length of Study: Two years.

Country of Study: Australia.

Closing Date: November.

Additional Information: A project must be proposed by the applicant in collaboration with a La Trobe University research worker or team. The approved project will be designated in the letter of offer and the major objectives of a Fellow's project shall not be altered without the written approval of the University.

*Postgraduate Scholarship

Subjects: Aboriginal studies: accountancy; agriculture; archaeology; art history; Asian studies; Australian studies; behavioural health sciences; biochemistry; botany; chemistry; cinema studies; communication disorders; computer science; drama; economic history; economics; econometrics; education; electronic and communication sciences; English; French; genetics and human variation; geology; gerontology; health administration; health education; history; history and philosophy of science; Italian; legal studies; linguistics; Latin American studies; mathematics; microbiology; music; nursing; North American studies; occupational therapy; orthoptics; pacific studies; peace studies; philosophy; philosophy of science; physics; physiotherapy; podiatry; politics; prosthetics and orthotics; psychology; religious studies; revolutionary studies; romance languages; social work; sociology; statistics; Spanish; women's studies; zoology.

Eligibility: Open to applicants of any nationality having qualifications deemed to be equivalent to a first class Australian honours degree. Scholarships may be awarded to persons holding a high H2A degree from an Australian institution.

Purpose: To provide financial assistance to masters and PhD candidates.

Type: Scholarship.

No. of awards offered: Approximately 45.

Frequency: Annual.

Value: Values for 1993: A$14,260 per annum, no spouse allowance, A$884 per annum per dependent child, a thesis allowance and partial removal and travel allowances; all dependent on funds available.

Length of Study: Up to 24 months for masters candidates and for up to 36 months for PhD candidates.

Country of Study: Australia.

Applications Procedure: Application forms available directly from the department offering the relevant course of study.

Closing Date: September 30th for candidates with overseas qualifications.

For further information contact:
La Trobe University, Bundoora Campus, Melbourne, Victoria, 3083, Australia
Tel: 03 479 2971
Fax: 03 479 1994
Contact: Admissions & Scholarships Officer

*Research Fellowship for Women with Family Responsibilities

Subjects: Unrestricted.

Eligibility: Open to women who have been awarded doctorates and are able to show that their research career has been significantly retarded because of family responsibilities.

Purpose: To assist women who have had their research careers interrupted or slowed by family responsibilities.

Type: Fellowship.

No. of awards offered: One.

Frequency: Annually; dependent on funds available.

Value: A$28,700-A$38,950 per annum, plus airfares and a resettlement allowance.

Length of Study: 12 months full-time study or 24 months part-time.

Country of Study: Australia.

Closing Date: June/July.

Additional Information: The University may terminate a Fellowship at any time if it is not satisfied with the progress or conduct of a Fellow. The Fellowship shall commence on a date specified by the University, this normally being the date upon which the Fellow commences work on the approved project at the University. The Fellowship must be taken up within three months from the date of offer.

LEAGUE FOR THE EXCHANGE OF COMMONWEALTH TEACHERS

Commonwealth House, 7 Lion Yard, Tremadoc Road, Clapham, London, SW4 7NF, England
Tel: 0171 498 1101
Fax: 0171 720 5403
Contact: League for the Exchange of Commonwealth Teachers

UK Government Grants

Subjects: Any subject.

Eligibility: Open to teachers (in all types of schools - primary, secondary, special, technical colleges, colleges of education) from the UK who are accepted for exchange with teachers in selected Commonwealth countries. Teachers should be 25 - 45 years of age and have not less than 5 years' teaching experience in the UK, with at least 2 years under the current employing authority.

Purpose: To facilitate the exchange of British teachers to other Commonwealth countries.

Type: Grant.

No. of awards offered: Approximately 300.

Frequency: Annual.

Value: Return air fare.

Length of Study: One academic year.

Study Establishment: Schools or colleges in selected Commonwealth countries.

Country of Study: Australia, Bahamas, Bermuda, Canada, India, Jamaica, Kenya (Nairobi), New Zealand, Sierra Leone and Trinidad.

Applications Procedure: Application form must be completed.

Additional Information: There is also a separate programme to support teacher exchanges between different parts of the UK.

LEEDS INTERNATIONAL PIANOFORTE COMPETITION

Leeds International Pianoforte Competition, Piano Competition Office, The University of Leeds, Leeds, LS2 9JT, England
Tel: 0113 244 6586
Fax: 0113 244 6586
Contact: Mrs Françoise Logan, Hon Administrator

Leeds International Pianoforte Competition

Subjects: Piano performance.

Eligibility: Open to professional pianists who were born on or after September 1st 1967.

Level of Study: Professional development.

Purpose: To promote the careers of talented professional pianists.

Type: Prize.

No. of awards offered: Varies.

Frequency: Every three years (next 1999).

Value: Total prizes £57,600, and a number of national and international engagements for all six finalists.

Country of Study: Any country.

Applications Procedure: Application forms by not later than March 15th 1999.

Closing Date: March 15th 1999.

PROFESSOR CHARLES LEGGETT TRUST

Leggett Awards, 16 Ogle Street, London, W1P 7LG, England
Tel: 0171 636 4481
Fax: 0171 637 4307
Contact: Valerie Beale, Administrator

*Leggett Awards

Subjects: Musical performance: 1998 horn, 1999 trombone, 1997 tuba.

Eligibility: Open to players of any nationality who have been resident in the UK for three years and are aged 18 to 26 years inclusive on closing date. The award is open to individual instrumentalists. Awards are intended for those in financial need.

Purpose: To provide annual awards for talented young brass players.

No. of awards offered: One or more.

Frequency: Annual.

Value: From a total of £4,000.

Study Establishment: Tuition, maintenance and the purchase of instruments.

Country of Study: Unrestricted.

Closing Date: December 1st.

Additional Information: Selected applicants are asked to audition in January and to play a specially commissioned piece.

LEPRA (THE BRITISH LEPROSY RELIEF ASSOCIATION)

Lepra, Fairfax House, Causton Road, Colchester, Essex, CO1 1PU, England
Tel: 01206 562286
Fax: 01206 762151
Contact: Information Officer

Grants

Subjects: Any relevant medical subject.

Purpose: To encourage an interest in leprosy among doctors and research workers.

Type: Grant.

No. of awards offered: Variable number of grants.

Frequency: Dependent on funds available.

Value: Dependent on funds available and the nature of the research or training.

Study Establishment: As appropriate to the nature of the research or training. Arrangements are made to enable interested medical students to spend their elective period anywhere in the world where a suitable project can be arranged, working on a specific leprosy research project.

Applications Procedure: For research, the applicant must submit a

programme considered useful by the Medical Board; for training, the applicant must submit a course deemed useful by the Board and will be expected to undertake work in leprosy after completion of training.

Closing Date: End of March, August/November.

Additional Information: Annual awards are also given to registered medical students in the UK for the best essay or essays on a specific subject in the field.

LEUKAEMIA RESEARCH FUND

Leukaemia Research Fund, 43 Great Ormond Street, London, WC1N 3JJ, England
Tel: 0171 405 0101
Fax: 0171 242 1488
Email: lrf@leukres.demon.co.uk
www: http://www/phoenix.jrz.ox.ac.uk/lrf/lrfhome.htm
Contact: Dr David Grant

Clinical Research Fellowship

Subjects: All life science disciplines. The research topic must be applicable to leukaemia.

Eligibility: Open to researchers of any nationality who work and reside in the UK.

Level of Study: Clinical.

Purpose: To train registrar-grade clinicians in research and allow them to submit for a higher degree (MD or PhD).

Type: Fellowship.

No. of awards offered: Four.

Frequency: Annual.

Value: Varies.

Length of Study: 2 or 3 years.

Study Establishment: Universities, medical schools, research institutes and teaching hospitals.

Country of Study: UK.

Applications Procedure: Application form must be completed.

Closing Date: March.

Clinical Training Fellowship

Subjects: Haematology, oncology.

Eligibility: Open to researchers of any nationality who work and reside in the UK.

Level of Study: Clinical.

Purpose: To train registrar-grade clinicians in the care and treatment of patients with a haematological malignancy.

Type: Fellowship.

No. of awards offered: 11.

Frequency: Annual.

Value: Varies.

Length of Study: Two years.

Study Establishment: Any UK centre of excellence for leukaemia medicine.

Country of Study: UK.

Applications Procedure: Application form must be completed.

Closing Date: March.

Gordon Piller Studentships

Subjects: All life science disciplines. The research topic must be applicable to leukaemia.

Eligibility: Open to graduates of any nationality who work and reside in the UK.

Level of Study: Postgraduate.

Purpose: To train graduates in life sciences in research and allow them to submit for a PhD degree.

Type: Studentships.

No. of awards offered: Four.

Frequency: Annual.

Value: £50,000, including fees.

Length of Study: Three years.

Study Establishment: At universities, medical schools and research institutes.

Country of Study: UK.

Applications Procedure: Application form to be completed.

Closing Date: August.

Research Grant Programme

Subjects: All life science disciplines.

Eligibility: Open to researchers who work and reside in the UK.

Level of Study: Unrestricted.

Purpose: To give long-term support to research groups studying the causes and treatment of haematological malignancies.

Type: Research Grant.

No. of awards offered: Varies.

Frequency: Three times yearly.

Value: Varies.

Study Establishment: Universities, medical schools, research institutes and teaching hospitals.

Country of Study: UK.

Applications Procedure: Application form to be completed only after discussion with Scientific Director.

Closing Date: Available on request.

Research Grant Project

Subjects: All life science disciplines.

Eligibility: Open to researchers of any nationality who work and reside in the UK.

Level of Study: Postgraduate, Unrestricted, Postdoctorate.

Purpose: To support laboratory and clinical based research into the causes and treatment of the haematological malignancies.

Type: Grant.

No. of awards offered: Varies.

Frequency: Three times yearly.

Value: Up to £200,000.

Length of Study: Varies.

Study Establishment: Universities, medical schools, research institutes and teaching hospitals.

Country of Study: UK.

Applications Procedure: Application form must be completed.

Closing Date: Available on request.

LEUKEMIA RESEARCH FUND

3768 Bathurst Street, Suite 300, Toronto, Ontario, M3H 3M7, Canada
Tel: 416 638 8522
Fax: 416 638 1495
Contact: Norma Barkin

Awards

Subjects: Research on leukemia and related blood diseases.

Eligibility: Open to postdoctorate students engaged in work in Canada in the field of leukemia and related blood diseases.

Purpose: To provide funds for researchers in the field of leukemia and blood diseases, and to provide a limited number of postdoctorate fellowships in the same field.

No. of awards offered: Varies.

Frequency: Annual.

Value: Varies.

Length of Study: One year.

Country of Study: Canada.

Applications Procedure: All applications must be prepared on the Fund's forms and submitted by the deadline for evaluation, on a merit basis, by the scientific review panel. Applications are available through Deans of Medicine or the LRF Office.

Closing Date: February 1st.

LEUKEMIA SOCIETY OF AMERICA

Leukemia Society of America, 600 Third Avenue, 4th Floor, New York, NY, 10016, USA
Tel: 212 573 8484
Fax: 212 856 9686
Email: BLERMAND@aol.com
Contact: Barbara P Lermand, Director of Research Administration

Scholarships, Special Fellowships and Fellowships

Eligibility: There are no restrictions.

Level of Study: Postdoctorate.

Purpose: To provide support for individuals pursuing careers in basic, clinical or translational research in leukemia and related diseases.

No. of awards offered: 64.

Frequency: Annual.

Value: US$26,000-US$40,000 per year for up to five years.

Length of Study: Three to five years, based on experience and training.

Study Establishment: Domestic or foreign non-profit organizations.

Country of Study: USA.

Applications Procedure: Application form must be completed. Please contact Leukemia Society of America.

Closing Date: September 16th for the preliminary (two page) application. October 1st for the complete application.

Translational Research Award

Eligibility: No restrictions.

Level of Study: Postdoctorate.

Purpose: To encourage and provide early stage support for clinical research on Leukemia and its related cancers, emphasising novel approaches and strategies.

No. of awards offered: 23.

Frequency: Annual.

Value: Annual maximum of US$100,000 in direct costs plus 8% overhead.

Length of Study: Two years (possibly three).

Study Establishment: Domestic or foreign non-profit organizations.

Country of Study: USA.

Applications Procedure: By application form, contact Leukemia Society of America.

Closing Date: February 15th for the preliminary (two page) application, and March 15th for the complete application.

Additional Information: Write to LSA for further details.

THE LEVERHULME TRUST

Research Awards Advisory Committee, The Leverhulme Trust, 15-19 New Fetter Lane, London, EC4A 1NR, England
Tel: 0171 822 6964
Fax: 0171 822 5084
Contact: Secretary

The grants made by the Leverhulme Trust are in two categories: grants to institutions, and awards to individuals on the recommendation of a Research Awards Advisory Committee

Emeritus Fellowships

Subjects: Any subject.

Eligibility: Open to persons who have retired during the last three years or are about to retire, who hold or have recently held full-time teaching and/or research posts in universities or institutions of similar status in the UK and who have an established record of research. Must be resident in the UK.

Level of Study: Senior experienced researchers.

Purpose: To assist experienced researchers who will have attained the age of 59 or above at the time of retirement in the completion of research already begun.

Type: Fellowship.

No. of awards offered: 38.

Frequency: Annual.

Value: By individual assessment, but not exceeding £15,050.

Length of Study: Between three months and two years.

Study Establishment: In the UK or abroad.

Country of Study: Worldwide.

Applications Procedure: Application form must be completed. Requests for application forms must be accompanied by an A4 size SAE.

Closing Date: Mid-November.

Additional Information: The awards are to meet incidental costs and do not provide a personal allowance or pension supplementation.

Research Fellowships and Grants

Subjects: Any subject.

Eligibility: Open to persons educated in the UK or in any other part of the Commonwealth who are permanent members of the UK scholarly community and who are normally resident in the UK. Awards are not normally made to those under 30 and are never made to those registered for first or higher degrees, professional or vocational qualifications.

Purpose: To assist experienced researchers pursuing investigations who are prevented by routine duties or other cause from undertaking or completing a research programme.

Type: Awards.

No. of awards offered: 80.

Frequency: Annual.

Value: By individual assessment, but not exceeding a total of £15,050.

Length of Study: For between three months and two years.

Country of Study: UK or abroad.

Applications Procedure: Application form must be completed. Requests for application forms must be accompanied by an A4 size stamped addressed envelope.

Closing Date: Mid-November.

Study Abroad Studentships

Subjects: Any subject, but students wishing only to improve knowledge of modern languages are not eligible.

Eligibility: At the time of application candidates must hold a first degree from a UK university, or be able to show evidence of equivalent education in the UK. They must also have been educated at a school or schools in the UK or other part of the Commonwealth. They must be normally resident in the UK and under 30 years of age on June 1st, or holder must at the time of application have completed a degree course (undergraduate or postgraduate) within the last five years.

Level of Study: Postgraduate, Doctorate, Postdoctorate, Professional development.

Purpose: To fund advanced study or research at a centre of learning.

Type: Studentships.

No. of awards offered: 20.

Frequency: Annual.

Value: £11,078 per annum plus return air passage and other allowances at the discretion of the Committee.

Length of Study: For one or two years.

Country of Study: Any, except UK and USA.

Applications Procedure: Application form must be completed. Requests for application must be accompanied by an A4 size stamped self addressed envelope.

Closing Date: Early January.

LIBRARY & INFORMATION TECHNOLOGY ASSOCIATION

Library & Information Technology Association, 50 East Huron Street, Chicago, IL, 60611, USA
Tel: 312 280 4270

*LITA/CLSI-GEAC Scholarship

Subjects: Library information science, with an emphasis on library automation.

Eligibility: Open to beginning students at the masters degree level in an ALA-accredited program.

Type: Scholarship.

No. of awards offered: One.

Frequency: Annual.

Value: US$2,500.

Study Establishment: An American Library Association-accredited program.

Country of Study: USA.

Additional Information: Factors considered in awarding the Scholarship are academic excellence, leadership, evidence of commitment to a career in library automation and information technology, and prior activity and experience in those fields.

*LITA/OCLO Minority Scholarship

Subjects: Library information science, with an emphasis on library automation.

Eligibility: Open to US and Canadian citizens who belong to one of the following minority groups: American Indian or Alaskan Native, Asian or Pacific Islander, African-American, and Hispanic.

Purpose: To encourage the entry of qualified minority persons into the library automation field who plan to follow a career in that field and who evidence potential leadership in, and a strong commitment to, the use of automated systems in libraries.

Type: Scholarship.

No. of awards offered: One.

Frequency: Annual.

Value: US$2,500.

Study Establishment: An American Library Association-accredited program.

Country of Study: USA.

MIRIAM LICETTE TRUST

Miram Licette Trust, 16 Ogle Street, London, W1P 7LG, England
Tel: 0171 636 4481
Fax: 0171 637 4307
Contact: Valerie Beale, Administrator

*Miriam Licette Scholarship

Subjects: Musical performance; song.

Eligibility: Open to soprano, mezzo-soprano or contralto singers for advanced study in Paris. Applicants should be under 30 years of age and British or have been resident in the UK for three years.

Purpose: To assist a student of French song.

Type: Scholarship.

No. of awards offered: One.

Frequency: Annual.

Value: £5,000.

Country of Study: France.

Applications Procedure: Selected students will be asked to audition.

Closing Date: Mid-February.

LIFE SCIENCES RESEARCH FOUNDATION

Life Sciences Research Foundation, Lewis Thomas Labs, Princeton University, Washington Road, Princeton, NJ, 08544, USA
Tel: 609 258 3551
www: http://wwwmolbio.princeton.edu
Contact: Susan DiRenzo, Assistant Director

Three-year Postdoctoral Fellowships

Eligibility: Open to all.

Level of Study: Postdoctorate.

Purpose: To offer research support for aspiring scientists.

Type: Fellowship.

No. of awards offered: 15.

Frequency: Annual.

Value: US$35,000 per year three years.

Length of Study: Three years.

Applications Procedure: Front page (form), CV, five-page research proposal, letter from sponsoring lab supervisor, and three letters of reference.

Closing Date: October 1st.

LIGHT WORK

Light Work, 316 Waverly Avenue, Syracuse, NY, 13244, USA
Tel: 315 443 1300
Fax: 315 443 9516
Email: cdlight@summon2.syr.edu
www: http://sumweb.syr.edu/summon2/com_dark/public/web/LI.html

Contact: Jeffrey Hoone, Director

Light Work is an artist-run space which focuses on providing direct support for artists working in photography

Artist-in-Residence Program

Subjects: Photography.

Eligibility: Open to artists of any nationality working in photography with a demonstrated, serious intent and experience in the field. Students are not eligible.

Level of Study: Professional development.

Purpose: To support and encourage the production of new work by emerging and mid-career artists.

Type: Residency.

No. of awards offered: 12-15.

Frequency: Annual.

Value: US$1,200 stipend plus darkroom and apartment.

Length of Study: One month; not renewable.

Country of Study: USA.

Applications Procedure: Write for guidelines: there are no application forms. Submit a cover letter, 20 slides, other support materials and an SASE.

Closing Date: Applications are accepted on a rolling basis.

Additional Information: The Residencies are non-academic. Artists will be asked to give one informal lecture about their work and to contribute work produced in Syracuse to the Light Work collection. Work by participating artists is published in the Contact Sheet. Light Work also curates two photography galleries at Syracuse University and accepts exhibition proposals.

THE CHARLES A. AND ANNE MORROW LINDBERGH FOUNDATION

The Charles A. and Anne Morrow Lindbergh Foundation, 708 South 3rd Street, Suite 110, Minneapolis, MN, 55415-1141, USA
Tel: 612 338 1703
Fax: 612 338 6826
Email: lindfdtn@mtn.org
www: http://www.mtn.org/lindfdtn
Contact: Marlene White, Grants Administrator

Lindbergh Grants

Subjects: Adaptive technology, waste minimization and management, agriculture, aviation/aerospace, conservation of natural resources, humanities/education, arts, intercultural communication, exploration, biomedical research, health and population sciences.

Eligibility: Open to nationals of any country.

Level of Study: Unrestricted.

Purpose: To provide grants to individuals whose initiative in a wide spectrum of disciplines seeks to actively further a better balance between technology and the natural environment.

Type: Research Grant.

No. of awards offered: Approximately 10 per year.

Frequency: Annual.

Value: Maximum of US$10,580.

Applications Procedure: Application form must be completed.

Closing Date: Second Tuesday in June.

THE LINNEAN SOCIETY OF NEW SOUTH WALES

Linnean Society of New South Wales, 6/24 Cliff Street, PO Box 457, Milsons Point, NSW, 2061, Australia
Tel: 9 929 0253 (Tuesdays only)
Contact: Mrs Barbara J Stoddard

Linnean Macleay Fellowship

Subjects: Animal and plant physiology and pathology, anthropology, biochemistry, botany, comparative anatomy and embryology, general biology, geography, geology, palaeontology and zoology; research.

Eligibility: Candidates must be residents of New South Wales, Australia, and must have taken a degree in science or agricultural science in the University of Sydney, and must be a Member of the Linnean Society of New South Wales.

Level of Study: Postgraduate.

Purpose: To encourage the study of natural history in New South Wales.

Type: Fellowship.

No. of awards offered: One.

Frequency: Annual.

Value: A$3,200.

Length of Study: One year.

Study Establishment: At the University of Sydney or elsewhere, subject to the approval of the Council of the Linnean Society.

Country of Study: Australia.

Closing Date: November 15th.

Joyce W Vickery Scientific Research Fund

Purpose: To support worthy research in natural history in Australia.

No. of awards offered: Dependent on funds available.

Frequency: Annual.

Value: Not exceeding A$600.

Length of Study: Up to 12 months.

Country of Study: Australia.

Applications Procedure: Please submit application form, plus references and a list of publications over the previous five years.

Closing Date: June 30th.

Additional Information: Subject matter must be Australian natural history, written in English.

THE LISTER INSTITUTE OF PREVENTIVE MEDICINE

The White House, 70 High Road, Bushey Heath, Herts, WD2 3JG, England
Tel: 0181 421 8808
Fax: 0181 421 8818
Contact: F K Cowey

Lister Institute Senior Research Fellowships

Subjects: Biomedicine.

Eligibility: Open to UK citizens with a PhD, DPhil, MD, or MB BCh with membership of the Royal College of Physicians, who must be aged under 34 years. Anyone aged between 34 and 40 years must request permission to make a full application.

Level of Study: Postdoctorate.

Purpose: To support postdoctoral scientific research into the causes and prevention of disease in man.

Type: Senior Postdoctoral Fellowships.

No. of awards offered: Five.

Frequency: Annual.

Value: Full salary plus employer's superannuation and national insurance costs reimbursed, together with up to £8,500 per annum consumables.

Length of Study: Five years.

Study Establishment: UK universities, research institutes and hospitals.

Country of Study: UK.

Applications Procedure: Application form should be submitted along with CV and two letters of reference on approved form.

Closing Date: End of January each year.

Additional Information: Fellowships are not awarded to full-time members of research council staffs or staffs of medical charities. An annual report is required and Fellows are from time to time invited to give talks on their research at Fellowship gatherings which are held once or twice a year. Topics of applicants own choosing, though must have implications for preventive medicine.

THE LONDON CHAMBER OF COMMERCE AND INDUSTRY

The London Chamber of Commerce and Industry Examinations Board, Marlow House, 109 Station Road, Sidcup, Kent, DA15 7BJ, England
Tel: 0181 302 0261
Fax: 0181 302 4169
Contact: The Chief Executive

LCCI Examinations Board Scholarships

Level of Study: Unrestricted.

Purpose: To award scholarships to suitable applicants desiring to pursue LCCIEB qualifications or to LCCIEB qualified candidates wishing to take higher level qualifications.

Type: Scholarship.

Frequency: Dependent on funds available.

Value: Varies according to students requirements.

Country of Study: Malaysia, Hong Kong, Indonesia, Vietnam, China and UK currently. Will extend to other countries later.

Applications Procedure: Application form to be completed by applicant subject to recommendation from an approved LCCIEB Examinations centre who must process the application on the applicant's behalf.

Closing Date: December.

THE LONDON SYMPHONY ORCHESTRA

The London Symphony Orchestra, Barbican Centre, Barbican, London, EC2Y 8DS, England
Tel: 0171 588 1116
Fax: 0171 374 0127
Contact: Helen Smith

Shell LSO Music Scholarship

Subjects: Musical performance.

Eligibility: The Scholarship is open to British nationals, or persons normally resident in the UK for at least the past three years aged 15-22 years.

Level of Study: Unrestricted.

Purpose: The Scholarship is to be used in the best interests of the winner's development, and to faciltate his or her entry into the musical profession.

No. of awards offered: 1 Scholarship, 3 cash prizes.

Frequency: Annually, in a four-year cycle covering each section of the orchestra.

Value: Scholarship £6,000, gold medal; 2nd Prize, £3,000, silver medal; 3rd Prize £1,500, bronze medal; 4th Gerald McDonald Prize £750.

Applications Procedure: Application forms plus two references.

Closing Date: December.

Additional Information: Frequency: 1997 Woodwind; 1998 Strings; 1999 Brass; 2000 Tinpani and Percussion.

ROBERTO LONGHI FOUNDATION

Roberto Longhi Foundation, Via Benedetto Fortini 30, Florence, 50125, Italy
Tel: 055 658 0794
Fax: 055 658 0794
Contact: Secretariat

Fellowships

Subjects: Art history.

Eligibility: Open to Italian citizens who possess a degree from an Italian university with a thesis in the history of art; and to non-Italian citizens who have fulfilled the preliminary requirements for a doctoral degree in the history of art at an accredited university or an institution of equal standing. The fellowships are designed for those who want seriously to dedicate themselves to research in the history of art. Students who have reached their thirtieth birthday before April 30th are not eligible.

Level of Study: Doctorate, Postgraduate.

Type: Fellowships.

No. of awards offered: Several.

Frequency: Annual.

Value: The monthly rate is 800,000 lire, and for residents of the city and provinces of Florence 400,000 lire.

Length of Study: Nine months.

Country of Study: Italy.

Applications Procedure: Applications should contain the candidate's biographical data (place and date of birth, domicile, citizenship); a transcript of the candidate's undergraduate and graduate records; a copy of the degree thesis (if available) and of other original works, published or unpublished; a 'curriculum studiorum', also indicating the knowledge of foreign languages, spoken and written; letters of reference from at least two persons of academic standing who are acquainted with the candidate's work; the subject of the research which the candidate is interested in pursuing within the range of the history of art; and two passport photographs.

Closing Date: April 30th.

Additional Information: A Fellowship will be offered by Daisaku Ikeda, President of the Soka Gakkai International, Tokyo. In particular, successful candidates must give the assurance that they can dedicate their full time to the research for which the Fellowship is assigned. They may not enter into any connection with other institutions; they must live in Florence for the duration of the Fellowship, excepting travels required for their research. They may not exceed the periods of vacations fixed by the Institute. They are required to attend seminars, lectures and other activities arranged by the Institute. The Fellows must in addition submit a written report at the end of their stay in Florence, relating the findings of their individual research undertaken at the Longhi Foundation. The non-observance of the above conditions will be considered sufficient grounds for the cancellation of a Fellowship.

PAUL LOWIN TRUST

Perpetual Trustee Company Limited, 39 Hunter Street, Sydney, NSW, 2000, Australia
Tel: 02 229 9866
Fax: 02 221 4885
Contact: Charitable Trusts Manager

*Paul Lowin Awards

Subjects: Music composition: orchestral works; song cycles.

Eligibility: Open to Australian citizens over 18 years of age.

Purpose: To recognize original composition.

Type: Prizes.

No. of awards offered: Two.

Frequency: Every three years (next in 1997).

Value: Orchestral prize A$45,000; song cycle prize A$20,000.

Closing Date: June 30th 1997.

CATHERINE MCCAIG'S TRUST

Clerk to the Governors, Catherine McCaig's Trust, c/o McLeish Carswell, 29 St Vincent Place, Glasgow, G1 2DT, Scotland
Tel: 0141 248 4134
Fax: 0141 226 3118
Contact: Anne F Wilson

McCaig Bursaries and Postgraduate Scholarships

Subjects: Gaelic studies.

Eligibility: Bursaries are open to students enrolling in a course of Gaelic studies at any Scottish university; Postgraduate Scholarships are open to MA students of any Scottish university who have studied Gaelic among their course subjects.

Level of Study: Postgraduate, Undergraduate.

Type: Scholarship.

Frequency: Annual.

Value: £250 per annum for the entire course of study (Bursaries); £750 per annum, renewable (Postgraduate Scholarships).

Length of Study: 1-3 years.

Country of Study: UK.

Applications Procedure: Application forms are available from the Clerk.

Closing Date: May.

MCDONNELL CENTER FOR THE SPACE SCIENCES

McDonnell Center for the Space Sciences, Physics Department, 1105, Washington University, One Brookings Drive, St Louis, MO, 63130-7899, USA
Tel: 314 935 6225
Fax: 314 935 4083
Email: rmw@howdy.wustl.edu
www: http://www.physics.wustl.edu/~astro
Contact: Professor Robert M Walker

McDonnell Astronaut Fellowship in the Space Sciences

Subjects: Space sciences; physics; earth sciences; astronomy; chemistry; planetary studies.

Eligibility: Open to US citizens who have received or are about to receive their bachelor's or master's degree and are able to demonstrate an excellent academic performance in an accredited institution of higher learning.

Level of Study: Doctorate.

Purpose: To encourage prospective graduate students with an interest in space science to participate in the active and growing research programs of the McDonnell Center for the Space Sciences.

Type: Fellowship.

No. of awards offered: Three.

Frequency: Annual.

Value: Full tuition.

Length of Study: Nine month academic year (three years).

Study Establishment: The Physics, Earth and Planetary Sciences, or Chemistry Department of Washington University.

Country of Study: USA.

Closing Date: January 15th.

Additional Information: Candidates must apply and be accepted to one of the standard science or engineering departments at the university (Physics, Chemistry, Earth & Planetary Sciences, Biology or Electrical Engineering). Optional summer employment at McDonnell Douglas Corporation.

McDonnell Fellowship in the Space Sciences

Subjects: Space sciences; physics; earth sciences; astronomy; chemistry; planetary studies.

Eligibility: Open to candidates who have received or are about to receive their bachelor's or master's degree and are able to demonstrate an excellent academic performance in an accredited institution of higher learning.

Level of Study: Doctorate.

Type: Fellowship.

No. of awards offered: Two.

Frequency: Annual.

Value: Full tuition.

Length of Study: One year.

Study Establishment: Washington University.

Country of Study: USA.

Closing Date: January 15th.

Additional Information: Candidates must apply and be accepted by one of the standard science or engineering departments at the university (Physics, Chemistry, Earth & Planetary Sciences, Biology or Electrical Engineering).

THE MACDOWELL COLONY

The MacDowell Colony, 100 High Street, Peterborough, NH, 03458, USA
Tel: 603 924 3886 or 212 966 4860
Fax: 603 924 9142
Contact: Admissions Coordinator

Residencies

Subjects: Creative writing; visual arts; musical composition; filmmaking; architecture.

Eligibility: Open to established and emerging artists in the above fields.

Purpose: To provide a place where creative artists can take advantage of uninterrupted work time and seclusion in which to work and enjoy the experience of living in a community of gifted artists.

No. of awards offered: A total of 31 studios are available each application period for individual residencies.

Frequency: Three application reviews per year.

Value: Accepted applicants are asked to contribute toward residency costs.

Length of Study: Up to 8 weeks.

Study Establishment: The Colony, for one of three seasons: summer, fall to winter and winter to spring.

Country of Study: USA.

Closing Date: 15 January, 15 April and 15 September for Residencies to become tenable in summer, fall to winter and winter to spring respectively.

Additional Information: The studios are offered for the independent pursuit of the applicants' art. No workshops or courses are given. There are no stipends. Requests for information should be accompanied by an SASE.

VERNE CATT MCDOWELL CORPORATION

Verne Catt McDowell Corporation, PO Box 1336, Albany, OR, 97321-0440, USA
Tel: 1 541 926 6829
Contact: Emily Killin, Business Manager

Verne Catt McDowell Scholarship

Subjects: Religion and theology; church administration.

Eligibility: All scholarship candidates must be ministers ordained or studying to meet the requirements to be ordained as a minister in the Christian Church (Disciples of Christ). Candidates must be a member of the Christian church (Disciples of Christ) denomination. Preference given to Oregon graduates.

Level of Study: Postgraduate.

Purpose: To provide supplemental financial grants to men and women for graduate theological education for ministry in the Christian Church (Disciples of Christ) Denomination.

Type: Scholarship.

No. of awards offered: Four to six per year.

Frequency: Annual, dependent on funds available.

Value: US$400 to US$500 per school month.

Length of Study: Through completion.

Country of Study: USA.

Applications Procedure: Candidates are required to complete an application form and provide details of qualifications, transcripts, three references and state where they obtained information about the scholarship. An interview will be requested.

Closing Date: May.

Additional Information: Must be accepted into a professional degree program at a graduate institution of theological education, accredited by the general assembly of the Christian church (Disciples of Christ).

MCGILL UNIVERSITY

McGill University, 3644 Peel Street, Montreal, Quebec, H3A 1W9, Canada
Tel: 514 398 6604
Fax: 514 398 4659
Contact: Dean, Faculty of Law

Maxwell Boulton QC Fellowship

Subjects: Any legal subject, especially those having significance to the Canadian legal system and legal community.

Eligibility: Open to candidates who have completed residency requirements for a doctoral degree in law.

Level of Study: Doctorate, Postdoctorate.

Purpose: To provide younger scholars with an opportunity to pursue a major research project or to complete the research requirement for a higher degree.

Type: Fellowship.

No. of awards offered: Two.

Frequency: Annual.

Value: C$30,000-C$35,000 per annum.

Length of Study: One year.

Country of Study: Canada.

Closing Date: March 1st.

MACKENZIE KING SCHOLARSHIP TRUST

Faculty of Graduate Studies, University of British Columbia, 180 63H Cresceant Road, Vancouver, British Columbia, V6T 1Z2, Canada
Tel: 604 822 4556
Fax: 604 822 5802
Contact: Dr Frieda Granot, Associate Dean

MacKenzie King Open Scholarship

Subjects: Any subject.

Eligibility: Open to graduates of any Canadian university. Applicants should be persons of unusual worth or promise. Awards are determined on the basis of academic achievement, personal qualities and demonstrated aptitudes. Consideration is also given to the applicant's proposed programme of postgraduate study.

Type: Travel Grant.

No. of awards offered: One.

Frequency: Annual.

Value: C$8,000.

Length of Study: One year.

Country of Study: Canada or elsewhere.

Closing Date: February 1st.

Additional Information: Applications must be submitted to the dean of graduate studies at the Canadian university from which the candidate most recently graduated.

For further information contact:
MacKenzie King Scholarship Trust, 180-63H Crescent Road, Vancouver, V6T 1Z2, Canada
Tel: 604 822 4556
Fax: 604 822 5802
Email: schmiesi@mercury.ubc.ca
Contact: Ms Suzann Schmiering, Award Administrator

MacKenzie King Travelling Scholarships

Subjects: International or industrial relations, including the international or industrial aspects of law, history, politics and economics.

Eligibility: Open to graduates of any Canadian university who propose to engage in postgraduate studies in the given fields.

Purpose: To give Canadian students the opportunity to broaden their outlook and sympathies and contribute in some measure to the understanding of the problems and policies of other countries.

No. of awards offered: Four to six months.

Frequency: Annual.

Value: C$13,000.

Study Establishment: Suitable institutions.

Country of Study: USA or UK.

Applications Procedure: Applications must be sumitted to the dean of

graduate studies at the Canadian university from which the candidate most recently graduated.

Closing Date: February 1st.

MACQUARIE HILL SAMUEL GRADUATE MANAGEMENT FOUNDATION

Macquarie Hill Samuel Graduate Management Foundation, Box H68, Australia Square, Sydney, NSW, 2000, Australia
Tel: 237 3333
Fax: 237 4090
Contact: The Secretariat

*Macquarie Hill Samuel Graduate Management Scholarship

Subjects: Business administration.

Eligibility: Open to citizens or permanent residents of Australia or New Zealand who have work experience which reflects management expertise or potential; who indicate a firm intention to reside in Australia or New Zealand within a reasonable period after completion of the course; and who are bona fide candidates for full-time study on an MBA course at an institution approved by the Trustees. The applicants must not have yet commenced the relevant course on either a full- or part-time basis. Successful applicants will be required to attend initial and final interviews in Australia in November/December.

Purpose: To encourage and contribute to a higher standard of management education and to the effectiveness of Australasia's future managers.

Type: Scholarship.

No. of awards offered: One.

Frequency: Annual.

Value: US$22,500, payable over the study period.

Length of Study: A maximum of two years, the normal term of an MBA course.

Study Establishment: Any Business School.

Closing Date: Last Friday in October.

MAMMAL RESEARCH INSTITUTE

Mammal Research Institute, University of Pretoria, Pretoria, 0002, South Africa
Tel: 27 112 420 2066
Fax: 27 112 420 2534
Email: JSkinner@scientia.kp.ac.za
Contact: Director

Postdoctoral Bursaries

Subjects: The physiology, ecology, ethology and systematics of South African mammals.

Eligibility: Open to South African and foreign scientists and students holding a PhD degree from universities other than Pretoria.

Level of Study: Postdoctorate.

Purpose: To further research.

Type: Bursary.

No. of awards offered: Varies.

Frequency: Annually; dependent on funds available.

Value: R20,000-R45,000 per annum. A part or the whole of running expenses may also be paid.

Length of Study: One year; renewable up to two years.

Study Establishment: The Institute.

Country of Study: South Africa.

Applications Procedure: Applicants should submit a full CV, transcript of academic record, list of publications, and names of referees together with their application.

Closing Date: March 31st of the year of the award.

MANHATTAN SCHOOL OF MUSIC

Manhattan School of Music, 120 Claremont Avenue, New York, NY, 10027, USA
Tel: 212 749 2802 ext.449
Fax: 212 749 5471
Contact: Amy A Anderson

Music Scholarships

Subjects: Professional music study at the bachelor's, master's and doctoral levels.

Eligibility: Open to all students who demonstrate through performance that they have attained excellence in the field of music and have the capacity for further development.

Level of Study: Unrestricted.

Purpose: To recognize outstanding talent, achievements and performance.

Type: Travel Grant.

No. of awards offered: 400.

Frequency: Annual.

Value: Tuition expenses only; awards range from US$1,000 to full tuition costs, payable in equal instalments by semester.

Length of Study: One academic year; renewable for a total of four years (undergraduates) or two years (graduates).

Study Establishment: At the School.

Country of Study: USA.

Applications Procedure: For US/permanent residents, PROFILE form and FAFSA. For international students 'International Application for MSM Scholarship' in house form.

Closing Date: March 15th for March auditions, April 15th for May auditions.

Additional Information: Students must demonstrate financial need and provide the necessary income documents in order to qualify.

MANIPUR UNIVERSITY

Manipur University, Canchipur, Imphal, Manipur, 795003, India
Tel: 220787,221429
Contact: Shri Th. Joychandra Singh, Registrar

Govt. of Manipur Research Fellowship

Eligibility: The scholar should not be in receipt or any other award, scholarship/fellowship from any other source.

Purpose: To support research in science subjects under PhD program.

Type: Fellowship.

No. of awards offered: 11.

Frequency: Annual.

Value: Rs800 (Rupees) per month - Fellowship. Rs2000 (Rupees) per month -Contingency.

Length of Study: Maximum three years.

Study Establishment: Manipur University.

Country of Study: India.

Applications Procedure: Advertisement is made during November-December every year. Applications should be addressed to The Director, Science, Techology and Environment Department, Imphal -785001, India.

Closing Date: One month after advertisement.

Manipur University Scholar

Eligibility: The scholar should not be in receipt of any other awards, scholarship/fellowship from any other source.

Level of Study: Doctorate.

Purpose: For research under the M.Phil/PhD programmes.

Type: Scholarship.

No. of awards offered: One in each department.

Frequency: Annual.

Value: Rs500 (Rupees) per month.

Length of Study: Two years.

Study Establishment: Manipur University.

Country of Study: India.

Applications Procedure: After expiry of the tenure of scholarship offered to the previous awardee, the university calls applications in plain paper from M.Phil/PhD students during any month of the year.

Closing Date: Generally about one month from the date of notice of award applications.

Additional Information: Information can be obtained from the information officer at the university.

THE KATHERINE MANSFIELD MEMORIAL FELLOWSHIP TRUST

Creative New Zealand, PO Box 3806, Wellington, New Zealand
Tel: 04 473 0880
Fax: 04 471 2865
Contact: Administrator, Programmes

The Katherine Mansfield Memorial Fellowship

Subjects: Writing.

Eligibility: Open to writers who are New Zealand citizens.

Purpose: To enable a New Zealand writer to work in Menton, France.

Type: Fellowship.

No. of awards offered: One.

Frequency: Annual.

Value: NZ$36,000.

Length of Study: For not less than four months.

Country of Study: France.

Closing Date: July 31st.

Additional Information: The Fellowship is sponsored by the Electricity Corporation of New Zealand Ltd.

MARCH OF DIMES BIRTH DEFECTS FOUNDATION

March of Dimes Birth Defects Foundation, 1275 Mamaroneck Avenue, White Plains, NY, 10605, USA
Tel: 914 997 4552
Fax: 914 997 4560
Contact: Grants Administration

Basil O'Connor Starter Scholar Research Award Program

Subjects: The research interests of the Foundation include the broader aspects of pregnancy outcome, i.e. factors underlying the birth and survival of a healthy infant; the cognitive development of low birthweight infants; as well as the function of chromosomes, their subunits, genes, supporting structures and the like.

Eligibility: Open to young investigators (MDs or PhDs) who are interested in embarking an independent research after completion of their doctoral and postdoctoral training.

Purpose: To encourage research into the prevention of birth defects. The Foundation defines birth defects as an abnormality of structure, function or metabolism, whether genetically determined or as a result of environmental interference during embryonic or fetal life. A congenital defect may cause disease from the time of conception through birth or later in life.

Type: Research award.

No. of awards offered: Varies.

Frequency: Annual.

Value: US$40,000.

Study Establishment: An appropriate institution.

Applications Procedure: Candidates interested in this program should submit a brief abstract, a copy of their curriculum vitae with a covering letter mentioning the BOC program and a letter of nomination, written by the chairman of the department, director of the institute, the dean, or an equivalent person. The Foundation will respond indicating whether he/she qualifies administratively for this program, or, if not, whether he/she should apply to one of the Foundation's other research programs. Please note that BOC applicants may not submit an application simultaneously for another MOD research grant program.

Closing Date: Abstract due by February 28th, application due by May 31st.

Research Grants

Subjects: Research subjects include, basic biological phenomena governing development, genetics, clinical studies, studies of reproductive health, environmental toxicology, and social and behavioral studies.

Eligibility: Open to qualified scientists from universities, hospitals and research institutions.

Purpose: Research into birth defects.

Type: Several different types previously known as Clinical, Basic and Social and behavioral are now together under this one heading, Research Grant.

Applications Procedure: Each potential applicant will write a letter of intent (in quadruplicate, limited to two pages) addressed to the vice-president for research, and also include two copies of CV.

Closing Date: September 30th.

MARINE CORPS HISTORICAL CENTER

History and Museums Division, Marine Corps Historical Center, Building 58, Washington Navy Yard, Washington, DC, 20734-0580, USA
Tel: 202 433 3839
Fax: 202 433 7265
Contact: Benis M Frank, Chief Historian

College Internships; Dissertation Fellowships; Masters Thesis Fellowships; Research Grants

Subjects: Topics in US military and naval history, as well as history and history-based studies in the social and behavioral sciences, with a direct relationship to the history of the US Marine Corps.

Eligibility: Open to students enrolled in programs at the appropriate academic level at recognized institutions. Other requirements may apply. Dissertation Fellowships and Masters Thesis Fellowships are restricted to US citizens.

Level of Study: Postgraduate, Doctorate.

Type: Internships, Dissertation Fellowships, Masters Thesis Fellowships, Research Grants.

Applications Procedure: Application form and other documentation required.

JOHN AND MARY R MARKLE FOUNDATION

John and Mary R Markle Foundation, 75 Rockefeller Plaza, Suite 1800, New York, NY, 10019, USA
Tel: 212 489 6655
Fax: 212 765 9690
Email: info@markle.org
Contact: Tracie L Sullivan, Grants Manager

Grants

Subjects: The current program of the Markle Foundation is focused on the following areas: the potential of communications and information technologies to enhance political participation; developments in interactive communications technology; and analysis of issues of public policy and public interest in the communications field.

Eligibility: Open to suitably qualified investigators.

Purpose: The purpose of the Foundation's program is the improvement of all media including services growing out of new technologies for the processing and transfer of information.

No. of awards offered: Varies.

Frequency: Three times yearly.

Value: Varies.

Country of Study: There are no geographical restrictions, but most of the Foundation's work is in the USA.

Applications Procedure: Grant proposals may be submitted in an informal letter and must include the following: the purpose for which aid is sought, resources needed, personnel involved and a description of methods to be used in completing the project.

Closing Date: Proposals are evaluated any time during the year and awarded in March, June and November.

MARSHALL AID COMMEMORATION COMMISSION

British Embassy, 3100 Massachusetts Avenue, NW, Washington, DC, 20008, USA
Tel: 202 898 4407
Fax: 202 898 4612
Contact: Cultural Department

British Marshall Scholarships

Subjects: Any subject.

Eligibility: Open only to United States citizens. Must be graduates of four-year accredited US college/university course with a minimum GPA of 3.7. Maximum age limit of 26.

Level of Study: Postgraduate, Undergraduate.

Purpose: To enable United States graduates of high ability to study for a degree - at either postgraduate or undergraduate level - at any UK university.

Type: Scholarship.

No. of awards offered: Up to 40.

Frequency: Annual.

Value: About £15,000 per year (includes full tuition fees and living allowance).

Length of Study: Two to three years.

Study Establishment: Any UK university.

Country of Study: United Kingdom.

Applications Procedure: Applications submitted to (and prospectus available from) the British Embassy in Washington DC, or British Consulates in Boston, Chicago, Atlanta, and San Francisco.

Closing Date: October (in year preceding take up of award).

For further information contact:
Marshall Aid Commemoration Commission, Association of Commonwealth Universities, 36 Gordon Square, London, WC1H OPF, England
Tel: 0171 387 8572
Fax: 0171 387 2655
Contact: Assistant Secretary

Marshall Scholarships

Subjects: Any subject.

Eligibility: Open to US citizens, under 26 years of age, who have graduated with a minimum grade point average of 3.7 or A- from an accredited US college at the time of taking up the Scholarship. Recipients are required to take a degree at their UK university. Preference is given to candidates who combine high academic ability with the capacity to play an active part in the UK university.

Purpose: To provide intellectually distinguished young Americans with the opportunity to study in the UK and thus to understand and appreciate the British way of life.

Type: Scholarship.

No. of awards offered: 40.

Frequency: Annual.

Value: Approximately £13,500 per annum, which comprises tuition fees, residence, travel and related costs.

Length of Study: Two academic years; with possible extension for a third year.

Study Establishment: Any UK university.

Country of Study: UK.

Applications Procedure: Please submit application form, university/college endorsement, and two references.

Closing Date: October 15th.

Additional Information: Information and application forms may be obtained from: Mid-Eastern Region: Cultural Department, British Embassy, 3100 Massachusetts Avenue, NW, Washington DC 20008, USA; or from the following British Consulates-General: Mid-Western Region: 33 North Dearborn Street, Chicago, IL 60602, USA; North-Eastern Region:Federal Reserve Plaza, 600 Atlantic Avenue, Boston, MA 02210, USA; Pacific Region: 1 Sansome Street, San Francisco, CA 94104, USA; Southern Region: Suite 2700, Marquis One Tower, 245 Peachtree Center Avenue, Atlanta, GA 30303, USA.

HILDA MARTINDALE EDUCATIONAL TRUST

Hilda Martindale Educational Trust, c/o Registry, Royal Holloway University of London, Egham, Surrey, TW20 0EX, England
Tel: 01784 434455
Fax: 01784 437520
Contact: The Secretary

*Hilda Martindale Exhibitions

Subjects: Any vocational training for a career likely to be of value to the community.

Eligibility: Open to women of the British Isles.

Purpose: To help girls and women of the British Isles to fit themselves for a profession or career.

No. of awards offered: Approximately 20.

Frequency: Annual.

Value: Varies, normally £250-£1,000.

Length of Study: One year.

Country of Study: UK.

Closing Date: March 1st, for the following academic year.

MARYLAND INSTITUTE COLLEGE OF ART

Maryland Institute College of Art, 1300 W Mt Royal Ave, Baltimore, MD, 21217, USA
Tel: 410 225 2306
Fax: 410 669 9206
Contact: Dr Leslie King-Hammond, Dean of Graduate Studies

Coca-Cola National Fellows Program for the MFA in Studio for Art Educators

Subjects: Painting, printmaking, photography, drawing.

Eligibility: Open to art educators committed to teaching in urban public schools and districts with populations of large numbers of people of color.

Type: Fellowship.

No. of awards offered: Four.

Frequency: Annual.

Value: To cover the cost of independent studio space.

Length of Study: A 4-summer, 6-week residency, plus winter seminar/critique.

Country of Study: USA.

Closing Date: April 15th.

MICA Fellowship

Subjects: Arts.

Eligibility: TOFBC score 500. One international fellowship available.

Level of Study: Masters of Fine Arts.

Purpose: To serve as a tuition scholarship.

Type: Fellowship.

No. of awards offered: Six.

Frequency: Annual.

Value: US$10,000.

Length of Study: Two years.

Study Establishment: Maryland Institute College of Art.

Country of Study: USA.

Closing Date: March 1st.

MASSEY UNIVERSITY

Massey University, Private Bag 11-222, Palmerston North, New Zealand
Tel: 64 6 3505549
Fax: 64 6 3505603

Contact: The Scholarships Officer

Massey Doctoral Scholarship

Subjects: Agriculture, forestry and fishery; architecture and town planning; arts and humanities; business administration and management; education and teacher training; engineering; commercial law; media studies; mathematics and computer science; nursing; midwifery; natural sciences; social welfare and social work; environmental studies; religious studies; tourism; social and behavioural studies; air transport.

Eligibility: Minimum qualification of a first class honours degree.

Level of Study: Doctorate.

Purpose: For research towards a PhD degree.

Type: Scholarship.

No. of awards offered: 20-30.

Frequency: Annual.

Value: NZ$12,000 per year.

Length of Study: Three years.

Study Establishment: University.

Country of Study: New Zealand.

Applications Procedure: Application form must be completed.

Closing Date: October 1st and July 1st.

THE MATSUMAE INTERNATIONAL FOUNDATION

c/o Tokai University, Yoyogi Campus, Tomigaya , Shibuyu-ku, Tokyo, 151, Japan
Tel: 81 3 5453 0861
Fax: 81 3 5453 0810

Research Fellowship

Subjects: Engineering, mathematics, medicine, natural sciences and agriculture.

Eligibility: Open to applicants under 40 years of age, of non-Japanese nationality, who hold a doctorate or have two years research experience after receipt of a masters degree, and who have not been in Japan previously.

Level of Study: Postgraduate, Professional development.

Purpose: To provide the opportunity for foreign scientists to conduct research at Japanese institutions.

Type: Fellowship.

No. of awards offered: 20.

Frequency: Annual.

Value: Covers the cost of an air ticket, research stipend, personal accident/sickness insurance up to a total of 450,000 yen.

Length of Study: 3-6 months.

Study Establishment: Unrestricted.

Country of Study: Japan.

Applications Procedure: Applicants should obtain the current issue of the Fellowship announcement from the Foundation.

Closing Date: July 31st.

Additional Information: Priority will be given to fields of science, engineering and medicine.

MEDICAL LIBRARY ASSOCIATION

Medical Library Association, Suite 300, Six North Michigan Avenue, Chicago, IL, 60602-4805, USA
Tel: 312 419 9094

Fax: 312 419 8950
Email: MLAPD@MLAHQ.ORG
Contact: Professional Development Department

Continuing Education Grants

Subjects: The theoretical, administrative and technical aspects of library and information science.

Eligibility: Candidates must be US or Canadian citizens or permanent residents who are medical librarians with a graduate degree in library science and at least two years of work experience at the professional level.

Level of Study: Professional development.

Purpose: To provide professional health science librarians with the opportunity to continue their education.

Type: Fellowship.

No. of awards offered: One or more.

Frequency: Annual.

Value: US$100-US$500.

Length of Study: One year.

Country of Study: USA.

Applications Procedure: Completed application, references (3), must identify a continuing education program, not to support work towards a degree or certificate.

Closing Date: December 1st.

Additional Information: Candidates must be members of the Association.

Cunningham Memorial International Fellowship

Subjects: Medical librarianship.

Eligibility: Open to those with a baccalaureate degree and a library degree and working in a medical library. The applicant must furnish a signed statement from a home country official that he/she is guaranteed a position in a medical library upon returning home. A satisfactory score must be achieved on the TOEFL English competency examination. Excludes nationals of the USA or Canada.

Level of Study: Professional development.

Purpose: To provide a foreign medical librarian with the opportunity to observe and perform specialized work in the USA or Canada.

Type: Fellowship.

No. of awards offered: One.

Frequency: Annual.

Value: US$3,000 to cover living expenses and travel within the USA and Canada.

Length of Study: Four months.

Study Establishment: Medical libraries.

Country of Study: USA or Canada.

Applications Procedure: Please submit a completed application form, three letters of reference in English, project overview, certificate of health, TOEFL exam results, and audio or video tape.

Closing Date: December 1st.

Doctoral Fellowship

Subjects: Medical librarianship or information science.

Eligibility: Open to citizens or permanent residents of the USA or Canada who are graduates of an ALA-accredited library school and are in a PhD program with an emphasis on biomedical and health-related information science.

Level of Study: Doctorate.

Purpose: To encourage superior students to conduct doctoral work.

Type: Fellowship.

No. of awards offered: One.

Frequency: Annual.

Value: US$1,000.

Length of Study: One year; not renewable.

Country of Study: USA or Canada.

Applications Procedure: Please submit a completed application form, two letters of reference, transcripts of graduate work completed, summary of project and detailed budget, and signed statement of terms and conditions.

Closing Date: December 1st.

Additional Information: The award supports research or travel applicable to the candidate's study and may not be used for tuition. The award is sponsored by the Institute for Scientific Information.

Research, Development and Demonstration Project Award

Subjects: Health science librarianship and the information sciences.

Eligibility: Open to members of the Association who have a graduate degree in library science, are practising medical librarians with at least two years' experience at the professional level, and are citizens or permanent residents of the USA or Canada.

Purpose: To provide medical librarians with the opportunity to promote excellence in their field.

Type: Award.

No. of awards offered: One or more.

Frequency: Annual.

Value: US$100-US$1,000.

Length of Study: One year.

Country of Study: USA or Canada.

Applications Procedure: Completed application form, names of three references, detailed description of project design and budget.

Closing Date: December 1st.

Additional Information: Grants will not be given to support an activity which is operational in nature or has only local usefulness.

Scholarship for Minority Students

Subjects: Medical librarianship.

Eligibility: Open to Black, Hispanic, Asian, Pacific Island or Native American students who are entering an ALA-accredited library school and have at least one half of the academic requirements of the program to finish in the Scholarship year.

Level of Study: Graduate.

Purpose: To provide a minority student with the opportunity to begin or continue graduate study.

Type: Scholarship.

No. of awards offered: One.

Frequency: Annual.

Value: US$2,000.

Length of Study: One academic year.

Study Establishment: ALA-accredited library school.

Country of Study: USA or Canada.

Applications Procedure: Applicants should submit a completed application form, two letters of reference, official transcripts and a statement of career objectives.

Closing Date: December 1st.

THE MEDICAL MISSIONARY ASSOCIATION

The Medical Missionary Association, 157 Waterloo Road, London, SE1 8XN, England
Tel: 0171 829 4636
Fax: 0171 620 2453
Contact: Dr David Clegg

Grants

Subjects: Medical mission (Church related or Christian Healthcare).

Eligibility: Open to committed Christians who have spent at least one tour working in a mission/church-related medical post and who will be going back to continue this work for at least one further tour of three years, and to committed Christian medical students who are going to the Developing World for their elective period in a mission/church-related medical work.

Purpose: To assist doctors and nurses and other paramedicals who have served at least one tour in a mission/church-related medical post in the Developing World to gain a postgraduate qualification, or to assist Christian medical students to spend their elective in a mission/church-related hospital in the Developing World.

Type: Varies.

Frequency: Varies.

Value: Varies, usually reimbursement of fees and, for electives, assistance towards travel costs (approximately £150); dependent on funds available.

Country of Study: UK/Developing World countries.

Applications Procedure: Write for application form.

Closing Date: At least six months before the course is due to start.

Additional Information: Each request is discussed on its own merit.

MEDICAL RESEARCH COUNCIL

Medical Research Council, 20 Park Crescent, London, W1N 4AL, England
Tel: 0171 636 5422
Fax: 0171 636 3427
Email: rtcginfo@hq.mrc.ac.uk
Contact: Research Career Awards

Advanced Course Studentships

Subjects: Any science relevant to medicine.

Eligibility: Candidates should have graduated with a good honours degree. A copy of the regulations governing residence eligibility may be obtained from the Council.

Purpose: To enable graduates to take an approved postgraduate course of instruction.

Type: Studentship.

No. of awards offered: 45.

Frequency: Annual.

Value: To include a tax-free maintenance grant depending on location and nature of living accommodation, compulsory university and college fees, certain travel expenses, additional allowances for dependents in certain circumstances and allowances for older students and those with approved experience.

Length of Study: A period corresponding to the duration of the course.

Study Establishment: A recognized institution.

Country of Study: UK.

Applications Procedure: Applications must be made by heads of department on behalf of candidates. Awards are made only in respect of full-time courses. Applications for a quota of awards should be submitted by departments by October 1st.

For further information contact:
Medical Research Council, 20 Park Crescent, London, W1N 4AL,
England
Tel: 0171 636 5422
Fax: 0171 636 3427
Contact: Training Awards Group

Career Development Award

Subjects: Biomedical science.

Eligibility: Residence requirements apply. Details governing these criteria may be obtained from Research Career Awards, MRC.

Level of Study: Postdoctorate.

Purpose: To award outstanding scientists (non-clinical, postdoctoral) wishing to become independent investigators.

Type: Fellowship.

No. of awards offered: Ten.

Frequency: Annual.

Value: Appropriate academic salary plus support for technician.

Length of Study: Up to four years.

Country of Study: Tenable in UK for up to four years, including one year in a recognized research establishment overseas or in UK industry.

Applications Procedure: Personal application. Forms and further details are available from MRC.

Closing Date: February.

Clinical Scientist Fellowship

Subjects: Biomedical science.

Eligibility: Open to nationals of any country.

Level of Study: Medical/dental.

Purpose: To provide the opportunity for clinicians to apply their research training in basic science to clinical problems.

Type: Fellowship.

Frequency: Annual.

Value: Comprises salary at appropriate point on clinical academic scale plus support for technician.

Length of Study: Up to four years.

Country of Study: Tenable in UK for up to four years, including one year in a recognized research establishment or in UK industry.

Applications Procedure: Personal application. Form and further details can be obtained from MRC.

Closing Date: September.

Clinical Training Fellowships

Subjects: Biomedical sciences.

Eligibility: Residence requirements apply. Details governing these criteria may be obtained from MRC.

Level of Study: Postgraduate.

Purpose: To enable medical and dental graduates, at any stage of their careers up to and including senior registrar, lecturer or equivalent levels, and science graduates with postgraduate experience up to lecturer or equivalent level, to gain specialized research training.

Type: Fellowship.

Frequency: Twice a year.

Value: Appropriate point on current NHS or university lecturer scale.

Length of Study: Up to three years.

Study Establishment: A suitable university department or similar institution.

Country of Study: UK.

Applications Procedure: Personal application. Forms and further details are available from MRC.

Closing Date: February/October.

Research Fellowship

Subjects: Biomedical sciences.

Eligibility: Residence requirements apply. Details governing these criteria may be obtained from MRC.

Level of Study: Postdoctorate.

Purpose: To enable science graduates to gain postdoctoral specialized research training in the UK.

Type: Fellowship.

No. of awards offered: c.10.

Frequency: Annual.

Value: Appropriate academic salary.

Length of Study: Up to three years.

Country of Study: UK.

Applications Procedure: Personal application. Form and further details are available from MRC.

Closing Date: February.

Research Studentships

Subjects: Any biomedical science.

Eligibility: Candidates should have graduated with a good honours degree. A copy of the regulations governing residence eligibility may be obtained from the Council.

Level of Study: Postgraduate.

Purpose: To enable individuals of special promise to receive full-time training in research methods in a biomedical field under suitable direction.

No. of awards offered: 220.

Frequency: Annual.

Value: To include a tax-free maintenance grant depending on location and nature of living accommodation, compulsory university and college fees, certain travel expenses, additional allowances for dependents in certain circumstances and allowances for older students and those with approved experience. In addition, a support grant is paid to the university as a contribution towards the incidental departmental costs incurred in the student's training.

Length of Study: Up to othree years.

Study Establishment: A recognized institution.

Country of Study: UK.

Applications Procedure: Applications must be made by heads of department on behalf of candidates. Applications for a quota of awards should be submitted by departments by the beginning of October. Application forms are available from July.

Closing Date: October 1st.

For further information contact:
Medical Research Council, 20 Park Crescent, London, W1N 4AL,
England
Tel: 0171 636 5422
Fax: 0171 636 3427
Email: rfcginfo@hq.mrc.ac.uk
www: http//www.mrc.ac.uk/mrc/
Contact: Training Awards Group

Senior Fellowship (clinical)

Subjects: Biomedical science.

Eligibility: Open to nationals of any country.

Level of Study: Postdoctorate.

Purpose: To provide support for clinical/dental graduates of exceptional ability who wish to concentrate on research before possibly taking up a permanent teaching appointment.

Type: Fellowship.

No. of awards offered: Two.

Frequency: Annual.

Value: Appropriate point of clinical academic scale plus support for post-doc/technician, consumables and some equipment.

Length of Study: Up to five years.

Country of Study: UK.

Applications Procedure: Personal application. Forms and further details are available from MRC.

Closing Date: September.

Additional Information: Possibility of a further five years of funding (renewal through open competition).

Senior Fellowship (non-clinical)

Subjects: Biomedical sciences.

Eligibility: Open to nationals of any country.

Level of Study: Postdoctorate.

Purpose: To provide support for non-clinical scientists of exceptional ability who are well qualified for academic or research careers.

Type: Fellowship.

No. of awards offered: c.10.

Frequency: Annual.

Value: Appropriate academic salary plus support for technician/postdoc, consumables and some equipment.

Length of Study: Up to five years.

Country of Study: UK.

Applications Procedure: Personal application. Forms and further details are available from MRC.

Closing Date: February.

Additional Information: Possibility of a further five years funding (renewal through open competition).

Travelling Fellowships

Subjects: Biomedical science.

Eligibility: Open to UK candidates who are either medically or dentally qualified and presently holding appointments of status comparable with that of NHS registrar, or senior registrar; or scientifically qualified with a PhD degree, preferably with two years' postdoctoral experience. A copy of the regulations governing residence eligibility may be obtained from the Council.

Level of Study: Postdoctorate.

Purpose: To enable clinical and non-clinical research workers in the bio-medical field to undertake a period of advanced specialized research training overseas.

Type: A variable number of Medical Research Council Travelling Fellowships, one French Fellowship, and one nomination for the Lilly International Fellowship Program.

No. of awards offered: Varies.

Frequency: Annual.

Value: Stipends are based on the appropriate UK university or NHS basic salary level, and will include a cost of living allowance, depending on circumstances and place of tenure. Stipends normally remain fixed for the duration of the Fellowship. Travel expenses are paid for the Fellow and spouse and/or children when the award is for one year; an internal travel allowance is paid for the Fellow only.

Length of Study: Up to a maximum of 12 months.

Study Establishment: Any recognized research or academic institution outside the UK.

Country of Study: Any country outside the UK.

Applications Procedure: Personal application in open competition. Forms and further details are available from the MRC.

Closing Date: March 1st (future of competition is currently under review).

Additional Information: Applicants should make the necessary provisional arrangements with the intended host institution prior to submitting an application. On the conclusion of awards, all Fellows must submit a short report on their activities and have an appointment to be taken up on return to the UK.

MEET THE COMPOSER, INC

Meet The Composer, Inc., 2112 Broadway, Suite 505, New York, NY, 10023, USA
Tel: 212 787 3601
Contact: Theodore Wiprud, Senior Program Manager

Commissioning Music/USA

Purpose: Supports the commissioning of new works by American composers in orchestral, chamber, opera, music theatre, choral, jazz, experimental and avant garde music.

Country of Study: USA.

Applications Procedure: Call or write to Meet The Composer for program deadlines and application materials.

Composer/Choreographer Project

Eligibility: Commissioned composers and choreographers must be citizens or permanent residents of the USA.

Purpose: Awards grants to American dance companies to commission collaborative works by composers and choreographers.

Country of Study: USA.

Applications Procedure: Call or write to Meet The Composer for program deadlines and application materials.

International Creative Collaborations

Eligibility: Experience in commissioning new work and familiarity with international exchange are required.

Purpose: Funds three year collaborations between USA based composers, choreographers, and dramatists, and their counterparts in Asia, Africa and Latin America.

Length of Study: Three years.

Country of Study: USA.

Applications Procedure: Call or write to Meet The Composer for program deadlines and applications.

New Residencies

Subjects: Works to celebrate local culture, organizing cultural events, teaching and making public appearances.

Level of Study: Professional development.

Purpose: Places composers in service to communities by creating residencies based in partnerships between arts organizations and community or human development agencies.

Type: Residencies.

Length of Study: Three years.

Country of Study: USA.

Applications Procedure: Call or write to Meet The Composer for program deadlines and application materials.

Additional Information: Applications to all Meet The Composer programs are submitted by non-profit organizations sponsoring individual composers.

NYC Composers Aids Fund

Purpose: Assists composers in the New York City area who, due to illness with HIV/AIDS and lack of adequate financial resources, need emergency financial assistance to complete specific musical projects.

Country of Study: USA.

Applications Procedure: Call or write to Meet The Composer for program deadlines and application materials.

THE GOLDA MEIR MOUNT CARMEL INTERNATIONAL TRAINING CENTRE

The Golda Meir Mount Carmel International Training Centre, PO Box 6111, Haifa, 31060, Israel
Tel: 972 4 8375904
Fax: 972 4 8375913
Email: MCTCI@actcom.co.il
Contact: Fannette Modek

Assistance for Courses

Subjects: Courses in community organization and management of human services; pre-school education; organization and management of income-generating projects and small-scale industries.

Eligibility: Open mainly to women aged 25-45 from developing countries. Male students are also accepted. Participants must have completed at least twelve years of schooling, have undergone relevant professional training, and have work experience. A good knowledge of the language in which the course will be given is essential.

Level of Study: Postgraduate, Professional development.

Purpose: To assist developing countries in training personnel engaged in community work.

No. of awards offered: 28 places on each course.

Frequency: Annual.

Value: Tuition, lodging and board, plus a monthly pocket money allowance, are covered by international fellowships.

Length of Study: 4 and 8 weeks, accordingly.

Study Establishment: The Centre.

Country of Study: Israel.

Applications Procedure: For admission to the course, candidates should apply to the Israeli diplomatic representative in their country.

Closing Date: Three months prior to commencement of the course.

Additional Information: Courses are given in English, French or Spanish and include lectures, discussion groups, study tours and fieldwork.

Tuition and Maintenance Scholarships

Eligibility: Open to nationals of developing countries and transitional societies.

Level of Study: Postgraduate, Professional development.

Purpose: Human resource development.

Type: Tuition and maintenance scholarships.

Frequency: Annual.

Value: $2,800 per month.

Length of Study: 4 or 8 weeks.

Study Establishment: The Centre.

Country of Study: Israel.

Applications Procedure: Application form must be completed (to include health form and copies of diplomas). These can be obtained from nearest Israel diplomatic representative.

Closing Date: Three months prior to course opening.

PAUL MELLON CENTRE FOR STUDIES IN BRITISH ART, LONDON

Paul Mellon Centre for Studies in British Art, 16 Bedford Square, London, WC1B 3JA, England
Email: bacinfo@minerva.cis.yale.edu
www: www.cis.yale.edu/yups/bac/entrance.html
Contact: Director

Paul Mellon Centre Fellowship

Subjects: Any aspect of British art, including architecture, before 1960.

Eligibility: Open to candidates of any nationality who are graduates of, or currently enrolled in a graduate program at, a US university. They must be ordinarily resident outside Britain. Graduates of US universities who are enrolled elsewhere or who are pursuing more advanced research in the field may also be considered.

Level of Study: Postgraduate.

Type: Fellowship.

No. of awards offered: One.

Frequency: Annual.

Value: US$13,000 and return airfare from the USA plus travelling expenses within the UK of up to US$500.

Length of Study: One academic year.

Country of Study: UK.

Closing Date: January 31st.

MEMORIAL FOUNDATION FOR JEWISH CULTURE

Memorial Foundation for Jewish Culture, Room 1703, 15 East 26th Street, New York, NY, 10010, USA
Contact: Executive Vice President

International Doctoral Scholarships

Subjects: Jewish studies.

Eligibility: Open to graduate students of any nationality who are specializing in a Jewish field and are officially enrolled or registered in a doctoral program at a recognized university.

Level of Study: Doctorate.

Purpose: To assist in the training of future Jewish scholars for careers in Jewish scholarship and research, and to enable religious, educational and other Jewish communal workers to obtain advanced training for leadership positions.

Type: Scholarship.

No. of awards offered: Varies.

Frequency: Annual.

Value: Varies depending on the country where study is undertaken; usually between US$2,000 and US$5,000 per annum.

Length of Study: One academic year; renewable for a maximum of four years.

Study Establishment: A recognized university.

Country of Study: Any country.

Applications Procedure: Applicants must write requesting an application.

Closing Date: October 31st.

International Fellowships in Jewish Studies

Subjects: A field of Jewish specialization which will make a significant contribution to the understanding, preservation, enhancement or transmission of Jewish culture.

Eligibility: Open to recognized and/or qualified scholars, researchers or artists of any nationality who possess the knowledge and experience to formulate and implement a project in a field of Jewish specialization.

Purpose: To assist well-qualified individuals to carry out independent scholarly, literary or artistic projects.

Type: Fellowship.

No. of awards offered: Varies.

Frequency: Annual.

Value: Variable, depending on the country in which the project is undertaken; usually US$1,000-US$4,000.

Length of Study: One academic year; renewable for one additional year in exceptional cases.

Country of Study: Any country.

Applications Procedure: Applicants must write requesting an application.

Closing Date: October 31st.

International Scholarship Program for Community Service

Subjects: The rabbinate; Jewish education; communal service or religious functionaries, e.g. shohatim, mohalim.

Eligibility: Open to any individual, regardless of country of origin, who is presently receiving, or plans to undertake training in his or her chosen field in a recognized Yeshiva, teacher training seminary, school of social work, university or other educational institution.

Purpose: To assist well-qualified individuals for career training.

Type: Scholarship.

No. of awards offered: Varies.

Frequency: Annual.

Value: Varies, depending on the country in which the recipient is trained and other considerations; usually US$1,000-US$4,000.

Length of Study: One year; renewable.

Study Establishment: In diaspora Jewish communities in need of such personnel.

Country of Study: Any country except the USA, Canada or Israel.

Closing Date: November 30th.

Additional Information: Recipients must commit themselves to serve a community of need. They should also be knowledgeable in the language and culture of that country or be prepared to learn it.

Scholarships for Post-Rabbinical Students

Subjects: Jewish studies.

Eligibility: Open to a recently ordained rabbi engaged in full-time studies at a Yeshiva, Kollel or rabbinical seminary.

Purpose: To assist in the training of future Jewish religious scholars and leaders, and to help newly ordained rabbis obtain advanced training for careers as head of Yeshivot, as Dayanim and in other leadership positions.

Type: Scholarship.

No. of awards offered: Varies.

Frequency: Annual.

Value: US$1,000-US$4,000.

Length of Study: One year.

Country of Study: Any country.

Closing Date: November 30th.

Additional Information: The following Institutional Support Programs are also available: Grants for Jewish Research and Publication: Grants are awarded to universities and recognized scholarly bodies for research and publication in Jewish fields; to universities and Jewish educational organizations for the preparation of textbooks and educational literature for children and youth. The Foundation also provides grants to bolster Jewish educational programs in areas of need. Grants are awarded on the understanding that the recipient institution will assume responsibility for the program following the initial limited period of Foundation support. Grants are made only for team or collaborative projects.

MENDELSSOHN SCHOLARSHIP FOUNDATION

Mendelssohn Scholarship Foundation, c/o Royal Academy of Music, Marylebone Road, London, NW1 5HT, England
Contact: Jean Shannon, Honorary Secretary

Mendelssohn Scholarship

Subjects: Musical composition.

Eligibility: Open to music students of any nationality under 30 years of age who are resident in the UK or Republic of Ireland.

Level of Study: Postgraduate.

Purpose: To enable postgraduate students to pursue their study.

Type: Scholarship.

No. of awards offered: One.

Frequency: Biennially (next in 1997).

Value: £5,000.

Country of Study: Unrestricted.

Applications Procedure: Application form must be completed and submitted with photocopy of applicant's birth certificate.

Closing Date: Usually first half of March in the Scholarship year.

Additional Information: Candidates compete for the Scholarship by submitting up to three compositions, which are assessed by independent judges. There is a small entrance fee for the competition.

SIR ROBERT MENZIES CENTRE FOR AUSTRALIAN STUDIES

Sir Robert Menzies Centre for Australian Studies, 28 Russell Square, London, WC1B 5DS, England
Tel: 0171 580 5876
Fax: 0171 580 9627
Email: k.mcintyre@sas.ac.uk
Contact: Kirsten McIntyre

Australian Bicentennial Scholarships and Fellowships

Subjects: Any subject.

Eligibility: Scholarship: open to candidates registered as a postgraduate student at a British tertiary institution or eligible for registration at an Australian tertiary institution and usually resident in the UK. Fellowship: open to holders of a good postgraduate degree or relevant experience who are seeking to further their education or professional experience but not through taking a further degree.

Level of Study: Postgraduate, Postdoctorate.

Purpose: To promote scholarship, intellectual links and mutual awareness and understanding between the UK and Australia and to enable UK graduates to study in approved courses or undertake approved research in Australia and to enable Australian graduates to study in approved courses to undertake approved research in the UK. To make allowance for disadvantaged persons.

Type: 1-4 Scholarships and/or Fellowships in each direction.

Frequency: Annual.

Value: Up to £4,000.

Study Establishment: Any approved Australian tertiary institution (UK applicants) or in any approved UK tertiary institution (Australian applicants).

Country of Study: Australia or the UK.

Applications Procedure: Application form and three references must be submitted.

Closing Date: June 18th for UK applicants; October 29th for Australian applicants.

For further information contact:
Australian Vice-Chancellors' Committee, GPO Box 1142, Canberra, ACT, 2601, Australia
Tel: 06 285 8200
Fax: 06 285 8211
Contact: Mr F S Hambly

Northcote Graduate Scholarship

Subjects: Any subject.

Eligibility: Open to applicants resident in the UK who are under 30 years old.

Level of Study: Postgraduate.

Purpose: To enable students to undertake a higher degree at an Australian University.

Type: Scholarship.

No. of awards offered: Up to two.

Frequency: Annual.

Value: Allowance of A$17,427 per annum, plus return economy air fare and payment of compulsory fees.

Length of Study: Up to three years.

Study Establishment: Any approved Australian tertiary institution.

Country of Study: Australia.

Applications Procedure: Application form, two references, and letter of acceptance from Australian university must be submitted.

Closing Date: August 30th.

Northcote Visiting Scholarship Scheme

Subjects: Any.

Eligibility: Open to applicants under the age of 30, normally resident in the UK, who have registered for a higher degree at a British university.

Level of Study: Postgraduate.

Purpose: To assist students registered for a higher degree to travel to Australia and carry out research necessary for their dissertation.

Type: Scholarship.

No. of awards offered: Up to four.

Frequency: Annual.

Value: Up to £4,000 to cover the cost of a return economy-class fare and reasonable maintenance costs for a maximum of six months.

Study Establishment: At any approved Australian tertiary institution.

Country of Study: Australia.

Applications Procedure: Application form, two references, and a letter from proposed host university in Australia must be submitted.

Closing Date: May 10th.

Postgraduate Visiting Fellowship

Subjects: No restriction, but usually modern languages and literatures.

Level of Study: Postgraduate.

Purpose: To allow postgraduate students from European universities to travel to Britain to consult material essential to their research on Australian topics.

Type: Fellowship.

No. of awards offered: Up to two.

Frequency: Annual.

Value: £600.

Country of Study: UK.

Applications Procedure: Application form must be completed and two references submitted.

Closing Date: May 10th (variable).

Visiting Fellowships

Subjects: Any subject.

Eligibility: Applicants should teach courses with Australian content or be prepared to introduce a significant and on-going Australian component into their teaching at a UK university.

Level of Study: Professional development.

Purpose: To encourage the teaching of Australian Studies in the UK.

Type: Fellowship.

No. of awards offered: Four.

Frequency: Annual.

Value: Up to a maximum of £1,200.

Study Establishment: Any approved Australian tertiary institution.

Country of Study: Australia.

Applications Procedure: Application form, three references, and a letter of invitation from host university in Australia must be submitted.

Closing Date: May 10th (variable).

Visiting Fellowships - European

Subjects: Modern languages and literatures, political science and government, international relations, sociology, women's studies, area and cultural studies.

Eligibility: Applicants should take courses with Australian content or be prepared to introduce a significant and on-going Australian component into their teaching at a European university.

Level of Study: Professional development.

Purpose: To encourage the teaching of Australian studies in Europe.

Type: Fellowship.

No. of awards offered: Up to four.

Frequency: Annual.

Value: £600-£1,200.

Country of Study: Australia or UK.

Applications Procedure: Application must be completed and two/three references submitted.

Closing Date: May 10th (variable).

Visual Arts Fellowship

Subjects: Drawing and painting; sculpture; handicrafts; photography; design. Some interest and experience in landscape representation would be an advantage.

Eligibility: Open to UK citizens.

Level of Study: Postgraduate, Postdoctorate.

Purpose: For appropriately qualified UK candidates to take up a fellowship at the Western Australian Academy of Performing Arts, Edith Cowan University, Australia, and its regional centres.

Type: Fellowship.

No. of awards offered: One.

Frequency: Annual.

Value: Up to £4,000.

Length of Study: Minimum of three months.

Study Establishment: WAAPA, Edith Cowan University, Western Australia.

Country of Study: Australia.

Applications Procedure: Application form, three references, and six slides of work.

Closing Date: June 18th.

Additional Information: This award is run in conjunction with the Australian Bicentennial Scholarships & Fellowships scheme.

SIR ROBERT MENZIES MEMORIAL TRUST

The Menzies Foundation, 210 Clarendon Street, East Melbourne, Victoria, 3002, Australia
Fax: 039 417 7049
Email: menzies@vicnet.net.au
Contact: National Executive Officer

Menzies Memorial Scholarships in Law

Subjects: Law.

Eligibility: Open to Australian citizens of five years standing, or British subjects permanently resident in Australia who hold a recognized degree, normally from an Australian university.

Purpose: To enable Australian citizens or British subjects permanently resident in Australia to pursue postgraduate studies in the UK generally leading to a higher degree.

Type: Scholarship.

No. of awards offered: Two.

Frequency: Annual.

Value: Payment of tuition fees, or a research grant equivalent, examination and other compulsory fees; a grant of £300 for books and equipment in the first year and £150 in the second year; a grant of up to £120 towards the typing and binding of a thesis; a quarterly living allowance of £1,250 plus addditional allowance of £150 per month for spouse and £30 per month each for dependant children under 16. Return airfares.

Length of Study: Usually two academic years.

Study Establishment: The universities of St Andrews, Edinburgh, Cambridge or Oxford, or occasionally elsewhere.

Country of Study: UK.

Applications Procedure: Application form must be completed.

Closing Date: August 31st.

Additional Information: The Selection Committee will seek individuals who are likely to attain prominence in Australia and, in their subsequent careers, make a contribution to British-Australian relations and understanding.

METROPOLITAN MUSEUM OF ART

Metropolitan Museum of Art, 1000 Fifth Avenue, New York, NY, 10028-0198, USA
Contact: Internship Programs/Education

*Nine-Month Internship

Subjects: Art history, art administration, conservation or art education.

Eligibility: Open to disadvantaged, especially minority, New Yorkers who are graduating seniors, recent graduates or graduate students and intend to pursue careers in art museums.

Frequency: Annual.

Value: US$12,000.

Length of Study: Nine months from September to June.

Study Establishment: The Museum.

Country of Study: USA.

Closing Date: February 4th.

Additional Information: The award is part funded by the Edward and Sally Van Lier Fund at the New York Community Trust.

*Six-Month Internship

Subjects: Art history or related fields.

Eligibility: Open to Black, Hispanic and other minority students who are graduating college seniors, recent graduates or graduate students in art history or related fields, and who intend to pursue careers in art museums.

Type: Internship.

Frequency: Annual.

Value: US$8,000.

Length of Study: Six months from June to December.

Study Establishment: The Museum.

Country of Study: USA.

Closing Date: February 4th.

Additional Information: The award is part funded by the National Endowment for the Arts.

*Summer Internships for College Students

Subjects: Art history.

Eligibility: Open to college juniors, seniors and recent graduates who have not yet entered graduate school. Candidates should have a strong background in art history and intend to pursue careers in art museums.

Type: Internships.

No. of awards offered: 14.

Frequency: Annual.

Value: US$2,200.

Length of Study: Ten weeks from June to August.

Study Establishment: The Museum.

Country of Study: USA.

Closing Date: January 21st.

Additional Information: The award is funded by the Ittleson Foundation.

*Summer Internships for Graduate Students

Subjects: Art history or an allied field.

Eligibility: Open to individuals who have completed at least one year of graduate work in art history or an allied field and who intend to pursue careers in art museums.

Type: Internships.

Frequency: Annual.

Value: US$2,500.

Length of Study: Ten weeks from June to August.

Study Establishment: The Museum.

Country of Study: USA.

Closing Date: January 28th.

Additional Information: The award is part funded by the Ittleson Foundation and the National Endowment for the Arts.

MICHIGAN SOCIETY OF FELLOWS

University of Michigan, Michigan Society of Fellows, 3030 Rackham Building, Ann Arbor, MI, 48109-1070, USA

Tel: 313 763 1259
Email: lbriefer@umich.edu
Contact: Luan McCarty-Briefer

Postdoctoral Fellowship

Subjects: Open to all fields of the University of Michigan.

Eligibility: Applicants must have completed the PhD or comparable professional or artistic degree within three and a half years of appointment.

Level of Study: Postdoctorate.

Purpose: To provide financial and intellectual support for individuals selected for outstanding achievement, professional promise, and interdisciplinary interests. All Fellows are expected to be in residence in Ann Arbor during the academic years of the Fellowship.

Type: Fellowship.

No. of awards offered: Four.

Frequency: Annual.

Value: Stipend of US$32,500 annually from 1997-2000.

Length of Study: Three years.

Study Establishment: University of Michigan.

Country of Study: USA.

Applications Procedure: Application form must be completed; please write to request application materials.

MIGRAINE TRUST

Migraine Trust, 45 Great Ormond Street, London, WC1N 3HZ, England
Tel: 0171 278 2676
Fax: 0171 831 5174
Contact: Director

Grants-in-Aid

Subjects: All aspects of migraine.

Eligibility: Grants are awarded on merit and not according to predetermined criteria.

Purpose: To fund research into migraine.

No. of awards offered: Varies.

Frequency: Annual.

Value: Varies.

Length of Study: Up to three years.

Study Establishment: Approved universities or research institutions.

Country of Study: Worldwide.

Closing Date: April 30th.

Additional Information: Applicants should write for a grant application form in the first instance.

THE MILLAY COLONY FOR THE ARTS, INC

The Millay Colony for the Arts, Inc, East Hill Road, PO Box 3, Austerlitz, NY, 12017-0003, USA
Tel: 518 392 3103
Email: application@millaycolony.org
Contact: Executive Director

Residencies

Subjects: Visual arts; musical composition; creative writing.

Eligibility: Open to professional visual artists, composers and writers.

Type: Residency.

No. of awards offered: Five residencies per month (60 annually).

Frequency: Monthly.

Value: Room, board and studio space for one month. No fees. The Millay Colony does not provide financial assistance of any kind. However, as the Colony depends on gifts for its existence, contributions are welcomed.

Length of Study: One month.

Study Establishment: The Colony.

Country of Study: USA.

Applications Procedure: SASE required for application form or can be accessed by Email.

Additional Information: Decisions are made by committees of professional artists. The Millay Colony is set in the 600-acre Steepletop estate, a National Historic landmark which was the home of Edna St Vincent Millay.

MINISTÈRE DES AFFAIRES ÉTRANGÈRES

Bureau des Boursiers Français a l'Etranger, 244 boulevard Saint-Germain, Paris, 75303, France
Tel: 43 17 72 22
Fax: 43 17 97 57
Contact: Serge François

Lavoisier Award

Subjects: All fields.

Eligibility: Reserved to French nationals going overseas.

Level of Study: Postgraduate, Doctorate, Postdoctorate.

Purpose: To encourage scientific cooperation abroad.

Type: Scholarship.

No. of awards offered: 250.

Frequency: Dependent on funds available.

Value: Between 40,000 and 80,000FF per year, depending on the cost of living in the host country.

Length of Study: One year.

Study Establishment: Unrestricted.

Country of Study: Unrestricted.

Applications Procedure: Please write for application forms between October and February.

Closing Date: March 1st.

MINISTRY OF AGRICULTURE, FISHERIES AND FOOD

Ministry of Agriculture, Fisheries and Food (R105), Nobel House, 17 Smith Square, London, SW1P 3JR, England
Tel: 0171 238 5598
Fax: 0171 238 5597
Contact: Mrs Barbara Keller

Postgraduate Agricultural and Food Studentships

Subjects: Crop and animal production; horticulture; farm management; agricultural economics; agricultural and horticultural marketing and rural estate management; agriculture statistics; agriculture and dairy engineering, farm mechanism and building; agricultural science and agricultural extension: formal courses or research training. A few awards are available for research training in the applied aspects of food science.

Eligibility: Full studentships are open to UK and Commonwealth citizens who are normally resident in the UK for the three-year period prior

425

to the date of application for an award. Studentships are also open to EC nationals who are or have been in employment in the UK or who are children of an EC national whose current or (if unemployed) last previous employment was on the date of the application in the UK and who have been resident in the EC for the three-year period prior to the date of application.

Purpose: To further the education of agriculturists and food scientists.

No. of awards offered: Up to 78 Studentships (including 10 Cooperative Awards in Science and Engineering) are awarded to universities for research training leading to a PhD and advanced courses leading to an MSc.

Frequency: Annual.

Value: To cover compulsory fees, and, in certain circumstances, travelling expenses and dependants' allowance, as well as maintenance allowance of up to £7,072 per annum (London area) or £5,638 per annum (elsewhere) for students living in college, hostel or lodgings. (Allowances are subject to change.).

Length of Study: Up to 2 years; possibly renewable for a third year for research training.

Study Establishment: Universities, colleges and polytechnics only.

Country of Study: UK.

Applications Procedure: Applicants should enquire at the institution where they wish to undertake postgraduate study about the possibility of being nominated.

Closing Date: July 31st for the UK.

Additional Information: The Ministry considers applications in agricultural science which relate to the more applied aspects of the subject, including projects requiring industrial participation.

MINISTRY OF CULTURE AND EDUCATION

Ministry of Culture and Education, Sölvholsgata 4, 150 Reykjavik, Iceland
Tel: 3541 609000
Fax: 3541 623068
Contact: University Section

Scholarships

Subjects: Icelandic language, literature and history.

Eligibility: Some knowledge of Icelandic is essential. Beneficiary countries are decided each year by the Ministry. One or two scholarships are awarded to students of Icelandic origin from Canada or the USA.

Type: Scholarship.

No. of awards offered: Approximately 20.

Frequency: Annual.

Value: 400,000 kronur, plus free tuition.

Length of Study: 8 months.

Study Establishment: University of Iceland, Reykjavik.

Country of Study: Iceland.

Applications Procedure: Candidates should apply to the relevant government department in their own country. US candidates should apply to the Institute of International Education, 809 United Nations Plaza, New York, New York 10017. UK candidates should apply to the Icelandic Embassy, 1 Eaton Terrace, London SW1. Candidates of Icelandic origin from Canada or the US should apply to the Icelandic National League, 699 Carter Avenue, Winnipeg, Manitoba R3M 2C3, Canada.

Closing Date: Nomination of candidates must reach the Ministry of Culture and Education, Iceland, before May 15th.

426

MINISTRY OF CULTURE AND PUBLIC EDUCATION

Embassy of the Republic of Hungary, 17 Beale Crescent, Deakin, ACT, 2600, Australia
Tel: 06 282 3226
Fax: 06 285 3012

*Hungarian Government Scholarships

Subjects: Music, fine arts or dance (advanced studies); or any subject (postgraduate study or research).

Eligibility: Open to Australian citizens who are graduates of an Australian tertiary institution; however, outstanding musicians, artists and dancers without tertiary qualifications will also be considered.

Type: Scholarship.

No. of awards offered: Limited.

Frequency: Annual.

Value: A monthly living allowance of 4,000 forints, payment of compulsory fees, free medical treatment, approved internal travel, and suitable accommodation.

Length of Study: Three to six months.

Country of Study: Hungary.

Closing Date: April 28th.

MINISTRY OF EDUCATION

Embassy of Greece, Cultural Department, 1a Holland Park, London, W11 3TP, England
Tel: 0171 229 3850
Fax: 0171 229 7221

Scholarships for British Students

Subjects: All disciplines.

Eligibility: Open to UK nationals who hold at least a bachelor's degree. Candidates graduating during the year of application will be considered.

Level of Study: Postgraduate, Doctorate, Postdoctorate.

Purpose: To pursue postgraduate research.

Type: Scholarship.

No. of awards offered: A maximum of ten.

Frequency: Annual.

Value: 100,000 drachmas monthly plus 20,000 drachmas to meet expenses on first arrival (or 30,000 for those who will settle out of Athens), plus 30,000 drachmas for scholars requiring to travel within Greece for their research.

Study Establishment: At any university or institution of higher education in Greece.

Country of Study: Greece.

Applications Procedure: Application forms may be requested from January.

Closing Date: 15 March.

Additional Information: Scholars are strongly recommended to acquire at least an elementary knowledge of modern Greek.

MINISTRY OF FOREIGN AFFAIRS (FRANCE)

French Embassy, 6 Perth Avenue, Yarralumla, ACT, 2600, Australia
Tel: 06 216 0137
Fax: 06 216 0156
Contact: Linguistic Service

*Bursaries

Subjects: Scientific topics: priority is given to environment, astronomy and biology.

Eligibility: Open to Australian citizens aged between 25 and 45. The candidates must provide evidence of an invitation from a French laboratory.

Purpose: To enable an Australian to have a training period in a French laboratory or research organization.

Type: Bursary.

No. of awards offered: Six.

Frequency: Annual.

Value: FF4,550-FF5,350 per month. Air fare is sometimes provided.

Length of Study: Three to six months.

Study Establishment: A laboratory, university, research center, or similar institution.

Country of Study: France.

Closing Date: June 30th.

*Visiting Senior Scientist Award

Subjects: Scientific topics: priority is given to environment, biology, geology, astronomy.

Eligibility: Open to Australian citizens or permanent residents at the postdoctoral level. The candidate must provide evidence of an invitation from a French laboratory.

Purpose: To enable a highly skilled research director to pursue research in a French host laboratory.

No. of awards offered: Four.

Frequency: Annual.

Value: FF8,000-FF12,000 per month. Air fare is not provided.

Length of Study: Three months to one year.

Study Establishment: A research organization or university laboratory.

Country of Study: France.

Closing Date: March/April.

Additional Information: The project must be in the context of French-Australian scientific cooperation.

MINNESOTA HISTORICAL SOCIETY

Minnesota Historical Society, Research Department, 345 Kellogg Bird West, St Paul, MN, 55102, USA
Tel: 612 297 4464
Fax: 612 297 1345
Contact: Deborah L. Miller

Minnesota Historical Society Research Grant

Eligibility: Facility with reading and writing English is necessary..

Level of Study: Unrestricted.

Purpose: To support original research and interpretive writing on the history of Minnesota by academicians, independent scholars and professional and non professional writers.

Type: Research support.

No. of awards offered: Varies.

Frequency: Dependent on funds available, three times per year.

Value: Varies, up to US$1,500 for research that will result in an article or up to US$5,000 for research that will result in a book.

Length of Study: Varies.

Country of Study: Varies.

Applications Procedure: Application form must be completed; other documentation is also required.

Closing Date: January 1st, March 1st, October 1st.

Additional Information: Guidelines and applications are available by writing to the given address.

MINTEK

Human Resources Division, Mintek, Private Bag X3015, Randburg, 2125, South Africa
Tel: 27 11 709 4111
Fax: 27 11 793 2413

*Bursaries

Subjects: Chemical engineering; electrical engineering (light current and electronics); metallurgical engineering; chemistry (with the emphasis on inorganic, physical, or analytical chemistry); metallurgy (extraction and physical); mineralogy; geology or physics.

Eligibility: Open to graduates of any nationality who possess an appropriate four-year degree or higher qualification. A knowledge of English is essential.

Level of Study: Postgraduate.

Purpose: To promote the training of research workers for the minerals industry in general.

Type: Bursary.

No. of awards offered: Varies.

Value: R17,000 per annum for a MSc degree; R21,000 per annum for a PhD degree (no commitment).

Length of Study: Up to two years; extension of this period can be granted by the President of Mintek.

Study Establishment: Any university.

Country of Study: South Africa.

THE MITTAG-LEFFLER INSTITUTE

The Mittag-Leffler Institute, Auravägen 17, Djursholm, S-182 62, Sweden
Tel: 46 8 755 18 09
Fax: 46 8 622 05 89
Contact: Marie-Louise Koskull

Grants

Subjects: Mathematics: specific topics vary each year.

Eligibility: Open to recent PhDs and advanced graduate students. Preference will be given to applications for long stays.

Type: Grant.

No. of awards offered: Varies.

Frequency: Annual.

Value: 12,000 Swedish crowns per month, or 108,000 Swedish crowns for those who stay for the full duration of the program.

Length of Study: One academic year, from September to May.

Country of Study: Sweden.

Closing Date: March 31st.

MONASH UNIVERSITY

Monash University, Wellington Road, Clayton, Victoria, 3168, Australia
Tel: 61 3 565 3009
Fax: 61 3 565 5042
Email: Simon.Liddle@adm.monash.edu.au
www: http://www.monash.edu.au
Contact: PhD and Scholarships Branch

Logan Research Fellowships

Subjects: Any subject.

Eligibility: PhD plus between two to six years of postdoctoral research experience. Must have gained either PhD or two years of postdoctoral experience at an institution other than Monash University.

Level of Study: Postdoctorate.

Purpose: To attract outstanding researchers with two to six years postdoctoral research experience..

Type: Fellowship.

No. of awards offered: Five per annum.

Frequency: Annual.

Value: Salary of research fellowship level B (A$45,362) per annum or above, plus research support grants of between A$5,000 and A$20,000 per annum depending on the nature of the research. Return air fare provided.

Length of Study: Three years with the possibility of an additional three years.

Study Establishment: Monash University.

Country of Study: Australia.

Applications Procedure: Application forms and referees report forms.

Closing Date: February 28th.

Additional Information: Electronic lodgement of application is preferred.

For further information contact:
Monash University, Wellington Road, Clayton, Victoria, 3168, Australia
Tel: 9905 9016
Fax: 9905 3831
Email: http://www.monash.edu.au
Telex: Christina.Perrett@adm.Monash.edu.au
Contact: Christina Perrett

Sir James McNeill Foundation Postgraduate Scholarship

Subjects: Engineering, medicine, music or science.

Eligibility: Open to graduates or graduands of any Australian or overseas university, who should hold at least an upper second class honours bachelor's degree or the equivalent, or should be completing the final year of a course leading to such a degree.

Purpose: To enable a PhD scholar to pursue a full-time program of research which is both environmentally responsible and socially beneficial to the community.

Type: Scholarship.

No. of awards offered: One.

Frequency: Annual.

Value: A$19,500 per annum, plus allowances (under review).

Length of Study: Up to four years.

Study Establishment: Monash University.

Country of Study: Australia.

Applications Procedure: Application kit available four months before closing date.

Closing Date: October 31st.

Additional Information: International; students must meet English proficiency requirements.

Monash Graduate Scholarships

Subjects: Any subject.

Eligibility: Open to graduates or graduands of any Australian or overseas university, who should hold at least an upper second class honours bachelor's degree or the equivalent, or should be completing the final year of a course leading to such a degree.

Level of Study: Postgraduate, Doctorate.

Purpose: To provide support for supervised full-time research at masters and doctoral level.

Type: Scholarship.

No. of awards offered: 110.

Frequency: Annual.

Value: A$14,000 stipend plus thesis preparation and other allowances.

Length of Study: Up to two years for the Master's degree; for up to three years with the possibility of an additional six-month extension for the PhD degree.

Study Establishment: Monash University.

Country of Study: Australia.

Applications Procedure: Application kit available four months before closing date.

Closing Date: October 31st.

Additional Information: International students must meet English language proficiency requirements.

Silver Jubilee Postgraduate Scholarship

Subjects: In 1997, Computing and Information Technology or Engineering; 1998, Law or Education or Business and Economics; 1999, Medicine or Pharmacy; 2000, Science.

Eligibility: Open to graduates or graduands of any Australian or overseas university, who should hold at least an upper second class honours bachelor's degree or the equivalent, or should be completing the final year of a course leading to such a degree.

Level of Study: Postgraduate, Doctorate.

Purpose: To provide supervised full-time research at masters and doctorate level.

Type: Research Scholarship.

No. of awards offered: One.

Frequency: Annual.

Value: Stipend: A419,827 pr annum plus establishment, relocation, incidentals and thesis allowance.

Length of Study: Up to two years for the Master's degree; for up to three years with the possibility of an additional six-month extension for the PhD.

Study Establishment: At Monash University.

Country of Study: Australia.

Applications Procedure: Application kit available four months before closing date.

Closing Date: October 31st.

Additional Information: International students must meet English proficiency requirements.

THE MONGOLIA SOCIETY, INC

The Mongolia Society, Inc, 322 Goodbody Hall, Indiana University,
Bloomington, IN, 47405-2401, USA
Tel: 812 855 4078
Fax: 812 855 7500
Email: MONSOC@Indiana.edu
Contact: Hangin Scholarship Committee

Dr Gombojab Hangin Memorial Scholarship

Subjects: Mongolian studies.

Eligibility: Open to students of Mongolian nationality (defined as a Mongolian individual who has permanent residency in the Mongolian People's Republic, the People's Republic of China, or the Commonwealth of Independent States).

Purpose: To give a student of Mongolian nationality a chance to pursue Mongolian studies in the USA.

Type: Scholarship.

No. of awards offered: One.

Frequency: Annual.

Value: US$2,500.

Length of Study: One year.

Country of Study: USA.

Applications Procedure: Application form must be completed.

Closing Date: January 1st.

MONTREAL INTERNATIONAL MUSIC COMPETITION

Concours international de musique de Montréal, Place des Arts, 1501 rue Jeanne-Mance, Montréal, Québec, H2X 1Z9, Canada
Tel: 514 285 4380
Fax: 514 285 4266

Montreal International Music Competition

Subjects: Violin (1998), piano (1999), voice (1997).

Eligibility: Open to young musicians of any nationality. Candidates must be 17-30 years old for violin and piano; and 20-35 years old for voice.

Purpose: To help launch an international career for young talented violinists, pianists and singers.

Type: Prizes.

No. of awards offered: Eight, six ranked prizes and two special prizes.

Frequency: Annual.

Value: Ranked prizes: C$18,000, C$10,000, C$6,000, C$3,000, C$2,000, C$1,500; special prizes: C$1,000.

Country of Study: Canada.

Applications Procedure: Rules and repertoire are available one year prior to each competition.

Closing Date: February 1st.

MONTREAL NEUROLOGICAL INSTITUTE

Montreal Neurological Institute, McGill University, 3801 University Street, Montréal, Québec, H3A 2B4, Canada
Tel: 514 398 1903
Fax: 514 398 8248
Contact: Director

Jeanne Timmins Costello Fellowships

Subjects: Neurology, neurosurgery or neuroscience: research and study.

Eligibility: Open to candidates of any nationality who have an MD or PhD degree. Those with MD degrees will ordinarily have completed clinical studies in neurology or neurosurgery.

Level of Study: Doctorate, Postgraduate.

Type: Fellowship.

No. of awards offered: Four.

Frequency: Annual.

Value: C$25,000 per annum.

Length of Study: One year; possibly renewable for 1 further year.

Study Establishment: The Institute.

Country of Study: Canada.

Closing Date: October 15th.

Preston Robb Fellowship

Subjects: Neurology, neurosurgery or neuroscience.

Level of Study: Postdoctorate.

Type: Fellowship.

No. of awards offered: One.

Frequency: Annual.

Value: C$25,000.

Length of Study: One year.

Country of Study: Canada.

MONTREAL SYMPHONY ORCHESTRA

Montreal Symphony Orchestra, 85 Ste-Catherine Street West #900, Montreal, Québec, H2X 3P4, Canada
Tel: 514 842 34 02
Fax: 514 842 07 28
Contact: Christine Vauchel

MSO Competitions

Subjects: Piano, singing, strings and winds.

Eligibility: Open to Canadian citizens/landed immigrants.

Level of Study: Unrestricted.

Purpose: To award best performances in piano, singing, strings and winds.

Type: Scholarships granted in money.

No. of awards offered: Ten.

Frequency: Every two years.

Applications Procedure: Applicants must complete a registration form showing proof of eligibility, and submit resumé and registration fee.

Closing Date: November 1st.

JENNY MOORE FUND FOR WRITERS

George Washington University, English Department, Washington, DC, 20052, USA
Tel: 202 9948223
Contact: Faye Moskowitz

Jenny Moore Writer-in-Washington

Subjects: Authorship.

Eligibility: There are no eligibility restrictions.

Level of Study: Professional development.

Purpose: To offer a free writing workshop.

Type: Residency.

No. of awards offered: One.

Frequency: Annual.

Applications Procedure: Please submit 25-page writing sample, CV and letters of recommendation.

Closing Date: November 15th each year.

PHILIP MORRIS SCHOLARSHIPS FOR ARTISTS OF COLOR

Philip Morris Scholarships for Artists of Color, Maryland Institute College of Art, 1300 West Mount Royal Avenue, Baltimore, MD, 21217, USA
Tel: 410 225 2255

Fax: 410 669 9206
Contact: Dr Leslie King-Hammond, Program Director

Minority Scholarships for Graduate Studies

Subjects: The visual arts, and architecture and interior architecture: art education; art and technology; ceramics; design; graphic design, and industrial design; drawing; fibers; film; glass; illustration; metalsmithing; painting; performance; photography; printmaking; sculpture; textile arts; time arts; video; and visual communication. Specific subjects vary depending on the institution.

Eligibility: Open to minority students who have gained admission to a graduate program at one of the consortium institutions who meet the GRADFAF guidelines.

Type: Scholarship.

No. of awards offered: A total of 20 Scholarships (4 at each institution).

Frequency: Annual.

Value: US$10,000 per annum.

Length of Study: Two years.

Study Establishment: At five schools.

Country of Study: USA.

Closing Date: California Institute of the Arts 1 February; Cranbrook Academy of Art 1 March; Maryland Institute College of Art 1 March; the School of the Art Institute of Chicago 15 February; Yale School of Art 1 February.

Additional Information: Additional information may be obtained by writing to the institutions.

MOTT MACDONALD CHARITABLE TRUST

Mott MacDonald Charitable Trust, St Anne House, 20-26 Wellesley Road, Croydon, CR9 2UL, England
Tel: 0181 686 5041
Fax: 0181 688 1814/0181 681 5706
Contact: Justine Attwell

Scholarships

Subjects: Disciplines of the Mott MacDonald Group.

Eligibility: Open to engineering students who wish to further their academic training at postgraduate level.

Level of Study: Doctorate, Postgraduate.

Purpose: To enable a recipient to pursue studies and thus contribute to the advancement of engineering technology.

Type: Scholarship.

No. of awards offered: Varies.

Frequency: Annual.

Value: £10,000 PhD Scholarship; £9,000 MSc Scholarship.

Study Establishment: Any UK university.

Country of Study: UK.

Applications Procedure: Application form must be completed; these are available from the address given.

Closing Date: March 31st each year.

MOUNT DESERT ISLAND BIOLOGICAL LABORATORY

Mount Desert Island Biological Laboratory, PO Box 35, Salisbury Cove, Maine, 04672, USA
Tel: 207 288 3605

Fax: 207 288 2130
Email: bkb@mdibl.org
www: http:/www.mdibl.org
Contact: Mrs Mary Rush

New Investigator Award

Eligibility: Open to US citizens and permanent residents. Afican Americans, Hispanic, Native American Indian and Native Pacific Islanders targeted.

Level of Study: Professional development.

Purpose: To support independent investigators spending one to two months in the summer doing physiological research on marine animals at MDIBL.

Type: Funds costs of lab. housing and research supplies.

No. of awards offered: 20.

Frequency: Annual.

Length of Study: One to two months.

Study Establishment: Mount Desert Island Biological Laboratory.

Country of Study: USA.

Applications Procedure: Application form obtained from MDIBL.

Closing Date: January 15th.

Additional Information: Summer Fellowships.

THE MOUNTBATTEN MEMORIAL TRUST

The Mountbatten Memorial Trust, 1 Grosvenor Crescent, London, SW1X 7EF, England
Tel: 0171 235 5231 ext.255
Contact: John Boyd-Brent, Secretary and Director

Mountbatten Grants

Subjects: Any subject.

Eligibility: Grants are open to organizations rather than individuals internationally.

Purpose: To assist technological research aimed at assisting handicapped and disabled people throughout the world.

Frequency: As funds permit.

Value: Varies; dependent on funds.

Additional Information: Grants supplement other funds rather than supplying continuous funding.

MULTIPLE SCLEROSIS SOCIETY OF CANADA

Multiple Sclerosis Society of Canada, 250 Bloor Street East, Suite 1000, Toronto, Ontario, M4W 3PG, Canada
Tel: 416 922 6065
Fax: 416 922 7538
Contact: Jacquie Munroe

Career Development Award

Subjects: Multiple sclerosis.

Eligibility: Open to individuals holding a doctorate degree who have recently completed their training in research and are capable of carrying out independent research relevant to MS on a full-time basis.

Purpose: To encourage full-time research.

No. of awards offered: Limited.

Frequency: Annual.

Value: The salary scale, conditions of remuneration and allowable involvement in non-research activities will be similar to Medical Research Council Scholarships.

Length of Study: Three years initially; with the opportunity for renewal twice.

Study Establishment: A Canadian school of medicine.

Country of Study: Canada.

Closing Date: October 1st.

Postdoctoral Fellowship

Subjects: Multiple sclerosis and allied diseases.

Eligibility: Open to qualified persons holding an MD or PhD degree and intending to pursue research work relevant to MS and allied diseases. The applicant must be responsible to an appropriate authority in the field he or she wishes to study.

Purpose: To encourage research.

Type: Fellowship.

No. of awards offered: Varies.

Frequency: Annual.

Value: Salary scales follow those suggested by the Medical Research Council for Fellowships, plus C$1,000.

Length of Study: Three years; may be extended for one additional year under exceptional circumstances.

Study Establishment: A recognized institution which deals with problems relevant to MS.

Country of Study: Applicants proposing to go abroad are encouraged to seek the advice of the panel members regarding suitable laboratories for advanced training.

Closing Date: October 1st.

Additional Information: Maximum funding three years, but under exceptional circumstances may be extended for one additional year.

Research Studentship

Subjects: Multiple sclerosis research.

Eligibility: Open to qualified persons holding other than an MD or PhD degree. Applicants directed towards understanding the pathogenesis and potential treatment of MS will receive priority.

Purpose: To provide further training in a specialized area related to research in multiple sclerosis and allied diseases.

Type: Studentship.

No. of awards offered: Varies.

Frequency: Annual.

Value: Salary scales follow those suggested by the Medical Research Council for Studentships.

Length of Study: Four years; under exceptional circumstances this may be extended. Renewal must be obtained each year.

Study Establishment: A recognized institution.

Closing Date: October 1st.

Research Grant

Subjects: Multiple sclerosis.

Eligibility: Open to researchers working in Canada or intending to return to Canada.

Purpose: To fund research projects.

Type: Research Grant.

No. of awards offered: Limited.

Frequency: Annual.

Value: Varies.

Length of Study: One, two or three years; if further funding is requested reapplication in full must be made.

Study Establishment: An approved institution.

Closing Date: October 1st.

MULTIPLE SCLEROSIS SOCIETY OF GREAT BRITAIN AND NORTHERN IRELAND

Multiple Sclerosis Society, 25 Effie Road, London, SW6 1EE, England
Tel: 0171 610 7171
Fax: 0171 736 9861
Email: LLayward@mssociety.org.uk
www: IFMSS.org.uk
Contact: Research Liaison Officer

Research Grants

Subjects: Multiple sclerosis.

Eligibility: Open to nationals of all countries.

Level of Study: Doctorate, Postdoctorate.

Purpose: To promote medical research into the cause and cure of multiple sclerosis.

Type: Research Grant.

No. of awards offered: Varies.

Frequency: Two or three times per year.

Value: Research Grants may be awarded in the form of fellowships and PhD studentships, to provide remuneration for research workers. They may also be awarded for the provision of scientific assistance in connection with some particular aspect of research by a qualified medical or graduate scientist, to meet the entire or part cost of technical laboratory assistance, equipment and materials, and also to meet the cost of travel in connection with attendance at regional or international conferences.

Length of Study: Three years.

Study Establishment: Suitable institutions.

Country of Study: UK.

Applications Procedure: Application form must be completed.

Closing Date: Two months before meeting of the Society's Review Committee.

Additional Information: Applications should, where applicable, be sponsored by the head of the hospital department or laboratory on which the work is to be carried out. The Society's Committee normally meets three times each year for consideration of applications.

GILBERT MURRAY TRUST

Gilbert Murray Trust, International Affairs Committee, 5 Warnborough Road, Oxford, OX2 6HZ, England
Tel: 01865 56633
Contact: Mrs Mary Bull, Secretary

Junior Awards

Subjects: International affairs or international law.

Eligibility: Open to persons of any nationality who are, or have been, undergraduate or postgraduate students at a university or similar institution in the UK. Candidates should be taking or should have taken part in a course of international affairs or international law, and must not be over 25 years of age, although consideration will be given to those over that age in special cases.

Level of Study: Postgraduate, Undergraduate.

Purpose: The study of the purposes and work of the United Nations.

Type: Awards.

No. of awards offered: Ten.

Frequency: Annual.

Value: £250.

Study Establishment: For carrying out a specific research project or experience to assist in the study of international affairs or law, such as a visit to a foreign country and/or international organisation, or attendance at a short course at an institution abroad.

Country of Study: Any country.

Applications Procedure: Application by letter enclosing relevant documents.

Closing Date: April 1st of year of application.

Additional Information: A letter of application should include a CV, outline of intention with regard to future career and full particulars of the purpose for which the Award would be used, and be accompanied by a supporting testimonial from a person capable of judging the candidate's ability to use the Award profitably.

HENRY A MURRAY RESEARCH CENTER OF RADCLIFFE COLLEGE

Henry A Murray Research Center of Radcliffe College, 10 Garden Street, Cambridge, MA, 02138, USA
Tel: 617 495 8140
Fax: 617 496 3993
Contact: Grants Administrator

Jeanne Humphrey Block Dissertation Award

Subjects: Social and behavioural sciences.

Eligibility: Applicants must be enrolled in a doctoral program in a relevant field and must have had their dissertation proposal approved by an advisor or committee before the grant application is made.

Level of Study: Doctorate.

Purpose: To enable a woman doctoral student to undertake research on sex and gender differences or some developmental issue of particular concern to girls or women. Projects drawing on Center data will be given priority, although this is not a requirement.

No. of awards offered: One.

Frequency: Annual.

Value: US$2,500.

Length of Study: One year.

Applications Procedure: The applicant's CV, including social security number, permanent home address, and the name of a referee who has been asked to send a letter of recommendation directly to the program, should be attached to the proposal. Four copies of all materials are requested, plus an application for the Use of Data form and a Computer Data Request form, if applicable.

Closing Date: April 1st.

Henry A Murray Dissertation Award Program

Subjects: Social and behavioural studies.

Eligibility: Applicants must be enrolled in a doctoral program in a relevant field and must have their dissertation proposal approved by an advisor or committee before the grant application is made.

Level of Study: Doctorate.

Purpose: To enable doctoral students to undertake projects which focus on some aspect of 'the study of lives', concentrating on issues in human development or personality. Priority will be given to projects drawing on Center data.

Type: Research Grant.

No. of awards offered: 3-4.

Frequency: Annual.

Value: US$2,500.

Length of Study: One year.

Applications Procedure: The applicant's CV, including social security number, permanent home address, and the name and address of a reference who has been asked to send a letter of recommendation directly to the program, should be attached to the proposal. Four copies of all the materials are requested. Also, an application for the Use of Data form and a Computer Data Request form, if applicable, must be completed.

Closing Date: April 1st.

Radcliffe Research Support Program

Subjects: Social and behavioural sciences.

Eligibility: Applicants must have received a PhD or equivalent degree prior to application.

Level of Study: Postdoctorate.

Purpose: To enable postdoctoral investigators to undertake research whilst drawing on the Center's data resources. Funds are provided for travel to the Center, duplication, computer time, assistance in coding data and other research expenses.

Type: Research Grant.

No. of awards offered: Six.

Frequency: Annual.

Value: US$5,000.

Length of Study: One year.

Study Establishment: The Center.

Country of Study: USA.

Applications Procedure: In addition to the proposal, applicants must complete an application form for the Use of Data form for each data set to be used in the proposed project, as well as a Computer Data Request form if applicable. Applicants should also submit a budget, CV with social security number, permanent home address, and reference.

Closing Date: April 15th and October 15th.

Additional Information: Applicants must submit seven copies of all proposed materials. A letter of reference should be sent directly to the program.

Visiting Scholars Program

Subjects: Social and behavioural studies.

Eligibility: Open to nationals of any country.

Level of Study: Doctorate.

Purpose: To offer space and access to the facilities of Radcliffe College and Harvard University each year to six to eight scholars who wish to investigate some aspect of women and social change or the study of lives over time.

Type: Scholar's appointment.

No. of awards offered: Ten.

Frequency: Annual.

Value: No stipend.

Length of Study: One semester/one year.

Applications Procedure: Applicants should submit a covering letter indicating when they would like to be at the Center, specifying the start and end dates, reasons for seeking affiliation with the Murray Center, a brief description of research plans for the period of residency, plus one example of published work related to the intended project. A CV should also be included.

Closing Date: March 1st, postmarked.

MUSCULAR DYSTROPHY ASSOCIATION

Muscular Dystrophy Association, 3300 East Sunrise Drive, Tucson, AZ, 85718, USA
Tel: 520 529 2000
Fax: 520 529 5300
Contact: Karen Mashburn, Grants Coordinator

Grant Programs

Subjects: The muscular dystrophies and related diseases which include spinal muscular atrophies and motor neuron diseases, peripheral neuropathies, inflammatory myopathies, metabolic myopathies and diseases of the neuromuscular junction.

Eligibility: Open to persons who are professional or faculty members at appropriate educational, medical, or research institutions and qualified to conduct and supervise programs of original research; who have access to institutional resources necessary to conduct the proposed research project; and who hold a Doctor of Medicine, Doctor of Philosophy, Doctor of Science or equivalent degree.

Level of Study: Postdoctorate.

Purpose: To support research into 40 diseases of the neuromuscular system to identify the causes of, and effective treatments for, the muscular dystrophies and related diseases.

Type: Grant.

No. of awards offered: Varies.

Frequency: Annual.

Value: Amount not specified; overhead limited to a maximum of 8% of the total amount of the grant requested.

Length of Study: One year; renewable for 2 or 3 years.

Closing Date: Varies; details available from the Association.

Additional Information: Proposals from applicants outside the USA will only be considered for projects of highest priority to MDA and when, in addition to the applicants having met the eligibility requirements noted above, one or more of the following conditions exist: the applicant's country of residence has inadequate sources of financial support for biomedical research; collaboration with an MDA-supported US investigator is required to conduct the project; or an invitation to submit an application has been extended by MDA. The research program, under which a full application may be invited, is determined at MDA's sole discretion. Research is sponsored under the following grant programs: Neuromuscular Disease Research; Neuromuscular Disease Research Development; Task Force on Genetics; Neuromuscular Disease Special Grants.

MUSCULAR DYSTROPHY GROUP OF GREAT BRITAIN AND NORTHERN IRELAND

Muscular Dystrophy Group of Great Britain and Northern Ireland, Strangeways Research Laboratory, Wort's Causeway, Cambridge, Cambs., CB1 4RN, England
Tel: 01223 411706
Fax: 01223 411609
Contact: Dr Sarah Yates, Director of Research Funding

Programme Grant

Subjects: Biomedicine.

Eligibility: Only awarded in exceptional circumstances - a site visit would be made prior to approval.

Level of Study: Postdoctorate.

Purpose: To provide continuity of funding for high quality research of central importance to the Muscular Dystrophy Group's research objectives.

Type: Programme grant.

No. of awards offered: Varies.

Value: Salary of research staff, equipment and consumables. Salary of grant holder is not funded.

Length of Study: Five years.

Study Establishment: University/hospital.

Country of Study: UK.

Applications Procedure: Individual applicants should contact the Director of Research Funding with a summary of proposed research.

Closing Date: To be announced.

Project Grant

Subjects: Biomedicine. Muscular dystrophy and allied neuromuscular diseases.

Eligibility: Open to research workers with appropriate qualification and experience. Grant holder must have tenured position. UK nationals (usually restricted).

Level of Study: Postdoctorate, Studentship.

Purpose: For the advancement of medical research into muscular dystrophy and allied neuromuscular conditions.

Type: Project grant.

No. of awards offered: Varies.

Frequency: Annual.

Value: Salary of research staff, equipment and consumables.

Length of Study: Three years.

Study Establishment: University/hospital.

Applications Procedure: Summary of proposal to Director of Research Funding in the first instance.

Closing Date: To be announced.

Additional Information: Grant holder must have tenured position.

Research Grants

Subjects: Muscular Dystrophy and allied neuro muscular diseases.

Eligibility: Open to UK nationals who have appropriate qualifications and experience.

Level of Study: Postdoctorate, Studentships.

Purpose: To support research into neuromuscular function in health and in disease, with particular reference to muscular dystrophy and related disorders.

Type: Research Grant.

No. of awards offered: Varies.

Frequency: Dependent on funds available.

Value: Varies according to the nature of the research and the qualifications and experience of the applicant.

Length of Study: Three years.

Study Establishment: Universities, hospitals and other research institutions.

Country of Study: UK.

Applications Procedure: Send summary of proposal to the Director of Research Funding, in first instance.

Additional Information: Grant holder must have tenured position.

MUSEUM OF COMPARATIVE ZOOLOGY

Museum of Comparative Zoology, 26 Oxford Street, Cambridge, MA, 02138, USA

Tel: 617 495 2460
Fax: 617 496 8308
Contact: The Director

Ernst Mayr Grants

Subjects: Zoology.

Eligibility: There are no restrictions on eligibility.

Level of Study: Unrestricted.

Purpose: To enable systematists to make short visits to museums in order to undertake research needed for the completion of taxonomic revisions and monographs.

Type: Travel Grant.

No. of awards offered: Varies.

Frequency: Twice a year.

Value: Typical expenses that may be covered by this award include travel, lodging, and meals for up to a few months whilst conducting research, services purchased from the host institution, research supplies etc.

Length of Study: Varies - short visits.

Study Establishment: Museums.

Applications Procedure: Applicants should submit three copies of a short proposal, budget, CV and three letters of support.

Closing Date: April 15th and September 15th.

NATIONAL ACADEMY OF DESIGN

National Academy of Design, 1083 Fifth Avenue, New York, NY, 10128, USA
Tel: 1 212 369 4880
Fax: 1 212 360 6795

Prizes for Painting in their Annual Exhibition

Subjects: Painting.

Eligibility: Open to US artists.

Level of Study: Unrestricted.

Type: Prize.

No. of awards offered: 22.

Frequency: Every two years.

Value: Varies; US$200-US$5,000.

Country of Study: USA.

Closing Date: Varies.

Additional Information: Further details may be obtained from the Academy.

Prizes for Prints, Drawings and Pastels in their Annual Exhibition

Subjects: Prints, drawings and pastels.

Eligibility: Open to artists of any nationality.

Type: Prize.

No. of awards offered: Six.

Frequency: Annual.

Value: Varies; US$200-US$400.

Additional Information: Further details may be obtained from the Academy.

Prizes for Sculpture in their Annual Exhibition Competition

Subjects: Sculpture.

Eligibility: Open to sculptors of any nationality.

Type: Prize.

No. of awards offered: 7-10.

Frequency: Annual.

Value: Varies; US$200-US$5,000.

Additional Information: Further details may be obtained from the Academy.

Prizes for Watercolor in their Annual Exhibition Competition

Subjects: Watercolor painting.

Eligibility: Open to US artists.

Type: Prize.

No. of awards offered: Seven.

Frequency: Annual.

Value: Varies: US$200-US$3,500.

Country of Study: USA.

Additional Information: Further details may be obtained from the Academy.

THE NATIONAL ACADEMY OF EDUCATION

Spencer Fellowship Program, The National Academy of Education, Stanford University School of Education, CERAS 108, Stanford, CA, 94305-3084, USA
Tel: 415 725 1003
Fax: 415 725 2165
Email: BITNET:EA.dlc@Forsythe.STANFORD.edu
Contact: Debbie Leong-Childs

Spencer Postdoctoral Fellowships

Subjects: Education.

Eligibility: Open to candidates who have had doctorate for less than six years and are doing research relevant to the improvement of education in all its forms. US citizenship is not required.

Level of Study: Postdoctorate.

Purpose: To promote scholarship on matters relevant to the improvement of education.

Type: Fellowship.

No. of awards offered: Up to 30.

Frequency: Annual.

Value: US$35,000.

Length of Study: One academic year (full-time) or two academic years (part-time).

Country of Study: Any country.

Closing Date: December 21st.

Additional Information: The Fellowship is non-residential. Application forms are available on request before December 15th.

NATIONAL AIR AND SPACE MUSEUM, SMITHSONIAN

National Air and Space Museum, Smithsonian, Room 3341, MRC313, Washington, DC, 20560, USA
Tel: 202 357 1529
Fax: 202 357 4579
Email: NASPL003@SIVM.SI.EDU
Contact: Cheryl Bauer

Garber Fellowship

Eligibility: There are no restrictions.

Level of Study: Doctorate, Postdoctorate.

Purpose: Intended for pre- and postdoctoral candidates interested in scientific research in astrophysics or in planetary and terrestrial geologic and geophysical studies.

Type: Fellowship.

Frequency: Annual, dependent on funds available.

Value: Competitive with the National Research Council Awards.

Length of Study: Six months to two years.

Study Establishment: In residence at National Air and Space Museum, Smithsonian.

Country of Study: USA.

Applications Procedure: Application form is required to be completed.

Closing Date: January 15th.

NATIONAL ALLIANCE FOR RESEARCH ON SCHIZOPHRENIA AND DEPRESSION

NARSAD, 208 South LaSalle Street, Suite 1431, Chicago, IL, 60604, USA
Tel: 312 641 1666
Fax: 312 641 3483
Contact: Brenda Berman

Established Investigator Awards

Subjects: Mental illness.

Eligibility: Open to senior researchers of any nationality who are of associate professor status or above (or equivalent).

Level of Study: Postdoctorate.

Purpose: To encourage experienced scientists to pursue innovative projects in diverse areas of mental illness research.

No. of awards offered: Varies.

Frequency: Annual.

Value: Up to US$100,000.

Closing Date: Mid-June.

Young Investigator Awards

Subjects: Mental illness.

Eligibility: Open to investigators of any nationality who have attained a doctorate or equivalent degree, are affiliated with a specific research institution and who have a mentor or senior collaborator who is performing significant research in an area relevant to schizophrenia, depression or other serious mental illnesses. Candidates should be at the postdoctoral through assistant professor level.

Level of Study: Postdoctorate.

Purpose: To encourage basic or clinical investigators in the beginning phase of a research career.

No. of awards offered: Varies.

Frequency: Annual.

Value: US$30,000 for up to two years, (e.g. may apply for US£60,000 @ US$30,000 a year).

Closing Date: October 25th.

NATIONAL ASSOCIATION FOR CORE CURRICULUM, INC

National Association for Core Curriculum, Inc, Suite #5, 1100 E. Summit Street, Kent, OH, 44240-4094, USA
Tel: 216 677 5008
Fax: 216 677 5008
Contact: Dr Gordon F Vars, Executive Secretary-Treasurer

Bossing-Edwards Research Scholarship Award

Subjects: Research on interdisciplinary approaches to education, with special emphasis on core curriculum.

Eligibility: Open to individuals who have previously been a core teacher for at least one year, and have been accepted to a graduate program leading to a master's, specialist's or doctor's degree at a university that has adequate resources for research in core curriculum.

Level of Study: Doctorate.

Purpose: To encourage research on core curriculum and other interdisciplinary/integrative approaches to education.

Type: Scholarship.

No. of awards offered: Varies.

Frequency: Throughout the year.

Value: Up to US$400.

Study Establishment: An appropriate institution.

Country of Study: USA.

Applications Procedure: Write explaining intended research and how you meet the criteria of eligibility.

Closing Date: Applications can be submitted at any time; Scholarships are awarded in October of each year.

NATIONAL ASSOCIATION OF BROADCASTERS

National Association of Broadcasters, 1771 North Street, NW, Washington, DC, 20036-2891, USA
Tel: 202 429 5389
Contact: Senior Vice President of Research and Information

*Grants for Research in Broadcasting

Subjects: Broadcast research, especially research on economic, business, social or policy issues of importance to the USA commercial broadcast industry.

Eligibility: Open to all academic personnel working in the several disciplines that relate to the social, cultural, political and economic aspects of broadcasting. Graduate students and senior undergraduates are invited to submit proposals.

Type: Grant.

No. of awards offered: Varies.

Frequency: Annual.

Value: Up to US$5,000.

Country of Study: USA.

Closing Date: January 3rd.

NATIONAL ASSOCIATION OF COMPOSERS

National Association of Composers, PO Box 49256 , Barrington Station, Los Angeles, CA, 90049, USA
Contact: Marshall Bialosky

Young Composers' Competition

Subjects: Music composition.

Eligibility: Open to nationals of any country between the ages of 18-30.

Level of Study: Postgraduate, Postdoctorate.

Purpose: To foster the creation of new American concert hall music.

Type: Cash and musical performance.

No. of awards offered: Two.

Frequency: Annual.

Value: US$200 first place; US$50 second place.

Applications Procedure: There are no application forms; contestants simply send in their music. Applicants must be members of NACUSA.

Closing Date: October 30th each year.

NATIONAL ASSOCIATION OF DENTAL ASSISTANTS

National Association of Dental Assistants, 900 South Washington Street, G-13, Falls Church, VA, 22046, USA
Tel: 703 237 8616
Contact: Scholarship Department

*Annual Scholarship Award

Subjects: Dental assistant certification, recertification, dental training, continuing dental education seminars or any course that is related to or required in the dental degree program. (All courses must be approved by the board.).

Eligibility: Open to dental assistants who have a minimum of two years' membership in good standing (members only). Applicants must submit one recommendation from their current or previous employer, one recommendation from someone other than a member (if a member's dependant), such as a school counselor or another dental assistant, and a completed application form and up-to-date student transcript. Applicants may also be a member's dependant, spouse or grandchild.

Purpose: To assist dental assistants to further their education.

Type: Scholarship.

No. of awards offered: One.

Frequency: Annual.

Value: US$250.

Closing Date: May 31st.

NATIONAL ASSOCIATION OF PURCHASING MANAGEMENT, INC

National Association of Purchasing Management, Inc, 2055 East Centennial Circle, PO Box 22160, Tempe, AZ, 85285-2160, USA
Tel: 602 752 2277
Fax: 602 752 7890
Email: rboyle@napm.org
Contact: Richard A Boyle, PhD, Doctoral Grant Committee

Doctoral Grants

Subjects: Purchasing and materials management.

Eligibility: Open to full time student candidates in the PhD or DBA program of an accredited United States university only, that offers doctoral-level studies in a discipline appropriate to the research project.

Level of Study: Doctorate.

Purpose: To provide financial assistance to PhD candidates at the dissertation stage in preparation for a career in the field or for university teaching; and to encourage research.

Type: Grant.

No. of awards offered: Four.

Frequency: Annual.

Value: Up to US$10,000.

Country of Study: USA.

Applications Procedure: Application form and documents (letters of recomendation and transcripts) and a research proposal.

Closing Date: January 31st.

Additional Information: Upon successful completion of the research, the Association will be interested in the publication of material from the study. Nominations are invited from departments of economics, management, marketing and business administration at US universities offering a doctoral degree in appropriate fields.

NATIONAL BACK PAIN ASSOCIATION

National Back Pain Association, 31-33 Park Road, Teddington, Middlesex, TW11 0AB, England
Tel: 0181 977 5474
Fax: 0181 943 5318
Contact: Executive Director

*Research Grants

Subjects: Studies related to back pain: causation and diagnosis of back pain; identification of those most susceptible to back pain; identification of the main environmental and occupational hazards; trials of different methods of treatment to alleviate back pain; methods of preventing back pain; reduction in back pain disability by influencing health education, lifestyles, patient behaviour and clinical practice; social and psychological factors relevant to back pain; back pain and primary care.

Eligibility: Open to appropriately qualified and experienced persons.

Purpose: To encourage and support scientific research into the causes, treatment and prevention of back pain. The objective is to reduce the incidence of and disability from back pain and improve its treatment by gaining through research a better understanding of its manifestation and causes.

Type: Research Grant.

Value: Varies; dependent on funds available. The Association is not a major funding organization.

Length of Study: Up to two years.

Study Establishment: Suitable establishments.

Applications Procedure: Applicants should write, in the first instance, for a copy of the detailed application procedure, as failure to comply with all conditions may diminish the success of an application.

Closing Date: June 1st and November 1st.

Additional Information: Applicants should first satisfy themselves that their proposed research falls within the remit of the National Back Pain Association as defined in the Grant Policy Statement. The Association is unable to fund educational courses, attendance at meetings or conferences, or the purchase of computers.

NATIONAL BLACK LAW STUDENTS ASSOCIATION

National Black Law Students Association, 1225 11th Street, NW, Washington, DC, 20001, USA
Contact: National Chairperson/Director of Community Service

Nelson Mandela Scholarship

Subjects: Law.

Eligibility: Open to pre-law students who are committed to uplifting the black community. Candidates must be of African descent, and be planning to enter law school in the following fall. Recipients are selected based on financial need, work experience, academic achievement, community service, references, and essay.

Purpose: To increase the number of African-American lawyers by reducing the financial burden of a legal education.

Type: Scholarship.

No. of awards offered: Six.

Frequency: Annual.

Value: US$1,000.

Country of Study: USA.

Closing Date: January 31st.

Additional Information: Requests for application forms should include a self-addressed stamped envelope.

NATIONAL BLACK MBA ASSOCIATION

National Black MBA Association, 1800 North Michigan, Suite 1515, Chicago, IL, 60601, USA
Contact: Lisa Collins, Program Manager

National MBA Scholarships

Subjects: An essay topic is selected annually by the Scholarship Committee.

Eligibility: Open to minority full-time students enrolled in an accredited US business program pursuing an MBA degree.

Level of Study: Postgraduate, Doctorate.

Type: Scholarship, Fellowship.

No. of awards offered: MBA-25; PhD-2.

Frequency: Annual.

Value: MBA - US$3,000 average; PhD - US$10,000 and US$5,000.

Applications Procedure: Application form must be completed, along with the submission of official transcripts.

Closing Date: March/April.

NATIONAL CANCER INSTITUTE

Cancer Training Branch, National Cancer Institute, EPN-Room 520, Bethesda, MD, 20892-4200, USA
Tel: 301 496 8580
Fax: 301 402 4472
Contact: Andrew Vargosko, PhD Coordinator

*Cancer Education Award

Subjects: Chronic disease prevention and control, especially cancer.

Eligibility: Open to US public or private non-profit research institutions. Trainees must be US citizens, nationals or permanent residents. Minority student participation is strongly encouraged.

Purpose: To prepare doctoral-level practitioners of chronic disease prevention and control with emphasis on cancer or to provide short term research experiences for medical, dental, nursing, public health and allied health students. An additional purpose is the creation, implementation and evaluation of a nutrition curriculum at professional schools.

No. of awards offered: Approximately 80.

Frequency: Annual.

Value: US$10,000 per annum for Predoctoral Awards; US$24,000-US$35,000 per annum for Postdoctoral Awards; plus other costs. Supplies, travel and equipment costs are paid for short-term research experiences and for nutrition curriculum projects.

Length of Study: Five years; renewable except for nutrition curriculum projects.

Study Establishment: An appropriate institution,.

Country of Study: USA.

Additional Information: There is no payback obligation.

Cancer Prevention Fellowship Program

Subjects: Primary prevention, nutrition, surveillance and special populations, early detection and health promotion and community interventions.

Eligibility: Open to holders of MD, DDS or DO from a US, territorial, or Canadian medical school. Foreign medical graduates must have current ECFMG, FMGEMS or USMLE certification and appropriate experience, or PhD, or other doctoral degree in a related discipline. Foreign education must be comparable to that received in accredited US institutions. All applicants should hold US citizenship or be resident aliens eligible for citizenship within four years.

Level of Study: Postdoctorate.

Purpose: To attract individuals from a multiplicity of health science disciplines into the field of cancer prevention and control. The program provides for Master of Public Health training, participation in the DCPC Cancer Prevention and Control Academic Course, working at NCI directly with individual preceptors, and field assignments in cancer prevention and control programs at other institutions.

Type: Fellowship.

No. of awards offered: Up to ten.

Frequency: Annual.

Value: Physicians: US$30,000-US$41,000; other doctoral degrees: US$22,000-US$35,000.

Length of Study: Up to three years of training; the first year may be spent obtaining MPH at an accredited school and two years at the National Cancer Institute.

Country of Study: USA.

Applications Procedure: Applicants should submit letter of interest, CV, transcripts, copies of permanent resident (if applicable) and copies USMLE (if applicable) plus four current letters of reference.

Closing Date: September 1st.

For further information contact:
Cancer Prevention Fellowship Program, Division of Cancer Prevention and Control, National Cancer Institute, Room T-41, Executive Plaza South, MSC 7105, 6130 Executive Blvd, Bethesda, MD, 20892-7105, USA
Tel: 301 496 8640
Fax: 301 402 4863
Email: ReddingB@dcpeps.nci.nih.gov
Contact: Coordinator Coordinator

Individual Postdoctoral Fellowships (F32 Grants)

Subjects: Research directly relevant to cancer.

Eligibility: Open to US citizens, nationals or permanent residents holding a PhD, MD, DDS, etc.

Level of Study: Postgraduate, Doctorate, Postdoctorate.

Purpose: To provide long-term basic or applied research training.

Type: Fellowship.

No. of awards offered: 212.

Frequency: Ongoing.

Value: US$19,600-US$32,300 per annum, plus an institutional allowance.

Length of Study: Up to three years.

Study Establishment: An appropriate institution.

Country of Study: USA.

Closing Date: Three cycles each year with closing dates of 5 April, 5 August, and 5 December.

Additional Information: Supplementation of funds is permitted. There is a payback obligation if the trainee does not continue biomedical research or teaching activities for at least one year after the first year of support.

Individual Predoctoral Fellowships for Oncology Nurses (F31 Grants)

Subjects: Any science relevant to cancer.

Eligibility: Open to registered nurses who are US citizens, nationals or permanent residents and have earned at least a bachelor's degree.

Level of Study: Predoctorate.

Purpose: To enable Fellows to earn the PhD degree.

Type: Fellowship.

No. of awards offered: 15.

Frequency: Annual.

Value: Stipend of US$10,000 per annum, plus an institutional allowance.

Length of Study: Up to five years.

Study Establishment: University.

Country of Study: USA.

Closing Date: Three cycles each year with closing dates of 5 April, 5 August, and 5 December.

Institutional Research Training Grants for Predoctoral and Postdoctoral Trainees (T32 Grants)

Subjects: Any science directly relevant to cancer. Areas of special interest include surgical oncology, radiotherapy, radiodiagnosis, preventive oncology and biostatistics.

Eligibility: Open to US public non-profit research institutions. Trainees must be US citizens, nationals or permanent residents.

Level of Study: Postgraduate, Doctorate, Postdoctorate.

Purpose: To provide support for long-term basic or applied research training programs for predoctoral and postdoctoral trainees.

No. of awards offered: C.180.

Frequency: Annual.

Value: US$8,800 per annum for predoctoral trainees; US$18,600-US$32,300 per annum for postdoctoral trainees; plus tuition, fees, travel expenses and an institutional allowance.

Length of Study: Up to 5 years (predoctoral); for up to 3 years (postdoctoral).

Country of Study: USA.

Closing Date: Three cycles each year with closing dates of 10 January, 10 May, and 10 September.

Additional Information: There is a one-year payback obligation for postdoctoral trainees. This may be satisfied by either serving in a position in which a combination of biomedical or behavioral research or teaching constitutes more than 20 hours per week for one year after the first year of training, or by financially recompensating the government in an amount of money determined in accordance with a recovery formula specified in the legislation. Trainees may supplement their NCI funds.

Mentored Clinical Scientist Development Awards (K08 Grants)

Subjects: Research directly relevant to cancer.

Eligibility: Open to US citizens, nationals and permanent residents who have a professional degree (MD, DVM, DDS, etc.) with more than two but less than seven years' postdoctoral experience at the time of application (a waiver is possible). Candidates must provide evidence of research potential and desire for an academic career.

Level of Study: Postgraduate.

Purpose: To provide long-term basic or clinical research training to MDs.

No. of awards offered: 111.

Frequency: Ongoing.

Value: Salary up to US$50,000 per annum, plus up to US$10,000 for research expenses and travel during the first two years and up to US$20,000 per annum thereafter. Fringe benefits are also paid and indirect costs up to 8% of total direct costs.

Length of Study: 3-5 years; not renewable.

Country of Study: USA.

Closing Date: Three cycles each year with closing dates of 1 February, 1 June, and 1 October.

Additional Information: Candidates must have one or more preceptors. There is no payback obligation.

Preventive Oncology Academic Award (K07 grants)

Subjects: The scope of this Award extends from the development and experimental testing of hypotheses about cancer prevention and control in people, through the stage of confirming results using defined populations, to the development and demonstration of cancer control technology. Some relevant disciplines are: epidemiology, human genetics, biostatistics, human nutrition, behavioral sciences, etc.

Eligibility: Open to US citizens, nationals or permanent residents who hold a doctorate from an accredited institution. The candidate must have at least two years' postdoctoral experience and must hold an appropriate teaching and/or research appointment in the sponsoring institution at the time the award is made.

Level of Study: Doctorate, Postdoctorate.

Purpose: To stimulate research and teaching in cancer prevention and control.

No. of awards offered: 31.

Frequency: Ongoing.

Value: Salary up to $50,000 per annum, plus fringe benefits, travel, miscellaneous expenses and indirect costs up to 8% of total direct costs.

Length of Study: Up to five years; non-renewable.

Study Establishment: An appropriate institution.

Country of Study: USA.

Closing Date: Three cycles each year with closing dates of 1 February, 1 June, and 1 October.

Additional Information: There is no payback obligation.

*Research Career Development Awards

Subjects: Cancer-related research.

Eligibility: Open to US citizens, nationals or permanent residents who are at least three years beyond a doctorate and are sponsored by a domestic institution. Candidates should not already be developed as independent investigators, i.e. they should have 6-30 publications and be of instructor or assistant professor rank, or have recently been appointed associate professor.

Purpose: To free investigators with high research potential from most teaching and administrative duties so they may spend their full time in research; to bring developing researchers to the status of fully independent investigators.

No. of awards offered: 30.

Frequency: Annual.

Value: Up to US$50,000 per annum, plus fringe benefits and indirect costs up to 8% of total direct costs.

Length of Study: Five years; not renewable.

Country of Study: USA.

Additional Information: There is no payback obligation.

Senior Individual Postdoctoral Fellowships (F33 Grants)

Subjects: Any science relevant to cancer.

Eligibility: Open to US citizens, nationals or permanent residents holding a PhD, MD, DNS, etc. Candidates must have had at least seven years of relevant research or professional experience.

Level of Study: Postdoctorate.

Purpose: To permit experienced scientists to make major changes in their research careers, to broaden their scientific background, acquire new research capabilities or enlarge a command of an allied research field.

Type: Fellowship.

No. of awards offered: 4-6.

Frequency: Annual.

Value: Negotiable up to US$32,500 per annum, plus an institutional allowance.

Length of Study: Up to two years.

Study Establishment: An appropriate institution.

Country of Study: USA.

Closing Date: Three cycles each year with closing dates of 5 April, 5 August, and 5 December.

NATIONAL CANCER INSTITUTE OF CANADA

National Cancer Institute of Canada, Suite 200, 10 Alcorn Avenue,
Toronto, Ontario, M4V 3B1, Canada
Tel: 416 961 7223
Fax: 416 961 4189
Email: ncic@cancer.ca
www: http://www.cancer.ca.ccsncic.htm
Contact: Research Awards, Manager or Assistant

Clinical Research Fellowships

Subjects: Clinical cancer research.

Eligibility: Open to Canadian citizens or residents who are graduates in medicine from a recognized institution and licensed to practise in Canada, who have normally qualified for admission to Fellowship of the Royal College of Physicians and Surgeons of Canada.

Level of Study: Doctorate, Professional development.

Purpose: To assist outstanding medically qualified individuals who seek specialized training.

Type: Research fellowship.

No. of awards offered: Varies.

Frequency: Annual.

Value: C$29,200 minimum, to a maximum of C$45,400 per annum.

Length of Study: One or two years; with the possibility of renewal for a third year.

Country of Study: Canada, or outside as approved.

Applications Procedure: Please write to the institute for application information.

Closing Date: February 1st.

Additional Information: Stipends are subject to annual review. Recipients of these Fellowships are eligible to apply for a contribution of C$1,000 towards the cost of conference travel per award year.

Research Fellowships

Subjects: Cancer research.

Eligibility: Open to Canadian citizens or residents who have graduated from universities approved by the Institute. Candidates must be accepted for postdoctoral training or research towards a PhD degree in a university laboratory or teaching hospital approved by the Institute, and be engaged in the field of cancer research.

Level of Study: Postdoctorate.

Type: Research Fellowships.

No. of awards offered: Varies.

Frequency: Annual.

Value: Minimum of C$29,200 per annum, to a maximum of C$45,400.

Study Establishment: A university laboratory or teaching hospital approved by the Institute. Fellowships will commence as soon as practicable after July 1st.

Country of Study: Canada or overseas, as approved.

Applications Procedure: Please contact the institute for application forms.

Closing Date: February 1st.

Additional Information: A Fellow may apply for a transportation grant to and from the laboratory where his training will take place, and if married, an amount to assist in the expense of moving his family. Research Fellowships are not awarded for the purpose of providing practical clinical training. For further details and conditions of Research Fellowships, consult the manual 'Support for Research and Training', which is available from the Institute.

Research Grants to Individuals

Subjects: Cancer research.

Eligibility: Open to persons with research experience and competence, holding appointments at Canadian universities or other institutions.

Type: Research Grant.

No. of awards offered: Varies.

Frequency: Annual.

Value: To cover the purchase and maintenance of animals, expendable supplies, minor items of equipment, and payment of graduate students, postdoctoral fellows, and technical and research assistants, but not personal support for the grantee.

Length of Study: Three years in the first instance; renewable for periods of one or two years.

Study Establishment: Universities or other institutions.

Country of Study: Canada.

Applications Procedure: Please contact the institute for application forms.

Closing Date: October 15th.

Additional Information: Grants will be awarded to projects deemed worthy of support, provided that the basic equipment and research facilities are available in the institution concerned and that it will provide the necessary administrative services. Grants are made only with the consent and knowledge of the administrative head of the institution at which they are to be held, and applications must be countersigned accordingly. The Institute also makes available to individuals engaged in studies related to cancer research, grants for purchase of permanent equipment, including specialized major equipment. For further information and conditions of application, consult the manual 'Support for Research and Training' which is available form the institute.

Research Scientist Awards

Subjects: Cancer research.

Eligibility: Open to trained investigators interested in careers in cancer research who hold a doctorate in medicine or in related science, and have completed three years of postdoctoral training in research, but not more than seven, and who intend to remain in Canada.

Purpose: To develop the abilities and research potential of candidates, and to enable them to work full-time on the research project without involvement in major teaching responsibilities.

Type: Research award.

No. of awards offered: Varies.

Frequency: Annual.

Value: Initial salary will depend on the experience and competence of the individual.

Length of Study: Six years for the initial appointment.

Country of Study: Canada.

Applications Procedure: Please contact the institute for application forms.

Closing Date: February 1st.

Additional Information: Senior Research Scientists should apply to the Institute for funds to carry out the research under the regulations set forth in 'Research Grants to Individuals'. Regarding eligibilty, receipt of an NCIC Operating Research Grant is seen as the base line requirement.

NATIONAL CENTER FOR ATMOSPHERIC RESEARCH

National Center for Atmospheric Research, PO Box 3000, Boulder, CO, 80307-3000, USA
Tel: 303 497 1601
Fax: 303 497 1400
Contact: Barbara Hansford, Administrator

Postdoctoral Appointments in the Advanced Study Program

Subjects: Atmosphere sciences.

Eligibility: Open to persons who have recently received their PhD, and to scientists with no more than four years' applicable experience since receiving their PhD. Foreign nationals may apply; NCAR is an equal opportunity employer with an affirmative action program.

Level of Study: Postdoctorate.

Purpose: To assist research.

Type: Fellowships.

No. of awards offered: Eight to ten.

Frequency: Annual.

Value: Minimum of US$33,415 per annum (for recent PhDs), US$34,645 for appointees with more than one year's experience. All appointees are eligible for life and health insurance. Travel expenses to the Center are reimbursed for the appointee and family.

Length of Study: Up to one year; renewable for one year.

Study Establishment: The Center.

Country of Study: USA.

Closing Date: January 7th.

THE NATIONAL CHAPTER OF CANADA IODE

Suite 254, 40 Orchard View Boulevard, Toronto, Ontario, M4R 1B9, Canada
Tel: 416 487 4416
Fax: 416 487 4417

The mission of IODE, a Canadian women's charitable organization, is to improve the quality of life for children, youth and those in need, through educational, social service and citizenship programs

War Memorial Doctoral Scholarship

Subjects: Any subject.

Eligibility: Open to Canadian citizens who hold a first degree from a recognized Canadian university. At the time of applying a candidate must be enrolled in a programme at the doctoral level or equivalent.

Level of Study: Doctorate.

Purpose: To honour the memory of the men and women who gave their

lives for Canada in World Wars One and Two, this memorial was established to provide scholarships for study at the doctoral level.

Type: Scholarship.

No. of awards offered: Eight.

Frequency: Annual.

Value: C$10,000 for study in Canada; C$12,500 for study overseas within the Commonwealth.

Country of Study: Canada or other Commonwealth countries.

Applications Procedure: Applications and supporting documents are available in September and must be submitted by December 1st.

Closing Date: December 1st.

THE NATIONAL COLLEGIATE ATHLETIC ASSOCIATION

The National Collegiate Athletic Association, 6201 College Boulevard, Overland Park, Kansas, 66211-2422, USA
Tel: 913 339 1906
Fax: 913 339 0035
Contact: Fannie Vaughan, Executive Assistant

NCAA Postgraduate Scholarship

Subjects: Sports.

Eligibility: Minimum GPA of 3.000 on a 4.000 scale or its equivalent; student athlete enrolled at an NCAA member institution must be in last year of intercollegiate competition.

Level of Study: Postgraduate.

Purpose: To honor outstanding student athletes from NCAA member institutions who are also outstanding scholars.

Type: Grant.

No. of awards offered: 154.

Frequency: Annual.

Value: Award (one time grant of US$5,000) is not earmarked for a specific area of postgraduate study but awardee must use as a full time graduate student in a graduate or professional school of an academically accredited institution.

Country of Study: USA.

Applications Procedure: Write for application materials.

Closing Date: Three deadlines - may vary slightly each year.

NATIONAL CONFERENCE OF POLITICAL SCIENTISTS

Department of Political Science, Morgan State University, 1700 East Cold Spring Lane & Hillen Road, Baltimore, MD, 21239, USA
Tel: 410 319 3277
Fax: 410 319 3837
Email: kgolden@moe.morgan.edu
Contact: Kathie Stromile Golden

Graduate Assistantship Fellowship

Subjects: Social and behavioural sciences.

Eligibility: African-American and other persons of African Descent.

Level of Study: Doctorate, Masters.

Purpose: To provide financial assistance to prospective black political science graduate students; to contribute to the improvement of political science by recruiting persons who will bring new perspectives, experiences, and creativity to the discipline.

Type: Monetary.

No. of awards offered: 1-2.

Frequency: Annual.

Value: US$1,000.

Study Establishment: Accredited institutions.

Country of Study: USA.

Applications Procedure: Application must include biographical essay, official transcripts, and three letters of recommendation.

Closing Date: February 1st, 1997.

NATIONAL CONSORTIUM FOR GRADUATE DEGREES FOR MINORITIES IN ENGINEERING SCIENCE

National Consortium for Graduate Degrees for Minorities in Engineering Science, PO Box 537, Notre Dame, IN, 46556, USA
Tel: 219 287 1097
Fax: 219 287 1486
Contact: Betty Jean Valdez

*GEM Graduate Fellowships

Subjects: Engineering; physical and life sciences.

Eligibility: Open to US citizens who are American Indian, Black American, Mexican American, or Puerto Rican, hold a junior, senior, or baccalaureate degree and have an academic record that indicates the ability to successfully pursue graduate studies in engineering and science (2.8 Masters, 3.2 PhD). Exceptions by committee.

Purpose: To identify potential minority graduate students and encourage them to make application to graduate school/fellowship programs; to promote graduate education to minority students as a career/life goal planning option.

Type: Fellowship.

No. of awards offered: Approximately 225 for a masters in engineering; 30 for a PhD in engineering; 30 for a PhD in science.

Frequency: Annual.

Value: To cover full tuition and fees, plus a stipend. Paid summer internships for masters and PhD science awards.

Study Establishment: One of 75 USA universities; masters and PhD science Fellows have an internship requirement.

Country of Study: USA.

Applications Procedure: Applications should include three letters of recommendation and a transcript.

Closing Date: December 1st.

Additional Information: The minimum academic load is 12 hours.

NATIONAL ENDOWMENT FOR THE HUMANITIES

Division of Research and Education, Room 318, National Endowment for the Humanities, 1100 Pennsylvania Avenue, NW, Washington, DC, 20506, USA
Tel: 202 606 8466
Fax: 202 606 8558
Email: fellowsuniv@neh.fed.us
www: http://www.neh.fed.us

Centers for Advanced Study Grants

Subjects: The humanities.

Eligibility: Open to independent research libraries and museums, American research centers overseas, and centers for advanced study.

Purpose: To support coordinated research in well-defined subject areas at centers for advanced study through block fellowship grants.

Type: Grant.

No. of awards offered: Varies.

Frequency: Annual.

Value: Varies.

Country of Study: USA or overseas.

Closing Date: October 1st.

Additional Information: Individuals should apply directly to the centers, a list of which is available from the Division of Research and Education.

For further information contact:
Room 318, National Endowment for the Humanities, 1100 Pennsylvania Avenue, NW, Washington, DC, 20506, USA
Tel: 202 000 8210
Fax: 202 606 8204
Contact: Division of Research and Education

Collaborative Research Program

Subjects: Collaborative research that will advance knowledge or deepen critical understanding of important topics in the humanities.

Eligibility: Open to institutions of higher education, non-profit professional associations and scholarly societies, and individuals.

Purpose: To support collaborative research in the humanities: history, literature, philosophy, fine arts and other disciplines.

Type: Research Program.

No. of awards offered: Varies.

Frequency: Annual.

Value: Dependent upon proposal.

Length of Study: Up to three years.

Country of Study: USA or overseas.

Closing Date: September 2nd.

Additional Information: For information, write or call the Division of Research and Education.

For further information contact:
Room 318, National Endowment for the Humanities, 1100 Pennsylvania Avenue, NW, Washington, DC, 20506, USA
Tel: 202 606 8210
Fax: 202 606 8204
Contact: Division of Research and Education

*Dissertation Grants

Subjects: The humanities.

Eligibility: Open to doctoral candidates in the humanities.

Purpose: To provide support for doctoral candidates in the humanities to complete the writing of their dissertation.

Type: Grant.

No. of awards offered: Varies.

Frequency: Annual.

Value: US$14,000.

Length of Study: Six to 12 months.

Applications Procedure: Applicants must be nominated by their graduate institutions.

Closing Date: November 15th.

Additional Information: Awardees are expected to work full-time on their dissertations during the tenure period.

Fellowships for College Teachers and Independent Scholars

Subjects: Projects which may contribute to scholarly knowledge, to the conception and substance of individual courses in the humanities, or to the general public's understanding of the humanities. Projects may address broad topics or consist of study and research in a specialized field.

Eligibility: Open to teachers in two-year, four-year and five-year colleges and universities, faculty members of university departments and programs that do not grant the PhD, individuals affiliated with institutions other than colleges and universities, and scholars and writers working independently. Applicants need not have advanced degrees, but candidates for degrees and persons seeking support for work leading toward degrees are not eligible. Applicants should be US citizens or foreign nationals who have resided in the USA for at least three years.

Level of Study: Postdoctorate.

Purpose: To encourage and support full-time independent advanced study and research by people of diverse interests, backgrounds and circumstances.

Type: Fellowship.

No. of awards offered: Approximately 85 Fellowships (in 1997).

Frequency: Annual.

Value: The maximum stipend is US$30,000.

Length of Study: 6-12 consecutive months.

Applications Procedure: Application form must be completed.

Closing Date: May 1st.

Additional Information: Application guidelines are available from the NEH Public Affairs Office, room 402 (202 606 8435).

For further information contact:
Division of Research and Education Programs, Room 318, National Endowment for the Humanities, 1100 Pennsylvania Avenue, NW, Washington, DC, 20506, USA
Tel: 202 606 8467
Fax: 202 606 8204
Email: fellowscollind@neh.fed.us
Contact: Joseph B Neville

Fellowships for University Teachers

Subjects: Projects which may contribute to scholarly knowledge, to the conception and substance of individual courses in the humanities, or to the general public's understanding of the humanities. Projects may address broad topics or consist of study and research in a specialized field.

Eligibility: Open to faculty members of departments and programs in universities that grant the PhD and faculty members of postgraduate professional US schools. Applicants need not have advanced degrees, but candidates for degrees and persons seeking support for work leading toward degrees are not eligible. Applicants should be US citizens or foreign nationals who have resided in the USA for at least three years.

Level of Study: Postdoctorate.

Purpose: To encourage and support full-time independent advanced study and research by people of diverse interests, backgrounds and circumstances.

Type: Fellowship.

No. of awards offered: Approximately 86 Fellowships (in 1996).

Frequency: Annual.

Value: The maximum stipend is US$30,000.

Length of Study: Periods of 6-12 consecutive months.

Applications Procedure: Applicants should submit NEH application forms, resume, detailed description (3-6 pages) one-page biography and two reference letters.

Closing Date: May 1st.

Additional Information: Application guidelines are available from the NEH Public Affairs Office, room 402 (202 606 8446).

For further information contact:
Division of Fellowships and Seminars, Room 318, National Endowment for the Humanities, 1100 Pennsylvania Avenue, NW, Washington, DC, 20506, USA
Tel: 202 606 8466
Fax: 202 606 8558
Email: fellowsuniv@neh.fed.us
www: http://www.neh.fed.us
Contact: Jane A Rosenberg

Graduate Study Fellowships for Faculty at Historically Black Colleges and Universities

Subjects: The humanities.

Eligibility: Open to faculty members of historically Black US colleges and universities.

Level of Study: Doctorate.

Purpose: To strengthen teaching at historically Black US colleges and universities.

Type: Fellowship.

No. of awards offered: Varies.

Frequency: Annual.

Value: Up to US$30,000.

Length of Study: 9-12 months.

Country of Study: USA.

Applications Procedure: Application materials are available from the NEH.

Closing Date: March 15th.

For further information contact:
Division of Research and Education, Room 318, National Endowment for the Humanities, 1100 Pennsylvania Avenue, NW, Washington, DC, 20506, USA
Tel: 202 606 8467
Fax: 202 606 8204
Email: fellowscollind@neh.fed.us
Contact: Joseph Neville

International Research Grants

Subjects: The humanities.

Eligibility: Open to research organizations and learned societies.

Purpose: To provide funds to national organizations and learned societies to enable American scholars to pursue research abroad and to collaborate with foreign colleagues.

Type: Research Grant.

No. of awards offered: Varies.

Frequency: Annual.

Value: Varies.

Closing Date: October 1st.

For further information contact:
Room 318, National Endowment for the Humanities, 1100 Pennsylvania Avenue, NW, Washington, DC, 20506, USA
Tel: 202 606 8210
Fax: 202 606 8204
Contact: Division of Research and Education

Preservation and Access Grants

Subjects: Arts and humanities.

Eligibility: Open to individuals, non-profit institutions, cultural organizations, state agencies and institutional consortia.

Purpose: To support projects that will describe, organize, preserve and increase the availability of resources supporting research, education and public programming in the humanities.

Frequency: Annual.

Value: Varies.

Applications Procedure: Application guidelines and instructions are available upon request.

Closing Date: July 1st.

*Reference Materials Program Guides Grants

Subjects: Projects that promise to assist researchers and scholars in becoming aware of and utilizing materials in all fields of the humanities. Priority is given to projects that provide access to materials that are national or international in scope or impact.

Eligibility: Open to institutions of higher education, non-profit professional associations and scholarly societies, and individuals.

Purpose: To provide support for projects that promise to facilitate research in the humanities by organizing essential resources for scholarship and by preparing reference works that can improve scholarly access to information and collections.

Type: Grant.

No. of awards offered: Varies.

Frequency: As required.

Value: Dependent upon proposal.

Country of Study: USA.

Applications Procedure: For information, write or call the Assistant Director, Reference Materials, room 318.

Closing Date: September 1st.

Additional Information: Support is provided for bibliographies, bibliographic data bases, descriptive catalogues, indexes, union lists, other guides to humanities information or documentation, and projects to improve the ways in which research materials are made available. The Endowment encourages proposals for the compilation of guides that will help researchers learn of new sources or locate materials.

*Reference Materials Program Tools Grants

Subjects: The creation of dictionaries, historical/linguistic atlases, encyclopedias, concordances, catalogues/raisonnés, linguistic grammars, descriptive catalogues, databases, and other materials that serve to codify information essential to research in the humanities.

Eligibility: Open to institutions of higher education, non-profit professional associations and scholarly societies, and individuals.

Purpose: To provide support for projects that promise to facilitate research in the humanities by organizing essential resources for scholarship and by preparing reference works that can improve scholarly access to information and collections.

Type: Grant.

No. of awards offered: Varies.

Frequency: As required.

Value: Dependent upon proposal.

Country of Study: USA.

Closing Date: September 1st.

Additional Information: For information, write or call the Assistant Director, Reference Materials, room 318.

*Study Grants for College and University Teachers

Subjects: All disciplines of the humanities and the humanistic social sciences.

Eligibility: Open to college or university teachers who have taught full-time for three years; and college or university administrators who also teach undergraduates.

Purpose: To support college and university teachers to undertake independent study in their own disciplines or related disciplines.

Type: Grant.

No. of awards offered: Approximately 95.

Frequency: Annual.

Value: US$3,000.

Length of Study: A study period of six consecutive weeks.

Applications Procedure: Application guidelines are available from the NEH Public Affairs Office, room 402 (202 606 8435).

Closing Date: August 15th.

For further information contact:
Division of Fellowships and Seminars, Room 316, National Endowment for the Humanities, 1100 Pennsylvania Avenue, NW, Washington, DC, 20506, USA
Tel: 202 606 8463
Fax: 202 606 8558
Contact: Clayton Lewis

Summer Seminars for College Teachers

Subjects: All disciplines of the humanities and the humanistic social sciences.

Eligibility: Open to individuals who primarily teach undergraduates and have not recently had the opportunity to use the resources of a major library. Independent scholars are also eligible. Applicants must have completed their professional training by 1 March. Candidates for degrees and persons seeking support for work leading towards a degree are ineligible. Applications from members of PhD-granting departments are not normally accepted. Applicants should be US citizens or foreign nationals who have resided in the USA for at least three years.

Level of Study: Postgraduate, Professional development.

Type: Summer seminar.

No. of awards offered: Approximately 35 Seminars, each with 12 members.

Frequency: Annual.

Value: US$4,000 (for 8 weeks) US$3,600 (for 7 weeks) US$3,200 (for 6 weeks), US$2,825 (for 5 weeks), US$2,450 (for 4 weeks) to cover travel expenses to and from the seminar center, books, and other research expenses and living expenses.

Length of Study: 4-8 weeks.

Study Establishment: Various institutions under the direction of distinguished scholars and teachers.

Country of Study: USA and abroad.

Applications Procedure: Applications are available from individual seminar directors. A list of directors and program description are available from NEH.

Closing Date: March 1st.

For further information contact:
Summer Seminars for College Teachers, Division of Research and Education, Room 318, 1100 Pennsylvania Avenue, NW, Washington, DC, 20506, USA
Tel: 202 606 8463
Fax: 202 606 8204
Email: jmalloy@neh.fed.us
www: http://www.neh.fed.us
Contact: John D Malloy

Summer Seminars for School Teachers

Subjects: The humanities.

Eligibility: Open to US citizens who are full-time teachers at US public, private or parochial schools, of grades K through 12. Other school personnel may also apply. An individual may apply to only one Seminar in any one year.

Level of Study: Professional development.

Purpose: To provide opportunities for US teachers of grades K through 12 to work with master teachers and distinguished scholars, studying

443

important works in a systematic and thorough way.

No. of awards offered: Approximately 50 Seminars, each with 15 members.

Value: US$2,450, US$2,825 or US$3,200, depending on the length of the Seminar; to cover travel expenses to and from the Seminar location, books, other research expenses and living expenses.

Length of Study: 4-6 weeks.

Country of Study: USA and abroad.

Applications Procedure: Application forms and essays are required.

Closing Date: March 1st.

Additional Information: A list of the Seminars is distributed widely in late fall and is also available from the Research and Education division. Interested school teachers should write directly to the Seminar director. Applications are then submitted to the director, and not to the NEH.

For further information contact:
Summer Seminars for School Teachers, Room 321, National Endowment for the Humanities, 1100 Pennsylvania Avenue, NW, Washington, DC, 20506, USA
Tel: 202 606 8463
Fax: 202 606 8558
www: http://www.neh.fed.us

*Summer Stipends

Subjects: The humanities; the work proposed may be within the applicant's special areas of interest, or in some field that will enable them to understand their own fields better and enlarge their competence.

Eligibility: Each college and university in the USA and its territorial possessions may nominate three members of its faculty and staff. No more than two of the nominees should be in the early stages of their careers, i.e. junior nominees; no more than two should be at a more advanced stage, i.e. senior nominees. For the purposes of the program, instructors and assistant professors will be considered junior nominees and associate professors and professors will be considered senior nominees. Writers and independent scholars may apply without nomination. All applicants should be USA citizens or foreign nationals who have resided in the USA for at least three years.

Purpose: To allow college and university staff to pursue two consecutive months of full-time study and research.

Type: Stipends.

No. of awards offered: Approximately 200.

Frequency: Annual.

Value: US$4,000.

Length of Study: Full-time study or research, for two consecutive months.

Country of Study: USA.

Applications Procedure: Application guidelines are available from the NEH Public Affairs Office, room 402 (202 606 8435).

Closing Date: October 1st.

For further information contact:
Summer Stipends, Division of Fellowships and Seminars, Room 316, National Endowment for the Humanities, 1100 Pennsylvania Avenue, NW, Washington, DC, 20506, USA
Tel: 202 606 8466
Fax: 202 606 8558
Contact: Thomas O'Brien

Texts Program Publication Subvention Grants

Subjects: The publication and dissemination of scholarly books of compelling importance in all fields of the humanities.

Eligibility: Open to established publishers or scholarly publishing entities (non-profit and commercial) in the USA. Presses whose place of business is not in the USA are not eligible.

Purpose: To provide support for the preparation for publication of works

that promise to make major contributions to the study of the humanities.

No. of awards offered: 50.

Frequency: Annual.

Value: US$7,000.

Closing Date: April 1st.

Additional Information: Applications must demonstrate that the work for which a subvention is sought is important and likely to be influential.

NATIONAL FEDERATION OF MUSIC SOCIETIES

National Federation of Music Societies, Francis House, Francis Street, London, SW1P 1DE, England
Tel: 0171 828 7320
Fax: 0171 828 5504
Email: postmaster@nfms.demon.co.uk
Contact: Russell Jones

NFMS Award for Young Concert Artists

Subjects: Mens' voices; Womens' voices; strings, wind and bass; piano.

Eligibility: Open to singers under 30 years of age, instrumentalists under 28 years of age. All applicants must be UK residents.

Level of Study: Professional development.

Purpose: To support young musicians at the start of their professional careers.

No. of awards offered: 3 or 4.

Frequency: Annually, in a 4-year cycle.

Value: 70 engagements with affiliated societies.

Applications Procedure: Please complete application form and submit with CV.

Closing Date: As advertised in the national press.

NATIONAL FEDERATION OF STATE POETRY SOCIETIES, INC

National Federation of State Poetry Societies, Inc, 4242 Stevens, Minneapolis, MN, 55409, USA
Tel: 612 824 1964
Fax: 612 872 3267
www: GEN@INTERNET.COM
Contact: Pj Doyle

Edna Meudt Memorial Scholarships

Subjects: Poetry.

Eligibility: Open to juniors or seniors of accredited universities or colleges who write poetry.

Purpose: To encourage the study and writing of poetry.

Type: Scholarship.

No. of awards offered: Two.

Frequency: Annual.

Value: US$500, plus publication.

Applications Procedure: Candidates should submit a ten-poem manuscript (titled) plus application form.

Closing Date: February 1st 1997.

Additional Information: Committee members will evaluate, judge and select scholarship winners on or before March 1st 1997.

NATIONAL FEDERATION OF THE BLIND

National Federation of the Blind Scholarship Committee, 814 Fourth Avenue, Suite 200, Grinnell, IA, 50112, USA
Tel: 515 236 3366
Contact: Miss Peggy Pinder, Chairman

*American Action Fund Scholarship

Eligibility: Open to legally blind persons pursuing, or planning to pursue, a full-time post-secondary (graduate or undergraduate) course of training. The Scholarship is awarded on the basis of academic excellence, service to the community and financial need. Candidates need not be members of the Federation.

Purpose: Any subject.

Type: Scholarship.

No. of awards offered: One.

Frequency: Annual.

Value: US$10,000.

Country of Study: USA.

Applications Procedure: Application forms are available on request.

Closing Date: March 31st.

*Hermione Grant Calhoun Scholarship

Subjects: Any subject.

Eligibility: Open to legally blind women pursuing, or planning to pursue, a full-time post-secondary (graduate or undergraduate) course of training. The Scholarship is awarded on the basis of academic excellence, service to the community and financial need. Candidates need not be members of the Federation.

Type: Scholarship.

No. of awards offered: One.

Frequency: Annual.

Value: US$2,000.

Country of Study: USA.

Applications Procedure: Application forms are available on request.

Closing Date: March 31st.

*Educator of Tomorrow Award

Subjects: Teaching.

Eligibility: Open to legally blind persons pursuing, or planning to pursue, a full-time post-secondary (graduate or undergraduate) course of training. The winner must be planning a career in elementary, secondary or post-secondary teaching. The Scholarship is awarded on the basis of academic excellence, service to the community and financial need. Candidates need not be members of the Federation.

No. of awards offered: One.

Frequency: Annual.

Value: US$2,500.

Country of Study: USA.

Applications Procedure: Application forms are available on request.

Closing Date: March 31st.

*Frank Walton Horn Memorial Scholarship

Subjects: Any subject; however, preference will be given to applicants in the fields of architecture and engineering.

Eligibility: Open to legally blind persons pursuing, or planning to pursue, a full-time post-secondary (graduate or undergraduate) course of training. The Scholarship is awarded on the basis of academic excellence, service to the community and financial need. Candidates need not

be members of the Federation.

Type: Scholarship.

No. of awards offered: One.

Frequency: Annual.

Value: US$2,500.

Country of Study: USA.

Applications Procedure: Application forms are available on request.

Closing Date: March 31st.

*Humanities Scholarship

Subjects: The traditional humanities such as art, English, foreign languages, history, philosophy or religion.

Eligibility: Open to legally blind persons pursuing, or planning to pursue, a full-time post-secondary (graduate or undergraduate) course of training. The Scholarship is awarded on the basis of academic excellence, service to the community and financial need. Candidates need not be members of the Federation.

Type: Scholarship.

No. of awards offered: One.

Frequency: Annual.

Value: US$2,500.

Country of Study: USA.

Applications Procedure: Application forms are available on request.

Closing Date: March 31st.

*Kuchler-Killian Memorial Scholarship

Subjects: Any subject.

Eligibility: Open to legally blind persons pursuing, or planning to pursue, a full-time post-secondary (graduate or undergraduate) course of training. The Scholarship is awarded on the basis of academic excellence, service to the community and financial need. Candidates need not be members of the Federation.

Type: Scholarship.

No. of awards offered: One.

Frequency: Annual.

Value: US$2,000.

Country of Study: USA.

Applications Procedure: Application forms are available on request.

Closing Date: March 31st.

*Melva T Owen Memorial Scholarship

Subjects: Any subject, except religion.

Eligibility: Open to legally blind persons pursuing, or planning to pursue, a full-time post-secondary (graduate or undergraduate) course of training. Individuals seeking only to further their general or cultural education are ineligible. The Scholarship is awarded on the basis of academic excellence, service to the community and financial need. Candidates need not be members of the Federation.

Type: Scholarship.

No. of awards offered: One.

Frequency: Annual.

Value: US$3,000.

Country of Study: USA.

Applications Procedure: Application forms are available on request.

Closing Date: 31 March.

*Howard Brown Rickard Scholarship

Subjects: Law, medicine, engineering, architecture or the natural sciences.

Eligibility: Open to legally blind persons pursuing, or planning to pursue, a full-time post-secondary (graduate or undergraduate) course of training. The Scholarship is awarded on the basis of academic excellence, service to the community and financial need. Candidates need not be members of the Federation.

Type: Scholarship.

No. of awards offered: One.

Frequency: Annual.

Value: US$2,500.

Country of Study: USA.

Applications Procedure: Application forms are available on request.

Closing Date: March 31st.

*Scholarships

Eligibility: Open to legally blind persons pursuing, or planning to pursue, a full-time post-secondary (graduate or undergraduate) course of training. The Scholarship is awarded on the basis of academic excellence, service to the community and financial need. Candidates need not be members of the Federation.

Purpose: Any subject.

Type: Scholarship.

No. of awards offered: 16.

Frequency: Annual.

Value: Two at US$4,000; five at US$2,500; nine at US$2,000.

Country of Study: USA.

Applications Procedure: Application forms are available on request.

Closing Date: March 31st.

*Ellen Setterfield Memorial Scholarship

Subjects: Social sciences.

Eligibility: Open to legally blind persons pursuing, or planning to pursue, a full-time graduate course of training. The Scholarship is awarded on the basis of academic excellence, service to the community and financial need. Candidates need not be members of the Federation.

Type: Scholarship.

No. of awards offered: One.

Frequency: Annual.

Value: US$2,000.

Country of Study: USA.

Applications Procedure: Application forms are available on request.

Closing Date: March 31st.

NATIONAL FOUNDATION FOR INFECTIOUS DISEASES

National Foundation for Infectious Diseases, 4733 Bethesda Avenue, Suite 750, Bethesda, MD, 20814, USA
Tel: 301 656 0003
Fax: 301 907 0878

Fellowship in Infectious Diseases

Subjects: Infectious diseases.

Eligibility: Open to physicians who are citizens of the USA and have satisfactorily completed three or more years of postgraduate medical training (internal medicine, surgery, pediatrics, epidemiology, etc.) The applicant must be sponsored by a university-affiliated medical center. This fellowship may not be awarded if the applicant has received or will receive a major fellowship, research grant or traineeship in excess of the amount of this award from the Federal government or another foundation. A letter from the Chairman of the Department of Infectious Diseases expressing a willingness to assume responsibility for training the applicant must accompany the application.

Level of Study: Postgraduate.

Purpose: To encourage and assist young qualified physicians to become specialists and investigators in the field of infectious diseases.

Type: Fellowship.

No. of awards offered: Varies.

Frequency: Annual.

Value: A stipend of US$17,000 for the year and an additional US$1,000 for travel and supplies. Although it is anticipated that the award will be tax-exempt, no guarantee of IRS rulings can be made. No overhead will be paid to the sponsoring institution.

Length of Study: One year.

Closing Date: Postmark 14 January for notification in April.

Additional Information: The fellowship will be awarded to individuals who do not or will not have training or research grant support during the period of this grant and who are seeking support for one of two or three years of postdoctoral fellowship experience. Preference will be given to those applying for the third year of such support. Support will be provided for one year only, commencing on 1 July.

Postdoctoral Fellowship in Infectious Disease Training and Herpes Virus Research

Subjects: Priority will be given to the study of Herpes viruses, especially as they might pertain to AIDS and HIV infections.

Eligibility: Open to physicians who are citizens of the USA. Candidates must demonstrate aptitude in and preparatory training for research, and must confirm arrangements for conduct of the proposed research in a recognized host laboratory. Applicants receiving or to be awarded grants in the same academic year in excess of the amount of this award are not eligible for funding under this proposal. Applicants with no grant support will receive priority consideration.

Level of Study: Postdoctorate.

Purpose: To encourage and assist a qualified physician researcher to become a specialist and investigator in the field of viral infections, notably those due to Herpes viruses.

Type: Fellowship.

No. of awards offered: Varies.

Frequency: Annual.

Value: A stipend of US$23,000 for the year, with an additional US$1,000 that may be used for travel and supplies (at investigator's discretion). Although it is anticipated that the award will be tax-exempt, no guarantee of IRS rulings can be made. No overhead to the sponsoring institution will be paid. The stipend may be supplemented by other monies to achieve salary levels consistent with other fellowships within the supporting institutions.

Length of Study: One year.

Closing Date: Postmark 14 January for notification in April.

Postdoctoral Fellowship in Medical Mycology

Subjects: Medical mycology.

Eligibility: The applicant must be a physician who is a citizen of the United States. He/she must demonstrate aptitude and accomplishment in research, and must confirm arrangements for conduct of the proposed research in a recognized host laboratory. The applicant must be sponsored by a university-affiliated medical center. The fellowship may not be awarded if the applicant has received or will receive a major fellowship, research grant or traineeship from the Federal government or another foundation in excess of the amount of this award. A letter from the Chairman of the Department of Infectious Diseases expressing a willingness to assume responsibility for training the applicant must accompany the application.

Level of Study: Postdoctorate.

Purpose: To encourage and assist a qualified physician to become a specialist and investigator in medical mycology.

Type: Fellowship.

No. of awards offered: Three.

Frequency: Annual.

Value: A stipend of US$17,000 for the year and an additional US$1,000 for travel and supplies. Although it is anticipated that the award will be tax-exempt, no guarantee of IRS rulings can be made. No overhead will be paid to the sponsoring institution.

Length of Study: One year.

Study Establishment: Approved research institutions.

Country of Study: USA.

Closing Date: Postmark 14 January for notification in April.

Additional Information: Detailed guidelines are available from the NFID.

Postdoctoral Fellowship in Nosocomial/Gram-Positive Infection Research and Training

Subjects: Priority will be given to the study of gram-positive nosocomial infections.

Eligibility: Open to physicians in training who are citizens of the USA. Applicants must demonstrate aptitude or accomplishments in research, and must confirm arrangements for conduct of the proposed research in a recognized host laboratory. Applicants receiving or to be awarded grants in the same academic year in excess of the amount of this award are not eligible for funding under this proposal. Applicants with no grant support will receive priority consideration.

Level of Study: Postdoctorate.

Purpose: To encourage and assist a qualified physician trainee researcher to become a specialist and investigator in the field of nosocomial infections.

Type: Fellowship.

No. of awards offered: Varies.

Frequency: Annual.

Value: A stipend of US$18,000 for the year, of which US$1,000 may be used for travel and supplies (at investigator's discretion). Although it is anticipated that the award will be tax-exempt, no guarantee of IRS rulings can be made. No overhead to the sponsoring institution will be paid. The stipend may be supplemented by other monies to achieve salary levels consistent with other fellows within the supporting institutions.

Length of Study: One year.

Closing Date: Postmark 14 January for notification in April.

NATIONAL GALLERY OF ART

Center for Advanced Study in the Visual Arts, National Gallery of Art, Washington, DC, 20565, USA
Tel: 202 842 6480
Fax: 202 408 8531
Contact: Dean

*Kress Fellowship in Art History

Subjects: Art history.

Eligibility: Open to PhD candidates in art history who have finished all their course work, residence requirements, and general or preliminary examinations and have devoted at least one full year's research to their proposed dissertation topic.

Type: Fellowship.

No. of awards offered: One.

Frequency: Annual.

Value: US$11,000 per annum.

Length of Study: Two years.

Study Establishment: The Center for Advanced Study in the Visual Arts.

Closing Date: November 15th.

NATIONAL HEADACHE FOUNDATION

National Headache Foundation, 428 West Street , James Place, 2nd Floor, Chicago, IL, 60614, USA
Tel: 312 388 6399
Fax: 312 525 7357
Contact: Suzanne E Simons, Director of Administration and Development

National Headache Foundation Research Grant

Subjects: Causes of and treatments for headache.

Eligibility: Open to researchers in neurology and pharmacology departments in US medical schools. Submissions from other departments and individual investigators are also welcome.

Level of Study: Doctorate, Postdoctorate.

Purpose: To encourage better understanding and treatment of headache and head pain.

No. of awards offered: Varies; dependent on funds available and worthy projects submitted.

Frequency: Annual.

Value: Amount is dependent on funds available. Grant covers only direct costs of carrying out research, no overhead or salaries.

Country of Study: USA.

Closing Date: December 1st for notification by the following March.

NATIONAL HEALTH AND MEDICAL RESEARCH COUNCIL

National Health and Medical Research Council, GPO Box 9848, Canberra, ACT, 2601, Australia
Tel: 06 289 8187
Fax: 06 289 6957
Contact: The Secretary

Australian Applied Health Sciences Fellowships

Subjects: Scientific research, including the social and behavioural sciences, which can be applied to any area of clinical or community medicine.

Eligibility: Open to Australian citizens or graduates from overseas with permanent Australian resident status, who are not under bond to any foreign government. Candidates should hold a doctorate in a health related field of research or have submitted a thesis for such by December of the year of application and be actively engaged in such research in Australia or overseas and have no more than two years postdoctoral experience at the time of application.

Level of Study: Postdoctorate.

Purpose: To provide training in scientific research methods.

Type: Fellowship.

No. of awards offered: Varies.

Frequency: Annual.

Value: Varies.

Length of Study: Four years.

Study Establishment: Institutions approved by the NHMRC, such as teaching hospitals, universities and research institutes.

Country of Study: Australia.

Closing Date: July 31st.

Australian Postdoctoral Fellowships

Subjects: Biomedical sciences.

Eligibility: Open to Australian citizens or graduates from overseas with permanent Australian resident status who are not under bond to any foreign government. Candidates should hold a doctorate in a medical, dental or related field of research or have submitted a thesis for such by December in the year of application, be actively engaged in such research in Australia or overseaes and have no more than two years' postdoctoral experience at the time of application.

Level of Study: Postdoctorate.

Purpose: To provide a vehicle for training in clinical and basic research in Australia, and to encourage persons of outstanding ability to make medical research a full-time career.

Type: Fellowship.

No. of awards offered: Varies.

Frequency: Annual.

Value: Varies.

Length of Study: Four years.

Study Establishment: Institutions approved by the NHMRC, such as teaching hospitals universities and research institutes.

Country of Study: Australia.

Applications Procedure: Application form.

Closing Date: July 31st.

Burnet Fellowships

Subjects: Any field of the Biomedical sciences.

Eligibility: Open to Australian citizens or permanent residents who are not under bond to any foreign government. Candidates should have a current academic or hospital appointment overseas equivalent to an Australian Professor/Associate Professor, and be actively engaged in research and apply in conjunction with a host institution which must undertake to provide infrastructural support and administer the award (normal access procedures for receipt of NHMRC funds will apply).

Purpose: To attract back to Australia medical researchers of a high calibre who have spent considerable time overseas (at least seven years) and who have not returned because of the lack of suitable opportunities.

Type: Fellowships.

No. of awards offered: Two.

Frequency: Annual.

Value: A setting up grant of up to A$250,000 p.a. to cover the senior investigator's salary at the appropriate level on the NHMRC Research Fellowship scales, maintenance/equipment and/or salaries for a limited number of associate investigators who wish to return with the senior investigator, plus appropriate travel/removal allowances.

Length of Study: Five years.

Country of Study: Australia.

Applications Procedure: There is no application form. Applications should be submitted in writing with CV attached.

Closing Date: None.

For further information contact:
National Health and Medical Research Council, GPO Box 9848, Canberra, ACT, 2601, Australia
Tel: 06 289 7662
Fax: 06 289 6957
Email: kerry.warren@hhlgcs.ausgovnncs.telememo.au
Contact: Ms R Skilling

448

Eccles Awards

Subjects: Any field of the biomedical sciences; preference will be given to fields recognized as high priority to the health of the nation.

Eligibility: Open to investigators with an outstanding record in research, who have potential for appointment at a level equivalent to Australian Professor/Associate Professor, and who are Australian citizens currently working overseeas or have permanent Australian resident status and are not under bond to any foreign government.

Purpose: To assist in the appointment of distinguished and productive expatriate medical and dental researchers, who have been overseas for at least seven years, to an academic position in Australia.

No. of awards offered: Up to two awards.

Frequency: Annual.

Value: No more than A$150,000 per annum to be used for equipment, maintenance and/or salaries for associate investigators, excluding the salary of the potential appointee. This grant must be matched by the appointing institution in an appropriate and adequate way.

Length of Study: Three years.

Study Establishment: Australian research institutions.

Country of Study: Australia.

Applications Procedure: There is no application form. Application should be submitted in writing with a full CV attached.

Closing Date: None.

For further information contact:
National Health and Medical Research Council, GPO Box 9848, Canberra, ACT, 2601, Australia
Tel: 06 289 7165
Fax: 06 289 8617
Email: kerry.warren@hhlgcs.ausgovhmcs.telememo.au
Contact: Ms R Skillings

Equipment Grants

Subjects: All fields of medicine and dentistry.

Eligibility: Open to individuals, groups or institutions which are normally eligible for NHMRC support. Grants will be made on the basis of scientific merit, taking into consideration factors including: whether the applicant(s) hold NHMRC grants; the institutional ranking of the application; institutional/regional availability of major equipment.

Purpose: To provide funding support for the purchase of items of equipment required for biomedical research costing in excess of A$10,000.

Type: Grant.

No. of awards offered: Varies.

Frequency: Annual.

Value: To cover the cost of equipment in excess of A$10,000.

Country of Study: Australia.

Applications Procedure: Application form required to be completed.

Closing Date: April 30th.

For further information contact:
National Health and Medical Research Council, GPO Box 9848, Canberra, ACT 2601, 2601, Australia
Tel: 06 289 7006
Fax: 06 289 8617
Contact: Ms L Anasson

Neil Hamilton Fairley Fellowships

Subjects: Scientific research, including the social and behavioural sciences, which can be applied to any area of clincial or community medicine.

Eligibility: Open to Australian citizens or graduates from overseas with permanent Australian resident status who are not under bond to any foreign government. Candidates should hold a doctorate in a health related field of research or have submittted a thesis for such by December of the year of application and be actively engaged in such research in Australia and have no more than two years postdoctoral experience at the time of application.

Level of Study: Postdoctorate.

Purpose: To provide training in scientific research methods.

Type: Fellowship.

No. of awards offered: Varies.

Frequency: Annual.

Value: Varies.

Length of Study: Four years, the first two of which are to be spent overseas and the final two in Australia.

Study Establishment: Institutions approved by the NHMRC, such as teaching hospitals, universities and research institutes.

Country of Study: Australia and abroad.

Applications Procedure: Application form required.

Closing Date: July 31st.

Dora Lush (Biomedical) Postgraduate Scholarships

Subjects: Biomedical sciences.

Eligibility: Australian citizens who have already completed a science degree (or equivalent) at the time of submission of the application. Science honours graduates and unregistered medical or dental graduates from overseas, who have permanent resident status and are currently residing in Australia.

Level of Study: Postgraduate.

Purpose: The purpose of the scholarship is to encourage science honours or equivalent graduates of outstanding ability to gain full-time medical research experience. All candidates must enrol for a higher degree.

Type: Scholarship.

No. of awards offered: Varies.

Frequency: Annual.

Value: A variable stipend per annum, plus an allowance of A$1,500 per annum, payable to the department where the Scholar is working.

Length of Study: One year; renewable for up to two further years.

Study Establishment: Institutions of higher learning.

Country of Study: Australia.

Closing Date: September 30th.

C J Martin Fellowships

Subjects: Biomedical sciences.

Eligibility: Open to Australian citizens or graduates from overseas with permanent Australian resident status who are not under bond to any foreign government. Candidates should hold a doctorate in a medical, dental or related field of research, be actively engaged in such research in Australia and have no more than two years' postdoctoral experience at the time of application.

Level of Study: Postdoctorate.

Purpose: To enable Fellows to develop their research skills and work overseas on specific research projects within the biomedical sciences under nominated advisers.

Type: Fellowship.

No. of awards offered: Varies.

Frequency: Annual.

Value: Varies.

Length of Study: Four years, of which the first two are to be spent overseas and the final two in Australia.

Study Establishment: Institutions approved by the NHMRC, such as teaching hospitals, universities and research institutes.

Country of Study: Australia and abroad.

Applications Procedure: Application form.

Closing Date: July 31st.

Medical and Dental Postgraduate Research Scholarships

Subjects: Medical or dental research.

Eligibility: Open to Australian citizens who are medical or dental graduates registered to practice in Australia, with the proviso that Dental Postgraduate Research Scholarships may be awarded prior to graduation provided that the evidence of high quality work is shown. Medical and dental graduates from overseas who hold a qualification that is registered for practice in Australia and who have permanent resident status and are currently residing in Australia. Evidence of residence status shall be provided. The scholarship shall be held within Australia.

Level of Study: Postgraduate.

Purpose: To encourage medical and dental graduates to gain full-time research experience.

Type: Scholarship.

No. of awards offered: Varies.

Frequency: Annual.

Value: Stipend varies per annum, plus an allowance of A$1,500 per annum payable to the department where the Scholar is working.

Length of Study: One year; renewable for up to two further years.

Study Establishment: Institutions of higher learning.

Country of Study: Australia.

Applications Procedure: Application form.

Closing Date: June 30th.

Medical Research Project Grants

Subjects: All fields of medicine and dentistry.

Eligibility: Open to Australian researchers.

Purpose: To provide support for work on problems which are likely to be capable of solution in a reasonably short period of time.

Type: Grant.

No. of awards offered: Varies.

Frequency: Annual.

Value: To cover salary, equipment, maintenance and other specific expenses.

Country of Study: Australia.

Applications Procedure: Application form required to be completed.

Closing Date: March 6th.

For further information contact:
National Health and Medical Research Council, GPO Box 9848, Canberra, ACT, 2601, Australia
Tel: 06 289 6974
Fax: 06 289 8617
Contact: Ms E Hoole

NHMRC/INSERM Exchange Fellowships

Subjects: Biomedical sciences.

Eligibility: Open to Australian citizens and permanent residents who hold a doctorate in a medical, dental or related field of research or have submitted a thesis for such by December in the year of application, are actively engaged in such research in Australia and have no more than two years' postdoctoral experience at the time of application.

Level of Study: Postdoctorate.

Purpose: To enable Fellows to work overseas on specific research projects.

Type: Fellowship.

No. of awards offered: One.

Frequency: Annual.

Value: Varies.

Length of Study: Two years, one of which is to be spent in France and one in Australia.

Study Establishment: Institutions approved by the NHMRC, such as teaching hospitals, universities and research institutes.

Country of Study: France and Australia.

Applications Procedure: Application form required.

Closing Date: July 31st.

Additional Information: This Fellowship is awarded in association with l'Institut National de la Santé et de la Recherche Médicale (INSERM), France.

Public Health Travelling Fellowships

Subjects: Public health, defined as the organized response by society to the need to protect and promote the people's health.

Eligibility: Open to all personnel working in the field of public health, who are suitably qualified at a level appropriate for fulfilment of the objectives of the study and for implementation of its benefits. The applicant may be employed in government or industry, or may be self-employed. Preference will be given to those applicants who would not normally, in the course of their employment, have the opportunity, as part of their normal duties, for overseas travel and experience.

Level of Study: Unrestricted.

Purpose: To enable Fellows to make postgraduate study tours abroad or within Australia, which relate to their work and specialty and which will be of benefit to public health in Australia.

Type: Travelling Fellowships.

No. of awards offered: Varies.

Frequency: Annual.

Value: Not exceeding A$19,240, plus an agreed annual allowance to cover cost increases.

Length of Study: Two to 12 months.

Country of Study: Australia or abroad.

Closing Date: June 30th.

Additional Information: Preference will be given to public health practitioners.

Research Program grants

Subjects: All fields of medicine and dentistry.

Eligibility: Open to research teams which would normally comprise several outstanding established investigators. The principal investigator or co-investigators should normally have held five or more Project Grants between them for much of the previous six years; the ratings achieved by these grants will be taken into account.

Purpose: To provide guaranteed support for a research team.

Type: Grant.

No. of awards offered: Varies.

Frequency: Annual.

Value: Varies.

Length of Study: Five years.

Country of Study: Australia.

Applications Procedure: Two stage application process: application forms and information kit available from Ms R Skilling.

Closing Date: August 31st.

For further information contact:
National Health and Medical Research Council, GPO Box 9848, Canberra, ACT, 2601, Australia
Tel: 06 289 7165
Fax: 06 289 8617
Email: kerry.warren@hhlgcs.ausgovhcs.telememo.au
Contact: Ms R Skilling

R Douglas Wright Awards

Subjects: Biomedical sciences.

Eligibility: Open to applicants who have completed postdoctoral research training or have equivalent experience, and are seeking to establish themselves in a career in medical research in Australia.

Purpose: To provide outstanding researchers at an early stage in their career with an opportunity for independent research together with improved security.

Type: Awards.

No. of awards offered: Varies.

Frequency: Annual.

Value: To provide a salary usually starting in the range of Senior Research Officer Level 1 to Senior Research Officer Level 4, with annual increments, plus an allowance of A$10,000 per annum payable to the department where the scholar is working.

Length of Study: Four years.

Country of Study: Australia.

Applications Procedure: Applications available from Ms R Skilling.

Closing Date: April 30th.

For further information contact:
National Health and Medical Research Council, GPO Box 9848, Canberra, ACT, 2601, Australia
Tel: 06 289 7165
Fax: 06 289 8617
Email: kerry.warren@mmlgcs.ausgovhcs.telemeo.au
Contact: Ms R Stilling

NATIONAL HEART FOUNDATION OF AUSTRALIA

National Heart Foundation of Australia, PO Box 2, Woden, ACT, 2606, Australia
Tel: 282 2144
Fax: 282 5147
Contact: Deidre Houston-Robey

Warren McDonald International Fellowship

Subjects: Cardiovascular research.

Eligibility: Open to senior research workers of proven ability in the cardiovascular field, whose normal employment is outside Australia.

Purpose: To add a special viewpoint or skill not available in Australia to an active Australian research group.

Type: Fellowship.

No. of awards offered: One.

Frequency: Annual.

Value: Up to A$47,500 per annum, plus allowances for travel and dependants. The Foundation also makes a grant of up to A$4,000 to cover departmental expenses.

Length of Study: Up to one year.

Study Establishment: Universities, hospitals or research institutions.

Country of Study: Australia.

Closing Date: May 31st.

Additional Information: Candidates must be nominated by the head of the host department or institution and may not apply directly to the Foundation.

Research Grants-in-Aid

Eligibility: Australian citizens only.

Purpose: To support research in the cardiovascular field.

Type: Grant.

No. of awards offered: 50-60.

Frequency: Annual.

Value: Dependent on project and funds available.

Country of Study: Australia.

Applications Procedure: Application must be submitted outlining research proposal. References and supervisor/departmental support.

Closing Date: April 30th.

Overseas Research Fellowships

Subjects: Clinical or basic medical sciences related to cardiovascular problems.

Eligibility: Open to persons normally resident in Australia with at least two years' postgraduate experience and significant achievement in research.

Purpose: To allow Fellows to obtain skills in cardiovascular research.

Type: Fellowship.

No. of awards offered: One to two per annum.

Frequency: Annual.

Value: A$37,345-A$45,362 per annum.

Length of Study: Three years.

Study Establishment: Approved institutions.

Country of Study: Overseas for the first two years and Australia for the third year.

Closing Date: May 31st.

Additional Information: Fellowships are awarded on the understanding that the Fellow will return to Australia to continue his or her career upon completion of the Fellowship.

Postgraduate Medical Research Scholarship

Eligibility: Australian citizens.

Level of Study: Postgraduate.

Purpose: To assist medical graduates to undertake a period of training in research under the full-time supervision and tuition of a responsible investigator.

Type: Scholarship.

No. of awards offered: Three.

Frequency: Annual.

Value: A$23,450.

Length of Study: Three years.

Study Establishment: University, hospitals, and research institutions.

Country of Study: Australia.

Applications Procedure: Application outlining research proposal must be accompanied by supervisor's reference and backing.

Closing Date: May 31st.

Postgraduate Research Science Scholarship

Eligibility: Australian nationals.

Level of Study: Postgraduate.

Purpose: To assist science graduates to undertake a period of training in cardiovascular research under the full-time supervision and tuition of a responsible investigator.

Type: Scholarship.

Frequency: Annual.

Value: A$17,161.

Length of Study: Three years.

Study Establishment: Universities, hospitals, research institutions.

Country of Study: Australia.

Applications Procedure: Application submission outlining research

proposal stating name of supervisor and host institution. References also required.

NATIONAL HEART FOUNDATION OF NEW ZEALAND

National Heart Foundation of New Zealand, PO Box 17-160, Greenlane, Newmarket, Auckland, New Zealand
Tel: 64 9 524 6005
Fax: 64 9 524 7854
Contact: Medical Director

Fellowships, Project Grants, Travel Grants and Grants-in-Aid

Subjects: Any aspect of cardiovascular disease including research, rehabilitation and education.

Eligibility: Normally open to New Zealand graduates only.

Level of Study: Postgraduate.

Purpose: To promote the aims of the National Heart Foundation of New Zealand.

No. of awards offered: A variable number of grants and fellowships.

Frequency: Annual.

Value: Varies according to the determination of the Scientific Committee and within an annual budget.

Study Establishment: New Zealand institutions.

Country of Study: New Zealand, but Travel Grants and Clinical Training Fellowships may be held abroad.

Applications Procedure: Candidates should apply to the Foundation for the publication 'A Guide to Applicants for Research and Other Grants'.

Closing Date: Fellowships 1 April; Project Grants 1 April; Grants-in-Aid 1 February, 1 April and 1 September; Travel Grants throughout the year.

NATIONAL HEART FOUNDATION (USA)

15825 Shady Grove Road, Suite 140, Rockville, MD, 20850, USA
Tel: 301 948 3244
Fax: 301 258 9454
Contact: Dr Sherry Marts

Grant

Eligibility: The principal investigator must hold the academic rank of assistant professor (or equivalent) and must be the head of an independent research lab group.

Level of Study: Professional development.

Purpose: Basic research on the causes of, or treatments for, heart disease and stroke.

Type: Grant.

No. of awards offered: Varies.

Frequency: Annual.

Value: Up to US$15,000.

Length of Study: One year.

Country of Study: Any.

Applications Procedure: Application form must be completed.

Additional Information: The National Heart Foundation starter grants program is intended to assist young investigators who are beginning independent research careers at the assistant professor level or equivalent.

NATIONAL HEMOPHILIA FOUNDATION

National Hemophilia Foundation, Room 303, 110 Greene Street, New York, NY, 10012, USA
Tel: 212 219 8180 ext.3052
Fax: 212 966 9247
Contact: Charla Andrews, MS

Judith Graham Pool Postdoctoral Research Fellowships in Hemophilia

Subjects: Clinical or basic research on the biochemical, genetic, hematologic, orthopedic, psychiatric, or dental aspects of the hemophilias or von Willebrand's Disease and their complications. Other permissible areas include research into rehabilitation, therapeutic modalities, AIDS research with respect to the hemophiliacs or social features of these diseases.

Eligibility: Open to US citizens or permanent residents with doctoral degrees who are currently engaged in, or intend to pursue, hemophilia research. Preference is given to investigators whose proposals aim to further the understanding of or improve the management of the hemophilias. Preference is also shown to candidates having prior experience in the areas of their proposal, but the JGP Fellowships are not intended for established investigators or faculty.

Level of Study: Postgraduate.

Purpose: To enhance research in hemophilia or von Willebrand's Disease by supporting studies of high scientific merit and relevance to hemophilia and stimulating the life-long interest in hemophilia of promising investigators.

No. of awards offered: Varies.

Frequency: Annual.

Value: Up to US$35,000 per annum. No institutional sharing; up to US$750 for domestic travel is included in the Fellowship. Payments are made to the sponsoring institution on a quarterly basis.

Length of Study: One year; Fellowships may be renewed for a second year of research if merited.

Study Establishment: Appropriate sponsoring institutions throughout the United States.

Country of Study: USA.

Applications Procedure: Application forms are available on request.

Closing Date: December 15th. Notification on or about May 1st.

NATIONAL HISTORICAL PUBLICATIONS & RECORDS COMMISSION

National Historical Publications & Records Commission, Room 607, National Archives Building (Archives 1), 7th & Pennsylvania Ave, NW, Washington, DC, 20408, USA
Tel: 202 501 5610
Fax: 202 501 5601
Email: nhprc@archl.nara.gov
www: http://www.nara.gov/nara/nhprc/nhprc.html
Contact: Laurie A Baty

Documentary Editing and Archival and Records Management Grants

Eligibility: Open to a state, tribal, local government, individual, not-for-profit organisation. Federal agencies are excluded.

Purpose: The NHPRC encourages efforts by government and private organizations to preserve and make accessible for use those records that further an understanding and appreciation of American History.

Type: Monetary, Travel Grant.

No. of awards offered: Varies.

Frequency: Three times a year depending on available funds.

Country of Study: USA.

Applications Procedure: Contact the agency for current guidelines and application materials.

Closing Date: February 1st, June 1st, October 1st, depending on the category under which applying.

Fellowship in Archival Administration

Eligibility: Individuals must have spent two to five years working as an archivist. Must be US citizens.

Level of Study: Professional development.

Purpose: To provide experience in management and administration for archivists with two to five years' experience.

Type: Fellowship.

No. of awards offered: One.

Frequency: Annual.

Value: Currently US$35,000 (+US$7,000 benefits).

Length of Study: 9-12 months.

Country of Study: USA.

Applications Procedure: Potential applicants should contact the commission for guidelines and host institution information. This information is available by December of the preceding year.

Closing Date: March 1st postmark.

Fellowship in Documentary Editing

Eligibility: Individuals must have completed coursework and examinations leading to the doctorate. Applicants may be working on their dissertation. Official transcripts must be submitted.

Level of Study: Doctorate, Postdoctorate.

Purpose: To provide individuals with training in the field of documentary editing.

Type: Fellowship.

No. of awards offered: One.

Frequency: Annual.

Value: Currently US$33,000 (+US$8,250 benefits).

Length of Study: 9-12 months.

Country of Study: USA.

Applications Procedure: Potential applicants should contact the commission for guidelines and host institution information. This information is available by December of the preceding year.

Closing Date: March 1st postmark.

NATIONAL HUMANITIES CENTER

National Humanities Center, PO Box 12256, Research Triangle Park, NC, 27709-2256, USA
Tel: 919 549 0661
Contact: Fellowship Program

Fellowships in the Humanities

Subjects: History, philosophy, languages and literature, classics, religion, history of the arts, and other fields in the liberal arts.

Eligibility: Open to scholars of any nationality. Social scientists, natural scientists, or professionals whose work has a humanistic dimension may also apply. Applicants must hold a doctorate or have equivalent professional accomplishments. Fellowships are awarded to senior scholars of recognized accomplishment and to promising young scholars engaged in research beyond the revision of their dissertations.

Level of Study: Postdoctorate.

Purpose: To support advanced postdoctoral scholarship in the humanities.

Type: Fellowship.

No. of awards offered: 35-40.

Frequency: Annual.

Value: Fellowship stipends are individually determined in accordance with the needs of each Fellow and the Center's ability to meet them. As the Center cannot in most instances replace full salaries, applicants are urged to seek partial funding in the form of sabbatical salaries or grants from other sources. In addition to stipends, the Center provides round-trip travel expenses for Fellows and their immediate families to and from North Carolina.

Length of Study: One academic year, although a few Fellowships may be awarded for a single semester.

Study Establishment: The Center.

Country of Study: USA.

Closing Date: October 15th.

Additional Information: Fellowships are supported by grants from the Andrew W Mellon Foundation, the National Endowment for the Humanities, the Research Triangle Foundation, Delta Delta Delta and the Rockefeller Foundation.

NATIONAL INSTITUTE OF MENTAL HEALTH THRU AMERICAN SOCIOLOGICAL SOCIETY

National Institute of Mental Health thru American Sociological Society, 1722 N Street NW, Washington, DC, 20036, USA
Tel: 202 833 3410
Fax: 202 785 0146
Email: ASA-Minority-Affairs@MCIMAIL.COM
Contact: Frances M Foster, Minority Affairs Program Manager

American Sociological Association Minority Fellowship Program

Subjects: Sociological research on mental health.

Eligibility: Candidates must be citizens or non citizen nationals of the USA and must be accepted or enrolled in a full time sociology doctoral program in the USA at the time of the appointment. In addition applicants must be of a racial or ethnic minority group.

Level of Study: Doctorate.

Purpose: To support the development and training of minority sociologists in mental health.

Type: Fellowship.

No. of awards offered: Approximately 10.

Frequency: Annual.

Value: US$10,008.

Length of Study: Up to three years possible without reapplying.

Country of Study: USA.

Applications Procedure: Contact the ASA and request application form (must be typed), will also need to prepare appropriate essays (see application form) ; must supply three letters of recommendation; transcripts of all institutions attended ; and may supply any other documentation to support application as necessary.

Closing Date: December 31st annually.

NATIONAL KIDNEY FOUNDATION

Research Fellowship Committee, National Kidney Foundation, 30 East 33rd Street, New York, NY, 10016, USA

*Postdoctoral Fellowships

Subjects: Kidney function and disease: research and training.

Eligibility: Open to qualified investigators of any nationality who are interested in a career in kidney research, and will not have had more than one year of research training at the start of the tenure of the Fellowship.

Type: Fellowship.

No. of awards offered: Approximately 40.

Frequency: Annual.

Value: US$25,000 per annum.

Length of Study: One year; renewable for one additional year.

Country of Study: USA.

Applications Procedure: Applications should be made in the form of a proposal (20 copies required) which should contain the following: a CV and list of publications of the principal investigators and other professional personnel involved; a concise description of the proposed research (including aims, significance, methodology and relevant research); a list of other current and pending financial support.

Closing Date: September 14th.

*Young Investigator Grants

Subjects: Nephrology, urology and related disciplines.

Eligibility: Open to holders of an MD or PhD degree who hold a full-time junior faculty appointment in a university-affiliated medical center in the USA, and who have completed research fellowship training in nephrology, urology or closely related fields.

Purpose: To support research.

Type: Grant.

No. of awards offered: Varies.

Frequency: Annual.

Value: Technician salary, equipment, supplies, clinical research costs or other expenses directly related to the proposed research.

Study Establishment: Faculty of a medical school.

Country of Study: USA.

Closing Date: Varies.

For further information contact:
National Kidney Foundation, 30 East 33rd Street, New York, NY, 10016, USA
Tel: 212 889 2210
Fax: 212 689 9261
Contact: Dolph Chianchiano

NATIONAL KIDNEY FOUNDATION OF SOUTH AFRICA

National Kidney Foundation of South Africa, PO Box 5706, Johannesburg, 2000, South Africa
Tel: 484 7547 am
Contact: Secretary

*Charlotte Roberts Trust Kidney Research Award

Subjects: Kidney disease.

Eligibility: Open to suitably qualified medical practitioners and allied medical workers registered in South Africa.

Purpose: To sponsor a suitable person on a short-term overseas visit devoted to research or study.

No. of awards offered: One.

Frequency: Biennially.

Value: R10,000, payable every second year.

Study Establishment: An appropriate research institute or university department.

Country of Study: Any country.

Applications Procedure: Applications should include summary of the proposed study; evidence of suitability to undertake the research programme and names and addresses of two referees.

Closing Date: End of March.

Additional Information: In determining the Award, the value of the proposed research project to kidney research in South Africa is taken into consideration. The Award will not be disbursed until the Foundation is satisfied that the successful applicant has been accepted by an appropriate research institute or university department, and the recipient must undertake to return to South Africa on the termination of the project.

NATIONAL KIDNEY RESEARCH FUND

National Kidney Research Fund, 3 Archers Court, Stukeley Road, Huntingdon, Cambridgeshire, PE18 6XG, England
Tel: 01480 454828
Fax: 01480 454683
Contact: Rick Holland

*NKRF Research Project Grants

Subjects: Renal research projects.

Eligibility: Open to suitably qualified researchers.

Frequency: Annual.

Value: Up to £65,000.

Length of Study: One to three years.

Applications Procedure: Applications forms are available from Department RG.

Closing Date: March 14th.

*NKRF Senior Fellowships

Subjects: Scientific aspects of renal medicine.

Eligibility: Open to postdoctoral researchers in the biomedical field with evidence of independent research, including two years' postdoctoral research.

Frequency: Annual.

Value: Salary will be at Registrar/Senior Registrar level or at the appropriate university scale. An allowance for consumables and minor equipment is available, and technical support.

Length of Study: Three to five years, subject to review in the third year.

Applications Procedure: Application forms are available from Department SF.

Closing Date: March 21st.

*NKRF Special Project Grants

Subjects: Renal disease.

Eligibility: Open to suitably qualified researchers.

Purpose: To provide support for substantial projects in scientific disciplines related to renal disease and its management.

Type: Grant.

No. of awards offered: Three.

Frequency: Annual.

Value: Up to £150,000.

Length of Study: Three years.

Applications Procedure: Applications forms are available from Department SP.

Closing Date: February 25th.

*NKRF Studentships

Subjects: Renal medicine.

Eligibility: Open to institutions.

Frequency: Annual.

Value: University fees are met by the NKRF, and a bench fee is available to the host institution. Student stipend of £9,000 per annum in London or £8,000 elsewhere.

Length of Study: Three years, subject to a satisfactory annual report.

Applications Procedure: Applications are available from Department S.

Closing Date: March 21st.

*NKRF Training Fellowships

Subjects: Renal medicine and related scientific studies.

Eligibility: Open to medical candidates of immediate post-registration to Registrar level and to science candidates with a PhD or DPhil.

Purpose: To enable medical or scientific graduates to undertake specialized training in the renal field.

Type: Fellowship.

Frequency: Annual.

Value: Level of financial support will be based on an appropriate point on current NHS or university pay scales. A training support allowance will be available to the host institution.

Length of Study: One to three years, subject to annual review.

Applications Procedure: Application forms are available from Department TF.

Closing Date: March 21st.

NATIONAL LEAGUE OF AMERICAN PEN WOMEN, INC

National League of American Pen Women, Inc, 1300 17th Street, NW, Washington, DC, 20036, USA
Tel: 202 785 1997
Contact: Shirley Holden Helberg, National Scholarship Chairperson

Scholarships for Mature Women

Subjects: Art, letters and music.

Eligibility: Open to non-Pen Women over 35 years of age who wish to pursue special work in their field of art, letters, and music.

Level of Study: Unrestricted.

Type: Scholarship.

No. of awards offered: One in each category.

Frequency: Biennially (even-numbered years).

Value: US$1,000. The award may be used for college, framing, research, etc.

Country of Study: USA.

Applications Procedure: There are no application forms.

Closing Date: January 15th.

For further information contact:
National League of American Pen Women, Inc, RD 4, Box 4245, Spring Grove, PA, 17362, USA

Tel: 717 225 3023/410 522 2557

NATIONAL LIBRARY OF AUSTRALIA

National Library of Australia, Canberra, ACT, 2600, Australia
Tel: 0162 62 1111
Fax: 0162 57 1703
Contact: Graeme Powell, Manuscript Librarian

Harold White Fellowships

Subjects: Any subject that involves materials in the Library's collections.

Eligibility: Open to established scholars, writers and librarians from any country. Fellowships are not normally offered to candidates working for a higher degree.

Purpose: To promote the Library as a centre of scholarly activity and research; to encourage scholarly and literary use of the collection and the production of publications based on them; to publicize the Library's collections.

Type: Fellowship.

No. of awards offered: Three.

Frequency: Annual.

Value: A$450 per week.

Length of Study: Three to six months.

Study Establishment: The Library.

Country of Study: Australia.

Applications Procedure: Application forms are available from the Library.

Closing Date: April 30th.

Additional Information: Normally Fellows will be expected to give a public lecture and at least one seminar during their tenure on the subject of their research. At least three-quarters of the Fellowship time should be spent in Canberra.

NATIONAL MEDICAL FELLOWSHIPS, INC

National Medical Fellowships, Inc, 254 West 31st Street, 7th Floor,
New York, NY, 10001, USA
Tel: 212 714 0933
Contact: Special Programs

William and Charlotte Cadbury Award

Subjects: Medicine.

Eligibility: Open to senior minority students enrolled in accredited US medical schools.

Purpose: To recognize outstanding superior scholastic achievement and leadership.

Type: Fellowship.

No. of awards offered: One.

Frequency: Annual.

Value: Certificate of Merit and US$2,000 stipend.

Length of Study: One year; not renewable.

Country of Study: USA.

Applications Procedure: Students must be nominated by medical school deans.

Closing Date: June.

Fellowship Program in Academic Medicine

Subjects: Biomedical research and academic medicine.

Eligibility: Open to minority students attending accredited US medical schools. Candidates must have demonstrated outstanding academic achievement and show promise for careers in research and academic medicine. Preference will be given to third-year students; however, second-year students may be considered under special circumstances. Applicant must be either African American, Mexican American, Native American, mainland Puerto Rico.

Purpose: To encourage academically outstanding minority medical students to pursue careers in biomedical research and academic medicine.

Type: Fellowships.

No. of awards offered: 35.

Frequency: Annual.

Value: US$6,000.

Length of Study: 8-12 weeks.

Study Establishment: A major research laboratory under the tutelage of a well-known, senior biomedical scientist, for eight-12 weeks; not renewable.

Country of Study: USA.

Applications Procedure: Application requirements - letter of nomination by Dean, letter of commitment by mentor, letter of recommendation by another faculty member, academic transcript, program application, personal essay, and description of research project.

Closing Date: November.

Additional Information: Candidates must be nominated by medical school deans. The program is co-sponsored by Bristol-Myers Squibb Company and the Commonwealth Fund.

For further information contact:
National Medical Fellowships, Inc, 110 West 32nd Street, 8th Floor, New York, New York, 10001, USA
Tel: 212 714 1007
Fax: 212 239 9718
Contact: Special Programs

Irving Graef Memorial Scholarship

Subjects: Medicine.

Eligibility: Open to rising, third-year minority medical students who received NMF financial assistance during their second year.

Purpose: To recognize outstanding academic achievement.

Type: Scholarship.

No. of awards offered: One.

Frequency: Annual.

Value: Certificate of Merit and annual stipend of US$2,000.

Length of Study: Two years; renewable in the fourth year if the award recipient continues in good academic standing.

Country of Study: USA.

Applications Procedure: Students must be nominated by medical school deans.

Closing Date: July.

Henry G Halladay Awards

Subjects: Medicine.

Eligibility: Open to African-American male students who have been accepted into the first-year classes of accredited US medical schools and who demonstrate exceptional financial need.

Purpose: To assist medical students who have overcome significant obstacles to obtain a medical education.

No. of awards offered: Five supplemental awards.

Frequency: Annual.

Value: US$760.

Length of Study: One year renewable.

Country of Study: USA.

Closing Date: August 31st.

*Franklin C McLean Award

Subjects: Medicine.

Eligibility: Open to senior minority students enrolled in accredited US medical schools.

Purpose: To recognize outstanding academic achievement, leadership and community service.

No. of awards offered: One.

Frequency: Annual.

Value: Certificate of Merit and US$3,000 stipend.

Length of Study: One year.

Country of Study: USA.

Closing Date: June.

*Metropolitan Life Foundation Awards Program for Academic Excellence

Subjects: Medicine.

Eligibility: Open to second- or third-year minority medical students attending medical schools or having legal residence in designated cities.

Purpose: To assist underrepresented minority students of outstanding academic achievement, leadership and potential for distinguished contributions to medicine, and documented financial need.

Type: Scholarship.

No. of awards offered: Up to ten.

Frequency: Annual.

Value: US$2,500 stipend.

Length of Study: One year not renewable.

Country of Study: USA.

Applications Procedure: Students must be nominated by medical school deans.

Closing Date: August.

*James H Robinson Memorial Prizes

Subjects: Surgical disciplines.

Eligibility: Open to senior minority students enrolled in accredited US schools of medicine graduating during the academic year in which the awards are made available.

Purpose: To recognize outstanding performance in surgical disciplines.

No. of awards offered: Two.

Frequency: Annual.

Value: Certificate of Merit and US$500 stipend.

Length of Study: One year.

Country of Study: USA.

Closing Date: December.

Additional Information: Students must be nominated by the medical school dean and the chairman of the department of surgery at the medical school in which they are enrolled and should be in good academic standing overall with no deficiency in their academic record.

*Scholarship Program

Subjects: Medicine.

Eligibility: Open to US citizens of the following groups: African-Americans/Blacks, Mexican Americans, mainland Puerto Ricans and American Indians, who have been admitted to a USA medical school

and are in need of financial assistance.

Purpose: To provide minorities currently underrepresented in the medical profession with the financial assistance to attend medical school for first or second year study, leading to an MD or DO degree.

Type: Scholarship.

No. of awards offered: Approximately 760.

Frequency: Annually, depending on funds available.

Value: US$500-US$4,000.

Study Establishment: A medical school.

Country of Study: USA.

Closing Date: May 31st for previous applicants; August 31st for new applicants.

Additional Information: NMF also offers various other similar awards to minority medical students from particular states or at specific medical schools.

THE NATIONAL MULTIPLE SCLEROSIS SOCIETY

National Multiple Sclerosis Society, 733 Third Avenue, New York, NY, 10017, USA
Tel: 212 986 3240
Fax: 212 986 7981
Email: NAT@NMSS.ORG
www: WWW.NMSS.ORG

Junior Faculty Awards

Subjects: Neurosciences related to multiple sclerosis.

Eligibility: Open to US citizens holding a doctoral degree who have had sufficient research training at the pre- or postdoctoral levels to be capable of independent research. Individuals who have already carried out independent research for more than five years are not eligible.

Level of Study: Professional development.

Purpose: To enable highly qualified persons who have concluded their research training and have begun academic careers as independent investigators to undertake independent research.

No. of awards offered: Varies.

Frequency: Annual.

Value: Approximately US$75,000 per year.

Length of Study: Five years.

Study Establishment: An approved US university, professional or research institute.

Country of Study: USA.

Applications Procedure: Application form must be completed.

Closing Date: February 1st for awards to become effective July 1st or September 1st.

Additional Information: The candidate will not be an employee of the Society, but rather of the institution. It is expected that the institution will develop plans for continuing the candidate's appointment and for continued salary support beyond the five-year period of the award. Fellows may not supplement their salary through private practice or consultation, nor accept another concurrent award. The grantee institution holds title to all equipment purchased with award funds.

Pilot Research Grants

Subjects: Multiple sclerosis.

Eligibility: Open to suitably qualified investigators.

Level of Study: Established Investigator.

Purpose: To provide limited short-term support of novel high-risk research.

Type: Research Grant.

No. of awards offered: Varies.

Frequency: Dependent on funds available.

Value: Up to US$25,000 in direct costs may be requested for the one-year period.

Length of Study: One year.

Applications Procedure: Application form must be completed.

Closing Date: Applications are accepted at any time.

Additional Information: Grants are awarded to an institution to support the research of the principal investigator. Progress reports are required.

Postdoctoral Fellowships

Subjects: Training in research applicable to multiple sclerosis.

Eligibility: Open to unusually promising recipients of MD and/or PhD degrees. The program of training to be supported by the grant must materially enhance the likelihood of the trainee performing meaningful and independent research on multiple sclerosis, and obtaining a suitable position which will enable him to do so. Foreign nationals are welcome to apply for Fellowships in the USA only. Besides its attention to younger researchers, the Society will also consider applications from established investigators who seek support to obtain specialized training in some field in which they are not expert, when such training will materially enhance their capacity to conduct more meaningful research on multiple sclerosis. US citizenship is not required for training in US institutions; applicants who plan to train in other countries must be US citizens.

Level of Study: Postdoctorate.

Purpose: To provide postdoctoral training which will enhance the likelihood of performing meaningful and independent research relevant to multiple sclerosis.

Type: Fellowship.

No. of awards offered: Varies.

Frequency: Annual.

Value: Varies according to professional status, previous training, accomplishments in research, and to the payscale of the institution in which the training is provided. Fellowships may be supplemented by other forms of support, with prior approval.

Length of Study: 1-3 years.

Study Establishment: An institution of the candidate's choice.

Country of Study: USA for foreign postdoctoral applicants.

Applications Procedure: Application form must be completed.

Closing Date: February 1st for grants to become effective July 1st or thereafter.

Additional Information: These Fellowships are awarded to support training in research and are not awarded to support clinical training directed towards the completion of internship and/or specialty board certification. Similarly, they cannot be used to provide support for individuals whose primary responsibility is teaching and/or service, although Fellows are encouraged to spend a reasonable amount of their time (up to 10%) in teaching. Fellows are not considered as employees of the Society, but rather of the institution where the training is provided; the Fellowship is to be administered in accordance with the prevailing policies of the sponsoring institution. It is the responsibility of the applicant to make all arrangement for his training with the mentor and institution of his choice.

Research Grants

Subjects: Multiple sclerosis: cause, prevention, alleviation and cure.

Eligibility: Open to suitably qualified investigators.

Level of Study: Established Investigator.

Purpose: To stimulate, coordinate and support fundamental or applied, clinical or non-clinical research.

Type: Research Grant.

No. of awards offered: Varies.

Frequency: Twice a year.

Value: Funds may be used to pay in whole or in part the salaries of associated professional personnel, technical assistants and other non-professional personnel in proportion to their time spent directly on the project. Salaries are in accordance with the prevailing policies of the grantee institution. If requested, other expenses, such as travel costs and fringe benefits, may also be paid.

Length of Study: Three years.

Country of Study: Unrestricted.

Applications Procedure: Application form must be completed.

Closing Date: February 1st and August 1st for grants to become effective October 1st and April 1st respectively.

Additional Information: Grants are awarded to an institution to support the research of the principle investigator. Scientific equipment and supplies bought with Grant funds become the property of the grantee institution. Progress reports are required, and appropriate publication is expected.

NATIONAL OPERA ASSOCIATION

National Opera Association, 6805 Tennyson Drive, McLean, VA, 22101, USA
Tel: 703 790 8426
Email: Arvidius@aol.com
www: http://www.wtamu.edu/academics/finearts/music/noa.html
Contact: Arvio Kautsen

Competitions

Subjects: Music theory and composition, singing and opera.

Eligibility: Open to anyone under the age of 35.

Level of Study: Professional development, Unrestricted.

Purpose: To promote singers and opera.

Type: Competition.

No. of awards offered: Eight.

Frequency: Annual.

Value: US$500-US$1,500.

Applications Procedure: Application for competition is required.

Closing Date: Different dates throughout the year.

NATIONAL OSTEOPATHIC FOUNDATION

National Osteopathic Foundation, 5775G Peachtree-Dunwoody Road, Ste.500, Atlanta, GA, 30342, USA
Tel: 404 705 9999
Fax: 404 252 0774
Email: nof@assnhg.com
Contact: Jacqueline Weiss

Zeneca Pharmaceuticals Underserved Healthcare Grant

Subjects: Osteopathy.

Eligibility: Only students in third year of study at US accredited colleges of osteopathic medicine are eligible to apply.

Level of Study: Doctorate.

Purpose: To support 4th year osteopathic medical students committed to practice in underserved or minority populations.

Type: Grant.

No. of awards offered: Two.

Frequency: Dependent on funds available, annually.

Value: Minimum of US$5,000 plus travel expenses.

Study Establishment: College of Osteopathic Medicine.

Country of Study: USA.

Applications Procedure: Please submit an application form, 500 word essay, and the names of three references.

Closing Date: January 31st.

NATIONAL POETRY SERIES

National Poetry Series, PO Box G, Hopewell, NJ, 08525, USA
Tel: 609 466 9712
Fax: 609 466 4706
Contact: Emily Wylie, Coordinator

National Poetry Series

Eligibility: NPS accepts entries from American citizens who have an unpublished book length manuscript in English to submit.

Level of Study: Unrestricted.

Purpose: To promote America's awareness of poetry and to ensure the trade publication of five new books of poetry in America each year.

Type: Book publication.

No. of awards offered: Five.

Frequency: Annual.

Value: US$1,000 book publication.

Country of Study: USA.

Applications Procedure: Interested poets should send an SASE by January of the year of the contest to receive submission guidelines.

Closing Date: January 1st.

NATIONAL RADIO ASTRONOMY OBSERVATORY

National Radio Astronomy Observatory, Edgemont Road,
Charlottesville, VA, 22903-2475, USA
Tel: 804 296 0221
Fax: 804 296 0385
Email: rebrown@NRAO.edu
www: http://www.nrao.edu/
Contact: Director

Jansky Postdoctorals

Subjects: Areas of present interest include: theoretical and observational studies of discrete radio sources, galaxies, the interstellar medium, planets; millimeter-wave instrumentation and research; interferometry, aperture, synthesis, large antenna arrays; radio astronomy instrumentation (HFET and SIS amplifiers, radiometer systems, cryogenics); data processing, information theory, computer system applications, digital and online techniques.

Eligibility: Open to astronomers, physicists, electrical engineers and computer specialists. Preference will be given to recent PhD recipients.

Level of Study: Postdoctorate.

Purpose: To provide outstanding opportunities to qualified young PhDs who wish to devote themselves full-time to research.

Type: Postdoctorals.

No. of awards offered: Five.

Frequency: Annual.

Value: US$33,000 per annum, plus liberal vacation allowance, authorized travel expenses, moving allowance, etc.

Length of Study: Two years; renewable for 1 further year.

Study Establishment: At the Observatory's centers: Charlottesville,

Virginia (headquarters); Green Bank, West Virginia; Tucson, Arizona; Socorro, New Mexico.

Applications Procedure: Applicants normally commence in September or October. There is no application form. The initial letter should include a statement of the individual's research interests together with his/her own appraisal of his/her qualifications for carrying out research. Special facilities including a 140-foot steerable telescope, a 12-metre millimetre-wave telescope, a 27-element variable baseline very large array interferometer, the Very Long Baseline Array (VLBA), a 10-element telescope with antenna sites spanning the US, Hawaii, and the Virgin Islands, various computers, a wide variety of radiometer systems and well-equiped electronics laboratories, as well as skilled technical supporting staffs, are available to Associates. The applicant should have three letters of recommendation sent directly to the NRAO.

Closing Date: 15 December.

Additional Information: Research Associates may formulate and carry out investigations either independently or in collaboration with others.

NATIONAL RESEARCH COUNCIL

National Research Council, Office for Central Europe and Eurasia,
2101 Constitution Ave NW FO2014, Washington, DC, 20418, USA
Tel: 202 334 3680
Fax: 202 334 2614
Email: ocee@nas.edu
www: http://www.NAS.EDU/OCEE

CAST Cooperation in Applied Science and Technology

Eligibility: US citizens or permanent residents, must possess PhD or equivalent.

Purpose: To support collaborative projects with commercial applications and/or potential to improve quality or life in USA or NIS. For specialists with defence related backgrounds to apply skills to civilian activities.

Type: Grant.

Frequency: Dependent on funds available.

Value: US$3,000 for travel and supplies, US$1,500 per month for living expenses.

Length of Study: 6-12 months.

Country of Study: Selected countries of the NIS and Eastern Europe; to be announced.

Applications Procedure: Submit originals plus five copies of application forms, resumes and publication lists, 1-3 pages of statement of technical basis, 1-2 page statement on how proposal fits into program, and budget.

Closing Date: January 3rd.

For further information contact:
National Research Council, Office for Central Europe and Eurasia,
2101 Constitution Ave NW FO 2014, Washington, DC, 20418, USA
Tel: 202 334 3680
Fax: 202 334 2614
Email: ocee@nas,edu
www: http://www.nas.edu.ocee

COBASE- Collaboration in Basic Science and Engineering (long term)

Subjects: History, philosophy of science, social science, science and technology policy.

Eligibility: Open to US citizens/permanent residents, but not to US Government employees. American and foreign colleagues must possess a PhD or equivalent. No more than two grants in a four year period.

Level of Study: Postdoctorate.

Purpose: Primarily to prepare new partnerships of American specialists with their colleagues from Central/Eastern Europe and the NIS for competition in the National Science Foundation Programs.

No. of awards offered: 15.

Frequency: Annual.

Value: US$3,000 to US$15,300.

Length of Study: 1-6 months.

Country of Study: Selected countries of the NIS and Eastern Europe; to be announced.

Applications Procedure: Please submit application forms, 3-4 page statement of objectives, resumes and publication list statement from collaborator, and a budget. Please submit original and four copies.

Closing Date: August 7th.

Additional Information: No proposals on agricultural production, drug testing or disease. Can fund visits by Americans to foreign countries or foreign specialists to the USA.

COBASE-Collaboration in Basic Science and Engineering

Eligibility: US Citizens/permanent residents, must possess PhD or equivalent, no more than two grants per applicant in four year period.

Purpose: To prepare new partnerships of American specialists with their colleagues from Eastern Europe and the NIS for competition in the National Science Foundation programs.

Type: Travel.

No. of awards offered: Approximately 40.

Frequency: Annual.

Value: US$2,200 to US$2,500.

Length of Study: Two weeks.

Country of Study: Selected countries of the NIS and Eastern Europe to be announced.

Applications Procedure: Application forms, 3-4 page statement of objectives, resumes and publication list statement from collaborator, budget, submit original and four copies.

Closing Date: August 4th, June 8th.

Additional Information: No proposals on agricultural production, drug testing or disease. Can fund visits by Americans to foreign countries or foreign specialists to the USA.

For further information contact:
National Research Council, 2101 Constitution Ave NW FO 2014, Washington, DC, 20418, USA
Tel: 202 334 3680
Fax: 202 334 2614
Email: ocee@nas.edu
www: http://www,nas.edu.ocee

CRSP-Collaborative Research in Sectoral Policy

Eligibility: Applicant must have PhD or equivalent, and must be engaged in teaching or a research career, be an American citizen/permanent resident, and have existing contacts with NIS researchers.

Level of Study: Postdoctorate.

Purpose: To facilitate collaborations which will lead to publications by Americans and NIS specialists in areas of pressing public policy concerns, to provide access to specialised facilities and to promote sustained cooperative research interactions between the USA and the NIS.

No. of awards offered: 30.

Frequency: Twice annually.

Value: US$2,200 to US$3,500.

Length of Study: Two weeks to two months.

Country of Study: Selected countries of the NIS and Eastern Europe; to be announced.

Applications Procedure: Please submit five copies of resume, list of

publications, two page statement of purpose, budget, list of foreign specialists who will be involved, correspondence from foreign colleagues, statement that the applicant's institution will charge no overhead against a grant, and two letters of recommendation.

Closing Date: March 15th.

Additional Information: Topics should have significant input from applied sciences.

Ford Foundation Postdoctoral Fellowships for Minorities

Subjects: Behavioral and social sciences, humanities, engineering, mathematics, physical sciences, and biological sciences, or interdisciplinary programs composed of two or more eligible disciplines. Not supported: medicine, law, social work, library science, business administration and management, fine arts, performing arts, speech pathology and audiology, education.

Eligibility: Open to US citizens and nationals who are members of one of the following minority ethnic groups: Native American, Alaskan Native, Black/African American, Mexican American/Chicano, Native Pacific Islander (Polynesian or Micronesian), and Puerto Rican. Applicants are required to have completed the PhD or ScD degree by the deadline date and may not have held the PhD or ScD for more than seven years as of that date.

Purpose: To identify individuals of high ability who are members of minority groups that have traditionally been underrepresented among the nation's behavioral and social scientists, humanists, engineers, mathematicians, physical scientists, and life scientists and to enable them to engage in postdoctoral research and scholarship in an environment free from the interference of their normal professional duties.

Type: Fellowships.

No. of awards offered: 25.

Frequency: Annual.

Value: A stipend of US$25,000; plus US$3,000 relocation allowance, US$2,000 cost-of-research allowance and US$2,500 grant-in-aid for Fellow's use afterwards.

Study Establishment: An appropriate not-for-profit institution of higher education or research, primarily in the USA.

Closing Date: January 5th.

Ford Foundation Predoctoral and Dissertation Fellowships for Minorities

Subjects: Behavioral and social sciences, humanities, engineering, mathematics, physical sciences, biological sciences, or interdisciplinary programs composed of two or more eligible disciplines.

Eligibility: Open to individuals who are citizens or nationals of the USA at the time of application, and who are members of the following minority groups: Alaskan Natives (Eskimo or Aleut), Native American Indians, Black/African Americans, Mexican Americans/Chicanos, Native Pacific Islanders (Polynesian or Micronesian), and Puerto Ricans.

Purpose: To increase the presence of underrepresented minorities on the nation's college and university faculties.

No. of awards offered: Approximately 55 Predoctoral and 20 Dissertation Fellowships.

Value: US$12,000 per annum for the Fellow, plus US$6,000 for the institution, for Predoctoral Fellowships; US$18,000 for Dissertation Fellowships.

Length of Study: Three years (Predoctoral Fellowships) or for 12 months (Dissertation Fellowships).

Study Establishment: For advanced study leading to the PhD or ScD degree, at any accredited non-profit institution of higher education offering PhDs or ScDs in the fields eligible for support.

Country of Study: USA.

Closing Date: November 3rd (postmark).

For further information contact:
National Research Council, 2101 Constitution Ave, Washington, DC, 20418, USA
Tel: 202 334 2872
Contact: The Fellowship Office

Howard Hughes Medical Institute Predoctoral Fellowships

Subjects: Biological sciences in the following fields: biochemistry, biophysics, biostatistics, cell biology and regulation, developmental biology, epidemiology, genetics, immunology, mathematical biology, microbiology, molecular biology, neuroscience, pharmacology, physiology, structural biology, and virology.

Eligibility: Open to individuals who are citizens or nationals of the USA or who are foreign citizens or nationals. Applicants should be at or near the beginning of their graduate study toward a PhD or ScD degree in the designated fields.

Purpose: To promote excellence in biomedical research by helping prospective researchers with exceptional promise to obtain high-quality graduate education.

Type: Fellowship.

No. of awards offered: 80 Fellowships.

Frequency: Annual.

Value: A stipend of US$14,500 per annum for the Fellow, and US$14,000 paid to the fellowship institution to cover fees.

Length of Study: Three years, with possible continuation for an additional two years; the fellowship must be consecutive.

Study Establishment: Any institution of higher education offering advanced degrees in biological sciences.

Country of Study: USA (all nationals); or USA or abroad (US nationals).

Closing Date: November 3rd (postmark).

For further information contact:
National Research Council, 2101 Constitution Ave, Washington, DC, 20418, USA
Tel: 202 334 2872
Contact: The Fellowship Office

RADWASTE- Radioactive Waste Management Program

Subjects: Radioactive Waste Management.

Eligibility: Open to American citizens/permanent residents. American and foreign colleagues must possess a PhD or equivalent. NIS colleagues must not be currently researching in the USA or planning to remain in the USA permanently.

Level of Study: Postdoctorate.

Purpose: To support American specialists wishing to host their colleagues from the NIS to conduct research on the management of radioactive waste.

No. of awards offered: Five.

Frequency: Annual, dependent on funds available.

Value: US$2,000 per month.

Length of Study: 6-12 months.

Country of Study: Selected countries of the NIS and Eastern Europe; to be announced.

Applications Procedure: Please submit application forms, a three page statement of purpose, resumes and publication lists, and proposed budget. Please submit four copies plus originals.

Closing Date: January 1st.

Additional Information: This award exists to fund visits by NIS specialists to USA only.

Twinning Program

Subjects: Fields supported by NSF. No disease related topics.

Eligibility: American citizen or permanent resident. Applicants may be graduate or doctoral students or may hold PhD.

Level of Study: Postdoctorate.

Purpose: To yield significant publications and long term sustained linkages between researchers in the USA and NIS.

Type: Travel Grant.

No. of awards offered: Varies.

Frequency: Annual, dependent on funds available.

Value: US$13,200.

Length of Study: Two years.

Country of Study: Selected countries of the NIS and Eastern Europe to be announced.

Applications Procedure: Five copies of description of proposed research, budget, resume, list of publications, resumes of foreign counterparts, letters of support from US applicants' institutions, correspondence with prospective twinning partner, and a list of potential peer reviewers.

Closing Date: TBA.

For further information contact:
National Research Council, Office for Central Europe and Eurasia , 2101 Constitution Ave NW F02014, Washington, DC, 20418, USA
Tel: 202 334 3680
Fax: 202 334 2614
Email: ocee@nas.edu
www: http://www.nas.edu/ocee

US Department of Energy Predoctoral Fellowships in Integrated Manufacturing

Subjects: Integrated manufacturing.

Eligibility: Open to US citizens or permanent residents who plan to work toward a PhD degree in a field related to integrated manufacturing.

Purpose: To create a pool of PhDs trained in the integrated approach to manufacturing, to promote academic interest in the field, and to attract talented professionals to this challenging area of engineering.

Type: Fellowships.

No. of awards offered: 12.

Frequency: Annual.

Value: US$20,000 stipend, US$15,000 cost-of-education allowance.

Length of Study: Three years.

Study Establishment: Any US non-profit educational institution which offers a PhD in fields related to integrated manufacturing.

Country of Study: USA.

Applications Procedure: Application forms are available on request.

Closing Date: December 1st for notification in April.

NATIONAL RESEARCH COUNCIL OF CANADA

Recruitment Unit, National Research Council of Canada, Montreal Road, M58, Ottawa, Ontario, K1A 0R6, Canada
Tel: 613 998 4126
Fax: 613 954 1471
Contact: Research Associates Coordinator

*National Research Council Laboratories Research Associateships

Subjects: Biological sciences; biotechnology; chemistry; molecular science; chemical engineering and process technologies; electrical engineering; astrophysics; industrial materials research; marine dynamics; construction; mechanical engineering; aeronautics; physics; photonics; microstructural sciences; plant biotechnology; biochemistry; microbiology; advanced structural ceramics.

Eligibility: Open to nationals of all countries although preference will be given to Canadians and permanent residents of Canada. Applicants should have acquired a PhD in natural science or a masters degree in an engineering field within the last five years or should expect to obtain the degree before taking up the Associateship. Selections will be made on a competitive basis. Demonstrated ability to perform original research of high quality in the chosen field will be the main criterion used in selecting candidates and in considering extensions of their term.

Purpose: To give promising scientists and engineers an opportunity to work on challenging research problems in fields of interest to NRC as a stage in the development of their research careers.

Type: Research Associateship.

No. of awards offered: Approximately 50.

Frequency: Annual.

Value: C$39,366 for a new PhD, i.e. no experience. Salaries are revised annually.

Study Establishment: The laboratories in the National Research Council of Canada only.

NATIONAL RIGHT TO WORK COMMITTEE

William B Ruggles Scholarship Selection Committee, National Right to Work Committee, 8001 Braddock Road, Suite 500, Springfield, VA, 22160, USA
Tel: 703 321 9820
Contact: Public Relations Department

William B Ruggles Right to Work Scholarship

Subjects: Journalism.

Eligibility: Open to students majoring in journalism or mass communication who exemplify the dedication to the principle and high journalistic standards of William B Ruggles.

Level of Study: Postgraduate, Doctorate, Undergraduate.

Type: Scholarship.

No. of awards offered: One.

Frequency: Annual.

Value: US$2,000.

Study Establishment: At an institution of higher learning.

Country of Study: USA.

Applications Procedure: Recent transcript of grades, application filled out, and a 500-word essay on the right to work.

Closing Date: 1 January to 31 March.

NATIONAL SCHOLARSHIP TRUST FUND OF THE GRAPHIC ARTS

National Scholarship Trust Fund of the Graphic Arts, 4615 Forbes Avenue, Pittsburgh, PA, 15213-3796, USA
Tel: 412 621 6941
Fax: 412 621 8107
Contact: Margaret Dimperio, Business Manager

*Fellowships

Subjects: Graphic communications.

Eligibility: Open to graduates of programs in graphic communications and/or related fields.

Type: Fellowship.

No. of awards offered: Varies.

Frequency: Annual.

Value: US$1,500-US$3,000.

Length of Study: One year.

Applications Procedure: Application packs are available on request.

Closing Date: January 10th.

NATIONAL SCIENCE FOUNDATION

Division of Earth Sciences, National Science Foundation, 4201 Wilson Boulevard, Arlington, VA, 22230, USA
Tel: 703 306 1550
Fax: 703 306 0382

*Earth Science Program

Subjects: Emphasis is on basic research aimed at an improved understanding of the earth's structure, properties, processes, and evolution, including basic research in areas of practical importance. Support is provided in most fields of the solid-earth sciences including geology, geophysics, geochemistry, and hydrology in response to unsolicited, investigator-initiated proposals. The Division is a participant in the National Earthquake Hazard Prevention Program and the USA Global Change Research Program.

Eligibility: Open to qualified US research scientists.

Purpose: To advance the state of knowledge in the solid-earth sciences and enhance the ability of USA colleges and universities to do research and education in these fields.

No. of awards offered: Approximately 600.

Value: Award sizes vary greatly depending on the project proposed, but most awards are US$50,000-US$100,000.

Study Establishment: Appropriate sites and institutions.

Applications Procedure: Persons planning to submit proposals should consult the following publications: 'NSF Guide to Programs', 'Grants for Research and Education in Science and Engineering', and 'Earth Sciences Research at NSF'. Latest editions of these publications may be requested by mail from the Forms and Publications Unit.

Closing Date: June 1st; December 1st.

*NSF-NATO Postdoctoral Fellowships in Science and Engineering

Subjects: Mathematics, physics, biology, engineering, social sciences and the history and philosophy of science.

Eligibility: Open to US citizens or permanent resident aliens of the USA who have received a PhD or equivalent degree within five years prior to the date of application.

Purpose: To promote the progress of science and closer collaboration among the scientists of various nations.

Type: Fellowship.

No. of awards offered: Approximately 40.

Frequency: Annual.

Value: US$33,000 stipend for a 12-month period, plus dependency and travel allowances.

Length of Study: Six to twelve months full-time study.

Study Establishment: Appropriate non-profit scientific institutions.

Country of Study: NATO member countries, except the USA, and the Cooperation Partner Countries of Eastern Europe and the former Soviet Union.

Applications Procedure: A detailed program description and guidelines for preparation of applications are contained in the brochure 'NATO Postdoctoral Fellowships in Science', available annually from the Foundation. Applicants should not previously have held an NSF-NATO Fellowship.

Closing Date: Early November for awards to be announced in March of the following year.

For further information contact:
Division of Research Career Development, NATO Postdoctoral Program, National Science Foundation, 4201 Wilson Boulevard, Arlington, VA, 22230, USA
Tel: 703 306 1696
Fax: 703 306 0468
Contact: Directorate for Education & Human Resources

*Oceanography Programs

Subjects: Oceanographic sciences: physics; chemistry; geology; biology.

Eligibility: Open to highly qualified research scientists.

Purpose: To fund a broad range of research projects.

Type: Grant.

No. of awards offered: Varies.

Value: Varies according to research proposed.

Length of Study: Ranging from several months to several years.

Additional Information: Grants are awarded on the basis of a competitive peer review of unsolicited research proposals. These proposals may be submitted throughout the year. Approximately six months are required for review and processing of a formal proposal. The NSF Oceanographic Facilities Support Program.

For further information contact:
National Science Foundation, Arlington, VA, 22230, USA
Tel: 703 306 1580
Fax: 703 306 0390
Contact: Division of Ocean Sciences

NATIONAL SPACE CLUB

National Space Club, 665 Fifteenth Street, NW, Suite 300, Washington, DC, 20005, USA

*Dr Robert H Goddard Scholarship

Subjects: Science or engineering.

Eligibility: Open to US citizens at or above the junior year of study at an accredited university, who intend to pursue graduate or undergraduate study in science or engineering during the interval of the award.

Purpose: To stimulate the interest of talented students in the fields of space research and exploration and therefore help to promote the advancement of scientific knowledge.

Type: Scholarship.

No. of awards offered: One.

Frequency: Annual.

Value: US$10,000.

Length of Study: One year; renewable for a further year if the circumstances and accomplishments are warranted.

Closing Date: January 10th.

Additional Information: Selection is based upon official school transcripts, faculty letters of recommendation, accomplishments demonstrating personal qualities of creativity and leadership, and scholastic plans leading to future participation in some phase of the aerospace sciences and technology. Personal need is considered, but not as a primary criterion.

NATIONAL SPELEOLOGICAL SOCIETY

Ralph W Stone Research Award Committee, 101 Geology Building, University of Missouri, Columbia, MO, 65211, USA
Tel: 573 882 3231
Fax: 573 882 5458
Email: geosccw@showme.missouri.edu
Contact: Carol Wicks

Ralph W Stone Graduate Research Award

Subjects: Speleology and related studies: research applicable to work on thesis or dissertation for MSc or PhD degree.

Eligibility: Open to duly registered graduate students of any nationality who are members of the Society.

Level of Study: Postgraduate.

Purpose: To encourage excellence in graduate-level research.

Type: Research Award.

No. of awards offered: One.

Frequency: Annual.

Value: US$1,000.

Study Establishment: Anywhere that research can be carried out.

Country of Study: Unrestricted.

Closing Date: Announced yearly in 'NSS News'.

For further information contact:
National Speleological Society, Cave Avenue, Huntsville, AL 35810, USA

NATIONAL TRUST FOR HISTORIC PRESERVATION

National Trust for Historic Preservation, 1785 Massachusetts Avenue, NW, Washington, DC, 20036, USA
Tel: 202 673 4038
Fax: 202 673 4200
Contact: Samuel W Friedman, Preservation Services Fund

Johanna Favrot Fund

Subjects: Historic preservation.

Purpose: To contribute to the preservation or recapture of an authentic sense of place.

Type: Grant.

No. of awards offered: One.

Frequency: Annual.

Value: Within the range of US$2,500 to US$25,000.

Country of Study: USA.

Applications Procedure: Application forms are available from National Trust regional offices.

Closing Date: Applications must be postmarked February 1st.

NATIONAL UNION OF TEACHERS

Central Co-ordinating Unit, National Union of Teachers, Hamilton House, Mabledon Place, London, WC1H 9BD, England
Tel: 0171 380 4704
Fax: 0171 387 8458
Contact: Angela Bush

Page Scholarship

Subjects: A specific aspect of American education relevant to the recipient's own professional responsibilities.

Eligibility: Open to teachers who are members of the National Union of Teachers or organizations affiliated to the NUT who are between 25 and 60 years of age.

Purpose: To promote the exchange of educational ideas between Britain and America.

Type: Scholarship.

No. of awards offered: One.

Frequency: Annual.

Value: £1,350 with complete hospitality in the USA provided by the English-Speaking Union of the United States.

Length of Study: For 3 weeks. The Scholarship must be taken during the American academic year, September to April, whilst the American educational institutions are in session.

Country of Study: USA.

Closing Date: 30 November.

Additional Information: The Scholarship is limited to the individual teacher and neither the spouse nor partner can be included in the travelling, accommodation or study arrangements. Recipients are required to report on their visit to teacher groups, educational meetings, etc. in the USA and on their return home.

NATIONAL UNIVERSITY OF SINGAPORE

Lower Kent Ridge Road, Singapore, 119260
Tel: 7723300
Fax: 7731462
Email: pmdonghw@nus.sg
www: http://www.nus.sg/nusinfo/med/webspms/spmsmain.html

Academy of Medicine Fellowship

Subjects: Surgery and O&G (1997).

Eligibility: Open to doctors from ASEAN member countries, who should have a first medical degree with a minimum of two years' postgraduate experience in the relevant field, be under 35 years of age, and be fluent in English. Singapore citizens and residents are ineligible.

Level of Study: Postgraduate.

Purpose: To provide the opportunity for postgraduate study.

Type: Fellowship.

No. of awards offered: One in each discipline.

Frequency: Annual.

Value: Approximately S$1,000.

Length of Study: For a maximum of one month.

Study Establishment: The National University of Singapore.

Country of Study: Singapore.

Closing Date: July 31st.

ASEAN Postgraduate Scholarships

Subjects: Non-research postgraduate studies by coursework and dissertation leading to the following degrees: MA in English language; Master of Business Administration; MMed in anaesthesia, internal medicine, obstetrics and gynaecology, paediatrics, psychiatry, or surgery; public health, or occupational medicine, or in civil, electrical, industrial or mechanical engineering: Master of Social Sciences (Economics), Building Science, Property Management and Property and Maintenance Management.

Eligibility: Open to citizens of ASEAN member countries (except Singapore).

Level of Study: Postgraduate.

Type: Scholarship.

No. of awards offered: Three.

Frequency: Annual.

Value: Varies.

Study Establishment: National University of Singapore.

Country of Study: Singapore.

Closing Date: November/December.

Lee Foundation and Tan Sri Dr Runme Shaw Foundation Fellowships in Orthopaedic Surgery

Subjects: Orthopaedic surgery, hand and reconstructive microsurgery.

Eligibility: Open to doctors from developing countries who have a first medical degree with a minimum of four years' postgraduate experience, of which at least two years must have been in orthopaedic surgery or at least one year must have been in orthopaedic surgery after the completion of basic surgical training. Applicants must be fluent in English.

Level of Study: Postgraduate.

Purpose: To offer the opportunity for clinical hospital attachment.

Type: Fellowship.

No. of awards offered: Two of each fellowship.

Frequency: Twice yearly.

Value: Approximately S$1,000.

Length of Study: Six months.

Study Establishment: National University Hospital or at Singapore General Hospital.

Country of Study: Singapore.

Applications Procedure: Applicants should write for application form.

Closing Date: July 31st.

Postgraduate Research Scholarship

Eligibility: Open to graduates of any nationality.

Level of Study: Postgraduate.

Purpose: To encourage qualified candidates to pursue postgraduate research in their fields of interest in NUS.

Type: Scholarship.

No. of awards offered: 410.

Frequency: Annual.

Value: S$1,500 per month over two to three years.

Length of Study: Two or three years.

Study Establishment: NUS.

Country of Study: Singapore.

Applications Procedure: Application form must be completed.

Closing Date: Available throughout the year.

NATIVE AMERICAN SCHOLARSHIP FUND, INC

Native American Scholarship Fund, Inc, 8200 Mountain Road NE, Suite 203, Albuquerque, NM, 87110, USA
Tel: 505 262 2351
Fax: 505 262 0534
Contact: Lucille Kelley, Recruitment Secretary

Scholarship Program

Subjects: All subjects.

Eligibility: Restricted to students enrolled in North American Indian tribe, with at least one quarter or more degree Indian blood.

Level of Study: Unrestricted.

Purpose: To provide scholarships to high-potential Native American students in the fields that are critical for the political, economic, social and business development of American Indian tribes.

Type: Scholarship.

No. of awards offered: 160.

Frequency: Three times per year.

Value: From US$500 to US$2,500 per academic year.

Length of Study: Four years.

Study Establishment: Accredited college or university.

Country of Study: USA.

Applications Procedure: Please write to request pre-application form. This will be screened and full application forms sent out when applicable.

Closing Date: September 15th for Spring, April 15th for Fall, and March 15th for Summer.

NATURAL ENVIRONMENT RESEARCH COUNCIL

Natural Environment Research Council, Polaris House, North Star Avenue, Swindon, SN2 1EU, England
Tel: 01793 411500
Contact: Awards and Training Section

Advanced Course Studentships

Subjects: Environmental sciences.

Eligibility: Open to persons who, at the closing date of application for an award, have been ordinarily resident in Great Britain or Northern Ireland throughout the three-year period preceding that date. 'Ordinarily resident' means that no period of the candidate's residence during those three years has been wholly, or mainly, for the purpose of receiving full-time education. Candidates must hold a first or second class honours degree in an appropriate branch of science or technology. An alternative qualification or combination of qualifications and experience which clearly demonstrate equivalent knowledge and ability may exceptionally be accepted at the Council's discretion. There is no age limit for Studentships but the Council reserves the right to decline an application from an older candidate it it considers that an award would not represent a good investment of public funds.

Purpose: To allow postgraduate students to take courses recognized by NERC and which usually lead to an MSc. These courses are essentially vocational and are designed to prepare students for employment in industry or the public sector.

Type: Studentship.

No. of awards offered: Varies.

Frequency: Annual.

Value: A maintenance grant, the payment of approved fees; assistance with travel and subsistence expenses under specified conditions (fieldwork).

Length of Study: One year.

Study Establishment: Any approved institution of higher education.

Country of Study: UK.

Applications Procedure: All applications for Studentships must be submitted by the head of the department in which the student proposes to work. Applications will not be accepted directly from individual candidates. Awards are tenable only for those courses which are currently recognized by NERC for the purposes of its Studentship scheme. The number of NERC awards given to each of these courses is detailed in the Display Notice which is widely circulated in March. Applications for

the recognition of new advanced courses should be submitted by heads of departments. A&T will be pleased to discuss any proposed application in advance of its formal submission. Recognition of a course does not guarantee the provision of a NERC award in any year. Application forms are available on request. Industrial studentships are available to enable scientists in industry to obtain further training on postgraduate courses recognized by NERC.

Closing Date: November 15th.

Fellowship Schemes

Subjects: Novel research within the sciences of the natural environment.

Eligibility: Candidates must hold a PhD and have had at least two years' research experience at postdoctoral level, not necessarily in the UK, at the time of application. They must also have proved their ability as individual research workers.

Purpose: To support outstanding research workers who are well qualified for academic careers, but who do not hold tenured posts at the time of application.

Type: Fellowship.

No. of awards offered: Varies.

Frequency: Annual.

Value: Awards are based on the UK universities non-clinical academic and related research staff scale and are related to age when taking up appointment. Increments are awarded on the anniversary of the day the award is taken up. NERC will determine the maximum point on the scale.

Length of Study: Depends on the individual scheme.

Country of Study: UK.

Applications Procedure: Application forms are available on request.

Closing Date: September 30th.

Research Grants

Subjects: Research projects concerned with the natural environment.

Eligibility: Open to research workers ordinarily resident in the UK who are also members of the academic staff of universities, colleges and similar institutions within the UK recognized by the NERC. Research assistants and technicians are not eligible to apply. Holders of Research Council fellowships at HEIs are eligible to apply for research grants.

Purpose: To support a specific investigation in which the applicant will be engaged personally; to enter promising new or modified fields of research; or to take advantage of developments in apparatus offering improved techniques in promising lines of research already established.

Type: Grant.

No. of awards offered: Varies.

Frequency: Annual.

Value: Standard Research Grant: for amounts over £25,000, and for periods not usually in excess of three years; Small Research Grant for a more rapid response to applications costing £2,000-£25,000. Applications for less than £2,000 will not be accepted.

Country of Study: UK.

Applications Procedure: Application forms are available on request.

Closing Date: Standard Research Grant: 1 July, 1 December; Small Research Grant : January 1st, April 1st, July 1st, October 1st.

Research Studentships

Subjects: Environmental sciences.

Eligibility: Open to persons who, at the closing date of application for an award, have been ordinarily resident in Great Britain or Northern Ireland throughout the three-year period preceding that date. 'Ordinarily resident' means that no period of the candidate's residence during those three years has been wholly, or mainly, for the purpose of receiving full-time education. Candidates must hold a first or upper second class honours degree in an appropriate branch of science or technology. An alternative qualification or combination of qualifications and experience which clearly demonstrate equivalent knowledge and ability may exceptionally be accepted at the Council's discretion. Possession of an MSc degree will not be accepted by itself as an adequate qualification for Research Studentship candidates who do not have at least an upper second class honours degree. Strong and specific reasons will still be needed for an exception to be made. There is no age limit for Studentships but the Council reserves the right to decline an application from an older candidate if it considers that an award would not represent a good investment of public funds.

Level of Study: Postgraduate.

Purpose: To enable postgraduate students to receive training in methods of research and to undertake research in particular scientific areas under the guidance of named supervisors. It is expected that the awards will lead to the submission of a PhD thesis.

Type: Studentships.

No. of awards offered: Varies.

Frequency: Annual.

Value: A maintenance grant, additional allowances, the payment of approved fees, assistance with travel and subsistence expenses under specified conditions (fieldwork).

Length of Study: Up to three years, part of which may be spent at an institution in Europe.

Study Establishment: Any approved institution of higher education.

Country of Study: UK and Europe.

Applications Procedure: All applications for Studentships must be submitted by the head of the department in which the student proposes to work. Applications will not be accepted directly from individual candidates. To encourage research students to gain additional experience outside the academic sphere some of these awards are made as Cooperative Awards in Sciences of the Environment (CASE Studentships). CASE awards involve the joint supervision of the student by a member of staff of an academic institution and a scientist from industry, a public authority or government research institute. Application forms are available on request.

NATURAL HISTORY MUSEUM

Natural History Museum, Cromwell Road, London, SW7 5BD, England
Tel: 0171 938 9013
Contact: Secretary of NHM Studentships

*Research Studentships

Subjects: Taxonomically oriented projects in the earth and life sciences.

Eligibility: Similar to the UK Research Councils' awards.

Purpose: To encourage study at the PhD level in the Natural History Museum.

Type: Studentships.

No. of awards offered: Two.

Frequency: Annual.

Value: Similar to the UK Research Councils' awards.

Length of Study: Three years.

Study Establishment: The Natural History Museum in South Kensington, London.

Country of Study: UK.

Closing Date: Usually February/March preceding the October in which the award commences.

Additional Information: Arrangements will be made with an appropriate university for higher degree registration and joint supervision of the student's research project. The main aim of scientific research at the Museum is to make available definitive accounts of the world's animals, plants and minerals in the form of monographs, taxonomic revisions and fauna and flora of particular areas (the Museum's taxonomic collections are the most comprehensive in the world).

NATURAL SCIENCES AND ENGINEERING RESEARCH COUNCIL

Natural Sciences and Engineering Research Council, 350 Albert Street, Ottawa, Ontario, K1A 1H5, Canada
Tel: 613 996 3769
Fax: 613 996 2589
Email: SCHOL@NSERC.CA
www: http://www.NSERC.CA
Contact: Scholarships and Fellowships Branch

Industrial Research Fellowships

Subjects: Science and engineering: industrial aspects.

Eligibility: Open to Canadian citizens or permanent residents who have recently completed a doctorate degree and who are seeking employment in industry in Canada for the first time.

Level of Study: Doctorate.

Purpose: To encourage highly qualified scientists and engineers to seek careers in Canadian industry.

Type: Fellowship.

No. of awards offered: 98.

Frequency: Every two months.

Value: A maximum of C$25,000 per annum towards the gross salary, which is set by the sponsoring company, plus travel costs.

Length of Study: Two years (maximum).

Study Establishment: Approved industrial organizations.

Country of Study: Canada.

Closing Date: Five weeks prior to each competition.

Additional Information: Nominating companies must contribute at least C$5,000 to the basic salary of the fellow in addition to NSERC's contribution of $25,000.

Postdoctoral Fellowships

Subjects: Natural sciences and engineering.

Eligibility: Open to Canadian citizens or permanent residents residing in Canada, who have recently received, or will shortly receive, a PhD.

Level of Study: Postdoctorate.

Purpose: To provide persons who have recently completed a doctorate with an opportunity to add to their experience through specialized training.

Type: Fellowship.

No. of awards offered: Approximately 200.

Frequency: Annual.

Value: C$29,000 per annum, plus a travel allowance.

Length of Study: One year; renewable for an additional year.

Study Establishment: A university or research institution of the Fellow's choice.

Country of Study: Canada or abroad.

Closing Date: November 15th; awards announced in late March. Earlier deadline (November 1st) in psychology.

Postgraduate Scholarships

Subjects: Natural sciences and engineering.

Eligibility: Open to Canadian citizens or permanent residents who will undertake a programme of postgraduate studies and research leading to an advanced degree. Specific eligibility conditions apply for PGSA and PGSB awards. Applicants must have obtained a first class average in the last two completed years of study.

Level of Study: Postgraduate, Doctorate, Postdoctorate.

Purpose: To assist in the training of highly qualified scientists and engineers by providing financial support to excellent students working towards a masters or doctoral degree in the natural sciences or engineering.

Type: Scholarship.

No. of awards offered: 1500.

Frequency: Annual.

Value: PGSA, masters: C$15,600; PGSB, Ph; C$17,400; plus a travel allowance, if required.

Length of Study: Two years; renewable for a further two years.

Study Establishment: Universities.

Country of Study: Canada. A maximum of 50 Scholarships are approved on a competitive basis for tenure in other countries.

Closing Date: December 1st. Earlier application deadline (November 15th) in psychology.

Research Reorientation Associateships

Subjects: Natural sciences or engineering.

Eligibility: Open to Canadian citizens or permanent residents living in Canada at the time of application, who must hold a doctoral degree in one of the natural sciences or in engineering, must have been away from active research for five or more years for reasons of family responsibilities, and must propose to carry out research in a field supported by NSERC.

Purpose: To provide support for a period of postdoctoral training to persons who hold a doctoral degree in one of the natural sciences or engineering but who have interrupted their research career for reasons of family responsibilities for a period of five or more years.

No. of awards offered: c.6.

Value: C$29,000.

Length of Study: One year; renewable for a second year.

Study Establishment: Canadian universities eligible for NSERC awards.

Country of Study: Canada.

Closing Date: Applications are accepted all year.

Additional Information: Award holders must work under supervision of faculty member who holds an NSERC research grant.

1967 Science and Engineering Scholarships

Subjects: Natural sciences or engineering.

Eligibility: Open to outstanding Canadian students and permanent residents of Canada who are in their final year of an honours course in a Canadian university or in the qualifying year after graduation from a general course in the natural sciences or engineering.

Purpose: To encourage outstanding students to undertake graduate studies and research leading to a doctorate and to take advantage of the best possible training opportunities.

No. of awards offered: c.55.

Frequency: Annual.

Value: C$21,300 per annum, plus travel expenses.

Length of Study: 24 months; renewable for a further 24 months.

Study Establishment: Universities.

Country of Study: Canada or abroad.

Applications Procedure: Candidates must first be invited by the chairman of the university's NSERC scholarship committee to submit an application.

FRIEDRICH NAUMANN FOUNDATION

Institut für Forschung und Begabtenförderung, Königswinterer Strasse 407, Königswinter, 53639, Germany
Tel: 02223 701 149
Fax: 02223 701 222
Contact: Friedrich-Naumann-Stiftung

Scholarships

Subjects: Subjects related to liberal philosophies.

Eligibility: Foreign applicants have to come from one of the countries where the Foundation has a project.

Level of Study: Postgraduate, Doctorate.

Purpose: To support the new liberal minded academics.

Type: Scholarship.

No. of awards offered: Varies.

Frequency: Annually depending on funds available.

Value: Up to DM1,030 per month (DM1,400 for graduates).

Length of Study: For the duration of studies after BA or German equivalent (up to 3 years for graduates).

Country of Study: Germany.

Applications Procedure: Application forms and information about the Friedrich Naumann Foundation Scholarship Programme are available on request.

Closing Date: 31 May and 30 November.

Additional Information: Applicants should have received an acceptance from a German university for doctorate or postgraduate studies. Fluency in German is required.

NAVAL RESEARCH LABORATORY (NRL)

American Society for Engineering Education (ASEE), 1818 N Street, NW, Suite 600, Washington, DC, 20036, USA
Tel: 202 331 3517
Fax: 202 265 8504
Email: projects@asee.org
www: http://www.asee.org
Contact: Luis Hernandez

NRL/ASEE Postdoctoral Fellowship Program

Subjects: Engineering.

Eligibility: Open to citizens of the United States.

Level of Study: Postdoctorate.

Purpose: To significantly increase the involvement of creative and highly trained scientists and engineers from academia and industry to scientific and technical areas of interest and relevance to the Navy.

Type: Fellowship.

No. of awards offered: Unlimited.

Frequency: Annual.

Value: US$36,000-US$49,000.

Length of Study: One to three years.

Study Establishment: Naval laboratory.

Country of Study: United States.

Applications Procedure: Requirement: application, research proposal and transcripts. The applicant must contact the research facility at which he/she is interested in working, in order to develop a suitable research proposal.

Closing Date: January 1st, April 1st, July 1st, October 1st.

Additional Information: The applicant must be sponsored by a Navy laboratory.

NDUS

NDUS, 600 East Boulevard, Bismarck, ND, 58505, USA
Tel: 701 328 2960
Contact: Rhonda Shaver

North Dakota Indian Scholarship

Eligibility: Must be a resident of North Dakota with one quarter degree Indian Blood. Must be accepted for admission at an institute of higher learning or state vocational program. Recipients must be enrolled full-time and have a grade point average above 2.00.

Level of Study: Postgraduate, Doctorate.

Purpose: To assist Native American Students in obtaining a basic college education.

Type: Scholarship.

No. of awards offered: 140.

Frequency: Annual.

Value: US$600-US$2,000.

Country of Study: USA.

Applications Procedure: Send completed forms to: North Dakota Indian Scholarship Program, North Dakota University System, 10th Floor State Capitol, 600 E Boulevard Avenue, Bismarck, ND 58505-0230.

Closing Date: July 15th.

NETHERLANDS GOVERNMENT

Royal Netherlands Embassy, 120 Empire Circuit, Yarralumla, ACT, 2600, Australia
Tel: 06 273 3111
Fax: 06 273 3206

*Scholarships

Subjects: Any subject.

Eligibility: Open to Australian citizens under 36 years of age who are university or college of advanced education graduates or tertiary students undertaking postgraduate study, have a good command of Dutch, English or German (or French if appropriate to the course of study), and are prepared to remain in the Netherlands for their studies for at least three months. Preference may be given to persons who have not recently studied in the Netherlands but each case will be considered on its merits.

Type: Scholarship.

No. of awards offered: Up to two.

Frequency: Annual.

Value: Varies.

Length of Study: 3-12 months.

Study Establishment: A university, art academy, school of music or other institute of tertiary education.

Country of Study: Netherlands.

Closing Date: December 15th.

NETHERLANDS ORGANIZATION FOR INTERNATIONAL COOPERATION IN HIGHER EDUCATION

NUFFIC, PO Box 29777, The Hague, 2502 LT, The Netherlands
Tel: 070 4260 260
Fax: 070 4260 229
www: http://www.nuffics.nl
Contact: Information Department

NFP: Netherlands Fellowships Programme of Development Cooperation (nationals from developing countries only)

Subjects: Most of the courses offered by the Institutes for International Education in the Netherlands.

Eligibility: Open to candidates who have the education and work experience required for the course, as well as an adequate command of the language in which it is conducted (usually English, sometimes French). The age limit is 40 for men and 45 for women. It is intended that candidates, upon completion of training, return to their home countries and resume their jobs. When several candidates with comparable qualifications apply, priority will be given to women. Candidates for a Fellowship must be nominated by their employer, and formal employment should be continued during the Fellowship period. As a rule the candidate's government is required to state its formal support, except in the case of certain development-oriented non-government organizations.

Level of Study: Postgraduate.

Type: Fellowships.

No. of awards offered: Variable number.

Value: Normal living expenses, fees and health insurances. International travel expenses are provided only when the course lasts three months or longer.

Length of Study: For the duration of the course in question.

Applications Procedure: For information on the nationality eligibility for these Fellowships and on the application procedure, candidates should contact the Netherlands embassy in their own country. Information on the courses for which the Scholarships are available can be found in the NUFFIC publication.

NETHERLANDS-SOUTH AFRICA ASSOCIATION

Netherlands-South Africa Association, PO Box 2363, Bloemfontein, 9300, South Africa
Tel: 0124 21313

*Study Fund

Subjects: Any subject.

Eligibility: Open to nationals of South Africa of all races.

Purpose: To support postgraduate study.

No. of awards offered: Five to ten.

Frequency: Twice yearly.

Value: 1,100 Dutch guilders per month.

Length of Study: Up to one year.

Country of Study: The Netherlands.

Closing Date: June 30th and November 30th.

For further information contact:
Department of Library Science, University of Stellenbosch, Dummerstraat 68, Somerset-Wes 7130, South Africa
Tel: 02231 774336
Contact: Professor P G J Overduin

THE NEWBERRY LIBRARY

The Newberry Library, 60 West Walton Street, Chicago, IL, 60610,
USA
Tel: 312 255 3610
Fax: 312 255 3666

American Society for Eighteenth Century Studies

Subjects: Arts and humanities.

Eligibility: Must be a member of the Society.

Level of Study: Postgraduate, Postdoctorate.

Purpose: For Scholars wanting to use the Newberry's collections to study the period 1660-1815.

Frequency: Annual.

Value: US$800.

Length of Study: From two weeks to two months.

Study Establishment: The Newberry Library.

Country of Study: USA.

Applications Procedure: Please submit completed application form, description of project, and three letters of reference.

Closing Date: March 1st.

For further information contact:
The Newberry Library, 60 West Walton Street, Chicago, IL, 60610,
USA
Tel: 312 255 3666
Fax: 312 255 3510
Contact: Michael Calvert, Assistant to the Vice President

Center for Renaissance Studies Fellowships

Subjects: Renaissance studies.

Eligibility: Open to faculty members and graduate students of the 32 member institutions of the Center.

Type: Fellowship.

No. of awards offered: Varies.

Frequency: Annual.

Value: Varies.

Study Establishment: Participation in seminars either at the Library or at the Folger Institute of Renaissance and Eighteenth-Century Studies.

Country of Study: USA.

Additional Information: Requests for information should be addressed to the Center or to the applicant's faculty representative. Funds are also available from the Folger Institute.

Center for Renaissance Studies Seminar and Summer Institute Fellowships

Subjects: Renaissance studies.

Eligibility: Open to postdoctoral scholars teaching in US colleges and universities.

Level of Study: Postdoctorate.

Purpose: To enable participation in a summer institute.

Type: Fellowship.

No. of awards offered: Ten.

Frequency: Annual.

Value: A stipend of US$3,000.

Length of Study: Six weeks.

Study Establishment: The Center.

Country of Study: USA.

Lloyd Lewis Fellowships in American History

Subjects: Any field of American history appropriate to the collections of the Newberry Library.

Eligibility: Open to established scholars, holding the PhD, who have demonstrated, through publications, excellence in the field.

Level of Study: Postdoctorate.

Type: Fellowship.

No. of awards offered: 2 - 3.

Frequency: Annual.

Value: Up to US$40,000.

Length of Study: 6 - 11 months.

Study Establishment: In residence at the Library with participation in the Library's scholarly community.

Country of Study: USA.

Closing Date: January 20th.

Additional Information: Applicants may combine grants with sabbaticals or other stipendiary support.

For further information contact:
The Newberry Library
Tel: 312 255 3666
Contact: Committee on Awards

Audrey Lumsden-Kouvel Fellowship

Subjects: Late medieval or Renaissance studies.

Eligibility: Open to postdoctoral scholars wishing to carry on extended research in late medieval or Renaissance studies.

Level of Study: Postdoctorate.

Type: Fellowship.

No. of awards offered: One.

Frequency: Annual.

Value: A stipend of up to US$3,000.

Length of Study: At least three months.

Study Establishment: The Newberry Library.

Country of Study: USA.

Closing Date: January 20th.

Additional Information: Preference is given to scholars who wish to come for longer periods or who may wish to use the award to extend a sabbatical.

For further information contact:
The Newberry Library, 60 West Walton Street, Chicago, IL, 60610,
USA
Tel: 312 255 3514
Contact: The Center for Renaissance Studies

D'Arcy McNickle Center Frances C Allen Fellowships

Subjects: Humanities and social sciences.

Eligibility: Open to women of American Indian heritage who are pursuing an academic program at any stage beyond the undergraduate degree.

Type: Fellowship.

No. of awards offered: Varies.

Frequency: Annual.

Value: Varies according to need.

Study Establishment: The Library.

Country of Study: USA.

Closing Date: February 1st.

Additional Information: Length of tenure varies according to need but Fellows are expected to spend a significant amount of their Fellowship term in residence at the Center.

For further information contact:
The Newberry Library, 60 West Walton Street, Chicago, IL, 60610, USA
Tel: 312 255 3666
Contact: The D'Arcy McNickle Center for the History of the American Indian

Monticello College Foundation Fellowship for Women

Subjects: Any field appropriate to the Library's collections.

Eligibility: Open to women who hold the PhD at the time of application.

Level of Study: Postdoctorate.

Purpose: To offer young women the opportunity to undertake work in residence at the Library and to significantly enhance their careers through research and writing.

Type: Fellowship.

No. of awards offered: One.

Frequency: Annual.

Value: US$12,500.

Length of Study: Six months.

Study Establishment: The Library.

Country of Study: USA.

Closing Date: January 20th.

Additional Information: The Award is designed especially for younger women whose work gives clear promise of scholarly productivity. Other things being equal, preference is given to the applicant whose proposed study is concerned with the study of women.

For further information contact:
The Newberry Library
Tel: 312 255 3666
Contact: Committee on Awards

National Endowment for the Humanities Postdoctoral Fellowships

Subjects: Any field appropriate to the Library's collections.

Eligibility: Open to US citizens or nationals and foreign nationals who have lived in the USA for at least three years and who are established scholars at the postdoctoral level or its equivalent.

Level of Study: Postdoctorate.

Purpose: To encourage scholarly research, and to deepen and enrich the opportunities for serious intellectual exchange through the active participation of Fellows in the Library community.

Type: Fellowship.

No. of awards offered: Varies.

Frequency: Annually, depending on funds available.

Value: Up to US$30,000 (for 11 months' residency).

Length of Study: 6 - 11 months.

Study Establishment: The Library.

Country of Study: USA.

Closing Date: January 20th.

Additional Information: Fellowships may be combined with sabbatical or other stipendiary support.

For further information contact:
The Newberry Library
Tel: 312 255 3666
Contact: Committee on Awards

Newberry Library-British Academy Fellowship for Study in the UK

Subjects: The humanities.

Eligibility: Open to established scholars at the postdoctoral level or equivalent. Preference is given to readers and staff of the Newberry Library and to established scholars who have previously used the Newberry Library.

Level of Study: Postdoctorate.

Type: Fellowship.

No. of awards offered: One.

Frequency: Annual.

Value: A stipend of £30 per day while the Fellow is in the UK.

Length of Study: Three months.

Country of Study: UK.

Closing Date: January 20th.

Additional Information: The home institution is expected to continue to pay the Fellow's salary.

For further information contact:
The Newberry Library
Tel: 312 255 3666
Contact: Committee on Awards

The Newberry Library - Ecole des Chartes Exchange Fellowship

Subjects: Renaissance studies.

Eligibility: Preference is given to graduate students at institutions in the Renaissance Center Consortium.

Level of Study: Doctorate.

Purpose: To enable a graduate student to study at the Ecole des Chartes in Paris.

Type: Fellowship.

Frequency: Annual.

Value: Varies.

Length of Study: Three months.

Study Establishment: Ecole des Chartes.

Country of Study: France.

Applications Procedure: Request an application form from the Center.

Closing Date: January.

Short-Term Resident Fellowships for Individual Research

Subjects: Any field appropriate to the Library's collections.

Eligibility: Open to nationals of any country who hold a PhD degree or have completed all requirements for the degree except the dissertation.

Level of Study: Postdoctorate, Doctorate.

Type: Fellowship.

Frequency: Twice yearly.

Value: US$800 per month.

Length of Study: Up to two months; three months for foreign applicants.

Study Establishment: The Library.

Country of Study: USA.

Closing Date: March 1st; October 15th.

Additional Information: Preference is given to those who particularly need the facilities of the Library and live outside Chicago.

For further information contact:
The Newberry Library
Tel: 312 255 3666
Contact: Committee on Awards

Harry and Sarah Zeltzer Fellowship and Prize

Subjects: Music research.

Eligibility: Musicians in the early stage of their career. Must be instrumentalists.

Purpose: Supports research in the Library's music collections.

Type: Fellowship and Prize.

Value: Cash prize of US$1,500 plus US$500 per week stipend and housing plus airfares.

Study Establishment: Newberry Library.

Country of Study: USA.

Additional Information: Applicants will be judged on their artistic merit (67%) and the quality of their research proposal.

For further information contact:
The Newberry Library, 60 West Walton Street, Chicago, IL, 60610, USA
Tel: 312 255 3610
Fax: 312 255 3666
Contact: Fred Leise

NEWBY TRUST LTD

Newby Trust Ltd, Hill Farm, Froxfield, Petersfield, Hampshire, GU32 1BQ, England
Tel: 01730 827 557
Contact: The Secretary

Awards

Subjects: Any subject.

Eligibility: Open to students of any nationality. Students not already in the UK are rarely considered. Foreign students must already be studying in the UK.

Level of Study: Postgraduate, Doctorate, Professional development.

Purpose: General educational purposes among others.

No. of awards offered: Varies.

Frequency: Annual.

Value: Up to £1,000 for fees or maintenance.

Country of Study: UK unless there are strong reasons for studying elsewhere.

Applications Procedure: No forms issued. Personal letter with CV, names and addressess of two referees, and SAE must be submitted.

Closing Date: None, but applications in September/October are rarely considered.

NEWCOMEN SOCIETY IN THE UNITED STATES

Newcomen Society in the United States, 412 Newcomen Road, Exton, PA, 19341, USA
Tel: 610 363 6600
Fax: 610 363 0612
Contact: Sandra Richter

Dissertation Fellowship in Business and American Culture

Subjects: American business history.

Level of Study: Doctorate.

Purpose: For doctoral students, to encourage them to pursue careers in studying and teaching the history of American business.

Type: Fellowship.

No. of awards offered: One.

Frequency: Annual.

Value: US$10,000.

Length of Study: Nine months full-time.

Country of Study: USA.

Applications Procedure: Applicants should submit five copies of their curriculum vitae and a research program not to exceed ten double spaced pages (including references). Faxed proposals cannot be accepted. University transcript and two letters of recommendation must be sent in support of applications.

Closing Date: February 15th.

Postdoctoral Fellowship

Subjects: Business history.

Eligibility: Open to scholars who have received the PhD in history, economics or a related discipline within the past ten years, and who would not otherwise be able to attend Harvard Business School.

Level of Study: Postdoctorate.

Purpose: To improve the Scholar's professional acquaintance with business and economic history, to increase his or her skills as they relate to this field, and to enable him or her to engage in research that will benefit from the resources of the Harvard Business School and the Boston scholarly community.

Type: Fellowship.

No. of awards offered: One.

Frequency: Annual.

Value: US$40,000.

Length of Study: One year.

Study Establishment: Harvard Business School, Cambridge, Massachusetts.

Country of Study: USA.

Closing Date: March 15th.

For further information contact:
Harvard University, Graduate School of Business Administration, Soldiers Field Road, Boston, MA, 02163, USA
Contact: Mr Thomas K McCraw, Straus Professor of Business History

NEW DRAMATISTS

Weissberger Award, New Dramatists, 424 West 44th Street, New York, NY, 10036, USA
Tel: 212 757 6960
Fax: 212 265 4738
Email: newdram@aol.com
www: http://www.itp.tsoq.nyu.edu/~diana/ndintro.html
Contact: L Arnold

L Arnold Weissberger Award

Subjects: Playwriting.

Level of Study: Professional development.

Purpose: To recognize outstanding achievement.

Type: Prize.

No. of awards offered: One.

Frequency: Annual.

Value: US$5,000.

Applications Procedure: Please submit script and letter of nomination.

Closing Date: May 30th.

Additional Information: Plays must be full length, unpublished and unproduced. Children's plays and musicals are not eligible. Plays must be nominated by an industry professional (ie. agent, literary manager, artistic director, or chairperson of accredited university, theatre or playwriters programs). Nominations will be limited to ONE per nominator. Nomination letters accompanying script submissions are recommended, but not required. All submitted scripts must include the name, address, phone number and letter of application of the nominator.

NEW ENGLAND THEATRE CONFERENCE

c/o Department of Theatre, 360 Huntington Avenue, Northeastern University, Boston, MA, 02115, USA
Tel: 617 424 9275
Fax: 617 424 9275
Contact: New England Theatre Conference

John Gassner Memorial Playwriting Award

Subjects: Playwriting (new full-length plays).

Eligibility: Open to all playwrights in New England, or NETC members, who wish to submit a full-length play which is both commercially unpublished and unproduced.

Type: Prize.

No. of awards offered: Two.

Frequency: Annual.

Value: First prize US$500; second prize US$250.

Applications Procedure: Send SASE for current guidelines. There is a processing fee of $10.

Closing Date: April 15th.

Additional Information: Portions of winning plays are given staged readings at an 'NETC New Scripts Showcase'. This is a competition and not a financial aid program.

NEW JERSEY STATE OPERA

New Jersey State Opera, 50 Park Place, 10th Floor, Newark, NJ, 07102, USA
Tel: 201 623 5757
Fax: 201 623 5761
Contact: Wanda Anderton

Vocal Competition

Subjects: Opera.

Eligibility: Open to singers aged 22-34, without restrictions on nationality, with a serious commitment to an operatic career.

Level of Study: Unrestricted, Professional development.

Purpose: To assist artists in furthering their career.

Type: Scholarship.

No. of awards offered: Three to five.

Frequency: Annual.

Value: A minimum of US$1,000 and attachment to an opera company performing world-class performances.

Country of Study: Unrestricted.

Applications Procedure: Completed application, two recommendations, proof of age, photo; if over 27, proof of operatic experience must be presented.

Closing Date: Varies.

THE NEW SCHOOL FOR MUSIC STUDY

The New School for Music Study, PO Box 360, Kingston, NJ, 08528-0360, USA
Tel: 609 921 2900
Fax: 609 924 2536

Contact: Ted Cooper

Assistantship in Piano Pedagogy

Level of Study: Postgraduate.

Purpose: To fund individuals enrolled in the Master of Music in Piano Performance and Pedagogy offered jointly by The New School and Westminster Choir College of Rider University.

Type: Assistantship.

No. of awards offered: Four.

Frequency: Annual.

Value: US$6,000.

Length of Study: Two years.

Country of Study: USA.

Applications Procedure: Application form is required along with college transcripts, letters of recommendation and performance and teaching auditions.

Closing Date: Rolling admissions.

Fellowship in Piano Pedagogy

Eligibility: Applicants must have a bachelors or masters degree in piano pedagogy, piano performance or music education (with a concentration in piano).

Purpose: To help fund qualified individuals enrolled in our Piano Teaching Certificate program.

Type: Fellowship.

No. of awards offered: 1-4.

Frequency: Annual.

Value: US$2,000-US$5,800.

Length of Study: One year.

Country of Study: USA.

Applications Procedure: Applicants are required to complete an application and submit college transcripts and letters of recommendation. Performance and teaching auditions will be required.

Closing Date: March 15th.

Additional Information: Private and/or group teaching experience is desirable. Awards must be applied to tuition fees at the at the New School. Fellows will be expected to undertake a teaching assistantship.

NEW SOUTH WALES CANCER COUNCIL

NSW Cancer Council, PO Box 572, Kings Cross, NSW, 2011, Australia
Tel: 61 2 334 1944
Fax: 61 2 358 1452
Contact: Manager Professional Education and Training

*Bicentennial Cancer Research Fellowship

Subjects: Cancer research.

Eligibility: Open to Australian citizens and permanent residents.

Purpose: To entice back to New South Wales a talented Australian cancer researcher who is currently working overseas.

Type: Fellowship.

No. of awards offered: One.

Frequency: Every five years.

Value: Varies.

Length of Study: Three years with a view to extending the fellowship to five years; potentially renewable.

Country of Study: Australia.

471

Closing Date: To be advised.

For further information contact:
NSW Cancer Council, 153-161 Dowling Street, Woolloomooloo, NSW, 2011, Australia

*Patient Care Research Awards

Subjects: Control of cancer through diminishing suffering from cancer: quality of life of cancer patients; coordination of domiciliary and instutitonal services for cancer patients; cost and effectiveness of such services; psychosocial needs of cancer patients, their families and carers; support services for cancer patients; and voluntary support groups. Studies including populations are ineligible.

Eligibility: Open to Australian residents who are health care professionals.

No. of awards offered: Varies.

Frequency: Annual.

Value: To cover salary and consumables.

Length of Study: Up to two years.

Study Establishment: Approved institutions in New South Wales.

Country of Study: Australia.

Applications Procedure: Application forms are available on request.

Closing Date: August 31st.

For further information contact:
NSW Cancer Council, 153-161 Dowling Street, Woolloomooloo, NSW, 2011, Australia

*Research Program Grant

Subjects: Cancer research.

Eligibility: Open to investigators with a sufficient record of research achievement in any field of cancer research. Individuals or groups of researchers are eligible.

Purpose: To provide longer-term, more flexible support than Research Project Grant.

Type: Research Grant.

No. of awards offered: Varies.

Frequency: Varies; dependent on other priorities.

Value: To cover salaries, consumables and equipment.

Length of Study: Three to five years; potentially renewable based on results.

Study Establishment: An approved institution in New South Wales.

Country of Study: Australia.

Closing Date: To be advised.

For further information contact:
NSW Cancer Council, 153-161 Dowling Street, Woolloomooloo, NSW, 2011, Australia

*Research Project Grants

Subjects: Research projects in all aspects of cancer which elucidate its origin, cause and control at a fundamental and applied level.

Eligibility: Open to Australian residents who are health care professionals. Recipients of tobacco sponsorship are ineligible.

Type: Research Grant.

No. of awards offered: Varies.

Frequency: Annual.

Value: Varies depending on requirements.

Length of Study: One to two years.

Study Establishment: An approved institution in New South Wales.

Country of Study: Australia.

Applications Procedure: Application forms are available on request.

Closing Date: June.

For further information contact:
NSW Cancer Council, 153-161 Dowling Street, Woolloomooloo, NSW, 2011, Australia

Travel Grants-in-Aid

Subjects: Cancer research.

Eligibility: Open to residents of New South Wales who are medical/scientific graduates or other health professionals currently working in cancer at an approved institute in New South Wales.

Level of Study: Postgraduate.

Purpose: To allow individuals to attend overseas or Australian conferences where abstracts have been accepted, and for attendance at an overseas or Australian institution to receive training.

No. of awards offered: Up to 15.

Frequency: Twice yearly.

Value: Up to a maximum of A$2,500 on the minimum air fare.

Length of Study: Up to three months.

Country of Study: Any country.

Closing Date: March 30th and September 30th.

For further information contact:
NSW Cancer Council, 153-161 Dowling Street, Woolloomooloo, NSW, 2011, Australia
Tel: 61 2 334 1900
Fax: 61 2 357 2670

NEW YORK STATE HISTORICAL ASSOCIATION

New York State Historical Association, PO Box 800, Lake Road, Cooperstown, NY, 13326, USA
Tel: 607 547 1481
Fax: 607 547 1405
Contact: Wendell Tripp

Manuscript Award

Subjects: History.

Eligibility: Open to nationals of any country - applicants must be of doctoral level.

Level of Study: Postgraduate, Doctorate, Postdoctorate, Professional development.

Purpose: To award the best unpublished book-length monograph dealing with the history of New York State. Manuscripts deal with any aspect of NYS history: biographies of individuals whose careers illuminate aspects of the history are eligible as are those dealing with such cultural matters as literature and the arts, provided that the methodology is historical.

No. of awards offered: One.

Frequency: Annual.

Value: US$1,500.

Length of Study: Book length.

Country of Study: USA/New York State.

Applications Procedure: Two copies of the manuscript are to be submitted, typed, double-spaced with at least 1" margins. Ribbon/photocopies on bond paper (no carbons).

Closing Date: January 20th.

NEW ZEALAND COMMONWEALTH SCHOLARSHIPS AND FELLOWSHIPS COMMITTEE

New Zealand Vice-Chancellors' Committee, PO Box 11-915,
Wellington, New Zealand
Tel: 64 04 801 5091
Fax: 64 04 801 5089
Contact: The Scholarships Officer

Commonwealth Scholarships

Subjects: Any subject.

Eligibility: Open to graduates who are citizens of a Commonwealth country and who graduated within the last five years.

Purpose: To enable persons of high intellectual promise to study in New Zealand in the expectation that they will make a significant contribution to life in their own countries on their return.

Type: Scholarship.

No. of awards offered: Approximately 15.

Frequency: Annual.

Value: NZ$950 per month, plus travel and allowances.

Length of Study: Up to three years.

Country of Study: New Zealand.

Applications Procedure: Nominations should be sent to the appropriate agency in the home country.

Closing Date: Differs from country to country. Applications close in New Zealand on August 1st.

Additional Information: Scholarships are provided by the New Zealand government and fall within the framework of the Commonwealth Scholarship and Fellowship Plan.

NEW ZEALAND FEDERATION OF UNIVERSITY WOMEN

New Zealand Federation of University Women, Fellowship Trust Board,
PO Box 13044, Hillcrest, Hamilton, New Zealand
Contact: The Secretary-Treasurer

Postgraduate Fellowships

Subjects: Any subject.

Eligibility: Open to graduates of a New Zealand university, or graduates of other universities who have resided in New Zealand for at least five years prior to application.

Level of Study: Postgraduate, Doctorate, Postdoctorate.

Purpose: To award fellowships to women graduates for the purpose of postgraduate study or research.

Type: Fellowship.

No. of awards offered: Up to 10, subject to resources.

Frequency: Annual.

Value: NZ$4,000-NZ$10,000 per annum.

Length of Study: One year.

Study Establishment: Any recognized university or research institution (under conditions to be approved by the Trust Board).

Country of Study: Any country.

Applications Procedure: Application forms are available from the Fellowship Trust Board.

Closing Date: July 31st each year.

Additional Information: Recipients must submit to the Federation a full report of research carried out during the tenure of the Fellowship.

NEW ZEALAND SOCIETY OF ACCOUNTANTS

New Zealand Society of Accountants, PO Box 11-342, Wellington, New Zealand
Tel: 64 4 474 7840
Fax: 64 4 473 6303
Email: harry_maltby@nzsa.co.nz
Contact: Harry Maltby, Admissions Director

Coopers & Lybrand Peter Barr Fellowship

Subjects: No particular topic.

Eligibility: Open to members and provisional members of the NZSA and to persons who have completed the examination requirement for admission to membership of the Society. Holders of such alternative qualifications as are deemed acceptable by the Award's Selection Committee for the purpose of a particular project are also eligible.

Level of Study: Postgraduate.

Purpose: To provide financial assistance for projects which will benefit the accountancy profession in New Zealand.

Type: Fellowship.

No. of awards offered: Unlimited.

Frequency: Annual.

Value: Maximum of NZ$10,000.

Country of Study: New Zealand or overseas.

Applications Procedure: There is no application form but full documentation must include a research proposal.

Closing Date: September 30th.

Additional Information: The award may be used to enable holders to extend their knowledge of developments in the accountancy profession, to undertake research on a particular topic chosen by the Selection Committee or to finance lecture tours in New Zealand by prominent overseas visitors.

PhD Scholarships

Subjects: Full-time or part-time PhD studies in any area of accounting, auditing, or closely related disciplines.

Eligibility: Open to applicants presently enrolled, or intending to enrol, for a PhD in a tertiary institution in New Zealand.

Level of Study: Doctorate.

Purpose: To help encourage candidates to pursue an accounting academic career in New Zealand.

Type: Scholarship.

No. of awards offered: Unlimited.

Frequency: Annual.

Value: Maximum of NZ$15,000 available annually to cover tuition fees, programme-related costs and living expenses.

Study Establishment: A New Zealand tertiary institution.

Country of Study: New Zealand.

Applications Procedure: Application form must be completed and full documentation on proposed programme of study submitted.

Closing Date: October 15th.

NEW ZEALAND VICE-CHANCELLORS COMMITTEE

New Zealand Vice-Chancellors Committee, PO Box 11-915,
Wellington, New Zealand
Tel: 64 4 801 5091
Fax: 64 4 801 5089
Contact: The Scholarships Officer

*William Georgetti Scholarships

Subjects: Any subject.

Eligibility: Open to graduates who have been resident in New Zealand for five years immediately before application and who are aged 21-28.

Level of Study: Postgraduate.

Purpose: To encourage postgraduate study and research in a field which is important to the social, cultural or economic development of New Zealand.

Type: Scholarship.

No. of awards offered: Varies.

Frequency: Annual.

Value: Up to NZ$5,100 for study in New Zealand; up to NZ$10,000 for study overseas.

Study Establishment: Universities in New Zealand or overseas.

Country of Study: Any country.

Closing Date: October 1st.

*Claude McCarthy Fellowships

Subjects: Literature; science; medicine.

Eligibility: Open to any graduate of a New Zealand university.

Purpose: To enable graduates of New Zealand universities to undertake original work or research.

Type: Fellowship.

No. of awards offered: Varies, depending upon available funds (usually 12-15).

Frequency: Annual.

Value: Varies, according to country of residence during tenure, and the project itself. Assistance for expenses incurred in travel, employment of technical staff, special equipment, etc. may be provided.

Length of Study: Normally for not more than one year.

Country of Study: New Zealand or overseas.

Closing Date: August 1st.

*Shirtcliffe Fellowship

Subjects: Arts; science; law; commerce; agriculture.

Eligibility: Open to graduates of New Zealand universities.

Purpose: To provide further aid for New Zealand doctoral students.

Type: Fellowship.

No. of awards offered: Three.

Frequency: Annual.

Value: NZ$2,000 as a supplement to the postgraduate scholarship emolument.

Length of Study: Up to three years.

Study Establishment: A suitable education institution.

Country of Study: New Zealand or a Commonwealth country overseas.

Closing Date: October 1st.

*Gordon Watson Scholarship

Subjects: International relationships or social and economic conditions.

Eligibility: Open to holders of an honours degree, or a degree in theology from a university in New Zealand. Candidates must undertake to return to New Zealand after the Scholarship period for not less than two years.

Purpose: To facilitate the study abroad of questions of international relationships or social and economic conditions.

Type: Scholarship.

No. of awards offered: One.

Frequency: Annual.

Value: NZ$10,200 per annum.

Length of Study: Three years.

Study Establishment: A university or universities.

Country of Study: UK, Europe, Asia or America.

Closing Date: October 1st.

*L B Wood Travelling Scholarship

Subjects: Any subject.

Eligibility: Open to all holders of postgraduate scholarships from any faculty of any university in New Zealand, provided that application is made within three years of the date of graduation.

Purpose: To assist graduates of New Zealand universities to undertake doctoral studies in the UK.

Type: Scholarship.

No. of awards offered: Two.

Frequency: Annual.

Value: NZ$3,000 per annum, as a supplement to another postgraduate scholarship.

Length of Study: Up to three years.

Study Establishment: University or institution of university rank.

Country of Study: UK.

Closing Date: October 1st.

NIEMAN FOUNDATION

Nieman Foundation, 1 Francis Avenue, Cambridge, MA, 02138, USA
Tel: 617 495 2237
Fax: 617 495 8976

Lucius W Nieman Fellowships for Journalists

Subjects: Fellows are customarily accorded auditing privileges in all Harvard faculties. Fellows select their own studies and pursue them through courses (undergraduate and graduate) or in more informal ways. Fellows have pursued courses in the central Faculty of Arts and Sciences; the Business, Divinity, Medical, and Law Schools; the Kennedy School of Government; and the School of Public Health, among others. No course credits are given or degree granted for work done during the Nieman year.

Eligibility: Open to full-time staff or freelance journalists working for the news or editorial department of newspapers, news services, radio, television or magazines of general public interest. Applicants must have at least three years of media experience (most Fellows have had five to ten), obtain the employer's consent for a leave of absence for the academic year (September to June), agree to return to the employer at the end of the Fellowship, and refrain from professional work during the period of the Fellowship.

Level of Study: Postgraduate.

Purpose: To provide a mid-career opportunity for journalists to study and broaden their intellectual horizons.

Type: Fellowships.

No. of awards offered: Approximately 12 to US journalists; 10-12 to foreign journalists.

Frequency: Annual.

Value: Tuition fees plus a monthly stipend for living expenses. Since income from the Nieman endowment is for the support of citizens of the USA, applicants from abroad must compete for restricted grants available to the program or secure their own financial backing.

Length of Study: One academic year.

Study Establishment: Harvard University, Cambridge, Massachusetts.

Country of Study: USA.

Applications Procedure: Application form will be supplied upon request. Also require professional endorsements and essays on proposed program and ambitions.

Closing Date: January 31st for US journalists; March 1st for foreign journalists.

Additional Information: Fellows are not candidates for degrees and receive no formal credit for studies; they are therefore free of the usual degree requirements. Fellows may select their own studies and pursue them through courses or in more informal ways. Each year the program includes 10-12 additional Nieman Fellows from foreign countries. These journalists must meet the same requirements as the American journalists. Since the Nieman Foundation is bound in general by the terms of its bequest to support only citizens of the US, foreign applicants must obtain funding by successfully competing for support from a few restricted grants available to the Nieman Foundation, or by securing their own financial backing from sources outside the University.

NORDIC AFRICA INSTITUTE

Nordic Africa Institute, PO Box 1703, Uppsala, S-751 47, Sweden
Tel: 46 18 56 22 00
Fax: 46 18 69 56 29
Email: nai@nai.uu.se
Contact: Mrs Ingrid Andersson

Guest Researchers Scholarship

Eligibility: Researchers at PhD level.

Level of Study: Professional development.

Purpose: To give researchers permanently affiliated to African research institutes a possibility to use the facilities of NAI.

Type: Scholarships covering travel, board and lodging.

No. of awards offered: Four.

Frequency: Annual.

Value: US$9,000.

Length of Study: Three months.

Study Establishment: NAI.

Country of Study: Sweden.

Applications Procedure: Application instructions available from NAI.

Closing Date: July 31st.

NAI Study Grant

Subjects: All development problems related to African studies.

Eligibility: Students in the Nordic countries only. Undergraduate students close to their MA.

Level of Study: Unrestricted.

Purpose: To give students in the Nordic countries (Denmark, Finland, Iceland, Norway and Sweden) an opportunity to use the library facilities of NAI.

Type: Funds covering travel and lodging, Travel Grant.

No. of awards offered: 18 spring term, 15 autumn term.

Frequency: Twice a year.

Value: US$700, on average.

Length of Study: One month.

Study Establishment: NAI.

Country of Study: Sweden.

Applications Procedure: Application forms available from NAI.

Closing Date: April 1st and November 1st.

For further information contact:
Nordic Africa Institute, PO Box 1703, Uppsala, S-751 47, Sweden
Tel: 46 18 56 22 00
Fax: 46 18 69 56 29

Email: nai@nai.uu.se
Contact: Ms Susanne Östman

NAI Travel Grant

Eligibility: Possession of a BA/MA degree. Must be students or researchers from the Nordic countries.

Level of Study: Postgraduate.

Purpose: To give possibilities for researchers in the Nordic countries (Denmark, Finland, Iceland, Norway and Sweden) to carry out field studies in Africa.

Type: Travel Grant.

No. of awards offered: 25-35.

Frequency: Annual.

Value: US$7,000 on average.

Length of Study: Varies.

Country of Study: Africa.

Applications Procedure: Application forms available from NAI.

Closing Date: September 30th.

NORTH ATLANTIC TREATY ORGANIZATION

NATO Information Service, NB 110, NATO, Brussels, B-1110, Belgium
Tel: 32 2 728 5014
Fax: 32 2 728 5457/4743
Contact: Academic Affairs Officer

*NATO Institutional Research Fellowships and NATO Research Fellowships

Subjects: Any relevant subject.

Eligibility: Open to citizens of any NATO member-state who are university graduates of established reputation. Candidates will be selected on the basis of their special aptitude and experience for carrying through a major project of research. In making this selection such factors as academic qualifications, professional experience and publications will be taken into account.

Purpose: To promote study and research leading to publication on aspects of the North Atlantic Alliance.

Type: Fellowship.

No. of awards offered: Varies.

Frequency: Varies.

Value: Individual 240,000 BEF; Institutional 250,000 BEF.

Study Establishment: One or more NATO member-countries.

Country of Study: Belgium, Canada, Denmark, France, Germany, Greece, Iceland, Italy, Luxembourg, Netherlands, Norway, Portugal, Spain, Turkey, UK, USA.

Additional Information: Fellows are required to submit to NATO before the expiration of their grant a final report in English or French on their studies. All studies are considered for publication, and manuscripts should be submitted in duplicate to NATO. Fellows are required to acknowledge the fact that their research was made possible through a NATO award. Further details may be obtained from the national authority in the relevant NATO member-country: Canada-Awards Committee, Royal Society of Canada, 344 Wellington Street, Ottawa, Ontario K1A 0N4; UK-The British Council, 65 Davies Street, London W1Y 2AA; US-Council for International Exchange of Scholars, 3400 International Drive, NW, Suite M-500, Washington DC 20008-3097.

NORTHERN TERRITORY UNIVERSITY

Research Management Unit, Northern Territory University, Darwin, NT, 0909, Australia
Tel: 089 466548
Fax: 089 270612
Email: rmu@banks.ntu.edu.au
www: www.ntu.edu.au
Contact: Dr C Berryman

One Year Postdoctoral University Fellowship

Subjects: African studies; natural sciences; special education; management systems and techniques; energy engineering; environmental studies.

Eligibility: Open competition. All applicants must have completed their PhD within three years of date of application.

Level of Study: Postdoctorate.

Purpose: To foster research in designated areas of research strength & developing priority.

Type: Fellowship.

Frequency: Annual.

Value: A$38,092 per year plus allowances; A$3,500 per year research support.

Length of Study: One year.

Study Establishment: Northern Territory University.

Country of Study: Australia.

Applications Procedure: Contact the Research Management Unit at the University for application forms.

Closing Date: October 31st.

Three Year Postdoctoral Fellowship

Subjects: African studies; natural sciences; special education; management systems and techniques; energy engineering; environmental studies.

Eligibility: Open competition. All applicants must have completed their PhD within three years of date of application.

Level of Study: Postdoctorate.

Purpose: To foster research in designated areas of research strength & developing priority.

Type: Fellowship.

Frequency: Every three years.

Value: A$38,092 per year plus allowances; A$3,500 per year research support.

Length of Study: Three years.

Study Establishment: Northern Territory University.

Country of Study: Australia.

Applications Procedure: Contact the Research Management Unit at the University for application forms.

Closing Date: October 31st.

NORWICH JUBILEE ESPERANTO FOUNDATION

Esperanto Centre, 140 Holland Park Ave, London, W11 4UF, England
Tel: 0171 727 7821
Fax: 0171 229 5784
Contact: The Secretary

Grants-in-Aid

Subjects: Esperanto.

Eligibility: Open to citizens of any country who are not more than 25 years of age, require financial assistance and have a high standard of competence in Esperanto. An efficiency test may be required. There are no set academic or age requirements for research grants.

Level of Study: Unrestricted.

Purpose: To encourage the thorough study of Esperanto by enabling young students to travel abroad, and to promote research into the teaching of Esperanto.

No. of awards offered: Varies according to funds.

Frequency: Varies according to funds.

Value: Normally £50-£200; maximum £1,000.

Length of Study: One week to several months.

Country of Study: Outside the UK (for UK applicants); UK (for other applicants).

Applications Procedure: A letter of application in Esperanto is necessary; an application form may be completed later.

Additional Information: Visitors to the UK will be expected to speak in Esperanto to schools or clubs.

For further information contact:
Norwich Jubilee Esperanto Foundation, 37 Granville Court, Cheney Lane, Oxford, OX3 0HS, England
Tel: 01865 245509
Contact: Dr Kathleen Hall, Secretary

NUFFIELD FOUNDATION

Nuffield Foundation, 28 Bedford Square, London, WC1B 3EJ, England
Tel: 0171 631 0566
Fax: 0171 323 4877
Contact: Ann Weber

Social Science Research Fellowships

Subjects: Social sciences and social studies.

Eligibility: Open to social scientists with some research experience.

Purpose: To enable teachers in UK universities to pursue their research interest on a full-time basis.

Type: Fellowship.

No. of awards offered: 10-15.

Frequency: Annual.

Value: Varies according to individual projects.

Length of Study: From three months to one year.

Study Establishment: Any university.

Country of Study: UK.

Closing Date: November 30th.

NURSES' EDUCATIONAL FUNDS, INC

Nurses' Educational Funds, Inc, 555 West 57th Street, New York, NY, 10019, USA
Tel: 212 582 8820 ext.806
Contact: Barbara Butler, Scholarship Coordinator

Fellowships and Scholarships

Subjects: Administration; supervision; education; clinical specialization and research.

Eligibility: Open to full-time masters degree students or full- or part-time doctoral students who are US citizens or have officially declared the intention of becoming US citizens. Applicants must be members of a professional nursing association.

Level of Study: Postgraduate, Doctorate.

Purpose: To provide the opportunity to registered nurses who seek to qualify through advanced study in a degree program.

Type: Fellowship.

No. of awards offered: Varies.

Frequency: Annual.

Value: US$2,500-US$10,000.

Length of Study: One year.

Study Establishment: Any college or university offering masters programs in nursing accredited by the National League for Nursing (NLN), or at an accredited University doctoral degree program.

Country of Study: USA.

Applications Procedure: Completed applications must be accompanied by official transcripts of academic records, GRE or MAT scores, references, proof of membership in a national professional nursing association, and proof of admission to an academic program.

Closing Date: March 1st preceding the academic year for which funds are sought.

Additional Information: Application forms are available from the Fund from August 1st to February 1st. Fellowships and Scholarships administered by the NEF include those donated by: American Journal of Nursing Company, Mead Johnson, F A Davis Company, BOC Group Award, Nurses' Scholarship and Fellowship Fund, National Student Nurses' Association, Edith M Pritchard Award, Isabel Hampton Robb Award, Leisel M Hiemenz Award, Bernhard J Springer Award, Isabel McIsaac Award, Lucy C Perry Award, Elizabeth Carnegie Award, Margaret G Tyson Award, Estelle Massey Osborne Award and others. Applicants are advised to apply to the school of nursing of their choice concerning fellowships and scholarships available there.

OFFICE OF NAVAL RESEARCH (ONR)

American Society of Engineering Education (ASEE), 1818 N Street, NW, Suite 600, Washington, DC, 20036, USA
Tel: 202 331 3517
Fax: 202 265 8504
Email: projects@asee.org
www: http://www.asee.org
Contact: Luis Hernandez

ONR/ASEE Postdoctoral Fellowship Program

Subjects: Engineering.

Level of Study: Postdoctorate.

Purpose: To significantly increase the involvement of creative and highly trained scientists and engineers from academia and industry to scientific and technical areas of interest and relevance to the navy.

Type: Fellowship.

No. of awards offered: Unlimited.

Frequency: Dependent on funds available.

Value: US$36,000-US$49,000.

Length of Study: One to three years.

Study Establishment: Naval laboratory.

Country of Study: United States.

Applications Procedure: Requirement: application, research proposal and transcripts. The applicant must contact the research facility at which he/she is interested in working, in order to develop a suitable research proposal.

Closing Date: January 1st, April 1st, July 1st, October 1st.

Additional Information: The applicant must be sponsored by a Navy laboratory.

OLFACTORY RESEARCH FUND LTD

Olfactory Research Fund Ltd, 145 e 32nd Street, New York, NY, 11354, USA
Tel: 212 725 2755
Fax: 212 779 9058

Awards

Eligibility: Applicants must possess a PhD in a related field.

Level of Study: Postdoctorate.

Purpose: Seeks talented investigators to conduct high quality research specializing in the study of olfaction.

Type: Research Grant.

Frequency: Annual.

Length of Study: One year.

Country of Study: USA.

Applications Procedure: Please send for criteria and guidelines booklet from ORFL; contains all application procedures.

Closing Date: First Monday of each January.

GEORGE AND CAROL OLMSTED FOUNDATION

The George and Carol Olmsted Foundation, 1515 North Courthouse Road, Arlington, VA, 22201, USA
Tel: 703 527 9070
Contact: Ms Barbara Schimpff, Executive Vice President

Olmsted Scholar Program

Subjects: Social and political sciences and international affairs are the preferred subject areas, but another choice by the Scholar is not precluded. Study must be in a foreign language.

Eligibility: Open to outstanding officers from each of the three US service academies and from each military department who have earned a regular commission through other officer training programs.

Purpose: To provide education for young career military officers in foreign universities in foreign languages.

Type: Fellowship.

No. of awards offered: Three.

Frequency: Annual.

Value: Varies.

Length of Study: Two years.

Study Establishment: A foreign university.

Country of Study: Outside the USA.

Closing Date: Military services set the date for their selection boards.

Additional Information: The Program also provides for assistance in obtaining an advanced degree at the conclusion of the overseas study, if approved by the Scholar's service. This study can take place at any accredited university in the USA approved by the Department of Defense for attendance by military officers immediately following the overseas study, or later if this is more convenient. A descriptive brochure on the Program is available from the Foundation.

OMAHA SYMPHONY GUILD

Omaha Symphony , 1605 Howard St, Omaha, NE, 68102, USA
Tel: 402 342 3836
Fax: 402 342 3819
Contact: Kimberly Mettenbrink

Omaha Symphony Guild International Music Competition

Subjects: Music theory and composition.

Eligibility: Open to composers of postgraduate age and above.

Level of Study: Postgraduate.

Purpose: The Omaha Symphony Guild is hosting an international music competition for composers with unpublished compositions which have never been performed by a professional orchestra.

No. of awards offered: One.

Frequency: Annual.

Value: US$2,000 Award and premiere performance.

Country of Study: USA.

Applications Procedure: Write for application form. Two copies of composition score must be submitted. Photocopies are acceptable. No tapes are accepted.

Additional Information: Composition must be no longer than 20 minutes. If you request the score to be returned please include US$10 postage.

ONCOLOGY NURSING FOUNDATION

Oncology Nursing Society, 501 Holiday Drive, Pittsburgh, PA, 15220-2749, USA
Tel: 412 921 7373 ext.257
Fax: 412 921 6565
Email: res_ons@nauticom.net
Contact: Research Department

Research Awards

Subjects: Oncology nursing research, including research proposals related to AIDS.

Eligibility: Open to nurses working in the field of oncology.

Level of Study: Unrestricted.

Type: Research Award.

No. of awards offered: 25.

Frequency: Annual.

Value: US$3,000-US$10,000.

Applications Procedure: Application form must be completed.

ONTARIO CHORAL FEDERATION

Ontario Choral Federation, 100 Richmond Street East, Suite 200, Toronto, Ontario, M5C 2P9, Canada
Tel: 416 363 7488
Fax: 416 363 8236
Contact: Bev Jahnke, Executive Director

Leslie Bell Prize

Subjects: Choral music: conducting.

Eligibility: Candidates must be Canadian citizens or landed immigrants who are permanent residents of the Province of Ontario.

Purpose: To reward an emerging new conductor.

Type: Prize.

No. of awards offered: One.

Frequency: Biennially (even-numbered years).

Value: C$5,000.

Closing Date: April 1st in even-numbered years.

THE ONTARIO INSTITUTE FOR STUDIES IN EDUCATION

Ontario Institute for Studies in Education, University of Toronto, 252 Bloor Street West, Toronto, Ontario, M5S 1V6, Canada
Tel: 416 923 6641
Fax: 416 323 9964
Email: gradstudy@oise.on.ca
Contact: Margaret Brennan

OISE Graduate Assistantships

Subjects: Adult education, applied psychology, curriculum, educational administration, higher education, history and philosophy of education, sociology in education.

Eligibility: Open to persons of any nationality who are suitably qualified for admission to a master's or doctoral degree programme in the Graduate Department of Education at the University of Toronto.

Level of Study: Postgraduate, Doctorate.

Purpose: To provide remuneration and financial assistance for graduate students who are engaged in research and/or field development oriented projects contributing to their academic and professional development.

Type: Assistantships.

No. of awards offered: 182.

Frequency: Annual.

Value: C$8,000 per annum (plus 4% vacation pay).

Length of Study: Eight months; renewable for one additional year in certain programmes.

Study Establishment: The Institute.

Country of Study: Canada.

Applications Procedure: Application form must be submitted along with application for admission.

Closing Date: January 15th.

Additional Information: Award is for employment - average of 10 hours per week.

OISE Scholarships

Subjects: Adult education, applied psychology, curriculum, educational administration, higher education, history and philosophy of education, sociology in education.

Eligibility: Open to persons of any nationality who are suitably qualified for admission to a master's or doctoral degree programme in the Graduate Department of Education at the University of Toronto.

Level of Study: Postgraduate, Doctorate.

Purpose: To support programs of full-time study. Offered for the first year of full-time study in master's programmes and for years of required academic residence (full-time study) in doctoral programs.

No. of awards offered: Up to 70 scholarships, depending on funds available.

Frequency: Annual.

Value: C$10,500 (does not include fees).

Length of Study: Eight months; renewable for an additional year in certain programmes.

Study Establishment: The Institute.

Country of Study: Canada.

Applications Procedure: Candidates may not apply: they are nominated by each OISE Department at the time of admission.

Closing Date: January 15th.

ONTARIO MINISTRY OF EDUCATION AND TRAINING

Ministry of Education and Training, PO Box 4500, 189 Red River Road, 4th Floor, Thunder Bay, Ontario, P7B 6G9, Canada
Tel: 1 800 465 3957/807 343 7257
Fax: 1 807 343 7278
Contact: Student Support Branch

Ontario Graduate Scholarship Programme

Subjects: Any subject.

Eligibility: Open to Canadian residents with an overall A- average or equivalent during the previous two years of study. Sixty awards may be allocated to students holding a 'student authorization'.

Purpose: To encourage excellence in graduate studies.

Type: Scholarships.

No. of awards offered: 1,300.

Frequency: Annual.

Value: Approximately C$3,953 per term.

Length of Study: Two or three consecutive terms of full-time graduate study; students must reapply each year and may receive a maximum of four awards.

Study Establishment: An Ontario university.

Country of Study: Canada.

Applications Procedure: Candidates currently registered in a university in Ontario must submit their applications and supporting documentation through that institution.

Closing Date: November 15th.

Additional Information: Students may hold another award up to C$5,000 and may accept research assistantships or part-time teaching or demonstrating appointments, providing that the total amount paid to the Scholars within the period of the award shall not interfere with their status as full-time graduate students. The total time spent by the student in connection with such an appointment, including preparation, marking examinations, etc., must not exceed an average of ten hours per week.

OPPENHEIM-JOHN DOWNES MEMORIAL TRUST

36 Whitefriars Street, London, EC4Y 8BH, England

Grants

Subjects: Arts.

Eligibility: Open to artists over 30 years of age, born in the British Isles of British parents and grandparents born after 1900. These qualifications are mandatory and applicants who do not qualify in all respects should not apply.

Purpose: To assist artists, musicians, writers, inventors, singers, actors and dancers of all descriptions who are unable to pursue their vocation by reason of their poverty.

No. of awards offered: Approximately 30-40.

Frequency: Annually in December.

Value: £50-£1,500 depending on requirement.

Closing Date: November 30th.

ORENTREICH FOUNDATION FOR THE ADVANCEMENT OF SCIENCE, INC

Orentreich Foundation for the Advancement of Science, Inc, RD2 Box 375, Biomedical Research Station, Cold Spring-on-Hudson, NY, 10516, USA
Tel: 914 265 4200
Fax: 914 265 4210
Contact: Nancy P Durr, Assistant Director

OFAS is an operating private Foundation that performs its own research and/or collaborates on projects of mutual interest

Grants

Subjects: Areas of interest to the Foundation, which include: ageing, dermatology, endocrinology, and serum markers for human diseases.

Eligibility: Recipients are typically at or above the postgraduate level in science or medicine at accredited research institutions in the USA. There are, however, no citizenship restrictions.

Level of Study: Postgraduate.

No. of awards offered: Varies.

Frequency: Occasionally, almost always at the grantor's initiation.

Value: Varies.

Country of Study: USA.

Closing Date: Applications for grants may be submitted at any time.

Additional Information: The Foundation is an operating one, conducting its own research.

ORGANIZATION OF AMERICAN STATES (OAS)

Organisation of American States , 1889 'F' Street NW, Washington, DC, 20006-3897, USA
Tel: 202 458 3446
Fax: 202 458 3897
Contact: Colin E Martinez, Information Officer

PRA Fellowships

Eligibility: Candidates must be a citizen or permanent resident of an OAS member state, and hold a university degree or have demonstrated ability to pursue advanced studies in the chosen field.

Level of Study: Postgraduate.

Purpose: To promote the economic, social scientific and cultural development of the member states in order to acheive a stronger bond and better understanding among the peoples of the Americas.

Type: There are two types of fellowship: a) those for advanced study at the graduate level and b) those for research, Fellowship.

Frequency: Annual.

Length of Study: From three months to two years.

Study Establishment: The candidate must choose the university or study centre in their chosen country of study and make the necessary contacts to secure acceptance.

Country of Study: Any member country of the OAS.

Applications Procedure: The fellowship form must be presented to the General Secretariat of the OAS through the official channels established by each government. US citizens can send applications directly to OAS headquarters in Washington, DC.

Closing Date: March 1st.

ORIENTAL CERAMIC SOCIETY

Oriental Ceramic Society, 30B Torrington Square, London, WC1E 7JL,
England
Tel: 0171 636 7985
Contact: Secretary

George De Menasce Memorial Trust Bursary

Subjects: Any aspect of oriental art.

Purpose: To promote research.

Type: Bursary.

No. of awards offered: One.

Frequency: Occasionally.

Value: £1,500.

Study Establishment: Applicants are required to complete a form giving complete academic qualifications. Research connected with a PhD degree is not normally considered adequate for the Bursary.

Additional Information: The recipient is required to read a paper on the research undertaken.

ORTHOPAEDIC RESEARCH AND EDUCATION FOUNDATION

Orthopaedic Research and Education Foundation, 6300 N River Road,
Suite 700, Rosemont, IL, 60018, USA
Tel: 847 698 9980
Fax: 847 698 9767
Contact: Katherine Walker, Director of Grants

AAOF/OREF Fellowship in Health Services

Subjects: Orthopaedics.

Eligibility: Applicant must be an orthopaedic surgeon in either Canada or USA.

Level of Study: Postdoctorate.

Purpose: To develop orthopaedic surgeons with research skills to manage health services and outcomes research.

Type: Clinical/educational.

No. of awards offered: One.

Frequency: Annual.

Value: US$70,000 per year, for up to two years.

Length of Study: Two years.

Study Establishment: At participating institutions.

Country of Study: USA.

Applications Procedure: Formal application is required.

Closing Date: May 31st.

Bristol-Myers Squibb/Zimmer Research Grant

Subjects: Treatment techniques, orthopaedics.

Eligibility: PI must be affiliated with a department or division of orthopaedic surgery with strong institutional commitment and competence in orthopaedic research.

Level of Study: Patient care.

Purpose: To support research which positively affects treatment of orthopaedic diseases leading to improved patient care.

Type: Clinical.

No. of awards offered: One.

Frequency: Annual.

Value: US$50,000 per year for up to five years.

Length of Study: Five years.

Country of Study: USA.

Applications Procedure: A formal application is required.

Closing Date: August 1st.

Career Development Award

Subjects: Orthopaedic surgery.

Eligibility: Applicants must be orthopaedic surgeons; not eligible if holders of NIHROI award.

Level of Study: Professional development.

Purpose: To encourage a commitment to scientific research in orthopaedic surgery.

Type: Basic/clinical research.

No. of awards offered: Three.

Frequency: Annual.

Value: Up to US$75,000 per year.

Length of Study: Three years.

Country of Study: USA or Canada.

Applications Procedure: Formal application is required with letters of recommendation.

Closing Date: August 1st.

Prospective Clinical Research

Subjects: Orthopaedics.

Eligibility: Applicant must be an orthopaedic surgeon.

Level of Study: Professional development.

Purpose: To provide funding for promising prospective clinical proposals in orthopaedics.

Type: Clinical.

No. of awards offered: Three.

Frequency: Annual.

Value: Up to US$50,000 per year.

Length of Study: Three years.

Study Establishment: Medical center.

Country of Study: USA or Canada.

Applications Procedure: Formal application is required.

Closing Date: August 1st.

Research Grants

Subjects: Sports medicine, surgery, rheumatology and treatment techniques.

Eligibility: Orthopaedic surgeon must be PI or co PI; PI cannot have NIH ROI award.

Level of Study: Postdoctorate.

Purpose: To encourage new investigators by providing seed money and start-up funding.

Type: Clinical Research.

No. of awards offered: 10-20.

Frequency: Annual.

Value: Up to US$50,000 per year.

Length of Study: Two years.

Study Establishment: A medical center.

Country of Study: USA or Canada.

Applications Procedure: Formal application is required.

Closing Date: August 1st.

Resident Research Award

Subjects: Orthopaedic research.

Eligibility: Applicants must be orthopaedic surgeon resident.

Level of Study: Professional development.

Purpose: To encourage development of research interests for residents.

Type: Basic research training.

No. of awards offered: Ten.

Frequency: Annual.

Value: US$15,000.

Length of Study: One year.

Study Establishment: Medical center.

Country of Study: USA or Canada.

Applications Procedure: Formal application is required.

Closing Date: August 1st.

PALOMA O'SHEA SANTANDER INTERNATIONAL PIANO COMPETITION

Paloma O'Shea Santander International Piano Competition, Calle Hernán Cortés 3, Santander, E-39003, Spain
Tel: 42 31 14 51
Fax: 42 31 48 16
Contact: Secretary General

Paloma O'Shea Santander International Piano Competition

Subjects: Piano performance.

Eligibility: Open to pianists of any nationality. Age limit: 29 years old.

Type: Competition.

Frequency: Triennially (next in 1998).

Value: Total amount approximately 17,000,000 Pesetas. Santander Grand Prize: 2,500,000 pesetas. Worldwide concert tours. CD Recording. A KAWAI Piano. Honour Prize: 1,800,000 Pesetas. Recitals and concerts in Europe. Finalist Prizes: 500,000 Pesetas. Recitals throughout Spain..

Additional Information: Representation in America: Mrs Brookes McIntyre, 1401 Brickell Avenue, Miami, FL 33131, USA. Tel: 1 305 530 29 10, Fax: 1 305 530 29 05.

OSTEOGENESIS IMPERFECTA FOUNDATION, INC

Osteogenesis Imperfecta Foundation, Inc, PO Box 24776, Tampa, FL, 33623-4776, USA
Tel: 813 282 1161
Fax: 813 287 8214
Contact: Leanna Jackson

Michael Geisman Memorial Fellowship Fund

Subjects: Osteogenesis Imperfecta.

Eligibility: Open to suitably qualified investigators.

Purpose: To encourage research scientists to study Osteogenesis Imperfecta.

Type: Fellowship.

No. of awards offered: 2-3 per year.

Frequency: Annual.

Value: US$25,000 per annum salary, plus US$10,000 per annum for supplies.

Length of Study: Two years.

Country of Study: Unrestricted.

Closing Date: November 25th.

Seed Research Grant

Eligibility: Open to respected researchers in the field of OI.

Level of Study: Postdoctorate.

Purpose: To fund seed projects which can then be submitted to larger funding bodies.

Type: Research Grant.

No. of awards offered: 1-2 each year.

Frequency: Annual.

Length of Study: One year.

Country of Study: Unrestricted.

Closing Date: RFPs are released in August, with deadline in November.

Additional Information: No PI salaries are allowed; no indirect cost allowed.

For further information contact:
Osteogenesis Imperfecta Foundation, Inc, 5005 W Laurel Street, Suite 210, Tampa, FL, 33607, USA
Tel: 813 282 1161
Fax: 813 287 8214
Email: BoneLink@aol.com
Contact: Leanna Jackson

OULU UNIVERSITY SCHOLARSHIP FOUNDATION

Finance Office, Oulu University, PO Box 191, Oulu, FIN-90101, Finland
Tel: 358 81 553 4135
Fax: 358 81 371 158
Contact: Juho Koivuniemi

Travel and Research Grants

Eligibility: Open to nationals of any country.

Level of Study: Unrestricted.

Purpose: For postgraduate research.

Type: Travel and research grants.

No. of awards offered: Varies.

Frequency: Annual.

Value: 400,000-500,000 FIM per year; 5,000-20,000 FIM per person.

Study Establishment: University of Oulu.

Country of Study: Finland.

Applications Procedure: Application forms are available from the Administrative Office, University of Oulu.

Closing Date: End of March.

PACIFIC CULTURAL FOUNDATION

Pacific Cultural Foundation, Suite 807, Palace Office Building, 346 Nanking East Road, Section 3, Taipei, Taiwan, Republic of China
Tel: 02 752 7424
Fax: 02 752 7429
Contact: Academic Section

*Grants in Chinese Studies

Subjects: Chinese culture, history and contemporary Chinese problems.

Eligibility: Open to candidates who hold at least a masters degree and who are residing in the free world outside Taiwan. Applicants for Writing Grants must have previously written in English at least one work of 30,000 words or more which has been published in book form or in a journal.

Purpose: To encourage foreign scholars in the free world to pursue further research.

Type: Grant.

No. of awards offered: Approximately 80.

Frequency: Annual.

Value: Up to US$5,000.

Length of Study: One year; not renewable, though an extension may be given.

Country of Study: Any country.

Closing Date: March 1st, September 1st.

NICOLO PAGANINI INTERNATIONAL VIOLIN COMPETITION

Nicolo Paganini International Violin Competition, Palazzo Tursi, Via Garibaldi 9, Genoa, 1-16124, Italy
Tel: 10 20981
Fax: 10 206235
Contact: Secretariat

*Nicolo Paganini International Violin Competition

Subjects: Violin.

Eligibility: Open to violinists of any nationality under 33 years of age.

Type: Prizes.

No. of awards offered: Six.

Frequency: Annual.

Value: A total of 40,000,000 lire. Paganini Prize: 15,000,000 lire; 2nd Prize: 10,000,000 lire; 3rd Prize: 6,000,000 lire; 4th Prize: 4,000,000 lire; 5th Prize: 3,000,000 lire; 6th Prize: 2,000,000 lire.

Closing Date: June 20th.

Additional Information: The Competition is held from late September to early October.

PAN-AMERICAN OPHTHALMOLOGICAL FOUNDATION

Pan-American Ophthalmological Foundation, 1301 S Bowen Road 365, Arlington, TX, 76013, USA
Tel: 817 265 2831
Fax: 817 275 3961
Contact: Teresa J Bradshaw

Fellowships and Research Grants

Subjects: Ophthalmology: continuing education, prevention of blindness and research.

Eligibility: Fellowships: open to post-residents; Research Grants: open to certified ophthalmologists practising in the western hemisphere.

Purpose: To encourage continuing education for ophthalmologists, the prevention of blindness, and the promotion of scientific and cultural exchange among ophthalmologists in the western hemisphere and beyond.

No. of awards offered: Varies.

Frequency: Annually, pending availability of funds.

Value: US$500-US$20,000, covering costs as stipulated.

Country of Study: Western hemisphere.

Closing Date: October 1st.

PARALYZED VETERANS OF AMERICA, SPINAL CORD RESEARCH FOUNDATION

Paralyzed Veterans of America, Spinal Cord Research Foundation, 801 18th Street, NW, Washington, DC, 20006, USA
Tel: 202 416 7656
Fax: 202 416 7641
Contact: Administrative Officer of Research

Research Grants; Fellowships; Design and Development Grants; Conference Support

Subjects: Spinal cord injury. Special consideration is given to proposals which benefit the spinal cord injured. Priority areas include: basic spinal cord regeneration; applied research in interdisciplinary medical, psychological and behavioural specialities; and technological and assistive devices.

Eligibility: Open to suitably qualified individuals who are seeking funds to develop a project in the field of spinal cord injury.

Level of Study: Postdoctorate.

Type: Research Grant.

No. of awards offered: Approximately 10-15.

Frequency: Twice yearly.

Value: US$20,000-US$50,000.

Length of Study: One year; renewable for a further two years.

Applications Procedure: A brochure, Guidelines and Procedures for Grant Request, is available from the Foundation.

Closing Date: January 9th, July 1st.

Additional Information: All grant recipients must submit biannual and annual progress reports and two articles in layman's language for publications in PVA's monthly publication, Paraplegia News.

PARAPSYCHOLOGY FOUNDATION, INC.

Parapsychology Foundation, Inc., 228 East 71st Street, New York, NY, 10021, USA
Tel: 212 628 1550
Fax: 212 628 1559
Contact: Lisette Coly, Vice President

Eileen J Garrett Scholarship

Subjects: Parapsychology.

Eligibility: Open to nationals of any country.

Purpose: To assist students attending an accredited college or university in pursuing the academic study of the science of parapsychology.

Type: Scholarship.

No. of awards offered: One.

Frequency: Annual.

Value: US$3,000.

Length of Study: One year.

Study Establishment: An accredited college or university.

Country of Study: Unrestricted.

Applications Procedure: Applicants should submit samples of writings on the subject with an application form from the Foundation. Letters of reference are required from three individuals, familiar with the applicant's work and/or studies in parapsychology.

Closing Date: July 15th for notification on August 1st.

Grant

Subjects: Parapsychology.

Eligibility: Open to nationals of any country.

Level of Study: Unrestricted.

Purpose: For original study, research and experiments in parapsychology.

Type: Grant.

No. of awards offered: Ten.

Frequency: Annual.

Value: Up to US$3,000.

Length of Study: One year.

Country of Study: Unrestricted.

Applications Procedure: Applicants should submit a proposal outlining the aims of the project, the time required to complete it, likely expenditure, educational background, references, past work and publications.

Closing Date: Applications are welcomed at any time.

D Scott Rogo Award for Parapsychological Literature

Subjects: Parapsychology.

Eligibility: Open to nationals of any country.

Level of Study: Unrestricted.

Purpose: To provide support to authors working on a manuscript pertaining to the science of parapsychology.

No. of awards offered: One.

Frequency: Annual.

Value: US$3,000.

Length of Study: One year.

Country of Study: Unrestricted.

Applications Procedure: Applicants should submit a brief synopsis of the proposed contents of manuscript, a list of previous writings and sample writing of assistance.

Closing Date: April 15th for notification on May 1st.

PARENTERAL DRUG ASSOCIATION FOUNDATION FOR PHARMACEUTICAL SCIENCES, INC

Parenteral Drug Association Foundation for Pharmaceutical Sciences, Inc, PO Box 242, Garden City, NY, 11530, USA
Tel: 516 248 6713
Contact: Awards and Grants Program

Foundation Grant in Biotechnology

Subjects: Biotechnology: research into developing analytical methodology for peptides, polypeptides and proteins. It is expected that the methodology will be used in formulation and stability studies on bioengineered products.

Eligibility: There are no geographic restrictions on grant recipients.

Purpose: To stimulate research.

No. of awards offered: One.

Frequency: Annual.

Value: US$15,000 per annum.

Length of Study: Up to three years.

Country of Study: Any country.

Applications Procedure: Full eligibility/application requirements are available on request. Candidates must submit a completed application form with eight copies of the proposal.

Closing Date: Early June.

Additional Information: First publication rights are reserved by the Foundation for possible publication in the Journal of Parenteral Science and Technology. The grant is funded by the Schering-Plough Corporation, the Nina Dale Demuth Fund, and John N Kapoor, PhD.

Foundation Research Grants

Subjects: Parenteral technology and related disciplines, including pharmaceutics; microbiology; biology; chemistry; pharmacy; quality assurance; pharmacology; manufacturing; engineering; formulation and stability studies.

Eligibility: Open to suitably qualified researchers.

Purpose: To stimulate research.

Type: Grant.

No. of awards offered: Two.

Value: US$15,000 each.

Length of Study: One year; renewable for a maximum of one additional year.

Country of Study: USA.

Closing Date: Early June.

Additional Information: Full eligibility/application requirements are available on request. The grants are funded by the PDA Foundation; Glaxo, Inc; The Pall Corporation; and the Parke Davis Division of Warner-Lambert.

Charles P Schaufus Grant

Subjects: Pharmaceutics; quality assurance; biotechnology processing; pharmaceutical process engineering; or other appropriate disciplines.

Eligibility: Open to suitably qualified researchers.

Purpose: To stimulate research in the area of parenteral processing technology.

Type: Grant.

No. of awards offered: One.

Value: US$10,000 per annum, plus an equipment grant of US$10,000 per annum.

Length of Study: Up to three years.

Country of Study: USA.

Applications Procedure: Full eligibility/application requirements are available on request.

Closing Date: Early June.

Additional Information: First publication rights are reserved by the Foundation for possible publication in the Journal of Parenteral Science and Technology. The grant is funded by the Millipore Corporation.

MANOUG PARIKIAN TRUST

Manoug Parikian Trust, 16 Ogle Street, London, W1P 7LG, England
Tel: 0171 636 4481
Fax: 0171 637 4307
Contact: Valerie Beale, Administrator

*Manoug Parikian Award

Subjects: Musical performance: violin.

Eligibility: Open to violinists under the age of 24 years of any nationality who have been resident in the UK for three years.

Purpose: To assist the studies of a talented young violinist.

No. of awards offered: One.

Frequency: Annual.

Value: £2,000.

Country of Study: Unrestricted.

Closing Date: Mid-February.

Additional Information: Selected students will be asked to audition.

PARIS INTERNATIONAL SINGING COMPETITION

Concours International de Chant de Paris, UFAM, 10 rue de Dome, Paris, 75116, France
Tel: 1 47047638
Fax: 1 47273503
Contact: Ms C de Bayser, President

*Paris International Singing Competition

Subjects: Singing.

Eligibility: Open to female singers of no more than 32 years of age and to male singers of no more than 34 years of age. The Competition is open to singers of all nationalities.

Purpose: To help young singers to start their careers.

Type: Various prizes.

Frequency: Biennially (even-numbered years).

Value: From a total fund of FF150,000, with a Grand Prix of FF50,000, plus free accommodation for competitors. Winners are also offered important singing engagements.

Applications Procedure: A brochure is available on request.

Closing Date: May 15th.

PARKINSON'S DISEASE FOUNDATION, INC

Parkinson's Disease Foundation, Inc, 650 West 168th Street, New York, NY, 10032, USA
Tel: 1 212 923 4700
Fax: 1 212 923 4778
Contact: Dinah T Orr

*Extramural Research Grants

Subjects: Parkinson's disease: research.

Eligibility: Open to PhDs and MDs.

Type: Grants.

No. of awards offered: 12-14.

Frequency: Annual.

Value: US$25,000.

Study Establishment: Any institution.

Closing Date: April 1st.

*H Houston Merritt Fellowship

Subjects: Parkinson's disease: research.

Eligibility: Open to established scientists at the level of associate professor or above.

Type: Fellowship.

No. of awards offered: One.

Frequency: Annual.

Value: US$15,000.

Length of Study: Six months to one year.

Study Establishment: The College of Physicians and Surgeons, Columbia University, New York.

Country of Study: USA.

Applications Procedure: There is no application form. Applications, including a CV, should be sent directly to Dr Stanley Fahn at the Foundation.

Closing Date: April 1st.

*Postdoctoral Fellowships

Subjects: Parkinson's disease: research.

Eligibility: Open to physicians who have completed their residency in neurology.

Level of Study: Postdoctorate.

Type: Fellowship.

No. of awards offered: Three.

Frequency: Annual.

Value: US$35,000.

Length of Study: One year.

Study Establishment: The College of Physicians and Surgeons, Columbia University, New York.

Country of Study: USA.

Applications Procedure: There is no application form. Applications, including a CV, should be sent directly to Dr Stanley Fahn at the Foundation.

Closing Date: April 1st.

*Summer Fellowships

Subjects: Parkinsons's disease: research.

Eligibility: Open to pre-med and medical students and to doctoral candidates.

Purpose: To allow students to study under the supervision of an established investigator.

Type: Fellowship.

No. of awards offered: 10-15.

Frequency: Annual.

Value: US$1,800-US$2,200.

Length of Study: Ten weeks.

Study Establishment: Any college or university.

Country of Study: USA.

Applications Procedure: Application forms are available from the Foundation.

Closing Date: April 1st.

PARKINSON'S DISEASE SOCIETY OF THE UNITED KINGDOM

Parkinson's Disease Society of the United Kingdom, 22 Upper Woburn Place, London, WC1H 0RA, England
Tel: 0171 383 3513
Fax: 0171 383 5754
Contact: The Research Coordinator

Medical Advisory Panel Research Grants

Subjects: Clinical, scientific and technological fields relating to PD, from neurology to pharmacology. All disciplines considered.

Eligibility: Open to suitably qualified researchers.

Purpose: To fund research committed to finding the cause and cure for Parkinson's disease (PD).

Type: Research Grant.

No. of awards offered: Varies.

Frequency: Annual.

Value: To cover salaries, consumables, equipment: from £20,000 over one year to £130,000 over three years.

Length of Study: Up to three years.

Study Establishment: At a recognized UK teaching, research or clinical institution.

Country of Study: UK.

Closing Date: November 30th.

Additional Information: The grants are advertised in the second week of October.

Welfare Advisory Panel/Research Committee Grants

Subjects: Counselling; nursing care; physio-, occupational or speech therapy.

Eligibility: Open to practitioners in the field of Parkinson's Disease.

Purpose: To fund research into improving the quality of life of those with PD and/or their carers.

No. of awards offered: Varies.

Frequency: Annual.

Value: To cover salaries, consumables, equipment: from £5,000 over one year to £50,000 over three years.

Study Establishment: At a recognized UK teaching, research or clinical institution.

Country of Study: UK.

PARTICLE PHYSICS AND ASTRONOMY RESEARCH COUNCIL

Particle Physics and Astronomy Research Council, Polaris House, North Star Avenue, Swindon, SN2 1SZ, England
Tel: 01793 442026
Fax: 01793 442036
Contact: E & T Section

Advanced Fellowships

Subjects: Particle physics, astronomy and astrophysics.

Eligibility: Candidates must hold a PhD or be of equivalent standing in their profession and have at least two years of research experience at postdoctoral level when the application is made.

Level of Study: Doctorate, Postdoctorate.

Purpose: To support a small number of outstanding research workers.

Type: Fellowship.

No. of awards offered: A small number of Fellowships.

Frequency: Annual.

Value: Awards are made on the first 14 points on the UFC scale for non-clinical academic and related staff in UK universities.

Length of Study: Up to five years.

Study Establishment: In the UK at any academic institution acceptable to PPARC.

Country of Study: UK.

Closing Date: November 15th.

Senior Fellowships

Subjects: Particle physics and astronomy.

Eligibility: Open to scientists who are already established in their careers, having proved their exceptional research and interpretative ability. Applicants must be members of permanent staff of UK universities, technical colleges or similar institutions. Fellows are expected to return to their normal employment at the termination of the Fellowship.

Purpose: To enable a small number of outstanding scientists at the peak of their capabilities to devote themselves full-time to research and scholarship, free of the restrictions imposed by their normal employment.

No. of awards offered: A small number of Fellowships.

Frequency: Annual.

Value: The Council will pay the salary, but not superannuation or National Insurance contributions, as if the Fellow is continuing in his/her normal employment at his/her home institution.

Length of Study: Up to three years.

Study Establishment: Any institution which has a firm working link with a university.

Country of Study: UK.

Closing Date: November 15th.

Additional Information: Fellowships are not intended to replace sabbatical leave.

ALICIA PATTERSON FOUNDATION

Alicia Patterson Foundation, 1730 Pennsylvania Ave NW #850, Washington, DC, 20006, USA
Tel: 202 393 5995
Fax: 301 951 8512
Email: apfengel@charm.net
www: http://www.charm.net/~apfengel/home.html
Contact: Margaret Engel

Alicia Patterson Journalism Fellowships

Subjects: Journalism.

Eligibility: Open to print journalists (reporters, editors, photographers etc) with at least five years of full-time professional experience. Must be US citizens.

Level of Study: Professional development.

Purpose: To give working print journalists a chance to spend a year researching and writing on a topic of their choosing.

Type: Fellowship.

No. of awards offered: Eight.

Frequency: Annual.

Value: US$30,000.

Length of Study: One year.

Applications Procedure: Use APF application - also required to submit three-page proposal, two-page autobiographical essay, three clips, four letters of reference and a budget.

Closing Date: October 1st each year - must be postmarked by this date.

PEACE RESEARCH CENTRE

Gujarat Vidyapith, Ashram Road, Ahmedabad, 380014, India
Tel: 91 272 429392/446148
Fax: 91 272 429547
Contact: Vice-Chancellor

*Fellowship for MPhil Course in Peace Studies

Subjects: Peace and global society; Ghandian thought; science and non-violence.

Eligibility: Open to holders of a second class master's degree (with a minimum 55% average) in a social science. Candidates should have a good knowledge of the English language.

Purpose: To promote studies in peace and non-violence.

Type: Fellowship.

No. of awards offered: One.

Frequency: Annual.

Value: 1,000 rupees per month.

Length of Study: On year.

Study Establishment: The Gujarat Vidyapith.

Country of Study: India.

Closing Date: March 31st.

PEDIATRIC AIDS FOUNDATION

Pediatric Aids Foundation, 1311 Colorado Avenue, Santa Monica, CA, 90404, USA
Tel: 310 395 9051
Fax: 310 395 5149
Contact: Trish Devine, Medical Programs Manager

Student Intern Awards

Eligibility: Open to highly motivated high-school, college, graduate and medical students who have a sponsor recognized for his or her contributions to pediatric AIDS. The program may be orientated to either fundamental research or clinical research and care.

Level of Study: Postgraduate, Doctorate, Undergraduate.

Purpose: To encourage students to enter clinical and research programs related to pediatric AIDS.

Applications Procedure: Applications procedure depends on progam; contact Trish Devine, Programs Manager for additional information.

PEN AMERICAN CENTER

PEN American Center, 568 Broadway, New York, NY, 10012, USA
Tel: 212 334 1660
Fax: 212 334 2181
Contact: India Amos

PEN Writers Fund

Subjects: Writing.

Eligibility: Open to US writers facing emergency situations.

Purpose: To assist professional literary writers facing emergency situations.

Frequency: Every two months.

Value: Grants and interest-free loans of up to US$500.

Applications Procedure: Application consists of a two-page form, published writing samples, documentation of financial emergency (bills etc.), and professional resumé.

Additional Information: Approximately 100 writers are assisted each year, and aid is extended within eight weeks of application. A separate fund exists for writers and editors with AIDS in need of emergency assistance. The funds are not for research purposes, to enable writers to complete unfinished projects, or to fund writing publications or organizations; grants and loans are for unexpected emergencies only, and not for the support of working writers. PEN also offers numerous annual awards to recognize distinguished writing, editing and translation.

PERMANENT INTERNATIONAL ASSOCIATION OF NAVIGATION CONGRESSES

Permanent International Association of Navigation Congresses, WTC, Tour 3, 26e étage, Boulevard Simon Bolivar 30, Brussels, B-1210, Belgium
Tel: 32 2 208 52 16/18
Fax: 32 2 208 52 15

Gustave Willems Prize

Subjects: Articles must deal with a subject in the field of the design, construction, improvement, maintenance or operation of inland and maritime waterways (rivers, estuaries, canals, port approaches), of inland and maritime ports and of coastal areas.

Eligibility: Open to members of PIANC or candidates sponsored by a member, who are under the age of 35.

Purpose: To encourage young engineers, research workers and others to pursue studies in fields of interest of the Association and to submit articles on these subjects suitable for publication in the PIANC Bulletin.

Type: Prize.

No. of awards offered: One.

Frequency: Annual.

Value: A monetary award (the amount of which shall be fixed each year by the Permanent International Commission), plus free membership of PIANC for a five-year period.

Closing Date: December 31st.

Additional Information: Articles must be written by a single author; not have been previously published elsewhere; not exceed 12,000 words; be in type-script and either in English or French with a summary in the alternate language: they may be accompanied by illustrations or diagrams. The prize will be awarded to the individual candidate who submits the most outstanding article in the calendar year preceding the PIC meeting at which the prize is awarded: provided the article is judged to be of sufficiently high standard. The prize-winner will be invited to present a commentary on his or her article either during the technical day following the General Assembly of the PIC or during the Congress and to take part in the technical excursions after the PIC meeting. Free hotel accommodation will be provided, together with an allowance towards the cost of travel to the venue of the General Assembly. In judging the articles the jury shall take into account their technical level, originality and practical value and the quality of presentation. Candidates are advised that the Bulletin is designed for readers with a wide range of engineering interests and highly specialized articles should be written with this in mind.

PERMANENT TRUSTEE COMPANY LTD

Permanent Trustee Company Ltd, Arts Management, 180 Goulburn Street, Darlinghurst, NSW, 2010, Australia
Tel: 02 283 2066
Fax: 02 264 8201
Contact: Aimee Said

The Marten Bequest Travelling Scholarships

Subjects: Fine and applied arts; drawing and painting; sculpture; singing; musical performance; drama; dancing.

Eligibility: Applicants must have been born in Australia, and be between the ages of 21 and 35 (17-35 for ballet).

Level of Study: Unrestricted.

Purpose: To augment a scholar's own resources towards affording them a cultural education by means of a travelling scholarship.

Type: Scholarship.

No. of awards offered: Six.

Frequency: Annual.

Value: A$15,000 over two years.

Length of Study: Two years.

Applications Procedure: Applicants should submit an application form, study outline and supporting material.

Closing Date: October 31st.

THE PERRY FOUNDATION

The Perry Foundation, 31 Rossendale, Chelmsford, Essex, CM1 2UA, England
Tel: 01245 260805
Fax: 01245 260805
Contact: D J Naylor, Secretary

Perry Postgraduate Scholarships

Subjects: The production and utilisation of crops for non-food uses; ecologically acceptable and sustainable farming systems, including in particular, water and nutrient balances, intergrated disease and pest control systems for both crops and livestock. Socio-economic studies in the occupation and use of land, the rural economy and infrastructure and developments in marketing. Scholarship may be linked to Perry Research Awards.

Eligibility: Open to holders of first and 2nd degrees in appropriate subjects, gained in the UK.

Level of Study: Postgraduate.

Purpose: To enable postgraduates to undertake research projects and investigative work into agriculture and related fields. To build and develop a pool of highly competent researchers in the UK.

Type: Scholarship.

No. of awards offered: Varies.

Frequency: Annually.

Value: Not less than MAFF postgraduate agriculture & food studentships.

Length of Study: Normally three years leading to a doctorate.

Study Establishment: Universities, colleges, institutes and research establishments in the UK.

Country of Study: United Kingdom.

Applications Procedure: Brochure and application forms with details of procedure are available from the Foundation Secretary. Applications submitted by individuals, must be supported by their university, college, institute or other establishment.

Closing Date: October 31st.

Perry Research Awards

Subjects: The production and utilisation of crops for non-food uses; ecologically acceptable and sustainable farming systems, including in particular, water and nutrient balances, integrated disease and pest control systems for both crops and livestock. Socio-economic studies in the occupation and use of land, the rural economy and infrastructure and developments in marketing. The Perry Foundation welcomes proposals for joint ventures with other organisations, particularly those that may be suitable for consideration by government sponsored Link Collaborative Research Programmes.

Eligibility: Open to suitably qualified individuals or research teams.

Purpose: For the promotion of the cause of agriculture in the shorter term by enabling research and investigative work into agriculture and related fields.

Type: Research Award.

No. of awards offered: Depends on the availability of funds.

Frequency: Annual.

Value: Varies.

Length of Study: Normally three years maximum.

Study Establishment: Universities, colleges, institutes and research establishments in the UK.

Country of Study: United Kingdom.

Applications Procedure: Brochure and application forms are available from the Foundation Secretary on request.

Closing Date: October 31st.

PETERHOUSE

Peterhouse, Cambridge, CB2 1RD, England
Tel: 01223 338200
Fax: 01223 337578
Contact: The Senior Tutor

Friends of Peterhouse Bursary

Subjects: All subjects except clinical medicine.

Eligibility: Open to those who are required to pay university fees at the overseas rate.

Level of Study: Postgraduate.

Purpose: For study for a postgraduate one- or two-year taught course as a registered graduate student.

Type: Bursary.

No. of awards offered: One.

Frequency: Annual.

Value: University fees only.

Length of Study: One or two years.

Study Establishment: Peterhouse.

Country of Study: United Kingdom.

Applications Procedure: Application form, CV and two references.

Closing Date: April 1st.

Peterhouse Research Fellowship

Subjects: All subjects.

Eligibility: Applicants must hold, or be studying for, a degree from Cambridge or Oxford universities.

Level of Study: Postdoctorate.

Purpose: To support a young scholar in postdoctoral research.

Type: Fellowship.

No. of awards offered: Two or three.

Frequency: Annual.

Value: Maintenance and allowances.

Length of Study: Three years.

Study Establishment: Peterhouse.

Country of Study: United Kingdom.

Applications Procedure: Application form must be completed.

Closing Date: Early February each year.

Peterhouse Research Studentship

Subjects: All subjects.

Eligibility: Unrestricted.

Level of Study: Postgraduate.

Purpose: To study for a PhD.

Type: Studentship.

No. of awards offered: Two or three.

Frequency: Annual.

Value: Full fees and maintenance.

Length of Study: Three years.

Study Establishment: Peterhouse.

Country of Study: United Kingdom.

Applications Procedure: Application form, CV and references.

Closing Date: April 1st.

THE PEW CHARITABLE TRUSTS

1388 Sutter Street, Suite 805, San Francisco, CA, 94109, USA

Pew Latin American Fellows Program

Subjects: Sciences.

Eligibility: Open to postdoctoral level students from any Central or South American country or Mexico.

Level of Study: Postdoctorate.

Purpose: To serve as a nucleus of scientific exchange and collaboration between investigators in the USA and Latin America.

No. of awards offered: Ten.

Frequency: Annual.

Value: US$75,000.

Length of Study: Two years.

Country of Study: USA.

Applications Procedure: Applications are available from the Regional Committee Chairman or the Program office.

Closing Date: October.

Pew Scholars Program in the Biomedical Sciences

Subjects: Medical sciences.

Eligibility: Applicants must be nominated by one of the invited US institutions.

Level of Study: Assistant Professor level or equivalent.

Purpose: To support young investigators of outstanding promise in basic and clinical sciences relevant to the advancement of human health.

Type: Research Grant.

No. of awards offered: Twenty.

Frequency: Annual.

Value: US$200,000 in total over four years.

Applications Procedure: Through nomination by their institution.

Closing Date: November 1st.

PHARMACEUTICAL MANUFACTURERS ASSOCIATION FOUNDATION

Pharmaceutical Manufacturers Association Foundation, 1100 Fifteenth Street, NW, Washington, DC, 20005, USA
Tel: 202 835 3565

*Advanced Predoctoral Fellowships in Pharmaceutics

Subjects: Pharmaceutics.

Eligibility: Candidates must be sponsored by the school or university at which the research is to be conducted.

Purpose: To support promising students during their thesis research.

Type: Fellowship.

No. of awards offered: Eight.

Frequency: Annual.

Value: US$10,000 per annum.

Length of Study: Two years.

Study Establishment: An appropriate institution.

Country of Study: USA.

Closing Date: October 1st.

*Advanced Predoctoral Fellowships in Pharmacology/Toxicology

Subjects: Pharmacology and toxicology.

Eligibility: Candidates must be sponsored by the school or university at which the research is to be conducted.

Type: Fellowship.

No. of awards offered: 12.

Frequency: Annual.

Value: US$10,000 per annum, plus US$500 per annum for expenses associated with thesis research.

Length of Study: One to two years.

Study Establishment: An appropriate institution.

Country of Study: USA.

Closing Date: September 15th (pharmacology); October 1st (pharmaceutics).

*Development Grants for Clinical Pharmacology Units

Subjects: Clinical pharmacology.

Eligibility: Candidates must be sponsored by the school or university at which the research is to be conducted.

Type: Grant.

No. of awards offered: One.

Frequency: Annual.

Value: US$100,000.

Length of Study: Three years.

Study Establishment: An appropriate institution.

Country of Study: USA.

Closing Date: January 15th.

*Faculty Awards in Basic Pharmacology/Toxicology

Subjects: Pharmacology and toxicology.

Eligibility: Candidates must be sponsored by the school or university at which the research is to be conducted.

No. of awards offered: Three.

Frequency: Annual.

Value: US$30,000 per annum.

Length of Study: Two years.

Study Establishment: An appropriate institution.

Country of Study: USA.

Closing Date: September 15th.

*Faculty Awards in Clinical Pharmocology

Subjects: Clinical pharmacology.

Eligibility: Candidates must be sponsored by the school or university at which the research is to be conducted.

Purpose: To meet the manpower needs in the field of clinical pharmacology.

No. of awards offered: Three.

Frequency: Annual.

Value: US$40,000 per annum.

Length of Study: Three years.

Study Establishment: An appropriate institution.

Country of Study: USA.

Closing Date: October 1st.

Faculty Awards in Toxicologic-Pathology

Subjects: Toxicologic-pathology.

Eligibility: Candidates must be sponsored by the school or university at which the research is to be conducted.

Purpose: To encourage veterinary and comparative pathologists in academic settings to pursue careers in drug toxicology research.

No. of awards offered: Two.

Frequency: Annual.

Value: US$30,000 per annum.

Length of Study: Two years.

Study Establishment: An appropriate institution.

Country of Study: USA.

Closing Date: September 1st.

Fellowships for Careers in Clinical Pharmacology

Subjects: Clinical pharmacology.

Eligibility: Candidates must be sponsored by the school or university at which the research is to be conducted.

Purpose: To assist those who are vitally interested in careers in clinical pharmacology.

Type: Fellowship.

No. of awards offered: 14.

Frequency: Annual.

Value: US$24,000 per annum.

Length of Study: Two years.

Study Establishment: An appropriate institution.

Country of Study: USA.

Closing Date: October 1st.

Fellowships in Pharmacology-Morphology

Subjects: Pharmacology-morphology, including cell biology.

Eligibility: Candidates must be sponsored by the school or university at which the research is to be conducted.

Purpose: To advance understanding of drug action through discovery of specifically related cellular and tissue changes and to uncover associations between normal and abnormal function in particular tissue and cellular structures.

Type: Fellowship.

No. of awards offered: Three.

Frequency: Annual.

Value: US$21,000 per annum.

Length of Study: Two years.

Study Establishment: An appropriate institution.

Country of Study: USA.

Closing Date: January 15th.

Medical Student Research Fellowships

Subjects: Clinical pharmacology.

Eligibility: Candidates must be sponsored by the school or university at which the research is to be conducted.

Purpose: To generate interest in research careers among medical students.

Type: Fellowship.

No. of awards offered: Six.

Frequency: Annual.

Value: US$10,000.

Length of Study: Three months to two years.

Study Establishment: An appropriate institution.

Country of Study: USA.

Closing Date: January 15th.

Postdoctoral Research Fellowships in Pharmaceutics

Subjects: Pharmaceutics.

Eligibility: Open to graduates from PhD programs in pharmaceutics.

Purpose: To encourage graduates to continue to refine their research skills through formal postdoctoral training.

Type: Fellowship.

No. of awards offered: Varies.

Frequency: Annual.

Value: US$25,000.

Length of Study: One year.

Study Establishment: An appropriate institution.

Country of Study: USA.

Closing Date: October 1st.

Research Starter Grants

Subjects: Pharmacology, clinical pharmacology, pharmaceutics and drug toxicology.

Eligibility: Candidates must be sponsored by the school or university at which the research is to be conducted.

Purpose: To offer support to new investigators beginning their careers.

Type: Grant.

No. of awards offered: 20.

Frequency: Annual.

Value: US$10,000 per annum.

Length of Study: Two years.

Study Establishment: An appropriate institution.

Country of Study: USA.

Closing Date: September 1st.

PHI BETA KAPPA SOCIETY

Phi Beta Kappa Society, 1811 Q Street, NW, Washington, DC, 20009, USA
Tel: 202 265 3808
Fax: 202 986 1601
Contact: Linda Surles

Mary Isabel Sibley Fellowship

Subjects: French language or literature (even years); Greek language, literature, history, or archaeology (odd years).

Eligibility: Open to unmarried women between the ages of 25 and 35 (inclusive) who have demonstrated their ability to carry out original research. Candidates must hold the doctorate or have fulfilled all the requirements for the doctorate except the dissertation. There are no restrictions as to nationality. Not restricted to members of Phi Beta Kappa.

Level of Study: Doctorate, Postdoctorate.

Purpose: To recognize women scholars who have demonstrated their ability to carry out original research.

Type: Fellowship.

No. of awards offered: One.

Frequency: Annual.

Value: US$10,000.

Length of Study: One year; not renewable.

Applications Procedure: Application, transcripts, references. Applications are available from Phi Beta Kappa.

Closing Date: January 15th.

PHI CHI THETA FOUNDATION

Phi Chi Theta Foundation, 8656 Totempole Drive, Cincinatti, OH, 45249, USA
Contact: Scholarship Chairman

Scholarship

Subjects: Business and administration management; social and behavioural sciences.

Eligibility: Open to women enrolled full-time in courses leading to a degree in business or economics at a US college. They must have completed two semesters.

Level of Study: Postgraduate, Doctorate, Undergraduate.

Purpose: To promote the cause of higher education for women in business and/or economics.

Type: Scholarship.

No. of awards offered: Three.

Frequency: Annual.

Value: US$1,000.

Length of Study: Degree program.

Study Establishment: US college or university.

Country of Study: USA.

Applications Procedure: Application form is required with official transcripts, two letters of recommendation and a financial statement.

Closing Date: May 1st.

Additional Information: Please send stamped self-addressed envelope for application. The award is based on leadership, scholastic achievement, motivation and financial need.

PHILLIPS EXETER ACADEMY

Phillips Exeter Academy, 20 Main Street, Exeter, NH, 03833-2460, USA
Contact: Chairman, Bennett Fellowship Committee

George Bennett Fellowship

Subjects: Creative writing.

Eligibility: Preference is given to writers who have not published a book with a major commercial publisher.

Purpose: To allow a person commencing a career as a writer the time and freedom from material considerations to complete a manuscript in progress.

Type: Fellowship.

No. of awards offered: One.

Frequency: Annual.

Value: US$5,000 per annum.

Study Establishment: Phillips Exeter Academy in Exeter, New Hampshire.

Country of Study: USA.

Closing Date: December 1st for the following academic year.

Additional Information: Duties include being in residence for one academic year while working on the manuscript, and informal availability to student writers. Requests for further information should be accompanied by an SSAE.

PHYSIOLOGICAL SOCIETY

Physiological Society, Administrative Office, PO Box 506, Oxford, OX1 3XE, England
Tel: 01865 798498
Fax: 01865 798092
Email: admin@physoc.org
Contact: The Administrator

Dale and Rushton Fund Travel Grants

Subjects: Physiological sciences.

Eligibility: Open to physiologists working in the British Isles. The applicants must be living in the British Isles. The Dale Fund is open to members and non-members, and the Rushton Fund only to non-members of the Society.

Purpose: To promote new physiological research in the British Isles, training and overseas collaboration.

Type: Travel Grant.

No. of awards offered: Varies.

Frequency: Throughout the year.

Value: Dale Fund: up to £800; Rushton Fund: up to £500.

Country of Study: British Isles.

Applications Procedure: Must use application form.

Eastern European and Third World Support Scheme

Subjects: Physiology.

Eligibility: Open to centres of physiological research in countries that currently have serious problems, with clear evidence of or well-documented potential for research excellence, where particular types of support, not currently available from other sources, can be identified which will make a real difference to the work of physiologists, particularly those in the early stages of their careers.

Purpose: To provide support for centres of scientific excellence in Eastern European and Third World countries, where the high quality of research in physiology is in danger of being eroded by severe financial problems or is threatened by severe lack of resources.

No. of awards offered: Three or four awards in the first instance.

Frequency: Every two months.

Value: £5,000-£10,000 per annum.

Length of Study: One year; renewable for two subsequent years, subject to annual review.

Applications Procedure: Applications must be made by sponsors who are resident in the British Isles and will normally be Members of the Physiological Society. Applicants will be required to present costed proposals, giving details of support secured from other sources, of the nature of the difficulties experienced, of the nature of the support required and of the proposed financial mechanism for administration of the grant by the beneficiary, and stating the benefit that the beneficiaries will derive from such support. Beneficiaries will be expected to have regular contact with their sponsor and with the Society during the period of the grant, and proposals for how these contacts would be maintained should be made in the application. Members of the Society wishing to recommend centres for support are encouraged to discuss the matter with the Foreign Secretary. Application forms are available on request.

Closing Date: End January, end March, end May, end July, end September, end November.

Eastern European and Third World Visitor Fund

Subjects: Physiology.

Eligibility: Open to persons engaged in physiological research in Eastern European and Third World countries who cannot obtain funds from other sources to enable them to visit laboratories in the British Isles.

Purpose: To provide support for Eastern European and Third World physiologists to visit institutions in the British Isles for short periods with a view to establishing research contacts that might lead in due course to more substantial joint grants. The overall object of the Fund is to benefit physiological work in the Eastern European and Third World countries.

Frequency: Every two months.

Value: Awards are intended to cover the cost of travel to the British Isles at Apex rates and living expenses (but not laboratory expenses) for a period of up to two months, and will not normally exceed £1,500. Awards will be payable to the host or host department.

Length of Study: For up to two months.

Country of Study: British Isles.

Applications Procedure: Applications should be submitted on the nominee's behalf by persons engaged in physiological research in a university department of physiology or a cognate science in the British Isles who will normally be Members of the Physiological Society and who seek opportunities for collaborative research with the beneficiaries and will act as hosts in providing laboratory facilities. Beneficiaries will not normally be eligible for more than one award from this Fund, but may be encouraged to seek subsequent funding under the Eastern European and Third World Support Scheme. Applicants will be required to present a costed proposal including air fares at Apex rate or less and a specified sum per week for living expenses. Applicants will also be required to state the benefit that the beneficiary will derive from the visit, including a succinct summary of the scientific work proposed and a description of how it is likely to lead to more substantial research collaboration. They will be asked for a report one year after the conclusion of the visit, including details of publications, of subsequent grants awarded from other sources and of other advances accruing from the visit. Application forms are available on request.

Closing Date: End January, end March, end May, end July, end September, end November.

Physiological Society Affiliate Travel Grant Scheme

Eligibility: Open to Affiliates of the Society resident in the British Isles. Former Affiliates will continue to be eligible for one year after being elected members of the Society. The meeting attended must be of clear relevance and grants will be made only to those actively participating in the scientific meeting. The applicant must be the first or presenting author of the abstract.

Purpose: To provide travel grants for Affiliates to attend scientific meetings.

Type: Travel Grant.

Frequency: Annual.

Value: The maximum award allowable is £600.

Applications Procedure: Applications must be made via the administration office and be accompanied by copies of the abstract to be submitted for the meeting.

Closing Date: Applications will be considered in competition at two-monthly intervals.

Physiological Society Bursaries

Subjects: MSc courses in physiology (including human and applied physiology, neurophysiology, etc.); or, for graduates in physiology, courses relevant to the development of their careers in physiological sciences.

Eligibility: Open to science graduates of institutions in the UK or the Republic of Ireland, especially those wishing to enter physiology as a new discipline, who are accepted for entry into courses leading to the award of the degree of MSc.

Level of Study: Postgraduate.

Type: Bursary.

No. of awards offered: Approximately 5 bursaries each year.

Frequency: Twice yearly.

Value: Up to £2,000 'seed funding'.

Applications Procedure: Application form must be completed.

Closing Date: May 31st, November 30th.

Physiological Society New Lectures Support Scheme

Eligibility: The fund is available to academic staff on their first appointment to an established university lectureship. The fund is intended to support research in physiology; applicants must be members of the Physiological Society. Applications must be made within 12 months of taking up an appointment.

Level of Study: Postgraduate.

Purpose: To assist young Physiologists in developing independent research programmes and establishing themselves as independent researchers.

Type: Grant.

Frequency: Twice yearly.

Value: Applicants may request up to £5,000 to be used for consumables, equipment, or in exceptional cases, technical help.

Applications Procedure: Applicants will be required to provide a full account of the background and plan of the proposed work (up to two sides of A4), together with a costing and justification of the support requested. Applications must be supported by a CV, and a copy of the advertisement of the post filled by the applicant, plus a letter from the head of the department providing confirmation of the appointment.

Postgraduate Support Fund

Subjects: Physiology.

Eligibility: Open to graduates in physiology, or a cognate science, engaged in research in the UK in a department of physiology or cognate science, when their supervisor is a Member of the Physiological Society. Applicants will need to demonstrate the progress of their research programme by submitting copies of abstracts that have been presented at Meetings of the Physiological Society and any other published material. Applicants will normally be registered for a PhD, although MPhil and MSc students may apply.

Level of Study: Postgraduate, Doctorate.

Purpose: To provide support for postgraduates in exceptional circumstances such as periods of ill-health, absence of essential facilities, disruption of supervision, etc., to assist in the completion of their research projects and to bridge the period between graduation and the availability of full-time posts for especially gifted students. The funds cannot be used to initiate a programme of research nor for a purpose normally supported by the Dale or Rushton Fund.

Type: Support fund.

Frequency: Annual.

Value: The maximum award allowable will be £1,000 and not more than one award will be permitted to an individual. (Since the funds available are small, it is proposed that, in the first instance, only a single award will be made to any one institution in any one calendar year.).

Applications Procedure: Applications must be supported by confidential letters of support from the supervisor and head of department. A simple application form will be completed with a standard curriculum vitae and sections requesting information on the purpose for which the support is requested, background to the project and accomplishments to date will be identified.

Closing Date: Normally July 31st.

PIRA INTERNATIONAL

Pira International, Randalls Road, Leatherhead, Surrey, KT22 7RU,
England
Tel: 01372 802000
Fax: 01372 802244
Email: Futures@Pira.co.uk
www: www.pira.co.uk/
Contact: Dr Averil Horton

Postgraduate Scholarship of the Education Charity of the Stationers' & Newspaper Makers' Company

Subjects: The subject must be relevant to the UK printing, publishing, packaging and paper and board manufacturing industries. The nature of the research idea and its inventive or innovative character are the critical factors on which awards will be made; research must be of a business nature.

Eligibility: Applicants must be under 25 years of age with an upper second or better from a recognized higher educational institute. English language required.

Level of Study: Postgraduate.

Purpose: To encourage the entry of well-qualified postgraduate staff into the printing, paper and board and packaging industries.

Type: Scholarship.

No. of awards offered: Several.

Frequency: Annual.

Value: Fees will be reimbursed and the student will become an employee of Pira (on an industrial salary) for the duration of the award.

Country of Study: UK.

Applications Procedure: Please apply directly to Pira International.

Closing Date: July 31st.

PITT RIVERS MUSEUM

Pitt Rivers Museum, University of Oxford, South Parks Road, Oxford,
OX1 3PP, England
Tel: 01865 270927
Fax: 01865 270943
Email: skye.jones@prm.ox.ac.uk
Contact: Dr Schuyler Jones, Director

James A Swan Fund

Subjects: Anthropology, archaeology, hunter-gatherer studies.

Eligibility: There are no set rules. Most of the successful applicants are graduates but all applications are considered. Two or three academic references are required.

Level of Study: Unrestricted.

Purpose: To provide support for research sponsored by the Pitt Rivers Museum on the archaeological, historical, physical and cultural nature of the Bushmen, Pygmies and other 'small peoples' of Africa (primarily field-work).

Type: Research Grant.

No. of awards offered: Varies.

Frequency: Varies.

Value: Varies, but usually in the £500-£2,000 range.

Length of Study: Varies.

Country of Study: Unrestricted.

Applications Procedure: There are no application forms. Applicants should write, stating their qualifications and giving a clear indication of the kind of research they propose to undertake, together with a budget of anticipated expenses.

Additional Information: The terms under which the fund operates restricts grants to those carrying out field research on pygmies, 'bushmen' & other 'small peoples' of Africa, i.e. hunter-gatherers.

PITTSBURGH NEW MUSIC ENSEMBLE

Pittsburgh New Music Ensemble, School of Music, Duquesne
University, Pittsburgh, PA, 15282, USA
Tel: 412 261 0554
Fax: 412 396 5479
Contact: David Stock, Conductor

Harvey Garl Composition Contest

Eligibility: US citizens only.

Level of Study: Professional Development, Unrestricted.

Purpose: Prize is a commission for The Pittsburgh New Music Ensemble.

Type: Commission.

No. of awards offered: One.

Frequency: Every two years.

Value: US$3,000.

Country of Study: USA.

Applications Procedure: Write for application form.

Closing Date: Next award April 1st 1998.

PLASTIC SURGERY EDUCATIONAL FOUNDATION

Plastic Surgery Educational Foundation, 444 East Algonquin Road,
Arlington Heights, IL, 60005, USA
Tel: 708 228 9900
Fax: 708 228 9131
Contact: Mary-Patricia McKeever

Plastic Surgery Basic Research Grant

Subjects: Clinical research in plastic surgery.

Eligibility: Open to plastic surgeons, and holders of an MD or PhD working in plastic surgery. Residents/Fellows and non-members of ASPRS/PSEF require sponsorship of a Member or Candidate for Membership of ASPRS/PSEF or the American Society for Aesthetic Plastic Surgery.

Level of Study: Postdoctorate, Doctorate.

Purpose: To encourage young investigators to perform clinical research.

Type: Research Grant.

No. of awards offered: Approximately 40.

Frequency: Annual.

Value: Research seed money US$5,000.

Length of Study: One year.

Closing Date: Mid-January.

Plastic Surgery Educational Foundation Essay Scholarship Contest

Subjects: Plastic surgery: junior and senior award categories in the basic science and clinical research areas; one award category to focus on theory, history, ethics, socio-economic issues relating to the art and science of plastic surgery; three prizes in the non-plastic surgeon category.

Eligibility: Open to persons involved in research in the field of plastic surgery.

Type: Prize.

No. of awards offered: Eight.

Frequency: Annual.

Value: US$500 to US$2,000.

Length of Study: One year.

Closing Date: March 1st for manuscript.

Additional Information: Manuscripts should contain the result of original clinical or basic science research in an area of importance to plastic and reconstructive surgery.

Plastic Surgery Research Fellowship Award

Subjects: Plastic surgery.

Eligibility: Open to surgical residents or fellows preparing for a plastic surgery residency, or plastic surgery residents planning to interrupt their training for a research experience, or recent residency graduates wishing to supplement their clinical training with a research experience. Residents/Fellows and non-members of ASPRS/PSEF require sponsorship of a Member or Candidate for Membership of ASPRS/PSEF.

Purpose: To encourage research and academic career development in plastic and reconstructive surgery.

No. of awards offered: Two.

Frequency: Annual.

Value: Each award underwrites the salary of the investigator for a one-year period US$30,000.

Length of Study: One year.

Closing Date: September 19th.

PLAYMARKET

Independent Newspapers Ltd/Playmarket, PO Box 9767, Wellington, New Zealand
Tel: 04 382 8462
Fax: 04 382 8461
Contact: Susan Wilson

The Sunday Star Times/Bruce Mason Playwriting Award

Subjects: Playwriting.

Eligibility: Open to New Zealand playwrights.

Level of Study: Unrestricted.

Purpose: To recognize achievement at the beginning of a career.

Type: Awards.

No. of awards offered: One.

Frequency: Annual.

Value: NZ$5,000.

Length of Study: One year.

Country of Study: New Zealand.

Applications Procedure: Name, address, plus two references. No scripts need to be submitted.

Closing Date: Announced annually.

Additional Information: It is expected that the Award will be used to write or complete a work for the theatre.

POLISH CULTURAL INSTITUTE

Polish Cultural Institute, 34 Portland Place, London, W1N 4HQ, England
Tel: 0171 636 6032/3
Fax: 0171 637 2190
Email: PCI-LOND@pcidir.demon.co.uk
Contact: Information Officer

Polish Cultural Institute Short-Term Bursaries

Subjects: Unrestricted.

Eligibility: Candidates must be British citizens with a university degree or equivalent qualification, who have some postgraduate research or lecturing experience; preference is given to those undertaking doctoral or postdoctoral work. Married candidates must indicate whether they are prepared to go unaccompanied. Candidates wishing to study Polish philology, Slavonic languages and the history and the geography of Poland must be conversant with Polish or the appropriate Slavonic language.

Level of Study: Postgraduate, Professional development.

Purpose: According to the Convention between the Government of the Republic of Poland and the Government of the United Kingdom of Great Britain and Northern Ireland on co-operation in the field of Culture, Education and Science, 1978.

Type: Bursary.

No. of awards offered: 15.

Frequency: Annual.

Value: A monthly allowance, free accommodation in student hostels (or possibly in hotels) or a monthly allowance towards accommodation found privately, free meals in a student canteen or a monthly allowance in lieu, a modest book grant, exemption from tuition fees, and free medical care. The Polish authorities will pay for necessary travel expenses within Poland from one academic centre to another; recipients will be required to pay their own fares to and from Poland.

Length of Study: From three to nine months.

Study Establishment: At universities and other institutions of higher education and research.

Country of Study: Poland.

Applications Procedure: Please submit completed application form, CV, copy of diploma, research proposal, medical statement, and two letters of recommendation.

Closing Date: January 31st.

Additional Information: The scheme is new under agreement between Poland and the UK on exchanges in the fields of science, humanities and arts. The length of the Scholarship is from three to nine months. Bursaries cannot normally be taken up during the university summer.

Postgraduate Scholarships

Subjects: Unrestricted. The following subjects in particular are taught to a high standard in Polish universities: sociology, mathematics, geography and geology, history of Polish architecture, music (performance and composition), the arts and scientific topics.

Eligibility: Candidates must be British citizens with a university degree or equivalent qualification; priority is given to candidates who hold an honours degree and have had some experience of research, laboratory techniques or teaching since graduation. Married candidates must indicate whether they are prepared to go unaccompanied. Candidates wishing to study Polish philology, Slavonic languages and the history and the geography of Poland must be conversant with Polish or the appropriate Slavonic language.

Level of Study: Postgraduate, Professional development.

Purpose: According to the Convention between the Government of the Republic of Poland and the Government of the United Kingdom of Great Britain and Northern Ireland on co-operation in the field of Culture, Education and Science, 1978.

Type: Scholarship.

No. of awards offered: 16.

Frequency: Annual.

Value: A monthly allowance, free accommodation in student hostels or a monthly allowance towards accommodation found privately, free meals in a student canteen or a monthly allowance in lieu, a modest book grant, exemption from tuition fees, and free medical care.

Length of Study: For periods of up to 10 months. Though applications for shorter periods of study may be considered, preference will be given to those wishing to study for periods of more than 6 months.

Study Establishment: Universities and other institutions of higher education and research.

Country of Study: Poland.

Applications Procedure: Completed application form, CV, copy of diploma, research proposal, medical statement, and two letters of recommendation must be submitted. Application forms are obtainable from the Education Officer and should be returned to the Institute by 31 December.

Closing Date: 31 December.

Additional Information: The scheme is run under agreement between Poland and the UK on exchange in the fields of science, humanities and arts. The length of the scholarship is from three to nine months.

PONTIFICAL INSTITUTE OF MEDIEVAL STUDIES

Pontifical Institute of Medieval Studies, 59 Queen's Park Crescent East, Toronto, Ontario, M5S 2C4, Canada
Tel: 416 926 1300
Fax: 416 926 7276
Email: scampbel@epas.utoronto.ca
Contact: Secretary

Council of the Institute Awards

Subjects: Medieval studies.

Eligibility: Open to junior associates engaged in mediaeval studies at the Institute.

Level of Study: Postdoctorate, Undergraduate.

Type: Bursaries and scholarships.

No. of awards offered: Variable.

Frequency: Annual.

Value: Varies, dependent on funds available.

Length of Study: One year.

Study Establishment: The Institute.

Country of Study: Canada.

Closing Date: March 31st.

Additional Information: The Institute also offers a small number of Research Associateships annually to postdoctoral students and senior scholars who wish to use the Institute library for their research. Candidates must apply in person. Applications must be received by January 15th.

THE POPULATION COUNCIL

The Population Council, One Dag Hammarskjold Plaza, New York, NY, 10017, USA
Tel: 212 339 0665/0671
Fax: 212 755 6052
Email: MDONOVAN@POPCOUNCIL.ORG or JLam@POPCOUNCIL.ORG
Telex: 9102900660 POPCO
Contact: Manager of Fellowship Program

Fellowships in the Social Sciences

Subjects: Advanced training in population studies (including demography and biostatistics), or for study plans in population in combination with a social science discipline, such as economics, sociology, anthropology, geography, and public health. Awards will be made only to applicants whose proposals deal with the developing world.

Eligibility: Predoctoral: open to persons who have completed all coursework requirements toward the PhD or an equivalent degree in one of the social sciences. Applications requesting support for either the dissertation fieldwork or the dissertation writing period will be considered. Postdoctoral: open to persons having a PhD or equivalent degree who wish to undertake postdoctoral training and research at an institution other than the one at which they received their PhD degree. Mid-career: open to persons with a minimum of five years of professional experience in the population field. Mid-career Academic Awards are open to scholars with a PhD or equivalent degree wishing to undertake specific study in connection with a research institution. Mid-career Professional Awards are open to population or development professionals with a keen interest in enhancing and strengthening their professional skills by participating in a one-year diploma, certificate, or master's degree program (no MPH candidates will be considered). Awards are open to all qualified persons, but strong preference will be given to applicants from developing countries who have a firm commitment to return home upon completion of their training programs. Applications by women are particularly encouraged.

Level of Study: Doctorate, Postdoctorate, Professional development.

Type: Fellowship.

No. of awards offered: 20-25.

Frequency: Annual.

Value: Predoctoral: US$24,000; postdoctoral: US$32,000; mid-career: varies. A monthly stipend (based on type of Fellowship and place of study), tuition payments and related fees, transportation expenses (for Fellow only), and health insurance. Some research-related costs may also be part of the award. Tuition at the postdoctoral and mid-career academic levels is not included in the award.

Length of Study: Up to one year.

Study Establishment: At a training or research institution with a strong program in population studies, regardless of geographic location. For graduate students, when a strong case can be made for continued support, a single extension, or a nonconsecutive second award, will be considered in competition with first-time applicants.

Country of Study: Any country.

Applications Procedure: Applicants must submit application and supporting documents. Application forms can be obtained from our Fellowship Office.

Closing Date: January 2nd of each year for notification in March.

Additional Information: Selection will be based on the recommendation of the Fellowship Committee, which consists of three distinguished scholars in the field of population. Selection criteria will stress academic excellence and prospective contribution to the population field. Application for independent research funds or for fieldwork not related to a dissertation will not be considered. Requests for application forms should include a brief description of candidates' academic and professional qualifications and a short statement about their research or study plans for the proposed Fellowship period.

POTATO MARKETING BOARD

Potato Marketing Board, Broad Field House, 4 Between Towns Road, Cowley, Oxford, OX4 3NA, England
Tel: 01865 714455
Fax: 01865 716418
Contact: Research & Development Department

Research Grants

Subjects: Preference is given to research into ways of increasing the efficiency of economic production and utilization of the crop, particularly the reduction of mechanical damage and bruising, seed health and the efficient use of nitrogen and water resources.

Eligibility: Grants will normally be made to the investigator's university or institution, and will require the institution to accept all the normal duties and responsibilities of employer, including those relating to national insurance and income tax, in relation to any person whose services are provided by means of a Grant.

Level of Study: Postgraduate, Doctorate, Unrestricted, Postdoctorate.

Purpose: To aid special projects or new developments considered likely to be of direct practical value to the potato industry in Great Britain.

Type: Research Grant.

No. of awards offered: Approximately 10.

Frequency: Submissions considered throughout the year.

Value: Covers employment of assistants specially needed for the purposes of the research; their travel expenses; apparatus not normally provided in a well-equipped laboratory; materials and services needed for the research on a scale which the institution is unable to supply; and other research and development purposes if the Board so decides.

Length of Study: Normally for a maximum period of 3 years; subject to annual review.

Study Establishment: Suitable universities and research institutions.

Country of Study: UK.

Applications Procedure: Concept note on research to be submitted, followed by full project proposal.

Closing Date: Announced annually.

Additional Information: R & B priorities document published by the Potato Marketing Board provides information on research topics and procedures for assessment of research proposals.

PRAGUE SPRING INTERNATIONAL MUSIC COMPETITION

Prague Spring International Music Competition, Hellichova 18, Prague 1, 11800, Czech Republic
Tel: 2 53 34 74
Fax: 2 53 60 40
Contact: J Nedvedova, Z Korbelova

Prague Spring International Music Competition

Subjects: Music: competitions categories are changing in five year cycles : 1996 flute, oboe, clarinet, bassoon; 1997 violin, french horn, trumpet, trombone; 1998 piano, string quartet, singing; 1999 violoncello, organ, harpsichord; 2000 conducting.

Eligibility: Open to musicians of any nationality who do not exceed the age limit (30 years, harpsichord 35 years, string quartet together 140 years, conducting 32).

Purpose: To encourage and assist outstanding young musicians.

Type: Financial and engagements.

No. of awards offered: Three main prizes.

Frequency: Annually (early May).

Value: Prizes range from 10,000-100,000 Czechoslovak crowns. Accommodation is paid for those who qualify for the second round and final.

Country of Study: Czech Republic.

Applications Procedure: The applicants should enclose an audio tape with recording of the setting compositions.

Closing Date: Varies from year to year.

Additional Information: There is an application fee of US$100.

PREHISTORIC SOCIETY

Prehistoric Society, University College London, Institute of Archaeology, 31-34 Gordon Square, London, WC1H 0PY, England
Fax: 0171 383 2572
Contact: Administrative Assistant

Conference Fund

Subjects: Archaeology, especially prehistory.

Eligibility: Preference is given first to scholars from developing countries, whether they are members of the Society or not, then to Members of the Society not qualified to apply for conference funds available to University staff etc. Other members of the Society are also eligible.

Purpose: To finance attendance at international conferences.

Type: Travel Grant.

No. of awards offered: Two.

Frequency: Annual.

Value: Up to £250.

Length of Study: One year only; renewals are considered.

Closing Date: December 31st.

Additional Information: Recipients are required to submit a short report on the conference to PAST, the society's newsletter, and their papers for the society's proceedingsif these are not to be included in a conference voulme. Forms are available from the Honarary Secretary.

Research Fund Grant

Subjects: Prehistoric archaeology.

Eligibility: Open to all members of the Society. The Society may make specific conditions relating to individual applications.

Purpose: To further research in prehistory by excavation or other means.

Type: Grant.

No. of awards offered: Varies.

Frequency: Annual.

Value: At the discretion of the Society.

Length of Study: One year only, but reapplications are considered.

Applications Procedure: Applications should include the names of two referees.

Closing Date: December 31st.

Additional Information: Awards are made on the understanding that a detailed report will be made to the Society as to how the grant was spent.

PREMIO MUSICALE 'CITTÀ DI TRIESTE'

Premio Musicale 'Città di Trieste', Palazzo Municipale, Piazza dell'Unità, D'Italia, 4, Trieste, 1-34121, Italy
Tel: 0039 40 366030
Fax: 0039 40 636969

International Competition for Musical Composition

Subjects: Orchestral or chamber music composition.

Eligibility: Open to composers of any age and from any country.

Type: Prize.

No. of awards offered: One.

Frequency: Biennially (1997, 1999).

Value: 1st prize and a public performance.

Country of Study: Italy.

Closing Date: April 30th.

For further information contact:
c/o Civico Museo Teatrale 'C Schmidl', via Imbriani 5, Trieste, 1-34122, Italy
Tel: 0039 40 366030
Fax: 0039 40 636 969
Contact: Dr Adriano Dugulin, General Secretary

PRINCETON UNIVERSITY

Procter Visiting Fellowships, University Registry, The Old Schools, Cambridge, CB2 1TN, England
Contact: The Secretary

Shelby Cullom Davies Center for Historical Studies Research Fellowships

Subjects: Animals and human society. From 1996-1998.
Eligibility: Open to highly recommended younger scholars and to senior scholars with established reputations.
Type: Fellowship.
No. of awards offered: Limited.
Frequency: Annual.
Value: Up to US$56,000.
Length of Study: One or two semesters.
Study Establishment: Princeton University.
Country of Study: USA.
Closing Date: December 1st.
Additional Information: Fellows are expected to live in Princeton and to take an active part in the intellectual interchange with other seminar members.

Procter Visiting Fellowships

Subjects: Liberal arts and sciences, excluding professional, technical or commercial subjects: advanced study and investigation.
Eligibility: Open to Commonwealth citizens who hold a first class honours BA or equivalent from a UK university and are able to prove 'exceptional scholarly power'. Preference is normally given to candidates who would be in their second or third year of postgraduate research when, if elected, they take up tenure of the award.
Type: Fellowship.
No. of awards offered: Two.
Frequency: Annual.
Value: US$10,450 plus tuition fees and health insurance.
Length of Study: One year.
Study Establishment: Princeton University, New Jersey.
Country of Study: USA.
Closing Date: Early December.

PURINA MILLS, INC

Purina Research Awards Committee, Purina Mills, Inc, PO Box 66812, St Louis, MO, 63166-6812, USA
Tel: 314 768 4614
Fax: 314 768 4433
Contact: Joan M Roslauski, 2E

Research Fellowships

Subjects: Dairy, poultry and animal science.
Eligibility: Open to persons qualified for graduate study in any US agricultural college.

Purpose: To assist in the training of exceptional personnel for leadership.
Type: Fellowship.
No. of awards offered: Four.
Frequency: Annual.
Value: US$12,500.
Length of Study: One year.
Study Establishment: Any agricultural college.
Country of Study: USA.
Closing Date: First Monday in February.

PYMATUNING LABORATORY OF ECOLOGY

Pymatuning Laboratory of Ecology, The University of Pittsburgh, Route 1 Box 7, Linesville, PA, 16424, USA
Tel: 814 683 5813
Fax: 814 683 2302
Email: pymatuning@gremlan.org
www: www.pitt.bio.edu
Contact: Brigitte Vandeneeden, Resident Manager

Darbaker Botany Prize

Subjects: Botany.
Eligibility: Applicants must conduct research and reside at Pymatuning Laboratory.
Level of Study: Doctorate, Postdoctorate.
Purpose: To award funds for the pursuit of excellent graduate and recent postdoctoral research in botany at Pymatuning Laboratory of Ecology.
Type: Research Grant.
No. of awards offered: 1-3.
Frequency: Annual.
Value: US$500-US$4,000.
Length of Study: One year.
Study Establishment: Pymatuning Laboratory of Ecology.
Country of Study: USA.
Applications Procedure: Please request guidelines from Pymatuning Laboratory of Ecology.
Closing Date: February 13th each year.

G M McKinley Research Fund

Subjects: Ecology.
Eligibility: Applicants must conduct research and reside at the Pymatuning Laboratory of Ecology.
Level of Study: Doctorate, Postdoctorate.
Purpose: To fund research at the graduate and recent postdoctoral level in ecological science at the Pymatuning Laboratory of Ecology.
Type: Research Grant.
No. of awards offered: 1-5.
Frequency: Annual.
Value: US$500-US$4,000.
Length of Study: One year.
Country of Study: USA.
Applications Procedure: Please request guidelines from Pymatuning Laboratory of Ecology.
Closing Date: February 13th each year.

THE QUEBEC DIABETICS ASSOCIATION

The Quebec Diabetics Association, 5635 Sherbrooke Street East, Montreal PQ, Quebec, H1N 1A3, Canada
Tel: 514 259 3422
Fax: 514 259 9286
Contact: Serge Langlois, President and Executive Director

Diabetaid for Diabetics/Health Professionals/Pharmacists and Doctors

Subjects: Social/preventative medicine, diatetics, ophthalmology, cardiology, endocrinology, gynaecology and obstetrics.

Eligibility: Open to anyone willing to work toward the organization's objectives in education and medical research. Must be nonprofit.

Level of Study: Postgraduate, Postdoctorate, Professional development.

Purpose: To provide educational and other services for diabetics and their families.

Type: Grant and fellowship.

No. of awards offered: Ten.

Frequency: Annual.

Value: Amount of support per award: C$2,400 and C$3,600 for university students grants. Up to C$27,500 for fellowships, depending on postgraduate experience.

Length of Study: One year renewable.

Country of Study: Canada.

Applications Procedure: Write for application information, released in November of each year.

Closing Date: March 1st for summer grant.

QUEEN ELISABETH INTERNATIONAL MUSIC COMPETITION OF BELGIUM

Concours musical international Reine Elisabeth de Belgique, 20 rue aux Laines, Brussels, B-1000, Belgium
Tel: 32 2 513 0099
Fax: 32 2 514 3297
Contact: Secrétariat

Queen Elisabeth International Music Competition of Belgium

Subjects: Piano and composition; 1996: singing, 1997: piano, violin, singing and composition; 1999.

Eligibility: Open to musicians of any nationality who are at least 17 years of age and not older than 30 (violin and piano) or 30 (singing).

Type: Prizes.

No. of awards offered: Twelve.

Frequency: A competition for each category is held at four-yearly intervals.

Value: From a total amounting to more than BF3,200,000.

Closing Date: January 15th.

Additional Information: Also master classes with jury members.

QUEEN MARIE JOSÉ PRIZE FOR MUSICAL COMPOSITION

Prix de Composition Musicale Prize Marie-José, Case Postale 19, CH 1252 Meinier, Geneva, Switzerland
Contact: Secretary

Queen Marie José Prize for Musical Composition

Subjects: Musical composition.

Eligibility: Open to composers of all nationalities and of any age.

Level of Study: Unrestricted.

Type: Prize.

No. of awards offered: One.

Frequency: Biennially (even-numbered years).

Value: SwFr10,000.

Applications Procedure: Subject and form are prescribed in advance by the Committee. All works submitted must be accompanied by a tape recording. The award-winning work remains its author's exclusive property, but, if possible, is performed as part of the Merlinge concerts.

Closing Date: May 31st.

QUEENSLAND UNIVERSITY OF TECHNOLOGY

Office of Research, Queensland University of Technology, GPO Box 2434, Brisbane, Queensland, 4001, Australia
Tel: 61 7 864 5053
Fax: 61 7 864 5165
www: http://www.qut.edu.au

Postdoctoral Research Fellowship

Subjects: All disciplines supported by research centres at QUT.

Eligibility: Open to holders of the PhD who have less than five years' full-time professional experience and have submitted their thesis for examination prior to closing date.

Level of Study: Postdoctorate.

Purpose: The fellowships serve both as a mechanism for fostering effective and productive interdisciplinary group research and for encouraging excellence in individual research.

Type: Fellowship.

No. of awards offered: Four.

Frequency: Twice yearly.

Value: A$36,000-A$39,000 (in 1995).

Length of Study: Up to two years.

Study Establishment: Queensland University of Technology in a specified centre or area of research concentration.

Country of Study: Australia.

Applications Procedure: The candidates must contact the centre prior to application; must contact office for research for application guidelines and list of research centres; must discuss research program with relevant acdemic area at QUT.

Closing Date: March 31st, September 30th.

Additional Information: Referee reports will be called only for applicants supported by QUT research centres.

THE QUEEN'S UNIVERSITY OF BELFAST

The Queen's University of Belfast, Belfast, BT7 1NN, Northern Ireland

Tel: 01232 245133
Fax: 01232 313537
Email: academic.council@qub.ac.uk
www: http://www.qub.ac.uk
Contact: Secretary to Academic Council

Musgrave Research Studentships

Subjects: Biology, chemistry, pathology, physics, physiology.

Eligibility: Open only to British subjects who are graduates, with preference being given to graduates of universities in the UK, a UK colony, protectorate, trust or mandated territory or any territory within or associated with the Commonwealth or Republic of Ireland. Candidates must be engaged in or show marked capacity for research in one of the subjects indicated above.

Level of Study: Postgraduate, Doctorate.

Purpose: For personal research.

Type: Studentship.

No. of awards offered: 2-3.

Frequency: Annual.

Value: Dependent upon trust income.

Length of Study: One year; may be renewed for 1 or 2 further years.

Study Establishment: Queen's University of Belfast.

Country of Study: UK.

Applications Procedure: Application form must be completed.

Closing Date: June 1st.

Additional Information: The selection panel will take into account other sources of funding for the research.

Research and Senior Visiting Research Fellowships

Subjects: Irish studies.

Eligibility: Open to all.

Level of Study: Postdoctorate.

Purpose: For personal research at the Institute of Irish Studies.

No. of awards offered: Three research fellowships and 1 or 2 senior visiting research fellowships.

Frequency: Annual.

Value: £12,500 (research); £16,500 (senior visiting research).

Length of Study: One year.

Study Establishment: Queen's University of Belfast.

Country of Study: UK.

Applications Procedure: Completion of application form required.

Closing Date: January 14th.

Visiting Fellowships

Subjects: Unrestricted.

Eligibility: Candidates should be of doctoral degree standing or have undertaken research to an equivalent standard.

Level of Study: Postdoctorate, Professional development.

Purpose: Awarded for personal research.

Type: Fellowship.

No. of awards offered: Two.

Frequency: Annual.

Value: Salary within the first 5 points on the Lecturer's scale.

Length of Study: One year.

Study Establishment: Queen's University of Belfast.

Country of Study: UK.

Applications Procedure: Application form must be completed.

Closing Date: January 10th each year.

Additional Information: Two references are also required at a later stage in the application.

Visiting Studentships

Subjects: Unrestricted.

Eligibility: Open only to persons holding a good honours degree from another university. Candidates must show aptitude for research or other original work.

Level of Study: Doctorate.

Purpose: For original research.

Type: Studentship.

No. of awards offered: Three.

Frequency: Annual.

Value: £6,060 plus fees.

Length of Study: Two years; renewable for one further year.

Study Establishment: Queen's University of Belfast.

Country of Study: UK.

Applications Procedure: Application form must be completed and two references submitted.

Closing Date: January 10th.

RAGDALE FOUNDATION

Ragdale Foundation, 1260 North Green Bay Road, Lake Forest, IL, 60045, USA
Tel: 847 234 1063
Fax: 847 234 1075
Contact: Sonja Carlborg, Executive Director

Residencies

Subjects: Creative writing, musical composition, film-making, visual artists.

Eligibility: Open to all creative writers, scholars, composers, film-makers, and visual artists. Professional recognition is helpful for admission, but it is not essential. Selections are based on the peer panel's rankings of work samples.

Purpose: To provide a peaceful place and uninterrupted time for writers, scholars and artists to do their work.

Type: Residency.

No. of awards offered: Up to 12 places.

Frequency: Throughout the year, except May and 15 December to 1 January.

Value: A charge of US$105 per week is made, although information regarding financial assistance is available on request. The charge covers the cost of all meals, use of linen and laundry facilities, a convenient, private work space and sleeping accommodation.

Length of Study: Periods of two weeks to two months.

Study Establishment: Ragdale House and Barnhouse.

Country of Study: USA.

Applications Procedure: Applicants are required to submit slides, tapes or samples of writing and three references.

Closing Date: January 15th for June to December; June 1st for January to May.

Additional Information: Couples are not accepted unless each qualifies independently. Ragdale is in Lake Forest, 30 miles north of Chicago on Lake Michigan. The Ragdale House and Barnhouse were designed by Howard Van Doren Shaw. Much of his landscaping also remains intact: a garden, lanes through meadow and prairie, a wide lawn and large trees. Ragdale is on the National Register of Historic Places and the property overlooks a large nature preserve. A new studio building was constructed in 1991.

CLIVE AND VERA RAMACIOTTI FOUNDATIONS

Clive and Vera Ramaciotti Foundations, c/o Perpetual Trustee Company Limited, 39 Hunter Street, Sydney, NSW, 2000, Australia
Tel: 229 9866
Fax: 221 4885
Contact: The Administrator

Wellcome-Ramaciotti Research Travel Grants

Subjects: Medical research or such related fields of experimental science as are approved by the Wellcome and Ramaciotti Boards of Trustees.

Eligibility: Open only to workers engaged in research. Travel undertaken solely to attend meetings or congresses or purely for educational or vocational purposes does not come within the scope of this scheme. The awards are not available for predoctoral workers or medical students during their elective period. Postdoctoral candidates must be able to demonstrate independent research experience.

Purpose: To enable medical researchers from the UK and the Republic of Ireland to travel to Australia (and possibly on to New Zealand) and for Australian researchers to visit the UK and the Republic of Ireland to undertake short-term collaborative research or to learn a new technique.

Type: Travel Grants.

Value: Decided by the relevant Board of Trustees in the light of the candidate's experience and current practice.

Length of Study: Up to 3 months.

Study Establishment: Candidates from the UK or Republic of Ireland who also wish to travel to New Zealand may apply to extend the duration of their visit by up to a maximum of one month.

Country of Study: UK and Republic of Ireland (Australia candidates) or Australia and New Zealand (UK and Republic of Ireland candidates).

Closing Date: At least two months prior to departure date.

Additional Information: Candidate wishing to consult with colleagues, or to work at a research centre overseas, should find out in advance that their visits will be welcomed by the colleagues in question, and that appropriate facilities can be made available, and should state this in their application. A letter from the institution to be visited, supporting the proposal, must be submitted with the application. If the host institution requires the research expenses to be covered, a note outlining these should be included in this letter. It is expected that recipients of a Grant will return to their country of origin on completion of the period of the Grant, and should submit a brief report of their visit. Applications must be supported by the Head or a Senior Member of the applicant's Department who should be requested by the applicant to assess the value of the visit, to certify that the applicant is engaged in bona fide research and that local resources are insufficient. Applications submitted without such support will not be considered.

RAMSAY MEMORIAL FELLOWSHIPS TRUST

Ramsay Memorial Fellowships Trust, University College London, Gower Street, London, WC1E 6BT, England
Tel: 0171 380 7815
Fax: 0171 380 7327
Contact: Executive Secretary

British (General) Fellowship

Subjects: Chemistry.

Eligibility: Usually open to British or Commonwealth citizens who have had training in research methods as evidenced by the possession of a PhD or its equivalent, preferably from a university within the Commonwealth, and who can demonstrate their capacity for original research in chemical science. Upper age limit of 35 years.

Level of Study: Postdoctorate.

Purpose: To assist postdoctoral research.

Type: Fellowship.

No. of awards offered: Normally one or two.

Frequency: Annual.

Value: Normally equivalent to the lower part of the Lecturer scale for UK universities, plus superannuation benefits and a maximum of £100 for research expenses.

Length of Study: Two years.

Study Establishment: A university, university college or other place of higher education.

Country of Study: UK or, exceptionally, elsewhere.

Applications Procedure: Application forms are available from August.

Closing Date: November 15th.

Additional Information: Recipients are encouraged to undertake a small amount of teaching work, not exceeding three hours per week.

REGIONAL ARTS BOARDS

Awards and Schemes for Artists

Subjects: The arts.

Eligibility: Open to individual writers, artists, composers, photographers, etc.

Level of Study: Professional development.

Purpose: To help artists to reach a new and wider audience.

Type: A variety of commissions, bursaries, fellowships and residencies.

No. of awards offered: Varies.

Value: Varies.

Country of Study: UK.

Applications Procedure: Contact relevant regional arts board for application form.

For further information contact:
Eastern Arts, Cherry Hinton Hall, Cherry Hinton Road, Cambridge, CB1 4DW, England
Tel: 01223 215355
Fax: 01223 248075
Email: info@eastern-arts.co.uk
www: http://www.metro-net.co.uk

or

East Midlands Arts, Mountfields House, Forest Road, Loughborough, LE11 3HU, England
Tel: 01509 218292
Fax: 01509 262214

or

London Arts Board, Elme House, 13 Long Acre, London, WC2E 9AF, England
Tel: 0171 240 1313
Fax: 0171 240 4580

or

Northern Arts, (Arts North Limited), 10 Osborne Terrace, Newcastle upon Tyne, NE2 1NZ, England
Tel: 0191 281 6334
Fax: 0191 281 3276

or

Arts Board: North West, 12 Harter Street, Manchester, M1 6HY, England

Tel: 0161 228 3062
Fax: 0161 236 1257

or

Southern Arts, 13 St Clement Street, Winchester, SO23 9DQ, England
Tel: 01962 855099
Fax: 01962 861186

or

South East Arts, 10 Mount Ephraim, Tunbridge Wells, TN4 8AS, England
Tel: 01892 515210
Fax: 01892 549383

or

South West Arts, Bradninch Place, Gandy Street, Exeter, EX4 3LS, England
Tel: 01392 218188
Fax: 01392 413554

or

West Midlands Arts, 82 Granville Street, Birmingham, B1 2LH, England
Tel: 0121 631 3121
Fax: 0121 643 7239

or

Yorkshire Arts, 21 Bond Street, Dewsbury, West Yorkshire, WF13 1AX, England
Tel: 01924 455555
Fax: 01924 466522

REGIONAL INSTITUTE FOR POPULATION STUDIES

Regional Institute for Population Studies, University of Ghana, PO Box 96, Legon, Accra, Ghana
Tel: 233 21 501070
Fax: 233 21 773899
Contact: Director

United Nations Fellowships

Subjects: Population studies.

Eligibility: Open to English-speaking Africans, nominated by their governments, who are capable of pursuing a course of study or research using English as a medium of expression. Candidates should have a good first degree in population studies for the master of arts degree course or the master of population studies degree; a master of arts in population studies or its equivalent for the course for the master of philosophy degree; a master of philosophy in population studies degree or its equivalent for the course for the PhD degree.

Level of Study: Postgraduate, Doctorate.

Purpose: To enable fellows to obtain advanced training through study or research leading to a master of arts, master of philosophy or PhD degree.

Type: Fellowship.

No. of awards offered: Twenty.

Frequency: Annual.

Value: Approximately US$12,250 per annum including stipend, fees, costs for books, minor equipment and production of dissertations and theses.

Length of Study: One year, renewable.

Study Establishment: Regional Institute for Population Studies at the University of Ghana.

Country of Study: Ghana.

500

Applications Procedure: Application forms are available at any United Nations Development Programme Office in the capital city of each English-speaking African country, through which all applications should be routed.

Closing Date: June 30th.

For further information contact:
PO Box 1423, Accra, Ghana
Tel: 233 21 772 829
Fax: 233 21 772 899
Contact: UNFPA

THE REID TRUST FOR THE HIGHER EDUCATION OF WOMEN

The Reid Trust for the Higher Education of Women, 53 Thornton Hill, Exeter, Devon, EX4 4NR, England
Contact: Mrs H M Harvey, MA

Awards

Subjects: Any subject.

Eligibility: Open to women educated in Britain who have appropriate academic qualifications and who wish to undertake further training or research.

Level of Study: Unrestricted.

Purpose: To assist in the higher education of women.

No. of awards offered: Usually 6-10.

Frequency: Annual.

Value: £50-£750.

Country of Study: UK.

Applications Procedure: Requests for application forms must be accompanied by an SAE.

Closing Date: May 31st.

Additional Information: This award is for women only.

For further information contact:
The Reid Trust for the Higher Education of Women, 24 Collins Road, Exeter, Devon, EX4 5DV, England
Contact: Mrs J Mimmack

REMEDI (REHABILITATION AND MEDICAL RESEARCH TRUST)

REMEDI (Rehabilitation and Medical Research Trust), The Old Rectory, Stanton Prior, Bath, BA2 9HT, England
Tel: 01761 472 662
Contact: Director

Research Grants

Subjects: Stroke, speech therapy, cerebral palsy, arthritis, meningitis, muscular dystrophy, Parkinson's disease, osteoporosis, and rehabilitation of the elderly.

Eligibility: Open to applicants living and working in the UK but does not cover students, their fees or travel.

Level of Study: Postgraduate.

Purpose: To support pioneering research into all aspects of disability, in the widest sense of the word, with special emphasis on handicap and the way in which it limits the activities and lifestyle of people of all ages.

Type: Research Grant.

No. of awards offered: Dependent on funding available.

Frequency: Throughout the year if funds are available.

Value: Grants normally do not exceed £10,000 and are often substantially less. They are awarded for a project. Administration costs and university overheads are not entertained.

Study Establishment: At a hospital or university.

Country of Study: UK.

Applications Procedure: Please submit two copies of the protocol, start date, name of supervisor/head of department, and a full breakdown of costs.

Closing Date: Applications are received throughout the year.

RESEARCH CORPORATION (USA)

Science Advancement Program, Research Corporation, 101 North Wilmot Road , Suite 250, Tucson, AZ, 85711-3332, USA
Tel: 602 571 1111
Fax: 602 571 1119
Email: AWARDS@RESCORP.ORG

Cottrell College Science Awards

Subjects: Astronomy, chemistry and physics.

Eligibility: Open to faculty members at public and private institutions of higher education in the USA; the principal investigator must have an appointment in a department of astronomy, chemistry or physics, and the department must offer at least baccalaureate, but not doctoral, degrees. The institution must show its commitment by providing facilities and opportunities for faculty and student research.

Level of Study: Professional development.

Purpose: To develop faculty research that includes undergraduates in meaningful roles, and research-oriented teaching that assists able students to pursue careers in science.

No. of awards offered: Varies.

Frequency: Twice yearly.

Value: Equipment and supplies, student summer stipends of up to US$3,000, and a faculty summer stipend of up to US$6,000.

Length of Study: 1-2 years; possibly renewable for a further 1-2 years.

Study Establishment: Public and private, predominantly undergraduate colleges.

Country of Study: USA.

Applications Procedure: Application form must be completed.

Closing Date: November 15th; May 15th.

Cottrell Scholars Awards

Subjects: Chemistry, physics and astronomy in graduate university departments.

Eligibility: Open to faculty in the third year of a first tenure-track position.

Level of Study: Professional development.

Purpose: To encourage excellence in both research and teaching.

No. of awards offered: Varies.

Frequency: Annual.

Value: US$50,000.

Study Establishment: Universities with graduate departments of physics, chemistry and astronomy.

Country of Study: USA.

Applications Procedure: Application form must be completed.

Closing Date: September 1st.

Additional Information: Candidates must provide both a research and teaching plan for peer review.

Research Opportunity Awards

Subjects: Basic research in physics, chemistry and astronomy.

Eligibility: Open to established faculty members in PhD departments in the USA.

Level of Study: Professional development.

Purpose: To assist mid-career faculty scientists in launching new research programs.

No. of awards offered: Varies.

Frequency: Twice yearly.

Value: US$25,000 (average).

Study Establishment: Universities with graduate departments of physics, chemistry and astronomy.

Country of Study: USA.

Applications Procedure: Application form must be completed.

Closing Date: May 1st and October 1st target dates.

Additional Information: The chair of each PhD-granting physics and chemistry department in the USA may make two nominations annually from tenured faculty without major research funding. Applications are invited from a selected group of these nominees.

THE RESEARCH COUNCIL OF NORWAY/THE SECRETARIAT FOR CULTURAL EXCHANGE PROGRAMMES

The Research Council of Norway, POB 2700 St Hanshaugen, Oslo, N-0131, Norway
Tel: 47 22 03 70 00
Fax: 47 22 03 70 01
Contact: Secretariat for Cultural Exchange Programmes

*Norwegian Government Scholarship for Foreign Students

Subjects: Any subject.

Eligibility: Open to advanced students from countries with which Norway has cultural agreements or other reciprocal scholarship agreements (most of the European countries and China, Egypt, India, Israel, Japan, Mexico).

Purpose: To establish contacts between Norwegian and foreign students and universities.

Type: Scholarship.

No. of awards offered: Varies according to each Cultural Agreement.

Frequency: Annual.

Value: NOK5,700 per month plus NOK2,000 to cover initial expenses.

Study Establishment: Norwegian universities, research institutes and other institutions at university level.

Country of Study: Norway.

Applications Procedure: Students must apply through the relevant authorities in their home country.

Closing Date: As published by the relevant authorities in the home country.

RESEARCH INTO AGEING

Research into Ageing, Baird House, 15-17 St Cross Street, London, EC1N 8UN, England
Tel: 0171 404 6878
Fax: 0171 404 6816
Contact: Administrator

Prize Studentships

Subjects: Geriatric medicine, gerontology and related disciplines.

Eligibility: Open to potential supervisors wishing to enable a postgraduate to obtain a further degree, usually to PhD standard, through work on a topic connected with age related illness or the ageing process. Applicants must be able to speak English and must be employed by a UK institution.

Level of Study: Postgraduate.

Purpose: To improve the health and quality of life of the elderly, through the initiation, funding and support of medical research relevant to the conditions that affect them.

Type: Studentship.

No. of awards offered: Five.

Frequency: Annual.

Value: Varies.

Study Establishment: At suitable UK establishments.

Country of Study: UK.

Applications Procedure: Initially a one page summary of proposed project should be sent in. Application will be sent if appropriate.

Closing Date: Mid September for consideration at November selection meeting. Candidates should apply to Administrator for further details.

Additional Information: Awards should be applied for by supervisors.

Research Fellowship

Subjects: Anaesthesiology; epidemiology; gastroenterology; geriatrics; neurology; ophthalmolgy; psychiatry and mental health; urology; biochemistry; neurosciences; pharmacology; physiology.

Eligibility: Applicants must be able to speak English. Award is only tenable at UK institutions.

Level of Study: Postdoctorate.

Purpose: To enable outstanding postdoctoral graduates to receive support to develop an independent research career whilst furthering research into the diseases and conditions which most affect the elderly.

Type: Fellowship.

No. of awards offered: One or two per year.

Frequency: Annual.

Value: Up to £140,000.

Length of Study: Three years.

Study Establishment: UK institution.

Country of Study: United Kingdom.

Applications Procedure: Application forms can be requested from Research into Ageing.

Closing Date: Early January.

Additional Information: Applicants should normally have a maximum of ten and a minimum of three years' postdoctoral research experience.

Research into Ageing Research Grants

Subjects: Geriatric medicine, gerontology and related disciplines.

Eligibility: Open to suitably qualified clinical or scientific workers who wish to undertake a project studying any aspect of age-related illness or infirmity, or fundamental research into the ageing process. Applicants must speak English.

Level of Study: Postdoctorate.

Purpose: To improve the health and quality of life of the elderly, through the initiation, funding and support of medical research relevant to the conditions that affect them.

No. of awards offered: Dependent on availability of funds.

Frequency: Twice yearly.

Value: Maximum grant £90,000 over three years except in exceptional circumstances.

Study Establishment: At UK Universities, medical colleges, hospitals and general practices.

Country of Study: UK.

Applications Procedure: Initially a one page summary of proposed project should be submitted. Application form will be sent if appropriate.

Closing Date: Twice yearly to coincide with the charity's council meetings. Candidates should apply to Administrator for further details.

RESOURCES FOR THE FUTURE

Resources for the Future, 1616 P Street, NW, Washington, DC, 20036, USA
Tel: 202 328 5067
Fax: 202 939 3460
Email: MORAN@RFF.ORG
www: INFO@RFF.ORG
Contact: Mary Moran

Joseph L Fisher Dissertation Award

Subjects: Economics, policy sciences, environment, natural resources.

Eligibility: Open to all nationalities. Students must be in the final year of dissertation research or writing.

Level of Study: Doctorate.

Purpose: To support PhD students in their last year of dissertation research in economics or other policy sciences on issues related to the environment, energy, or natural resources.

Type: Dissertation Award.

No. of awards offered: Five.

Frequency: Annual.

Value: US$12,000.

Length of Study: One year.

Applications Procedure: Applicants should submit a letter of application, a resumé, graduate transcripts, a one-page abstract of the dissertation, a technical summary of the dissertation, a letter from the department chair, and two letters of recommendation.

Closing Date: March 1st each year.

Gilbert F White Postdoctoral Fellowship

Subjects: Social and policy sciences, environmental studies, energy and natural resources.

Eligibility: A strong economics background is required; applicants must be of postdoctorate level.

Level of Study: Postdoctorate.

Purpose: To enable postdoctoral researchers to spend a year in residence conducting research in the social or policy sciences in areas related to the environment, energy, or natural resources.

Type: Fellowship.

No. of awards offered: Two each year.

Frequency: Annual.

Value: US$35,000 plus living expenses.

Length of Study: One year.

Country of Study: USA.

Applications Procedure: Application form must be completed and should be submitted with a proposal relating to budget, and three letters of recommendation.

Closing Date: March 1st each year.

REUTER FOUNDATION

Reuter Foundation, 85 Fleet Street, London, EC4P 4AJ, England

Tel: 0171 542 7015
Fax: 0171 542 8599
Email: rtrfoundation@easynet.co.uk

*Fellowships

Subjects: Journalism.

Eligibility: Open to full-time journalists employed by newspapers, news agencies, general circulation magazines, radio or television in the developing world or Eastern Europe. Applicants must have a minimum of five years' full-time experience and are unlikely to be less than 28 or more than 45 years of age. They must be committed to a career in journalism in the country in which they work. If applying for Oxford or Stanford, English must be proficient, or French if applying for Bordeaux.

Frequency: Annual.

Length of Study: From three months to one academic year.

Study Establishment: Oxford, Stanford or Bordeaux.

Applications Procedure: Application forms are available on request.

*Journalism Training for Former Soviet Bloc Countries

Subjects: Journalism; writing international news; writing business news.

Eligibility: Open to full-time journalists from former Soviet Bloc countries of Central and Eastern Europe and Central Asia, between the ages of 23 and 45, with a sound working knowledge of the English language.

Length of Study: Two to four weeks.

Additional Information: The awards are made for visits to media organizations as well as practical work in a classroom situation.

Robert Mauthner Memorial Fellowship

Subjects: Journalism.

Eligibility: Open to nationals of European Union countries.

Type: Fellowship.

No. of awards offered: One.

Frequency: Annual.

Length of Study: One term.

Study Establishment: Oxford University.

Country of Study: UK.

Applications Procedure: Application form must be completed and submitted with work examples and references.

Closing Date: April 30th.

*Television Journalism Programme

Subjects: International television journalism.

Eligibility: Open to television journalists, under the age of 35, from developing countries or the former Soviet Bloc countries of East and Central Europe and Asia. Applicants must be fluent in English and have a minimum of three years' experience.

No. of awards offered: Up to six.

Frequency: Annual.

Length of Study: Eight weeks.

Applications Procedure: Application forms are available on request.

Additional Information: The awards are made for visits to major broadcasters and other organizations concerned with world dialogue and communications, in Europe and North America, visiting cities such as London, New York, Washington and Toronto.

University Fellowship

Subjects: Journalism.

Type: Fellowship.

No. of awards offered: Up to 12.

Frequency: Annual.

Length of Study: One term.

Study Establishment: University.

Country of Study: UK, USA or France.

Applications Procedure: Application form must be completed, in addition to work examples and references.

Closing Date: January 31st.

University Fellowship for US Journalists

Subjects: Journalism.

Eligibility: Open to US journalists.

Type: Fellowship.

No. of awards offered: One.

Frequency: Annual.

Length of Study: One term.

Country of Study: UK.

Applications Procedure: Application form must be submitted with work examples and references.

Closing Date: April 15th.

THE RHODES TRUST

The Rhodes Trust, Rhodes House, Oxford, OX1 3RG, England
Tel: 01865 270902
Fax: 01865 270914
Contact: Sir Anthony Kenny

Rhodes Scholarships

Subjects: Adult education.

Eligibility: Open to citizens from Australia, Bermuda, Commonwealth Caribbean, Canada, Germany, Hong Kong, India, Jamaica, Kenya, Malaysia, New Zealand, Pakistan, Singapore, South Africa, Uganda, USA, Zambia, Zimbabwe. Candidates must be between the ages of 19 and 25 (in Kenya and Southern Africa the upper age limit is 27).

Level of Study: Postgraduate.

Purpose: To enable overseas students from specified countries to study at Oxford University.

Type: Scholarship.

No. of awards offered: 86.

Frequency: Annual.

Value: £6,708 per year, plus college and university fees. Average value per scholar £16,000 per year.

Length of Study: Two or three years.

Study Establishment: Oxford University.

Country of Study: England.

Applications Procedure: Candidates must apply to local secretaries in own countries for individual memorandum of regulations.

Closing Date: Various.

RHODES UNIVERSITY

Rhodes University, PO Box 94, Grahamstown, 6140, South Africa
Tel: 01461 318102
Fax: 01461 25049
Contact: Registrar's Office

Hobart Houghton Research Fellowship

Subjects: Social and behavioural sciences, and economics.

Eligibility: Open to English speakers who must hold at least a masters degree in Economics and exhibit successful research experience.

Level of Study: Doctorate, Postdoctorate.

Purpose: To promote work of scientific value relevant to the economic problems of the Eastern Cape Province, Republic of South Africa, which could contribute to the upliftment of the people of the region.

Type: Fellowship.

No. of awards offered: One.

Frequency: Annual.

Value: R20,000.

Length of Study: One year.

Country of Study: South Africa.

Applications Procedure: Application form must be completed (available from registrars office). Enquiries may also be addressed to either Professor G G Antrobus, or Professor A C M Webb, Department of Economics and Economic History. EMail: ecogga@sable.ru.ac.za or ecoacmw@sable.ru.ac.za.

Closing Date: September 14th.

Hugh Kelly Fellowship

Subjects: Biochemistry and microbiology, botany, chemistry, computer science, statistics, mathematics (pure and applied), microbiology, pharmaceutical sciences, physics and electronics, psychology, zoology and entomology.

Eligibility: Open to suitable postdoctoral scientists. Preference is given to candidates willing to accept appointment for at least six months.

Level of Study: Postdoctorate.

Purpose: To enable senior scientists to devote themselves to advanced (postdoctoral) work.

Type: Fellowship.

No. of awards offered: One.

Frequency: Biennially (odd-numbered years).

Value: R2,200 per month, plus the cost of a return economy class air fare or first class rail fare from the Fellow's place of residence. If the Fellow accepts appointment for at least six months and is accompanied by a spouse, the spouse's air or rail fares will also be paid. University accommodation will be provided free of charge, but the provision of a telephone (if available) at the place of residence will be for the Fellow's personal account.

Length of Study: Up to one year.

Study Establishment: Rhodes University, Grahamstown.

Country of Study: South Africa.

Applications Procedure: Forms of application may be obtained from the Registrar.

Closing Date: July 31st of the year before the award.

Additional Information: The Fellow will be required to present a concise report on the work completed at the conclusion of the term of the Fellowship.

Hugh Le May Fellowship

Subjects: Philosophy; theology; classics; ancient, modern or mediaeval history; classical, biblical, mediaeval or modern languages; political theory; law.

Eligibility: Open to any postdoctoral scholars of standing with research publications to their credit.

Level of Study: Postdoctorate.

Purpose: To enable scholars to devote themselves to advanced (postdoctoral) work.

Type: Fellowship.

No. of awards offered: One.

Frequency: Biennially (even-numbered years).

Value: Return economy air ticket, furnished accommodation, and small monthly cash stipend.

Length of Study: Three to four months. May be extended by mutual agreement, subject to availability of funds.

Study Establishment: Rhodes University.

Country of Study: Republic of South Africa.

Closing Date: July 31st of the year before the award.

Additional Information: Fellows are not expected to undertake teaching duties.

RICHARD III SOCIETY, AMERICAN BRANCH

Richard III Society, American Branch, Physical address not available at time of publication, Philadelphia, PA, USA
Email: lblanchard@aol.com
www: http://www.webcom.com/blanchard/edu.html#schallek
Contact: Laura V Blanchard

William B Schallek Memorial Graduate Fellowship Award

Eligibility: Applicants must be US citizens.

Level of Study: Doctorate.

Purpose: To support graduate study of fifteenth century English history and culture.

Type: Cash.

No. of awards offered: Varies.

Frequency: Annual.

Value: In multiples of US$500 to a maximum of US$2000.

Length of Study: One year.

Study Establishment: Recognised and accredited degree granting institutions.

Applications Procedure: Guidelines, lists of past awards and their topics, and a downloadable application form may be found at the Society's World Wide Web site.

Closing Date: February 28th for the following academic year.

Additional Information: Physical address not available at time of publication. Web address and E-mail are currently the only form of contact.

SIR HENRY RICHARDSON TRUST

Sir Henry Richardson Trust, 16 Ogle Street, London, W1P 7LG, England
Tel: 0171 636 4481
Fax: 0171 647 4307
Contact: Valerie Beale, Administrator

*Sir Henry Richardson Award

Subjects: Musical performance: repetiteurs in even-numbered years; accompanists in odd-numbered years.

Eligibility: Open to postgraduates of up to 30 years.

Level of Study: Postgraduate.

Purpose: To assist a young accompanist and repetiteur in alternate years.

No. of awards offered: One.

Frequency: Annual.

Value: £5,000.

Country of Study: Unrestricted.

Applications Procedure: Selected students will be asked to audition.

Closing Date: Mid-February.

MARY ROBERTS RINEHART FUND

Mary Roberts Rinehart Fund, MSN 3E4, English Department, George Mason University, Fairfax, VA, 22030-4444, USA
Tel: 703 993 1185

Mary Roberts Rinehart Grants

Subjects: Literary composition: fiction and poetry, or non-fiction and drama. Only works in English will be read.

Eligibility: Open to new and relatively unknown writers, without regard to citizenship, sex, color or creed. Published writers are ineligible.

Purpose: To encourage young writers who need financial assistance not otherwise available to complete works-in-progress.

Type: Grant.

No. of awards offered: Two.

Frequency: Annual.

Value: Varies; approximately US$900.

Country of Study: Any country.

Applications Procedure: There are no formal application forms. The only way to have a work considered is to have it submitted, in manuscript form, by a sponsoring writer, agent, writing teacher or editor who is familiar with the author.

Closing Date: November 30th for announcement the following March.

FOREST ROBERTS THEATRE

Panowski Playwriting Competition, Forest Roberts Theatre, Northern Michigan University, 1401 Presque Isle, Marquette, MI, 49855-5364, USA
Tel: 906 227 2082
Fax: 906 227 2567
Contact: Award Coordinator

Mildred and Albert Panowski Playwriting Award

Subjects: Playwriting.

Eligibility: Open to amateur, pre-professional, and professional playwrights. Plays must be written in English.

Level of Study: Unrestricted.

Purpose: To encourage and stimulate artistic growth among educational and professional playwrights and to provide the students and faculty of Northern Michigan University the unique opportunity to mount and produce an original work on the university stage.

No. of awards offered: One.

Frequency: Annual.

Value: US$2,000 cash award and production of the winning script.

Country of Study: USA.

Applications Procedure: Applicants should send SASE for rules and application form.

Closing Date: Plays must be received by the Friday before Thanksgiving.

Additional Information: There is no restriction as to theme or genre. Entries must be original, full-length plays. Musicals, one-act plays, and previously submitted works are unacceptable. Submissions must not have been previously produced or published. Please write for a complete copy of the rules.

ROCHE RESEARCH FOUNDATION

F Hoffmann-La Roche Ltd, Bldg.71/502, Basel, CH-4070, Switzerland
Tel: 41 61 688 21 82
Fax: 41 61 688 14 60

Contact: Prof. A Fischli, PhD

Roche Research Foundation

Subjects: Biology, medicine.

Eligibility: Open to all qualified researchers for fellowships at Swiss universities or hospitals; and to qualified Swiss students for fellowships abroad.

Purpose: To promote scientific research at Swiss universities and hospitals in the biomedical field; and to sponsor experimental research of Swiss fellows in biology and medicine working at universities and laboratories abroad.

Type: Fellowship.

No. of awards offered: 100 each year.

Frequency: Quarterly.

Value: Living and travelling costs.

Country of Study: Switzerland and abroad.

Closing Date: 15 January, 15 April, 15 July, 15 October.

ROCKEFELLER ARCHIVE CENTER

Rockefeller Archive Center, 15 Dayton Avenue, Pocantico Hills, North Tarrytown, NY, 10591-1598, USA
Tel: 914 631 4505
Fax: 914 631 6017
Contact: Darwin H Stapleton, Director

Research Grant Program

Subjects: Developments and issues of the 20th century in the USA and throughout the world.

Eligibility: Open to applicants of any discipline, usually graduate students or postdoctoral scholars, who are engaged in projects which require substantial use of the collections.

Level of Study: Unrestricted.

Purpose: To foster research in the records of the Rockefeller Foundation, Rockefeller University, the Rockefeller Brothers Fund, the Rockefeller family, and in collections of other institutions and individuals deposited at the Rockefeller Archive Center.

Type: Grants.

No. of awards offered: 35-40.

Frequency: Annual.

Value: Up to US$1,500 for applicants within the USA; US$2,000 for applicants from outside the USA; depending upon travel, lodging and research expenses of the applicant.

Length of Study: One year; renewable through application.

Study Establishment: The Center.

Country of Study: USA.

Applications Procedure: Application form must be completed.

Closing Date: November 30th for notification in March.

THE ROEHER INSTITUTE

The Roeher Institute, Kinsmen Building, 4700 Keele Street, North York, Ontario, M3J 1P3, Canada
Tel: 416 661 9611
Fax: 416 661 5701
Contact: Secretary of Bursaries and Grants Adjudicating Committee

*Research Grants

Subjects: A broad range of fields relating to human services and intellectual impairment.

Eligibility: Open to Canadian citizens or landed immigrants who are graduate students enrolled in graduate programs at Canadian universities.

Purpose: To enable researchers to examine issues affecting people with an intellectual impairment and other disabilities.

Type: Research Grant.

No. of awards offered: Varies.

Frequency: Annual.

Value: Up to C$8,000.

Length of Study: One year; renewable if research project shows results and can be published in related journals.

Study Establishment: A university.

Country of Study: Canada.

Closing Date: April 30th.

Additional Information: Candidates must state intent to pursue a career in Canada and must have definite research projects supported by an academic advisor or an Institute associate or consultant. Applicants must be prepared to forward progress reports and/or publish their results. Research Grants are also offered to associates, associations and agencies.

*Major Research Grants

Subjects: A broad range of academic disciplines where the study itself has implications for the field of mental impairment, including Alzheimer's Disease.

Eligibility: Open to Canadian citizens or landed immigrants who hold a postgraduate degree in a field related to the proposed research. Applicants must have their research projects approved by a Canadian academic or research Institute.

Type: Research Grant.

No. of awards offered: Varies.

Frequency: Annual.

Value: Up to US$35,000.

Length of Study: One to three years; renewal is contingent on a progress report of the work and research results.

Country of Study: Canada.

Closing Date: April 30th.

FRANKLIN AND ELEANOR ROOSEVELT INSTITUTE

Franklin and Eleanor Roosevelt Institute, Franklin D Roosevelt Library, 511 Albany Post Road, Hyde Park, NY, 12538, USA
Tel: 914 229 5321
Fax: 914 229 9046

Roosevelt Institute Grant-in-Aid

Subjects: The Roosevelt years and clearly related subjects.

Eligibility: Open to qualified researchers of any nationality with a viable plan of work. Proposals are recommended for funding by an independent panel of scholars which reports to the Institute Board.

Level of Study: Unrestricted.

Purpose: To encourage younger scholars to expand our knowledge and understanding of the Roosevelt period and to give continued support to more experienced researchers who have already made a mark in the field.

Type: Grant.

No. of awards offered: 15-20.

Frequency: Twice yearly.

Value: Up to US$2,500.

Country of Study: USA.

Applications Procedure: Two copies - application face sheet, research proposal, relevance of holdings, travel plans, time estimate, CV and budget.

Closing Date: March 15th and October 15th.

ROSWELL MUSEUM AND ART CENTRE FOUNDATION (USA)

100 West 11th Street, Roswell, NM, 88201, USA
Tel: 505 622 6037
Fax: 505 623 5603
Email: ROSWELLAiR@aol.com
Contact: Stephen Fleming, Program Director

Roswell Artists in Residence Program

Subjects: Drawing, painting, sculpture, photography, printmaking, and other fine art media.

Eligibility: Open, no performance based work or production crafts.

Level of Study: Postgraduate, Professional development.

Purpose: To provide time for artists to focus on their work.

Type: Residency.

No. of awards offered: Five per year.

Frequency: Annual.

Value: US$500 per month, plus housing, studio and utilities.

Length of Study: 6-12 months.

Country of Study: USA.

Applications Procedure: Applicants must complete current application. Send SASE for application materials.

Additional Information: No dogs; families welcome.

For further information contact:
409 E College Avenue, Roswell, NM, 88201, USA
Tel: 505 623 5600
Contact: Marina Mahan

ROTARY FOUNDATION

The Rotary Foundation, 1560 Sherman Avenue, Evanston, IL, 60201, USA
Tel: 847 866 3320
www: http://www.rotary.org

Academic-Year Ambassadorial Scholarships

Subjects: Any subject.

Eligibility: Open to undergraduates, graduates and those wishing to undertake vocational study. Applicants must have completed two years of university work or appropriate professional experience before starting scholarship studies. Scholarships are available to individuals of all ages. Spouses or descendents of Rotarians may not apply. Applicants must be citizens of countries in which there are Rotary clubs.

Level of Study: Unrestricted.

Purpose: To further international understanding and friendly relations among people of different countries.

Type: Scholarship.

No. of awards offered: Varies.

Frequency: Annual.

Value: Up to US$22,000 in 1997-8 to help cover tuition, fees, room and board, and round-trip transportation.

Length of Study: One academic year.

Country of Study: Any country other than that in which the Scholar resides, providing there are Rotary clubs there.

Applications Procedure: Applicants must submit a completed application form, two recommendations, college transcripts, an autobiographical essay, statement of purpose, and a language ability form verifying applicant's background in the language of the proposed host country, if different from his/her native language.

Closing Date: Varies according to local Rotary club, but between March and July.

Additional Information: Scholars will not be assigned to study in areas of a country where they have previously lived or studied for more than six months. During the study year, scholars are expected to be outstanding ambassadors of goodwill through appearances before Rotary clubs, schools, civic organizations and other forums. Upon completion of the scholarship, scholars are expected to share the experiences of understanding acquired during the study year with the people of their home countries. Candidates should contact local Rotary clubs for information on the availability of particular scholarships.

Cultural Ambassadorial Scholarships

Subjects: For cultural immersion and intensive language study: available languages may vary each year.

Eligibility: Open to students who have completed two years of university work or appropriate professional experience before starting scholarship studies, and who have studied the proposed language for at least one year at the college level. Scholarships are available to individuals of all ages. Spouses or descendants of Rotarians may not apply. Applicants must be citizens of countries in which there are Rotary clubs.

Level of Study: Unrestricted.

Purpose: To further international understanding and friendly relations among people of different countries.

Type: Scholarship.

No. of awards offered: Varies.

Frequency: Annual.

Value: To cover tuition, room and board, and round-trip transportation up to a maximum of US$10,000 for 3-month awards and US$17,000 for 6-month awards. All other expenses are the responsibility of the scholars.

Length of Study: 3 or 6 months.

Country of Study: Determined by the Rotary Foundation, according to the language of study.

Applications Procedure: Applicants must submit a completed application form, two recommendations, college transcripts, an autobiographical essay and statement of purpose.

Closing Date: Varies according to local Rotary club, but between March and July.

Additional Information: Wherever possible, Scholars will reside with host families. Candidates should contact local Rotary clubs for information on the availability of particular scholarships.

Multi-Year Ambassadorial Scholarships

Subjects: Any subject.

Eligibility: Open to undergraduates and graduates who have completed two years of university work or appropriate professional experience before starting scholarship studies. Scholarships are available to individuals of all ages. Spouses or descendents of Rotarians may not apply. Applicants must be citizens of countries in which there are Rotary clubs.

Level of Study: Unrestricted.

Purpose: To further international understanding and friendly relations among people of different countries and help defray the cost of pursuing a degree.

Type: Scholarship.

No. of awards offered: Varies.

Frequency: Annual.

Value: In addition to the ambassadorial nature of the scholarship, the award is intended to assist in the cost of degree-oriented study in another country. In 1997-98 the scholarship will provide a flat award of US$11,000 or its equivalent per annum. All additional costs must be absorbed by scholars.

Length of Study: 2 or 3 years.

Country of Study: Any country other than that in which the Scholar resides, providing there are Rotary clubs there.

Applications Procedure: Applicants must submit a completed application form, two recommendations, college transcripts, an autobiographical essay and a statement of purpose.

Closing Date: Varies according to local Rotary club, but between March and July.

Additional Information: Scholars will not be assigned to study in areas of a country where they have previously lived or studied for more than six months. During the study year, scholars are expected to be outstanding ambassadors of goodwill through appearances before Rotary clubs, schools, civic organizations and other forums. Upon completion of the scholarship, scholars are expected to share the experiences of understanding acquired during the study year with the people of their home countries. Candidates should contact local Rotary clubs for information on the availability of particular scholarships.

Rotary Grants for University Teachers to Serve in Developing Countries

Subjects: Fields taught must have practical use to the host country.

Eligibility: Applicants must hold a college or university appointment for 3 or more years, and must be proficient in the language of their prospective host country.

Purpose: To build international undersatnding while strengthening higher education in low-income countries.

Type: Grant.

No. of awards offered: Varies.

Frequency: Annual, dependent on funds available.

Value: US$10,000 for 3-5 months; US$20,000 for 6-10 months of service.

Length of Study: 3-10 months.

Country of Study: Countries with a per capita GNP of US$5,000 or less in which there are Rotary clubs.

Applications Procedure: Teachers must apply through a local Rotary club. Applications should include a completed application form, current CV, statement of intent and two letters of recommendation.

Closing Date: Varies according to club; between March and July 15th.

Additional Information: Grant recipients are expected to be outstanding ambassadors of goodwill to the people of their host and home countries through appearances to Rotary clubs.

For further information contact:
Rotary Foundation, 1560 Sherman Avenue, Evanston, IL, 60201, USA
Tel: 847 866 3320
Fax: 847 328 8554
www: http://www.rotary.org
Contact: Sharon Gerlach

ROTARY YONEYAMA MEMORIAL FOUNDATION, INC

Rotary Yoneyama Memorial Foundation, Inc., abc Building 8F, 6-3 Shiba Koen 2-chome, Minato-ku, Tokyo, 105, Japan
Tel: 03 3434 8681
Fax: 03 3578 8281
Contact: The Secretary

Rotary Yoneyama Scholarship

Subjects: All subjects.

Eligibility: Applicants must come from countries where there is at least one Rotary Club and must be non-Japanese nationals who have entered Japan with a 'college student' visa for the purpose of studies and researches.

Level of Study: Postgraduate, Doctorate, Unrestricted.

Purpose: Rotary Yoneyama Foundation, Inc., supported by all the Rotary Clubs and Rotarians in Japan, offers its scholarships to those non-Japanese national overseas students who are resident in Japan studying at colleges/universities and other higher educational institutions as 'regular' (full-time degree courses) students at their own expense.

Type: Scholarship.

Frequency: Annual.

Value: Yen 150,000 per month (postgraduate); Yen 120,000 per month (undergraduate).

Length of Study: Two years maximum.

Study Establishment: Colleges, universities, and other institutions of higher education.

Country of Study: Japan.

Applications Procedure: All the procedures of selection are to be carried out in Japanese.

Closing Date: October 1st.

Additional Information: It is recommended to contact the Foundation directly, since requirements for certain applicants can be conditional. Selection is extremely competitive, with the number of awards very limited.

ROTCH TRAVELING SCHOLARSHIP

52 Broad Street, 4th Floor, Boston, MA, 02109, USA

Rotch Traveling Scholarship

Subjects: Architecture.

Eligibility: Open to US architects who are under 35 years of age on 10 March of the year of competition and have a degree from an accredited school of architecture plus one full year of professional experience in an architectural office.

Level of Study: Professional development.

Purpose: To provide the opportunity for travel and study in foreign countries.

Type: Fellowship.

No. of awards offered: One or two.

Frequency: Annual.

Value: A stipend of US$30,000.

Length of Study: Eight months.

Country of Study: Outside the USA.

Applications Procedure: Please submit a written request for an application form.

Closing Date: January 1st for application requests.

Additional Information: The Scholar is selected through a two-stage design competition. The one year of professional experience required should be completed prior to the beginning of the preliminary competition. Scholars are required to return to the USA after the duration of the Scholarship and submit a report of their travels.

ROTHMANS FOUNDATION

Rothmans Foundation, 13th Floor, 309 Kent Street, Sydney, NSW, 2000, Australia

Tel: 02 299 2500
Fax: 02 299 2464
Contact: Mr A K Davidson AM MBE, Executive Director

*Fellowships

Subjects: Any subject.

Eligibility: Open to men and women of any nationality. Applicants must have held a doctoral degree for no more than three years at the closing date for receipt of applications.

Purpose: To assist in the development of postdoctoral studies in Australian universities.

Type: Fellowship.

No. of awards offered: One.

Frequency: Annual.

Value: A$39,000 per annum, plus A$11,000 for institutional overheads including superannuation.

Length of Study: One year; renewable for a second year and in exceptional cases for a third year.

Study Establishment: Any university.

Country of Study: Australia.

Applications Procedure: Candidates must complete five applications forms and obtain referees' reports.

Closing Date: June 30th.

Additional Information: No Fellowships will be awarded to an applicant who is proceeding on sabbatical, study or other leave (including leave without pay), or to a permanent member of academic staff.

ROYAL ACADEMY OF ARTS

British Institution Fund, Royal Academy of Arts, Piccadilly, London, W1V 0DS, England
Tel: 0171 439 7438
Fax: 0171 434 0837
Contact: The Secretary

British Institution Fund Awards

Subjects: Painting, sculpture, printmaking and architecture.

Eligibility: Open to full- or part-time students, normally not over 25 years of age, who are currently enrolled in recognized courses in an art school, university or architectural institution in the UK or the Republic of Ireland. Student members of the Royal Institute of British Architects studying for their Part 3 examination are also eligible.

Level of Study: Postgraduate, Undergraduate.

Purpose: To encourage the study of the fine arts, subject to discretionary conditions set by the Trustees.

Type: Grant.

No. of awards offered: Varies.

Frequency: Annually, usually in February.

Value: Up to £1,000.

Length of Study: One year.

Country of Study: UK or Republic of Ireland.

Applications Procedure: Applicants should submit with their works a certified statement of their study of art, either whole or part-time, for a period of not less than one year in a recognized school of art in the UK, and their current attendance at such a school. Application forms are distributed to all Art Schools in January.

THE ROYAL ACADEMY OF ENGINEERING

The Royal Academy of Engineering, 29 Great Peter Street, London, SW1P 3LW, England
Tel: 0171 222 2688
Fax: 0171 233 0054
Contact: Manager of Research Fellowships and Secondments

Athlone-Vanier Engineering Fellowships

Subjects: All disciplines of engineering.

Eligibility: Open to graduates under 30 years of age, with high academic qualifications and two years' work experience in engineering. Fellows are to find their own placements in Canada.

Purpose: To allow high calibre British engineers to undertake postgraduate studies or gain industrial experience in Canada.

Type: Fellowship.

No. of awards offered: Two.

Frequency: Annual.

Value: All reasonable expenses, including travel, tuition fees and a subsistence allowance.

Length of Study: One year.

Study Establishment: At recognized engineering establishments.

Country of Study: Canada.

Closing Date: January.

Additional Information: Applicants are expected to return to the UK at the completion of the Fellowship and to submit interim and final reports and give one public lecture. In addition applicants are to undertake an in-depth investigation of an aspect of Canadian industry.

Engineering Secondments Overseas

Subjects: All fields of engineering.

Eligibility: Open to suitably experienced engineers. Preference is given to candidates of 25-35 years of age who are employed in industry, commerce, local government or institutions of higher learning.

Purpose: To allow experienced professional engineers to work in areas of advanced engineering in organizations in developed overseas countries.

Type: Grant.

No. of awards offered: Varies.

Value: Approximately 50% of the total cost of the Secondment.

Length of Study: Six months to a year.

Study Establishment: In advanced industrial firms or research and development organizations in a foreign country.

Country of Study: Outside the UK.

Applications Procedure: There is no application form. A written proposal must be submitted. Applicants should contact the scheme manager prior to submitting a proposal.

Additional Information: Awards are made on the basis of the applicant's experience and ability, and on the benefit to be gained by the seconded engineer, his or her firm and the country. Applicants must be supported by their employer and undertake to return to the UK upon completion of the Secondment.

*Engineers to Japan Scheme

Subjects: Japanese technology, research and development.

Eligibility: Open to British-based engineers and technologists destined for senior management.

No. of awards offered: Varies.

Frequency: Rolling programme.

Value: Usually 50% towards salary and other expenses.

Length of Study: Six to 12 months.

Country of Study: Japan.

Additional Information: The project must be agreed by the two companies concerned. The Scheme is provided in conjunction with the Department of Trade and Industry.

ESSO Engineering Teaching Fellowships

Subjects: Chemical, petroleum, or mechanical engineering.

Eligibility: Open to graduates, preferably with industrial experience, who hold full-time lecturing posts at a UK university and teach chemical, petroleum or mechanical engineering to undergraduates on courses accredited by the Engineering Council. Age limit is typically 32 years.

Purpose: To encourage able young engineering lecturers to remain in the education sector in their early years.

Type: Fellowship.

No. of awards offered: Six.

Frequency: Annual.

Value: £9,000 over four years.

Length of Study: Four years.

Study Establishment: At the applicant's current university in the UK; two weeks will be spent at an ESSO site.

Country of Study: UK.

Applications Procedure: Application form to be completed.

Closing Date: 1 October.

Additional Information: A brochure is available on request.

ICI Fellowship Scheme for Young Academic Chemical Engineers

Subjects: Chemical engineering relevant to ICI.

Eligibility: Open to lecturers or assistant lecturers in a chemical engineering department of a UK university (or have the offer of such a post) accredited by the Institution of Chemical Engineers or undergoing academic training and having the offer of an academic post in chemical engineering; or to young industrialists with the offer of an academic post in chemical engineering. Candidates should not normally be over 35 years of age.

Purpose: To assist the UK chemical engineering community by promoting the recruitment and retention of outstanding young faculty members and encouraging appropriate industrial contact.

Type: Fellowship.

No. of awards offered: One.

Frequency: Annual.

Value: £24,700 over five years.

Length of Study: Over five years.

Study Establishment: At an ICI site or in ICI related work for a few weeks each year.

Country of Study: UK.

Applications Procedure: There is no form. CV and statement of research, and interests to be submitted.

Closing Date: April 1st (initial applications by December 31st).

Additional Information: Nominations must be made by the Head of the relevant UK Department of Chemical Engineering.

Industrial Secondment Scheme

Subjects: All fields of engineering.

Eligibility: Open to academic engineering staff. There are no limitations on age or seniority, however preference will be given to applications from more junior staff and to those without previous industrial experience.

Purpose: To provide financial support for the secondment of academic engineering staff to industrial companies within the UK.

Type: Grant.

No. of awards offered: Varies.

Frequency: Varies depending on funds available.

Value: Varies.

Length of Study: Normally three to six months.

Study Establishment: At an industrial company within the UK.

Country of Study: UK.

Applications Procedure: Contact Mr A Eades for more information.

Closing Date: Offered all year round, subject to availability of funds.

Additional Information: The main objective is to obtain up-to-date industrial experience, to improve teaching capabilities and generally to foster academic industrial links.

International Travel Grants

Subjects: Engineering, materials technology, computing.

Eligibility: Open to postgraduate students, postdoctoral researchers, HEI lecturers involved in research, and chartered engineers, who are UK nationals. There is no age limit and no restrictions.

Purpose: To facilitate study visits overseas, generally for attendance at conferences, research institutions and/or industrial sites.

Type: Travel Grant.

No. of awards offered: Varies.

Frequency: Varies depending on funds available.

Value: 30-50% of approved costs.

Country of Study: Outside the UK.

Closing Date: Offered all year round.

MacRobert Award

Subjects: The successful development of innovation in engineering or the other physical sciences.

Eligibility: Open to individuals, independent teams, or teams working for a firm, organization or laboratory (no more than five members in a team).

Purpose: To recognize and reward outstanding contributions by way of innovation in engineering.

Type: Award.

No. of awards offered: One.

Frequency: Annual.

Value: £50,000 and a gold medal.

Country of Study: UK.

Closing Date: 31 March.

Management Fellowship Scheme

Subjects: Engineering.

Eligibility: Open to UK citizens with chartered engineer status who are aged between 26 and 34 years at the commencement of the proposed MBA course.

Purpose: To enable young chartered engineers of the highest career potential to undertake MBA courses at European business schools.

Type: Fellowship.

No. of awards offered: 14.

Frequency: Annual.

Value: To cover course fees.

Study Establishment: For an MBA course at INSEAD, IMD, EAP, ENPC or Theseus and Erasmus Business Schools.

Closing Date: None.

Panasonic Trust

Subjects: Engineering, particularly new engineering developments and new technologies.

Eligibility: Open to persons working at the professional level in engineering in the UK, with several years' experience at this level. There are no age restrictions.

Purpose: To encourage the technical updating and continuous professional development of qualified engineers through courses provided by UK institutions of higher education at masters level.

No. of awards offered: Varies.

Frequency: Varies depending on funds available.

Value: Usually to cover 50% of course fees up to a maximum of £1,000.

Length of Study: For the duration of the course.

Country of Study: UK.

Closing Date: Offered all year round.

Additional Information: Preference is given to those undertaking part-time modular masters courses. The intended course of study must be relevant to the applicant's current or future career plans.

Senior Research Fellowships

Subjects: Engineering research projects of direct relevance to the sponsoring industrial company.

Eligibility: Open to individuals holding qualifications commensurate with those required for a senior research post.

Purpose: To provide additional funds for a Senior Research Fellow working in a higher education institution in the United Kingdom on a research project of direct relevance to the sponsoring company, and the industry as a whole.

Type: Fellowship.

No. of awards offered: Varies.

Frequency: Proposals considered throughout the year.

Value: One-third of gross salary to spend on equipment.

Length of Study: 3-5 years.

Country of Study: UK.

Applications Procedure: Written proposal is required. Candidates are encouraged to contact the scheme manager prior to submitting an application. Applications must be submitted by the appropriate Head of Department of the higher education institution.

Additional Information: Fellows are required to submit written annual progress reports and may be invited to give a presentation of their work to Fellows of the Royal Academy of Engineering.

ROYAL ACADEMY OF MUSIC

Royal Academy of Music, Marylebone Road, London, NW1 5HT, England
Tel: 0171 873 7393
Fax: 0171 873 7394
Contact: Philip White, Academic Registrar

General Bursary Awards

Subjects: All relevant branches of music education and training.

Eligibility: Any student offered a place at the Academy, irrespective of race, creed, gender, etc.

Level of Study: Postgraduate.

Purpose: To assist towards tuition fees and general living expenses for study at the Royal Academy of Music.

Type: Bursary.

No. of awards offered: Varies.

Frequency: Annually, funds often available on continuing basis.

Value: According to need and availability of funds.

Length of Study: Normally for a complete academic year. Individual requirements may be imposed.

Study Establishment: Royal Academy of Music.

Country of Study: UK.

Applications Procedure: Application forms are sent automatically to all postgraduate students who are offered places.

Closing Date: January 31st for the following academic year.

ROYAL AERONAUTICAL SOCIETY

Handley Page Award, Royal Aeronautical Society, 4 Hamilton Place, London, W1V 0BQ, England
Tel: 0171 499 3515
Fax: 0171 499 6230
Contact: Secretary

*Handley Page Award

Subjects: Aeronautics, with special reference to safety and reliability in air transport. The Award can also be given to encourage interest in aerospace technology in schools and colleges and by young people generally.

Eligibility: Open to citizens of the British Commonwealth who are suitably qualified to undertake the proposed work.

No. of awards offered: One.

Frequency: Annual.

Value: Approximately £5,000 to be awarded in whole or in part to an individual or group.

Country of Study: Any country.

Closing Date: May 31st.

Additional Information: The Award is for original work leading to advancement and progress in the art and science of aeronautics, with special reference to the practical application of a device, or the long-term implications of a new concept, directed towards the safety of those who work with or travel in aircraft.

THE ROYAL AUSTRALASIAN COLLEGE OF RADIOLOGISTS

The Royal Australasian College of Radiologists, Level 9, 51 Druitt Street, Sydney, NSW, 2000, Australia
Tel: 02 264 3555
Fax: 02 264 7799
Contact: Honorary Secretary

Thomas Baker Memorial Fellowship

Subjects: The study and advancement of diagnostic radiology and radiation oncology.

Eligibility: Open to Australian or New Zealand members of the College of less than five years standing.

Purpose: To assist in travelling expenses for visiting centres.

Type: Fellowship.

No. of awards offered: One.

Value: Up to a maximum of A$10,000.

Length of Study: From 3-18 months.

Country of Study: Any country in the Northern Hemisphere.

Applications Procedure: Applicants are required to submit details of the proposed plan of study with application.

Closing Date: June 30th.

Additional Information: A report to the Council is expected on the Fellow's return, and he or she must remain resident in Australasia for two years thereafter. The College also offers a number of smaller awards for travel assistance to the Annual General Meeting of the College, best presentations by student members, etc.

ROYAL AUSTRALIAN COLLEGE OF GENERAL PRACTITIONERS

South Australia Faculty, Royal Australian College of General Practitioners, 15 Gover Street, North Adelaide, South Australia, 5006, Australia
Contact: Dr Max Dunstone, Francis Hardy-Faulding Awards Committee

*Francis Hardy-Faulding Memorial Fellowship

Subjects: Medicine: general practice.

Eligibility: Open to general practitioners registered and working in Australia.

Purpose: To reward a completed research project relevant to general practice.

Type: Fellowship.

No. of awards offered: One.

Frequency: Annual.

Value: A$5,000.

Country of Study: Australia.

Closing Date: February 28th.

ROYAL COLLEGE OF MUSIC

Royal College of Music, Prince Consort Road, London, SW7 2BS, England
Tel: 0171 589 3643
Fax: 0171 589 7740
Contact: Kevin Porter, Academic Registrar

Scholarships and Exhibitions

Subjects: Music performance, composition or conducting.

Eligibility: Unrestricted, but only for study at the College.

Level of Study: Unrestricted.

Purpose: To recognize merit in music performance, composition or conducting.

Type: Scholarship.

No. of awards offered: c.50.

Frequency: Annual.

Value: Up to £10,000 (ie. full or part-time fees).

Length of Study: 1-4 years.

Study Establishment: Music conservatoire.

Country of Study: UK.

Applications Procedure: Application by application for place of study.

Closing Date: October 1st.

ROYAL COLLEGE OF ORGANISTS

The Royal College of Organists, 7 St Andrew Street, Holborn, London, EC4A 3LQ, England
Tel: 0171 936 3606
Fax: 0171 353 8244
Contact: Clerk

RCO Grants and Travel Scholarships

Subjects: Organ playing.

Eligibility: Open to promising pupils of any nationality who are training to be organists. Some of the Grants are restricted to applicants under 20 years of age.

Type: Grants and travel scholarships.

No. of awards offered: Varies.

Frequency: Annually renewable.

Value: Not less than £50.

Length of Study: One year, renewable.

Applications Procedure: Write for applications.

Closing Date: May 1st.

RCO Grants & Trusts

Eligibility: Open.

Level of Study: Postgraduate, Professional development, Unrestricted.

Purpose: Study of organ playing.

Type: Grants and trusts.

No. of awards offered: Varies.

Frequency: Annual.

Value: Not less than £50.

Length of Study: One year renewable.

Study Establishment: Varies.

Applications Procedure: Write for application form.

Closing Date: May 1st.

For further information contact:
Royal College of Organists, 7 St Andrew Street, Holborn, London, EC4A 3LQ, United Kingdom
Tel: 0171 936 3606
Fax: 0171 353 8244
Contact: Dr Micheal Nicholas

THE ROYAL COLLEGE OF PHYSICIANS AND SURGEONS OF CANADA

The Royal College of Physicians and Surgeons of Canada, Office of Fellowship Affairs, 774 Echo Drive, Ottawa, Ontario, K1S 5N8, Canada
Tel: 613 730 8177 ext.355
Fax: 613 730 8260
Email: diane.sarrazin@rcpsc.edu
Contact: Mrs Diane C Sarrazin, Awards and Grants Coordinator

International Travelling Fellowship

Subjects: Medicine and surgery.

Eligibility: Open to Fellows of the Royal College.

Level of Study: Postgraduate.

Purpose: To enable fellows residing outside of Canada to study in a medical centre in Canada or gain experience in the application of new knowledge or skills for direct application to clinical practices or to the pursuit of a clinical research problem or, to enable fellows residing in Canada to practice and teach in a lesser developed country.

Type: Fellowship.

No. of awards offered: One.

Frequency: Annual.

Value: C$1,750 per month for up to 12 months (maximum C$21,000).

Length of Study: 6-12 months.

Country of Study: Fellows residing outside of Canada study in Canada, whilst Fellows residing in Canada practice and teach in a lesser developed country.

Applications Procedure: Application form must be completed; please write or call to receive the guidelines and form.

Closing Date: September 30th for the Fellowship to be taken up in the following year.

Additional Information: The RCPSC Awards Committee acts as a selection committee. The selection is based upon an assessment of the overall merit of the application. The criteria for this assessment are: a) the benefits to the individual and to the community; b) the quality of the program to be undertaken; and c) the financial need and funds available to the applicant.

ROYAL COLLEGE OF PHYSICIANS OF EDINBURGH

Royal College of Physicians, 9 Queen Street, Edinburgh, EH2 1JQ, Scotland
Tel: 0131 225 7324/5
Fax: 0131 220 3939
Contact: Treasurer

Hill Pattison-Struthers Bursary

Subjects: Internal medicine.

Eligibility: Open to suitably qualified persons.

Type: Bursary.

No. of awards offered: One.

Frequency: Annually or as funds allow.

Value: Up to £300.

Study Establishment: For a course organised by the Lister Postgraduate Institute.

Country of Study: UK.

Applications Procedure: Applicants should submit details of their age, marital status, children, career and an indication of their plans for their future career after they have attended the course. They should also give the names of two referees, not necessarily medically qualified, to whom application can be made. It would be of help to the selection committee if applicants offered details of any financial hardship caused by attendance at the course. Applications are expected after the start of the course.

ROYAL COLLEGE OF SURGEONS FOUNDATION INC, NEW YORK

Royal College of Surgeons of England, 35-43 Lincoln's Inn Fields, London, WC2A 3PN, England
Tel: 0171 405 3474 ext.4004
Fax: 0171 831 9438
Contact: Secretary

Travelling Fellowships

Subjects: Surgery, dentistry.

Eligibility: Open to UK surgeons, usually between 30-36 years of age, who are qualified practitioners in their speciality and Fellows of the Royal College of Surgeons of England.

Level of Study: Professional development.

Purpose: To enable young surgeons and dental surgeons to visit the USA to observe first-hand medical procedures.

Type: Fellowship.

No. of awards offered: Three.

Frequency: Annual.

Value: Up to US$5,000.

Length of Study: Four to six weeks.

Country of Study: USA.

Applications Procedure: Application must include CV, proposal, letters of support from the applicant's present consultant and a statement of expenses to be incurred.

Closing Date: February.

ROYAL COLLEGE OF SURGEONS OF ENGLAND

Royal College of Surgeons of England, 35-43 Lincoln's Inn Fields, London, WC2A 3PN, England
Tel: 0171 405 3474
Fax: 0171 831 9438
Contact: Secretary

Norman Capener Travelling Fellowships

Subjects: Surgery.

Eligibility: Open to medical practitioners. Preference is given to candidates enrolled for Higher Surgical Training or who have recently completed a course in orthopaedic or hand surgery.

Purpose: To provide travel expenses to and from the UK for the study of orthopaedic surgery and surgery of the hand.

Type: Fellowship.

No. of awards offered: Varies.

Frequency: Biennially.

Value: Varies according to travel costs; paid in one lump sum.

Country of Study: Any country.

Closing Date: July.

Lionel Colledge Memorial Fellowship in Otolaryngology

Subjects: Surgery.

Eligibility: Open to candidates who are Fellows of the Royal College of Surgeons and between 25-35 years of age. Candidates must be senior trainees or recently appointed consultants, or of similar status, in otolaryngology, rhinology, or otology.

Purpose: To encourage research in the area of head and neck surgery with an emphasis on laryngology, rhinology or otology.

Type: Fellowship.

No. of awards offered: One.

Frequency: Annual.

Value: Up to £3,000.

Study Establishment: Appropriate research institutions outside the UK.

Closing Date: April.

Ethicon Foundation Fund

Subjects: Surgery.

Eligibility: Open to Fellows of the Royal College of Surgeons of England.

Purpose: To promote international goodwill in surgery and to assist Fellows travelling abroad for research or training purposes.

Type: Grant.

No. of awards offered: One.

Frequency: Twice yearly.

Value: Varies according to number of awards and travel costs.

Country of Study: Any country.

Closing Date: February and August.

Sir Alexander McCormick Travelling Fellowship

Subjects: Surgery.

Eligibility: Open to Fellows of the Royal College of Surgeons of England who are enrolled by an SAC for Higher Surgical Training.

Purpose: To further specialist clinical training or research in Australia.

No. of awards offered: One.

Frequency: Annual.

Value: £5,000.

Length of Study: One year.

Country of Study: Australia.

Closing Date: End of September.

Porritt Fellowship

Subjects: Sports medicine.

Eligibility: Candidates must be a registered medical practitioner.

Purpose: To aid research into accidents and injuries which have relevance to sporting activities.

Type: Fellowship.

No. of awards offered: One.

Frequency: Annual.

Value: £7,500.

Closing Date: August.

Regent Travelling Scholarship

Subjects: Surgery.

Eligibility: Open to Fellows of Royal College of Surgeons of England, born in the UK and between 25 and 35 years of age.

Purpose: To enable one or two young surgeons to study abroad to acquire surgical expertise not readily available to them in the UK.

No. of awards offered: 1-2.

Frequency: Annual.

Value: Total of £7,000.

Length of Study: 3-12 months.

Country of Study: Any country outside the UK.

Closing Date: End of February.

ROYAL COMMISSION FOR THE EXHIBITION OF 1851

Sherfield Building, Imperial College, London, SW7 2AZ, England
Tel: 0171 594 8790
Fax: 0171 594 8794
Contact: Mr JPW Middleton

1851 Research Fellowships

Subjects: Natural sciences.

Eligibility: Open to citizens of the British Commonwealth, Ireland or Pakistan.

Level of Study: Postdoctorate.

Purpose: To give young scientists or engineers of exceptional promise the opportunity to conduct research for a further period of two years.

Type: Fellowship.

No. of awards offered: About 6.

Frequency: Annual.

Value: c.£14,000 per year.

Length of Study: Two years.

Study Establishment: Any approved university.

Country of Study: Unrestricted.

Applications Procedure: Application forms are available from all UK universities.

Closing Date: February 23rd.

Industrial Design Studentship

Subjects: Industrial design.

Eligibility: Open to UK nationals only.

Level of Study: Postgraduate.

Purpose: To fund engineering/science graduates for a postgraduate industrial design course.

Type: Studentship.

No. of awards offered: About 6.

Frequency: Annual.

Value: Tuition and c.£8,000 per year.

Length of Study: 1-2 years.

Study Establishment: UK/universities abroad.

Country of Study: Unrestricted.

Applications Procedure: Application form must be completed.

Closing Date: April.

Royal Commission Industrial Fellowships

Subjects: Industrial and management engineering.

Eligibility: Open to UK nationals only.

Level of Study: Postgraduate.

Purpose: To allow able science or engineering graduates working in industry to carry out R&D leading to a higher degree or other career milestone.

Type: Fellowship.

No. of awards offered: Approximately 6.

Frequency: Annual.

Value: c.£15,000 per year.

Length of Study: Three years.

Study Establishment: UK company.

Country of Study: UK.

Applications Procedure: Application form must be completed.

Closing Date: January.

ROYAL GEOGRAPHICAL SOCIETY (WITH THE INSTITUTE OF BRITISH GEOGRAPHERS)

Royal Geographical Society-1BG, 1 Kensington Gore, London, SW7 2AR, England
Tel: 0171 589 5466
Fax: 0171 584 4447
Email: grants@rgs.org
Contact: Expedition Grants Secretary

Monica Cole Research Grant

Subjects: Natural Sciences (Geography).

Level of Study: Postgraduate, Undergraduate.

Purpose: To enable a female physical geographer to undertake original fieldwork overseas.

Type: Grant.

No. of awards offered: One.

Frequency: Every three years (next 1998).

Value: £1,000.

Country of Study: Outside United Kingdom.

Applications Procedure: Application form required.

Violet Cressey-Marcks Fisher Travel Scholarship

Subjects: Natural sciences (geography).

Level of Study: Postgraduate, Undergraduate.

Purpose: To finance geographical research in the field that is likely to last for over six months, with preference given to younger applicants.

Type: Grant.

No. of awards offered: One.

Frequency: Every three years - next 1998.

Value: £500.

Length of Study: Over six months.

Country of Study: Outside United Kingdom.

Applications Procedure: No application form, formal proposal following guidelines.

Closing Date: March 31st.

Gilchrist Expedition Award

Subjects: Natural sciences, social sciences.

Eligibility: Open to teams of up to ten members, the majority of which must have established posts in university departments.

Level of Study: Doctorate, Postdoctorate.

Purpose: To finance the best senior overseas research proposal to enable original and challenging research to take place, preferably of potential applied benefit to the host.

Type: Grant.

No. of awards offered: One.

Frequency: Every two years.

Value: £10,000.

Length of Study: Over 6 weeks.

Country of Study: Outside the UK.

Applications Procedure: There is no application form. Please submit proposal, following the guidelines, to the Director by the closing date.

Closing Date: January 31st.

Additional Information: Further details can be obtained from The Secretary, Gilchrist Educational Trust, Mary Trevelyan Hall, 10 York Terrace East, London, NW1 4PT; Tel: 0171 631 8300 ext.773.

Henrietta Hutton Memorial Travel Award

Subjects: Natural Sciences (geography).

Eligibility: Female members of Oxford University, under 25 years of age.

Level of Study: Unrestricted.

Purpose: To allow female members of Oxford University, under 25 years of age, to travel overseas to undertake fieldwork, not necessarily connected to their academic syllabus.

Type: Grant.

No. of awards offered: Two to six.

Frequency: Annual.

Value: £2,500 total.

Study Establishment: Oxford University.

Country of Study: Outside United Kingdom.

Applications Procedure: Application form required.

Closing Date: January 29th.

Royal Geographical Society Expedition Grants

Subjects: Geographical, earth, life and human sciences.

Eligibility: Open to multi-disciplinary teams, rather than individuals, the majority of which must be British and over 19 years of age.

Level of Study: Unrestricted.

Purpose: To fund expeditions with scientific objectives related to geography and exploration outside Europe (not mountaineering expeditions).

Type: Grant.

No. of awards offered: 60-70.

Frequency: Twice yearly.

Value: £500-£2,000.

Length of Study: Must be over five weeks.

Country of Study: Usually outside Europe.

Applications Procedure: Application form required.

Closing Date: January 25th , August 25th.

Whiteley Award for Animal Conservation

Subjects: Natural Sciences.

Eligibility: Multi-disciplinary teams, rather than individuals. Applicant may be from any nation but must be over 25 years of age.

Level of Study: Postgraduate, Doctorate, Postdoctorate.

Purpose: Aa annual award that will make a substantial contribution to field projects directly concerned with the protection and conservation of animals in their habitat.

Type: Grant.

No. of awards offered: One.

Frequency: Annual.

Value: £15,000.

Country of Study: Anywhere in the world.

Applications Procedure: Application form required.

Closing Date: January 10th.

ROYAL HOLLOWAY, UNIVERSITY OF LONDON

Royal Holloway, University of London, Egham Hill, Surrey, TW20 0EX, England
Tel: 01784 434455
Fax: 01784 473662
Email: graduateoffice@rhbnc.ac.uk
Contact: Academic Registrar

Jubilee Research Fellowship

Subjects: Arts and music, classics, drama and theatre studies, Economics, English, French, German, history, Italian, management studies, social policy and social sciences; sciences, biology, biochemistry, chemistry, computer science, geography, geology, mathematics, physics and psychology.

Eligibility: Open to suitably qualified candidates who hold a PhD degree or equivalent. There are no restrictions, but a good standard in the English language is essential.

Level of Study: Postdoctorate.

Purpose: To promote research in subjects within the scope of the Faculty of Arts and Music or the Faculty of Science.

Type: Fellowship.

No. of awards offered: One.

Frequency: As funds permit, usually every three or four years.

Value: Normally equivalent to the lower end of the lecturer scale.

Length of Study: For three years.

Study Establishment: At the College.

Country of Study: UK.

Applications Procedure: Details may be obtained from the academic registrar.

Closing Date: As advertised.

Additional Information: The College is part of the University of London.

Royal Holloway Studentship

Subjects: The classics and historical studies, alternately.

Eligibility: Open to graduates with at least a good second class honours degree in the classics, Greek, Latin, or in history.

Level of Study: Postgraduate.

Purpose: To enable a graduate in classics or historical studies to complete research for a higher degree.

Type: Studentship.

No. of awards offered: One.

Frequency: As funds permit.

Value: Equal to a British Academy Major Studentship.

Length of Study: One year.

Study Establishment: At the College.

Country of Study: UK.

Applications Procedure: Details may be obtained from the academic registrar.

Closing Date: As advertised.

Additional Information: The College is part of the University of London.

Caroline Spurgeon Research Fellowship

Subjects: English literature.

Eligibility: Open to candidates who have obtained a higher degree or completed at least two years of research towards a higher degree. There are no restrictions but a good standard in English language is essential.

Level of Study: Postgraduate, Postdoctorate.

Purpose: To enable either a postdoctoral student to undertake research in English or a postgraduate student to complete his/her research.

Type: Fellowship.

No. of awards offered: One.

Frequency: As funds permit, usually every 3 or 4 years.

Value: Equal to a British Academy Major Studentship.

Length of Study: For one year.

Study Establishment: At the College.

Country of Study: UK.

Applications Procedure: Details may be obtained from the academic registrar.

Closing Date: As advertised.

Additional Information: The College is part of the University of London.

ROYAL HORTICULTURAL SOCIETY

Royal Horticultural Society, Wisley, Woking, Surrey, GU23 6QB, England
Tel: 01483 224 234
Fax: 01243 211 750
Contact: Mr P F Ryland

The Expo '90 Osaka Travel Bursary

Subjects: Horticulture: study tours, horticulturally related travel programmes, minor research projects-possibly working with an acknowledged expert (i.e. short-term research), taxonomic studies, specialized courses and programmes of study (e.g. specific subject symposia).

Eligibility: Open to British and Japanese citizens with a horticultural background. Applicants should preferably be within the age bracket of 20-35 years. Financial sponsorship will be available to both professional and amateur horticulturists and consideration for an award is not restricted to RHS Members.

Level of Study: Unrestricted.

Purpose: To allow young people from the UK and Japan to study in each other's country and benefit from a cross-cultural exchange of ideas.

Type: Bursary.

No. of awards offered: One.

Frequency: Twice yearly.

Value: Funds are limited. High-cost projects are expected to receive supplementary finance from other sources, including personal contributions.

Country of Study: Japan; Britain.

Applications Procedure: Application form to be completed. Successful applicants are required to attend an interview.

Closing Date: 31 December, 30 June.

Additional Information: The awards are made to individuals, not to groups or expeditions. Recipients must submit a factual report within six weeks of completion, along with an outline of achievements/difficulties and an account of expenses. Application forms are available on request.

The Queen Elizabeth the Queen Mother Bursary

Subjects: Horticulture: study tours, horticulturally related expeditions, minor research projects-possibly working with an acknowledged expert (i.e. short-term research), taxonomic studies, specialized courses and programmes of study (e.g. specific subject symposia).

Eligibility: Submissions are welcomed from applicants worldwide but preference is given to UK and Commonwealth citizens. Applicants should preferably be within the age bracket of 20-35 years and satisfy the Society that their health enables them to undertake the project proposed. Financial sponsorship will be available to both professional and amateur horticulturists and consideration for an award is not restricted to RHS Members.

Level of Study: Unrestricted.

Purpose: To help young horticulturists finance specific projects.

Type: Bursary.

No. of awards offered: One to three per year.

Frequency: Twice yearly.

Value: Funds are limited. High-cost projects are expected to receive supplementary finance from other sources, including personal contributions.

Country of Study: Any country.

Applications Procedure: Application form to be completed and candidates may be called for an interview.

Closing Date: December 31st, June 30th.

Additional Information: The awards are made to individuals, not to groups or expeditions. Recipients must submit a brief factual report within six weeks of completion, along with an outline of achievements/difficulties, including any unusual problems (e.g. medical/political) and an account of expenses.

ROYAL INCORPORATION OF ARCHITECTS IN SCOTLAND

The Royal Incorporation of Architects in Scotland, 15 Rutland Square, Edinburgh, EH1 2BE, Scotland
Tel: 0131 229 7545
Fax: 0131 228 2188
Contact: Alice J Aitchison

*The Sir Rowand Anderson Silver Medal

Subjects: Architecture.

Eligibility: Open to student members of the RIAS within a year of passing Part II.

Purpose: To recognize the best student member in Scotland.

No. of awards offered: One.

Frequency: Annual.

Value: £300, a silver medal, and a certificate.

Country of Study: Scotland.

Closing Date: October 31st.

Additional Information: The RIAS Awards Committee may require to interview candidates before making their selection. The Award and Presentation will be made at the RIAS Annual Convention, for which the winner may be asked to make available a selection of his or her portfolio for exhibition.

*The Sir John Burnet Memorial Award

Subjects: Architecture.

Eligibility: Competitors must be student members of the RIAS, and should be first year full-time post-Part I.

Purpose: To test a student's skill in architectural design in communicating by drawings, prepared within a predetermined time limit, their proposals in response to a client's brief.

No. of awards offered: One.

Frequency: Annual.

Value: £150 and a certificate.

Additional Information: Submissions will be judged by the RIAS Awards Committee. The Committee may be assisted by distinguished critics, co-opted by the Committee. The judges will consider: skills in interpreting a brief within a time deadline; flair in architectural design; and skill in methods of communication and presentation. The drawings will remain the property of the Royal Incorporation.

*The Sir Robert Lorimer Memorial Award

Subjects: Architecture.

Eligibility: Open to student members, and members of the RIAS under the age of 29.

Purpose: To encourage students to keep sketch books or notebooks 'as in Lorimer's time'.

No. of awards offered: One.

Frequency: Annual.

Value: A book voucher to the value of £125, and a certificate.

Closing Date: End of January.

Additional Information: The assessors prefer working sketch book(s), which are a record of study and travel, and will look for careful observation and sensitive draughtsmanship. Adjudication will normally take place in March; if confirmed by the RIAS council, the result of the competition will be notified to the competitors. The presentation of the award will be made at the RIAS Annual Convention.

*RIAS Award for Measured Drawing

Subjects: Architecture: measured drawing.

Eligibility: Open to student members and members of the RIAS.

Purpose: To encourage and recognize original hand-measured drawing as essential to an architect's training.

No. of awards offered: One.

Frequency: Annual.

Value: Premier Award for student members £200; Prize for full members £100.

Closing Date: End of January.

Additional Information: The Committee will judge competitors on the following points: the choice of architectural fabric for the measured study, such as buildings under threat (the building need not be old); the clarity of understanding and accuracy revealed by the drawing; and the elegance with which the analysis is presented. Adjudication will normally take place in March; if confirmed by the RIAS council, the result of the competition will be notified to the competitors. The presentation of the award will be made at the RIAS Annual Convention; the winning drawing will form part of a travelling exhibition of RIAS Awards and Prizes, and may at the Incorporation's discretion form part of the RIAS Archive subsequently.

*RIAS John Maclaren Travelling Fellowship

Subjects: Architecture.

Eligibility: Applicants must be on the Register of Registered Architects, and Corporate Members of the Royal Incorporation.

Purpose: To assist study at a School of Architecture or Engineering, or in taking up a paid position in practice in the country chosen for study, or to reward work which has involved study overseas.

Type: Fellowship.

No. of awards offered: One.

Frequency: Biennially.

Value: £600 and a certificate.

Study Establishment: A study of contemporary architectural design and construction.

Country of Study: Outside the UK.

Closing Date: End of January.

Additional Information: It is the preference of the RIAS that the outcome of the Fellowship should be a presentation at the RIAS Convention of the results of the study with a lodgement in the RIAS Library of such manuscript and slides or photographs as may be appropriate. The Fellowship requires both scholarship and analysis, and submission to the RIAS of evidence of lasting value. Applicants, both in their proposal and in the subsequent presentation, are expected to have adopted an investigative and critical attitude towards their proposed subject of study in the manner of a learned society dissertation. The option of presenting the results orally at the Convention (with the deposit of the material in the Library), or the simple deposit of written material in the Library, will be a matter for determination between the Fellow and the RIAS Awards Committee.

*RIAS/Whitehouse Studios Award for Architectural Photography

Subjects: Architectural photography: 'A building and its people'.

Eligibility: Open to student members and members of the RIAS.

Purpose: To recognize that architectural photography is a distinct art, and to encourage its appreciation and development.

No. of awards offered: One.

Frequency: Annual.

Value: Certificate and £250.

Closing Date: January 31st.

Additional Information: At the Incorporation's discretion, the winning photograph may also form part of the RIAS Archives.

*The Thomas Ross Award

Subjects: Architecture pertaining particularly to Scotland, Scottish architecture and/or environment, or the study of ancient Scottish buildings or monuments.

Eligibility: Candidates must be members of the RIAS, be otherwise of graduate status or possess and produce evidence of such other qualifications as may satisfy the requirements of the RIAS.

Purpose: To recognize post-qualification research into architecture and/or the environment.

No. of awards offered: One.

Frequency: Biennially.

Value: £600, a certificate, and the possibility of additional help towards publication.

Study Establishment: The production of a thesis or report resulting from research or study.

Closing Date: End of January.

Additional Information: The Committee will judge applicants upon the clarity of the proposal or completed work, upon the candidates' ability to write and to present material, and upon the extent to which the study covers ground not covered by existing material. The Committee may require applicants to attend an interview. The Committee, at its discretion, may make more than one Award, provided that the total number of Awards in a six-year period does not exceed three.

THE ROYAL INSTITUTE OF BRITISH ARCHITECTS

The Royal Institute of British Architects, 66 Portland Place, London, W1N 4AD, England
Tel: 0171 580 5533 ext.4241/4245
Fax: 0171 255 1541
Contact: John Veal

Research Awards

Subjects: Those fields which are relevant to the contemporary or historical study of architecture, architectural education or practice, town planning or building. Historical Architecture Research Trust Bursaries: architecture, other than contemporary and recent architecture, including the decoration and furnishing of buildings in any part of the world; Modern Architecture and Town Planning Trust Bursaries: contemporary and recent architecture, including the decoration and furnishing of buildings and the arrangement and landscaping of land adjacent to buildings in any part of the world, and including research into architectural education.

Eligibility: Open to young persons (whether or not they are graduates or have completed a normal course of architectural studies) who are pursuing a scheme of architectural education or research; but in special circumstances, the Institute may, if it thinks fit, award bursaries to older candidates.

Purpose: To help the education of young people embarked on a course of architectural studies, to understand the role of research therein.

No. of awards offered: Varies.

Frequency: Annual.

Value: To be determined by the estimated requirements of each project; applications for up to £5,000 will be considered, although a number of smaller awards will be made.

Country of Study: UK.

Closing Date: January 31st.

Additional Information: Projects must normally be supervised and supported by a school of architecture or research institution, and results of research should be presented in publishable form; successful work will be placed on open access in the British Architectural Library at 66 Portland Place, London. The awards are funded by The Historical

Architecture Research Trust and The Modern Architecture & Town Planning Research Trust.

ROYAL INSTITUTION OF CHARTERED SURVEYORS

Royal Institution of Chartered Surveyors, 12 Great George Street, London, SW1P 3AD, England
Tel: 0171 222 7000
Fax: 0171 222 9430
Email: S6@rics.co.uk
Contact: Research Officer

RICS Education Trust Award

Subjects: The theory and practice of surveying in any of its disciplines (General Practice, Quantity Surveying, Building Surveying, Rural Practice, Planning and Development, Land Surveying and Minerals Surveying).

Eligibility: Open to chartered surveyors and others carrying out research studies in relevant subjects.

Level of Study: Unrestricted.

Type: Award.

No. of awards offered: One.

Value: Normally up to £5,000.

Country of Study: Unrestricted.

Applications Procedure: Application form to be completed.

Closing Date: End February, end September.

THE ROYAL INSTITUTION OF GREAT BRITAIN

The Royal Institution, 21 Albemarle Street, London, W1X 4BS, England
Tel: 0171 409 2992
Fax: 0171 629 3569
Contact: The Director

Dewar Research Fellowship

Subjects: Chemical and physical sciences.

Eligibility: Open to holders of a PhD.

Purpose: To fund independent research related to the chemical and physical sciences.

Type: Fellowship.

No. of awards offered: One.

Frequency: Periodically: as and when advertised.

Value: Approximately £400.

Study Establishment: At the Davy Faraday Research Laboratory of the Royal Institution.

Country of Study: UK.

Closing Date: Infrequently available: date as advertised.

THE ROYAL INSTITUTION OF NAVAL ARCHITECTS

The Royal Institution of Naval Architects, 10 Upper Belgrave Street, London, SW1X 8BQ, England
Tel: 0171 235 4622
Fax: 0171 245 6959

Contact: Education and Training Officer

*Froude Research Scholarship in Naval Architecture

Subjects: Research into hydrodynamic or other problems connected with marine technology.

Eligibility: Open to British subjects and citizens of EEC countries, normally under 30 years of age, who have shown unusual promise in the study of naval architecture and are members of RINA.

No. of awards offered: Usually one as funds permit.

Frequency: Applications considered annually.

Value: As for CASE awards.

Length of Study: Two years; possibly renewable for a third year.

Study Establishment: An approved institution.

Closing Date: July 31st prior to commencement.

*Sir William White Postgraduate Scholarship in Naval Architecture

Subjects: Research into problems connected with the design and construction of ships and their machinery, or a postgraduate course of study relevant to ship technology.

Eligibility: Open to British subjects and citizens of EEC countries, under 30 years of age, who have passed with merit through an approved course of study and have at some time been employed in the industry.

No. of awards offered: Usually one as funds permit.

Frequency: Applications considered annually.

Value: £1,250 per annum plus fees.

Length of Study: One or two years.

Study Establishment: An approved university, college or research establishment.

Closing Date: July 31st prior to commencement.

ROYAL IRISH ACADEMY

Royal Irish Academy, 19 Dawson Street, Dublin, 2, Republic of Ireland
Tel: 353 1 676 2570
Fax: 353 1 676 2346
Contact: Executive Secretary

Senior Visiting Fellowships

Subjects: Scientific research other than in social sciences, dentistry and theoretical and clinical medicine.

Eligibility: Open to senior researchers from OECD countries only.

Level of Study: Postdoctorate, Professional development.

Purpose: To enable a new scientific research technique or development to be introduced into Ireland.

Type: Fellowship.

No. of awards offered: Varies.

Frequency: Annual.

Value: Varies.

Country of Study: Ireland or other OECD countries.

Applications Procedure: Application form to be completed.

Closing Date: December 31st.

Additional Information: The Academy participates in the Royal Society European Science Exchange Programs in pure and applied science, in the British Academy European Exchange Programs in the humanities, in the Austrian, Hungarian, or Polish academy exchange schemes in science and the humanities. Small grants for work in all disciplines are available annually from the Academy's own funds. The Senior Visiting Fellowship Awards are made on behalf of the Irish government.

ROYAL OVER-SEAS LEAGUE

Cultural Affairs Department, Royal Over-Seas League, Over-Seas House, Park Place, St James's Street, London, SW1A 1LR, England
Tel: 0171 408 0214 ext.219
Fax: 0171 499 6738
Contact: Roderick Lakin, Director

Annual Open Exhibition

Subjects: Painting and drawing.

Eligibility: Open to citizens of Commonwealth (including the UK) and former Commonwealth countries, who are up to 35 years of age.

Purpose: To support and promote young Commonwealth artists.

No. of awards offered: Varies.

Frequency: Annual.

Value: 1st Prize: £3,000 and a trophy commissioned from the Royal College of Art; Art Travel Scholarship worth £1,000; further awards totalling over £2,000.

Closing Date: July.

Additional Information: Each artist may be represented by one recent work only, in oil or comparable media, watercolour or mixed media, including drawings. Editioned, multiple and free-standing works will not be accepted. Works must not exceed 152cm in their largest dimension, inclusive of frame.

Music Competition

Subjects: Musical performance, in four solo classes: strings (including harp and guitar), woodwind/brass, keyboard, singers; and an ensemble class, plus major composition award.

Eligibility: Open to citizens of Commonwealth (including the UK) and former Commonwealth countries, who are no more than 28 years of age (instrumentalists) or 30 years of age (singers and composers).

Purpose: To support and promote young Commonwealth musicians.

No. of awards offered: Varies.

Frequency: Annual.

Value: Over £20,000 in prizes, including £3,000 in awards, and a £2,500 award for composers.

Closing Date: February.

ROYAL PHARMACEUTICAL SOCIETY OF GREAT BRITAIN

Royal Pharmaceutical Society of Great Britain, 1 Lambeth High Street, London, SE1 7JN, England
Tel: 0171 735 9141
Fax: 0171 735 7629
Contact: Education Division

Leverhulme Scholarships

Subjects: Pharmaceutical sciences.

Eligibility: Open to candidates who have been awarded the Pharmaceutical Chemists' Qualifying Diploma or a pharmacy degree approved for the purposes of registration in Great Britain by the Council of the Royal Pharmaceutical Society of Great Britain.

Level of Study: Postgraduate, Doctorate.

Purpose: To allow students to take up postgraduate research on a full-time basis. Only in exceptional circumstances might an award be made to a student following a full-time taught postgraduate course.

Type: Scholarship.

No. of awards offered: One.

Frequency: Normally every three years.

Value: Minimum annual value of £6,520 for students attending establishments within the City of London and the Metropolitan Police District; minimum annual value of £5,260 for students attending any other establishment. Payment is made in equal monthly instalments. Tuition fees up to the Home/EC student rate are paid directly to the Scholar's school of pharmacy.

Length of Study: One year; renewable for up to a total of 3 years, subject to satisfactory progress.

Study Establishment: Any UK school of pharmacy or other establishment.

Country of Study: UK.

Applications Procedure: Application form with sections for completion by a) the applicant, b) the proposed supervisor, c) the head of the school of pharmacy (where applicable), d) the applicant's undergraduate tutor. The applicant should append a one-page CV to the form.

Closing Date: March 1st.

Additional Information: Awards can be made to overseas students, but tuition fees can only be paid at home/EC rate. Overseas applicants should consult their prospective supervisor about possible sources of top-up funding.

Redwood Scholarship, Ransom Fellowship, Rammell Studentship, Lewis Edwards Memorial Scholarship, Jacob Bell Memorial Scholarship

Subjects: Pharmaceutical sciences.

Eligibility: Open to candidates who have been awarded the Pharmaceutical Chemists' Qualifying Diploma or a United Kingdom degree in pharmacy approved for the purpose of registration in Great Britain by the Council of the Royal Pharmaceutical Society of Great Britain.

Level of Study: Doctorate.

Purpose: To allow students to take up postgraduate research on a full-time basis.

No. of awards offered: A variable number of Scholarships and Fellowships.

Frequency: Annual.

Value: Minimum annual value of £6,520 for students attending establishments within the City of London and the Metropolitan Police District; minimum annual value of £5,260 for students attending any other establishment. Exact value is dependent on student's age and experience. Payment is made in equal monthly instalments. Awards can be made to overseas (i.e. other than home/EC) students, but tuition fees can only be paid up to the Home/EC student rate and paid directly to the Scholar's school of pharmacy. Overseas applicants should consult their prospective supervisor about sources of top up funding.

Length of Study: For one year; renewable for up to a total of three years, subject to satisfactory progress.

Study Establishment: Any UK school of pharmacy.

Country of Study: UK.

Applications Procedure: Application form with sections for completion by a) the applicant; b) the applicant's proposed supervisor; c) the head of the school of pharmacy; d) the applicant's undergraduate tutor. The applicant should append a one page CV to the form.

Closing Date: March 1st.

Additional Information: Applications for the awards should be made on behalf of the candidate by the head of the school of pharmacy at which the research is to be undertaken. The awardee may not teach or engage in any other form of employment for more than six hours in a week. The awardee should submit a copy of his/her thesis not more than one year after the end of the total period of research funded by the Society.

Victor Reed Scholarships

Subjects: Pharmaceutical sciences.

Eligibility: Open to candidates who have been awarded the Pharmaceutical Chemists' Qualifying Diploma or a degree in pharmacy approved for the purpose of registration in Great Britain by the Council of the Royal Pharmaceutical Society of Great Britain.

Level of Study: Postgraduate, Doctorate.

Purpose: To allow students to take up postgraduate research on a full-time basis.

No. of awards offered: One.

Frequency: Normally every three years.

Value: Minimum annual value of £6,520 for students attending establishments within the City of London and the Metropolitan Police District; minimum annual value of £5,260 for students attending any other establishment. Exact value is dependent on a student's age and experience. Payment is made in equal monthly instalments. Tuition fees up to the Home/EC student rate are paid directly to the Scholar's school of pharmacy. Overseas students should consult their proposed supervisor about possible sources of top-up funding.

Length of Study: One year; renewable for up to a total of 3 years subject to satisfactory progress.

Study Establishment: Any UK school of pharmacy or other establishment.

Country of Study: UK.

Applications Procedure: Application form with sections for completion by a) the applicant, b) the proposed supervisor, c) the head of the school of pharmacy (where applicable), d) the applicant's undergraduate tutor. The applicant should append a one-page CV to the form.

Closing Date: March 1st.

Additional Information: Applications should be submitted on behalf of the candidate by the head of the school of pharmacy, or in the case of some other establishment, by the supervisor, who should be a pharmacist registered in Great Britain. The awardee may not teach or engage in any other form of employment for more than six hours in a week. The awardee should submit a copy of his/her thesis not more than one year after the end of the total period of research funded by the Society.

Royal Pharmaceutical Society/CRISP Scholarships

Subjects: Pharmaceutical sciences.

Eligibility: Open to candidates who have been awarded the Pharmaceutical Chemists' Qualifying Diploma or a United Kingdom degree in pharmacy approval for the purposes of registration in Great Britain by the Council of the Royal Pharmaceutical Society of Great Britain.

Level of Study: Doctorate.

Purpose: To allow students to take up postgraduate research on a full-time basis.

Type: Scholarship.

No. of awards offered: Varies.

Frequency: Annual.

Value: Minimum annual value of £6,520 for students attending establishments within the City of London and the Metropolitan Police District; minimum annual value of £5,260 for students attending any other establishment. The exact value is dependent on the student's age and experience. Payment is made in equal monthly instalments. Tuition fees up to the Home/EC student rate are paid directly to the Scholar's school of pharmacy.

Length of Study: One year; renewable for up to a total of three years, subject to satisfactory progress.

Study Establishment: Any UK school of pharmacy.

Country of Study: UK.

Applications Procedure: Application form with sections for completion by a) the applicant, b) the applicant's proposed supervisor, c) the head of the school of pharmacy, d) the applicant's undergraduate tutor. The applicant should append a one-page CV to the form.

Closing Date: March 1st.

Additional Information: Applications for the awards should be made on behalf of the candidate by the head of the school of pharmacy at which the research is to be undertaken. The awardee may not teach or engage in any other form of employment for more than six hours in a week. The awardee should submit a copy of his/her thesis not more than one year after the end of the total period of research funded by the Society. Each CRISP (Collaborative Research Investment Studentship Programme for Pharmacy) Scholarship is co-sponsored by the Royal Pharmaceutical Society and a pharmaceutical company.

THE ROYAL PHILHARMONIC SOCIETY

10 Stratford Place, London, W1N 9AE, England
Tel: 0171 491 8110
Fax: 0171 493 7463
Contact: General Administrator

Kathleen Ferrier Awards and Decca Prize

Subjects: Singing.

Eligibility: Open to singers of either sex who are British born, or holders of British, Commonwealth or Republic of Ireland passports, are between 21 and 28 years of age on the day of the Finals, and are sponsored by 2 musicians of repute.

Level of Study: Unrestricted.

Purpose: To provide awards for singers.

Type: Prize.

No. of awards offered: Varies.

Frequency: Annual.

Value: Varies; £17,500 in 1996.

Applications Procedure: Application form to be completed and two references are required.

Closing Date: March 1st for selection in April.

Julius Isserlis Scholarship

Subjects: Musical performance (1997 violin and viola).

Eligibility: Open to students of any nationality domiciled in the UK, who are 15-25 years of age.

Level of Study: Unrestricted.

Purpose: To facilitate musical study abroad, starting within sixteen months of the award being made.

Type: Scholarship.

No. of awards offered: One.

Frequency: Biennially (next 1997).

Value: £20,000.

Length of Study: Two years.

Country of Study: Outside the UK.

Applications Procedure: Application form must be completed.

Closing Date: Spring 1997.

Additional Information: Winner must take up residence for period of study in country designated on the application.

Royal Philharmonic Society Composition Prize

Subjects: Musical composition.

Eligibility: Open to past and present registered students of any Conservatoire or university within the UK of any nationality, under the age of 26. Former winners are not eligible.

Purpose: To encourage young composers.

No. of awards offered: One.

Frequency: Annual.

Value: £2,000.

Applications Procedure: Application form must be completed.

Closing Date: As announced, usually in December.

THE ROYAL SCOTTISH ACADEMY

The Royal Scottish Academy, The Mound, Edinburgh, EH2 2EL,
Scotland
Tel: 0131 225 6671
Contact: The Secretary

Annual Student Competition

Subjects: Painting, sculpture, architecture and printmaking.

Eligibility: Candidates should be residents of Scotland. Painting, print-making and sculpture students should be in their penultimate, final or postgraduate years of study at a college of art in Scotland; others, not being students or graduates of such a college, may submit work to the Competition provided they are proposed and seconded by painter or sculptor members of the Academy. Applicants should submit one work. Architecture students should be in their final year and present work normally related to the requirements of the RIBA Part II syllabus.

Level of Study: Postgraduate.

No. of awards offered: Varies.

Frequency: Annual.

Value: Varies: The Macallan Award of £1,000; Royal Scottish Academy Awards £400 for Printmaking, Painting, Sculpture, Architecture; Carnegie Travelling Scholarship of £200;.

Closing Date: February.

Additional Information: The Academy also sponsors an Annual Exhibition of painting (oil, water-colour, pastel, black and white), sculpture, architectural drawings and prints. Various monetary awards are made.

The John Kinross Memorial Fund Student Scholarships

Subjects: Painting, sculpture, printmaking and architecture.

Eligibility: Painting, printmaking and sculpture: open to students in final or postgraduate years of study at one of the Scottish Colleges of Art; Architecture: open to senior students at one of the six Scottish Schools of Architecture presenting work which would normally be related to the requirements of RIBA Part 1 or Part 2 Syllabus. Group work is not acceptable.

Level of Study: Postgraduate.

Purpose: To assist young artists from the established training centres in Scotland, within the disciplines of painting, sculpture and architecture, to spend three months in Italy.

Type: Scholarship.

No. of awards offered: Varies.

Frequency: Annual.

Value: Varies.

Length of Study: Three months.

Study Establishment: Florence (or in that area of Italy) to make drawings etc. to make up a portfolio which is afterwards inspected by the RSA Award Committee, and to acquire a working knowledge of Italian.

Country of Study: Italy.

Closing Date: Late April each year.

THE ROYAL SOCIETY

The Royal Society, 6 Carlton House Terrace, London, SW1Y 5AG,
England

Tel: 0171 839 5561 ext.2579
Fax: 0171 930 2170
Contact: Ms C R Davis

Conference Grants

Subjects: Natural and applied sciences and technology.

Eligibility: Open to non-government scientists of PhD status who are normally resident in the UK. Must be working at a UK institution.

Level of Study: Postdoctorate.

Purpose: To assist with expenses in participating at a conference overseas.

Type: Grant.

No. of awards offered: Varies.

Frequency: Applications considered four times yearly.

Value: Partial cost of travel expenses and subsistence.

Length of Study: Up to seven days, to attend scientific meetings directly related to the recipient's own research.

Country of Study: Any country outside the UK.

Applications Procedure: Application form to be completed.

Closing Date: March 1st, June 1st, October 1st, or December 1st; special closing dates apply in respect to certain major conferences.

For further information contact:
The Royal Society, 6 Carlton House Terrace, London, SW1Y 5AG,
England
Tel: 0171 839 5561 ext.2540
Fax: 0171 930 2170
Contact: Executive Secretary, (Ref: SG)

European Science Exchange Programme

Subjects: Natural sciences, including mathematics, engineering, non-clinical medical research and the scientific research aspects of psychology, archaeology, geography and the history of science.

Eligibility: Fellowships: preference is given to recently qualified post-doctoral applicants but candidates holding a permanent post are eligible. Study visits: applicants should normally be of postdoctoral status and should not have received an award under the Programme in the previous 12 months.

Level of Study: Postdoctorate.

Purpose: To establish closer contacts between laboratories in the UK and other European countries.

Type: Exchange programme.

No. of awards offered: Varies.

Frequency: Fellowships annually; study visits throughout the year.

Value: Fellowships: candidates receive an award in line with that of a young postdoctoral researcher in a UK university. Study visits: candidates receive a subsistence allowance and the cost of an APEX or similar fare.

Length of Study: Preferably twelve months, but periods from 6-24 months will be considered for fellowships (rarely renewable). Study visits are tenable for 10 days to six months.

Country of Study: UK, Austria, Belgium, Bulgaria, the Czech Republic, Denmark, Estonia, Finland, France, Germany, Greece, Hungary, the Republic of Ireland, Italy, Latvia, the Netherlands, Poland, Portugal, the Slovak Republic, Slovenia, Spain, Sweden, Switzerland and Turkey. Applications for visits to Iceland, Greenland and Norway may also be considered.

Closing Date: Fellowships: January 12th. Study visits: no closing date but applications should be made at least three months in advance of the proposed starting date of visit.

For further information contact:
The Royal Society, 6 Carlton House Terrace, London, SW1Y 5AG,
England

Tel: 0171 839 5561 ext.2555
Fax: 0171 925 2620
Contact: The Executive Secretary (Ref: VC)

Exchanges with Albania, Bulgaria, Croatia, Macedonia, Romania and the other Republics of the former Yugoslavia and the former Soviet Union

Subjects: Natural sciences, including mathematics, engineering, non-clinical medical research and the scientific research aspects of psychology, archaeology, geography and the history of science.

Eligibility: Open to UK scientists and those of the countries listed above, of postdoctoral status.

Level of Study: Postdoctorate.

Purpose: To establish closer scientific cooperation between laboratories in the UK and the countries concerned.

Type: Exchange.

No. of awards offered: Varies.

Frequency: Throughout the year.

Value: To cover accommodation and a subsistence allowance (and in some instances, the cost of an APEX or similar fare).

Length of Study: Generally from one week to six months, depending on the scheme.

Country of Study: UK and countries listed above.

Applications Procedure: Applications should be made at least three months before the proposed starting date of the visit.

Henry Head Research Fellowship

Subjects: Neurology: research.

Eligibility: Open to persons of any nationality who are suitably experienced in independent research.

Purpose: To encourage original independent scientific research.

Type: Fellowship.

No. of awards offered: One.

Frequency: As advertised in Nature and other scientific journals; about every five years.

Value: Salary on the university lecturers' scale for academic and academic-related staff.

Length of Study: Up to a maximum of 5 years.

Study Establishment: At approved institutions.

Country of Study: Normally UK.

For further information contact:
The Royal Society, 6 Carlton House Terrace, London, SW1Y 5AG, England
Tel: 0171 451 2547
Fax: 0171 930 2170
Contact: Research Appointments Department

History of Science Grants

Subjects: History of science (including mathematics), medicine and technology.

Eligibility: Applicants must be domiciled in the UK and must be working in association with an eligible institution.

Level of Study: Postdoctorate.

Purpose: To meet specified costs entailed in undertaking a research project in the history of science.

Type: Grant.

No. of awards offered: Varies.

Frequency: Twice yearly.

Value: Varies according to requirements.

Applications Procedure: Application forms are available on request.

Closing Date: November 15th, April 1st.

Additional Information: Grants are not given to meet the costs of publishing results, of a stipend for a principal investigator, of paying staff or for a project undertaken for a higher degree. The History of Science Research Grants are part of the Royal Society's Research grants Scheme.

Mr and Mrs John Jaffé Donation Research Fellowships

Subjects: Practical sciences (e.g. chemistry, physics, medicine) and the application of scientific discoveries to industry: original research.

Eligibility: Open to persons of any nationality who are suitably experienced in independent research. Awards may not be made to Nobel Prize winners.

Purpose: To encourage original, independent scientific research.

Type: Fellowship.

No. of awards offered: One or more.

Frequency: As advertised in Nature and other scientific journals.

Value: Salary on the university lecturers' scale for academic and academic-related staff.

Length of Study: Five years in the first instance; with two possible further renewals for three and then two years.

Study Establishment: Approved institutions.

Country of Study: Normally UK.

For further information contact:
The Royal Society, 6 Carlton House Terrace, London, SW1Y 5AG, England
Tel: 0171 451 2547
Fax: 0171 930 2170
Contact: Research Appointments Department

Japan Programme

Subjects: Natural sciences, including mathematics, engineering, non-clinical medical research and the scientific research aspects of psychology, archaeology, geography, agriculture and the history of science.

Eligibility: Open to British scientists of postdoctoral status.

Purpose: To establish closer contacts between laboratories and universities in the UK and Japan.

Type: Fellowships; study visits.

No. of awards offered: Varies.

Frequency: Fellowships annually. Study visits throughout the year.

Value: Fellowships: return fare, monthly allowance, housing, health insurance and other allowances; study visits: return fare plus a subsistence allowance.

Length of Study: Fellowships: for 6-24 months, depending on programme. Study visits: normally 10 days to three months.

Country of Study: Japan.

Closing Date: Fellowships: September 20th. Study visits: no closing date but applications should be made at least three months in advance of the proposed visit.

Additional Information: Joint Research Projects are also offered - funding is available for projects between British and Japanese groups over a two-year period. Awards cover international travel and some local costs overseas. Deadline for applications: October 7th (annually).

For further information contact:
The Royal Society, 6 Carlton House Terrace, London, SW1Y 5AG, England
Tel: 0171 839 5561 ext.2557
Fax: 0171 925 2620
Contact: Executive Secretary (Ref: VC)

E Alan Johnston Research Fellowship

Subjects: Research in biomedicine.

Eligibility: Open to persons of any nationality. Candidates must have a PhD or equivalent research experience.

Level of Study: Postdoctorate.

Purpose: To encourage original, independent scientific research.

Type: Fellowship.

No. of awards offered: One.

Frequency: As advertised in 'Nature' and other scientific journals.

Value: Salary on the university lecturers' scale for academic and academic-related staff.

Length of Study: Five years in the first instance; with two possible further renewals for three and then two years.

Study Establishment: Approved institutions.

Country of Study: Normally UK.

Latin American Science Exchange Programme

Subjects: Natural and applied sciences and technology.

Eligibility: Open to UK and Latin American scientists of postdoctorate or similar level.

Level of Study: Postdoctorate.

Purpose: To establish closer contacts between laboratories working in the UK and Latin America.

Type: Grants.

No. of awards offered: Varies.

Frequency: Throughout the year.

Value: The sending institution pays the return fare between capitals of its visitors; the receiving side arranges and pays for local accommodation and travel.

Length of Study: For short periods of not less than 3 weeks, usually with the aim of visiting a number of laboratories in the host country (study visits); or for longer periods of not less than 4 months, to carry out research projects (fellowships).

Country of Study: UK and Latin America, particularly Argentina, Brazil, Chile, Mexico and Venezuela, where special arrangements have been agreed upon between the Royal Society and the corresponding organizations for exchange visits. Prospective visitors from these countries should contact these organizations rather than the Royal Society.

Horace Le Marquand and Dudley Bigg Research Fellowship

Subjects: Medical research.

Eligibility: Open to persons of any nationality.

Purpose: To further the application of physiological principles to medicine, or such other research of a biological nature, in relation to the problems of health or disease.

Type: Fellowship.

No. of awards offered: One.

Frequency: As advertised in 'Nature' and other scientific journals.

Value: Salary on the university lecturers' scale for academic and academic-related staff.

Length of Study: Five years in the first instance; with two possible further renewals for three and then two years.

Study Establishment: Approved institutions.

Country of Study: Normally UK.

Leverhulme/Amersham International Trust Senior Research Fellowships

Subjects: Natural sciences including mathematics and engineering.

Eligibility: Open to applicants aged between 35 and 55, who hold a PhD or have equivalent research experience and hold a post in a British university.

Purpose: To enable scientists to be relieved of all teaching and administrative duties to do full-time research for up to one year.

Type: Fellowship.

No. of awards offered: Up to seven.

Value: The Fellow's employing institution will be reimbursed for the full salary costs of a younger academic employed to take over the Fellow's teaching and administrative duties for the period of the Fellowship. Additional grants for travel to conferences or overseas laboratories may also be made.

Length of Study: One academic term to one year.

Country of Study: UK.

Closing Date: Late December.

Additional Information: Employees of Research Councils or those in governmental or other research institutions are not eligible.

Locke Research Fellowship

Subjects: Experimental physiology and pharmacology.

Eligibility: Open to persons of any nationality who are experienced in independent research.

Purpose: To encourage original, independent scientific research.

Type: Fellowship.

No. of awards offered: One.

Frequency: As advertised in Nature and other scientific journals.

Value: Salary on the university lecturers' scale for academic and academic-related staff.

Length of Study: Five years in the first instance; with two possible further renewals for three and then two years.

Study Establishment: Approved institutions.

Country of Study: Normally UK.

For further information contact:
The Royal Society, 6 Carlton House Terrace, London, SW1Y 5AG, England
Tel: 0171 839 5561 ext.301
Fax: 0171 930 2170
Contact: Research Appointments Department

Bruno Mendel Fellowship

Subjects: Experimental medical research or biomedical sciences.

Eligibility: Open to suitably qualified postgraduate candidates who are normally resident in the UK, the Netherlands or Israel.

Level of Study: Postgraduate.

Type: Fellowship.

No. of awards offered: One (dependent on availability of funds).

Frequency: Irregularly. As advertised in Nature and other scientific journals.

Value: Dependent on qualifications and place and duration of visit; normally at the level of a junior research fellowship. Additional allowances for travel and superannuation may be provided as appropriate.

Study Establishment: At universities, medical research centres or medical schools.

Country of Study: Any country, preferably in either The Netherlands or Israel (for applicants from the UK).

Applications Procedure: Candidates are kindly requested to apply only when the award has been publicly advertised.

Closing Date: Normally mid-February every third or fourth year only.

For further information contact:
The Royal Society, 6 Carlton House Terrace, London, SW1Y 5AG, England
Tel: 0171 451 2547
Fax: 0171 930 2170
Contact: Research Appointments Department

Moseley Research Fellowship

Subjects: Research in physics.

Eligibility: Open to persons of any nationality. Candidates must have a PhD or equivalent research experience.

Level of Study: Postdoctorate.

Purpose: To encourage original, independent scientific research.

Type: Fellowship.

No. of awards offered: One.

Frequency: As advertised in Nature and other scientific journals.

Value: Salary on the unversity lecturers' scale for academic and academic-related staff.

Length of Study: Five years in the first instance; with two possible further renewals for three and then two years.

Study Establishment: Approved institutions.

Country of Study: Normally UK.

For further information contact:
The Royal Society, 6 Carlton House Terrace, London, SW1Y 5AG, England
Tel: 0171 451 2547
Fax: 0171 930 2170
Contact: Research Appointments Department

R W Paul Instrument Fund Grants

Subjects: Pure or applied physical science: instrument development.

Eligibility: Open to British subjects or persons domiciled or ordinarily resident in the UK who are working in Great Britain and whose qualifications in physical research are supported by the signed recommendation of one of the following persons: President of the Royal Society (if a physicist) or alternatively, the Secretary of the Royal Society dealing with physical subjects; President of the Institute of Physics; President of the Institution of Electrical Engineers.

Level of Study: Postdoctorate.

Purpose: For the design, construction and maintenance of novel, unusual or much improved types of physical instruments and apparatus for investigations, particularly in cases where a relatively large expenditure may be justified on experimental apparatus.

Type: Grant.

No. of awards offered: Varies.

Frequency: Three times yearly.

Value: Varies.

Country of Study: UK.

Applications Procedure: Application form to be completed.

Closing Date: January 15th, May 15th and, September 15th.

Additional Information: Applications may be submitted by any worker or group of workers of Great Britain. Grants, however, may not be used to relieve expenditure in any establishment controlled by the government, or to relieve any university or other educational establishment of its normal financial obligations.

For further information contact:
The Royal Society, 6 Carlton House Terrace, London, SW1Y 5AG, England
Tel: 0171 839 5561 Ext 2538
Fax: 0171 930 2170
Contact: Executive Secretary, (Ref: JECL/PIF)

Pickering Research Fellowship

Subjects: Chemistry (especially physical and inorganic) or botany.

Eligibility: Open to candidates of PhD or equivalent research experience. There is no restriction on nationality.

Purpose: To encourage original, independent scientific research.

Type: Fellowship.

No. of awards offered: One to three.

Frequency: As advertised in Nature and other scientific journals.

Value: Salary on the university lecturers' scale for academic and academic-related staff.

Length of Study: Five years in the first instance; with two possible further renewals for three and then two years.

Study Establishment: At approved institutions.

Country of Study: Normally UK.

Applications Procedure: Candidates are kindly requested to apply only when these Fellowships are publicly advertised.

For further information contact:
The Royal Society, 6 Carlton House Terrace, London, SW1Y 5AG, England
Tel: 0171 451 2547
Fax: 0171 930 2170
Contact: Research Appointments Department

Postdoctoral Fellowship Programmes with the former Soviet Union and Central/East Europe

Subjects: Natural sciences, including mathematics, engineering, non-clinical medical research and the scientific research aspects of psychology, archaeology, geography and the history of science.

Eligibility: Open to nationals of the countries listed above of postdoctoral status. Candidates must be under 40 years of age at the time of taking up the award.

Level of Study: Postdoctorate.

Purpose: To enable outstanding young scientists from the countries listed above to undertake one year's research in a British laboratory. The schemes are generously supported by NATO, the Foreign and Commonwealth Office, The Wolfson Foundation and other private sources.

Type: Fellowships.

No. of awards offered: Varies.

Frequency: Annual.

Value: Subsistence at £900 per month. Research expenses of £1,500 for the year (and in some instances, the cost of an APEX or similar fare).

Length of Study: 12 months.

Study Establishment: A British laboratory.

Country of Study: UK.

Closing Date: Varies.

Additional Information: A good command of the English language is essential.

For further information contact:
The Royal Society, 6 Carlton House Terrace, London, SW1Y 5AG, England
Tel: 0171 839 5561
Fax: 0171 925 2620
Contact: Executive Secretary (Ref: SGK)

Public Understanding of Science Grants

Subjects: Natural sciences, including mathematics, technology and engineering.

Eligibility: Open to residents of the UK who are able to show clearly how their proposal relates to the stated aim of the award.

Purpose: To encourage new or continuing activities or initiatives directly concerned with the promotion of the public understanding of science.

No. of awards offered: Varies.

Frequency: Twice yearly.

Value: Up to £3,000.

Closing Date: March 31st and September 30th.

For further information contact:
The Royal Society, 6 Carlton House Terrace, London, SW1Y 5AG, England
Tel: 0171 839 5561 ext. 2579
Fax: 0171 930 2170
Contact: Ms C R Davis

Research Grants

Subjects: Any scientific or technological discipline within the remit of the Royal Society, i.e. the natural sciences, including mathematics, engineering science, agricultural and medical research, the scientific aspects of archaeology, geography, experimental psychology and the history of science.

Eligibility: Applicants should normally either be holding or have been appointed to permanent posts in recognized institutions or hold or have been appointed to limited-tenure postdoctoral research posts, obtained in open competition, and held in such establishments. Applications from retired scientists may also be accepted where the individual conducts his/her research in, or directly associated with, an eligible organization. Non-tenured researchers working in association with an eligible institution may apply for support for research in the history of science. No age restriction or preference applies.

Level of Study: Postdoctorate.

Purpose: To meet certain specified costs entailed in undertaking a research project in which the applicant is personally engaged. Such costs are envisaged as normally arising through an applicant initiating or developing specific investigations, entering a promising new or modified field of research, or taking advantage of developments in apparatus offering improved techniques in a promising line of research.

Type: Research Grant.

No. of awards offered: Varies.

Frequency: Twice yearly.

Value: Up to £10,000.

Country of Study: UK, except field research, research at sea, research at a marine biological laboratory or research in the history of science.

Applications Procedure: Application form to be completed.

Closing Date: November 15th, April 1st.

Additional Information: Grants are for one or more specific items of expenditure in a given 12-month period. Provision is intended to complement that provided by the host department/institution where an individual's research capacity can be significantly enhanced by such provision. Grants will be made through host institutions. Academic workers in UK universities, or other institutions of higher education or in certain associated, independent non-governmental, non-commercial research institutions recognized by the Royal Society are eligible.

Rosenheim Research Fellowship

Subjects: Biological chemistry.

Eligibility: Open to persons of any nationality who are suitably experienced in independent research.

Purpose: To encourage original, independent scientific research.

Type: Fellowship.

No. of awards offered: One.

Frequency: As advertised in Nature and other scientific journals.

Value: Salary on the university lecturers' scale for academic and academic-related staff.

Length of Study: Five years in the first instance; with two possible further renewals for three and then two years.

Study Establishment: Approved institutions.

Country of Study: Great Britain.

For further information contact:
The Royal Society, 6 Carlton House Terrace, London, SW1Y 5AG, England
Tel: 0171 451 2547
Fax: 0171 930 2170
Contact: Research Appointments Department

*The Royal Society/Academy of Science and Technology of the Philippines Study Visits and Fellowships

Subjects: Natural science and technology.

Eligibility: Open to UK and Filipino postdoctoral scientists.

Purpose: To promote research collaboration between the UK and the Philippines.

No. of awards offered: Four.

Value: Fellowships: at the expense of the sending side; Study Visits: the sending side pays international fares and the host side pays local costs.

Country of Study: UK and the Philippines.

Applications Procedure: Applications are accepted at any time.

For further information contact:
The Royal Society, 6 Carlton House Terrace, London, SW1Y 5AG, England
Tel: 0171 839 5561 ext.293
Fax: 0171 930 2170
Contact: Executive Secretary (Ref: FGM)

The Royal Society/Academy of Scientific Research and Technology Egyptian Scientific Exchange Programme

Subjects: Natural sciences and technology.

Eligibility: Open to British and Egyptian scientists working in their respective countries who wish to undertake research in a laboratory in the other country. Applicants should normally have several years' postdoctoral experience.

Level of Study: Postdoctorate.

Purpose: To promote Anglo-Egyptian scientific interchange.

Type: Study Visits.

No. of awards offered: Varies.

Value: The Egyptian Academy pays all costs for British visitors and international fares for Egyptian scientists; the Society pays local costs of Egyptian scientists.

Length of Study: Short periods of not less than two weeks.

Study Establishment: Laboratory.

Country of Study: UK and Egypt.

Applications Procedure: While the sending institution usually nominates recipients, the application procedure allows host institutions to take the initiative and request visitors either by name or by field of specialization.

The Royal Society/Indian National Science Academy Study Visits and Fellowships

Subjects: Natural sciences and technology.

Eligibility: Open to British and Indian scientists at the postdoctoral level who wish to pursue research in a laboratory in the other country. Applicants are expected to have several years' experience.

Level of Study: Postdoctorate.

Purpose: To promote scientific collaboration between India and the UK.

Type: Study Visits and Fellowships.

No. of awards offered: Varies.

Value: The annual financial limit is decided each year in advance. The sending side pays international fares and the host side pays local costs. No provision is made for research fees or accompanying dependants.

Study Establishment: Laboratory.

Country of Study: India and the UK.

Applications Procedure: Applications are accepted at any time.

For further information contact:
The Royal Society, 6 Carlton House Terrace, London, SW1Y 5AG, England
Tel: 0171 839 5561 ext.2564
Fax: 0171 930 2170
Contact: Executive Secretary (Ref: FGM)

The Royal Society/Israel Academy of Sciences and Humanities Scientific Exchange Programme

Subjects: Natural sciences, including mathematics, engineering, non-clinical medical research and the scientific research aspects of psychology, archaeology, geography, agriculture and the history of science.

Eligibility: Open to UK postdoctoral scientists.

Level of Study: Postdoctorate.

Purpose: To further relations between research scientists and scientific institutions in the UK and Israel.

Type: Fellowships and Study Visits.

No. of awards offered: Varies.

Frequency: Fellowships annually; Study visits throughout the year.

Value: Fellowships: candidates receive an award in line with that of a young postdoctoral researcher in a UK university. Study visits: candidates receive a subsistence allowance and the cost of an APEX or similar fare.

Length of Study: Fellowships: preferably for 12 months but periods of 6-24 months will be considered. Study visits: from 10 days to 6 months.

Country of Study: Israel.

Closing Date: Fellowships: January 12th. Study visits: no closing date but applications should be made at least three months in advance of the proposed visit.

Additional Information: A separate progamme exists for research professorships. All enquiries should be made to the address cited.

For further information contact:
The Royal Society, 6 Carlton House Terrace, London, SW1Y 5AG, England
Tel: 0171 839 5561 ext.2564
Fax: 0171 930 2170
Contact: Executive Secretary (Ref: FGM)

*The Royal Society/Korea Science and Engineering Foundation Study Visits and Fellowships

Subjects: Natural sciences and technology.

Eligibility: Open to UK and South Korean scientists at the postdoctoral level.

Purpose: To promote scientific collaboration between the UK and South Korea.

No. of awards offered: Six.

Value: The sending institution pays the return fare between capitals of its visitors; the receiving side arranges and pays for local accommodation and travel.

Country of Study: UK and South Korea.

Applications Procedure: Applications are accepted at any time.

Additional Information: Visits in connection with joint research projects are especially favoured.

For further information contact:
The Royal Society, 6 Carlton House Terrace, London, SW1Y 5AG, England
Tel: 0171 839 5561 ext.293
Fax: 0171 930 2170
Contact: Executive Secretary (Ref: FGM)

The Royal Society/The Pakistan Science Foundation Study Visits and Fellowships

Subjects: Natural sciences and technology.

Eligibility: Open to UK and Pakistani scientists at the postdoctoral level.

Level of Study: Postdoctorate.

Purpose: To promote scientific collaboration between the UK and Pakistan.

Type: Study Visits and Fellowships.

No. of awards offered: Four persons per month.

Frequency: Annual.

Value: Fellowships: at the expense of the sending side; Study Visits: the sending side pays international travel fares and the host side pays local costs.

Country of Study: UK and Pakistan.

For further information contact:
The Royal Society, 6 Carlton House Terrace, London, SW1Y 5AG, England
Tel: 0171 839 5561 ext.2564
Fax: 0171 930 2170
Contact: Executive Secretary (Ref: FGM)

Rutherford Scholarship

Subjects: Experimental research in any branch of the natural sciences, with preference to experimental physics.

Eligibility: Open to UK or Commonwealth university graduates who are under 26 years of age on May 1st in the year of application and have not previously held a senior research award.

Type: Scholarships.

No. of awards offered: Normally two.

Frequency: Biennially (dependent on availability of funds).

Value: £7,050 per annum if held in the UK, plus travel allowance, university fees, etc.

Length of Study: Three years.

Country of Study: Some part of the Commonwealth other than that in which the candidate graduated.

Closing Date: Mid-February.

Stothert Research Fellowship

Subjects: Medicine, including the sciences on which medical knowledge is based, particularly with a view to increasing knowledge useful to the investigation or treatment of disease and relief of suffering in human beings and animals.

Eligibility: Open to UK citizens who are suitably experienced in independent research.

Type: Fellowship.

No. of awards offered: One.

Frequency: As advertised in 'Nature' and other scientific journals; approximately every four years.

Value: Varies.

Length of Study: Three years; renewable for a further two years.

Study Establishment: Approved institutions.

Country of Study: Normally UK.

Study Visits and Fellowships to Australia and New Zealand

Subjects: Natural sciences, including engineering, mathematics, non-clinical medical research and the scientific research aspects of psychology, archaeology, geography and the history of science.

Eligibility: Open to scientists of postdoctoral status from the UK.

Level of Study: Postdoctorate.

Purpose: To promote collaboration between scientists in the UK and in Australia and New Zealand.

Type: Fellowships and Study Visits.

No. of awards offered: Varies.

Frequency: Fellowships annually. Study visits throughout the year.

Value: Awards cover a subsistence allowance and the cost of an APEX or similar fare.

Length of Study: Fellowships: for 6-12 months. Study Visits: for two weeks to six months.

Country of Study: Australia and New Zealand.

Closing Date: Fellowships: May 17th. Study visits: no closing date but applications should be made at least three months prior to the date of departure.

For further information contact:
The Royal Society, 6 Carlton House Terrace, London, SW1Y 5AG, England
Tel: 0171 839 5561 ext.2564
Fax: 0171 930 2170
Contact: Executive Secretary (Ref: FGM)

Study Visits to Canada

Subjects: Natural sciences, including engineering, mathematics, non-clinical medical research and the scientific research aspects of psychology, archaeology and geography.

Eligibility: Open to UK postdoctoral scientists.

Level of Study: Postdoctorate.

Purpose: To promote scientific collaboration between the UK and Canada.

Type: Study Visits.

No. of awards offered: Varies.

Frequency: Throughout the year.

Value: Return air fare and subsistence.

Length of Study: From three weeks to six months.

Country of Study: Canada.

Closing Date: Applications should be made at least three months in advance of the proposed starting date of the visit.

For further information contact:
The Royal Society, 6 Carlton House Terrace, London, SW1Y 5AG, England
Tel: 0171 839 5561 ext.305
Fax: 0171 930 2170
Contact: Executive Secretary (Ref: LM)

University Research Fellowships

Subjects: Science (including agriculture, medicine, mathematics, engineering and technology).

Eligibility: Open to outstanding young scientists between 26 and 40 years of age (or older in exceptional circumstances) of PhD status with between two to seven years postdoctoral experience. Persons holding tenured posts in UK universities will not normally be considered. Candidates must be European Union citizens who are either employed in or who have been resident in the UK for a continuous period of three years other than for the sole purpose of receiving full-time education.

Level of Study: Postdoctorate.

Purpose: To provide support for young, high-quality research workers to work in university departments, possibly leading to a permanent post.

Type: Fellowship.

No. of awards offered: Varies.

Frequency: Annual.

Value: Salaries on the university lecturers' A/B scale for non-clinical academic and related staff.

Length of Study: Five years in the first instance; with two possible further renewals for three and then two years.

Study Establishment: Appropriate departments of universities.

Country of Study: UK.

Closing Date: Late January.

Warren Research Fellowships

Subjects: Metallurgy, engineering, physics, sometimes with close industrial contact.

Eligibility: Candidates must be British citizens or citizens of independent Commonwealth countries and have a PhD or equivalent research experience.

Level of Study: Doctorate.

Purpose: To encourage original, independent scientific research.

Type: Fellowship.

Frequency: As advertised in Nature and other scientific journals.

Value: To be decided according to age and experience, at a point on the national university scale for non-clinical staff.

Length of Study: Five years; possibly renewable for one further year.

Study Establishment: Any university department, industrial research laboratory or research institution.

Country of Study: UK.

Applications Procedure: Please write for details.

For further information contact:
The Royal Society, 6 Carlton House Terrace, London, SW1Y 5AG, England
Tel: 0171 451 2547
Fax: 0171 930 2170
Contact: Research Appointments Department

ROYAL SOCIETY FOR THE ENCOURAGEMENT OF ARTS, MANUFACTURE AND COMMERCE (RSA)

RSA, 8 John Adam Street, London, WC2N 6EZ, England
Tel: 0171 930 5115
Fax: 0171 839 5805
Email: RSA@RSA.FTECH.CO.UK
www: http://www.cs.mdx.ac.uk/rsa/

RSA Art for Architecture

Subjects: Art and architecture.

Eligibility: Open to visual artists who are to be employed at the earliest stage of a building project as part of the design team. This award is open to British citizens only.

Purpose: To promote collaboration between visual artists and architects and other design professionals at the early stage of a building project or development.

Type: Varies.

Frequency: Approximately four times a year.

Value: £2,000-£15,000. Awards are in the form of payment towards the consultancy fees of artists appointed.

Applications Procedure: Application form needs to be completed. Other documentation such as slides, plans, letters of support should be submitted with all applications.

RSA Student Design Awards

Subjects: Design.

Eligibility: Open to students who have studied for at least one term at a recognized college of design within the UK, and some in other EC countries.

Level of Study: Postgraduate, Undergraduate.

Purpose: Annual competition offering winning students the opportunity to undertake research or study abroad, or to undertake periods of attachment in industry.

No. of awards offered: Varies.

Frequency: Annual.

Value: £250 to £4,250.

Study Establishment: At an appropriate institution or in industry.

Country of Study: Travel awards may be used to fund study tours abroad.

Applications Procedure: Project briefs and details for application are published each year in the 'SDA Projects Book' available from September.

Closing Date: November.

Additional Information: The Student Design Awards Scheme is not a grant giving body, but an annual competition open to design students. The majority of periods of attachment are with companies in the UK but some are with companies abroad.

ROYAL SOCIETY OF CANADA

Royal Society of Canada, 225 Metcalfe Street , Suite 308, Ottawa, Ontario, K2P 1P9, Canada
Tel: 613 991 6990
Fax: 613 991 6996

Fellowships

Subjects: Related to the natural and social environment.

Eligibility: Open to citizens of NATO countries who have demonstrated research interest and/or experience in a subject area related to one of the on-going CCMS pilot studies, and willingness to work under the guidance of the respective pilot study Director. Candidates must have a suitable background which is acceptable to the pilot study Director; connection with a research unit or government agency having an active interest in the subject with a view to ensuring the useful application of the experience gained to the needs of the home country; and a good working knowledge of the language of the CCMS pilot study Director with whom the Fellow will be working, or English or French, if either of them is sufficient and mutually convenient.

Purpose: To allow Fellows to contribute to the work of CCMS pilot studies. The purpose of these studies is to suggest, on the basis of existing knowledge, solutions to problems relating to the natural and social environment. To achieve this objective, the Programme provides support to Fellows who wish to conduct research under the guidance of pilot study Directors and/or to work as members of the CCMS pilot study teams.

Type: Fellowship.

No. of awards offered: Varies.

Frequency: Annual.

Applications Procedure: Application forms and a list of pilot studies are available on request. Consultation with the pilot study Director prior to the preparation of the application is recommended.

Closing Date: February 28th.

For further information contact:
Royal Society of Canada, 225 Metcalfe Street, Suite 308, Ottawa, Ontario, K2P 1P9, Canada
Tel: 613 991 6990
Fax: 613 991 6996
Email: lvachon@rsc.ca
Contact: Dr Howard Alper, CCMS Program Chair

Sir Arthur Sims Scholarship

Subjects: Humanities, social sciences or natural sciences.

Eligibility: Open to graduates of Canadian universities who have completed one year of postgraduate study at a British institution and display outstanding merit and promise in their field of study.

Level of Study: Postgraduate.

Purpose: To encourage Canadian students to undertake postgraduate work in Great Britain.

Type: Scholarship.

No. of awards offered: One.

Frequency: Dependent on funds available.

Value: £700 per annum.

Length of Study: Two years.

Study Establishment: Approved institutions.

Country of Study: UK.

Closing Date: February 15th (odd-numbered years).

For further information contact:
Royal Society of Canada, 225 Metcalfe Street, Suite 308, Ottawa, Ontario, K2P 1P9, Canada
Tel: 613 991 6990
Fax: 613 991 6996
Email: lvachon@rsc.ca
Contact: Linda Vachon, Awards Coordinator

THE ROYAL SOCIETY OF CHEMISTRY

The Royal Society of Chemistry, Burlington House , Piccadilly, London, WIV OBN, England
Tel: 0171 437 8656
Fax: 0171 734 1227
Email: RAFFA@RSC.ORG
www: http://chemistry.rsc.org/rsc/
Contact: Mr S S Langer

Corday-Morgan Memorial Fund

Subjects: Chemistry.

Eligibility: Open to citizens of, and domiciled in, any Commonwealth country.

Level of Study: Professional development.

Purpose: To assist members of any established Chemical Society/Institute in the Commonwealth to visit chemical establishments in another Commonwealth country. The visits must be clearly of benefit to the country concerned.

Type: Grant.

No. of awards offered: Approximately ten per year.

Frequency: Throughout the year.

Value: Up to £500. The grants will complement, where appropriate, those for visits to developing countries available from the International Committee's fund, and funding would cover the additional travel costs involved, together with appropriate subsistence.

Applications Procedure: Applications should be submitted on the official form and will normally be considered within one month of receipt.

Additional Information: Applicants must be travelling to another country (not necessarily in the Commonwealth) and would normally stop en route to visit a third country which must be in the Commonwealth.

Hickenbottom/Briggs Fellowship

Eligibility: Domiciled in the UK or Republic of Ireland.

Level of Study: Postdoctorate.

Purpose: Research in organic chemistry.

Type: Fellowship.

No. of awards offered: One.

Frequency: Annual.

Value: Approximately £10,000.

Length of Study: Two years.

Study Establishment: British university or college.

Country of Study: UK or Republic of Ireland.

Applications Procedure: Nomination/application form.

Closing Date: April 1st.

J W T Jones Travelling Fellowship

Subjects: Chemistry.

Eligibility: Open to members of the Royal Society of Chemistry who hold at least a Masters or PhD degree in chemistry or a related subject and are already actively engaged in research. Candidates must produce evidence that the theoretical and practical knowledge or training to be acquired in the foreign laboratory will be beneficial to their scientific development and must also return to their country of origin upon termination of the Fellowship.

Level of Study: Professional development.

Purpose: To promote international cooperation in chemistry; to enable chemists to carry out short-term studies in well-established scientific centres abroad and to learn and use techniques not accessible to them in their own country.

Type: Fellowship.

No. of awards offered: Three to five per year.

Frequency: Annual.

Value: A lump sum of up to £5,000, designed to cover part or all of an economy class air/rail ticket and a subsistence allowance. It is expected that the institute of origin and/or the host institution will contribute to defray any remaining expenses incurred by the Fellowship holder.

Applications Procedure: Application forms, together with full details, may be obtained from the International Affairs Officer.

Closing Date: September 12th.

Additional Information: Fellowships will not be awarded to attend scientific meetings. Applications will be considered by a Fellowship Committee and the holder will be required to submit a formal report on the work accomplished.

Research Fund

Subjects: Chemistry research and chemical education.

Eligibility: Open to members of the Society.

Level of Study: Professional development.

Type: Grant.

No. of awards offered: 30-40.

Frequency: Annual.

Value: Up to £1,000 for the purchase of chemicals, equipment or for running expenses of research.

Length of Study: One year.

Country of Study: Worldwide.

Closing Date: November 1st.

Additional Information: Funds are limited, so preference will be given to those working in less well-endowed institutions. Council is especially anxious to see inventive applications of a 'pump priming' nature. Members in developing countries should note particularly that additional funds have been made available by the Society's International Committee, to provide grants for successful applicants from such countries. Preference will be given to those able to cite collaborative research projects with UK institutions.

Visits to Developing Countries

Subjects: Chemistry.

Eligibility: Open to members of the Royal Society of Chemistry, who hold at least a masters or PhD degree in chemistry or a related subject and are already actively engaged in research. Candidates must produce evidence that the theoretical and practical knowledge or training to be acquired in the foreign laboratory will be beneficial to their scientific development and must also return to their country of origin upon termination of the Fellowship.

Level of Study: Professional development.

Purpose: To promote international cooperation in chemistry; specifically, to enable chemists to carry out short-term studies in well-established scientific centres abroad and to learn and use techniques not accessible to them in their own country.

Value: A lump sum to a maximum value of £5,000, designed to cover part or all of an economy class air/rail ticket and a subsistence allowance. It is expected that the institute of origin and/or the host institution will contribute to defray any remaining expenses incurred by the Fellowship holder.

Applications Procedure: Applications should be submitted on the official form and will normally be considered within one month of receipt.

Closing Date: None.

THE ROYAL SOCIETY OF EDINBURGH

The Royal Society of Edinburgh, 22-24 George Street, Edinburgh, EH2 2PQ, Scotland
Tel: 0131 225 6057
Fax: 0131 220 6889
Contact: The Research Fellowships Secretary

BP Research Fellowships

Subjects: Mechanical engineering, chemical engineering, control engineering, solid state sciences, information technology, chemistry (non-biological) and geological sciences.

Eligibility: Open to persons of all nationalities who have a PhD or equivalent qualification. Applicants should normally be aged under 35 on the date of appointment (October 1st) and must show they have a capacity for innovative research and have a substantial volume of published work relevant to their proposed field of study.

Purpose: For independent research in specific fields.

Type: Fellowships.

No. of awards offered: Two.

Frequency: Annual.

Value: Salaries within the scales RGIA-2 for research and analogous staff in Higher Education Institutions (£16,986-£26,430 in 1995) with annual increments and superannuation benefits. Financial support towards expenses involved in carrying out the research is available, including a start-up grant of £1,000 in the first year only and a further allowance of up to £1,500 for travel and subsistence each year. Fellows are also eligible to bid annually for equipment and consumables, usually up to a value of £2,500, from a research support pool.

Length of Study: Up to three years.

Study Establishment: Any Higher Education Institution in Scotland approved for the purpose by the Council of the Society.

Country of Study: Scotland.

Applications Procedure: Application forms are available from the Research Fellowships Secretary. Candidates must negotiate directly with the relevant Head of Department of the proposed host institution.

Closing Date: Mid-March.

Additional Information: The Fellowships are offered with the support of British Petroleum (BP). Fellows will be expected to devote their full time to research and will not be allowed to hold other paid appointments without the express permission of the Council of the RSE.

CRF European Visiting Research Fellowships

Subjects: Within one of the following arts and letters subjects: archaeology, art and architecture, economics and economic history, geography, history, jurisprudence, linguistics, literature and philology, philosophy, religious studies.

Eligibility: Applicants must be aged 60 or under on date of appointment, which is variable but must be within sixteen months of date of award. Applicants from continental Europe must be nominated by members of staff from a Scottish Higher Education Institution.

Purpose: To create a two-way flow of visiting scholars in arts and letters between Scotland and continental Europe.

No. of awards offered: Up to six Fellowships in each direction.

Frequency: Annual.

Value: Up to £5,000 for visits of six months (reduced pro-rata for shorter visits) to cover actual costs of travel, subsistence and relevant study costs.

Length of Study: Up to six months.

Study Establishment: A Scottish Higher Education Institution or a recognized centre of higher education in a continental European country.

Country of Study: Scotland and any continental European country.

Closing Date: November.

Additional Information: Successful applicants will be required to submit a report within two months of the end of the visit.

CRF Personal Research Fellowships

Subjects: Biological, biochemical, physical and clinical sciences.

Eligibility: Open to students of all nationalities, who have a PhD and are aged 32 or under on the date of appointment.

Purpose: To aid independent research in the biomedical sciences.

Type: Fellowship.

No. of awards offered: Two.

Frequency: Annual.

Value: Salary according to age, qualifications and experience. Salaries within the scales RGIA-2 for research staff in Higher Education Institutions (£15,986-£24,132). Financial support towards expenses involved in carrying out the research is available, including a start-up grant of £1,000 in the first year only. Fellows receive £1,500 for travel and subsistence each year and are also eligible to make bids annually for equipment and consumables, usually up to a value of £5,000, from a research support pool.

Length of Study: Up to three years.

Study Establishment: Any Higher Education Institution in Scotland.

Country of Study: Scotland.

Applications Procedure: Application forms are available from the Research Fellowships Secretary. Candidates must negotiate directly with the relevant Head of Department of the proposed host institution.

Closing Date: Mid-March.

Additional Information: The Fellowships are offered with the support of the Caledonian Research Foundation (CRF). Fellows will be expected to devote their full time to research and will not be allowed to hold other paid appointments without the express permission of the Council of the RSE.

CRF Support Research Fellowship

Subjects: Biology, biochemical, physical and clinical sciences related to medicine.

Eligibility: Open to existing members of academic staff (aged 40 or under on date of appointment and employed on the lecturer scale) who have held a permanent appointment for at least five years in any Scottish Higher Education Institution.

Purpose: To enable support fellows to take study leave, either in their own institution or elsewhere, whilst remaining in continuous employment with their present employer.

Type: Fellowship.

No. of awards offered: One.

Frequency: Annual.

Value: The actual cost for non-clinical staff will be reimbursed according to the lecturer 'A' scale (maximum RGI-4) with the placement determined by the employer. If clinically qualified, salary will be within clinical senior lecturer grade. Provision of £1,000 is made for a start-up grant. Also a grant of £1,500 for travel and subsistence. Fellows are also eligible to make a bid for equipment and consumables, usually up to a value of £2,000, from a research support pool.

Length of Study: One year.

Study Establishment: Any Higher Education Institution in Scotland.

Country of Study: Scotland.

Closing Date: Mid-March.

Henry Dryerre Scholarship

Subjects: Medical or veterinary physiology.

Eligibility: Open to EC citizens holding a first class honours degree from a Scottish university.

Purpose: To support postgraduate research.

Type: Scholarship.

No. of awards offered: One.

Frequency: Every four years.

Value: Covers the cost of fees; provides for research costs and travel expenses up to £750 per year and a maintenance grant of £5,800 (1995/96) if living away from home.

Length of Study: Three years full-time research.

Study Establishment: A Scottish institution.

Country of Study: Scotland.

Applications Procedure: Applicants must be nominated by a professor, reader or lecturer in a Scottish university.

Closing Date: March 15th.

Additional Information: The Scholarships are administered by the Carnegie Trust.

For further information contact:
Carnegie Trust for the Universities of Scotland, Cameron House, Abbey Park Place, Dunfermline, Fife, KY12 7PZ, Scotland
Tel: 01383 622148
Fax: 01383 622149
Contact: Professor J T Coppock

John Moyes Lessells Scholarships

Subjects: Engineering: mechanical, electrical, civil and chemical (in that order of preference).

Eligibility: Applicants must be graduates of a Scottish Higher Education Institution.

Purpose: To enable well-qualified engineers to study some aspect of their profession overseas.

No. of awards offered: Varies.

Frequency: Annual.

Value: Normally up to a maximum of £7,500 per annum. Additional research or travel expenditure may be sanctioned.

Length of Study: Initially for 12 months, but shorter periods or extension for a second year may be considered. Acceptance of a Scholarship implies a willingness to spend at least two years in the UK following the period of tenure.

Country of Study: Outside the UK.

Applications Procedure: Application forms are provided by the Society.

Closing Date: January 31st.

Auber Bequest

Subjects: Any subject.

Eligibility: Open to naturalized British citizens or individuals wishing to acquire British nationality who are over 60 years of age, resident in Scotland or England and are bona fide scholars engaged in academic (but not industrial) research.

Purpose: To provide assistance in academic reseach.

No. of awards offered: Varies.

Frequency: Biennially.

Value: Varies; not normally exceeding £3,000.

Country of Study: Scotland or England.

Applications Procedure: Application forms are available from the Society and may be submitted at any time. Consideration of applications is made quarterly.

Closing Date: Mid-January.

Additional Information: Applicants should not at birth have been British nationals nor held dual British nationality.

SOED Personal Research Fellowships

Subjects: All subjects. A proportion of the Fellowships are awarded in fields likely to enhance the development of industry and encourage better uses of resources in Scotland.

Eligibility: Open to persons of all nationalities who have a PhD or equivalent qualification. Candidates must be aged 32 or under on the date of appointment (October 1st) and must show they have a capacity for innovative research and have a substantial volume of published work relevant to their proposed field of study.

Level of Study: Doctorate.

Purpose: To encourage independent research in any discipline.

Type: Fellowship.

No. of awards offered: Normally two.

Frequency: Annual.

Value: Annual stipends are within the scales RGIA-2 for reseach and analogous staff in Higher Education Institutions (£15,986-£24,132 as at April 1st 1995) with annual increments and superannuation benefits. Expenses to a maximum of £2,500 in year one; £1,000 in years two and three, for travel and attendance at meetings or incidentals may be reimbursed. No support payments are available to the institution but Fellows may seek support for their research from other sources.

Length of Study: Up to three years full-time research.

Study Establishment: Any Higher Education Institution, research institution or industrial laboratory approved for the purpose by the Council of the Society.

Country of Study: Scotland.

Applications Procedure: Candidates should negotiate directly with the proposed host institution. The Fellowships are offered with the support of the Scottish Office Education Department (SOED).

Closing Date: Mid-March.

Additional Information: Fellows may not hold other paid appointments without the express permission of the Council, but teaching or seminar work appropriate to their special knowledge may be acceptable.

SOED Support Research Fellowships

Subjects: All subjects. A proportion of the Fellowships are awarded in fields of research likely to enhance the development of industry and encourage better use of resources in Scotland.

Eligibility: Candidates must be existing members of staff who have held a permanent appointment for not less than five years in any Higher Education Institution in Scotland. Applicants should normally be aged under 40 on the date of appointment (October 1st) and employed on the lecturer (or equivalent) grade.

Purpose: To enable support fellows to take study leave, either in their own institution or elsewhere, whilst remaining in continuous employment with their present employer.

Type: Fellowship.

No. of awards offered: Two.

Frequency: Annual.

Value: The actual cost of replacement staff will be reimbursed according to the Lecturer A scale (maximum RGI-3) with the placement determined by the employer. Superannuation costs and employer's NI contributions will also be reimbursed.

Length of Study: Up to 12 months full-time research.

Study Establishment: Any Higher Education Institution, research institution or industrial laboratory in Scotland approved for the purpose by the Council of the Society.

Country of Study: Scotland.

Applications Procedure: Application forms are available from the Research Fellowships Secretary. Candidates should negotiate directly with the proposed host institution. The Fellowships are offered with the support of the Scottish Office Education Department (SOED).

Closing Date: Mid-March.

Additional Information: Awards will take the form of funding for the appointment of a temporary replacement to enable fellows to take study leave. There is provision for reimbursement of approved expenses for support fellows to a maximum of £500 per annum, in respect of actual expenses associated with the research, including travel and attendance at meetings.

THE ROYAL SOCIETY OF MEDICINE

Royal Society of Medicine, 1 Wimpole Street, London, W1M 8AE, England
Tel: 0171 290 2985
Fax: 0171 290 2989
Contact: Section Administrator

John of Arderne Medal

Subjects: Coloproctology.

Level of Study: Professional development.

Purpose: To award the presenter of the best paper presented at the short papers meeting of the section of Coloproctology. Applicants have to submit an abstract for presentation at the meeting.

Type: Medal and travelling fellowship to the overseas meeting.

No. of awards offered: One.

Frequency: Annual.

Colyer Prize

Subjects: Odontology.

Eligibility: Open to dental surgeons educated at a UK dental school who have not been qualified more than 10 years: awarded for the best original work in dental science completed during the previous five years.

Type: Research Prize.

No. of awards offered: One.

Frequency: Triennially.

Value: Varies; at least £100.

Country of Study: UK.

Applications Procedure: Candidates should submit a general brief account of their research of not more than 800 words.

Closing Date: March 31st.

Dowling Endowment

Subjects: Dermatology.

Eligibility: Open to British dermatologists.

Purpose: To further study.

Type: Travel Grant.

No. of awards offered: One.

Frequency: Dependent on funds available.

Value: Varies.

Country of Study: UK or abroad.

Norman Gamble Fund and Research Prize

Subjects: Otology.

Eligibility: Open to British nationals.

Level of Study: Unrestricted.

Purpose: To support specific research projects in otology.

No. of awards offered: One.

Frequency: Every four years.

Value: £300 for research prize; £1,000 for grant-in-aid.

Closing Date: May 31st.

Medical Insurance Agency Prize

Subjects: Surgery.

Eligibility: Open to surgeons in training, holding the post of up to the grade of registrar or senior registrar.

Level of Study: Professional development.

Purpose: To enable the recipient to travel to a recognized institution (in the UK or overseas) to further his or her knowledge of surgery, or to attend an overseas conference in the speciality.

No. of awards offered: One.

Frequency: Annual.

Study Establishment: A recognized institution in the UK or overseas.

Country of Study: Unrestricted.

Additional Information: The winner will be required to submit a brief report on the visit, within three months of his or her return.

Mental Health Foundation Essay Prize

Subjects: Psychiatry.

Eligibility: Open to candidates practising medicine in the UK or the Republic of Ireland who are in training at any grade from senior house officer to senior registrar or equivalent.

Type: Essay Prize.

No. of awards offered: One.

Frequency: Annual.

Value: Varies: £500, but depends on available finance. Also, subscription to RSM (if funds available).

Country of Study: UK.

Applications Procedure: Applicants need not be members of RSM. The prize is awarded for an essay on psychiatry, submitted to the RSM Section of Psychiatry (in triplicate).

Closing Date: March 1st.

Additional Information: The subject is left to the candidate. Essays should be approximately 5,000 words in length.

MSc Bursaries

Subjects: Primary health care, general practice.

Eligibility: Open to UK general practitioners who are undertaking MSc courses.

Level of Study: Postgraduate.

Purpose: To assist GPs undertaking MSc courses related to general practice or primary health care.

Type: Bursary.

No. of awards offered: Six.

Frequency: Annual.

Value: £500.

Country of Study: UK.

Applications Procedure: Application form must be completed and submitted with project statement.

Closing Date: August 30th.

Nichols Fellowship

Subjects: Obstetrics and gynaecology.

Eligibility: Open to suitably qualified UK citizens.

Purpose: To encourage research.

Type: Fellowship.

No. of awards offered: One.

Frequency: Triennially (1999).

Value: £500.

Length of Study: Two years.

Country of Study: UK or abroad.

Closing Date: May 31st.

Ophthalmology Travelling Fellowship

Subjects: Ophthalmology.

Eligibility: Open to ophthalmologists in the British Isles of any nationality who have not attained an official consultant appointment, nor undertaken professional clinical work or equivalent responsibility for any substantial period before or during the execution of original work.

Type: Fellowship.

No. of awards offered: Varies.

Frequency: Twice yearly.

Value: Varies.

Country of Study: Unrestricted.

Closing Date: Entries are evaluated in December and May.

President's Prize

Subjects: Neurology.

Level of Study: Professional development.

Purpose: Summaries of cases for clinical presentation.

Type: Prize.

No. of awards offered: One.

Frequency: Annual.

Closing Date: April.

Karl Storz Travelling Scholarship

Subjects: Laryngology/rhinology.

Eligibility: Open to senior registrars or consultants of not more than two years standing.

Purpose: To assist with the cost of travel to overseas centres.

Type: Scholarship.

No. of awards offered: One.

Frequency: Annual.

Value: £1,000.

Country of Study: Unrestricted.

Applications Procedure: The Scholarship is awarded for a paper to be submitted to the RSM Section of Laryngology and Rhinology (in triplicate).

Closing Date: January 31st.

Additional Information: A report is required of the recipient within three months of his/her return to the UK.

Norman Tanner Medal and Prize

Subjects: Surgery.

Level of Study: Professional development.

Purpose: To enable the recipient to travel to a recognized institution (in the UK or overseas) to further his or her knowledge of surgery, or to attend an overseas conference in the speciality.

Type: Medal and travel.

No. of awards offered: One.

Frequency: Annual.

Applications Procedure: Papers must be presented at a meeting.

Travelling Fellowship

Subjects: Urology.

Level of Study: Professional development.

Purpose: To enable the holder to enhance his or her knowledge and experience by visiting an overseas unit.

Type: Travelling fellowship.

No. of awards offered: Varies.

Frequency: Annual.

Value: £1,000.

ROYAL TOWN PLANNING INSTITUTE

Royal Town Planning Institute, 26 Portland Place, London, W1N 4BE, England
Tel: 0171 636 9107
Fax: 0171 323 1582
Contact: Judy Woollett

George Pepler International Award

Subjects: Town and country planning, or some particular aspect of planning theory and practice.

Eligibility: Open to persons under 30 years of age of any nationality.

Level of Study: Professional development.

Purpose: To enable young people of any nationality to visit another country for a short period to study the theory and practice of town and country planning.

No. of awards offered: One.

Frequency: Annual.

Value: Up to £750.

Length of Study: Short-term travel outside the UK (for UK residents) or for visits to the UK (for applicants from abroad).

Country of Study: Unrestricted.

Applications Procedure: Applicants are required to submit a statement showing the nature of the study visit proposed, together with an itinerary. Application forms are available from the RTPI.

Closing Date: March 31st.

Additional Information: At the conclusion of the visit the recipient must submit a report. Application forms are available on request.

RP FOUNDATION FIGHTING BLINDNESS

RP Foundation Fighting Blindness, 1401 Mount Royal Avenue, 4th Floor, Baltimore, MD, 21217-4245, USA
Tel: 410 225 9400
Fax: 410 225 3936
Contact: Jeanette S Felix PhD, Director of Science

*Research Career Development Awards

Subjects: The field of hereditary retinal degenerations: retinitis pigmentosa, macular degeneration, Usher's syndrome, etc.

Eligibility: Open to recent MDs who have completed their residency, have an interest in clinical retinal disease and can provide evidence of research potential.

Purpose: To support the training of young research clinicians.

No. of awards offered: One to four.

Frequency: Annual.

Value: Usually US$30,000-US$40,000 per annum to include salary and limited travel.

Length of Study: One year; renewable.

Study Establishment: RP Research Centers.

Country of Study: USA (occasionally elsewhere).

Closing Date: Usually April 1st.

RUSSELL SAGE FOUNDATION

Russell Sage Foundation, 112 East 64th Street, New York, NY, 10021, USA
Tel: 212 750 6012
Fax: 212 371 4761
Email: info@rsage.org
www: http://epn.org/sage.html
Contact: Ms Madeline Spitaleri

Visiting Fellowships

Subjects: Social sciences.

Eligibility: Open to scholars in the social sciences. The Foundation particularly welcomes groups of visiting scholars who wish to collaborate on a specific project during their residence at the Foundation; in order to develop these projects fully, support is sometimes provided for working groups prior to their arrival at the Foundation. Awards are not made for the support of undergraduate or graduate degree work, nor for institutional support.

Type: Fellowship.

No. of awards offered: 15 visiting scholar appointments.

Frequency: Annual.

Value: Varies.

Length of Study: One academic year.

Study Establishment: The Foundation in New York City.

Country of Study: USA/International.

Applications Procedure: 4-5 page project description, plus CV.

Closing Date: November 15th prior to the year of residence.

Additional Information: Awardees are expected to offer the Foundation the right to publish any book-length manuscripts resulting from Foundation support.

SAINT ANDREW'S SOCIETY OF THE STATE OF NEW YORK

The Royal Bank of Scotland plc, 42 St Andrew Square, Edinburgh, EH2 2YE, Scotland
Tel: 0131 523 2049
Fax: 0131 557 9178
Telex: 72230 RBSCOT
Contact: The Rt Hon Lord Younger of Prestwick KT KCVO TD DL

Scholarship Fund

Subjects: Any subject.

Eligibility: Open to newly qualified graduates or undergraduates of a Scottish university or of Oxford or Cambridge. Candidates are required to have a Scottish background by way of birth or descent. The possession of an honours degree is not essential. Personality and other qualities will influence the selection.

Level of Study: Postgraduate.

Purpose: To support advanced study exchanges between the USA and Scotland by individuals with Scottish backgrounds.

Type: Scholarship.

No. of awards offered: Two.

Frequency: Annually; dependent on funds.

Value: US$15,000 to cover university tuition fees, room and board, and transportation expenses.

Length of Study: One academic year.

Study Establishment: A University in the USA, restricted to the New England states, New York, New Jersey and Pennsylvania, and only if there is an unusual reason and justification will the Society consider other locations for students who cannot find courses for their specialities within the boundaries outlined: thereafter, the scholar is expected to spend a little time travelling in America before returning to Scotland.

Country of Study: USA (restricted to the New England states, New York, New Jersey and Pennsylvania).

Closing Date: Early January.

Additional Information: Each Scottish University will vet its own applicants and nominate one candidate to go forward to the Final Selection Committee to be held in Edinburgh in early March.

For further information contact:
The Royal Bank of Scotland, plc, 42 St Andrew Square, Edinburgh, EH2 2YB, Scotland
Tel: 0131 523 2049
Fax: 0131 557 6565
Telex: 72230 RBSCOT
Contact: Tony Smith, Executive Assistant

SAN ANGELO SYMPHONY SOCIETY

San Angelo Symphony Society, PO Box 5922, San Angelo, TX, 76902, USA
Tel: 915 658 5877
Contact: Mr Gene Smith, Music Director

Sorantin Young Artist Award

Subjects: Piano performance, vocal performance and instrumental performance.

Eligibility: Open to instrumentalists and pianists under 28 years of age and vocalists under 31 years of age by 19 November in the year of the competition.

Purpose: To recognize and reward talent.

Type: Competition.

No. of awards offered: Varies.

Frequency: Annual.

Value: Overall Winner US$1,500 plus his/her division prize and a guest appearance with the San Angelo Symphony Orchestra; Division Winner US$500; Division Runner-Up US$250.

Closing Date: Thirty days before the competition is held (in November).

SAN BERNARDINO COUNTY DEPARTMENT OF MENTAL HEALTH

San Bernardino County Department of Mental Health, 700 East Gilbert Street, San Bernardino, CA, 92415, USA
Contact: Christopher Ebbe, PhD, Psychology Training Coordinator

*Psychology Internship Program

Subjects: Clinical or counseling psychology.

Eligibility: Open to candidates holding a master's degree in psychology or having at least three years graduate work in psychology, and who are enrolled in a recognized doctoral program in clinical or counseling psychology and have at least 500 hours of practicum training or clerkship experience.

Purpose: To provide internship training opportunities for doctoral candidates.

Type: Full-time and half-time internships.

No. of awards offered: Eight.

Value: US$13,148 per annum full-time; US$6,920 per annum part-time.

Length of Study: One year of on-site work; not renewable.

Study Establishment: San Bernardino, California.

Country of Study: USA.

Closing Date: Mid-December.

SANDOZ FOUNDATION FOR GERONTOLOGICAL RESEARCH AND THE INTERNATIONAL ASSOCIATION OF GERONTOLOGY

Official Coordinator for the Sandoz Prize, Consulting Physician, Department of Geriatric Medicine, The Victoria Infirmary, Glasgow, G42 9TY, Scotland
Contact: Dr John L C Dall, MD

Sandoz Prize for Gerontological Research

Subjects: All areas of gerontology and geriatrics, including biological, medical, psychological, social and other relevant aspects.

Eligibility: Open to individuals and groups directly engaged in research in some area of gerontology or geriatrics. Candidates may also be nominated by third parties.

Level of Study: Postgraduate, Doctorate, Postdoctorate.

Purpose: To encourage research in the field of gerontology, with special emphasis on multidisciplinary research programs.

No. of awards offered: One prize, which may be shared.
Frequency: Biennially.
Value: A total of SwFr50,000.
Country of Study: Any country.
Applications Procedure: Application forms are available in the Brochure from Sandoz Pharma Company worldwide.
Closing Date: October 18th (Basel). May 31st (Regional committees).
Additional Information: New submissions for individuals /groups to Sandoz Foundation regional committees by May 31st. Reapplications Direct to the secretary at the given address. Regional committees are based in - Australasia, Japan, Europe, North America and Latin America.

For further information contact:
Sandoz Foundation for Gerontological Research and the International Association of Gerontology, PO Box 4043, Basel, CH 400Z, Switzerland
Contact: Mr Charles Studer, Secretary

SAN FRANCISCO CONSERVATORY OF MUSIC

San Francisco Conservatory of Music, 1201 Ortega Street, San Francisco, CA, 94122, USA
Tel: 415 759 3422
Fax: 415 759 3499
Contact: Office of Student Services

Performance Scholarships in Music

Subjects: Musical performance.
Eligibility: Open to US and foreign nationals who will be attending the Conservatory on a full-time basis. Candidates must have had considerable experience in musical performance.
Level of Study: Postgraduate.
Type: Scholarship.
No. of awards offered: Varies.
Frequency: Varies.
Value: US$300-US$14,500.
Length of Study: One year; renewable.
Study Establishment: At the Conservatory.
Country of Study: USA.
Applications Procedure: Candidates must complete both admission and scholarship applications, and must audition.
Closing Date: March 1st.

SCHOLARSHIP FOUNDATION OF THE LEAGUE OF FINNISH-AMERICAN SOCIETIES

Mechelininkatu 10, Helsinki, 0010, Finland
Tel: 9 0 440 711
Fax: 9 0 408 794
Email: sayl@walrus.megabaud.fi
www: http://www.megabaud.fi/~sayl
Contact: Sisko Rauhala

Scholarship

Eligibility: Open to Finns only.
Level of Study: Postgraduate.
Purpose: To enable Finns to study in the United States.

Type: Scholarship.
No. of awards offered: 2-3.
Frequency: Annual.
Value: US$3,000-US$5,000.
Length of Study: One academic year.
Study Establishment: University.
Country of Study: USA.
Applications Procedure: Application form and references must be submitted.
Closing Date: First Monday in October.
Additional Information: The Scholarship Foundation also handles awards given to Finns by the American-Scandinavian Foundation and Thanks to Scandinavia Inc, both based in New York.

SCHOOL OF AMERICAN RESEARCH

School of American Research, PO Box 2188, Santa Fe, NM, 87504-2188, USA
Tel: 505 982 3583
Fax: 505 989 9809

Resident Scholar Fellowships

Subjects: Anthropology or research from anthropologically informed perspectives in allied fields such as history, sociology, art, law and philosophy.
Eligibility: Open to pre- and postdoctoral scholars (National Edowment for the Humanities Fellowships are for holders of the PhD only). Both humanistically and scientifically oriented scholars are encouraged to apply. Must speak and write English fluently.
Level of Study: Doctorate, Postdoctorate.
Purpose: To fund research into topics important to our understanding of the human species.
Type: Fellowship.
No. of awards offered: Six.
Frequency: Annual.
Value: A stipend, library assistance and accommodation.
Length of Study: For 9 months from 1 September to 31 May.
Study Establishment: At the School.
Applications Procedure: Application composed of proposal, curriculum vitae, and three letters of recommendation.
Closing Date: December 1st for notification in March.
Additional Information: Application details are available on request. These Fellowships are funded by the Weatherhead Foundation, the National Endowment for the Humanities and the Katrin H Lamon Endowment for Native American Art and Education.

SCHOOL OF ORIENTAL AND AFRICAN STUDIES

School of Oriental and African Studies, University of London, Thornhaugh Street, Russell Square, London, WC1H OXG, England
Tel: 0171 637 2388
Fax: 0171 436 4211
Telex: 262433 W6876

SOAS Bursary

Eligibility: No restrictions.
Level of Study: Postgraduate.
Purpose: Bursary for taught Masters course (full-time) at SOAS.

Type: Bursary.

No. of awards offered: Nine.

Frequency: Annual.

Value: £6,540.

Study Establishment: SOAS.

Country of Study: UK.

Applications Procedure: Application form (obtainable from registrar SOAS), two references plus 500 word submission.

Closing Date: March 31st.

SOAS Research Student Fellowships

Eligibility: No restrictions.

Level of Study: Doctorate.

Purpose: Scholarships for new research students (full-time) at SOAS.

No. of awards offered: Two.

Frequency: Annual.

Value: £5,180.

Length of Study: Three years.

Study Establishment: SOAS.

Country of Study: UK.

Applications Procedure: Application form (obtainable from registrar SOAS), two references plus 500 word submission.

Closing Date: March 31st.

SCOPE

SCOPE, 16 Fitzroy Square, London, W1P 6LP, England
Tel: 0171 387 9571
Fax: 0171 383 3205
Contact: Mr Richard Parnell

Scope Grants

Subjects: Biomedical, social, educational, epidemiological and technological studies in cerebral palsy.

Eligibility: Open to experienced researchers within the UK.

Purpose: To fund research into cerebral palsy and associated conditions and to provide grants for travel. To encourage the dissemination of information by assisting with specialist meetings.

Type: Grant.

No. of awards offered: Varies.

Frequency: Varies.

Value: Travel grants £1,000 maximum. £25,000 per research project per year.

Length of Study: Up to three years.

Country of Study: UK.

Applications Procedure: Initial application followed by full application if project helps to meet Scope's mission.

Closing Date: Project grants are considered twice a year. Travel grants are considered throughout the year.

Additional Information: SCOPE (for people with cerebral palsy). Formerly 'The Spastics Society'.

THE SCOTTISH AGRICULTURAL COLLEGE

Scottish Agricultural College, Auchincruive, Ayr, KA6 5HW, Scotland
Tel: 01292 520331
Fax: 01292 521119

Contact: Secretary and Treasurer

William John Thomson Scholarship

Subjects: Agriculture, horticulture and related areas in which the College can provide appropriate resources.

Eligibility: Open to any graduate in agricultural science from a UK university who is qualified to carry out research for a higher degree from either Glasgow or Strathclyde University.

Purpose: To fund students who would benefit from training in methods of research.

Type: Scholarship.

No. of awards offered: One.

Frequency: Triennially.

Value: Varies.

Length of Study: Three years.

Study Establishment: The Scottish Agricultural College, Auchincruive, or any of its out-stations.

Country of Study: UK.

Additional Information: The College also offers the Colin Thomson Research Scholarship to enable members of its staff to make a study tour overseas.

SCOTTISH OPERA

Scottish Opera, 39 Elmbank Crescent, Glasgow, G2 4PT, Scotland
Tel: 0141 248 4567
Fax: 0141 221 8812
Contact: Auditions/Planning Department

John Noble Bursary Award

Subjects: Singing.

Eligibility: Minimum entry age is 18, no upper age limit but the competition is intended for singers at the early stage of their professional careers. Scottish connections required through birth, training, residency, or two years of permanent residence in Scotland before the closing date of entry.

Level of Study: Professional development.

Purpose: To encourage and help young singers of Scottish origin, at the early stage of their professional careers. The winner will represent Scotland in the Cardiff Singer of the World competition 1999, subject to the appropriate standard being acheived.

No. of awards offered: One.

Frequency: Every two years.

Value: £2,000.

Country of Study: United Kingdom.

Applications Procedure: Application form and other relevant documents to be submitted.

Closing Date: May 1998.

THE SCOULOUDI FOUNDATION

The Scouloudi Foundation Historical Awards, c/o The Institute of Historical Research, University of London, Senate House, London, WC1E 7HU, England
Tel: 0171 636 0272
Fax: 0171 436 2183
Contact: Secretary

Historical Awards

Subjects: History or a related subject.

Eligibility: Open to graduates of UK universities who possess a relevant honours degree or UK citizens with a similar qualification from a university outside the UK. These awards are not made for study or research towards a postgraduate qualification.

Level of Study: Postgraduate, Doctorate, Postdoctorate.

Purpose: To provide subsidies towards the cost of publishing a book or article in the field of history, incorporating an academic thesis or other scholarly work, already accepted by a reputable publisher or learned journal; or to pay for special expenses incurred in the completion of advanced historical work (except theses for higher degrees) such as the cost of fares and subsistence during visits to libraries or record repositories.

Type: Varies.

Frequency: Annual.

Value: £100-£1,000. Applicants should not ask for more than their minimum requirements for the year concerned.

Country of Study: International.

Applications Procedure: Application form to be completed.

Closing Date: March 1st.

HERBERT SCOVILLE JR PEACE FELLOWSHIP

110 Maryland Avenue, Suite 211, Washington, DC, 20002, USA
Tel: 202 546 0795
Fax: 202 546 5142
Email: scoville@clw.org
www: http://www.clw.org/pub/clw/scoville/scoville.html
Contact: Paul Revsine

Herbert Scoville Jr Peace Fellowship

Eligibility: Open to college graduates with experience/interest in arms control, disarmament, international security and/or peace issues. A Fellowship to a foreign national from a country of proliferation concern to the USA is awarded periodically.

Level of Study: Postgraduate.

Purpose: To provide a unique arms control educational experience to outstanding college graduates; to develop leadership skills that can serve the fellow throughout a career in arms control or a related area of public service: to contribute to the work of the participating arms control and disarmament organizations and to continue the work of Herbert Scoville Jr.

Type: Fellowship.

Frequency: Twice yearly.

Value: US$1,400 per month; includes health insurance and travel to Washington DC.

Length of Study: Four to six months.

Country of Study: USA.

Applications Procedure: There is no application form. For application requirements, see www home page, or call or write to receive information.

Closing Date: March 15th for fall semester, October for spring.

SHASTRI INDO-CANADIAN INSTITUTE

Room 1402 Education Tower, 2500 University Drive NW, Calgary, AB, T2N 1N4, Canada
Tel: 403 220 7467
Fax: 403 289 0100
Email: sici@acs.ucalgary.ca

India Studies Fellowship Competition

Subjects: Subjects relating to India.

Eligibility: Applicants must be Canadian or Indian citizens/landed immigrants.

Level of Study: Doctorate.

Purpose: To support candidates wishing to undertake research or training in India.

Type: Fellowship.

No. of awards offered: Varies from year to year.

Frequency: Annual.

Value: Varies.

Length of Study: 3-12 months.

Study Establishment: Varies.

Country of Study: India.

Applications Procedure: Please contact the head office for application procedure.

Closing Date: June 30th.

Language Training Fellowship

Subjects: Social sciences and humanities.

Eligibility: Open to Canadian or Indian citizens/landed immigrants.

Level of Study: Doctorate, Postdoctorate.

Purpose: To support students in Canadian universities.

Type: Fellowship.

No. of awards offered: 6.

Frequency: Annual.

Value: C$2,500.

Length of Study: Varies.

Study Establishment: Varies.

Country of Study: Canada.

Applications Procedure: Please contact the head office for application procedure.

Closing Date: January.

Summer Programme

Subjects: Development and the environment, women's development, economic growth and business development.

Eligibility: Applicants must be Canadian or Indian citizens/landed immigrants.

Level of Study: Postgraduate, Doctorate, Postdoctorate.

Purpose: To support a course of study in India.

No. of awards offered: 15.

Frequency: Dependent on funds available.

Value: Course for credit.

Length of Study: Nine weeks.

Study Establishment: Varies.

Country of Study: India.

Applications Procedure: Please contact the head office for application procedure.

Closing Date: October 25th.

Women and Development Fellowships

Subjects: Subjects relating to Indo-Canadian relations.

Eligibility: Open to Canadian or Indian citizens/permanent residents/landed immigrants.

Level of Study: Doctorate.

Type: Fellowship.

No. of awards offered: Varies from year to year.
Frequency: Annual.
Value: Varies.
Length of Study: 3-12 months.
Study Establishment: Varies.
Country of Study: India.
Applications Procedure: Please contact the head office for application procedure.
Closing Date: October 31st.

SHEFFIELD HALLAM UNIVERSITY

Sheffield Hallam University, 100 Napier Street, Sheffield, S11 8HD, England
Tel: 0114 253 3169
Fax: 0114 253 3161
Email: http://www.shu.ac.uk/schools/research/mitri/crc/crc.htm
Telex: H.SCOTT@SHU.AC.UK
Contact: Heather Scott

Research Bursary

Subjects: Statistics, computer science, artificial intelligence and systems analysis.
Eligibility: Open to European Union nationals only.
Level of Study: Postgraduate.
Purpose: To support study towards an MPhil or PhD degree.
Type: Bursary.
No. of awards offered: Nine.
Frequency: Dependent on funds available.
Value: £5,000 bursary plus fees.
Length of Study: 2-3 years.
Study Establishment: SHU.
Country of Study: UK.
Applications Procedure: Please submit CV and subject areas of interest to Heather Scott at the School of Computing and Management Sciences at SHU.
Closing Date: Varies.

SHELBY CULLOM DAVIS CENTER FOR HISTORICAL STUDIES

Shelby Cullom Davis Center for Historical Studies, Department of History, G-13 Dickinson Hall, Princeton University, Princeton, NJ, 08544-1017, USA
Tel: 609 258 4997
Fax: 609 258 5326
Contact: Kari Hoover

Research Projects; Research Fellowships

Subjects: Animals and human society.
Eligibility: There are no restrictions, although applicants must have completed a PhD.
Level of Study: Postdoctorate.
Purpose: To explore material, ethical and symbolic dimensions of the role of animals in human culture.
Type: Research Grant, Fellowship.
No. of awards offered: Varies.
Frequency: Annual.

Value: Up to US$56,000 per year.
Applications Procedure: Application form must be completed.
Closing Date: December 1st each year.

JEAN SIBELIUS INTERNATIONAL VIOLIN COMPETITION

Jean Sibelius International Violin Competition, PB 31, Helsinki, SF-00101, Finland
Fax: 358 0 400 3382

Jean Sibelius International Violin Competition

Subjects: Musical performance: violin.
Eligibility: Open to violinists of any nationality born in 1970 or later.
Level of Study: Unrestricted.
Type: Prize.
No. of awards offered: Nine.
Frequency: Every five years (2000).
Value: First prize US$15,000; second prize US$10,000; third prize US$7,000; plus five prizes of US$2,000. A further prize of US$2,000 is given by the Finnish Broadcasting Company for the best performance of Sibelius' Violin Concerto.
Closing Date: August 18th.
Additional Information: The next competition will be held on November 18th to December 2nd 2000. For further information please contact the competition secretary.

SIDNEY SUSSEX COLLEGE, CAMBRIDGE

Sidney Sussex College, Cambridge, CB2 3HU, England
Tel: 44 1223 338800
Fax: 44 1223 338884
www: http://www.sid.com.ac.uk

Research Studentship

Subjects: Non specific.
Eligibility: No restriction.
Level of Study: Doctorate.
Purpose: To provide full support (fees & maintenance) for one student to do three years of research leading to the degree of PhD at the University of Cambridge.
Type: Studentship.
No. of awards offered: One.
Frequency: Two years in three.
Value: £5,050 (maintenance) per annum + fees.
Length of Study: Three years.
Study Establishment: University of Cambridge.
Country of Study: United Kingdom.
Applications Procedure: Application form available from the tutor for graduate studies.
Closing Date: March 1st.
Additional Information: Applicants must also apply for a postgraduate place at the University of Cambridge. Preference for candidates under 26 years of age and for candidates who have nominated Sidney Sussex as college of first preference.

Evan Lewis Thomas Law Studentships

Eligibility: No restriction.

Level of Study: Postgraduate, Doctorate.

Purpose: To support students doing research or taking advanced courses in law or cognate subjects at the University of Cambridge.

Type: Studentship.

No. of awards offered: Three to four.

Frequency: Annual.

Value: £1,000 to £4,000 per annum.

Length of Study: One to three years.

Study Establishment: University of Cambridge.

Country of Study: United Kingdom.

Applications Procedure: Application form obtainable from the tutor for graduate studies.

Closing Date: February 1st.

Additional Information: Applicants must also apply for a postgraduate place at the University of Cambridge. Preference for candidates under 26 years of age and for candidates who have nominated Sidney Sussex as college of first preference.

SIGMA ALPHA IOTA

Inter-American Music Awards, Sigma Alpha Iota, 165 West 82nd Street, New York, NY, 10024, USA
Tel: 212 724 2809
Contact: Eugenie Dengel, Director

Inter-American Music Awards

Subjects: Musical composition (specifications vary).

Eligibility: Open to any composer from North, Central or South America.

Type: Award.

No. of awards offered: One.

Frequency: Triennially.

Value: US$750, publication by C F Peters Corporation and first performance at the National Convention.

Applications Procedure: A candidate may enter more than one work for the competition and an entry fee of US$20 must accompany each manuscript submitted.

Closing Date: April 30th.

SIGMA DELTA EPSILON/GRADUATE WOMEN IN SCIENCE

Sigma Delta Epsilon/Graduate Women in Science, Inc, PO Box 19947, San Diego, CA, 92159, USA

*Eloise Gerry Fellowships

Subjects: Chemical or biological science.

Eligibility: Open to women of any race, nationality, creed, national origin or age who can show evidence of outstanding ability and promise in research and hold a degree in science from a recognized institution of higher learning.

Purpose: To encourage research in science by women.

Type: Fellowship.

No. of awards offered: 3-6.

Frequency: Annual.

Value: US$2,000-US$3,000, depending on the income generated by the Fund.

Length of Study: Usually for one year, determined when the Fellowship is awarded.

Country of Study: Any country.

Closing Date: December 1st.

Additional Information: The Fellowships are for research or research support broadly defined, not for tuition or scholarship support. Eloise Gerry Fellowships and Grants-in-Aid are mutually exclusive; no one may apply for both in the same year. Applications are available in September. Requests should be accompanied by a self-addressed stamped envelope.

SIGMA PHI ALPHA SUPREME CHAPTER NATIONAL DENTAL HYGIENE HONOR SOCIETY

Institute for Oral Health, American Dental Hygienists' Association, Suite 3400, 444 North Michigan Street, Chicago, IL, 60611, USA
Tel: 312 440 8900
Fax: 312 440 8929
Contact: Beatrice Pedersen

Sigma Phi Alpha Scholarship

Subjects: Dental hygiene.

Eligibility: Open to US dental hygiene students only. Candidates should have a minimum grade average of 3.0 and be able to demonstrate financial need.

Purpose: To promote scholarship, leadership and service in a student.

Type: Scholarship.

No. of awards offered: One.

Frequency: Annual.

Value: Approximately US$1,000.

Study Establishment: Institutions that have a dental hygiene curriculum.

Country of Study: USA.

Closing Date: June 1st.

For further information contact:
Sigma Phi Alpha Supreme Chapter, 205 Oak Street, Frankfort, IL, 60423, USA
Contact: Virginia Stankiewicz, Executive Secretary

SIGMA THETU TAU INTERNATIONAL

Sigma Thetu Tau International, 550 W. North Street, Indianapolis, IN, 46202, USA
Tel: 317 634 8171

STTI Corporate Sponsored Research Grants

Eligibility: 1) Must be a registered nurse with a current licence 2) must have received a masters degree 3) must have submitted an application package 4) must be ready to start the research project 5) must have signed a Sigma Thetu Tau research agreement.

Level of Study: Doctorate, Professional development.

Purpose: Various researches into nursing practice.

Type: Research Grant.

No. of awards offered: Four.

Frequency: Annual.

Value: Varies depending on the award from US$3,000 to US$10,000.

Study Establishment: Not specified.

Country of Study: Not specified.

Applications Procedure: Write for information booklet and application form.

Closing Date: Varies with each award.

Additional Information: The Awards are: Glaxo Wellcome Prescriptive Practice Grant; Glaxo Wellcome New Investigator Grant; Mead Johnson Nutritional Perinatal Grant.

For further information contact:
Sigma Thetu Tau International, 550 W.North Street, Indianapolis, IN, 46202, USA
Tel: 317 634 8171

STTI Co-Sponsored Research Grants

Eligibility: 1) Must be a registered nurse with a current licence 2) must have received a masters degree 3) must have submitted an application package 5) must have signed a Sigma Thetu Tau research agreement.

Level of Study: Postgraduate.

Purpose: Researches into nursing practice.

Type: Research Grant.

No. of awards offered: Five.

Frequency: Annual.

Value: Depending on the award from US$6,000 to US$10,000.

Applications Procedure: Write for information booklet and application form.

Closing Date: Varies with award.

Additional Information: The awards are: American Association of Critical Care Nurses Critical Care Grant; American Association of Diabetes Educators Grant; American Nurses Foundation Grant; Emergency Nurses Foundation Grant; Oncology Nursing Society Grant.

STTI Research Grant Opportunities

Eligibility: 1) Must be a registered nurse with a current licence 2) must have received a masters degree 3) Must have submitted an application package 4) are ready to start the research project 5) Must have signed a Sigma Thetu Tau research agreement.

Level of Study: Postgraduate.

Purpose: To encourage qualified nurses to contribute to the advancement of nursing through research. Multidisciplinary and international research is encouraged.

Type: Grant.

No. of awards offered: 10-15.

Frequency: Annual.

Value: Up to US$3,000.

Study Establishment: Not specified.

Country of Study: Not specified.

Applications Procedure: Write for information booklet and application form.

Closing Date: March 1st.

Additional Information: Preference is given to STTI Members.

SIGMA XI, THE SCIENTIFIC RESEARCH SOCIETY

Sigma Xi Headquarters, Box 13975, 99 Alexander Drive, Research Triangle Park, NC, 27709, USA
Contact: Committee on Grants-in-Aid of Research

*Grants-in-Aid of Research

Subjects: Scientific investigation in any field: physical sciences and engineering; behavioral and life sciences.

Eligibility: Open to graduate and undergraduate students in degree programs.

Level of Study: Postgraduate, Undergraduate.

Frequency: Three times yearly.

Value: No part of an award may be used for the payment of indirect costs to the recipient's institution. All funds must be expended directly in support of the proposed investigation. Any equipment purchased shall be the property of the institution. Awards are made in amounts up to a maximum of US$1,000 except in the fields of astronomy and eye or vision research where special funds allow for awards up to a maximum of US$2,500. At the present time, awards will not normally exceed US$600.

Applications Procedure: Candidates should request an application form and up-to-date guidelines.

Closing Date: February 1st, May 1st, November 1st.

Additional Information: The following are not granted support: educational programs and curriculum development; stipends for applicants or assistants; manuscript preparation and publication costs; purchase of standard equipment and supplies that should normally be available in an institutional research laboratory; travel to scientific meetings or symposia; requests for a third year of support. The Committee attaches low priority to support for use of institutional and departmental equipment and facilities.

SILSOE COLLEGE, CRANFIELD UNIVERSITY

Student Recruitment Executive, Silsoe College, Cranfield University, Silsoe, Bedford, MK45 4DT, England
Tel: 01525 863318
Fax: 01525 863316
www: http://www.cranfield.ac.uk/silsoe/prospect/pgpcpdp.htm
Telex: 826838 SILCAMG
Contact: Mrs M Merredy

Awards

Subjects: Any MSc programme option offered by Silsoe College. In the area of marketing and management, land and water management, applied remote sensing, information technology, agricultural engineering, postharvest technology.

Eligibility: Open to EC citizens who are graduates with honours degrees and have been offered a place on a 1-year MSc programme at Silsoe College.

Level of Study: Postgraduate.

No. of awards offered: Approximately 50.

Frequency: Annual.

Value: Tuition fees; varies according to available funds.

Study Establishment: Silsoe College, School of Agriculture, Food & Environment, Cranfield University.

Country of Study: UK.

Closing Date: July of each year.

PERCY SLADEN MEMORIAL FUND

Percy Sladen Memorial Fund, c/o The Linnean Society, Burlington House, Piccadilly, London, W1V 0LQ, England
Tel: 0171 434 4479
Fax: 0171 287 9364
Email: gina@linnean.demon.co.uk
Contact: Secretary to the Trustees

Percy Sladen Memorial Fund Grants

Subjects: Natural and earth sciences, including botany, zoology, geology, anthropology, archaeology, experimental physiology, pathology and therapeutics.

Eligibility: No restrictions.

Purpose: To assist field research or investigations overseas.

Type: Grant.

No. of awards offered: Varies.

Frequency: Twice yearly.

Value: £100-£500.

Study Establishment: Within one year of allocation; progress must be reported or final return submitted within one year.

Country of Study: Any, provided it is not the applicant's native country.

Applications Procedure: Application form and two referees forms. Available from the Secretary to the Trustees by post or e-mail.

Closing Date: January 30th and September 30th.

Additional Information: Funds are not provided for undergraduate expeditions or for major support towards fieldwork costs as part of a postgraduate qualification, or, in general, for UK-based fieldwork. No retrospective grants are made, trustees usually meet in mid-March or mid-November.

ALFRED P SLOAN FOUNDATION

Sloan Research Fellowships, Alfred P Sloan Foundation, Suite 2550, 630 Fifth Avenue, New York, NY, 10111, USA
Tel: 212 649 1649
Fax: 212 757 5117
Contact: Program Administrator

Research Fellowships

Subjects: Physics, chemistry, computer science, mathematics, economics, neuroscience and certain interdisciplinary fields such as geochemistry and astrophysics.

Eligibility: Open to young (no more than six years from completion of PhD) regular faculty members of a university or college in the USA or Canada who hold a PhD or equivalent degree in one of the named subjects.

Level of Study: Doctorate, Postdoctorate.

Purpose: To provide especially promising young scientists with flexible research support at an early stage of their academic careers.

Type: Fellowship.

No. of awards offered: 100.

Frequency: Annual.

Value: Approximately US$35,000, payable in two annual instalments.

Length of Study: Two years, with the possibility of renewal.

Study Establishment: Recognized universities and colleges.

Country of Study: USA or Canada.

Closing Date: September 15th.

Additional Information: The Fellow's institution is required to report annually on expenditures and the Fellow must submit a brief annual scientific progress report and a final report. Reprints or preprints of scientific papers may be submitted in lieu of such reports.

SME EDUCATION FOUNDATION

SME Education Foundation, PO Box 930, Dearborn, MI, 48121-0930, USA
Tel: 313 271 1500 ext.512
Fax: 313 240 6095

Email: murrdor@SME.org
Contact: Dora Murray, Grants Coordinator

SME Education Foundation Grants

Subjects: Capital equipment, student development, faculty development, curricula development, and research initiation.

Eligibility: Open to full-time university faculty representing engineering programs which offer manufacturing courses.

Level of Study: Postgraduate.

Purpose: 1) To draw together the talents, needs, and resources of education, industry, and SME as partners to improve the quality and development of institutional curricular training, and resources oriented towards increasing manufacturing productivity through university-industry-society cooperation; 2) To act as a catalyst to provide financial and technical support to a wide range of educational institutions with coursework, curricular, or a committment to the creation of new programs in manufacturing engineering or manufacturing engineering technology and 3) to foster trust in manufacturing engineering and enhance the technical competence and professionalism of the manufacturing engineer.

No. of awards offered: Varies.

Frequency: Annual.

Value: Funds are reimbursed upon receipt of an invoice and narrative report.

Country of Study: USA, Canada. Mexico.

Closing Date: February 1st.

Additional Information: One proposal per campus location is allowed. Capital equipment and research initiation grants must be matched dollar-for-dollar by the educational institution.

THE SMITH AND NEPHEW FOUNDATION

The Smith and Nephew Foundation, 2 Temple Place, Victoria Embankment, London, WC2R 3BP, England
Tel: 0171 836 7922
Fax: 0171 240 7088
Contact: Secretary to the Trustees

*Medical Research Fellowships

Subjects: Any branch of medicine.

Eligibility: Open to registrars and senior registrars who are citizens of the UK between 25 and 35 years of age who have had three years' general clinical experience. Normally, candidates should have held a residential hospital appointment in general medicine or surgery.

Type: Fellowship.

No. of awards offered: Varies.

Frequency: Annual.

Value: A minimum of £20,000.

Length of Study: One year.

Country of Study: UK.

Closing Date: Varies according to specific awards offered.

Additional Information: Conditions of Fellowships may change from year to year.

*Nursing Fellowships, Scholarships and Bursaries

Subjects: Postgraduate education and research in nursing. The areas of nursing for Scholarships vary each year.

Eligibility: Open to nurses and midwives, including those holding or aspiring to leadership positions in clinical, management or education spheres in the nursing professions.

541

Level of Study: Postgraduate.

Purpose: To enable the nursing professions to better serve the needs of society.

Frequency: Annual.

Value: Fellowships: up to £2,000; Scholarships: up to £5,000; Bursaries: up to £1,000.

Country of Study: Any country.

Applications Procedure: Application guidelines are available on request.

SMITHSONIAN INSTITUTION

Smithsonian Institution, 955 L'Enfant Plaza, Suite 7000, Washington, DC, 20560, USA
Tel: 202 287 3271
Email: siofg@sivm.si.edu
www: www.si.edu/youandsi/ofg/ofgintro.html
Contact: Office of Fellowships and Grants

*Conservation Analytical Laboratory Materials Analysis Fellowship

Subjects: Research on problems in the application of techniques of the physical sciences to problems in art history, anthropology, archaeology, and the history of technology.

Eligibility: Open to all qualified individuals without reference to race, color, religion, sex, national origin, condition of handicap or age. Pre- and postdoctoral fellowships are available; applications will also be accepted from persons with a degree or certificate of advanced training in the conservation of artefacts or art objects.

Type: Fellowship.

No. of awards offered: One to two.

Frequency: Annually if funds are available.

Value: US$14,000 for Predoctoral Fellows; US$25,000 for Postdoctoral Fellows.

Length of Study: 12 months.

Study Establishment: The Smithsonian Institution.

Country of Study: USA.

Closing Date: January 15th.

For further information contact:
Conservation Analytical Laboratory, Smithsonian Institution, Washington, DC, 20560, USA
Contact: Lambertus van Zelst, Director

Graduate Student Fellowships

Subjects: Animal behaviour, ecology, environmental science, anthropology, archaeology, astrophysics, astronomy, earth sciences, paleobiology, evolutionary and systematic biology, history of science and technology, history of art, and folklife.

Eligibility: Open to graduate students of any nationality who are formally enrolled and engaged in a graduate program of study at a degree-granting institution and who have completed at least one semester before the appointment period and have not yet been advanced to candidacy. Fluency in English is required.

Level of Study: Graduate.

Purpose: To enable graduate students to conduct individual research under the guidance of Smithsonian staff members.

Type: Fellowship.

No. of awards offered: Varies.

Frequency: Annual.

Value: US$3,000.

Length of Study: 10 weeks.

Study Establishment: Smithsonian facilities.

Country of Study: USA.

Applications Procedure: Applications are available via the world wide web or directly from the office.

Closing Date: January 15th.

Postdoctoral Fellowships

Subjects: American social and cultural history; history of science and technology; history of art; anthropology; biological sciences; earth sciences; history of African art and culture.

Eligibility: Open to candidates of any nationality who have received the PhD or equivalent within seven years of the application date. Recipients must have completed the degree or certificate at the time the Fellowship commences. Fluency in English is required.

Level of Study: Postdoctorate.

Purpose: To offer appointments to those who wish to pursue postdoctoral research training at the Smithsonian Institution in collaboration with a member of the professional staff of the institution.

Type: Fellowship.

No. of awards offered: Three.

Frequency: Annual.

Value: US$35,000 per annum, plus research and travel allowances.

Length of Study: 3-12 months, with the majority of appointments being for one year.

Study Establishment: Smithsonian Institution facilities, including museums on the Mall and elsewhere in Washington, DC, at its Astrophysical Observatory in Cambridge, Massachusetts, and at its Tropical Research Institute, Panama.

Country of Study: USA.

Applications Procedure: Application form can be obtained from the Secretary.

Closing Date: December 15th annually.

For further information contact:
Smithsonian Astrophysical Observatory, 60 Garden Street, Mail Stop 47, Cambridge, MA, 02138, USA
Tel: 617 495 7103
Fax: 617 495 7105
Email: dalianiello@cfa.harvard.edu
Contact: Dale A Alianiello, Fellowship Program Coordinator

Postdoctoral Fellowships at the Smithsonian Astrophysical Observatory

Subjects: Various fields of astrophysics and astronomy, including atomic and molecular physics, the solar system, stars, galaxies and cosmology.

Eligibility: Open to recent PhD recipients of any nationality in a relevant field with interests in theory, observation, instrumentation and/or laboratory research. Only applicants who receive their degrees in the academic year preceding application will be considered unless there are special circumstances such as illness or national service. A short postdoctoral period, especially at the PhD institution, is not a disqualification.

Level of Study: Postdoctorate.

Type: Fellowship.

No. of awards offered: Three.

Frequency: Annual.

Value: US$35,000 per annum, plus US$8,000 research allowance.

Length of Study: Two years; renewable for a third year.

Study Establishment: Smithsonian Astrophysical Observatory in Cambridge, Massachusetts.

Country of Study: USA.

Applications Procedure: Formal application form is required.

Closing Date: December 15th for notification by February 15th.

Additional Information: Techniques used ranged from computer simulations through observations in the radio, infrared, optical, ultraviolet, X- and gamma-ray bands, to instrument development and laboratory experiments. Facilities include the Multiple Mirror Telescope, many local computers, an image processing laboratory, the Einstein Observatory data archive, the EUV/Skylab solar data archive, a number of specialized laboratories, and an outstanding astronomical library, but above all a large and vigorous staff involved in almost every branch of astrophysical and solar-system research.

Predoctoral Fellowships

Subjects: Anthropology; biological sciences; earth sciences; history of art; history of science and technology; American social and cultural history; history of African art and culture.

Eligibility: Open to students of any nationality who are enrolled in a university as candidates for the PhD or equivalent. At the time of appointment, the university must approve the undertaking of dissertation research at the Smithsonian Institution and indicate that requirements for the doctorate, other than dissertation, have been met. Fluency in English is required.

Level of Study: Postgraduate, Predoctoral.

Type: Fellowship.

No. of awards offered: Approximately 25.

Frequency: Annual.

Value: US$14,000 per annum, plus research and travel allowances.

Length of Study: 3-12 months.

Study Establishment: Smithsonian Institution facilities.

Country of Study: USA.

Applications Procedure: Application form must be completed.

Closing Date: January 15th.

Additional Information: Projects proposed will be approved in advance by a Smithsonian staff member who will serve as the appointee's advisor. Projects must be related to the research and interest of the Institution's professional staff.

Predoctoral Fellowships at the Smithsonian Astrophysical Observatory

Subjects: Fields of astronomy, astrophysics, atomic and molecular physics, and planetary science, including theory, observation, instrument development (especially detectors and interferometers), and laboratory experiments.

Eligibility: Open to individuals who show promise in relevant fields. Applicants must have completed preliminary course work and examinations and be ready to begin dissertation research at the time of the award.

Level of Study: Doctorate.

Purpose: To allow students from other institutions throughout the world to do their thesis research at SAO working with SAO scientists.

Type: Fellowship.

No. of awards offered: 3-5.

Frequency: Annual.

Value: US$14,000; some funds may also be available for relocation, travel and other expenses.

Length of Study: One year; renewable for up to a total of three years.

Study Establishment: SAO.

Country of Study: Majority of period of appointment to be spent in Cambridge, MA.

Applications Procedure: Applicants should contact directly Smithsonian scientists in their area of interest to discuss possible research topics. Applicants' degrees will be awarded by their home insti-

tutions; therefore they must have the approval of their institutions to conduct their thesis research at SAO.

Closing Date: April 15th for notification by June 15th.

Additional Information: Research facilities include the Multiple Mirror Telescope and other telescopes at Mount Hopkins, Arizona, and elsewhere; radio telescopes; computer facilities including a 12-processor VAX Cluster, a Sun server and facility-wide ethernet connectivity, an image processing facility, a large number of minicomputers and workstations, and connections to major research networks providing on-line links to larger computers; and laboratories for determining atomic and molecular parameters, for petrographic and isotopic analysis of meteorites, and for instrument development. Data is available for analysis from X-ray satellites, Skylab (the Extreme Ultraviolet Telescope), and from the International Ultraviolet Explorer.

For further information contact:
Smithsonian Astrophysical Observatory, 60 Garden Street, Mail Stop 47, Cambridge, MA, 02138, USA
Tel: 617 495 7103
Fax: 617 495 7105
Email: dalianiello@cfa.harvard.edu
Contact: Dale A Alianiello, Fellowship Program Coordinator

Senior Fellowships

Subjects: Anthropology; biological sciences; American social and cultural history; history of science and technology; history of art; history of African art and culture.

Eligibility: Open to applicants of any nationality who are seven or more years beyond the degree of PhD or equivalent. Fluency in English is required.

Level of Study: Senior.

Purpose: To offer appointments to senior scholars who wish to pursue research at the Smithsonian Institution.

Type: Fellowship.

No. of awards offered: Varies.

Frequency: Annual.

Value: US$25,000 per annum, plus allowances.

Length of Study: 3-12 months.

Study Establishment: Smithsonian facilities.

Country of Study: USA.

Applications Procedure: Applications are available via the world wide web or directly from the office.

Closing Date: January 15th.

STANLEY SMITH (UK) HORTICULTURAL TRUST

Stanley Smith Horticultural Trust, Cory Lodge, PO Box 365, Cambridge, CB2 1HR, England
Tel: 01223 336299(am)/01223 60100(pm)
Fax: 01223 336278
Contact: Director

Awards

Subjects: Horticulture.

Eligibility: Open to institutions and individuals. All projects are judged entirely on merit, and there are no eligibility requirements.

Purpose: To support amenity horticulture and horticultural education.

No. of awards offered: Varies.

Frequency: Twice yearly.

Value: Varies.

Length of Study: For a period dependent on the nature of the project.

Country of Study: Any country.

Applications Procedure: The Trust invites applications for awards, but they are not awarded to students for academic or diploma courses. Trustees allocate awards in spring and autumn.

Closing Date: March 15th, September 15th.

W EUGENE SMITH MEMORIAL FUND, INC

W Eugene Smith Memorial Fund, Inc (US), c/o International Center of Photography, 1130 Fifth Avenue, New York, NY, 10128, USA

Smith (W Eugene) Grant in Humanistic Photography

Subjects: Photojournalism.

Eligibility: Open to outstanding photographers of any nationality.

Type: Grant.

No. of awards offered: Two.

Frequency: Annual.

Value: One grant for US$20,000, with a possible second grant for US$5,000.

Applications Procedure: For further information send a self addressed envelope to the given adddress.

Closing Date: July 15th.

THE SOCAN FOUNDATION

The SOCAN Foundation, 41 Valleybrook Drive, Don Mills, Ontario, M3B 2S6, Canada
Tel: 416 445 8700
Fax: 416 445 7108
Contact: Nancy Gyokeres, Administrator

The Gorden F Henderson/SOCAN Copyright Competition

Subjects: Copyright law and related issues such as performing and reproduction rights.

Eligibility: Open to Candian citizens or landed immigrants registered in law faculties in Canadian universities or graduates while articling in law in Canada at the date of the competition deadline.

Purpose: To encourage and support studies dealing with copyright law as it relates to music.

Type: Competition.

Frequency: Annual.

Value: C$2,000.

Country of Study: Canada.

Applications Procedure: Application form required to be completed.

Closing Date: April 1st.

Additional Information: The paper must address subjects of copyright law and related issues in music such as performing and reproduction rights. The essay or paper may be purely theoretical or related to the solving of a particular problem. It may be written in either French or English and there is no word limit. A paper may be submitted only once and must not have been published prior to the announcement of the winner.

*SOCAN Awards For Young Composers

Subjects: The Sir Ernest MacMillan Awards for orchestral compositions; The Serge Garant Awards for chamber music compositions; The Pierre Mercure Awards for solo or duet compositions; The Hugh Le Caine

Awards for compositions realized on tape with electronic means; The Godfrey Ridout Awards for choral compositions of any variety.

Eligibility: Open to candidates under 30 years of age on the closing date of the competition. Competition is open to SOCAN members or to composers who are not members of a performing right society but are Canadian citizens. Works submitted must be original and unpublished.

Purpose: To support and encourage Canadian composers.

Frequency: Annual.

Value: Three prizes offered in the Sir Ernest MacMillan, Serge Garant and Pierre Mercure categories of C$2,000 (1st prize), C$1,000 (2nd prize) and C$500 (3rd prize). Two prizes offered in the Hugh Le Caine and Godfrey Ridout categories: C$2,000 (1st prize) and C$1,000 (2nd prize).

Country of Study: Canada.

Closing Date: October 31st.

SOCIAL SCIENCE RESEARCH COUNCIL

Fellowships and Grants, Social Science Research Council, 810 Seventh Avenue, New York, NY, 10019, USA
Tel: 212 377 2700
Fax: 212 377 2727

Abe Fellowship Program

Subjects: Research in the social sciences and humanities relevant to any one or combination of the following themes: global issues, problems common to advanced industrial societies, and issues that relate to improving US-Japanese relations.

Eligibility: Open to Japanese and American citizens, and other scholars, who are involved in professional research at an American or Japanese institution at the time of application. Applicants must hold the PhD or have attained an equivalent level of professional experience, as evaluated in their country of residence. Applications from researchers in non-academic professions are welcome.

Level of Study: Postdoctorate.

Type: Fellowship.

Frequency: Annual.

Value: To include a base award and supplementary research and travel expenses as necessary for completion of the research project.

Length of Study: Up to 12 months.

Study Establishment: An appropriate American or Japanese institution.

Country of Study: USA or Japan.

Applications Procedure: References are required; optional language evaluation form.

Closing Date: September 1st.

Additional Information: In addition to receiving fellowship awards, fellows will attend annual conferences and other events sponsored by the program, which will promote the development of an international network of scholars concerned with research on contemporary policy issues. Funds are provided by the Japan Foundation's Center for Global Partnership.

For further information contact:
Abe Fellowship Program, Social Science Research Council, 810 Seventh Avenue, 31st Floor, New York, NY, 10019, USA
Tel: 212 377 2700
Fax: 212 377 2727

The Africa Program: Advanced Research Grants

Subjects: African studies. Applicants working in literature, philosophy, religion and art history, which are previously under-represented, are especially encouraged to apply.

Eligibility: Open to citizens and permanent residents of the USA for at least three consecutive years, who hold the PhD or an equivalent degree.

Level of Study: Postdoctorate.

Purpose: To support field research in Africa and comparative, theoretical research that proposes more than the analysis of previously gathered materials.

Type: Research Grant.

No. of awards offered: Varies.

Frequency: Annual.

Value: Up to US$15,000.

Country of Study: Africa.

Closing Date: December 1st.

Additional Information: If travel to Africa is planned, applicants must try to arrange for affiliation with an African university or research institute. Grants are for Sub-Saharan regions. North Africa is included in the Near and Middle East program.

Africa Program Dissertation Fellowships

Subjects: Doctoral dissertation work in the social sciences and humanities in Africa south of the Sahara.

Eligibility: Open to full-time students, regardless of citizenship, who are enrolled in doctoral programs in the USA; and to US citizens and permanent residents enrolled in full-time doctoral programs abroad.

Level of Study: Doctorate.

Type: Fellowship.

No. of awards offered: Varies.

Frequency: Annual.

Value: Varies.

Length of Study: 9-18 months.

Country of Study: Africa.

Applications Procedure: Application form must be completed - requested by SSRC.

Closing Date: November 1st.

Additional Information: Applicants are expected to have achieved a level of fluency in African and European languages sufficient to enable them to accomplish the goals of their project satisfactorily. Limited support for additional language training and dissertation write-up support may be included in awards. Please contact SSRC in May for further information.

The Japan Program: Fellowships for Dissertation Write-Up

Subjects: Japanese studies.

Eligibility: Open to full-time students, regardless of nationality, who are enrolled in doctoral programs in the USA.

Purpose: To support advanced graduate students during the writing of their dissertations in the USA.

Frequency: Annual.

Length of Study: Up to nine months.

Applications Procedure: Applications will be accepted from students working towards the PhD who have completed research on a Japan-related topic and who are now writing their dissertations, as well as from students who will have begun writing their dissertations by the time they propose to begin the Fellowship.

Closing Date: January 1st.

The Japan Program: Grants for Research Planning Activities

Subjects: Incorporation and exclusion in society, polity, economy, and culture: the structure and dynamics of inclusion and marginality in past and present Japan; orality and literacy: the relationship between the creation and transmission of written, spoken, and illustrated texts in Japanese literary, artistic, and dramatic history; peace and security in East Asia: actors, forces, and regimes in contemporary East-Asian international affairs; Japan and the developing world: Japanese perceptions and images of the developing world; its countries, international role, migrants, relationship to Japan; and/or the developing world's reciprocal view of Japan. Proposals for research outside the four themes are also welcomed.

Eligibility: Open to teams of scholars. The program especially encourages innovative projects at the planning stage which promote comparative or interdisciplinary perspectives, and involve the participation of scholars from outside North America

Purpose: To advance research concerning Japan in the social sciences and humanities.

Frequency: Annual.

Closing Date: Varies.

Additional Information: Some research planning activities are initiated by the Joint Committeee on Japanese Studies; however, the committee is especially interested in encouraging collaborative activities by teams of scholars outside the committee structure. These research planning activities seek to identify and bring together groups of scholars working on questions of particular interest and significance in advancing scholarship on Japan. Applicants must contact the Japan program for guidelines for the submission of proposals.

The Korea Program: Advanced Research Grants

Subjects: The social sciences and humanities relating to Korea. Researchers in disciplines previously underrepresented in this competition are especially encouraged; these include literature, philosophy, religion, art history, and performance studies.

Eligibility: Open to citizens or permanent residents of the USA who have either PhD or equivalent research or analytical experience, whose competence in the field of Korean studies has been demonstrated and whose proposed research promises to contribute to the further development of scholarship in Korea.

Type: Research Grant.

No. of awards offered: Varies.

Frequency: Annual.

Value: Up to US$15,000.

Length of Study: Two to 12 months, subject to funding.

Country of Study: Korea, the USA and/or other countries.

Closing Date: December 1st.

Additional Information: Proposals to revise doctoral dissertations for publication are also eligible for support.

The Korea Program: Dissertation Fellowships

Subjects: Doctoral dissertation research on Korea in the social sciences and humanities.

Eligibility: Open to full-time students, regardless of citizenship, who are enrolled in doctoral programs in the USA; and to US citizens and permanent residents enrolled in full-time doctoral programs abroad.

Frequency: Annual.

Length of Study: Nine to 18 months.

Country of Study: Where justified by the nature of the proposed research, the application may be for research both in Korea and in another foreign area.

Closing Date: January 1st.

Additional Information: Applicants are expected to be proficient in Korean. The program is supported in part by the Korea Foundation and the Korea Research Foundation.

The Korea Program: Grants for Planning Activities

Subjects: The social sciences and humanities relating to Korea.

Eligibility: There are no citizenship requirements. Grants are available to scholars with either a PhD or equivalent research experience.

Level of Study: Postdoctorate.

Frequency: Twice yearly.

Closing Date: November 1st, February 1st.

Additional Information: The Korea program is interested in promising new ideas or questions whose discussion offers considerable potential for advancing the state of theory or methodology in the social sciences and humanities; and topics where substantial new research is under way and where a comprehensive review can advance future studies. A 10--15-page proposal should describe the substantive problem, broad trends found in the literature on the topic, the particular research questions to be addressed, the theoretical and methodological approaches to be taken, a budget, and a list of the scholars to be involved.

The Latin America and Caribbean Program: Advanced Research Grants

Subjects: All aspects of the societies and cultures of Latin America or the Caribbean. Research proposals on any topic are eligible for support, including those involving more than one area or country within Latin America or the Caribbean. Projects involving a Latin American and a non-Latin American country are also accepted.

Eligibility: Open to scholars who hold the PhD or an equivalent degree and are US citizens or have been resident in the USA for at least three consecutive years at the time of application.

Level of Study: Postdoctorate.

Purpose: To facilitate research by social scientists and humanists.

Type: Research Grant.

No. of awards offered: Varies.

Frequency: Annual.

Value: Varies; a maximum of US$15,000.

Length of Study: 2-12 months, proposals for major projects as well as shorter visits to research sites will be considered.

Applications Procedure: Application form must be completed.

Closing Date: December 1st. Application forms are available from August 15th.

Additional Information: Regardless of the length of the grant, it is expected that grantees will devote all or a major part of their time during the grant period to research. This usually involves partial or full-time leave from a university or other institution. Other proposed arrangements for allocating research time will be considered, provided they include the commitment of at least two months of the applicant's own time. The grants vary in amount according to project requirements. While some awards cover only travel expenses, others provide financial support for maintenance and research as well. Travel expenses of dependants may be funded only for field stays of six months or more. In all cases, applicants are encouraged to seek additional support from other sources. While grants may be held concurrently with other funding, the program reserves the right to reduce the level of support if substantial overlap occurs. Scholars who have held an Advanced Research Grant from the Council in the previous five years may not submit an application, although individuals who have received a Doctoral Fellowship are eligible.

For further information contact:
Latin America and the Caribbean Program, Social Science Research Council, 810 Seventh Avenue, New York, NY, 10019, USA
Tel: 212 377 2700
Fax: 212 377 2727

The Latin America and the Caribbean Program: Dissertation Fellowships

Subjects: Doctoral dissertation research in the social sciences and the humanities relating to Latin America and the Caribbean. Proposals on any topic are eligible for support, including projects comparing Latin American or Caribbean countries to others located outside this region.

Eligibility: Open to full-time students, regardless of citizenship, who are enrolled in doctoral programs in the USA. Students should have completed all PhD requirements, except the dissertation, before going into the field.

Level of Study: Doctorate.

Type: Fellowship.

Frequency: Annual.

Value: Varies.

Length of Study: 9-18 months.

Study Establishment: A university, research institute or other appropriate institution in the foreign country.

Country of Study: In a country or countries relevant to the proposal.

Applications Procedure: Application form must be submitted with proposal, three letters of recommendation, graduate and undergraduate transcripts, and language evaluation forms.

Closing Date: November 1st. Application forms are available from August 1st.

Additional Information: Support for dissertation write-up is available to Fellows for up to six months after return from the field.

The Near and Middle East Program: Advanced Research Grants

Subjects: Doctoral dissertation research on the Near and Middle East (North Africa, the Middle East, Afghanistan, Iran and Turkey) in the humanities and social sciences. Research projects must be concerned with the period since the beginning of Islam. Researchers in disciplines previously underrepresented in this competition are especially encouraged; these include literature, economics, sociology, demographics, philosophy, religion, art history, and performance studies.

Eligibility: Open to citizens or permanent residents of the USA who are scholars whose competence for research on the area has been demonstrated by their previous work and who intend to make continuing contributions to the field.

Level of Study: Postdoctorate.

Type: Research Grant.

No. of awards offered: Varies.

Frequency: Annual.

Value: Up to US$15,000 for partial maintenance, travel, and research expenses.

Country of Study: One or more countries in the Near and Middle East.

Closing Date: December 1st.

Additional Information: Preference will be given to individuals without access to other major research support and to projects which are in the early stages of preparation and which require substantial field research.

The Near and Middle East Program: Dissertation Fellowships

Subjects: Doctoral dissertation research on the Near and Middle East (North Africa, the Middle East, Afghanistan, Iran, and Turkey) in the humanities and the social sciences. Research projects must be concerned with the period since the beginning of Islam.

Eligibility: Open to full-time students, regardless of citizenship, who are enrolled in doctoral programs in the USA; and to US citizens and permanent residents enrolled in full-time doctoral programs abroad.

Frequency: Annual.

Length of Study: Nine to 18 months.

Country of Study: One or more countries in the Near or Middle East.

Closing Date: November 1st.

Additional Information: Support for dissertation write-up cannot exceed six months. Successful applicants to the dissertation fellowship program may be eligible for the Louis Dupree Prize for Research on Afghanistan and/or Central Asia.

Sexuality Research Fellowship Program

Level of Study: Postdoctorate, Doctorate.

Purpose: To fund social and behavioural research on sexuality topics/issues at the dissertation and postdoctoral level.

Type: Fellowship.

No. of awards offered: Ten.

Frequency: Annual.

Length of Study: Two years.

Applications Procedure: Please write for details.

The South Asia Program: Advanced Research Grants

Subjects: All aspects of the societies and cultures of historical and contemporary South Asia, including politics, economics, culture and society.

Eligibility: Open to US citizens or persons who have been resident in the USA for three years at the time of application, who hold the PhD degree or an equivalent degree.

Level of Study: Postdoctorate.

Purpose: To enable humanists and social scientists to conduct research or to analyse previously gathered research materials on Bangladesh, Bhutan, India, Maldives, Nepal, Pakistan and Sri Lanka.

Type: Research Grant.

No. of awards offered: Varies.

Frequency: Annual.

Value: Up to US$15,000 for maintenance, travel and research expenses, and to supplement sabbatical salaries or awards from other sources.

Length of Study: Up to 12 months.

Study Establishment: At a major collection of South Asian materials or at any other appropriate locale.

Country of Study: Bangladesh, Bhutan, Maldives, Nepal, Pakistan and Sri Lanka.

Closing Date: December 1st.

Additional Information: Applicants should not request support for travel to or research within India, since funds for these purposes are available from the American Institute of Indian Studies, Foster Hall, University of Chicago, 1130 East 59th Street, Chicago, IL 60637, USA. Summer Awards will not be granted if the applicant is remaining at his/her home institution. Funds are limited and all applicants are encouraged to seek other support as well.

The South Asia Program: Bangladesh Predissertation Fellowships

Subjects: Bangladesh- or Bengal-related studies.

Eligibility: Open to students of any nationality who, at the time of application, have completed at least one year of graduate study in a program leading to a PhD in the social sciences or humanities at a North American university.

Level of Study: Doctorate.

Purpose: To support short-term field trips to Bangladesh designed for preliminary dissertation field activities, such as investigating potential research sites, archival and other research materials, development of language skills and establishing local research contacts.

Type: Fellowship.

Frequency: Annual.

Value: US$5,200.

Length of Study: 3-4 months.

Country of Study: Bangladesh.

Closing Date: November 1st.

Additional Information: The program is funded by the Ford Foundation.

For further information contact:
South Asia Program, Social Science Research Council, 810 Seventh Avenue, New York, NY, 10019, USA
Tel: 212 377 2700
Fax: 212 377 2727

The South Asia Program: Dissertation Fellowships

Subjects: Doctoral dissertation research in the social sciences and humanities relating to Nepal, Pakistan, Sri Lanka, Bhutan, Maldives and Bangladesh.

Eligibility: Open to full-time students, regardless of citizenship, who are enrolled in doctoral programs in the USA; and to US citizens and permanent residents enrolled in full-time doctoral programs abroad. Citizens of Bangladesh anywhere in the world are eligible to apply for Bangladesh dissertation grants. Applicants must expect to complete all requirements for the PhD except the dissertation by the spring of the year of the Fellowship.

Level of Study: Doctorate.

Type: Fellowship.

Frequency: Annual.

Length of Study: Up to 18 months.

Closing Date: November 1st.

Additional Information: Applicants seeking support for research in India should contact the American Institute of Indian Studies, Foster Hall, University of Chicago, 1120 East Street, Chicago, IL 60637, USA.

The South Asia Program: Predissertation Fellowships

Subjects: South Asian studies.

Eligibility: Open to US nationals only.

Level of Study: Doctorate.

Purpose: To support short-term field trips designed for preliminary dissertation field activities, such as investigating potential research sites and research materials, development of language skills and establishing local research contacts. Students in under-represented disciplines in South Asian studies, as well as students seeking language training in Bangladesh, Nepal, Pakistan or Sri Lanka, are encouraged to apply.

Type: Fellowship.

Frequency: Annual.

Length of Study: 3-9 months.

Country of Study: Nepal, Pakistan, Bhutan, Maldives, Bangladesh, Sri Lanka, India.

Closing Date: November 1st.

Additional Information: This program is funded by the United States Information Agency Near and Middle East Research and Training Act.

For further information contact:
South Asia Program, Social Science Research Council, 810 Seventh Avenue, New York, NY, 10019, USA
Tel: 212 377 2700
Fax: 212 377 2727

The Southeast Asia Program: Advanced Research Grants

Subjects: All aspects of the societies and cultures of historical and contemporary Southeast Asia. Comparative research between countries in the region is also encouraged.

Eligibility: Open to holders of the PhD or an equivalent degree who are US citizens or have been resident in the USA for at least three consecutive years at the time of application.

Level of Study: Postdoctorate.

Purpose: To enable social scientists, humanists, and other professionals to conduct research or analyse previously gathered research materials on Brunei, Burma, Indonesia, Cambodia, Laos, Malaysia, the Philippines, Thailand, Singapore and Vietnam.

Type: Research Grant.

No. of awards offered: Varies.

Frequency: Annual.

Value: Up to US$15,000 for travel, research expenses, and maintenance.

Length of Study: Up to 12 months.

Study Establishment: In Southeast Asia, at major collections of Southeast Asian materials, or at any other appropriate locale.

Country of Study: Any country.

Closing Date: December 1st.

Additional Information: Collaboration and team research projects among scholars of different disciplines, nationalities or levels of seniority are encouraged. Summer Awards will not be granted for those remaining at their home institution. Maintenance and travel of dependants may also be included if full-time research will be conducted outside the grantee's home country for more than six months. Funds are limited and all applicants are encouraged to seek other support as well.

The Southeast Asia Program: Dissertation Fellowships

Subjects: Doctoral dissertation research in the social sciences and humanities in Southeast Asia (Brunei, Burma, Indonesia, Cambodia, Laos, Malaysia, the Philippines, Thailand, Singapore and Vietnam).

Eligibility: Open to full-time students, regardless of citizenship, who are enrolled in doctoral programs in the USA; and to US citizens and permanent residents enrolled in full-time doctoral programs abroad.

Level of Study: Doctorate.

Type: Fellowship.

Frequency: Annual.

Length of Study: 9-18 months.

Country of Study: Southeast Asia.

Closing Date: November 1st.

The Soviet Union and its Successor States Program: Dissertation Fellowships

Subjects: The humanities and social sciences relating to the Soviet Union and its successor states.

Eligibility: Open to US citizens who have completed research for their doctoral dissertation and who expect to complete the writing of their dissertation during the next academic year.

Level of Study: Doctorate, Postdoctorate.

Type: Varies.

Frequency: Annual.

Value: Up to US$15,000.

Length of Study: Up to one year.

Applications Procedure: Application form; three letters of recommendation; one official copy of all relevant post secondary study; language self evauation; narrative statement.

Closing Date: December 1st.

For further information contact:
Social Science Research Council, 810 Seventh Ave, New York, NY, 10019, USA
Tel: 212 377 2700
Fax: 212 377 2727

548

Contact: JCSSS (Soviet Union & Successor States)

The Soviet Union and its Successor States Program: Graduate Training Fellowships

Subjects: Post-Soviet studies.

Eligibility: Open to US citizens currently enrolled in a graduate program who have strong training in the study of the Soviet Union and its successor states and propose related disciplinary or methodological training; or previous training in a discipline and wish to acquire competence in the study of the Soviet Union and its successor states.

Level of Study: Postgraduate.

Purpose: To support students in their third, fourth or fifth year of graduate study.

Type: Fellowship.

Frequency: Annual.

Value: Up to US$15,000.

Length of Study: 12 months subject to performance review at the end of the first six months.

Applications Procedure: Application forms; three letters of recommendation; one official copy of all relevant post-secondary study; language self evauation; description of program of study.

Closing Date: December 1st.

Additional Information: Fellowship applications must present a coherent program of training outside of the normal course of study that may include support for intensive training in the languages of the former Soviet Union. Successful applicants to the graduate training fellowship program may be eligible for the Louis Dupree Prize for Research on Afghanistan and/or Central Asia.

The Soviet Union and its Successor States Program: Postdoctoral Fellowships

Subjects: The social sciences and humanities relating to the Soviet Union and its successor states.

Eligibility: Open to US citizens who have defended their dissertations by September 1st, and who are untenured.

Purpose: To improve the academic employment and tenure opportunities of new PhDs.

Type: Fellowship.

Frequency: Annual.

Value: A stipend of US$27,000 to provide three years of summer support plus one semester free of teaching for scholars.

Closing Date: December 1st.

For further information contact:
JCSSS , Social Science Research Council, 810 Seventh Ave, New York, NY, 10019, USA
Tel: 212 377 2700

SSRC - MacArthur Foundation Dissertation Fellowships

Subjects: Training and research on peace and security in a changing world.

Eligibility: Open to researchers who are finishing course work, examinations, or similar requirements for the PhD or its equivalent. There are no citizenship, residency or nationality requirements.

Level of Study: Doctorate.

Purpose: To support innovative and interdisciplinary research on the implications for security issues of worldwide cultural, social, economic, military and political changes.

Type: Fellowship.

No. of awards offered: Approximately eight.

Frequency: Annual.

Value: Stipend appropriate for the cost of living in the area where the Fellow will be working. It will rarely exceed US$17,500 per annum.

Length of Study: Two years.

Country of Study: Unrestricted.

Applications Procedure: Official application form must be completed. Please send request to SSRC office.

Closing Date: December 1st for announcement in April.

Additional Information: The program is directed by the Committee on International Peace and Security. Successful applicants to the dissertation fellowship program may be eligible for the Louis Dupree Prize for Research on Afghanistan and/or Central Asia.

SSRC - MacArthur Foundation Postdoctoral Fellowships

Subjects: Training and research on peace and security in a changing world.

Eligibility: Open to persons who hold the PhD or its equivalent, and who are in the first ten years of their postdoctoral careers, and to lawyers, public servants, journalists or others who can demonstrate comparable research experience and an ability to contribute to the research literature. There are no citizenship, residency or nationality requirements.

Level of Study: Postdoctorate.

Purpose: To support innovative and interdisciplinary research on the implications for security issues of worldwide cultural, social, economic, military and political changes.

Type: Fellowship.

No. of awards offered: Approximately eight.

Frequency: Annual.

Value: Stipend appropriate for the Fellow's salary and the cost of living in the area where the Fellow will be working. It will rarely exceed US$36,000 per annum.

Length of Study: Two years.

Country of Study: Unrestricted.

Applications Procedure: Official application form must be completed - these can be obtained from the SSRC office.

Closing Date: December 1st for announcement in April.

Additional Information: Additional Support for Area Studies Specialists: at the time of application, both dissertation and postdoctoral applicants who are already qualified as area studies researchers may request a three- to twelve-month extension of the term of the Fellowship for field work in the nation or region of their expertise. The Council will purchase one round-trip ticket for the fellow's travel to the area, in addition to other Council funding. Applicants for such extensions must clearly demonstrate the substantive importance of conducting this field work as well as their special qualifications for it. This support is not available simply for short-term visits, for the use of European or US archives, or for taking one's training or maintaining residence in a foreign country. Conducting field work in one's native country or usual country of residence will ordinarily not qualify for this support.

The Japan Program: Advanced Research Grants

Subjects: Traditional, area-studies-oriented research in the humanities and the social sciences, as well as projects which are comparative and contemporary in nature, and have long-term applied policy implications, or which engage Japan in wider regional and global debates.

Eligibility: Open to holders of the PhD or an equivalent degree who are US citizens or have been resident in the USA for at least three consecutive years at the time of application.

Level of Study: Postdoctorate.

No. of awards offered: Varies.

Frequency: Annual.

Value: Grants are disbursed in dollars and/or yen depending on the location of the research.

Length of Study: Two to 12 months.

Country of Study: Japan, the USA and/or other countries.

Closing Date: December 1st.

Additional Information: Special attention will be given to Japanists who are interested in broadening their skills and expertise through additional training or comparative work in an additional geographic area; and to non-Japanists who use Japan as a case study or those who draw Japan into wider global debates.

Western Europe Program: Berlin Program for Advanced German and European Studies

Subjects: German and European studies.

Eligibility: Open to citizens and permanent residents of the USA who, at the dissertation level, have completed all requirements (except the dissertation) for the PhD at the time the Fellowship begins, or at the postdoctoral level, have received the PhD or its equivalent in the last two years.

Level of Study: Doctorate, Postdoctorate.

Purpose: To encourage the comparative and interdisciplinary study of the economic, political, and social aspects of modern and contemporary German and European affairs by supporting anthropologists, economists, political scientists, sociologists, and all scholars in germane social science and cultural studies fields, including historians working on the period since the mid-19th century.

No. of awards offered: 12.

Frequency: Annual.

Value: 2,000DM per month.

Length of Study: 9-12 months.

Study Establishment: The Free University of Berlin.

Country of Study: Germany.

Closing Date: January 1st.

Additional Information: Fellows are expected to produce a research monograph dealing with some aspect(s) of German or European affairs, including US-European relations. The program is funded by the Berlin government, the Volkswagen Foundation, and the German Marshall Fund of the United States.

SOCIAL SCIENCES AND HUMANITIES RESEARCH COUNCIL OF CANADA

Social Sciences and Humanities Research Council of Canada, PO Box 1610, Ottawa, Ontario, K1P 6G4, Canada
Tel: 613 992 0530
Fax: 613 992 1787
Contact: Fellowships Program

Thérèse F Casgrain Fellowship

Subjects: Women and social change in Canada: research.

Eligibility: Applicants must be Canadian citizens or permanent residents and maintain permanent residence in Canada for the duration of the award. At the time of taking up the Fellowship, the successful candidate must have obtained a doctorate or an equivalent advanced professional degree.

Purpose: To encourage research on any subject which falls within the broadly defined area of 'Women and Social Change in Canada'.

Type: Fellowship.

No. of awards offered: One.

Frequency: Biennially (even-numbered years).

Value: C$40,000 of which an accountable amount of C$10,000 may be used for travel and research expenses.

Length of Study: Twelve months; not renewable.

Country of Study: Canada.

Closing Date: June 15th.

Additional Information: The Fellowship was created by the Thérèse F Casgrain Foundation and is administered by the Social Sciences and Humanities Research Council.

Doctoral Fellowships

Subjects: Social sciences and humanities.

Eligibility: Open to persons who, by the time of taking up the Fellowship, will have completed one year of graduate study or all the requirements for the master's degree beyond the honours BA or its equivalent, and will be registered in a program of studies leading to the PhD or its equivalent. Fellowships are available to Canadian citizens and nationals of other countries who have obtained permanent resident status.

Purpose: To develop research skills and to assist in the training of highly qualified personnel.

No. of awards offered: Approximately 600 new Fellowships and 1,000 renewals.

Frequency: Annual.

Value: Up to C$14,436 per annum.

Length of Study: For a full 48 months, or for a shorter period of not less than 6 months; renewable.

Country of Study: Canada, or elsewhere under certain conditions.

Applications Procedure: On application form.

Closing Date: Completed application forms must be mailed to the Council by November 15th for applicants not registered at a Canadian university and by January 15th for Canadian universities. Each Canadian university must submit application for students registered at their university.

General Research Grants

Subjects: Social sciences, humanities.

Eligibility: Open to Canadian universities.

Purpose: To enable Canadian universities to meet modest research requirements of their teaching staff.

Type: Research Grant.

No. of awards offered: Varies.

Frequency: Annual.

Value: Varies: calculated on the number of faculty in each university. Universities may award not more than C$5,000 to individual researchers to help cover small research expenses, cost of travel to conferences and other similar costs.

Closing Date: October 1st.

For further information contact:
Social Sciences and Research Council of Canada, 255 Albert Street, PO Box 1610, Ottawa, Ontario, K1P 6G4, Canada
Tel: 613 992 3131
Fax: 613 992 1787
Contact: Research Communication and International Relations Division

Bora Laskin National Fellowship in Human Rights Research

Subjects: Human rights, as relevant to Canada.

Eligibility: Open to Canadian citizens or permanent residents of Canada who have a graduate degree or equivalent in one or more of the fields addressed.

Purpose: To encourage research and development of expertise in the field of human rights.

Type: Fellowship.

No. of awards offered: One.

Frequency: Annual.

Value: C$45,000, plus a research and travel allowance of C$10,000.

Length of Study: 12 months; not renewable.

Country of Study: Canada; travel abroad will be permitted for research purposes.

Closing Date: October 1st.

Jules and Gabrielle Léger Fellowship

Subjects: The Crown and Governor General in a parliamentary democracy.

Eligibility: Applicants must be Canadian citizens or permanent residents of Canada, of demonstrated scholarly competence, who will be able to devote their full time to this research.

Purpose: To encourage research and writing on the historical contribution of the Crown and its representatives, federal and provincial, to the political, constitutional, cultural, intellectual and social life of the country, including comparison between Canadian and Commonwealth systems.

Type: Fellowship.

No. of awards offered: One.

Frequency: Biennially (odd-numbered years).

Value: C$40,000, plus C$10,000 for research and travel costs.

Study Establishment: A recognized university or research institute.

Country of Study: Unrestricted.

Closing Date: October 1st.

Master's Scholarships in Science Policy

Subjects: Science policy.

Eligibility: Open to Canadian citizens or permanent residents of Canada living in Canada. At the time of taking up the award, the successful applicants must hold a bachelor's degree in any discipline.

Purpose: To encourage students to undertake studies at the master's level in science policy.

Type: Scholarship.

No. of awards offered: Six.

Frequency: Annual.

Value: C$14,436, plus a travel allowance.

Length of Study: One year; renewable for a second year.

Study Establishment: At any recognized university.

Country of Study: Any country.

Closing Date: December 1st.

Postdoctoral Fellowships

Subjects: Social sciences and humanities.

Eligibility: Open to Canadian citizens or permanent residents of Canada who have been awarded a doctoral degree no earlier than three years prior to the competition deadline (or who have fulfilled all requirements for a doctorate before the Fellowship period), and who intend to engage in full-time postdoctoral research for one year while affiliated with a recognized university or research institute.

Purpose: To support the most promising new scholars and to assist them in establishing a research base at an important time in their research career.

Type: Fellowships.

No. of awards offered: Approximately 100.

Frequency: Annual.

Value: Up to C$27,984, plus a personal allowance of up to C$5,000.

Length of Study: For a full 24 months.

Country of Study: Canada or elsewhere.

Closing Date: October 1st.

Queen's Fellowships

Subjects: Canadian studies.

Eligibility: Open to Canadian citizens and permanent residents who, by the time of taking up the Fellowship, will have completed one year of graduate study or all the requirements for the master's degree beyond the honours BA or its equivalent, and will be registered in a program of studies leading to the PhD or its equivalent. This award is offered to one or two outstanding successful Doctoral Fellowship candidates.

Purpose: To assist a candidate who intends to enter a doctoral program in Canadian studies at a Canadian university.

Type: Fellowship.

No. of awards offered: One to two.

Frequency: Annual.

Value: C$14,436, plus an allowance to cover tuition fees and travel.

Length of Study: One year; not renewable.

Study Establishment: At a recognized university.

Country of Study: Canada.

Closing Date: October 15th for candidates not registered at a Canadian university; November 20th for candidates registered at a Canadian university.

Additional Information: The Queen's Fellowship is not a program but a special award given to a Doctoral Fellow. Candidates cannot apply for this award but are automatically eligible if they intend to study Canadian studies at a Canadian university.

Research Grants (Major)

Subjects: Social sciences; humanities.

Eligibility: Open to career scholars who are Canadian citizens or permanent residents of Canada affiliated with a Canadian university, or a recognized post-secondary institution.

Purpose: To support large-scale advanced research and editorial projects and programs.

Type: Research Grant.

No. of awards offered: Varies.

Frequency: Annual.

Value: A minimum of C$100,000 for one year; C$250,000 for three years; C$400,000 for five years. The ceiling is C$500,000 in any given year.

Length of Study: Five years maximum.

Study Establishment: At an institution and for a duration appropriate to the nature of the research.

Closing Date: October 15th.

For further information contact:
Social Sciences and Humanities Research Council of Canada, 255 Albert Street, PO Box 1610, Ottawa, Ontario, K1P 6G4, Canada
Tel: 613 992 3145
Fax: 613 992 1787
Contact: Communications Division

Research Grants (Standard)

Subjects: Social sciences; humanities.

Eligibility: Open to career scholars who are Canadian citizens or permanent residents of Canada affiliated with a Canadian university or a recognized post-secondary institution.

Purpose: To support advanced research.

Type: Research Grant.

No. of awards offered: Varies.

Frequency: Annual.

Value: Less than C$100,000 per annum or less than C$250,000 over a three year period. A minimum of C$5,000 in at least one of the years is

required unless the applicant is at an institution not receiving a General Research Grant.

Length of Study: Grants in support of research programs will ordinarily be expected to cover three-year periods.

Study Establishment: At an institution and for a duration appropriate to the nature of the research.

Closing Date: October 15th.

Strategic Research Grants, Research Networks, Research Workshops, Partnership Development Grants

Subjects: Any subject relevant to the current five themes: Women and Change; Education and Work in a Changing Society; Applied Ethics; Managing for Global Competitiveness; Science and Technology Policy in Canada; mature themes are replaced after a period of five years.

Eligibility: Open to teams headed by career scholars who are Canadian citizens or permanent residents of Canada and who are affiliated with an eligible post-secondary institution in Canada.

Purpose: To support research projects and research related activities in areas of national importance.

Type: Research Grant.

No. of awards offered: Varies.

Frequency: Annual.

Value: Up to C$100,000 for one year or C$250,000 for three years (Strategic Research Grants); Up to C$40,000 per annum (Research Networks); Up to C$15,000 per event (Research Workshops); Up to C$5,000 (Partnership Development).

Length of Study: Up to three years (Strategic Research Grants); normally for three years (Research Networks); for single events held in Canada only (Research Workshops); for 1 year or less (Partnership Development).

Study Establishment: At an appropriate institution.

Country of Study: Canada.

Closing Date: October 15th; Partnership Development, any time.

Additional Information: An applicant may be principal investigator on only one Strategic Research Grant but may also participate in a Network or Workshop. Research Networks should be centred in Canada but may include non-Canadian members. Only the Canadian participants' expenses will be supported by the SSHRC.

SOCIAL WORKERS EDUCATIONAL TRUST

16 Kent Street, Birmingham, B5 6RD, England
Contact: British Association of Social Workers

*Award

Subjects: Competitive submission of research and practice development in social work, health care, mental health.

Eligibility: Open to qualified social workers who have completed two years' work post qualification.

No. of awards offered: One.

Frequency: Annual.

Value: £1,000.

Country of Study: UK.

Closing Date: End of January.

SOCIÉTÉ DES PROFESSEURS FRANÇAIS ET FRANCOPHONES D'AMÉRIQUE

Société des Professeurs Français et Francophones d'Amérique, 140 East 95th Street (1 E), New York, NY, 10128, USA
Tel: 212 996 2376
Fax: 212 996 2367
Contact: Dr J Macary

*Jean and Marie-Louise Dufrenoy Scholarship

Subjects: Graduate study in biology, biochemistry, botany, chemistry, diatetics, geology, mathematics, physics, plant pathology, zoology or any other scientific discipline. If there are no candidates in the above mentioned fields the Scholarship could be awarded to a student who, after getting a Bachelor of Arts degree, would start a career in the field of education or diplomacy.

Eligibility: Open to holders of a Bachelor of Sciences or a Bachelor of Arts degree.

No. of awards offered: One.

Frequency: Annual.

Value: US$8,000.

Length of Study: One year; renewable for a further year in exceptional circumstances.

Study Establishment: A French university.

Country of Study: France.

Applications Procedure: Applications should include a letter in French stating the applicant's reasons for studying in a French university, two copies of his/her academic transcript(s), and three letters of recommendation. Applicants are advised to contact the university of their choice as soon as possible, as well as the French General Consulate of their region to determine the requirements for obtaining a student visa. A certificate of admission to a French university or a certified copy of it must be received at the SPFFA before July 1st.

Closing Date: February 1st.

Additional Information: The student's knowledge of French must be at a level which will allow studies to be undertaken at the university.

*Jeanne Marandon Scholarships

Subjects: All disciplines will be considered, the following ones in particular: literature, history, social sciences, arts and music.

Eligibility: Open to scholars holding a doctorate; graduate students (preferably ABD); and students enrolled for an MA, MHA or MAT.

Type: Scholarship.

No. of awards offered: Varies.

Frequency: Annual.

Value: Varies according to academic level and length of stay: researchers US$12,000 per annum; graduate students US$10,000 per annum; MA, MHA and MAT students US$2,500-US$8,000.

Length of Study: One semester, or for a full academic year.

Country of Study: France or Canada (Quebec).

Applications Procedure: Researchers: the application file must include a resume, a proposal, a bibliography, and three letters of recommendation. Graduate students: the application file must include the thesis proposal, a resume, complete transcripts, three letters of recommendation, one of which must be from the dissertation director. MA, MHA or MAT students: the application file must include complete transcripts, three letters of recommendation and a copy of the candidate's matriculation certificate. All candidates must have a sufficient knowledge of both oral and written French to allow them to continue their studies in France or Quebec.

Closing Date: January 1st.

*Scholarships in Quebec

Subjects: Any subject offered at the universities of Montreal and Laval.

Eligibility: Open preferably to US citizens who are undergraduate students, graduate students who specialize in French or whose major necessitates a sound knowledge of French, and professors who teach French in High Schools.

Type: Scholarship.

No. of awards offered: Varies.

Frequency: Annual.

Value: US$1,200 to cover fees and most living expenses.

Length of Study: Six weeks from July to August.

Study Establishment: The University of Montreal or the University Laval, in Quebec.

Country of Study: Canada.

Applications Procedure: Application requirements vary according to academic level.

Closing Date: November 15th.

SOCIETY FOR ITALIAN HISTORICAL STUDIES

Society for Italian Historical Studies, History Department, Boston College, Chestnut Hill, MA, 02167, USA
Tel: 617 552 3814
Contact: Alan J Reinerman

Award for the Best Unpublished Dissertation

Eligibility: US or Canadian citizens who have received PhD within two years of closing date.

Level of Study: Doctorate.

Purpose: To encourage the study of Italian History.

Type: Cash.

No. of awards offered: One.

Frequency: Annual.

Value: US$200.

Applications Procedure: Submit CV and three copies of dissertation to award committee.

Closing Date: August 1st.

THE SOCIETY FOR THEATRE RESEARCH

The Society for Theatre Research, c/o The Theatre Museum, 1E Tavistock Street, London, WC2 7PA, England
Contact: The Chairman of Research Awards Sub-Committee

*Research Awards

Subjects: Research substantially concerned with the history and practice of the British theatre, including music hall, opera, dance and other associated performing arts; exclusively literary topics are not eligible.

Eligibility: Applicants should normally be aged 18 or over but there is no other restriction on their status, nationality, or the location of the research.

No. of awards offered: Two major awards and a number of lesser awards.

Frequency: Annual.

Value: From a total of approximately £5,000: major awards normally £1,000-£2,000, other awards normally £200-£500.

Closing Date: February 1st.

Additional Information: While applications will need to show evidence of the value of the research and a scholarly approach, they are by no means restricted to professional academics. Many awards, including major ones, have previously been made to 'amateur' researchers, who are encouraged to apply. The Society also welcomes proposals which in their execution extend methods and techniques of historiography. In coming to its decisions, the Society will consider the progress already made by the applicants and the possible availability of other grants.

SOCIETY FOR THE PROMOTION OF HELLENIC STUDIES

Society for the Promotion of Hellenic Studies, 31-34 Gordon Square, London, WC1H 0PP, England
Tel: 0171 387 7495
Fax: 0171 307 7495
Email: helsoc@clus1.ulcc.ac.uk
Contact: Miss F Jane Fisher

Dover Fund

Subjects: Greek language and papyri.

Eligibility: Open to currently registered research students, and, within the first five years of their appointment, to lecturers, teaching fellows, research fellows, postdoctoral fellows and research assistants.

Level of Study: Postgraduate, Doctorate, Postdoctorate.

Purpose: To further the study of the history of the Greek language in any period from the Bronze Age to the 15th century AD and to further the edition and exegesis of Greek texts, including papyri and inscriptions, from any period within those same limits.

Value: Grants will be made for such purposes as books, photography (including microfilm and xeroxing), and towards the costs of visits to libraries, museums and sites. The sums awarded will vary according to the needs of the applicant, but most grants will be in the range £50-£250; larger grants may be made from time to time at the discretion of the awards committee.

Applications Procedure: Application form (including section for a referee) available from the society.

Additional Information: February 14th of the year in which the award is sought.

SOCIETY FOR THE PROMOTION OF ROMAN STUDIES

Society for the Promotion of Roman Studies, 31-34 Gordon Square, London, WC1H 0PP, England
Tel: 0171 387 8157
Email: romansoc@sas.ac.uk
Contact: Dr Helen M Cockle

Hugh Last and Donald Atkinson Funds Committee Grants

Subjects: Italy and the Roman Empire: history, archaeology, literature and art.

Eligibility: Open to applicants of postdoctoral status or the equivalent, usually of UK nationality.

Level of Study: Postdoctorate.

Purpose: To assist in the undertaking, completion or publication of work that relates to any of the general scholarly purposes of the Roman Society, which are to promote the study of the history, archaeology, literature and art of Italy and the Roman Empire, from the earliest times down to about AD 700.

Type: Grant.

No. of awards offered: 20.

Frequency: Annually; dependent on funds available.

Value: Varies, but usually £200-£1,000.

Country of Study: Not specified but usually a country formerly in the Roman Empire.

Applications Procedure: Completion of application form is not essential, but all applicants must ensure that two references are sent directly to the Society.

Closing Date: January 15th.

Additional Information: Awards not normally made towards expenses incurred in preparation of a thesis.

SOCIETY FOR THE PSYCHOLOGICAL STUDY OF SOCIAL ISSUES

SPSSI Central Office, PO Box 1248, Ann Arbor, MI, 48106-1248, USA
Tel: 313 662 9130
Fax: 313 662 5607
Email: spssi@umich.edu
www: http://www.apa.org/division.html

Gordon Allport Intergroup Relations Prize

Subjects: Intergroup relations. Originality of the contribution, whether theoretical or empirical, will be given special weight. The research area of intergroup relations includes such dimensions as age, sex, and socioeconomic status, as well as race.

Eligibility: Open to non-members, as well as members of SPSSI. Graduate students are especially urged to submit papers.

Level of Study: Postgraduate.

Purpose: To recognize the best paper or article of the year on intergroup relations.

Type: Prize.

No. of awards offered: One.

Frequency: Annual.

Value: US$1,000.

Closing Date: December 31st.

Additional Information: Entries can be either papers published during the current year or unpublished manuscripts. Entries cannot be returned. Four copies of entries must be sent. Please include contact information for all authors.

Grants-in-Aid Program

Subjects: Scientific research in social problem areas related to the basic interests and goals of SPSSI and particularly those that are not likely to receive support from traditional sources.

Eligibility: Open to students at least at the dissertation stage of a graduate career.

Level of Study: Postgraduate.

Type: Grant.

No. of awards offered: Varies.

Frequency: Twice yearly.

Value: Up to US$2,000. Up to US$1,000 for graduates, which must be matched by the graduate's university. Funds are not normally provided for travel to conventions, travel or living expenses while conducting research, stipends of principal investigators, or costs associated with manuscript preparation.

Closing Date: April 1st, November 13th.

Additional Information: There are no formal application blanks; interested persons should submit three copies of a statement that includes a cover sheet stating title of proposal, name of investigator, address, phone, and fax number; an abstract of 100 words or less summarizing the proposed research; project purposes, theoretical rationale, and specific procedures to be employed; relevance of research to SPSSI goals and Grants-in-Aid criteria; resume of investigator (a faculty sponsor's recommendation must be provided if the investigator is a graduate student; support is seldom awarded to students who have not yet reached the dissertation stage); specific amount requested including a budget. A recommended length for the entire proposal is 5-7 double-spaced, typed pages. The entire submission should be sent in triplicate to the Chair of the Grants-in-Aid Program: Dr Virgil Sheets, Department of Psychology, Indiana State University, Terre Haute, IN 47809. The Grants-in-Aid Program is sponsored in part by the Sophie and Shirley Cohen Memorial Fund and through membership contributions.

James Marshall Public Policy Fellowship

Subjects: Public policy research.

Eligibility: Open to holders of a PhD or PsyD who are either members of SPSSI and APA or eligible to be members. The selected Fellow must join SPSSI before the appointment date. Candidates must demonstrate interest in or involvement in the application of social science to social issues and policy, have a sound scientific and/or clinical background, and demonstrate sensitivity toward policy issues. Candidates should be interested in and knowledgeable about at least one current social issue such as homelessness, violence, adolescent pregnancy, child abuse, etc. Candidates must be able to communicate effectively both orally and in writing. Individual initiative is critical as well as the ability to work cooperatively with others having diverse viewpoints. Knowledge of policy processes at the national level is desirable, but not essential.

Level of Study: Postdoctorate.

Type: Fellowship.

No. of awards offered: One.

Frequency: Every two years.

Value: The stipend is projected to be US$37,000 the first year, plus health and vacation benefits. The stipend will be modestly increased the second year.

Length of Study: One or two years.

Study Establishment: The Public Policy Office of the American Psychological Association, in Washington, DC.

Country of Study: USA.

Closing Date: Postmarked January 15th.

Additional Information: The Fellow will participate in supervised activities including using psychological research to analyse specific social policies and develop policy advocacy. In addition to policy work, the Fellow will serve in various capacities as directed by SPSSI, including but not limited to: serving on SPSSI committees and/or task forces; monitoring APA boards, committees, and/or task forces relevant to the Fellow's main policy area; reporting to and attending SPSSI's semi-annual Council meetings; writing a public policy column for the SPSSI newsletter; and meeting regularly with the Fellow Oversight Committee. The public policy activities and issues vary from year to year as opportunities and circumstances change, as SPSSI and APA priorities shift, and as the interests and expertise of the Fellows differ. Candidates for the Fellowship are required to submit a detailed vita: a 1000-word biographical statement of past experience and interest in policy activities and/or social issues, career goals, interest in the Fellowship and objectives desired from the Fellowship; a 600-word briefing statement using social science data and related information to inform a legislator about a specific social issue; three letters of reference addressing his/her abilities, experience, and interests as related to this Fellowship; and a statement indicating a preference for either a one- or two-year commitment to the Fellowship. Preference will be given to those making a two-year commitment. This award is not available until 1998.

Otto Klineberg Intercultural and International Relations Award

Subjects: Intercultural or international relations. Originality of the contribution, whether theoretical or empirical, will be given special weight.

Eligibility: Open to non-members, as well as members of SPSSI. Graduate students are especially urged to submit papers.

Level of Study: Postgraduate.

Purpose: To recognize the best paper or article of the year on intercultural or international relations.

No. of awards offered: One.

Frequency: Annual.

Value: US$1,000.

Closing Date: February 1st.

Additional Information: Entries can be either papers published during the current year or unpublished manuscripts. Entries cannot be returned. Five copies of entries must be sent. Please include contact information for all authors.

Sages Program

Subjects: Proposals are invited for applying social science principles to social issues in cooperation with a community, city, state or federal organization or other not-for-profit group. Projects may also be done in cooperation with universities or colleges throughout the world or with the UN.

Eligibility: Open to senior researchers who have retired from a previous research or teaching position in psychology, social science, or a related discipline.

Purpose: To encourage intervention projects, non-partisan advocacy projects, applied research, writing about the psychological study of social issues, and implementing public policy by social scientists over the age of 60.

Type: Grant.

No. of awards offered: Varies.

Frequency: Annual.

Value: Varies; up to US$2,000 for direct costs.

Applications Procedure: Candidates should send three copies of a brief (two- to five-page) proposal for the project they would like to do to the committee chair: Dr George Levinger, Chair, SAGES Committee, University of Massachusetts, Department of Psychology, Amhurst, MA, 01003. The proposal should also include a timetable and a request for any needed funds or other resources. Applications should include a copy of the candidate's CV and a letter from the sponsoring organization, if relevant.

Closing Date: April 15th.

Social Issues Dissertation Award

Subjects: Doctoral dissertations on social issues in psychology (or in a social science with psychological subject matter).

Eligibility: Open to doctoral dissertations on a relevant topic accepted between 1 March of the year preceding the year of application and 1 March of the year of application.

Level of Study: Postgraduate.

Type: Prize.

No. of awards offered: Two.

Frequency: Annual.

Value: First prize US$300; second prize US$200.

Additional Information: Dissertations will be judged according to scientific excellence and potential application to social problems. Applications should include four copies of a 500 word dissertation summary with all identification deleted; one copy of the summary with identification including the candidate's name, address, phone, school, and dissertation title; and certification by the dissertation advisor of the acceptance date of the dissertation.

THE SOCIETY FOR THE SCIENTIFIC STUDY OF SEXUALITY

The Society for the Scientific Study of Sexuality, PO Box 208, Mount Vernon, IA, 52314-0208, USA
Tel: 319 895 8407
Fax: 319 895 6203
Contact: Howard J Ruppel, Executive Director

SSSS Student Research Grant Award

Subjects: Related to the field of human sexuality from any discipline: psychology, anthropology, social work, biology, theology, medical research, etc.

Eligibility: Open to students of any nationality who are enrolled in a degree granting program.

Type: Grant.

No. of awards offered: Three.

Frequency: Twice yearly.

Value: US$750.

Study Establishment: At an appropriate institution.

Closing Date: February 1st; September 1st.

Additional Information: The purpose of the research can be a masters thesis or doctoral dissertation, but this is not a requirement. Funds to support these grants are provided by the Foundation for the Scientific Study of Sexuality.

SOCIETY FOR THE STUDY OF FRENCH HISTORY

Society for the Study of French History, History Department, Keele University, Keele, ST5 5BG, England
Tel: 01782 583199
Fax: 01782 583145
Email: hia10@keele.ac.uk
Contact: Dr Malcolm Crook

Bursaries

Subjects: Any aspect of French history.

Eligibility: Open to students registered for a higher degree at a UK university.

Level of Study: Postgraduate, Doctorate.

Type: Bursaries.

No. of awards offered: Two.

Frequency: Annual.

Value: £500.

Length of Study: One year.

Country of Study: UK.

Applications Procedure: Applications, giving details of the research being pursued and the use to which the money would be put, should be sent to the address shown, together with the names of two referees.

Closing Date: June 30th.

THE SOCIETY OF ANTIQUARIES OF LONDON

The Society of Antiquaries of London, Burlington House, Piccadilly, London, W1V 0HS, England
Tel: 0171 734 0193/437 9954
Fax: 0171 287 6967
Email: soc.antiq.lond@bacnc.org.uk

Contact: General Secretary

William Lambarde Memorial Fund Travelling Scholarships

Subjects: Archeology and other antiquarian subjects.

Eligibility: Open to academically well-qualified applicants who have demonstrated their ability to accomplish a particular project and publish the results.

Level of Study: Unrestricted.

Purpose: To enable scholars to travel abroad to pursue archaeological, or other antiquarian, research projects.

Type: Scholarship.

No. of awards offered: Around six.

Frequency: Triennially (1998).

Value: £200-£800.

Country of Study: Any country.

Applications Procedure: Form and further information available.

Closing Date: December 31st.

Joan Pye Award

Subjects: British archaeology.

Eligibility: Open to professional archaeologists who have recently been awarded a doctorate.

Level of Study: Unrestricted, Postdoctorate.

Purpose: To assist promising young archaeologists to follow a particular field of research.

No. of awards offered: One.

Frequency: Annual.

Value: At present £250.

Country of Study: UK.

Applications Procedure: Form and further information available.

Closing Date: December 31st.

Research Fund

Subjects: Archaeological and documentary research.

Eligibility: Open to academically well-qualified applicants who have demonstrated their ability to accomplish a particular project and publish the results.

Level of Study: Postdoctorate.

Purpose: To assist projects of a substantial nature aimed at increasing knowledge of a particular aspect of the past in any country or region.

No. of awards offered: Varies.

Frequency: Annual.

Value: Up to £2,000.

Country of Study: Any country.

Applications Procedure: Form and further information available.

Closing Date: December 31st.

SOCIETY OF APOTHECARIES OF LONDON

Society of Apothecaries of London, Black Friars Lane, London, EC4V 6EJ, England
Tel: 0171 236 1180
Fax: 0171 329 3177
Contact: The Clerk

Gillson Scholarship in Pathology

Subjects: Pathology.

Eligibility: Open to candidates under 35 years of age who are either Licenciates or Freemen of the Society, or who obtain the Licence or the Freedom within six months of election to the Scholarship.

Purpose: To encourage original research in any branch of pathology.

Type: Scholarship.

No. of awards offered: One.

Frequency: Triennially.

Value: £1,800 (£600 per annum). Payments are made twice annually for the duration of the Scholarship.

Length of Study: For 3 years; renewable for a second term of 3 years.

Applications Procedure: Candidates should submit two testimonials and present evidence of their attainments and capabilities as shown by any papers already published, and/or a detailed record of any pathological work already done. Candidates should also state where the research will be undertaken.

Closing Date: December 1st.

Additional Information: Preference is given to the candidate who is engaged in the teaching of medical science or in its research. Scholars are required to submit an interim report at the end of the first six months of tenure, and a complete report one month prior to the end of the third year. Any published results should also be submitted to the Society.

SOCIETY OF ARCHITECTURAL HISTORIANS

Society of Architectural Historians, 1365 North Astor Street, Chicago, Illinois, 60610-2144, USA
Tel: 312 573 1365
Fax: 312 573 1141

Annual Tour Scholarship

Subjects: Architectural history.

Eligibility: Open to SAH members who are students engaged in graduate work in architecture, or architectural history, city planning or urban history, landscape or the history of landscape design.

Level of Study: Postgraduate.

Purpose: To enable an outstanding student to participate in the annual SAH domestic tour.

Type: Scholarship.

No. of awards offered: One.

Frequency: Annual.

Value: A surcharge on non-student participants' registrations is applied toward such tour scholarships to defray the cost of the tour itself.

Applications Procedure: Write to SAH for SAH guidelines.

Additional Information: Application forms are available on request.

Rosann Berry Fellowship

Subjects: Architectural history or an allied field (e.g. city planning, landscape architecture, decorative arts or historic preservation).

Eligibility: Open to persons of any nationality who have been members of SAH for at least one year prior to the meeting; are currently engaged in advanced graduate study (i.e. normally beyond the masters level) that involves some aspect of the history of architecture or of one of the fields closely allied to it.

Level of Study: Postgraduate.

Purpose: To enable a student engaged in advanced graduate study to attend the annual meeting of the Society.

Type: Fellowship.

No. of awards offered: One.

Frequency: Annual.

Value: All fees and charges connected with the meeting itself are waived; plus reimbursement for travel, lodging, and meals directly related to the meeting, up to a combined total of US$500.

Applications Procedure: Write to SAH for application guidelines.

Additional Information: Application forms are available on request.

Edilia de Montequin Fellowship in Iberian and Latin American Architecture

Subjects: Spanish, Portuguese or Ibero-American architecture, including colonial architecture produced by the Spaniards in the Philippines and what is today the USA.

Eligibility: Open to SAH members who are junior scholars, including graduate students, or senior scholars.

Level of Study: Graduate.

Purpose: To fund travel for research on Spanish, Portuguese, or Ibero-American architecture.

Type: Fellowship.

No. of awards offered: One.

Frequency: Annual.

Value: US$1,000.

Applications Procedure: Write to SAH for application guidelines.

Additional Information: Application forms are available on request.

Sally Kress Tompkins Fellowship

Subjects: Architectural history.

Eligibility: Open to architectural history students.

Level of Study: Graduate.

Purpose: To enable an architectural history student to work as a summer intern on an Historic American Buildings Survey project during the summer.

Type: Fellowship.

No. of awards offered: One.

Frequency: Annual.

Value: US$7,000.

Country of Study: USA.

Applications Procedure: Write to SAH for application guidelines.

Additional Information: Applications should include a sample of work, a letter of recommendation from a faculty member, and a US Government Standard Form (171 available from HABS or most US Government personnel offices). Applications should be sent to The Sally Kress Tompkins Fellowship, c/o HABS/HAER, National Park Service, PO Box 37127, Washington, DC 20013-7127, USA. Applicants not selected for the Tomkins Fellowship will be considered for other HABS summer employment opportunities. For more information, please contact Robert J Kapsch, Chief, HABS/HAER.

SOCIETY OF CHILDREN'S BOOK WRITERS AND ILLUSTRATORS

Society of Children's Book Writers and Illustrators, 22736 Vanowen Street, West Hills, CA, 91306, USA
Contact: Stephen Mooser, President

Don Freeman Memorial Grant-in-Aid

Subjects: Children's picture-books.

Eligibility: Open to both full and associate members of the Society who, as artists, seriously intend to make picture-books their chief contribution to the field of children's literature.

Purpose: To enable picture-book artists to further their understanding, training and work in the picture-book genre.

Type: Grant.

No. of awards offered: Two.

Frequency: Annual.

Value: US$1,000.

Applications Procedure: Application to be submitted to the Society. Receipt of application will be acknowledged.

Closing Date: Application requests June 15th; completed application February 10th.

General Work-in-Progress Grant

Subjects: Children's literature.

Eligibility: Open to both full and associate members of the Society. The grant is not available for projects on which there is already a contract. Recipients of previous US$1,000 SCBWI Grants are not eligible to apply for any further SCBWI Grants.

Purpose: To assist children's book writers in the completion of a specific project.

Type: Grant.

No. of awards offered: One full grant and one runner-up grant.

Frequency: Annual.

Value: Full grant: US$1,000; runner-up grant: US$500.

Closing Date: May 1st.

Grant for a Contemporary Novel for Young People

Subjects: Children's literature.

Eligibility: Open to both full and associate members of the Society. The grant is not available for projects on which there is already a contract. Recipients of previous US$1,000 SCBWI Grants are not eligible to apply for any further SCBWI Grants.

Purpose: To assist children's book writers in the completion of a specific project.

Type: Grant.

No. of awards offered: One full grant and one runner-up grant.

Frequency: Annual.

Value: Full grant: US$1,000; runner-up grant: US$500.

Closing Date: May 1st.

Grant for Unpublished Authors

Subjects: Children's literature.

Eligibility: Open to both full and associate members of the Society who have never had a book published. The grant is not available for a project on which there is already a contract. Recipients of previous SCBWI Grants are not eligible to apply for any further SCBWI Grants.

Purpose: To assist children's book writers in the completion of a specific project.

Type: Grant.

No. of awards offered: One full grant and one runner-up grant.

Frequency: Annual.

Value: Full grant: US$1,000; runner-up grant: US$500.

Closing Date: May 1st.

Barbara Karlin Grant

Subjects: Children's picture-books.

Eligibility: Open to both full and associate members of the Society who have never had a picture-book published. The grant is not available for a project on which there is already a contract.

Purpose: To assist picture-book writers in the completion of a specific project.

Type: Grant.

No. of awards offered: One.

Frequency: Annual.

Value: US$1,000.

Closing Date: May 15th.

Non-Fiction Research Grant

Subjects: Children's literature.

Eligibility: Open to both full and associate members of the Society. The grant is not available for projects on which there is already a contract. Recipients of previous US$1,000 SCBWIGrants are not eligible to apply for any further SCBWI Grants.

Purpose: To assist children's book writers in the completion of a specific project.

Type: Grant.

No. of awards offered: One full grant and one runner-up grant.

Frequency: Annual.

Value: Full grant: US$1,000; runner-up grant: US$500.

Closing Date: May 1st.

SOCIETY OF EXPLORATION GEOPHYSICISTS FOUNDATION

Society of Exploration Geophysicists Foundation, Box 702740, Tulsa, OK, 74170, USA
Tel: 918 497 5530
Fax: 918 497 5558
Contact: Marge Gerhart

SEG Scholarships

Subjects: Geophysics and related earth sciences.

Eligibility: Open to citizens of any country who are entering freshman, undergraduate or graduate level and have above-average grades and an aptitude for physics, mathematics and geology.

Level of Study: Postgraduate, Undergraduate.

No. of awards offered: A variable number of Scholarships, depending on funds available.

Frequency: Annual.

Value: Usually US$500-US$3,000 per academic year. (Average awards approximately US$1,000.).

Length of Study: One academic year; renewable.

Study Establishment: Any college offering a course of study in geophysics.

Country of Study: USA.

Closing Date: March 1st of the year in which the award is made.

SOCIETY OF NAVAL ARCHITECTS AND MARINE ENGINEERS

Society of Naval Architects and Marine Engineers, 601 Pavonia Avenue , Suite 400, Jersey City, NJ, 07306, USA
Tel: 201 798 4800 ext.3033
Fax: 201 798 4975
Contact: Francis M Cagliari, Executive Director

Graduate Scholarships

Subjects: Awards are primarily for advanced study in naval architecture; marine engineering and ocean engineering, but are not necessarily limited to these subjects.

Eligibility: Open to citizens of the USA or Canada who are college graduates of a recognized technical institution.

Level of Study: Postgraduate.

Purpose: To encourage young men and women to enter the field of naval architecture, marine engineering and ocean engineering.

Type: Scholarship.

No. of awards offered: Five.

Frequency: Annual.

Value: Varies; usually to cover tuition costs at the selected school.

Length of Study: One year.

Applications Procedure: Applicants should write for details.

Closing Date: February 1st.

Additional Information: The Society also awards some Scholarships of US$1,000 for undergraduates.

SOCIETY OF WOMEN ENGINEERS

Society of Women Engineers, 120 Wall Street, 11th floor, New York, NY, 10005-3902, USA
Tel: 212 509 9577
Fax: 212 509 0224

General Motors Foundation Graduate Scholarship

Eligibility: All SWE scholarships are open only to women majoring in engineering or computer science in a college or university with an ABET-accredited program.

Level of Study: Postgraduate.

Purpose: To encourage woman engineers to attain high levels of education and professional achievement.

Type: Scholarship.

Frequency: Annual.

Value: US$1,000.

Country of Study: USA.

Applications Procedure: Applications and information can be obtained from the Dean of Engineering or from SWE Headquaters in New York. Requests must be accompanied by an SSAE.

Additional Information: The Society of Women Engineers also offer an extensive range of undergraduate scholarships. Information can be obtained form the appropriate Dean in October and March of each year.

Microsoft Corporation Scholarships

Eligibility: All SWE Scholarships are open only to women majoring in engineering or computer science in a college or university with an ABET-accredited program.

Level of Study: Postgraduate.

Purpose: To encourage women engineers to attain a high level of education and professional acheivement.

Type: Scholarship.

Frequency: Annual.

Value: US$1,000.

Country of Study: USA.

Applications Procedure: Application and information can be obtained form the Dean of Engineering or from the SWE headquarters in New York.

Olive Lynn Salembier Scholarship

Eligibility: This Scholarship is restricted to women who have neither been practising engineering within the past two years nor been enrolled in an engineering or other university/college program in the past two years.

Level of Study: Postgraduate, Undergraduate, Doctorate, Professional development.

Purpose: To aid women who have been out of the engineering market and out of school for a minimum of two years to obtain the credentials necessary to re-enter the job market as an engineer.

Type: Scholarship.

Frequency: Annual.

Value: US$2,000.

Country of Study: USA.

Applications Procedure: Applications and information can be obtained from SWE headquarters in New York.

FREDERICK SODDY TRUST

Frederick Soddy Trust, 7 The Drive, Hove, Sussex, BN3 3JS, England
Contact: Chairman

Grants

Subjects: Sociological sciences preferred.

Eligibility: Open to groups studying the whole life of a particular area in Great Britain or elsewhere with major emphasis on the human community therein. Preference is given to students of the sociological sciences and particularly to younger men and women, both teachers and students. Grants are not made to individuals or to individuals to take part in group expeditions.

Purpose: To encourage group study of the whole life of a specified area.

Type: Grant.

No. of awards offered: Up to eight.

Frequency: Annual.

Value: £200-£350.

Country of Study: UK or overseas.

SOIL AND WATER CONSERVATION SOCIETY

7515 Northeast Ankeny Road, Ankeny, Iowa, 50021-9764, USA
Tel: 515 289 2331
Fax: 515 289 1227
Email: swcs@netins.net
Contact: Mary Stoddard

Kenneth E Grant Research Scholarship

Subjects: Soil conservation.

Eligibility: Open to members of the SWCS who have demonstrated integrity, ability and competence to complete the specified study topic.

Level of Study: Postgraduate.

Purpose: To provide financial aid to members of SWCS for graduate-level research on a specific topic that will help SWCS carry out its mission of advocating the protection, enhancement, and wise use of soil, water, and related natural resources.

Type: Research Grant.

No. of awards offered: One.

Frequency: Annual.

Value: Up to US$1,300.

Length of Study: One year.

Applications Procedure: There are no specific application forms. Applicants should submit a proposal and evidence of the ability to meet eligibility requirements.

Closing Date: March 1st.

SONS OF THE REPUBLIC OF TEXAS

Sons of the Republic of Texas, 1717 8th Street, Bay City, TX, 77414, USA
Tel: 409 245 6644
Fax: 409 245 6644
Contact: Melinda Williams, Executive Secretary

Presidio La Bahia Award

Subjects: History.

Eligibility: Open to all persons interested in the Spanish colonial influence on Texas culture.

Level of Study: Unrestricted.

Purpose: To promote suitable preservation of relics, appropriate dissemination of data, and research into Texas heritage, with particular emphasis on the Spanish colonial period.

Type: Cash award.

No. of awards offered: Three.

Frequency: Annual.

Value: 1st place is a minimum of US$1,200; 2nd and 3rd place divide balance from the total amount available of US$2,000 at the discretion of the judges.

Applications Procedure: Published writings must be submitted in quadruplicate to the office. Galley proofs are not acceptable.

Closing Date: Entries are accepted from June 1st until September 30th.

Additional Information: Research writings have, in the past, proved to be the most successful type of entry. However, consideration will be given to other literary forms, art, architecture and archaeological discovery. For projects other than writing, contestants should furnish a description of the proposed entry, so the Chairman may issue specific instructions.

Summerfield G Roberts Award

Subjects: History.

Eligibility: Open to all writers.

Level of Study: Unrestricted.

Purpose: To encourage literary effort and research about historical events and personalities during the days of the Republic of Texas (1836-1846), and to stimulate interest in the period.

Type: Cash award.

No. of awards offered: One.

Frequency: Annual.

Value: US$2,500.

Applications Procedure: Manuscripts must be written or published during the calendar year for which the award is given. There is no word limit.

Closing Date: January 15th.

SOROPTIMIST INTERNATIONAL OF GREAT BRITAIN AND IRELAND

Golden Jubilee Fellowship, 127 Wellington Road South, Stockport, Cheshire, SK1 3TS, England
Tel: 0161 480 7686

Fax: 0161 477 6152
Contact: The Chairman

Golden Jubilee Fellowship

Subjects: Any subject, but preference is given to women seeking to train or retrain for a business or profession as mature students. However all applications will be considered by the Committee.

Eligibility: Open to women residing within the boundaries of Soroptimist International of Great Britain and Ireland, who need not be Soroptimists. The countries are Anguilla, Antigua and Barbuda, Bangladesh, Barbados, Cameroon, Gambia, Grenada, Hong Kong, India, Isle of Man, Jamaica, Republic of Ireland, Malta, Mauritius, Nigeria, Pakistan, Sierra Leone, South Africa, Sri Lanka, St Vincent and the Grenadines, Thailand, Trinidad and Tobago, Turks and Caicos Islands, Uganda, United Kingdom, Zimbabwe.

Type: Fellowship.

No. of awards offered: Approximately 30.

Frequency: Annual.

Value: Normally within range £100-£500 per annum, from a fund of £6,000.

Study Establishment: Any agreed institution, providing the residential stipulation is met.

Country of Study: International.

Closing Date: April 30th for the academic year beginning the following autumn.

Additional Information: Please enclose SAE or IRCs for details.

SOROPTIMIST INTERNATIONAL OF THE AMERICAS

Soroptimist International of the Americas, 1616 Walnut Street, Philadelphia, PA, 19103, USA
Tel: 215 732 0512
Fax: 215 732 7508
Contact: Training Awards Program

Training Awards Program (TAP)

Subjects: Vocational training.

Eligibility: Open to mature female heads of household who need additional skills, training and education to upgrade their employment status. Only women working toward a vocational or undergraduate degree are eligible. The award is not given to women working toward a graduate degree. Soroptomists and their families are not eligible.

Purpose: To aid the mature woman who, as the head of a household, must enter or return to the job market or further her skills and training to upgrade her employment status.

No. of awards offered: 54.

Frequency: Annual.

Value: US$3,000, plus an extra US$10,000 to one of the 54 recipients.

Applications Procedure: Applications are available from local participating Soroptimist clubs or by writing to SIA Headquarters, with a self-addressed, stamped envelope enclosed. The applicant must then forward the completed forms to the nearest participating club as instructed. Applicants must not send completed applications to the Headquarters.

Closing Date: TAP applications become available in the late summer of each year and must be completed and sent to the local participating Soroptimist club by 15 December. Winners receive the TAP Award the following April.

Additional Information: Recipients are chosen on the basis of financial need, as well as the statement of clear career goals.

SOUTH AFRICAN ASSOCIATION OF UNIVERSITY WOMEN

South African Association of University Women, PO Box 6638, Johannesburg, 2000, South Africa
Tel: 011 884 2748 or 011 836 2027
Fax: 011 784 1338 or 011 836 0029
Contact: Mrs J A Bell, Fellowships Secretary

Hansi Pollak Fellowship

Subjects: Any branch of the social sciences.

Eligibility: Open to South African women graduates of all races who are, or become, members of the Association.

Level of Study: Postgraduate, Doctorate.

Purpose: To assist study or research devoted to the practical purpose of ameliorating social conditions in South Africa.

Type: Fellowship.

No. of awards offered: One.

Frequency: Biennially.

Value: R6,000 paid in six-month instalments.

Length of Study: Two years; not renewable.

Study Establishment: At any recognized university.

Country of Study: South Africa or abroad.

Closing Date: October 1st for applications and proof of Association membership.

Additional Information: Fellows must spend at least two years in South Africa after completing a master's or doctorate degree, in order to put into practice the results of the research.

SAAUW International Fellowship

Subjects: Any subject: postgraduate research.

Eligibility: Open to members of the International Federation of University Women.

Level of Study: Postgraduate.

Type: Fellowship.

No. of awards offered: One.

Frequency: When advertised.

Value: R1,000.

Length of Study: For not less than 6 months.

Country of Study: South Africa.

Closing Date: August 31st.

Isie Smuts Research Award

Subjects: Any subject: postgraduate research.

Eligibility: Open to members of the South African Association of University Women.

Level of Study: Postgraduate.

Type: Award.

No. of awards offered: One.

Frequency: Annual.

Value: R1,000.

Study Establishment: Any South African university.

Country of Study: South Africa.

Closing Date: October 31st.

Bertha Stoneman Memorial Award for Botanical Research

Subjects: Botany.

Eligibility: Open to members of the South African Association of University Women.

Level of Study: Postgraduate.

Type: Research award.

No. of awards offered: One.

Frequency: Annual.

Value: R1,000.

Study Establishment: Any South African university.

Country of Study: South Africa.

Closing Date: October 31st.

SOUTH AFRICAN COUNCIL FOR ENGLISH EDUCATION

Director of Bursaries, SA Council for English Education, PO Box 660, Pretoria, 0001, South Africa
Tel: 012 218207
Contact: (Transvaal)

*In-Service Training Bursaries

Subjects: English and subjects in English.

Eligibility: Open to residents of the Republic of South Africa in the Transvaal, the vicinity of Cape Town or the vicinity of Port Elizabeth. Candidates must be teachers with three years' post-matriculation study and at least four years' teaching experience, intending to teach English or other subjects in English. Preference will be given to teachers with leadership potential.

Purpose: To assist teachers in service who wish to improve their qualifications.

No. of awards offered: Varies.

Value: Varies depending upon type of course taken.

Country of Study: South Africa.

Closing Date: July 31st preceding the year for which the bursary is required.

For further information contact:
The Bursary Officer, SACEE: Western Cape Branch, PO Box 32912, Claremont 7735, South Africa
Contact: (Western Cape)

or

The Bursary Officer, SACEE--Eastern Cape Branch, PO Box 12097, Centrahil 6001, South Africa
Contact: (Eastern Cape)

*Norah Taylor Bursary

Subjects: Speech training; oral communication; the teaching of English as a second language.

Eligibility: Open to qualified teachers teaching English or other subjects in English, with three years' post-matriculation study, at least four years' teaching experience and leadership potential.

Purpose: To assist qualified teachers to further their training.

No. of awards offered: Varies.

Value: Varies depending on type of course taken.

Study Establishment: Any educational institution for correspondence, part-time or full-time studies; renewable annually.

Country of Study: South Africa.

Closing Date: July 31st preceding the year for which the bursary is required.

Additional Information: Applicants not conforming to the requirements cannot be considered and will not be replied to.

For further information contact:
South African Council for English Education, PO Box 660, Pretoria, 0001, South Africa
Tel: 012 218207
Contact: Director of Bursaries

SOUTH AFRICAN COUNCIL FOR THE AGED

South African Council for the Aged, PO Box 2335, Cape Town, 8000, South Africa
Tel: 021 246270
Fax: 021 232168
Contact: Director

*Zerilda Steyn Memorial Trust

Subjects: Needs and care of the aged.

Eligibility: Open to researchers in all disciplines caring for the aged.

Purpose: To advance postgraduate research in South Africa and Namibia.

No. of awards offered: Several grants are made for a variety of small and large projects.

Frequency: Annual.

Value: R1,500 per annum.

Length of Study: One year; renewable only in exceptional cases.

Country of Study: South Africa or Namibia.

Closing Date: August 15th.

SOUTH AFRICAN MEDICAL RESEARCH COUNCIL

Research Grants Administration, South African Medical Research Council, PO Box 19070, Tygerberg, 7505, South Africa
Tel: 021 938 0227
Fax: 021 938 0368
Contact: Mrs M Jenkins

Dentistry Scholarships

Subjects: Dentistry.

Eligibility: Open to persons who have just obtained their bachelor's degree in dentistry and have registered with the South African Medical and Dental Council.

Level of Study: Postgraduate.

Purpose: To assist the recipient to do biomedical research.

Type: Scholarship.

No. of awards offered: Varies.

Frequency: Annual.

Value: To be determined by the MRC from time to time.

Length of Study: One year.

Study Establishment: At an established biomedical research environment.

Country of Study: South Africa.

Applications Procedure: There is no prescribed application form. Applications, in writing, must be directed to the administrative head of the institution where the research will be undertaken, for submission to the MRC. The applicant's study record, proposed research programme and the name of the person under whose supervision the research will be undertaken must be furnished.

Closing Date: March 15th.

Distinguished Visiting Scientists Awards

Subjects: Medical sciences.

Eligibility: Open to distinguished foreign scientists.

Purpose: To provide funds to support distinguished scientists from abroad to visit local researchers.

No. of awards offered: Varies.

Frequency: Annual.

Value: Varies; including funds for travel and a daily allowance.

Length of Study: Two weeks up to a maximum of three months.

Country of Study: South Africa.

Applications Procedure: Applications for support must be made by local scientists, in writing, providing the following information: a complete curriculum vitae of the visitor; his work programme; duration of the visit; and funds required for travel.

Closing Date: August 31st.

Post-Intern Scholarships

Subjects: Medical sciences.

Eligibility: Open to persons who have obtained a bachelor's degree in medicine and have just completed their internship.

Level of Study: Postgraduate.

Purpose: To assist the recipient to do research.

Type: Scholarship.

No. of awards offered: Varies.

Frequency: Annual.

Value: To be determined by the MRC from time to time.

Length of Study: One year.

Study Establishment: At an established biomedical research environment.

Country of Study: South Africa.

Applications Procedure: There is no prescribed application form. Applications, in writing, must be directed to the administrative head of the institution where the research will be undertaken, for submission to the MRC. The applicant's study record, proposed research programme and the name of the person under whose supervision the research will be undertaken must be furnished.

Closing Date: August 15th.

Scholarships for Research and Study Overseas

Subjects: Medical and related sciences.

Eligibility: Open to South African scientists under 50 years of age and holding at least a master's degree.

Level of Study: Postgraduate.

Purpose: To support research where facilities are not available or are inadequate in South Africa.

Type: Scholarship.

No. of awards offered: Varies.

Frequency: Annual.

Value: To be determined by the MRC from time to time.

Length of Study: Two years.

Study Establishment: At approved institutions.

Country of Study: Europe; UK; North America; Canada.

Closing Date: March 31st.

Additional Information: Holders of MRC grants must sign an undertaking that they will return to South Africa for at least three years for every year of support or for five years for two years of support.

Scholarships for Study in South Africa

Subjects: Medical sciences.

Eligibility: Open to candidates in the faculties of medicine, dentistry and engineering who hold a BSc honours degree. Applicants must be South African citizens or in receipt of a permanent residence permit issued by the state department concerned before the Scholarship, if granted, becomes operative. For the purposes of this condition, citizens of the TVBC states and self-governing states within the Republic of South Africa are deemed to be citizens of the Republic of South Africa.

Purpose: To assist students who have obtained an honours degree and wish to obtain an advanced degree in a biomedical research area.

Type: Scholarship.

No. of awards offered: Varies.

Frequency: Annual.

Value: To be determined by the MRC from time to time.

Study Establishment: At an appropriate institution.

Country of Study: South Africa.

Closing Date: October 31st.

Short-term Research Grants

Subjects: Medical sciences.

Eligibility: Open to South African scientists.

Purpose: To enable recipients to undertake advanced research.

Type: Research Grant.

No. of awards offered: Varies.

Frequency: Annual.

Value: Varies.

Length of Study: Up to three years.

Study Establishment: At approved research institutions.

Country of Study: South Africa.

Closing Date: May 15th.

SOUTH AFRICAN NURSING ASSOCIATION

South African Nursing Association, PO Box 1280, Pretoria, 0001, South Africa
Tel: 343 2315/6/7
Fax: 344 0750
Contact: Executive Director

*Bursaries, Scholarships and Grants

Subjects: Nursing.

Eligibility: Open to members in good standing of the Association who hold the required registered nursing qualifications.

Purpose: To encourage post-basic studies at a South African teaching institution.

No. of awards offered: Varies.

Frequency: Annual.

Value: Varies.

Length of Study: One year.

Study Establishment: A South African teaching institution.

Country of Study: South Africa.

Closing Date: January 31st.

SOUTHDOWN TRUST

Southdown Trust, Canbury School, Kingston Hill, Kingston upon Thames, Surrey, KT2 7LN, England
Contact: Mr J G Wyatt

Awards

Subjects: All subjects except medicine, law, drama and music, dance and journalism.

Eligibility: Open mainly to UK citizens but other nationalities are considered.

Purpose: To encourage personal initiative and concern for others.

No. of awards offered: A variable number of awards.

Frequency: Varies according to funds available.

Value: Varies, but limited. Ranges between £25-£200.

Country of Study: UK/International.

Closing Date: May 1st, November 1st.

Additional Information: Stamped addressed envelopes must always be enclosed.

SOUTHEAST ASIAN MINISTERS OF EDUCATION ORGANIZATION

Southeast Asian Ministers of Education Secretariat, Darakarn Building, 920 Sukhumvit Road, Bangkok, 10110, Thailand
Tel: 66 2 391 0144
Fax: 66 2 381 2587
Email: exseames@emailhost.ait.ac.th
Contact: Director

SEAMEO Scholarships

Subjects: Any subject offered at one of the regional centres.

Eligibility: Open to candidates nominated by the Ministry of Education of the member-country who must then obtain subsequent acceptance by the SEAMEO centre or project.

Purpose: To develop and upgrade the professional competence of nationals of member-countries: Brunei Darussalam, Cambodia, Indonesia, Laos, Malaysia, Philippines, Singapore, Thailand and Vietnam.

Type: Scholarship.

No. of awards offered: Varies.

Frequency: Varies.

Value: Varies according to requirements and courses offered. Usually allowances are made for tuition, food, accommodation, books and supplies, out-of-pocket allowances, international and domestic travel, and research and thesis support.

Study Establishment: SEAMEO regional centres and regional projects.

Additional Information: Courses depend on offers or requests by member-countries. Most of the programme activities are implemented through SEAMEO's regional centres/project: Regional Centre for Tropical Biology, Bogor, Indonesia; Regional Centre for Educational Innovation and Technology, Quezon City, the Philippines; Regional Centre for Education in Science and Mathematics, Penang, Malaysia; Regional Language Centre, Singapore; Regional Centre for Graduate Study and Research in Agriculture, Los Baños, the Philippines; Project for Tropical Medicine and Public Health (national centres in Indonesia, Malaysia, the Philippines and Thailand, with headquarters in Bangkok, Thailand); Regional Centre for Archaeology and Fine Arts, Bangkok, Thailand; Regional Centre for Vocational and Technical Education, Bandar Seri Begawan, Brunei Darussalam; SEAMEO Regional Institute of Higher Education (RIHED), Bangkok, Thailand.

SOUTHERN AFRICAN MUSIC RIGHTS ORGANIZATION

Southern African Music Rights Organization, PO Box 9292, Johannesburg, 2000, South Africa
Tel: 27 11 403 6635
Fax: 27 11 403 1934
Contact: The Cultural Officer

*Bursaries

Subjects: Any branch of music.

Eligibility: Open to citizens of South Africa, Botswana, Lesotho, Swaziland, Bophuthatswana, Ciskei, Transkei and Venda who have met the requirements for entering the first year or for proceeding to the second year of study at a tertiary institute.

Purpose: To encourage music study at tertiary level.

Type: Bursaries, 10 each for 'serious music' and for 'contemporary popular' music.

No. of awards offered: 20.

Frequency: Annual.

Value: R4,000 per annum.

Study Establishment: Any recognized tertiary institute of learning in SAMRO's territory of operation.

Country of Study: Southern Africa.

Closing Date: January 31st.

*Overseas Scholarship

Subjects: Music.

Eligibility: Open to citizens of South Africa, Botswana, Lesotho, Swaziland, Bophuthatswana, Ciskei, Transkei, Venda.

Purpose: To encourage music study at graduate level in a country outside SAMRO's territory of operation.

Type: Scholarship.

No. of awards offered: Two.

Frequency: Annual.

Value: R15,000 per annum.

Length of Study: Two years.

Study Establishment: An institute approved by SAMRO's Board of Directors.

Country of Study: Europe; North America.

Closing Date: January 31st.

Additional Information: These awards rotate on a quadrennial basis.

SOUTHERN CALIFORNIA UNIVERSITY

University Park, Mail Code 4012, University of Southern California, Los Angeles, CA, 90089, USA
Tel: 213 740 5294
Fax: 213 740 8607
Contact: Joseph Aonn, Dean of Faculty

*All-University Predoctoral Merit Fellowships; William M Keck Fellowships; All-University International Predoctoral Merit Scholarships

Subjects: Any subject.

Eligibility: Open to outstanding seniors and graduates of any nationality who present evidence of achievement and promise as scholars.

Purpose: To provide an opportunity for students working towards a PhD degree in any field who intend to pursue a career in university teaching and research.

Type: Fellowship.

No. of awards offered: Varies.

Frequency: Annual.

Value: US$14,000 per annum, plus full tuition and mandatory fees.

Length of Study: Up to three years.

Study Establishment: The University of Southern California.

Country of Study: USA.

Closing Date: February 1st.

Additional Information: All three Fellowships are awarded through the same competition.

For further information contact:
The Graduate School, University of Southern California, Los Angeles, CA, 90089-0282, USA
Tel: 213 740 9033
Fax: 213 740 9048
Contact: Barbara Solomon, Dean of Graduate Studies

*All-University Predoctoral Minority Fellowships

Subjects: Any subject.

Eligibility: Open to outstanding seniors and graduates who present evidence of achievement and promise as scholars, are US citizens and members of the following underrepresented minority groups: American Indians and Alaskan Natives (Eskimo or Aleut), Black/African Americans, US Hispanic/Latinos, and Native Pacific Islanders (Micronesians and Polynesians).

Purpose: To provide opportunities for minority students working towards the PhD degree who intend to pursue a career in university teaching and research.

Type: Fellowship.

No. of awards offered: Varies.

Frequency: Annual.

Value: US$14,000 per annum, plus full tuition and mandatory fees.

Length of Study: Three years.

Study Establishment: The University of Southern California.

Country of Study: USA.

Closing Date: February 1st.

Andrew W Mellon Postdoctoral Fellowships in the Humanities

Subjects: The humanities.

Eligibility: Open to Scholars who received their PhD within the past seven years and do not hold tenure at an academic institution.

Level of Study: Postdoctorate.

Purpose: To encourage junior scholars to develop their research.

Type: Fellowship.

No. of awards offered: Two per year.

Frequency: Annual.

Value: Approximately US$27,500, plus full faculty fringe benefits and modest research expense support.

Study Establishment: University of Southern California.

Country of Study: USA.

Closing Date: Varies each year with each search.

SOUTHERN CROSS UNIVERSITY

Graduate Research College, PO Box 157, Lismore, NSW, 2480,
Australia
Tel: 066 203705
Fax: 066 223180
Email: jrussell@scu.edu.au
Contact: John Russell

Postgraduate Research Scholarships

Subjects: Most subjects.

Eligibility: There are no eligibility restrictions.

Level of Study: Postgraduate.

Purpose: To support a student while undertaking postgraduate research study.

Type: Scholarship.

No. of awards offered: 5-10.

Frequency: Twice a year.

Value: Up to A$14,000.

Length of Study: Up to three years.

Study Establishment: Southern Cross University.

Country of Study: Australia.

Applications Procedure: Application form must be completed.

Closing Date: October 31st and May 31st.

SOUTH PLACE SUNDAY CONCERTS

South Place Sunday Concerts, Fernside, Copthall Green, Upshire,
Waltham Abbey, Essex, EN9 3SZ, England
Contact: Raymond Cassidy, Honorary Secretary

Clements Memorial Prize

Subjects: Musical composition.

Eligibility: Previous prize-winners may not re-enter.

Purpose: To encourage the composition of Chamber music.

Type: Prize.

No. of awards offered: One.

Frequency: Biennially (1998).

Value: £500.

Applications Procedure: Conditions and entry forms are available on request.

Closing Date: October 1st in the year of the award.

Additional Information: Entries should be for three to eight unmodified non-electronic musical instruments and should not have been publicly performed or have won a prize in any other competition. The winning composition will remain the copyright of its author.

SPACE COAST WRITERS GUILD, INC

Space Coast Writers Guild, Inc, PO Box 804, Melbourne, FL, 32902,
USA
Tel: 407 727 0051
Contact: Dr Edwin J Kirschner

Writers' Contests/Awards

Subjects: Writing, in six categories: book manuscript (fiction and non-fiction), short story, poetry, short story for children, short play, and feature article.

Eligibility: Open to attendees of the two-day conference.

Type: Contest/award.

No. of awards offered: One award in each category.

Frequency: Annual.

Value: US$100 and a plaque.

Applications Procedure: Registration/application to November SCWG Writers' Conference. Program/registration available after September 1st.

Closing Date: October 11th; contest submission with conference registration.

Additional Information: The awards are associated with the Guild's annual writers' conference in November.

SPALDING TRUSTS

Spalding Trusts, Fox Farm, Wetherden, Stowmarket, Suffolk, IP14
3NE, England
Tel: 01359 240364
Contact: Mrs T Rodgers, General Secretary

Grants-in-Aid of Research

Subjects: World religions other than that of the holder. Such study should be the principal, not a subsidiary, object.

Eligibility: Open to those engaged in academic studies or in study which will have practical benefit in promoting inter-religious understanding.

Level of Study: Postgraduate, Doctorate, Postdoctorate.

Purpose: To promote a better understanding between the great cultures of the world by encouraging the study of the religious principles on which they are based.

Value: Limited amounts in the form of grants for subsistence, purchase of books or for travel.

Length of Study: For short periods.

Country of Study: Usually UK.

Applications Procedure: Candidates are requested to submit a research proposal, budget, reference (academic), and CV.

Closing Date: Applications are considered throughout the year but major applications in April.

SPECIAL LIBRARIES ASSOCIATION

Special Libraries Association, 1700 18th Street, NW, Washington, DC,
20009, USA
Tel: 202 234 4700
Fax: 202 265 9317
Contact: Scholarship Committee

Affirmative Action Scholarship

Subjects: Library and information sciences.

Eligibility: Open to minority group members who are college graduates, college seniors or matriculated graduate library school students with an interest in special librarianship. Applicants must be citizens of the USA or Canada.

Level of Study: Postgraduate.

Purpose: To assist minority group members financially with their graduate study in librarianship.

Type: Scholarship.

No. of awards offered: One.

Frequency: Annual.

Value: US$6,000.

Study Establishment: Any accredited school of library or information science.

Country of Study: USA or Canada.

Closing Date: Postmarked October 31st.

Institute for Scientific Information Scholarship

Subjects: Special librarianship.

Eligibility: Open to US and Canadian citizens who are beginning PhD programs. Candidates must have a strong academic record and show financial need.

Purpose: To encourage doctoral research in a recognized program in library science, information science or a related field.

Type: Scholarship.

No. of awards offered: One.

Frequency: Annual.

Value: US$1,000.

Study Establishment: Any accredited school of library or information science.

Country of Study: USA or Canada.

Applications Procedure: Trsnscripts, essay, three letters of recommendation, personal interview.

Closing Date: Postmarked October 31st.

Plenum Scholarship

Subjects: Library or information science: preferably special librarianship.

Eligibility: Open to PhD candidates with an interest in special librarianship who are citizens of the USA or Canada and whose dissertation topics have been approved.

Level of Study: Doctorate.

Purpose: To assist the recipient financially with study for a doctoral degree.

Type: Scholarship.

No. of awards offered: One.

Frequency: Annual.

Value: US$1,000.

Length of Study: One academic year.

Study Establishment: A recognized school of library or information science.

Country of Study: USA or Canada.

Applications Procedure: Transcripts, essay, three letters of recommendation, personal interview.

Closing Date: Postmarked October 31st.

Scholarships

Subjects: Library or information science.

Eligibility: Open to college graduates working in a special library or with experience in a special library, and to recent college graduates wishing to enter special librarianship.

Level of Study: Postgraduate.

Purpose: To assist students financially with their graduate study in librarianship.

Type: Scholarship.

No. of awards offered: Three.

Frequency: Annual.

Value: Varies: approximately US$6,000.

Length of Study: One academic year of graduate study or an alternative plan of study acceptable to the Committee.

Study Establishment: A recognized school of library or information science.

Country of Study: USA or Canada.

Applications Procedure: Transcripts, essay, three letters of reference, personal interview.

Closing Date: October 31st.

SPINAL CORD INJURY EDUCATION & TRAINING FOUNDATION

Paralyzed Veterans of America Education & Training Foundation, 801 18th Street, NW, Washington, DC, 20006, USA
Tel: 202 416 7655
Fax: 202 416 7641
Contact: Patricia Audick

*Grants

Subjects: Spinal cord injury: continuing education and training, post-professional traineeships, patient/client education, conferences.

Eligibility: Open to suitably qualified persons working in the field of spinal cord injury.

Purpose: To provide funds for grants to institutions, agencies and organizations that will improve the knowledge and abilities of health professionals, people with SCI or disease and those significant to them.

No. of awards offered: Varies.

Frequency: Twice yearly.

Value: Varies.

Closing Date: December 1st, June 1st.

SPORT FISHING INSTITUTE

Sport Fishing Institute, 1010 Massachusetts Avenue, NW, Washington, DC, 20001, USA
Tel: 202 898 0770
Fax: 202 371 2085
Contact: Christine Altman

Sport Fishery Research Program

Subjects: Fish life history, fisheries management, and aquatic ecology pertinent to recreational fishing. Proposals for graduate student level support and/or faculty research are also considered.

Eligibility: Open to graduate students. All applications must be submitted by a supervising professor; no direct applications by students will be considered.

No. of awards offered: Varies.

Frequency: Annual.

Value: US$500-US$5,000.

Country of Study: USA.

Closing Date: March 1st.

JOHN F AND ANNA LEE STACEY SCHOLARSHIP FUND

Stacey Scholarship Fund, c/o National Cowboy Hall of Fame, 1700 North East 63rd Street, Oklahoma City, OK, 73111, USA
Contact: Ed Muno

Scholarships

Subjects: Painting and drawing in the classical or conservative tradition of Western culture.

Eligibility: Open to US citizens of 18-35 years of age who are skilled in and devoted to the classical or conservative tradition of Western culture.

Type: Scholarship.

No. of awards offered: One or more.

Frequency: Annual.

Value: A total of approximately US$3,000.

Length of Study: One year.

Country of Study: Any country.

Applications Procedure: Application form must be completed.

Closing Date: February 1st.

ST ANDREW'S SOCIETY OF THE STATE OF NEW YORK

St Andrew's Society of the State of New York, 3 West 51st Street, New York, NY, 10019, USA
Tel: 212 807 1730
Fax: 212 807 1877
Contact: Karen Jaehne, Executive Director

Scholarship

Subjects: General, no field of endeavour requirement.

Eligibility: Students who have graduated from an American university, of Scottish/American descent, and New York area address.

Level of Study: Postgraduate.

Purpose: To promote cultural and intellectual interchange and goodwill between Scotland and the USA.

Type: Scholarship.

No. of awards offered: Two.

Frequency: Annual.

Value: US$13,000.

Length of Study: One year.

Study Establishment: Any university in Scotland.

Country of Study: Scotland.

Applications Procedure: Application form, documentation of transcripts, and letters of recommendation.

Closing Date: December 1st yearly.

STANFORD HUMANITIES CENTER

Stanford Humanities Center, Mariposa House, Stanford University, Stanford, CA, 94305-8630, USA
Tel: 415 723 3052
Fax: 415 723 1895
Contact: Fellowship Program

External Faculty Fellowships

Subjects: Humanities.

Eligibility: External fellowships fall into two categories: senior fellowships for well-established scholars; junior fellowships for scholars who during the fellowship year will be at least three years beyond receipt of the PhD and normally no more than ten. Selection is based on the specific research project proposed, the intellectual distinction of the candidate's previous work, the research project's potential interest to scholars in varying fields within the humanities, and the potential contribution of the applicant to humanistic studies at Stanford.

Level of Study: Postdoctorate.

Purpose: To offer research opportunities to scholars in the humanities.

Type: Fellowship.

No. of awards offered: Up to six.

Frequency: Annual.

Value: Up to US$20,000 for junior scholars and up to US$30,000 for senior scholars. In addition, US$2,500-US$5,000 (depending on size of family) will be offered as a housing/travel subsidy. Applicants are expected to seek supplementary financial support and are required to contribute this support, together with any sabbatical earnings, to their stipend.

Length of Study: One year residency, not renewable.

Study Establishment: At the Center.

Country of Study: USA.

Applications Procedure: Application form must be completed.

Closing Date: November 15th.

SIR RICHARD STAPLEY EDUCATIONAL TRUST

Sir Richard Stapley Educational Trust, PO Box 57, Tonbridge, Kent, TN9 1ZT, England
Contact: M H Bushby, BA, Secretary

Grants

Subjects: Any subject.

Eligibility: Open to graduates holding a first or upper second class honours degree who are over the age of 24 on 1 October of the proposed academic year. Students in receipt of an award from local authorities, Research Councils, the British Academy or other similar public bodies will not receive a grant from the Trust.

Level of Study: Postgraduate.

Purpose: To award grants to graduate students on an approved course at a UK university, leading to a higher degree or to a medical, dental or veterinary science degree.

Type: Grants.

No. of awards offered: Approximately 230.

Frequency: Annual.

Value: £200-£800 according to individual assessment.

Length of Study: One year in the first instance.

Country of Study: UK.

Applications Procedure: Enquiries should include a stamped addressed C5 envelope. Application forms will be sent and should arrive between March 1st and March 31st, complete with two academic references in sealed envelopes. The address shown is a convenience address so allow seven days for forwarding.

Closing Date: March 31st.

Additional Information: Applications must be accompanied by SAE.

STATE HISTORICAL SOCIETY OF WISCONSIN

State Historical Society of Wisconsin, 816 State Street, Madison, WI, 53706, USA
Tel: 608 264 6464
Fax: 608 264 6486
Contact: Michael E Stevens, State Historian

John C Geilfuss Fellowship

Subjects: Wisconsin's business and economic history.

Eligibility: Open to graduate students and beyond.

Level of Study: Doctorate, Postdoctorate.

Type: Fellowship.

No. of awards offered: One.

Frequency: Annual.

Value: US$2,000.

Length of Study: One year; not renewable.

Country of Study: USA.

Applications Procedure: Applicants must submit four copies of a two-page letter detailing their research, and four copies of a current resume.

Closing Date: February 1st.

Additional Information: Usually awarded to candidates working on doctoral dissertations or postdoctoral research.

Amy Louise Hunter Fellowship

Subjects: American history.

Eligibility: Open to graduate students and beyond.

Level of Study: Doctorate, Postdoctorate.

Purpose: To promote research on topics related to the history of women and public policy, with preference given to Wisconsin topics or research using the collections of the State Historical Society.

Type: Fellowship.

No. of awards offered: One.

Frequency: Biennially (even-numbered years).

Value: US$2,500.

Length of Study: One year; not renewable.

Country of Study: USA.

Applications Procedure: Applicants must submit four copies of a two-page letter describing their research and four copies of current resume.

Closing Date: May 1st (even-numbered years).

Additional Information: Usually awarded to candidates working on doctoral dissertations or postdoctoral research.

Alice E Smith Fellowship

Subjects: American history.

Eligibility: Open to women undertaking research in American history, with preference given to those applicants doing graduate research in the history of Wisconsin or the Middle West.

Level of Study: Doctorate.

Purpose: To encourage and support research by women.

Type: Fellowship.

No. of awards offered: One.

Frequency: Annual.

Value: US$2,000 paid in a lump sum.

Length of Study: One year; not generally renewable.

Country of Study: USA.

Applications Procedure: Applicants should send four copies of a two page letter detailing their current research.

Closing Date: July 15th.

Additional Information: Usually awarded to candidates working on doctoral dissertations.

STATE LIBRARY OF NEW SOUTH WALES

State Library of New South Wales, Macquarie Street, Sydney, NSW, 2000, Australia
Tel: 02 230 1414
Fax: 02 233 2003
Email: library@ilanet.slnsw.gov.au
Contact: State Librarian

C H Currey Memorial Fellowship

Subjects: Australian history.

Eligibility: Open to individuals of any nationality.

Level of Study: Unrestricted.

Purpose: To promote the writing of Australian history from original sources.

Type: Fellowship.

No. of awards offered: One.

Frequency: Annual.

Value: Approximately A$10,000.

Country of Study: Australia.

Applications Procedure: An application form is obtained by contacting the state librarian. An original and two copies of the application should be provided.

Closing Date: October 1st.

Additional Information: Proposed work must conform to the purpose of the award. The award may be divided between two or more applicants.

STATE SCHOLARSHIPS FOUNDATION

Greek Embassy, Cultural Department, 1a Holland Park, London, W11 3TP, England
Tel: 0171 229 3850
Fax: 0171 229 7221

Scholarships for Postgraduate Studies in Greece

Subjects: Any subject.

Eligibility: Open to nationals of countries which are part of the Council of Europe who hold a graduate degree from a foreign university, have a good knowledge of English or French and are not more than 35 years of age.

Level of Study: Postgraduate, Doctorate, Postdoctorate.

Purpose: To fund postgraduate studies.

Type: Scholarship.

No. of awards offered: Ten.

Frequency: Annual.

Value: 70,000 drachmas monthly plus 50,000 drachmas for initial expenses; up to 60,000 drachmas for typing of PhD dissertation, up to 60,000 drachmas to cover mandatory laboratory expenses; exemption from tuition fees; free medical care in case of emergency.

Length of Study: For 1 academic year; renewable for 2 further years.

Study Establishment: At any university or institution of higher education.

Country of Study: Greece.

Applications Procedure: Application forms may be requested from January.

Closing Date: 31 March.

Additional Information: Scholars are strongly recommended to acquire at least an elementary knowledge of Modern Greek.

SIR HALLEY STEWART TRUST

Sir Halley Stewart Trust, 88 Long Lane, Willingham, Cambridge, CB4 5LD, England
Tel: 01954 260707
Fax: 01954 261623
Contact: Mrs Fawcitt

Grants

Subjects: Medical, social or religious research.

Eligibility: There are no restrictions as to who can apply.

Level of Study: Postgraduate, Doctorate, Postdoctorate.

Purpose: To assist pioneering research aimed at the prevention of human suffering (not the relief or alleviation).

Type: Research Grant.

Frequency: Trustees meet 3 times a year to agree grants.

Value: Salaries and relevant costs for young research students from PhD level to about £12,000 per annum.

Study Establishment: Under the auspices of a charitable institution, e.g. a hospital, laboratory, university department or charitable organization.

Country of Study: Worldwide.

Applications Procedure: There is no application form.

Closing Date: Applications taken at any time.

STIFTELSEN LAS HIERTAS MINNE

Stiftelsen Las Hiertas Minne, Eriksburgsg 3,2tr, Stockholm, S-11430, Sweden
Tel: 08 611 6401
Contact: Elisabeth Norlander

Scientific Research Award

Subjects: Any scientific field can be researched.

Eligibility: Open to all nationalities other than Swedish.

Level of Study: Postgraduate, Doctorate, Postdoctorate.

Purpose: For scientific research.

No. of awards offered: Varies.

Frequency: Annual.

Value: 5-2500SEK.

Study Establishment: Any institution.

Country of Study: Sweden.

Applications Procedure: Application form must be completed (in Swedish).

Closing Date: October 1st.

STOUT RESEARCH CENTRE, VICTORIA UNIVERSITY OF WELLINGTON

Stout Research Centre, Victoria University of Wellington, PO Box 600, Wellington, New Zealand
Tel: 0164 4 721 0000
Fax: 0164 4 496 5439
Contact: Director

J D Stout Fellowship

Subjects: New Zealand society, history or culture.

Eligibility: Open to distinguished scholars from New Zealand and abroad.

Level of Study: Postdoctorate.

Purpose: To encourage research.

Type: Fellowship.

No. of awards offered: One.

Frequency: Annually, depending on funds available.

Value: Up to NZ$56,000.

Length of Study: One year.

Study Establishment: Stout Research Centre.

Country of Study: New Zealand.

Closing Date: August 1st of year preceding the Fellowship.

STROKE ASSOCIATION

Stroke Association, CHSA House, Whitecross Street, London, EC1Y 8JJ, England
Tel: 0171 490 7999
Fax: 0171 490 2686
Contact: Secretary

Stroke Research Awards

Subjects: Stroke: applied research in epidemiology, prevention, acute treatment, assessment and rehabilitation.

Eligibility: Open to medically qualified and other clinically active researchers in the UK in the relevant fields. Applications are judged by peer review on their merit without limitations of age.

Purpose: To advance research into stroke.

No. of awards offered: Up to 22.

Frequency: Twice yearly.

Value: Awards cover salaries for researchers and support staff, some equipment costs, consumables and essential travel. No other overheads, advertising etc. covered. Maximum award normally £150,000.

Length of Study: One to three years.

Study Establishment: A university or hospital in the UK.

Country of Study: UK.

Applications Procedure: Application forms are available on request.

Closing Date: As advertised; usually July and November.

WALTER C SUMNER FOUNDATION

Walter C Sumner Foundation, PO Box 2187, Halifax, Nova Scotia, B3J 3C5, Canada
Tel: 902 420 2978
Fax: 902 420 7119
Contact: Susan Byrne, Vice-President

Fellowships

Subjects: Chemistry, physics and electronics.

Eligibility: Open to Canadian citizens who reside in Canada and hold a degree from a Canadian university other than the one at which the Fellowship will be taken up. Applicants holding only the bachelor's degree are required to have had at least two years experience in either teaching or industry in their chosen field of study.

Level of Study: Postgraduate.

Purpose: To assist doctoral students in chemistry, physics and electronics.

Type: Fellowship.

No. of awards offered: Varies; dependent on number of applications and funds available.

Frequency: Annual.

Value: C$4,000 - C$5,000 per annum.

Length of Study: One year; renewable for one year, upon application.

Study Establishment: The following universities: Dalhousie, McGill, Queen's, Saskatchewan, Toronto and British Columbia.

Country of Study: Canada.

Closing Date: 15 April.

SWEDISH HEART LUNG FOUNDATION

Swedish Heart Lung Foundation, Kungsgatan 30, Stockholm, S-111 35, Sweden
Tel: 08 411 0174
Fax: 08 723 1725

*Scholarships

Subjects: Cardiology, pneumonology.

Eligibility: Open to non-Swedish cardiologists or pneumonologists under 45 years of age, who have proven ability for research, are engaged in actual research in the field, and are interested in studying a special problem in Sweden. Applications must be endorsed by the candidate's institute or clinic, which should ensure a post and research facilities for the recipient after tenure of the award.

Type: Scholarship.

No. of awards offered: Three.

Frequency: Annual.

Value: 72,000 Swedish crowns.

Length of Study: One year.

Study Establishment: A hospital or medical institution.

Country of Study: Sweden.

Applications Procedure: Applications should contain a detailed CV including education and qualifications, experience, positions held, etc. and knowledge of language (the applicant's mother-tongue and other languages, which the applicant is able to read, write and speak); research project, i.e. title, methodology to be used, proposed place of study, relevance to the national health programme; a supporting letter from the director of the applicant's institution; and copies of relevant publications (maximum five).

Closing Date: October 1st.

SWEDISH INFORMATION SERVICE

The Swedish Government 'SASS' Travel Grants, Swedish Information Service, 1 Dag Hammarskjöld Plaza, 45th Floor, New York, NY, 10017-2201, USA
Tel: 212 751 5900 ext.3145
Fax: 212 752 4789
Email: swedeninfo@ix.netcom.com
www: http://www.swedeninfo.com/sis

The Swedish Government 'SASS' Travel Grants

Subjects: Study of, or research in, Swedish language, literature or linguistics.

Eligibility: Open to members in good standing of the Society for the Advancement of Scandinavian Studies (SASS). Priority will be given to graduate students and untenured faculty. Applicants must be nationals or permanent residents of the USA.

Level of Study: Postgraduate, Doctorate, Postdoctorate, Professional development.

Type: Travel Grant.

No. of awards offered: Varies.

Frequency: Annual.

Value: A sum of US$6,000 will be divided among the grantees. Awards vary depending upon individual need.

Country of Study: Sweden or USA.

Applications Procedure: Self-written application form must follow specific pattern. Project description is required in addition to two letters of recommendation.

Closing Date: March 15th to be taken up during the calendar year.

Additional Information: Graduate students in the social sciences may use the grants for intensive Swedish language study in Sweden. Otherwise grants may be used for projects either in North America or Sweden.

SWEDISH NATURAL SCIENCE RESEARCH COUNCIL (NFR)

Swedish Natural Science Research Council (NFR), Box 6711, Stockholm, S-113 85, Sweden
Tel: 46 8 610 07 00
Fax: 46 8 610 07 40

*NFR Programme for Visiting Scientists

Subjects: Natural sciences and mathematics.

Eligibility: Open to foreign senior scientists.

Purpose: To support the initiation of new research projects or participation in the development of existing work.

No. of awards offered: Varies.

Frequency: Annual.

Value: Either an amount equivalent to the salary reduction during the visiting scientist's absence from his home institution, or an amount equivalent to the salary of a Swedish scientist of corresponding status.

Study Establishment: A research institute.

Country of Study: Sweden.

Applications Procedure: Invitations to participate must be arranged between the Swedish host institution and the visiting scientist, who should not contact the NFR directly.

Closing Date: October 1st.

*Postdoctoral Fellowships

Subjects: Natural sciences and mathematics.

Eligibility: Open to postdoctorate researchers who have held their doctoral degree for no more than three years.

Purpose: To provide young researchers with the opportunity to conduct research at foreign institutions.

No. of awards offered: Varies.

Frequency: Annual.

Value: SEK120,000-280,000.

Length of Study: One year.

Study Establishment: Appropriate institutions.

Country of Study: Sweden or abroad.

Applications Procedure: Foreign applicants must be nominated by a senior scientist at the Swedish host institution. Swedish citizens may apply directly.

Closing Date: January 15th.

SWISS FEDERAL INSTITUTE OF TECHNOLOGY ZURICH

Eidgenössische Technische Hochschule Zürich, Austauschdienst, ETH Zentrum, Zürich, CH, 8092, Switzerland
Tel: 01 632 20 86/87
Fax: 01 632 12 64

Exchange Scholarships

Subjects: Architecture, engineering (civil, mechanical, electrical, production, rural and surveying), computer science, materials science, chemistry, physics, mathematics, biology, environmental sciences, earth sciences, pharmacy, agriculture, forestry.

Eligibility: Open primarily but not exclusively to nationals of Canada, Germany, Italy, Japan, Poland, Spain, the UK and the USA. Candidates should be 20-30 years of age, have had at least two years of university study, and have a good working knowledge of German.

Level of Study: Unrestricted.

Type: Scholarship.

No. of awards offered: Twenty.

Frequency: Annual.

Value: SwFr1,150 - SwFr1,350 per month, plus tuition.

Length of Study: One academic year.

Study Establishment: The Institute.

Country of Study: Switzerland.

Applications Procedure: Applications should be made to the following addresses, as appropriate: Canada - Office of the Rector, Laval University, Quebec City, Quebec; Dean of Graduate Studies, University of New Brunswick, Fredericton, New Brunswick. Germany - German Academic Exchange Service, Kennedyallee 50, D-53175 Bonn. Italy - Ministerio degli Affari Esteri, Direzione Generale delle Relazioni Culturali, Piazza Firenze 27, Roma. Japan - Dean of Students, Tokyo Institute of Technology, O-okoyama, Meguro-ku, Tokyo. Poland - Warsaw University of Technology, Warsaw. Spain - Consejo Superior de Investigaciones Cientificas, Serrano 117, Madrid-6. UK - Registrar, Imperial College of Sciences, Technology and Medicine, London SW7 2AZ. USA - Exchange Coordinator, Rensselaer Polytechnic Institute, Troy, NY 12180; World Student Fund, 756 West Peachtree Street, Atlanta, GA 30308 (Georgia Institute of Technology); Dean of Graduate School, Michigan Technological University, Houghton, MI 49931; International Student Adviser, Worcester Polytechnic Institute, Worcester, MA 01609; Exchange Coordinator, Union College, Schenectady, NY 12308; Office of Study Abroad, University of Kansas, Lawrence, KS 66045; Office of International Programs, Kansas State University, Manhattan, KS 66506.

Closing Date: 15 March; except USA: 31 January.

SWISS GOVERNMENT

Embassy of Switzerland, 7 Melbourne Avenue, Forrest, ACT, 2603, Australia
Tel: 06 273 3977
Fax: 06 273 3428

*Scholarships

Subjects: Any subject.

Eligibility: Open to Australian citizens who are either postgraduates with a clearly defined plan of study or students who are well advanced in their courses and for whom the sojourn in Switzerland would serve as complementary education. Candidates who have practised a profession for several years since completion of their studies or who are over 35 years of age are ineligible. A sufficient knowledge of French or German is required.

Type: Scholarships.

No. of awards offered: Two.

Frequency: Annual.

Value: An allowance of SwFr1,450-SwFr1,650 per month, tuition fees, medical insurance, and travel from Switzerland to Australia.

Length of Study: One year.

Study Establishment: An institution of higher education.

Country of Study: Switzerland.

Closing Date: November 10th.

*Scholarships for Art Studies

Subjects: Art studies.

Eligibility: Open to Australian students who are well advanced in their courses and for whom the sojourn in Switzerland would serve as complementary education. Students over 35 years of age are ineligible. A sufficient knowledge of French or German is required.

Type: Scholarships on a multilateral basis: Australia may nominate one candidate.

No. of awards offered: 12.

Frequency: Annual.

Value: An allowance of SwFr1,650 per month, medical insurance, travel from Switzerland to Australia.

Length of Study: One academic year.

Study Establishment: Any Swiss Art School or conservatory.

Country of Study: Switzerland.

Applications Procedure: Applications are available at Australian universities.

Closing Date: November 10th.

SYMPHONY ORCHESTRA ASSOCIATION OF KINGSPORT

Kingsport Symphony Orchestra, Renaissance Center, Box 13, 1200 East Center Street, Kingsport, TN, 37660, USA
Tel: 423 392 8423
Fax: 423 392 8428
Contact: Linda Windle, Assistant Manager

Elizabeth Harper Vaughn Concerto Competition

Subjects: Three categories alternating annually in the following sequence: percussion, winds and brass; strings; piano.

Eligibility: Open to American musicians 26 years old and younger.

No. of awards offered: One.

Frequency: Annual.

Value: US$1,000, plus a concert performance with the orchestra and accommodation.

Closing Date: December 31st.

Additional Information: The Competition is held in March. Applications must be accompanied by a letter of recommendation from a qualified teacher, the entrance fee (US$20, make checks payable to Kingsport Symphony Orchestra), and a cassette tape. The tape recording must be a concerto, or work of similar importance, written with orchestral accompaniment.

SYRACUSE UNIVERSITY

Syracuse University, SU Graduate School , 303 Bowne Hall, Syracuse, NY, 13244-1200, USA
Tel: 315 443 4492
Fax: 315 443 3423
Email: GRADSCHL@suadmin.syr.edu
www: http://cwis.syr.edu/
Contact: Kristin Sciortino

African American Fellowship

Eligibility: Open to nationals of any country.

Level of Study: Unrestricted.

Purpose: To provide support to African American students who will tie African American studies in with their programs of study.

Type: Fellowship.

Frequency: Annual.

Value: US$25,359.

Length of Study: One to six years.

Study Establishment: Syracuse University.

Country of Study: USA.

Applications Procedure: Application for fellowship is done through admission application.

Closing Date: July 2nd.

Syracuse University Fellowship

Subjects: All subjects.

Eligibility: Open to nationals of any country.

Level of Study: Unrestricted.

Purpose: To provide a full support package during a student's term of study.

Type: Fellowship.

No. of awards offered: 101.

Frequency: Annual.

Value: US$25,359.

Length of Study: One to six years.

Study Establishment: Syracuse University.

Country of Study: USA.

Applications Procedure: Application for fellowship is done through admission application.

Closing Date: July 2nd.

MURIEL TAYLOR SCHOLARSHIP FUND FOR CELLISTS

Muriel Taylor Scholarship Fund for Cellists, The Warehouse, 13 Theed Street, London, SE1 8ST, England
Tel: 0171 928 9251
Fax: 0171 928 9252
Contact: The Hon. Competition Secretary

Muriel Taylor Cello Scholarship

Subjects: Cello.

Eligibility: Open to candidates of any nationality and qualifications who are between no more than 17-23 years of age on March 31st in the year of competition.

Level of Study: Unrestricted.

Purpose: To help talented young cellists continue their studies, usually following study at a recognized tertiary college of music, i.e. RAM or RCM.

Type: Scholarship.

No. of awards offered: One.

Frequency: Annual.

Value: £2,000 for tuition fees.

Study Establishment: A recognized tertiary college of music.

Country of Study: Any country.

Closing Date: January 31st.

Additional Information: The competition is held annually, usually mid-April.

TEAGASC (AGRICULTURAL & FOOD DEVELOPMENT AUTHORITY)

Teagasc, 19 Sandymount Avenue, Dublin, 4, Republic of Ireland
Tel: 353 1 6688 188
Fax: 353 1 6688 023
Email: corourke@hq.teagsa.ie
Contact: Dr C O'Rourke

Teagasc Research Grants

Subjects: Any subject relevant to food and agriculture: animal sciences, plant sciences, physical/earth sciences, economics and rural development.

Eligibility: Open to full-time academic staff at third-level colleges in Ireland or abroad.

Purpose: To support projects in universities on topics relevant to the overall Teagasc research programme on agriculture and food.

Type: Research grants.

No. of awards offered: Approximately 25.

Frequency: Annual.

Value: Average IR£8,500 per annum to cover all costs (including fees, travel, materials).

Length of Study: One to three years.

Study Establishment: Any third-level college, in association with a Teagasc Research Centre,.

Country of Study: Usually Ireland.

Closing Date: April/May.

Additional Information: Grants are awarded to college staff members, who then take on graduate students to undertake the project, usually as an MSc or PhD project.

TECHNICAL UNIVERSITY OF LUBLIN

Dept. of Environmental Protection Engineering, Technical University of Lublin, Lublin, 20-618, Poland
Tel: 4881 554124
Fax: 4881 556948
Email: Gracywd@akropolis.pol
Contact: Professor Lucian Pawlowski

Scholarship

Subjects: Environmental engineering, incineration and hazardous waste.

Eligibility: Open to nationals of any country.

Level of Study: Unrestricted.

Purpose: To enable participation in research projects on the incineration of wastes in cement kilns.

Type: Scholarship.

No. of awards offered: One.

Frequency: Dependent on funds available.

Value: 400PLZ per month.

Length of Study: One year approximately.

Country of Study: Poland.

Applications Procedure: Please submit application form, CV and references.

Closing Date: March 30th.

TELLURIDE ASSOCIATION

Telluride Association, 217 West Avenue, Ithaca, NY, 14850, USA

Contact: Matthew Trail

Telluride Scholarship

Subjects: Any offered by the University.

Eligibility: Open to students at Cornell University.

Purpose: To provide room and board Scholarships to gifted students who attend Cornell University.

Type: Scholarship.

No. of awards offered: Up to 10.

Frequency: Annual.

Value: To cover room and board.

Study Establishment: Telluride House, Cornell.

Country of Study: USA.

Applications Procedure: Applicants must submit essays and attend an interview.

Closing Date: January.

THE TEXTILE INSTITUTE

The Textile Institute, International Headquarters, 10 Blackfriars Street, Manchester, M3 5DR, England
Tel: 0161 834 8457
Fax: 0161 835 3087
Contact: Catherine Cockburn, Qualifications Officer

*Lord Barnby Foundation Bursaries

Subjects: Textile technology.

Eligibility: Open to UK nationals previously employed for two years in the UK textile industry.

Purpose: To assist those who have been employed in the UK textile industry for at least two years and who are registered on or have recently completed a course of study leading to a qualification.

Type: Bursary.

No. of awards offered: Varies.

Frequency: Throughout the year.

Value: Varies; up to £500.

Country of Study: UK.

Applications Procedure: Applications must be made through the Head of Department.

*Cotton Industry War Memorial Trust Scholarships

Subjects: Textile technology or design.

Eligibility: All candidates must undertake to be employed in and for the benefit of the UK textile industry. Particular attention is paid to students transferring to an ATI course after completing a previous qualification who are not eligible for mandatory grants.

Purpose: To assist students to study full-time or part-time for the Associateship of the Textile Institute or for a textile degree in technology or design or to assist professionally qualified people and degree holders in textile technology or design, related sciences or other disciplines to undertake a full-time course for a Master's degree or PhD.

Type: Scholarship.

No. of awards offered: Varies.

Frequency: Annual.

Value: Up to £500.

Country of Study: UK.

Closing Date: Last Friday in July.

*William Lee Bursary

Subjects: Textiles.

Eligibility: Open to textile students.

Frequency: Annual.

Value: Varies.

Closing Date: End of July.

*Textile Institute Scholarship

Subjects: Any textile-related subject.

Eligibility: Open to students or professionally qualified individuals wishing to undertake further study in the fields of textile technology or design.

Purpose: To assist students to study full-time or part-time for the Associateship of the Textile Institute or for a textile degree in technology or design or to assist professionally qualified people and degree holders in textile technology or design, related sciences or other disciplines to undertake a full-time course for a Master's Degree or PhD.

Type: Scholarship.

No. of awards offered: Varies.

Frequency: Annual.

Value: Generally £100-£400, larger scholarships may be made in certain circumstances.

Country of Study: Any country.

Closing Date: Last Friday in July.

*Weavers' Company Scholarships

Subjects: Any subject relevant to weaving, including design.

Eligibility: All candidates must undertake to be employed in and for the benefit of the UK textile industry.

Purpose: To assist students to study full-time or part-time for the Associateship of the Textile Institute or for a textile degree in technology or design or to assist professionally qualified people and degree holders in textile technology or design, related sciences or other disciplines to undertake a full-time course for a Master's degree or PhD.

Type: Scholarship.

No. of awards offered: Varies.

Frequency: Annual.

Value: Varies; up to £500.

Country of Study: UK.

Closing Date: Last Friday in July.

THAILAND NATIONAL COMMISSION FOR UNESCO

Thailand National Commission for UNESCO, Ministry of Education, Bangkok, 10300, Thailand
Tel: 281 6370
Fax: 281 0953
Contact: Secretary General

Thailand Fellowships, Scholarships and Junior Scholarships

Subjects: Any subject offered by the universities in Thailand.

Eligibility: Open to members of UNESCO. Candidates are nominated by the UNESCO National Commission in their own country and should check other eligibility requirements through it.

Level of Study: Postgraduate, Undergraduate.

Purpose: To promote international understanding and enhance cultural exchange.

No. of awards offered: 6 Fellowships, 4 Scholarships and 4 Junior Scholarships.

Frequency: Annual.

Value: Fellowships 80,000 Baht; Scholarships 50,000 Baht; Junior Scholarships 40,000 Baht; from an annual total of 840,000 Baht.

Length of Study: One academic year (10 months) with the possibility of an extension.

Study Establishment: A college or university in Thailand.

Country of Study: Thailand.

Applications Procedure: Application form can be obtained from the Thai National Commission for UNESCO.

Closing Date: December 31st for nominations. Confirmation of the grant acceptance available in March.

Additional Information: The recipient government is requested to conduct the preliminary screening of candidates in cooperation with its UNESCO National Commission or with appropriate organizations. If possible, the selecting committee of recipient governments should include a person familiar with conditions in Thailand who is able to render suggestions as the situation requires. The recipient country is also asked to nominate only those candidates suitable to undertake their studies in Thailand, and who upon their return would render valuable service in their selected fields to their countries. Awardees must stay in Thailand for ten months and cover all their own international travelling costs.

THE THOMSON FOUNDATION

The Thomson Foundation, 68 Park Place, Cardiff, CF1 3AS, Wales
Tel: 01222 874 873
Fax: 01222 225 194
Email: Thomfound@Cardiff.AC.UK
Contact: Gareth Price

Thomson Foundation Scholarship

Eligibility: Open to professional journalists and broadcasters with at least three years full-time experience.

Level of Study: Professional development.

Purpose: To enable recipients to attend Thomson Foundation Training courses in Britain.

Type: Scholarship.

No. of awards offered: Varies.

Value: Variable.

Length of Study: Variable.

Study Establishment: The Thomson Foundation.

Country of Study: United Kingdom.

Applications Procedure: Application form from Thomson Foundation.

THIRD WORLD ACADEMY OF SCIENCES

Third World Academy of Sciences, c/o International Centre for Theoretical Physics, PO Box 586, Trieste, 34136, Italy
Tel: 39 40 2240 327
Fax: 39 40 224559
Contact: Mohamed H A Hassan, Executive Secretary

*Prizes to Young Scientists in Developing Countries

Subjects: Biology; chemistry; mathematics or physics; rotated annually.

Eligibility: Open to academies and research councils in developing countries.

Purpose: To enable academies and research councils in over 20 Third World countries to institute Prizes and Medals for young scientists in their countries.

Type: Prizes.

No. of awards offered: At least 20.

Frequency: Annual.

Value: Usually US$2,000.

Country of Study: Developing countries.

*Support for International Scientific Meetings

Subjects: Biological, chemical, agricultural and geological sciences, biochemistry, biotechnology, engineering and medical sciences.

Eligibility: Open to organizers of international scientific meetings in developing countries. Special consideration is given to those meetings which are likely to benefit the scientific community in the Third World and to promote regional and international cooperation in developing science and its applications to the problems of the Third World.

Purpose: To encourage the organization of international scientific meetings in Third World countries.

Type: Travel Grant.

No. of awards offered: Varies.

Value: To assist with the travel expenses of principal speakers from abroad and/or participants from the region.

Country of Study: Developing countries.

Closing Date: June 1st for meeting to be held during January and June of the following year; December 1st for meeting to be held during July and December of the following year.

*TWAS Awards in Basic Sciences

Subjects: Biology, chemistry, mathematics, physics, basic medical science.

Eligibility: Open to nationals of developing countries, working and living in these countries. Consideration is given to proven achievements judged particularly by their national and international impact.

Purpose: To reward individual scientists who have made outstanding contributions to the advancement of science.

No. of awards offered: Five.

Frequency: Annual.

Value: US$10,000.

Country of Study: Developing countries.

Closing Date: March 1st.

Additional Information: The Awards are usually presented on a special occasion, normally coinciding with the general meeting of the Academy and/or a general conference organized by the Academy. Recipients of Awards are expected to give lectures about the work for which the Awards have been made.

*TWAS Fellowship Scheme

Subjects: Mathematics, physics, biology, chemistry.

Eligibility: Open to nationals of developing countries, normally with some research experience, and with permanent positions in universities or research institutes in developing countries.

Purpose: To facilitate and promote mutual contacts of research scientists in the Third World and to further relations between their scientific institutions.

Type: Fellowship.

No. of awards offered: Varies.

Value: Travel support. Living expenses are usually obtained from local sources.

Length of Study: One month.

Country of Study: Developing countries.

Closing Date: None.

Additional Information: Special consideration will be given to visits which can be expected to promote cooperation among scientists of the same region and yield substantial benefits to the visitors, their host and their respective scientific communities.

*TWAS Research Grants

Subjects: Biology, chemistry, mathematics, physics.

Eligibility: Open to nationals of Third World countries who hold an applicable advanced academic degree and are employed by a university or research institute in the Third World. Applicants must refer to a specific research project to be carried out at a university or research institute in the Third World. Grants are awarded on the basis of scientific merit and priority is given to young scientists at an early stage of their career.

Purpose: To support Third World scientists of outstanding merit in their research.

Type: Grant.

No. of awards offered: Varies.

Value: Up to US$10,000.

Length of Study: One year.

Country of Study: Developing countries.

Additional Information: The Academy also provides additional funds for scientific equipment and the provision of books and journals, as well as for upgrading scientific institutions in the South.

THIRD WORLD NETWORK OF SCIENTIFIC ORGANIZATIONS

c/o International Centre for Theoretical Physics, PO Box 586, Trieste, 34100, Italy

*Prizes in Applied Sciences

Subjects: Major Third World problems related to agriculture and technology.

Eligibility: Open to individuals (living) or institutions whose scientific and technological innovations have had, or will have, a beneficial effect on the nations of the Third World in the fields of agriculture or technology. Nominees may be from either developing or developed countries. Fellows and Associate Fellows of the Third World Academy of Sciences (TWAS) are not eligible.

Purpose: To honour and support distinguished individuals or institutions whose scientific and technical innovations have provided significant and sustainable solutions to some important economic and social problems in the Third World and have brought, or will bring, substantial benefits to the well-being of the people.

Type: Prize.

No. of awards offered: Varies.

Frequency: Annual.

Value: US$10,000 per prize, plus a TWNSO Medal on which major contributions of the prize winner will be mentioned.

Closing Date: March 1st.

Additional Information: Nominations for the TWNSO prizes are invited from all members of TWNSO and TWAS as well as from Science Academies, National Research Councils, Universities and Research Institutions in developing and developed countries. They should be made on special TWNSO forms (available from the TWNSO Secretariat) and should clearly state the contributions made in one of the fields of applied science for which the prize would be given. The nomination should be accompanied by a one- or two-page profile of the nominated individual or institution, and a list of significant publications relevant to the award. For nominated individuals a complete list of publications and the biodata of the candidate are required. Nominations must be submitted in the English language. A nomination is normally considered for a period

of three years, after which a new nomination will be required. Nominations for each of these prizes are judged by an international committee of distinguished scientists and technologists appointed by the President of the Network.

THE ERIC THOMPSON TRUST

The Eric Thompson Trust, c/o The Royal Philharmonic Society, 10 Stratford Place, London, W1N 9AE, England
Tel: 0171 491 8110
Fax: 0171 493 7463
Contact: Clerk To the Trustees

Grants-in-Aid

Subjects: Organ.

Eligibility: Open to professional organists.

Purpose: To provide aspiring professional organists with financial assistance with special studies such as summer schools, travel and subsistence for auditions or performance, or other incidental costs incurred in their work.

No. of awards offered: Varies.

Frequency: Annual.

Value: Determined by Trustees, but normally limited to a contribution towards costs.

Country of Study: Any, but probably largely UK in practice.

Applications Procedure: Applicants (usually young professional organists) should send full details of their needs, together with information on their training and career and, where available, references and other relevant material, to the Clerk to the Trustees.

Closing Date: December 31st for notification at the end of February.

THOURON-UNIVERSITY OF PENNSYLVANIA FUND FOR BRITISH-AMERICAN STUDENT EXCHANGE

Thouron Awards, University of Glasgow, Glasgow, G12 8QQ, Scotland
Email: j.m.black@mis.gla.ac.uk
Contact: Registrar

Thouron Awards

Subjects: Any subject.

Eligibility: Open to UK citizens who are graduates and unmarried. Postdoctoral candidates are ineligible unless their proposed study is in a field different from that in which they undertook their previous postgraduate study. No application will be considered from a student already in the USA.

Level of Study: Postgraduate.

Purpose: To promote better understanding between the people of the UK and the USA.

No. of awards offered: Approximately 12.

Frequency: Annual.

Value: US$1,247 per month, plus tuition and fees of US$13,800 per annum.

Length of Study: One or two years.

Study Establishment: The University of Pennsylvania, Philadelphia.

Country of Study: USA.

Applications Procedure: Two application forms with two passport size photographs and three referee forms.

Closing Date: October 20th.

Additional Information: American citizens interested in studying in the UK should write to the University of Pennsylvania for further details.

THRASHER RESEARCH FUND

Thrasher Research Fund, 50 East North Temple, 8th floor, Salt Lake City, UT, 84150, USA
Tel: 801 240 4753
Fax: 801 240 1964
Contact: Robert M Briem, EdD, Associate Director

Research and Field Demonstration Project Grants

Subjects: Child health.

Eligibility: Open to research scientists and private voluntary organizations. Pre- and postdoctoral students may be employed on Thrasher-funded projects, but the principal investigator is expected to take an active role in the project and assume full responsibility for it. The principal investigator must have a connection with a university, research institution, or appropriate private voluntary organization.

Level of Study: Postdoctorate.

Purpose: To promote international and national child health research and child health-related projects. Emphasis is on practical and applied interventions with the potential to improve the health of children worldwide.

Type: Grant.

No. of awards offered: Varies.

Frequency: Twice yearly.

Value: Up to US$50,000 per year.

Length of Study: Up to three years.

Country of Study: Unrestricted.

Applications Procedure: Instructions for sending initial prospectus available upon request. Applicants are encouraged to consult with Fund staff prior to submitting a prospectus.

Closing Date: Proposals for which review is complete at the time of the semi-annual meetings are considered at those meetings.

Additional Information: The Thrasher Research Fund supports two programs. The Scientific Program supports research primarily in the areas of maternal and child health, infectious and parasitic diarrheal diseases, acute respiratory disease, and major nutritional deficiency. The Innovative Program supports projects that bridge the gap between formal research in the areas of children's health and field application of research findings. Research in the areas of abortion, reproductive physiology, contraceptive technology, and sexually transmitted disease is not supported. Grants are not given for conferences, workshops, or symposia; general operations; or construction or renovation of buildings. Material detailing the policy guidelines, application procedures, and the review process are available on request. Investigators are encouraged to call or write to consult with Fund staff before submitting a prospectus.

TIERÄRZTLICHE HOCHSCHULE HANNOVER

Postfach 71 11 80, Hannover, D-30545, Germany
Tel: 49 511 9536
Fax: 49 511 953 8050
Email: daltva@vw.tiho-hannover.de
www: http://www.tiho-hannover.de
Contact: Hans Linneman

Karl-Enigk-Stiftung

Subjects: Veterinary parasitology.

Eligibility: Applicants must not be aged more than 32 and must be from European countries where German is spoken.

Level of Study: Postdoctorate.

Purpose: To support research in experimental veterinary parasitology.

Type: Scholarship.

No. of awards offered: 1-2 each year.

Frequency: Annual.

Length of Study: 1-3 years.

Country of Study: European countries with German language.

Applications Procedure: Please submit CV, publication list, short research proposal and references from the head of the research institute.

Closing Date: December 1st.

TOKYO FOUNDATION FOR INBOUND STUDENTS

Tokyo Foundation for Inbound Students, 1-12-2 Dogenzaka, Shibuya Ku, Tokyo, 150, Japan
Tel: 03 3461 0844
Fax: 03 5458 1696
Contact: Shigeaki Yamamoto, Secretary General

Tokyo Scholarship

Subjects: Any subject in a Japanese university postgraduate course.

Eligibility: Asia and pacific regions.

Level of Study: Postgraduate.

Purpose: To promote international exchange. Fostering the development of international goodwill between Japan and her neighbours in the Pacific and Asia, and contributing to international cooperation and cultural exchange in the broadest possible sense.

Type: Scholarship.

No. of awards offered: 24.

Frequency: Annual.

Value: 160,000 Yen per month per student.

Country of Study: Japan.

Applications Procedure: Please write for application form.

Closing Date: From October 20th to November 15th.

Additional Information: 1) travel to Japan at own cost 2) must be admitted to enter university postgraduate school 3) it is worth noting that with over 700 applicants for these awards, competition for places is very high.

TOTAL SOUTH AFRICA PTY LTD

University of the Orange Free State, PO Box 339, Bloemfontein, 9300, South Africa
Tel: 0151 4012479/051 4012599
Fax: 0151 4012117
Contact: The Director of Student and Research Administration

*Frost Combating Bursary

Subjects: Agricultural meteorology: frost combating.

Eligibility: Open to postgraduates; in the event of suitable postgraduate students not being available, the Bursary Committee may consider advanced undergraduate students.

Type: Bursary.

No. of awards offered: One.

Frequency: Annual.

Value: R500 per annum.

Study Establishment: The University of the Orange Free State.

Country of Study: South Africa.

Closing Date: None.

Additional Information: There are a number of additional Bursaries available towards the master's and doctoral degrees.

TOURETTE SYNDROME ASSOCIATION, INC

Tourette Syndrome Association, Inc, 42-40 Bell Boulevard, Bayside, NY, 11361-2861, USA
Tel: 718 224 2999
Fax: 718 279 9596
Email: spear@ix.netcom.com
www: http://neuro-www2.mgh,harvard.edu/TSA/tsamain.html
Contact: Sue Levi-Pearl, Liaison for Medical and Scientific Programs

Research Grants

Subjects: Grants are awarded in three categories: basic neuroscience specifically relevant to Tourette Syndrome; clinical studies; training of postdoctoral Fellows.

Eligibility: Open to candidates who have an MD, PhD or equivalent qualifications. Previous experience in the field of movement disorders is desirable, but not essential. Fellowships are intended for young post-doctoral investigators in the early stages of their careers.

Purpose: To foster basic and clinical research related to the causes or treatment of Tourette Syndrome.

No. of awards offered: Varies.

Frequency: Annual.

Value: Varies depending upon category, and experience within that category: US$5,000-US$40,000.

Length of Study: One to two years.

Study Establishment: Any institution with adequate facilities.

Country of Study: Unrestricted.

Closing Date: October.

Additional Information: The Association provides up to 10% of overhead or indirect costs within the total amount budgeted.

THE TRANS-ANTARCTIC ASSOCIATION

The Trans-Antarctic Association, c/o Scott Polar Research Institute, Lensfield Road, Cambridge, CB2 1ER, England
Tel: 01223 337100
Fax: 01223 276604
Contact: Dr D I M MacDonald, Grants Secretary

TAA Grants

Subjects: Any Antarctic research, usually in the natural sciences, or Antarctic exploration.

Eligibility: Open only to nationals of the UK, Australia, New Zealand and South Africa (being those nations which supported the Trans-Antarctic Expedition, 1955-58). Grants are not available for research or exploration in the Arctic or any other geographical areas.

Level of Study: Unrestricted.

Purpose: To assist Antarctic research and exploration.

Type: Cash grants.

No. of awards offered: Normally 10-15 grants.

Frequency: Annual.

Value: Normally up to £1,000; does not normally include course fees or living expenses.

Study Establishment: For attendance at scientific meetings, for scientific research, or for Antarctic expeditions.

Applications Procedure: No application form; write to grants secretary.

Closing Date: January 31st.

TRANSPORTATION ASSOCIATION OF CANADA

Secretariat, Transportation Association of Canada, 2323 St Laurent Boulevard, Ottawa, Ontario, K1G 4K6, Canada
Tel: 613 736 1350
Fax: 613 736 1395
Contact: Mr Marc Comeau, Public Communications Manager

TAC Scholarships

Subjects: Highway sciences: highway engineering, transport economics, administration, etc.

Eligibility: Open to Canadian citizens and landed immigrants who hold university degrees and are acceptable to the university at which they plan to carry out postgraduate studies in the transportation field.

Purpose: To promote transportation-related disciplines at the postgraduate level.

Type: Scholarship.

No. of awards offered: Five.

Frequency: Annual.

Value: C$3,000-C$5,000.

Length of Study: One year.

Study Establishment: At universities.

Country of Study: Canada, the USA, or worldwide.

Closing Date: March. Applicants should call for the exact date, which varies yearly.

Additional Information: Scholarships currently offered are from the DELCAN Corporation, Stanley Engineering Group, Inc/Pavement Management Systems Ltd, Provincial/Territorial Governments of Canada, John Emery Geotechnical Engineering Limited, Lea Associates Group.

THE HARRY S TRUMAN LIBRARY INSTITUTE

The Harry S Truman Library Institute, U.S. Highway 25 and Delaware Street, Independence, MO, 64050, USA
Contact: The Secretary

Dissertation Year Fellowships

Subjects: The public career of Harry S Truman and the history of the Truman administration.

Eligibility: Open to individuals who have completed their dissertation research and are ready to begin writing.

Level of Study: Postgraduate, Postdoctorate.

Purpose: To encourage historical scholarship in the Truman era.

Type: Fellowship.

No. of awards offered: Two.

Frequency: Quarterly.

Value: US$16,000.

Study Establishment: One year.

Country of Study: USA.

Applications Procedure: Write for application form.

Closing Date: February 1st for notification in April.

Additional Information: Recipients will not be required to come to the Truman Library but will be expected to furnish the Library with a copy of their dissertation.

Research Grants

Subjects: The public career of Harry S Truman and the history of the Truman administration.

Eligibility: Open to graduate students and postdoctoral scholars who are working on a project pertaining to Truman's public career or to some facet of his administration.

Level of Study: Postgraduate, Postdoctorate.

Purpose: To enable graduate students and postdoctoral scholars to come to the library for one to three weeks to use its archival facilities.

Type: Research Grant.

No. of awards offered: Varies.

Frequency: Quarterly.

Value: Up to US$2,500, to cover round-trip air fare between the applicant's home and Independence, and a modest sum to cover living expenses while working at the Library.

Length of Study: 1-3 weeks.

Study Establishment: The Library.

Country of Study: USA.

Closing Date: 1 January, 1 April, 1 July, 1 October.

Scholar's Award

Subjects: The public career of Harry S Truman or some aspect of the history of the Truman administration or of the USA during that administration.

Eligibility: Open to established scholars and scholars about to embark on their careers.

No. of awards offered: One.

Frequency: Biennially (1998).

Value: Based primarily on a proposed budget submitted by the applicant and may amount to as much as one-half the applicant's academic-year salary.

Study Establishment: Recipients will be expected to spend a major portion of their research time utilizing the resources of the Truman Library.

Country of Study: USA.

Closing Date: December 15th.

Additional Information: The research should result in a book-length manuscript intended for publication; one copy of the publication resulting from work done under the award is to be provided by the author to the Library.

TRUSTEES OF THEODORA BOSANQUET BURSARY

Trustees of Theodora Bosanquet Bursary, c/o 28 Great James Street, London, WC1N 3ES, England
Tel: 0171 404 6447
Fax: 0171 404 6505

Bosanquet (Theodora) Bursary

Eligibility: Open to women only.

Level of Study: Postgraduate, Doctorate.

Purpose: To provide accommodation in London for up to four weeks for women students or women postgraduates carrying out research in English literature or history.

Type: Accommodation.

No. of awards offered: 1-2.

Frequency: Annual.

Value: £600.

Length of Study: Up to four weeks.

Study Establishment: A London college.

Country of Study: UK.

Applications Procedure: Application form to be completed.

Closing Date: November 22nd.

Additional Information: Requests for application forms should be accompanied by a stamped, self addressed envelope or International reply coupons and sent to the Clerk of the Trustees at the main award address.

RICHARD TUCKER MUSIC FOUNDATION

Richard Tucker Music Foundation, 1790 Broadway, Suite 715, New York, NY, 10019, USA
Tel: 212 757 2218
Fax: 212 757 2347
Contact: Ellen C Moran, Executive Director

Robert M Jacobson Study Grant

Subjects: Operatic singing.

Eligibility: Open to opera singers who are US citizens and are at an early level of their career. Candidates must be recommended for the grant and should be completing an apprentice program, or have recently graduated from a conservatory. Candidates may not have held any major roles prior to receiving the grant.

Level of Study: Postgraduate.

Purpose: To help an artist at the earliest stage of his or her career.

Type: Grant.

No. of awards offered: One or more.

Frequency: Annual.

Value: US$5,000.

Length of Study: One year; not renewable.

Country of Study: Any country.

Applications Procedure: By recommendation only.

Closing Date: November 10th of the year preceding the award.

Richard Tucker Award

Subjects: Operatic singing.

Eligibility: Open to male and female opera singers who are US citizens and are recommended to the Foundation by a person other than the artist or the artist's manager. The award is conferred rather than competed for.

Level of Study: Professional development.

Purpose: To further career development of an artist on the brink of international acclaim.

No. of awards offered: One award.

Frequency: Annual.

Value: US$30,000.

Length of Study: One year, not renewable.

Country of Study: Any country.

Applications Procedure: By recommendation only.

Closing Date: November 10th of the year preceding the award.

Richard Tucker Foundation Career Grants

Subjects: Operatic singing.

Eligibility: Open to male and female opera singers who are US citizens. Candidates must be recommended by a professional in the operatic field with whom they have worked. Singers cannot apply.

Level of Study: Professional development.

Purpose: To further the career of young American artists.

No. of awards offered: Five grants, including one to a tenor.

Frequency: Annual.

Value: At least US$7,500.

Length of Study: One year; renewable.

Country of Study: Any country.

Applications Procedure: By recommendation only.

Closing Date: November 10th of the year preceding the award.

TURKU CENTRE FOR COMPUTER SCIENCE/GRADUATE SCHOOL, TUCS

DataCity, Lemminkäisenkatu 14A, Turku, FIN-20520, Finland
Tel: 358 21 2654 204
Fax: 358 21 2410 154
Email: http://www.utu.fi/org/tucs/
Telex: TUCS@abo.fi
Contact: TUCS Office

Postgraduate Grant

Subjects: Computer Science.

Eligibility: Applicants should have a TOEFL score of at least 550 points or a corresponding level of English proficiency.

Level of Study: Postgraduate.

Purpose: To support students studying for a doctoral degree in Computer Science.

Type: Grant.

No. of awards offered: Varies.

Frequency: Annual.

Value: FIM5,500.

Length of Study: 4-6 years.

Study Establishment: Graduate school.

Country of Study: Finland.

Applications Procedure: No specific application form exists. Applicants should write with a free form application.

Closing Date: April 30th.

SYBIL TUTTON TRUST

Sybil Tutton Trust, 16 Ogle Street, London, W1P 7LG, England
Tel: 0171 636 4481
Fax: 0171 637 4307
Contact: Valerie Beale, Administrator

*Sybil Tutton Awards

Subjects: Musical performance: opera.

Eligibility: Open to opera students of 18-30 years who have been resident in the UK for three years.

Purpose: To assist exceptionally talented opera students.

No. of awards offered: Two.

Frequency: Annual.

Value: From a total of £15,000.

Country of Study: Unrestricted.

Closing Date: Mid-February.

Additional Information: Selected students will be asked to audition.

UCLA CENTRE FOR MEDIEVAL AND RENAISSANCE STUDIES

UCLA Centre for Medieval and Renaissance Studies, Box 951485, Los Angeles, CA, 90095-1485, USA
Tel: 310 825 1880
Fax: 310 825 0655
Email: cmrs@humntet.ucla.edu
www: http://www.humnet.ucla.edu/humnet/cmrs/default.html
Contact: John Hendra, Project Coordinator

Summer Fellowships

Subjects: Medieval and early modern history, culture, literature, philosophy and religion.

Eligibility: No restriction except applicant must have a PhD or similar from a recognised and accredited university.

Level of Study: Postdoctorate.

Purpose: To defray expenses for a scholar doing research at UCLA during July, August or September. The scholar should have a particular need to use UCLA and/or surrounding resources.

Type: Stipend.

No. of awards offered: One.

Frequency: Annual.

Value: US$500.

Length of Study: Not to exceed three months.

Study Establishment: UCLA.

Country of Study: USA.

Applications Procedure: Curriculum Vitae, two page project description, Biography for Academic Personnel form available through the centre, one letter of recommendation.

Closing Date: Early February 1997 for Summer 1997.

For further information contact:
UCLA Centre for Medieval and Renaissance, Studies, Box 951485, Los Angeles, CA, 90095-1485, USA
Tel: 310 825 1880
Fax: 310 825 0655
Email: cmrs@humntet.ucla.edu
www: http://www.humnet.ucla.edu/humnet/cmrs/default.html
Contact: John Hendra, Project Coordinator

UCLA INSTITUTE OF AMERICAN CULTURE/AMERICAN INDIAN STUDIES

UCLA Institute of American Culture/American Indian Studies, Box 951548, 3220 Campbell Hall, Los Angeles, CA, 90095-1548, USA
Tel: 310 825 7315
Fax: 310 206 7060
Email: aisc@ucla.edu
www: http://www.sscnet.ucla.edu/indian/
Contact: Lynn Gamble

Postdoctoral/Visiting Scholar Fellowships

Subjects: Arts and humanities, education and teacher training, fine and applied arts, law.

Eligibility: Open to nationals of any country.

Level of Study: Postgraduate, Postdoctorate.

Purpose: To advance knowledge of American Indians.

Type: Fellowship.

No. of awards offered: One.

Frequency: Annual.

Value: US$23,000-US$28,000.

Length of Study: 9 months to one year.

Country of Study: USA.

Applications Procedure: Application form must be completed.

Closing Date: December 31st each year.

UNESCO

UNESCO, 7 place de Fontenoy, Paris, 75352, France
Tel: 33 1 4568 1000
Fax: 33 1 4567 1690
Telex: 204461 PARIS
Contact: Mr N Noguchi, Director - Equipment and Fellowships Division

Aid to Refugees, National Liberation Movements and Organizations

Subjects: As per UNESCO Fellowships.

Eligibility: Open to refugees sponsored by the national liberation movements; refugees registered with the UNRWA for Palestine refugees in the Near East or sponsored by Palestine, recognized by the League of Arab States.

Level of Study: Unrestricted.

Purpose: To contribute to the specialized training of qualified personnel for their future integration and participation in the economic and social development of their respective countries after independence.

Frequency: Dependent on funds available.

Value: A monthly allowance, based in general on the scale adopted by the UN, plus travel expenses, tuition fees and books.

Length of Study: Usually 3-9 months.

Country of Study: UNESCO Member or Associate Member States.

Applications Procedure: Application through the national liberation movements and organizations, or through Palestine recognized by the Arab League of States.

Fellowships donated by Member States and sponsored by UNESCO

Subjects: Food science and production, architectural restoration, arts and humanities, business studies, education and teacher training, engineering, fine and applied arts, law, mathematics, natural sciences and social sciences.

Eligibility: Open to nationals of UNESCO member states and associate members, particularly from developing countries identified by the donor/sponsoring country.

Level of Study: Dependent on the donor country.

Purpose: To provide opportunities for Fellows to further primarily higher education or research abroad, and to acquire international experience in fields of study for which appropriate facilities are not available in the country of origin.

Type: Fellowship.

Frequency: Dependent on the donor country.

Value: Financial responsibilities in the country of study are undertaken by the sponsoring country; international travel costs must be borne by the benficiary or his/her governmental authorities.

Length of Study: Varies.

Country of Study: Donor/sponsoring country.

Applications Procedure: Application through the national authorities specially designated by UNESCO Member States (usually National Commission for UNESCO or appropriate Ministry).

Individual Fellowships

Subjects: Food science and production, architectural restoration, interpretation and translation, business studies, education and teacher training, fine and applied arts, law, natural sciences, social and behavioural science, and mathematics.

Eligibility: Open to nationals of UNESCO member states and associate members.

Level of Study: Postgraduate, Doctorate, Postdoctorate, Professional development.

Purpose: To provide opportunities to further primarily higher education or research generally abroad, and to acquire international experience in fields of study for which appropriate facilities are not available in the country of origin.

Type: Fellowship.

Frequency: Dependent on funds available.

Value: Monthly allowance usually based on UN stipend scale, plus travel, tuition, books and small equipment costs.

Length of Study: No more than nine months.

Country of Study: UNESCO member states as well as USA, UK and Singapore.

Applications Procedure: Application through national authorities specially designated by UNESCO member states (usually National Commission for UNESCO or appropriate Ministry). Direct applications will not be considered.

Study Grants

Subjects: As per UNESCO Fellowships.

Eligibility: Open to nationals of Member States of UNESCO who occupy positions of high professional responsibility in their country.

Level of Study: Professional development.

Purpose: To give Member States the opportunity to organize short study journeys, tours or visits abroad for nationals occupying posts of high professional responsibility.

Frequency: Dependent on funds available.

Value: Covers economy travel expenses and daily allowance based on UN subsistence rate.

Length of Study: Maximum of 2 months.

Country of Study: Several countries or in several places within one country, on observation or consultation visits.

Applications Procedure: Applications must be presented by the competent national authorities designated by the governments of UNESCO Member States.

Travel Grants for Leaders in Workers' and Cooperative Education

Subjects: Adult education.

Eligibility: Open to workers' education leaders nominated by workers' organizations in UNESCO Member States with the endorsement of the National Commission for UNESCO of the country concerned.

Level of Study: Professional development.

Purpose: To provide opportunities to acquire knowledge in the organization of adult education programmes and exchange of experience in this field.

Type: Travel Grant.

Frequency: Dependent on funds available.

Value: Travel costs are borne by UNESCO, other costs are to be covered by the sponsoring organization.

Length of Study: As required by the study programme.

Country of Study: UNESCO Member States.

Applications Procedure: Application from sponsoring organizations through National Commissions for UNESCO of the country concerned. Direct applications will not be considered.

UNION OF JEWISH WOMEN OF SOUTH AFRICA

Union of Jewish Women of South Africa, PO Box 87556, Houghton, 2041, South Africa
Contact: The Bursary Officer

The Toni Saphra Bursary and the Fanny and Shlomo Backon Bursary

Subjects: Any subject.

Eligibility: Open to any woman student, irrespective of race or creed, who already holds an undergraduate degree and whose proposed postgraduate course of study will qualify her to render some form of social service in the South African community. Applicants who have not completed a first degree but are in the final year of study may also apply. These applicants will only be considered for the bursary once they have furnished our office with their final year marks. Applicants must be South African citizens.

Type: Bursary.

No. of awards offered: Two.

Frequency: Annual.

Value: Saphra Bursary: R12,000 per annum; Backon Bursary: R6,000 per annum.

Length of Study: One year renewable.

Study Establishment: A university.

Country of Study: South Africa.

Applications Procedure: An application form with an allocated reference number will be sent for completion by the student. Any photocopied application forms will be disqualified. Proof of acceptance by the university for the proposed course must be submitted by the applicant as soon as possible, as well as a copy of receipt of registration for the proposed course and an official student number.

Closing Date: August 31st.

UNITED DAUGHTERS OF THE CONFEDERACY

United Daughters of the Confederacy, 328 North Boulevard, Richmond, VA, 23220-4057, USA
Tel: 804 355 1636
Fax: 804 353 1396
Contact: Chairman of the Awards Committee

Mrs Simon Baruch University Award

Subjects: Southern US history in or near the period of the Confederacy or bearing upon the causes that led to secession and the War Between the States. The life of an individual, a policy or a phase of life may be eligible.

Eligibility: Open to individuals who have graduated with an advanced degree from a US university or college within the previous 15 years, or whose thesis or dissertation has been accepted by such institutions as

part of graduation requirements. Book-length manuscripts should contain at least 75,000 words; monographs 25,000-50,000 words.

Level of Study: Postgraduate.

Purpose: To encourage research in Southern history and to assist scholars in the publication of their theses, dissertations and other writings on the Confederate period.

No. of awards offered: One.

Frequency: Biennially (even-numbered years).

Value: US$2,000 to aid in defraying the costs of publication, US$500 to the author.

Closing Date: May 1st of the award year.

UNITED NATIONS

African Institute for Economic Development and Planning, BP 3186, Dakar, Senegal
Tel: 221 23 10 20
Fax: 221 22 29 64
Contact: The Director

*African Institute for Economic Development and Planning-Fellowships and Grants

Subjects: Economic development and planning.

Eligibility: Open to persons holding a BA degree or its equivalent in economics, who are nationals of African member or associate member countries of the Economic Commission for Africa: Algeria, Benin, Botswana, Burundi, Cameroon, Cape Verde, Central African Republic, Chad, Congo, Arab Republic of Egypt, Ethiopia, Gabon, Gambia, Ghana, Guinea, Ivory Coast, Kenya, Lesotho, Liberia, Libya, Madagascar, Malawi, Mali, Mauritania, Morocco, Namibia, Niger, Nigeria, Rwanda, Senegal, Sierra Leone, Somalia, Sudan, United Republic of Tanzania, Togo, Tunisia, Uganda, Republic of Zaire, Zambia and Zimbabwe. Candidates should, preferably, have had some experience in working with a planning organization and must have the support of their governments or be formally nominated by them.

Purpose: To train participants in techniques of macroeconomic management, economic development and planning.

Value: A stipend of CFA210,600 per month, plus the cost of transportation and books.

Length of Study: Nine to 18 months.

Study Establishment: The Institute, for 9-18 months; for the nine-month programme (on macroeconomic policy analysis, management and planning), for the three-month specialization programmes (on industrial development; agriculture and rural development; population, human resources and development; and energy, environment and development) and for the six-month training programme.

Country of Study: Senegal.

Closing Date: June 30th.

Additional Information: These Fellowships and Grants are funded by various aid agencies such as UNDP, USAID, UNFPA, CFTC, World Bank, etc. No Fellowships or Grants are awarded by IDEP; IDEP depends on external donors for all Fellowships for its programs.

UNITED NATIONS DEPARTMENT FOR DEVELOPMENT SUPPORT AND MANAGEMENT SERVICES

United Nations, Department for Development Support and Management Services, Training and Fellowships Section, One UN Plaza, New York, NY, 10017, USA

*Fellowships and Awards

Subjects: The broad and general fields of energy, minerals, water, cartography, remote sensing, public works, development planning, statistics, development administration, population, rural development, ocean economics and technology, science and technology and social development.

Eligibility: Open primarily to nationals of developing countries upon specific request of the government concerned to the Resident Representative of the United Nations Development Programme in the home country within an approved project.

Purpose: To enable persons who are already or are soon to be entrusted with functions important for the development of their countries, to broaden their professional knowledge and operational experience by acquainting themselves with more advanced methods and techniques.

No. of awards offered: Approximately 4,000 individual awards.

Value: To include a monthly stipend based on the cost of living (fixed by the United Nations), tuition, book allowance and travel costs to the country of study)

Length of Study: Three to 12 months.

Study Establishment: Countries where special facilities exist for higher training or advanced study of a kind which will benefit the country of the Fellow on his/her return home.

Applications Procedure: Applications are made by Governments on behalf of candidates nominated for a specific fellowship within an approved project. A particular training programme may include attendance at an academic institution where a Fellow may take examinations and prepare a thesis or dissertation; however, the main purpose is to enable Fellows to derive from their training an increased ability to solve concrete problems when they return to their home country.

UNITED NATIONS ECONOMIC COMMISSION FOR AFRICA

United Nations Economic Commission for Africa, Box 3001, Addis Ababa, Ethiopia
Tel: 251 1 517200
Fax: 251 1 514416
Contact: Executive Secretary

*ECA Postdoctoral Fellowship in the Economics of African Development

Subjects: Economic development planning: history strategies, techniques and process (sectoral development), agriculture, industry, environment, etc.); macro-economic development: money and banking institutions, and public finance in developing African countries (short-term market fluctuations, structural adjustment with transformation); international trade and finance in Africa.

Eligibility: Open to young African nationals holding a PhD in Economics who have substantive knowledge of one or more relevant subjects, the ability to conduct qualitative and quantitative research involving large data base, and good writing and communication skills. Candidates should be interested in policy-oriented research in current issues related to social and economic development in Africa.

Purpose: To encourage young PhD graduates to conduct research which will stimulate, foster, advance and promote a better understanding, appreciation and resolution of significant, contemporary or emerging African common economic problems as they relate to development and to allow them to acquire professional experiences that will be beneficial to their future careers.

Type: Fellowship.

No. of awards offered: Three.

Frequency: Annual.

Value: US$20,000-US$25,000 per annum, payable monthly.

Length of Study: Up to 10 months from September to June; non-renewable.

Study Establishment: The United Nations Economic Commission for Africa under the supervision of the Social-Economic Research and Planning Division.

Country of Study: One or several African countries.

Applications Procedure: Application letter must be accompanied by a detailed CV, research interest project proposal and two letters of reference.

Closing Date: December 31st.

UNITED NATIONS POPULATION FUND

International Institute for Population Sciences, Govendi Station Road, Deonar, Bombay, 400088, India
Tel: 5562062, 5563254 or 5563255
Fax: 5563257
Contact: Professor K B Pathak, Director

*Diploma Course in Population Studies

Subjects: Population studies.

Eligibility: Open to those who have a bachelor's degree with some experience of handling population data. Generally, two types of students are admitted to this course: United Nations sponsored Fellows, usually from countries of Asia and the Pacific region, and sponsored candidates from various departments of the Government of India, States and other research organizations.

Purpose: To provide a higher level of understanding of the population sciences and to provide in-depth understanding of the links between population and various socio-economic phenomena.

Type: Fellowship.

No. of awards offered: 20.

Frequency: Annual.

Value: A stipend of 10,764 rupees per month, plus a taxi grant of US$20 and a book allowance of US$50 per month.

Length of Study: Two semesters beginning on the second Monday of July until mid-May of the following year.

Country of Study: India.

Closing Date: April.

UNITED NEGRO COLLEGE FUND, INC

United Negro College Fund, Inc, 500 East 62nd Street, New York, NY, 10021, USA
Tel: 1 800 331 2244
Fax: 1 212 326 1143
Contact: Educational Services Department

*UNCF Scholarships

Subjects: Any subject.

Eligibility: Candidates must have an unmet need, a 2.5 GPA and must file an FAF form. Eligibility is not based on race, color or creed.

Purpose: To provide scholarships to students who attend one of the member colleges/universities.

Type: Scholarship.

No. of awards offered: Varies.

Frequency: Varies, depending on availability of funds.

Country of Study: USA.

Applications Procedure: Candidates must apply through the UNCF college/university.

UNITED STATES EDUCATIONAL FOUNDATION IN INDIA

United States Educational Foundation in India, Fulbright House, 12
Hailey Road, New Delhi, 110001, India
Tel: 3328944 48
Contact: Program Officer

Fulbright Junior Postdoctoral Research Fellowship

Subjects: American studies, including international relations, law, literature and art; education (issues relating to the New Education Policy, e.g. distance education and curriculum development at the undergraduate level); development economics; women's studies; information technology/library science; communication/media; anthropology/sociology; and English teaching, e.g. English for Special Purposes (ESP)/English for Science and Technology (EST) and Teaching of English as a Foreign Language.

Eligibility: Open to Indian scholars in colleges, universities and research institutions, who have a PhD degree or equivalent published work in the subject concerned, are permanently employed as a full-time faculty member and eligible for leave, have not been in the USA during the last four years on a teaching or research assignment for a continuous period of three or more months. Candidates must be Indian citizens and be present in India at the time of application; be proficient in English; be in good health; and be under 45 years of age.

No. of awards offered: Varies.

Frequency: Annual.

Value: A monthly stipend of approximately US$2,000, return travel, university affiliation fees, health insurance and a small research or travel allowance where necessary.

Length of Study: Four to six months.

Study Establishment: Universities.

Country of Study: USA.

Closing Date: July 13th.

Additional Information: Subjects vary. Announcements are made in March after Board decision.

Hubert H Humphrey Fellowships

Subjects: Academic study and training for managers and administrators at decision-making levels in the fields of agriculture, planning, resource management, and public health and public administration. Subject to availability of funds, Fellowships may also be offered to working journalists and to medical practitioners (MD/PhD) in the area of drug abuse.

Eligibility: Open to Indian citizens present in India at the time of application and interview. Candidates should be preferably not over 40 years of age; have at least five years of professional experience in the respective field, and be eligible for leave; not have studied in the USA earlier; give an undertaking to return to India on completion of the grant; be in good health; be proficient in English, and be prepared to take the Test of English as a Foreign Language (TOEFL) and other tests that may be required for admission to American universities. Candidates should preferably have first class degrees at both bachelor's and master's level.

Type: Fellowship.

No. of awards offered: Varies.

Frequency: Annual.

Value: To cover tuition and fees, a monthly maintenance allowance, modest allowance for books and supplies, and round-trip international travel to the host institution.

Length of Study: Ten months.

Country of Study: USA.

Applications Procedure: Requests for application forms must state the candidate's academic/professional qualifications, date of birth and present position, and be accompanied by a large sae.

Closing Date: Early June.

Internships in Art History

Subjects: Art history: Asian and Western art.

Eligibility: Open to Indian citizens present in India at the time of the application and interview, who are permanently employed at an educational institution or museum and directly involved in teaching or research in art and art history.

Frequency: Annual.

Value: Stipend.

Study Establishment: Non-degree courses.

Applications Procedure: Requests for application forms must state the candidate's academic/professional qualifications, date of birth and present position, and should be accompanied by a large SAE.

Closing Date: Early July.

Internships in Communication Technology

Subjects: Communication technology.

Eligibility: Open to Indian citizens under 45 years of age, who should: be full-time professionals with at least three years' experience in the field; be employed at the time of application and be eligible for leave from the employer for a period of nine months; have a specific well-defined training program in mind and be prepared to submit a detailed project with the application as to what they wish to accomplish during the internship; be in India at the time of application and interview; not have studied at college level in the USA; be proficient in English; give an undertaking to return to India on completion of the Internship; and be in good health.

Purpose: To provide an opportunity to persons presently employed in television (in software and production) or to faculty engaged in teaching mass communications/journalism courses at recognized institutions to take academic courses and gain practical experience in the modern techniques of production in television.

Type: Internships.

No. of awards offered: Three.

Frequency: Annual.

Value: A monthly stipend, return travel, university affiliation fees and health insurance.

Length of Study: Two semesters.

Study Establishment: An appropriate institution.

Country of Study: USA.

Applications Procedure: Requests for application forms must state the name and full address of the candidate's employer, the candidate's present position and the nature of his/her duties, as well as date of birth and qualifications, and should be accompanied by a large SAE.

Closing Date: Early June.

Internships in Library Science/Library Management

Subjects: Library science.

Eligibility: Open to Indian citizens under 45 years of age, present in India at the time of application, who have a degree or postgraduate diploma in library science. Applicants should be permanently employed as an Assistant Librarian (or equivalent in rank) in an educational/research institution or Public Library which has a holding of at least 20,000 volumes, be eligible for leave with pay, have a good command of the English language and be prepared to take the Test of English as a Foreign Language, be in good health, and not have visited the USA for study purposes.

Purpose: To give recipients the opportunity to observe and learn the use of modern technology in an American library.

Type: Internships.

No. of awards offered: Three.

Frequency: Annual.

Value: Maintenance and round-trip travel.

Length of Study: Six months.

Study Establishment: A library.

Country of Study: USA.

Applications Procedure: Requests for application forms must be accompanied by a list of the candidate's academic/professional qualifications, his/her date of birth and present position, as well as by a large SAE.

Closing Date: Early June.

Additional Information: This is not a degree program but it may be possible for an intern to audit a course in library science. The emphasis of this program is on practical training.

*Postdoctoral Research Scholar Fellowships

Subjects: American studies, environmental studies, economic reforms, social development and change.

Eligibility: Open to Indian citizens permanently employed as full-time faculty members at Indian universities who teach courses on American studies or guide research on the USA. Applicants should: have a PhD degree or equivalent published work in the subject; be permanently engaged as a full-time faculty member, and be eligible for leave; not have been in the USA during the last four years for a teaching or research assignment for a continuous period of three months or more; be in good health; and be under 55 years of age.

Purpose: To enable senior scholars to renew contracts and consult the latest resources.

Type: Fellowship.

No. of awards offered: Limited.

Frequency: Annual.

Value: International and internal travel for self and spouse, and maintenance in the USA a per-diem of US$100 for a period.

Length of Study: Nine months.

Study Establishment: Libraries and centers of excellence.

Country of Study: USA.

Applications Procedure: Requests for application forms must state the area of research, the candidate's date of birth and present position, and be accompanied by a large SAE.

Closing Date: Early July.

Additional Information: Scholars will have to arrange their own USA university affiliation for their visit.

*Postdoctoral Travel-Only Grants

Subjects: Research or teaching assignments; faculty engaged in inter-institutional collaboration, with Indian government approval; candidates in the field of social sciences, humanities, fine arts and performing arts.

Eligibility: Open to Indian scholars present in India at the time of application. Candidates should be proficient in English and be in good health, and should not have been in the USA during the last four years to teach, to do research or on a professional assignment. Research applicants must have a PhD or equivalent published work.

Type: Travel Grant.

No. of awards offered: Limited.

Frequency: Twice yearly.

Value: Return air fare.

Study Establishment: Travel only, for varying periods.

Country of Study: USA.

Applications Procedure: Applicants should have letters of invitation/sponsorship and have secured financial support.

Closing Date: February 1st, August 1st.

*Predoctoral Scholarships at the East-West Center

Subjects: Culture and communication; environment and policy; population studies; resource systems; international relations.

Eligibility: Open to Indian citizens under 35 years of age, who have a postgraduate degree or diploma, are permanently employed and have two years of continuous experience in the field of specialization, are in India at the time of application and interview, are prepared to give an undertaking to return to India on completion of studies in this program, are proficient in English, are in good health, have not made three unsuccessful attempts in the past to secure this Scholarship and are prepared to take the Test of English as a Foreign language (TOEFL) and the Graduate Record Examination (GRE).

Purpose: To enable highly promising predoctoral students to participate in the research and professional development projects of the Center's four problem-oriented Institutions or in Open Grants activities, while studying for advanced degrees in a wide variety of disciplines offered at the University of Hawaii.

Frequency: Annual.

Value: Housing in an East-West dormitory or a housing allowance; a monthly stipend of US$472; a book allowance of US$220 per semester; health and accident insurance; partial tuition costs.

Length of Study: One year.

Study Establishment: The Institutes of the East-West Center, Honolulu, Hawaii.

Country of Study: USA.

Closing Date: June 8th.

Additional Information: The final decision and selection are made by EWC.

*United States Government Predoctoral Scholarships

Subjects: Topics relating to 'Life and Society in the USA'.

Eligibility: Open to Indian citizens, preferably no more than 45 years of age, who have a postgraduate degree; have registered for a PhD degree at an Indian university on a topic related to American studies, at least 12 months prior to the date of application, and should have already done considerable work in the field in India; not have studied in the USA earlier; be proficient in English; give an undertaking to return to India on completion of studies in the program; be in good health; and produce a certificate from the PhD supervisor stating that in his/her opinion the scholar must be given an opportunity to go to the USA.

Purpose: To enable doctoral students to consult the latest resources for their dissertation research.

Type: Scholarship.

No. of awards offered: Varies.

Frequency: Annual.

Value: Full tuition, maintenance and round-trip travel.

Length of Study: Nine months.

Study Establishment: Non-degree programs.

Country of Study: USA.

Applications Procedure: Requests for application forms must state the topic of research proposed, the university where the Scholar is registered for research and the date of registration, as well as the Scholar's date of birth and present position, if any, and should be accompanied by a large SAE.

Closing Date: Early June.

UNITED STATES FOUNDATION
Fondation des États-Unis, 15 boulevard Jourdan, Paris, Cedex 14, 75690, France

Tel: 45 89 35 77
Fax: 45 89 41 50
Contact: The Director

*Harriet Hale Woolley Scholarships

Subjects: Art and music. Grants are for persons doing painting, print-making, sculpture, and for instrumentalists; not for research in art history, musicology or composition, not for students of dance or of theater.

Eligibility: Open to US citizens, 21-29 years of age, who have graduated with high academic standing from an American college, university, or professional school of recognized standing. Preference is given to mature students who have already done graduate study. Applicants should provide evidence of artistic or musical accomplishment. Applicants should have a good working knowlege of French, sufficient to enable the student to benefit at once from study in France; good moral character, personality and adaptability; and good physical health and emotional stability.

Type: Scholarship.

No. of awards offered: Four to five.

Frequency: Annual.

Value: A stipend of US$8,500, payable in French francs.

Length of Study: One academic year.

Study Establishment: Paris.

Country of Study: France.

Closing Date: January 31st.

UNITED STATES INFORMATION AGENCY

600 Maryland Avenue SW, Room 140, Washington, DC, 20024, USA
Tel: 800 726 0479
Fax: 202 401 7203
Email: cbuttram@grad.usda.gov
www: http://www.grad.usda.gov/international/exchange.html
Contact: RGA/Teacher Exchange

Fulbright Teacher Exchange Program

Subjects: Education and teacher training.

Eligibility: Open to administrators and educators of all subjects and levels from elementary through to community college.

Level of Study: Professional development.

Purpose: To promote the mutual understanding between peoples of other countries and the people of the USA through educational exchange.

Type: Grant.

No. of awards offered: Varies.

Frequency: Annual.

Value: Varies.

Length of Study: Varies.

Country of Study: Unrestricted.

Applications Procedure: Application must be submitted prior to October 15th in order to be considered for the following year's program.

Closing Date: October 15th.

Additional Information: Applicants must be fluent in English.

UNITED STATES INSTITUTE OF PEACE

United States Institute of Peace, 1550 M Street, NW, Suite 700, Washington, DC, 20005-1708, USA
Tel: 202 429 3886
Fax: 202 429 6063
Contact: Jennings Randolph Program for International Peace

*Distinguished Fellows

Subjects: Research and other kinds of communication that will improve understanding and skills on the part of policy-makers and the public regarding important problems of international peace and conflict management.

Eligibility: Open to scholars, diplomats, public leaders, and professionals who have achieved exceptional international stature and recognition by virtue of their extraordinary academic or practical contributions to one or more fields. The award allows such individuals the freedom to undertake educational or research activities that draw on their wealth of experience and knowledge. There are no nationality restrictions for the awards and anyone who has specific interest or experience in international peace and conflict management may be nominated.

Type: Fellowship.

No. of awards offered: Two to three.

Frequency: Annual.

Value: A stipend based upon the recipients earned income in the year preceding the Fellowship, up to a maximum of US$86,589 per annum.

Study Establishment: The Institute in Washington, DC.

Country of Study: Unrestricted.

Closing Date: October 15th.

Additional Information: The Program does not support work involving partisan political and policy advocacy or policy-making for any government or private organization.

*Peace Fellows

Subjects: Research and other kinds of communication that will improve understanding and skills on the part of policy-makers and the public regarding important problems of international peace and conflict management.

Eligibility: Open to individuals who demonstrate both substantial accomplishment and promise of exceptional leadership. There are no nationality restrictions for the awards and anyone who has specific interest or experience in international peace and conflict management may apply.

Purpose: To use the recipient's existing knowledge and skills toward a fruitful endeavour in the international peace and conflict management field, and to help bring the perspectives of this field into the Fellow's own career.

Type: Fellowship.

No. of awards offered: Eight to ten.

Frequency: Annual.

Value: A stipend based upon the Fellow's earned income during the year preceding the Fellowships, up to a maximum of US$66,609 per annum.

Study Establishment: The Institute, in Washington, DC.

Country of Study: Unrestricted.

Closing Date: October 15th.

Additional Information: The Program does not support work involving partisan political and policy advocacy or policy-making for any government or private organization.

*Peace Scholars

Subjects: Research and other kinds of communication that will improve understanding and skills on the part of policy-makers and the public regarding important problems of international peace and conflict management.

Eligibility: Open to outstanding students in recognized American university doctoral programs who have demonstrated a clear interest in issues of international peace and conflict management and have completed by the beginning of the Scholarship all required course work for the doctorate except the dissertation. There are no nationality restrictions for the awards.

Purpose: To encourage outstanding doctoral students to undertake dissertation research and writing on vital subjects that concern the sources and nature of violent international conflict and the full range of ways to end or prevent conflict and to sustain peace.

Type: Fellowship.

No. of awards offered: 10-12.

Frequency: Annual.

Value: Stipend of US$14,000 per annum.

Study Establishment: The student's home university.

Country of Study: Unrestricted.

Closing Date: November 15th.

Additional Information: The Program does not support work involving partisan political and policy advocacy or policy-making for any government or private organization.

UNITED STATES PHARMACOPEIAL CONVENTION

United States Pharmacopeial Convention, 12601 Twinbrook Parkway, Rockville, MD, 20852, USA
Tel: 301 881 0666
Fax: 301 816 8299
Contact: Jacqueline L Eng

*Drug Standards and Drug Information Awards

Subjects: Pharmacopeia.

Eligibility: The applicant must be endorsed by a faculty member in the university who currently serves on the USP Committee of Revision or a USP Advisory Panel, although the Committee or Panel member need not be the major professor supervising the Fellow. The applicant shall have completed two years of full-time study in the doctoral program, have a Master of Science degree and be enrolled in a doctoral program, or have a postdoctoral research (non-faculty) appointment. The proposed research to be conducted by the Fellow must be related to the development or improvement of standards for product quality; or the development, dissemination or use of drug information, and the information processes involved in the use of drugs or other articles recognized in the USP-NF, or USP DI. Clinical studies would be considered only if they had such applications. A USP Fellow applying for a second year must submit, along with the new application, a progress report for the first months of research.

Purpose: Drug Standards Awards: to promote advanced graduate or postgraduate research in areas related to compendial standards; thereby encouraging education and training of Fellows in the sciences applicable to the standardization of drugs or other articles recognized in USP-NF and thus providing recognition and encouragement to university faculty members elected to the USP Committee of Revision and its Advisory Panels. Drug Information Awards: to promote advanced graduate or postgraduate research in areas related to drug use information; thereby encouraging education and training of Fellows in the sciences and practices applicable to the uses, information handling, and practitioner/patient use of information about drugs and other articles recognized in USP DI; and thus providing recognition and encouragement to university faculty members elected to the USP Committee of Revision and its Advisory Panels.

Type: Fellowship.

No. of awards offered: Ten.

Frequency: Annual.

Value: US$15,000.

Length of Study: One year; renewable for one further year.

Country of Study: USA.

Closing Date: February 1st.

UNITED STATES TROTTING ASSOCIATION

United States Trotting Association, 750 Michigan Avenue, Columbus, Ohio, 43215, USA
Tel: 614 224 2291
Fax: 614 228 1385
Email: JPawlak@u.s.trotting.com
www: www.ustrotting.com
Contact: John Pawlak

John Hervey and Broadcasters Awards

Subjects: Journalism, radio and television broadcasting.

Eligibility: Must be published or aired in North America.

Level of Study: Unrestricted.

Purpose: To honour the best media stories on harness racing. The categories are newspaper, magazines, radio, and television.

Type: Cash prize.

No. of awards offered: 12.

Frequency: Annual.

Value: US$500 for 1st prize; US$250 for 2nd; and US$100 for 3rd.

Applications Procedure: Please submit entries to the address shown.

Closing Date: January 19th.

UNIVERSAL ESPERANTO ASSOCIATION

Universal Esperanto Association, Nieuwe Binneweg 176, Rotterdam, 3015 BJ, The Netherlands
Tel: 31 10 4361044
Fax: 31 10 4361751
Email: uea@inter.nl.net
Contact: Mr P Zapelli

Universal Esperanto Association Awards

Subjects: Esperanto.

Eligibility: Open to individuals of all nationalities who are between 18 and 29 years of age. A fluent knowledge of Esperanto, both written and spoken, is an essential prior qualification.

Purpose: To train young volunteer workers for the advancement of the language and literature of Esperanto.

Type: Award.

No. of awards offered: One to two.

Frequency: Annual.

Value: A monthly stipend of 600 Dutch Florins, plus other expenses.

Length of Study: Up to one year; not renewable.

Study Establishment: The Head Office of the Association.

Country of Study: The Netherlands.

Closing Date: All year round.

UNIVERSITA' PER STRANIERI DI SIENA

Universita' Per Stranieri Di Siena, Via Pantaneto N.45, Siena, 53100, Italy
Tel: 577 240 111
Fax: 577 283 163

Unstra Grants-P.V.S Grants-Cils Grants

Eligibility: P.V.S Students from developing countries, Cils and Unstra - world students with a general certificate of education.

Level of Study: Postgraduate.

Purpose: For attendance at regular courses.

Type: Grant.

No. of awards offered: 90.

Frequency: Dependent on funds available.

Value: Unstra - cover the course fees, P.V.S and Cils grants - cover fees and lodging.

Length of Study: 2 or 3 months.

Country of Study: Italy.

Applications Procedure: Students should apply to the Italian Cultural Institute in their own countries.

Closing Date: Depends on the institutes.

UNIVERSITÉ DE NANTES

Université de Nantes, 1 quai de Tourville, Nantes, 44035, France
Tel: 33 99 83 32
Fax: 33 40 99 83 00
Contact: Jean-Pierre Boisrond

Bourse du Conseil Scientifique

Eligibility: Open to nationals of any country, who have a sound knowledge of French.

Level of Study: Postdoctorate.

Purpose: To assist young researchers who wish to study at the University of Nantes.

Type: Grant.

No. of awards offered: Three.

Frequency: Annual.

Value: 5,000 francs per month.

Length of Study: Six months.

Study Establishment: Nantes University.

Country of Study: France.

Applications Procedure: Candidates are chosen by the Scientific Council of the University of Nantes on the recommendation of the directors of the laboratories concerned.

UNIVERSITIES FEDERATION FOR ANIMAL WELFARE

Universities Federation for Animal Welfare, 8 Hamilton Close, South Mimms, Potters Bar, Herts, EN6 3QD, England
Tel: 01707 658202
Fax: 01707 649279
Contact: The Secretary

Grants for Animal Welfare Projects

Subjects: Zoology, biology, marine biology, toxicology, environmental management.

Eligibility: Open to nationals of any country.

Level of Study: Unrestricted.

Purpose: To improve the welfare of farm, laboratory, companion, wild or zoo animals by providing full or part funding for small self-contained projects; to initiate projects/research which may lead to further investigation/welfare benfits; to supplement current work; or as a follow up to a project elsewhere.

Type: Grant.

No. of awards offered: Varies.

Frequency: Dependent on funds available.

Value: Varies.

Country of Study: UK and abroad for the duration of approved works.

Applications Procedure: Application form must be completed. Forms are available from the Secretary and must be completed prior to application.

UNIVERSITY FOR FOREIGNERS (ITALY)

Universita' per Stranieri, Palazzo Gallenga, Piazza Fortebraccio 4, Perugia, 06122, Italy
Tel: 0039 75 57461
Fax: 0039 75 574 6213, 0039 573 2014
Contact: Rector

University for Foreigners Scholarships

Subjects: Italian language and culture.

Eligibility: Open to foreign citizens and Italians resident abroad. Preference is given to students of Italian at schools and universities abroad and to teachers of the Italian language.

Type: Scholarship.

No. of awards offered: Varies.

Frequency: Annual.

Value: To cover one month's study and living expenses.

Study Establishment: The University.

Country of Study: Italy.

Applications Procedure: Application for Scholarships must be made through the Italian Institutes of Culture in the country of residence. Direct application to the University for Foreigners may be made only by applicants residing in countries where there are no Italian Institutes of Culture or, independently of this, applicants holding particular qualifications who intend to specialize in linguistic, literary, historical or artistic studies begun in their own countries and applicants who have attended courses at the University for Foreigners for at least three months in the past. Special Scholarships are awarded to the best qualified applicants wishing to attend the Course for Teachers of Italian abroad. Applications must be made before September 30th for the winter course/January; March 31st for the summer course/August. Forms containing details about qualification requirements and application procedures may be requested from the University for Foreigners or the Italian Institutes.

Closing Date: At least four months before the start of the course.

UNIVERSITY INSTITUTE OF EUROPEAN STUDIES

University Institute of European Studies, Via Sacchi, 28 bis, Torino, 10128, Italy
Tel: 011 5625458

Fax: 011 53 02 35
Email: IUSE@ARPNET.IT
www: http://www.ARPNET.IT/~IUSE
Contact: Course Secretariat

Postgraduate Scholarships

Subjects: International trade law.

Eligibility: Open to Italian and foreign graduates in law, business or economics, or undergraduates in their final year.

Level of Study: Postgraduate.

Purpose: To allow students to attend specialization courses.

Type: Scholarship.

No. of awards offered: Varies.

Frequency: Annual.

Value: To cover part of the accommodation expenses.

Length of Study: Three months (one term)

Study Establishment: The ILO Turin Centre.

Country of Study: Italy.

Applications Procedure: Application form should be completed in all its parts; copy of the university degree or certificate (with examinations) is required, and certificate showing knowledge of the English language.

Closing Date: Mid-January.

Additional Information: The course aims to provide the candidates with specialized knowledge in international trade law and contracts drafting. The lecturers are professors from Italy and other countries, senior officials from international bodies and experts from financial and industrial fields. The course, usually held in spring, is in English. The number of participants is limited. Full-time attendance is required throughout the programme.

UNIVERSITY OF ALBERTA

Faculty of Graduate Studies & Research, University of Alberta, 2-8 University Hall, Edmonton, Alberta, T6G 2J9, Canada
Tel: 403 492 3499
Fax: 403 492 0692
Email: susan.buchsdruecker@UAlberta.CA
Contact: Scholarship Coordinator

The Alberta Research Council Karl A Clark Memorial Scholarship

Subjects: Engineering, natural sciences, economics, or business, especially related to energy resources and their utilization; geological soil; water resources; chemical and biological processing; transportation and industrial development; technical and economic evaluations.

Eligibility: Open to students of any nationality who are enrolled in a graduate degree program and engaged in thesis research at the master's or doctoral level.

Level of Study: Postgraduate.

Type: Scholarship.

No. of awards offered: One.

Frequency: Annual.

Value: C$15,000 (master's); C$16,700 (doctoral).

Length of Study: One year; renewable for one further year through open competition.

Applications Procedure: Application forms are available from university departments.

Closing Date: Applicants must be nominated by the department in which they plan to pursue their studies. February 1st for submission of nominations from departments. Check with the department for internal deadline.

Izaak Walton Killam Memorial Postdoctoral Scholarships

Subjects: Any subject.

Eligibility: Open to candidates of any nationality who have recently completed a PhD program or will do so in the immediate future. Applicants who have received their PhD degree from the University of Alberta or who will be on sabbatical leave or who have held (or will have held) postdoctoral fellowships at other institutions for two years are not eligible.

Level of Study: Postdoctorate.

Type: Scholarship.

No. of awards offered: Five.

Frequency: Annual.

Value: C$29,000 per annum. A non-renewable, one-time research grant of C$3,000 accompanies the award, plus incoming and return airfare.

Length of Study: For two years.

Study Establishment: At the University.

Country of Study: Canada.

Closing Date: January 2nd.

For further information contact:
Faculty of Graduate Studies & Research, University of Alberta, 2-8 University Hall, Edmonton, Alberta, T6G 2J9, Canada
Tel: 403 492 3499
Fax: 403 492 0692
Contact: Secretary, Killam Scholarship Committee

Izaak Walton Killam Memorial Scholarships

Subjects: Any subject.

Eligibility: Open to candidates of any nationality who are registered in, or are admissible to, a doctoral program at the University. Scholars must have completed at least one year of graduate work prior to beginning the Scholarship.

Type: Scholarship.

No. of awards offered: Approximately 10.

Frequency: Annual.

Value: C$16,750 per annum, plus a non-renewable, one-time C$1,500 research grant.

Length of Study: For two years (from 1 May or 1 September); subject to review after the first year.

Study Establishment: At the University.

Country of Study: Canada.

Closing Date: Applicants must be nominated by the department in which they plan to pursue their doctoral studies. 1 February for submission of nominations from departments. Check with the department for internal deadline.

For further information contact:
Faculty of Graduate Studies & Research, University of Alberta, 2-8 University Hall, Edmonton, Alberta, T6G 2J9, Canada
Tel: 403 492 3499
Fax: 403 492 0692
Contact: Secretary, Killam Scholarship Committee

Grant Notley Memorial Postdoctoral Fellowship

Subjects: Research in the politics, history, economy or society of Western Canada, or related fields.

Eligibility: Open to persons who have recently completed a PhD program or will do so in the immediate future. Applicants should be active and promising young scholars who will perform significantly in fields associated with Grant Notley's broad interests in the politics, history, economy or society of Western Canada or related fields. Applicants who have received their PhD degree from the University of Alberta or who will be on sabbatical leave or who have held (or will have held) postdoctoral fellowships at other institutions for two years are not eligible.

Level of Study: Postdoctorate.

Type: Fellowship.

No. of awards offered: One.

Frequency: Annual.

Value: C$32,000 per annum, plus a research grant of C$3,000.

Length of Study: Two years.

Study Establishment: At the University.

Closing Date: 2 January.

Province of Alberta Graduate Fellowships

Subjects: Any subject.

Eligibility: Open to Canadian citizens or permanent residents at the date of application who have completed at least one year of graduate study and are registered in a full-time doctoral program.

Type: Fellowships.

No. of awards offered: Approximately 40.

Frequency: Annual.

Value: C$10,500 (May commencement); C$7,000 (September commencement).

Length of Study: For one year (from 1 May or 1 September).

Applications Procedure: Applicants must be nominated by the department in which they plan to pursue their doctoral studies.

Closing Date: February 1st for submission of nominations from departments. Check with the department for internal deadline.

Additional Information: Recipients must carry out a full-time research program during the summer months.

Province of Alberta Graduate Scholarships

Subjects: Any subject.

Eligibility: Open to Canadian citizens or permanent residents at the date of application who are entering or continuing in a full-time master's program. Students registered as qualifying graduate students are not eligible.

Type: Scholarships.

No. of awards offered: Approximately 50.

Frequency: Annual.

Value: C$9,300 (May commencement); C$6,200 (September commencement).

Length of Study: For 12 months (from 1 May) or for 8 months (from 1 September); partial awards may be recommended at a reduced value and the award may be terminated earlier by either the student or the University and the amount reduced proportionately.

Applications Procedure: Application forms are available from university departments.

Closing Date: Applicants must be nominated by the department in which they plan to pursue their studies. 1 February for submission of nominations from departments. Check with the department for internal deadline.

UNIVERSITY OF AUCKLAND

University of Auckland, Private Bag, Auckland, 1000, New Zealand
Tel: 64 9 373 7999
Fax: 64 9 373 7407
Email: appointments@auckland.ac.nz
Contact: M V Lellman, Assistant Registrar

AURC Postdoctoral Fellowships

Subjects: Any academic discipine represented at this University.

Eligibility: Must have completed a PhD not more than four years previously. Open to any suitably qualified applicant who has been the holder of a doctorate from an institution other than the University of Auckland for not more than four years.

Level of Study: Postdoctorate.

Purpose: To foster research.

Type: Fellowship.

No. of awards offered: Three.

Frequency: Annual.

Value: NZ$42,500 per annum, plus allowance for air fare of up to NZ$4,000.

Length of Study: Two years; not renewable.

Study Establishment: The University.

Country of Study: New Zealand.

Applications Procedure: All vacancies are advertised and application details are given in the advertisement.

Closing Date: Around June each year.

Additional Information: Fellowships are assigned to university staff members on a competitive basis. Graduates of the University of Auckland are not eligible for the Fellowships.

Foundation Visiting Fellowships

Subjects: Any offered at the University.

Eligibility: Open to suitably qualified scholars of high academic standing.

Level of Study: Postdoctorate, Professional development.

Purpose: To bring visiting scholars of high standing in their academic field to the University of Auckland.

Type: Fellowship.

No. of awards offered: Up to 15.

Frequency: Annual.

Value: Varies.

Length of Study: For variable periods of up to one year.

Study Establishment: University of Auckland.

Country of Study: New Zealand.

Applications Procedure: Recipients must be nominated by a staff member at the University of Auckland.

Closing Date: June 30th.

Literary Fellowship

Subjects: Creative writing.

Eligibility: Open to writers of proven merit who are New Zealand residents. Not available to staff of the University of Auckland.

Level of Study: Unrestricted.

Purpose: To foster New Zealand writing.

Type: Fellowship.

No. of awards offered: One.

Frequency: Annual.

Value: NZ$40,000.

Length of Study: One year.

Study Establishment: The University.

Country of Study: New Zealand.

Applications Procedure: A 'method of application' is detailed when the vacancy is advertised, there is no specific application form.

Closing Date: As advertised, usually in September/October each year.

Additional Information: Appointee must reside in Auckland for the duration of the award.

UNIVERSITY OF BIRMINGHAM

Office of the Academic Secretary, The University of Birmingham, Edgbaston, Birmingham, B15 2TT, England
Tel: 0121 414 3344
Fax: 0121 414 3907
Telex: 333762 UOBHAM G
Contact: Academic and Student Division

Neville Chamberlain Scholarship

Subjects: Humanities, including social and economic history, with preference given to studies in the political and social history of Great Britain, the British Empire and the Commonwealth, circa 1850.

Eligibility: Open to (preferably) non-UK students with a good honours degree who have been offered (either conditionally or unconditionally) and have accepted admission to study for a higher degree in a humanities subject.

Purpose: To provide financial assistance to students wishing to study for a higher degree in either the Faculty of Arts or the Faculty of Commerce and Social Science.

Type: Scholarship.

No. of awards offered: One.

Frequency: Annually, but subject to availability of funds.

Value: Supplement to student's resources should these be inadequate for taking the degree. An award may be given towards both tuition fees and maintenance but normally should not exceed a figure amounting to 130% of the standard British Academy maintenance rate.

Length of Study: One year; renewable as funds permit.

Study Establishment: The University.

Country of Study: UK.

Closing Date: Applicants should consult Faculties.

Additional Information: Proficiency in English is essential.

Kenward Memorial Fellowship

Subjects: Engineering production.

Eligibility: Open to graduates of British and other Commonwealth universities, or of universities in the Republic of Ireland and the USA.

Level of Study: Doctorate.

Purpose: To provide financial assistance to undertake research in manufacturing and mechanical engineering at the University of Birmingham.

Type: Fellowship.

No. of awards offered: Depends on funds available.

Frequency: As funds permit.

Value: Varies; dependent on funds available.

Length of Study: One year; possibly renewable for a further one or two years.

Study Establishment: The University.

Country of Study: UK.

Applications Procedure: Through recommendation by school and evidence of academic achievement.

Closing Date: Advertised with vacancies.

For further information contact:
The Engineering Division, Office of the Academic Secretary, The University of Birmingham, Edgbaston, Birmingham, B15 2TT, England
Tel: 0121 414 7007
Fax: 0121 414 6378
Contact: Administrative Assistant

UNIVERSITY OF BRITISH COLUMBIA

University of British Columbia, Faculty of Graduate Studies, 180-6371 Crescent Road, Vancouver, British Columbia, V6T 1Z2, Canada
Tel: 604 822 4556
Fax: 604 822 5802
Email: schmiesi@mercury.ubc.ca
Contact: Graduate Awards Officer

Izaak Walton Killam Postdoctoral Fellowships

Subjects: All areas of academic reearch.

Eligibility: Open to candidates who show superior ability in research and have obtained, within two academic years of the anticipated commencement date of the Fellowship, a doctorate at a university other than the University of British Columbia. Graduates of the University of British Columbia are not normally eligible.

Level of Study: Postdoctorate.

Type: Fellowship.

No. of awards offered: 8-12.

Frequency: Annual.

Value: C$31,000.

Length of Study: Two years, subject to satisfactory progress at the end of the first year.

Study Establishment: The University.

Country of Study: Canada.

Applications Procedure: Application form, academic transcripts and three reference letters must be submitted to the appropriate department.

Closing Date: November 15th.

Additional Information: Candidates are responsible for contacting the appropriate department at the University to ensure their proposed research project is acceptable and may be undertaken under the supervision of a member of the department. Travel/research grant of C$2,000 is available during the tenure of the fellowship.

For further information contact:
Faculty of Graduate Studies, University of British Columbia, 180-6371 Crescent Road, Vancouver, British Columbia, V6T 1Z2, Canada
Tel: 604 822 2933
Fax: 604 822 5802
Email: KILLAM@MERCURY.UBC.ca
Contact: The Secretary of the Killam Program

Killam Predoctoral Fellowship

Subjects: All disciplines offered by UBC at the graduate level.

Eligibility: Open to students of any nationality, discipline, age or sex. This award is given at the PhD level only and is strictly based on academic merit. Students must have a first class standing in their last two years of study.

Level of Study: Doctorate.

Purpose: To assist doctoral students to devote their full time to their studies and research.

Type: Fellowship.

No. of awards offered: Approximately 20.

Frequency: Annual.

Value: C$18,200 per annum.

Study Establishment: University of British Columbia.

Country of Study: Canada.

Applications Procedure: Top-ranked students are selected from the University Graduate Fellowship competition. Application forms can be obtained from departments or the Faculty of Graduate Studies.

Closing Date: January 26th.

Additional Information: Students must submit their applications to the departments, not to Graduates Studies; please check for internal departmental deadlines.

University Graduate Fellowship

Subjects: All disciplines offered by UBC at the graduate level.

Eligibility: Open to students of any nationality, discipline, age or sex. This award is strictly based on academic merit. Students must have a first class standing in their last two years of study.

Level of Study: Graduate.

Purpose: To assist graduate students to devote their full time to their studies and research.

Type: Fellowship.

No. of awards offered: Approximately 400.

Frequency: Annual.

Value: C$13,500 per annum for full UGFs; C$4,500 for partial UGFs.

Study Establishment: The University of British Columbia.

Country of Study: Canada.

Applications Procedure: Applicants are nominated by their departments based on academic merit. Students must submit their applications to the departments, not to Graduate Studies.

Closing Date: January 26th.

Additional Information: Please check for internal departmental deadlines.

For further information contact:
Faculty of Graduate Studies, University of British Columbia, 180-6371 Crescent Road, Vancouver, British Columbia, V6T 1Z2, Canada
Tel: 604 822 4556
Fax: 604 822 5802
Contact: Graduate Awards Officer

THE UNIVERSITY OF CALGARY

The University of Calgary, Earth Sciences Building, Room 720, 2500 University Drive NW, Calgary, Alberta, T2N 1N4, Canada
Tel: 403 220 5690
Fax: 403 207 7635
Email: 220110@ucdasvm1.admin.ucalgary.ca
Contact: Connie Busch, Graduate Scholarship Assistant

Alberta Art Foundation Graduate Scholarships in The Department of Art

Subjects: Major fields of study in the Department of Art.

Eligibility: Open to students entering the second year of the MFA program in the specializations of painting, printmaking, sculpture, drawing and photography.

Level of Study: Postgraduate.

Type: Scholarship.

No. of awards offered: Three.

Frequency: Annual.

Value: C$6,000.

Study Establishment: University of Calgary.

Country of Study: Canada.

Applications Procedure: Apply through nomination by the Department of Art.

Izaak Walton Killam Memorial Scholarships

Subjects: Unrestricted.

Eligibility: Open to qualified graduates of any university who are admissable to a dcotoral program at the University of Calgary. Applicants

must have completed at least one year of graduate study prior to taking up the award.

Level of Study: Postgraduate, Doctorate.

Type: Scholarship.

No. of awards offered: Four to five.

Frequency: Annual.

Value: C$16,000. If approved, award holders may also receive up to C$2,100 over the full term of appointment for special equipment and/or travel in direct connection with the PhD research.

Length of Study: One year.

Study Establishment: University of Calgary.

Country of Study: Canada.

Applications Procedure: Apply for application from The Graduate Scholarship Secretary at the university.

Additional Information: One year duration renewable once upon presentation of evidence of satisfactory progress. Further renewal in open competition.

UNIVERSITY OF CAMBRIDGE

University Registry, The Old Schools, Cambridge, CB2 1TN, England
Contact: The Registrar

Barrow and Geraldine S Cadbury Trust-Institute of Criminology Cropwood Programme

Subjects: Criminology and related fields.

Eligibility: There are no formal qualifications other than that candidates should be experienced practitioners in their field.

Purpose: To enable practitioners in the British criminal justice system to undertake research or study under the guidance of experienced academic researchers.

Type: Fellowship.

No. of awards offered: 3-4.

Frequency: Annual.

Value: £200 per week lodging allowance.

Length of Study: For one year with up to a maximum of 12 weeks in Cambridge; not renewable.

Study Establishment: The Institute of Criminology, Cambridge University.

Country of Study: UK.

Closing Date: September 30th.

For further information contact:
Institute of Criminology, University of Cambridge, 7 West Road, Cambridge, CB3 9DT, England
Tel: 01223 335364
Fax: 01223 335356
Contact: Mrs Helen Ruddy

Broodbank Fellowship

Subjects: Biochemistry or biophysics, with special reference to the principles and practice of food preservation. These terms will be interpreted broadly to include fundamental research including molecular processes.

Eligibility: Open to graduates of any university, but preference will be given to postdoctoral applicants.

Level of Study: Postdoctorate.

Purpose: To further research.

Type: Fellowship.

No. of awards offered: 1-2.

Frequency: When available.

Value: Determined according to a Fellow's experience and qualifications, from £12,690-£16,827 (under review) plus possible grants to cover expenses incurred by the Fellow in his or her work.

Length of Study: For not more than three years as determined by the managers.

Study Establishment: The University.

Country of Study: UK.

Closing Date: April 31st.

For further information contact:
The Broodbank Fund, The Physiological Laboratory, Downing Street, Cambridge, CB2 3EG, England
Contact: Secretary of the Managers

Churchill College Research Studentships

Subjects: Any subject for which research supervision can be provided at the University.

Eligibility: Open to any person who has graduated from a university or, if not a graduate, can show evidence of exceptional qualifications for research.

Level of Study: Doctorate.

Purpose: To assist research for candidates who intend to register for the degree of PhD of the University of Cambridge.

No. of awards offered: Varies according to funds available.

Frequency: Annual.

Value: University and College fees, plus maintenance (based on recommended rates).

Length of Study: Three years.

Study Establishment: Churchill College.

Country of Study: UK.

Applications Procedure: Application forms available from the given address.

Closing Date: February 15th.

For further information contact:
Churchill College, Cambridge, CB3 0DS, England
Tel: 01223 336157
Fax: 01223 336177
Contact: Tutor for Advanced Students

Clare Hall Foundation Fellowship

Subjects: Any subject.

Eligibility: Open to persons who already hold academic posts in their own country; have not previously studied in the UK or North America, and are able to demonstrate that a period of study in Cambridge would be of special benefit. There is no restriction as to sex or age, although preference may be given to applicants under the age of 40.

Level of Study: Postdoctorate.

Purpose: To help a rising scholar from either a developing country or a centrally planned economy.

Type: Fellowship.

No. of awards offered: One.

Frequency: Annual.

Value: Normally sufficient for three months residence in Cambridge.

Length of Study: Three months; although by supplementing other funds the Fellowship would possibly permit a longer stay of up to six months.

Study Establishment: Normally Clare Hall, but probably attached to one of the University departments.

Country of Study: UK.

Applications Procedure: Applications, accompanied by a curriculum vitae, should be sent to the Chairman of the Fellowship Committee at the College, to whom three referees should write direct. One reference should be from a referee whose work is recognized in the UK.

Additional Information: The Fellowship is awarded on the grounds of academic suitability.

For further information contact:
Clare Hall, Herschel Road, Cambridge, CB3 9AL, England
Tel: 01223 332360
Fax: 01223 332333
Contact: College Secretary

Corpus Christi College Research Scholarships

Subjects: Any subject.

Eligibility: Open to holders of a first class honours degree or equivalent. Candidates eligible for UK state awards are not eligible.

Purpose: To enable the successful candidate to pursue, as a member of the College, a course of study in any subject leading to a research-based higher degree, normally the PhD.

Type: Scholarship.

No. of awards offered: One or more.

Frequency: Annual.

Value: Awards are made usually in collaboration with the Cambridge Commonwealth and Overseas Trusts. The amount of the awards varies but substantial contributions (£6,000) towards fees or maintenance costs are made.

Study Establishment: Corpus Christi College.

Country of Study: UK.

Applications Procedure: All applications to the Board of Graduate Studies which name Corpus Christi College as their first preference on CIGAS form A will be considered for these Scholarships, provided they reach the College by the closing date. Separate application to the College is not required.

Closing Date: End of March.

For further information contact:
Corpus Christi College, Cambridge, CB2 1RH, England
Tel: 01223 339391
Fax: 01223 338057
Contact: The Tutor for Advanced Students

E D Davies Scholarship

Subjects: All subjects.

Eligibility: Open to graduates of any university who have been admitted to a course of research.

Level of Study: Doctorate.

Purpose: To enable graduates to undertake a course of research in any subject area.

Type: Scholarship.

No. of awards offered: One.

Frequency: Annual.

Value: £1,250 per annum. The award is designed to supplement funding from other sources.

Length of Study: Three years.

Study Establishment: Fitzwilliam College.

Country of Study: England.

Applications Procedure: Application forms are available on request.

Closing Date: June 14th.

For further information contact:
Fitzwilliam College, Cambridge, CB3 0DG, England
Tel: 01223 332 035
Fax: 01223 332 082
Contact: Tutor for Graduate Students

Downing College Research Fellowships

Subjects: As advertised, but generally arts and science subjects in alternate years.

Eligibility: Open to graduates who have completed or are on the point of completing a PhD. Must be under 30 on taking up award, or if over 30, must not have completed more than 12 terms research as a registered research student.

Level of Study: Postdoctorate.

Purpose: To enable promising young scholars to undertake research, undistracted by other duties, to consolidate their reputations.

Type: Fellowship.

No. of awards offered: One.

Frequency: Annually (at present).

Value: Resident pre-PhD £10,413, resident post-PhD £11,080; living out allowance £2,217.

Length of Study: Three years.

Study Establishment: Normally based in Cambridge.

Country of Study: UK.

Applications Procedure: Application forms are available follwing advertisements.

Closing Date: As advertised.

Additional Information: Application form indicates that candidates must get referees to write to the college.

For further information contact:
Downing College, Cambridge, CB2 1DQ, England
Tel: 01223 334811
Fax: 01223 467934
Contact: Senior Tutor

Evans Fund

Subjects: All aspects of anthropology and archaeology of Southeast Asia, especially in relation to Borneo, the Malay Peninsula, Singapore, and Thailand.

Eligibility: Open to graduates of any university who intend to engage in research in the above areas.

Type: Fellowship.

No. of awards offered: One or more.

Frequency: Annual.

Value: Up to £6,000 per annum.

Length of Study: One year in the first instance; up to a maximum of three years.

Study Establishment: For research and travel.

Country of Study: UK/International.

Closing Date: Usually mid-March.

Additional Information: It is intended that the successful candidate will either be based in Cambridge, or will spend a substantial period of time in Cambridge during or after the period of research.

For further information contact:
Department of Social Anthropology, University of Cambridge, Free School Lane, Cambridge, CB2 3RF, England
Tel: 01223 334592
Fax: 01223 334748
Contact: The Secretary, Evans Fund Advisory Committee

Fitzwilliam College J R W Alexander Studentship in Law

Subjects: Law (LLM degree).

Eligibility: Open to graduates of any university who will have graduated by the time they come into residence.

Level of Study: Postgraduate.

Type: Studentship.

No. of awards offered: One.

Frequency: Annual.

Value: £1,000 per annum. The award is designed to supplement funding from other sources.

Length of Study: One year.

Study Establishment: At the College.

Country of Study: UK.

Applications Procedure: The awards are only available to candidates who have applied for admission to the University through the Board of Graduate Studies (4 Mill Lane, Cambridge CB2 1RZ, England) and subsequently satisfied the conditions of admission made by the Board. Candidates should also place Fitzwilliam College as their first preference in their application.

Closing Date: June 14th.

Additional Information: Application forms are available on request.

For further information contact:
Fitzwilliam College, Cambridge, CB3 0DG, England
Tel: 01223 332 035
Fax: 01223 322 082
Contact: Tutor for Graduate Students

Fitzwilliam College Leathersellers' Graduate Scholarship

Subjects: Physical or biological sciences, mathematics or engineering.

Eligibility: Open to home graduates from any British university who have been admitted to a course of research in one of the appropriate faculties.

Type: Scholarship.

No. of awards offered: One.

Frequency: Annual.

Value: £2,000 per annum. The award is designed to supplement funding from other sources.

Length of Study: Three years.

Study Establishment: At the College.

Country of Study: UK.

Applications Procedure: Application forms are available on request.

Closing Date: June 14th.

For further information contact:
Fitzwilliam College, Cambridge, CB3 0DG, England
Tel: 01223 332 035
Fax: 01223 332 082
Contact: Tutor for Graduate Students

Fitzwilliam College Research Fellowship

Subjects: To be advised in further particulars.

Eligibility: Open to candidates who are carrying out research for the PhD at any British or Irish university, or who have recently completed their course of study for this degree. Candidates should not have completed four years of full-time research by the April preceding the commencement of the Fellowship.

Level of Study: Doctorate.

Purpose: To enable scholars to carry out a programme of new research.

Type: Fellowship.

No. of awards offered: Varies.

Frequency: Annual.

Value: £8,515- £10,841 (1995 figures, rising annually by general increase in stipend) with an additional allowance of £1,500 for any Research Fellow not resident in College. Non-stipendiary also offered.

Study Establishment: Fitzwilliam College.

Country of Study: UK.

Closing Date: Early September.

Additional Information: Fellowships are awarded for new research only, not to enable candidates to complete their PhD dissertation.

For further information contact:
Fitzwilliam College, Cambridge, CB3 0DG, England
Tel: 01223 332029
Fax: 01223 332074
Contact: Master's Secretary

Fitzwilliam College Shipley Studentship

Subjects: Theology.

Eligibility: Open to graduates of any university who have been admitted to a course of research in the Faculty of Divinity (or exceptionally a course of research on a theological topic in some other Faculty). The awards are only available to candidates who have applied for admission to the University through the Board of Graduate Studies (4 Mill Lane, Cambridge CB2 1RZ, England) and subsequently satisfied the conditions of admission made by the Board. Candidates should also place Fitzwilliam College as their first preference in their application.

Type: Studentship.

No. of awards offered: One.

Frequency: Annual.

Value: £1,250 per annum. The award is designed to supplement other funds.

Length of Study: One year.

Study Establishment: At the College.

Country of Study: UK.

Applications Procedure: Application forms are available on request.

Closing Date: June 14th.

For further information contact:
Fitzwilliam College, Cambridge, CB3 0DG, England
Contact: Tutor for Graduate Students

Oliver Gatty Studentship

Subjects: Physical and colloid science.

Eligibility: Open to graduates of all universities, preference being given to graduates of universities outside the UK. Both graduate and postdoctoral students may apply.

Purpose: To assist full-time study and training for research.

Type: Studentship.

No. of awards offered: One.

Frequency: When available.

Value: In line with the remuneration of a research assistant, currently £13,941 at age 25.

Length of Study: For one year; renewable for up to two additional years.

Study Establishment: The University.

Country of Study: UK.

Closing Date: April 30th.

Girton College Research Fellowships

Subjects: Any subject.

Eligibility: Open to qualified graduates of any university who are able to provide evidence of their research abilities.

Level of Study: Postdoctorate.

Purpose: To provide the opportunity for graduate students to conduct research in their chosen field of study.

Type: Fellowship.

No. of awards offered: Two to four.

Frequency: Annual.

Value: £9,245 per annum for predoctoral Fellows; £11,605-£12,220 per annum for postdoctoral Fellows, over three years. The stipend is reviewed annually.

Length of Study: Up to three years.

Study Establishment: Girton College.

Country of Study: UK.

Applications Procedure: Candidates must submit a completed application form.

Closing Date: Differs each year, but generally in early October.

For further information contact:
Girton College, Cambridge, CB3 0JG, England
Tel: 01223 338999
Fax: 01223 338896
Email: chk1@esc.cam.ac.uk
www: http://www.cl.cam.ac.uk/users/ckh/infidel/Fellowship_comp/Cover.html
Contact: Secretary to the Research Fellowship Electors

Gonville and Caius College Gonville Bursary

Subjects: Any offered by the University.

Eligibility: Open to candidates who have been accepted by the College through its normal admissions procedures, and who are classified as overseas students for fees purposes. A statement of financial circumstances is required.

Level of Study: Postgraduate, Doctorate, Undergraduate.

Purpose: To help outstanding students from outside the EC to meet the costs of degree courses at the University of Cambridge.

Type: Bursary.

No. of awards offered: Up to 6.

Frequency: Annual.

Value: Reimbursement of College fees: £2,646 for undergraduates, £1,596 for graduates (in 1995/96).

Length of Study: Up to three years, (renewable dependent on satisfactory progress).

Study Establishment: Gonville amd Caius College.

Country of Study: UK.

Applications Procedure: There are no application forms.

Closing Date: The same as for the University's courses.

For further information contact:
Gonville and Caius College, Cambridge, CB2 1TA, England
Tel: 01223 332447
Fax: 01223 332456
Email: ADMISSIONS@CAI.CAM.AC.UK
www: http://www.cai.cam.ac.uk
Contact: Dr M D Bailey, Tutor for Admissions

Gonville and Caius College Tapp Studentship in Law

Subjects: Law.

Eligibility: Open to candidates who are not already members of the College, but who propose to register as graduate students in the University of Cambridge. Candidates must be under 30 years of age as of 1 October of the Studentship year, and be graduates or expect to graduate no later than August of the same year. First consideration will be shown to applicants nominating Gonville and Caius College as their first preference when applying under the Cambridge Intercollegiate Graduate Application Scheme.

Level of Study: Postgraduate, Doctorate.

Type: Studentship.

No. of awards offered: Approximately six per annum.

Frequency: Annual.

Value: A stipend similar to that of a State Studentship for research (£5,050 in 1995-96), plus fees and certain allowances, dependant allowance, allowance for period of approved postgraduate experience, travelling contribution for foreign students, and a research allowance for research students.

Length of Study: One year; renewable for up to a maximum of three years.

Study Establishment: Gonville and Caius College.

Country of Study: UK.

Applications Procedure: Application forms are available from the admissions tutor.

Closing Date: January 15th.

Additional Information: Applications may be made at any time.

For further information contact:
Gonville and Caius College, Cambridge, CB2 1TA, England
Tel: 01223 332447
Fax: 01223 332456
Email: ADMISSIONS@CAI.CAM.AC.UK
www: http://www.cai.cam.ac.uk
Contact: The Admissions Tutor

Magdalene College Leslie Wilson Research Scholarships

Subjects: Any subject offered by the University.

Eligibility: Open to graduates from the UK and overseas who will be studying in Cambridge for a PhD degree. Consideration is normally restricted to those who have obtained, or who have a strong prospect of obtaining, a 1st class honours (bachelor's) degree. Preference is given to those nominating Magdalene as their first choice college.

Level of Study: Doctorate.

Purpose: To assist study leading to the degree of Doctor of Philosophy.

Type: Scholarship.

No. of awards offered: One.

Frequency: Annual.

Value: A maximum of £9,160 (1995-96 values) for a scholar who has no other sources of finance (maintenance grant £5,060, university fees £2,430, and college fees £1,670). Rented accommodation in or near Magdalene College will be made available during the first year of residence for unmarried scholars. Married scholars will be offered rented accommodation near to the College.

Length of Study: Up to three years.

Study Establishment: Magdalene College and the University of Cambridge.

Country of Study: UK.

Applications Procedure: Leslie Wilson Scholarship applicants should obtain a CIGAS form from the Board of Graduate Studies, 4 Mill Lane, Cambridge. UK candidates are expected to apply, if eligible, for State or Research Council Studentships. Overseas candidates are expected to apply for UK government support as well as Overseas Student Bursaries awarded by the University of Cambridge and administered by the Board of Graduate Studies. In addition, all candidates should obtain a Leslie Wilson Research Scholarship form from the address below.

Closing Date: March 31st.

For further information contact:
Magdalene College, University of Cambridge, Cambridge, CB3 0AG, England
Tel: 01223 332 135
Fax: 01223 462 589
Contact: Admissions Tutor for Graduates

Isaac Newton Studentship

Subjects: Astronomy (especially gravitational astronomy, but also including other branches of astronomy and astronomical physics) and those branches of physical optics which, in the opinion of the Electors, have a direct bearing on astronomy or astronomical techniques.

Eligibility: Open to graduates of any university who should normally be under 26 years of age on January 1st prior to the beginning of tenure.

Purpose: To further advanced study and research.

Type: Studentship.

No. of awards offered: Two.

Frequency: Annual.

Value: Currently £4,910. Married students will receive marriage allowance under EPSRC conditions. The Electors may also award grants for fees, books or other expenses incurred by the student in the course of study or research.

Length of Study: Two years.

Study Establishment: The University.

Country of Study: UK.

Closing Date: February 12th.

Pembroke College Graduate Awards

Subjects: Any subject offered by the University.

Eligibility: Open to candidates of any nationality who are accepted by Pembroke College, and who intend to register for a PhD degree at the University of Cambridge.

Type: Studentship.

No. of awards offered: One.

Frequency: Annual.

Value: Full support.

Length of Study: Three years.

Study Establishment: Pembroke College.

Country of Study: UK.

Closing Date: April 1st.

Additional Information: There are also a number of scholarships (fees only) and bursaries available.

For further information contact:
Pembroke College, Cambridge, CB2 1RZ, England
Tel: 01223 338100
Fax: 01223 338163
Contact: Graduate Admissions Tutor

Queens' College Research Fellowships

Subjects: Subjects announced each year.

Eligibility: Open to graduates of any university who should normally be under 30 years of age and who are well advanced in their doctoral research or who have recently begun postdoctoral research.

Level of Study: Postdoctorate.

Purpose: To provide the opportunity for postdoctoral research in various fields of study.

Type: Fellowship.

No. of awards offered: Two.

Frequency: Annual.

Value: Approximately £10,000.

Length of Study: Three years.

Study Establishment: Queen's College.

Country of Study: UK.

Applications Procedure: Application form must be completed and research proposal submitted.

Closing Date: Usually October 8th.

For further information contact:
Queens' College, Cambridge, CB3 9ET, England
Tel: 01223 335601
Fax: 01223 335522
Contact: Clerk to the Tutors

St John's College Benefactors' Scholarships for Research

Subjects: Any subject offered by the University.

Eligibility: Open to candidates of any nationality with a first class honours or equivalent degree.

Level of Study: Postgraduate.

Purpose: To fund candidates for the PhD and MPhil degrees.

Type: Scholarship.

No. of awards offered: Six.

Frequency: Annual.

Value: £5,050; plus approved College & University fees, book allowance of £300 and other expenses.

Length of Study: Up to three years.

Study Establishment: At the college.

Country of Study: UK.

Closing Date: May 1st.

Additional Information: For further particulars see Cambridge University Graduate Studies Prospectus.

For further information contact:
St John's College, Cambridge, CB2 1TP, England
Tel: 01223 338600
Fax: 01223 337720
Contact: Tutor for Graduate Affairs

*St John's College Harper-Wood Studentship

Subjects: Creative writing within the field of English poetry and literature.

Eligibility: Open to graduates of any university of Great Britain, Ireland, the Commonwealth, or the USA who are not over 30 years of age.

No. of awards offered: One.

Frequency: Annual.

Value: £4,450, depending on status.

Length of Study: One year; not renewable.

Country of Study: UK and/or overseas.

Applications Procedure: Applications should include: the candidate's curriculum vitae; a plan of the proposed study or research and of the proposed travel; and the names and addresses of not more than two referees. Short-listed candidates may be invited to submit examples of their work, up to a limit of 5,000 words. Details of any other research plans or applications which might relate to the tenure of the Harper-Wood Studentship should also be supplied.

Closing Date: End of May.

For further information contact:
St John's College, Cambridge, CB2 1TP, England
Tel: 01223 338635
Fax: 01223 338707
Contact: The Master

*St John's College Meres Senior Studentship

Subjects: Medical research.

Eligibility: Open to candidates holding a PhD degree or having other substantial research experience.

No. of awards offered: One.

Frequency: Occasionally.

Value: Up to £23,739, depending on status.

Length of Study: 1-3 years.

Study Establishment: University of Cambridge or in some place in the neighbourhood of Cambridge approved by the Council.

Country of Study: UK.

Applications Procedure: Applications should include: the applicant's full name and the date and place of birth; degrees or other academic qualifications, with dates, other awards and distinctions, professional qualifications, if any, the nature of any research previously undertaken, published work, and any appointments held; the nature of the research to be pursued, if elected; if possible the laboratory or institution in which the research will be carried out; the approximate date on which the Studentship will be taken up, and any circumstances the Council should take into consideration in determining the period of tenure; the names and addresses of not more than three persons to whom the Council may refer.

Closing Date: End of March.

For further information contact:
St John's College, Cambridge, CB2 1TP, England
Tel: 01223 338635
Contact: The Master

Westminster College Lewis and Gibson Scholarship

Subjects: Theology.

Eligibility: Open to graduates of a recognized university who are members of the United Reformed Church in the UK or of any church which is a member of the World Alliance of Reformed Churches and has a Presbyterian form of government. Applicants must have been recognized by their churches as candidates for the Ministry of Word and Sacrament, but should not yet have been ordained.

Purpose: To enable the Scholar to study for a theology degree of the University of Cambridge as an integral part of his or her training for the ministry of a church in the Reformed tradition which has a Presbyterian order.

Type: Scholarship.

No. of awards offered: One or two.

Frequency: Annually, except when the current holder(s) is/are likely to have the award renewed for the following year.

Value: One Scholarship of £6,000 or two Scholarships of £3,000 (approximately).

Length of Study: One year; renewable for up to two further years.

Study Establishment: University of Cambridge.

Country of Study: UK.

Applications Procedure: If it is the intention to study at the postgraduate level, an application should be made at the same time to the Board of Graduate Studies of the University. The Scholar will study for one of the following degrees: BA or MPhil in theology; MLitt; or PhD. He or she will be a member of both Westminster College and one of the University's constituent colleges.

Closing Date: December 31st.

Additional Information: Scholars from outside the United Reformed Church have usually been theology graduates and have used the scholarship for postgraduate work.

For further information contact:
Lewis and Gibson Scholarships, Westminster College, Cambridge, CB3 0AA, England
Tel: 01223 353997
Fax: 01223 300765
Contact: The Secretary to the Electors

UNIVERSITY OF CANTERBURY

University of Canterbury, Private Bag 4800, Christchurch, New Zealand
Tel: 03 364 2808
Fax: 03 364 2325
Email: staffing.acad.appts@regy.canterbury.ac.nz
Contact: Assistant Registrar (Staffing)

University of Canterbury and the Arts Council of New Zealand Toi Aoteoroa Writer in Residence

Subjects: Creative writing: fiction, drama and poetry.

Eligibility: Open to authors of proven merit who are normally resident in New Zealand and to New Zealand nationals temporarily resident overseas.

Level of Study: Unrestricted.

Purpose: To foster New Zealand writing by providing a full-time opportunity for a writer to work in an academic environment.

Type: Fellowship.

No. of awards offered: One.

Frequency: Annually, depending on the continued availability of funding.

Value: Emolument at the rate of NZ$36,000 per annum.

Length of Study: Up to one year.

Study Establishment: At the university.

Country of Study: New Zealand.

Applications Procedure: Send details of published writings and work in progress, and proposal of work during appointment. Conditions of appointment are available from the university in July.

Closing Date: Usually 31 October.

Additional Information: The appointment will be made on the basis of published or performed writing of high quality. Conditions of appointment should be obtained from the Registrar before applying.

UNIVERSITY OF COLORADO AT BOULDER

Graduate School/ CU - Boulder, Regent Administrative Center RM 308, Campus Box 26, Boulder, CO, 80309-0026, USA
Tel: 303 492 7401
Fax: 303 492 5777
Email: Barabara.Kraus@Colorado.EDU
www: http://www.colorado.edu/
Contact: Barbara Kraus

Kenneth Boulding Postdoctoral Research Fellowship

Eligibility: This position requires a PhD.

Level of Study: Postdoctorate.

Purpose: The Program on Political and Economic change is accepting applications for a postdoctoral fellowship to work with an interdisciplinary group on the topic of Globalization and Democratization (GAD Program).

Type: Fellowship.

Frequency: Annual.

Value: US$31,000.

Length of Study: Ten months (renewable).

Study Establishment: University of Colorado at Boulder.

Country of Study: USA.

Applications Procedure: Candidates are requested to send a covering letter with their applications including, curriculum vitae, three letters of reference, a writing sample, and an E-Mail address for acknowledgement.

Closing Date: April 15th.

Additional Information: Some teaching will be required.

For further information contact:
University of Colorado at Boulder, Department of Geography and Institute of Behavioral Science, Campus Box 487, Boulder, Colorado, 80309-0487, USA
Tel: 303 492 1619

Fax: 303 492 3609
Email: postdoc@isere.colorado.edu
www: http://adder.colorado.edu/~gad.html
Contact: John O'Loughlin

Chancellors Postdoctoral Fellowship Program for Academic Diversity

Eligibility: Applicants must have received a doctorate within two years of the start of the appointment on or after August 1, 1997. Applicants must be US citizens or permanent residents who are members of underrepresented groups in higher education, especially racial and ethnic minorites (American Indian, African American, Asian American, Hispanic, Native Alaskan or Native Pacific Islander), or women in engineering, computer science, mathematics, or physical science fields.

Level of Study: Postdoctorate.

Purpose: The Chancellors Postdoctoral Fellowship Program offers postdoctorate research fellowships to members of groups underrepresented as US faculty members who show promise for tenure-track appointments at CU-Boulder.

Type: Fellowship.

No. of awards offered: Two.

Frequency: Annual.

Value: US$31,000 plus benefits per year.

Length of Study: 1-2 years.

Study Establishment: CU-Boulder.

Country of Study: USA.

Applications Procedure: Applicants should submit two copies of the following: cover letter describing proposed research, career plans, qualifications, and diversity information; curriculum vitae; certified graduate transcript; detailed statement of proposed research (maximum: five pages); sample publications and dissertation chapters. In addition, applicants should arrange to have three letters of recommendation sent; one letter must be from the dissertation advisor. A mentor need not be selected prior to applying.

Additional Information: Fellows will be selected on the basis of their proposed research and their scholarly promise and achievemnents. Applicants are encouraged to disscuss the proposed plan of study or research with the academic unit of interest.

UNIVERSITY OF DELAWARE

Department of History, University of Delaware, Newark, DE, 19716, USA
Tel: 302 831 8226
Fax: 302 831 1358
Email: PATRICIA.ORENDORF@MVS.UDEL.EDU
Contact: Coordinator

Fellowships in the University of Delaware - Hagley Program

Subjects: The history of industrialization, broadly defined to include business, economic, labor, and social history and the history of science and technology.

Eligibility: Open to graduate students of any nationality seeking degrees in American or European history or the history of science and technology.

Level of Study: Doctorate, Masters.

Purpose: To provide a program of graduate study leading to the MA or PhD degree for students who seek careers in college teaching and public history.

Type: Fellowship.

No. of awards offered: Approximately two to three.

Frequency: Annual.

Value: US$9,500 per annum for masters candidates; US$10,700 per annum for doctoral candidates. All tuition fees for university courses are paid.

Length of Study: One year; renewable once for those seeking a terminal MA, and up to three times for those seeking the doctorate.

Study Establishment: University of Delaware, Newark.

Country of Study: USA.

Applications Procedure: Fellows are selected upon GRE scores, recommendations, undergraduate grade index, work experience, and personal interviews.

Closing Date: January 30th.

Additional Information: This is an in-residence program.

E. Lyman Stewart Fellowship

Subjects: History.

Eligibility: Open to nationals of any country.

Level of Study: Doctorate, Masters.

Purpose: To provide a program of graduate study leading to a MA or PhD degree for students who plan careers as museum professionals, historical agency administrators, or seek careers in college teaching and public history.

Type: Fellowship.

No. of awards offered: Two.

Frequency: Annual.

Value: US$9,500 plus tuition.

Study Establishment: University of Delaware.

Country of Study: USA.

Applications Procedure: University of Delaware application, transcripts, GRE scores, TOEFL where applicable, three letters of recommendation and a writing sample.

Closing Date: January 30th.

For further information contact:
Department of History, University of Delaware, Newark, DE, 19716, USA
Tel: 302 831 8226
Fax: 302 831 1358
Email: PATRICIA.ORENDORF@MVS.UDEL.EDU
Contact: Graduate Studies Committee

UNIVERSITY OF DUNDEE

The University, Dundee, DD1 4HN, Scotland
Tel: 01382 23181 ext.4035
Fax: 01382 201604
Contact: Postgraduate Office

University of Dundee Research Awards

Subjects: Medicine, dentistry, science, engineering, law, arts, social sciences, environmental studies.

Eligibility: Open to holders of a 1st or upper 2nd class honours degree or equivalent.

Level of Study: Postgraduate.

Purpose: To assist full-time research leading to a PhD.

Type: Studentship.

No. of awards offered: Approximately 4-6 depending on funds available.

Frequency: Annual.

Value: £5,300 plus tuition fees at the home rate.

Length of Study: One year; renewable annually for up to a maximum of two additional years.

Study Establishment: University of Dundee, Tayside.

Country of Study: UK.

Closing Date: March 31st.

UNIVERSITY OF EAST ANGLIA

University of East Anglia, Norwich, NR4 7TJ, England
Tel: 01603 592734
Fax: 01603 593522
Email: dean.eas@uea.ac.uk
Contact: Director of Personnel & Registry Services

UEA Writing Fellowship

Subjects: Creative writing.

Eligibility: Open to practising, published writers in fiction and poetry. Applicants must be English-speaking.

Level of Study: Professional development.

Purpose: To enable a creative writer to work in a university atmosphere and with a regional arts board on a reciprocal basis.

Type: Fellowship.

No. of awards offered: One.

Frequency: Annual.

Value: £5,000, plus free accommodation.

Length of Study: The spring semester of each academic year (January to June).

Study Establishment: University of East Anglia.

Country of Study: UK.

Applications Procedure: Applicants should submit at least two examples of recent work, application form and CV.

Closing Date: November 17th (for exact dates each year, see advertisements in the press, or telephone). Interviews take place in December.

Additional Information: A driving licence and access to a car would be an advantage.

For further information contact:
School of English and American Studies, University of East Anglia, University Plain, Norwich, NR4 7TJ, England
Tel: 01603 592274
Fax: 01603 507728
Contact: Dean

UNIVERSITY OF EDINBURGH

Old College, South Bridge, Edinburgh, EH8 9YL, Scotland
Tel: 0131 650 2159
Fax: 0131 650 2147
Email: postgrad@ed.ac.uk

Postgraduate Research Studentships

Subjects: Any subject.

Eligibility: Open to individuals of any nationality with a first or upper second class honours degree or its equivalent. Candidates must have applied, or been accepted, for study for a research degree. Candidates liable to pay fees at overseas rate must also apply for Government-funded Overseas Research Student (ORS) award.

Level of Study: Postgraduate.

Purpose: To provide funds for students wishing to pursue research leading to a research degree (MPhil, MLitt or PhD).

Type: Studentships.

No. of awards offered: Approximately 12 in 1995-96.

Frequency: Annual.

Value: £5,050 (1995/96 rate), fees at home rate and research expenses up to £400 each year.

Length of Study: One year in the first instance; renewable for one or two years thereafter.

Study Establishment: Edinburgh University.

Country of Study: UK.

Applications Procedure: Application forms to be completed, evidence of academic qualifications, English proficiency, funding and two academic references.

Closing Date: April 30th.

Additional Information: Studies must be based at the University of Edinburgh, but leave of absence for essential study elsewhere is permitted (subject to approval). When writing, potential applicants should indicate the Faculty in which they wish to study, or the subject.

UNIVERSITY OF GLASGOW

University of Glasgow, Bearsden, Glasgow, G61 1QH, Scotland

William Barclay Memorial Scholarship

Subjects: Biblical studies, theology and church history.

Eligibility: Open to any suitably qualified graduate of theology from a university outside the UK.

Purpose: To provide an opportunity for a scholar from outside the UK to do research or graduate study.

Type: Scholarship.

No. of awards offered: One.

Frequency: Annual.

Value: Up to £2,000 approximately.

Length of Study: One year.

Study Establishment: In the Faculty of Divinity, University of Glasgow.

Country of Study: Scotland.

Closing Date: March 31st.

For further information contact:
Faculty of Divinity, University of Glasgow, Glasgow, G12 8QQ, Scotland
Tel: 0141 339 8855 ext.4363/6525
Fax: 0141 330 4943
Email: gvmx04@udcf.gla.ac.uk
Contact: Mr T W Mathieson

John Crawford Scholarship

Subjects: Veterinary medicine.

Eligibility: Open to university graduates of veterinary medicine and qualified veterinary surgeons.

Level of Study: Postgraduate.

Purpose: To assist the advanced study or research into equine animals, with particular reference to bloodstock breeding and its improvement.

Type: Scholarship.

No. of awards offered: One.

Frequency: Biennially.

Value: Approximately £7,200.

Length of Study: One year; with the possibility of renewal for up to two additional years.

Study Establishment: University of Glasgow.

Country of Study: UK.

Closing Date: February 28th.

Additional Information: Preference is given to graduates in veterinary medicine of the University of Glasgow.

For further information contact:
Faculty of Veterinary Medicine, University of Glasgow Veterinary School, Bearsden, Glasgow, G61 1QH, Scotland
Email: gvmx04@udcf.gla.ac.uk
Contact: Mr T W Mathieson

James Houston Scholarship

Subjects: Veterinary medicine.

Eligibility: Open to university graduates of veterinary medicine and qualified veterinary surgeons.

Purpose: To assist the advanced study or research into bovine animals, with particular reference to bloodstock breeding and its improvement.

Type: Scholarship.

No. of awards offered: One.

Frequency: Biennially.

Value: Approximately £7,200.

Length of Study: One year; with the possibility of renewal for up to two additional years.

Study Establishment: University of Glasgow.

Country of Study: UK.

Closing Date: February.

Additional Information: Preference is given to graduates in veterinary medicine of the University of Glasgow.

For further information contact:
Faculty of Veterinary Medicine, University of Glasgow Veterinary School, Bearsden, Glasgow, G61 1QH, Scotland
Email: gvmx04@udcf.gla.ac.uk
Contact: Mr T W Mathieson

University of Glasgow Postgraduate Scholarships

Subjects: Unrestricted.

Eligibility: Open to candidates of any nationality who are proficient in English and who have obtained at least an upper second class honours or equivalent degree.

Level of Study: Postgraduate.

Purpose: To assist with research toward a PhD degree.

Type: Scholarship.

No. of awards offered: 26.

Frequency: Annual.

Value: £5,050 maintenance allowance, plus home fees of £2,430.

Length of Study: Three years; subject to satisfactory progress.

Study Establishment: University of Glasgow.

Country of Study: Scotland.

Applications Procedure: Application form must be completed.

Closing Date: February 28th.

Additional Information: Scholars from outside the European Community will be expected to make up the difference between the home fee and the overseas fee.

For further information contact:
University of Glasgow, Glasgow, G12 8QQ, Scotland
Tel: 0141 330 6474
Fax: 0141 330 4021
Contact: Clerk to the Senate Office (Postgraduate Scholarships)

UNIVERSITY OF ILLINOIS

328A DKH, 1407 West Gregory, Urbana, IL, 61801, USA

Tel: 217 333 8153
Email: rdufrane@commerce.cba.uiuc.edu

The Kate Neal Kinley Memorial Fellowships

Subjects: Art; music; architecture.

Eligibility: Open to graduates of the College of Fine and Applied Arts of the University of Illinois at Urbana-Champaign or graduates of similar institutions of equal educational standing, whose principal or major studies have been in any branch of art or music, or in the design or history of architecture. Preference is given to applicants under 25 years of age.

Level of Study: Postgraduate.

Purpose: To encourage advanced study.

Type: Fellowship.

No. of awards offered: 2 or 3.

Frequency: Annual.

Value: US$7,000 towards expenses.

Length of Study: One academic year.

Study Establishment: An approved institution.

Country of Study: USA or abroad.

Applications Procedure: Application forms are available on request.

Closing Date: February 15th.

Additional Information: The Fellowship is awarded upon the basis of unusual promise in the fine arts as attested by: academic grades in major field of study as well as related cultural fields; quality of work submitted or performed; character, merit and suitability of the proposed program; personality, seriousness of purpose and moral character of the applicant. Other awards may be held simultaneously with the Fellowship.

For further information contact:
c/o Kinley Fellowship Committee, College of Fine and Applied Arts, 110 Architecture Building, University of Illinois, 608 East Lorado Taft Drive, Champaign, IL, 61820, USA
Tel: 217 333 1661
Contact: Dean

John E Rovensky Fellowships

Subjects: Business and economic history.

Eligibility: Open to US and Canadian citizens, working towards a PhD in American history or business. Preference is given to applicants who are preparing for a career in teaching and research.

Level of Study: Doctorate.

Purpose: To enable doctoral thesis research in American business and economic history.

Type: Fellowship.

No. of awards offered: Up to two.

Frequency: Annual.

Value: US$4,500.

Study Establishment: An accredited college/university in the United States.

Country of Study: USA.

Applications Procedure: Applications will be judged by the Rovensky Fellowship Selection Committee.

Closing Date: February.

For further information contact:
Department of Economics, 328A DKH, 1407 West Gregory, Urbana, IL, 61801, USA
Tel: 217 333 8153
Email: rdufrane@commerce.cba.uiuc.edu
Contact: Professor Larry Neal

UNIVERSITY OF KEELE

Keele University, Staffs, ST5 5BG, England
Tel: 01782 621111
Fax: 01782 632343
Email: aabol@admin.keele.ac.uk
Contact: Director of Academic Affairs

University of Keele Graduate Teaching Assistantships

Subjects: Any subject.

Eligibility: Candidates should hold a good honours degree and are required to register as full-time candidates for a higher degree at the University of Keele.

Level of Study: Postgraduate.

Purpose: To assist research and give teaching experience.

Type: Studentship.

No. of awards offered: 2-3.

Frequency: Annual.

Value: £5,050 per annum.

Length of Study: For one year; may be extended for an unspecified additional period.

Study Establishment: Keele University.

Country of Study: UK.

Closing Date: March 15th.

For further information contact:
Department of Academic Affairs, Keele University, Staffs, ST5 5BG, England
Contact: Postgraduate Admissions Office

UNIVERSITY OF KENT

Computing Laboratory, University of Kent, Canterbury, Kent, C2T 7NF, England
Tel: 44 1227 827 656
Fax: 44 1227 762 811
Email: S.A.Hill@ukc.ac.uk
www: www.ukc.ac.uk
Contact: Dr S A Hill

History of Science Studentship

Subjects: History of Science.

Level of Study: Postgraduate.

Purpose: To fund research in history of science to PhD level.

Type: Studentship.

No. of awards offered: One.

Frequency: Annual.

Length of Study: Three years.

Study Establishment: University of Kent.

Country of Study: UK.

For further information contact:
Centre for History and Cultural Studies of Science, Rutherford College, University of Kent, Canterbury, Kent, C2T 7NF, England
Tel: 01227 764 000
Fax: 01227 827 258
Email: cs28@ukc.ac.uk
www: http://www.ukc.ac.uk
Contact: Dr Crosbie Smith

Institute Studentships

Subjects: Mathematics, Statistics, Operational Research.

599

Eligibility: The candidates for the scholarships should hold (or are expected to obtain) a first class Honours degree in Mathematics or a related subject.

Level of Study: Doctorate.

Purpose: To support the PhD studies at The Institute of Mathematics.

Type: Studentship.

No. of awards offered: Three.

Frequency: Dependent on funds available.

Value: The tuition fees plus the maintenance bursary at the same rate as provided by the EPSRC.

Length of Study: Three years.

Study Establishment: University of Kent.

Country of Study: UK.

Applications Procedure: Application form available.

Closing Date: April 19th.

Additional Information: Holders of the studentships are required to undertake a small amount of teaching assistance.

For further information contact:
Institute of Mathematics and Statistics, University of Kent, Canterbury, Kent, C2T 7NF, England
Tel: 01227 823 983
Fax: 01227 827 932
Email: S.Burke@ukc.ac.uk
www: http://www.ukc.ac.uk
Contact: Mr Stephen Burke

EB Spratt Bursary

Eligibility: Global eligibility, but fees component is sufficient for home fee only. Non EC citizens require further monies for overseas fees.

Level of Study: Postgraduate.

Purpose: Support postgraduate studies towards PhD.

Type: Bursary.

No. of awards offered: 2-5.

Frequency: Annual.

Value: £7,500.

Length of Study: Three years.

Study Establishment: University of Kent.

Country of Study: UK.

Applications Procedure: Applicants should enclose covering letter and make note on postgraduate application indicating their area of interest.

Closing Date: June each year.

Additional Information: Recipients of award are expected to perform light teaching duties for the laboratory, for which there is no further remuneration.

UNIVERSITY OF LEEDS

Research Degrees & Scholarships Office, University of Leeds, Leeds, LS2 9JT, England
Tel: 0113 233 4007
Fax: 0113 233 3941
Email: RSDNH@central.admin.leeds.ac.uk
Contact: Mrs J Y Findlay

ARUP-Leeds University Scholarship

Subjects: Engineering.

Eligibility: Open to candidates who have obtained a first degree of similar standard to at least a UK second class honours degree. Nationality requirements may vary each year.

Level of Study: Postgraduate.

Purpose: To provide postgraduate scholarships to students of high academic calibre.

Type: Scholarship.

No. of awards offered: Two.

Frequency: Annual.

Value: To cover academic fees and living expenses.

Length of Study: One year taught mastership courses.

Study Establishment: The University of Leeds.

Country of Study: UK.

Applications Procedure: By application form and acceptance onto taught course, both application forms available from the university address.

Closing Date: March 11th.

Guinness-Leeds University Scholarship

Subjects: Business and economic studies, development studies, education, international studies, politics, sociology, communication studies, development studies, development economics, economics, economics and finance, industrial and labour studies, modern international studies, politics of international resources and development.

Eligibility: Open to candidates who have obtained or are about to obtain a first degree of similar standard to at least a UK upper second class honours degree and who are nationals of Indonesia, Kenya, Malaysia or Nigeria.

Purpose: To provide postgraduate scholarships to students of high academic calibre.

Type: Scholarship.

No. of awards offered: Six.

Frequency: Annual.

Value: Grant towards travel to Britain and return, tuition fees, living expenses and pre-course English language tuition if required.

Length of Study: One year Masters course.

Study Establishment: University of Leeds.

Country of Study: UK.

Closing Date: February 7th.

For further information contact:
Research Degrees & Scholarships Office, University of Leeds, Leeds, LS2 9JT, England
Tel: 0113 233 4007
Fax: 0113 233 3941
Email: RDSNH@central.admin.leeds.ac.uk
Contact: Mrs J Y Findlay

Tetley and Lupton Scholarships for Overseas Students

Subjects: Any subject.

Eligibility: Open to candidates liable to pay tuition fees for undergraduate courses, masters' degrees, research degrees or diplomas at the 'full-cost' rate for overseas students. Applicants must be of a high academic standard.

Level of Study: Postgraduate, Undergraduate.

Purpose: To provide awards to overseas students of high academic calibre.

Type: Scholarship.

No. of awards offered: 70.

Frequency: Annual.

Value: £1,800 per annum to be credited towards academic fees.

Length of Study: One year; may be renewed for second or third year according to duration of course. May be held concurrently with other awards except those providing full payment of fees.

Study Establishment: University of Leeds.

Country of Study: UK.

Applications Procedure: Apply for a course and then apply for scholarship. Research candidates need to apply with national DRS competition.

Closing Date: Postgraduates are required to submit applications by June 1st.

For further information contact:
Research Degrees & Scholarships Office, University of Leeds, Leeds, LS2 9JT, England
Tel: 0113 233 4007
Fax: 0113 233 3941
Contact: Mrs J Y Findlay

UNIVERSITY OF LONDON

University of London, Senate House, Malet Street, London, WC1E 7HU, England
Tel: 0171 636 8000
Fax: 0171 636 0373

*Postgraduate Studentships

Subjects: Any subject.

Eligibility: Normally open only to graduates of the University of London.

Purpose: To assist postgraduate research leading to an MPhil or PhD degree of the University.

Type: Studentships.

No. of awards offered: Varies.

Frequency: Annual.

Value: Maintenance at DES rate for students living away from home in London and fees at Home Students rate.

Length of Study: Maximum of three years.

Study Establishment: The University.

Country of Study: UK.

Closing Date: March 1st.

For further information contact:
Room 21A, Senate House, Malet Street, London, WC1E 7HU, England
Tel: 0171 636 8000 ext.3042
Fax: 0171 636 0373
Contact: Secretary, Central Research Fund and Scholarships Committee

*Queen Mary and Westfield College Drapers' Company Research Studentships

Subjects: Arts, science, engineering, social sciences and law.

Eligibility: Open to suitably qualified candidates who hold at least an upper second class honours at first degree level.

Purpose: To provide the opportunity for full-time research leading towards an MPhil or PhD.

Type: Studentships.

No. of awards offered: Varies.

Frequency: Annual.

Value: Maintenance at the current research council rate, plus tuition fees.

Length of Study: One year; may be renewed only if other sources of funding cannot be obtained.

Study Establishment: Queen Mary and Westfield College.

Country of Study: UK.

Closing Date: June 30th.

For further information contact:
Queen Mary and Westfield College, University of London, Mile End Road, London, E1 4NS, England
Tel: 0181 975 5555
Fax: 0181 975 5500
Contact: Academic Registrar

SOAS Bursaries

Subjects: Oriental and African studies in archaeology, area studies, economics, geography, history, law, languages, linguistics, phonetics, politics, religious studies, social anthropology, development studies.

Eligibility: Open to holders of a good honours degree from a UK university, or equivalent qualification.

Type: Bursary.

No. of awards offered: 9.

Frequency: Annual.

Value: Approximately £6,510.

Length of Study: One year; not renewable.

Study Establishment: SOAS in London.

Country of Study: UK.

Closing Date: March 31st.

Additional Information: Bursaries are only available for a taught masters course.

For further information contact:
School of Oriental and African Studies, University of London, Thornhaugh Street, Russell Square, London, WC1H 0XG, England
Tel: 0171 637 2388
Fax: 0171 436 4211
Contact: Terry Harvey, Registrar

*SOAS Ouseley Memorial Scholarship

Subjects: Any subject which needs to use library facilities and archival records in Oriental languages.

Eligibility: Open to research students registered at the School of Oriental and African Studies.

Purpose: To encourage research into or studies involving the use of language facilities and archival records in Oriental languages. The Scholarship is not intended for language acquisition. The award holder must be registered for a degree at SOAS.

Type: Scholarship.

No. of awards offered: One.

Frequency: Annual.

Value: £6,115, plus fees at home/EC rate.

Length of Study: One academic year initially.

Study Establishment: The School of Oriental and African Studies, University of London.

Country of Study: UK.

Closing Date: May 1st.

For further information contact:
School of Oriental and African Studies, University of London, Thornhaugh Street, Russell Square, London, WC1H 0XG, England
Tel: 0171 637 2388
Fax: 0171 436 4211
Contact: Terry Harvey, Registrar

UNIVERSITY OF MANCHESTER

Awards & Examinations Office, University of Manchester, Oxford Road, Manchester, M13 9PL, England
Tel: 0161 275 2084
Fax: 0161 275 2407

Contact: Sara Duncalf

Frederick Craven Moore Awards

Subjects: Clinical medicine.

Eligibility: Open to graduates of any approved university, or other suitably qualified persons, who can furnish satisfactory evidence of their qualifications to pursue research in clinical medicine.

Level of Study: Postgraduate.

Purpose: Principally to support postgraduate research.

Type: Scholarships and Fellowships.

No. of awards offered: Variable number.

Frequency: As funds permit; Scholarships are awarded annually.

Value: The value of the Scholarship varies, but is normally less than the annual value of a State or Research Council Postgraduate Award in Medicine. The value of the Fellowship is determined on an individual basis in accordance with the qualifications and experience of the Fellow.

Length of Study: One year; the Scholarships only are renewable for up to a maximum of two additional years.

Study Establishment: The University.

Country of Study: UK.

Closing Date: May 1st.

University Research Studentships

Subjects: Any area of study within the purview of the faculties of arts, economic and social studies, education, law, medicine, science, and engineering.

Eligibility: Open to graduates of any approved university, or other suitable qualified persons, who can furnish satisfactory evidence of their qualifications to pursue research.

Level of Study: Postgraduate.

Purpose: To support postgraduate research, and provide funding for high quality UK, European overseas graduates wishing to study for PhD.

Type: Studentships. Maintenance stipend and tuition fees.

No. of awards offered: 40.

Frequency: Annual.

Value: Normally equivalent to the annual value of a State or Research Council Studentship. In 1996-97 Maintenance fee; £5,190 Pa, Home fee: £2,490 pa.

Length of Study: Normally three years.

Study Establishment: At the University.

Country of Study: UK.

Applications Procedure: Application forms available on request from Awards and Examinations Office.

Closing Date: May 1st.

UNIVERSITY OF MANITOBA

Faculty of Graduate Studies, 500 University Centre, University of
Manitoba, Winnipeg, Manitoba, R3T 2N2, Canada
Tel: 204 474 9836
Fax: 204 275 6488
Email: IKRENTZ@BLDGUMSU.LANI.UMANITOBA.CA
www: http://www.umanitoba.ca/gradstud/gradstud.htm/
Contact: Ilse Krentz, Awards Officer

Graduate Fellowships

Subjects: Any discipline taught at the graduate level at the University.

Eligibility: At the time of application, students do not need to have been accepted by the Department/Faculty, but at the time of taking up the award must be regular full-time graduate students who have been admit-

ted to and registered in advanced degree programs (masters or PhD, but not pre-masters) in any field of study or Faculty of the University of Manitoba. Students beyond the second year in the masters program or beyond the fourth year in the PhD program are not eligible to apply for or hold a University of Manitoba Graduate Fellowship. Students whose previous study at the masters level has been part-time will be eligible for a University of Manitoba Graduate Fellowship for a period of one year from the date of registration as full-time students.

Level of Study: Postgraduate.

Purpose: To award academic excellence for graduate study.

Type: Fellowship.

No. of awards offered: 100-110.

Frequency: Annual.

Value: C$10,000 for PhD; C$8,000 for masters (thesis-based); C$6,000 masters (course-based).

Study Establishment: The University of Manitoba in either a masters (not pre-masters) or a PhD program.

Country of Study: Canada.

Applications Procedure: Application forms may be requested from the department applicants are applying to at the University of Manitoba. Forms are available from the beginning of December.

Closing Date: February 15th, or earlier departmental deadline.

UNIVERSITY OF MARYLAND

NOI/Rossborough Festival, 4321 Hartwick Road, Suite 220, College
Park, MD, 20740, USA
Tel: 301 403 8370
Fax: 301 403 8375
Contact: Don Reinhold

International Music Competitions

Subjects: Major international competitions for piano (William Kapell), cello (Leonard Rose) and voice (Marian Anderson).

Eligibility: Open to musicians of all nationalities: piano 18-33 years of age; cello 18-30 years of age; voice 21-39 years of age.

Level of Study: Professional development.

Purpose: To recognize and assist the artistic development of young musicians at the highest levels of achievement in piano, cello, and voice.

Type: Competition.

No. of awards offered: 3 Finalist and 9 Semi-Finalist Prizes.

Frequency: Annually, in rotation: piano biennially (1998, 2000); cello every four years (1997); voice every four years (next in 1999).

Value: Finalist prizes US$20,000, US$10,000 and US$5,000; Semi-Finalists US$1,000.

Applications Procedure: Applicants should submit application form, fee, cassette recording, repertoire list, resume, photos, and letters of recommendation.

Closing Date: March 15th.

Additional Information: The competition is held in July. Concurrent Festivals offer master classes, recitals, symposia.

For further information contact:
c/o Rossborough Festival, 4321 Hartwick Road, Suite 220, College
Park, MD, 20740, USA
Tel: 301 403 8370
Fax: 301 403 8375
Email: intlcomp@umdacc.umd.edu
Contact: Don Reinhold

National Orchestral Institute Scholarships

Subjects: Orchestral performance.

Eligibility: Open to advanced musicians between 18 and 30 years of age. Primarily for students and postgraduates of American universities, conservatories and colleges; others, however, are welcome to apply but must appear at an audition center.

Level of Study: Professional development.

Purpose: To provide an intensive three-week orchestral training program to enable musicians to rehearse and perform under internationally acclaimed conductors and study with principal musicians of America's foremost orchestras.

Type: Scholarship.

No. of awards offered: Approximately 90.

Frequency: Annual.

Value: Full tuition, room and board.

Length of Study: Three weeks.

Study Establishment: The university.

Country of Study: USA.

Closing Date: Before regional auditions.

Additional Information: Applicants must submit application, fee, resume and letters of recommendation. Personal auditions are required at one of the audition centers throughout the country.

For further information contact:
NOI/Rossborough Festival, 4321 Hartwick Road, Suite #220, College Park, MD, 20740, USA
Tel: 301 403 8370
Fax: 301 403 8375
Email: noi@umdacc.umd.edu
Contact: Don Reinhold

UNIVERSITY OF MELBOURNE

University of Melbourne, Parkville, Victoria, 3052, Australia
Tel: 61 3 344 6099
Fax: 61 3 347 6739
Contact: Assistant Registrar (Research)

*Grants-in-Aid

Subjects: Any subject offered by the University.

Eligibility: Open to suitably qualified academics.

Purpose: To enable senior academics on sabbatical or other types of leave to conduct full-time research.

Type: Grant.

No. of awards offered: 20 each year.

Frequency: Annual.

Value: Varies according to individual circumstances; maximum grants, including travel, are A$8,500.

Length of Study: For a period of not less than six months.

Study Establishment: The University of Melbourne.

Country of Study: Australia.

Closing Date: January 31st and August 31st each year.

Additional Information: Interested parties should contact the head of the department they wish to visit.

*Postgraduate Scholarships

Subjects: Any subject offered by the University.

Eligibility: Open to candidates from Australia and foreign countries.

Purpose: To enable graduates to undertake research.

Type: Scholarship.

No. of awards offered: 50 for Australian citizens and residents and 30 for overseas students.

Frequency: Annual.

Value: A$12,880 per annum, payable fortnightly.

Length of Study: Up to two years at the master's level; for up to three years at the PhD level, with the possibility of extension for an additional six months.

Study Establishment: The University of Melbourne.

Country of Study: Australia.

Closing Date: October 31st.

UNIVERSITY OF MICHIGAN

University of Michigan, Mike and Mary Wallace House, 620 Oxford Road, Ann Arbor, MI, 48104, USA
Tel: 313 998 7666
Fax: 313 998 7979
Email: drath@umich.edu
www: http://www.umich.edu/~mjfellow
Contact: Charles R Eisendrath, Director

Michigan Journalism Fellows

Subjects: Journalism.

Eligibility: Open to full-time print or broadcast journalists, including freelancers, who have a minimum of five years' experience.

Level of Study: Professional development.

Purpose: To enable the most talented mid-career professional US journalists to attain peak performance.

Type: Fellowship.

No. of awards offered: 10-12.

Frequency: Annual.

Value: US$30,000 plus tuition, paid directly to the University.

Length of Study: From September to April.

Study Establishment: On campus.

Country of Study: USA.

Closing Date: February 1st.

Additional Information: The Fellow's work must appear regularly in US-controlled news organizations.

UNIVERSITY OF NEW ENGLAND

Research Services, University of New England, Armidale, NSW, 2351, Australia
Tel: 067 73 3571
Fax: 067 73 3543
Email: lmccabe3@mets.une.edu.au
www: http://www.une.edu.au/~researchservices/research.htm
Contact: Postgraduate Scholarships Officer

Research Scholarships

Subjects: Arts, education, economics, sciences, social science, resource sciences.

Eligibility: Open to candidates of any nationality having at least a bachelor's degree at one honours level or equivalent.

Level of Study: Postgraduate.

Purpose: To provide assistance toward the completion of a research master's degree or PhD.

Type: Scholarship.

No. of awards offered: 20.

Frequency: Annual.

Value: Approximately A$15,000.

Length of Study: Two years (master's degree) or for an initial period of three years which may be renewed for six months (PhD).

Study Establishment: The University.

Country of Study: Australia.

Applications Procedure: Application form with certified copies of academic transcripts and academic referees.

Closing Date: October 31st.

Additional Information: Candidates who are not permanent residents or citizens of Australia must provide evidence of additional financial support of at least A$10,000. The research proposal must be approved by the head of the relevant department. Initial enquiries from overseas students should be directed to the International Students Officer at the University.

UNIVERSITY OF NOTTINGHAM

University of Nottingham, University Park, Nottingham, NG7 2RD, England
Tel: 0115 9515792
Fax: 0115 9513666
Contact: Dr R Masterman

University Postgraduate Studentships

Subjects: Any subject offered by the University.

Eligibility: Open to graduates of all nationalities. The Studentships are allocated to departments to whom students should apply for further information.

Level of Study: Postgraduate.

Purpose: To promote research.

No. of awards offered: Varies.

Frequency: Annual.

Value: £5,100 per annum, plus University fees at the HEC rate.

Length of Study: One year; renewable for up to 2 additional years.

Study Establishment: University of Nottingham.

Country of Study: UK.

Closing Date: May 1st.

For further information contact:
University of Nottingham, The Graduate School, University Park, Nottingham, NG7 2RD, England
Tel: 0115 951 4664
Fax: 0115 951 4668
Email: LINDA.CUNLIFF@nottingham.ac.uk
www: http://www.nott.ac.uk
Contact: Linda Cunniff

UNIVERSITY OF OSLO

International Summer School, University of Oslo, Box 3, Blindern, Oslo, 01313, Norway
Tel: 22 85 63 85/6/8
Fax: 22 47 85 41 99

*International Summer School Scholarships

Subjects: General courses: Norwegian art; Nordic folklore; Norwegian language; history and literature of Norway; Scandinavian literature; Norwegian economics, politics, culture and society; Norway and Scandinavia in international relations. Graduate courses: special education in Norway; peace research; international development studies; analysis and planning of development projects; medical care and health services in Norway; energy planning and the environment.

Eligibility: Open to students with good academic records as evidenced by an official transcript (US students should have completed their sophomore year; non-US students must present evidence of matriculation at a recognized university in their own country or abroad); teachers with a

good professional record as evidenced by a statement from the teacher's present supervisor, principal or headmaster; and members of graduate courses who have good professional records and/or other qualifications listed on the relevant application form.

Purpose: To impart knowledge about various aspects of Norwegian and Scandinavian culture or topics of international interest, comparatively presented, and to increase international understanding.

Type: Scholarship.

No. of awards offered: Limited.

Frequency: Annual.

Value: Normally covers room and board and incidental expenses. There is no tuition fee.

Length of Study: For six weeks, from late June to early August.

Study Establishment: Oslo.

Country of Study: Norway.

Applications Procedure: Candidates should apply directly to the International Summer School office or to the Norwegian embassy in their country. Prospective participants from the USA and Canada should make formal application for admission on special forms from Oslo International Summer School, North American Admissions Office, c/o Saint Olaf College, 1520 Saint Olaf Ave, Northfield, MN 55057-1098, USA.

Closing Date: March 1st.

Additional Information: All lectures, except Norwegian language classes, are given in English.

UNIVERSITY OF OXFORD

*Christ Church Senior Scholarships

Subjects: Any subject.

Eligibility: Open to candidates who will have been reading for a higher degree in the University of Oxford for one year by October 1st of the year in which the award is sought.

Purpose: To enable graduate scholars to undertake some definite course of literary, educational, scientific or professional study or training.

Type: Scholarship.

No. of awards offered: Two.

Frequency: Annual.

Value: £4,450, subject to deductions if other funding is acquired, plus housing or £450 per annum in lieu of accommodation.

Length of Study: Two years; renewable for a further year.

Study Establishment: Christ Church.

Country of Study: UK.

Closing Date: May 1st.

Additional Information: Normally, the Scholarship is held in conjunction with an award from a government agency which pays the university fees.

For further information contact:
The Deanery, Christ Church, Oxford, OX1 1DP, England
Contact: The Dean's Secretary

Exeter College Usher-Cunningham Studentship

Subjects: Medical science and modern history, alternately.

Eligibility: The Modern History Studentship is only open to graduates of Irish Universities.

Level of Study: Postgraduate.

Purpose: To support graduate study.

Type: Studentship.

No. of awards offered: One.

Frequency: Triennially (1997 for medical science).

Value: Similar to a Research Council Studentship.

Length of Study: One year, renewable for up to two additional years.

Study Establishment: Exeter College.

Country of Study: UK.

For further information contact:
Exeter College, Oxford, OX1 3DP, England
Tel: 01865 279660
Fax: 01865 279630
Contact: College Secretary

*James Ingram Halstead Scholarship in Music

Subjects: Music.

Eligibility: Open to graduates of any University who intend to proceed to one of the University's advanced degrees in Music (MLitt, MPhil or DPhil) or are intending to supplicate for the DMus or DMus.

Type: Scholarship.

No. of awards offered: One or more.

Frequency: Annually, but dependent on funds available.

Value: Normally £300 per annum.

Length of Study: One year.

Study Establishment: University of Oxford, in the first instance.

Country of Study: UK.

Closing Date: March 1st.

For further information contact:
Board of the Faculty of Music, University Offices, Wellington Square, Oxford, OX1 2JD, England
Tel: 01865 270001
Fax: 01865 270708
Contact: Secretary

Lady Margaret Hall EPA Cephalosporin Research Fellowship

Subjects: Biological, chemical or medical sciences.

Eligibility: Open to qualified persons who hold, or will have obtained, a doctorate or equivalent degree by the start of tenure, and are engaged in advanced scientific research in Oxford.

Purpose: To provide an opportunity for academic postdoctoral research.

Type: Fellowship.

No. of awards offered: One.

Frequency: Varies, but usually every 2-3 years.

Value: Not less than £3,000 per annum; but may be held with other post-doctoral awards.

Length of Study: Two years; not renewable.

Study Establishment: Lady Margaret Hall.

Country of Study: UK.

Closing Date: As advertised.

Additional Information: Terms and conditions may be varied according to the decisions of the Governing Body. The Fellowship may sometimes be offered as a supplementary award.

For further information contact:
Lady Margaret Hall, Norham Gardens, Oxford, OX2 6QA, England
Tel: 01865 274300
Fax: 01865 511069
Contact: Principal's Secretary

Lady Margaret Hall Talbot Research Fellowship

Subjects: Various arts subjects, as advertised.

Eligibility: Open to qualified persons who hold or will have obtained a postdoctoral or equivalent degree by the start of tenure.

Purpose: To provide an opportunity for academic postdoctoral research.

Type: Fellowship.

No. of awards offered: One.

Frequency: Triennially.

Value: Approximately £10,000 per annum plus residence (for single persons only).

Length of Study: Three years; not renewable.

Study Establishment: Lady Margaret Hall.

Country of Study: UK.

Closing Date: As advertised.

For further information contact:
Lady Margaret Hall, Norham Gardens, Oxford, OX2 6QA, England
Tel: 01865 274300
Fax: 01865 511069
Contact: Principal's Secretary

Linacre College Domus Studentships

Subjects: Any subject.

Eligibility: Open to students with a good first degree.

Level of Study: Postgraduate.

Purpose: To assist postgraduate study.

Type: Studentship.

No. of awards offered: Four.

Frequency: Annual.

Value: £250 per annum.

Length of Study: Up to three years.

Study Establishment: Linacre College.

Country of Study: UK.

Closing Date: January 31st of preceding academic year.

For further information contact:
Linacre College, St Cross Road, Oxford, OX1 3JA, England
Tel: 01865 271657
Fax: 01865 271668
Email: jane.edwards@linacre.ox.ac.uk
Contact: The College Secretary

Linacre College EPA Cephalosporin Junior Research Fellowships

Subjects: Biology, biochemistry, medicine, organic chemistry, psychology.

Eligibility: Open to persons with a postdoctoral qualification.

Level of Study: Postdoctorate.

Purpose: To assist postdoctoral research.

Type: Fellowship.

No. of awards offered: Three.

Frequency: Annual.

Value: £250 per annum.

Length of Study: Up to two years.

Study Establishment: Linacre College.

Country of Study: UK.

Closing Date: January 31st.

For further information contact:
Linacre College, St Cross Road, Oxford, OX1 3JA, England
Tel: 01865 271657
Fax: 01865 271668
Email: jane.edwards@linacre.ox.ac.uk
Contact: The College Secretary

Linacre College Junior Research Fellowship

Subjects: Any subject.

Eligibility: Open to students with a doctorate or equivalent degree.

Level of Study: Postdoctorate.

Purpose: To assist postdoctoral research.

Type: Fellowship.

No. of awards offered: Three.

Frequency: Annual.

Value: £250 per annum.

Length of Study: Up to two years.

Study Establishment: Linacre College.

Country of Study: UK.

Closing Date: January 31st.

For further information contact:
Linacre College, St Cross Road, Oxford, OX1 3JA, England
Tel: 01865 271657
Fax: 01865 271668
Email: jane.edwards@linacre.ox.ac.uk
Contact: The College Secretary

Lincoln College Berrow Scholarship

Subjects: Any subject.

Eligibility: Open to graduates of the following Swiss universities: Berne, Geneva, Lausanne, Fribourg, Neuchâtel, or the Ecole Polytechnique Fédérale de Lausanne.

Level of Study: Postgraduate.

Purpose: To permit graduates of Swiss universities to undertake postgraduate study at Oxford.

Type: Scholarship.

No. of awards offered: Three.

Frequency: Annual.

Value: All University and College fees are covered, together with a maintenance allowance (equal to that of Rhodes Scholarship).

Study Establishment: Lincoln College, Oxford, for any recognized postgraduate degree course.

Country of Study: UK.

Closing Date: December 1st of the year preceding admission.

For further information contact:
Lincoln College, Oxford, OX1 3DR, England
Tel: 01865 279836
Fax: 01865 279802
Contact: Tutor for Graduates

Lincoln College Keith Murray Senior Scholarship

Subjects: The humanities (may vary from year to year).

Eligibility: Open to holders of a very good first degree, who are citizens of any country outside the EC.

Level of Study: Postgraduate.

Purpose: To permit students from outside the EC to undertake postgraduate study at Oxford University.

Type: Scholarship.

No. of awards offered: One or more, depending on the availability of funds.

Frequency: Biennially, depending on the adequacy of the Fund (next 1998).

Value: All University and College fees are covered, plus a maintenance allowance (equal to that of Rhodes Scholarship).

Study Establishment: Lincoln College, Oxford.

Country of Study: UK.

Closing Date: December of the year preceding commencement of study.

For further information contact:
Lincoln College, Oxford, OX1 3DR, England
Tel: 01865 279836
Fax: 01865 279802
Contact: Tutor for Graduates

Violet Vaughan Morgan Commonwealth Studentship in English Literature

Subjects: English literature.

Eligibility: Open to graduate students of a designated Commonwealth country (different Commonwealth countries are invited in rotation to make nominations).

Type: Studentship.

No. of awards offered: One.

Frequency: Triennially.

Value: £7,500 per annum (under review).

Length of Study: Up to 3 years, depending upon the course chosen.

Study Establishment: The University.

Country of Study: UK.

For further information contact:
Board of the Faculty of English Language and Literature, University Offices, University of Oxford, Wellington Square, Oxford, OX1 2JD, England
Tel: 01865 270081
Fax: 01865 270708
Contact: The Secretary

Nuffield College Funded Studentships

Subjects: Social sciences; political science; economics.

Eligibility: Open to persons with at least an upper second first degree, or equivalent.

Level of Study: Postgraduate.

Purpose: To assist students on a postgraduate degree course.

Type: Studentship.

No. of awards offered: Varies.

Frequency: Annual.

Value: University and College fees plus maintenance.

Study Establishment: Nuffield College.

Country of Study: UK.

Applications Procedure: Applicants are required to complete Nuffield application form and submit two pieces of recent academic written work. They must apply to the relevant faculty board of the university via the Graduate admissions office of the university.

Closing Date: January 31st.

Additional Information: Requests for information should be addressed to the Admissions Secretary. The Studentships are offered in August for commencement in October. Candidates are advised to apply as early as possible.

For further information contact:
Nuffield College, Oxford, OX1 1NF, England
Tel: 01865 278515
Fax: 01865 278621
Email: glynis.baleham@ox.ac.uk
www: http://www.hicks.nuff.ox.ac.uk/
Contact: The Admissions Secretary

Nuffield College Guardian Research Fellowship

Subjects: Media/broadcasting.

Eligibility: Open to journalists or management staff members from fields of newspaper press, periodicals and broadcasting.

Purpose: To support research on projects directly related to the media.

Type: Fellowship.

No. of awards offered: One.

Frequency: Annual.

Value: Varies according to the Fellow's financial circumstances and proposed research.

Length of Study: One academic year.

Study Establishment: Nuffield College.

Country of Study: UK.

Applications Procedure: Applicants are required to submit CV, research proposal, and names and addresses of three referees.

Closing Date: Mid-January.

Additional Information: Preference will be given to proposals directly related to the applicant's experience of working in the media. The Fellow will be asked to give the annual Guardian Lecture to members of the University and the public at some time during tenure. Requests for information should be addressed to the Warden's Secretary.

For further information contact:
Nuffield College, Oxford, OX1 1NF, England
Tel: 01865 278520
Fax: 01865 278676
Email: marion.rogers@nuf.ox.ac.uk
Contact: Warden's Secretary

Nuffield College Gwilym Gibbon Research Fellowships

Subjects: Problems of government, the subject having been approved by the College.

Eligibility: Preference will be given to candidates with experience in some form of public service.

Level of Study: Postgraduate, Postdoctorate, Professional development.

Purpose: To support the study of problems of government, especially by cooperation between academic and non-academic persons.

Type: Fellowship.

No. of awards offered: Varies.

Frequency: Annual.

Value: To cover accommodation, necessary travel costs and some secretarial and other assistance.

Length of Study: One year.

Study Establishment: Nuffield College.

Country of Study: UK.

Applications Procedure: Write for application form.

Closing Date: Mid-April.

Additional Information: It is hoped that the results of the research will be published or made available in some way to interested persons. Requests for information should be addressed to the Admissions Secretary.

For further information contact:
Nuffield College, Oxford, OX1 1NF, England
Tel: 01865 278515
Fax: 01865 278621
Email: glynis.baleham@nuf.ox.ac.uk
Contact: Admissions Secretary

Nuffield College Norman Chester Senior Research Fellowship

Subjects: Social studies.

Eligibility: Open to fairly senior scholars in social studies. Preference is given to candidates holding academic posts in the UK.

Level of Study: Postdoctorate.

Purpose: To allow a scholar to obtain leave from his or her academic post so that a defined piece of academic work may be advanced or completed.

Type: Fellowship.

No. of awards offered: One.

Frequency: Annual.

Value: Varies according to the Fellow's financial circumstances.

Length of Study: Three months.

Study Establishment: Nuffield College.

Country of Study: UK.

Applications Procedure: Please submit a list of publications, CV, proposed research synopsis and names and addresses of three referees.

Closing Date: Mid-January.

Additional Information: Requests for information should be addressed to the Warden's Secretary.

For further information contact:
Nuffield College, Oxford, OX1 1NF, England
Tel: 01865 278520
Fax: 01865 278676
Email: marion.rogers@nuf.ox.ac.uk
Contact: Warden's Secretary

*Nuffield College Prize Research Fellowships

Subjects: Social sciences; political science; economics.

Eligibility: Open to men and women no more than five years beyond first degree graduation, or at a comparable stage in their academic careers. Candidates will not be subject to any test of a religious, political or racial character.

Purpose: To allow young scholars to continue research.

Type: Fellowship.

No. of awards offered: Three to five.

Frequency: Annual.

Value: £6,922 per annum for Predoctoral Fellows; £11,724 per annum for Postdoctoral Fellows; plus accommodation or housing allowance, children's allowance and essential travel expenses.

Length of Study: Two years; extendable for one year provided a doctorate is completed within an appropriate time.

Study Establishment: The College.

Country of Study: UK.

Applications Procedure: Requests for information should be addressed to the Admissions Secretary.

Closing Date: End October.

For further information contact:
Nuffield College, Oxford, OX1 1NF, England
Tel: 01865 278524
Fax: 01865 278621
Contact: Assistant Domestic Bursar

Plant Sciences Department Claridge Druce Scholarship

Subjects: Any aspect of plant taxonomy.

Eligibility: Candidates should have a first or upper second class bachelor of science degree in botany or biology.

Level of Study: Postgraduate.

Type: Scholarship.

No. of awards offered: One.

Frequency: Every 5 years.

Value: Equal in value to an SRC studentship, plus £50 and fees.

Length of Study: Three years not renewable.

Study Establishment: The University.

Country of Study: UK.

Closing Date: Usually advertised in or near December.

For further information contact:
Plant Sciences Department, South Parks Road, Oxford, OX1 3RB, England
Tel: 01865 275800
Fax: 01865 275805
Contact: Professor H G Dickinson

Joanna Randall-MacIver Junior Research Fellowship

Subjects: Fine arts, music or literature of any nation: research.

Eligibility: Open to women candidates only.

Type: Fellowship.

No. of awards offered: One.

Frequency: Annual.

Value: Approximately £10,000 per year renewed annually.

Length of Study: Two years in rotation; not renewable.

Study Establishment: Lady Margaret Hall, Somerville College, St Hugh's College, St Hilda's College and St Anne's College.

Country of Study: UK.

Applications Procedure: Information can be obtained by writing to the individual college.

For further information contact:
University Offices, University of Oxford, Wellington Square, Oxford, OX1 2JD
Tel: 01865 270111
Fax: 01865 270708
Contact: P J Smith

*Sir John Rhys Studentship in Celtic Studies

Subjects: Celtic studies.

Eligibility: Open to persons engaged in graduate research in Celtic Studies who need financial support in respect of living expenses or fees. The award is not intended for those who hold full-time university posts.

Purpose: To enable the successful candidate to complete a research programme on which he or she is already engaged.

Type: Studentships.

No. of awards offered: One or two.

Frequency: Normally annually.

Value: Dependent on circumstances; normally similar to a graduate studentship from a UK research council.

Length of Study: One year; renewable only in exceptional circumstances.

Study Establishment: The University.

Country of Study: UK.

Applications Procedure: Applications should be sent to the Secretary to the Trustees of the Rhys Fund, 37 Wellington Square, Oxford OX1 2JF, and should include: a CV; a brief outline of the research proposed; an indication of the size of grant required (i.e. any necessary expenses in addition to the normal living costs of a graduate student) and of other sources of financial support (if any); brief details of any other awards or appointments for which the candidate is applying; the names of two academic referees; and the candidate's address for the Easter period if different from the term-time address.

Closing Date: March 1st.

Additional Information: The successful applicant, if not already a member of the University of Oxford, would normally become a member of Jesus College and would be expected to reside in Oxford for the greater part of the academic year.

For further information contact:
37 Wellington Square, Oxford, OX1 2JF, England

Tel: 01865 270753
Fax: 01865 270757
Contact: Secretary to the Trustees of the Rhys Fund

St Anne's College Biegun Warburg Junior Research Fellowship

Subjects: Research in the human and social sciences, including sociology, social anthropology (not African), socio-legal studies, social psychology and the cognitive sciences, economics, politics and geography.

Eligibility: Open to graduates in their second or subsequent year of research, and to candidates registered for doctorates at other universities.

Purpose: To fund research.

Type: Fellowship.

No. of awards offered: One.

Frequency: Biennially (next 1998/99).

Value: £7,300, plus free accommodation or living allowance of £1,871 per annum.

Length of Study: One year in the first instance; renewable for up to one additional year.

Study Establishment: The College.

Country of Study: UK.

Closing Date: Further particulars and closing date available in Michaelmas term one year before the award.

For further information contact:
St Anne's College, Oxford, OX2 6HS, England
Tel: 01865 274825
Fax: 01865 274899
Contact: The Senior Tutor's Secretary

St Anne's College Drapers' Company Junior Research Fellowship

Subjects: Mathematics or the sciences; Chemistry, biochemistry, or molecular biophysics in 1997-98.

Eligibility: Open to graduates in their second or subsequent year of research, and to candidates registered for doctorates at other universities.

Level of Study: Doctorate, Postdoctorate.

Purpose: To fund research.

Type: Fellowship.

No. of awards offered: One.

Frequency: Biennially (next 1998/99).

Value: £7,300 plus free accommodation or living allowance of £1,871 per annum.

Length of Study: For one year in the first instance; may be renewed for up to one additional year.

Study Establishment: The College.

Country of Study: UK.

Closing Date: Further particulars and closing date available in Michaelmas term one year before the award.

For further information contact:
St Anne's College, Oxford, OX2 6HS, England
Tel: 01865 274825
Fax: 01865 274899
Contact: The Senior Tutor's Secretary

St Anne's College Fulford Junior Research Fellowship

Subjects: Any arts subject offered by the University; philosophy, theology, archeology, classical languages, classical studies 1998-9.

Eligibility: Open to graduates in their second or subsequent year of research, and to candidates registered for doctorates at other universities.

Level of Study: Postdoctorate, Doctorate.

Purpose: To fund research.

Type: Fellowship.

No. of awards offered: One.

Frequency: Biennially (next 1998/99).

Value: £7,300, plus free accommodation or living allowance of £1,871 per annum.

Length of Study: One year in the first instance; may be renewed for up to one additional year.

Study Establishment: The College.

Country of Study: UK.

Closing Date: Further particulars and closing date available in Michaelmas term the year before the award

For further information contact:
St Anne's College, Oxford, OX2 6HS, England
Tel: 01865 274825
Fax: 01865 274899
Contact: The Senior Tutor's Secretary

St Anne's College Ioma Evans-Pritchard Junior Research Fellowship

Subjects: Social anthropology in Africa.

Eligibility: Open to graduates who are normally resident in the British Isles and to members of African universities.

Level of Study: Doctorate, Postdoctorate.

Purpose: To fund research.

Type: Fellowship.

No. of awards offered: One.

Frequency: Every two years, next 1998-9.

Value: £7,300, plus free accommodation or living allowance of £1,871 per annum.

Length of Study: One year in the first instance; may be renewed for up to one additional year.

Study Establishment: The College.

Country of Study: UK.

Closing Date: Further particulars and closing date available in Michaelmas term one year before the award.

For further information contact:
St Anne's College, Oxford, OX2 6HS, England
Tel: 01865 274825
Fax: 01865 274899
Contact: The Senior Tutor's Secretary

St Anne's College Irene Jamieson Research Scholarship

Subjects: Any arts or social science subject offered by the University.

Eligibility: Open to men and women who are UK or EC citizens and who are graduates of any university, or individuals who can show some other proof of their ability to undertake advanced work. Candidates who are graduates of a British university must have obtained first or good second class honours. All candidates must be accepted by the University of Oxford to read for a higher degree, and by the College. No further application is then necessary.

Level of Study: Postgraduate, Doctorate.

Type: Scholarship.

No. of awards offered: Two.

Frequency: Annual.

Value: Equal to the College fee.

Length of Study: Up to two years.

Study Establishment: The College.

Country of Study: UK.

Closing Date: June 1st.

For further information contact:
St Anne's College, Oxford, OX2 6HS, England
Tel: 01865 274825
Fax: 01865 274899
Contact: Registrar

St Anne's College Kathleen Bourne Junior Research Fellowship

Subjects: Primarily French language and literature, architecture, art, history, music or philosophy.

Eligibility: Open to graduates who are citizens of one of the countries or territories of the British Commonwealth or the Republic of Ireland

Level of Study: Postdoctorate, Doctorate.

Purpose: To fund research in a French subject.

Type: Fellowship.

No. of awards offered: One.

Frequency: Biennially (next 1998/99).

Value: £7,300 plus free accommodation or living allowance of £1,871 per annum.

Length of Study: One year in the first instance; may be renewed for up to one additional year.

Study Establishment: The College.

Country of Study: UK.

Closing Date: Further particulars and closing date available in Michaelmas term one year before the award.

For further information contact:
St Anne's College, Oxford, OX2 6HS, England
Tel: 01865 274825
Fax: 01865 274899
Contact: The Senior Tutor's Secretary

St Anne's College Olwen Rhys Research Scholarship

Subjects: Medieval romance language and literature; medieval history.

Eligibility: Open to men and women who are UK or EC citizens and who are graduates of any university, or individuals who can show some other proof of their ability to undertake advanced work. Candidates who are graduates of a British university must have obtained first or good second class honours. All candidates must be accepted by the University of Oxford to read for a higher degree, and by the College. No further application is then necessary.

Type: Scholarship.

No. of awards offered: One.

Frequency: Annual.

Value: Equal to the College fee.

Length of Study: Up to two years.

Study Establishment: At the College.

Country of Study: UK.

Closing Date: June 1st.

For further information contact:
St Anne's College, Oxford, OX2 6HS, England
Tel: 01865 274825
Fax: 01865 274899
Contact: Registrar

St Anne's College Overseas Scholarship

Subjects: Any subject offered by the University.

609

Eligibility: Open to graduates of any university who are not UK or EC citizens. All candidates must be accepted by the University of Oxford to read for a higher degree, and by the College. No further application is then necessary.

Level of Study: Postgraduate.

Type: Scholarship.

No. of awards offered: Three.

Frequency: Annual.

Value: Equal to the College fee.

Length of Study: Up to two years.

Study Establishment: At the College.

Country of Study: UK.

Closing Date: June 1st.

For further information contact:
St Anne's College, Oxford, OX2 6HS, England
Tel: 01865 274825
Fax: 01865 274899
Contact: Registrar

St Anne's College Schoolteacher Fellowship

Subjects: Unrestricted.

Eligibility: Open to persons engaged in sixth-form teaching and preferably in mid-career.

Level of Study: Professional development.

Purpose: To enable sixth form teachers to spend a term in Oxford engaged in writing or research, or studying recent work or new methods.

Type: Fellowship.

No. of awards offered: One.

Frequency: Annual.

Value: Free room and board is provided, as well as library facilities.

Length of Study: Usually for eight weeks, however limited residences may be arranged.

Study Establishment: The College.

Country of Study: UK.

For further information contact:
St Anne's College, Oxford, OX2 6HS, England
Tel: 01865 274825
Fax: 01865 274899
Contact: The Senior Tutor

St Anne's College Una Goodwin Research Scholarship

Subjects: Any science subject offered by the University.

Eligibility: Open to men and women who are UK or EC citizens and who are graduates of any university, or individuals who can show some other proof of their ability to undertake advanced work. Candidates who are graduates of a British university must have obtained first or good second class honours. All candidates must be accepted by the University of Oxford to read for a higher degree, and by the College. No further application is then necessary.

Level of Study: Postgraduate, Doctorate.

Type: Scholarship.

No. of awards offered: One.

Frequency: Annual.

Value: Equal to the College fee.

Length of Study: Up to two years.

Study Establishment: At the College.

Country of Study: UK.

Closing Date: June 1st.

For further information contact:
St Anne's College, Oxford, OX2 6HS, England
Tel: 01865 274825
Fax: 01865 274899
Contact: Registrar

St Catherine's College Graduate Scholarship

Subjects: Varies, please write for details.

Eligibility: Open to research students, normally in first year of graduate study.

Level of Study: Postgraduate.

Purpose: To assist graduates studying for a research degree, usually in their first year at the University of Oxford.

Type: Scholarship.

No. of awards offered: One.

Frequency: Annual.

Value: £2,000.

Length of Study: Two years.

Study Establishment: St Catherine's College, University of Oxford.

Country of Study: UK.

Closing Date: May 5th.

St Catherine's College Graduate Scholarship for Overseas Students

Subjects: Any subject.

Eligibility: Open to qualified individuals who are citizens of non-EC countries.

Level of Study: Postgraduate.

Purpose: To assist graduates studying for a research degree, usually in their first year at the University of Oxford.

Type: Scholarship.

No. of awards offered: One.

Frequency: Annual.

Value: £2,000.

Length of Study: Two years in the first instance.

Study Establishment: St Catherine's College, University of Oxford.

Country of Study: UK.

Closing Date: July 1st.

For further information contact:
St Catherine's College, Oxford, OX1 3UJ, England
Tel: 01865 271732
Fax: 01865 271768
Contact: Tutor for Graduates

St Cross College F C Osmaston Scholarship

Subjects: Forestry.

Eligibility: Open to students from Oxford or from other institutions of higher education who intend to study or are studying for a postgraduate degree.

Level of Study: Postgraduate.

Purpose: To support postgraduate study.

Type: Scholarship.

No. of awards offered: One.

Frequency: Annual.

Value: £500 per annum.

Study Establishment: St Cross College.

Country of Study: UK.

Closing Date: March.

Additional Information: Students already working for higher degrees at other colleges in Oxford are not eligible to apply for this award.

For further information contact:
St Cross College, Oxford, OX1 3LZ, England
Tel: 01865 278490
Contact: Tutor for Admissions

St Cross College Major College Scholarships

Subjects: Any subject.

Eligibility: Open to students from Oxford or from other institutions of higher education who intend to study or are studying for a postgraduate degree.

Level of Study: Postgraduate.

Purpose: To support postgraduate study.

Type: Scholarship.

No. of awards offered: Up to 2.

Frequency: Annual.

Value: £1,650 per annum.

Study Establishment: St Cross College.

Country of Study: UK.

Closing Date: March.

For further information contact:
St Cross College, Oxford, OX1 3LZ, England
Tel: 01865 278490
Contact: Tutor for Admissions

St Cross College Paula Soans O'Brian Scholarships

Subjects: Any subject.

Eligibility: Open to students from Oxford or from other institutions of higher education who intend to study or are studying for a postgraduate degree.

Level of Study: Postgraduate.

Type: Scholarship.

No. of awards offered: Up to 2.

Frequency: Varies.

Value: £1,650 per annum.

Length of Study: 1-3 years.

Study Establishment: St Cross College.

Closing Date: March.

For further information contact:
St Cross College, Oxford, OX1 3LZ, England
Tel: 01865 278490
Contact: Tutor for Admissions

St Cross College Unilever Scholarship

Subjects: Engineering or an area of science, particularly biochemistry.

Eligibility: Open to any student from Oxford or from other institutions of higher education who intends to study, or are studying, for a postgraduate degree.

Level of Study: Postgraduate.

Purpose: To support postgraduate study.

Type: Scholarship.

No. of awards offered: One.

Frequency: Annual.

Value: £500 per annum.

Study Establishment: St Cross College.

Country of Study: UK.

Closing Date: March.

Additional Information: Students already working for higher degrees at other colleges in Oxford are not eligible to apply for this award.

For further information contact:
St Cross College, Oxford, OX1 3LZ, England
Contact: Tutor for Admissions

St Hilda's College E P Abraham Junior Research Fellowship

Subjects: Chemistry, medicine or the biological sciences.

Eligibility: Open to women of any nationality who have completed their doctorate, or are within sight of submission.

Level of Study: Postdoctorate.

Type: Fellowship.

No. of awards offered: One.

Frequency: As vacancy occurs (next not before 1997).

Value: £9,485 per annum, plus free board and lodging.

Length of Study: Two years; renewable for one additional year.

Study Establishment: St Hilda's College.

Country of Study: UK.

Closing Date: January.

For further information contact:
St Hilda's College, Oxford, OX4 1DY, England
Tel: 01865 276815
Fax: 01865 276816
Contact: The College Officers' Secretary

St Hilda's College Graduate Studentships

Subjects: Any subject offered by the University.

Eligibility: Open to women graduates from the UK and other EC countries working for a higher degree.

Level of Study: Postgraduate.

Type: Studentship.

No. of awards offered: Normally two.

Frequency: Annual.

Value: Up to £1,000 per annum.

Length of Study: One year; renewable.

Study Establishment: St Hilda's College.

Country of Study: UK.

Applications Procedure: Applicants must have been accepted by the relevant University Faculty before applying for a Studentship.

Closing Date: June 1st.

For further information contact:
St Hilda's College, Oxford, OX4 1DY, England
Tel: 01865 276815
Fax: 01865 276816
Contact: College Officers' Secretary

St Hilda's College Julia Mann Junior Research Fellowship

Subjects: Any subject offered by the University.

Eligibility: Open to women of any nationality who have completed their doctorate or are within sight of submission.

Level of Study: Postdoctorate.

Type: Fellowship.

No. of awards offered: One.

Frequency: As the Fellowship becomes available (next not before 1998).

Value: £9,485 per annum, plus free board and lodging.

Length of Study: Two years; renewable for one additional year.

Study Establishment: St Hilda's College.

Country of Study: UK.

Closing Date: January.

For further information contact:
St Hilda's College, Oxford, OX4 1DY, England
Tel: 01865 276815
Fax: 01865 276816
Contact: The College Officers' Secretary

St Hilda's College Randall-MacIver Junior Research Fellowship

Subjects: Fine art, music or literature of any nation and of any period.

Eligibility: Open to women of any nationality who have completed their doctorate or are within sight of submission.

Level of Study: Postdoctorate.

Type: Fellowship.

No. of awards offered: One.

Frequency: As the Fellowship becomes available (next 1998).

Value: £9,485, plus free board and lodging.

Length of Study: One year, renewable for one additional year.

Study Establishment: St Hilda's College.

Country of Study: UK.

Closing Date: January 1998.

Additional Information: The Fellowship is awarded to five Oxford Colleges in rotation.

For further information contact:
St Hilda's College, Oxford, OX4 1DY, England
Tel: 01865 276815
Fax: 01865 276816
Contact: The College Officers' Secretary

St Hilda's College Raymond Bursary

Subjects: Any subject offered by the University.

Eligibility: Open to women students who are New Zealand citizens.

Level of Study: Postgraduate, Undergraduate.

No. of awards offered: Varies.

Frequency: Occasionally, as needed.

Value: Up to £1,700 per annum.

Length of Study: One year; renewable.

Country of Study: UK.

Closing Date: June 1st.

Additional Information: Available for undergraduate or postgraduate degrees and diplomas.

For further information contact:
St Hilda's College, Oxford, OX4 1DY, England
Tel: 01865 276815
Fax: 01865 276816
Contact: The College Officer's Secretary

St Hilda's College Rhodes Visiting Fellowship for Women

Subjects: Any subject offered by the University.

Eligibility: Open to women.

Level of Study: Postdoctorate.

Type: Fellowship.

No. of awards offered: One.

Frequency: As the Fellowship becomes available.

Value: £10,500 per annum, plus free board and lodging.

Length of Study: Two years; renewable for one additional year.

Study Establishment: The College.

Country of Study: UK.

Closing Date: Early February.

Additional Information: The Fellowship is restricted to specific countries in different years.

For further information contact:
St Hilda's College, Oxford, OX4 1DY, England
Tel: 01865 276815
Fax: 01865 276816
Contact: The College Officer's Secretary

St Hilda's College Schoolmistress Fellowships

Subjects: Any subject offered by the University.

Eligibility: Open to schoolmistresses, engaged in sixth form teaching.

Purpose: To enable the Fellow to undertake private study in Oxford.

Type: Fellowship.

No. of awards offered: Two.

Frequency: Annual.

Value: To cover room and board; there is no stipend.

Length of Study: One term up to eleven weeks.

Study Establishment: The College.

Country of Study: UK.

Closing Date: February of the preceding year.

Additional Information: Preference will normally be given to applicants who are not graduates of Oxford University.

For further information contact:
St Hilda's College, Oxford, OX4 1DY, England
Tel: 01865 276815
Fax: 01865 276816
Contact: The College Officer's Secretary

St Hugh's College Graduate Scholarships

Subjects: A wide range of subjects.

Eligibility: Open to British nationals and candidates from overseas.

Purpose: To provide further financial support to graduates already in receipt of funding, at any stage in their course.

Type: Scholarship.

No. of awards offered: Up to 15.

Frequency: Annual.

Value: Varies.

Length of Study: Usually for the fee-paying duration of the course followed.

Study Establishment: The College.

Country of Study: UK.

Closing Date: March 1st.

Additional Information: Scholars are entitled to accommodation in College for up to 2 years at the standard charge.

For further information contact:
St Hugh's College, Oxford, OX2 6LE, England
Tel: 01865 274918
Fax: 01865 274912
Contact: Tutor for Graduates/The College Secretary

St John's College Junior Research Fellowship

Subjects: Any subject offered by the College.

Eligibility: Open to candidates who obtained their first degree not more than 6 years previously.

Level of Study: Postgraduate, Doctorate.

Purpose: To assist research.

Type: Fellowship.

No. of awards offered: Four.

Frequency: Annual.

Value: £12,700 per annum, plus any University fees, plus room and board.

Length of Study: Three years; renewable for one further year.

Study Establishment: St John's College.

Country of Study: UK.

Applications Procedure: Application form.

Closing Date: January.

Additional Information: Junior Research Fellowships are advertised nationally during the autumn of the year preceding appointment. Prospective candidates should contact the College in September/October.

For further information contact:
St John's College, Oxford, OX1 3JP, England
Tel: 01865 277300
Fax: 01865 277435
Email: THORNTON@FYFIELD.sjc.ox.ac.uk
Contact: College Secretary

St John's College North Senior Scholarships

Subjects: Any subject offered by the College.

Eligibility: Open to graduates, not normally over 25 years of age, who are in receipt of a UK graduate award.

Level of Study: Postgraduate.

Purpose: To assist research.

Type: Scholarship.

No. of awards offered: Two.

Frequency: Annual.

Value: Equivalent to a graduate award, plus academic fees and accommodation.

Length of Study: Two years.

Study Establishment: St John's College.

Country of Study: UK.

Applications Procedure: Application form.

Closing Date: Early January.

Additional Information: North Senior Scholarships are advertised nationally at the end of the year preceding appointment. Prospective candidates should contact the College in November/December.

For further information contact:
St John's College, Oxford, OX1 3JP, England
Tel: 01865 277300
Fax: 01865 277435
Email: THORNYON@FYFIELD.sjc.ox.ac.uk
Contact: College Secretary

*Donald Tovey Memorial Prize

Subjects: The philosophy, history or understanding of music.

Eligibility: Open to men or women, without regard to nationality, age or membership of a university.

Purpose: To assist in the furtherance of research or in the publication of work already done.

Type: Prize.

No. of awards offered: One.

Frequency: Infrequently (dependent on funds available).

Value: £1,000.

Closing Date: June (to be announced).

For further information contact:
Board of the Faculty of Music, University Offices, Wellington Square, Oxford, OX1 2JD, England
Tel: 01865 270001
Fax: 01865 270708
Contact: Secretary

or

Faculty of Music, St Aldate's, Oxford, OX1 1DB, England
Contact: Heather Professor of Music

Trinity College Junior Research Fellowship

Subjects: Biological sciences, history, geography, theology and music, law, philosophy, economics, politics, physical sciences, English, classics, modern languages.

Eligibility: Open to suitably qualified candidates having some research experience (e.g., a completed doctoral thesis).

Level of Study: Doctorate, Postdoctorate.

Purpose: To promote and encourage research among those at the start of an academic career.

Type: Fellowship.

No. of awards offered: One.

Frequency: Annual.

Value: Approximately £11,000 per annum.

Length of Study: Three years; not renewable.

Study Establishment: Trinity College.

Country of Study: UK.

Closing Date: Early October of the year preceding the start of the appointment.

For further information contact:
Trinity College, Oxford, OX1 3BH, England
Tel: 01865 279910
Fax: 01865 279911
Contact: The Academic Administrator

Wolfson College Stipendiary Junior Research Fellowships

Subjects: Social anthropology/indology (in rotation); history and/or philosophy of science history and philosophy of mathematics (in rotation); humanities (six fields in rotation); intellectual history (as funds permit).

Eligibility: Open to persons with at least 2 years of research experience who are normally under 30 years of age at commencement of the Fellowship and have not held any other junior research fellowship.

Level of Study: Postgraduate.

Purpose: To facilitate research in six given fields.

No. of awards offered: Four or five.

Frequency: Triennially.

Value: £9,797 per annum and single accommodation in College without charge and Common Table meals (£24.50/week) in Hall.

Length of Study: Three years.

Study Establishment: Wolfson College.

Country of Study: UK.

Applications Procedure: Application form required, CV, details of proposed research, and specimens of written work.

Closing Date: Variable.

Additional Information: Interview in Oxford required.

For further information contact:
Wolfson College, Linton Road, Oxford, OX2 6UD, England
Tel: 01865 274102

Fax: 01865 274125
Email: david.smith@wolfson.ox.ac.uk
Contact: Sue Hales, President's Secretary

UNIVERSITY OF PENNSYLVANIA

School of Arts and Sciences, 16 College Hall, University of
Pennsylvania, Philadelphia, PA, 19109-6378, USA
Tel: 215 898 7156
Fax: 215 898 0821
Email: tcheek@mail.sas.upenn.edu
Contact: Humanities Coordinating Committee c/o Tracey L Cheek,
Program Coordinator

Mellon Postdoctoral Fellowships in the Humanities

Subjects: Humanities; educational curriculum; performing arts, graphic arts.

Eligibility: Open to persons who received the PhD degree at least three years, but not more than eight years, before September 30th of the Fellowship year.

Level of Study: Postgraduate.

Type: Fellowships.

No. of awards offered: Four.

Frequency: Annual.

Value: US$32,000, plus a limited allowance for travel and research.

Length of Study: One academic year and possibly the summer term before or after; not renewable.

Study Establishment: The University of Pennsylvania.

Country of Study: USA.

Closing Date: October 15th.

Additional Information: Fellows may not normally hold other concurrent awards.

THE UNIVERSITY OF QUEENSLAND

Office of Research and Postgraduate Studies, The University of
Queensland, Queensland, 4072, Australia
Tel: 073 365 2033
Fax: 073 365 4455
Contact: Mrs Jill Hillman-Marks, The Scholarships Officer

Postdoctoral Research Fellowship

Subjects: Any subject offered at the Univerity.

Eligibility: Open to candidates of any nationality. An applicant must not have had more than five years' full-time professional experience since the award of a doctoral degree as at 30 June of the year before the Fellowship commences. Fellowships may be offered to applicants who do not hold a doctoral degree provided that evidence is given that a doctoral thesis has been submitted by 30 June (for candidates from Australia, New Zealand or Papua New Guinea) or 1 September (for all other candidates), and that the selection committee is satisfied that the degree will be awarded by 30 June of the Fellowship year.

Type: Fellowship.

No. of awards offered: Approximately six.

Frequency: Annual.

Value: A$35,974-A$40,088 per annum, plus excursion return air fare for the recipient only.

Length of Study: Two years; not normally renewable. In exceptional circumstances, shorter appointments may be considered.

Study Establishment: The University.

Country of Study: Australia.

Applications Procedure: Application forms are available from the heads of the relevant departments or from the Director, Research Services.

Closing Date: February 28th of the year preceding the award.

Postgraduate Research Scholarships

Subjects: Field of study unrestricted.

Eligibility: Open to candidates of any nationality who are acceptable as full-time internal students for a postgraduate research degree at the University. Applicants should hold an Australian first class honours or masters degree, or the equivalent. Candidates must have a sound knowledge of both written and spoken English.

Level of Study: Postgraduate.

Type: Varies.

No. of awards offered: Approximately 56.

Frequency: Annual.

Value: A$14,482.

Length of Study: Two years for the masters degree, and for up to three years for the PhD degree.

Study Establishment: The University.

Country of Study: Australia.

Applications Procedure: International students must apply for the university's International Education Office.

Closing Date: September 31th.

Additional Information: To assist with tuition fee expenses International students may apply for the Overseas Research Scholarships (OPRS) which are administered through tthe International Education Office.

For further information contact:
Office of Research and Postgraduate Studies, The University of
Queensland, Queensland, 4072, Australia
Tel: 073 365 2033
Fax: 073 365 4455
Contact: For Australian citizens and permanent residents, The Scholarships Officer

or

The University of Queensland, International Education Office,
Queensland, 4072, Australia
Tel: 07 3365 1960
Fax: 07 3365 1794
Contact: For International students, The Coordinator

Travel Awards for International Collaborative Research

Subjects: Any subject offered at the University.

Eligibility: Open to any scholar actively engaged in academic work who will be able to contribute substantially to research activity in the department to which he or she is attached at the University of Queensland.

Purpose: To facilitate visits by scholars from institutions in other countries.

Type: Grant.

No. of awards offered: Approximately 10.

Frequency: Annual.

Value: Return economy air fare.

Length of Study: Eight weeks or longer during semester periods in the year of the award.

Study Establishment: The University.

Country of Study: Australia.

Applications Procedure: Application forms are available from the head of the relevant department or from the Director, Research Services, at the University of Queensland.

Closing Date: August 1st of the year preceding the award year.

UNIVERSITY OF READING

University of Reading, Whiteknights, PO Box 219, Reading, RG6 2AW, England
Tel: 01734 318182
Fax: 01734 313856
Email: DAStannard@Reading.ac.uk
Contact: Mr D A Stannard

Otway Cave Scholarship

Subjects: Land management.

Eligibility: Open to candidates who hold a first degree and are, at the time of the award, ordinarily resident in the UK.

Level of Study: Postgraduate.

Purpose: To assist students who would otherwise be unable financially to follow the MSc course in land management.

Type: Scholarship.

No. of awards offered: One or two.

Frequency: Annual.

Value: £1,000 (sometimes more).

Length of Study: One year.

Study Establishment: The University.

Country of Study: UK.

Applications Procedure: Submission of CVs by invitation.

Additional Information: Scholars must intend to remain resident in the UK after the term of the Scholarship has ended. Awarded only to students accepted to study Msc Land Management.

For further information contact:
Faculty of Urban and Regional Studies, University of Reading, Whiteknights, PO Box 219, Reading, RG6 6AU, England
Tel: 01734 318181
Fax: 01734 313856
Contact: N Samman, Sub Dean

or
Department of Land Management and Development, University of Reading, Whiteknights, PO Box 219, Reading, RG6 6AW, England
Tel: 01734 875123 ext.7360
Fax: 01734 313856
Contact: Mr N S French, Course Director

University of Reading Postgraduate Studentships

Subjects: No restriction, subject to availability of appropriate supervision at the University.

Eligibility: Candidates must hold a first degree qualification.

Level of Study: Postgraduate, Doctorate.

Purpose: To enable students to obtain a doctoral degree.

Type: Studentships.

No. of awards offered: Four.

Frequency: Annual.

Value: Composition fee (at home standard rate), plus maintenance award as for Research Council Postgraduate Studentships, plus £1,000.

Length of Study: For a course of directed research, for up to three years.

Country of Study: UK.

Applications Procedure: An application form (available from Mr D A Stannard) should be completed, and a confidential academic reference should also be submitted.

Closing Date: A date to be arranged in March of the year of entry.

Additional Information: At present the Studentships are awarded on the nomination of the Head of Department.

For further information contact:
Faculty of Urban and Regional Studies, The University, Whiteknights, PO Box 219, Reading, RG6 2AW, England
Tel: 01734 318182
Fax: 01734 313856
Email: DAStannard@Reading.ac.uk
Contact: Mr D A Stannard

UNIVERSITY OF REGINA

Faculty of Graduate Studies & Research, University of Regina, Regina, Saskatchewan, S4S OA2, Canada
Tel: 306 585 4161
Fax: 306 585 4893
Email: urgrad@cc.max.uregina.ca
www: http://www.uregina.ca
Contact: Doris Morrow

Regina Graduate Scholarships

Eligibility: Must be accepted by the Graduate Faculty as fully-qualified for admission to Masters or PhD degree program at the University of Regina. Must be registered as full-time student and must not receive any other scholarship(s).

Level of Study: Postgraduate, Doctorate.

Purpose: These scholarships are awarded to students of high academic standing who wish to work full-time on program requirements.

Type: Scholarship.

No. of awards offered: Approximately 120 annually.

Frequency: Three times a year.

Value: Masters level: C$3,000 per semester, Doctoral level: C$3,600 per semester.

Country of Study: Canada.

Applications Procedure: Application forms are available from the Faculty of Graduate Studies and Research.

Closing Date: March 1st, June 15th, October 15th.

For further information contact:
Faculty of Graduate Studies & Research, University of Regina, Regina, Saskatchewan, S4S OA2, Canada
Tel: 306 585 4161
Fax: 306 585 4893
Email: urgrad@cc.max.uregina.ca
www: http://wwwuregina.ca
Contact: Doris Morrow

Regina Teaching Assistantships

Eligibility: Candidates must meet appropriate qualifications to participate in the instructional program in the assigned academic unit. Must be accepted by the Graduate Faculty at the University of Regina as fully qualified for admission to masters or PhD degree.

Level of Study: Postgraduate, Doctorate.

Purpose: Teaching assistants to assist with the instructional program of undergraduate courses or laboratories.

Type: Assistantship.

No. of awards offered: Approximately 88 annually.

Frequency: Two times a year.

Value: Masters level: C$3,518 per semester, Doctoral level C$4,020 per semester.

Country of Study: Canada.

Closing Date: March 1st, October 15th.

UNIVERSITY OF ROCHESTER

Eastman School of Music, University of Rochester, 26 Gibbs Street,
Rochester, NY, 14604, USA
Tel: 716 274 1060
Contact: Director of Admissions

Eastman School of Music Graduate Awards

Subjects: Music.

Eligibility: Open to nationals of all countries. Candidates should have the qualifications necessary for admission to the Eastman School of Music. Non-US citizens are usually offered service scholarships in ensemble work at the graduate level.

Level of Study: Postgraduate.

Purpose: To support the School's academic programs.

No. of awards offered: Approximately 200.

Frequency: Annual.

Value: Up to US$23,450.

Length of Study: One academic year; renewable.

Study Establishment: At the School.

Country of Study: USA.

Closing Date: January 15th.

UNIVERSITY OF ST ANDREWS

University of St Andrews, St Salvators College, Development Office,
North Street, St Andrews, Fife, KY16 9AL, Scotland
Tel: 01334 462 111
Fax: 01334 462 030
Email: gwd@ st-andrews.ac.uk
www: http://www.st-and.ac.uk/
Contact: Secretary to the Special Lectureships Committee

Gifford Research Fellowship

Subjects: Philosophy or natural theology.

Eligibility: Open to suitably qualified candidates having a doctorate in a relevant subject.

Level of Study: Postdoctorate.

Type: Fellowship.

No. of awards offered: One.

Frequency: Every one or two years.

Value: £14,317-£16,628.

Length of Study: One year; may be renewable for one further year.

Study Establishment: University of St Andrews.

Country of Study: UK.

Applications Procedure: Curriculum Vitae, outline of proposed research-as advertised in the press.

Closing Date: January/February for appointment the following academic year.

Additional Information: When applications are required adverts usually appear in The Times, Church Times and The Tablet.

UNIVERSITY OF SHEFFIELD

University of Sheffield, 85 Wilkinson Street, Sheffield, S10 2GJ,
England
Tel: 0114 282 6086
Fax: 0114 279 5227
Contact: Graduate Office

Hossein Farmy Scholarships

Subjects: Mining, which expression shall include the geological, engineering, scientific and technological aspects of mining, and the archaeological, economic, historical, legal and social aspects of mining and the mining industry.

Eligibility: Open to persons born in the UK. Candidates must hold a good honours degree from a recognized institution.

Level of Study: Postgraduate.

Purpose: To pursue a higher degree by research.

Type: Scholarship.

No. of awards offered: Four.

Frequency: Annual.

Value: Fees and maintenance at Research Council rates.

Length of Study: Up to 3 years.

Study Establishment: One of the departments of the University of Sheffield.

Country of Study: UK.

Closing Date: March 31st.

UNIVERSITY OF SOUTHAMPTON

University of Southampton, Highfield, Southampton, SO9 5NH,
England
Tel: 01703 593623
Fax: 01703 593037
Contact: Academic Registrar

*Studentships

Subjects: All subjects offered by the University.

Eligibility: Open to candidates who hold a good honours first degree and are eligible for admission to the department in which they intend to study.

Purpose: To support postgraduate research study.

No. of awards offered: Varies.

Frequency: Annual.

Value: Based on Research Council Studentship rates.

Length of Study: The duration of the course of study and research.

Study Establishment: The University.

Country of Study: UK.

Applications Procedure: Initial enquiries to head of academic department in which research is to be undertaken.

Closing Date: Varies; enquiries should be made by January for the following October.

UNIVERSITY OF STIRLING

University of Stirling, Stirling, FK9 4LA, Scotland
Tel: 01786 407041
Fax: 01786 466699
Email: GEMI@STIRLING.AC.UK
Contact: Assistant Secretary

Research Studentships

Subjects: All subjects which are available for research at the University of Stirling.

Eligibility: Open to candidates who hold a good honours degree or equivalent and are eligible for fees at the home student rate.

Level of Study: Postgraduate, Doctorate.

Purpose: To assist full-time research leading towards a master's by research or the PhD degree.

Type: Scholarship.

No. of awards offered: Six.

Frequency: Annual.

Value: Standard Research Council maintenance allowance and tuition fees.

Length of Study: Up to three years.

Study Establishment: The University of Stirling.

Country of Study: UK.

Closing Date: March 31st.

UNIVERSITY OF SUSSEX/ASSOCIATION OF COMMONWEALTH UNIVERSITIES

International Office, Sussex House, Falmer, Brighton, East Sussex, BN1 9RH, England
Tel: 01273 678422
Fax: 01273 678545
Email: International.off@sussex.ac.uk
Contact: Dr Philip Baker

Overseas Development Administration Shared Scholarship Scheme

Subjects: Social and behavioural sciences, science and technology, policy studies.

Eligibility: Candidates must be below the age of 35, have sufficient fluency in English, not have studied in the UK before, be a national of a developing Commonwealth country, not be living in a developed country and not be employed by a government department.

Level of Study: Postgraduate.

Purpose: To help students in developing Commonwealth countries who, though of high academic calibre, would not be eligible for awards to study in the UK under existing British Government schemes, and would themselves not be able to afford to pay for the cost themselves.

Type: Scholarship.

No. of awards offered: 2.

Frequency: Annual.

Value: Fees and maintenance grant.

Length of Study: One year.

Study Establishment: Sussex University.

Country of Study: UK.

Applications Procedure: Application form is required to be completed and submitted with academic transcripts and references.

Closing Date: Usually mid-March.

Additional Information: Only applicants from targeted countries are eligible to apply and this information is usually known in the January preceding the start of the academic year; targeted countries are decided annually. Successful applicants must agree to return to their home country on completion of studies.

Sasakawa Scholarship

Subjects: Social and behavioural science, science and technology, policy studies.

Eligibility: Applications are usually accepted from students from UK, China, Vietnam, Eastern Europe, and former Soviet Republics.

Level of Study: Postgraduate.

Purpose: To educate graduate students with high potential for future leadership in international life as well as in private endeavour.

Type: Scholarship.

No. of awards offered: Six.

Frequency: Annual.

Value: Fees and maintenance award.

Length of Study: One year.

Study Establishment: Sussex University.

Country of Study: UK.

Applications Procedure: Application form is required to be submitted with transcripts and academic references.

THE UNIVERSITY OF SYDNEY

The Research and Scholarships Office, Main Quadrangle A14, Sydney, NSW, 2006, Australia
Tel: 02 351 3250
Fax: 02 351 3256
Email: scholars@reschols.usyd.edu.au

Australian Postgraduate Award

Subjects: All areas.

Eligibility: Open to Australian citizens & permanent residents (resident in Australia continuously for 12 months).

Level of Study: Postgraduate, Doctorate.

No. of awards offered: 200.

Frequency: Annual.

Value: Stipend is A$15,364.

Length of Study: Two to three years.

Study Establishment: University of Sydney.

Country of Study: Australia.

Applications Procedure: Forms are available from the scholarships office.

Closing Date: October 31st.

Overseas Postgraduate Research Award

Subjects: All areas.

Eligibility: Unrestricted.

Level of Study: Postgraduate, Doctorate.

Purpose: To pay tuition for overseas students, possibly awarded in conjunction with a UPA for overseas students.

Value: Varies, covers tuition fees.

Country of Study: Australia.

Applications Procedure: Application forms from the International Office.

Additional Information: The UPA Stipend is for A$12,000 for overseas nationals.

For further information contact:
The University of Sydney, The International Office, Margeret Telfer Building KO7, Sydney, NSW, 2006, Australia
Tel: 02 351 4161
Fax: 02 351 4013

University Postgraduate Award (UPA)

Subjects: All areas.

Eligibility: Open to Australian citizens and permanent residents.

Level of Study: Postgraduate, Doctorate.

Frequency: Annual.

Value: Stipend is A$15,364 per annum.

Length of Study: Two to three years.

Study Establishment: University of Sydney.

Country of Study: Australia.

Applications Procedure: Forms are available from the scholarships office.

Closing Date: October 31st.

UNIVERSITY OF TASMANIA

University of Tasmania, GPO Box 252C, Hobart, Tasmania, 7001, Australia
Tel: 002 202766
Fax: 002 202765
Contact: Office for Research

*Merle Weaver Postgraduate Scholarship

Subjects: Any subject.

Eligibility: Open to women graduates from South East Asia and the Pacific region.

Purpose: To fund research leading to a higher degree.

Type: Scholarship.

No. of awards offered: One.

Frequency: As funding permits.

Value: A$14,500 per annum.

Length of Study: Up to three years.

Study Establishment: The University of Tasmania.

Country of Study: Australia.

Closing Date: October 31st.

Additional Information: Unlikely to be availabe before 1998.

UNIVERSITY OF TORONTO

Admissions and Awards, 315 Bloor Street West, Toronto, Ontario, M5S 1A3, Canada

Taylor Statten Memorial Fund

Subjects: Any professional field or career related to youth services.

Eligibility: Open to graduates of a Canadian university who are under 25 years of age. Candidates should have high academic standing with previous experience in the youth field.

Level of Study: Postgraduate.

Purpose: To assist Post-baccalaureate study in any professional field or career related to youth services, such as but not restricted to, physical and health education, psychology, teaching, the ministry and social work.

Type: Fellowship.

No. of awards offered: One.

Frequency: Annual.

Value: Approximately C$1,800 per annum.

Length of Study: One year.

Study Establishment: Any appropriate university.

Country of Study: Canada.

Closing Date: 28 February.

THE UNIVERSITY OF WAIKATO

The University of Waikato, Te Whare Wananga o Waikato, Private Bag 3105, Hamilton, Waikato, New Zealand
Tel: 07 856 0135

Fax: 07 856 2889
Contact: Jeanette Dyer, Graduation & Scholarship Administrator

TW Adams Scholarship in Forestry

Subjects: Forestry, Agriculture, Engineering and Science.

Eligibility: Open to nationals of New Zealand.

Level of Study: Postgraduate.

Purpose: Postgraduate Studies at the School of Forestry.

Type: Scholarship.

Frequency: Annual.

Value: NZ$2,652 for MForSc - NZ$5,304 for two years for PhD.

Study Establishment: University of Canterbury.

Country of Study: New Zealand.

Applications Procedure: Write for Application.

Closing Date: November 1st.

For further information contact:
The University of Waikato, University of Canterbury, Private Bag, Christchurch, New Zealand
Contact: The Scholarships Officer

Advanced School of Planning Science, Rome - Bursary

Subjects: Administration, political, sociological, urban, ecological, geographic and systems sciences.

Eligibility: Applicants must hold a Bachelors degree.

Level of Study: Postgraduate.

Purpose: Offers Bursaries to undertake the Individual Study Programme in Planning Science.

Type: Bursary.

Frequency: Annual.

Value: NZ$35,000 includes programme and attendance fees and is subject to tax.

Study Establishment: The Centre for Economic Studies and Planning-Rome.

Country of Study: Italy.

Applications Procedure: Write for application form.

Closing Date: October 31st.

For further information contact:
The University of Waikato, Segretaria della Scuola, CO Centro di Studiepiani Economici, Via Federico Gassitto 110,00131, Roma, 110,00131, Italy
Tel: 06 713 54200
Fax: 06 713 54200

AGC Young Achievers Award

Subjects: Academic, Arts, Enterprise, Sport.

Level of Study: Professional development.

Purpose: The grants are awarded to support projects, either in New Zealand or overseas, that will take place between September in the year of the award and December in the following year.

Frequency: Annual.

Value: Varies.

Applications Procedure: Write for application form.

Closing Date: July 8th.

For further information contact:
The University of Waikato, AGC young Achievers Award, PO Box 7130, Wellesley Street, Auckland, 1000, New Zealand
Tel: 09 377 3615

Agricultural & Marketing Research and Development Trust (AGMARDT)

Level of Study: Professional development.

Purpose: To support research leading to the development of greater efficiency in agricultural, pastoral and horticultural industries (new products, marketing strategies, etc.).

Type: Research Grant.

Frequency: Annual.

Country of Study: New Zealand.

Applications Procedure: Further information and application forms are available from the Fees and Allowances Office.

Closing Date: May 20th.

For further information contact:
The University of Waikato, AGMARDT, PO Box 6941, Auckland, 1000, New Zealand

ALAC Research Project Grants

Subjects: Alcohol related research, health education and social policies.

Level of Study: Unrestricted.

Purpose: For alcohol related research which could have practical application in designing more effective social and legislative control policies; health education and promotion treatment.

Type: Research Grant.

Frequency: Annual.

Study Establishment: University of Waikato.

Country of Study: New Zealand.

Applications Procedure: Write for application form.

Closing Date: March 1st, September 1st.

Additional Information: Travel grants available, no fixed closing dates. Postgraduate scholarships are also available - closing date November 1st.

For further information contact:
(The University of Waikato), Alcoholic Liquor Advisory Council, PO Box 5023, Wellington, New Zealand
Contact: Research Advisor

Alberta Research Council (Karl A Clark) Memorial Scholarship

Eligibility: Must be a student in a graduate degree engaged in thesis research at masters or doctoral level.

Level of Study: Postgraduate, Doctorate.

Purpose: Awarded to a student in a graduate degree engaged in thesis research at masters or doctorate level in engineering, economics or business, especially related to energy resources and their utilisation, geological soil, water resources, chemical and biological processing, transportation and industrial development, technical and economic evaluations.

Type: Scholarship.

Frequency: Annual.

Value: C$15,000 (Masters) C$16,700 (Doctoral).

Country of Study: Canada.

Applications Procedure: Nominated by department in which student intends to study.

Closing Date: February 1st.

For further information contact:
(The University of Waikato), Faculty of Graduate Studies and Research, 2-8 University Hall, Edmonton, Alberta, T6G 2J9, Canada

Aorere Scholarship

Subjects: No restriction.

Eligibility: Must be New Zealand Maori.

Level of Study: Postgraduate.

Purpose: The Scholarships are open to Maori students who are completing their final year of a postgraduate, honours, or a conjoint degree.

Type: Scholarship.

Frequency: Annual.

Value: NZ$4,000.

Study Establishment: University of Waikato.

Country of Study: New Zealand.

Applications Procedure: Write for application form.

Closing Date: March 31st.

For further information contact:
(The University of Waikato), Personnel Division, Ministry of Foreign Affairs and Trade, Private Bag, Wellington, New Zealand
Tel: 04 472 8877
Contact: Aorere Scholarships Officer

Association of Rhodes Scholars in Australia

Eligibility: Open to nationals of Commonwealth countries.

Level of Study: Postgraduate.

Purpose: The Association has established a scholarship fund for the purpose of bringing a Commonwealth student to Australia for postgraduate study.

Type: Stipend, Scholarship.

Frequency: Annual.

Value: A$15,000.

Length of Study: Two years.

Study Establishment: University of Melbourne.

Country of Study: Australia.

Applications Procedure: Write for application.

Closing Date: December 15th.

For further information contact:
(The University of Waikato), Association of Rhodes Scholars in Australia, Office for Research, University of Melbourne, Parkville, Victoria, 3052, Australia
Contact: The Secretary

Australian Federation Of University Women

Subjects: Arts, science, law, medicine, dentistry, home science, commerce, theology, physical education.

Eligibility: Open to nationals of New Zealand.

Level of Study: Postgraduate.

Purpose: Open to women graduates or final year honour students, who wish to carry out some short project, in any field, that would benefit from a short stay in Canberra. Preference may be given to to applicants who are members of the International Federation of University Women.

Type: Free board and lodging for up to four weeks preferably during summer vacation at Ursula College, Grant.

Frequency: Annual.

Length of Study: Four weeks.

Study Establishment: Australian National University, Canberra.

Country of Study: Australia.

Applications Procedure: Write for application form.

Closing Date: September 15th.

For further information contact:
(The University of Waikato), Australian Federation Of University Women-ACT Inc, GPO Box 520, Canberra, ACT, 2601, Australia
Contact: Fellowship Convener

Australian National University - Kodak Research Scholarship

Eligibility: Candidates must hold, or have applied for an Australian Commonwealth Scholarship or an ANU PhD Scholarship.

Level of Study: Doctorate.

Purpose: The Kodak Research Scholarship in Chemistry at ANU is a supplementary scholarship for PhD Study.

Type: Scholarship.

Frequency: Annual.

Value: A$5,000 p.a.

Study Establishment: Australian National University.

Country of Study: Australia.

Applications Procedure: Write for application form.

Closing Date: Otober 31st.

For further information contact:
(The University of Waikato), Australian National University , Kodak Research Scholarship, GPO Box 4, Canberra, ACT, 2601, Australia
Contact: Dean Research Scholarship

Australian National University - PhD Research Scholarship

Subjects: Scholarships available for PhD research in fields of Organic and Biological, Inorganic Chemistry, and Physical and Theoretical Chemistry.

Eligibility: Applicants should hold a Bachelors with honours degree.

Level of Study: Doctorate.

Type: Scholarship.

Frequency: Every two years.

Value: A$14,260 p.a. (tax free) airfares and a grant towards removal expenses.

Length of Study: Three years.

Study Establishment: Australian National University.

Country of Study: Australia.

Applications Procedure: Write for application form.

Closing Date: January 31st, September 30th.

For further information contact:
(The University of Waikato), Australian National University, GPO Box 4, Canberra, ACT, 2601, Australia
Contact: Professor L N Mander, Dean, Research Scholarship of Chemistry

Australian National University Research Scholarship in Astronomy

Subjects: Astronomy.

Eligibility: Applicants must have an MSc of at least second class division one standard in the fields of Mathematics and Physics.

Level of Study: Doctorate.

Type: Scholarship.

Frequency: Annual.

Length of Study: Four years.

Study Establishment: Mt Stromlo and Siding Springs Observatories.

Country of Study: Australia.

Applications Procedure: Write for application form.

Closing Date: None Specified.

For further information contact:
(The University of Waikato), Graduate Studies Section, Australian National University , GPO Box 4, Canberra, ACT, 2601, Australia
Contact: The Registrar

Austrian Federal Ministry Scholarship

Eligibility: Knowledge of German required.

Level of Study: Postgraduate.

Purpose: Applications are invited for Austrian Federal Ministry Scholarships, and also for Guest Researcher Scholarships. A knowledge of German is required for those wishing to enrol at an Austrian University.

Type: Scholarship.

Frequency: Annual.

Country of Study: Austria.

Applications Procedure: Write for application form.

Closing Date: April 15th.

For further information contact:
(The University of Waikato), Austrian Embassy, Canberra, ACT, 2601, Australia

Bank of New Zealand Graduate Scholarship

Eligibility: Applicants must be graduates of a New Zealand university and be New Zealand citizens or hold permanent resident status.

Level of Study: Postgraduate.

Purpose: Study of social, economic, or cultural value to New Zealand.

Type: Scholarship.

No. of awards offered: Four.

Frequency: Annual.

Length of Study: Up to three years.

Study Establishment: University of Waikato.

Country of Study: New Zealand.

Applications Procedure: Write for application forms.

Closing Date: October 1st.

Additional Information: Up to three scholarships awarded for masters study. Tenure up to two years. One or more awards for study in an area different to the subject of the applicant's first degree. Tenure up to three years.

For further information contact:
The University of Waikato, Fees and Allowances Office, Private Bag 3105, Hamilton, Waikato, New Zealand
Tel: 07 856 2889
Fax: 07 856 0135

Bank of New Zealand Research Fellowship

Subjects: Topics relating to the banking industry.

Purpose: To assist specific research projects which may, but need not necessarily be, part of the requirements for a degree.

Type: Fellowship.

Frequency: Annual.

Value: Maximum of NZ$4,000.

Study Establishment: University of Waikato.

Country of Study: New Zealand.

Applications Procedure: Write for application form.

Closing Date: December 1st.

For further information contact:
(The University of Waikato), Sponsorships Marketing and Product Development, Bank of New Zealand, PO Box 2392, Wellington, New Zealand

Contact: Product Manager

Bank of Thailand Scholarship

Subjects: New Zealand Economics.

Eligibility: Applicants must be Thai citizens and under the age of 25 as of January 1st.

Level of Study: Postgraduate, Doctorate.

Type: Scholarship.

Frequency: Annual.

Study Establishment: University of Waikato.

Country of Study: New Zealand.

Applications Procedure: Write for application form.

Closing Date: March 10th.

Additional Information: The scholarships are tenable for masters or PhD study in New Zealand economics. The awardees will be employed by the Bank of Thailand after their graduation.

For further information contact:
(The University of Waikato), Training and Development, Bank of Thailand, Bangkok, 10500, Thailand
Contact: The Director

Bings Scholarship

Subjects: Medicine, Veterinary Science, Agriculture, Psychology, Psychiatry, or Theology.

Eligibility: Open to students enrolled full-time in the thesis year of a masters degree.

Level of Study: Postgraduate.

Purpose: Tenable for one year to students enrolled full-time in the thesis year of a masters degree.

Type: Scholarship.

Frequency: Annual.

Value: NZ$2,000.

Study Establishment: University of Waikato.

Country of Study: New Zealand.

Applications Procedure: Write for application forms.

For further information contact:
The University of Waikato, Fees and Allowances Office, School of Education, Private Bag 3105, Hamilton, Waikato, New Zealand
Tel: 07 856 2889
Fax: 07 856 0135

E J Brenan Memorial Trust

Purpose: To support research in New Zealand and overseas.

Type: Grant.

Frequency: Annual.

Applications Procedure: Write for information.

Closing Date: July 30th.

For further information contact:
The University of Waikato, E J Brenan Memorial Trust, c/o New Zealand Road Transport Association Inc., PO Box 1778, Wellington, New Zealand

British Telecom Cambridge Scholarship

Eligibility: Preference may be given to candidates applying for one year taught postgraduate courses. Preference given to those under 26.

Level of Study: Postgraduate.

Purpose: In collaboration with British Telecom, these scholarships are offered for study at the University of Cambridge.

Type: Scholarship.

Frequency: Annual.

Value: Maintenance allowance for a single student, contribution to return air fare. Covers University Composition Fee and approved college fees.

Length of Study: Up to three years.

Study Establishment: University of Cambridge.

Country of Study: United Kingdom.

Applications Procedure: Write for application form.

Closing Date: November 30th.

For further information contact:
(The University of Waikato), Cambridge Commonwealth Trust/Cambridge Overseas Trust, PO Box 252, Cambridge, CB2 1TZ, England

Bursaries for Maori to study Postgraduate Clinical Psychology

Subjects: Clinical Psychology.

Eligibility: Open to Maoris only.

Level of Study: Postgraduate.

Purpose: Offers bursaries to support Maori who are undertaking a postgraduate clinical psychology course at any New Zealand university.

Type: Bursary.

Frequency: Annual.

Study Establishment: Any New Zealand university.

Country of Study: New Zealand.

Applications Procedure: Write for application form.

Closing Date: November 20th.

For further information contact:
(The University of Waikato), Psychological Services, Department of Justice, Private Box 180, Wellington, New Zealand
Contact: Director

Cambridge Commonwealth Trust - Prince of Wales Scholarship

Subjects: Non-specific.

Eligibility: Applicants are required to be of high academic ability. Usually reserved for PhD candidates.

Level of Study: Doctorate.

Type: Scholarship.

Frequency: Annual.

Value: £4,908.

Length of Study: Tenure for up to three years.

Study Establishment: University of Cambridge.

Country of Study: United Kingdom.

Applications Procedure: Write for application form.

Closing Date: October 1st.

For further information contact:
(The University of Waikato), Cambridge Commonwealth Trust, Prince of Wales Scholarship, Fees and Allowances Office, School of Education, Private Bag 3105, Hamilton, Waikato, New Zealand
Tel: 07 856 2889
Fax: 07 856 0135

Canterbury Frozen Meat Company Postgraduate Scholarship in Business Administration

Eligibility: Open to NZ nationals.

Level of Study: Postgraduate.

Purpose: Open to graduates pursuing postgraduate studies in business administration.

Type: Scholarship.

Frequency: Annual.

Value: NZ$2,000 p.a for one year for full-time students; NZ$1,000 for four years for part-time students.

Length of Study: Up to four years.

Study Establishment: Canterbury University.

Country of Study: New Zealand.

Applications Procedure: Write for application forms.

Closing Date: November 1st.

For further information contact:
(The University of Waikato), Canterbury University, Private Bag, Christchurch, New Zealand
Contact: Scholarships Officer

Chartered Institute of Transport in New Zealand Scholarship & BP Travel Award

Subjects: New Zealand Transport.

Eligibility: Applicants must be under 40.

Purpose: Assists any person working on a research project related to transport in New Zealand.

Type: Scholarship.

Frequency: Annual.

Value: Up to NZ$8,000 for 12 months. In addition the BP Travel Award may be given for travel expenses to a maximum of NZ$6,000 where the research involves international travel.

Country of Study: New Zealand.

Applications Procedure: Write for application forms.

Closing Date: September 30th.

For further information contact:
(The University of Waikato), Chartered Institute of Transport in New Zealand, PO Box 13-635, Christchurch, New Zealand
Tel: 03 365 4920

Commonwealth Scholarship - Australia

Subjects: Non-specific.

Eligibility: Must be between 22-30 years of age. For graduates of any New Zealand university who have completed four years of university study.

Level of Study: Postgraduate.

Type: Scholarship.

Frequency: Annual.

Length of Study: Two to four years.

Country of Study: Australia.

Applications Procedure: Write for application form.

Closing Date: June 1st.

For further information contact:
The University of Waikato, Private Bag 3105, Hamilton, Waikato, New Zealand
Tel: 07 856 2889
Fax: 07 856 0135

Commonwealth Scholarship/Fellowship - Trinidad & Tobago

Level of Study: Postgraduate.

Type: Scholarship.

Frequency: Annual.

Value: Various rates and allowances.

Length of Study: Two to four years.

Study Establishment: University of the West Indies, St Augustine.

Country of Study: Trinidad & Tobago.

Applications Procedure: Write for application form.

Closing Date: October 1st.

For further information contact:
The University of Waikato, Fees and Allowances Office, School of Education, Private Bag 3105, Hamilton, Waikato, New Zealand
Tel: 07 856 2889
Fax: 07 856 0135

Commonwealth Scholarship/Fellowship Canada

Level of Study: Postgraduate.

Type: Scholarship.

Frequency: Annual.

Value: The Scholarship covers all expenses of travel, living and study.

Length of Study: Tenure normally for two years.

Study Establishment: At both English and French speaking universities in Canada.

Country of Study: Canada.

Applications Procedure: Write for application forms.

Closing Date: October 1st.

For further information contact:
The University of Waikato, Fees and Allowances Office, School of Education, Private Bag 3105, Hamilton, Waikato, New Zealand
Tel: 07 856 2889
Fax: 07 856 0135

Commonwealth Scholarship/Fellowship - Hong Kong

Eligibility: Must be under 35 years of age.

Level of Study: Postgraduate.

Type: Scholarship.

Frequency: Annual.

Value: Various rates and allowances.

Length of Study: Two to four years.

Applications Procedure: Write for application form.

Closing Date: October 1st.

For further information contact:
The University of Waikato, Fees and Allowances Office, School of Education, Private Bag 3105, Hamilton, Waikato, New Zealand
Tel: 07 856 2889
Fax: 07 856 0135

Commonwealth Scholarship - India

Level of Study: Postgraduate.

Purpose: These awards are normally offered for postgraduate study in India and are not offered every year. The terms vary from time to time.

Type: Scholarship.

Country of Study: India.

Closing Date: March.

Additional Information: Write for information.

For further information contact:
The University of Waikato, Fees and Allowances Office, Private Bag 3105, Hamilton, Waikato, New Zealand
Tel: 07 856 2889
Fax: 07 856 0135

Commonwealth Scholarship - Nigeria

Level of Study: Postgraduate.

Type: Scholarship.

Frequency: Annual.

Value: Various rates and allowances.

Length of Study: Two to four years.

Country of Study: Nigeria.

Applications Procedure: Write for application form.

Closing Date: October 1st.

For further information contact:
The University of Waikato, Fees and Allowances Office , School of Education, Private Bag 3105, Hamilton, Waikato, New Zealand
Tel: 07 856 2889
Fax: 07 856 0135

Commonwealth Scholarship - United Kingdom

Subjects: Non specific.

Eligibility: The scholarships are normally for PhD study and applicants must have at least a first class honours degree. Age limit is 35, some flexibility.

Level of Study: Doctorate.

Purpose: For graduates of any New Zealand University for tenure at a university within the United Kingdom.

Type: Scholarship.

Frequency: Annual.

Value: Varies.

Country of Study: United Kingdom.

Applications Procedure: Write for application form.

Closing Date: October 1st.

For further information contact:
The University of Waikato, Fees and Allowances Office, School of Education, Private Bag 3105, Hamilton, Waikato, New Zealand
Tel: 07 856 2889
Fax: 07 856 0135

Country Calendar Scholarship

Subjects: Rural studies.

Eligibility: Open to New Zealand citizens who are undertaking Masters degree study.

Level of Study: Postgraduate.

Purpose: Open to any student in any subject who is engaged in innovative research into the rural sector.

Type: Scholarship.

Frequency: Annual.

Value: NZ$7,500 per year.

Length of Study: Two years.

Study Establishment: University of Waikato.

Country of Study: New Zealand.

Applications Procedure: Write for application form.

Closing Date: October 1st.

For further information contact:
The University of Waikato, Fees and Allowances Office, Private Bag 3105, Hamilton, Waikato, New Zealand
Tel: 07 856 2889
Fax: 07 856 0135

DAAD Scholarship for Study in Germany

Subjects: German, fine arts and music.

Eligibility: Applicants must have been studying in New Zealand within the last two years. German knowledge required, must not be more than 32 years of age.

Level of Study: Postgraduate.

Purpose: Study in Germany from April 1st to March 31st.

Type: Scholarship.

Frequency: Annual.

Value: A monthly allowance, exemption from enrolment and tuition fees, return airfares, book allowance and a payment towards initial expenses.

Length of Study: One year.

Country of Study: Germany.

Applications Procedure: Write for application form.

Closing Date: June 1st & September 1st.

For further information contact:
The University of Waikato, Fees And Allowances Office, School of Education, Private Bag 3105, Hamilton, Waikato, New Zealand
Tel: 07 856 2889
Fax: 07 856 0135

DAAD Short Term Grants - PhD and Junior Scientists

Subjects: Science, German.

Level of Study: Doctorate.

Purpose: A scheme of study grants which will provide for PhD candidates and junior scientists to spend up to six months in Germany to collect material for their dissertation or to undertake a short-term education course or research visit.

Type: Short-term Grant, Research Grant.

Frequency: Annual.

Value: A monthly payment of DM1,490 and a travel grant of DM2,000.

Length of Study: Up to six months.

Country of Study: Germany.

Applications Procedure: Write for application form.

Closing Date: August 15th/December 15th.

Additional Information: Embassy of The Federal Republic of Germany, PO Box 1214, Wellington, New Zealand.

For further information contact:
The University of Waikato, Fees And Allowances Office, Private Bag 3105, Hamilton, Waikato, New Zealand
Tel: 07 856 2889
Fax: 07 856 0135

Earthquake and War Damage Commission - Research Grant

Purpose: To support research in the fields of seismic and geotechnical engineering.

Type: Research Grant.

Frequency: Annual.

Study Establishment: University of Waikato.

Country of Study: New Zealand.

Applications Procedure: Write for information.

Closing Date: October 31st.

For further information contact:
The University of Waikato, Research Committee, Earthquake and War Damage Commission, PO Box 31-342, Lower Hutt, Wellington, New Zealand
Tel: 04 699 771

Earthwatch - Private Grants for Field Research

Eligibility: Postdoctoral scholars are invited to apply; research teams must include qualified volunteers from Earthwatch.

Level of Study: Postdoctorate.

Purpose: Earthwatch Centre for Field Research considers applications for funding of any field research in the humanities or sciences which needs volunteer assistance and funds.

Type: Research Grant.

Frequency: Annual.

Value: Grants range form NZ$5,000 to NZ$85,000.

Country of Study: New Zealand.

Applications Procedure: Preliminary application forms are available from the Fees and Allowances Office, School of Education.

Closing Date: No fixed date.

For further information contact:
The University of Waikato, Earthwatch, 39 Lower Fort Street, Sydney, NSW, 2000, Australia
Tel: 02 251 2928

Fanny Evans Postgraduate Scholarship for Women

Eligibility: Women only.

Level of Study: Doctorate, Postgraduate.

Purpose: To encourage postgraduate study and research in disciplines in which women are under-represented.

Type: Scholarship.

Frequency: Annual.

Value: Covers tuition fees plus an annual emolument (currently NZ$10,200 for a PhD student or NZ$6,390 for a masters student).

Length of Study: Three years.

Study Establishment: University of Otago.

Country of Study: New Zealand.

Applications Procedure: Write for application form.

Closing Date: October 1st.

Additional Information: In exceptional circumstances a Scholarship may be awarded to a masters candidate.

For further information contact:
The University of Waikato, c/o The University of Otago, PO Box 56, Dunedin, New Zealand
Contact: The Registrar

Family Violence Prevention Committee Grant

Level of Study: Postgraduate.

Purpose: To encourage research into aspects of family violence.

Type: Research Grant.

Frequency: Annual.

Study Establishment: University of Waikato.

Country of Study: New Zealand.

Applications Procedure: Application forms are available form the Fees and Allowances Office, School of Education.

Closing Date: March 9th.

For further information contact:
The University of Waikato, Family Violence Prevention Committee, PO Box 9732, Te Aro, Wellington, New Zealand
Contact: The Administration Officer

Fleming Conservation Scholarship

Eligibility: Open to nationals of New Zealand.

Level of Study: Postgraduate.

Purpose: Previously called the Queen Elizabeth II Scholarship, this award provides funds for postgraduate research on plants, animals and relevant topics falling within the objectives of the Society.

Type: Scholarship.

Frequency: Annual.

Value: NZ$7,000.

Country of Study: New Zealand.

Applications Procedure: Applicants are required to provide an outline of the planned project.

Closing Date: October 1st.

For further information contact:
(The University of Waikato), Royal Forest and Bird Protection Society, PO Box 631, Wellington, New Zealand

Foundation for Research, Science and Technology-Research Grant

Eligibility: Projects are assessed according to scientific merit, need and feasibility.

Purpose: To increase the knowledge and understanding of New Zealand society and people.

Type: Research Grant.

Frequency: Annual.

Country of Study: New Zealand.

Applications Procedure: Write for information.

Closing Date: December 15th.

Additional Information: Application for research grants that involve relevant research to New Zealand will be considered. Preference will be given to research likely to make an important new contribution to the knowledge or understanding of New Zealand society and people.

For further information contact:
(The University of Waikato), Foundation For Research, Science and Technology, PO Box 12-240, Thorndon, Wellington, New Zealand
Tel: 04 499 2559
Contact: The Programme Manager

Foundation for Research, Science and Technology-Social Science Research Grant

Subjects: New Zealand history, society, culture and Te Aro Maori. Social and personal development, relationships and well being. Political, economic and international relationships. Knowledge, education and training.

Eligibility: Grants are based on the full costs of undertaking the research and disseminating the results.

Purpose: Funding for programmes carried out by a senior social scientist working with a group of researchers over a number of years and projects undertaken by one researcher over 1-2 years.

Type: Research Grant.

Frequency: Annual.

Country of Study: New Zealand.

Applications Procedure: Write for information.

Closing Date: January 31st.

For further information contact:
The University of Waikato, Foundation for Research, Science and Technology, PO Box 12-240, Thorndon, Wellington, New Zealand
Tel: 04 499 2559
Contact: The Programme Manager

Freyberg Scholarship

Subjects: National Security; Strategic Studies.

Level of Study: Postgraduate.

Purpose: Applications invited for two postgraduate scholarships tenable on the Graduate Programme in Strategic Studies at the Australian National University, Canberra.

Type: Scholarship.

No. of awards offered: Two.

Frequency: Annual.

Value: NZ$25,000 for Masters candidates - NZ$21,000 for the Graduate Diploma Course.

Length of Study: 12 months for Masters and 10 months for Graduate Diploma course.

Study Establishment: Australian National University, Canberra.

Country of Study: Australia.

Applications Procedure: Write for information.

Closing Date: September 1st.

For further information contact:
The University of Waikato, Fees and Allowances Office, School of Education, Private Bag 3105, Hamilton, Waikato, New Zealand
Tel: 07 856 2889
Fax: 07 856 0135

Fulbright Programme Fellowship

Eligibility: Open to nationals of New Zealand.

Level of Study: Postdoctorate, Postgraduate.

Purpose: Awards travel grants to New Zealand citizens who intend to begin study in the USA during the next academic year and who undertake to return to New Zealand.

Type: Travel Grant.

No. of awards offered: Up to 20.

Frequency: Annual.

Length of Study: Up to five years.

Study Establishment: An American university.

Country of Study: USA.

Applications Procedure: Enquiries should be directed to the Academic Staff Unit.

Closing Date: July 31st.

For further information contact:
(The University of Waikato), NZ - USA Educational Foundation, PO Box 3465, Wellington, New Zealand
Tel: 04 472 2065

Fulbright Graduate Student Award

Eligibility: Open to nationals of New Zealand.

Level of Study: Postgraduate.

Purpose: Offers grants to New Zealand citizens who intend to undertake postgraduate study in the USA.

Type: Grant.

No. of awards offered: Twelve.

Frequency: Annual.

Value: Grants cover return airfares plus a supplementary grant of NZ$500.

Length of Study: One year.

Study Establishment: An American university.

Country of Study: USA.

Applications Procedure: Write for information.

Closing Date: July 31st.

For further information contact:
(The University of Waikato), NZ - USA Educational Foundation , PO Box 3465, Wellington, New Zealand
Tel: 04 472 2065

General Accident/NZI Waitangi Scholarship to Edinburgh University

Eligibility: Open to New Zealand university graduates.

Level of Study: Postgraduate.

Purpose: To enable recipients to study economics or business studies at Edinburgh University in Scotland.

Type: Scholarship.

Frequency: Annual.

Value: Includes all full cost foreign tuition fees, airfares and a living allowance of £5,500.

Length of Study: Initially one year.

Study Establishment: University of Edinburgh.

Country of Study: Scotland.

Applications Procedure: Write for application.

Closing Date: October 1st.

For further information contact:
The University of Waikato, Fees And Allowances Office, Private Bag 3105, Hamilton, Waikato, New Zealand
Tel: 07 856 2889
Fax: 07 856 0135

Getty Centre for the History of Art and the Humanities - Predoctoral Fellowship

Subjects: Fields such as Anthropology, Cultural, Economic, Intellectual, Political and Social History; the History of Art, Architecture, Music, Religion, Science & Technology, Literary Criticism & Theory and Philosophy.

Level of Study: Doctorate.

Purpose: The Getty Centre provides support for students enrolled for doctorates.

Type: Stipend, Fellowship.

Frequency: Annual.

Value: US$15,000.

Length of Study: Nine months.

Country of Study: USA.

Applications Procedure: Write for information.

Closing Date: None specified.

Additional Information: These fellowships are not renewable.

For further information contact:
(The University of Waikato), Visiting Scholars and Conferences, Getty Centre For The History Of Art and The Humanities, 401 Wilshire Boulevard, Suite 700, Santa Monica, CA, 90401-1455, USA
Contact: Dr Herbert H Hymans, Assistant Director

Griffith University Scholarship - Australia

Subjects: Not specified.

Eligibility: Applicants need to have completed an honours degree at second class honours, division 1 level or higher.

Level of Study: Doctorate, Postgraduate.

Type: Scholarship.

Frequency: Annual.

Study Establishment: Griffith University.

Country of Study: Australia.

Applications Procedure: Write for information.

Closing Date: October 31st.

For further information contact:
(The University of Waikato), Griffith University, Queensland, 4111, Australia
Contact: Postgraduate Studies Officer

625

Health Research Council of New Zealand

Type: Grant.

Frequency: Annual.

Country of Study: New Zealand.

Applications Procedure: Application forms can be obtained from the Fees and Allowances Office, School of Education.

Closing Date: Project Grants February 1st and August 1st; Scholarships and Fellowships April 1st; Travel Grants February 15th, August 15th and November 15th.

For further information contact:
(The University of Waikato), Health Research Council of New Zealand, PO Box 5541, Wellesley Sreet, Auckland, 1000, New Zealand
Tel: 09 379 8227
Fax: 09 377 9988
Contact: The Secretary

Health Research Council Summer Scholarship

Subjects: Biological sciences related to human health.

Eligibility: Open to students who wish to undertake research in the biological sciences related to human health.

Type: Scholarship.

Frequency: Annual.

Country of Study: New Zealand.

Applications Procedure: Write for application form.

For further information contact:
(The University of Waikato), Fees and Allowances Office, School Of Education, Private Bag 3105, Hamiton, Waikato, New Zealand
Tel: 07 856 0135
Fax: 07 856 2889

C R F Heinhold Memorial Award

Eligibility: Student must hold a BSc(Tech) or MSc(Tech).

Level of Study: Postgraduate.

Purpose: The Award is made to a student to allow him/her to carry out project work as part of the requirement for a degree in the area of meat production.

Frequency: Annual.

Value: Value reviewed annually.

Study Establishment: Ruakura Agricultural Centre.

Country of Study: New Zealand.

Applications Procedure: Application for the award should be made in writing and should include a brief CV and an outline of the proposed project.

Closing Date: October 1st.

For further information contact:
(The University of Waikato), Fees and Allowances Office, School of Education, Private Bag 3105, Hamilton, Waikato, New Zealand
Tel: 07 856 2889
Fax: 07 856 0135

Harriette Jenkins Award

Subjects: Not specific.

Level of Study: Postgraduate.

Purpose: For members of NZFUW to carry out research in New Zealand.

Type: Grant.

Frequency: Twice a year.

Value: Between NZ$200 and NZ$1,000.

Country of Study: New Zealand.

Applications Procedure: Write for information.

Closing Date: March 31st and September 30th.

For further information contact:
(The University of Waikato), New Zealand Federation of University Women, PO Box 2006, Wellington, New Zealand

Alan Lomas Memorial Grant

Subjects: Oncology treatment and research.

Level of Study: Professional development, Postgraduate.

Purpose: Assists senior graduates to further their knowledge in cancer related fields of patient care, treatment or research.

Type: Research Grant.

Frequency: Annual.

Value: Up to NZ$10,000 annually.

Country of Study: New Zealand.

Applications Procedure: Write for application form.

Closing Date: December 31st.

For further information contact:
The University of Waikato, Waikato/Bay of Plenty Division Cancer Society of New Zealand Inc., PO Box 134, Hamilton, Waikato, New Zealand

Betty Loughhead Soroptimist Trust Scholarship

Eligibility: Women only.

Level of Study: Unrestricted.

Purpose: The award has been established to help women attain further qualifications to advance their career in business, the arts, or the professions.

Type: Scholarship.

Frequency: Annual.

Study Establishment: University of Waikato.

Country of Study: New Zealand.

Applications Procedure: Write for application form.

Closing Date: October 1st.

Additional Information: This Scholarship is offered by Soroptimist International, a worldwide organisation of service clubs for women. There is no age limit. Courses considered include summer schools, seminars, diploma, certificate or degree courses.

For further information contact:
(The University of Waikato), Soroptomist International of New Zealand, PO Box 2127, Wellington, New Zealand
Contact: The Secretary

Claude McCarthy Fellowship

Subjects: Science, Medicine or Literature.

Eligibility: Candidates must have graduated from a New Zealand university.

Level of Study: Postgraduate.

Purpose: To enable graduates of any New Zealand university to conduct research in any area of literature, science, or medicine either in New Zealand or overseas.

Type: Fellowship.

Frequency: Annual.

Length of Study: One year.

Country of Study: Any.

Applications Procedure: Write for application form.

Closing Date: August 1st.

Additional Information: Not for research to be credited towards qualification.

For further information contact:
The University of Waikato, Private Bag 3105, Hamilton, Waikato, New Zealand
Tel: 07 856 2889
Fax: 07 856 0135

Don Sinclair Research Fellowship - NZ Apple and Pear Board

Subjects: Horticulture.

Eligibility: Open to graduates in horticulture.

Level of Study: Doctorate.

Purpose: To promote further development of the New Zealand pip-fruit industry.

Type: Fellowship.

Frequency: Annual.

Value: Up to NZ$16,000 p.a. plus tuition fees, a thesis allowance and an allowance for dependants.

Length of Study: Three years.

Study Establishment: University of Waikato.

Country of Study: New Zealand.

Applications Procedure: Write for application form.

Closing Date: October 31st.

For further information contact:
(The University of Waikato), New Zealand Apple and Pear Board, PO Box 3328, Wellington, New Zealand

Dame Catherine Tizard Scholarship

Eligibility: Only women may apply.

Level of Study: Postgraduate.

Purpose: The Scholarship has been estalished in honour of Dame Catherine Tizard as the first woman Governor-General, to enable women to undertake tertiary or postgraduate study in a discipline which is of value to local government.

Type: Scholarship.

Frequency: Annual.

Value: Up to NZ$5,000.

Length of Study: One year.

Study Establishment: University of Waikato.

Country of Study: New Zealand.

Applications Procedure: Write for application form.

Closing Date: November 6th.

For further information contact:
(The University of Waikato), New Zealand Local Government Association Inc., PO Box 1214, Wellington, New Zealand
Tel: 04 472 6437

Vacation Scholarship

Eligibility: Applicants must be completing the third or fourth year of a four year honours degree.

Purpose: The ANU offers, each year, a number of vacation scholarships in most research schools and centres of the Institute of Advanced Studies during the summer vacation period.

Type: Scholarship.

Frequency: Annual.

Value: Weekly (tax free) allowance of A$100, also covers return airfares, accommodation, and meals.

Length of Study: Eight to twelve weeks.

Study Establishment: Australian National University.

Country of Study: Australia.

Applications Procedure: Application is by letter, there is no specific application form.

Closing Date: August 15th.

For further information contact:
(The University of Waikato), Australian National University, GPO Box 4, Canberra, ACT, 2061, Australia
Contact: The Registrar

Gordon Watson Scholarship

Subjects: Arts, Social Sciences, Theology, Economics.

Eligibility: Applicants must have an honours degree or degree in theology and must return to New Zealand for at least two years at the end of the period of tenure.

Level of Study: Postgraduate.

Purpose: Postgraduate study or research in the area of international relations or social and economic conditions.

Type: Scholarship.

Frequency: Dependent on funds available.

Value: NZ$10,200.

Length of Study: Two years.

Study Establishment: Tenable overseas.

Country of Study: Not specific.

Applications Procedure: Write for information.

Closing Date: October 1st.

Additional Information: Not available every year.

For further information contact:
The University of Waikato, Fees and Allowances Office, School of Education, Private Bag 3105, Hamilton, Waikato, New Zealand
Tel: 07 856 2889
Fax: 07 856 0135

Gordon Williams Postgraduate Fellowship - Lincoln University

Eligibility: Preference given to fields related to Ecology and/or Wildlife Management. The basic criterion for the award is academic merit.

Level of Study: Doctorate, Postdoctorate, Postgraduate.

Purpose: Lincoln University offers this fellowship for Masters, PhD or Postdoctoral research in the biological sciences.

Type: Fellowship.

Frequency: Annual.

Study Establishment: Lincoln University.

Country of Study: New Zealand.

Applications Procedure: Write for information.

Closing Date: October 1st.

For further information contact:
(The University of Waikato), Lincoln University, PO Box 94, Lincoln, Canterbury, New Zealand
Contact: The Registrar

UNIVERSITY OF WALES

Academic Registry, University of Wales College of Cardiff, PO Box 495, Cardiff, CF1 3XD, Wales
Tel: 01222 874413
Fax: 01222 874130
Contact: Senior Assistant Registrar

*College of Cardiff University Postgraduate Research Studentships

Subjects: Any subject offered at the University (on a rotation basis).

Eligibility: Candidates must possess at least an upper second class honours degree from an approved university. For purposes of fee payment, applicants must be a 'home student' ordinarily resident in the UK (or the European Community provided he or she is an EC national) throughout the period of three years immediately preceding the date on which the course of study is due to begin. Heads of department at the College select recipients from among the applicants for admission.

Purpose: To enable nominated students to pursue doctoral research to PhD level.

Type: Studentships.

No. of awards offered: 10-15.

Frequency: Annual.

Value: £2,260 (fees), plus up to £4,720 maintenance allowance.

Length of Study: One year; renewable annually to a maximum of three years.

Study Establishment: The College.

Country of Study: UK.

Closing Date: June 30th.

UNIVERSITY OF WALES, ABERYSTWYTH

University of Wales, Aberystwyth, King Street, Aberystwyth, Dyfed, SY23 2AX, Wales
Tel: 01970 622 270
Fax: 01970 622 921
Email: ctj@aber.ac.uk
Contact: The Postgraduate Admissions Office

Postgraduate Research Studentships

Subjects: Any research course (MPhil/PhD/LLM by research).

Eligibility: Open to UK/EU candidates who have obtained at least upper second class honours or equivalent in their degree examination.

Level of Study: Postgraduate, Doctorate.

Purpose: To enable UK/EU students to undertake postgraduate research at University of Wales, Aberystwyth.

Type: Studentships.

No. of awards offered: Varies.

Frequency: Annual.

Value: UK fees plus a subsistence allowance based on research council rates.

Length of Study: One year; usually renewable for up to two additional years, subject to satisfactory academic progress.

Study Establishment: The College.

Country of Study: UK.

Applications Procedure: Completion of application form is required.

Closing Date: March 1st.

UNIVERSITY OF WALES, BANGOR

Academic Office, University of Wales, Bangor, Bangor, Gwynedd, LL57 2DG, Wales
Tel: 01248 382025
Fax: 01248 370451
Email: (kiio)@bangor.ac.uk
Contact: Dr J C T Perkins, Assistant Registrar

Postgraduate Studentships

Subjects: Any subject offered at the University.

Eligibility: Open to candidates classified as Home/EC for fees payment purposes who have attained a first or exceptional upper second class honours degree (or equivalent).

Level of Study: Postgraduate, Doctorate.

Purpose: To fund research training to PhD level.

Type: Studentships.

No. of awards offered: 12-15.

Frequency: Annual.

Value: Equal to that of a British public-funded Research Studentship.

Length of Study: One year; renewable for up to two additional years.

Study Establishment: The University.

Country of Study: Wales.

Closing Date: June 1st.

Mr and Mrs David Edward Roberts Memorial Award

Subjects: Any subject offered at University of Wales, Bangor.

Eligibility: Open to holders of relevant first or, exceptionally, upper second class honours degree, who are of any nationality classified as a 'home/EC' student for fees purposes.

Level of Study: Postgraduate, Doctorate.

Purpose: To aid postgraduate research.

Type: Research Studentship.

No. of awards offered: One.

Frequency: Triennially.

Value: No less that of a Research Council or British Academy Research Studentship, including fees.

Length of Study: One year; renewable for a further two years if satisfactory progress is maintained.

Study Establishment: University of Wales, Bangor.

Closing Date: May 1st.

Sir William Roberts Scholarship

Subjects: Agriculture, agricultural science.

Eligibility: Open to candidates classified as "home based' who have attained a first or upper second class honours degree.

Level of Study: Postgraduate, Doctorate.

Purpose: To fund research training to PhD level.

Type: Scholarship.

No. of awards offered: One.

Frequency: Annual.

Value: Equal to that of a British Research Council Research Studentship.

Length of Study: One year; renewable for up to two additional years.

Study Establishment: The University.

Closing Date: June 1st.

Llewellyn and Mary Williams Scholarship

Subjects: All biological sciences, including marine biology.

Eligibility: Open to first class honours degree holders who are classified as home/EC for fees purposes.

Level of Study: Postgraduate, Doctorate.

Purpose: To support doctoral studies and research training in the biological sciences.

Type: Scholarship.

No. of awards offered: One.

Frequency: Triennially.

Value: Same basic value as a British Research Council Studentship.

Study Establishment: University of Wales, Bangor.

Country of Study: Wales/UK.

Closing Date: May 1st.

UNIVERSITY OF WESTERN AUSTRALIA

University of Western Australia, Nedlands, Perth, Western Australia, 6009, Australia
Tel: 09 380 3838
Fax: 09 382 4071
Contact: Brian Cleary, Scholarships Officer

*James and Sith Annie Chesters Scholarship

Subjects: Medicine and surgery.

Eligibility: Open to recent medical graduates with limited research experience.

Purpose: To encourage younger graduates to conduct research and establish themselves as research workers.

Type: Scholarship.

No. of awards offered: One.

Frequency: Annual.

Value: Up to A$36,285 per annum, depending upon qualifications; specific travel expenses may be met.

Length of Study: One year.

Study Establishment: The University of Western Australia.

Country of Study: Australia.

Closing Date: June 30th of the year preceding tenure.

Additional Information: Except with the consent of the Vice-Chancellor a Scholar shall not be permitted to undertake any employment for payment during the tenure of the Scholarship.

*Richard Walter Gibbon Medical Research Fellowship

Subjects: Research into the causes and treatment of cancer and Parkinson's disease.

Eligibility: Open to Australian residents who are medical graduates of a recognized tertiary institution.

Purpose: To promote research by facilitating and encouraging students to pursue postgraduate research in the Faculty of Medicine at the University.

Type: Fellowship.

No. of awards offered: Varies.

Frequency: Varies according to funds available and standard of the applications.

Value: Determined on an individual basis. Out of surplus income the Vice-Chancellor may make travel grants to Fellows to attend conferences or visit colleagues in other universities or institutions in Australia and provide a grant to a host department towards the cost of necessary minor equipment and consumables.

Length of Study: Up to three years.

Study Establishment: The University.

Country of Study: Australia.

Closing Date: June 30th.

Additional Information: Except by permission a Fellow may not engage in any work during tenure of the Fellowship other than that for which it was awarded. A full report is required at the end of tenure. Resulting publications must acknowledge that the work was done under a Gibbon Fellowship.

*Gledden Postgraduate Studentships

Subjects: Applied science, particularly relating to engineering, mining, surveying, and cognate subjects.

Eligibility: Open to postgraduates with a first class honours degree or its equivalent in an applied science, with research experience included in the degree course.

Purpose: To enable the holder to conduct research in applied science leading to a higher qualification.

Type: Studentship.

No. of awards offered: One.

Frequency: As vacancies occur.

Value: A$18,679 per annum (tax free); thesis allowance of A$395 (master's) or A$790 (doctoral).

Length of Study: Up to three years.

Study Establishment: The University, depending on the approved study plan. Permission may exceptionally be given for part of the research to be conducted at another university or recognized institution in Australia.

Country of Study: Australia.

Closing Date: October 31st of the year preceding tenure.

*Gledden Visiting Senior Fellowships

Subjects: Applied science, more particularly relating to surveying, engineering, mining and cognate subjects.

Eligibility: Open to graduates from outside Western Australia who have doctoral degrees or qualifications or experience equivalent to doctorate.

Purpose: To provide travel costs, or travel costs and living expenses, for scholars from outside Western Australia to visit the University and contribute to its work and activities in applied science.

Type: Fellowship.

No. of awards offered: Varies.

Frequency: Annual.

Value: Determined on an individual basis.

Length of Study: From one academic term (defined as a minimum of three months) to two years.

Study Establishment: The University.

Country of Study: Australia.

Applications Procedure: Applications are invited by advertisement as and when directed by the Vice-Chancellor of the University.

Closing Date: March 31st.

Postdoctoral Research Fellowship

Subjects: All areas covered by UWA departments. Please see UWA www home page for details.

Eligibility: Open to all nationalities. Applicants should hold a PhD for all appointments. The appointment of an overseas Fellow is subject to Australian Department of Immigration and Ethnic Affairs' approval of UWA's sponsorship for residence, and the Fellow's successful application for appropriate visa.

Level of Study: Postdoctorate.

Purpose: To provide a two-year appointment to a postdoctoral Research Fellow bringing special new expertise and a high level of relevant experience which is not otherwise available at the UWA department, to carry out a research project in a UWA department.

Type: Fellowship.

No. of awards offered: Three.

Frequency: Annual.

Value: A$37,345-A$40,087 per year salary plus A$3,500-A$5,000 per year fellowship support grant. A relocation allowance is also included.

Length of Study: Two years.

Study Establishment: UWA.

Country of Study: Australia.

Applications Procedure: Applications are accepted from UWA departments only.

Closing Date: Generally March 1st.

*Saw Medical Research Fellowship

Subjects: The causation, prevention and cure of disease, primarily diabetes mellitus.

Eligibility: Candidates need not have medical qualifications.

Purpose: To promote personal research.

Type: Fellowship.

No. of awards offered: One.

Frequency: Annually, or as vacancies occur.

Value: Up to A$36,285 per annum depending on qualfications. May be held concurrently with other awards.

Length of Study: One year; renewable for one further year.

Study Establishment: The University.

Country of Study: Australia.

Closing Date: June 30th of the year preceding tenure.

Additional Information: During the tenure of the Fellowship a Fellow may not engage in any work other than that for which the Fellowship has been awarded except by permission of the Vice-Chancellor.

*Ernest and Evelyn Havill Shacklock Scholarships

Subjects: The arts; science; or civil engineering.

Eligibility: Open to graduates who possess at least an upper second class honours degree.

Purpose: To promote study or research leading to a higher degree.

Type: Scholarship.

No. of awards offered: Up to three.

Frequency: As vacancies occur.

Value: A$13,500 per annum (tax free); relocation allowance of up to A$1,140; thesis allowance of A$395 (master's) or A$790 (doctoral).

Length of Study: One year; renewable for one year (master's) or for two years (doctoral).

Study Establishment: The University.

Country of Study: Australia.

Closing Date: October 31st of the year preceding tenure.

Additional Information: Scholarships may not be held concurrently with other awards but appropriate employment is permitted to a maximum of 240 hours in a calendar year.

*Wyn Spence Fellowships in Medical Research

Subjects: A proposed programme of medical research which is suitable to be undertaken in the department of the Medical School.

Eligibility: Open to any candidate holding a medical degree from a recognized university whose proposed programme of research is suitable to be undertaken in a department of the Medical School. It is not necessary for a Fellow to complete a postgraduate degree.

Purpose: To enable the Fellow to carry out medical research work within the School of Medicine of the University of Western Australia.

Type: Fellowship.

No. of awards offered: One.

Frequency: Annual.

Value: Up to A$36,285 depending on qualifications.

Length of Study: One year; renewable for a further year or, exceptionally, for two years.

Study Establishment: The University.

Country of Study: Australia.

Closing Date: June 30th.

Additional Information: The Fellowship may not be held concurrently with other awards or sources of income except with the approval of the Vice-Chancellor.

*University Research Studentships

Subjects: Any subject offered at the University.

Eligibility: Open to graduates who possess at least an upper second class honours degree.

Purpose: To enable students to conduct research leading to a master's or doctoral degree.

Type: Studentships.

No. of awards offered: 40.

Frequency: Annual.

Value: A$13,500 per annum (tax free); plus travel costs; relocation allowance of up to A$1,140; thesis allowance of A$395 (master's) or A$790 (doctoral).

Length of Study: One year; renewable for one year (master's) or for two years (doctoral).

Study Establishment: The University.

Country of Study: Australia.

Closing Date: October 15th.

Additional Information: Scholarships may not be held concurrently with other awards but appropriate employment is permitted to a maximum of 240 hours in a calendar year.

THE UNIVERSITY OF WESTERN ONTARIO

Centre for Interdisciplinary Studies in Chemical Physics, The University of Western Ontario, London, Ontario, N6A 3K7, Canada
Tel: 519 679 2111 ext.6860
Contact: Dr I V Mitchell

*Senior Visiting Fellowship

Subjects: Current research programmes are focused on problems in condensed matter; properties of isolated atoms and molecules; surface studies; and biological applications.

Eligibility: Open to senior scientific researchers of established standing. There are no nationality restrictions.

Purpose: To bring established senior scientists to the Centre for Interdisciplinary Studies in Chemical Physics to work on problems that are interdisciplinary in nature and of interest to Centre members, who are drawn from the departments of applied mathematics, physics, chemistry, geology, materials engineering, cancer research, and the Robarts Institute.

Type: Fellowships.

No. of awards offered: Two to four.

Frequency: Annual.

Value: Estimated living expenses for the period involved, plus travel expenses. Fellowships may be held concurrently with other awards or income.

Length of Study: Three to 12 months.

Study Establishment: The Centre.

Country of Study: Canada.

Applications Procedure: Application forms are available from the Centre.

Closing Date: July of year preceding tenure.

UNIVERSITY OF WESTERN SYDNEY

University of Western Sydney, Nepean, Postgraduate Studies Office, PO Box 10, Kingswood, NSW, 2747, Australia
Tel: 61 2 685 9127
Fax: 61 2 685 9021
Email: c.stevenson@nepean.uws.edu.au
Contact: Catherine Stevenson

Nepean Postgraduate Research Award

Subjects: All subjects offered at the University.

Eligibility: Applicants must hold or be eligible for the award of B(Hons) Degree Class 1, from an Australian university, or an equivalent award.

Level of Study: Postgraduate, Doctorate.

Purpose: To support students of high academic merit in undertaking postgraduate research degrees at UWS Nepean.

No. of awards offered: 12.

Frequency: Annual.

Value: A$15,131 stipend plus allowances.

Length of Study: Two years-Masters/three years-Doctorate.

Study Establishment: UWS Nepean.

Country of Study: Australia.

Applications Procedure: Please submit application form, certified copies of all academic records and two academic referee reports (submitted by referees).

Closing Date: October 31st.

Additional Information: Other than Australian Nationals may apply and may be awarded a scholarship in exceptional circumstances.

UNIVERSITY OF THE WITWATERSRAND

University of the Witwatersrand, Private Bag 3, Wits, 2050, South Africa
Tel: 011 716 3256
Fax: 011 339 4387
Contact: Financial Aid and Scholarships Office, Senior Assistant Registrar

Herbert Ainsworth Scholarship

Subjects: Modern history.

Eligibility: Open to distinguished graduates of approved universities in South Africa.

Level of Study: Postgraduate.

Purpose: To assist with study towards an honours degree.

Frequency: Annual.

Value: R2,000 per annum.

Length of Study: One year of full-time study.

Study Establishment: At the University.

Country of Study: South Africa.

Closing Date: January 10th.

Backeberg Research Scholarship

Subjects: Chemistry.

Eligibility: Open to graduates of any approved university or institution; judged on academic merit and achievement.

Purpose: To assist with full-time PhD study.

Frequency: Annual.

Value: R5,000 per annum.

Length of Study: For one year; renewable upon reapplication.

Study Establishment: The University.

Country of Study: South Africa.

Closing Date: January 10th.

E P Bradlow/John Lemmer Scholarship

Subjects: Any subject.

Eligibility: Open to candidates showing appropriate academic merit. A student who accepts a Scholarship shall be required to remain in South Africa for a period of time equal to that for which the Scholarship was held after completing all the requirements for the postgraduate degree.

Purpose: To assist with full-time masters or PhD degree study.

Type: Scholarship.

Frequency: Annual.

Value: R5,000 per annum.

Study Establishment: The University.

Country of Study: South Africa.

Closing Date: January 10th.

*Bradlow Foundation Bursaries for MBA Study

Subjects: Business administration.

Eligibility: Open to candidates with a first degree from any recognised University. If subjects taken do not include mathematics or science, the student will normally have to complete a preliminary course, MAP or PLATO, before being admitted to the MBA programme. Financial need must be demonstrated.

Purpose: To assist with full-time study towards the MBA degree.

Type: Bursary.

No. of awards offered: Varies.

Frequency: Annual.

Value: At the discretion of the Trustees.

Study Establishment: The University.

Country of Study: South Africa.

Closing Date: January 10th.

Henry Bradlow Scholarship

Subjects: Any subject offered by the University.

Eligibility: Open to distinguished graduates of approved universities in South Africa.

Purpose: To assist in postgraduate study towards a full-time masters or PhD degree.

Type: Scholarship.

Frequency: Annual.

Value: R5,000 per annum; paid in four equal instalments.

Length of Study: For one year of full-time study.

Study Establishment: The University.

Country of Study: South Africa.

Closing Date: January 10th.

Carnovski Postgraduate Scholarship

Subjects: African studies, i.e. African languages, social anthropology and African government, African literature.

Eligibility: Open to distinguished graduates of approved universities in South Africa.

Level of Study: Postgraduate.

Purpose: To assist with full-time honours degree studies.

Type: Scholarship.

Frequency: Annual.

Value: R1,500 per annum; paid in equal instalments.

Length of Study: One year of full-time study.

Study Establishment: University of the Witwatersrand.

Country of Study: South Africa.

Closing Date: January 10th.

G A Denny Postgraduate Research Scholarship

Subjects: The broad field of social relations including civics, municipal administration and race relations.

Eligibility: Open to distinguished graduates of approved universities in South Africa.

Purpose: To assist with full-time postgraduate studies.

Type: Scholarship.

Frequency: Annual.

Value: R1,700 per annum; paid in four equal instalments.

Length of Study: For one year of full-time study renewable for a maximum of two years.

Study Establishment: At the University.

Country of Study: South Africa.

Closing Date: January 10th.

Freda Lawenski Scholarship Fund Grants

Subjects: All fields of study offered at the University.

Eligibility: Open to distinguished graduates of approved universities in South Africa.

Purpose: To assist with full-time postgraduate studies.

Type: Scholarship.

Frequency: Annual.

Value: From R500 to a maximum of R2,500 per annum.

Length of Study: For one year of full-time study.

Study Establishment: The University.

Country of Study: South Africa.

Closing Date: January 10th.

Mones Michaels Bursary

Subjects: Geophysics.

Eligibility: Open to distinguished graduates of approved universities in South Africa.

Purpose: To assist with postgraduate degree study in research.

Frequency: Annual.

Value: Up to R2,000 per annum; paid in four equal instalments.

Length of Study: For one year of full-time study; renewable for additional periods of study.

Study Establishment: The University.

Country of Study: South Africa.

Closing Date: January 10th.

Bernard Price Scholarships in Power Engineering

Subjects: Electrical engineering.

Eligibility: Open to distinguished graduates of approved universities in South Africa.

Purpose: To assist with study and research.

Frequency: Annual.

Value: Up to R2,000 per annum; paid in four equal instalments.

Length of Study: For one year of full-time study; renewable for maximum of two years.

Study Establishment: The University.

Country of Study: South Africa.

Closing Date: January 10th.

Raikes Scholarships

Subjects: Arts or sciences.

Eligibility: Open to distinguished graduates of approved universities in South Africa.

Purpose: To assist with full-time study towards an honours degree.

Frequency: Annual.

Value: R700-R1,000 per annum.

Length of Study: For one year of full-time study.

Study Establishment: The University.

Country of Study: South Africa.

Closing Date: January 10th.

J Arthur Reavell Foundation Scholarship

Subjects: Chemical engineering.

Eligibility: Open to distinguished graduates of approved universities in South Africa.

Purpose: To assist with full-time postgraduate study.

Type: Scholarship.

Frequency: Annual.

Value: At the discretion of the Selection Committee.

Length of Study: For one year of full-time study; renewable for additional periods of study.

Study Establishment: The University.

Country of Study: South Africa.

Closing Date: January 10th.

For further information contact:
University of the Witwatersrand, Private Bag 3, Wits, 2050, South Africa
Tel: 011 716 3256
Fax: 011 716 8030
Contact: The Head, Department of Chemical Engineering

Adolph Wagner Scholarships

Subjects: Engineering; preference will be given to applicants studying mining engineering.

Eligibility: Open to distinguished graduates of approved universities in South Africa.

Purpose: To assist with postgraduate research.

Type: Scholarship.

Frequency: Annual.

Value: Approximately R1,200 per annum; paid in four equal instalments.

Length of Study: For one year of full-time study; renewable for a maximum of two years.

Study Establishment: The University.

Country of Study: South Africa.

Closing Date: January 10th.

UNIVERSITY OF WOLLONGONG

University of Wollongong, Northfields Avenue, Wollongong, NSW, 2522, Australia
Contact: Kim Roser

University of Wollongong Postgraduate Awards

Subjects: Any subject offered by the University.

Eligibility: Open to graduates with at least a second class honours degree.

Purpose: To provide financial support for full-time study leading to a masters or PhD degree.

No. of awards offered: Varies.

Frequency: Annual.

Value: A$14,474.

Length of Study: Two years for the masters or for 3 years for the PhD; renewable subject to satisfactory progress.

Study Establishment: The University.

Country of Study: Australia.

Closing Date: 31 October.

Additional Information: Holders of the Award must pursue studies on a full time basis and submit an annual report.

UNIVERSITY OF YORK

Registrar's Department, University of York, Heslington, York, YO1 5DD, England
Tel: 01904 432143
Fax: 01904 432092
Contact: Philip Simisan

Access Awards

Subjects: Any full-time degree (graduate or undergraduate), diploma or certificate of the university.

Eligibility: Open to full-time home students only. Also, only self-financing students are eligible: students whose fees and maintenance are covered by awards from EGA Research Council or an LEA are not eligible.

Purpose: To assist home candidates of high academic standard.

Type: Grant.

No. of awards offered: Approximately 15 awards.

Frequency: Annually if funds available.

Value: Up to £1,000.

Length of Study: One year; not renewable.

Study Establishment: The University.

Country of Study: UK.

Closing Date: Mid-August.

Scholarships for Overseas Students

Subjects: Any full-time degree (graduate or undergraduate), diploma or certificate of the University.

Eligibility: Open to students who have been accepted for registration as a full-time student for a degree, diploma or certificate course of the University of York and are liable to pay tuition fees at the 'full-cost' rate for overseas (non-EC) students.

Level of Study: Postgraduate, Undergraduate.

Purpose: To assist overseas candidates of high academic standard.

Type: Scholarship.

No. of awards offered: Approximately 30.

Frequency: Annual.

Value: One-third or one-sixth of the value of tuition fees.

Study Establishment: The University.

Country of Study: UK.

Applications Procedure: Application form available for completion, contact international office.

Closing Date: May 1st.

For further information contact:
International Office, University of York, Heslington, York, YO1 5DD, England
Tel: 01904 433534
Fax: 01904 433538
Email: international@york.ac.uk

UNIVERSITY OF THE ORANGE FREE STATE

University of the Orange Free State, PO Box 339, Bloemfontein, 9300, South Africa
Tel: 4012479/4012599
Fax: 4012117
Contact: The Director of Student and Research Administration

*Bursary for Doctoral Study

Subjects: Any discipline in the human, natural and medical sciences.

Eligibility: Open to those who wish to pursue full-time doctoral study or part-time study; dependent upon merit.

Purpose: To give a student the opportunity to study full-time at the university. Bursaries for part-time study are awarded in exceptional cases only.

Type: Bursary.

No. of awards offered: One.

Frequency: Annual.

Value: Varies.

Length of Study: Two years depending on progress; renewable.

Study Establishment: University of the Orange Free State.

Country of Study: South Africa.

Closing Date: Mid-October.

Dr Edward (Jiffy) King Scholarship

Subjects: Any discipline in the human, natural and medical sciences.

Eligibility: Open to deserving foreign postgraduate students intending to study at the University and who will be attached to a department.

Level of Study: Postgraduate.

Type: Scholarship.

No. of awards offered: One.

Frequency: Annual.

Value: Varies; may be supplemented to provide for residence and tuition fees.

Length of Study: 1-2 years.

Study Establishment: University of the Orange Free State.

Country of Study: South Africa.

Applications Procedure: Application form must be completed and relevant documents attached.

Closing Date: September 30th.

Additional Information: In considering applications the following categories, in order of priority, will be taken into account: full-time study for the degree of doctor; part-time study for the degree of doctor; postdoctoral study; study for the master's degree.

*National Scholarship

Subjects: Any discipline in the human, natural and medical sciences.

Eligibility: Open to persons registered at the UOFS, who wish to study with a view to obtaining a doctorate, or who wish to do postdoctorate study or to study for a master's degree.

Type: Scholarship.

No. of awards offered: Two.

Frequency: Annual.

Value: R3,000 for local and R4,000 for overseas study.

Length of Study: Two years depending on progress; renewable for a further two years.

Study Establishment: University of the Orange Free State.

Country of Study: South Africa.

Closing Date: Mid-July.

Additional Information: These Scholarships are funded by the Department of National Education.

US ARMY CENTER OF MILITARY HISTORY

Dissertation Fellowship Program, US Army Center of Military History, 1099 14th St., NW, Washington, DC, 20005-3402, USA
Tel: 202 761 5402/5364
Fax: 202 761 5390
Contact: Andrew J. Birtle

Dissertation Fellowships

Subjects: For the purposes of this program, the history of war on land is broadly defined, including such areas as biography, military campaigns, military organization and administration, policy, strategy, tactics, weaponry, technology, training, logistics, and evolution of civil military relations.

Eligibility: Open to civilian graduate students of the USA who have completed by September all requirements for the PhD degree except the dissertation.

Level of Study: Doctorate.

Purpose: To support scholarly research and writing among qualified civilian graduate students preparing dissertations in the history of war on land, especially the history of the US Army.

Type: Fellowship.

No. of awards offered: Two.

Frequency: Annual.

Value: US$8,000 stipend, plus access to the Center's facilities and technical expertise.

Applications Procedure: Each applicant must submit a completed application form, a proposed plan of research, a statement of approval from the academic director of the dissertation, two other letters of recommendation, an official graduate transcript, and a writing sample: 10-25 pages.

Closing Date: February 1st.

Additional Information: Fellows visit the Center at the beginning and end of the Fellowship period. On the first visit, the Fellow meets key individuals at the Center and is consulted on ways CMH can help him/her. On the second visit, the Fellow presents an oral report on his/her progress. A brief written report and a copy of the completed dissertation are also required. Candidates who have previously held or accepted an equivalent Fellowship from any other US Department of Defense agency are not eligible.

US ARMY RESEARCH INSTITUTE

US Army Research Institute, PERI-BR, 5001 Eisenhower Avenue, Alexandria, VA, 22333-5600, USA
Tel: 703 617 8641
Fax: 703 617 5162
Email: DRILLINGS@ARI.FED.US
www: http://www.ARI.FED.US/

Contact: Michael Drillings

Basic Research Program

Subjects: Psychology, cognitive sciences and social institutions.

Eligibility: Most awards go to US scientists, but there are no definite restrictions.

Purpose: To enable basic research in the behavioural and social sciences to support the Army's mission.

No. of awards offered: 4-10.

Frequency: Annual.

Value: US$10,000 to US$150,000 per year.

Length of Study: Up to three years.

Country of Study: Unrestricted.

Applications Procedure: A full proposal is required with a budget.

Closing Date: Varies from year to year.

US DEPARTMENT OF DEFENSE

Air Force Office of Scientific Research, Air Force Systems Command, USAF, Bolling Air Force Base, Washington, DC, 332-6448, USA
Tel: 202 767 4945
Contact: AFOSR/PKO

*Air Force Office of Scientific Research Grants and Contracts

Subjects: Sciences of direct interest to strengthening Air Force operating capabilities: chemical sciences, mathematical and information sciences, electronics and solid state sciences, aerospace sciences, life sciences, general physics, geophysics, and atmospheric sciences.

Eligibility: AFOSR principal investigators are predominantly at the postdoctoral level. Awards are not restricted by citizenship.

Purpose: To stimulate high quality scientific research on problems of Air Force interest.

No. of awards offered: Current research program consists of about 1,125 individual work efforts.

Value: Varies.

Study Establishment: Colleges and universities and industrial or non-profit research laboratories.

Country of Study: Any country.

Applications Procedure: Prior to formal submission of a proposal, investigators should write for the Proposer's Guide to the AFOSR Research Program.

US DEPARTMENT OF EDUCATION

US Department of Education, 400 Maryland Avenue, SW, Room 2177, Mail Stop 6335, Washington, DC, 20202, USA
Contact: Indian Fellowship Program

*Indian Fellowship Program

Subjects: Postbaccalaureate degree: business administration; clinical psychology; education; engineering; law; medicine; natural resources and related fields; psychology. Undergraduate degree: business administration; engineering; natural resources and related fields.

Eligibility: Open to US citizens who meet the following definition of Indian: a member of a tribe, band or other organized group of Indians, including those terminated since 1940 and those recognized by the state in which they reside, or a descendant in the first or second degree of any individual described above; or considered by the Secretary of the Interior to be an Indian for any purpose; or an Eskimo or Aleut or other Alaska native. In addition, applicants must be full-time degree candidates who have not yet obtained a terminal graduate or post-baccalaureate degree in any of the above-mentioned fields of study.

Purpose: To enable American Indians to pursue a course of study leading to a post-baccalaureate degree or an undergraduate degree.

No. of awards offered: Varies.

Frequency: Annual.

Value: An amount up to, but not more than, the difference between the student's educational resources and the student's expenses.

Length of Study: Two years (master's degree) or for four years (undergraduate and doctorate degrees).

Study Establishment: An accredited institution of higher learning.

Country of Study: USA.

Applications Procedure: Applications are available on request during open season, which varies annually.

USIA FULBRIGHT PROGRAM

Institute of International Education, 809 United Nations Plaza, New York, NY, 10017-3580, USA
Tel: 212 984 5330
Contact: US Student Programs

Hubert H Humphrey Fellowship Program

Subjects: Natural resources and environmental management; public policy analysis and public administration; economic development; agricultural development/agricultural economics; finance and banking; human resource management/personnel; urban and regional planning; public health policy and management; technology policy and management; educational planning; communications/journalism.

Eligibility: Open to mid-career professionals in public service from developing countries and Central Eastern Europe (low and middle income), with at least a first university degree, five years of substantive professional experience, demonstrated leadership qualities, and fluency in English (TOEFL required for all applicants); English refresher course available.

Level of Study: Postgraduate, Professional development.

Purpose: To increase mutual understanding between the people of the USA and the people of other countries by means of sharing work-related experience.

Type: Fellowship.

No. of awards offered: 150.

Frequency: Annual.

Value: International and domestic travel, tuition and books, monthly stipend, professional development allowance, health insurance.

Study Establishment: Selected universities throughout the USA.

Country of Study: USA.

Applications Procedure: Applications are available through USIS posts or Fulbright Commissions in their home countries.

For further information contact:
Institute of International Education, 1400 K Street, NW, Washington, DC, 20005-2403, USA
Tel: 202 326 7701
Fax: 202 326 7702
Email: hhh@iie.org
Contact: Humphrey Fellowship Program

Study and Research Grants for US Citizens

Subjects: Study and research in all fields, as well as professional training in the creative and performing arts.

Eligibility: Open to US citizens who have a bachelor's degree or equivalent qualification. Candidates must have a high scholastic record, have

an acceptable plan of study, demonstrate proficiency in the language of the host country, and be in good health. In some cases special language training is provided as part of a grant. Preference is given to persons who have not had prior experience of, or opportunity for, extended foreign study, residence or travel.

Level of Study: Postgraduate.

Purpose: To increase mutual understanding between the people of the USA and the people of other countries by means of educational and cultural exchange.

No. of awards offered: Varies.

Frequency: Annual.

Value: To cover international transportation, language or orientation course (where appropriate), tuition, book, and maintenance allowances, and health and accident insurance. Some grants, however, will consist of travel expenses only, supplementing maintenance allowances and tuition scholarships which are granted to students by universities and other organizations. An applicant who has received a doctoral degree since applying, or has been admitted to doctoral candidacy having completed all requirements except the writing of the dissertation may, upon arrival in certain countries, receive a higher stipend.

Length of Study: One academic year.

Study Establishment: Institutions of higher learning.

Country of Study: Outside the USA. A list of participating countries in a given year may be obtained from the Institute of International Education.

Applications Procedure: Applicants enrolled in a college or university should apply to the Fulbright Program Adviser on their campus. Applicants not enrolled in a college or university should apply to the Institute of International Education. Applications should be requested at least 15 days prior to the closing date.

Closing Date: October 23rd.

*Teachers Program for US Citizens

Subjects: The program is open to educators in most fields.

Eligibility: Open to secondary and elementary level educators, college instructors, and assistant, associate, and full professors. Applicants must be currently employed in a full-time teaching position, be a US citizen, and have at least a bachelor's degree. Three years' full-time teaching experience is required for an exchange, two years' full-time teaching experience is required for seminars. For most countries, competency in the host nation language is not required.

Purpose: To promote mutual understanding between the people of the USA and the people of other countries through educational exchange.

No. of awards offered: Varies, depending on funds available.

Frequency: Annual.

Value: Direct exchange of teaching assignment requires that the US teacher obtain a leave of absence with pay from school authorities. The US school agrees to accept a teacher from an exchange country who also has secured a leave of absence with pay. In some cases there is an award to cover transportation costs. For seminars, tuition and other participation fees may be provided by the host nation.

Length of Study: 3-8 weeks.

Country of Study: Argentina, Belarus, Bulgaria, Canada, Chile, Colombia, Cyprus, Czech Republic, Denmark, Egypt, Estonia, Finland, France, Germany, Hungary, Italy, Latvia, Lithuania, Mexico, Morocco, Netherlands, Norway, Poland, Portugal, Romania, Russia, Senegal, Slovak Republic, South Africa, Switzerland, Turkey, Ukraine and UK.

Closing Date: October 15th.

For further information contact:
Fulbright Teacher Exchange Branch, E/ASX, United States Information Agency, 301 4th Street SW, Washington, DC, 20547, USA
Tel: 202 619 4555
Fax: 202 401 1433

or

Fulbright Teacher Exchange, 600 Maryland Avenue, SW, Room 142, Washington, DC 20024, USA
Tel: 202 382 8586

US-ISRAEL BINATIONAL SCIENCE FOUNDATION

US-Israel Binational Science Foundation, PO Box 7677, Jerusalem, 91076, Israel
Tel: 02 617 314
Fax: 02 633 287

Research Grants

Subjects: Health sciences, life sciences, physics, chemistry, mathematical sciences, atmospheric and earth sciences, oceanography and limnology, materials research, environmental research, energy research, biomedical engineering, economics, sociology, anthropology. social and developmental psychology.

Eligibility: Scientists who wish to apply for grants must submit their applications through an institution or agency with legal status. The BSF accepts research proposals from institutions of higher learning, government research institutions, hospitals and other non-profit research organizations. Proposals originating in industry are not considered. Although proposals cannot be submitted by for-profit or industrial organizations, the US principal investigator may be affiliated with such an organization. In such cases the investigators must be familiar with BSF patent policy before completing the collaborative arrangements. Israeli and American principal investigators must hold a doctoral degree or its equivalent. Graduate students are not eligible to submit applications.

Purpose: To encourage cooperation between US and Israeli scientists.

Type: Research Grants.

No. of awards offered: Varies.

Frequency: Annual.

Value: Varies.

Country of Study: US or Israel.

Applications Procedure: Prior to formal submission, the proposal may be discussed with the BSF staff either by letter, telephone or in person.

Closing Date: 15 November.

Additional Information: Investigators may submit only one proposal to each annual competition. Further, since an investigator may hold only one BSF award at a time, an Israeli grantee may submit a new proposal only during the last year of the award.

THE US-UK FULBRIGHT COMMISSION

US-UK Fulbright Commission, Fulbright House, 62 Doughty Street, London, WC1N 2LS, England
Tel: 0171 404 6880
Fax: 0171 404 6834
Email: education@fulbright.co.uk
Contact: Programme Director

Academic Administrator in Veterinary Education

Subjects: Veterinary education.

Eligibility: Applicants must hold a veterinary degree and be actively involved in veterinary education.

Level of Study: Professional development.

Purpose: To enable an administrator to conduct research into an aspect of veterinary education in the UK.

No. of awards offered: One.

Frequency: Every two years.

Value: £7,500 (inclusive of round-trip travel).

Length of Study: A minimum of four months.

Study Establishment: One of the six UK veterinary schools.

Country of Study: UK.

Applications Procedure: Please apply to CIES with four references and a proposal.

Closing Date: November 1st.

Fulbright Fellowship in Securities Law

Subjects: Securities law.

Eligibility: Open to qualified and practising British solicitors or barristers.

Level of Study: Professional development.

Purpose: To enable a qualified and practising British solicitor or barrister, working in the field of Securities Law, the opportunity to spend 4-6 months following postgraduate courses at Georgetown University, Washington DC, and gain practical experience with the US law firm Morgan, Lewis and Bockius in DC.

Type: Fellowship.

No. of awards offered: One.

Frequency: Annual.

Value: US$4,000 plus round-trip travel and tuition.

Length of Study: 4-6 months.

Study Establishment: Georgetown University, Washington DC.

Country of Study: USA.

Applications Procedure: Formal application and interview are required.

Closing Date: March 31st.

Fulbright Graduate Student Awards

Subjects: All subjects. Some special funding exists for MBA or related studies.

Eligibility: Open to US citizens, normally resident in the USA. Minimum GPA:3.5; must demonstrate evidence of leadership qualities.

Level of Study: Postgraduate.

Purpose: To enable US students to follow postgraduate study or research in the UK.

No. of awards offered: Approximately 20.

Frequency: Annual.

Value: Maintenance allowance, approved tuition fees and round-trip travel are covered.

Length of Study: A minimum of nine months.

Study Establishment: Any UK institution of higher education.

Country of Study: UK.

Applications Procedure: Formal application is required, with four references and a telephone interview for shortlisted candidates.

Closing Date: October.

For further information contact:
Institute of International Education, 809 United Nations Plaza, New York, NY, 10017, USA
Tel: 212 984 5466
Fax: 212 984 5465
Contact: Student Program Division

Fulbright Louise Buchanan Fellowship in Cancer Research

Subjects: Oncology.

Eligibility: Open to British scientists or clinicians.

Level of Study: Postdoctorate.

636

Purpose: To enable a scientist or clinician to carry out research into cancers of the lymph glands.

Type: Fellowship.

No. of awards offered: One, dependent on funds available.

Frequency: Annual.

Value: £4,000 plus round-trip travel.

Length of Study: A minimum of four months.

Study Establishment: An approved US institution of higher education.

Country of Study: USA.

Applications Procedure: Formal application is required.

Closing Date: April 30th.

Fulbright Police Studies Fellowship

Subjects: Policing.

Eligibility: Open to British police officers.

Level of Study: Professional development.

Purpose: To enable serving police officers to spend three months in the USA researching an aspect of policing.

Type: Fellowship.

No. of awards offered: Two.

Frequency: Annual.

Value: £3,000 (includes round-trip travel).

Length of Study: 3 months.

Study Establishment: An approved US institution of higher education.

Country of Study: USA.

Applications Procedure: Formal application and interview are required.

Closing Date: Early April.

Fulbright Postgraduate Student Awards

Subjects: Any subject.

Eligibility: Applicants must be UK citizens normally resident in the UK. Must hold, prior to departure, a minimum of a 2:i honours degree. Must demonstrate leadership qualities.

Level of Study: Postgraduate.

Purpose: To enable students to carry out postgraduate study or research in the USA.

No. of awards offered: 20-25 each year.

Frequency: Annual.

Value: Maintenance for nine months and round-trip travel (projected level for 1997/8 ranges between £6,488-£8,325 for maintenance, slightly more if accompanied by a dependant).

Length of Study: Minimum of nine months.

Study Establishment: An approved US institution of higher education.

Country of Study: USA.

Applications Procedure: Please submit a formal application with two references.

Closing Date: Late October.

Additional Information: Shortlisted candidates will be interviewed.

Fulbright-Robertson Visiting Professorship in British History

Subjects: British History.

Eligibility: Open to scholars of British History, with 1-2 years' experience of teaching undergraduates.

Level of Study: Professional development.

Purpose: To enable a British scholar to spend ten months at Westminster College, Fulton, Missouri, lecturing in British History.

Type: Professorship.

No. of awards offered: One.

Frequency: Annual.

Value: Up to US$40,000 plus round-trip travel for grantee and up to four accompanying dependants.

Length of Study: Ten months.

Study Establishment: Westminster College, Fulton, Missouri.

Country of Study: USA.

Applications Procedure: Please submit formal application and two references.

Closing Date: December 31st.

Additional Information: Shortlisted candidates will be interviewed.

Fulbright Scholar Grants

Subjects: Any subject, with particular interest in topics which address problems shared by the USA and UK.

Eligibility: Open to US scholars who took their first degree more than five years ago.

Level of Study: Postdoctorate.

Purpose: To enable US scholars to carry out lecturing or research in the UK.

No. of awards offered: Two Distinguished Scholar awards, and eight Scholar awards.

Frequency: Annual.

Value: Distinguished Scholar: £9,750; Scholar: £1,500 per month.

Length of Study: 3-12 months.

Study Establishment: Any approved UK institution of higher education.

Country of Study: UK.

Applications Procedure: Application and four references should be submitted to the CIES.

Closing Date: August 1st.

For further information contact:
Council for International Exchange of Scholars, 3007 Tilden Street NW, Suite 5M, Washington, DC, 20008-3009, USA
Tel: 202 686 6245
Email: we1@ciesnet.cies.org

Fulbright Scholarship Grants

Subjects: All subjects - although subjects where there is an opportunity for collaborative innovation of international significance or a focus on Anglo-American relations are preferred.

Eligibility: Candidates must demonstrate academic or artistic excellence.

Level of Study: Postdoctorate.

Purpose: To enable Visiting Lecturers, Junior and Senior Postdoctoral Research Scholars, to lecture or carry out research in the USA for a minimum of three months.

Type: Scholarship.

No. of awards offered: 12 each year.

Frequency: Annual.

Value: £1,750; proof of additional dollar support is required.

Length of Study: 3-12 months.

Study Establishment: An approved US institution of higher education.

Country of Study: USA.

Applications Procedure: Please submit a formal application and two references.

Closing Date: Early April.

Fulbright TEB Clarke Fellowship in Screenwriting

Subjects: Screenwriting.

Eligibility: Open to young British screenwriters under the age of 35.

Level of Study: Professional development.

Purpose: To enable a young British screenwriter to spend nine months developing his/her screenwriting skills at a major US film school.

Type: Fellowship.

No. of awards offered: One, dependent on funds available.

Frequency: Annual.

Value: £18,000 maintenance allowance, approved tuition fees and round-trip travel.

Length of Study: Nine months.

Study Establishment: A major US film school.

Country of Study: USA.

Applications Procedure: Please submit one full feature-length screenplay, synopsis and two further story treatments.

Closing Date: February 28th.

Additional Information: Shortlisted candidates will be interviewed.

Humphrey-Fulbright Fellowship for Civil Servants

Subjects: Public policy.

Eligibility: Open to British civil servants.

Level of Study: Professional development.

Purpose: To enable a British civil servant to spend 12 months at the Hubert Humphrey Institute of Public Affairs at the University of Minnesota.

Type: Fellowship.

No. of awards offered: One.

Frequency: Annual.

Value: US$10,000 plus round-trip travel (confirmation is required that salary will still be paid during the award period).

Length of Study: 12 months.

Study Establishment: Hubert Humphrey Institute of Public Affairs, University of Minnesota.

Country of Study: USA.

Applications Procedure: Please submit formal application, research proposal and departmental reference.

Closing Date: December 1st.

Additional Information: Shortlisted candidates will be interviewed.

THE VAN CLIBURN FOUNDATION

The Van Cliburn Foundation, 2525 Ridgmar Boulevard, Ste 307, Fort Worth, Texas, 76116, USA
Tel: 817 738 6536
Fax: 817 738 6534
Contact: Patricia O'Neill, Development Director

Van Cliburn Medals

Subjects: Piano.

Eligibility: Open to young classical pianists between 18-30 years, of any nationality.

Level of Study: Professional development.

Purpose: To discover and reward the world's finest young pianists. Additionally to nurture and oversee the professional debuts of the Cliburn medallists, and ensure their proper introduction to the professional concert world.

Type: Cash, career management, Carnegie Hall debut, CD recording contract.

No. of awards offered: Three.

Frequency: Every four years.

Value: First (Gold) US$20,000, 2nd (Silver) US$15,000, 3rd (Bronze) US$10,000.

Country of Study: USA.

Applications Procedure: Application form required; available from the given address.

Closing Date: October 15th, postmark deadline.

TIBOR VARGA INTERNATIONAL COMPETITION FOR VIOLIN

Tibor Varga International Competition for Violin, PO Box 954, Sion, CH-1951, Switzerland
Tel: 0041 27 23 43 17
Fax: 0041 27 23 46 62

Tibor Varga International Competition for Violin

Subjects: Violin: interpretive performance.

Eligibility: Open to violinists of any nationality aged 15 to 32.

Level of Study: Unrestricted.

Type: Prize.

No. of awards offered: Four prizes and several special prizes.

Frequency: Annual.

Value: 1st prize SwFr10,000; 2nd prize SwFr7,500; 3rd prize SwFr5,000; 4th prize SwFr2,000; special prizes totalling approximately SwFr30,000.

Length of Study: August 5th to 15th.

Country of Study: Switzerland.

Applications Procedure: Application form fully filled in, plus three passport photographs (4*5 cm) and curriculum vitae with details.

Closing Date: May 1st.

Additional Information: Participants will compete in Sion during August. Prize-winners are obliged to remain in Sion for the awards presentation at the end of the competition. They will also be expected to perform in the presentation concert. The first prize-winner will be presented as soloist with a symphony orchestra at the Festival. There is an application fee of SwFr100.

VICTORIA UNIVERSITY

Emmanuel College, Victoria University, 75 Queen's Park Crescent East, Toronto, Ontario, M5S 1K7, Canada
Tel: 416 585 4539
Fax: 416 585 4516
Contact: Director for Advanced Degree Studies

Bridge Street United Church Foundation Scholarship

Subjects: Biblical studies, theology, pastoral studies or church history.

Eligibility: Open to third-world candidates who are enrolled in or who have graduated from a degree program of a university in a third-world country.

Level of Study: Postgraduate.

Purpose: To enable a third-world student to do a year of postgraduate work at Emmanuel College, possibly leading to a masters degree.

Type: Scholarship.

No. of awards offered: One.

Frequency: Annual.

Value: To be determined.

Length of Study: One year; renewable for a second year.

Study Establishment: Emmanuel College, Victoria University, and the Toronto School of Theology, University of Toronto.

Country of Study: Canada.

Applications Procedure: Application form available.

Closing Date: December 31st.

VIRGINIA CENTER FOR THE CREATIVE ARTS

Virginia Center for the Creative Arts, Sweet Briar, VA, 24595, USA
Tel: 804 946 7236
Fax: 804 946 7239
Email: VCCA@SBC.EDU
Contact: William Smart, Director

Fellowships

Subjects: Writing; painting; sculpture; musical composition; photography.

Eligibility: Open to artists with professional competence and promise, regardless of age, sex, citizenship or academic background.

Purpose: To provide the proper environment for creative work for extended periods of time.

No. of awards offered: Approximately 300 Fellowships in any given year.

Frequency: Fellowships are available simultaneously.

Value: Subsidized residence at the Center. No cash stipends or travel allowances are provided.

Length of Study: One to three months each year; renewable.

Study Establishment: The Center.

Country of Study: USA.

Closing Date: January 31st.

VITUKI TRAINING

International Postgraduate Course on Hydrology, Vituki Training, H-1453 Budapest, Pf 27, Hungary
Tel: 361 215 3043
Fax: 361 215 3043
Contact: The Director

*Financial Support for Course Participants

Subjects: Hydrology base subjects: mathematics; hydraulics; geosciences; hydrological studies; hydrological processes; observation processing; analysis; forecasting; application; environment water management.

Eligibility: Open to nationals of any country who are under 40 years of age. A degree from a recognized institution is required in applied mathematics, mathematical statistics, systems analysis, hydrology, fluid mechanics, geology or meteorology.

Purpose: To make a contribution towards raising the level of hydrological sciences in developing countries.

Type: Financial support.

No. of awards offered: 20.

Frequency: Annual.

Value: US$10,000.

Study Establishment: The premises of Vituki, Budapest, for the duration of the course (January to July).

Country of Study: Hungary.

Closing Date: October 31st.

Additional Information: The Course's finances are essentially based on applicants holding fellowships granted by international organizations, or their own government, or applicants paying for themselves. The Course's admission board may be able to propose Fellowship applicants to sponsoring national/international agencies, but disposes no Fellowships of its own.

VOLZHSKY INSTITUTE OF HUMANITIES

Volgograd State University (VIH), 40 Years of Victory Street 11, Volzhsky, Volgograd, 404132, Russia
Tel: 8443 29 84 60
Fax: 8443 29 17 78
Email: bat@vgumi.tsaritsyn.su
Contact: Gennady Babkov, Director

Awards

Subjects: Environmental management, management systems and techniques, applied mathematics, ecology, natural resources, statistics, criminal law, Russian language and literature, philosophy, computer science, econometrics, soil conservation.

Eligibility: Applicants must be of at least postgraduate standard and have a sound knowledge of Russian.

Level of Study: Postgraduate, Professional development.

Purpose: A variety of awards are offered to allow recipients to acquire new skills and undertake research.

No. of awards offered: Two in each subject area.

Frequency: Dependent on funds available.

Value: Tuition fees.

Length of Study: 2-4 months.

Study Establishment: VIH.

Country of Study: Russia.

Applications Procedure: Please contact the VIH for details.

Closing Date: November 30th.

ALEXANDER VON HUMBOLDT FOUNDATION

Alexander von Humboldt-Stiftung, Jean-Paul Strasse 12, Bonn, Bad Godesberg, D-53173, Germany
Tel: 228 833 0126
Fax: 228 833 212
Telex: 885 627

Konrad Adenauer Research Award

Subjects: Humanities, social sciences.

Eligibility: Open to highly qualified Canadian scholars, whose research work in the humanities or in the social sciences has brought them international recognition and who belong to the group of leading scholars in their respective area of specialization. The award will be made regardless of the age, race, religion or sex of the applicants.

Level of Study: Postdoctorate.

Purpose: To promote academic relations between Canada and the Federal Republic of Germany.

Type: Research award.

No. of awards offered: One.

Frequency: Annual.

Value: Up to DM100,000. The Humboldt Foundation will pay the return travel costs once only for award winners and family members (provided the latter stay with them in Germany for at least three months) between Canada and Germany. Medical and accident insurance may be provided for the award winners (and family members) if requested.

Length of Study: One year.

Study Establishment: German Research Institutes.

Country of Study: Germany.

Applications Procedure: Self-application cannot be accepted. Candidates should be nominated by their universities and the dossiers should be sent to the Executive Director, Royal Society of Canada, PO Box 9734, Ottawa, Ontario K1G 5J4, Canada. Nominations should include a letter from the candidate's institution regarding the candidate's academic qualifications; a list of publications; a detailed statement of the candidate's research proposal; at least three names, complete with addresses, of internationally recognized scholars who can provide information of the nominee's academic qualifications; the names of German scholars who would provide expert guidance to the Canadian scholar during his/her stay in Germany.

Closing Date: December 1st.

Additional Information: Nominations will be made jointly by the Royal Society of Canada and the University of Toronto, and submitted to the Humboldt Foundation. At least two candidates should be nominated each year.

For further information contact:
Alexander von Humboldt-Stiftung, Jean-Paul Strasse 12, Bonn, Bad Godesberg, D-53173, Germany
Tel: 228 8330
Fax: 228 833 199
Telex: 885 627

or
The Royal Society of Canada, 225 Metcalfe Street, Suite 308, Ottawa, ON, K2P 1P9, Canada
Tel: 613 991 6990
Fax: 613 991 6996
Email: lvachon@rsc.ea
Contact: Linda Vachon

*Federal Chancellor Scholarship

Subjects: Arts and humanities; business administration and management; fine and applied arts; mass communication and information science; medicine; recreation, welfare, protective services; religion and theology; social and behavioural sciences.

Eligibility: Open to US citizens only.

Level of Study: Postgraduate.

Purpose: To maintain and foster a close relationship between the USA and Germany by sponsoring individuals who demonstrate the potential of playing a pivotal role in the future development of this relationship.

Type: Scholarship.

No. of awards offered: Ten.

Frequency: Annual.

Value: DM2,500-DM5,000 per month plus travel costs.

Length of Study: 12 months.

Study Establishment: Academic or other research institutions.

Country of Study: Germany.

Applications Procedure: Application form must be completed; available from Bonn or Washington office.

Closing Date: October 31st of each year, for next academic year.

For further information contact:
Alexander von Humboldt Foundation, 1055 Thomas Jefferson St., NW, Suite 2020, Washington, DC, 20007, USA
Tel: 202 296 2990
Fax: 202 833 8514
Email: humboldt@umail.umd.edu
Contact: US Liaison Office

or
Alexander von Humboldt-Stiftung, Jean-Paul Strasse 12, Bonn, Bad Godesberg, D-53173, Germany
Tel: 011 49 228 833 0
Fax: 011 49 228 833 199
Telex: 885 627

Humboldt Research Prize for Foreign Scholars

Subjects: All subjects.

Eligibility: Open to all nationalities except Germans.

Level of Study: Postdoctorate.

Purpose: To enable internationally recognized foreign scholars to conduct research on a project of their choice in Germany.

Type: Research prize.

No. of awards offered: Up to 200.

Frequency: Three times a year.

Value: Between DM20,000 and DM120,000 plus travel costs.

Length of Study: 4-12 months.

Study Establishment: Universities, research institutions.

Country of Study: Germany.

Applications Procedure: Eminent German scholars propose candidates directly to the Foundation in Bonn. Direct applications are not accepted.

Closing Date: No deadline; nominations are accepted throughout the year.

Additional Information: Selection committee meetings are held three times per year, usually in March, June/July and November. Nominations should be submitted at least five months before the selection committee meeting at which a decision is to be made.

For further information contact:
Alexander von Humboldt Foundation, US Liaison Office, 1055 Thomas Jefferson St., NW, Suite 2020, Washington, DC, 20007, USA
Tel: 202 296 2990
Fax: 202 833 8514
Email: humboldt@umail.umd.edu
Contact: Dr Bernard Stein

or
Alexander von Humboldt Stiftung, Jean-Paul Strasse 12, Bonn, Bad Godesberg, D-53173, Germany
Tel: 011 49 228 833 0
Fax: 011 49 228 833 199
Telex: 885 627

Japan Society for the Promotion of Science (JSPS) and the Science and Technology Agency (STA) Research Fellowships

Subjects: All academic fields except for Japanese.

Eligibility: Open to German nationals only.

Level of Study: Postdoctorate.

Purpose: To enable highly-qualified German scholars up to the age of 35 to carry out research projects of their own choice at universities or non-university research institutions in Germany.

Type: Fellowship.

No. of awards offered: Thirty.

Frequency: Annual.

Value: 270,000 yen plus travel and housing allowance.

Length of Study: 12-24 months (JSPS) and 6-24 months (STA).

Study Establishment: University or other research institution.

Country of Study: Japan.

Applications Procedure: Application form must be completed.

Closing Date: No deadline.

For further information contact:
Alexander von Humboldt Foundation, 1055 Thomas Jefferson St., NW, Suite 2020, Washington, DC, 20007, USA
Tel: 202 296 2990
Fax: 202 833 8514
Email: humboldt@umail.umd.edu
Contact: US Liaison Office

or

Alexander von Humboldt-Stiftung, Jean-Paul Strasse 12, Bonn, Bad Godesberg, D-53173, Germany
Tel: 011 49 228 833 0
Fax: 011 49 228 833 199
Telex: 885 627

Feodor Lynen Research Fellowships for German Scholars

Subjects: All academic fields.

Eligibility: Open to German nationals.

Level of Study: Postgraduate.

Purpose: To enable highly-qualified German scholars (of not more than 38 years of age) to conduct research of their choice at home institutions of non-German recipients of Humboldt fellowships and prizes.

Type: Fellowship.

No. of awards offered: Up to 200.

Frequency: Three times per year.

Value: DM3,200-DM4,000 per month (joint financing by Humboldt Foundation and host institute is required).

Length of Study: 1-4 years.

Study Establishment: Research institutions.

Country of Study: Any, except Germany.

Applications Procedure: Application form is required, available from Bonn and Washington addresses.

Closing Date: Five months before the selection committee meeting, but applications are accepted at any time.

For further information contact:
Alexander von Humboldt Foundation, 1055 Thomas Jefferson St., NW, Suite 2020, Washington, DC, 20007, USA
Tel: 202 296 2991
Fax: 202 833 8514
Email: humboldt@umail.umd.edu
Contact: US Liaison Office

or

Alexander von Humboldt-Stiftung, Jean-Paul Strasse 12, Bonn, Bad Godesberg, D-53173, Germany
Tel: 011 49 228 833 0
Fax: 011 49 228 833 199
Telex: 885 627

Max-Planck Cooperative Research Prize

Subjects: All academic fields.

Eligibility: Open to scholars of all disciplines and nations.

Level of Study: Postdoctorate, Professional development.

Purpose: To enable internationally recognized US and German scholars to conduct long-term cooperative research.

Type: Research prize.

No. of awards offered: Twelve.

Frequency: Annual.

Value: Up to DM250,000.

Length of Study: 3-5 years.

Country of Study: Germany.

Applications Procedure: Nomination by presidents of German universities, academies of sciences, Max-Planck Society, corp. of large research establishments, Fraunhofer Society, German Research Association, former prize holders, and selection committee members.

Closing Date: Middle of April/end of March.

Additional Information: Selection occurs once per year.

For further information contact:
Alexander von Humboldt Foundation, 1055 Thomas Jefferson St., NW, Suite 2020, Washington, DC, 20007, USA
Tel: 202 296 2990
Fax: 202 833 8514
Email: humboldt@umail.umd.edu
Contact: US Liaison Office

or

Alexander von Humboldt-Stiftung, Jean-Paul Strasse 12, Bonn, Bad Godesberg, D-53173, Germany
Tel: 011 49 228 833 0
Fax: 011 49 228 833 199
Telex: 885 627

Postdoctoral Humboldt Research Fellowships

Subjects: Postdoctoral academic research in any subject.

Eligibility: Open to persons of any nationality other than German, up to 40 years of age, who have obtained a PhD degree or equivalent, who can furnish proof of independent research and can submit academic publications. Candidates in the arts and humanities should possess sound German language ability. Those in the natural, medical and engineering sciences should possess English language ability. (German language courses at the Goethe Institute for 2-4 months may be available prior to commencement of the Research Fellowship.) Candidates should already have established relations with a German research institute where the project can be realized.

Level of Study: Postdoctorate.

Purpose: To provide opportunities for young, highly qualified scholars from abroad to carry out research projects of their own choice in Germany.

Type: Research fellowship.

No. of awards offered: Approximately 500.

Frequency: Annual.

Value: DM3,200-DM4,000 per month, plus travel allowance for Research Fellow only, and dependant's allowance.

Length of Study: 6-12 months, with the possibility of renewal for a further 12 months.

Study Establishment: Universities or research institutions in Germany.

Country of Study: Germany.

Applications Procedure: Application form must be completed (available from Bonn or Washington office); submit completed forms to Bonn office at least five months before selection committee meeting, during which the decision is to be made.

Closing Date: No specified deadline, applications can be accepted at any time.

Additional Information: Applications should be forwarded directly to the Foundation or through diplomatic or consular offices of the Federal Republic of Germany in the candidates' respective countries. Candidates must submit a detailed research plan in German or English. The Foundation also offers up to 200 Feodor Lynen Research Fellowships to German postdoctoral researchers to foster cooperation with former Humboldt Fellows and Award-holders abroad.

For further information contact:
Alexander von Humboldt-Stiftung, Jean-Paul Strasse 12, Bonn, Bad Godesberg, D-53173, Germany
Tel: 228 8330
Fax: 228 833 199

Telex: 885 627

or

Alexander von Humboldt Foundation, 1055 Thomas Jefferson St.,NW, Suite 2020, Washington, DC, 20007, USA
Tel: 202 296 2990
Fax: 202 833 8514
Email: humboldt@umail.umd.edu
Contact: Dr Bernhard Stein, Director of the North American Office

or

German Academic Exchange Service (DAAD), 11-15 Arlington Street, London, SW1 1RD, England

VON KARMAN INSTITUTE

Von Karman Institute, Chausse de Waterloo 72, Rhode-Saint-Genese, 1640, Belgium
Tel: 32 2 358 1901
Fax: 32 2 358 2885
Email: wendt@vki.ac.be
www: http://www.vki.ac.be
Contact: J Wendt

VKI Fellowship

Subjects: Fluid dynamics.

Eligibility: Open to citizens of NATO countries with the equivalent of a five-year engineering degree (MS or, for UK, BSc honours, upper second). Applicants must have a working knowledge of English.

Level of Study: Postgraduate.

Purpose: To support the living costs of recipients who attend the VKI Diploma Course.

Type: Fellowship.

No. of awards offered: 25.

Frequency: Annual.

Value: Approximately US$1,000 per month.

Length of Study: Nine months.

Study Establishment: VKI.

Country of Study: Belgium.

Applications Procedure: Two forms, one to be endorsed by AGARD National Delegate (NATO Advisory Group for Aerospace Research and Development), copy of college transcripts and three references are required.

Closing Date: March 1st.

For further information contact:
Von Karman Institute, Chausse de Waterloo, 72, Rhode-Saint-Genese, 1640, Belgium
Tel: 32 2 358 1901
Fax: 32 2 358 2885
Email: wendt@vki.ac.be
www: http://www.vki.ac.be
Contact: J Wendt, Director

WALSH MEMORIAL SCHOLARSHIP TRUST

Walsh Memorial Scholarship Trust, 3/2 Marine Parade, Herne Bay, Auckland, New Zealand
Contact: Sheila T Quirk, Secretary

*Scholarships

Subjects: Aeronautical engineering and flying.

Eligibility: Open only to New Zealanders interested and qualified in the field of aviation.

Purpose: To promote and benefit aviation in New Zealand, usually by furthering education in engineering and flying.

No. of awards offered: Varies according to number of applicants and funds available.

Frequency: Annual.

Value: NZ$500-NZ$5,000.

Closing Date: October.

THE WARBURG INSTITUTE

The Warburg Institute, Woburn Square, London, WC1H 0AB, England
Tel: 0171 580 9663
Fax: 0171 436 2852
Email: warburg@sas.ac.uk
www: http://www.sas.ac.uk/warburg
Contact: Secretary and Registrar

Brian Hewson Crawford Fellowship

Subjects: The classical tradition.

Eligibility: Applicants must normally be under 35 years of age on 1 October of the academic year prior to which the Fellowship is taken up, and have completed at least two years' research towards a doctorate.

Level of Study: Doctorate, Postdoctorate.

Purpose: To support research in any aspect of the classical tradition.

Type: Short-term Fellowship.

No. of awards offered: One.

Frequency: Annual.

Value: £800-£1,800.

Length of Study: One to three months.

Study Establishment: At the Institute.

Country of Study: UK.

Applications Procedure: Further information should be obtained form the Secretary and the Registrar.

Closing Date: Beginning December.

Henri Frankfort Fellowship

Subjects: The intellectual and cultural history of the ancient Near and Middle East.

Eligibility: Open to individuals under 35 years of age on 1 October of the academic year prior to which the Fellowship is taken up, and have completed at least two years of postgraduate study.

Level of Study: Doctorate, Postdoctorate.

Purpose: To promote research.

Type: Fellowship.

No. of awards offered: One.

Frequency: Annual.

Value: £800-£1,800.

Length of Study: For one to three months.

Study Establishment: At the Institute.

Country of Study: UK.

Applications Procedure: Further information should be obtained from the Secretary and Registrar.

Closing Date: December.

Frances A Yates Fellowships

Subjects: Cultural and intellectual history.

Eligibility: Applicants must normally be under 35 years of age on 1 October of the academic year prior to which the Fellowship is taken up, and have completed at least two years of postgraduate study.

Level of Study: Doctorate, Postdoctorate.

Purpose: To promote research.

No. of awards offered: One long-term Fellowship, six to ten short-term Fellowships.

Frequency: Annually. The long-term Fellowship is not available every year.

Value: £13,500-£14,500 (long-term); £800-£1,800 (short-term).

Length of Study: For one to three years (long-term Fellowship, not normally renewable) or for one to three months (short-term Fellowships, not renewable).

Study Establishment: At the Institute.

Country of Study: UK.

Applications Procedure: Further information should be obtained from the Secretary and Registrar.

Closing Date: December.

WASHINGTON UNIVERSITY

Graduate School of Arts & Sciences, Campus Box 1187, Washington University, 1 Brookings Drive, St Louis, MO, 63130, USA
Tel: 314 935 6821
Fax: 314 935 4887
Email: c43000je@wuvmd.wustl.edu
Contact: Joyce Edwards

Chancellor's Graduate Fellowship Program for African Americans

Subjects: Any of Washington University's PhD or DSc programs in Arts and Sciences, Business, Engineering, or Social Work. The Fellowship includes other Washington University programs providing final disciplinary training for prospective college professors.

Eligibility: Open to African-American doctoral candidates.

Level of Study: Doctorate.

Purpose: To encourage African Americans who are interested in becoming college or university professors.

Type: Fellowship.

No. of awards offered: 5-6.

Frequency: Annual.

Value: Doctoral candidates will receive full tuition plus US$16,000 stipend and allowances.

Length of Study: Five years, subject to satisfactory academic progress.

Study Establishment: Washington University.

Country of Study: USA.

Applications Procedure: Application form must be completed.

Closing Date: January 25th.

Mr and Mrs Spencer T Olin Fellowships for Women

Subjects: Any discipline offered in the University.

Eligibility: Open to female graduates of a baccalaureate institution in the USA who plan to prepare for a career in higher education or the professions. Applicants must meet the admission requirements of the graduate or professional school of Washington University. Preference will be given to those who wish to study for the highest earned degree in their chosen field, do not already hold an advanced degree, and who are not currently enrolled in a graduate or professional degree program.

Level of Study: Postgraduate.

Purpose: To encourage women of exceptional promise to prepare for careers in higher education and the professions.

Type: Fellowship.

No. of awards offered: Approximately ten.

Frequency: Annual.

Value: Full tuition and, in most cases, a living expense stipend.

Length of Study: One year; renewable up to four years, or until completion of degree program, whichever comes first.

Study Establishment: Washington University.

Country of Study: USA.

Closing Date: February 1st.

Additional Information: Candidates must also make concurrent application to the department or school of Washington University in which they plan to study.

For further information contact:
Olin Fellowship Program for Women, Graduate School of Arts & Sciences, Campus Box 1187, Washington University, 1 Brookings Drive, St Louis, MO, 63130, USA
Tel: 314 935 0848
Fax: 314 935 4887
Email: mmwatkin@artsci.wustl.edu
Contact: Margaret Watkins, Coordinator

THE KURT WEILL FOUNDATION FOR MUSIC

The Kurt Weill Foundation for Music, 7 East 20 Street, 3rd Floor, New York, NY, 10003, USA
Tel: 212 505 5240
Fax: 212 353 9663
Email: kwf@panix.com
www: http://www.kwf.org
Contact: Joanna C Lee, Associate Director for Business Affairs

Kurt Weill Foundation Music Grant

Subjects: Any subject related to the perpetuation of Kurt Weill's artistic legacy.

Eligibility: Open to music and theater scholars and professionals.

Level of Study: Postgraduate, Doctorate, Postdoctorate, Professional development.

Purpose: The Kurt Weill Foundation for Music is a non-profit corporation which promotes public understanding and appreciation of the musical works of Kurt Weill. To this end, the Foundation solicits proposals from individuals and non-profit organizations for funding of projects related to the perpetuation of Kurt Weill's artistic legacy.

Type: Research Grants; Publication Assistance Grants; Dissertation Fellowships; Travel Grants; Professional Performance and Production Grants; College and University Performance Production Grants; Recording Projects; Broadcasts.

No. of awards offered: Varies.

Frequency: Annual.

Value: For college and university production and performances, caps of US$3,000 and US$1,500 respectively; otherwise, no restrictions on requested amounts.

Country of Study: Any country.

Applications Procedure: Application forms must be completed for all but performances over US$5,000.

Closing Date: November 1st (no date for professional proposals over US$5,000).

Kurt Weill Prize

Subjects: Music.

Eligibility: Open to nationals of any country.

Level of Study: Unrestricted.

Purpose: To encourage scholarship relating to the musical theater in the 20th century.

Type: Cash.

No. of awards offered: One.

Frequency: Annual.

Value: US$2,500.

Applications Procedure: Applicants must submit five copies of their work.

Closing Date: April 1st.

Additional Information: Works must have been published within the previous year.

WEIZMANN INSTITUTE OF SCIENCE

Feinberg Graduate School, Weizmann Institute of Science, PO Box 26, Rehovot, 76100, Israel

*MSc Fellowships

Subjects: Life sciences (biology, biochemistry, biophysics), chemistry (physical, theoretical, organic, geological, biological and material sciences), physics (theoretical, experimental and applied), mathematics (pure and applied), computer science, science teaching.

Eligibility: Open to holders of a BSc degree from an accredited Institute of Higher Learning in Israel or of an equivalent degree from a recognized overseas university.

Frequency: Annual.

Value: To cover living expenses.

Study Establishment: The Institute.

Country of Study: Israel.

Closing Date: July 1st.

*PhD Fellowships

Subjects: Life sciences (biology, biochemistry, biophysics), chemistry (physical, theoretical, organic, geological, biological and material sciences), physics (theoretical, experimental and applied), mathematics (pure and applied), computer science, science teaching.

Eligibility: Open to holders of an MSc or MD degree.

Frequency: Throughout the year.

Value: To cover living expenses.

Study Establishment: The Institute.

Country of Study: Israel.

Additional Information: A special program is offered to students wishing to take a direct BSc to PhD route.

*Postdoctoral Fellowships Program

Subjects: Life sciences (biology, biochemistry, biophysics), chemistry (physical, theoretical, organic, geological, biological and material sciences), physics (theoretical, experimental and applied), mathematics (pure and applied), computer science, science teaching.

Eligibility: Open to holders of a PhD degree.

Frequency: Twice yearly.

Value: To cover living expenses.

Study Establishment: The Institute.

Country of Study: Israel.

Closing Date: January 1st, May 15th.

ROB AND BESSIE WELDER WILDLIFE FOUNDATION

Rob and Bessie Welder Wildlife Foundation, PO Drawer 1400, Sinton, TX, 78387, USA
Tel: 512 364 2643
Fax: 512 364 2650
Contact: Dr James G Teer, Director

Welder Wildlife Fellowship, Winnie Smith Fellowship

Subjects: Wildlife ecology and management.

Eligibility: Open to US citizens or aliens registered in a US university for a graduate degree.

Level of Study: Graduate.

Purpose: To provide support of graduate student research and education programs.

Type: Fellowship.

No. of awards offered: 20 fellowships at any given time; approximately 10 each year.

Frequency: Annual.

Value: According to individual needs; but up to US$15,000 per annum.

Length of Study: The duration of a graduate degree program.

Country of Study: USA.

Closing Date: October 1st for fellowships to begin in January.

Additional Information: Priority is given to students who wish to work at the Welder Foundation Refuge or in the Coastal Bend Region of Texas.

WELLBEING

WellBeing, 27 Sussex Place, London, NW1 4SP, England
Tel: 0171 262 5337
Fax: 0171 724 7725
Email: mary.stanton@wellbeing.org.uk
Contact: Research Administrator

Grants

Subjects: Obstetrics, gynaecology, and related disciplines.

Eligibility: No restrictions. Open to all qualified candidates, with the emphasis on clinicians.

Level of Study: Unrestricted.

Purpose: For research into all matters of women's obstetric and gynaecological health and the health of their babies, particularly all aspects of pregnancy, birth and care of newborns, gynaecological cancers including ovarian, cervical, endometrial and breast and quality of life issues such as menstrual problems, the menopause, infertility and incontinence.

Type: Grant.

No. of awards offered: 15-20.

Frequency: Annual.

Value: Varies; up to £75,000.

Length of Study: From one to three years.

Study Establishment: At appropriate institutions.

Country of Study: No restrictions but usually UK.

Applications Procedure: Application form and full instructions are available from the Research Administrator.

Closing Date: December 6th or nearest Monday each year.

THE WELLCOME TRUST

The Wellcome Trust, 183 Euston Rd, London, NW1 2BE, England
Tel: 0171 611 8888
Fax: 0171 611 8545
Contact: Grants Section

Awards, Fellowships and Studentships

Subjects: Biomedical sciences, from the basic sciences related to medicine to the clinical aspects of medicine and veterinary medicine, and the history of medicine.

Eligibility: Open to academic staff in universities, medical and veterinary schools and other institutions of higher education, who are engaged in all types of research.

No. of awards offered: A large number of Awards, Fellowships and Studentships.

Value: Varies.

Country of Study: Mostly UK, but also Eastern and Western Europe and limited schemes available in other countries.

Closing Date: Varies.

Additional Information: The Wellcome Trust is the most richly endowed of all charitable institutions that fund general medical research in the UK. The Governors review their policy annually in response to proposals from their advisory panels and professional staff.

WESLEYAN UNIVERSITY

Center for the Humanities, Wesleyan University, Middletown, CT, 06459-0069, USA
Tel: 860 685 2170
Fax: 860 685 2171
Email: PCAMDEN@Wesleyan.edu
Contact: The Director

Andrew W Mellon Postdoctoral Fellowship

Subjects: Cultural studies.

Eligibility: Open to persons who have received their PhD within the last four years.

Level of Study: Postdoctorate.

Purpose: To promote interdisciplinary interests among younger scholars.

Type: Fellowship.

No. of awards offered: One.

Frequency: Annual.

Value: US$31,000, plus US$500 reserve.

Applications Procedure: No formal application form. Request brochure detailing application process.

Closing Date: November 15th.

Additional Information: The Fellow must reside in Middletown during the tenure of the Fellowship, give one public lecture and teach one course (20 students).

WHITEHALL FOUNDATION, INC

Whitehall Foundation, Inc, 251 Royal Palm Way, Suite 211, Palm Beach, FL, 33480, USA
Tel: 407 655 4474
Fax: 407 659 4978
Contact: Laurel Baker

Grants-in-Aid

Subjects: The Foundation's current interest is in the field of neurobiology, defined as follows: invertebrate and vertebrate (exclusive of human beings) neurobiology, specifically investigations of neural mechanisms involved in sensory, motor and other complex functions of the whole organism as these relate to behavior.

Eligibility: Open to young PhD investigators who have not yet established themselves and who, for this reason, experience difficulty in competing for funds. Criteria upon which applications are judged include an abstract of the doctoral dissertation, published reprints if available and letters of recommendation from three experts in the specified field. Grants-in-Aid are also made to senior scientists. In addition to scientific merit, the major criteria upon which these applications are judged include past performance and evidence of continued productivity.

Level of Study: Postdoctorate.

Purpose: To assist scholarly research in dynamic areas of the life sciences that are not already heavily supported by other funding agencies.

Type: Grants-in-Aid.

No. of awards offered: Six to nine per review session.

Frequency: 3 review sessions annually.

Value: Stipend of up to US$15,000. Funds are not offered for replacement of PI's regular salary or summer salary; living expenses while working at home; travel to conferences or for consultation; secretarial services; publication costs; overhead or indirect costs.

Length of Study: One year; not renewable.

Country of Study: USA.

Applications Procedure: A letter of intent is required prior to application form being sent. There is no deadline for the letter.

Research Grants

Subjects: The Foundation's current interest is in the field of neurobiology, defined as follows: invertebrate and vertebrate (exclusive of human beings) neurobiology, specifically investigations of neural mechanisms involved in sensory, motor and other complex functions of the whole organism as these relate to behavior.

Eligibility: Open to scientists of all ages at the PhD/assistant professor level who are affiliated with recognized institutions. Applications are judged on the scientific merit of the proposal and evidence of the competence of the applicant.

Level of Study: Postdoctorate.

Purpose: To assist scholarly research in dynamic areas of the life sciences that are not already heavily support by other funding agencies.

Type: Research Grant.

No. of awards offered: Six to nine per review session. Some of these are awarded as Grants-in-Aid.

Frequency: Three review sessions annually.

Value: US$10,000-US$40,000 per annum. Funds may not be used for purchase of major items of permanent equipment; travel unless it is to unique field areas essential to the research; replacement of PI's regular salary or summer salary; consultant's fees.

Length of Study: One to three years, with the possibility of renewal.

Country of Study: USA only.

Applications Procedure: Applications are not accepted from investigators who already have, or expect to receive, substantial support from other sources even though the support may be for an unrelated project. A letter of intent is required prior to application form being sent. There is no deadline for the letter.

MRS GILES WHITING FOUNDATION

Writers' Program, Mrs Giles Whiting Foundation, 22nd Floor, 1133 Avenue of the Americas, New York, NY, 10036-6710, USA
Contact: Director

*Whiting Fellowships in the Humanities

Subjects: Humanities.

Eligibility: Open to students selected by their participating institutions: Bryn Mawr, University of Chicago, Columbia, Harvard, Princeton, Stanford and Yale. Direct applications are not accepted by the Foundation.

Purpose: To award outstanding doctoral candidates in the humanities during the final year of dissertation-writing.

Type: Fellowship.

No. of awards offered: Varies.

Frequency: Annual.

Value: Varies; the amount of the stipend is set by each school (normal range US$12,500-US$13,600).

Whiting Writers' Awards

Subjects: Writing.

Eligibility: Nominated candidates may be writers of fiction, poetry or non-fiction; they may be essayists, literary scholars, playwrights, novelists, poets or critics. Selections are based on the quality of nominee writing accomplishment and the likelihood of outstanding future work. The program places special emphasis on promising emerging talent; to qualify, writers need not be 'young', given that new talent may emerge at any age. Occasionally, the program also considers proven authors for whom a Whiting Award would provide further recognition and encouragement at a critical stage of their careers.

Purpose: To identify and support deserving writers of exceptional promise.

No. of awards offered: Ten.

Frequency: Annual.

Value: US$30,000.

Applications Procedure: Direct applications and informal nominations are not accepted by the Foundation. Recipients are nominated by writers, educators and editors from communities across the USA whose experience and vocations bring them into contact with individuals of unusual talent. The nominators and selectors are appointed by the Foundation and serve anonymously.

PETER WHITTINGHAM TRUST

Whittingham Awards, 16 Ogle Street, London, W1P 7LG, England
Tel: 0171 636 4481
Fax: 0171 637 4307
Contact: Administrator

*Whittingham Award

Subjects: Popular music or jazz; applications should bear in mind the chosen idiom of such artists as Gershwin, Cole Porter, Jerome Kern, Bernstein, Hamlisch, Sondheim, George Shearing, Art Tatum and Oscar Peterson.

Eligibility: Open to individuals, ordinarily resident in the UK, of any age group, for work independently or with a project-group of any size. The project should be in creation, performance, teaching or research in the field of quality popular music or jazz.

Purpose: To promote both composition and performance in the field of popular music or jazz.

No. of awards offered: One or more.

Frequency: Annual.

Value: From a total of £3,000.

Applications Procedure: Selected applicants are asked to attend an interview.

Closing Date: Mid-September.

VERNON WILLEY TRUST

New Zealand Guardian Trust, PO Box 9, Christchurch, New Zealand
Tel: 03 379 0644
Fax: 03 366 7616
Contact: Frances Cattermole

Awards

Subjects: The sheep and wool industry of New Zealand.

Eligibility: Open normally to residents of New Zealand, but others are welcome to apply. Candidates may be of widely varying seniority.

Level of Study: Unrestricted.

Purpose: To assist with research and education into the production, processing and marketing of wool and the general development of the industry for the national benefit of New Zealand.

No. of awards offered: Varies; dependent on funds available.

Frequency: Annual.

Value: Amount varies annually, usually between NZ$3,000-NZ$5,000.

Country of Study: New Zealand.

Applications Procedure: Application form required.

Closing Date: Usually second week in November.

Additional Information: Applicants for financial grants must satisfy the Committee that their activities are of general or public benefit. The results of the research or studies are expected to be covered by material suitable for publication in recognized scientific or technical journals.

DR WILLIAMS'S TRUST

Dr Williams's Trust, 14 Gordon Square, London, WC1H 0AG, England
Tel: 0171 387 3727
Fax: 0171 388 1142
Contact: Secretary

Glasgow Bursary

Subjects: Religious studies: theology, Christian history, etc.

Eligibility: Open to Protestant Dissenting ministers wishing to take refresher courses; graduate Protestant Dissenting ministers for a course leading to the degree of MTh; and mature students intending to enter the Protestant Dissenting ministry after training. Applicants must be from England or Wales.

Type: Bursary.

No. of awards offered: One.

Frequency: Annual.

Value: Normally £13,500 per annum, plus fees, paid each term.

Length of Study: One year; renewable for a second year.

Study Establishment: University of Glasgow Faculty of Divinity.

Country of Study: UK.

Closing Date: March 31st.

WILSON ORNITHOLOGICAL SOCIETY

Wilson Ornithological Society, Research Awards, c/o Museum of Zoology, University of Michigan, Ann Arbor, MI, 48109-1079, USA

*Louis Agassiz Fuertes Awards, Margaret Morse Nice Award

Subjects: Any aspect of ornithology.

Eligibility: Fuertes Awards are open to all ornithologists, although graduate students and young professionals are preferred; Nice Awards are limited to applicants who are not associated with a college or university, being intended for the encouragement of the independent researcher without access to funds and facilities generally available at the College. High school students are also eligible.

Purpose: To encourage and stimulate research on birds, by amateurs and students.

No. of awards offered: Two.

Frequency: Annual.

Value: Nice Award: US$200; Fuertes Award: several hundred dollars.

Country of Study: Unrestricted.

Closing Date: January 15th.

Additional Information: Each proposal is considered primarily on the basis of possible contribution to ornithological knowledge. It is hoped, though not required, that Awardees submit a manuscript detailing their results to the editor of the Wilson Bulletin for consideration.

*Paul A Stewart Awards

Subjects: Ornithology, especially studies of bird movements based on banding and analyses of recoveries and returns, and investigations pertaining to economic ornithology.

Eligibility: Open to students, amateurs and professionals without preference.

Purpose: To support research on birds.

No. of awards offered: Several.

Frequency: Annual.

Value: US$200.

Country of Study: Unrestricted.

Closing Date: January 15th.

Additional Information: Each proposal is considered primarily on the basis of possible contribution to ornithological research. It is hoped, though not required, that awardees submit a manuscript detailing their results to the editor of the Wilson Bulletin for consideration.

THE WOODROW WILSON NATIONAL FELLOWSHIP FOUNDATION

The Woodrow Wilson National Fellowship Foundation, CN 5281, Princeton, NJ, 08543-5281, USA
Tel: 609 542 7007
Fax: 609 542 0066
Email: maryh@wwnff.org

Grants in Women's Studies

Subjects: Women's studies; the history, education, psychology, etc. of women.

Eligibility: Open to doctoral candidates at American universities who have completed all the requirements for the degree course except the dissertation.

Level of Study: Doctorate.

Purpose: To assist men and women writing doctoral dissertations.

Type: Grant.

No. of awards offered: 15.

Frequency: Annual.

Value: Grants average US$1,500.

Length of Study: One year.

Closing Date: Early November.

Charlotte W Newcombe Doctoral Dissertation Fellowships

Subjects: Topics of religious or ethical values in all fields.

Eligibility: Open to students enrolled in doctoral programs in the humanities and social sciences at an American university. Must have completed all pre-dissertation requirements by November 30th.

Level of Study: Doctorate.

Purpose: To encourage new and significant research.

Type: Fellowship.

No. of awards offered: 30-35.

Frequency: Annual.

Value: US$14,000.

Study Establishment: At any appropriate graduate school in the USA.

Country of Study: USA.

Closing Date: Early December.

The Andrew W Mellon Fellowships in Humanistic Studies

Eligibility: College senior or recent graduate- US citizen or permanent resident entering into a progam leading to a PhD in the humanities. Must not be enrolled in graduate, or professional study or hold the MA degree.

Level of Study: Doctorate.

Purpose: To attract exceptionally promising students to prepare for careers of teaching and scholarship in humanistic studies by providing top level, competitive, portable awards, and to contribute thereby to the continuity of teaching and research of the highest order in America's colleges and universities.

Type: Fellowship.

No. of awards offered: 80.

Frequency: Annual.

Value: US$13,750 plus tuition and mandated fees.

Length of Study: One year.

Country of Study: USA and Canada.

Applications Procedure: The following must be provided by mail, phone, fax or E-Mail; Full name, current address and telephone and physical address in March 1997. Details of undergraduate institution, major and year of graduation. Intended Discipline in graduate school. Details of mailing address US mail or E-mail.

For further information contact:
The Woodrow Wilson National Fellowship Foundation, CN5329, Princeton, NJ, 08543-5329, USA
Tel: 609 452 7007
Fax: 609 452 0066
Email: jacquie@woodrow.org
Contact: Alvin Kernan, Director

THE HAROLD HYAM WINGATE FOUNDATION

Wingate Scholarships, 38 Curzon Street, London, W1Y 8EY, England
Contact: Jane Reid

Wingate Scholarships and Young Artists Awards

Subjects: Almost any subject.

Eligibility: Open to British, Commonwealth, ex-Commonwealth or Israeli citizens over 24 years of age who are resident in British Isles when applying. No qualifications are necessary.

Level of Study: Postgraduate, Doctorate, Unrestricted, Postdoctorate.

Purpose: To fund study, research or creative endeavour and to identify and reward the best talent of the emerging generation of artists in Britain.

Type: Cash and exhibition for young artists, Scholarship.

No. of awards offered: 36-40.

Frequency: Annual.

Value: £500-£30,000, according to need (average £8,000) for scholarships.

Applications Procedure: Application forms available from the administrator.

Closing Date: February 15th, for scholarships: October 1st for young artists awards.

Additional Information: The Scholarships are not intended for professional qualifications or standard courses, electives, etc., or the completion of courses.

THE WOLFSON FOUNDATION

The Wolfson Foundation, 18-22 Haymarket, London, SW1Y 4DQ, England
Tel: 0171 930 1057
Fax: 0171 930 1036
Contact: The Director

Wolfson Foundation Grants

Subjects: Areas supported by the Trustees are: medicine and health care, including the prevention of disease and the care and treatment of the sick, disadvantaged and disabled; research, science, technology and education, particularly where benefits may accrue to the development of industry or commerce in the UK; arts and the humanities, including libraries, museums, galleries, theatres, academies and historic buildings.

Eligibility: Open to registered charities and to exempt charities such as universities. Eligible applications from registered charities for contributions to appeals will normally be considered only when at least 50% of that appeal has already been raised. Grants to universities for research and scholarship are normally made under the umbrella of designated competitive programmes in which vice-chancellors and principals are invited to participate from time to time. Applications from university researchers are not considered outside these programmes. Grants are not made to private individuals.

Type: Grant.

No. of awards offered: Varies.

Frequency: The trustees meet twice a year.

Value: The Trustees make several types of grant which are not necessarily independent of each other. Capital Projects: grants may contribute towards the cost of erecting a new building or extension, or of renovating and refurbishing existing buildings; Equipment Grants: the supply of equipment for specific purposes, and/or furnishing and fittings; Recurrent Costs: grants in this category are not normally provided unless they form part of a designated programme.

Applications Procedure: Before embarking on a detailed proposal, prospective applicants are encouraged to explore its eligibility by submitting in writing a brief outline of the project with one copy of the organisation's most recent audited accounts.

THE WOLFSONIAN RESEARCH CENTER

The Wolfsonian Research Center, 1001 Washington Avenue, Miami Beach, FL, 33139, USA
Tel: 305 535 2650
Fax: 305 531 2133
Email: researchctr@neptune.com
Contact: Program Officer

Senior Fellowship; Visiting Scholar; Assoc. Fellowship

Subjects: History and philosophy of art.

Eligibility: Funded fellowships are available to those who have held a master's degree for five years or who possess an outstanding record of professional accomplishment. All fellowships are awarded without regard to race, color, gender, religion, national origin, sexual orientation, age, or disability of applicants.

Level of Study: Professional development.

Purpose: To conduct research on the Wolfsonian's collection of 70,000 objects from the period 1885-1945, including decorative arts, works on paper, books and ephemera. Senior Fellowships are also available for joint study at the Wolfsonian and either the Victoria and Albert in London, or the American Academy in Rome.

Type: Fellowship.

No. of awards offered: Varies.

Frequency: Annual.

Value: Varies.

Length of Study: Six weeks to six months.

Study Establishment: Either: the Wolfsonian, the Victoria and Albert, or the American Academy in Rome.

Country of Study: USA, UK or Italy.

Applications Procedure: Application form must be completed and submitted with three recommendations. Contact the program officer for details and application materials.

Closing Date: Varies.

WOMAN'S NATIONAL FARM AND GARDEN ASSOCIATION, INC

Woman's National Farm and Garden Association, Inc, 13 Davis Drive, Saginaw, MI, 48602, USA
Contact: Mrs Elmer Braun, Chairwoman

Sarah Bradley Tyson Memorial Fellowship

Subjects: Agriculture, horticulture and related subjects.

Eligibility: Open to properly qualified young women and men who have proved their abilities by several years' experience.

Purpose: To assist with advanced study.

Type: Fellowship.

No. of awards offered: One.

Frequency: Annual.

Value: US$500.

Length of Study: One year.

Study Establishment: An educational institution of recognized standing approved by the Fellowship Committee.

Country of Study: USA.

Closing Date: April 15th.

Additional Information: The acceptance of the Fellowship implies an obligation on the part of the student to devote herself or himself unreservedly to study or research as outlined in the application and to submit any proposed change in plans to the chairman for approval. The student must also send to the chairman at least two reports on work done, one at the end of the first semester and another upon the completion of the year's work. The Committee regards the acceptance of the Fellowship as creating a contract requiring the fulfilment of these conditions.

WOMEN BAND DIRECTORS NATIONAL ASSOCIATION

Women Band Directors National Association, 10,000 Garrett Street, Vienna, VA, 22181, USA

Tel: 203 281 1770
Contact: Noreen Linnemann

*Scholarship Awards

Subjects: Music education.

Eligibility: Open to women band instrument majors enrolled in a university and working towards a degree in music education.

Purpose: To support young college women presently preparing to be band directors.

Type: Scholarship.

No. of awards offered: Two.

Frequency: Annual.

Value: US$300.

Country of Study: USA.

Closing Date: December 1st.

For further information contact:
Women Band Directors National Association, 345 Overlook Drive, West Lafayette, IN, 47906-1249, USA
Tel: 317 463 1738
Contact: Gladys Wright

WOMEN'S RESEARCH & EDUCATION INSTITUTE

Women's Research & Education Institute, 1700 18th Street, NW, 400, Washington, DC, 20009, USA
Tel: 202 328 7070
Fax: 202 328 3514
Contact: Fellowship Program

WREI is an independent, national public policy research and education center whose mission is to inform and help shape the public policy debate on issues affecting women and their roles in the family, workplace, and public arena

WREI Congressional Fellowships on Women and Public Policy

Subjects: Policy issues affecting women.

Eligibility: Open to students currently enrolled in a graduate program anywhere in the USA. Applicants must have the approval of their academic advisor to register for six hours of Fellowship credit at the home institution. It is recommended that students complete at least nine hours of graduate work prior to commencement and have a demonstrated interest in research and political activity relevant to women's social and political status.

Level of Study: Postgraduate.

Purpose: To train women as potential leaders in public policy formation and to examine issues from the perspective and experiences and needs of women.

Type: Fellowship.

No. of awards offered: Varies.

Frequency: Annual.

Value: A stipend of US$9,500 for the academic year. An additional sum of US$500 is provided for the purchase of health insurance. WREI will also reimburse Fellows up to a maximum of US$1,500 for the cost of six hours of tuition at their home institutions.

Length of Study: One academic year, from September through May.

Country of Study: USA.

Applications Procedure: Applications can be obtained by sending a written request along with a self-addressed, stamped envelope.

Closing Date: Mid-March.

Additional Information: The Fellow will work 30 hours per week in a Congressional office as a legislative aide on policy issues affecting women. Fellows meet once a week in issue seminars directed by the WREI staff.

WOMEN'S STUDIO WORKSHOP

Women's Studio Workshop, PO Box 489, Rosendale, NY, 12472, USA
Tel: 1 914 658 9133

Artists' Book Residencies

Subjects: Art: books.

Eligibility: Open to women artists.

Purpose: To enable artists to produce a limited edition of a book work at WSW.

Type: Residency.

No. of awards offered: Varies.

Frequency: Annual.

Value: A stipend of US$1,800, materials of up to US$450, and housing at the WSW.

Length of Study: Six weeks.

Study Establishment: The Workshop.

Country of Study: USA.

Applications Procedure: Applications should include a one-page description of the proposed project, the medium or media used to print the book, number of pages, page size, edition number, a structural dummy, a materials budget, a resume, six to ten slides and a SASE for return of materials. Applications are reviewed by past grant recipients and a WSW staff artist.

Closing Date: November 15th.

Artists' Fellowships

Subjects: Intaglio, water-based silkscreen, photography and papermaking.

Eligibility: Open to women artists.

Purpose: To provide a time for artists to explore new ideas in a dynamic and cooperative community of women artists in a rural environment.

Type: Fellowship.

No. of awards offered: Varies.

Frequency: Annual.

Value: US$200 per week, including housing.

Length of Study: Two to four weeks between September and June.

Study Establishment: At the WSW.

Country of Study: USA.

Applications Procedure: Applicants should write for details.

Internships

Subjects: Book arts, specialized papermaking and printmaking techniques.

Eligibility: Open to young women artists/students who are aged between 20 and 30.

Level of Study: Unrestricted.

Type: Internship.

No. of awards offered: Nine.

Frequency: Three times per year.

Length of Study: Three to five months.

Country of Study: USA.

Applications Procedure: Send resume, 10-20 slides, three current letters of reference, letter of interest which addresses why an internship at WSW would be important, what applicants have to offer and SASE.

Closing Date: Summer - March 15th; Fall - July 15th; Spring - November 15th.

For further information contact:
Women's Studio Workshop, PO Box 489, Rosendale, NY, 12472, USA
Tel: 914 658 9133
Fax: 914 658 9031
www: www.webmark.com/wsw/wswhome.htm
Contact: Ann Kalmbach

Production Grants

Subjects: Art: books.

Eligibility: Open to all artists.

Purpose: To assist artists working in their own studios with the publication of small-scale book works.

Type: Grant.

No. of awards offered: Varies.

Frequency: Annual.

Value: To cover production costs, up to US$750.

Applications Procedure: Applications should include a one-page description of the proposed project, the medium or media used to print the book, number of pages, page size, edition number, a structural dummy, a materials budget, a resume, six to ten slides and a SASE for return of materials. Applications are reviewed by past grant recipients and a WSW staff artist.

Closing Date: November 15th.

WOODS HOLE OCEANOGRAPHIC INSTITUTION

Fellowship Committee, Education Office, Clark Laboratory, Woods Hole Oceanographic Institution, Woods Hole, MA, 02543, USA
Tel: 508 548 1400
Fax: 508 457 2188

Postdoctoral Awards in Ocean Science and Engineering

Subjects: Oceanography; oceanographic engineering.

Eligibility: Open to US citizens and foreign nationals who have earned the PhD degree in biology, molecular biology, chemistry, geology, geophysics, oceanography, meteorology, engineering or mathematics. Scientists with more than three years' postdoctoral experience are not eligible.

Level of Study: Postdoctorate.

Purpose: To further the education and training of recent recipients of doctoral degrees.

No. of awards offered: 7-10.

Frequency: Annual.

Value: US$36,000 per annum, plus limited additional support for equipment, supplies and travel.

Length of Study: 12-18 months.

Study Establishment: Woods Hole.

Country of Study: USA.

Applications Procedure: Application form must be completed.

Closing Date: January 15th for notification in March.

Additional Information: Award holders work in the laboratory, and under the general supervision of an appropriate member of the staff, but are expected to work independently on research problems of their own choice.

WORLD HEALTH ORGANIZATION

World Health Organization, Regional Office for the Americas/Pan-American Sanitary Bureau, 525, 23rd Street, NW, Washington, DC, 20037, USA
Tel: 1 202 861 3200
Fax: 1 202 223 5971

WHO Fellowships, Research Training Grants and Visiting Scientist Grants

Subjects: Medical and health studies. The most common subjects of study are in the various areas of public health, teacher training in health sciences, postgraduate studies in medicine and surgery. Fellowships are awarded to attend formal courses or to study the services and practice in other countries. As a general rule, WHO does not organize regular courses.

Eligibility: Open to nationals of Member States and Associate Members of WHO and to nationals of trust and other territories for whose international relations WHO Member States are responsible, or which are administered by international authorities established by the United Nations.

Purpose: To promote the international exchange of scientific knowledge and techniques relating to health, for the purpose of improving standards of teaching and training in the health, medical and related fields; and to strengthen national health services.

Type: Grants and fellowships.

No. of awards offered: Varies.

Frequency: As required.

Value: To cover the cost of travel, maintenance, tuition fees and other expenses in special cases.

Study Establishment: For attendance of formal courses or to study the services and practices of the countries concerned.

Country of Study: As appropriate, according to the subject of study and the origin of the candidate.

Applications Procedure: The World Health Organization only awards Fellowships through the governments of its Member States, and candidates should contact the Ministry of Health, or the corresponding national health administration, of their country of origin, which will advise them on the procedure for application. Applicants are discouraged from applying to the Geneva address. At the Headquarters level, the World Health Organization only awards Research Training Grants and Visiting Scientist Grants to candidates from institutions working in collaboration with the Special Programme of Research, Development and Research Training in Human Reproduction, and the Special Programme for Research and Training in Tropical Diseases. However, the WHO regional offices award grants in other fields and further information can be requested from the WHO regional office of the region of origin of the candidate.

Closing Date: At least six months prior to study.

For further information contact:
World Health Organization, Regional Office for Africa, PO Box No 6, Brazzaville, Congo
Tel: 242 83 38 60 64
Fax: 242 83 18 79
Contact: (Research Training Grants)

or
World Health Organization, Regional Office for the Eastern Mediterranean, PO Box No 1517, Alexandria, 21511, Egypt
Tel: 203 48 202 23/4 or 203 48 300 90/6/7
Fax: 203 48 38 916

or
World Health Organization, Regional Office for Europe, 8 Scherfigsvej, 2100 Copenhagen, Denmark
Tel: 45 39 17 17 17
Fax: 45 39 17 18 18

or

World Health Organization, Regional Office for South-East Asia, Indraprastha Estate, Mahatma Gandhi Road, New Delhi, 110002, India
Tel: 91 11 331 7804 or 91 11 331 7823
Fax: 91 11 331 8607 or 91 11 332 7972

or

World Health Organization, Regional Office for the Western Pacific, PO Box 2932, Manila, 1099, Philippines
Tel: 632 521 84 21
Fax: 632 59 11 036 or 632 59 68 13

WORLD LEARNING

School for International Training, Kipling Road, PO Box 676, Brattleboro, VT, 05302 0676, USA
Tel: 800 451 4465 or 802 257 7751
Fax: 802 258 3296
www: http://www.worldlearning.org

Master of Arts in Teaching Program

Subjects: Teaching of French, Spanish or English as a second language.

Eligibility: Open to persons of any nationality who are preparing for a language teaching career.

Level of Study: Postgraduate.

Purpose: To prepare language teachers committed to professional development and service in their field.

Type: Scholarship.

No. of awards offered: Small number.

Frequency: Annual.

Value: Varies.

Length of Study: A period which includes a period of student teaching and homestay.

Study Establishment: The School for International Training for a masters of arts degree.

Country of Study: USA and overseas.

Applications Procedure: Institutional Financial Aid application.

Closing Date: June 15th.

Additional Information: Applicants must be registered students.

For further information contact:
MAT Admissions, School for International Training, Kipling Road, PO Box 676, Brattleboro, VT, 05302-0676, USA
Tel: 800 451 4465 or 802 257 7751
Fax: 802 258 3296
www: http://www.worldlearning.org
Contact: Fiona Cook

Master's Program in Intercultural Management

Subjects: Participants concentrate on sustainable development, international education, or training and human resource development.

Eligibility: Open to persons of any nationality.

Level of Study: Postgraduate.

Purpose: To provide competency-based, professional-level training for intercultural managers.

Type: Scholarship.

No. of awards offered: Varies.

Frequency: Annual.

Value: Varies.

Study Establishment: The School for International Training, and a period of overseas working experience with an international organization, leading to a Master's degree.

Country of Study: USA and overseas.

Applications Procedure: Institutional Financial Aid form must be completed.

Closing Date: June 15th.

Additional Information: In order to receive an award, the individual must be a registered student.

WORLD METEOROLOGICAL ORGANIZATION

World Meteorological Organization, 41 Av Guiseppe-Motta, Case Postale No.2300, Geneva, 1211, Switzerland
Tel: 4122 730 8111
Fax: 4122 734 2326
www: www.wmo.ch
Telex: 414199 OMMCH
Contact: Secretary-General

Education and Training Fellowships

Subjects: Atmospheric science/meteorology.

Eligibility: Fellowships are awarded to candidates designated by their respective governments, through the Permanent Representative with WMO.

Level of Study: Professional development.

Purpose: To educate and train meteorological personnel on individually tailored or group study training programmes.

Type: Fellowship.

No. of awards offered: Approximately 300 per year.

Frequency: Dependent on funds available.

Value: According to UN rates.

Length of Study: Variable.

Study Establishment: WMO.

Country of Study: Switzerland.

Applications Procedure: Candidates are to be designated officially through the Permanent Representative with WMO (normally the Director of the National Meteorological Service in the requesting country concerned).

WORLD PATHOLOGY FOUNDATION

In der Fina 21 A, Schaan, FL-9494, Liechtenstein
Tel: 41 75 2320424
Fax: 41 75 2320437
Contact: Professor Thomas Krech

Gordon Signy Foreign Fellowship

Subjects: Clinical pathology.

Eligibility: Open to young pathologists of any nationality, who are completing, or have recently completed, training in pathology.

Purpose: To provide young pathologists with the means to travel to another country for short periods in order to acquire skills which will be advantageous upon their return home.

Type: Fellowship.

No. of awards offered: One.

Value: US$3,000.

Length of Study: 2-4 months.

Country of Study: Any country.

Closing Date: May 31st.

THE WORLD PRESS INSTITUTE

World Press Institute, 1635 Summit Avenue, St Paul, MN, 55105, USA
Tel: 612 696 6360
Fax: 612 696 6306
Email: hodowanic@macalstr.edu
Contact: John Hodowanic

Fellowship

Subjects: Journalism.

Eligibility: Open to foreign national full-time professional journalists with a minimum of five years' experience. They must be fluent in spoken and written English and should be between 25 and 35 years of age.

Level of Study: Professional development.

Purpose: To provide the opportunity for international journalists to study, work and travel in the United States.

Type: Fellowship.

No. of awards offered: Ten.

Frequency: Annual.

Value: US$25,000.

Length of Study: Four months.

Study Establishment: Macalester College.

Country of Study: USA.

Applications Procedure: Applications will be sent upon request and must be completed by December 31st each year.

Closing Date: December 31st.

WORLD UNIVERSITY SERVICE (WUS)

World University Service (UK), 20-21 Compton Terrace, London, N1 2UN, England
Tel: 0171 226 6747
Fax: 0171 226 0482
Contact: The Small Grants Programme

Small Grants Programme

Subjects: Any subject.

Eligibility: Open to refugees, including people with exceptional leave to remain and asylum seekers, who have been residing in the UK for no more than three years since their application for asylum.

Purpose: To assist refugees, including people with exceptional leave to remain and asylum seekers, whose financial difficulties stem from political, racial or religious discrimination. WUS also offers an educational advisory service.

No. of awards offered: Varies.

Frequency: Dependent on funds.

Value: A one-off payment not normally exceeding £500. Cheques will normally be made out in the name of the educational institution.

Country of Study: UK.

Applications Procedure: Prospective applicants should write to the Small Grants Programme, stating their status in the UK, the nature of the course they are pursuing, and why they are in financial need. They will subsequently be requested to fill out an application form and produce evidence of their income. Applicants will also be requested to produce evidence of a definitive offer from the educational institution.

WORLD WITHOUT WAR COUNCIL

World Without War Council, Fellows Program Coordinator, 1730 Martin Luther King Jr. Way, Berkeley, CA, 94709-2140, USA
Tel: 510 845 1992
Fax: 510 845 5721
Email: wwwc@igc.apc.org
Contact: Robert Pickus, President

Americans and World Affairs Fellows Program

Eligibility: Fellows are generally expected to have completed academic work for an MA or its equivalent. Individuals with a BA and demonstrated commitment to the goals and values of the program will also be considered.

Level of Study: Postgraduate.

Purpose: The program is designed to give participants a better understanding of the role nongovernmental organisations play in shaping our engagements with the world.

Type: Stipend, Fellowship.

Frequency: Annual.

Value: Fellows who work full-time may receive stipends ranging from US$3,600 to US$10,000 a year. Payments depend on the financial resources of the organisation to which the fellow applies. Many fellows receive only a small stipend, or no stipend at all, they have to use their own resources or hold a second, part-time job to support themselves.

Country of Study: USA.

Applications Procedure: Completed applications should be submitted.

Closing Date: June 1st.

Additional Information: The Program accomplishes its purposes by providing participating fellows with: work experience, seminars, encounters, individual study and skills training.

THE WORSHIPFUL COMPANY OF MUSICIANS

The Worshipful Company of Musicians, 2nd Floor, St Dunstan's House, 2/4 Carey Lane, London, EC2V 8AA, England
Tel: 0171 600 4636
Fax: 0171 606 7269
Contact: The Clerk

Allcard Grants

Subjects: Music.

Eligibility: Open to individuals wishing to undertake a relevant training or research programme. The grants are not available for courses leading either to a first degree at a university or to a diploma at a college of music, and only in exceptional circumstances will assistance towards the cost of a fourth or fifth year at a college of music be considered. Grants are not available towards the purchase of instruments.

Type: Grant.

No. of awards offered: A limited number.

Frequency: Annual.

Value: Up to £1,000.

Study Establishment: For advanced training for performers (at home or abroad) or for significant projects of a special nature (e.g. in the field of musicology).

Country of Study: Any country.

Applications Procedure: Written applications only.

Closing Date: Applications to be made after 1 January and before 1 April.

W T Best Memorial Scholarships

Subjects: Music.

Eligibility: Open to advanced students of the organ.

Type: Scholarship.

No. of awards offered: One.

Frequency: Trienially (1999).

Value: £3,000 per annum.

Length of Study: Up to three years.

Country of Study: UK.

Applications Procedure: Nominations must be made by any one of the following: professors of music at Oxford, Cambridge or London Universities; directors, Royal College of Music and Royal College of Organists; principals, Royal Academy of Music, Guildhall School of Music and Drama, Royal Northern College of Music, and Royal Scottish Academy of Music and Drama; directors, Edinburgh, Cardiff and Belfast Universities. No application should be made directly to the Worshipful Company of Musicians.

Closing Date: June 1st in the year of the award.

Carnwath Scholarship

Subjects: Music.

Eligibility: Open to any person of either sex permanently resident in the UK and 21-25 years of age. The Scholarship is intended only for the advanced student who has successfully completed a solo performance course at a college of music.

Type: Scholarship.

No. of awards offered: One.

Frequency: Biennially (1998).

Value: £3,000.

Length of Study: Up to two years.

Country of Study: UK.

Applications Procedure: Nominations must be made by any one of the following: principals, Royal Academy of Music, Guildhall School of Music and Drama, Royal Northern College of Music, Royal Scottish Academy of Music, Trinity College of Music, London College of Music, Welsh College of Music and Drama, Birmingham School of Music; director, Royal College of Music. No application should be made directly to the Worshipful Company of Musicians.

Closing Date: June 1st in the year of the award.

John Clementi Collard Fellowship

Subjects: Music.

Eligibility: Open to professional musicians of standing and experience who show excellence in one or more of the higher branches of musical activity, i.e. composition, research, and performance (including conducting).

Type: Fellowship.

No. of awards offered: One.

Frequency: Approximately triennially (1998).

Value: £5,000 per annum.

Length of Study: Up to three years.

Country of Study: UK.

Applications Procedure: Nominations must be made by any one of the following: professors of music at Oxford, Cambridge or London Universities; director, Royal College of Music; principals, Royal Academy of Music, Guildhall School of Music and Drama, Royal Northern College of Music. No application should be made directly to the Worshipful Company of Musicians.

Closing Date: March 31st in the year of the award.

Gemini Fellowship

Subjects: Musical composition.

Eligibility: Open to candidates aged not less than 20 and not more than 35 on the closing date and who are at the time permanently resident in the UK.

Type: Fellowship.

No. of awards offered: One.

Frequency: Annual.

Value: £5,000 on selection and £5,000 on delivery of completed score.

Length of Study: Two years, during which time the Fellow will be expected to compose a major work for performance.

Country of Study: UK.

Closing Date: May 1st.

Additional Information: The Fellowship is administered by the Worshipful Company of Musicians on behalf of the Gemini Foundation, and awarded upon the recommendation of an adjudication panel of distinguished composers. Subject to the work attaining the required standard, the Company will arrange the first performance of the work composed during the Fellowship.

Maisie Lewis Young Artists Fund

Subjects: Musical performance.

Eligibility: Open to instrumentalists (including organists) up to 25 years of age and to singers of up to 30 years of age.

Purpose: To assist young artists of outstanding ability who wish to acquire experience on the professional soloist concert platform.

No. of awards offered: Six half-recitals per annum.

Frequency: Annual.

Value: Reimbursement of recitalists' expenses.

Country of Study: UK.

Applications Procedure: Application forms are available from January 1st.

Closing Date: May 1st.

Additional Information: Auditions are normally held in September.

WRITER'S DIGEST

Writer's Digest, 1507 Dana Avenue, Cincinnati, OH, 45207, USA
Contact: Category Judge

Writer's Digest Writing Competition

Subjects: Creative writing: literary short stories and mainstream/genre works (up to 2,000 words); feature articles and personal essays (2,000 words); stage plays and television/movie scripts (the first 15 pages segment of script in standard script format); rhyming poetry and non-rhyming poetry (one poem up to 16 lines).

Eligibility: Open to authors of any nationality; works must be written in English.

Type: Grand prize and awards for first through fifth place winners; sixth through 100th place receive a certificate, Competition.

Frequency: Annual.

Value: Cash prizes for first to fifth prizewinners.

Closing Date: May 31st.

Additional Information: Contestants may enter as many categories and as many times in each category as they wish. Manuscripts will not be returned and each entry must be made on an official entry form and accompanied by a US$8 entry free. Entries must be original and unprinted.

YALE CENTER FOR BRITISH ART

Yale Center for British Art, PO Box 208280, New Haven, CT, 06520-8280, USA
Tel: 203 432 2822
Fax: 203 432 4538
Email: bacinfo@minerva.cis.yale.edu
www: www.cis.yale.edu/yups/bac/entrance.html
Contact: Director

Fellowships

Subjects: British art from the Elizabethan period onwards.

Eligibility: Open to scholars in postdoctoral or equivalent research related to British art.

Level of Study: Postdoctorate.

Purpose: To allow scholars of either literature, history, the history of art or related fields, to study the Center's holdings of paintings, drawings, prints and rare books, and to make use of its research facilities.

Type: Fellowship.

No. of awards offered: Limited.

Frequency: Annual.

Value: Cost of travel to and from New Haven, plus accommodation and a living allowance.

Length of Study: Normally four weeks.

Study Establishment: The Center.

Country of Study: USA.

Closing Date: January 31st.

Additional Information: Applications are also welcomed from museum professionals whose responsibilities and research interests include British art.

Andrew W Mellon Fellowship

Subjects: History and philosophy of art.

Eligibility: Open to foreign students enrolled for a higher degree at a British or other non-American university.

Level of Study: Postgraduate.

Type: Fellowship.

No. of awards offered: One.

Frequency: Annual.

Value: US$13,500 plus return airfare from London, health benefits and travel expenses up to US$1,000.

Length of Study: One year.

Study Establishment: Yale Center for British Art.

Country of Study: USA.

Applications Procedure: No application form. Please submit name, address, telephone number, CV listing professional experience, education and publications, three-page outline of research proposal, and two confidential letters of recommendation.

Closing Date: January 31st.

Lewis Walpole Library Fellowship

Subjects: History and philosophy of art; English.

Eligibility: Applicants must be pursuing an advanced degree and must be engaged in postdoctoral research or equivalent research.

Level of Study: Postgraduate, Doctorate, Postdoctorate.

Purpose: To enable one month of study in the Library's collection of eighteenth-century British prints, paintings, books and manuscripts.

Type: Fellowship.

No. of awards offered: Two per year.

Frequency: Annual.

Value: US$1,500 plus modest travel allowance.

Length of Study: One month.

Study Establishment: Walpole Library.

Country of Study: USA.

Applications Procedure: Please submit CV, brief outline of research proposal (no more than three pages) and two confidential letters of recommendation.

Closing Date: January 31st.

For further information contact:
Lewis Walpole Library, 154 Main Street, Farmington, CT, 06032-2958, USA
Tel: 203 432 2822
Fax: 203 432 4538
Email: bacinfo@minerva.cis.yale.edu
www: www.cis.yale.edu/yups/bac/entrance.html
Contact: The Librarian

YALE UNIVERSITY PRESS

Yale University Press, 302 Temple Street, PO Box 209040, New Haven, CT, 06520-9040, USA
Tel: 203 432 0960
Fax: 203 432 0948
Contact: Richard Miller

Yale Series of Younger Poets

Eligibility: All poems must be original; translations are not acceptable. Writers who have had volumes of poetry printed privately or printed in limited editions of no more than 300 copies are eligible. Manuscripts submitted in previous years may be resubmitted.

Purpose: The series is an annual competition held in the month of February for poets who have not yet published a book of poetry.

Type: Publication.

Frequency: Annual.

Country of Study: USA.

Applications Procedure: There is no application form. Please write for more information on entry criteria.

Closing Date: Submissions must be postmarked for the month of February.

VERA YELVERTON ACADEMY OF MUSIC

Vera Yelverton Academy of Music, 39 Wood Vale, London, N10 3DJ, England
Tel: 0181 372 0295
Contact: Vera Yelverton, ARCM

Fritz Gottlieb Memorial Scholarship

Subjects: Piano and theory.

Eligibility: Open to talented students of any nationality up to 25 years of age.

Level of Study: Professional development.

Purpose: To enable gifted students to improve their playing and win further awards.

Type: Scholarship.

No. of awards offered: One.

Frequency: Biennially.

Value: Lessons to a value of at least £2,500. No money is given.

Length of Study: For two years.

Country of Study: UK.

Applications Procedure: Please submit a tape of piano playing.

Closing Date: Open any time.

Additional Information: The tuition leads finally to a performance on the South Bank if possible.

LOREN L ZACHARY SOCIETY FOR THE PERFORMING ARTS

The Loren L Zachary Society, 2250 Gloaming Way, Beverly Hills, CA, 90210, USA
Tel: 310 276 2731
Contact: Nedra Zachary, Director of Auditions

National Vocal Competition

Subjects: Operatic singing.

Eligibility: Open to female singers between 21 and 33 years of age and male singers between 21 and 35 years of age who have completed operatic training and are fully prepared to pursue professional stage careers.

Level of Study: Professional development.

Purpose: To assist in the careers of young opera singers through competitive auditions and monetary awards.

Type: Competition.

No. of awards offered: Ten.

Frequency: Annual.

Value: US$10,000 plus a round-trip flight to Vienna, Austria, for the top winner for opera auditioning purposes. Approximately US$33,000 was distributed amongst the finalists (1995).

Applications Procedure: Application forms need to be completed and accompanied by proof of age and application fee of US$30.

Closing Date: New York auditions: February. Los Angeles auditions: early April.

Additional Information: Applicants must be present at all phases of the auditions. Tapes are not acceptable. Auditions take place in New York and in Los Angeles, March to May. For application forms and exact dates, interested singers should send a stamped business-size envelope to the Society.

ZONTA INTERNATIONAL FOUNDATION

Zonta International Foundation, 557 West Randolph Street, Chicago, IL, 60661-2206, USA
Tel: 312 930 5848
Fax: 312 930 0951
Contact: Ana L Ubides

Amelia Earhart Fellowship Awards

Subjects: Aerospace-related science and engineering.

Eligibility: Open to women of any nationality who have a bachelors degree in an area of science or engineering relating to advanced studies in aerospace studies, a superior academic record and evidence of potential and who have been accepted by a graduate school offering accredited courses and degrees in aerospace studies.

Level of Study: Postgraduate.

Purpose: To enable women to undertake graduate study.

Type: Fellowship.

No. of awards offered: Approximately 40.

Frequency: Annual.

Value: US$6,000.

Study Establishment: Any institution offering accredited graduate courses and degrees in aerospace studies.

Country of Study: No restrictions.

Closing Date: November 1st.

INDEX OF AWARDS

INDEX OF DISCONTINUED AWARDS

The following is a list of awards previously included in The Grants Register which are no longer being offered, have been replaced by another program, or are no longer relevant to the publication.

AFI/NEA Independent Film/Videomaker Program
American Academy for Jewish Research Publication Grants
American Academy of Neurology Research Fellowship Award
American College of Physicians International Scholarships
Anglo-German Journalism Prize
Arab-British Chamber Charitable Foundation Scholarship
Architects Registration Council Education Fund Award
Arthritis Society Clinical Assistantships
Arthritis Society Studentships
Australian Awards for Research in Asia (AARA)
Australian War Memorial Special Project Fellowships
Baron (Bernhard) Travelling Scholarships
Bean (Charles) Postgraduate Scholarship
Bensinger-Liddell Salmon Fellowship
Blaxall/Valentine Bursary
Bogie (Donald) Prize
Boyle (Edward) Banff Award
Boyle (Edward) Medical Elective Bursaries
Boyle (Edward) Music Award
British Gas plc Research Scholarships
Building Feasibility Studies Scheme
Burroughs Wellcome STD Postdoctoral Research Fellowship
CLEO Scholarships
Cambridge Overseas Trust Grants to Americans
Canadian Career Awards for National Health Scientists
Canadian Career Awards for Visiting National Health Scientists
Canadian Law Foundation Legal Research Scholarship
Canadian Liver Foundation Bridging Operating Grants
Cater Fellowship
Colella (Filomena) Scholarships and Laurito (Rosa Angela) Scholarships
Commonwealth Youth Programme Bursaries and Study Fellowships
Commonwealth Youth Service Awards Scheme
Coulter Electronics Scholarship
Department of National Defence Postdoctoral Fellowships in Military History
Department of National Education (South Africa) Research Scholarship
EPSRC Studentships Tenable Outside the UK
Eberhard Student Writing Competition
Eden Travelling Fellowship
Edgar Research Fellowship
Fellowship in Paediatric Orthopaedic Surgery
German Historical Institute Summer Program
Grains Research and Development Corporation Postgraduate Research Scholarships
Green-Armytage and Spackman Travelling Scholarship
Hannigan (Jane Anne) Research Award
Hayek Fund for Scholars
Hoiles (RC) and IHS Postdoctoral Fellowships
Honeybee Research and Development Council Grants
Horniman (Emslie) Anthropological Scholarship Fund
IARC Visiting Scientist Award
IEE Clayton Grants for Diploma in Engineering Management
IEE Manville Fellowship
IEE Measurement Prize
IEE Prize
IEE Robinson Research Fellowship
IEE Vodafone Scholarships
IEE Younger Members Conference Bursary
IHS Summer Faculty Fellowships
ISAS Research Fellowship in Australian-Southeast Asian Relations
ISAS Research Fellowship in Canadian-Southeast Asian Relations
Indiana University English-Speaking Union Fellowship

Indo-American Research Fellowships
Institute for Humane Studies Assistance Fund for Professionals
JCB Travel Grants; Maria-Elena Cassiet Travel Grants
Jackson (John Hughlings) Clinical Research Fellowship
Leslie Vacation Scholarships
Li (KT) Predoctoral Fellowships on the Newly Industrialized Countries
Liberty and Society Week-Long Summer Conferences
Live Art Commissions Scheme
McKenzie (JR) Senior Fellowship in Educational Research
March of Dimes Basic Research Grants
March of Dimes Chapter Grants
March of Dimes Clinical Research Grants
March of Dimes Social and Behavioral Sciences Research Grants
Menopause Travel Award
Mental Health Foundation Career Development Fellowships
Mental Health Foundation Grants for Scientific Assistance and Expenses
Mental Health Foundation Grants in Aid of Travel During Medical Students Elective Periods
Menuhin (Yehudi) International Violin Competition Prizes
Ministry of Agriculture and Natural Resources Scholarships
Moore (Vera) Junior Research Fellowship
Morley (Felix) Memorial Journalism Competition
Muscular Dystrophy Association Fellowship Programs
Mweka Wildlife Management Scholarships
NCAR Graduate Fellowships
NCIC Blair Awards
NCIC Fonyo (Steve) Research Studentship
NCIC Senior Research Scientist Grants
Newberry Library Resident Fellowships for Unaffiliated Scholars
New Collaborations Fund
New Jersey Historical Commission Grants and Prizes
Olin (John M) Fellowships
Potato Marketing Board Postgraduate Studentships
Price Waterhouse (Shaw) Leonard Scholarship
Radcliffe-Brown Memorial Fund for Social Anthropological Research
Research Corporation Partners in Science
Road Haulage Association Travelling Scholarship
Robinson (Julius) Postgraduate Scholarship
Royal Society of Edinburgh Research Workshops
Ruggles-Gates Grant for Research in Biological Anthropology
SSRC Africa Program: Predissertation Fellowships
SSRC Soviet Union and its Successor States Program: Workshops
SSRC Western Europe Program: Dissertation Fellowships
St Hilda's College McIlrath Junior Research Fellowship
Scholarships for Postgraduate Soil Scientists
Scimed Award
Selkirk (William) Scholarship
Smith (Hermon Dunlap) Center for the History of Cartography Fellowships
Soviet Union and its Successor States Program: Research and Development Grants
Soviet Union and its Successor States Program: Summer Postdoctoral Retraining Grants
Staley (JI) Prize
Stuart (JM) Fellowship
FRD University Development Programme: Grants
FRD University Development Programme: Honours Bursaries
University of Bath Studentships
Waring Bowen Memorial Scholarship Fund
Wellcome Trust-RSE Senior Research Fellowship
Women's Studio Workshop Residencies
Woods Hole Postdoctoral Awards in Marine Policy and Ocean Management